MARKETING RESEARCH

An Applied Orientation

Second Edition

Naresh K. Malhotra

Georgia Institute of Technology

Prentice Hall, Upper Saddle River, New Jersey 07458

Library of Congress Cataloging-in-Publication Data

Malhotra, Naresh K.
    Marketing research : an applied orientation / Naresh K. Malhotra.
    —2nd ed.
        p.   cm.
    Includes bibliographical references and index.
    ISBN 0-13-125733-1 (hard cover)
    1. Marketing research.   2. Marketing research—Methodology.
    I. Title.
HF5415.2.M29   1996   95–36703
658.8'3—dc20   CIP

The assistance of James Agarwal with the international marketing research
example, the assistance of Mark Leach and Gina Miller in writing the
ethics section, and the assistance of Mark Peterson in writing the computer
applications section is gratefully acknowledged.

Acquisitions Editor: David Borkowsky
Associate Editor: Melissa Steffens
Production Editor: Edith Pullman
Marketing Manager: John Chillingworth
Interior Design: Rosemarie Paccione Votta
Cover Design: Lorraine Costellano
Cover Illustration: Paul Schulenburg
Design Director: Patricia H. Wosczyk
Manager of Production Services: Lorraine Patsco
Electronic Page Formatter: Christy Mahon
Electronic Interior Line Art: Warren Fischbach
Prepress and Manufacturing Buyer: Vincent Scelta
Editorial Assistant: Theresa Festa
Production Assistants: Annie Bartell and David Cotugno

©1996, 1993 by Prentice Hall, Inc.
A Simon & Schuster Company
Upper Saddle River, New Jersey 07458

Printed in the United States of America

10 9 8 7 6 5 4 3 2 1

ISBN 0-13-125733-1

Prentice-Hall International (UK) Limited, *London*
Prentice-Hall of Australia Pty. Limited, *Sydney*
Prentice-Hall Canada Inc., *Toronto*
Prentice-Hall Hispanoamericana, S.A., *Mexico*
Prentice-Hall of India Private Limited, *New Delhi*
Prentice-Hall of Japan, Inc., *Tokyo*
Simon & Schuster Asia Pte. Ltd., *Singapore*
Editora Prentice-Hall do Brasil, Ltda., *Rio de Janeiro*

To my parents,
Mr. and Mrs. H. N. Malhotra
and
To my wife, Veena, and my
children, Ruth and Paul

Brief Contents

Contents

PART II: RESEARCH DESIGN FORMULATION   83

PART III: DATA COLLECTION   441

PART IV: DATA PREPARATION AND ANALYSIS 469

PART V: COMMUNICATING THE RESEARCH PROJECT   765

PART VI: INTERNATIONAL AND ETHICAL DIMENSIONS   798

Preface

The motivation in writing *Marketing Research* was to provide a college text that is comprehensive, practical, applied, and managerial and that presents a balanced coverage of both qualitative and quantitative material. This book is written from the perspective of users of marketing research, and it reflects the current trends in international marketing, ethics, and the integration of microcomputers and mainframes into this field. Several unique features in terms of the content and presentation of the material make this book distinctive from others.

The response to the first edition was truly gratifying, and more than 100 universities adopted the book. I want to express my sincere thanks and appreciation to all the professors and students who, as users, reviewers, and providers of valuable feedback and encouragement, have contributed to the success of the book. This second edition attempts to build on this success to make the book even more current, contemporary, illustrative, and sensitive to user needs.

AUDIENCE

This book is suitable for use at both the undergraduate and graduate levels. This positioning is confirmed by the response to the first edition, which included adoptions at both levels. The coverage is comprehensive and the depth and breadth of topics encompass both levels. Yet the material is presented in a manner that is easy to read and understand. Diagrams, tables, pictures, illustrations, and examples explain the basic concepts. Special features designed for undergraduate students include acronyms, extensive exercises (questions, problems, and microcomputer and mainframe exercises), and activities (role playing, field work, and group discussion). Features that will appeal to graduate students include extensive notes and comprehensive coverage. An *Instructor's Manual* offers specific suggestions for teaching each chapter at the undergraduate and graduate levels. Activities (role playing, field work, and group discussion) have been moved to the *Instructor's Manual*. Not only is the book suitable for use in courses on marketing research, but it can also be effectively used in courses on marketing data analysis. All the commonly used univariate and multivariate data analysis techniques are discussed extensively yet simply.

ORGANIZATION

The book is organized into six parts, based on a six-step framework for conducting marketing research. Part I provides an introduction and discusses problem definition, the first and the most important step. The nature and scope of research undertaken to develop an approach to the problem, the second step in the marketing research process, is also described. Part II covers research design, the third step, and describes in detail exploratory, descriptive, and causal research designs. The types of information commonly obtained in marketing research and the appropriate scales for obtaining such information are described. Several guidelines for designing questionnaires and explaining the procedures, techniques, and statistical considerations involved in sampling are also presented. Part III presents a practical and managerially oriented discussion of field work, the fourth step in the marketing research process.

Part IV is devoted to data preparation and analysis, the fifth step of the marketing research process. Here the basic and advanced statistical techniques are discussed in detail, with emphasis on explaining the procedures, interpreting the results, and uncovering the managerial implications, rather than on statistical elegance. Communicating the research by preparing and presenting a formal report constitutes the sixth step in the marketing research process and forms the subject of Part V. Finally, Part VI is devoted to the complex process of international marketing research and the ethical issues that arise in marketing research. Throughout the book, the orientation is applied and managerial.

NEW FOR THE SECOND EDITION

While retaining the desirable features, this second edition of *Marketing Research* contains major revisions. Several significant changes, identified by conducting surveys of professors (users and nonusers) and students and by obtaining critical reviews and detailed evaluations, were made, including the following.

1. *Integrated coverage of international marketing research.* A section on international marketing research has been added to each chapter. This section discusses and illustrates how the concepts in that chapter can be applied when conducting international marketing research. This section takes the form of a major heading, including at least one blocked example, in each of Chapters 1 through 14, 22, and 24. The data analysis chapters, 15 through 21, each contain a Research in Practice box that illustrates the use of the technique in an international context. The capstone chapter on international marketing research has been retained from the first edition, although in modified form. It now appears as Chapter 23 and presents only material not covered elsewhere in the text.

2. *Integrated coverage of ethics in marketing research.* A section on ethics in marketing research has been added to each chapter. This section discusses and illustrates the ethical issues that arise when implementing the concepts in the chapter. This section also takes the form of a major heading and includes one blocked example in each of Chapters 1 through 14, 22, and 23. The data analysis chapters, 15 through 21, each contain a Research in Practice box that illustrates the use of the technique in a marketing research ethics context. A capstone chapter on ethics in marketing research has been added as Chapter 24, which presents the various codes of ethics and develops a framework for ethics in marketing research. This framework incorporates various approaches: teleology—egoism and utilitarianism, deontology, hybrid, and objectivism.

3. *Newly revised sections entitled "Computer Applications."* These sections have been rewritten for Chapters 1 through 14, 22, and 23. Each section now discusses in detail a major software program and illustrates its use with one or more exhibits. The data analysis chapters, 15 through 21, retain the emphasis on the microcomputer and mainframe programs for SPSS, SAS, and BMDP packages.

4. *New figures, tables, exhibits, Research in Practice boxes, and text.* Where appropriate, new material has been added to either present new ideas (e.g., the changing nature of marketing research in Chapter 1, database marketing in Chapter 4) or clarify the subject (e.g., problem definition and approach development process in Chapter 2, cohort analysis in Chapter 3, a comparative evaluation of observation methods in Chapter 6). Such additions have been made throughout the text.

5. *New and updated examples and cases*. Several new examples have been added, some old ones have been deleted, and the remaining examples have been updated as appropriate. Some new cases have been added, and all the rest have been updated to reflect the current marketing and marketing research environment.

6. *Updated references*. Each chapter contains at least some references from 1993 or later.

KEY FEATURES OF THE TEXT

The book has several salent and unique features, both in terms of content and pedagogy.

Content Features

1. A separate chapter has been devoted to problem definition and developing an approach. These important steps in the marketing research process are discussed thoroughly and extensively (Chapter 2).

2. A separate chapter covers secondary data analysis. In addition to the traditional sources, computerized databases and syndicate sources are also covered in some detail (Chapter 4).

4. Qualitative research is discussed in a separate chapter. Focus groups, depth interviews, and projective techniques are discussed in detail, with emphasis on the applications of these procedures (Chapter 5).

5. A separate chapter presents survey and observation methods (Chapter 6), and another discusses experimentation (Chapter 7). Thus, descriptive and causal designs are covered in detail.

6. Two chapters have been devoted to scaling techniques. One chapter is devoted to the fundamentals and comparative scaling techniques (Chapter 8), and another covers noncomparative techniques, including multiitem scales, and procedures for assessing their reliability, validity, and generalizability (Chapter 9).

7. A separate chapter discusses questionnaire design. A step-by-step procedure and several guidelines are provided for constructing questionnaires (Chapter 10).

8. Two chapters cover sampling techniques. One chapter discusses the qualitative issues involved in sampling and the various nonprobability and probability sampling techniques (Chapter 11). The other chapter explains statistical issues as well as final and initial sample size determination (Chapter 12).

9. A separate chapter presents field work. It provides several guidelines on interviewer training, interviewing, and supervision of field workers (Chapter 13).

10. The book is unique in the treatment of marketing research data analysis. Separate chapters have been devoted to:
    a. Frequency distribution, cross-tabulation, and hypothesis testing (Chapter 15)
    b. Analysis of variance and covariance (Chapter 16)
    c. Regression analysis (Chapter 17)
    d. Discriminant analysis (Chapter 18)
    e. Factor analysis (Chapter 19)
    f. Cluster analysis (Chapter 20)
    g. Multidimensional scaling and conjoint analysis (Chapter 21)

11. To supplement the discussions throughout the text, an additional chapter explains international marketing research. The environment in which international marketing research is conducted is described, followed by a discussion of some advanced concepts (Chapter 23).

12. In addition to discussions throughout the text, another chapter has been devoted to ethics in marketing research. Some of the guidelines that aid managers and researchers alike in ethical decision making are described. A framework for ethics in marketing research is then proposed. The way in which ethics influence each step of the marketing research process is explained (Chapter 24).

Pedagogical Features

1. Scholarship is appropriately blended with a highly applied and managerial orientation. The application of marketing research findings by managers to improve marketing practice is illustrated throughout.

2. Several real-life examples, which have been boxed for clarity and impact, are given. These examples describe in some detail the kind of marketing research used to address a specific managerial problem and the decision that was based on the findings. Where appropriate, the sources cited have been supplemented by additional marketing research information to enhance the usefulness of these examples. Additional examples have been integrated throughout the text to explain and illustrate the concepts in each chapter further.

3. In addition, a real-life project is used as a running example to illustrate various concepts throughout the text. These illustrations, entitled "Department Store Patronage Project," are highlighted using a colored background. To make the running example comprehensive so that it covers all aspects of marketing research, an actual department store project is supplemented with other similar projects with which I was involved, although several aspects of these projects have been disguised. In other instances, as in the case of causal research design, how the relevant concepts can be applied in a department store setting are shown. Thus, the department store example spans the whole book and is easy to pick up in any chapter.

4. Each chapter contains Research in Practice boxes. These provide a further illustration of how marketing research concepts are being implemented in practice.

5. Another way in which a contemporary focus is achieved is by integrating the coverage of international marketing research and ethics in marketing research throughout the text. Discussions include how the concepts discussed in each chapter can be applied in an international setting and the ethical issues that may arise when implementing those concepts domestically and internationally.

6. The use of microcomputers and mainframes has also been integrated throughout the text. Each chapter has a section entitled "Computer Applications," which shows how microcomputers and mainframes can be integrated in each step of the marketing research process. Both types of computers are considered because both systems are used in practice, and abundant software has been developed to facilitate interaction between both.

7. Data analysis procedures are illustrated with respect to mainframes as well as microcomputers. SPSS, SAS, and BMDP mainframe and microcomputer packages are used, along with other popular programs. Thus, this book can be used as a text, regardless of the statistical package being used by the instructor.

8. Each chapter contains one or more helpful acronyms that summarize the salient concepts. Acronyms are the most popular mnemonic technique used by college students. Theoretical and empirical evidence supporting the effectiveness of mnemonic techniques and their usefulness as a pedagogical tool has been discussed in a paper I published in the *Journal of the Academy of Marketing Science* (Spring 1991): 141–150.

9. Each part contains Practitioner Viewpoints that feature articles by some of the leading marketing research practitioners, including practitioners from Market Facts, Burke, and Elrick and Lavidge. These articles complement the material in the chapters and further strengthen the applied orientation of the book.

10. Short and long real-life cases. Each part of the book contains some short cases that illustrate the concepts discussed. The conciseness of the cases will allow for their use in examinations. Some long cases are also provided, including some cases with statistical data. These cases are current and deal with topics of interest to students.

11. Extensive exercises and activities sections include questions, problems, microcomputer and mainframe exercises, role playing, field work, and group discussion and are found at the conclusion of each chapter. These provide ample opportunities for learning and testing the concepts covered in the chapter.

12. A complete set of learning aids, including an *Instructor's Manual*, tailor-made *Instructional and Tutorial Software* (for presentation of materials in class and for tutorials), *Test Item File*, and *Study Guide* have been provided.

INSTRUCTIONAL SUPPORT

- *Instructor's Manual.* Personally written by me, the entire *Instructor's Manual* is very closely tied to the text. The manual shows how to tailor the material in each chapter to the undergraduate and graduate levels. Each chapter contains transparency masters, chapter objectives, author's notes, a chapter outline, teaching suggestions, and answers to all end-of-chapter exercises and activities (questions, problems, microcomputer and mainframe exercises, role playing, field work, and group discussion). In addition, solutions are provided to all the questions in the cases, including those that involve data analysis. A disk containing statistical data for some of the cases is provided.

- *Test Item File.* Available for both IBM and Macintosh computers, this valuable test item file contains a wide variety of tests for each chapter that allow instructors to "create" their own exams.

- *Instructional and Tutorial Software.* This software, available for both IBM and Macintosh computers, covers the key material in each chapter including examples, figures, tables, and Research in Practice boxes. It can be used by the instructor for presenting the book material in the class as well as by students in the computer lab or at home as a tutorial.

- *Exercises in Marketing Research.* Written by Naresh K. Malhotra and Chulwan Kim, this guide is designed to give students practice in marketing research. It presents four real-life scenarios, with exercises framed on all the phases of the marketing research process, from problem definition to report presentation. A questionnaire and statistical data are provided for each case, and solutions to exercises are discussed.

ACKNOWLEDGMENTS

Several people have been extremely helpful in writing this textbook. I would like to acknowledge Professor Arun K. Jain (State University of New York at Buffalo), who taught me marketing research in a way that I will never forget. My students, particularly former doctoral students (James Agarwal, Imad Baalbaki, Dan McCort, Gina Miller, and Mark Peterson) and current doctoral students (Charla Allen, Mark Leach, Tyra Mitchell, Rick McFarland, and Jamie Pleasant), have been very helpful in many ways. I particularly want to acknowledge the assistance of Mark Leach and Gina Miller in writing the ethics sections and chapter, the assistance of Mark Peterson in writing the computer applications sections, and the assistance of James Agarwal with the international marketing research examples. The students in my marketing research courses have provided useful feedback as the material was class-tested for several years. My colleagues at Georgia Tech, especially Fred Allvine, have been very supportive. I would also like to thank Ronald L. Tatham (Burke Marketing Research), Lawrence W. Labash (Market Facts, Inc.), Roger L. Bacik (Elrick and Lavidge, Inc.), and the other practitioners who have contributed to this book.

The reviewers have provided many constructive and valuable suggestions. Among others, the help of the following reviewers is gratefully acknowledged.

Reviewers for the second edition

Rick Andrews, University of Delaware
Holland Blades, Jr., Missouri Southern State College
Sharmila Chatterjee, Santa Clara University
Rajshekhar Javalgi, Cleveland State University
Mushtaq Luqmani, Western Michigan University

Jeanne Munger, University of Southern Maine
Audesh Paswan, University of South Dakota.
Venkatram Ramaswamy, University of Michigan
Gillian Rice, Thunderbird University
Paul L. Sauer, Canisius College
Hans Srinivasan, University of Connecticut

Reviewers for the first edition

David M. Andrus, Kansas State University
Joe Ballenger, Stephen F. Austin State University
Joseph D. Brown, Ball State University
Thomas E. Buzas, Eastern Michigan University
Rajendar K. Garg, Northeastern Illinois University
Lawrence D. Gibson, Consultant
Ronald E. Goldsmith, Florida State University
Rajshekhar G. Javalgi, Cleveland State University
Charlotte H. Mason, University of North Carolina
Kent Nakamoto, University of Colorado
Thomas J. Page, Jr., Michigan State University
William S. Perkins, Pennsylvania State University
Sudhi Seshadri, University of Maryland at College Park
David Shani, Baruch College

The team at Prentice Hall provided outstanding support. Special thanks are due to James C. Boyd, editor in chief; David Borkowsky, senior marketing editor; Sandra Steiner, director of marketing for Prentice Hall Business Publishing Division; John Chillingworth, marketing manager; Edie Pullman, production editor; Theresa Festa, administrative assistant; and Carole Horton, field editor. Special recognition is due to the several field representatives and salespeople, who have done an outstanding job in marketing the book.

I want to acknowledge with great respect my parents, Mr. and Mrs. H. N. Malhotra. Their love, encouragement, support, and the sacrificial giving of themselves have been exemplary. My heartfelt love and gratitude go to my wife, Veena, and my children, Ruth and Paul, for their faith, hope, and love.

Most of all, I want to acknowledge and thank my Savior and Lord, Jesus Christ, for the many miracles He has performed in my life. This book is, truly, the result of His grace. "This is the Lord's doing; it is marvelous in our eyes" (Psalm 118:23).

Naresh K. Malhotra

About The Author

NARESH K. MALHOTRA is Regents' Professor at the Georgia Institute of Technology. He is President of the Academy of Marketing Science, Distinguished Fellow of the Academy of Marketing Science, and Fellow of the Decision Sciences Institute. He has published more than 60 papers in major refereed journals including the *Journal of Marketing Research*, *Journal of Consumer Research*, *Marketing Science, Journal of Marketing, Journal of the Academy of Marketing Science, Journal of Retailing, Journal of Health Care Marketing*, and other leading journals in the fields of statistics, management science, and psychology. In addition, he has also published numerous refereed articles in the proceedings of major national and international conferences.

Malhotra has published nine papers in the prestigious *Journal of Marketing Research*. In an article by Wheatley and Wilson (*AMA Educators' Proceedings,* 1987), Malhotra was ranked first in the United States based on articles published in the *Journal of Marketing Research* from 1980 to 1985. He is also ranked first in the country based on articles published in the *Journal of Health Care Marketing* from its inception to 1994. (This analysis was conducted by William Gombeski, Jr., editor of that journal.) Malhotra is the recipient of numerous awards for research, teaching, and service to the profession.

He is also an active marketing and marketing research consultant and has consulted for private, public, nonprofit, and government organizations in the United States and abroad. He has served as an expert witness in regulatory and legal proceedings.

Dr. Malhotra is a member and deacon of the First Baptist Church of Atlanta. He lives in the Atlanta area with his wife, Veena, and children, Ruth and Paul.

Introduction and Early Phases of Marketing Research

In this part, we discuss the nature and scope of marketing research and explain its role in decision support systems. We describe the marketing research industry and the many exciting career opportunities in this field. We set out a six-step marketing research process and discuss problem definition, the first and the most important step, in detail. Finally, we describe the development of an approach to the problem, the second step in the marketing research process, and discuss in detail the various components of the approach. The perspective given in these chapters should be useful to both the decision maker and the marketing researcher.

CHAPTER ONE

Introduction to Marketing Research

The task of marketing researchers is to provide management with the information needed to identify and solve marketing problems.

◆

OBJECTIVES

After reading this chapter, the student should be able to:

1. Understand the nature and scope of marketing research and its role in designing and implementing successful marketing programs.
2. Explain the role of marketing research in decision support systems in providing data, marketing models, and specialized software.
3. Discuss the types and roles of research suppliers including internal and external, full-service, and limited-service suppliers.
4. Describe careers available in marketing research and the backgrounds and skills needed to succeed in them.
5. Describe a conceptual framework for conducting marketing research as well as the six steps of the marketing research process.
6. Acquire an appreciation of the international dimension and the complexity involved in international marketing research.
7. Gain an understanding of the ethical aspects of marketing research and the responsibilities that marketing research stakeholders have to themselves, each other, and to the research project.
8. Explain how microcomputers and mainframes can facilitate the marketing research process.

OVERVIEW

Marketing research comprises one of the most important and fascinating facets of marketing. In this chapter, we describe the nature of marketing research, emphasizing its role of providing information for marketing decision making and provide several real-life examples to illustrate the basic concepts of marketing research. We give a formal definition of marketing research and subdivide marketing research into two areas: problem identification and problem-solving research. We show that marketing research is also an integral part of marketing information systems or decision support systems. Next, we provide an overview of marketing research suppliers and services, along with guidelines for selecting a supplier. Because of demand for well-executed marketing research, there are many exciting career opportunities in this field. We discuss these opportunities, along with ethical issues, and describe the stages of the marketing research process. To illustrate this process, we examine the department store patronage project, which was an actual marketing research project conducted by the author, and use it as a running example throughout the book. The topic of international marketing research is introduced and discussed systematically in the subsequent chapters. The ethical aspects of marketing research and the responsibilities that marketing research stakeholders have to themselves, each other, and to the research project are presented and developed in more detail throughout the text. This chapter concludes with an applications-oriented discussion on the use of mainframe and microcomputers in marketing research, another emphasis that pervades the entire book.

WHAT DOES MARKETING RESEARCH ENCOMPASS?

The term *marketing research* is broad in meaning; it is related to all aspects of marketing. The following examples provide a flavor of the varied nature of marketing research.

EXAMPLE
Baby Bell Grows Up

The breakup of America's telecommunications industry in 1983 put the burden of building public understanding and support on the resulting "Baby Bell" companies. The St. Louis–based Southwestern Bell uses marketing research to measure customer perceptions of its services. The company has been successful in building public support with the help of a telephone survey called the customer attitude survey (CAS). This periodic survey has helped Southwestern Bell identify and address customer concerns. For example, when customers complained about difficulty with the billing format, a new, easier to read and understand format was implemented. As a result of CAS, positive customer attitudes toward the company are at an all-time high.[1] ◆

Southwestern Bell
Telephone

"The One to Call On"®

Customer attitude surveys have helped Southwestern Bell to establish a favorable image—"The one to call on." ◆ Southwestern Bell.

EXAMPLE
The Making of a President _____

President Bill Clinton used market research to develop policies and to polish those policies once they were in place. Clinton and his team made extensive use of focus groups (group interviews), telephone and personal surveys, and interview-style meetings to understand what people were expecting from the policies that are developed. In the eyes of the President, the taxpayers of the country were his administration's "customers."

His first big test came during his first State of the Union address when he unveiled his "product of uncertain demand," a new economic package that included higher taxes. The White House used market research to smooth the rough edges of the new package and to sell it to the American people. The raising of taxes was the ultimate hard sell. Clinton made use of focus groups and telephone surveys to determine how to make the new package palatable. The research indicated that the public was willing to pay higher taxes so as to reduce the national debt, but the research also revealed that it expected both the president and Congress to deal with wasteful federal spending. Thus, deficit reduction was an important aspect of this package.

One advertising executive noted that "instituting a new policy is the same as offering a new product. When you market anything you need to concentrate on the end benefit." Bill Clinton attempted to do just that by making extensive use of marketing research.[2]◆

EXAMPLE
Marketing Research Gives NEC a Tall Neck _____

When redesigning its personal computer notebook, NEC, a Japanese electronics company, first went to business users rather than its engineers. Many users were observed as to how they use their notebook computers. This observation process revealed that people using a notebook are generally performing multiple tasks when they open the machine. Therefore, a two-handed latch was inconvenient. With this information in hand, the company designed a latch system that required only one hand to operate.

Further research was conducted using focus groups and computer-assisted personal interviewing (CAPI). It was found that versatility and modularity were important features to most businesspeople. NEC redesigned their notebook to have snap-off parts to allow versatility in configuration, including a screen that could be disconnected and turned around for others to see. Modularity was also very important, and many consumers needed extended battery life when traveling long distances without access to an electrical outlet. NEC's new design incorporated several battery packs to allow for extended battery use. Other findings that emerged from focus groups and CAPI were that people were increasingly taking their notebooks with them everywhere they went and that the machines were becoming more a part of the normal businessperson's life. With this in mind, NEC designed the UltraLite Versa to have more rounded features than other notebooks and to give the notebook the look and feel of a consumer appliance rather than an office product.

The redesign seems to have worked well for NEC. In just four months after the introduction of the UltraLite Versa, NEC's share of the notebook market rose 2.5% and the Versa grabbed approximately 10% of its market within a year. In contrast, Zenith went to an industrial design consultant to redesign its notebook. While the consultant turned out a product that has won many design awards, it did not take customer needs into consideration. Consequently, the sales of the redesigned computer sank to a dismal 1% of the market.[3]◆

EXAMPLE
Ford "Probes" the Car Market

Ford Motor Company runs a marketing research clinic to test the design of its new car models. Invited guests test drive the prototype models through a predetermined route. A

trained observer rides along, making notes on the driver's reactions to the car. After putting the car through its paces, each participant is given a six-page questionnaire and asked to rate every aspect of the car from poor to excellent. Information provided by the participants enables Ford to assess consumer reaction to the new models and to make the models more appealing to the target consumers. For example, the 1996 Probe was introduced with improved rear lights to address a safety concern identified in the marketing research clinic.[4] ◆

Marketing research by the Ford Motor Company has resulted in successful models such as the 1996 Probe. ◆ Ford Motor Company.

EXAMPLE
Century City Hospital Moves into New Century of Health Care

When most hospitals across the country were emphasizing cost cutting, the Century City Hospital in Los Angeles opened its deluxe Century Pavilion offering luxurious private accommodations. This action was based on extensive marketing research, including analysis of published data and a large survey that indicated that nearly 50% local residents had high incomes, were accustomed to the best in food and accommodation, and valued privacy and exclusiveness. Thus, the Century City Hospital was able to carve a niche in a profitable market segment.[5] ◆

EXAMPLE
The Jury Is in for Marketing Research

Lawyers are now turning to marketing research to better understand their juries. Lawyers find target marketing research to be beneficial, especially when the case is difficult, the jury pool is diverse, and the facts are controversial.

Jury research consultants use such techniques as focus groups and demographic and psychographic databases. One such marketing research device is Percep'Trac, a juror database. The device is used by mock jurors to determine their positive or negative responses to facts presented in the trial. Jurors record their response changes as the trial is presented. The lawyer can then review the responses to determine if the presentation of the facts is being received well. The response data can be sorted by demographic and psychographic profiles so that a lawyer will have a better understanding of the reactions of the actual jury. The device was successfully used in a Florida Department of Transportation case seeking to secure land for a road-widening project. The device pointed out a legal term for condemning land, a *taking*, that was causing large negative responses from the mock jury. When the case went to court, the lawyer avoided the legal term that had caused such a negative response in mock jurors and subsequently won the case.[6] ◆

EXAMPLE
FIND is a Real Find for Marketing Researchers

Do you want to know the recent trends in the juvenile furniture market? How much of Australia's dairy products are exported to the United States? What new frozen cookie is being test marketed by a major food manufacturer? The answers to these questions can be obtained from FIND/SVP, a New York–based, worldwide information and research service and the largest business information center in America. Its goal is to meet the information and research needs of American businesses by providing a convenient, fast, cost-efficient service that is literally a phone call away. More than half of the Fortune 100 firms use FIND as an adjunct to in-house marketing research departments. By providing information suited to the client's specific needs at a low cost, FIND/SVP enhances the effectiveness and efficiency of the marketing research conducted by these firms.[7] ◆

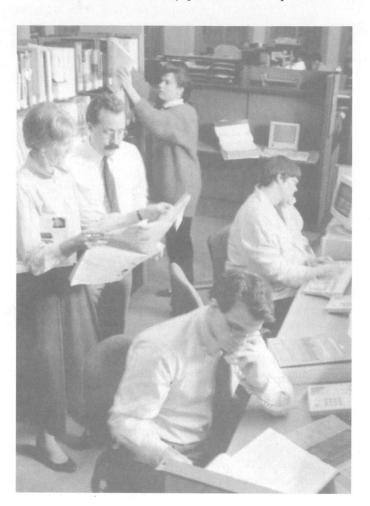

FIND/SVP is a worldwide information and research service and the largest business information center in America. ◆ FIND/SVP.

THE NATURE OF MARKETING RESEARCH

The previous examples illustrate only a few of the methods used to conduct marketing research: one-on-one participatory surveys, questionnaires to a limited sample, large surveys, published sources of information, and focus groups. This book will introduce you to the full complement of marketing research techniques. These examples also illustrate the crucial role played by marketing research in designing and implementing successful marketing programs.[8] Perhaps the role of marketing research can be better understood in light of the basic marketing paradigm depicted in Figure 1.1.

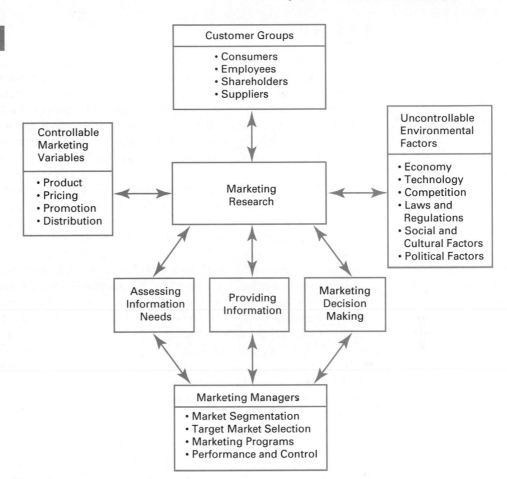

FIGURE 1.1

*The Role of
Marketing Research*

The emphasis in marketing is on the identification and satisfaction of customer needs. To determine customer needs and to implement marketing strategies and programs aimed at satisfying those needs, marketing managers need information about customers, competitors, and other forces in the marketplace. In recent years, many factors have increased the need for more and better information. As firms have become national and international in scope, the need for information on larger, and more distant, markets has increased. As consumers have become more affluent and sophisticated, marketing managers need better information on how they will respond to products and other marketing offerings. As competition has become more intense, managers need information on the effectiveness of their marketing tools. As the environment is changing more rapidly, marketing managers need more timely information.[9]

The task of marketing research is to assess the information needs and provide management with relevant, accurate, reliable, valid, and current information. Today's competitive marketing environment and the ever-increasing costs attributed to poor decision making require that marketing research provide sound information. Sound decisions are not based on gut feeling, intuition, or even pure judgment. In the absence of sound information, an incorrect management decision may result, as illustrated by the case of Johnson & Johnson baby aspirin.

EXAMPLE
J & J's Gentleness Could Not Handle Pain _____

Johnson & Johnson's attempt to use its company name on baby aspirin proved to be unsuccessful. Johnson & Johnson products are perceived as gentle, but gentleness is not what people want in a baby aspirin. Although baby aspirin should be safe, gentleness per se is not a desirable feature. Rather, some people perceived that a gentle aspirin may not be effective enough. So here is an example of what seemed, intuitively, to be a natural move but turned out to be an incorrect decision.[10] ◆

As indicated by the Johnson & Johnson example, marketing managers make numerous strategic and tactical decisions in the process of identifying and satisfying customer needs. As shown in Figure 1.1, they make decisions about potential opportunities, target market selection, market segmentation, planning and implementing marketing programs, marketing performance, and control. These decisions are complicated by interactions between the controllable marketing variables of product, pricing, promotion, and distribution. Further complications are added by uncontrollable environmental factors such as general economic conditions, technology, public policies and laws, the political environment, competition, and social and cultural changes. Another factor in this mix is the complexity of the various customer groups: consumers, employees, shareholders, suppliers, and so forth. Marketing research helps the marketing manager link the marketing variables with the environment and the customer groups. It helps remove some of the uncertainty by providing relevant information about the marketing variables, environment, and consumers. In the absence of relevant information, consumers' response to marketing programs cannot be predicted reliably or accurately. Ongoing marketing research programs provide information on controllable and noncontrollable factors and consumers; this information enhances the effectiveness of decisions made by marketing managers.[11]

Traditionally, marketing researchers were responsible for assessing information needs and providing the relevant information but marketing decisions were made by the managers. These roles are changing, however, and marketing researchers are becoming more involved in decision making whereas marketing managers are becoming more involved with research. This trend can be attributed to better training of marketing managers, advances in technology, and a shift in the marketing research paradigm where more and more marketing research is being undertaken on an ongoing basis rather than in response to specific marketing problems or opportunities.[12]

This crucial role of marketing research is recognized in its definition, which is given in the next section.

DEFINITION OF MARKETING RESEARCH

The American Marketing Association's formal definition of marketing research is given in Research in Practice 1.1.[13] For the purpose of this book, which emphasizes the need for information for decision making, marketing research is defined as follows:

> **Marketing research** is the systematic and objective identification, collection, analysis, and dissemination of information for the purpose of improving decision making related to the identification and solution of problems and opportunities in marketing.

marketing research The systematic and objective identification, collection, analysis, and dissemination of information for the purpose of improving decision making related to the identification and solution of problems and opportunities in marketing.

Several aspects of this definition are noteworthy. First, marketing research is systematic. Thus, systematic planning is required at all stages of the marketing research process. The procedures followed at each stage are methodologically sound, well documented, and, as much as possible, planned in advance. Marketing research uses the scientific method in that data are collected and analyzed to test prior notions or hypotheses.

Marketing research is objective. It attempts to provide accurate information that reflects a true state of affairs. It should be conducted impartially. Although research is always influenced by the researcher's research philosophy, it should be free from the personal or political biases of the researcher or the management. Research motivated by personal or political gain involves a breach of professional standards. Such research is deliberately biased so as to result in predetermined findings. The motto of every researcher should be, "Find it and tell it like it is."

RESEARCH IN PRACTICE 1.1

The American Marketing Association Redefines Marketing Research

The Board of Directors of the American Marketing Association has approved the following as the new definition of marketing research:

Marketing research is the function that links the consumer, customer, and public to the marketer through information—information used to identify and define marketing opportunities and problems; generate, refine, and evaluate marketing actions; monitor marketing performance; and improve understanding of marketing as a process.

Marketing research specifies the information required to address these issues, designs the method for collecting information, manages and implements the data collection process, analyzes the results, and communicates the findings and their implications.

Marketing research involves the identification, collection, analysis, and dissemination of information. Each phase of this process is important. We identify or define the marketing research problem or opportunity and then determine what information is needed to investigate it. Because every marketing opportunity translates into a research problem to be investigated, the terms *problem* and *opportunity* are used interchangeably here. Next, the relevant information sources are identified and a range of data collection methods varying in sophistication and complexity are evaluated for their usefulness. The data are collected using the most appropriate method; they are analyzed and interpreted, and inferences are drawn. Finally, the findings, implications and recommendations are provided in a format that allows the information to be used for marketing decision making and to be acted upon directly. The next section elaborates on this definition by classifying different types of marketing research.[14]

A CLASSIFICATION OF MARKETING RESEARCH

problem identification research Research under-taken to help identify problems that are not necessarily apparent on the surface and yet exist or are likely to arise in the future.

Our definition states that organizations engage in marketing research for two reasons: (1) to identify and (2) to solve marketing problems. This distinction serves as a basis for classifying marketing research into problem identification research and problem-solving research, as shown in Figure 1.2.

Problem identification research is undertaken to help identify problems that are, perhaps, not apparent on the surface and yet exist or are likely to arise in the future. Examples of problem identification research include market potential, market share, brand or company image, market characteristics, sales analysis, short-range forecasting, long-range forecasting, and business trends research. A survey of companies conducting marketing research indicated that 97 percent of those who responded were conducting market potential, market share, and market characteristics research.[15] About 90 percent also reported that they were using other types of problem identification research. Research of this type provides information about the marketing environment and helps diagnose a problem. For example, a declining market potential indicates that the firm is likely to have a problem achieving its growth targets. Similarly, a problem exists if the market potential is increasing but the firm is losing market share. The recognition of economic, social, or cultural trends, such as changes in consumer behavior, may point to underlying problems or opportunities. The importance of undertaking problem identification research for the survival and long-term growth of a company is exemplified by the case of PIP printing company.

FIGURE 1.2

A Classification of Marketing Research

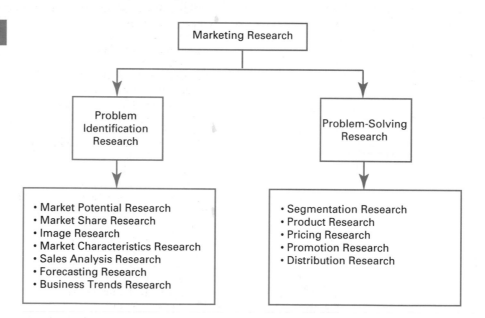

EXAMPLE
Image Research Helps PIP Become VIP (Very Important Printer) _____

Sales at PIP Printing had never been higher. The company remained the undisputed market leader. Yet an image study indicated a potential problem. The two major segments of the printing market are the low-end copy shops and the higher, more profitable commercial printers who do annual reports and multicolor printing. The image survey revealed that customers thought of PIP as a low-end copy shop. They did not know that PIP could do almost any type of commercial printing. Marketing research further indicated that the increasing number of competitors in the copy market segment would create price wars that would be detrimental to profit margins, if not to survival. This information led PIP to pursue the more profitable commercial market aggressively and to reposition itself as "the world's largest business printer." ◆

problem-solving research
Research undertaken to help solve specific marketing problems.

Once a problem or opportunity has been identified, as in the case of PIP, **problem-solving research** is undertaken to arrive at a solution. The findings of problem-solving research are used in making decisions that will solve specific marketing problems. More than two-thirds of companies conduct problem-solving research.[16] Table 1.1 shows the different types of issues that are addressed by problem-solving research, including segmentation, product, pricing, promotion, and distribution research. An example of problem-solving research is provided by the repositioning of Ovaltine.

TABLE 1.1 *Problem-Solving Research*	
	Segmentation Research
	determine basis of segmentation
	establish market potential and responsiveness for various segments
	select target markets and create lifestyle profiles: demography, media, and product image characteristics
	Product Research
	test concept
	determine optimal product design
	package tests
	product modification
	brand positioning and repositioning
	test marketing
	control store tests
	Pricing Research
	importance of price in brand selection
	pricing policies
	product line pricing
	price elasticity of demand
	initiating and responding to price changes
	Promotional Research
	optimal promotional budget
	sales promotion relationship
	optimal promotional mix
	copy decisions
	media decisions
	creative advertising testing
	claim substantiation
	evaluation of advertising effectiveness
	Distribution Research
	determine type of distribution
	attitudes of channel members
	intensity of wholesale and retail coverage
	channel margins
	location of retail and wholesale outlets

EXAMPLE

Ovaltine Wakes Up the Chocolate Drink Mix Market

Originally popular during the World War II era as a prebedtime drink, Ovaltine hot chocolate mix began losing market share in the 1960s. The first response of management was to bring back the popular characters used in the wartime advertisements. These outdated characters, however, did not fit in well with the period and only served to reinforce the image of Ovaltine as a prebedtime drink.

Management employed marketing research to help develop their product. Brand repositioning research revealed several opportunities. As it had only natural ingredients, Ovaltine could be positioned as a health-food drink, targeted at mothers twenty to thirty-five years of age. In addition, the demand for instant beverages was increasing, and a low-calorie version was well received in concept testing in which respondents provided their evaluations of different hot chocolate mixes and drinks. The company developed an instant hot chocolate mix and a reduced-calorie Ovaltine drink to meet these needs. This helped Ovaltine to regain some of its lost share.[17] ◆

Classifying marketing research into two main types is useful from a conceptual as well as a practical viewpoint. The Ovaltine example is clearly one of problem-solving research. A problem-solving perspective enabled management to focus on the product development of Ovaltine. Problem identification research and problem-solving research go hand-in-hand, however, and a given marketing research project may combine both types of research. A marketing research project for Scott Paper Company that investigated loss of market share identified the cause as increased local competition (problem identification) and the solution as the introduction of new products designed to meet this competition (problem solving).

THE ROLE OF MARKETING RESEARCH IN MIS AND DSS

marketing information systems (MIS) A formalized set of procedures for generating, analyzing, storing, and distributing pertinent information to marketing decision makers on an ongoing basis.

Earlier, we defined marketing research as the systematic and objective identification, collection, analysis, and dissemination of information for use in marketing decision making.[18] The information obtained through marketing research and sources such as internal records and marketing intelligence becomes an integral part of the firm's marketing information system (MIS). A **marketing information system (MIS)** is a formalized set of procedures for generating, analyzing, storing, and distributing pertinent information to marketing decision makers on an ongoing basis. Note that the definition of MIS is similar to that of marketing research except that MIS provides information continuously rather than on the basis of ad hoc research studies. The design of an MIS focuses on each decision maker's responsibilities, style, and information needs. Information gathered from various sources—such as invoices and marketing intelligence, including marketing research—is combined and presented in a format that can be readily used in decision making. More information can be obtained from MIS than from ad hoc marketing research projects, but MIS is limited in the amount and nature of information it provides and the way this information can be used by the decision maker because the information is rigidly structured and cannot be easily manipulated.

decision support systems (DSS) An information system that enables decision makers to interact directly with both databases and analysis models. The important components of a DSS include hardware and a communication network, database, model base, software base, and the DSS user (decision maker).

Developed to overcome the limitations of MIS, decision support systems (DSS) enable decision makers to interact directly with databases and analysis models.[19] A **decision support system (DSS)** is an integrated information system including hardware, communications network, database, model base, software base, and the DSS user (decision maker) that collects and interprets information for decision making. Marketing research contributes research data to the database, marketing models and analytical techniques to the model base, and specialized programs for analyzing marketing data to the software base. DSSs differ from MISs in various ways (see Figure 1.3).[20] They combine the use of models or analytical techniques with the traditional access and retrieval functions of an MIS. They are easier to use in an interactive mode and can adapt to changes in the environment as well as to the decision-making approach of the user. In addition to improving efficiency, a DSS can also enhance decision-making effectiveness by using "what if" analysis, as illustrated by the Rose Medical Center example.[21]

FIGURE 1.3

Management Information Systems versus Decision Support Systems

MIS	DSS
• Structured Problems • Use of Reports • Rigid Structure • Information Displaying Restricted • Can Improve Decision Making by Clarifying Raw Data	• Unstructured Problems • Use of Models • User-Friendly Interaction • Adaptability • Can Improve Decision Making by Using "What If" Analysis

EXAMPLE
Medical Center Uses DSS to Diagnose Marketing Maladies

Rose Medical Center, a 420-bed acute care teaching hospital in Denver, negotiated and won 42 contracts with managed-care organizations (Preferred Provider Organizations and Health Maintenance Organizations) in 18 months. Rose used the DSS contract simulation model to run several permutations of contracts before making bids. The model sorted cost data in a variety of ways and simulated costs and profitability using groups of varying sizes. The resulting information was invaluable to Rose's decision about which contract to propose.

After negotiating a contract, Rose used its DSS to measure changes in its markets and compared utilization rates and patterns among various insured groups. Analysis by zip codes indicated where cases were coming from and whether activity from a certain area was increasing or decreasing. Further cross-classification by insurance types indicated whether these changes were the result of one of the negotiated contracts. This information was useful not only in monitoring and controlling negotiated contracts but also as feedback in preparing future bids.[22] ◆

As shown by the experience of Rose Medical Center, MIS and DSS can greatly enhance the information available to management. In making specific marketing decisions, management may also rely on marketing research suppliers and services.

MARKETING RESEARCH SUPPLIERS AND SERVICES

Marketing research suppliers and services provide most of the information needed for making marketing decisions. Figure 1.4 classifies marketing research suppliers and services. Broadly, research suppliers can be classified as internal or external. An

internal suppliers
Marketing research departments located within a firm.

internal supplier is a marketing research department within a firm. Many firms—particularly the big ones, ranging from automobile companies (GM, Ford, Chrysler)—to consumer products firms (Procter & Gamble, Colgate Palmolive, Coca-Cola) to banks (Citicorp, Bank of America)—maintain in-house marketing research departments. A marketing research department's place in the organizational structure may vary considerably. At one extreme, the research function may be centralized and located at the corporate headquarters. At the other extreme is a decentralized structure in which the marketing research function is organized along divisional lines. In a decentralized scheme, the company may be organized into divisions by products, customers, or geographical regions, with marketing research personnel assigned to the various divisions. These personnel generally report to a division manager rather than to a corporate-level executive. In addition, between these two extremes is a variety of types of organization. The best organization for a firm depends on its marketing research needs and the structure of marketing and other functions, although in recent years there has been a trend toward centralization and a trimming of the marketing research staff.[23] Internal suppliers often rely on external suppliers to perform specific marketing research tasks. Research in Practice 1.2 illustrates the organization of the marketing research function at Oscar Mayer.[24]

external suppliers
Outside marketing research companies hired to supply marketing research datum of services.

full-service suppliers
Companies that offer the full range of marketing research activities.

External suppliers are outside firms hired to supply marketing research data. These external suppliers, which collectively comprise the marketing research industry, range from small (one or a few persons) operations to very large global corporations.[25] Research in Practice 1.3 lists the top 50 marketing research suppliers in the United States.[26] External suppliers can be classified as full-service or limited-service suppliers. **Full-service suppliers** offer the entire range of marketing research services, from defining a problem, developing an approach, designing questionnaires, sampling, collecting, analyzing, and interpreting data, to preparing and presenting reports. The services provided by these suppliers can be further broken down into syndicated services, standardized services, and customized services (see Figure 1.4).

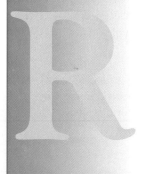

RESEARCH IN PRACTICE 1.2

Organization of Marketing Research at Oscar Mayer

The Oscar Mayer marketing research department is organized into two functional areas: brand research and marketing systems and analytics (MSA). The brand research group has the following responsibilities:

- Conducting primary and secondary research
- Serving as marketing consultants
- Analyzing market trends
- Advancing the state-of-the-art in marketing research

Researchers in the MSA group fulfill three main roles:

- Performing sales analysis based on shipment and store-scanner data
- Supporting computer end users within the marketing department
- Serving as a source of marketing information

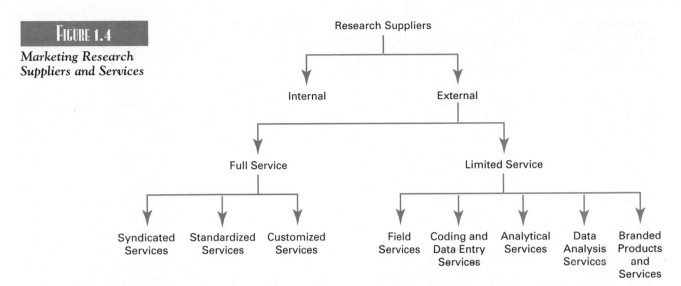

FIGURE 1.4

*Marketing Research
Suppliers and Services*

RESEARCH IN PRACTICE 1.3

Top 50 U.S. Research Organizations

Rank 1994	Rank 1993	Organization	Total research revenue[a] ($ in millions)	Percent change from 1993[b]	Percent from outside U.S.	revenues from outside U.S. ($ in millions)
1	1	D & B Marketing Information Services	$2,042.9	6.0%	63.8%[c]	$1,303.8[c]
2	2	Information Resources Inc.	376.6	12.6	16.0	60.3
3	3	The Arbitron Co.	121.3	5.4		
4	5	Westat Inc.	119.0	6.3		
5	6	Maritz Marketing Research Inc.	107.2	14.9	19.0	20.4
6	4	Walsh International/PMSI	104.8	-8.4	53.4	56.0
7	7	The NPD Group	80.8	15.3	28.6	23.1
8	8	NFO Research Inc.	61.5	6.2		
9	10	Market Facts Inc.	55.5	13.2	7.0	3.9
10	11	The M/A/R/C Group	50.5	13.0		
11	9	Elrick and Lavidge Inc.	47.8	1.5		
12	13	Abt Associates Inc.	46.8	28.6	2.1	1.0
13	—	Audits & Surveys, Inc.	43.9	10.0	20.0	8.8
14	20	Opinion Research Corp.	39.8	12.8	29.0	11.5
15	12	Walker Group	38.6	2.2	0.8	0.3
16	15	The National Research Group Inc.	37.0	7.2	15.0	5.5
17	17	Intersearch Corp.	36.6	13.7		
18	16	MAI Information Group	34.0	3.0		
19	18	The BASES Group	32.7	5.5	6.0	2.0
20	—	Macro International Inc.	32.5	8.3	40.3	13.1
21	19	Milward Brown Inc.	32.0	10.3		
22	14	MRB Group Ltdd.	31.1	-11.1		
23	21	Burke Marketing Research, Inc.	29.0	11.1	2.7	0.8
24	23	J.D. Power & Associates	28.5	16.3		
25	22	Roper Starch Worldwide Inc.	26.3	5.6	4.9	1.3

(continued)

RESEARCH IN PRACTIC 1.3   (CONTINUED)

Top 50 U.S. Research Organizations

Rank 1994	Rank 1993	Organization	Total research revenue[a] ($ in millions)	Percent change from 1993[b]	Percent and revenues from outside U.S. ($ in millions)	
26	28	Mercer Management Consulting/ Marketing Group	26.1	10.0	2.3	0.6
27	24	Creative & Response Research Services, Inc.	25.1	5.5		
28	25	Research International USA	23.4	3.1	26.0	6.1
29	27	Chilton Research Services	22.0	No Change		1.6
30	29	Yankelovich Partners Inc.	20.6	3.0	3.0	0.6
31	30	ASI Market Research Inc.	19.7	13.9		
32	33	Lieberman Research West Inc.	19.5	28.3	9.7	1.9
33	31	M.O.R.-PACE	18.4	10.2	4.9	0.9
34	32	The Wirthlin Group	18.4	13.6		
35	38	Market Strategies Inc.	18.1	39.2		
36	34	Custom Research Inc.	16.9	11.3		
37	35	Data Development Corp.	16.8	13.7		
38	40	ICR Survey Research Group	16.7	32.5		
39	36	Total Research Corp.	16.2	12.7	9.8	1.6
40	37	Response Analysis Corp.	15.4	14.9		
41	41	Research Data Analysis Inc.	13.0	8.3		
42	39	National Analysis Inc.	12.9	0.6		
43	45	Market Decisions	12.1	7.0		
44	43	Conway/Milliken & Assocs.	11.6	14.5		
45	—	Matrixx Marketing Inc.	10.9	17.9	52.0	5.7
46	49	Gordon S. Black Corp.	10.1	20.1		
47	48	BAI (Behavioral Analysis Inc.)	9.7	11.4	22.1	2.1
48	44	Guideline Research Corp.	9.7	-3.0		
49	47	Newman-Stein Inc.	8.9	No Change	5.0	0.4
50	—	Nordhaus Research Inc.	8.5	24.1		
Subtotal, top 50			$4,057.4	7.6%	37.08%	$1,531.7
All other (111 CASRO member companies not included in top)			380.9	5.4		
[d]Total (161 organizations)			$4,438.3	7.4%		

[a]*Total revenues that included nonresearch activities for some companies are significantly higher.*

[b]*Rate of growth from year to year has been adjusted so as not to include revenue gains from acquisition.*

[c]*Estimate.*

[d]*Total revenues of 111 survey research firms—beyond those listed in the Top Fifty—that provided financial information, on a confidential basis, to the council of American Survey Research Organizations (CASRO).*

syndicated services
Companies that collect and sell common pools of data designed to serve information needs shared by a number of clients.

Syndicated services collect information that they provide to subscribers. Surveys, diary panels, scanners, and audits are the main means by which these data are collected. For example, the Nielsen Television Index provides information on the audience size and the demographic characteristics of households watching specific television programs. Scanner volume tracking data, such as those generated by electronic scanning at check-out counters in supermarkets, are also provided by the A. C. Nielsen Company. The Stanford Research Institute, on the other hand, conducts an annual survey of consumers that is used to classify persons into homogeneous groups for segmentation purposes. The National Purchase Diary panel maintains the largest diary panel in the United States. Syndicated services are discussed in more detail in Chapter 4.[27]

standardized services
Companies that use standardized procedures to provide marketing research to various clients.

customized services
Companies that tailor research procedures to best meet the needs of each client.

limited-service suppliers
Companies that specialize in one or a few phases of a marketing research project.

field services Companies whose primary service offering is their expertise in collecting data for research projects.

coding and data entry services Companies whose primary service offering is their expertise in converting completed surveys or interviews into a usable database for conducting statistical analysis.

analytical services
Companies that provide guidance in the development of the research design.

data analysis services
Firms whose primary service is to conduct statistical analysis of quantitative data.

branded marketing research products
Specialized data collection and analysis procedures developed to address specific types of marketing research problems.

Standardized services are research studies conducted for different clients but in a standard way. For example, procedures for measuring advertising effectiveness have been standardized so that the results can be compared across studies and evaluative norms can be established. The Starch Readership Survey is the most widely used service for evaluating print advertisements; another well-known service is the Gallup and Robinson Magazine Impact Studies. These services are also sold on a syndicated basis.

Customized services offer a wide variety of marketing research services specifically designed to suit a client's particular needs. Each marketing research project is treated uniquely. Some marketing research firms that offer these services include Burke Marketing Research, Market Facts, Inc., and Elrick & Lavidge.

Limited-service suppliers specialize in one or a few phases of a marketing research project. Services offered by such suppliers are classified as field services, coding and data entry, data analysis, analytical services, and branded products. **Field services** collect data through mail, personal interviews, or telephone interviews, and firms that specialize in interviewing are called field service organizations. These organizations may range from small proprietary organizations that operate locally to large multinational organizations with WATS line interviewing facilities. Some organizations maintain extensive interviewing facilities across the country for interviewing shoppers in malls. Many offer qualitative data collection services such as focus group interviewing (discussed in Chapter 5). Some firms that offer field services are Field Facts, Inc., Field Work Chicago, Inc., Quality Controlled Services, and Survey America.

Coding and data entry services include editing completed questionnaires, developing a coding scheme, and transcribing the data onto diskettes or magnetic tapes for input into a computer. NRC Data Systems provides such services.

Analytical services include designing and pretesting questionnaires, determining the best means of collecting data, and designing sampling plans, as well as other aspects of the research design. Some complex marketing research projects require knowledge of sophisticated procedures, including specialized experimental designs (discussed in Chapter 7) and analytical techniques such as conjoint analysis and multidimensional scaling (discussed in Chapter 21). This kind of expertise can be obtained from firms and consultants specializing in analytical services.

Data analysis services are offered by firms, also known as tab houses, that specialize in computer analysis of quantitative data such as those obtained in large surveys. Initially, most data analysis firms supplied only tabulations (frequency counts) and cross tabulations (frequency counts that describe two or more variables simultaneously). Now, many firms, such as Sophisticated Data Research, Inc., offer sophisticated data analysis using advanced statistical techniques. With the proliferation of microcomputers and software, many firms now have the capability to analyze their own data, but data analysis firms are still in demand.

Branded marketing research products and services are specialized data collection and analysis procedures developed to address specific types of marketing research problems. These procedures are patented, given brand names, and marketed like any other branded product. Magic Wand by DigiData Entry System is an example of a branded product that transcribes data from printed questionnaires into a computer-readable format. It uses a hand-held scanner to pick up respondent-completed checkmarks, interprets them, and writes them to a disk.

SELECTING A RESEARCH SUPPLIER

A firm that cannot conduct an entire marketing research project in-house must select an external supplier for one or more phases of the project. The firm should compile a list of prospective suppliers from such sources as trade publications, professional directories, and word of mouth. When deciding on criteria for selecting an outside supplier, a firm should ask itself why it is seeking outside marketing research support. For example, a small firm that needs one project investigated may find it economically efficient to employ an outside source. Or a firm may not have the technical expertise to undertake certain phases of a project, or political conflict-of-interest issues may determine that a project be conducted by an outside supplier.

When developing criteria for selecting an outside supplier, a firm should keep some basics in mind. What is the reputation of the supplier? Does the supplier complete projects on schedule? Is the supplier known for maintaining ethical standards? Is the firm flexible? Are the research projects of high quality? What kind and how much experience does the supplier have? Has the firm had experience with projects similar to this one? Does the supplier's personnel have both technical and nontechnical expertise? In other words, in addition to technical skills, are the personnel assigned to the task sensitive to the client's needs, and does the firm share the client's research ideology? Can the supplier communicate well with the client?

Remember that the cheapest bid is not always the best one. Competitive bids should be obtained and compared on the basis of quality as well as price. A good practice is to get a written bid or contract before beginning the project. Decisions about marketing research suppliers, just like other management decisions, should be based on sound information.

CAREERS IN MARKETING RESEARCH

Promising career opportunities are available with marketing research firms (e.g., Arbitron, Burke Marketing Research Inc., M/A/R/C). Equally appealing are careers in business and nonbusiness firms and agencies with in-house marketing research departments (e.g., Procter & Gamble, Coca-Cola, AT&T, the Federal Trade Commission, the U. S. Census Bureau). Advertising agencies (e.g., BBDO International, Ogilvy & Mather, J. Walter Thompson, Young & Rubicam) also conduct substantial marketing research and employ professionals in this field. Some of the positions available in marketing research include vice-president of marketing research, research director, assistant director of research, project manager, statistician/data processing specialist, senior analyst, analyst, junior analyst, and field work director. Figure 1.5 lists job titles in marketing research and describes their accompanying responsibilities.[28] Research in Practice 1.4 gives several examples of job ads one might see in newspapers, journals, and trade magazines.[29]

The most common entry-level position in marketing research for people with bachelor's degrees (e.g., a B.B.A.) is as operational supervisor. These people are responsible for supervising a well-defined set of operations, including field work, data editing, and coding, and may be involved in programming and data analysis. Another entry-level position for those with B.B.A.s is assistant project manager. An assistant project manager will learn and assist in questionnaire design, will review field instructions, and will monitor timing and costs of studies. In the marketing research industry, however, there

FIGURE 1.5

Selected Marketing Research Job Descriptions

1. **Vice-President of Marketing Research:** The senior position in marketing research. The vice-president (VP) is responsible for the entire marketing research operation of the company and serves on the top management team. This person sets the objectives and goals of the marketing research department.
2. **Research Director:** Also a senior position. The research director has the overall responsibility for the development and execution of all the marketing research projects.
3. **Assistant Director of Research:** Serves as an administrative assistant to the director and supervises some of the other marketing research staff members.
4. **(Senior) Project Manager:** Has overall responsibility for design, implementation, and management of research projects.
5. **Statistician/Data Processing Specialist:** Serves as an expert on theory and application of statistical techniques. Responsibilities include experimental design, data processing, and analysis.
6. **Senior Analyst:** Participates in the development of projects and directs the operational execution of the assigned projects. The senior analyst works closely with the analyst, junior analyst, and other personnel in developing the research design and data collection and prepares the final report. The primary responsibility for meeting time and cost constraints rest with the senior analyst.
7. **Analyst:** Handles the details involved in executing the project. The analyst designs and pretests the questionnaires and conducts a preliminary analysis of the data.
8. **Junior Analyst:** Handles routine assignments such as secondary data analysis, editing and coding of questionnaires, and simple statistical analysis.
9. **Field Work Director:** Responsible for the selection, training, supervision, and evaluation of interviewers and other field workers.

is a growing preference for people with master's degrees. Those with with an M.B.A. or equivalent degrees are likely to be employed as project managers. In marketing research firms such as Elrick and Lavidge, the project manager works with the account director in managing the day-to-day operations of a marketing research project. The typical entry-level position in a business firm would be junior research analyst (for B.B.A.s) or research analyst (for M.B.A.s). The junior analyst and the research analyst learn about the particular industry and receive training from a senior staff member, usually the marketing research manager. The junior analyst position includes a training program to prepare individuals for the responsibilities of a research analyst, including coordinating with the marketing department and sales force to develop goals for product exposure. The research analyst's responsibilities include checking all data for accuracy, comparing and contrasting new research with established norms, and analyzing primary and secondary data for the purpose of market forecasting.

As these job titles indicate, people with a variety of backgrounds and skills are needed in marketing research. Technical specialists such as statisticians obviously need strong backgrounds in statistics and data analysis. Other positions, such as research director, call for managing the work of others and thus require more general skills. To prepare for a career in marketing research you should:

- Take all the marketing courses you can.
- Take courses in statistics and quantitative methods.
- Acquire computer skills for both mainframe computers and microcomputers. Knowledge of programming languages is an added asset.
- Take courses in psychology and consumer behavior.

A Sample of Marketing Research Jobs

Marketing

Apple Computer has created an environment as progressive and breakthrough as the products we bring to market. Here, your ideas are heard. And your ability to shape the industry is as unlimited as your ambition. Join us, and we'll give you the freedom to inspire the kind of change that can impact our future—and yours.

Senior Customer Research Analyst

Using custom market research, you'll be responsible for answering a wide range of complex marketing and strategic questions, and for advocating the customer's perspective in key Apple decisions. Working with product marketing and corporate decision-makers, you'll assist in setting priorities, and in defining/refining corporate objectives. You'll also design and manage research projects, including studies of positioning, new product benefits, concept testing, etc. Then, you'll present results and make recommendations.

The ideal candidate will have a relevant advanced degree and 5+ years' experience, a BA and 8 years' experience, or an equivalent combination of training and experience, including the management of projects using the full range of research methodology. Superior verbal and written communication skills, and the ability to synthesize research results into persuasive recommendations, are absolutely essential. Fluency in a foreign language and direct experience with PC customers in a non-research capacity are also desirable assets.

Send your resume to: Apple Computer, Inc., 1 Infinite Loop, MS 75-2CE, Dept. YCMN01313, Cupertino, CA 95014. Or fax to: (408) 974-5691. Principals only, no phone calls, please.

Apple Computer has a corporate commitment to the principle of diversity. In that spirit, we welcome applications from all individuals.

Apple

Market Research Manager

Hilti, a worlwide leader in the manufacturing and marketing of construction tools and fasteners for nearly half a century, is presently seeking a Marketing Research Manager for our Tulsa, Oklahoma corporate facility.

Responsible for all primary and secondary Market Research functions, the candidate for this position must be able to perform all functions; surveys, focus groups, analysts, database management and presentation of results. In addition, the incumbent must be able to work with outside suppliers of services.

Qualified candidates must possess:
- Bachelor's degree plus five years of industrial market research
- Specific experience writing and conducting both phone and written surveys including analysis and presentation of the results.
- Complete competency conducting focus groups with customers with responsibility for the entire process.
- Experience utilizing secondary sources such as supplier databases (i.e. Dodge and D&B).
- Absolute wizardry with database programs such as D-base and Access.
- Experience gathering intelligence on competitors from traditional and non-traditional sources.
- Highly developed business writing and presentation skills.

Individuals meeting our requirements and seeking a career with an industry leader offering a competitive salary and excellent benefits should send a resume complete with salary history to:

HILTI INC.
Attn: Personnel Manager, Corporate Division
P.O. Box 21148, Tulsa, OK 74121
Or fax your resume to (918) 250-8089.
Our job line number is (918) 252-6001.

No phone calls or agencies please! Hilti is proud to be an Equal Opportunity Employer MF/V/

INCORPORATED

MARKET RESEARCH

Smith Hanley Associates is the premier resource for the market research professional nationwide. Below is a sample of current openings:

•**Consumer Research**—Financial services, publishing and packaged goods companies seek Master's/MBA with 3-8 yrs. quantitative research experience. Multivariate statistics & project management skills desired. Many locations: NY, CA, D.C., MA, IL, MI, TX, NE, KS, UT, KY, IN, NC. Salary $45-75K.

•**Directors, Market Analysis**—Interactive media, entertainment software or telecommunication ind. exp. desired for high profile opportunities. Stellar MBA w/3-4 yrs. exp. in bus. modeling & sales forecasting E. Coast Salary $60-80K + Bonus.

•**Management Consulting**—Top tier consulting firms seek PhD/Master's in quantitative discipline for strategic mkt research groups. Survey research and statistical modeling exp. required. Projects include product positioning, market entry, sales force strategy. Boston and New York. Salary $50-100K.

•**Direct Marketing**—Red hot field for researchers with a strong technical bent. Positions in publishing, catalogues, ad agencies, financial services, and consulting firms. Segmentation modeling and experience with neural nets desired. Dozens of positions nationwide! Salary $40-90K + Bonus.

SMITH HANLEY
Associates, Inc.

Please call or write:

Linda Burtch
312-629-2400
200 W. Madison, Chicago, IL 60606

Sandra Rupp
212-687-9696
99 Park Ave., New York, NY 10016

EXECUTIVE RECRUITERS

- Acquire effective written and verbal communication skills.
- Think creatively. Creativity and common sense command a premium in marketing research.

Marketing researchers should be liberally educated so that they can understand the problems confronting managers and address them from a broad perspective.[30] The following example shows what managers look for in entry-level employees.

EXAMPLE
Amoco Digs for the Right Stuff

Abdul Azhari, marketing research director for Amoco, Chicago, looks for the following credentials when hiring new members for his department:

"It's essential that they know how to dig into the analytical matters, that they know how to analyze things. Also, it's essential that they know how to analyze data with an eye to practicality and application to marketing needs. It is also essential that they can communicate verbally and in writing to the various client departments that we have and also adjust communication to these various departments so that when they are with R&D people, they talk the language of scientists. When the client is the director of sales, they have to be able to speak 'marketingese.' Their written word as well as their presentation must be appropriate to the audience.

"They must look at the broad picture. They must see the forest—not only the trees. They must also understand that marketing research is one element of the process and is not the end itself."[31]◆

MARKETING RESEARCH PROCESS

marketing research process A set of six steps that defines the tasks to be accomplished in conducting a marketing research study. These are problem definition, development of an approach to the problem, research design formulation, field work, data preparation and analysis, and report preparation and presentation.

We conceptualize the **marketing research process** as consisting of six steps. Each of these steps is discussed in great detail in the subsequent chapters; thus, the discussion here is brief.

Step 1: Problem Definition   The first step in any marketing research project is to define the problem. In defining the problem, the researcher should take into account the purpose of the study, the relevant background information, what information is needed, and how it will be used in decision making. Problem definition involves discussion with the decision makers, interviews with industry experts, analysis of secondary data, and perhaps some qualitative research, such as focus groups. Once the problem has been precisely defined, the research can be designed and conducted properly. (See Chapter 2.)

Step 2: Development of an Approach to the Problem   Development of an approach to the problem includes formulating an objective or theoretical framework; preparing analytical models, research questions, and hypotheses; and identifying characteristics or factors that can influence the research design. This process is guided by discussions with management and industry experts, analysis of secondary data, qualitative research, and pragmatic considerations. (See Chapter 2.)

Step 3: Research Design Formulation   A research design is a framework or blueprint for conducting a marketing research project. It details the procedures necessary for obtaining the required information, and its purpose is to design a study that will test the hypotheses of interest, determine possible answers to the research questions, and provide the information needed for decision making. Conducting exploratory research, precisely defining the variables, and designing appropriate scales to measure them are also a part of the research design. The issue of how the data should be obtained from the respondents (for example, by conducting a survey or an experiment) must be addressed. It is also necessary to design a questionnaire and a sampling plan to select respondents for the study. More formally, formulating the research design involves the following steps:

1. Secondary data analysis
2. Qualitative research
3. Methods of collecting quantitative data (survey, observation, and experimentation)
4. Definition of the information needed
5. Measurement and scaling procedures
6. Questionnaire design
7. Sampling process and sample size
8. Plan of data analysis

These steps are discussed in detail in Chapters 3 through 12.

Step 4: Field Work or Data Collection   Data collection involves a field force or staff that operates either in the field, as in the case of personal interviewing (in-home, mall intercept, or computer-assisted personal interviewing), from an office by telephone (telephone or computer-assisted telephone interviewing), or through mail (traditional mail or mail panel surveys with prerecruited households). Proper selection, training, supervision, and evaluation of the field force help minimize data collection errors. (See Chapter 13.)

Step 5: Data Preparation and Analysis   Data preparation includes the editing, coding, transcription, and verification of data. Each questionnaire or observation form is inspected or edited and, if necessary, corrected. Number or letter codes are assigned to represent each response to each question in the questionnaire. The data from the questionnaires are transcribed or keypunched onto magnetic tape or disks or are inputted directly into a computer. Verification ensures that the data from the original questionnaires have been accurately transcribed, whereas data analysis gives meaning to the data that have been collected. Univariate techniques are used for analyzing data when there is a single measurement of each element or unit in the sample, or if there are several measurements of each element, each variable is analyzed in isolation. On the other hand, multivariate techniques are used for analyzing data when there are two or more measurements on each element and the variables are analyzed simultaneously. (See Chapters 14 through 21.)

Step 6: Report Preparation and Presentation   The entire project should be documented in a written report that addresses the specific research questions identified; describes the approach, research design, data collection, and data analysis procedures adopted; and presents the results and major findings. The findings should be presented in a comprehensible format so that they can be readily used in the decision-making process. In addition, an oral presentation to management should be made using tables, figures, and graphs to enhance clarity and impact. (See Chapter 22.)

As indicated by Research in Practice 1.5, our description of the marketing research process is fairly typical of the research being done by major corporations.[32]

RESEARCH IN PRACTICE 1.5

Marketing Research at Marriott Corporation

Marriott functions in three main areas: lodging (Marriott Hotels and Resorts, Marriott Suites, Residence Inns, Courtyard Hotels, and Fairfield Inns), contract services (Marriott Business Food and Services, Education, Health Care, In-Flight Services, and Host International, Inc.) and restaurants (family restaurants, Travel Plazas, and Hot Shoppes). It is probably best known, however, for its lodging operations.

Marketing research at Marriott is done at the corporate level through the Corporate Marketing Services (CMS). CMS's goals include providing the management of the different areas of Marriott with the information that they need to understand the market and the customer better. CMS conducts many different types of research. They use quantitative and qualitative research approaches such as telephone and mail surveys, focus groups, and customer intercept to gain more information on market segmentation and sizing, product testing, price sensitivity of consumers, consumer satisfaction, and the like.

The process of research at Marriott is a simple stepwise progression. The first steps are to define the problem to be addressed and the objectives of the client unit better and to develop an approach to the problem. The next step is to formulate a research design and design the study. CMS must decide whether to conduct its own research or buy it from an outside organization. If the latter option is chosen, CMS must decide whether or not to use multiple firms. Once a decision is made, the research is carried out by collecting and analyzing the data. Then, CMS presents the study findings. The final step in the research process is to keep a constant dialogue between the client and CMS. During this stage, CMS may help explain the implications of the research findings or may make suggestions for future actions.

THE DEPARTMENT STORE PATRONAGE PROJECT

A department store patronage project conducted by the author is used as a running example throughout this text to illustrate concepts and data analysis procedures. The purpose of this project was to assess the relative strengths and weaknesses of a major department store, relative to a group of direct and indirect competitors. This store will be referred to as Sears; the true identity of the actual store has been disguised. The goal was to formulate marketing programs designed to boost the declining sales and profits of Sears. Ten major stores, including prestigious department stores (e.g., Saks Fifth Avenue, Neiman-Marcus), national chains (e.g., J.C. Penney), discount stores (e.g., Kmart, Woolworth), and some regional chains (e.g., Belk) were considered in this study. A nondisguised questionnaire was designed and administered, using in-home personal interviews, to a convenience sample of 271 households drawn from a major metropolitan area. A six-point scale was used (subjects were asked to check a number from 1 to 6) whenever ratings were obtained. The following information was solicited:

Some Americans were born to shop in department stores. ◆ Sears Department Stores.

1. Familiarity with the ten department stores.
2. Frequency with which household members shopped at each of the ten stores.
3. Relative importance attached to each of the eight factors selected as the choice criteria used in selecting a department store. The eight factors identified as influencing the choice of a department store were quality of merchandise, variety and assortment of merchandise, returns and adjustment policy, service of store personnel, prices, convenience of location, layout of store, and credit and billing policies.
4. Evaluation of the ten stores on each of the eight factors of the choice criteria.
5. Preference ratings for each store.
6. Rankings of the ten stores (from most preferred to least preferred).
7. Degree of agreement with 21 lifestyle statements.
8. Standard demographic characteristics (age, education, etc.).
9. Name, address, and telephone number.

The study helped the sponsor determine consumer perceptions of and preferences for the department store. Areas of weakness were identified in terms of specific factors influencing consumers' choice criteria and in terms of specific product categories. Appropriate marketing programs were designed to overcome these weaknesses. Finally, a positioning strategy was developed to attain a desirable store image.

INTERNATIONAL MARKETING RESEARCH

The United States accounts for only 39% of worldwide marketing research expenditures. About 40% of all marketing research is conducted in Western Europe and 9% in Japan. Most of the research in Europe is done in Germany, the United Kingdom, France, Italy, and Spain.[33] With the globalization of markets, marketing research has assumed a truly international character, and this trend is likely to continue. Several U.S. firms conduct international marketing research, including D & B Marketing Information Services, Information Resources, and Walsh International/PMSI (see Research in Practice 1.3). Foreign-based firms include IMS International, AGB (United Kingdom), Infratest, and GfK (Germany).

Conducting international marketing research (research for true international products), foreign research (research carried out in a country other than the country of the research-commissioning organization), or multinational research (research conducted in all countries or in all important countries where the company is represented) is much more complex than domestic marketing research. All research of this kind, including cross-cultural research, will be discussed under the broad rubric of international marketing research. The environment prevailing in the countries, cultural units, or international markets that are being studied influences the way the six steps of the marketing research process should be performed. These environmental factors and their impact on the marketing research process are discussed in detail in subsequent chapters. In addition, Chapter 23 is devoted exclusively to this topic.

Despite the complexity involved, international marketing research is expected to grow at a faster rate than domestic research. A major contributing factor is that markets for many products in the United States are approaching saturation. In contrast, the markets for these products in other countries are in the early stages of development. This point is well illustrated by the case of mobile phones.

EXAMPLE
Mobile Phones Gain Mobility in Europe

The mobile phone market in Europe is still in its infancy, although the market seems to offer promising potential. Meanwhile, European mobile phone marketers are dialing for consumer dollars. Unlike the business segment, which has a limited market, the consumer market is expected to mean big business for both the hardware marketers and service providers. According to the data provided by Ericsson, the cellular phone penetration rates for each major country in Europe are as follows: Belgium, 0.57%; Denmark, 3.77%; Finland, 6.51%; France, 0.74%; Germany, 0.87%; Hungary, 0.13%; Italy, 1.10%; Norway, 6.12%; Spain, 0.36%; Sweden, 7.51%; and the United Kingdom, 2.26%. The figures indicate that cellular phones have not yet taken off in these countries and that there is a big market potential. Notice that the figures are relatively higher for the Nordic countries such as Norway, Finland, Denmark, and Sweden than for other European countries.

Swatch, a Swiss company, attempted to take advantage of this vast untapped market potential. In November 1992, Swatch made its debut in Italy with a print and poster campaign from Farner Publicis, Zurich. In 1993, Swatch rolled out mobile phones in the United Kingdom, Germany, Switzerland, Sweden, and other international markets. Just like any new product introduction, cellular phones will have to exceed a certain minimum threshold penetration rate before the usage can take off. Takeoff seems to happen when the market has reached 1% to 1.5% penetration.

Marketing research shows that market awareness is the key to growth in the mobile phone category. Therefore, Swatch developed TV spots emphasizing the safety and security aspects of owning a cellular phone. Germany and France are likely to take off next, with the growth rate in Germany doubling to nearly two million users by 1995. It is also expected that with dropping prices, the number and size of the distributors will grow. Market projections indicate that the number of mobile phone users in Europe will nearly triple to sixteen million by 1997. Mobile phone companies like Swatch, which base their marketing strategies on sound marketing research, are the ones most likely to capitalize on this growth potential.[34] ◆

ETHICS IN MARKETING RESEARCH

Ethical issues arise in marketing research for several reasons. Marketing research often involves contact with the respondents and the general public, usually by way of data collection, dissemination of the research findings, and marketing programs such as advertising campaigns based on these findings. Thus, there is the potential to abuse or misuse marketing research by taking advantage of these people, for example by misrepresenting the research findings in advertising. As explained earlier, marketing research is generally conducted by commercial (i.e., for-profit) firms which are either independent research organizations (external suppliers) or departments within corporations (internal suppliers). Most marketing research is conducted for clients representing commercial firms. The profit motive may occasionally cause researchers or clients to compromise the objectivity or professionalism associated with the marketing research process, as the following example illustrates.

EXAMPLE
"Sugging" and "Frugging" are Unethical

A direct marketing company selling insurance and financial products has developed a life insurance policy targeted at the low-income family. A concise survey, which fits on the back of a check for two dollars, is developed with the motive of generating sales leads. It asks for information about life insurance policies, demographics, and concludes with a question on whether more information is desired. The survey is mailed with a letter to residents in targeted communities. The letter begins by announcing, "Two dollars for two minutes of your time." The respondent is requested to answer the survey questions and cash the check. The company collects the returned checks. Salespeople armed with pertinent information gathered from the survey are sent to respondents who checked the more information box. The real purpose of this survey was not scientific investigation but generating sales leads. This practice is unethical and is called "sugging" in the trade language. A similar unethical practice is "frugging" and involves fund raising under the guise of research. The American Marketing Association (AMA) ethical guidelines state, "No individual or organization will undertake any activity which is directly or indirectly represented to be marketing research, but which has as its real purpose the attempted sale of merchandise or services to some or all of the respondents interviewed in the course of the research."[35] ◆

Marketing research has often been described as having four stakeholders. These stakeholders are (1) the marketing researcher, (2) the client, (3) the respondent, and (4) the public. Ethical issues can be understood in terms of the responsibilities these stakeholders have to each other and to the research project. Questions of ethics arise when the interests of these stakeholders are in conflict. When conflict occurs it becomes the responsibility of the stakeholders involved to behave honorably. Sometimes accepted codes of conduct, such as the AMA code of ethics in the preceding example, help guide this behavior. Often, decisions rely solely on the character of the stakeholder. These ethical issues are discussed in more detail in the subsequent chapters and in Chapter 24 which is devoted to ethical theories and models and which presents a framework for incorporating ethics in marketing research.

COMPUTER APPLICATIONS

Computers—mainframes and microcomputers—have had a profound impact on marketing and marketing research. In this book, we show how microcomputers and mainframes can be integrated in each step of the marketing research process. We focus on both types of computers because both systems are used in practice, and abundant software has been developed to facilitate interaction between microcomputers and mainframes. For example, EPSILON INSIGHT by Epsilon Inc. retrieves information from a mainframe database for further analysis and formatting with a PC spreadsheet, database, or statistics package.[36] The processed data can be transferred to the mainframe, transcribed on a tape or disk, or printed. It is available for IBM PCs and compatibles as well as Apple microcomputers. Part IV of this book illustrates the use of the mainframe and microcomputer versions of the three popular statistical packages, SPSS, SAS, and BMDP.

Developers of software programs have targeted marketing research as an area ready for the benefits of software application. Numerous marketing research software products have become available in recent years. One such program is STATPAC GOLD IV developed by StatPac, Inc. of Minneapolis. This program was developed to have multiple uses in the marketing research process. STATPAC GOLD IV represents one of the most comprehensive survey and marketing research software systems available today. It is a valuable tool in each step of the market research process. With add-on modules to the basic system, STATPAC GOLD IV can handle all aspects of study design, sampling, data management, basic statistics, advanced statistics, and graphics. In short, such a software system can help in just about every step of collecting data and transforming these data into relevant information.

Questions for a research survey can be created with the STATPAC GOLD IV study design program. The program offers assistance in designing the questionnaire itself. The resulting questionnaire can be loaded into a word processor for final editing and enhancements or can appear as entry screens in computer-assisted telephone interviewing (CATI) or computer-assisted personal interviewing (CAPI).

STATPAC GOLD IV can determine the sample size needed for any desired confidence level or margin of error. The telephone manager module allows the importation of a list of names and phone numbers from another source. The program can also automatically dial these numbers and track completed interviews.

After data collection, answers to questions on the survey can be entered into a data matrix for tabulation and analysis by the STATPAC GOLD IV program. This data entry process will be expedited by the screen templates or snapshots of the actual questionnaire with branching in the questionnaire controlled by skip patterns. Errors in data entry are reduced by STATPAC GOLD IV's range checking for acceptable values for each question.

Most of the statistical techniques discussed in this book are available in STATPAC GOLD IV. The preview editor can be used to review and edit results of analyses prior to printing. In effect, each report can be customized in appearance to a degree.

As an example of problem-solving research, fast-food restaurant chains such as McDonald's and Arby's interview consumers on a regular basis to evaluate new product offerings these firms have in development. Taste tests are part of such evaluations. To tabulate responses from these taste tests, a statistical software program, such as STATPAC GOLD IV, can be used.

Suppose McDonald's develops a new veggie burger sandwich. A survey of consumers is conducted in which the respondents are asked to taste the veggie burger and evaluate it on the dimensions of taste, smell, texture, appearance and package design.

Exhibit 1.1 shows a STATPAC GOLD IV output file featuring the tabulations of taste test results for one segment of the survey sample, the 16–20 year age group, which accounts for 10% of the sample. The number of responses for the values of each question are included along with the corresponding percentages to which these responses account. Here, the evaluated veggie burger receives only middling ratings on the various dimensions from this age group as at least 65% of the frequency counts for each question are in the "good" or "fair" categories. The results indicate that research with another larger sample is in order because the other age groups in the sample gave much higher ratings to the veggie burger. STATPAC GOLD IV's ability to conduct subgroup analysis identifies an important question for future research: in general, do 16–20 year olds view the veggie burger differently than other age groups?

Although STATPAC GOLD IV provides the market researcher a nearly complete tool kit for conducting survey research, it must be compared on cost, training required, and adaptability with the specialized needs of the industry or market area to be studied. There is no doubt that integrated software packages such as STATPAC GOLD IV should continue to evolve to provide more user-friendliness in the Windows environment for the PC, which will reduce required training for the program. Despite years of improvements, and more than 15,000 users, a competitive market for marketing research software should push the makers of programs such as STATPAC GOLD IV to offer even more adaptability and reasonable prices to attract more users to their systems.

EXHIBIT 1.1

A STATPAC GOLD IV Output File

General Attribute Ratings

(N=31)	Excellent 1	Good 2	Fair 3	Poor 4	Total
How would you rate the taste?	7 24.1	8 27.6	11 37.9	3 10.3	29 100.0
How would you rate the smell?	4 13.8	9 31.0	12 41.4	4 13.8	29 100.0
How would you rate the texture?	1 3.4	13 44.8	14 48.3	1 3.4	29 100.0
How would you rate the appearance?	4 13.8	10 34.5	11 37.9	4 13.8	29 100.0
How would you rate the package design?	6 20.7	11 37.9	8 27.6	4 13.8	29 100.0

Page 1 Of 1   Press [F1] For Help

SUMMARY

Marketing research provides information about consumers, channel members, competitors, changes and trends in the marketplace, and other aspects of the firm's environment. The purpose of marketing research is to assess information needs and provide the relevant information in a systematic and objective manner so as to improve marketing decision making. Marketing research may be classified into problem identification research and problem-solving research. Information obtained using marketing research becomes an integral part of the MIS and DSS. Marketing research contributes to the DSS by providing research data to the database, marketing models and analytical techniques to the model base, and specialized marketing research programs to the software base.

Marketing research may be conducted internally (by internal suppliers) or may be purchased from external suppliers. Full-service suppliers provide the entire range of marketing research services, from problem definition to report preparation and presentation. The services provided by these suppliers can be classified as syndicated services, standardized services, or customized services. Limited-service suppliers specialize in one or a few phases of the marketing research project. Services offered by these suppliers can be classified as field services, coding and data entry, data analysis, analytical services, or branded products.

Due to the need for marketing research, attractive career opportunities are available with marketing research firms, business and nonbusiness firms and agencies with marketing research departments, and advertising agencies. The marketing research process consists of six steps that must be followed systematically. International marketing research is much more complex than domestic research because the researcher must consider the environment prevailing in the international markets being researched. Marketing research makes extensive use of microcomputers and mainframes.[37]

ACRONYMS

The role and salient characteristics of marketing research may be described by the acronym RESEARCH:

R   ecognition of information needs
E   ffective decision making
S   ystematic and objective
E   xude/disseminate information
A   nalysis of information
R   ecommendations for action
C   ollection of information
H   elpful to managers

EXERCISES

QUESTIONS

1. Describe the task of marketing research.
2. What decisions are made by marketing managers? How does marketing research help in making these decisions?
3. Define marketing research.

4. Describe one classification of marketing research.
5. What is a marketing information system?
6. How is a DSS different from an MIS?
7. Explain one way to classify marketing research suppliers and services.
8. What are syndicated services?
9. What is the main difference between a full-service and a limited-service supplier?
10. What are branded products?
11. List five guidelines for selecting an external marketing research supplier.
12. What career opportunities are available in marketing research?
13. Discuss the ethical issues in marketing research that relate to the (1) client, (2) the supplier, and (3) the respondent.
14. Describe the steps in the marketing research process.

PROBLEMS

1. Look through recent issues of newspapers and magazines to identify five examples of problem identification research and five examples of problem-solving research.
2. List one kind of marketing research that would be useful to each of the following organizations:
   a. Your campus bookstore
   b. The public transportation authority in your city
   c. A major department store in your area
   d. A restaurant located near your campus
   e. A zoo in a major city

COMPUTER EXERCISES

1. Examine recent issues of magazines such as *Marketing News, Advertising Age, Quirk's Marketing Research Review*, and *Marketing Research: A Magazine of Management and Applications* to identify one mainframe or one microcomputer application in each of the following areas:
   a. Identification of information needs
   b. Collection of information
   c. Analysis of information
   d. Provision of information (report preparation)

NOTES

1. "Attitude Surveys Keep Phone Company in Touch," *Quirk's Marketing Research Review* (June–July 1988): 6, 22–24.
2. Susan Garland, Richard Dunham, and Laura Zinn, "Polling for policy, How Clinton Uses Whiz-Bang Marketing to Make Decisions," *Business Week* (February 22, 1993): 34–35.
3. G. McWilliams, "A Notebook that Puts Users Ahead of Gimmicks," *Business Week* (September 27, 1993): 92–93.
4. Rich Ceppos, "Is Anybody Out There Listening?" *Car and Driver* (October 1987): 24–25.
5. "Hospital Puttin' on the Ritz to Target High-End Market," *Marketing News* (January 17, 1986): 14.
6. Joe Schwartz, "Marketing the Verdict," *American Demographics* (February 1993): 52–54.
7. "Research Service Satisfies Businesses' Information Needs," *Quirk's Marketing Research Review* (June–July 1988): 8–10, 24.

8. For the strategic role of marketing research, see Noel B. Zabriskie and Alan B. Huellmantel, "Marketing Research as a Strategic Tool," *Long-Range Planning* 27 (February 1994): 107–18.

9. For relationship among information processing, marketing decisions, and performance, see Rashi Glazer and Allen M. Weiss, "Marketing in Turbulent Environments: Decision Process and the Time-Sensitivity of Information," *Journal of Marketing Research* 30 (November 1993): 509–21.

10. Rebecca Fannin, "More Marketers Are Using Creative Brand Extensions to Expand Their Franchises. The Question Is: Can the Practice Be too Much of a Stretch?" *Marketing and Media Decisions* (January 1987): 22–28.

11. For the role of marketing research in marketing management, see Anthony Freeling, "Marketing is in Crisis—Can Marketing Research Help?," *Journal of the Market Research Society* 36 (April 1994): 97–104.

12. N.K. Malhotra, "Shifting Perspective on the Shifting Paradigm in Marketing Research," *Journal of the Academy of Marketing Science* 20 (Fall 1992): 379–87; and William Perreault "The Shifting Paradigm in Marketing Research," *Journal of the Academy of Marketing Science* 20 (Fall 1992): 367–75.

13. Reported in "New Marketing Research Definition Approved," *Marketing News* 21 (January 2, 1987): 1, 14.

14. For a historical discussion and an assessment of marketing research, see L. McTier Anderson, "Marketing Science: Where's the Beef?" *Business Horizons* 37 (January–February 1994): 8–16; Alvin J. Silk, "Marketing Science in a Changing Environment," *Journal of Marketing Research* 30 (November 1993): 401–4; and Frank M. Bass, "The Future of Research in Marketing: Marketing Science," *Journal of Marketing Research* 30 (February 1993): 1–6.

15. Dick Warren Twedt, *Survey of Marketing Research* (Chicago: American Marketing Association, 1983).

16. Dick Warren Twedt, *Survey of Marketing Research* (Chicago: American Marketing Association, 1983).

17. "Say Goodnight Ovaltineys," *Marketing* (November 27, 1986): 25–27.

18. David Cowan, "Good Information—Generals Can't Do Without It. Why Do CEOs Think They Can?" *Journal of the Market Research Society* 36 (April 1994): 105–14.

19. E. Turban, *Decision Support and Expert Systems* (New York: Macmillan, 1990); John McCann, Ali Tadlaoui, and John Gallagher, "Knowledge Systems in Merchandising: Advertising Designs," *Journal of Retailing* (Fall 1990): 257–77.

20. Sunil Gupta and Rajeev Kohli, "A Knowledge-Based System for Advertising Design." *Marketing Science* (Summer 1990): 212–29.

21. Giuseppe A. Forgionne, "Using Decision Support Systems to Market Prepaid Medical Plans," *Journal of Health Care Marketing* (December 1991): 22–38; Ralph H. Sprague, Jr., and Hugh J. Watson, *Decision Support Systems: Putting Theory into Practice* (Englewood Cliffs, NJ: Prentice Hall, 1986), p. 1.

22. Naresh K. Malhotra, "Decision Support Systems for Health Care Marketing Managers," *Journal of Health Care Marketing* 9 (June 1989): 20–28.

23. Lee Adler and Charles S. Mayer, eds., *Readings in Managing the Marketing Research Function* (Chicago: American Marketing Association, 1980). See also Rashi Glazer, "Marketing in an Information-Intensive Environment: Strategic Implications of Knowledge as an Asset," *Journal of Marketing*, 55 (October 1991): 1–19.

24. Charlie Etmekjian and John Grede, "Marketing Research in a Team-Oriented Business: The Oscar Mayer Approach," *Marketing Research: A Magazine of Management and Applications* (December 1990): 6–12.

25. A complete listing and description of the individual firms in the marketing research industry is provided in Ryan P. Green, *International Directory of Marketing Research Houses and Services* (New York Chapter, American Marketing Association, annual).

26. Jack Honomichl, "The Honomichl 50," *Marketing News*, 29 (June 5, 1995): H1–H43. Copyright ©1995 by the American Marketing Association. Reprinted by permission.

27. For a historical note and future directions in syndicated services, see Mike Penford, "Continuous Research—Art Nielsen to AD 2000," *Journal of the Market Research Society* 36 (January 1994): 19–28; and Edward C. Dittus, "Marketing Research Directions in the USA," *Journal of the Market Research Society* 36 (January 1994): 29–40.

28. Thomas C. Kinnear and Ann R. Root, *1988 Survey of Marketing Research* (Chicago: American Marketing Association, 1989).

29. A discussion of the characteristics of successful researchers and typical career paths is provided by John R. Blair, "Marketing Research Offers Highly Visible Action-Oriented Career with Growth Potential," by Emanuel H. Demby, "The Marketing Researcher: A Professional Statistician, Social Scientist—Not Just Another Business Practitioner," and by Lawrence D. Gibson, "Confused New Marketing Researchers Soon Feel Confidence, Then Challenge," in *Student Edition Marketing News* 2 (March 1984): 1, 3, and 7. Some suggestions for preparing for a career in marketing research are made by Michael Boudreaux, "Prepare for Your Future in Marketing, Your Interviews, and Something 'Extra,'" *Student Edition Marketing News* 2 (March 1984): 3.

30. Ralph W. Giacobbe and Madhav N. Segal, "Rethinking Marketing Research Education: A Conceptual, Analytical, and Empirical Investigation," *Journal of Marketing Education* 16 (Spring 1994): 43–58.

31. "AMR Interviews Abdul Azhari, on Today and the Future of Marketing Research at a Major Corporation," *Applied Marketing Research* (Spring 1989): 3–8.

32. "Listening to Customers: The Market Research Function at Marriott Corporation," *Marketing Research: A Magazine of Management and Applications* (March 1989): 5–14.

33. E. H. Demby, "ESOMAR Urges Changes in Reporting Demographics, Issues Worldwide Report," *Marketing News* 24(1) (January 8, 1990): 24–25.

34. Elena Bowes and David Bartal, "Mobile Phones Call to Consumers, " *Advertising Age* (January 18, 1993). Copyright ©1993 by Crain Communications, Inc.

35. Gene R. Lacyniak and Patrick E. Murphy, "Marketing Research Code of Ethics of the American Marketing Association," *Ethical Marketing Decision: The Higher Road* (Needham Heights, MA: Allyn and Bacon, 1993), pp. 76–7. Reprinted with permission from the American Marketing Association, Chicago, IL 60606.

36. Nancy J. Merritt and Cecile Bouchy, "Are Microcomputers Replacing Mainframes in Marketing Research Firms?" *Journal of the Academy of Marketing Science* 20 (Winter 1992): 81–85. Information about the software cited in this book, if not referenced, can be obtained from recent issues of *Marketing News* and *Marketing Research: A Magazine of Management and Applications*, published by the American Marketing Association, or from a software vendor directory.

37. The assistance of James Agarwal with the international marketing research example, the assistance of Mark Leach and Gina Miller in writing the ethics section, and the assistance of Mark Peterson in writing the computer applications section is gratefully acknowledged.

CHAPTER TWO

Defining the Marketing Research Problem and Developing an Approach

Problem definition is the most important step in a marketing research project. An incorrect approach to a problem will, at best, lead to wasted resources. At worst, it may lead to wrong decisions.

◆

OBJECTIVES

After reading this chapter, the student should be able to:

1. Understand the importance of and process used for defining the marketing research problem.
2. Describe the tasks involved in problem definition, including discussions with decision makers, interviews with industry experts, secondary data analysis, and qualitative research.
3. Discuss the environmental factors affecting the definition of the research problem: past information and forecasts, resources and constraints, objectives of the decision maker, buyer behavior, legal environment, economic environment, and marketing and technological skills of the firm.
4. Clarify the distinction between the management decision problem and the marketing research problem.
5. Explain the structure of a well-defined marketing research problem, including the broad statement and the specific components.
6. Discuss in detail the various components of the approach: objective/theoretical framework, analytical models, research questions, hypotheses, and characteristics or factors influencing the research design.

7. Acquire an appreciation of the complexity involved and gain an understanding of the procedures for defining the problem and developing an approach in international marketing research.
8. Understand the ethical issues and conflicts that arise in defining the problem and developing the approach.
9. Explain how microcomputers and mainframes can facilitate the process of defining the problem and developing an approach.

OVERVIEW

This chapter covers the first two of the six steps of the marketing research process described in Chapter 1: defining the marketing research problem and developing an approach to the problem. Defining the problem is the most important step, since only when a problem has been clearly and accurately identified can a research project be conducted properly. Defining the marketing research problem sets the course of the entire project. In this chapter, we allow the reader to appreciate the complexities involved in defining a problem by identifying the factors to be considered and the tasks involved. Additionally, we provide guidelines for appropriately defining the marketing research problem and avoiding common types of errors. We also discuss in detail the components of an approach to the problem: objective/theoretical framework, analytical models, research questions, hypotheses, and characteristics or factors influencing the research design. The special considerations involved in defining the problem and developing an approach in international marketing research are discussed. Several ethical issues that arise at this stage of the marketing research process are considered. Finally, we discuss the use of microcomputers and mainframes in defining the problem and developing an approach.

We introduce our discussion with examples from *Tennis* magazine, which needed specific information about its readers, and Standard Drug's attempt to create a new standard of personal pharmacy.

EXAMPLE
Research Serves *Tennis* Magazine

Tennis magazine, a publication of the New York Times Company, is as hard-core about its readers as its readers are about the sport of tennis. The management wanted to obtain information about the readers and hired Signet Research, Inc., an independent research company in Cliffside Park, New Jersey, to conduct marketing research.

The marketing research problem was defined as gathering information about the subscribers of *Tennis* magazine. Specific components of the problem included the following:

1. *Demographics.* Who are the men and women who subscribe to the magazine?
2. *Psychological characteristics and lifestyles.* How do the subscribers spend their money and their free time? Lifestyle indicators to be examined were fitness, travel, car rental, apparel, consumer electronics, credit cards, and financial investments.
3. *Tennis activity.* Where and how often do subscribers play tennis? What are their skill levels?
4. *Relationship to* Tennis *magazine.* How much time do subscribers spend with the issues? How long do they keep them? Do they share the magazine with other tennis players?

Because the questions were so clearly defined, the information provided by this research helped management design specific features on tennis instruction, equipment,

Vital information about its readers, obtained by correctly defining marketing research problems, has helped Tennis magazine "turn defense into offense" in protecting its market share. ◆ Churchill & Klehr.

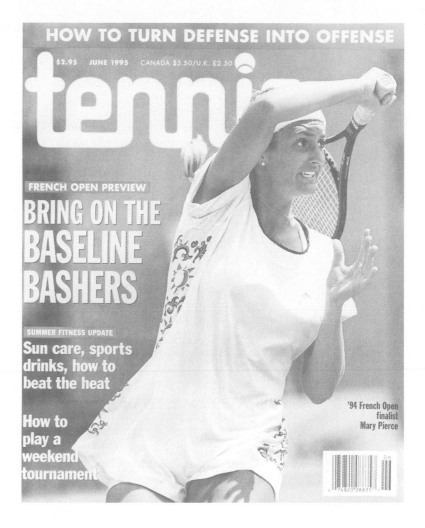

famous tennis players, and locations to play tennis to meet readers' specific needs. These changes made *Tennis* magazine more appealing to readers.[1] ◆

EXAMPLE

Standard Creates a New Standard: Personal Pharmacy

Richmond-based research firm Southeastern Institute of Research (SIR) conducted qualitative research and subsequent quantitative research for Standard Drug, a 60-unit chain of retail drugstores operating throughout Virginia and Washington, D.C. Richmond, Virginia's Edelman Scott advertising agency used the results from these studies to produce an effective communication campaign for Standard.

Because Standard had already undertaken a major renovation of its stores, SIR excluded physical appearance and store aesthetics from its market research study. Instead, the marketing research problem was defined as determining the image and shopping preference for Standard Drug relative to competing drugstores. A major research question was:

RQ: How do consumers perceive service levels of retail drugstores?

The related hypothesis was:

H: There are no significant differences in perceptions of service levels of competing retail drugstores.

SIR gave shopping assignments in competing Richmond pharmacies (and cash) to focus group participants prior to the focus group interviews. The striking finding from this first qualitative research effort was a common misattribution of shopping experience to drugstore. In other words, no competitor's service stood out in the minds of focus group participants. This finding was congruent with industrywide perceptions of retail drugstore service being lower than many other retail establishments. The focus group shoppers also responded to 16 drugstore concepts. Based on these results, 12 were eliminated from further consideration.

Quantitative research, a telephone survey of 300 households using random-digit dialing, helped to identify which of the remaining four concepts would provide Standard with a differentiated position for competition. The findings disclosed that customers most wanted to shop at drugstores with a caring pharmacist.

Based on these results, Edelman Scott designed a TV campaign for Standard. The campaign featured the caring pharmacist of Standard (played by actor William Christopher, known for his long-running portrayal of Father Mulcahy on the TV show M*A*S*H) along with the tagline "We're creating a whole new Standard." In addition to the broadcast media campaign, Standard added pharmacy-related information to the company's newspaper advertising inserts, which rarely mentioned the pharmacy in its printed price/item advertising. Standard also undertook a direct mail campaign to newcomers and residents near renovated stores that specifically asked customers to come in and meet the pharmacist, by name, at the Standard Drug closest to them. This effort resulted in increased pharmacy and drug store sales.[2] ◆

These examples shows the importance of correctly defining the marketing research problem and developing an appropriate approach.

IMPORTANCE OF DEFINING THE PROBLEM

problem definition A broad statement of the general problem and identification of the specific components of the marketing research problem.

Although each step in a marketing research project is important, problem definition is the most important step. As mentioned in Chapter 1, for the purpose of marketing research, problems and opportunities are treated interchangeably. **Problem definition** involves stating the general problem and identifying the specific components of the marketing research problem. Only when the marketing research problem has been clearly defined can research be designed and conducted properly. "Of all the tasks in a marketing research project, none is more vital to the ultimate fulfillment of a client's needs than an accurate and adequate definition of the research problem. All the effort, time, and money spent from this point on will be wasted if the problem is misunderstood and ill-defined."[3] This point is worth remembering, since inadequate problem definition is a leading cause of failure of marketing research projects. Further, a survey of 183 of the largest consumer goods and services companies revealed that better communication and more involvement in problem definition were the most frequently mentioned ways of improving the usefulness of research.[4] These results lead to the conclusion that the importance of clearly identifying and defining the marketing research problem cannot be overstated. Research in Practice 2.1 cites an episode from the author's personal experience to illustrate this point. Further insights on the difficulty involved in appropriately defining the problem are provided by the problem definition process.

RESEARCH IN PRACTICE 2.1

Chain Restaurant Study

One day I received a telephone call from a research analyst who introduced himself as an alumnus of my university. He was working for a restaurant chain in town and wanted help in analyzing the data he had collected while conducting a marketing research study. When we met, he presented me with a copy of the questionnaire and asked how he should analyze the data. My first question to him was, "What is the problem being addressed?" When he looked perplexed, I explained that data analysis was not an independent exercise. Rather, the goal of data analysis is to provide information related to the problem components. I was surprised to learn that he did not have a clear understanding of the marketing research problem and that a written definition of the problem did not exist. So, before proceeding any further, I had to define the marketing research problem. Once that was done, I found that much of the data collected was not relevant to the problem. In this sense, the whole study was a waste of resources. A new study had to be designed and implemented to address the problem identified.

THE PROCESS OF DEFINING THE PROBLEM AND DEVELOPING AN APPROACH

The problem definition and approach development process is shown in Figure 2.1. The tasks involved in problem definition consist of discussions with the decision makers, interviews with industry experts and other knowledgeable individuals, analysis of secondary data, and sometimes qualitative research. These tasks help the researcher to understand the background of the problem by analyzing the environmental context. Certain essential environmental factors bearing on the problem should be evaluated. Understanding of the environmental context facilitates the identification of the management decision problem. Then, the management decision problem is translated into a marketing research problem. Based on the definition of the marketing research problem, an appropriate approach is developed. The components of the approach consist of objective/theoretical framework, analytical models, research questions, hypotheses, and characteristics or factors influencing the research design. Further explanation of the problem definition process begins with a discussion of the tasks involved.

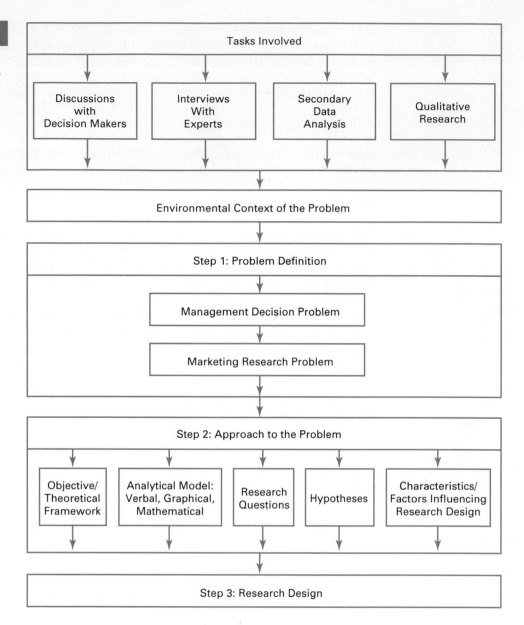

FIGURE 2.1

The Process of Defining the Problem and Developing an Approach

TASKS INVOLVED

The tasks involved in problem definition include discussions with the decision makers, interviews with industry experts, secondary data analysis, and qualitative research. The purposes of these tasks are to obtain information on the environmental context of the problem and to help define the marketing research problem.

Discussions with Decision Makers

Discussions with the decision makers (DMs) are extremely important. The DM needs to understand the capabilities and limitations of research.[5] Research provides information relevant to management decisions, but it cannot provide solutions, because solutions require managerial judgment. Conversely, the researcher needs to understand the nature of the decision the managers face—the management problem—and what they hope to learn from the research.

To identify the management problem, the researcher must possess considerable skill in interacting with the DM. Several factors may complicate this interaction. Access to the DM may be difficult, and some organizations have complicated protocols for access to top executives. The organizational status of the researcher or the research department may make it difficult to reach the key DM in the early stages of the project. Finally, there may be more than one key DM and meeting collectively or individually may be difficult. Despite these problems, it is necessary that the researcher interact directly with the key decision makers.[6]

problem audit A comprehensive examination of a marketing problem to understand its origin and nature.

The problem audit provides a useful framework for interacting with the DM and identifying the underlying causes of the problem. The **problem audit**, like any other type of audit, is a comprehensive examination of a marketing problem with the purpose of understanding its origin and nature.[7] The problem audit involves discussions with the DM on the following issues:

1. The events that led to the decision that action is needed, or the history of the problem.
2. The alternative courses of action available to the DM. The set of alternatives may be incomplete at this stage, and qualitative research may be needed to identify the more innovative courses of action.
3. The criteria that will be used to evaluate the alternative courses of action. For example, new product offerings might be evaluated on the basis of sales, market share, profitability, return on investment, and so forth.
4. The actions that are suggested based on the research findings.
5. The information needed to answer the DM's questions.
6. The manner in which the DM will use each item of information in making the decision.
7. The corporate culture as it relates to decision making.[8] In some firms, the decision-making process is dominant; in others, the personality of the DM is more important. Awareness of corporate culture may be one of the most important factors that distinguishes researchers who affect strategic marketing decisions from those who do not.[9]

It is important to perform a problem audit because the DM, in most cases, has only a vague idea of what the problem is. For example, the DM may know that the firm is losing market share but may not know why, because DMs tend to focus on symptoms rather than on causes. Inability to meet sales forecasts, loss of market share, and decline in profits are all symptoms. The researcher should treat the underlying causes, not merely address the symptoms. For example, loss of market share may be caused by a superior promotion by the competition, inadequate distribution of the company's products, or any number of other factors. Only when the underlying causes are identified can the problem be successfully addressed, as exemplified by the effort of the California Almond Growers Exchange to penetrate the Japanese market.

EXAMPLE

Coca-Cola Goes Nuts in Japan

For five years, the California Almond Growers Exchange (CAGE) was unable to penetrate the almond market in Japan. Management focused on how to increase sales and market share in the Japanese market. Low sales and market share were merely symptoms, however.

Then a problem audit was conducted. An examination of possible underlying causes and alternative courses of action indicated that the Japanese were satisfied with the quality of CAGE almonds. The almonds were competitively priced. The Japanese also viewed the advertising for CAGE almonds, which was handled by a Japanese advertising agency, favorably. The real cause for lack of penetration was that CAGE lacked a distribution system. A decision was then made to use the Coca-Cola distribution system. Coca-Cola had in place 15,000 salespeople, 500 sales offices, and 1.1 million sales locations throughout Japan. CAGE has since captured 70% of the almond market in Japan.[10] ◆

Its intensive distribution system in Japan has not only helped the Coca-Cola company to capture a large share of the soft drink market, it has also assisted partners such as the California Almond Growers Exchange to penetrate the Japanese market. ◆ Photo Researchers Inc.

As in the case of the California Almond Growers Exchange, a problem audit, which involves extensive interaction between the DM and the researcher, can greatly facilitate problem definition by determining the underlying causes. The interaction between the researcher and the DM is facilitated when one or more people in the client organization serve as a liaison and form a team with the marketing researcher. To be fruitful, the interaction between the DM and the researcher should be characterized by the seven Cs:

1. *Communication.* Free exchange of ideas between the DM and researcher is essential.
2. *Cooperation.* Marketing research is a team project in which both parties (DM and researcher) must cooperate.
3. *Confidence.* Mutual trust should underlie the interaction between the DM and the researcher.
4. *Candor.* There should not be any hidden agendas, and an attitude of openness should prevail.
5. *Closeness.* Feelings of warmth and closeness should characterize the relationship between the DM and the researcher.
6. *Continuity.* The DM and the researcher must interact continually rather than sporadically.
7. *Creativity.* The interaction between the DM and the researcher should be creative rather than formulaic.

Interviews with Industry Experts

In addition to discussions with the DM, interviews with industry experts, individuals knowledgeable about the firm and the industry, may help formulate the marketing research problem.[11] These experts may be found both inside and outside the firm. Typically, expert information is obtained by unstructured personal interviews, without administering a formal questionnaire. It is helpful, however, to prepare a list of topics to be covered during the interview. The order in which these topics are covered and the questions to ask should not be predetermined. Instead, they should be decided as the interview progresses, which allows greater flexibility in capturing the insights of the experts. The purpose of interviewing experts is to help define the marketing research problem rather than to develop a conclusive solution. Unfortunately, two potential difficulties may arise when seeking advice from experts:

1. Some individuals who claim to be knowledgeable and are eager to participate may not really possess expertise.
2. It may be difficult to locate and obtain the help from experts who are outside the client organization.

For these reasons, interviews with experts are more useful in conducting marketing research for industrial firms and for products of a technical nature, where it is relatively easy to identify and approach the experts. This method is also helpful in situations where little information is available from other sources, as in the case of radically new products. Experts can provide valuable insights in modifying or repositioning existing products, as illustrated by the repositioning of Pontiac.

EXAMPLE
Pontiac Gears Up for Excitement

During the 1960s and early 1970s, the Pontiac Motor Division of General Motors was very successful. Then the gas crunch and increasing imports of cars hurt the division badly. It lost sales as well as market share. In the early 1980s, Pontiac set out to regain, redefine, and rebuild its products and customer base. The first order of business was to determine what Pontiac was and what it could become. When outside consultants were brought in, the real problem was identified: Pontiac had no image. These experts emphasized that brand image was a key factor influencing automobile sales. Subsequent research on brand image led Pontiac to embrace the "We build excitement" theme and position its cars to younger, better-educated, higher-income buyers. This marketing strategy helped Pontiac become GM's "top import conquester."[12] ◆

The Pontiac example points to the key role of industry experts. Information obtained from the DM and the industry experts should be supplemented with the available secondary data, however.

Secondary Data Analysis

secondary data Data collected for some purpose other than the problem at hand.

primary data Data originated by the researcher specifically to address the research problem.

Secondary data are data collected for some purpose other than the problem at hand. **Primary data**, on the other hand, are originated by the researcher for the specific purpose of addressing the research problem. Secondary data include information made available by business and government sources, commercial marketing research firms, and computerized databases. Secondary data are an economical and quick source of background information. Analysis of available secondary data is an essential step in the problem definition process: primary data should not be collected until the available secondary data have been fully analyzed. Given the tremendous importance of secondary data, this topic will be discussed in detail in Chapter 4, which also further discusses the differences between secondary and primary data. Research in Practice 2.2 illustrates the role of secondary data in problem definition.[13]

RESEARCH IN PRACTICE 2.2

Splice *Splices the Female Teenage Market*

As more new magazines entered the youth market, new marketing problems arose to haunt the magazine industry. Because of increased competition, youth magazines began experiencing a decline in advertising revenues and loss of market share in the late 1980s. In attempting to increase its revenues, *Splice* magazine was guided by secondary data. Research by the U.S. Census Bureau revealed that the number of young adults should decline by 1995, while the number of teenagers will hold steady. Secondary data also indicated that 80% of 15- to 17-year-old girls decide for themselves what brands of hair-care products to buy and most use shampoo seven days a week. Based on this information and internal management discussions, *Splice* determined that its marketing research problem was to target the magazine to a specific market, female teenagers. This target positioning helped *Splice* elicit higher advertising revenues from the cosmetic and personal care industry.

Although valuable insights may be obtained from secondary data, as in the *Splice* magazine targeting study, the findings from secondary data often must be enriched by conducting qualitative research.

Qualitative Research

qualitative research An unstructured, exploratory research methodology based on small samples intended to provide insight and understanding of the problem setting.

Information obtained from the DM and industry experts, along with secondary data may not be sufficient to define the research problem. Sometimes qualitative research must be undertaken to gain an understanding of the problem and its underlying factors. **Qualitative research** is unstructured, exploratory in nature, based on small samples, and may utilize popular qualitative techniques such as focus groups (group interviews), word association (asking respondents to indicate their first responses to stimulus words), and depth interviews (one-on-one interviews that probe the respondents' thoughts in detail). Other exploratory research techniques, such as pilot surveys with small samples of respondents, may also be undertaken. Exploratory research is discussed in more detail in Chapter 3, and qualitative research techniques are discussed in detail in Chapter 5. Although research undertaken at this stage may not be conducted in a formal way, it can provide valuable insights, as illustrated by Avon's attempt to penetrate the Hispanic market.

EXAMPLE

The Many Faces of Hispanic Females

Avon Products Inc., which markets cosmetics to women, was attempting to capture an increased share of the Hispanic market. Secondary data from the U.S. Census Bureau treated Hispanic females as one cultural group. Qualitative research in the form of depth interviews, pilot surveys and observations of the Hispanic community, however, indicated that the Hispanic population has many segments that differ in cultural and historic background as well as in attitudes and beliefs. Based on these findings, the marketing research problem was redefined and narrowed to one of how best to segment the Hispanic female market.[14] ◆

The insights gained from qualitative research, along with discussions with decision maker(s), interviews with industry experts, and secondary data analysis, help the researcher to understand the environmental context of the problem.

ENVIRONMENTAL CONTEXT OF THE PROBLEM

environmental context of the problem The factors that have an impact on the definition of the marketing research problem, including past information and forecasts, resources and constraints of the firm, objectives of the decision maker, buyer behavior, legal environment, economic environment, and marketing and technological skills of the firm

To understand the background to a marketing research problem, the researcher must understand the client's firm and industry. In particular, the researcher should analyze the factors that have an impact on the definition of the marketing research problem. These factors, encompassing the **environmental context of the problem**, include past information and forecasts pertaining to the industry and the firm, resources and constraints of the firm, objectives of the decision maker, buyer behavior, legal environment, economic environment, and marketing and technological skills of the firm, as shown in Figure 2.2. Each of these factors is now discussed briefly.[15]

Past Information and Forecasts

Past information and forecasts of trends with respect to sales, market share, profitability, technology, population, demographics, and lifestyle can help the researcher to understand the underlying marketing research problem. Where appropriate, this kind of analysis should be carried out at the industry and firm levels. For example, if a firm's sales

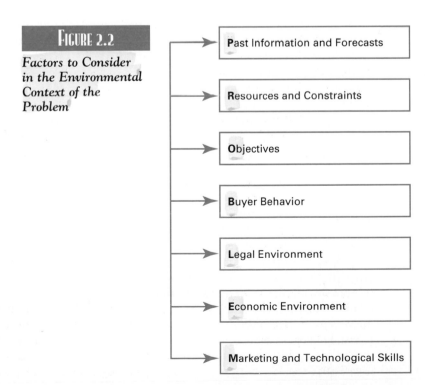

FIGURE 2.2

Factors to Consider in the Environmental Context of the Problem

- Past Information and Forecasts
- Resources and Constraints
- Objectives
- Buyer Behavior
- Legal Environment
- Economic Environment
- Marketing and Technological Skills

have decreased but industry sales have increased, the problems will be very different than if the industry sales have also decreased. In the former case, the problems are likely to be specific to the firm.[16]

Past information and forecasts can be valuable in uncovering potential opportunities and problems, as the fast-food industry has discovered. The following example shows how fast-food chains, pizza restaurants, and other outlets for take-out food have sought to exploit potential opportunities in the recent trend toward take-out food and home delivery.

EXAMPLE
Take-Out Market Takes Off

In recent years, there has been a significant trend toward take-out food. A study by Liberman Research, New York, found that an average of 81% of households buy take-out food at least once every four weeks and that many individuals take out food once a week, at an average weekly cost of $16.50 a person. Traditional fast-food outlets remain the most popular, with 76% of consumers buying take-out food there, followed by 66% preferring take-out pizza. The study forecasts that home delivery will be the future of take-out food. Up-scale entrees, soups, salads, and sandwiches will be added to the home delivery repertoire. Also, the study forecasts that one day snacks and candy will be home delivered. This presents problems for fast-food marketers that emphasize dine-in service but offers tremendous opportunities for those catering to the take-out and home delivery segments. Pizza Hut has successfully capitalized on this trend by emphasizing take-out and home delivery services. For example, it opened several take-out only (with no dine-in service) outlets to better serve this market.[17] ◆

This example illustrates the usefulness of past information and forecasts, which can be especially valuable if resources are limited and other constraints on the organization exist.

Resources and Constraints

To formulate a marketing research problem of appropriate scope, it is necessary to consider both the resources available, such as money and research skills, and the constraints on the organization, such as cost and time. Proposing a large-scale project that would cost $100,000 when only $40,000 has been budgeted obviously will not meet management approval. In many instances, the scope of the marketing research problem may have to be reduced to accommodate budget constraints. This might be done, as in the department store patronage project, by confining the investigation to major geographical markets rather than conducting the project on a national basis.

It is often possible to extend the scope of a project appreciably with only a marginal increase in costs. This can considerably enhance the usefulness of the project, thereby increasing the probability that management will approve it. Time constraints can be important when decisions must be made quickly.[18] A project for Fisher-Price, a major toy manufacturer, involving mall-intercept interviews in six major cities (Chicago, Fresno, Kansas City, New York, Philadelphia, and San Diego) had to be completed in six weeks. Why this rush? The results had to be presented at an upcoming board meeting where a major (go/no go) decision was to be made about a new product introduction.[19]

Other constraints, such as those imposed by the client firm's personnel, organizational structure and culture, or decision-making styles, should be identified to determine the scope of the research project. Yet constraints should not be allowed to diminish the value of the research to the decision maker or to compromise the integrity of the research process. If a research project is worth doing, it is worth doing well. In instances where the resources are too limited to allow a high-quality project, the firm should be advised not to undertake formal marketing research. Thus it becomes necessary to identify resources and constraints, a task that can be better understood when examined in the light of the objectives of the organization and the decision maker.

Objectives

objectives To conduct successful marketing research, goals of the organization and of the decision maker must be considered.

Decisions are made to accomplish **objectives**. The formulation of the management decision problem must be based on a clear understanding of two types of objectives: the organizational objectives (the goals of the organization) and the personal objectives of the decision maker. For the project to be successful, it must serve the objectives of the organization and of the DM. This, however, is not an easy task.

The decision maker rarely formulates personal or organizational objectives accurately. Rather, it is likely that these objectives will be stated in terms that have no operational significance, such as "to improve corporate image." Direct questioning of the DM is unlikely to reveal all the relevant objectives. The researcher needs skill to extract these objectives. An effective technique is to confront the DM with each of the possible solutions to a problem and ask whether he or she would follow that course of action. If the answer is no, use further probing to uncover objectives that are not served by the course of action.

Buyer Behavior

buyer behavior A body of knowledge that tries to understand and predict consumers' reactions based on an individual's specific characteristics.

Buyer behavior is a central component of the environmental context. In most marketing decisions, the problem can ultimately be traced to predicting the response of buyers to specific actions by the marketer. An understanding of the underlying buyer behavior can provide valuable insights into the problem. Buyer behavior factors that should be considered include:

1. The number and geographical location of the buyers and nonbuyers
2. Demographic and psychological characteristics
3. Product consumption habits and the consumption of related product categories
4. Media consumption behavior and response to promotions
5. Price sensitivity
6. Retail outlets patronized
7. Buyer preferences

The following example shows how changes in buyer behavior may pose both threats and opportunities.

EXAMPLE
Coffee Isn't Just the Same Old Grind

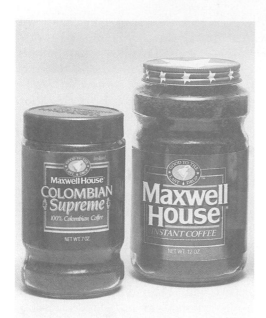

Coffee consumption in the United States has been declining since the early 1960s. Most experts think that coffee will never again be the all-purpose, all-meal, adult drink it once was. By the early 1990s, the average age of coffee drinkers was above 40, and it was continuing to increase. Another notable change in the behavior of consumers was that different kinds of coffee were being used for different occasions. These changes in consumer behavior and the decline in the coffee market posed a threat for coffee marketers, especially the market leader, General Foods (GF). This company, however, saw this threat as an opportunity to entrench its competitive position. After substantial research, GF segmented the market based on coffee usage behavior and introduced a much larger variety of coffee brands and types than its competitors. Furthermore, GF attempted to position each brand for a different usage situation. The Maxwell House brand of regular coffee was positioned as the morning breakfast beverage to be consumed at home. Although both Sanka and Brim are decaffeinated brands, Sanka was marketed primarily as dinner coffee, and Brim for the office. Finally, General Foods International Coffees were positioned as special-occasion beverages. This strategy strengthened the leadership position of GF in the coffee market.[20] ◆

General Foods has successfully segmented the market based on changes in coffee consumption. ◆ Teri Stratford.

The increase in the average age of the coffee drinker and the decline in coffee consumption could be attributed to changes in the sociocultural environment, which includes demographic trends and consumer tastes. In addition, the legal environment and the economic environment can impact the behavior of the consumers and the definition of the marketing research problem.

Legal Environment

legal environment
Regulatory policies and norms within which organizations must operate.

The **legal environment** includes public policies, laws, government agencies, and pressure groups that influence and regulate various organizations and individuals in society. Important areas of law include patents, trademarks, royalties, trade agreements, taxes, and tariffs. Federal laws have an impact on each element of the marketing mix. In addition, laws have been passed to regulate specific industries. The legal environment can have an important bearing on the definition of the marketing research problem.

Economic Environment

economic environment
The economic environment consists of income, prices, savings, credit, and general economic conditions.

Along with the legal environment, another important component of the environmental context is the **economic environment**, composed of purchasing power, gross income, disposable income, discretionary income, prices, savings, credit availability, and general economic conditions. The general state of the economy (rapid growth, slow growth, recession, or stagflation) influences the willingness of consumers and businesses to take on credit and spend on big-ticket items. Thus, the economic environment can have important implications for marketing research problems.

Marketing and Technological Skills

A company's expertise with each element of the marketing mix as well as its general level of marketing and technological skills affect the nature and scope of the marketing research project. For example, introducing a new product that requires sophisticated technology may not be a viable course if the firm lacks the skills to manufacture or market it.

A firm's marketing and technological skills greatly influence the marketing programs and strategies that can be implemented. At a broader level, other elements of the technological environment should be considered. Technological advances such as the continuing development of computers have had a dramatic impact on marketing research. To illustrate, computerized checkout lanes allow supermarkets to monitor daily consumer demand for products and make the data available to the researcher. It is possible to obtain precise information on retail sales, not only of the firm's brands but also of competing brands. The speed and accuracy of data collection enable the researcher to investigate intricate problems such as the daily changes in market share during a promotion.

After gaining an adequate understanding of the environmental context of the problem, the researcher can define the management decision problem and the marketing research problem.

MANAGEMENT DECISION PROBLEM AND MARKETING RESEARCH PROBLEM

management decision problem The problem confronting the decision maker, which asks what the decision maker needs to do.

marketing research problem A problem that entails determining what information is needed and how it can be obtained in the most feasible way.

The management decision problem asks what the DM needs to do, whereas the marketing research problem asks what information is needed and how it can best be obtained.[21] Research can provide the necessary information to make a sound decision.[22] The **management decision problem** is action oriented. It is concerned with the possible actions the DM can take. How should the loss of market share be arrested? Should the market be segmented differently? Should a new product be introduced? Should the promotional budget be increased?

In contrast, the **marketing research problem** is information oriented. It involves determining what information is needed and how that information can be obtained effectively and efficiently. Consider, for example, the loss of market share for a particular product line. The DM's decision problem is how to recover this loss. Alternative courses of action include modifying existing products, introducing new products, changing other elements in the marketing mix, and segmenting the market. Suppose that the DM and the researcher (R) believe that the problem is caused by inappropriate segmentation of the market and wanted research to provide information on this issue. The research problem would then become the identification and evaluation of an alternative basis for segmenting the market. Note that this process is interactive. The department store patronage project example illustrates further the distinction between the management decision problem and the marketing research problem as well as the interactive nature of the problem definition process.

DEPARTMENT STORE PATRONAGE PROJECT
Defining the Problem

DM: We have seen a decline in the patronage of our store.

  R: How do you know that?

DM: Well, it is reflected in our sales and market share.

  R: Why do you think that your patronage has declined?

DM: I wish I knew!

  R: What about competition?

DM: I suspect we are better than competition on some factors and worse on others.

  R: How do the customers view your store?

DM: I think most of them positively, although we may have a weak area or two.

After a series of dialogues with the DM and other key managers, analysis of secondary data, and qualitative research, the problem was identified as follows:

Management Decision Problem

What should be done to improve the patronage of Sears?

Marketing Research Problem

Determine the relative strengths and weaknesses of Sears, vis-à-vis other major competitors, with respect to factors that influence store patronage. ◆

The department store patronage project shows the interactive nature of the process to identify the management decision problem and the marketing research problem. The following examples further distinguish between the management decision problem and the marketing research problem:

Management decision problem	Marketing research problem
Should a new product be introduced?	To determine consumer preferences and purchase intentions for the proposed new product
Should the advertising campaign be changed?	To determine the effectiveness of the current advertising campaign
Should the price of the brand be increased?	To determine the price elasticity of demand and the impact on sales and profits of various levels of price changes

DEFINING THE MARKETING RESEARCH PROBLEM

The general rule to be followed in defining the research problem is that the definition should (1) allow the researcher to obtain all the information needed to address the management decision problem and (2) guide the researcher in proceeding with the project. Researchers make two common errors in problem definition. The first arises when the research problem is defined too broadly. A broad definition does not provide clear guidelines for the subsequent steps involved in the project. Some examples of overly broad marketing research problem definitions are: developing a marketing strategy for the brand, improving the competitive position of the firm, or improving the company's image. These are not specific enough to suggest an approach to the problem or a research design.

The second type of error is just the opposite: the marketing research problem is defined too narrowly. A narrow focus may preclude consideration of some courses of action, particularly those that are innovative and not obvious. It may also prevent the researcher from addressing important components of the management decision problem. For example, in a project conducted for a major consumer products firm, the management problem was how to respond to a price cut initiated by a competitor. The alternative courses of action initially identified by the firm's research staff were (1) to decrease the price of the firm's brand to match the competitor's price cut; (2) to maintain price but increase advertising heavily; (3) to decrease the price somewhat, without matching the competitor's price, and moderately increase advertising. None of these alternatives seemed promising. When outside marketing research experts were brought in, the problem was redefined as improving the market share and profitability of the product line. Qualitative research indicated that in blind tests, consumers could not differentiate products offered under different brand names. Furthermore, consumers relied on price as an indicator of product quality. These findings led to a creative alternative: increase the price of the existing brand and introduce two new brands: one priced to match the competitor and the other priced to undercut it.

The likelihood of committing either error of problem definition can be reduced by stating the marketing research problem in broad, general terms and identifying its specific components (see Figure 2.3). The **broad statement of the problem** provides perspective and acts as a safeguard against committing the second type of error. The **specific components of the problem** focus on the key aspects and provide clear guidelines on how to proceed further. Examples of appropriate marketing research problem definitions are provided in the two following examples.

broad statement of the problem The initial statement of the marketing research problem that provides an appropriate perspective on the problem.

specific components of the problem The second part of the marketing research problem definition that focuses on the key aspects of the problem and provides clear guidelines on how to proceed further.

FIGURE 2.3

Proper Definition of the Marketing Research Problem

EXAMPLE
Chi-Chi's Grabs the Bull by the Horns, Mexican Style _____

A Chi-Chi's Mexican restaurant in Peoria, Illinois, was having difficulties attracting customers. The marketing research problem was defined as determining Chi-Chi's weaknesses within the total market. Specifically, the following issues had to be addressed:

1. What is the nature of the local economy?
2. What restaurants are patronized in the market area?
3. What factors cause customers to patronize restaurants other than Chi-Chi's?

Research revealed that the local economy was depressed. The perception was that Chi-Chi's was taking local money out of the community and hurting local restaurants. Chi-Chi's countered this perception by setting up a Community Network Plan involving public relations–oriented ideas such as tours of the restaurant by local Brownie troops and fund-raiser sponsorship. Eventually, sales began to pick up.[23] ◆

A Chi-Chi's Mexican restaurant.
◆ Chi-Chi's Mexican Restaurants.

In the Chi-Chi's example, the broad statement of the problem focused on examining Chi-Chi's weaknesses within the total market, and the specific components dealt with the local economy, restaurant patronage, and factors that caused consumers to patronize competing restaurants. An appropriate definition of the problem helped Chi-Chi's to address the underlying problem and attract more customers. Problem definition in the department store patronage project followed a similar pattern.

DEPARTMENT STORE PATRONAGE PROJECT
Problem Definition

In the department store patronage project, the marketing research problem was to determine the relative strengths and weaknesses of Sears, vis-à-vis other major competitors, with respect to factors that influence store patronage. Specifically, research provided information on the following questions:

1. What criteria do households use when selecting department stores?
2. How do households evaluate Sears and competing stores in terms of the choice criteria identified in question 1?
3. Which stores are patronized when shopping for specific product categories?
4. What is the market share of Sears and its competitors for specific product categories?
5. What is the demographic and psychological profile of the customers of Sears? Does it differ from the profile of customers of competing stores?
6. Can store patronage and preference be explained in terms of store evaluations and customer characteristics? ◆

Once the marketing research problem has been broadly stated and its specific components identified, the researcher is in a position to develop a suitable approach.

COMPONENTS OF THE APPROACH

In the process of developing an approach, we must not lose sight of the goal: the outputs. The outputs of the approach development process should include the following components: objective/theoretical framework, analytical models, research questions, hypotheses, and identification of characteristics influencing the research design (see Figure 2.1). Each of these components is discussed in the following sections.

Objective/Theoretical Framework

theory A conceptual scheme based on foundational statements, or axioms, that are assumed to be true.

objective evidence Unbiased evidence that is supported by empirical findings.

In general, research should be based on objective evidence and supported by theory. A **theory** is a conceptual scheme based on foundational statements called axioms that are assumed to be true. **Objective evidence** (evidence that is unbiased and supported by empirical findings) is gathered by compiling relevant findings from secondary sources. Likewise, an appropriate theory to guide the research might be identified by reviewing academic literature contained in books, journals, and monographs. The researcher should rely on theory to determine which variables should be investigated. Past research on theory development and testing can provide important guidelines on determining dependent variables (those whose values depend on the values of other variables) and independent variables (those whose values affect the values of other variables). Furthermore, theoretical considerations provide information on how the variables should be operationalized and measured, as well as how the research design and sample should be selected. A theory also serves as a foundation on which the researcher can organize and interpret the findings: "nothing is so practical as a good theory."[24] Conversely, by neglecting theory, the researcher increases the likelihood that he or she will fail to understand the data obtained or be unable to interpret and integrate the findings of the project with findings obtained by others. The role of theory in the various phases of an applied marketing research project is summarized in Table 2.1.

	Research Task	Role of Theory
TABLE 2.1 *The Role of Theory in Applied Marketing Research*	1. Conceptualizing and identifying key variables	Provides a conceptual foundation and understanding of the basic processes underlying the problem situation. These processes will suggest key dependent and independent variables.
	2. Operationalizing key variables	Theoretical constructs (variables) can suggest independent and dependent variables occurring naturally in the real world.
	3. Selecting a research design	Causal or associative relationships suggested by the theory may indicate whether a causal or descriptive design should be adopted (see Chapter 3).
	4. Selecting a sample	The theoretical framework may be useful in defining the population and suggesting variables for qualifying respondents, imposing quotas, or stratifying the population (see Chapter 11).
	5. Analyzing and interpreting data	The theoretical framework (and the models, research questions and hypotheses based on it) guide the selection of a data analysis strategy and the interpretation of results (see Chapter 14).
	6. Integrating findings	The findings obtained in the research project can be interpreted in the light of previous research and integrated with the existing body of knowledge.

Theory also plays a vital role in influencing the research procedures adopted in basic research. Applying a theory to an applied marketing research problem requires creativity on the part of the researcher, however. A theory may not specify adequately how its abstract constructs (variables) can be embodied in a real-world phenomenon. Moreover, theories are incomplete; they deal with only a subset of variables that exist in the real world. Hence, the researcher must also identify and examine other, nontheoretical, variables.[25]

The department store patronage project illustrates how theory can be used to develop an approach. A review of the literature in consumer behavior, economics, and biostatistics reveals broad support for the concept of threshold effects in consumer response. This concept states that the consumer will not make a response unless the value of the underlying variable exceeds a certain threshold or critical level. The threshold approach was adopted to explain store patronage behavior. A consumer, when considering a store, must decide whether to patronize it. A consumer generally prefers one store over another. If the degree of preference is above the threshold value for that consumer, that person will patronize the store under consideration. If it is below the threshold, the person will not choose it. The threshold value varies from individual to individual for a given store and may vary from one store to another. Also, the degree of preference for a store may be affected by several variables, the more important ones being the factors that influence the choice criteria.[26]

Review of the retailing literature revealed that the modeling of store patronage in terms of choice criteria had received considerable support. Furthermore, as many as 42 choice criteria had been identified in the literature, and guidelines on operationalizing these variables were provided. This provided an initial pool from which the final eight characteristics included in the questionnaire were selected. Theoretical considerations also suggested that store patronage behavior based on the threshold effect could be examined via a survey of respondents familiar with department store shopping. The theoretical framework also serves as a foundation for developing an appropriate analytical model.

Analytical Model

analytical model An explicit specification of a set of variables and their interrelationships designed to represent some real system or process in whole or in part.

An **analytical model** is a set of variables and their interrelationships designed to represent, in whole or in part, some real system or process. Models can have many different forms. The most common are verbal, graphical, and mathematical structures. In **verbal models**, the variables and their relationships are stated in prose form. Such models may be mere restatements of the main tenets of a theory. **Graphical models** are visual. They are used to isolate variables and to suggest directions of relationships but are not designed to provide numerical results. They are logical, preliminary steps to developing mathematical models.[27] **Mathematical models** explicitly specify the relationships among variables, usually in equation form.[28] These models can be used as guides for formulating the research design and have the advantage of being amenable to manipulation.[29] The different models are illustrated in the context of the department store patronage project.

verbal models Analytical models that provide a written representation of the relationships between variables.

graphical models Analytical models that provide a visual picture of the relationships between variables.

mathematical models Analytical models that explicitly describe the relationships between variables, usually in equation form.

DEPARTMENT STORE PATRONAGE PROJECT
Model Building
Verbal Model

A consumer first becomes aware of a department store. That person then gains an understanding of the store by evaluating the store in terms of the factors comprising the choice criteria. Based on the evaluation, the consumer forms a degree of preference for the store. If preference exceeds a certain threshold level, the consumer will patronize the store.

Graphical Model

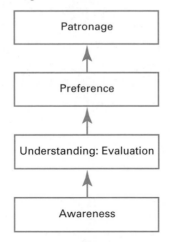

Patronage

↑

Preference

↑

Understanding: Evaluation

↑

Awareness

Mathematical Model

$$y = a_0 + \sum_{i=1}^{n} a_i x_i$$

where

y = degree of preference

a_0, a_i = model parameters to be estimated statistically

x_i = store patronage factors that constitute the choice criteria ◆

As can be seen from this example, the verbal, graphical, and mathematical models depict the same phenomenon or theoretical framework in different ways. The phenomenon of threshold effect stated verbally is represented for clarity through a figure (graphical model) and is put in equation form (mathematical model) for ease of statistical estimation and testing. Graphical models are particularly helpful in conceptualizing an approach to the problem, as the following new car purchase model illustrates.

EXAMPLE
Out-and-Out Pleasure Is in for Buick

The following graphical model illustrates the decision-making process for purchasing a new car. A person starts as a passive consumer ("I am not now interested in considering the purchase of a new vehicle"). When the consumer is actively interested in purchasing a new car, the consumer creates a consideration set (limits the brands to be considered). This is followed by shopping, buying (sale), and assessing the value of products and services. Automobile firms such as Buick have used the new car purchase model to formulate marketing strategies that are consonant with consumers' underlying decision-making process. In this model, Buick is part of the consideration set for a certain group of consumers who are comfort- and quality-oriented. Therefore, the marketing theme of the 1995 Buick Regal, "Regal's all-new interior is an out-and-out pleasure," was based on this model.[30] ◆

New Car Purchase Model

Passive Population
↓
Active Consumers
↓
Consideration Set
↓
Shopping
↓
Sale
↓
Assessment of Product/Services

The verbal, graphical, and mathematical models complement each other and help the researcher identify relevant research questions and hypotheses.

Research Questions

Research questions (RQs) are refined statements of the specific components of the problem. Although the components of the problem define the problem in specific terms, further detail may be needed to develop an approach. Each component of the problem may have to be broken down into subcomponents or research questions. Research questions ask what specific information is required with respect to the problem components. If the research questions are answered by the research, then the information obtained should aid the decision maker. The formulation of the research questions should be guided not only by the problem definition, but also by the theoretical framework and the analytical model adopted. For a given problem component, there are likely to be several research questions, as in the case of the department store patronage project.

DEPARTMENT STORE PATRONAGE PROJECT
Research Questions

The fifth component of the research problem was the psychological profile of Sears' customers. In the context of psychological characteristics, several research questions were asked about the customers of Sears.

- Do they exhibit store loyalty?
- Are they heavy users of credit?
- Are they more conscious of personal appearance as compared to customers of competing stores?
- Do they combine shopping with eating out?

The research questions were then further refined by precisely defining the variables and determining how they were to be operationalized. To illustrate, how should the use of Sears credit be measured? It could be measured any of the following ways:

1. Whether the customer holds a Sears credit card
2. Whether the customer uses the Sears credit card
3. The number of times the Sears credit card was used in a specified time period
4. The dollar amount charged to the Sears credit card during a specified time period ◆

The theoretical framework and the analytical model play a significant role in the operationalization and measurement of variables specified by the research questions. So, although in the department store patronage project the literature reviewed did not provide any definitive measure of store credit, the mathematical model could incorporate any of the alternative measures. Thus, it was decided to include all four measures of store credit in the study. Research questions may be further refined into one or more hypotheses.

Hypotheses

A **hypothesis** (H) is an unproven statement or proposition about a factor or phenomenon that is of interest to the researcher. It may, for example, be a tentative statement about relationships between two or more variables as stipulated by the theoretical framework or the analytical model. Often, a hypothesis is a possible answer to the research question.[31] Hypotheses go beyond research questions because they are statements of relationships or propositions rather than merely questions to which answers are sought. Research questions are interrogative, hypotheses are declarative and can be tested empir-

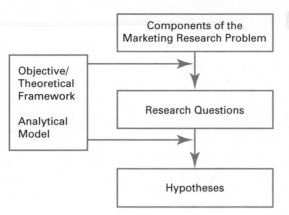

FIGURE 2.4

*Development
of Research Questions
and Hypotheses*

ically (see Chapter 15). An important role of a hypothesis is to suggest variables to be included in the research design.[32] The relationship between the marketing research problem, research questions, and hypotheses, along with the influence of the objective/theoretical framework and analytical models, is described in Figure 2.4 and illustrated by the following example from the department store patronage project.[33]

DEPARTMENT STORE PATRONAGE PROJECT
Hypotheses

The following hypotheses were formulated in relation to the research question on store loyalty:[34]

H1: Customers who are store loyal are less knowledgeable about the shopping environment.
H2: Store-loyal customers are more risk-averse than are nonloyal customers.

These hypotheses guided the research by ensuring that variables measuring knowledge of the shopping environment and propensity to take risks were included in the research design. ◆

Unfortunately, it may not be possible to formulate hypotheses in all situations. Sometimes sufficient information is not available to develop hypotheses. At other times, the most reasonable statement of a hypothesis may be a trivial restatement of the research question. For example:

RQ: Do customers of Sears exhibit store loyalty?
H: Customers of Sears are loyal.

Hypotheses are an important part of the approach to the problem. When stated in operational terms, as H1 and H2 in the department store example, they provide guidelines on what, and how, data are to be collected and analyzed. When operational hypotheses are stated using symbolic notation, they are commonly referred to as statistical hypotheses. A research question may have more than one hypothesis associated with it, as in the case of Chanel. Chanel Inc. was considering advertising its Chanel brand of perfume in magazines it formerly considered too pedestrian for its prestigious brand, such as *Working Woman, Savvy, Rolling Stone, Omni* and *Interview*. The Chanel brand had a 2.8% share of department store sales (the leader is Estée Lauder with a 20.9% share). By expanding its advertising beyond high-fashion magazines, Chanel Inc. hoped to improve its share of department store sales. The following research question and hypotheses may be posed:[35]

RQ: Does Chanel have an upscale image?
H1: Chanel is perceived to be an expensive brand.

H2: Users of Chanel have higher-than-average incomes.

H3: Users of Chanel associate this perfume with status.

Note that to test H1, the researcher would have to operationalize and measure the perceived price associated with Chanel. Empirical testing of H2 would require that the respondents be classified as users or nonusers of Chanel and provide information on their incomes. Finally, H3 tells us that we need to operationalize another variable or a set of variables that measure the status associated with Chanel. The results of this research provided support for H1 and H3 but not for H2. Although Chanel did have an up-scale image, its appeal was not limited to the up-scale segment. Broadening the target market by advertising in magazines formerly considered pedestrian led to improved department store sales of Chanel.

Chanel has broadened its target market by advertising in magazines formerly considered pedestrian. ◆ Teri Stratford.

Relevant Characteristics

As mentioned earlier, a useful way of conceptualizing the development of an approach is to view it as a bridge between step 1 (problem definition) and step 3 (research design) of the marketing research process. Specifically, we focus here on one important aspect of research design: developing a questionnaire. The key question to ask—given the problem definition, research questions, and hypotheses—is what additional characteristics, factors, product attributes, or variables should be identified so that a questionnaire can be constructed? The answer to this question will result in the identification of the **relevant characteristics**. Let us consider the department store patronage project and focus on the components of the problem identified earlier in this chapter.

relevant characteristics
Characteristics, factors, product attributes, or variables that may affect a research design.

DEPARTMENT STORE PATRONAGE PROJECT
Relevant Characteristics

Component 1

Component 1 involves the criteria households use to select a department store. Unless the specific factors comprising this criteria are identified, we cannot formulate a question asking the respondents which of these are important to them.

Based on the process outlined earlier, the following characteristics were identified: quality of merchandise, variety and assortment of merchandise, returns and adjustment policy, service of store personnel, prices, convenience of location, layout of store, credit and billing policies.

Component 2

Component 2 is concerned with competition. Unless the competing stores are identified, it would be impossible to obtain information related to this component. Nine department stores were identified as competitors to Sears.

Component 3

Specific product categories are the focus of component 3. Sixteen different product categories were selected, including women's dresses, women's sportswear, lingerie and body fashion, junior merchandise, men's apparel, cosmetics, jewelry, shoes, sheets and towels, furniture and bedding, and draperies.

Component 4

No additional characteristics or variables need to be identified.

Component 5

The standard demographic characteristics were included in component 5. The specific psychological characteristics selected were store loyalty, credit use, appearance consciousness, and combining shopping with eating.

Component 6

No additional characteristics or variables need to be identified. ◆

Similar analyses should be performed for all the research questions and hypotheses. The process identifying the relevant characteristics was illustrated in Figure 2.1. We use the example of the S.C. Johnson Company to show how the identification of relevant characteristics can aid the formulation of research design and subsequent research. When S.C. Johnson Company was considering the introduction of a new instant hair conditioner, it needed a better understanding of the market and the competitive positioning of the various brands. To develop a research design, it was necessary to determine what variables were important in differentiating hair conditioners. These variables were identified as conditioning, cleaning, manageability, and fragrance. Subsequent research based on these variables provided insights into the competitive structure of the instant hair conditioner market. For example, Agree and Breck Creme Rinse had achieved the "cleaning" position, whereas Clairol conditioner was perceived as a "conditioning" brand. Wella Balsam appeared to have virtually no image and thus might be vulnerable to a new entry.[36]

The process of identifying the relevant characteristics and the other components of the approach to the problem lead to a specification of the information needed. By focusing on each component of the problem and the related theory, models, research questions, hypotheses, and characteristics that have been identified in developing an approach, the researcher can determine what information should be obtained. This facilitates the formulation of an appropriate research design.

INTERNATIONAL MARKETING RESEARCH

The precise definition of the marketing research problem is more difficult in international marketing research than in domestic marketing research. Unfamiliarity with the environmental factors of the country where the research is being conducted can greatly increase the difficulty of understanding the problem's environmental context and uncovering its causes.

EXAMPLE
Heinz Ketchup Couldn't Catch-Up in Brazil _____

Despite good track records inland and overseas, H.J. Heinz Company failed in Brazil, a market that seemed to be South America's biggest and most promising market. Heinz entered into a joint venture with Citrosuco Paulista, a giant orange juice exporter, because of the future possibility of buying the profitable company. Yet the sales of its products, including ketchup, did not take off. Where was the problem? A problem audit revealed that the company lacked a strong local distribution system. Heinz lost control of the distribution because it worked on consignment. Distribution could not reach 25% penetration. The other related problem was that Heinz concentrated on neighborhood shops because this strategy was successful in Mexico. The problem audit, however, revealed that 75% of the grocery shopping in São Paulo is done in supermarkets and not the smaller shops. Although Mexico and Brazil may appear to have similar cultural and demographic characteristics, consumer behavior can vary greatly. A closer and intensive look at the Brazilian food distribution system and the behavior of consumers could have averted this failure. Heinz, however, is watching more closely at Asia, especially China, where the company markets baby food and where 22 million babies are born every year.[37] ◆

As the Heinz example illustrates, many international marketing efforts fail not because research was not conducted but because the relevant environmental factors were not taken into account. Generally this leads to a definition of the problem that is too narrow. Consider, for example the consumption of soft drinks. In many Asian countries such as India, water is consumed with meals, and soft drinks are generally served to guests and on special occasions. Therefore, the management problem of increasing the market share of a particular soft drink would translate to different marketing research problems in India than in the United States. Before defining the problem, the researcher must isolate and examine the impact of the **self-referent culture** (SRC), or the unconscious reference to one's own cultural values. The following steps help researchers account for environmental and cultural differences when defining the problem in an international marketing context: [38]

self-referent culture The unconscious reference to one's own cultural values.

1. Define the marketing research problem in terms of domestic environmental and cultural factors. This involves an identification of relevant American (or Western) traits, economics, values, needs or habits.

2. Define the marketing research problem in terms of foreign environmental and cultural factors. Make no judgments. This involves an identification of the related traits, economics, values, needs, or habits in the proposed market culture. This task requires input from researchers familiar with the foreign environment.

3. Isolate the self-referent culture influence on the problem and examine it carefully to see how it complicates the problem. Examine the differences between steps 1 and 2. The SRC can be seen to account for these differences.

4. Redefine the problem without the SRC influence and address it for the foreign market situation. If the differences in steps 3 are significant, the impact of the SRC should be carefully considered.

Consider the broad problem of the Coca-Cola Company trying to increase its penetration of the soft drink market in India. In Step 1, the problem of increasing the market penetration in the United States would be considered. In the United States, virtually all the households consume soft drinks, and the problem would be to increase the soft drink consumption of existing consumers. Furthermore, soft drinks are regularly consumed with meals and as thirst quenchers. So the problem of increasing marketing penetration would involve getting the consumers to consume more soft drinks with meals and at other times. In India, on the other hand (step 2), a much smaller percentage of households consumes soft drinks, and soft drinks are not consumed with meals. Thus, in step 3, the SRC can be identified as the American notion that soft drinks are an all-purpose, all-meal beverage. In step 4, the problem in the Indian context can be defined as how to get a greater percentage of the Indian consumers to consume soft drinks (Coca-Cola products) and how to get them to consume soft drinks (Coca-Cola products) more often for personal consumption.

While developing theoretical frameworks, models, research questions, and hypotheses, remember that differences in the environmental factors, especially the sociocultural environment, may lead to differences in the formation of perceptions, attitudes, preferences, and choice behavior. For example, orientation toward time varies considerably across cultures. In Asia, Latin America, and the Middle East, people are not as time conscious as Westerners. This influences their perceptions of and preferences for convenience foods such as frozen foods and prepared dinners. In developing an approach to the problem, the researcher should consider the equivalence of consumption and purchase behavior and the underlying factors that influence them. This is critical to the identification of the correct research questions, hypotheses, and characteristics/factors that influence the research design.

EXAMPLE

Surf Superconcentrate Faces a Super Washout in Japan

Unilever attempted to break into the Japanese detergent market with Surf Superconcentrate. It initially achieved 14.5% of the market share during test marketing but fell down to a shocking 2.8% when the product was introduced nationally. Where did they go wrong? Surf was designed to have a distinctive premeasured packet as in tea bag–like sachets, joined in pairs because convenience was an important attribute to Japanese consumers. It also had a "fresh smell" appeal. Japanese consumers, however, noticed that the detergents did not dissolve in the wash, partly because of weather conditions and also because of the popularity of low-agitation washing machines. Surf was not designed to work in the new washing machines. Unilever also found that the "fresh smell" positioning of new Surf had little relevance since most consumers hang their wash out in the fresh air. The research approach was certainly not without flaw as Unilever failed to identify critical attributes that are relevant in the Japanese detergent market. Furthermore, it identified factors such as "smell fresh" that had no relevance in the Japanese context. Appropriate qualitative research such as focus groups across samples from the target market could have revealed the correct characteristics or factors leading to a suitable research design.[39] ◆

ETHICS IN MARKETING RESEARCH

Ethical situations arising from the process of problem definition and developing an approach are likely to occur between the market researcher and the client. As explained earlier, identifying the correct marketing research problem is crucial to the success of the project. This process can, however, be compromised by the personal agendas of the researcher or the client (DM). For example, the researcher, after performing the tasks involved in problem definition and analyzing the environmental context of the problem, realizes that the correct marketing research problem may be defined in a way that makes primary research unnecessary. This would reduce the cost of the project and the research firm's profit margin substantially. Does the researcher define the problem correctly, fabricate a research problem that involves primary data collection, or does the researcher refuse to proceed with this project in lieu of those more profitable? The researcher is faced with an ethical dilemma, as in the following example.

EXAMPLE
Taste (Profits) or Image (Ethics)?

A marketing research firm is hired by a soft drink company to conduct taste tests to determine why its newly introduced soft drink brand has not captured the expected market-share. The researcher, after following the process outlined in this chapter, determines that the problem is not one of taste but of the image and its positioning. The client, however, has already defined the problem as a taste problem and not as the more broad market share problem. The researcher must also weigh the relatively high profit margin of taste test research to the less lucrative survey research needed to answer questions pertaining to soft drink image. What should the researcher do? Should he simply conduct the research the client wants rather than the research he feels the client needs? The guidelines indicate that "the researcher has a professional obligation to indicate to the client that, in his or her judgment, the research expenditure is not warranted. If, after this judgment has been clearly stated, the client still desires the research, the researcher should feel free to conduct the study. The reason for this is that the researcher can never know for certain the risk preferences and strategies that are guiding the client's behavior."[40] ◆

Such ethical situations would be satisfactorily resolved if the client/researcher relationship developed with both the client and the researcher adhering to the seven Cs discussed earlier: communication, cooperation, confidence, candor, closeness, continuity, and creativity. This would provide a relationship of mutual trust that would check any unethical tendencies.

Ethical situations affecting the researcher and the client may also arise in developing an approach to the problem. When researchers conduct studies for different clients in related industries (i.e., banking and financial services) or in similar research areas (i.e., customer satisfaction) they may be tempted to cut corners in theoretical framework and model development. Take an example where a grocery chain client (e.g., Kroger) has on its board of directors the chairman of a bank (e.g., NationsBank). The bank had recently conducted customer satisfaction research using a client specific model and the bank affiliated board member has access to this research. The researcher feels that a customer satisfaction model for NationsBank could be easily adapted to work for Kroger grocery stores. The client (Kroger) feels that it would not be a good business decision to have access to this information and not use it. Is it ethical for the client and researcher to obtain and use this model developed for another company (NationsBank) by another research firm? There is an underlying trust between the researcher and the client that the research firm is honor bound not to reuse client specific models or findings for other projects.

The client also has an ethical responsibility not to solicit proposals merely to gain the expertise of the research firms without pay. It is unethical for a client to solicit proposals from a few research firms and then adopt one or a combination of the approaches suggested in them and conduct the project in-house. The client must respect the rights of a research firm by realizing that an unpaid proposal belongs to the research firm that generated it. However, if the client firm pays for the development of the proposal, it has a right to use the information contained in it.

COMPUTER APPLICATIONS

Microcomputers and mainframes can be used to define the problem and develop an approach. The literature review could be conveniently conducted by examining, among other sources, on-line information about catalogs, books, and articles. Databases such as *Books in Print, Management Contents,* and *Economic Literature Index,* provided by the Dialog corporation, are very useful in this respect. The benefits of using computers for library research extend far beyond automating the tedious manual search process. On-line databases enhance reliability and quality while decreasing the cost of information acquisition. The information received on-line can be conveniently stored on a microcomputer or mainframe. For conducting a literature review, programs such as INQUIRE/TEXT by Infodata Systems Inc. can be used. INQUIRE/TEXT is a full-featured text and database management system that uses powerful search commands, based on recognition of key words and word combinations, to index, retrieve, access, maintain, and manipulate textual data with a high degree of flexibility.

Spreadsheet software packages such as LOTUS 1-2-3 and EXCEL are effective managerial tools in developing and testing simple simulation models. The microcomputer and mainframe versions of three popular statistical packages—SPSS, SAS, and BMDP—can be used for developing and estimating mathematical models.[41]

Specialized marketing software is also available. MARKSTRAT2 is a management training computer software program that can be customized by its maker Strat*X of Paris and Boston to feature the competitive circumstances of a selected industry. The MARKSTRAT2 model incorporates an extensive number of variables involved in the operation of most business enterprises. In this way, the environmental context of the problem can be analyzed.

The software consists of six to eight periods of simulated time. Choices about a firm's business activities must be made for the upcoming period. Past information and forecasts, available resources, objectives of the firm, and the economic environment are some of the variables which can be altered by the marketer. All such choices are then entered into the MARKSTRAT2 model. After running the simulation software, results for each period's activities for the companies are returned.

As an example, marketers at the firm of Conrad Machine Tools are interested in analyzing the environmental context of the problem facing their firm, which manufactures cutting inserts for high-speed lathes used for shaping steel pieces in the metal fabrication industry. One of the inserts, Sama, is made of a tungsten-carbide alloy with a cutting life of medium length, but the other, Salt, has a tungsten steel base and a diamond tip giving it a relatively long cutting life even when used to shape very hard steel.

Exhibit 2.1 shows a MARKSTRAT2 decision form completed prior to initiating MARKSTRAT2's computations for the period's activities. The two brands of machine cutting tools, Sama and Salt, are featured. Here, Conrad marketers allocate 66% more on the advertising and sales effort of Salt ($2.5 million versus $1.5 million) and list Salt for $420 per unit. As for Sama, it receives a list price of $278.

EXHIBIT 2.1

*A MARKSTRAT2
Decision Form*

MARKSTRAT DECISION FORM - PART 1
A
DEFAULT DECISIONS DISPLAYED FOR PERIOD 1

* Incomplete R&D projects continued with modified unit costs and required budgets
* Other decisions similar to last period.
* Note that these decisions can result in total marketing expenditures in excess of your budget

PRODUCT MANAGEMENT

Brand names	Name of R&D project	Product. planning KU	Advert. budget K$	Advert. research %	Rec. retail price $	Percep. obj. (-20 to +20, or 99) Axis 1	Axis 2
SAMA		150	1500	4	278	99	99
SALT		120	2500	4	420	99	99

The inputs for Exhibit 2.1 are based on past results from Conrad's previous marketing efforts. The resource limitations of Conrad Machine Tools are addressed by Conrad's inability to allocate more than $4 million to the promotional effort for its two inserts. The objective for Conrad is understood to be the improvement of market share for Salt in the short term. The buyer behavior of purchasing managers in five different segments in the metal fabrication industry received inputs at another stage of the MARKSTRAT2 simulation, as did the economic environment for each of these segments.

Exhibit 2.2 shows outcomes for the period based on the inputs of the first figure. As can be seen, Sama would account for more than 45% of sales in segment 5, the specialized machine industry (which comprises the manufacture of such capital equipment as printing presses, food processing equipment, and textile machinery) whereas Saltwould account for only slightly more than 3%. As can be seen from Exhibit 2.2, the more profitable and higher-priced Salt has a substantially lower share in the two most important segments (segments 2 and 5). The problem could thus be broadly defined as

EXHIBIT 2.2

*A MARKSTRAT2
Outcome: Sales
Estimates*

Brand share of market segments (% Units)

		SAMA	SALT
Segment 1	% Units	5.1	4.9
Segment 2	% Units	16.9	7.1
Segment 3	% Units	1.3	4.1
Segment 4	% Units	1.3	7.7
Segment 5	% Units	45.3	3.2
Total market share	% U	15.7	5.2
Total units sales	U	158509	52299
Total retail sales	K $	44066	21966

determining what marketing strategies should be adopted to increase the market share of Salt in each of the five segments and to improve the overall profitability of Sama and Salt across the five segments.

One specific component of this problem would be to determine the attitude of purchasing managers in the specialized machine industry toward diamond-tipped cutting tools. Perhaps these purchasing managers are too price sensitive for their own good. It is possible that these managers consider products with any type of diamond to be an extravagant purchase, despite the longer life and added uses of such cutting tools.

SUMMARY

Defining the marketing research problem is the most important step in a research project. Problem definition is a difficult step, because frequently management has not determined the actual problem or has only a vague notion about it. The researcher's role is to help management identify and isolate the problem.

The tasks involved in formulating the marketing research problem include discussions with the key decision makers including a problem audit, interviews with industry experts, analysis of secondary data, and qualitative research. These tasks should lead to an understanding of the environmental context of the problem. The environmental context of the problem should be analyzed and certain essential factors evaluated. These factors include past information and forecasts about the industry and the firm, objectives of the DM and the organization, buyer behavior, resources and constraints of the firm, the legal and economic environment, and marketing and technological skills of the firm.

Analysis of the environmental context should assist in the identification of the management decision problem, which should then be translated into a marketing research problem. The management decision problem asks what the DM needs to do, whereas the marketing research problem asks what information is needed and how it can be obtained effectively and efficiently. The researcher should avoid defining the marketing research problem either too broadly or too narrowly. An appropriate way of defining the marketing research problem is to make a broad statement of the problem and then identify its specific components.

Developing an approach to the problem is the second step in the marketing research process. The components of an approach consist of objective/theoretical framework, analytical models, research questions, hypotheses, and relevant characteristics influencing the research design. It is necessary that the approach developed be based on objective evidence or empirical evidence and be grounded in theory. The relevant variables and their interrelationships may be neatly summarized via an analytical model. The most common kinds of model structures are verbal, graphical, and mathematical. The research questions are refined statements of the specific components of the problem that ask what specific information is required with respect to the problem components. Research questions may be further refined into hypotheses. Finally, given the problem definition, research questions, and hypotheses, characteristics or factors needed to construct a questionnaire should be identified.

When defining the problem in international marketing research, the researcher must isolate and examine the impact of the self-referent culture (SRC), or the unconscious reference to one's own cultural values. Likewise, when developing an approach, the differences in the environment prevailing in the domestic market and the foreign markets should be carefully considered. Several ethical issues that have an impact on the client and the researcher can arise at this stage but can be resolved by adhering to the seven Cs: communication, cooperation, confidence, candor, closeness, continuity, and creativity. Microcomputer and mainframe software can be useful in the process of defining the problem and developing an approach.[42]

ACRONYMS

The factors to be considered while analyzing the environmental context of the problem may be summed up by the acronym PROBLEM:

P   ast information and forecasts
R   esources and constraints
O   bjectives of the decision maker
B   uyer behavior
L   egal environment
E   conomic environment
M   arketing and technological skills

EXERCISES

QUESTIONS

1. What is the first step in conducting a marketing research project?
2. Why is it important to define the marketing research problem appropriately?
3. What are some reasons why management is often not clear about the real problem?
4. What is the role of the researcher in the problem definition process?
5. What is a problem audit?
6. What is the difference between a symptom and a problem? How can a skillful researcher differentiate between the two and identify a true problem?
7. What are some differences between a management decision problem and a marketing research problem?
8. What are the common types of errors encountered in defining a marketing research problem? What can be done to reduce the incidence of such errors?
9. How are the research questions related to components of the problem?
10. What are the differences between research questions and hypotheses?
11. Is it necessary for every research project to have a set of hypotheses? Why or why not?
12. What are the most common forms of analytical models?
13. Give an example of an analytical model that includes all the three major types.
14. Describe a microcomputer software program that can be used to assist the researcher in defining the research problem.

PROBLEMS

1. State the research problems for each of the following management decision problems.
   a. Should a new product be introduced?
   b. Should an advertising campaign that has run for three years be changed?
   c. Should the in-store promotion for an existing product line be increased?
   d. What pricing strategy should be adopted for a new product?
   e. Should the compensation package be changed to motivate the sales force better?
2. State management decision problems for which the following research problems might provide useful information.
   a. Estimate the sales and market share of department stores in a certain metropolitan area.
   b. Determine the design features for a new product that would result in maximum market share.
   c. Evaluate the effectiveness of alternative TV commercials.
   d. Assess current and proposed sales territories with respect to their sales potential and workload.

e. Determine the prices for each item in a product line so as to maximize total sales for the product line.

3. Identify five symptoms and a plausible cause for each one.

4. For the first component of the department store patronage project, identify the relevant research questions and develop suitable hypotheses. (Hint: Closely follow the example given in this chapter for the fifth component of the department store project.)

5. Suppose that you are doing a project for Delta Airlines. Identify, from secondary sources, the attributes or factors passengers consider when selecting an airline.

COMPUTER EXERCISES

1. You are a consultant to Coca-Cola USA working on a marketing research project for Diet Coke. Use the on-line databases in your library to compile a list of articles related to the Coca-Cola Company, Diet Coke, and the soft drink industry published during the past year.

2. Select any firm. Using secondary sources, obtain information on the annual sales of the firm and the industry for the last ten years. Use a spreadsheet package, such as LOTUS 1-2-3 or EXCEL, or any microcomputer or mainframe statistical package, to develop a simple model relating the firm's sales to the industry sales.

NOTES

1. "Readership Survey Serves *Tennis* Magazine's Marketing Needs," *Quirk's Marketing Research Review* (May 1988): 75–76.

2. *Quirk's* editorial staff, "The pharmacist is foremost," *Quirk's Marketing Research Review* 6 (3) (March 1992): 8–9, 34–35.

3. Robert W. Joselyn, *Designing the Marketing Research Project* (New York: Mason/Charter, 1977), p. 46.

4. *Consumer Market Research Techniques, Usages, Patterns, and Attitudes in 1983* (Arlington Heights: Market Facts, Inc.), p. 20.

5. Mary T. Curren, Valerie S. Folkes, and Joel H. Steckel, "Explanations for Successful and Unsuccessful Marketing Decisions: The Decision Maker's Perspective," *Journal of Marketing* 56 (April 1992): 18–31; L. Adler and C. S. Mayer, *Managing the Marketing Research Function* (Chicago: American Marketing Association, 1977), pp. 89–110.

6. Sue, Jones "Problem-Definition in Marketing Research: Facilitating between Clients and Researchers," *Psychology and Marketing* (Summer 1985): 83–93.

7. Leonard L. Berry, Jeffrey S. Conant, and A. Parasuraman, "A Framework for Conducting a Services Marketing Audit," *Journal of the Academy of Marketing Science* 19 (Summer 1991): 255–268; Russell L. Ackoff, *Scientific Method* (New York: Wiley, 1961), p. 71; Russell L. Ackoff, *The Art of Problem Solving* (New York: Wiley, 1978).

8. See also Bernie Whalen, "Researchers Stymied by 'Adversary Culture' in Firms," *Marketing News* (September 17, 1982): 1, 7.

9. Joel Levine, "Six Factors Mark Researchers Who Sway Strategic Decisions," *Marketing News* (February 4, 1983): 1.

10. Vernon R. Alden, "Who Says You Can't Crack the Japanese Market?" *Harvard Business Review* (January–February 1987): 52–56.

11. J. Scott Armstrong, "Prediction of Consumer Behavior by Experts and Novices," *Journal of Consumer Research* 18 (September 1991): 251–56; Phillip Kotler, "A Guide to Gathering Expert Estimates," *Business Horizons* 13 (October 1970): 79–87.

12. "Excitement Image Helps Pontiac to Become GM's 'Top Import Conquester,'" *Marketing News* (July 31, 1987): 18, 31.

13. "Teen Mags Dive In," *American Demographics* (June 1987): 23–24.

14. Maisie Wong, Ayn Gelinas, and Phyllis Rocha, "Avon Researchers Find That Normal Rules Don't Apply When Testing among Hispanic Women," *Quirk's Marketing Research Review* (June–July 1990): 8–10, 38–39.

15. Mary T. Curren, Valerie S. Folkes, and Joel H. Steckel, "Explanations for Successful and Unsuccessful Marketing Decisions: The Decision Maker's Perspective," *Journal of Marketing* 56 (April 1992): 18–31; J. Scott Armstrong, "Prediction of Consumer Behavior by Experts and Novices," *Journal of Consumer Research* 18 (September 1991): 251–56; and William B. Locander and A. Benton Cocanougher (eds.),

Problem Definition in Marketing (Chicago: American Marketing Association, Marketing Research Techniques, Ser. 2, 1975).

16. C. L. Jain, "Myths and Realities of Forecasting," *Journal of Business Forecasting* 9 (Fall 1990): 18–22.

17. "Takeout Food Turns Up Heat," *Marketing News* (May 6, 1987): 31.

18. Ron Sanchez and D. Sudharshan, "Real-Time Market Research," *Marketing Intelligence and Planning* 11 (1993): 29–38.

19. Based on a marketing research project conducted by the author.

20. J. Sheth and G. Morrison, "Winning Again in the Marketplace: Nine Strategies for Revitalizing Mature Products," *The Journal of Consumer Marketing* (1984): 19.

21. Paul W. Conner, "Research Request Step Can Enhance Use of Results," *Marketing News* 19 (January 4, 1985): 41.

22. See Paul D. Boughton, "Marketing Research and Small Business: Pitfalls and Potential," *Journal of Small Business Management* 21 (July 1983): 36–42, for a list of questions small business managers (and decision makers) can ask to make sure they get the most from their research.

23. Joe Agnew, "Local Involvement Helps Franchisees 'Dechain the Chain,'" *Marketing News* (November 21, 1986): 1, 30.

24. Jacob Jacoby, "Consumer Research: A State of the Art Review," *Journal of Marketing* 42 (April 1978): 87–96. See also Shelby D. Hunt, "Truth in Marketing Theory and Research," *Journal of Marketing* 54 (July 1990): 1–15; Shelby D. Hunt, "For Reason and Realism in Marketing," *Journal of Marketing* 56 (April 1992): 89–102.

25. Bobby. J. Calder, Lynn W. Phillips, and Alice M. Tybout, "Designing Research for Applications," *Journal of Consumer Research* 8 (September 1981): 197–207. A positivist perspective on research is used here. Positivism encompasses logical positivism, logical empiricism, and all forms of falsificationism. This is the dominant perspective adopted in commercial marketing research. More recently, a relativist perspective has been offered. See, for example, Shelby D. Hunt, *Modern Marketing Theory* (Cincinnati: South-Western, 1991).

26. N. K. Malhotra, "A Threshold Model of Store Choice," *Journal of Retailing* (Summer 1983): 3–21.

27. For an illustration of a graphical model of software piracy, see Figure 1 of Moshe Givon, Vijay Mahajan, and Eitan Muller, "Software Piracy: Estimation of Lost Sales and the Impact on Software Diffusion," *Journal of Marketing* 59 (January 1995): 29–37.

28. For an example of developing a theoretical framework and a mathematical model based on it, see Christopher M. Miller, Shelby H. McIntyre, and Murali K. Mantrala, "Toward Formalizing Fashion Theory," *Journal of Marketing Research* 30 (May 1993): 142–157.

29. G. L Lilien, Philip Kotler, and K. Sridhar Moorthy, *Marketing Models* (Englewood Cliffs, NJ: Prentice Hall, 1992).

30. Douglas Scott and Flaurel English, "Tracking Automotive Intentions and Imagery: A Case Study," *Journal of Advertising Research* (February–March 1989): RC-13–RC-20.

31. For a recent example of hypotheses formulation, see Gregory T. Gundlach, Ravi S. Achrol, and John T. Mentzer, "The Structure of Commitment in Exchange," *Journal of Marketing* 59 (January 1995): 78–92.

32. Fred N. Kerlinger, *Foundations of Behavioral Research* 3rd ed. (New York: Holt, Rinehart, and Winston, 1986). See pp. 17–20 for a detailed discussion of the characteristics and role of hypotheses in research. For an alternative view, see Raymond J. Lawrence, "To Hypothesize or Not to Hypothesize? The Correct 'Approach' to Survey Research," *Journal of the Market Research Society* 24 (October 1982): 335–343. For a recent example of model development and hypotheses formulation see Mary Jo Bitner, "Servicescapes: The Impact of Physical Surroundings on Customers and Employees," *Journal of Marketing* 56 (April 1992): 57–71.

33. The integrated role of theory, models, research questions, and hypotheses in marketing research can be seen in Robert E. Morgan and Shelby D. Hunt, "The Commitment-Trust Theory of Relationship Marketing," *Journal of Marketing* 58 (July 1994): 20–38.

34. A. K. Jain, C. Pinson, and N. K. Malhotra, "Customer Loyalty as a Construct in the Marketing of Banking Services," *International Journal of Banking* (1987): 49–72.

35. "Chanel Plans to Run Ads in Magazines with Less Cachet," *Wall Street Journal* (January 27, 1988): 30.

36. Darral G. Clarke, *Marketing Analysis and Decision Making* 2nd ed. (South San Francisco: Scientific Press, 1992).

37. Dagnoli Judann, "Why Heinz Went Sour in Brazil," *Advertising Age* (December 5, 1988).

38. James A. Lee, "Cultural Analysis of Overseas Operations," *Harvard Business Review* 44 (March–April 1966): 106–14; and Susan P. Douglas and C. Samuel Craig, *International Marketing Research* (Englewood Cliffs, NJ: Prentice Hall, 1983).

39. David Kilburn, "Unilever Struggles with Surf in Japan," *Advertising Age* (May 6, 1991).

40. G. R. Laczniak and P. E. Murphy, *Ethical Marketing Decisions, the Higher Road* (Boston: Allyn and Bacon, 1993), p. 64.

41. For mainframe packages see:
  SPSS Base Systems User's Guide (Englewood Cliffs, NJ: Prentice Hall, 1994).
  SAS Language and Procedure: Usage, V 6 (Cary, NC: SAS Institute, 1989).
  SAS Language and Procedure: Usage 2, V 6 (Cary, NC: SAS Institute, 1991).
  SAS Procedures Guide, V 6, 3rd ed. (Cary, NC: SAS Institute, 1990).
  SAS Language: Reference, V 6 (Cary, NC: SAS Institute, 1990).
  BMDP Statistical Software Manual, Vols. 1 and 2 (Berkeley: University of California Press, 1990).

  For microcomputer packages see:
  SPSS/PC+™ V 4.0 BASE MANUAL (Englewood Cliffs, NJ: Prentice Hall, 1990).
  SPSS/PC+ Advanced Statistics™, V 4.0 (Englewood Cliffs, NJ: Prentice Hall, 1990).
  SAS/STAT™ User Guide, V 6, 4th ed., Vols. 1 and 2 (Cary, NC: SAS Institute, 1990).
  The BMDP manual for microcomputers is the same as that for the mainframe.

42. The assistance of James Agarwal with the international marketing research example, the assistance of Mark Leach and Gina Miller in writing the ethics section, and the assistance of Mark Peterson in writing the computer applications section is gratefully acknowledged.

PROFESSIONAL PERSPECTIVES

The Profession of Marketing Research: A Strategic Assessment

The profession of marketing research is being redefined. To understand this redefinition, we must take a hard look at the current state of both the industry and the profession, because they are so intertwined. However, before examining the status of the profession we will consider the research purchasers, advertising agencies, and research agencies.

RESEARCH PURCHASERS

Dramatic changes are taking place in the corporate environment that have a direct effect on the research function. One is the impact of new technologies. Powerful personal computers are fostering hands-on access to marketing data throughout the corporate environment. Scanning and single-source data systems are flooding packaged goods marketers with an overflow of data. Advanced, extremely fast communications capabilities are accelerating the marketing process. This technology is having the effect of "flattening" the traditional corporate organization. Corporations no longer need a battalion of middle managers to prepare and filter information for senior corporate decision making.

For similar reasons, large corporate research departments are often seen as incompatible with today's lean and mean, fast-moving corporate environment. In many cases, corporate research departments are being reorganized, redeployed, downsized, and, in some cases, wiped out altogether. In many firms, the nature of corporate investments in marketing research is also changing. We are seeing major new investments in single-source data systems, product tracking panels, audience measurement systems, and service quality measurement systems. These systems tend to be tactical. Constrained budgets have forced firms to invest in the quick-payoff research that such systems seem to represent.

William D. Neal[1]

William D. Neal is the founder and senior executive officer of Sophisticated Data Research (SDR), Inc., in Atlanta. He has also served as vice-president of the Marketing Research Division and chairman of the board of the American Marketing Association. Mr. Neal oversees all marketing and customer satisfaction programs at SDR. In addition, he conducts seminars and provides consulting services to clients in the areas of market segmentation and strategic positioning

These tactical systems, which are often very promotion-oriented, are being purchased and installed at the expense of the more strategic and long-term research that supports long-term planning.

However, emerging sectors of the economy are approaching marketing research in a different way than do the traditional packaged goods companies that have been our corporate model for so many years. The services sector is a major bright spot for our profession and the industry of marketing research. Especially noteworthy are the areas of communications, health care, travel and tourism, financial services, and professional services. All are making major investments in marketing research, but few are using the packaged goods model. High technology marketers, for the most part, continue to ignore traditional marketing research, though there are a few notable exceptions. Retailing seems to be slowly emerging as a major area for research investigations especially in service quality measurement.

ADVERTISING AGENCIES

In many advertising agencies, the trend is toward severe downsizing of research departments. Research professionals in many advertising agencies are experiencing lower status. They are being viewed as technicians rather than as consultants and managers. Agency research professionals have reduced in-house capabilities and they are becoming less involved in high-level client consulting and advisory services. Many are simply brokering marketing research to full-service commercial firms—and, most recently, they are doing precious little of

[1]From "The Profession of Marketing Research," by William D. Neal, in *Marketing Research* (September 1989): pp. 13–23. Reprinted with permission from the American Marketing Association, Chicago, IL.

that. In general, the research professional in the advertising agency is being directed toward concept development and promotional pretesting and directed away from assessment, evaluation, and strategy development functions.

RESEARCH AGENCIES

Large, traditional marketing research firms are typically taking one of three paths:

1. They are building and selling huge databases, such as transaction measurement products and services, specialized panels, audience measurement systems, or service-quality measurement systems.
2. They are building and selling technology-based solutions to marketing problems, such as consumer behavior models, pricing models, marketing effectiveness/efficiency models, or market forecasting models.
3. They are very efficiently providing the operational end of custom research services, namely data collection, data processing, and computer analysis services.

All three of these avenues require ever-increasing capital investments, and this requirement for capital is fueling much of the consolidation and buyout activity that is flourishing in the marketing research industry. It is becoming increasingly difficult for these larger, operationally oriented firms to compete in the custom research and expert consulting arenas because of (1) their typically high overhead and operating costs, (2) extreme pressure to "keep the plant operating at full capacity," and (3) a management philosophy directed toward operating efficiency and not scientific investigation.

Among the smaller research agencies and consultancies, we see ever-expanding numbers, increased fragmentation, and a tendency toward "custom" research services in both strategic and tactical arenas. These smaller firms are moving toward product and service category areas of specialization, and their low operational overhead makes them very price competitive. In many cases, they are putting the custom research departments of the large, full-service research companies at an extreme price and expertise disadvantage.

STATUS OF THE PROFESSION

The crossroads at which the profession finds itself is best described by the role of the professional marketing researcher in the corporate environment, which is often ill-defined. Is it the role of the marketing researcher to be the consummate critic of new things and new ideas, who subjects those new ideas to some acid test of dispassionate analysis, or is it that of the advocate of the new and faddish? Is our role that of the high-level consultant who has a finger on the pulse of the consumer or customer, or is it that of a technician who needs only to react to the demands and whims of the marketer? Is the professional marketing researcher a specialist or a generalist, an artist or a technocrat?

Another problem facing our industry and detracting severely from our professional image is the lack of specific requirements for entry into our profession. There are no explicit educational requirements, though the vast majority of us have at least one college degree. There are no requirements in terms of either field of training or experience. Literally anyone can hang out a shingle and claim to be a qualified marketing researcher.

Current professional development programs do not seem to be adequate for advancing the knowledge and expertise of the majority of marketing researchers. For the most part, colleges and universities are not providing a sufficient technical or business foundation for entry-level professionals in our field. Until very recently, there was no generally-agreed upon curriculum for a career in marketing research, but the American Marketing Association now has published a draft curriculum. Few opportunities are available for independent training of marketing research professionals. Far fewer investments in professional training are being made by either client firms or research agencies, mainly because of both the expense and the lack of pertinent programs. Finally, few quality publications are targeted to the professional practitioner, though this situation is rapidly changing. Where will this lead us in the future?

FUTURE DIRECTIONS

In the future, the corporate research staff is likely to be more decentralized and dispersed into the operating units. The research staff will become smaller, because there will be fewer technical and analytical staff people. In many firms, the research function will become more "managerial" in that the corporate research department will become procurers and managers of business research information and information systems, not collectors and detailed analyzers of data. They will have a major role in integrating business information from divergent sources—market scanning and transaction measurement systems, secondary sources, internal sources, and custom studies. More research emphasis will be on service quality research and measurement, customer satisfaction research and measurement, pricing research and pricing experiments, and explaining measured market behavior with sophisticated models that simulate the purchase environment. We can expect to see more true experimentation, with less emphasis on ad hoc, disjointed market analysis. Given the foregoing observations, we can expect that the corporate research staff will rely more heavily on outside, independent service companies for both market measurement and consulting services for particular product or service areas.

For the research providers, the future for business research seems bright—but it will be different! First, the split will continue to accelerate between the larger, more traditional marketing research companies and the smaller, consultancy-based research organizations. On one side, the major research firms will invest heavily in the operational aspect of the business, either providing very efficient custom data collection and data processing services or providing highly specialized database and technology-based services. The survivors will be those that continue to provide extremely efficient or unique services and have the capital resources to exploit their position.

On the other side will be an ever-expanding set of small, specialized firms that will combine custom research services with product- and service-category-specific consulting services. The secret to survival for these firms will be a top-notch reputation in a particular product/service category, a considerable capability to execute custom research studies rapidly, and a broad utilization of the newer analytical procedures.

It may be nearly impossible for any research firm to fill both roles. Each side requires a unique management philosophy and management skills. The two sides require different financial structures and radically different marketing philosophies. Therefore, the larger, traditional "general services" research firms that have been a basic strength in our industry may be forced to jump to one side or the other of this split or, alternatively, to put an entirely separate corporate entity in each camp. Either way, marketing research professionals and firms must look toward the future, if they expect to be in it and be viable.

The Marketing Research Problem: From the DM's Desk to Study Execution

As a practicing researcher, I find that much of the satisfaction of this profession comes from the sense of discovery and achievement that arises because there are so many unique and interesting problems waiting to be solved. It is this uniqueness that prevents the development of a simple cookbook approach to problem solving and allows creativity in our professional lives. Still, we must have foundations for how we define or examine marketing research problems.

The decision maker (DM) tends to focus on the symptoms and usually defines problems in terms of a desired outcome, such as why are my sales down (desired outcome = high levels of sales) or how I choose the best of the two test products (desired outcome = product which produces the largest share and/or revenue). To a researcher, on the other hand, a problem is appropriately defined when it states the needed information such that a level of measurement is specified. For example:

DM: Our sales are going down. What can we do?
Researcher: Declining sales are symptoms of problems in the marketplace in general (all products in our category are declining in popularity) or problems with our product. The resolution is sequential:

1. What are the causes of the decline? (A research issue)
2. What actions are we capable of taking against these causes once identified? (A management issue)
3. Which of these actions produces the optimal result for us? (A research issue)
4. How do we monitor the impact of these actions once they are taken? (A research issue)
5. How do we implement ongoing modifications to continue to improve sales? (Another sequence of management and research issues)

Thus, from the researcher's point of view, the problem definition has to result in a specific set of components.

In the simplest case, a DM asks: "Which of these two proposed new products is better?" The researcher must now define "better" in such a way that specific components of the marketing research problem can be identified and appropriate measurements made. The definition stage could result in defining "better" as some combination of:

1. Has an image most consistent with that sought by our company in terms of specific measurable image characteristics
2. Has the greatest appeal when measured in a concept test prior to product creation (appeal defined in terms of a purchase interest scale)
3. Has the highest sales forecast in a simulated test market that includes a home use period
4. Results in the highest net sales when accounting for cannibalization in a minitest market

Each of these four definitions of "better" implies a specific measurement to be taken by the researcher. However, the researcher must address the more specific issues of:

1. There are many components of image. Which are appropriate to this occasion and how do we assess them?
2. Which purchase interest scale do we use, and how do we evaluate the results?
3. There are several approaches to simulated test markets. Which do we select?
4. How do we measure cannibalization in a test market?

These do not exhaust the components of the problem that must be addressed, but they show that the researcher must eventually define the problem in terms of specific components and measurements. At the exploratory stages of problem development the measures may be "expert opinion." However, at later stages the measures will likely be obtained from the eventual purchasers or purchase deciders for the product or service.

A general statement of proper problem definition is as follows: "When the problem is properly defined the researcher knows all of the possible answers, but the researcher simply has not counted the answers yet." In other words, the best problem definition, from the researcher's point of view, leads to such a precise definition of measurement that the nature of the answers are known: only their frequencies are unknown. For example, problem definition meetings may have led the researcher to measure the following characteristics of a sample of current users of a product:

1. Age
2. Number of times the product was purchased in the past seven days
3. Number of items purchased at each purchase occasion (past seven days)
4. Number of times competitive products were purchased in past seven days
5. Number of competitive items purchased at each purchase occasion (past seven days)

Ronald L. Tatham

Ronald L. Tatham is president and chief executive officer, Burke Marketing Research, an employee-owned company, Dr. Tatham is actively involved in both the general management of the corporation and the design and analysis of research. Burke operates with the concept of the "producing manager." Every senior manager is involved in client-related activities and the delivery of Burke's research efforts.

6. Ratings of client's product and competitive products on five ten-point image questions

For each of the six information areas listed above, the researcher knows the form of the answer and the limits within which acceptable answers can be given. That is, we know the population distribution of ages and we know the specific units (years of age) we will get for answers; we know that only answers of the numbers 1 through 10 are permitted on information item six, and so forth. We do not know the actual values of the answers among our target population. This may sound naively simple, but it illustrates the point that you must know what you are measuring before you attempt to gather information.

If the problem is defined rigorously, the usefulness of the information can be tested with the DM. The basic question to be asked of the DM is: "If the data the respondents give us take the following forms, what would you or could you do?" The researcher can show the DM hypothetical results based on the researcher's conjecture. If the DM says, "I'm not sure what I would do with that information," the researcher must stop and ask, "What additional information would you need to make this information more useful or what about this information limits its usefulness to you?" Because you know the form of all of the possible answers, you must test the likely results for usefulness with the DM even if you do not know the outcome of the study. A proper definition of the problem will provide the DM with the relevant information needed for decision making and guide the researcher in proceeding with the research project.

Defining the Research Problem

Most marketing researchers will agree that defining the research problem is the most important step in the marketing research process. This part in the marketing research process is essentially the translation of the management decision information needs into the marketing research objectives or components of the problem, which collectively state the research problem. The execution of a study will always be enhanced by articulating the components of the marketing research problem in the most explicit and specific terms possible.

To accomplish this goal, first get the client to sign off on the information needs in writing. If the client hasn't already written them down, you should write them when presenting the research proposal. This is to make sure that you have a clear understanding of the DM's needs so that an appropriate set of components of the problem can be stated.

Also, before beginning the development of a questionnaire, specify the components of the marketing research problem. Sometimes, however, some additional components of the problem emerge during the development of the questionnaire. If this happens, it is necessary to restate all the components of the problem after the research design has been developed.

One way to ensure that you have incorporated all the marketing research problem components into the questionnaire is to develop a questionnaire-components grid. The grid consists of cells defined by columns and rows; each column represents a component of the problem further broken down by research questions and hypotheses, and each row represents a question. At the intersection of each row and column where a question addresses a com-

Albert G. Swint

Albert Swint is Vice President, Marketing Workshop, Inc. At the time of writing this article he was an account director responsible for all aspects of the design and execution of marketing research studies at Elrick and Lavidge, Inc.

ponent of the problem, you put an "X"; otherwise leave a cell blank. When completed, the grid gives a vivid picture of what problem components are not addressed by any questions, or what questions do not address any problem component, research question, or hypothesis.

The problem definition process also includes discussions with decision makers, interviews with industry experts and other knowledgeable individuals, analysis of secondary data, and (sometimes) qualitative research. From the perspective of a research firm like Elrick and Lavidge, these activities often take place internally within the client's organization before a proposal is requested. We encourage our clients to do as much of the process internally as possible, at least up to the qualitative research phase (if it is needed), because it enables the research firm to deliver results faster and cheaper. Another benefit of doing the qualitative research internally is that it forces the client to think about the problem in depth. Consequently, the client will understand the underlying issues much better, will give better guidance to the research firm, and will be able to act upon the research findings more decisively.

In addition, the client should not hesitate to seek input from the research firm regarding cost and time constraints. Elrick and Lavidge is eager to have close relationships with clients so that our input is sought before a formal proposal is issued. It gives us a head start and a better understanding of the issues. On the client side, the informal preproposal input regarding cost and time constraints helps ensure that the client research manager gives realistic cost and turnaround estimates to the decision makers, thus facilitating realistic expectations on the part of the decision makers.

Life in the Fast Lane:
Fast-Food Chains Race to Be Number One

Fast-food restaurants have been characterized by their limited menus, self-service, high turnover, and high percentage of take-out orders. The fast-food hamburger spectrum is comprised of many popular chains, although McDonald's, Burger King, Hardee's/Roy Rogers, and Wendy's are the four largest. These chains and other fast-food restaurants had sales of more than $90 billion in 1994 in the United States alone and accounted for 30% of the U.S. food service industry, which totaled about $300 billion in 1994. The largest, McDonald's, had U.S. systemwide sales exceeding $15 billion in 1994, up more than $1 billion from 1993. It has approximately 10,000 restaurants domestically. In contrast, Burger King is number 2 with U.S. sales exceeding $6 billion in 1994, up from about $5.5 billion in 1993. It has about 6,000 restaurants in the United States. Advertising is a major competitive weapon, with McDonald's spending more than $100 million in 1995.

In coming years, all the major chains will have to deal with the aging U.S. population. As the average age of the American consumer increases, a shift away from fast-food restaurants toward midscale restaurants is a possibility, if the fast-food industry does not meet the needs of this group. According to a recent National Restaurant Association study, 79% of customers aged 18 to 24 visited quick-service restaurants, but only 60% of the 40 to 60 age group did. This probably reflected the disparity of disposable incomes between these two age groups and a desire for better services among older customers. With the number of Americans aged 50 or older expected to rise over 15% by the year 2000, combined with a decline among members of the 15 to 34 age group, the fast-food industry will have to adapt to the changing population structure.

One way the industry might do this is to focus on nutrition. An important aspect of America's lifestyle has been its increasing focus on becoming a healthier nation. Mainstream America has become obsessed with health to the point of eschewing their old lifestyles and discriminating against those who do not share their view. Since the mid-1980s, the average life span of Americans increased from 72 to 81 years. This change may be due to exercise and better eating habits. As all areas of society have changed to reflect this new awareness about health, so too must the fast-food industry reposition itself. The industry must have concrete information on what the new health-conscious society will expect from it.

Therefore, it is not surprising that McDonald's researched, tested, and introduced the McLean Deluxe in 1990. The hamburger is 91% fat free and has only 325 calories. Hardee's followed suit and introduced the Lean 1, while Burger King and Wendy's introduced skinless, boneless breasts of grilled chicken sandwiches . Upon the launch of Burger King's grilled chicken sandwich, the BK Broiler, sales of the sandwich were reported at over one million per day. Today this 265 calorie sandwich has captured a market of its own. In addition to its lighter sandwich, Burger King tested Weight Watchers products in its restaurants and debuted salad bars nationally. Over the years in response to the changing lifestyles of its consumers, Wendy's has introduced baked potatoes; five new, fresh prepackaged salads each served with a breadstick; cholesterol-free all-vegetable cooking oil for frying; and reduced-calorie, low- and no-fat salad dressings. All the new items are meant to combine nutrition with carryout convenience.

Although customers report that they desire more healthy foods, their purchases have failed to uphold that premise. In 1993, the biggest new introductions were high in both fat and calories. The Big Bacon Classic offered by Wendy's includes a quarter-pound beef pattie topped with three strips of bacon, a slice of cheese, and a dollop of mayonnaise. Each of these sandwiches averages about 700 calories and is loaded with fat. McDonald's is joining the fray by test marketing fried chicken in several markets. The Hardee's fried chicken has fared well. Burger King's Whopper sandwich with its increased weight still remains a favorite despite its high caloric and fat content. Recent estimates show that more than seven hundred million Whopper sandwiches are sold each year. The reason for this backlash against low-fat and low-calorie foods has been revealed by market research that shows that the American public is sick of being chastised about eating the food they love. Moreover, customers are craving a variety of selections.

Experts have predicted that the number of menu items will continue to grow as all fast-food restaurateurs offer new items to avoid consumer boredom and maintain growth and market share. As a spokesman for Burger King said, "We'll stay with what we know best, but we have to add items to meet consumer preferences." Therefore, while Burger King made a deal with Domino's in the early 1990s to offer personal pizzas, McDonald's has offered its own brand of pizza along with chicken fajitas, and Arby's has opened its own sub shop. In a further effort to attract customers, some restaurants have been teaming with prepackaged food brands. McDonald's had teamed with Quaker Oats to offer oatmeal to its customers for breakfast. More recently, some McDonald's franchises have teamed with Good Humor brand ice cream products to offer its customers a wider variety of desserts. Burger King has teamed with Newman's Own to provide its customers with branded salad dressing. Upon the alliance with Newman's Own, Burger King's salad sales doubled.

The most recent trend in fast-food restaurants has been toward value pricing. This trend was ushered in by Taco Bell, which dropped prices and boosted system wide sales by 18.5% in only two years. Although it was a novelty for a short time, value pricing has become a part of almost every major competitor. McDonald's offers its Extra Value Menu, Wendy's has a 99¢ Super Value Menu that emphasizes variety by offering items ranging from ready-to-go Side Salads to a Country Fried Steak Sandwich, and Burger King and Hardee's offer similar plans to that of McDonald's.

Although many restaurants have been focusing on cost, a recent survey taken by the National Restaurant Association revealed that according to customers, cleanliness of the dining area is the most important attribute to customer satisfaction, followed by accuracy of filling the order. Reasonable prices ranked a distant sixth which was two spots below receiving the correct change. From these findings many restaurants have begun targeting customer service rather than strictly focusing on price. For example, Wendy's has adopted a special "M.B.A.," which stands for "A Mop Bucket Attitude." This represents Wendy's "commitment to the traditional definition of customer satisfaction which means putting customer service (cleanliness, quality food, and atmosphere) before numbers and computer printouts." Wendy's maintains that this is one of the major reasons for their success. Burger King has long recognized the importance of creating a favorable and memorable dining experience. Burger King was the first fast-food restaurant to introduce dining rooms that allowed its customers to dine inside its facilities. In 1992, Burger King became the first fast-food restaurant to introduce table

service and an expanded dinner menu to enhance the customer's dining experience. Burger King Corporation states that it has "always taken great care in the design and construction of its restaurants so they will be attractive features of the communities in which they are located." Burger King Corporation plans to introduce the Double Drive-Thru, Kiosk, and In-Line restaurants in the 1990s to meet the challenges that the fast-food market will present.

In a further effort to expand the fast-food market, the industry has looked overseas. Because Asian and European markets are at the stage of fast food that America reached in 1960, American chains have a substantial competitive advantage there. Marketing experts have predicted that it will be easier for established American chains to expand overseas than at home. McDonald's is expected to realize more than 30% of its operating profits outside the United States in 1995, as compared with 21% in 1990.

Burger King has also focused on Japan as a wide open market for its burgers. Almost 22 years after the opening of McDonald's first restaurant in Japan, by 1993, Burger King had opened its own restaurant to compete. Burger King cites the $4.22 billion hamburger market in Japan as incentive for operating in the country. The competition among Japanese companies in the business has grown fierce, however. Home companies own about half of the market while McDonald's controls the rest. Burger King has turned much attention to the Eastern European market. It has recently opened up restaurants in Poland, the former East Germany, and Hungary while at the same time establishing a training academy in London to service its European franchises. In 1995, Burger King had over 7,000 restaurants in 50 countries worldwide.

Wendy's has recently been recognized as a serious competitor in the international fast-food market. Wendy's is currently contracted with 43 countries outside of the United States and has approximately 28 markets that are already open for business. Sixty-two percent of Wendy's international stores are located in the Pacific Region, which includes Japan, Korea, Taiwan, Hong Kong, the Philippines, Indonesia, New Zealand, and Guam. The company's fastest growing market in 1994 was Saudi Arabia. Eastern Europe currently offers an untapped market on which Wendy's is concentrating. In these countries, some locations have needed 12 to 15 registers to keep up with demand for the company's products. Transactions have varied between 5,000 and 10,000 per day, when 5,000 transactions per week is considered good in the United States. Currently, systemwide sales total over $3.6 billion (this amount includes U.S. locations as well as international locations). Given the stiff competition, it remains to be seen if McDonald's can continue to be the leader in the domestic fast-food race, as well as become the front runner in the international fast-food race.

QUESTIONS

1. Describe the marketing information needs of the fast-food industry.

2. What role can marketing research play in providing the information needed?

3. Give some examples of problem identification research that McDonald's can undertake to ensure their continued leadership in the fast-food industry.

4. Describe the kinds of problem solution research that Hardee's might undertake to improve its sales and market share.

5. Given the market potential overseas, should fast-food chains conduct marketing research in foreign countries? What kind of opportunities and challenges will fast-foods chains encounter while conducting international marketing research?

REFERENCES

1. Whalen, Jeanne. "Fast-Food Hungers for Fresh Approach." *Advertising Age* (November 8, 1993): 3.

2. Stern, Gabriella. "In a Turnabout, Fast-Food Fare Becomes Fattier." *Wall Street Journal* (August 23, Monday 1993): B1.

3. "Burger King Opens First Store in Japan, 22 Years after Rival." *Wall Street Journal* (September 23, 1993): A10.

4. Sellers, Patricia. "Look Who Learned About Value." *Fortune* (October 18, 1993): 75–76.

5. Bartlett, Michael and Lisa Bertagnoli. "'93 R&I Forecast: Operations Work to Keep Business Costs in Line as Economy Slowly Perks Up." *Restaurants and Institutions* (January 1, 1993): 14.

6. Carlino, Bill. "Fast Food Tops '94 Forecast; Passes Full Service; NRA Predicts 2% Growth for Industry." *Nation's Restaurant News* (December 6, 1993): 1.

7. Goldman, Kevin. "McDonald's Mixes Past with New Slogan." *Wall Street Journal* (February 17, 1995): B4.

CASE 1.2 Nike Sprints Ahead of the Competition, Yet Has a Long Way to Run

Recently, Nike Inc., located in Beaverton, Oregon, entered its third decade of business as the number one U.S. athletic footwear company and the number two American brand in terms of name recognition among foreign consumers, a status shared with IBM and second only to Coca-Cola. This high degree of recognition is probably one of the main reasons Nike has been so immensely successful. For the 1993 fiscal year Nike continued to soar and earned $365 million with sales of $3.93 billion, up from $3.41 billion in 1992. Nike held a tight grip on the athletic shoe market with a 24% share of the market, followed by Reebok and Adidas with 16% and 14% shares, respectively. Furthermore, Nike held a market share exceeding 50% in some shoe channels.

Perhaps such success should be attributed in part to Nike's decision to marry marketing to athletic performance in 1987, when it was overtaken by Reebok International Ltd. as the industry leader. One of the first offsprings of this marriage were shoes with air bags that were visible in a tiny window in the heel. Nike developed and tested these shoes with their target market's needs in mind by soliciting volunteers to wear the shoes and then return them to Nike to see how well they held up. This product, perfected through market testing and pushed through extensive advertising, represented the beginning of Nike's successful Air line, which enabled Nike to surpass Reebok in market share and sales.

With the marketing success story of the Air line, the slow unit growth in the athletic footwear market, and the notorious fickleness of buyers, Nike felt that advertising was increasingly important. Its 1991 advertising budget was $100 million, a significant increase over the $52 million the company spent in 1990. Also, when deciding how to spend advertising dollars, Nike realized that with a 28.6% share of the overall U.S. sneaker market in 1991, as well as a 45% share of the men's niche, it was significantly skewed to performance sneakers. For this reason, Michael Jordan, Andre Agassi, Bo Diddley, Bo Jackson, and Butch Reynolds were chosen to promote the new lines. Nike found out that their target market wanted "authenticity," and to convey this image, Nike wanted advertising that communicated that Nike wearers played sports—they did not just watch others play them.

During 1992, Nike has also made a push for the woman's athletic shoe market. Reebok International has held the lead in that market for some time. While most of Nike's advertising is very male dominated, 1992 saw a very aggressive ad campaign directed toward women. Jennie Garth of *Beverly Hills, 90210* fame put out an exercise video with the sponsorship of Nike. In conjunction with Lady Foot Locker stores, Nike paired the video with jazzercise shoes for the Christmas 1992 season. Nike supplied Lady Foot Locker with posters of Jennie Garth to give away with shoe purchases.

Nike also hoped to repeat their U.S. success in Europe, with similar advertising campaigns focusing on performance. Nike had good reason to want a successful advertising campaign in Europe, since Europe is a market with vast potential. Sales of sneakers in Europe in 1993 rose to $4.5 billion. It is estimated that Nike and Reebok combined had 50% of the market in 1993, up from only 5% only a decade ago. For the fiscal year ended May 31, 1993, Nike sneaker sales in Europe were $1.1 billion, up 25% from 1992 and about six times the sales in 1987. Rather than strictly compete with Adidas and Puma in Europe for the athletic market, Nike and Reebok have instituted strong marketing programs to sell street sneakers to the European masses. Nike and Reebok each spend between $80 and $100 million per year in Europe on advertising and promotions. This compares with a smaller budget of only $60 million for Adidas. Recent Nike and Reebok advertising has capitalized on the surging European popularity of basketball spurred on by the 1992 Olympic dream team. NBA stars have been used extensively for advertising and personal appearances promoting Nike and Reebok products.

After six years of rapid growth, Nike has emerged as the most powerful force in the world of sports and sportswear. Annual sales have stalled at $4 billion, however, and Nike is currently trying to find a way to restart itself. Today, one out of three pairs of sneakers that are sold in the United States are Nike. Sixty percent of all the basketball shoes sold are Nike. Despite these impressive figures, Nike's revenues decreased by an estimated 6% for the fiscal year ending May 31, 1994. This translated into a revenue of about $3.7 billion. Profits decreased by 22% to a level of $283 million. In addition, the price of Nike stock had dropped by approximately 41%. The sale of basketball shoes had dropped sharply, and the key growth markets of Europe and Japan had also "tanked." The situation, however, was not all discouraging. On the brighter side, analysts feel that Nike had touched the bottom, and earnings should jump approximately 12% by 1995 and reach $316 million. New model shoes including redesigned basketball shoes should be catching on with retailers.

At the heart of the problem were many of the teenagers and twenty-somethings who drove Nike's incredible sales over the past years. These consumers had turned away from sneakers in masses. This segment was looking for shoes that are fresh and less commercial in nature. This desire has been fulfilled in the form of increasingly popular outdoor hiking boots.

To resolve Nike's problems, chairman Phil Knight replaced Nike's 66-year-old president with 42-year-old Tom Clarke. Nike will also attempt to battle the saturation of the U.S. market. It will redesign its "air" technology to present a new line of running shoes, basketball shoes, and cross-training shoes. It will also push the expansion of its outdoor division, which will be selling hiking boots and other rugged shoes. The outdoor division recently doubled the number of products that it offers, and as a result it is posting double-digit growth rates. Nike is confident that by 1996 this division will be at the top of Nike and will have sales that will exceed $500 million. Nike realizes that to achieve this $500 million sales goal it will have to revamp its advertisements to reach yuppies and Xers who will wear its outdoor products. These groups are too skeptical to respond well to the celebrity endorsements that Nike has used in the past. Nike plans to introduce the biggest print campaign in its history "to lure them in."

Also at the heart of Nike's new strategy is the international arena. That may prove to be the most difficult element for Nike to undertake. According to one source there seems to be strong recognition that in a few years Nike will be larger outside of the U.S. than inside. The problem that the company faces is that even though international sales currently are one-third of Nike's business, international business still pales in comparison with the domestic sales of Nike. Nike would like expand into the soccer and international sports arena, but to do so it will have to refocus is marketing and distribution to reestablish itself as an authentic, technically superior sports shoe. Most recently Nike has bought out many of its worldwide distribution centers to achieve greater control of its operations. In the future, Nike would like to build up its presence in the key markets of China, Germany, Mexico, and Japan. Nike will focus its advertising on sports and will feature sports that are of a particular interest in a specific region. Nike and its chairman, Knight, realize that although Nike is ahead of competition, they still have a long, long way to run.

QUESTIONS

1. How would you describe the buying behavior of consumers with respect to athletic footwear?
2. What is the management decision problem facing Nike as it attempts to restart itself?
3. Define the marketing research problem facing Nike, given the management decision problem you have identified.
4. Develop two suitable research questions and formulate two hypotheses for each.

REFERENCES

1. Magiera, M. "Nike Has Women in Mind." *Advertising Age* (January 4, 1993): 36.
2. "Off and Running; Catchy Ads, Basketball Stars and Slick Designs Make Inroads Against Rivals; Don't Trash Those Wingtips." *Wall Street Journal* (July 22, 1993): A1.
3. Yang, Dori J., Michael Oneal, Charles Hoots, and Robert Neff. "Can Nike Just Do It?" *Business Week* (April 18, 1994): 86–90.
4. Tedeschi, Mark. "Looking Out for No. 1." *Footwear News* (July 26, 1993): 30.
5. Silverstein, Michael J. "Innovators Have Edge in War of the Brands." *Advertising Age* (August 9, 1993): 14.

CASE 1.3
Lexus: Imparting Value to Luxury or Luxury to Value?

In the 1980s, Toyota developed a concept for a new car that was destined to be a success. The concept of the car, to be called Lexus, was based on the observation that there was a large, affluent market for cars that could boast exceptional performance. A significant portion of that market, however, ranked value highly. Thus, they were loathe to pay the extraordinary prices that Mercedes charged for its high-performance vehicles. Toyota planned to target this market by creating a car that matched Mercedes on the performance criteria but was priced much more reasonably, providing consumers the value they desired and making them feel that they were smart buyers.

Toyota introduced the Lexus in 1989 with much fanfare. A clever advertising campaign announced the arrival of this new car. One ad showed the Lexus next to a Mercedes with the headline, "The First Time in History That Trading a $73,000 Car for a $36,000 Car Could Be Considered Trading Up." Of course, Lexus had all the detail that the Mercedes did: a sculptured form, a quality finish, and a plush interior. The detail was not, however, limited to the car. Separate dealerships were created that had the type of atmosphere that affluent consumers expected from a luxury carmaker, including a grand showroom, free refreshments, and professional salespeople.

Toyota placed a strong emphasis on the performance of the new car. A package was sent to potential customers that included a 12-minute video displaying Lexus's superior engineering. The video showed that when a glass of water was placed on the engine block of a Mercedes and a Lexus, the water shook on the Mercedes while the Lexus had a virtually still glass of water. This visually told the viewer that the stability of Lexus was far more extraordinary than even one of the most expensive cars around. Another video showed a Lexus making a sharp turn with a glass of water on its dashboard. The glass remained upright; again, the Lexus proved itself. These videos were successful in bringing in customers, whose expectations were surpassed.

The luxury carmakers noticed and realized that they had to respond somehow. They could either lower their prices, admitting they were overpriced to begin with, or they could increase prices, adding more extras and reinforcing the image of the rich person's vehicle. They chose the former strategy and decided to beat Toyota at its own game. Since 1992, Mercedes, BMW, and Jaguar, which is now owned by Ford Motor Company, have kept prices low and have increased quality. This has led to significant sales growth for all three auto manufacturers. Mercedes and Jaguar saw 20% increases, each, in 1994 from the previous year.

As a result of its success, Lexus decided to raise prices from $30,000 to $50,000 in 1994. This strategy has not worked out as well as Lexus had hoped. Sales dropped 10% to 72,000 cars in the first ten months of 1994 compared with 1993 sales. Lexus has since realized that it lacks the heritage for prestige that European luxury cars command and that people are once again willing to pay extra for it. As a result, it has turned to a new advertising campaign to inspire an emotional response to its cars. The campaign must be exceptionally powerful because it also has to combat the decrease in growth of the luxury car market compared to the auto industry's overall growth. Partly responsible for this decline, the "near luxury" autos have skimmed away potential luxury auto consumers. Included in this group are the Toyota Avalon, the Nissan Maxima, the Mazda Millenia. BMW and Mercedes have also introduced products for this segment: the BMW 3 Series and the Mercedes C Class.

The $50 million advertising effort by Lexus is the most expensive campaign since the introduction of the LS 400. Created by Team One Advertising, a unit of California based Saatchi & Saatchi, the TV ads, as reported in the *Wall Street Journal*, feature "majestic shots of fast-running schooners and endless rippling sand dunes. The images build a feeling of speed, performance and timelessness before the car is finally revealed at the end of the ads." Team One did not limit itself in finding the appropriate places to shoot the ad. Maine's coast was chosen to portray the smooth boating scenes while the desert scenes were shot in Africa's Namibia.

The imagery and the style of the ads are 180 degrees from the campaign that launched the LS 400. Those ads spoke of Lexus' "relentless pursuit of perfection" by showing images of the car with those of a ball bearing rolling smoothly down an engineered groove and a balancing act of champagne glasses over the hood. The ads clearly emphasized that the car was extremely well engineered. The focus was on tangible aspects of the vehicle. In contrast, the recent advertising campaign focuses on feeling and emotion, those intangibles that are worth big bucks to some consumers. The intangible aspects of aspiration and luxury also appear in the new ad campaigns of Mercedes and BMW. To promote its position as leader, Lexus portrays them as a pack of barking dogs in dealer advertising ads that account for 25% of the total budget.

Lexus is also launching a print campaign in which ads will focus more on the car's physical attributes rather the intangibles. Readers of news magazines will receive a 12-page insert, and 78 magazines will carry monochromatic ads that promote features of the product. Current Lexus owners, which total about 400,000, will also be targeted with mailed invitations to test-drive the new LS 400.

QUESTIONS

1. Describe the management decision problem facing Lexus as it seeks to fight competition from other luxury car manufacturers such as Mercedes, BMW, and Jaguar as well competition from the "near luxury" autos like the Nissan Maxima and the Mazda Millenia.

2. Formulate the marketing research problem corresponding to the management decision problem you have identified in (1).

3. Develop a graphical model explaining the consumer choice process for luxury cars.

4. Identify two research questions based on the definition of the marketing research problem and the graphical model.

5. Develop at least one hypothesis for each research question you have identified in (4).

REFERENCES

1. Warner, Fara. "Lexus, Sales Skidding 10%, Hopes Campaign Can Retool Its Identity." *Wall Street Journal* (November 14, 1994): B4.

2. Kotler, Philip. *Marketing Management: Analysis, Planning, Implementation and Control.* 8th ed. Englewood Cliffs, NJ: Prentice Hall, 1994, p. 490.

CASE 1.4 Marketing Research Lights the Way for Electric Utilities

In the late 1980s, the electric utility industry was in a turmoil. Utility companies were being challenged internally and externally as deregulation set in. International and low-cost competition entered the industry. While the electric utility companies looked like prime targets for mergers and takeovers, alternative energy sources were becoming a hot item on Wall Street. In 1988, revenues were up 4.6% from the previous year, but earnings per share dropped 10% that same year. According to the Edison Electric Institute, nuclear suppliers generated 15% more electricity in 1988 than the year before, yet their operating costs increased 22%. In 1989, revenues were up only 2.28%. In 1990, slight gains in revenues were also made. With deregulation, increased competition, alternative energy suppliers, and customer sensitivity to rates, the industry was forced to develop a marketing orientation.

In the 1990s, the electric utility market has once again become a tumultuous market. Recent threats to companies include weak earnings growth and the possibility of rising interest rates. The biggest threat perceived today is a new law that would allow large-scale industrial and municipal customers to purchase power on the open market. The National Energy Policy Act, passed in the fall of 1992, currently affects only the larger customers, however, it is expected to become more encompassing in the next few years. The result is likely to be an all-out free-for-all competition for customers. This competition will serve to weed out the winners from the losers in a market that had previously had little direct competition for customers.

Market segmentation has become the buzzword in the industry. The industry has realized that there was not a single market; rather, there were several markets that were inherently segmented. Marketing research has allowed utilities to target growth industries, industries that often were already customers. Utilities that could identify such industries could plan for regional expansion of their services to better meet their needs. Conversely, if a maturing industry could be identified, the utility could estimate how much demand would slack off and work out a way to redirect the excess electrical load to a growing area.

Marketing research has benefited utilities in their residential markets, where information is gathered mainly from direct measurement of consumer needs, opinions, and behavior. This prevents the utility from making erroneous assumptions about its customers. This information is often not enough, however, and electric utilities also acknowledge their need for other benchmark information to help interpret consumer responses. For example, if a utility discovered that its consumers thought that 50% of its meter readers were "friendly," what would this mean? Would it be good or bad? One utility interpreted this kind of result by examining how the 50% compared with its competitors and to a previous period.

By storing and analyzing huge amounts of consumer data in computers, utilities can carry out targeted advertising campaigns. For example, a software program called RECAP (residential end-use consumption analysis program), offered by Xenergy Inc., itemized the cost and usage of each major household appliance by incorporating utility billing data, information about a customer's household, weather data, and setup assumptions on appliance usage. In addition to providing utilities with a fast way to respond to "high bill inquiries" in a way that was satisfying to the customer, this software can improve understanding of customers and help utilities project which customers might have an interest in new cogeneration technologies. These projections can be used to plan a promotional campaign encouraging customers to adopt the new technologies or remain with the current system, depending on the needs of the individual utility.

In particular, several utilities have demonstrated the power of marketing research for generating new or additional business. In the late 1980s, Florida Power and Light Company of Miami started focusing its efforts on issues beyond conservation marketing. The marketing department fine-tuned its market segmentation strategies. The commercial customer segment was broken down further into hotel, hospital, and office subsegments. One of the most successful programs involved a residential outdoor security light program targeted toward the senior citizen community. The program helped increase the use of outdoor lights and helped the older community feel safer and more secure. Florida Power and Light found that its customers were more concerned with value than price.

The Milwaukee-based Wisconsin Electric Power Company spent $84 million to market a "Smart Money" program that allows customers to use energy more efficiently. The program provided rebates for customers who purchased more efficient appliances. As of 1995, the program resulted in more than $350 million in customer energy improvements and more than $85 million in rebates. The key to the market was to propose a more efficient use of energy rather than a decrease in the use of energy (conservation).

These examples show that marketing research can serve as a powerful tool in the electrical utility industry. Marketing research can generate new customers for the industry and light the way for more sophisticated marketing techniques.

Questions

1. Discuss the role of marketing research in the electric utilities industry.
2. Discuss the role of computers (microcomputers and mainframes) in conducting marketing research and providing decision support in the electric utilities industry.
3. Given the success of the outdoor security light program, Florida Power and Light would like to identify the other needs of the senior citizen community. Define the management decision problem.
4. Define the marketing research problem, given the management decision problem identified above.
5. Develop two research questions and two hypotheses.
6. Develop a simple graphic model explaining how outdoor light meets the security needs of senior citizens.

References

1. "Electric Utilities Finally Discover Marketing." *Marketing News* (November 20, 1989): 1–2.
2. Brokaw, Leslie. "Pay as You Glow." *Inc.* (January 1991): 21.
3. Pearl, Lewis J., and J. Falk. "What's the Best Way to Price Electricity?" *Electrical World* (December 1990): 23–24.
4. Bary, Andrew. "High Voltage." *Barron's* (July 12, 1993): 12–13.

CASE 1.5

Quaker Oats: Marketing Its Way to Success

Founded in 1891, the Quaker Oats Company woke up to show its true powers in the 1980s. Quaker has continued its success into the early 1990s, with 1992 sales at $5,576.4 million and 1993 sales at $5,730.6 million. Quaker Oats is a strong company touting many products which lead their categories in market share. In fact, in 1993, over 77% of Quaker's worldwide sales came from products that were in the number one or two position in their respective categories. Quaker is not sitting still with older, maturing products, however. Actually, over 80% of their 1993 sales came from brands in growing categories. This leads Quaker to believe that they are well positioned for growth in the future.

Since its founding, Quaker has grown into a diversified, well-managed company. Product development and aggressive marketing have played a key role in safeguarding its market share from competitors. In 1993, Quaker invested nearly 26% of sales back into the marketing and advertising of their brands. The reinvestment raised awareness of their current brands and helped establish a strong foundation for new products while actually revitalizing the more mature product arenas. Quaker believes in providing good marketing support to strong products.

In 1993, Quaker had a 7.3% share of the growing $9 billion ready-to-eat cereal market. Sales in 1993 grew 7%, which was ahead of the average while the past five years have shown a compounded annual rate of 5% growth. The core cereals for Quaker are Cap'n Crunch, Life, Quaker 100% Natural and Quaker Oat Squares. Each of these businesses holds approximately a 1% share in the market and is poised for long-term future growth. Life cereal's market share increased somewhat in 1993 with the advertising campaign asserting, "Your Kids Will Eat It." Quaker 100% Natural and Quaker Oat Squares cereals' shares declined slightly in 1993. Cap'n Crunch continued to grow in market share in 1993 and is currently the number two brand in the presweetened cereal segment. Brand extensions such as Cap'n Crunch's Deep Sea Crunch and Cap'n Crunch's Christmas Crunch were seasonal additions to the Quaker cereal line in 1993. The line extensions served to spice up the cereal line for a short period of time and gain more product recognition for the main brands. In the third quarter of 1993, Quaker Toasted Oatmeal cereal was introduced. The new cereal is intended to capitalize on the Quaker name and the health benefits derived from oatmeal.

Hot cereals are Quaker's oldest and best-known products. Quaker held a leading 66% market share in this $810 million category in 1993. For the first time since 1989 the hot cereal market grew in 1993 by 4%. In conjunction with this growth, Quaker's 1993 growth in this category was 5% over 1992. This growth was fueled by the improved performance of older brands and the introduction of new brands such as Quaker MultiGrain hot cereal.

In the convenience breakfast market, Quaker patented a process that removed one-third of the calories from pancake syrup and used it to introduce Aunt Jemima Lite in 1980 and later Aunt Jemima Butter Lite. Eventually, Quaker introduced Lite pancake mix to accompany the syrup. The success of both products led to an Aunt Jemima frozen breakfast line in 1988, a response to the fast-food industry's success in the convenience breakfast market. Unfortunately, sales were initially disappointing, and it could only be speculated how far Quaker would go to produce growth in this new field when the breakfast foods arena has been so competitive. More recently, Quaker has added French toast and waffles to their frozen breakfast offerings, and in 1993, market share increased for both frozen waffles and French toast. Sales were aided by reformulations in the product producing improved taste.

In 1994 Quaker submitted a bid for Snapple Beverage Corporation offering $1.7 billion (see Figure 1). The addition of Snapple makes Quaker the largest soft-drink producer behind Coca-Cola and PepsiCo. Teaming Gatorade, which boasts sales of $1.2 billion, with Snapple, which brings in $700 million a year, is a strategy that Quaker is relying on to combat Coke and Pepsi's moves into the sports drink market. Gatorade once had a market share of 95%, but products such as PowerAde and Allsport have cut it to 88%. Quaker plans to use Snapple's marketing expertise to boost Gatorade's market share to previous levels. It also plans on using Snapple's distribution network to sell Gatorade through smaller retail outlets that have not been tapped.

The synergies acquired by the addition of Snapple to Quaker may also be applied to the advantage of Snapple. Quaker's strength in supermarkets may be used to increase Snapple distribution. Currently, Snapple's grocery store sales account for only 20% of its total sales. Snapple may also be introduced to the international market. Gatorade now claims $200 million in sales from 25 countries, but with Snapple abroad also, Quaker could reach international sales of $1 billion, estimates Quaker's CEO, especially if Snapple makes the same inroads as it did domestically in the tea market. In the first half of 1994, Snapple's share in the ready-to-drink tea market was 27%, second to Lipton, which had 38% share. Thus, Quaker Oats hopes to translate the success that it has experienced in cereals to sports drinks and other product categories.

FIGURE 1

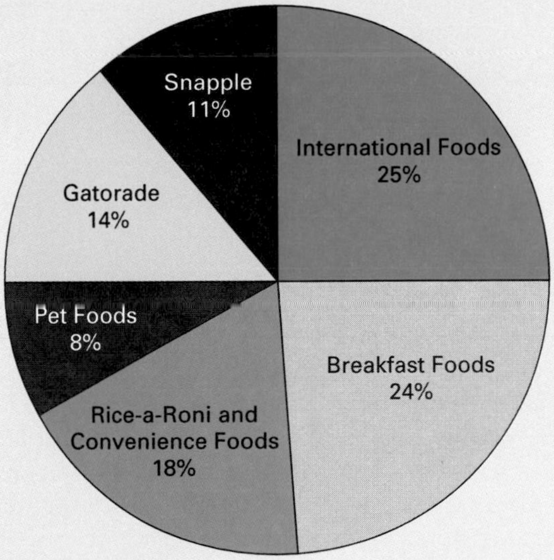

Snapple 11%
International Foods 25%
Gatorade 14%
Pet Foods 8%
Breakfast Foods 24%
Rice-a-Roni and Convenience Foods 18%

QUESTIONS

1. Based on an analysis of relevant secondary data:
   a. Present a forecast of cereal sales for next three years.
   b. Describe the buyer behavior factors influencing cereal consumption.
2. Create a graphic model of consumer choice for cereals.
3. Describe the management decision problem facing Quaker Oats with respect to the Aunt Jemima frozen breakfast line.

4. Define the marketing research problem emerging from the management decision problem identified above.

5. Based on the marketing research problem identified in (4), develop three suitable research questions with a corresponding hypothesis for each.

6. When Quaker Oats was in the process of acquiring Snapple, how do you think the marketing research problem was defined?

REFERENCES

1. Miller, A., D. Tsiantar, K. Springen, M. Hager, and K. Robins. "Oat-Bran Heartburn." *Newsweek* (January 29, 1990): 50–52.

2. The Quaker Oats Company, 1993 Annual Report.

3. McCarthy, Michael J. "Quaker Oats to Buy Snapple for $1.7 Billion." *Wall Street Journal* (November 3, 1994): A3–A4.

PART II

Research Design Formulation

A research design (step 3) is formulated after the problem has been defined (step 1) and the approach developed (step 2). This part of the text describes in detail exploratory, descriptive, and causal research designs. We describe the primary scales of measurement and the comparative and non-comparative scaling techniques commonly used. We present several guidelines for designing questionnaires and explain the procedures, techniques, and statistical considerations involved in sampling. Managers and researchers should find this material helpful.

CHAPTER THREE

Research Design

There is never a single, perfect research design that is the best for all marketing research projects, or even for a specific type of marketing research task.

OBJECTIVES

After reading this chapter, the student should be able to:

1. Define research design, classify various research designs, and explain the differences between exploratory and conclusive research designs.
2. Compare and contrast the basic research designs: exploratory, descriptive, and causal.
3. Describe the major sources of errors in a research design including random sampling error and the various sources of nonsampling error.
4. Discuss managerial aspects of coordinating research projects, particularly budgeting and scheduling.
5. Describe the elements of a marketing research proposal and show how it addresses the steps of the marketing research process.
6. Explain research design formulation in international marketing research.
7. Understand the ethical issues and conflicts that arise in formulating a research design.
8. Discuss the use of microcomputers and mainframes in research design formulation.

OVERVIEW

Chapter 2 discussed how to define a marketing research problem and develop a suitable approach. These first two steps are critical to the success of the entire marketing research project. Once they have been completed, attention should be devoted to designing the formal research project by formulating a detailed research design (see Figure 2.1).

This chapter defines and classifies research designs. We describe the two major types of research designs: exploratory and conclusive. We further classify conclusive research designs as descriptive or causal and discuss both types in detail. We then consider the differences between the two types of descriptive designs—cross-sectional and longitudinal—and identify sources of errors. We cover budgeting and scheduling of a research project and present guidelines for writing a marketing research proposal. The special considerations involved in formulating research designs in international marketing research are discussed. Several ethical issues that arise at this stage of the marketing research process are considered. Finally, we discuss the use of microcomputers and mainframes in formulating research designs. The reader can develop a better appreciation of the concepts presented in this chapter by first considering the following examples, which illustrate cross-sectional and longitudinal research designs.

EXAMPLE
Cross-Sectional Research Prevents Airlines from "Flying by the Seat of Their Pants"

An international survey of airline passengers, employing a cross-sectional design in which each respondent was interviewed only once, found that convenient schedules and seating comfort were passengers' most important considerations in selecting an airline. Lots of leg room, wide seats, and general spaciousness were desirable characteristics for a trip that lasted between two and five hours. Travelers who reside outside of North America were more likely than their North American peers to rate safety and security, punctuality, and in-flight service as features influencing their choice of airline. In keeping with the results of this survey, Lufthansa, a German international airline, emphasizes convenient schedule to a large number of destinations, seating comfort, and "unparalleled on-board service" in its advertising, which uses the theme, "A passion for perfection."[1] ◆

Airlines such as Lufthansa frequently make use of surveys based on cross-sectional designs. ◆ Lufthansa Airlines.

EXAMPLE
Longitudinal Research Shows Combustion Engineering the Benefits of Shows

To measure the effectiveness of its exhibits in the Instrument Society of America (ISA) trade show, Combustion Engineering adopted a three-phase longitudinal design in which some respondents were interviewed repeatedly. Phase 1, executed just before the four-day show, involved 109 interviews. Phase 2, conducted immediately after the show, and phase 3, conducted five months after the show, each involved 60 interviews with respondents who had participated in phase 1. Analysis of phase 1 and phase 2 data indicated that 82% of the attendees had refined their buying plans by attending the ISA show. Aided and unaided recall of Combustion's ISA exhibit in phases 2 and 3 were higher than that for any other supplier. Based on this information, Combustion Engineering shifted most of its promotional dollars to trade show promotions, with the major chunk going to the ISA show.[2] ◆

As these examples indicate, two main types of research designs are employed in marketing research. An understanding of the fundamentals of research design and its components enables the researcher to formulate a design that is appropriate for the problem at hand.

RESEARCH DESIGN: DEFINITION

research design A framework or blueprint for conducting the marketing research project. It specifies the details of the procedures necessary for obtaining the information needed to structure or solve marketing research problems.

A **research design** is a framework or blueprint for conducting a marketing research project. It details the procedures necessary for obtaining the information needed to structure or solve marketing research problems. Although a broad approach to the problem has already been developed, the research design specifies the details—the nuts and bolts—of implementing that approach. A research design lays the foundation for conducting the project. A good research design will ensure that the marketing research project is conducted effectively and efficiently. Typically, a research design involves the following components, or tasks:

1. Define the information needed (Chapter 2).
2. Design the exploratory, descriptive, or causal phases of the research (Chapters 3 through 7).
3. Specify the measurement and scaling procedures (Chapters 8 and 9).
4. Construct and pretest a questionnaire (interviewing form) or an appropriate form for data collection (Chapter 10).
5. Specify the sampling process and sample size (Chapters 11 and 12).
6. Develop a plan of data analysis (Chapter 14).

exploratory research One type of research design that has as its primary objective the provision of insights into and comprehension of the problem situation confronting the researcher.

Each component will be discussed in great detail in the subsequent chapters. But first, we must further our understanding of research design with a classification of the different types.

RESEARCH DESIGN: CLASSIFICATION

Research designs may be broadly classified as exploratory or conclusive (see Figure 3.1). The differences between exploratory and conclusive research are summarized in Table 3.1. The primary objective of **exploratory research** is to provide insights into and an

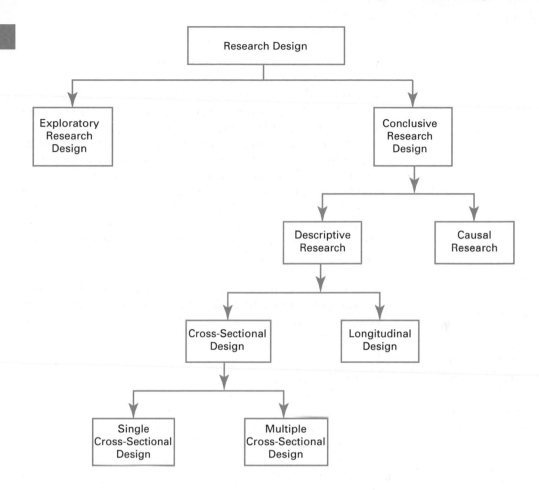

FIGURE 3.1

A Classification of Marketing Research Designs

understanding of the problem confronting the researcher.[3] Exploratory research is used in cases when you must define the problem more precisely, identify relevant courses of action, or gain additional insights before an approach can be developed. The information needed is only loosely defined at this stage, and the research process that is adopted is flexible and unstructured. For example, it may consist of personal interviews with industry experts. The sample, selected to generate maximum insights, is small and non-

TABLE 3.1

Differences between Exploratory and Conclusive Research

	Exploratory	Conclusive
Objective:	To provide insights and understanding.	To test specific hypotheses and examine relationships.
Characteristics:	Information needed is defined only loosely.	Information needed is clearly defined.
	Research process is flexible and unstructured.	Research process is formal and structured.
	Sample is small and nonrepresentative.	Sample is large and representative.
	Analysis of primary data is qualitative.	Data analysis is quantitative.
Findings/Results:	Tentative.	Conclusive.
Outcome:	Generally followed by further exploratory or conclusive research.	Findings used as input into decision making.

representative. The primary data are qualitative in nature and are analyzed accordingly. Given these characteristics of the research process, the findings of exploratory research should be regarded as tentative or as input to further research. Typically, such research is followed by further exploratory or conclusive research. Sometimes, exploratory research, particularly qualitative research, is all the research that is conducted. In these cases, caution should be exercised in utilizing the findings obtained. Exploratory research will be discussed in more detail in the next section.

The insights gained from exploratory research might be verified by conclusive research because the objective of conclusive research is to test specific hypotheses and examine specific relationships. This requires that the information needed is clearly specified.[4] **Conclusive research** is typically more formal and structured than exploratory research. It is based on large, representative samples, and the data obtained are subjected to quantitative analysis. The findings from this research are considered to be conclusive in nature in that they are used as input into managerial decision making. (It should be noted, however, that from the perspective of the philosophy of science, nothing can be proven and nothing is conclusive.) As shown in Figure 3.1, conclusive research designs may be either descriptive or causal, and descriptive research designs may be either cross-sectional or longitudinal. Each of these classifications is discussed further, beginning with exploratory research.

conclusive research
Research designed to assist the decision maker in determining, evaluating, and selecting the best course of action to take in a given situation.

EXPLORATORY RESEARCH

As its name implies, the objective of exploratory research is to explore or search through a problem or situation to provide insights and understanding (Table 3.2). Exploratory research could be used for any of the following purposes:

- Formulate a problem or define a problem more precisely.
- Identify alternative courses of action.
- Develop hypotheses.
- Isolate key variables and relationships for further examination.[5]
- Gain insights for developing an approach to the problem.
- Establish priorities for further research.

In general, exploratory research is meaningful in any situation where the researcher does not have enough understanding to proceed with the research project. Exploratory research is characterized by flexibility and versatility with respect to the methods because formal research protocols and procedures are not employed. It rarely involves structured questionnaires, large samples, and probability sampling plans. Rather, researchers are alert to new ideas and insights as they proceed. Once a new idea or insight is discovered, they may redirect their exploration in that direction. That new direction is pursued until its possibilities are exhausted or another direction is found. For this reason, the focus of the investigation may shift constantly as new insights are discovered. Thus, the creativity and ingenuity of the researcher play a major role in exploratory research. Yet, the abilities of the researcher are not the sole determinants of good exploratory research. Exploratory research can greatly benefit from use of the following methods (see Table 3.2):

Survey of experts (discussed in Chapter 2)
Pilot surveys (discussed in Chapter 2)

TABLE 3.2

A Comparison of Basic Research Designs

	Exploratory	Descriptive	Causal
Objective:	Discovery of ideas and insights	Describe market characteristics or functions	Determine cause and effect relationships
Characteristics:	Flexible, versatile	Marked by the prior formulation of specific hypotheses	Manipulation of one or more independent variables
	Often the front end of total research design	Preplanned and structured design	Control of other mediating variables
Methods:	Expert surveys	Secondary data	Experiments
	Pilot surveys	Surveys	
	Secondary data	Panels	
	Qualitative Research	Observational and other data	

Analysis of secondary data (discussed in Chapter 4)
Qualitative research (discussed in Chapter 5)

The use of exploratory research in defining the problem and developing an approach was discussed in Chapter 2. The advantages and disadvantages of exploratory research are further discussed in Chapter 4 (Secondary Data) and Chapter 5 (Qualitative Research). To aid the reader in visualizing the applications of exploratory research, we now consider the department store patronage project, which might employ the following types of exploratory studies:

A review of academic and trade literature to identify the relevant demographic and psychographic factors that influence consumer patronage of department stores

Interviews with retailing experts to determine trends, such as emergence of new types of outlets and shifts in consumer patronage patterns

A comparative analysis of the three best and three worst stores of the same chain to gain some idea of the factors that influence store performance

Focus groups to determine the factors that consumers consider important in selecting department stores

Further illustration of exploratory research is provided by the following example.

EXAMPLE
Fountain Pens as Signature of Style

How do you revive a semiobsolete and dying product category? Montblanc found the answer through exploratory research. Montblanc Simplo GmbH conducted focus groups and in-depth interviews that provided the following insights: (1) many consumers had a desire to view fountain pens as fashion accessories, much like jewelry, rather than inexpensive, utilitarian, and disposable; (2) "the power of the pen" notion was still lingering in the minds of consumers; and (3) the prestige pricing phenomenon was applicable to fountain pens (many consumers associated higher price with higher prestige). When these findings were confirmed by descriptive survey research, Montblanc positioned its fountain pens as a fashionable and prestigious item, a way of self-expression in a tech-

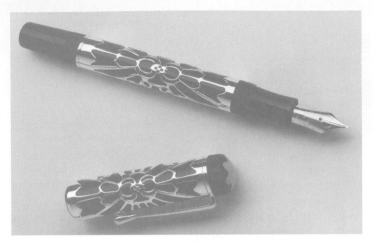

Valuable insights obtained through exploratory research using focus groups and depth interviews have enabled Montblanc to position its fountain pens as "signature of style." ◆ Nike Communications.

nological age. Bill Brown, president and chief executive of U.S. operations of Montblanc Simplo GmbH, explained that in the 1950s, the typed business letter represented power, but with the arrival of the word processor everyone has the ability to produce perfectly typed documents. In the 1990s, a "note, hand-written with a fountain pen and appended to the bottom of a letter, ... will indicate power."[6]

Montblanc, whose fountain pen line varies from $225 for the Meisterstuck to $100,000 for the Royale, has also taken the lead in developing the lucrative "limited edition" pen market. One example of a limited edition pen is Montblanc's Octavian pen. At $1650 each, the 4180 pens issued will be in demand by collectors. Aggressive marketing, aimed at satisfying underlying consumer needs discovered by exploratory research, has enabled Montblanc to position its fountain pens as "signature of style." ◆

Note that Montblanc did not rely exclusively on exploratory research. Once new positioning ideas were identified, they were further tested by descriptive research in the form of customer surveys. This example points to the importance of descriptive research in obtaining more conclusive findings.

DESCRIPTIVE RESEARCH

descriptive research A type of conclusive research that has as its major objective the description of something, usually market characteristics or functions.

As the name implies, the major objective of **descriptive research** is to describe something, usually market characteristics or functions (see Table 3.2). Descriptive research is conducted for the following reasons:

1. To describe the characteristics of relevant groups, such as consumers, salespeople, organizations, or market areas. For example, we could develop a profile of the "heavy users" (frequent shoppers) of prestigious department stores like Saks Fifth Avenue and Neiman Marcus.
2. To estimate the percentage of units in a specified population exhibiting a certain behavior. For example, we might be interested in estimating the percentage of heavy users of prestigious department stores who also patronize discount department stores.
3. To determine the perceptions of product characteristics. For example, how do households perceive the various department stores in terms of salient factors of the choice criteria?
4. To determine the degree to which marketing variables are associated. For example, to what extent is shopping at department stores related to eating out?
5. To make specific predictions. For example, what will be the retail sales of Neiman Marcus (specific store) for fashion clothing (specific product category) in the Dallas area (specific region)?

The Lufthansa and Combustion Engineering examples at the beginning of the chapter both employed descriptive research. These examples show that descriptive research assumes that the researcher has much prior knowledge about the problem situation.[7] In fact, a major difference between exploratory and descriptive research is that descriptive research is characterized by the prior formulation of specific hypotheses. Thus, the information needed is clearly defined. As a result, descriptive research is preplanned and structured. It is typically based on large representative samples. A formal research design specifies the methods for selecting the sources of information and for collecting data from those sources. A descriptive design requires a clear specification of the who, what, when, where, why, and way (the six Ws) of the research.[8] (It is interesting to note that news reporters use similar criteria for describing a situation.) We illustrate this in the context of the department store patronage project.

DEPARTMENT STORE PATRONAGE PROJECT
The Six Ws

1. *Who*: Who should be considered a patron of a particular department store? Some of the possibilities are:
   a. Anyone who enters the department store, whether or not he or she purchases anything
   b. Anyone who purchases anything from the store
   c. Anyone who makes purchases at the department store at least once a month
   d. The person in the household most responsible for department store shopping

2. *What*: What information should be obtained from the respondents? A wide variety of information could be obtained, including:
   a. Frequency with which different department stores are patronized for specific product categories
   b. Evaluation of the various department stores in terms of the salient choice criteria
   c. Information pertaining to specific hypotheses to be tested
   d. Psychographics and lifestyles, media consumption habits, and demographics

3. *When*: When should the information be obtained from the respondents? The available options include:
   a. Before shopping
   b. While shopping
   c. Immediately after shopping
   d. Sometime after shopping to allow time for evaluation of the shopping experience

4. *Where*: Where should the respondents be contacted to obtain the required information? Possibilities include contacting the respondents:
   a. In the store
   b. Outside the store but in the shopping mall
   c. In the parking lot
   d. At home

5. *Why*: Why are we obtaining information from the respondents? Why is the marketing research project being conducted? Possible reasons could be:
   a. To improve the image of the sponsoring store
   b. To improve patronage and market share
   c. To change the product mix
   d. To develop a suitable promotional campaign
   e. To decide on the location of a new store

6. *Way*: In what way are we going to obtain information from the respondents? The possible ways could be:
   a. Observe respondents' behavior
   b. Conduct personal interviews
   c. Conduct telephone interviews
   d. Conduct mail interviews ◆

These and other similar questions should be asked until the information to be obtained has been clearly defined.

In summary, descriptive research, in contrast to exploratory research, is marked by a clear statement of the problem, specific hypotheses, and detailed information needs. The survey conducted in the department store patronage project, which involved personal interviews, is an example of descriptive research. Other examples of descriptive studies are as follows:

- Market studies describe the size of the market, buying power of the consumers, availability of distributors, and consumer profiles.
- Market share studies determine the proportion of total sales received by a company and its competitors.
- Sales analysis studies describe sales by geographic region, product line, type of the account, and size of the account.
- Image studies determine consumer perceptions of the firm and its products.
- Product usage studies describe consumption patterns.
- Distribution studies determine traffic flow patterns and the number and location of distributors.
- Pricing studies describe the range and frequency of price changes and probable consumer response to proposed price changes.
- Advertising studies describe media consumption habits and audience profiles for specific television programs and magazines.

These examples demonstrate the range and diversity of descriptive research studies. A vast majority of marketing research studies involve descriptive research, which incorporates the following major methods:

Secondary data (discussed in Chapter 4)
Surveys (Chapter 6)
Panels (Chapters 4 and 6)
Observational and other data (Chapter 6)

cross-sectional design A type of research design involving the collection of information from any given sample of population elements only once.

Although the methods shown in Table 3.2 are typical, it should be noted that the researcher is not limited to these methods. For example, surveys can involve the use of exploratory (open-ended) questions, or causal studies (experiments) are sometimes administered by surveys. Descriptive research using the methods of Table 3.2 can be further classified into cross-sectional and longitudinal research (Figure 3.1).

Cross-Sectional Designs

single cross-sectional design A cross-sectional design in which one sample of respondents is drawn from the target population and information is obtained from this sample once.

The cross-sectional study is the most frequently used descriptive design in marketing research. **Cross-sectional designs** involve the collection of information from any given sample of population elements only once. They may be either single cross-sectional or multiple cross-sectional (Figure 3.1). In **single cross-sectional designs**, only one sample of respondents is drawn from the target population, and information is obtained from this sample only once. These designs are also called sample survey research designs. In **multiple cross-sectional designs**, there are two or more samples of respondents, and information from each sample is obtained only once. Often, information from different samples is obtained at different times. The following examples illustrate single and multiple cross-sectional designs.

multiple cross-sectional design A cross-sectional design in which there are two or more samples of respondents, and information from each sample is obtained only once.

EXAMPLE
Designing Coupons from Cross-Sections

A cross-sectional study was conducted by NPD////MARKETRAX, a consumer panel service, to determine the effectiveness of coupons in stimulating sales as well as to assess coupon user and nonuser profiles. The data were collected from 8,000 households in New York, St. Louis, and Los Angeles. The results showed that 31% of all coupon-redeeming households account for 72% of all redemptions. Demographically, heavy coupon redeemers are large households with children and annual incomes exceeding $30,000, with female heads of household aged 35 to 54 who work part-time and have a high school education. Light users of coupons are smaller households with female heads who are younger and work full-time. Such information is useful to consumer products firms like Procter & Gamble that rely heavily on coupon promotion, as it enables them to target their promotions to heavy coupon redeemers.[9] ◆

EXAMPLE
Chase and Grabbits Multiply Like Rabbits

Eating behavior trends were examined in a marketing research project by the Pillsbury Company, conducted with the assistance of SRI International and Creative Research Associates, Inc. This project involved data from food diaries collected at three points since 1980. Each wave had a different sample of 1,000 households for a total sample size of 3,000 in the multiple cross-sectional design. The data were collected by Market Research Corporation of America. Based on an analysis of eating patterns, the market was divided into five segments: Chase and Grabbits, Functional Feeders, Down Home Stokers, Careful Cooks, and Happy Cookers. The changes in composition of these segments were examined over time. For example, the Chase and Grabbits experienced the biggest increase over the 15-year period (+136%). Currently, this group represents 26% of the total sample. Their desire for more convenience has also increased over time. Says one Chase and Grabbit, "Someday all you'll have to do is take a pill and it'll give you everything you need." This information enabled the Pillsbury Company to target different products for different segments. For example, the Chase and Grabbit represented a prime segment for prepared foods and TV dinners.[10] ◆

The survey of coupon use, a single cross-sectional design, involved only one group of respondents who provided information only once. On the other hand, the Pillsbury study involved three different samples, each measured only once, with the measures obtained five years apart. Hence, the latter study illustrates a multiple cross-sectional design. A type of multiple cross-sectional design of special interest is cohort analysis.

cohort analysis A multiple cross-sectional design consisting of a series of surveys conducted at appropriate time intervals. The cohort refers to the group of respondents who experience the same event within the same time interval.

Cohort Analysis **Cohort analysis** consists of a series of surveys conducted at appropriate time intervals, where the cohort serves as the basic unit of analysis. A cohort is a group of respondents who experience the same event within the same time interval.[11] For example, a birth (or age) cohort is a group of people who were born during the same time interval, such as 1951–60. The term *cohort analysis* refers to any study in which there are measures of some characteristics of one or more cohorts at two or more points in time.

It is unlikely that any of the individuals studied at time one will also be in the sample at time two. For example, the age cohort of people between 8 and 19 years was selected, and their soft drink consumption was examined every ten years for 30 years. In other words, every ten years a different sample of respondents was drawn from the population of those who were then between 8 and 19 years old. This sample was drawn independently of any previous sample drawn in this study from the population of 8 to 19 years. Obviously, people who were selected once were unlikely to be included again in the same age cohort (8 to 19 years), as these people would be much older at the time of subsequent sampling. This study showed that this cohort had increased consumption of soft drinks over time. Similar findings were obtained for other age cohorts (20–29, 30–39, 40–49, and 50+). Further, the consumption of each cohort did not decrease as the cohort aged. These results are presented in Table 3.3 in which the consumption of the various age cohorts over time can be determined by reading down the diagonal. These findings contradicted the common belief that the consumption of soft drinks will decline with the graying of the United States. This common but erroneous belief was based on single cross-sectional studies. Note that if any column of Table 3.3 is viewed in isolation (as a single cross-sectional study) the consumption of soft drinks declines with age, thus fostering the erroneous belief.[12]

Cohort analysis is also used to predict changes in voter opinions during a political campaign. Well-known marketing researchers like Louis Harris or George Gallup, who specialize in political opinion research, periodically question cohorts of voters (people with similar voting patterns during a given interval) about their voting preferences to predict election results. Thus, cohort analysis is an important cross-sectional design. The other type of descriptive design is longitudinal design.

Longitudinal Designs

longitudinal design A type of research design involving a fixed sample of population elements measured repeatedly. The sample remains the same over time, thus providing a series of pictures that, when viewed together, portray a vivid illustration of the situation and the changes that are taking place.

In **longitudinal designs**, a fixed sample (or samples) of population elements is measured repeatedly. A longitudinal design differs from a cross-sectional design in that the sample or samples remain the same over time. In other words, the same people are studied over time. In contrast to the typical cross-sectional design, which gives a snapshot of the variables of interest at a single point in time, a longitudinal study provides a series of pictures that give an in-depth view of the situation and the changes that take place over time. For example, the question, How did the American people rate the performance of President George Bush immediately after Desert Storm? would be addressed using a cross-sectional design. A longitudinal design, however, would be used to address the

TABLE 3.3	Age	1950	1960	1969	1979	
Consumption of Soft Drinks by Various Age Cohorts (Percentage Consuming on a Typical Day)	8–19	52.9	62.6	73.2	81.0	
	20–29	45.2	60.7	76.0	75.8	C8
	30–39	33.9	46.6	67.7	71.4	C7
	40–49	23.2	40.8	58.6	67.8	C6
	50+	18.1	28.8	50.0	51.9	C5
			C1	C2	C3	C4

C1: cohort born prior to 1900   C5: cohort born 1931–40
C2: cohort born 1901–10   C6: cohort born 1940–49
C3: cohort born 1911–20   C7: cohort born 1950–59
C4: cohort born 1921–30   C8: cohort born 1960–69

CONSUMER MAIL PANEL
P.O. Box 4602   North Suburban, IL 60197-4602

WHAT IS CONSUMER MAIL PANEL?

Consumer Mail Panel, a facility of Market Facts, is more than thirty years old and is nationally recognized as a reliable and accurate means of learning consumer reactions and attitudes. It was established to give people like you the chance to say what you think, with privacy, about the products you buy. And, it provides the opportunity for your opinions to be heard by the people who make these products.

Members are asked to express their opinions about products and services they use. Their opinions about different things are asked on a questionnaire sent through the mail. From time to time, a product to try may be sent.

WHAT DOES IT COST?

Nothing at all. Postage is paid both ways on everything. You are never asked to buy anything.

All information received is absolutely confidential. Answers become a part of general statistics. The questionnaires ask for your frank opinions just as they occur to you. Households of all sizes, including persons living alone, are equally important. I may be interested in the opinions of the whole family. Occasionally, I have some questions about gasoline or tires on the family car, or I may ask what the children think of products they use.

TO BECOME A MEMBER OF CONSUMER MAIL PANEL . . .

Just answer all the questions on the enclosed questionnaire. I am looking for representatives of every kind of household in the country; that is, members of all ages and all income categories.

After completing my questionnaire, please use the postage paid envelope to return it to me. That is all there is to it.

Does it sound to you as though Consumer Mail Panel might be interesting? Members tell me it's fun -- and I think you'll find it fun too. I hope to hear from you soon.

If you have any questions, please call 1-800-745-4267.

Cordially,

Marie Brighton
for Consumer Mail Panel

P.S. If you are already a member of Consumer Mail Panel, or if for some reason you are not in a position to join now, please pass along the questionnaire and return envelope to any friend, neighbor or relative you feel might enjoy panel membership.

A mail panel recruitment letter. ◆ Market Facts, Inc.

panel A sample of respondents who have agreed to provide information at specified intervals over an extended period.

question, How did the American people change their view of Bush's performance during his presidency?

Often, the term *panel* is used interchangeably with the term *longitudinal design*. A **panel** consists of a sample of respondents, generally households, that have agreed to provide information at specified intervals over an extended period. Panels are maintained by syndicated firms, and panel members are compensated for their participation with gifts, coupons, information, or cash.[13] Panels are discussed further in Chapter 4. An example of a mail panel recruitment letter is shown here.

A panel design was used to understand the coffee market, as illustrated in the following example.

EXAMPLE
What Is Coffee Taster's Choice?

Choice map is a procedure that infers a product market map from traditional panel data. Panel data obtained from the Kansas City area contained information on household purchases of regular ground coffee over a 60-week period. These purchases were analyzed for three major brands, Folgers, Maxwell House, and Butternut, which accounted for more than 90% of all purchases in the market. In the choice map, Maxwell House and Butternut were about equidistant from Folgers, which indicated that the relative probabilities of buying Maxwell House and Butternut were nearly independent of the probability of buying Folgers. By estimating choice maps every quarter, coffee marketers like General Foods can monitor changes in the different brands over time.[14] ◆

Data obtained from panels not only provide information on market shares that are based on an extended period of time (60 weeks in the case of this example) but also allow the researcher to examine changes in market share over time.[15] As the following section explains, these changes cannot be determined from cross-sectional data.

Relative Advantages and Disadvantages of Longitudinal and Cross-Sectional Designs

The relative advantages and disadvantages of longitudinal versus cross-sectional designs are summarized in Table 3.4. A major advantage of longitudinal design over the cross-

TABLE 3.4	Evaluation Criteria	Cross-Sectional Design	Longitudinal Design
Relative Advantages and Disadvantages of Longitudinal and Cross-Sectional Designs	Detecting change	–	+
	Large amount of data collection	–	+
	Accuracy	–	+
	Representative sampling	+	–
	Response bias	+	–

Note: A + indicates a relative advantage over the other design, whereas a - indicates a relative disadvantage.

sectional design is the ability to detect change as a result of repeated measurement of the same variables on the same sample.

Tables 3.5 and 3.6 demonstrate how cross-sectional data can mislead researchers about changes over time. The cross-sectional data reported in Table 3.5 reveal that the purchases of Brands A, B, and C remain the same in time periods 1 and 2. In each survey, 20% of the respondents purchase Brand A, 30% Brand B, and 50% Brand C. The longitudinal data presented in Table 3.6 show that substantial change, in the form of brand switching, occurred in the study period. For example, only 50% (100/200) of the respondents who purchased Brand A in period 1 also purchased it in period 2. The corresponding repeat purchase figures for Brands B and C are, respectively, 33.3% (100/300) and 55% (275/500). Hence, during this interval Brand C experienced the greatest loyalty and Brand B the least. Table 3.6 provides valuable information on brand loyalty and brand switching. (Such a table is called a turnover table or a brand-switching matrix.[16])

Longitudinal data enable researchers to examine changes in the behavior of individual units and to link behavioral changes to marketing variables, such as changes in advertising, packaging, pricing, and distribution. Since the same units are measured repeatedly, variations caused by changes in the sample are eliminated and even small changes are apparent.[17]

Another advantage of panels is that relatively large amounts of data can be collected. Because panel members are usually compensated for their participation, they are willing to participate in lengthy and demanding interviews. Yet another advantage

TABLE 3.5	Brand purchased	Time Period	
Cross-Sectional Data May Not Show Change		Period 1 Survey	Period 2 Survey
	Brand A	200	200
	Brand B	300	300
	Brand C	500	500
	Total	1,000	1,000

TABLE 3.6	Brand Purchased in Period 1	Brand Purchased in Period 2			
Longitudinal Data May Show Substantial Change		Brand A	Brand B	Brand C	Total
	Brand A	100	50	50	200
	Brand B	25	100	175	300
	Brand C	75	150	275	500
	Total	200	300	500	1,000

is that panel data can be more accurate than cross-sectional data.[18] A typical cross-sectional survey requires the respondent to recall past purchases and behavior; these data can be inaccurate because of memory lapses. Panel data, which rely on continuous recording of purchases in a diary, place less reliance on the respondent's memory. A comparison of panel and cross-sectional survey estimates of retail sales indicates that panel data give more accurate estimates.[19]

The main disadvantage of panels is that they may not be representative. Nonrepresentativeness may arise because of:

1. *Refusal to cooperate.* Many individuals or households do not wish to be bothered with the panel operation and refuse to participate. Consumer panels requiring members to keep a record of purchases have a cooperation rate of 60% or less.

2. *Mortality.* Panel members who agree to participate may subsequently drop out because they move away or lose interest. Mortality rates can be as high as 20% per year.[20]

3. *Payment.* Payment may cause certain types of people to be attracted, making the group unrepresentative of the population.

Another disadvantage of panels is response bias. New panel members are often biased in their initial responses. They tend to increase the behavior being measured, such as food purchasing. This bias decreases as the respondent overcomes the novelty of being on the panel, so it can be reduced by initially excluding the data of new members.[21] Seasoned panel members may also give biased responses because they believe they are experts or they want to look good or give the "right" answer. Bias also results from boredom, fatigue, and incomplete diary entries.

CAUSAL RESEARCH

causal research A type of conclusive research where the major objective is to obtain evidence regarding cause-and-effect (causal) relationships.

Causal research is used to obtain evidence of cause-and-effect (causal) relationships (see Table 3.2). Marketing managers continually make decisions based on assumed causal relationships. These assumptions may not be justifiable, and the validity of the causal relationships should be examined via formal research.[22] For example, the common assumption that a decrease in price will lead to increased sales and market share does not hold in certain competitive environments. Causal research is appropriate for the following purposes:

1. To understand which variables are the cause (independent variables) and which variables are the effect (dependent variables) of a phenomenon

2. To determine the nature of the relationship between the causal variables and the effect to be predicted

Like descriptive research, causal research requires a planned and structured design. Although descriptive research can determine the degree of association between variables, it is not appropriate for examining causal relationships. Such an examination requires a causal design, in which the causal or independent variables are manipulated in a relatively controlled environment. A relatively controlled environment is one in which the other variables that may affect the dependent variable are controlled or checked as much as possible. The effect of this manipulation on one or more dependent variables is then measured to infer causality. The main method of causal research is experimentation.[23]

Due to its complexity and importance, Chapter 7 has been devoted to causal designs and experimental research. Some examples are given here, however. In the context of the department store patronage project, a researcher wishes to determine whether the presence and helpfulness of salespeople (causal variable) will influence the sales of housewares (effect variable). A causal design could be formulated in which two groups of otherwise comparable housewares departments of a particular chain are selected. For four weeks, trained salespeople are stationed in one group of housewares departments but not in the other. Sales are monitored for both groups, while controlling for other variables. A comparison of sales for the two groups will reveal the effect of salespeople on housewares sales in department stores. Alternatively, instead of selecting two groups of stores, the researcher could select only one set of department stores and carry out this manipulation for two comparable time periods: salespeople are present in one time period and absent in the other. As another example, consider the following.

EXAMPLE
Advertising Your Way to Profits _____

A causal study was undertaken to measure the effect of business-to-business advertising on the sales of a variety of products as well as to evaluate the effects of ad frequency schedules and varying media weight. The study involved a participating manufacturer, the publishers of the magazines used in the study, and a tightly controlled stratification of the magazine's circulation into three cells, which were to receive light, medium, and heavy levels of advertising. Four products in the growth stage of the product life cycle were chosen for advertisement. To obtain clear sales data on these products, distribution channel restrictions were necessary, so that sales could be linked to the balanced advertising cells. After the four products and the participating magazines had been selected, the advertising cells and levels for each product were defined. At the conclusion of the one-year study, findings supported the hypothesis that more advertising caused an increase in sales. The study also concluded that if a product is sold through dealers, both dealers and end users should be targeted for ads. Further, increased advertising frequency can increase sales leads and result in higher profits.[24] ◆

In this experiment, the causal (independent) variable was advertising, which was manipulated to have three levels: light, medium, and heavy. The effect (dependent) variable was sales, and the influence of distribution on sales had to be controlled. Although the preceding example distinguished causal research from other types of research, causal research should not be viewed in isolation. Rather, the exploratory, descriptive, and causal research designs often complement each other.

RELATIONSHIPS AMONG EXPLORATORY, DESCRIPTIVE, AND CAUSAL RESEARCH

We have described exploratory, descriptive, and causal research as major classifications of research designs, but the distinctions among these classifications are not absolute. A given marketing research project may involve more than one type of research design and thus serve several purposes.[25] Which combination of research designs to employ depends on the nature of the problem. We offer the following general guidelines for choosing research designs:

1. When little is known about the problem situation, it is desirable to begin with exploratory research. Exploratory research is appropriate when the problem needs to be defined more

precisely, when alternative courses of action need to be identified, when research questions or hypotheses need to be developed, and when key variables need to be isolated and classified as dependent or independent.

2. Exploratory research is the initial step in the overall research design framework. It should, in most instances, be followed by descriptive or causal research (see Research in Practice 3.1).[26] For example, hypotheses developed via exploratory research should be statistically tested using descriptive or causal research.

3. It is not necessary to begin every research design with exploratory research. It depends on the precision with which the problem has been defined and the researcher's degree of certainty about the approach to the problem. A research design could well begin with descriptive or causal research. To illustrate, a consumer satisfaction survey that is conducted annually need not begin with or include an exploratory phase.

4. Although exploratory research is generally the initial step, it need not be. Exploratory research may follow descriptive or causal research. For example, descriptive or causal research results in findings that are hard for managers to interpret. Exploratory research may provide more insights to help understand these findings.

RESEARCH IN PRACTICE 3.1

Research Design to Detect Trends in Women's Attitudes

Langer Associates Inc., New York, employs a research design consisting of exploratory and descriptive phases to detect new and long-range trends in women's attitudes toward beauty, fashion, and fitness. In the exploratory phase, focus groups are used to obtain "a sense of the real woman." They help identify changing consumer lifestyles and attitudes reflected in all aspects of beauty and fashion. In the descriptive phase, the findings of focus groups are used to structure a questionnaire. The questionnaire is administered to a sample of 800 women, 16 to 64 years old, using in-home personal interviews.

The relationship between exploratory, descriptive, and causal research is further illustrated by the department store patronage project.

DEPARTMENT STORE PATRONAGE PROJECT
Exploratory, Descriptive, and Causal Research

In the store patronage project, exploratory research, including secondary data analysis and qualitative research, was first conducted to define the problem and develop a suitable approach. This was followed by a descriptive study consisting of a survey in which a questionnaire was constructed and administered by personal interviews.

Suppose that the patronage study was to be repeated after two years to determine if any changes had taken place. At that point, exploratory research would probably be unnecessary and the research design could begin with descriptive research.

Assume that the survey is repeated two years later and that some unexpected findings are then obtained. Management wonders why the store's ratings of in-store service have declined when the sales staff has increased. Exploratory research in the form of focus groups might be undertaken to probe the unexpected findings. The focus groups may reveal that although the salespeople are easy to find, they are not perceived to be friendly or helpful. This may suggest the need for training the sales staff. ◆

This example involves the use of exploratory and descriptive research but not causal research. This reflects that exploratory and descriptive research are frequently used in commercial marketing research but causal research is not as popular. It is possible to combine exploratory, descriptive, and causal research, however, as demonstrated by Citibank (Research in Practice 3.2).[27]

Regardless of the kind of research design employed, the researcher should attempt to minimize the potential sources of error.

POTENTIAL SOURCES OF ERROR

total error The variation between the true mean value in the population of the variable of interest and the observed mean value obtained in the marketing research project.

Several potential sources of error can affect a research design. A good research design attempts to control the various sources of error. Although these errors are discussed in great detail in subsequent chapters, it is pertinent at this stage to give brief descriptions.

The **total error** is the variation between the true mean value in the population of the variable of interest and the observed mean value obtained in the marketing research project. As shown in Figure 3.2, total error is composed of random sampling error and nonsampling error.

FIGURE 3.2

Potential Sources of Error in Research Designs

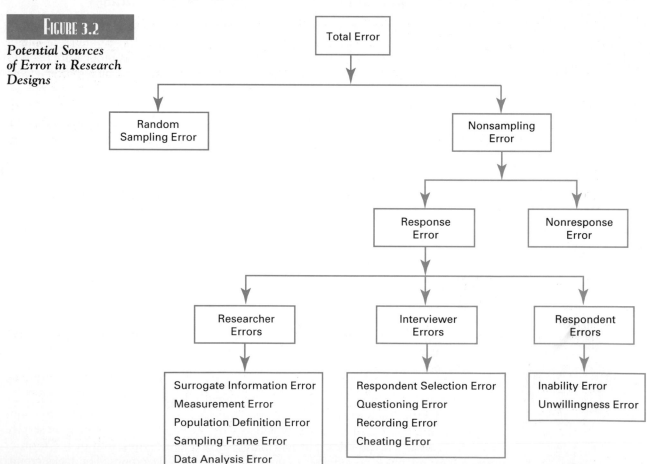

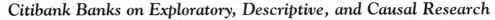

Citibank Banks on Exploratory, Descriptive, and Causal Research

Marketing research at Citicorp/Citibank is typical in that it is used to measure consumer awareness of products, to monitor their satisfaction and attitudes associated with the product, to track product usage, and to diagnose problems as they occur. To accomplish these tasks, Citibank makes extensive use of exploratory, descriptive, and causal research.

Often it is advantageous to offer special financial packages to specific groups of customers. In this case, a financial package is being designed for senior citizens. The following seven-step process was taken by marketing research to help in the design.

1. A task force was created to better define the market parameters to include all the needs of the many Citicorp/Citibank branches. A final decision was made to include Americans 55 years of age or older, retired, and in the upper half of the financial strata of that market.

2. Exploratory research in the form of secondary data analysis of the mature or older market was then performed, and a study of competitive products was conducted. Exploratory qualitative research involving focus groups was also carried out to determine the needs and desires of the market and the level of satisfaction with the current products. In the case of senior citizens, a great deal of diversity was found in the market. This was determined to be due to such factors as affluence, relative age, and the absence or presence of a spouse.

3. The next stage of research was brainstorming. This involved the formation of many different financial packages targeted for the target market. In this case, a total of ten ideas was generated.

4. The feasibility of the ten ideas generated in step 3 was then tested. The ideas were tested on the basis of whether they were possible in relation to the business. The following list of questions was used as a series of hurdles that the ideas had to pass to continue on to the next step.
    - Can the idea be explained in a manner that the target market will easily understand it?
        - Does the idea fit into the overall strategy of Citicorp/Citibank?
        - Is there available a description of a specific target market for the proposed product?
        - Does the research conducted so far indicate a potential match for target market needs, and is the idea perceived to have appeal to this market?
        - Is there a feasible outline of the tactics and strategies for implementing the program?
        - Have the financial impact and cost of the program been thoroughly evaluated and determined to be in line with company practices?

In this study, only one idea generated from the brainstorming session made it past all the listed hurdles and on to step 5.

5. A creative work plan was then generated. This plan was to emphasize the competitive advantage of the proposed product as well as to delineate the specific features of the product better.

6. The previous exploratory research was now followed with descriptive research in the form of mall intercept surveys of people in the target market range. The survey showed that the list of special features was too long, and it was decided to drop the features more commonly offered by competitors.

7. Finally, the product was test-marketed in six of the Citicorp branches within the target market. Test marketing is a form of causal research. Given successful test marketing results, the product was introduced nationally.

Banks undertake exploratory, descriptive, and causal research to understand the financial services needs of consumers. ◆ Stock Boston.

Random Sampling Error

random sampling error
The error because the particular sample selected is an imperfect representation of the population of interest. It may be defined as the variation between the true mean value for the sample and the true mean value of the population.

Random sampling error occurs because the particular sample selected is an imperfect representation of the population of interest. Random sampling error is the variation between the true mean value for the population and the true mean value for the original sample. Random sampling error is discussed further in Chapters 11 and 12.

Nonsampling Error

nonsampling error An error that can be attributed to sources other than sampling and that can be random or nonrandom.

Nonsampling errors can be attributed to sources other than sampling, and they may be random or nonrandom. They result from a variety of reasons, including errors in problem definition, approach, scales, questionnaire design, interviewing methods, and data preparation and analysis. Nonsampling errors consist of nonresponse errors and response errors.

A **nonresponse error** arises when some of the respondents included in the sample do not respond. The primary causes of nonresponse are refusals and not-at-homes (see Chapter 12). Nonresponse will cause the net or resulting sample to be different in size or composition from the original sample. Nonresponse error is defined as the variation between the true mean value of the variable in the original sample and the true mean value in the net sample.

nonresponse error A type of nonsampling error that occurs when some of the respondents included in the sample do not respond. This error may be defined as the variation between the true mean value of the variable in the original sample and the true mean value in the net sample.

Response error arises when respondents give inaccurate answers or their answers are misrecorded or misanalyzed. Response error is defined as the variation between the true mean value of the variable in the net sample and the observed mean value obtained in the marketing research project. Response errors can be made by researchers, interviewers, or respondents.

Errors made by the researcher include surrogate information, measurement, population definition, sampling frame, and data analysis errors.

response error A type of nonsampling error arising from respondents who do respond but who give inaccurate answers or whose answers are misrecorded or misanalyzed. It may be defined as the variation between the true mean value of the variable in the net sample and the observed mean value obtained in the marketing research project.

Surrogate information error may be defined as the variation between the information needed for the marketing research problem and the information sought by the researcher. For example, instead of obtaining information on consumer choice of a new brand (needed for the marketing research problem), the researcher obtains information on consumer preferences because the choice process cannot be easily observed.

Measurement error may be defined as the variation between the information sought and information generated by the measurement process employed by the researcher. While seeking to measure consumer preferences, the researcher employs a scale that measures perceptions rather than preferences.

Population definition error may be defined as the variation between the actual population relevant to the problem at hand and the population as defined by the researcher. The problem of appropriately defining the population may be far from trivial, as illustrated by the case of affluent households.

EXAMPLE
How Affluent Is Affluent? _____

In a recent study, the population of the affluent households was defined in four different ways: (1) households with income of $50,000 or more; (2) the top 20% of households, as measured by income; (3) households with net worth over $250,000; and (4) households with spendable discretionary income 30% higher than that of comparable households. The number and characteristics of the affluent households varied depending on the definition, underscoring the need to avoid population definition error.[28] ◆

As may be surmised, depending upon the way the population of affluent households was defined, the results of this study would have varied markedly.

Sampling frame error may be defined as the variation between the population defined by the researcher and the population as implied by the sampling frame (list) used. For example, the telephone directory used to generate a list of telephone numbers does not accurately represent the population of potential consumers due to unlisted, disconnected, and new numbers in service.

Data analysis error encompasses errors that occur while raw data from questionnaires are transformed into research findings. For example, an inappropriate statistical procedure is used, resulting in incorrect interpretation and findings.

Response errors made by the interviewer include respondent selection, questioning, recording, and cheating errors.

Respondent selection error occurs when interviewers select respondents other than those specified by the sampling design or in a manner inconsistent with the sampling design. For example, in a readership survey, a nonreader is selected for the interview but classified as a reader of the *Wall Street Journal* in the 15- to-19-years-old category in order to meet a difficult quota requirement.

Questioning error denotes errors made in asking questions of the respondents or in not probing, when more information is needed. For example, while asking questions an interviewer does not use the exact wording given in the questionnaire.

Recording error arises due to errors in hearing, interpreting, and recording the answers given by the respondents. For example, a respondent indicates a neutral response (undecided) but the interviewer misinterprets that to mean a positive response (would buy the new brand).

Cheating error arises when the interviewer fabricates answers to a part or whole of the interview. For example, an interviewer does not ask the sensitive questions related to respondent's debt but later fills in the answers based on personal assessment.

Response errors made by the respondent are composed of inability and unwillingness errors.

Inability error results from the respondent's inability to provide accurate answers. Respondents may provide inaccurate answers because of unfamiliarity, fatigue, boredom, faulty recall, question format, question content, and other factors. For example, a respondent cannot recall the brand of yogurt purchased four weeks ago.

Unwillingness error arises from the respondent's unwillingness to provide accurate information. Respondents may intentionally misreport their answers because of a desire to provide socially acceptable answers, to avoid embarrassment, or to please the interviewer. For example, to impress the interviewer, a respondent intentionally misreports reading *Time* magazine.

These sources of error are discussed in more detail in subsequent chapters; what is important here is that there are many sources of error. In formulating a research design, the researcher should attempt to minimize the total error, not just a particular source. This admonition is warranted by the general tendency among students and unsophisticated researchers to control sampling error with large samples. Increasing the sample size does decrease sampling error, but it may also increase nonsampling error, for example by increasing interviewer errors.

Nonsampling error is likely to be more problematic than sampling error. Sampling error can be calculated, whereas many forms of nonsampling error defy estimation. Moreover, nonsampling error has been found to be the major contributor to total error, whereas random sampling error is relatively small in magnitude.[29] The point is that total error is important. A particular type of error is important only in that it contributes to total error.

Sometimes, researchers deliberately increase a particular type of error to decrease the total error by reducing other errors. For example, suppose that a mail survey is being conducted to determine consumer preferences for purchasing fashion clothing from department stores. A large sample size has been selected to reduce sampling error. A response rate of 30% may be expected. Given the limited budget for the project, the selection of a large sample size does not allow for follow-up mailings. Past experience, however, indicates that the response rate could be increased to 45% with one follow-up mailing and to 55% with two follow-up mailings. Given the subject of the survey, non-respondents are likely to differ from respondents in terms of salient variables. Hence, it may be desirable to reduce the sample size to make money available for follow-up mailings. While decreasing the sample size will increase random sampling error, the two follow-up mailings will more than offset this loss by decreasing nonresponse error. Research in Practice 3.3 gives a practitioner's viewpoint on errors in marketing research.[30]

RESEARCH IN PRACTICE 3.3

Errors in Marketing Research: A Practitioner's Viewpoint

Here are the views of Alan Roberts, former manager of market research, Wayne Seed Division of Continental Grain Company, Chicago.

While it is useful to assess sampling errors, of critical concern are the nonsampling errors. In the real world, the difficult, often messy process of assessing nonsampling errors is all too easily overlooked. However, at least the following dozen nonsampling errors should be closely examined in any marketing research project.

1. *Nonprobability sampling.* If nonprobability sampling is employed, the degree to which the sample of convenience actually used reflects or fails to reflect the universe (or market) of interest should be examined.
2. *Nonresponse.* Even a low nonresponse rate of 15 or 20% creates doubts as to how the survey results would have changed if all nonrespondents had, in fact, participated.
3. *Response by a nontargeted individual.* This can arise in mail surveys when the questionnaire is answered by or influenced by a person other than the addressee, such as a family member.
4. *Interrespondent bias.* This bias arises from interaction between respondents. For example, during one-on-one interviewing in a public area, a subsequent respondent may overhear questions and answers from the interview with a prior respondent.
5. *Yea-saying.* This is the desire to please the interviewer by answering according to how the respondent senses the interviewer would like to have the questions answered.
6. *Respondent fatigue.* Respondent fatigue or unrest may arise early or late in the interview, but more likely toward the end.
7. *Questionnaire bias.* The questionnaire can be biased in terms of sequence or phrasing. Professional researchers are usually competent enough to avoid the more obvious types of questionnaire bias. However, when operating management starts hanging "whistles and bells" on the professional's questionnaire draft, much bias can creep in.
8. *"Iffy" questions.* Any question that asks for more than a respondent's actual (past) behavior or current opinions tends to be "iffy."
9. *Unfamiliar questions.* These are questions outside the respondent's qualified range of personal knowledge or interests.
10. *Interviewer bias.* This error can be insidious, especially in surveys where interviewing is not centrally controlled.
11. *Interviewer cheating.* The extent of cheating can vary from reporting many totally fictitious interviews to more limited forms, such as skipping a few questions or including nonqualified respondents.
12. *Incompetent interviewing.* Sloppy interviewing techniques can take many forms, such as misrecording answers, failure to probe, or rephrasing questions.

BUDGETING AND SCHEDULING THE PROJECT

budgeting and scheduling
Management tools needed to help ensure that the marketing research project is completed within the available resources.

critical path method A management technique of dividing a research project into component activities, determining the sequence of these components, and estimating the time that each activity will require.

Once a research design, appropriately controlling the total error, has been specified, the budgeting and scheduling decisions should be made. **Budgeting and scheduling** help to ensure that the marketing research project is completed within the available resources: financial, time, labor, and so forth. By specifying both the time parameters within which each task should be completed and the costs of each task, the research project can be effectively managed. A useful approach for managing a project is the **critical path method** (CPM), which involves dividing the research project into component activities, determining the sequence of these activities, and estimating the time required for each activity. These activities and time estimates are diagrammed in the form of a network flowchart. The critical path, the series of activities whose delay will hold up the project, can then be identified.

An advanced version of the CPM, the **program evaluation and review technique (PERT)**, is a probability-based scheduling approach that recognizes and measures the uncertainty of the project completion times.[31] An even more advanced scheduling technique is the **graphical evaluation and review technique (GERT)**, in which both the completion probabilities and the activity costs can be built into a network representation.

MARKETING RESEARCH PROPOSAL

program evaluation and review technique (PERT) A sophisticated critical path method that accounts for the uncertainty in project completion times.

graphical evaluation and review technique (GERT) A sophisticated critical path method that accounts for both the completion probabilities and the activity costs.

marketing research proposal The official layout of the planned marketing research activity for management. It describes the research problem, the approach, the research design, data collection methods, data analysis methods, and reporting methods.

Once the research design has been formulated and budgeting and scheduling of the project accomplished, a written research proposal should be prepared. The **marketing research proposal** contains the essence of the project and serves as a contract between the researcher and management. The research proposal covers all phases of the marketing research process. It describes the research problem, the approach, the research design, and how the data will be collected, analyzed, and reported. It gives a cost estimate and a time schedule for completing the project. Although the format of a research proposal may vary considerably, most proposals address all the steps of the marketing research process and contain the following elements.

1. *Executive summary.* The proposal should begin with a summary of the major points from each of the other sections, presenting an overview of the entire proposal.
2. *Background.* The background to the problem, including the environmental context, should be discussed.
3. *Problem definition/objectives of the research.* Normally, a statement of the problem, including the specific components, should be presented. If this statement has not been developed (as in the case of problem identification research), the objectives of the marketing research project should be clearly specified.
4. *Approach to the problem.* At a minimum, a review of the relevant academic and trade literature should be presented, along with some kind of an analytical model. If research questions, hypotheses, and factors influencing the research design have been identified, then these should be included in the proposal.
5. *Research design.* The research design adopted—whether exploratory, descriptive, or causal—should be specified. Information should be provided on the following components: (1) kind of information to be obtained; (2) method of administering the questionnaire (mail, telephone, or personal interviews); (3) scaling techniques; (4) nature of the questionnaire (type of questions asked, length, and average interviewing time); and (5) sampling plan and sample size.
6. *Field work/data collection.* The proposal should discuss how the data will be collected and who will collect it. If the field work is to be subcontracted to another supplier, this should be stated. Control mechanisms to ensure the quality of data collected should be described.

7. *Data analysis.* The kind of data analysis that will be conducted (simple cross-tabulations, univariate analysis, multivariate analysis) and how the results will be interpreted should be described.

8. *Reporting.* The proposal should specify whether intermediate reports will be presented and at what stages, what will be the form of the final report, and whether a formal presentation of the results will be made.

9. *Cost and time.* The cost of the project and a time schedule, broken down by phases, should be presented. A CPM or PERT chart might be included. In large projects, a payment schedule is also worked out in advance.

10. *Appendices.* Any statistical or other information of interest to only a few people should be contained in appendices.

Preparing a research proposal has several advantages. It ensures that the researcher and management agree about the nature of the project, and it helps sell the project to management. As preparation of the proposal entails planning, it helps the researcher conceptualize and execute the marketing research project.

INTERNATIONAL MARKETING RESEARCH

While conducting international marketing research, it is important to realize that given the environmental differences (see Chapter 23), the research design appropriate for one country may not be suitable in another. Consider the problem of determining household attitudes toward major appliances in the United States and Saudi Arabia. While conducting exploratory research in the United States, it is appropriate to conduct focus groups jointly with male and female heads of households. It would be inappropriate to conduct such focus groups in Saudi Arabia, however. Given the traditional culture, wives are unlikely to participate freely in the presence of their husbands. It would be more useful to conduct one-on-one depth interviews with both male and female heads of households being included in the sample. Procter & Gamble encountered a similar situation in Japan.

EXAMPLE
P & G Wooing and Exploring Japanese Women

The consumer market in Japan is one of the toughest, most competitive, fastest-moving markets in the world. Japan represents the cutting edge of worldwide product technology in many product categories. When Procter & Gamble started business in Japan, it conducted a detailed study of market characteristics and market profile. The target market for P & G was housewives who were largely responsible for the consumption of several products such as diapers, household cleaners, soaps, and detergents. Exploratory research followed by descriptive research was undertaken for this purpose. Although focus groups are most popular in the United States, exploratory research in Japan emphasized individual depth interviews. Given the Japanese cultural tendency to not openly disagree in group settings, one-on-one in-depth interviews were preferred. The descriptive surveys emphasized in-home personal interviews. Results showed that an average Japanese housewife was very uncompromising in her demands for high quality, value, and service. She was a paragon of conservation and efficiency in the management of her household. About half the adult women in Japan were employed. They generally worked before marriage and after children were raised. Child rearing was the number one priority for Japanese mothers. When it came to foreign versus domestic brands, Japanese women preferred foreign name brand products that had style and status symbol, such as fashionable clothing, French perfumes, wines, liquors, and Gucci bags. They did not prefer functional products that were made in foreign countries, however, because they usually did not meet their exacting and demanding quality standards. Japanese women greatly preferred commercials that conserved traditional social and family values and roles rather than the typical Western examples. Although P & G initially made a few mistakes by misjudging Japanese nuances such as the introduction of Camay toilet soap and Pampers diaper, this market profile study helped them to avoid costly mistakes later.[32] ◆

In many countries, particularly developing countries, consumer panels have not been developed, making it difficult to conduct descriptive longitudinal research. Likewise, in many countries the marketing support infrastructure—that is, retailing, wholesaling, advertising, and promotional infrastructure—is lacking, making it infeasible to implement a causal design involving a field experiment. In formulating a research design, considerable effort is required to ensure the equivalence and comparability of secondary and primary data obtained from different countries. In the context of collecting primary data, qualitative research, survey methods, scaling techniques, questionnaire design, and sampling considerations are particularly important. These topics are discussed in more detail in subsequent chapters.

ETHICS IN MARKETING RESEARCH

During the research design stage, not only are the concerns of the researcher and the client involved, but the rights of the respondents also must be respected. Although normally there is no direct contact between the respondents and the other stakeholders (client and researcher) during the research design phase, this is the stage when decisions, such as using hidden video or audio tape recorders, with ethical ramifications are made.

The basic question of the type of research design which should be adopted (i.e., descriptive or causal, cross-sectional or longitudinal) has ethical overtones. For example, when studying brand switching in toothpaste purchases, a longitudinal design is the only actual way to assess changes in an individual respondent's brand choice. A research firm that has not conducted many longitudinal studies may try to justify the use of a cross-sectional design. Is this ethical?

The researchers must ensure that the research design utilized will provide the information needed to address the marketing research problem which has been identified. The client should have the integrity not to misrepresent the project and should describe the constraints under which the researcher must operate and not make unreasonable demands. Longitudinal research takes time. Descriptive research might require interviewing customers. If time is an issue, or if customer contact has to be restricted, the client should make these constraints known at the start of the project. Finally, the client should not take undue advantage of the research firm to solicit unfair concessions for the current project by making false promises of future research contracts by holding out the carrot.

EXAMPLE
Holding Out the Carrot

Ethical dilemmas may arise due to the strong desire of marketing research firms to become suppliers to large business firms who are heavy users of marketing research. Take for example, American Express, American Airlines, or Coca-Cola. Such firms frequently hire external marketing research suppliers. These large clients can manipulate the price for the current study or demand unreasonable concessions in the research design (e.g., a larger sample size or the examination of more variables) by suggesting the potential for the marketing research firm to become a regular supplier. This may be considered just business, but it becomes unethical when there is no intention to follow up with a larger study or to use the research firm in the future. This has been labeled "holding out the carrot" and is considered a client transgression.[33] ◆

Equally important, the responsibilities to the respondents must not be overlooked. The researcher should design the study so as not to violate the respondents' right to safety, right to privacy, or right to choose. Furthermore, the client must not abuse power to jeopardize the anonymity of the respondents. These respondent related issues are discussed in more detail in Chapters 4, 5, 6 and 7.

COMPUTER APPLICATIONS

The formulation of a research design and the preparation of a proposal are greatly facilitated by the use of microcomputers and mainframes. The use of microcomputers and mainframes in exploratory research for secondary data analysis and qualitative research is discussed in Chapters 4 and 5. Their use in descriptive cross-sectional and causal research is discussed in Chapters 6 and 7. These later chapters discuss in detail the role of computers in each component of research design. Here we discuss the role of microcomputers in longitudinal designs and in controlling potential sources of error.

When deciding to initiate a panel study, the researcher should consider the deeper insights into the problem area that a repeated measures design can bring. To obtain such insights, analysis of longitudinal data can be performed with FORECAST PRO for Windows by Business Forecast Systems, Inc. of Belmont, Massachusetts. Data in spreadsheets (such as those created with LOTUS 1-2-3) or in ASCII files can be used as the source for data used by FORECAST PRO.

FORECAST PRO enables the user to discern seasonality in data collected repeatedly over regular periods. In addition, FORECAST PRO can help identify trends in data over periods longer than seasons in a year. Understanding seasonality and trends in a data set cannot be gained with a single cross-sectional research design.

Suppose that in December 1995 the marketing research manager for the dairy division of Borden Foods—a national manufacturer of food products—is faced with the problem of estimating the relative preference for milk as compared with other beverages during 1996–98. Should the researcher adopt a longitudinal research design to obtain a forecast of milk consumption during 1996–98, or can this information be reasonably obtained from longitudinal data obtained in the past (i.e., May 1994 to November 1995)?

In Exhibit 3.1, the purchases of milk from May 1994 to November 1995 by members of a panel of grocery store shoppers are presented. The broad line denotes the main sample, and the narrow line denotes a holdout sample of panel members in the study. During the period of the study, seasonal fluctuation occurred each July, as purchases of milk (labeled as "sales" of milk to the panel in the exhibit) declined markedly. By looking at these repeated measures of panel member purchases as one set, a slight upward trend can be discerned.

The Peek and Poke utility of FORECAST PRO can be used to adjust data or forecasts on the screen. This utility allows the user to post alternative forecasts by using the mouse to click and drag the graphic plot of the forecasted variable to new positions repeatedly, as in the right side of Exhibit 3.1. In the three forecasts presented, the cen-

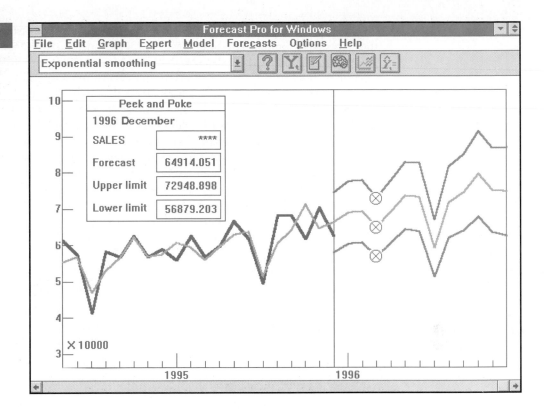

EXHIBIT 3.1

*Forecasting Milk
Consumption Using
FORECAST PRO*

ter line denotes the actual forecast made by the software, and the upper and lower lines denote the forecast when different samples of the targeted population of milk purchasers at convenience stores are considered. In this way, estimates of sampling frame error in the study can be included. This is a more expedient approach to sensitivity analysis, where best- and worst-case scenarios for sampling frame error can be readily depicted.

Forecasting by automated methods such as those in FORECAST PRO is not fool-proof. Important assumptions are made in such forecasts, particularly that relevant business conditions will continue to prevail or that a change in one condition can be anticipated and predicted with some accuracy. For best results, the user must understand the different forecasting techniques. Fortunately, FORECAST PRO includes an expert system that can automatically select a forecasting method and explain its logic in ordinary English.

With software such as FORECAST PRO, the researcher has a means to derive valuable insights that only longitudinal data can provide. Seasonality, trends, and consideration of total error are three of these important insights. This can help the researcher to determine whether a longitudinal design is appropriate for the problem at hand.

Microcomputers and mainframes can also help control total error. By using computers, it is possible to understand how the various sources of error will affect the results and what levels of errors might be acceptable. It is relatively easy to estimate random sampling error when probability sampling schemes are used. The formulas for estimating these errors can be easily programmed using a database manager such as dBASE IV. The author has developed several programs of this type.

Estimating the impact of various nonsampling errors, however, is much more problematic. Simulation can be conducted to determine how the distributions and levels of various nonsampling errors will affect final results.[34] This would indicate the acceptable levels of error, and the research design could be adjusted to contain these errors within the acceptable limits. The simulations provide only an indication, and considerable judgment on the part of the researcher is needed. Software like MONTE CARLO SIMULATIONS (MCS) by Actuarial Micro Software is useful for these purposes. MCS consists of three program modules for statistical analysis, simulation, and long-term projections. MCS can analyze and simulate a variety of systems for a wide variety of applications. Its statistical analysis module permits evaluation of sample data with up to 13 different probability distributions. The statistical analysis module can be used as a "front end" for the simulation module by helping to pick the appropriate distribution of error variable or other model variables. The statistical module can also be used to evaluate results generated by both the simulation and long-term projection modules.

MACPROJECT is an example of PERT/CPM software. The program provides several charts, including a schedule, resource timeline, cash flow table, and project table. "What if" questions can be answered quickly, and unit cost of personnel and materials can be automatically calculated from the number of hours set for normal working days and holidays. Other popular scheduling software include TIMELINE, HARVARD PROJECT MANAGER, MICROSOFT PROJECT, and CATEGORY PERTMASTER.

SUMMARY

A research design is a framework or blueprint for conducting the marketing research project. It specifies the details of how the project should be conducted. Research designs may be broadly classified as exploratory or conclusive. The primary purpose of exploratory research is to provide insights into the problem. Conclusive research is conducted to test specific hypotheses and examine specific relationships. The findings from conclusive research are used as input into managerial decision making. Conclusive research may be either descriptive or causal.

The major objective of descriptive research is to describe market characteristics or functions. A descriptive design requires a clear specification of the who, what, when, where, why, and way of the research. Descriptive research can be classified into cross-sectional and longitudinal research. Cross-sectional designs involve the collection of information from a sample of population elements at a single point in time. These designs can be further classified as single cross-sectional or multiple cross-sectional designs. In contrast, in longitudinal designs repeated measurements are taken on a fixed sample. Causal research is designed for the primary purpose of obtaining evidence about cause-and-effect (causal) relationships.

A research design consists of six components. Error can be associated with any of these components. The total error is composed of random sampling error and nonsampling error. Nonsampling error consists of nonresponse and response errors. Response error encompasses errors made by researchers, interviewers, and respondents. A written marketing research proposal including all the elements of the marketing research process should be prepared. In formulating a research design when conducting international marketing research, considerable effort is required to ensure the equivalence and comparability of secondary and primary data obtained from different countries. In terms of ethical issues, the researchers must ensure that the research design used will provide the information sought and that the information sought is the information needed by the client. The client should have the integrity not to misrepresent the project and should describe the situation within which the researcher must operate and must not make unreasonable demands. Every precaution should be taken to ensure the respondents' or subjects' right to safety, right to privacy, or right to choose. Microcomputers can be usefully employed to aid the process of formulating a research design.[35]

ACRONYMS

The components of a research design may be summarized by the acronym DESIGN:

D ata analysis plan
E xploratory, descriptive, causal design
S caling and measurement
I nterviewing forms, questionnaire design
G enerate the information needed
N Sample size and plan

EXERCISES

QUESTIONS

1. Define *research design* in your own words.
2. How does formulating a research design differ from developing an approach to a problem?
3. Differentiate between exploratory and conclusive research.
4. What are the major purposes for which descriptive research is conducted?
5. List the six Ws of descriptive research and give an example of each.
6. Compare and contrast cross-sectional and longitudinal designs.
7. Describe cohort analysis. Why is it of special interest?
8. Discuss the advantages and disadvantages of panels.
9. What is a causal research design? What is its purpose?
10. What is the relationship between exploratory, descriptive, and causal research?
11. List the major components of a research design.
12. What potential sources of error can affect a research design?
13. Why is it important to minimize total error rather than any particular source of error?

PROBLEMS

1. Sweet Cookies is planning to launch a new line of cookies and wants to assess the market size. The cookies have a mixed chocolate-pineapple flavor and will be targeted at the premium end of the market. Discuss the six Ws of a descriptive research design that may be adopted.
2. Express each of the following types of error as an equation:
   a. Total error
   b. Random sampling error
   c. Nonresponse error
   d. Response error
3. Welcome Inc. is a chain of fast-food restaurants located in major metropolitan areas in the South. Sales have been growing very slowly for the last two years. Management has decided to add some new items to the menu, but first they want to know more about their customers and their preferences.
   a. List two hypotheses.
   b. What kind of research design is appropriate? Why?

COMPUTER EXERCISES

1. Obtain one of the CPM/PERT programs listed in the book. Using this program, develop a schedule for the research project described in Problem 3.

NOTES

1. *ITAPA International Survey of Passenger Preferences* (Arlington, VA: International Airline Passengers Associations, 1987).

2. Kate Bertrand, "Talking Turkey on Trade Shows," *Business Marketing* (March 1987): 94–103.

3. Claire Selltiz, Lawrence S. Wrightsman, and Stuart W. Cook, *Research Methods in Social Relations*, 3rd ed. (New York: Holt, Rinehart and Winston, 1976).

4. Fred N. Kerlinger, *Foundations of Behavioral Research*, 3rd ed. (New York: Holt, Rinehart and Winston, 1986), pp. 17–20.

5. For an example of exploratory research, see David H. Furse, M. R. Burcham, R. L. Rose, and R. W. Oliver, "Leveraging the Value of Customer Satisfaction Information," *Journal of Health Care Marketing* 14 (Fall 1994): 16–20.

6. Laura Bird, "Marketers Sell Pen as Signature of Style," *Wall Street Journal* (November 9, 1993): B1, B7.

7. For an example of descriptive research, see Stanley F. Slater and John C. Narver, "Does Competitive Environment Moderate the Market Orientation-Performance Relationship?" *Journal of Marketing* 58 (January 1994): 46–55.

8. See Harper W. Boyd, Jr., Ralph Westfall, and Stanley F. Stasch, *Marketing Research: Text and Cases*, 7th ed. (Homewood, IL: Richard D. Irwin, 1989), p. 286; and Gilbert A. Churchill, Jr., *Marketing Research*, 5th ed. (Chicago: Dryden Press, 1991), p. 145, for a similar discussion.

9. "Coupon Use Low Among Young, Working Women," *Marketing News* (April 10, 1987): 24.

10. "Eating Behavior Trends Revealed in Pillsbury Study," *Quirk's Marketing Research Review* (June–July 1988): 14–15, 39, 44.

11. Norval D. Glenn, *Cohort Analysis* (Beverly Hills: Sage Publications, 1981). For a recent application see Joseph O. Rentz and Fred D. Reynolds, "Forecasting the Effects of an Aging Population on Product Consumption: An Age-Period-Cohort Framework," *Journal of Marketing Research* (August 1991): 355–60.

12. Joseph O. Rentz, Fred D. Reynolds, and Roy G. Stout, "Analyzing Changing Consumption Patterns with Cohort Analysis," *Journal of Marketing Research*, 20 (February 1983): 12–20.

13. For a recent application, see Terry Elrod and Michael P. Keane, "A Factor-Analytic Probit Model for Representing the Market Structure in Panel Data," *Journal of Marketing Research*, 32 (February 1995): 1–16.

14. Terry Elrod, "Choice Map: Inferring a Product-Market Map from Panel Data," *Marketing Science* 7 (Winter 1988): 21–41.

15. Gregory B. Markus, *Analyzing Panel Data* (Beverly Hills: Sage Publications, 1979). For recent applications of panel data, see Pradeep K. Chintagunta, Dipak C. Jain, and Naufel J. Vilcassim, "Investigating Heterogeneity in Brand Preferences in Logit Models for Panel Data," *Journal of Marketing Research* (November 1991): 417–28; and Barbara E. Kahn and Jagmohan S. Raju, "Effects of Price Promotions on Variety-Seeking and Reinforcement Behavior," *Marketing Science* (Fall 1991): 316–37.

16. Table 3.6 can also be viewed as a transition matrix. It depicts the brand-buying changes from period to period. Knowing the proportion of consumers who switch allows for early prediction of the ultimate success of a new product or change in market strategy. See Seymour Sudman and Robert Ferber, *Consumer Panels* (Chicago: American Marketing Association, 1979), pp. 19–27.

17. Mark W. Johnston, A. Parasuraman, Charles M. Futrell, and William C. Black, "A Longitudinal Assessment of the Impact of Selected Organizational Influences on Salespeople's Organizational Commitment during Early Employment," *Journal of Marketing Research* (August 1990): 333–44.

18. See Seymour Sudman and Robert Ferber, "A Comparison of Alternative Procedures for Collecting Consumer Expenditure Data for Frequently Purchased Products," and Robert A. Wright, Richard H. Beisel, Julia D. Oliver, and Michelle C. Gerzowski, "The Use of a Multiple Entry Diary in a Panel Study on Health Care," both in Robert Ferber (ed.), *Readings in Survey Research* (Chicago: American Marketing Association, 1978), pp. 487–502 and 503–12; Yoram Wind and David Lerner, "On the Measurement of Purchase Data: Surveys Versus Purchase Diaries," *Journal of Marketing Research* 16 (February 1979): 39–47; and John McKenzie, "The Accuracy of Telephone Call Data by Diary Methods," *Journal of Marketing Research* 20 (November 1983): 417–27.

19. Seymour Sudman and Robert Ferber, *Consumer Panels* (Chicago: American Marketing Association, 1979), pp. 19–27. See also Birger Wernerfelt, "Brand Loyalty and Market Equilibrium," *Marketing Science* (Summer 1991): 229–45.

20. Russell S. Winer, "Attrition Bias in Econometric Models Estimated with Panel Data," *Journal of Marketing Research* 20 (May 1983): 177–86.

21. William H. Motes, "How to Solve Common Problems in Longitudinal Studies," *Marketing News* (January 6, 1984): 3.

22. Keith K. Cox and Ben M. Enis, *Experimentation for Marketing Decisions* (Scranton, PA: International Textbook, 1969), p. 5.

23. For an application of causal research, see H. Rao Unnava, Robert E. Burnkrant, and Sunil Erevelles, "Effects of Presentation Order and Communication Modality on Recall and Attitude," *Journal of Consumer Research* 21 (December 1994): 481–90.

24. Michael J. Naples and Rolf M. Wulfsberg, "The Bottom Line: Does Industrial Advertising Sell?" *Journal of Advertising Research* (August–September, 1987): RC4–RC16.

25. Philip J. Cooper, Ian Diamond, and Sue High, "Choosing and Using Contraceptives: Integrating Qualitative and Quantitative Research Methods in Family Planning," *Journal of the Market Research Society* 35 (October 1993): 325–40.

26. "Study to Probe Attitudes about Fashion, Beauty," *Marketing News* (August 28, 1987): 60.

27. Sabra Brock, Sara Lipson, and Ron Levitt, "Trends in Marketing Research and Development at Citicorp/Citibank," *Marketing Research: A Magazine of Management and Applications* 1 (4) (December 1989): 3–8.

28. *Marketing News* (April 10, 1987): 3.

29. Henry Assael and John Keon, "Nonsampling vs. Sampling Errors in Survey Research," *Journal of Marketing* 46 (Spring 1982): 114–23.

30. "Understanding Data Requires Recognition of Types of Error," *Quirk's Marketing Research Review* (May 1987): 20, 58, 59.

31. Frederick S. Hillier and Gerald J. Lieberman, *Introduction to Operations Research*, 4 (Oakland, CA: Golden-Day, 1986), pp. 295–331.

32. Edwin Artzt, "Winning in Japan: Keys to Global Success," *Business Quarterly* (Winter 1989); Copyright © 1989 by *Business Quarterly*. Reprinted with permission of Business Quarterly, published by the Western Business School, The University of Western Ontario, London, Canada.

33. R. Bezilla, J. B Haynes, and C. Elliot, *Ethics in Marketing Research* (Business Horizons, 1976), pp. 83–86.

34. Naresh K. Malhotra, "An Approach to the Measurement of Consumer Preferences Using Limited Information," *Journal of Marketing Research* 23 (February 1986): 33–40; and Naresh K. Malhotra "Analyzing Marketing Research Data with Incomplete Information on the Dependent Variable," *Journal of Marketing Research* 24 (February 1987): 74–84.

35. The assistance of James Agarwal with the international marketing research example, the assistance of Mark Leach and Gina Miller in writing the ethics section, and the assistance of Mark Peterson in writing the computer applications section is gratefully acknowledged.

CHAPTER FOUR

Exploratory Research Design: Secondary Data

Examination of available secondary data is a prerequisite to the collection of primary data.

OBJECTIVES

After reading this chapter, the student should be able to:

1. Define the nature and scope of secondary data and distinguish secondary data from primary data.

2. Analyze the advantages and disadvantages of secondary data and their uses in the various steps of the marketing research process.

3. Evaluate secondary data using the criteria of specifications, error, currency, objectives, nature, and dependability.

4. Describe, in detail, the different sources of secondary data including internal sources and external sources in the form of published materials, computerized databases, and syndicated services.

5. Discuss in detail the syndicated sources of secondary data including household and consumer data obtained via surveys, mail diary panels, and electronic scanner services as well as institutional data related to retailers, wholesalers, and industrial or service firms.

6. Explain the need to use multiple sources of secondary data and describe single-source data.

7. Discuss applications of secondary data in constructing a buying power index and in computer mapping.

8. Identify and evaluate the sources of secondary data useful in international marketing research.
9. Understand the ethical issues involved in the use of secondary data.
10. Discuss the use of microcomputers and mainframes in researching secondary data.

OVERVIEW

As mentioned in the previous chapters, analysis of secondary data helps define the marketing research problem and develop an approach (Chapter 2). Also, before the research design for collecting primary data is formulated (Chapter 3), the researcher should analyze the relevant secondary data. In some projects, particularly those with limited budgets, research may be largely confined to the analysis of secondary data because some routine problems may be addressed based only on secondary data. This chapter discusses the distinction between primary and secondary data. The advantages and disadvantages of secondary data are considered, and criteria for evaluating secondary data are presented, along with a classification of secondary data. Internal secondary data are described, and major sources of external secondary data—such as published materials, on-line and off-line databases, and syndicated services—are also discussed. We consider applications of secondary data in calculating the buying power index and computer mapping. The sources of secondary data useful in international marketing research are discussed. Several ethical issues that arise in the use of secondary data are identified. Finally, we discuss the use of microcomputers and mainframes in conducting secondary data analysis.[1]

We begin by citing several examples to give you a flavor of secondary data.

EXAMPLE
High Touch Goes High Tech _____

The U.S. Department of Labor says that the average age of the American workforce will increase from 35 to 39 by the year 2000. This is in part the result of the maturation of the "baby bust" generation (those born between 1965 and 1976), which will cause a decline in the number of young (aged 16–24) workers available to fill entry-level positions.[2] This potential shortage of young workers has caused many marketers, such as Arby's, to switch from a "high-touch" to a "high-tech" service orientation. Many services formerly rendered by workers are now performed by consumers using high-tech equipment. ◆

EXAMPLE
Top Five Hits under the Convenience Label _____

A report by the National Association of Convenience Stores shows that the top five items in planned purchases (nonimpulse buying) from convenience stores are (1) soft drinks, (2) tobacco products, (3) gasoline, (4) dairy products (milk, eggs, margarine), and (5) reading material. This information can be valuable to convenience stores in determining their product mix. It is also useful to marketers of these products in designing sales promotional activities such as sampling, coupons, and point-of-sale displays.[3] ◆

EXAMPLE
Hard Data on Soft Drinks

Do you want to determine the market shares of different categories of soft drinks? There is no need to collect your own data. Here is the information provided by *Advertising Age*, a leading advertising publication.[4] ◆

Total Soft Drink Market: Share by Category

Category	Percent Share
Cola	66.6
Lemon-lime	13.0
Pepper	5.7
Orange	5.5
All others	9.2
Total	100.0

Secondary data on soft drinks are almost as readily available as soft drinks themselves. ◆ Teri Stratford.

EXAMPLE
Secondary Data Helps Samsonite to Establish a "Travel Expert" Image

Samsonite Corporation uses a consumer database and an 800-number Consumer Link program as well as an in-house consumer database. These activities are an effort to build stronger consumer relationships, to increase satisfaction, to establish a "travel expert" image for Samsonite, and to help sell products directly to consumers.

Information from consumers comes from consumer response cards and the 800 number used to elicit information calls from potential customers. This information becomes a part of the database and provides Samsonite with a great deal of planning data. By analyzing purchasers of specific types of luggage, Samsonite is better able to plan for future product offerings. By analyzing the response data, new product planning and product modifications can be researched. Research can also be done to estimate customer satisfaction with existing products by performing quarterly studies of past customers using the database information. Samsonite used this type of study to determine repurchase intent in the mid-1990s for new owners of the Piggyback Carry-On recently introduced.[5] ◆

As these examples illustrate, government departments (U.S. Department of Labor), industry associations (National Association of Convenience Stores), trade publications (*Advertising Age*), and in-house databases are only a few of the sources from which secondary data may be obtained. The nature and role of secondary data become clear when we understand the distinction between primary and secondary data.

PRIMARY VERSUS SECONDARY DATA

Primary data are originated by a researcher for the specific purpose of addressing the problem at hand. The collection of primary data involves all six steps of the marketing research process (Chapter 1). Obtaining primary data can be expensive and time con-

primary data Data originated by the researcher for the specific purpose of addressing the research problem.

secondary data Data collected for some purpose other than the problem at hand.

suming. The department store patronage project cited in Chapter 1 is an example of primary data collection.

Secondary data are data that have already been collected for purposes other than the problem at hand. These data can be located quickly and inexpensively. In the department store patronage project, secondary data on the criteria used by households to select department stores were obtained from marketing journals (*Journal of Retailing, Journal of Marketing,* and *Journal of Marketing Research*). Several other examples of secondary data were provided in the preceding section. The differences between primary and secondary data are summarized in Table 4.1. As compared with primary data, secondary data are collected rapidly and easily, at a relatively low cost, and in a short time. These differences between primary and secondary data lead to some distinct advantages and uses of secondary data.

TABLE 4.1		Primary Data	Secondary Data
A Comparison of Primary and Secondary Data	Collection purpose	For the problem at hand	For other problems
	Collection process	Very involved	Rapid and easy
	Collection cost	High	Relatively low
	Collection time	Long	Short

ADVANTAGES AND USES OF SECONDARY DATA

As can be seen from the foregoing discussion, secondary data offer several advantages over primary data. Secondary data are easily accessible, relatively inexpensive, and quickly obtained. Some secondary data, such as those provided by the U.S. Bureau of the Census, are available on topics where it would not be feasible for a firm to collect primary data. Although it is rare for secondary data to provide all the answers to a nonroutine research problem, such data can be useful in a variety of ways.[6] Secondary data can help you:

1. Identify the problem
2. Better define the problem
3. Develop an approach to the problem
4. Formulate an appropriate research design (for example, by identifying the key variables)
5. Answer certain research questions and test some hypotheses
6. Interpret primary data more insightfully

Given these advantages and uses of secondary data, we state the following general rule:

Examination of available secondary data is a prerequisite to the collection of primary data. Start with secondary data. Proceed to primary data only when the secondary data sources have been exhausted or yield marginal returns.

The rich dividends obtained by following this rule are exemplified by the Frost National Bank example.

EXAMPLE
Bank "Zips" Up the Market

Frost National Bank was considering modifying its Young Leaders Club (YLC) account to enhance its appeal to San Antonians between the ages of 21 and 35. The YLC offered members a checking account with enhancements such as life insurance, discount movie tickets, store coupons, tours, and social events, all for a monthly membership fee. Extensive analysis of secondary data was conducted. Using internal secondary data, club members were evaluated by zip code and account activity. The results of zip code analysis helped attract advertising and discount coupons from merchants in areas of San Antonio where large numbers of YLC members lived. External secondary data available on this age group provided additional insights in redeveloping the YLC package. Census information allowed Frost National Bank to estimate the size of the potential market for YLC. This secondary data analysis was followed by focus groups and survey research. After completing their marketing research, which began with the examination of secondary data, Frost National Bank was able to increase the number of YLC accounts in the target market significantly.[7] ◆

This example shows that analysis of secondary data can provide valuable insights and lay the foundation for conducting qualitative research, such as focus groups and surveys. The researcher should be cautious in using secondary data, however, because they have some limitations and disadvantages.

DISADVANTAGES OF SECONDARY DATA

Because secondary data have been collected for purposes other than the problem at hand, their usefulness to the current problem may be limited in several important ways, including relevance and accuracy. The objectives, nature, and methods used to collect the secondary data may not be appropriate to the present situation. Also, secondary data may be lacking in accuracy or may not be completely current or dependable. Before using secondary data, it is important to evaluate them on these factors.[8] These factors are discussed in more detail in the following section.

CRITERIA FOR EVALUATING SECONDARY DATA

The quality of secondary data should be routinely evaluated, using the criteria of Table 4.2 discussed in the following sections.[9]

Specifications: Methodology Used to Collect the Data

The specifications or the methodology used to collect the data should be critically examined to identify possible sources of bias. Such methodological considerations include size and nature of the sample, response rate and quality, questionnaire design and administration, procedures used for field work, and data analysis and reporting procedures. These checks provide information on the reliability and validity of the data and help determine whether they can be generalized to the problem at hand. The reliability and validity can be further ascertained by an examination of the error, currency, objectives, nature, and dependability associated with the secondary data.

Error: Accuracy of the Data

The researcher must determine whether the data are accurate enough for the purposes of the present study. Secondary data can have a number of sources of error or inaccuracy, including errors in the approach, research design, sampling, data collection, analysis,

TABLE 4.2

Criteria for Evaluating Secondary Data

Criteria	Issues	Remarks
Specifications and methodology	Data collection method. Response rate. Quality of data. Sampling technique. Sample size. Questionnaire design. Field work. Data analysis.	Data should be reliable, valid, and generalizable to the problem at hand.
Error and accuracy	Examine errors in approach, research design, sampling, data collection, data analysis, and reporting.	Assess accuracy by comparing data from different sources.
Currency	Time lag between collection and publication. Frequency of updates.	Census data are periodically updated by syndicated firms.
Objective	Why were the data collected?	The objective will determine the relevance of data.
Nature	Definition of key variables. Units of measurement. Categories used. Relationships examined.	Reconfigure the data to increase their usefulness, if possible.
Dependability	Expertise, credibility, reputation, and trustworthiness of the source.	Data should be obtained from an original rather than an acquired source.

and reporting stages of the project. Moreover, it is difficult to evaluate the accuracy of secondary data because the researcher did not participate in the research. One approach is to find multiple sources of data and compare them using standard statistical procedures. The accuracy of secondary data can also be verified by conducting field investigations, as recommended by the International Council of Shopping Centers.

EXAMPLE

Population Dynamics and the Accuracy of Secondary Data

The International Council of Shopping Centers conducted a study to evaluate the quality of small area estimates and projections provided by private vendors of demographic information. Six vendors (CACI, Claritas, Donnelley Marketing Information Services, National Decision Systems, National Planning Data Corporation, and Urban Decision Systems) participated in the research performed in three market areas: Baltimore, Detroit, and Phoenix. The vendors supplied the council with statistics and demographic data for each market area. The council analyzed the divergence among the vendors' reports using standard statistical procedures. The results indicated that there was little variation in the data provided by the vendors at the metropolitan and county levels with regard to household demographics and population statistics when these data reflected relatively stable population dynamics. The vendor-supplied demographic data varied considerably in areas with rapidly changing populations, however. In such cases, the council recommended that users verify vendor data findings with field investigations of their own.[10] ◆

As this example indicates, the accuracy of secondary data can vary, particularly if they relate to phenomena that are subject to change. Moreover, data obtained from different sources may not agree. In these cases, the researcher should verify the accuracy of secondary data by conducting pilot studies or by other appropriate methods. Often, by exercising creativity this can be done without much expense or effort.

Currency: When the Data Were Collected

Secondary data may not be current, and the time lag between data collection and publication may be long, as is the case with much census data. Moreover, the data may not be updated frequently enough for the purpose of the problem at hand. Marketing research requires current data; therefore, the value of secondary data is diminished as they become dated. For instance, although the 1990 *Census of Population* data are comprehensive, they may not be applicable to a metropolitan area whose population has changed rapidly during the last two years. Likewise, in the department store, patronage project, the *Census of Population* data had to be updated to reflect demographic changes that had subsequently taken place. Fortunately, several marketing research firms update census data periodically and make the current information available on a syndicated basis.

Objective: The Purpose for Which the Data Were Collected

Data are invariably collected with some objective in mind, and a fundamental question to ask is why the data were collected in the first place. The objective for collecting data will ultimately determine the purpose for which that information is relevant and useful. Data collected with a specific objective in mind may not be appropriate in another situation. As explained in more detail later in the chapter, scanner volume tracking data are collected with the objective of examining aggregate movement of brands, including shifts in market shares. Such data on sales of orange juice, for example, would be of limited value in a study aimed at understanding how households select specific brands.

Nature: The Content of the Data

The nature, or content, of the data should be examined with special attention to the definition of key variables, the units of measurement, categories used, and the relationships examined. If the key variables have not been defined or are defined in a manner inconsistent with the researcher's definition, then the usefulness of the data is limited. Consider, for example, secondary data on consumer preferences for TV programs. To use this information, it is important to know how preference for programs was defined. Was it defined in terms of the program watched most often, the one considered most needed, most enjoyable, most informative, or the program of greatest service to the community?

Likewise, secondary data may be measured in units that may not be appropriate for the current problem. For example, income may be measured by individual, family, household, or spending unit and could be gross or net after taxes and deductions. Income may be classified into categories that are different from research needs. If the researcher is interested in high-income consumers with gross annual household incomes of over $90,000, secondary data with income categories of less than $15,000, $15,001–$35,000, $35,001–$50,000, and more than $50,000 will not be of use. Determining the measurement of variables such as income may be a complex task, as illustrated by Research in Practice 4.1.[11] Finally, the relationships examined should be taken into account in evaluating the nature of data. If, for example, actual behavior is of interest, then data inferring behavior from self-reported attitudinal information may have limited usefulness. Sometimes it is possible to reconfigure the available data—for example, to convert the units of measurement—so that the resulting data are more useful to the problem at hand.

Dependability: How Dependable Are the Data?

An overall indication of the dependability of data may be obtained by examining the expertise, credibility, reputation, and trustworthiness of the source. This information can be obtained by checking with others who have used the information provided by

RESEARCH IN PRACTICE 4.1

The Elusive Median Income

There are 15 different definitions of income published by the U.S. government. According to the Census Bureau, the official median income of American households in 1991 was $30,100. If you add capital gains, returns on home equity, and other sources of income, however, the median income rises to $30,500. On the other hand, if you subtract taxes and government cash payments and add capital gains and health-insurance supplements the median falls to $24,200. The official definition measures money income before taxes, excluding capital gains. The impact of taxes and noncash benefits has a tremendous impact on income figures.

The following chart exemplifies the differences in the definitions. The different sources added or subtracted in the definitions can make a big impact in determining the median income. For instance, America's median household income declined 3.5% from 1990 to 1991 under the official definition. Under definition 15, however, the median income only fell 1.3% over the same period.

	Definition 1	Definition 3	Definition 8	Definition 15
Median household income in 1991	$30,126	$27,427	$24,212	$30,536
Married couples with children	42,583	41,840	36,751	39,896
Single mothers	14,556	11,783	12,298	17,724
Households with members aged 65 or older	18,183	8,129	7,853	25,440
White households	31,569	29,183	25,475	31,895
Black households	18,807	15,897	14,908	20,664
Hispanic households	22,691	20,862	19,276	24,108
Percent change in median household income (90–91)	−3.5%	−3.9%	−2.8%	−1.3%
Average household income in 1991	$37,992	$35,588	$29,551	$36,583

Definition 1 is the official Bureau of Census measure of income including before-tax money income, but excluding capital gains. Definition 3 deducts government cash transfers but adds in capital gains. Definition 8 adds health-insurance supplements and earned income tax credits and subtracts Social Security and federal and state income taxes. Definition 15 includes government cash and noncash transfer payments, Medicare and Medicaid, the value of school lunches, and the net imputed return on home equity.

the source. Data published to promote sales, to advance specific interests, or to carry on propaganda should be viewed with suspicion. The same may be said of data published anonymously or in a form that attempts to hide the details of the data collection methodology and process. It is also pertinent to examine whether the secondary data came from an original source, one that generated the data, or an acquired source, one that procured the data from an original source. For example, the *Census of Population* is an original source, whereas *Statistical Abstracts of the United States* is an acquired source. As a general rule, secondary data should be secured from an original rather than an acquired source. There are at least two reasons for this rule. First, an original source is the one that specifies the details of the data collection methodology, and second, an original source is likely to be more accurate and complete than a secondary source.

CLASSIFICATION OF SECONDARY DATA

internal data Data available within the organization for whom the research is being conducted.

external data Data that originate outside the organization.

Figure 4.1 presents a classification of secondary data. Secondary data may be classified as either internal or external. **Internal data** are those generated within the organization for which the research is being conducted. This information may be available in a ready-to-use format, such as information routinely supplied by the management decision support system. On the other hand, these data may exist within the organization but may require considerable processing before they are useful to the researcher. For example, a variety of information can be found on sales invoices. Yet this information may not be easily accessed; further processing may be required to extract it. **External data**, on the other hand, are those generated by sources outside the organization. These data may exist in the form of published material, on-line databases, or information made available by syndicated services. Before collecting external secondary data, it is useful to analyze internal secondary data.

FIGURE 4.1

A Classification of Secondary Data

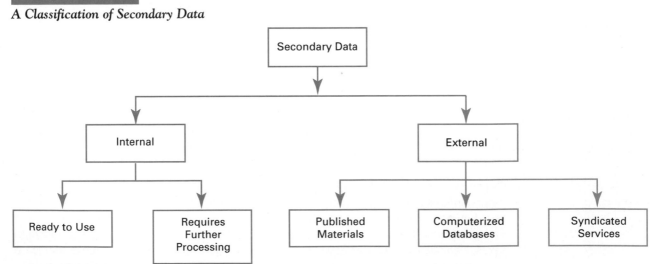

INTERNAL SECONDARY DATA

Internal sources should be the starting point in the search for secondary data. Most organizations have a wealth of in-house information, so some data may be readily available. For example, sales and cost data are compiled in the regular accounting process. Other information may be less readily available but may be compiled without difficulty, as illustrated by the department store example.

DEPARTMENT STORE PATRONAGE PROJECT
Internal Secondary Data

Extensive analysis was conducted on internal secondary data in the department store patronage project. This provided several rich insights. For example, sales were analyzed to obtain:

database marketing The use of computers to capture and track customer profiles and purchase detail.

- Sales by product line
- Sales by major department (e.g., menswear, housewares)
- Sales by specific stores
- Sales by geographical region
- Sales by cash versus credit purchases
  - Sales in specific time periods
  - Sales by size of purchase

Sales trends in many of these classifications were also examined. ◆

Secondary internal data have two significant advantages: they are easily available and they are inexpensive. In fact, internal secondary sources are generally the least costly of any source of marketing research information; yet these data often are not fully exploited. This trend is changing with the increased popularity of database marketing, however.

Database Marketing

Database marketing involves the use of computers to capture and track customer profiles and purchase details. This secondary information serves as the foundation for marketing programs or as an internal source of information related to customer behavior. For many companies, the first step in creating a database is to transfer raw sales information, such as that found on sales call reports or on invoices, to a microcomputer. This information can then be analyzed in terms

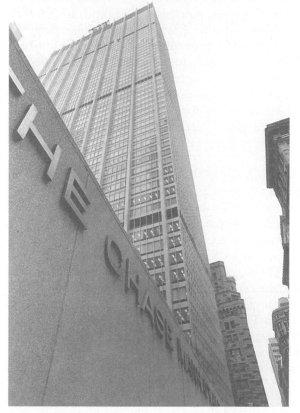

Chase Manhattan Bank is able to chase away its competitors by making heavy use of internal data. ◆ Chase Manhattan Bank.

of a customer's activity over the life of the business relationship. A profile of heavy versus low users, signs of change in the usage relationships, or significant "customer life cycle" events such as anniversaries can be identified and acted upon. These databases provide the essential tool needed to nurture, expand, and protect the customer relationship.[12]

To remain competitive, companies have come to realize the importance of providing customized service and product solutions. To operate at the individual customer level (sometimes called "micromarketing" level) requires an understanding of the significant differences in various customer groups. Direct mail is the promotional tool that most heavily relies on internal, secondary databases for program design and evaluation. Segmenting a customer base to offer and measure response to customized promotional messages, product offerings, or payment and pricing packages is the foundation of direct marketing techniques used in business today.

For example, suppose that a retail department store is concerned about falling sales in its housewares department. It wants to test whether an emphasis on payment plans or product line will generate the greatest response. The marketing director creates three direct mail pieces. The first is to announce the sale, emphasizing credit terms and easy payment plans. The second piece announced the sale, with an emphasis on the brand names that will be featured. The third piece was designed to operate as the experimental control; its message simply gave the date and time of the sale.

Each announcement was mailed to one-third of a sample of 3,000 current customers. For the past two years, the research department had been building and maintaining a database of customers. The customer's phone number, name, and address was entered into the register once, along with the items purchased. Once the customer file was established, future purchases were associated with that individual by matching the customer phone number, which was always the first item entered. In addition to name, address, and phone number, the system built a history file of items purchased, department shopped, dollar amount spent, dates of shopping trips, and method of payment. Direct marketing and research lists could be drawn from this customer purchase file by selecting zip code, items purchased or department visited, date of last shopping trip, or dollars spent within a specified time. For this direct marketing program, customers who had shopped in the housewares department in the past six months were defined as the sample frame.

In all cases, customers were asked to bring in the direct mail postcard they had received when they came to the store to receive a $10.00 discount. The postcard had been precoded with their specific customer identification code, thus enabling the measurement of the response to the various sale messages.

In analyzing the results, the marketing director was interested in whether there was a significant difference in the level of response to the three offers. Additionally, she was interested in knowing if the customer characteristics of the responders to the various offers, differed significantly. The emphasis on the product line generated the greatest response. These customers were significantly higher in terms of income, education, and age compared with the other two groups. These results enabled a department store to launch a marketing program built on an expanded product line and aimed at older customers and potential customers with high income.

As this example illustrates, database marketing can lead to quite sophisticated and targeted marketing programs.

PUBLISHED EXTERNAL SECONDARY SOURCES

Sources of published external secondary data include federal, state, and local governments, nonprofit organizations (e.g., Chambers of Commerce), trade associations and professional organizations, commercial publishers, investment brokerage firms, and professional marketing research firms.[13] In fact, so much data are available that the researcher can be overwhelmed. Therefore, it is important to classify published sources (see Figure 4.2). Published external sources may be broadly classified as general business data or government data. General business sources are comprised of guides, directories, indexes, and statistical data. Government sources may be broadly categorized as census data and other publications. These data types are discussed further, and specific sources in each category are listed in Appendix 4A.[14]

General Business Data

Businesses publish much information in the form of books, periodicals, journals, newspapers, magazines, reports, and trade literature. This information can be located by using guides, directories, and indexes. Sources are also available for identifying statistical data.[15]

Guides   Guides are an excellent source of standard or recurring information. A guide may help identify other important sources of directories, trade associations, and trade publications. Guides are one of the first sources a researcher should consult. Some of the most useful are the *American Marketing Association Bibliography Series, Business Information Sources, Data Sources for Business and Market Analysis,* and *Encyclopedia of Business Information Sources.* Information on these and other guides is provided in Appendix 4A.

Directories   Directories are helpful for identifying individuals or organizations that collect specific data. Some of the important directories include *Consultants and Consulting Organizations Directory; Directories in Print, Encyclopedia of Associations; FINDEX: The Directory of Market Research Reports, Studies and Surveys;* and *Research Services Directory* (see Appendix 4A).

FIGURE 4.2

A Classification of Published Secondary Sources

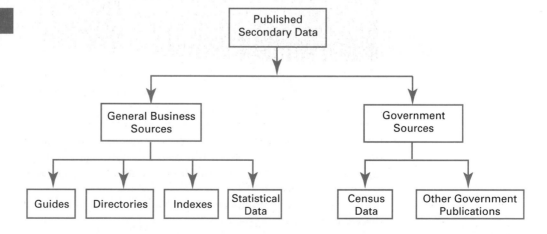

Indexes   It is possible to locate information on a particular topic in several different publications by using an index. Indexes can, therefore, increase the efficiency of the search process. Several were used in the department store project.

DEPARTMENT STORE PATRONAGE PROJECT
Data Search

In addition to reviewing the theoretical literature, as discussed in Chapter 2, it was also necessary to identify the nonacademic sources of secondary data related to the factors considered in selecting department stores and other aspects of store patronage. *Business Periodicals Index*, the *New York Times Index*, and the *Wall Street Journal Index* were used to generate a list of relevant articles that had appeared since 1990. *Business Periodicals Index* classifies articles by specific industries and firms, making it easy to locate articles of interest. Several articles obtained in this manner proved useful. One pointed to the tendency of people to combine shopping with eating out. Therefore, as discussed in Chapter 2, a specific research question was framed to investigate this behavior. ◆

As illustrated by this example, indexes greatly facilitate a directed search of the relevant literature. Several indexes are available for both academic and business sources. Some of the more useful business indexes are *Business Index*, *Business Periodicals Index*, *Predicasts F & S Index: United States*, *Social Sciences Citation Index*, and the *Wall Street Journal Index*, as described in Appendix 4A.

Nongovernment Statistical Data   Published statistical data are of great interest to researchers. Graphic and statistical analyses can be performed on these data to draw important insights. Important sources of nongovernmental statistical data include *A Guide to Consumer Markets*, *Predicasts Forecasts*, *Sales and Marketing Management Survey of Buying Power*, *Standard and Poor's Statistical Service*, and *Standard Rate and Data Service*.

Government Sources

The U.S. government also produces large amounts of secondary data. Its publications may be divided into census data and other publications.[16]

Census Data   The U.S. Bureau of the Census is the world's largest source of statistical data. Its monthly catalog lists and describes its various publications.[17] More convenient, however, is the *Guide to Economic Census*. The quality of census data is high and the data are often extremely detailed. Furthermore, one can purchase computer tapes or diskettes from the Bureau of the Census for a nominal fee and recast this information in a desired format.[18] Many private sources update the census data at a detailed geographic level for the between census years.[19] Important census data are described in Appendix 4A. They include *Census of Housing*, *Census of Manufacturers*, *Census of Population*, *Census of Retail Trade*, *Census of Service Industries*, and *Census of Wholesale Trade*. Research in Practice 4.2 gives some insights into the *Census of Population* data.[20]

Other Government Publications   In addition to the census, the U.S. collects and publishes a great deal of statistical data. The more useful publications are *Business America*, *Business Conditions Digest*, *Business Statistics*, *Index to Publications*, *Statistical Abstract of the United States*, and *Survey of Current Business* (Appendix 4A).

RESEARCH IN PRACTICE 4.2

Comments from the Census Director

Barbara Everitt Bryant, former director of the U.S. Bureau of the Census, reflects on her tenure and the 1990 census. She found the position to be both rewarding and challenging. The rewards were based on the researcher's dream of dealing with such a large budget and resources. The challenges pertain to the legal issues that stemmed from the data collected. She describes the position as a mountain top being both "rocky and exhilarating."

The design of the 1990 census was a repeat of the previous two censuses, 1980 and 1970. The census took place in three phases. The first phase was to develop a comprehensive mailing list. The second phase was to send a questionnaire to every household on the list. The third phase was to send enumerators to interview households that were missed by the mailings or did not return a mailing. The problem with the census was a decline in the number of returned questionnaires, 75% in 1980 versus 63% in 1990. The decline in questionnaire response will make it very difficult for the 2000 census. With this problem in mind, early research and development is under way to study 14 proposed new designs. Trial tests of the top two designs occurred in 1995. Mailing questionnaires will still be the major element of the 2000 census, but the procedure will be vastly different from the past census.

Bryant described the 1990 census as "an operational triumph bordering on a public relations disaster." She is proud that the census counted over 98% of the population. The media, however, focused on the 1.6% undercount. The legal questions regarding the census developed even before the 1990 census was started when the first of 18 lawsuits was filed. Her biggest disappointment was not being able to adjust statistically the 1990 census or the 1992 population estimates. Statistical adjustment would be sufficient to improve the count at the state and national level but would be problematic below the state level. The problem below the state level is that some communities would be overestimated while others underestimated; the two could not be distinguished, however. The political consequences of the survey were also apparent. Elected officials fought to maximize the counts and population shares in their own areas.

COMPUTERIZED DATABASES

Computerized databases consist of information that has been made available in computer-readable form for electronic distribution. Since the 1980s, the number of databases, as well as the vendors providing these services, has grown phenomenally. Most published information is also available in this form. Computerized databases offer a number of advantages over printed data, including the following:[21]

1. The data are current and up-to-date because, publishers and data compilers are now using computers as the primary production technology.
2. The search process is more comprehensive, quicker, and simpler than before. On-line vendors provide ready access to hundreds of databases. Moreover, this information can be

accessed instantaneously, and the search process is simplified as the vendors provide uniform search protocols and commands for accessing the database.

3. The cost of accessing these databases is low because information can be transferred at high speed.

4. It is convenient and easy to access these data using a personal computer fitted with an appropriate communication device, such as a modem or a communication network.

Although computerized database information can be helpful, it is vast and can be confusing. Thus, a classification of computerized databases is helpful.

Classification of Computerized Databases

Computerized databases may be classified as on-line or off-line, as shown in Figure 4.3. **On-line databases** consist of a central data bank that is accessed with a computer (or dumb terminal) via a telecommunications network.[22] **Off-line databases** make the information available on diskettes and CD-ROM disks. Thus, off-line databases can be accessed at the user's location without the use of an external telecommunications network.[23] For example, the U.S. Bureau of the Census makes computer data files available on CD-ROM disks. These disks contain detailed information organized by census track or zip code. In the department store patronage project, this type of information was used in sample selection.[24]

Both on-line and off-line databases may be further classified as bibliographic, numeric, full-text, directory, or special-purpose databases. **Bibliographic databases** are composed of citations to articles in journals, magazines, newspapers, marketing research studies, technical reports, government documents, and the like.[25] They often provide summaries or abstracts of the material cited. Examples of bibliographic databases include ABI/Inform and the Predicasts Terminal System. Another bibliographic database, Management Contents, provided by the Dialog Corporation, was used to enhance the literature search in the department store patronage project.

Numeric databases contain numerical and statistical information. For example, some numeric databases provide time series data (data arranged in relation to time) about the economy and specific industries produced by vendors like Boeing Computer Services Company, Data Resources, Evans Economics, and the Office of Economic

---

on-line databases
Databases, stored in computers, that require a telecommunications network to access.

off-line databases
Databases that are available on diskette or CD-ROM.

bibliographic databases
Databases composed of citations to articles in journals, magazines, newspapers, marketing research studies, technical reports, government documents, and the like. They often provide summaries or abstracts of the material cited.

numeric databases
Databases containing numerical and statistical information that may be important sources of secondary data.

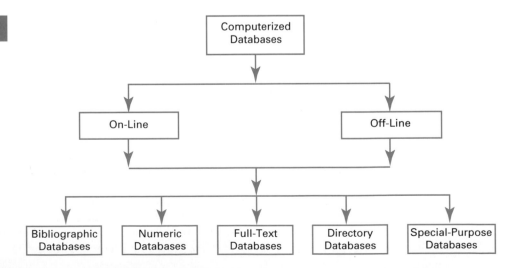

FIGURE 4.3

A Classification of Computerized Databases

full-text databases
Databases that contain the complete text of secondary source documents comprising the database.

directory databases
Databases that provide information on individuals, organizations, and services.

special-purpose databases
Databases that contain information of a specific nature, e.g., data on a specialized industry.

Coordination and Development. Census-based numeric databases that use the 1980 and 1990 censuses of population and housing with proprietary updating to provide data at the census tract and zip code level are also available. Vendors providing these databases include the U. S. Bureau of the Census, Donnelley Marketing Information Services, CACI Inc., and National Decision Systems.

Full-text databases contain the complete text of the source documents comprising the database. Vu/Text Information Systems, Inc., provides electronic full-text delivery and search capabilities for a number of newspapers (*Washington Post, Boston Globe, Miami Herald*). Mead Data Central, through its Nexis service, provides full-text access to hundreds of business databases, including selected newspapers, periodicals, company annual reports, and investment firm reports.

Directory databases provide information on individuals, organizations, and services. Economic Information Systems, Inc., through its database EIS Nonmanufacturing Establishments, provides information on location, headquarters, name, percent of industry sales, industry classification, and employment size class for about 200,000 nonmanufacturing establishments that employ 20 or more people. As another example, the national electronic Yellow Pages directories of manufacturers, wholesalers, retailers, professionals, and service organizations provide the names, addresses and Standard Industrial Classification numbers of numerous organizations.

Finally, there are **special-purpose databases**. For example, the Profit Impact of Market Strategies (PIMS) database is an ongoing database of research and analysis on business strategy conducted by the Strategic Planning Institute in Cambridge, Massachusetts. This database is composed of more than 250 companies, which provide data on over 2,000 businesses.[26] Virtually all libraries of major universities maintain computerized databases of management and related literature that students can access free of charge. Special-purpose databases have become popular in the health care industry, as illustrated by the following example.

EXAMPLE

BaseLine Helps Hospitals Maintain a Healthy Bottom Line

BaseLine is an on-line interactive and comparative data system from the Commission on Professional and Hospital Activities (CPHA). The system provides users in the health care field with on-line access to CPHA's in-house data and to normative data from CPHA's large national base of hospital discharge data. Hospitals can conveniently compare their own performance with CPHA's norms, look for overall trends and patterns, and analyze patient records and physician activities.

Analyses can be performed on BaseLine in the ad hoc mode, on a microcomputer after downloading from BaseLine, or by using a flexible menu system. The menus include severity-of-illness reports, length-of-stay reports, total charges reports, and comparative performance reports. BaseLine is used by over 100 hospitals and nine hospital associations all over the United States. BaseLine information has helped these hospitals conduct competitive analysis, manage their product portfolios, and determine which services should be provided on an outpatient basis, leading to increased profits.[27] ◆

Although computerized databases are numerous and varied, their sheer number can be overwhelming, and locating a particular database may seem difficult. How, then, do you locate specific bibliographic, numeric, full-text, directory, or special-purpose databases? Directories of databases provide the needed help.[28]

Directories of Databases

There are numerous sources of information on databases. Perhaps the best way to obtain information about databases is to consult a directory. Some of the useful directories which are periodically updated are:

- Directory of On-Line Databases
  Santa Monica, CA: Cuadra Associates, Inc.
- Encyclopedia of Information System and Services
  Detroit: Gale Research Company
- Information Industry Marketplace
  New York: R. R. Bowker

SYNDICATED SOURCES OF SECONDARY DATA

syndicated services (sources) Information services offered by marketing research organizations that provide information from a common database to different firms that subscribe to their services.

In addition to published data or data available in the form of computerized databases, syndicated sources constitute the other major source of external secondary data. **Syndicated sources**, also referred to as **syndicated services**, are companies that collect and sell common pools of data designed to serve information needs shared by a number of clients (see Chapter 1). These data are not collected for the purpose of marketing research problems, but the data and reports supplied to client companies can be personalized to fit specific needs. For example, reports could be organized on the basis of the clients' sales territories or product lines. Using syndicated services is frequently less expensive than collecting primary data. Figure 4.4 presents a classification of syndicated sources. Syndicated sources can be classified based on the unit of measurement (households and consumers or institutions). Household and consumer data may be obtained from surveys, diary panels, or electronic scanner services. Information obtained through surveys consists of values and lifestyles, advertising evaluation, or general information related to preferences, purchase, consumption and other aspects of behavior. Diary panels emphasize information on purchases or media consumption. Electronic scanner services might provide scanner data only, scanner data linked to diary panels, or scanner data linked to diary panels and (cable) TV. When institutions are the unit of measurement, the data may be obtained from retailers, wholesalers, or industrial firms. An overview of the various syndicated sources is given in Table 4.3. Each of these sources will be discussed.

SYNDICATED DATA FROM HOUSEHOLDS

Surveys

surveys Interviews with a large number of respondents using a pre-designed questionnaire.

Various services regularly conduct **surveys**, which involve interviews with a large number of respondents using a predesigned questionnaire. Surveys may be broadly classified on the basis of their content as psychographics and lifestyles, advertising evaluation, or general surveys.

psychographics uantified psychological profiles of individuals.

Psychographics and Lifestyles   Psychographics refer to the psychological profiles of individuals and to psychologically based measures of lifestyle. **Lifestyles** refer to the distinctive modes of living of a society or some of its segments. Together, these measures are generally referred to as activities, interest, and opinions, or simply AIOs. The Yankelovich Monitor provides an application.

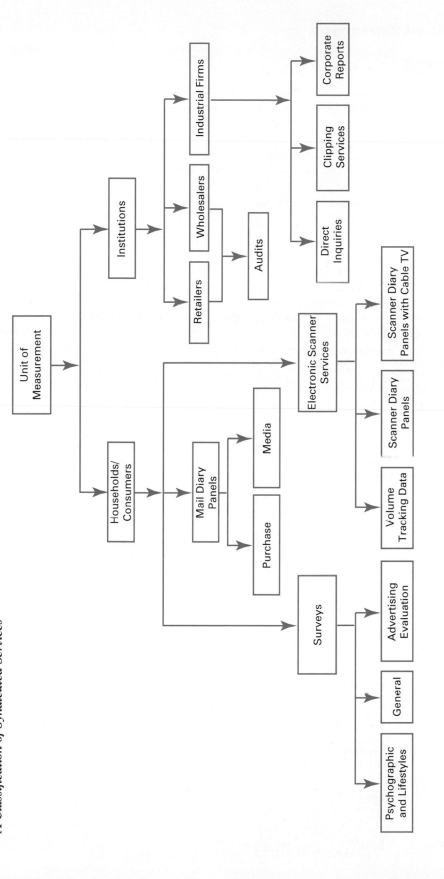

FIGURE 4.4

A Classification of Syndicated Services

TABLE 4.3

Overview of Syndicated Services

Type	Characteristics	Advantages	Disadvantages	Uses
Surveys	Surveys conducted at regular intervals	Most flexible way of obtaining data; information on underlying motives	Interviewer errors; respondent errors	Market segmentation, advertising theme selection, and advertising effectiveness
Diary Purchase Panels	Households provide specific information regularly over an extended period of time; respondents asked to record specific behaviors as they occur	Recorded purchase behavior can be linked to the demographic/ psychographic characteristics	Lack of representativeness; response bias; maturation	Forecasting sales, market share, and trends; establishing consumer profiles, brand loyalty and switching; evaluating test markets, advertising, and distribution
Diary Media Panels	Electronic devices automatically recording behavior, supplemented by a diary	Same as diary purchase panel	Same as diary purchase panel	Establishing advertising rates; selecting media program or air time; establishing viewer profiles
Scanner Volume Tracking Data	Household purchases are recorded through electronic scanners in supermarkets	Data reflect actual purchases; timely data less expensive	Data may not be representative; errors in recording purchases; difficult to link purchases to elements of marketing mix other than price	Price tracking, modeling, effectiveness of in-store modeling
Scanner Diary Panels with Cable TV	Scanner panels of households that subscribe to cable TV	Data reflect actual purchases; sample control; ability to link panel data to household characteristics	Data may not be representative; quality of data limited	Promotional mix analyses, copy testing, new-product testing, positioning
Audit Services	Verification of product movement by examining physical records or performing inventory analysis	Relatively precise information at the retail and wholesale levels	Coverage may be incomplete; matching of data on competitive activity may be difficult	Measurement of consumer sales and market share, competitive activity, analyzing distribution patterns: tracking of new products
Industrial Product Syndicated Services	Data banks on industrial establishments created through direct inquiries of companies, clipping services, and corporate reports	Important source of information in industrial firms, particularly useful in initial phases of the projects	Data are lacking in terms of content, quantity, and quality	Determining market potential by geographic area, defining sales territories, allocating advertising budget

EXAMPLE

Campbell Makes Sure AIOs Are in Its Alphabet Soup

lifestyles Distinctive patterns of living described by the activities people engage in, the interests they have, and the opinions they hold of themselves and the world around them (AIOs).

Yankelovich Partners Inc. provides the Yankelovich Monitor, a survey that contains data on lifestyles and social trends. The survey is conducted at the same time each year among a nationally projectable sample of 2,500 adults, 16 years of age or older, including a special sample of 300 college students living on campus. The sample is based on the most recent census data. All interviews are conducted in person at the respondent's home and take approximately 2-1/2 hours to complete. Advertising agencies use the

Yankelovich Monitor to discern changes in lifestyles and to design advertising themes that reflect these trends. For example, a Campbell Soup campaign that shows a husband fixing soup was designed when a significant trend toward reversal of traditional roles was discovered.[29] ◆

Another example is the Needham, Harper and Steers Lifestyle Study, which has been tracking consumer attitudes and behaviors for a number of years.[30] The Stanford Research Institute conducts an annual survey of consumers that is used to classify persons into VALS-2 (values and lifestyles) types for segmentation purposes.[31] Information on specific aspects of consumers' lifestyles is also available. Audits and Surveys, Inc., conducts an annual survey of 5,000 consumers who participate in leisure sports and recreational activities.

Advertising Evaluation   The purpose of advertising evaluation surveys is to assess the effectiveness of advertising using print and broadcast media. Two well-known surveys are the Gallup and Robinson Magazine Impact Studies and the Starch Readership Survey. The following example shows how Starch is used.

EXAMPLE
Starch Stiffens Ad Effectiveness Evaluations

Starch provides evaluation for most consumer magazines and selected business and industrial publications. This assessment can be provided for individual advertisements as well as for campaigns over time. As a measure of an advertisement's effectiveness, Starch classifies magazine readership into three groups: (1) those who remember seeing a particular advertisement ("noted"), (2) those who associate the sponsor's name with the advertisement ("seen-associated"), and (3) those who read half its copy ("read most"). Such results are particularly important to heavy advertisers, such as Procter & Gamble, General Motors, Sears, PepsiCo, Eastman Kodak, and McDonald's, who are greatly concerned about how well their advertising dollars are spent.[32] ◆

Evaluation of effectiveness is even more critical in the case of TV advertising. Television commercials are evaluated using either the recruited audience method or the in-home viewing method. In the former method, respondents are recruited and brought to a central viewing facility, such as a theater or mobile viewing laboratory. The respondents view the commercials and provide data regarding knowledge, attitudes, and preferences related to the product being advertised and the commercial itself. McCollum/ Spielman Company Audience Studies (ASI), Burgoyne, Inc., PACE (Personation and Communication Effectiveness), and Tele-Research, Inc., are among the syndicated services that use this method.

In the in-home viewing method, consumers evaluate commercials at home in their normal viewing environment. New commercials can be pretested at the network level or in local markets. A survey of viewers is then conducted to assess the effectiveness of the commercials. Services that use this method include AdTel, Ltd., Television Testing Company, ARS Division, Research Systems, Inc., and Audience Studies/Com. Lab, Inc.

General Surveys   Surveys are also conducted for a variety of other purposes, including examination of purchase and consumption behavior. The Gallup Organization, Inc., surveys 15,000 households annually about their purchase of consumer products. The

National Menu Census conducted by Marketing Research Corporation of America asks about consumption of food products in the home. Data are provided about meals, snack items, carry-out foods, and so forth. Trendex, Inc., surveys 15,000 households quarterly about ownership and acquisition of consumer durables. These surveys can be customized to suit the needs of specific clients, as the following example shows.

EXAMPLE
Customization via Syndication _____

Roper Reports, prepared by the Roper Organization, is a syndicated service offering customization. This service provides public opinion and behavior concerning a broad range of social, economic, and political issues, as well as various kinds of products and lifestyles. The data are collected every five weeks through personal interviews with a national sample of 2,000 adults aged 18 or older. In addition to the standard questions, a tack-on custom question service is also available to clients. The Roper Organization claims that this service offers a unique combination of frequency, speed of report delivery, quality, low cost, large sample size and extensive demographic breaks.[33] ◆

Uses of Surveys   Because a wide variety of data can be obtained, survey data have numerous uses. They can be used for market segmentation, as with psychographic and lifestyle data, and for establishing consumer profiles. Surveys are also useful for determining product image, measurement and positioning, and conducting price perception analysis. Other notable uses include advertising theme selection and evaluation of advertising effectiveness.

Advantages and Disadvantages of Surveys   Surveys are the most flexible means of obtaining data from respondents. The researcher can focus on only a certain segment of the population, such as teenagers, owners of vacation homes, or housewives between age 30 and 40. Surveys are the primary means of obtaining information about consumers' motives, attitudes, and preferences. A variety of questions can be asked, and visual aids, packages, products, or other props can be used during the interviews. Properly analyzed, survey data can be manipulated in many ways so that the researcher can look at intergroup differences, examine the effects of independent variables such as age or income, or even predict future behavior.

On the other hand, survey data may be limited in several significant ways. The researcher has to rely primarily on the respondents' self-reports. There is a gap between what people say and what they actually do. Errors may occur because respondents remember incorrectly or give socially desirable responses. Furthermore, samples may be biased, questions poorly phrased, interviewers not properly instructed or supervised, and results misinterpreted.

Diary Panels

Often, survey data can be complemented with data obtained from diary panels. Panels were discussed in Chapter 3 in the context of longitudinal research designs. Diary panels are samples of respondents who provide specified information at regular intervals over an extended period of time. These respondents may be organizations, households, or individuals, although household diary panels are most common. The distinguishing feature of diary panels is that the respondents record specific behaviors as they occur in a diary. Typically, the diary is returned to the research organization every one to four weeks. Panel members are compensated for their participation with gifts, coupons, information, or cash. Based on the content of information recorded, diary panels can be classified as diary purchase panels or diary media panels.

diary purchase panels A data gathering technique in which respondents record their purchases in a diary.

Diary Purchase Panels   In **diary purchase panels**, respondents record their purchases of a variety of different products, as in the National Purchase Diary Panel.

EXAMPLE
Information in These Diaries Is No Secret _____

The National Purchase Diary Panel (NPD) maintains the largest diary panel in the United States. More than 14,500 households use preprinted diaries to record their monthly purchases in about 50 product categories. Respondents provide detailed information regarding the brand and amount purchased, price paid, whether any special deals were involved, the store where purchased, and intended use. The total panel includes 29 miniature panels, each representative of a local market. The composition of the panel is representative of the U.S. population as a whole. Information provided by the National Purchase Diary Panel is used by soft drink firms like the Coca-Cola Company to determine brand loyalty and brand switching and to profile heavy users of various brands.[34] ◆

Other organizations that maintain diary purchase panels include National Family Opinion (NFO) and Market Research Corporation of America (MRCA). These organizations also maintain special-purpose diary panels. For example, NFO has a beverages panel consisting of 12,000 households that provide quarterly information on beverage consumption. MRCA's Funds panel reports information on the day-to-day financial decisions of America's most active retail consumers of financial services. The Funds panel is based on a national sample selected to represent households with annual incomes above $25,000, with a special concentration in the $75,000-and-up category.

diary media panels A data gathering technique composed of samples of respondents whose television viewing behavior is automatically recorded by electronic devices, supplementing the purchase information recorded in a diary.

Diary Media Panels   In **diary media panels**, electronic devices automatically record viewing behavior, thus supplementing a diary. Perhaps the most familiar diary media panel is Nielsen Television Index (NTI).

EXAMPLE
Be Careful What You Watch: A.C. Nielsen Is Watching You _____

The Nielsen Television Index consists of a representative sample of approximately 1,200 households. Each of these households has an electronic device called a storage instantaneous audimeter attached to its television sets. The audimeter continuously monitors television viewing behavior, including when the set is turned on, what channels are viewed, and for how long. These data are stored in the audimeter and transmitted via telephone lines to a central computer. The data collected by the audimeter are supplemented with diary panel records, called audilogs. The audilog contains information on who was watching each program, so that audience size and demographic characteristics can be calculated.

Using these data, Nielsen estimates the number and percentage of all TV households viewing a given show. Their popular report, issued biweekly, is available to clients

A Nielsen audimeter that continuously monitors television viewing behavior. ◆ Eric Mencher/Picture Group.

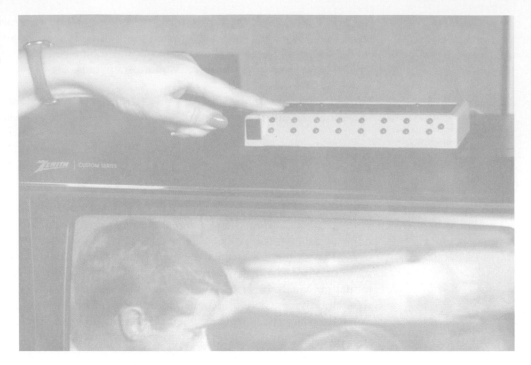

within two weeks after a measurement period. For those requiring information more frequently, Nielsen installs a terminal in the client's office that permits receipt of national household ratings within 24 hours of a broadcast. This information is also disaggregated by ten demographic and socioeconomic characteristics, such as household income, education of head of house, occupation of head of house, household size, age of children, age of women, age of men, and geographical location. The Nielsen Television Index is useful to firms such as AT&T, Kellogg Company, J.C. Penney, Pillsbury, and Unilever in selecting specific TV programs on which to air their commercials.[35] ◆

In addition to the Nielsen Television Index, other services provide diary media panels. Arbitron maintains local and regional radio and TV diary panels.[36] In the ScanAmerica people-meter ratings system, continuous detailed measures of television set tuning for every set in the home—including normal on-air programming, cable, and VCR usage—are automatically collected by an electronic meter.[37]

Uses of Diary Panels   Diary purchase panels provide information useful for forecasting sales, estimating market shares, assessing brand loyalty and brand switching behavior, establishing profiles of specific user groups, measuring promotional effectiveness, and conducting controlled store tests. Diary media panels yield information helpful for establishing advertising rates by radio and TV networks, selecting appropriate programming, and profiling viewer or listener subgroups. Advertisers, media planners, and buyers find panel information to be particularly useful.

Advantages and Disadvantages of Diary Panels   As compared with sample surveys, diary panels offer certain distinct advantages.[38] Panels can provide longitudinal data (data can be obtained from the same respondents repeatedly). People who are willing to serve on panels may provide more and higher-quality data than sample respondents. In purchase diary panels, information is recorded at the time of purchase, eliminating recall errors.[39] Information recorded by electronic devices is accurate because it eliminates human errors.

The disadvantages of diary panels include lack of representativeness, maturation, and response biases. Most diary panels are not representative of the U.S. population. They underrepresent certain groups such as minorities and those with low education levels. This problem is further compounded by refusal to respond and attrition of panel members. Over time, maturation sets in, and the panel members must be replaced (see Chapter 7). Response biases may occur, since simply being on the panel may alter behavior. Because purchase or media data are entered by hand, recording errors are also possible (see Chapter 3).

Electronic Scanner Services

scanner data Data obtained by passing merchandise over a laser scanner that reads the UPC code from the packages.

Although information provided by surveys and diary panels is useful, electronic scanner services are becoming increasingly popular. **Scanner data** reflect some of the latest technological developments in the marketing research industry. Scanner data are collected by passing merchandise over a laser scanner that optically reads the bar-coded description (universal product code, or UPC) printed on the merchandise. This code is then linked to the current price held in the computer memory and used to prepare a sales slip. Information printed on the sales slip includes descriptions as well as prices of all items purchased. Checkout scanners, now used in many retail stores, are revolutionizing packaged goods marketing research.

volume tracking data Scanner data that provide information on purchases by brand, size, price, and flavor or formulation.

Three types of scanner data are available: volume tracking data, scanner diary panels, and scanner diary panels with cable TV. **Volume tracking data** provide information on purchases by brand, size, price, and flavor or formulation, based on sales data collected from the checkout scanner tapes. This information is collected nationally from a sample of supermarkets with electronic scanners. Scanner services providing volume tracking data include National Scan Track (A. C. Nielsen), NABSCAN (The Newspaper Advertising Bureau), and TRIM (Tele-Research, Inc.).[40] In **scanner diary panels**, each household member is given an ID card that looks like a credit card. Panel members present the ID card at the checkout counter each time they shop. The checker keys in the ID numbers and each item of that customer's order. The information is stored by day of week and time of day.[41]

scanner diary panels Scanner data where panel members are identified by an ID card, allowing information about each panel member's purchases to be stored with respect to the individual shopper.

scanner diary panels with cable TV The combination of a scanner diary panel with manipulations of the advertising that is being broadcast by cable television companies.

An even more advanced use of scanning, **scanner diary panels with cable TV**, combines diary panels with new technologies growing out of the cable TV industry. Households on these panels subscribe to one of the cable TV systems in their market. By means of a cable TV "split," the researcher targets different commercials into the homes of the panel members. For example, half the households may see test commercial A during the 6:00 P.M. newscast while the other half see test commercial B. These panels allow researchers to conduct fairly controlled experiments in a relatively natural environment.[42]

EXAMPLE
Using Total TV Households for Testing Total Advertising _____

Testsight (ERIM, A. C. Nielsen) allows transmission of advertising into participating households without the use of a cable TV system. Because the panels can be selected from all available TV households, not just those with cable TV, the bias of cable-only testing is eliminated. Using this type of system, General Mills can test which one of four test commercials for Total cereal results in the highest sales. Four groups of panel members are selected, and each receives a different test commercial. These households are monitored via scanner data to determine which group purchased the most Total cereal. ◆

This example shows how scanner services incorporate advanced marketing research technology, which results in some advantages over survey and diary panel data.

Uses of Scanner Data   Scanner data are useful for a variety of purposes.[43] National volume tracking data can be used for tracking sales, prices, and distribution; for modeling, and for analyzing early warning signals. Scanner diary panels with cable TV can be used for testing new products, repositioning products, analyzing promotional mix, and making advertising decisions, including budget, copy and media, and pricing. These panels provide marketing researchers with a unique controlled environment for the manipulation of marketing variables.

Advantages and Disadvantages of Scanner Data   Scanner data have an obvious advantage over surveys and diary panels; they reflect purchasing behavior that is not subject to interviewing, recording, memory, or expert biases. The record of purchases obtained by scanners is complete and unbiased by price sensitivity, because the panelist is not required to be overly conscious of price levels and changes. Another advantage is that in-store variables such as pricing, promotions, and displays are part of the data set. The data are also likely to be current and can be obtained quickly. Finally, scanner panels with cable TV provide a highly controlled testing environment.

A major weakness of scanner data is lack of representativeness. National volume tracking data may not be projectable on to the total population, because only large supermarkets have scanners. Also, certain types of outlets such as food warehouses, drugstores, and mass merchandisers are excluded. Likewise, scanners have limited geographical dispersion and coverage.

The quality of scanner data may be limited by several factors. All products may not be scanned. For example, to avoid lifting a heavy item, a clerk may use the register to ring it up. If an item does not scan on the first try, the clerk may key in the price and ignore the bar code. Sometimes a consumer purchases many flavors of the same item, but the clerk scans only one package and then rings in the number of purchases. Thus, the transaction is inaccurately recorded. With respect to scanner panels, the available technology permits the monitoring of only one TV set per household. Hence, there is a built-in bias if the household has more than one TV set. Also, the system provides information on TV sets in use rather than actual viewing behavior. Although scanner data provide behavioral and sales information, they do not provide information on underlying attitudes and preferences and the reasons for specific choices.

SYNDICATED DATA FROM INSTITUTIONS

Retailer and Wholesaler Audits

As Figure 4.4 shows, syndicated data are available for retailers and wholesalers as well as industrial firms. The most popular means of obtaining data from retailers and wholesalers is an audit. An **audit** is a formal examination and verification of product movement carried out by examining physical records or analyzing inventory. Retailers and

audit A data collection process derived from physical records or performing inventory analysis. Data are collected personally by the researcher, or by representatives of the researcher and the data are based on counts usually of physical objects rather than people.

wholesalers who participate in the audit receive basic reports and cash payments from the audit service. Audit data focus on the products or services sold through the outlets or the characteristics of the outlets themselves, as illustrated by the following example.

Retail Auditing for Retailing Information

The largest retail audit service for consumer packaged goods is the Nielsen Retail Index. This index involves a biweekly store audit of supermarkets, drugstores, and mass merchandisers. Nielsen makes over 76,000 separate audits annually in over 11,350 different retail outlets.

Another major service is Audits and Surveys' National Total Market Audit, which uses different product categories than the Nielsen service. Retail audit data can be useful to consumer product firms. For example, Colgate-Palmolive is contemplating the introduction of a new toothpaste brand. A retail audit can help determine the size of the total market and distribution of sales by type of outlet and by different regions.[11]

Wholesale audit services, the counterpart of retail audits, monitor warehouse withdrawals. Participating operators, which include supermarket chains, wholesalers, and frozen-food warehouses, typically account for over 80% of the volume in the area.

Uses of Audit Data   The uses of retail and wholesale audit data include (1) determining the size of the total market and the distribution of sales by type of outlet, region, or city; (2) assessing brand shares and competitive activity; (3) identifying shelf space allocation and inventory problems; (4) analyzing distribution problems; (5) developing sales potentials and forecasts; and (6) developing and monitoring promotional allocations based on sales volume. Thus, audit data were particularly helpful in obtaining information on the environmental context of the problem in the department store patronage project.

Advantages and Disadvantages of Audit Data   Audits provide relatively accurate information on the movement of many different products at the wholesale and retail levels. Furthermore, this information can be broken down by a number of important variables, such as brand, type of outlet, and size of market.

Audits have limited coverage, however. Not all markets or operators are included. Also, audit information may not be timely or current, particularly compared with scanner data. Typically, there is a two-month gap between the completion of the audit cycle and the publication of reports. Another disadvantage is that, unlike scanner data, audit data cannot be linked to consumer characteristics. In fact, there may even be a problem in relating audit data to advertising expenditures and other marketing efforts. Some of these limitations are overcome in computerized audit panels, such as ELCAP.

EXAMPLE
Hats Off to ELCAP

Elrick and Lavidge has developed ELCAP, a computerized audit panel, for the highly volatile consumer electronics industry. It allows manufacturers and retailers to track consumer acceptance of new features and new technology, strengths and weaknesses in the distribution system, trends in retail pricing, and sales of the competition. The panel consists of about 1,000 retail stores—including department stores, discount stores, specialty stores, stores selling major home appliances, and superstores—that sell consumer electronic products.

Data are collected and tabulated electronically from the computerized sales records of each participating retailer. This data collection method is not prone to errors common to physical audits, such as failure to include all sales transactions, incorrect recording, or double counting.[45] ◆

Industry services

industry services
Secondary data derived from industrial sources and intended for industrial use.

Industry services provide syndicated data about industrial firms, businesses, and other institutions. These data are collected by making direct inquiries, from clipping services and corporate reports. The range and sources of syndicated data available to industrial goods firms are more limited than those available to consumer goods firms. Services available include Dun and Bradstreet's Market Identifiers, *Fortune* magazine's Input/Output Matrix Reports, and McGraw-Hill's Dodge Reports.

EXAMPLE
Women Make the Cut but Not the Decisions

Trinet, Inc., and Dunn's Marketing Services are two U.S. companies that provide a database of in-depth information on businesses. Trinet provides three basic information services: a database of seven million U.S. business locations, application services, and business-to-business telemarketing services. Recently, Trinet conducted a telephone survey of 100,000 U.S. businesses to assess the role of women in business. This study found that although more and more women are assuming management positions, the number of women with decision-making responsibility continues to lag far behind men.[46] ◆

Uses of Industry Services   Information provided by industrial services is useful for sales management decisions, including identifying prospects, defining territories, setting quotas, and measuring market potential by geographic areas. It can also aid in advertising decisions such as targeting prospects, allocating advertising budgets, selecting media, and measuring advertising effectiveness. This kind of information is useful for segmenting the market and for designing custom products and services for important segments.

Advantages and Disadvantages of Industry Services   Industry services represent an important source of secondary information on industrial firms. The information they provide can be valuable in the initial phases of a marketing project. They are limited in the nature, content, quantity, and quality of information, however.

COMBINING INFORMATION FROM DIFFERENT SOURCES: SINGLE-SOURCE DATA

It is desirable to combine secondary information obtained from different sources. Combining data allows the researcher to compensate for the weakness of one method with the strengths of another. One outcome of the effort to combine data from different sources is **single-source data**. Single-source research follows a person's TV, reading, and shopping habits. After recruiting a test panel of households, the research firm meters each home's TV sets and periodically surveys family members on what they read. Their

single-source data An effort to combine data from different sources by gathering integrated information on household and marketing variables applicable to the same set of respondents.

grocery purchases are tracked by UPC scanners. For background, most systems also track retail data, such as sales, advertising, and promotion. Thus, single-source data provide integrated information on household variables, including media consumption and purchases and marketing variables, such as product sales, price, advertising, promotion, and in-store marketing effort.[47] An application of single-source data is illustrated by the Campbell Soup Company.

EXAMPLE
Soaps Shed a *Guiding Light* on V-8 Consumption _____

The Campbell Soup Company used single-source data to target its advertising for V-8 juice. By obtaining single-source data on product consumption, media consumption, and demographic characteristics, Campbell found that demographically similar TV audiences consume vastly different amounts of V-8. For example, on an index of 100 for the average household's V-8 consumption, *General Hospital* had a below-average 80 index while *Guiding Light* had an above-average 120 index. These results were surprising because *General Hospital* actually had a slightly higher percentage of women 25 to 54 years old, the demographic group most predisposed to buy V-8, than *Guiding Light* and so would be expected to be a better medium to reach V-8 drinkers. Using this information, Campbell rearranged its advertising schedule to raise the average index.[48] ◆

Single-source data revealed that demographically similar TV audiences consume vastly different amounts of V-8 enabling Campbell Soup Company to select the right TV programs for advertising V-8. ◆ Klehr & Associates.

This example shows the usefulness of combining secondary information from different sources. The following example shows the various sources of secondary data on the department store industry used in the department store patronage project. (Refer to Appendix 4A for detailed information about each source.)

DEPARTMENT STORE PATRONAGE PROJECT
Sources of Industry Data
PUBLISHED EXTERNAL SECONDARY SOURCES

GENERAL BUSINESS SOURCES

GUIDES

Business Information Sources
Encyclopedia of Business Information Sources
Marketing Economics Guide

DIRECTORIES

Directories in Print
FINDEX: The Directory of Market Research Reports, Studies and Surveys

INDEXES

Business Index

PRIZM (Potential Rating Index by Zip Market)

TRADE JOURNALS

Retail and Distribution Management
Provides key trends in the industry, industry statistics, and relevant research results.
Chain Store Age (General Merchandise Edition)
Provides background information on trends and developments in the industry, statistics related to the retail industry, and current business practices.
Stores
Provides current trends in the industry, new retailing concepts and promotional ideas, and industry statistics.

NONGOVERNMENTAL STATISTICAL DATA

A Guide to Consumer Markets
Dealerscope Merchandising: Statistical and Marketing Report
Merchandising, "Statistical and Marketing Report"
Moody's Manuals
Predicasts Forecasts
Rand McNally Commercial Atlas and Marketing Guide
Sales and Marketing Management Survey of Buying Power
Sourcebook of Demographics and Buying Power for Every Zip Code in the USA

GOVERNMENT SOURCES

CENSUS DATA

Census of Retail Trade
County and City Databook

OTHER GOVERNMENT PUBLICATIONS

Economic Indicators
State and Metropolitan Area Databook

COMPUTERIZED DATABASES

DIRECTORIES OF DATABASES

ABI/Inform Ondisc
(Ann Arbor, MI: University Microfilms International)
This index on compact disc includes references and abstracts to articles from over 800 business and management journals.

SYNDICATED SOURCES OF SECONDARY DATA
RETAIL AUDIT SERVICES
Nielsen Retail Index
(A. C. Nielsen Co.)
Information on inventory levels, in-store promotions, prices, purchases, sales and special displays can be obtained. Nielsen also provides individualized reports.

DIARY PANELS
National Purchase Diary Panel
(New York: NPD Research, Inc.)
Provides details on key questions such as store patronage for different products and number and types of items purchased. ◆

Although we have already discussed several applications of secondary data in describing the various sources, we next consider two additional applications.

APPLICATIONS OF SECONDARY DATA

Secondary data have numerous applications in a variety of marketing research problems. Hence, we illustrate the applications of constructing a buying power index and computer mapping.

Buying Power Index

Sales and Marketing Management publishes an annual survey of buying power. This survey contains data for the United States on population, income, and retail sales, as well as a buying power index (BPI). These data are available at the metropolitan area, county, and city levels and are compiled from federal government statistics.

buying power index An indicator of the relative market potential between geographic territories.

The **buying power index** is an indicator of the relative market potential of different geographic areas. It is widely used for measuring market potential, evaluating new products, determining distribution channels, and long-range planning. It is also useful for measuring sales performance, setting sales goals and quotas, selecting test markets, and allocating media. In Research in Practice 4.3 we illustrate how a customized BPI is constructed and how it can be used for measuring market potential.

Computer Mapping

computer mapping Maps that solve marketing problems are called thematic maps. They combine geography with demographic information and a company's sales data or other proprietary information and are generated by a computer.

Computer mapping combines geography with demographic information and a company's sales data or other proprietary information to develop thematic maps. Marketers now routinely make decisions based on these color-coded maps. Mapping systems allow users to download geographically detailed demographic data supplied by vendors. The user can then draw a map that color codes neighborhoods in Dallas, for example, by the relative density of households with heads aged 35 to 45 with incomes of $50,000 or more. These systems allow users to add proprietary information to the downloaded data. Firms such as Equifax Marketing-Decision Systems, Inc. and the Demographic Research Company specialize in illustrating secondary data according to county lines, metropolitan areas, zip codes, and other geographical regions. The information is displayed so that patterns in the data can be easily recognized.[49]

RESEARCH IN PRACTICE 4.3

Applications of the Buying Power Index

CREATING YOUR OWN BPI

Suppose that your firm markets men's dress shirts mainly through department stores. The following steps are involved in creating a customized BPI that reflects the market's ability to purchase this specific product. We illustrate these steps by constructing a BPI for Boston.

Step 1. Specify the customer profile. Typically, the factors considered are demographic, economic, and distribution. For men's dress shirts we specify these factors as follows:

Demographic: Men 35 years and older

Economic: Household income $50,000 and over

Distribution: Department stores

Step 2. For each market, calculate the following percentages:

$$\text{Demographic} = \frac{\text{Market's men 35 years and older}}{\text{U.S. men 35 years and older}}$$

$$= x\%$$

$$\text{Economic} = \frac{\text{Market's households with income \$50,000 and over}}{\text{U.S. households with income \$50,000 and over}}$$

$$= y\%$$

$$\text{Distribution} = \frac{\text{Market's department store sales}}{\text{U.S. department store sale}}$$

$$= z\%$$

Step 3. Determine the importance of each factor. For men's dress shirts these factors could be:

Demographic: 20%
Economic: 50%
Distribution: 30%

Step 4. Calculate the BPI as follows:

$$\text{BPI} = 0.2 \, (\text{demographic \%}) + 0.5 \, (\text{economic \%}) + 0.3 \, (\text{distribution \%})$$

For Boston, these calculations are as follows:

Step 2.   Demographic $= \dfrac{744{,}410}{48{,}336{,}957} \times 100$

$$= 1.5400$$

(continued)

$$\text{Economic} \quad = \frac{299{,}291}{11{,}656{,}668} \times 100$$

$$= 2.5676$$

$$\text{Distribution} \quad = \frac{2{,}389{,}522{,}000}{127{,}230{,}971{,}000} \times 100$$

$$= 1.8781$$

Step 4:

$$\text{BPI for Boston} = 0.2 \times 1.5400 + 0.5 \times 2.5676 + 0.3 \times 1.8781$$

$$= 0.3080 + 1.2838 + 0.5634$$

$$= 2.1552$$

MEASURING MARKET POTENTIAL

The retail volume for men's dress shirts for the total United States is $2 billion. Suppose that your firm does $140 million, or 7% market share in dollar volume. The following steps are involved in measuring market potential.

Step 1. Estimate the total industry sales for that market. This can be done by multiplying the total industry sales by custom BPI and dividing by 100.

Step 2. Obtain the firm's actual sales in that market.

Step 3. Estimate the firm's market share by dividing the result of step 2 and step 1's results.

Step 4. Estimate the firm's sales potential in that market. This can be done by multiplying the firm's total sales by the market's BPI and dividing by 100.

Step 5. Estimate the market's performance index. This can done by dividing the actual sales (step 2) by the sales potential in that market (step 4).

For Boston, these calculations are as follows:

Step 1.   Estimate of industry sales in Boston $= \dfrac{2 \times 10^9 \times 2.1552}{100}$

Step 2.   Firm's actual sales in Boston $= \$2{,}678{,}760$

Step 3.   Firm's market share in Boston $= \dfrac{2{,}678{,}760}{4.3104 \times 10^7} \times 100 \ = 6.2146\%$

Step 4.   Sales potential in Boston $= \dfrac{\$140 \times 10^6 \times 2.1552}{100} = 3.01728 \times 10^6$

Step 5.   Performance Index for Boston $= \dfrac{2{,}678{,}760}{3.01728 \times 10^6} \times 100 = 88.78\%$

Although sales in Boston may be higher than in many other regions, they are below the potential.

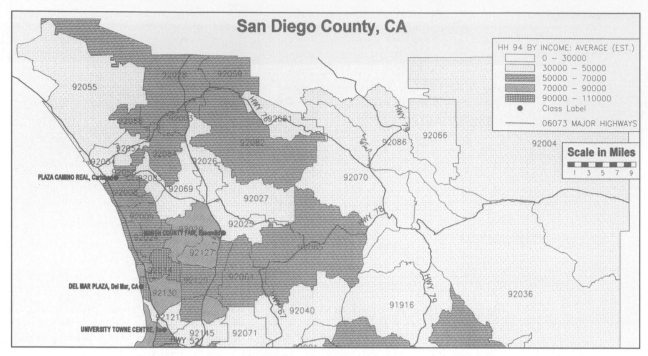

Computer mapping, which combines geographic, demographic, and company information, can be a valuable tool for marketing and marketing research. ◆ Equifax Marketing-Decision Systems, Inc.

INTERNATIONAL MARKETING RESEARCH

A wide variety of secondary data are available for international marketing research.[50] As with domestic research, the problem is not one of lack of data but one of the plethora of information available, and it is useful to classify the various sources (Figure 4.5). Domestic organizations in the United States, both government and nongovernment sources, can provide valuable secondary international data. The important government sources are the Department of Commerce, the Agency for International Development, the Small Business Administration, the Export-Import Bank of the United States, the Department of Agriculture, the Department of State, the Department of Labor, and the Port Authority of New York and New Jersey. The Department of Commerce offers not only a number of publications but also a variety of other services, such as the foreign buyer program, matchmaker events, trade missions, export contact list service, the foreign commercial service, and custom statistical service for exporters. The following example illustrates the use of the latter service.

EXAMPLE
Export Information Brings Profits Into Port

The U.S. Department of Commerce developed the Comparison Shopping Service (CSS) in 1986 to offer exporters custom export market research. It is now available for 52 countries, including Russia and other emerging markets. The fee ranges from $500 to

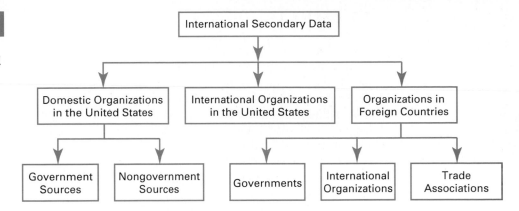

FIGURE 4.5

Sources of Secondary Data for International Marketing Research

$1,500, depending on the country surveyed. The final survey report is usually completed within 60 days.

Vestil Manufacturing of Angola, Indiana, is just one of many companies that have made use of CSS. Vestil, which makes dock and materials handling equipment for ports, says the surveys revealed "critically valuable information." Because the survey results were discouraging about the export of its bulky equipment, the company did not waste time pursuing that plan. The survey also pointed to other possible business relationships that proved profitable, including licensing agreements with local fabricators who could manufacture dock or materials handling equipment.[51] ◆

Nongovernment organizations, including international organizations located in the United States, can provide information about international markets. These include the United Nations, the Organization for Economic Cooperation and Development (OECD), the International Monetary Fund (IMF), the World Bank, International Chambers of Commerce, the Commission of the European Community to the United States, and the Japanese External Trade Organization (JETRO). Finally, sources in foreign countries include governments, international organizations located abroad, trade associations, and private services, such as syndicate firms. While conducting a review of the literature, one could use directories, indexes, books, commercially produced reference material, and magazines and newspapers .

Evaluation of secondary data is even more critical for international than for domestic projects. Different sources report different values for a given statistic, such as the gross domestic product (GDP), because of differences in the way the unit is defined. Measurement units may not be equivalent across countries. In France, for example, workers are paid a thirteenth monthly salary each year as an automatic bonus, resulting in a measurement construct that is different than other countries.[52] The accuracy of secondary data may also vary from country to country. Data from highly industrialized countries like the United States are likely to be more accurate than those from developing countries. Business and income statistics are affected by the taxation structure and the extent of tax evasion. Population censuses may vary in frequency and year in which the data are collected. In the United States, the census is conducted every ten years, whereas in the People's Republic of China, there was a 29-year gap between the censuses of 1953 and 1982. This situation, however, is changing quickly. Several countries such as China are developing huge sources of secondary data.

EXAMPLE

Secondary Data Gaining Primary Importance in China

Near a dreary concrete building in Beijing, Gao Yuxian is building what will be the largest database in China. Gao is the 48-year-old president of the newly formed All China Marketing Research Company. This company's purpose is to crunch numbers from millions of stores, factories, and farms in China and to create statistics that will become the basis for a massive information service that will be equated to a smaller version of Dun and Bradstreet.

China's fixation with counting and recording all aspects of the government owned businesses tends to favor the purpose of All China. These businesses provide All China with detailed and accurate quarterly statements on finance, production, employment, and other aspects that are relevant to the public. Then, Gao and All China's staff develop the numbers into a meaningful statistical database.

The All China database serves as an information reservoir not only to Chinese businesses but also to multinational corporations seeking to do business in China. For example, Coca-Cola used this database to determine that in 1993, although China had a population of 1.2 billion people, each person on the average drank only 1-1/2 cans or bottles of Coke per year! In comparison, in the United States each person typically consumed 1-1/2 cans or bottles of Coke per day. Thus, there was a tremendous potential to increase the consumption of Coke in China. Based on this finding, in 1993 Coca-Cola signed an agreement with the Chinese government to build or upgrade ten bottling plants in the interior of China. This deal allowed Coke to move well beyond the coastal regions of China, where it remains in a strong competitive position. Although this deal required the investment of $150 million in China through 1998, it would enable Coca-Cola to manufacture and sell more than 75 million cases of Coke per year.[53] ◆

ETHICS IN MARKETING RESEARCH

Possible ethical dilemmas exist when using internal or external secondary data. Some ethical issues that are pertinent include the unnecessary collection of primary data when the problem can be addressed based on secondary data alone, the use of only secondary data when primary data are needed, the use of secondary data that are not applicable, and the use of secondary data that have been gathered through morally questionable means.

As was discussed in Chapter 2, the unnecessary collection of expensive primary data when the research problem can be addressed using only secondary data is unethical. In this case, the researcher is using a more expensive method which is less appropriate. Similarly, the exclusive reliance on secondary data when the research problem requires primary data collection could raise ethical concerns, particularly if the researcher is billing the client a fixed fee for the project and the research methodology was not specified in advance. Here again, the researcher's profit goes up, but at the expense of the client.

The researcher is ethically obligated to ensure the relevance and usefulness of secondary data to the problem at hand. The secondary data should be evaluated by the criteria discussed earlier in this chapter. Only data judged to be appropriate should be used. It is also important that the data were collected using procedures which are morally appropriate. Data can be judged unethical if they were gathered in a way that harms the respondents. Take, for example, information on credit card holders' buying patterns with accompanying demographics available from a syndicated service. These data were collected without the consent of the card holders and may be considered an invasion of respondents' privacy. Although neither the client (a major bank) nor the researcher was involved in the unethical treatment of the respondents, should they use such research? This ethical dilemma becomes more complicated given the competition in the banking industry. A client with a moral objection to using such data realizes that these data are available also to competitors and that by not using them, the client firm can be at a competitive disadvantage. Clearly researchers and syndicate firms should not engage in any questionable or unethical practices, such as abuse of respondents' privacy, while generating secondary data. Privacy has, indeed, become a burning issue, as the following example indicates.

EXAMPLE
Privacy Issue Goes Public

The legal environment is becoming increasingly hostile toward marketing research. Government is considering more legislation that will cover a list of alleged privacy abuses in marketing research. Lately some 500 bills that cover a list of privacy abuses and protections have been introduced around the United States. The privacy issue has gone public with a wave of consumer complaints against many forms of marketing research. Two main issues are involved. First, consumers feel that they should not have to cope with unsolicited sales pitches that flood their mailboxes and phones. The second issue concerns the sophisticated databases that maintain enormous amounts of information about consumers ranging from the names of the consumers to their specific lifestyles and product consumption habits. Although this information is useful to researchers, many consumers argue that there is too much information of a personal nature available in the various databases. In a privacy survey conducted by Equifax, 78% of the respondents said that they were concerned about the personal privacy issue. A majority of the respondents said that though it was reasonable for companies to check public record information such as creditor checks, auto insurance checks or job checks, the public should be able to opt out of all other transactions.[54] ◆

COMPUTER APPLICATIONS

Microcomputers and mainframes can be used to access, analyze, and store information available from on- and off-line databases. Several syndicated services make information available for use on microcomputers and mainframes. Consider CompuServe, which is an on-line database with shopping and games for those who have a modem connected to their personal computers. CompuServe also holds deep reservoirs of data valuable to the market researcher. Census data, reports on geographic or market areas, industry reports, and full text articles from U.S. and international business newspapers and magazines, along with articles from a variety of daily newspapers in the United States and the United Kingdom are just some of the offerings that provide value to the market researcher using CompuServe.

CompuServe's Marketing/Management Research Center module contains nine databases containing national and international business magazine articles, market studies, and statistical reports. The Business Database Plus module contains articles from more than 450 regional, national, and international trade publications. Searching by word or phrase can provide the user with sales and marketing ideas, product news, industry trends, and analysis. The Business Dateline module holds articles from more than 115 regional business publications in the United States and Canada beginning from 1985.

Exhibit 4.1 shows the results of searching the Business Database Plus module for "consumer and automobile and attitude." Here, the abstract and the full text of the April 11, 1994 article "Automakers Recognizing Value of Women's Market" from *Marketing News* appear.

Consumer marketing research can be boosted by accessing the Consumer Reports module containing the issues of *Consumer Reports* magazine with product ratings for appliances, autos, electronics and cameras, and items for the home. The Neighborhood Report module provides demographic information on any zip code in the United States on such variables as population, race, age, occupation, and housing patterns. In addition, locating potential survey respondents can be facilitated by CompuServe's Phone*File, which offers access to the name, address, length of residence and phone number of 75 million households. Searches can be made by zip code, city, state, or telephone number.

CompuServe also can help the business-to-business market researcher. Biz*File provides directory information for over ten million U.S. and Canadian businesses. The European Company Library module holds directory and financial information on more than two million European companies. Searches can be made by company name, industry codes, or geographic region. CompuServe can claim a low price in comparison to other on-line databases, along with user-friendliness. Both of these aspects make it a database to consult first when conducting marketing research.

Given the sheer volume of available scanner data, software has been developed to process and repackage such data to user specifications. Cover Story by Information Resources Inc. is an expert system that extracts key information (sales, category volume, trend, and brand share) from large syndicated grocery scanner databases and delivers it in memo format. Sparscan—Scanner Data Analysis by Spar Inc. calculates base consumer demand, incremental volume, and estimated profit for Infoscan, Scantrac, Samscan, or other scanner data. It can also calculate incremental consumption from promotions based on scanner sales at the key account, market, and national levels.

EXHIBIT 4.1

Output from CompuServe Search

```
Business and Trade Journals                                      Article Selection Menu 1
Automakers recognizing value of women's market,        Marketing News, April 11, 1994 v28 n8 p1(2).
Reference # A15382739        Text: Yes (1592 words)              Abstract: Yes
1 Citation: Marketing News, April 11, 1994 v28 n8 p1(2)
Title: Automakers recognizing value of women's market.
Authors: Triplett, Tim
Subjects: Automobile industry—Marketing; Women consumers—Evaluation: Automobile dealers—Marketing
SIC Codes: 3711; 4411                                            Reference #: A15382739
=============================================================================
Abstract: The automobile industry has finally come to recognize the importance of women as a consumer
segment after decades of viewing them as mere passengers rather than purchasers. This change is
attitude has been brought about by changing demographics. Statistics show that women make up half of
the US labor force, as well as of the total number of single adult Americans. Over 6.5 million women
have their own businesses and nearly the same number have an annual income of $75,000 or more. More
importantly, women account for close to 505 of all vehicles sales and many influence up to 80% of all
buying decisions in the US automobile market every year. Automakers are responding to the growing power
of these consumers by creating marketing-to-women committees and by recruiting more female engineers
and executives. Unfortunately, the value of this market has yet to dawn on auto dealers, many of whom
continue to treat women condescendingly and patronizingly. Some dealers, however, still cling to
stereotypes. Women buy nearly half the vehicles sold and may influence up to 80% of the purchasing
decisions in the U.S. automobile market each year, but until recently the industry viewed women chiefly
as passengers, not purchasers. Most automakers now recognize the value of marketing their products to
women, but auto dealers appear to be lagging behind in the race to win the hearts and the purses of
female buyers.
=============================================================================
Full Text COPYRIGHT American Marketing Association 1994              Press CR for more (? for help)
Citation: Marketing News, April 11, 1994 v28 n8 p1(2)
- - - - - - - - - - - - - - - - - - - - - - - - - - - - - - - - - - - - - - - -
Title: Automakers recognizing value of women's market.
Authors: Triplett, Tim
```

Using desktop demographic systems, businesses can bring market analysis in-house on a personal computer. Desktop demographic systems allow businesses to integrate, manipulate, and analyze data from a variety of databases. These systems then summarize the merged data in the form of reports, charts, or maps. Most desktop systems allow businesses to incorporate their own data into the analysis, making them a powerful tool for linking internal and external secondary data. Desktop demographic systems include Market*America by CACI Market Analysis, Compass by Claritas Corp., Conquest by Donnelley Marketing Information Services, and Infomark by National Decision Systems.

Mainframe computers have been mapping demographic data since the mid-1970s. Companies like FedEx use mainframe programs because they need to make many nationwide geographically based decisions simultaneously. Firms like Geographic Systems Inc. (GSI) market mainframe mapping products. SPSS/PC+ Mapping Version features Map-Master from Ashton-Tate. It designates variables to be mapped and aggregates and transfers the data from SPSS/PC+ along with specifications for the base map on which the data are to be displayed.

SUMMARY

In contrast to primary data, which originate with the researcher for the specific purpose of the problem at hand, secondary data are data originally collected for other purposes. Secondary data can be obtained quickly and are relatively inexpensive. They have limitations, however, and should be carefully evaluated to determine their appropriateness for the problem at hand. The evaluation criteria consist of specifications, error, currency, objectivity, nature, and dependability.

A wealth of information exists in the organization for which the research is being conducted. This information constitutes internal secondary data. External data are generated by sources outside the organization. These data exist in the form of published (printed) material, on-line and off-line databases, or information made available by syndicated services. Published external sources may be broadly classified as general business data or government data. General business sources comprise guides, directories, indexes, and statistical data. Government sources may be broadly categorized as census data and other data. Computerized databases may be on-line or off-line. Both on-line and off-line databases may be further classified as bibliographic, numeric, full-text, directory, or specialized databases.

Syndicated sources are companies that collect and sell common pools of data designed to serve a number of clients. Syndicated sources can be classified based on the unit of measurement (households and consumers or institutions). Household and consumer data may be obtained via surveys, diary purchase or media panels, or electronic scanner services. When institutions are the unit of measurement, the data may be obtained from retailers, wholesalers, or industrial firms. It is desirable to combine information obtained from different secondary sources.

Several specialized sources of secondary data are useful for conducting international marketing research. The evaluation of secondary data becomes even more critical, however, because the usefulness and accuracy of these data can vary widely. Ethical dilemmas that can arise include the unnecessary collection of primary data, the use of only secondary data when primary data are needed, the use of secondary data that are not applicable, and the use of secondary data that have been gathered through morally questionable means. Microcomputers and mainframes can be used to access, analyze, and store information available from on- and off-line databases.[55]

ACRONYMS

The criteria used for evaluating secondary data may be described by the acronym SECOND:

S pecifications: methodology used to collect the data
E rror: accuracy of the data
C urrency: when the data were collected
O bjective: purpose for which data were collected
N ature: content of the data
D ependability: overall, how dependable the data are

EXERCISES

QUESTIONS

1. What are the differences between primary and secondary data?
2. Why is it important to obtain secondary data before primary data?
3. Differentiate between internal and external secondary data.
4. List the various sources of published secondary data.
5. What are the different forms of computerized databases?
6. What are the advantages of computerized databases?
7. List and describe the various syndicated sources of secondary data.
8. What is the nature of information collected by surveys?
9. How can surveys be classified?
10. Explain what a diary panel is. What is the difference between diary purchase panels and diary media panels?
11. What are relative advantages of diary panels over surveys?
12. What kinds of data can be gathered through electronic scanner services?
13. Describe the uses of scanner data.
14. What is an audit? Discuss the uses, advantages, and disadvantages of audits.
15. Describe the information provided by industrial services.
16. Why is it desirable to use multiple sources of secondary data?
17. What are the advantages of secondary data?
18. What are the disadvantages of secondary data?
19. What are the criteria to be used when evaluating secondary data?

PROBLEMS

1. Research in Practice 4.3 illustrates the construction of a customized buying power index (BPI) for men's dress shirts in Boston. Following the same steps, construct a BPI for men's dress shirts in your metropolitan area. Construct another BPI for women's dresses in your area.
2. Select an industry of your choice. Using secondary sources, obtain industry sales and the sales of the major firms in that industry for the past year. Estimate the market shares of each major firm. From another source, obtain information on the market shares of these same firms. Do the two estimates agree?

COMPUTER EXERCISES

1. Conduct an on-line data search to obtain background information on an industry of your choice (e.g., sporting goods). Your search should encompass both qualitative and quantitative information.
2. Using census or other data, obtain a demographic profile of the Zip code in which you live.

NOTES

1. David W. Stewart, *Secondary Research: Information Sources and Methods* (Beverly Hills: Sage Publications, 1984), pp. 23–33.

2. This example is taken from *Sales and Marketing Management* (July 1987): 56–57.

3. This example is taken from *Sales and Marketing Management* (July 1987): 56–57.

4. "Testing Juices Up Slice's Performance," *Advertising Age* (August 24, 1987): S2-S4.

5. Robert Bengen, "Teamwork: It's in the Bag," *Marketing Research: A Magazine of Management and Applications* 5 (Winter 1993).

6. For a recent application of secondary data, see Dipak Jain, Vijay Mahajan, and Eitan Muller, "Innovation Diffusion in the Presence of Supply Restrictions," *Marketing Science* (Winter 1991): 83–90.

7. Debra K. Johnson, "When 'Gut Feel' Is Not Enough," *Bank Marketing* (August 1986): 30–35.

8. Herbert Jacob, *Using Published Data: Errors and Remedies* (Beverly Hills: Sage Publications, 1984).

9. David W. Stewart, *Secondary Research: Information Sources and Methods* (Beverly Hills: Sage Publications, 1984), pp. 23–33.

10. John Chapman, "Cast a Critical Eye: Small Area Estimates and Projections Sometimes Can Be Dramatically Different," *American Demographics* 9 (February 1987): 30.

11. Judith Waldrop, "Choose the Income That's Right for You," *American Demographics* (December 1993): 9–10.

12. Paul Wang and Ted Splegel, "Database Marketing and Its Measurement of Success: Designing a Managerial Instrument to Calculate the Value of a Repeat Customer Base," *Journal of Direct Marketing* 8 (Spring 1994): 73–81.

13. James R. Fries, "Library Support for Industrial Marketing Research," *Industrial Marketing Management* 11 (February 1982): 47–51.

14. Jac L. Goldstucker, *Marketing Information: A Professional Reference Guide* (Atlanta: Georgia State University, College of Business Administration, 1982).

15. H. Webster Johnson, Anthony J. Faria, and Ernest L. Maier, *How to Use the Business Library: With Sources of Business Information*, 5th ed. (Cincinnati: South-Western, 1984), pp. 29–57.

16. G. May, *A Handbook for Business on the Use of Federal and State Statistical Data* (Washington, DC: U.S. Department of Commerce, 1979).

17. T. A. Nelson, *Measuring Markets: A Guide to the Use of Federal and State Statistical Data* (Washington, DC: U.S. Department of Commerce, 1979).

18. Martha Farnsworth Riche, "Choosing 1980 Census Data Products," *American Demographics* 3 (December 1981): 12–16.

19. C. Marshall, "PRIZM Adds Zip to Consumer Research," *Advertising Age* (November 10, 1980): 22.

20. Barbara Everitt Bryant, "Reflections of the Census Director," *American Demographics* (March 1993): 13–15.

21. C. L. Borguran, *Effective Online Searching* (New York: Marcel Dekker, 1984).

22. C. R. Milsap, "On-Line and On Target," *Business Marketing* (October 1985): 52–63.

23. Robert Donah, "Decision Analysis for Selecting Online Databases to Answer Business Questions," *Database* (December 1981): 49–63.

24. Katherine S. Chiang, "How to Find On-line Information," *American Demographics* 15 (September 1993): 52–55. This article shows how to perform a thorough search for information, then gives basic information about how to join an on-line service.

25. J. L. Hall and H. J. Brown, *Online Bibliographic Databases* (Detroit: Gale Research, 1980), pp. 17–19.

26. M. Lubatkin, and M. Pitts, "PIMS: Fact or Folklore," *Journal of Business Strategy* (Winter 1983): 38–43. For a recent application of PIMS database, see Venkatram Ramaswamy, Hubert Gatignon, and David J. Reibstein, "Competitive Marketing Behavior," *Journal of Marketing* 58 (April 1994): 45–56.

27. "Comparative Data Retrieved with On-Line System," *Quirk's Marketing Research Review* (June–July 1987): 6, 54.

28. For a recent application of computerized databases, see Vicki Lane, and Robert Jacobson, "Stock Market Reactions to Brand Extension Announcements: The Effects of Brand Attitude and Familiarity," *Journal of Marketing* 59 (January 1995): 63–77.

29. "The MonitorTM Service," brochure originally prepared by Yankelovich, Skelly, and White/Clancy, Shulman Inc., 8 Wright Street, Westport, CT 06880.

30. William D. Wells, "Attitudes and Behavior: Lessons from the Needham Life Style Study," *Journal of Advertising Research*, 25 (February–March 1985): 40–44.

31. William L. Wilkie, *Consumer Behavior*, 2nd. ed. (New York: Wiley, 1990), chapter 4 and appendix 4A.

32. *Starch Readership Report: Scope, Method, and Use* (Mamaroneck, NY: Starch INRA Hooper, undated).

33. "Roper Custom Question Service: A Unique Omnibus Research Facility," brochure prepared by the Roper Organization, Inc., 1 Park Avenue, New York, NY 10016.

34. Panel descriptions supplied by Rita E. Turgeon, We Make the Market Perfectly Clear (New York: NPD Research, Inc. undated).

35. A. C. Nielsen.

36. Peter J. Danaher and Trevor Sharot, "Cover Analysis: A New Tool for Monitoring Peoplemeter Panels," *Journal of the Market Research Society* 36 (April 1994): 133–38.

37. Roland Soong, "The Statistical Reliability of People Meter Ratings," *Journal of Advertising Research* (February–March 1988): 50–56.

38. "Why Consumer Mail Panel Is the Superior Option" (Chicago: Market Facts, Inc. undated); and Venkatram Ramaswamy and Wayne S. DeSarbo, "SCULPTURE: A New Methodology for Deriving and Analyzing Hierarchical Product-Market Structures from Panel Data," *Journal of Marketing Research* 27 (November 1990): 418–27.

39. S. Sudman, "On the Accuracy of Recording of Consumer Panels I," *Journal of Marketing Research* (August 1964): 69–83; S. Sudman, and M. Bradburn, "Response Effects in Surveys," *Journal of Marketing Research* (May 1964): 14–20; S. Sudman and R. Ferber, *Consumer Panels* (Chicago: American Marketing Association 1978); and S. Sudman, "On the Accuracy of Recording of Consumer Panels II," *Learning Manual* (New York: Neal-Schumen Publishers, 1981).

40. A recent study investigating the accuracy of UPC scanner pricing systems found that both underring and overring rates were significantly higher than retailers' expectations. See Ronald C. Goodstein, "UPC Scanner Pricing Systems: Are They Accurate?" *Journal of Marketing* 58 (April 1994): 20–30.

41. Rick L. Andrew and T. C. Srinivasan, "Studying Consideration Effects in Empirical Choice Models Using Scanner Panel Data," *Journal of Marketing Research* 32 (February 1995): 30–41; and Randolph E. Bucklin, Sunil Gupta, and Sangman Han, "A Brand's Eye View of Response Segmentation in Consumer Brand Choice Behavior," *Journal of Marketing Research* 32 (February 1995): 66–74.

42. It is possible to combine store-level scanner data with scanner panel data to do an integrated analysis. See, for example, Gary J. Russell and Wagner A. Kamakura, "Understanding Brand Competition Using Micro and Macro Scanner Data," *Journal of Marketing Research* 31 (May 1994): 289–303.

43. Examples of recent applications of scanner data include Peter S. Fader, and Leigh McAlister, "An Elimination by Aspects Model of Consumer Response to Promotion Calibrated on UPC Scanner Data," *Journal of Marketing Research* 27 (August 1990): 322–32; Eric Waarts, Martin Carree, and Berend Wierenga, "Full-Information Maximum Likelihood Estimation of Brand Positioning Maps Using Supermarket Scanning Data," *Journal of Marketing Research* 28 (November 1991): 483–490.

44. Based on information obtained from the suppliers.

45. M. A. Hardin, "Electronics Industry Offered `Early Alert' Sales Tracking," *Marketing News* (August 14, 1987): 10.

46. "Decision Makers Mostly Males, Study Shows," *Quirk's Marketing Research Review* (June–July, 1988): 45–46.

47. For an application of single-source data, see John Deighton, Caroline M. Henderson, and Scott A. Neslin, "The Effects of Advertising on Brand Switching and Repeat Purchasing," *Journal of Marketing Research* 31 (February 1994): 28–43.

48. Joanne Lipman, "Single-Source Ad Research Heralds Detailed Look at Household Habits," *Wall Street Journal* (February 16, 1988): 39.

49. David J. Cowen, "Computer Mapping," *Business and Economic Review* 34 (April–June 1988): 26–29.

50. For an example of research based on secondary data, see Hirokazu Takada and Dipak Jain, "Cross-National Analysis of Diffusion of Consumer Durable Goods in Pacific Rim Countries," *Journal of Marketing* 55 (April 1991): 48–54.

51. "Comparison Shopping Service Offers Custom Export Market Research," *Business America* (March 26, 1990): 14–15.

52. Susan P. Douglas, and C. Samuel Craig, *International Marketing Research* (Englewood Cliffs, NJ: Prentice Hall, 1983).

53. John E. Keller, "Firm Aims to be China's Dun & Bradstreet," *Wall Street Journal* (April 6, 1994).

54. Howard Schlossberg, "Marketing Researchers Face 'Increasingly Hostile' Legislation," *Marketing News* (August 16, 1993): 1, 8.

55. The assistance of James Agarwal with the international marketing research example, the assistance of Mark Leach and Gina Miller in writing the ethics section, and the assistance of Mark Peterson in writing the computer applications section is gratefully acknowledged.

APPENDIX 4A

PUBLISHED SOURCES OF SECONDARY DATA

General Business Sources

GUIDES

A Handbook on the Use of Government Statistics
(Charlottesville, VA: Taylor Murphy Institute)
Pamphlet designed to aid in understanding government statistics.

American Marketing Association Bibliography Series
(Chicago: American Marketing Association)
Detailed annotated bibliography of topics of interest to the AMA.

Business Information: How to Find It, How to Use It
(Phoenix, AZ: Oryx Press)
Guidebook on searching for business information and using statistical information, offering different strategies to find the desired information. Contains detailed descriptions of business publications.

Business Information Sources
(Berkeley: University of California Press)
Guide to sources of business information. Organized by subject; includes subjects useful for marketers (statistical sources, marketing research sources).

Business Services and Information: The Guide to the Federal Government
(New York: Management Information Exchange)
Guide for identifying U.S. government publications, including an annotated list of publications and agency phone numbers and addresses.

Data Sources for Business and Market Analysis
(Metuchen, NJ: Scarecrow Press)
Annotated guide to original sources indexed by source (e.g., *Fortune* magazine, *Census of Housing*).

Editor and Publisher Market Guide
(New York: *Editor and Publisher* magazine)
Annual guide for publishers on major metropolitan areas, giving demographic and descriptive information helpful for planning.

Encyclopedia of Business Information Sources
(Detroit: Gale Research)
Guide to information available to businesses from statistical sources, directories, periodicals, associations, bibliographies, and general works.

The Federal Database Finder
(Chevy Chase, MD: Information USA, Inc.)
Guide to over 4,200 databases available through the federal government.

Guide to American Directories
(Coral Springs, FL: B. Klein Publications)
Guide to published directories under 300 different headings.

How to Find Information about Companies: The Corporate Intelligence Source Book
(Washington, DC: Washington Researchers)
Guide containing statistical and summary information about specific companies.

The Library and Information Manager's Guide to Online Services
(White Plains, NY: Knowledge Industry Publication)
Guide to on-line information sources useful to business.

Management Information Guides
(Detroit: Gale Research Co.)
Bibliography of business information sources, including general reference publications, film strips, and government reports.

Marketing Economics Guide
(New York: Marketing Economics Institute)
Annual guide to 1,500 retailing centers containing information aggregated by city, county, state, and region. Contains demographic information on populations and economic information on retail operations.

Marketing Information
(Atlanta: Business Publishing Division, Georgia State University)
Comprehensive guide to books, periodicals, and other sources pertaining to 22 different areas of marketing. Lists marketing organizations, associations, government agencies, libraries, and private consulting organizations.

Surveys, Polls, Censuses, and Forecasts Directory
(Detroit: Gale Research Co.)
Guide to studies conducted in economics, business, science, and technology.

Washington Researchers
(Washington, DC)

Where to Find Business Information: A Worldwide Guide to Everyone Who Needs Answers to Business Questions
(New York: Wiley)
Guide to over 5,000 books, periodicals, and databases of business information.
How to Find Information about Companies: The Corporate Intelligence Source Book

DIRECTORIES

American Marketing Association International Membership Directory and Marketing Services Guide
(Chicago: American Marketing Association)
Annual directory of AMA members, both individuals and companies, and guide to firms offering marketing services.

Bradford's Directory of Marketing Research Agencies and Management Consultants in the U.S. and the World
(Fairfax, VA: Bradford)
Biannual booklet listing research agencies and consultants by geographic area and service offered.

Business Organizations, Agencies and Publications Directory
(Detroit: Gale Research Co.)
Directory listing over 20,000 business and trade organizations, agencies, professional societies, government agencies, educational institutions, and publications. Includes specific listings for accounting, administration, human resources, finance, and marketing organizations.

Consultants and Consulting Organizations Directory
(Detroit: Gale Research Co.)
Directory of over 14,000 consultants, listing their fields of expertise.

Directories in Print
(Detroit: Gale Research Co.)
Directory of more than 10,000 directories in print, including directories of industries, trades, professions, manufacturing, and professional societies. Includes brief descriptions, frequency of publication, and price.

Directory of American Research and Technology
(New York: R. R. Bowker)
Directory of organizations involved in research and development in the United States listing their fields of interest.

Directory of Corporate Affiliations
(Skokie, IL: National Register Publishing Co.)
Annual directory of over 4,000 American public and private companies and their subsidiaries, divisions, and affiliates. Information is broken out by Standard Industrial Classification code, state, and alphabetically.

Directory of Industry Data Sources
(Cambridge, MA: HARFAX)
Three-volume directory, containing more than 15,000 annotated entries for 60 industries, including general reference sources, industry data sources, and a directory of all publishers mentioned.

Directory of Online Databases
(Santa Monica, CA: Cuadra Associates, Inc.)
Quarterly directory of over 4,000 bibliographic and other databases available to on-line computer access.

Dun's Consultants Directory
(Parsippany, NJ: Dun's Marketing Service, Inc.)
Annual listing of more than 25,000 consulting firms by geographic area, service offered, and alphabetic order. Entries include sales volume, number of employees, and principal officers.

Encyclopedia of Associations
(Detroit: Gale Research Co.)
Annual encyclopedia of trade, business, and professional associations.

Encyclopedia of Information Systems and Services
(Detroit: Gale Research Co.)
Encyclopedia of over 2,500 database producers, data banks, information centers, on-line vendors, and research centers.

Federal Statistical Directory: The Guide to Personnel and Data Sources
(Phoenix, AZ: Oryx Press)
Directory of the key personnel in federal agencies who handle statistical information. Includes addresses and phone numbers.

FINDEX: The Directory of Market Research Reports, Studies and Surveys
(Bethesda, MD: Cambridge Information Group)
Directory of over 10,000 research reports written by research firms worldwide.

Fortune 500 Directory
(New York: Time, Inc.)
Annual directory of the 500 largest U.S. corporations, with information on assets, employees, invested capital, profits, and sales.

International Directory of Corporate Affiliations
(Wilmette, IL: National Register Publishing Co.)
Annual directory of the national and international corporate holdings of U.S. firms and the American holdings of non-U.S. firms.

International Directory of Marketing Research Houses and Services
(New York: American Marketing Association, New York Chapter)
Directory of marketing research firms around the world, indexed by both location and principal personnel.

Million Dollar Directory
(New York: Dun and Bradstreet)
Annual directory of over 160,000 American companies with net worth of over $500,000, including information on office location, products, sales, and number of employees.

Moody's Manuals
(New York: Moody's Investors Service)
Eight annual manuals giving background information and detailed financial information on companies (*Industrial, OTC Industrial, OTC Unlisted, Municipal and Government, Public Utility, Transportation, International* and *Banks and Finance*).

Research Services Directory
(Detroit: Gale Research Co.)
Directory of research firms, including marketing research firms, listing their areas of expertise.

Standard and Poor's Register of Corporations, Directors and Executives
(New York: Standard and Poor's Corp.)
Annual listing of addresses, employees, officers, products, sales, and telephone numbers for U.S. and Canadian corporations.

Standard Directory of Advertisers
(Wilmette, IL: National Register Publishing Co.)
Annual directory of over 25,000 companies that spend more than $75,000 on advertising, including such information as type of business, advertising agency relationships, media utilized, and products advertised.

Standard Directory of Advertising Agencies
(Wilmette, IL: National Register Publishing Co.)
Directory, published every four months, of over 5,000 advertising agencies, listing key accounts, addresses, and phone numbers.

Thomas Register of American Manufacturers
(New York: Thomas Publishing)
Annual multivolume directory of manufacturers of specific products and services, providing addresses, branch offices and subsidiaries. Indexed by alphabetic listing, brand names, and telephone directories for cities.

Who's Who in Consulting
(Detroit: Gale Research Co.)
Directory of prominent consultants, in marketing and other fields, including biographical sketches, location, and areas of expertise.

INDEXES

ABI/Inform Ondisc
(Ann Arbor, MI: University Microfilms International)
Index on compact disc that includes references and
abstracts to articles from over 800 business and management journals.

American Statistics Index
(Washington, DC: Congressional Information Service)
Annual comprehensive index to all statistical informa-
tion provided to the public by the federal government.

*Bibliographic Index: A Cumulative Bibliography of
Bibliographies*
(New York: H. W. Wilson Co.)
A listing published every four months of bibliographies
containing 50 or more citations of books and periodicals.

Business Index
(Foster City, CA: Information Access Co.)
Microform index to over 800 business magazines and
newspapers and relevant articles from general and legal
periodicals.

Business Periodicals Index
(New York: H. W. Wilson Co.)
Monthly index to approximately 350 business periodicals by field of business. Supplemented by quarterly
and annual updates.

Communications Abstracts
(Beverly Hills: Sage Publications, Inc.)
Quarterly index to articles, reports, and books from the
communications industry covering advertising, marketing, and mass communications.

Conference Board Cumulative Index
(New York: Conference Board)
Index of past studies from the Conference Board, covering a wide variety of areas, including economics and
marketing.

Dissertation Abstracts International
(Ann Arbor, MI: University Microfilms International)
Monthly index to over 30,000 annual doctoral dissertation abstracts from major universities around the
world. Marketing-related abstracts are included under
the Humanities and Social Sciences division or the
European division.

Index of Economic Articles
(Homewood, IL: Richard D. Irwin, Inc.)
Annual index of articles, papers, and proceedings from
over 200 economic journals.

Information Catalog
(New York: FIND/SVP)
Bimonthly index to directories, reports, and other ref-
erences in periodicals and private reports.

New York Times Index
(New York: New York Times)
Published every two weeks, a detailed subject index of
articles from the *New York Times.*

Predicasts F & S Index: United States
(Cleveland: Predicasts)
Weekly index (with monthly, quarterly, and annual
aggregations) of company, product, and industry infor-

mation, including new product updates, corporate
acquisitions and mergers, and technological developments. Over 750 sources are referenced.

Predicasts F & S Index: Europe
(Cleveland: Predicasts)
Same as above, covering only Europe.

Predicasts F & S Index: International
(Cleveland: Predicasts)
Same as above, covering Asia, Africa, Australia,
Central America, and South America.

PRIZM (Potential Rating Index by Zip Market)
(Claritas Corp.)
Descriptive profiles of residents in each zip code.
Originates from a compilation of demographic data
from the *Census of Population and Housing* and lifestyle
data for each region.

Social Sciences Citation Index
(Philadelphia: Institute for Scientific Information)
Index published every four months of all articles in
over 1,400 social science periodicals. Marketing-
related topics include economics and management.

Statistical Reference Index
(Washington, DC: Congressional Information Service)
Monthly index to statistical publications from educational,
industrial, and government sources, with annual compilations from both governmental and private sources.

*Statistics Sources: A Subject Guide to Data on Industrial,
Business, Social, Educational, Financial and Other Topics*
(Detroit: Gale Research Co.)
Guide to statistical indexes from both national and
international sources.

University Research in Business and Economics
(Morgantown: Bureau of Business Research, West
Virginia University)
Annual compilation of books, articles, working papers,
and monographs produced by universities. Indexed by
author, subject, and institution.

Wall Street Journal Index
(Princeton, NJ: Dow Jones Books)
Monthly index to articles, with annual compilations,
related to both corporate news and general news found
in the *Wall Street Journal.*

NONGOVERNMENTAL STATISTICAL DATA

Almanac of Business and Industrial Financial Ratios
(Englewood Cliffs, NJ: Prentice Hall)
Collection of sales and operating ratios organized to
allow for the comparison of companies of similar size
within industries.

BAR/LNA Multi-Media Service
(New York: Leading National Advertisers)
Series of quarterly reports providing advertising expenditures in six major media, including television, radio,
and print. Ad expenditures for specific brands are
listed as well.

Commodity Yearbook
(New York: Commodity Research Bureau)
Annual listing of prices, production volume, stocks,
exports, and other statistics for major commodities.

Dealerscope Merchandising: Statistical and Marketing Report
(Philadelphia: North American Publishing Co.)
The March issue of this trade publication reports on shipments, sales, product saturation, replacement and trade-in, and import and export figures for consumer goods; the April issue covers major appliances.

Fortune Double 500 Directory
(New York: Time Inc.)
Sales, assets, profits, and other descriptive statistics for the 500 largest American industrial corporations and the 500 largest American service organizations as published in *Fortune*.

Guide to Consumer Markets
(New York: Conference Board)
Annual compilation of data on consumer behavior, including information on employment, consumer expenditures, income, and prices.

Merchandising Statistical and Marketing Report
(New York: Billboard Publications)
Annual report of sales, shipments, imports, exports, and other statistics for major consumer durables; appears in the March issue of *Merchandising*.

Moody's Manuals
(New York: Moody's Investors Service)
Set of manuals for different industries, published annually, containing balance sheets and income statements for companies and government units.

Predicasts Forecasts
(Cleveland: Predicasts, Inc.)
Quarterly publication giving short- and long-term forecasts for economic indicators, industries, and products and basic statistical information on companies and industries.

Rand McNally Commercial Atlas and Marketing Guide
(Chicago: Rand McNally Co.)
Annual publication of maps and demographic, retail, and home-purchase data for over 100,000 cities in the United States.

Sales and Marketing Management Survey of Buying Power
(New York: Sales and Marketing Management)
Annual survey of household income, population, and retail sale data for cities, counties, and metropolitan statistical areas in North America. Includes a buying power index for the metropolitan statistical areas.

Sourcebook of Demographics and Buying Power for Every Zip Code in the USA
(Fairfax, VA: CACI, Inc.)
Listing of all zip codes, arranged by state, and associated demographic information (population size, population profile, income and employment statistics, housing profile). Also includes the purchasing potential index, a statistic measuring the likelihood that residents of a zip code will purchase various categories of goods and services.

Standard and Poor's Corporate Record
(New York: Standard and Poor's Corp.)
Listing of current financial statistics, background information, and news items for corporations.

Standard and Poor's Industry Survey
(New York: Standard and Poor's Corp.)
Surveys analyzing the major domestic industries and reporting current trends, statistical tables and charts, and industry outlook.

Standard and Poor's Statistical Service
(New York: Standard and Poor's Corp.)
Historic statistical data on a variety of industrial topics, including finance, production and labor, and income and trade.

Standard Rate and Data Service
(Skokie, IL: National Register Publication Co.)
Monthly listing of advertising rates for American radio and TV stations, consumer magazines, business publications, newspapers, and other periodicals.

State Data and Database Sourcebook
(Chevy Chase, MD: Information USA, Inc.)
How to obtain information from state offices, with specifics on available data and their cost for each state.

Statistical Reference Index: Worldcasts
(Cleveland: Predicasts, Inc.)
Quarterly forecasts for both products and regions around the world.

Survey of World Advertising Expenditures
(Mamaroneck, NY: Starch INRA Hooper)
Annual estimates of expenditures in different media categories for countries around the world.

Government Sources
CENSUS DATA

Publications by the U.S. Bureau of the Census: Government Printing Office, Washington, DC, include:

Census Catalog and Guide
Annual catalog of all information available from the Census Bureau since 1980, with phone numbers included.

Census Data Index
Quarterly index of data available from the Census Bureau listed under publications, data files, and special tabulations.

Census of Agriculture
Statistics on the number of farms, farm types, acreage, land-use practices, employment, livestock produced and products, and the value of products by state and county. The census, published every five years, is supplemented by the annual publication, *Agriculture Statistics and Commodity Yearbook*.

Census of Construction Industries
Statistics of the value of inventories, employment, and total assets of firms engaged in contract construction, construction for sale, or subdividing real property into lots.

Census of Government
Statistics on state and local government pertaining to local employment, size of payroll, operating budgets, and amount of indebtedness.

Census of Housing
A census published every ten years containing structural, financial, economic, and home furnishing data on housing (including homes and apartments) in the United States. Data are presented geographically and for major metropolitan areas, and are provided by city block. Supplemented by the annual *American Housing Survey.*

Census of Manufacturers
A census of manufacturing companies, classified by product classes and geographic location, containing statistics on the number of companies, quantity of output and value added in production, employment, capital expenditures, inventories, sales by customer class, and other statistics. Supplemented by the *Annual Survey of Manufactures and Current Industrial Reports.*

Census of Mineral Industries
Detailed information on the mining industry broken out by geographical area for approximately 50 segments of the industry. Statistics include level of production, value of shipments, capital expenditures, power equipment, cost of supplies, and other statistics. Supplemented by the *Minerals Yearbook* published by the Department of the Interior, although the two are not comparable.

Census of Population
A census of the population reported by geographic region. It provides a detailed breakdown of many types of social and demographic information. It is supplemented annually by the *Current Population Reports.*

Census of Population and Housing
Based on the *Census of Population*, three publications related to housing and demographics for groups of consumers are released: (1) *Block Statistics* contains data from individual city blocks; (2) *Census Tracts*, including data on tracts (neighborhoods) for each state; and (3) *Summary Characteristics for Governmental Units* on data pertaining to the government.

Census of Retail Trade
Statistics on retail stores, classified by type of business, including total sales, employment, and number of stores by counties, cities, and standard metropolitan statistical areas. Supplemented by *Monthly Retail Trade.*

Census of Service Industries
A census of service establishments providing information on type of business, number of units, and total receipts by geographic area.

Census of Transportation
A census of establishments in the transportation industry, broken out by various types of carriers and including information on passenger travel, truck and bus inventory, and use and the transport of commodities.

Census of Wholesale Trade
A census covering over 150 types of wholesale establishments containing information on business function, total sales, expenses, warehouse space, and other statistics broken out by county, city, and standard metropolitan area. Supplemented by *Monthly Wholesale Trade.*

County and City Databook
Statistics from various censuses aggregated by city and county. Includes demographic, educational, and financial, data manufacturing, retail, and wholesale sales; and agricultural production statistics.

County Business Patterns
Annual listing of employment and payroll business statistics indexed by county. A separate report exists for each state and one for the nation as a whole.

Directory of Federal Statistics for Local Areas: A Guide to Sources
Guide to the sources of federal statistics for cities and counties.

Directory of Federal Statistics for States: A Guide to Sources
Guide to the sources of federal statistics for states.

Directory of Nonfederal Statistics for State and Local Areas: A Guide to Sources
Guide to private, local, and state sources of statistics for cities and counties.

Factfinder for the Nation
Series of publications detailing the materials that are available from the Census Bureau on topics such as population, housing, and race.

Guide to Industrial Statistics
Guide to programs and statistical information available from the Census Bureau applicable to industrial uses.

Guide to 1990 Census Data on the Elderly
Guide detailing where to locate information from the 1990 census pertaining to the elderly.

Guide to the 1987 Economic Censuses and Related Statistics
A guide to the 1987 economic censuses, including information on possible uses, content, scope, classification system, and geographic detail. Descriptions of each census and its related surveys.

Highlights of U.S. Export and Import Trade
Monthly tables from the Bureau of Customs that give the unadjusted and seasonally adjusted data on U.S. international trade, listed by commodity group, nation, product use, U.S. customs region, and method of shipment.

Other Government Publications

Aging America—Trends and Projections
(Washington, DC: U.S. Senate Special Committee on Aging and the American Association of Retired Persons, U.S. Government Printing Office)
Report on the growth and characteristics of the elderly population over the next 30 years. Graphs and tables provide information on demographics, employment, health, and income.

Agricultural Statistics
(Washington, DC: U.S. Department of Agriculture, U.S. Government Printing Office)
Annual statistics on costs, consumption, prices, and production of U.S. agricultural productions.

A User's Guide to BEA Information
(Washington, DC: U.S. Bureau of Economic Analysis, U.S. Government Printing Office)

Directory of Bureau of Economic Analysis Information.

Business America
(Washington, DC: U.S. Department of Commerce, U.S. Government Printing Office)
Biweekly magazine of domestic and international commercial news.

Business Conditions Digest
(Washington, DC: U.S. Government Printing Office)
A monthly publication of indicators of current business activity in chart and table form.

Business Statistics
(Washington, DC: U.S. Department of Commerce, U.S. Government Printing Office)
Biannual publication giving the historical trends for data appearing in the *Survey of Current Business.*

Economic Indicators
(Washington, DC: Council of Economic Advisers, U.S. Government Printing Office)
Monthly publication of general economic statistics useful for measuring trends in business conditions.

Federal Reserve Bulletin
(Washington, DC: Federal Reserve System Board of Governors)
Monthly publication of financial data, including banking, department store sales, interest rates, prices, and savings.

Handbook of Basic Economic Statistics
(Washington, DC: Economic Statistics Bureau)
Monthly publication of data on the national economy compiled from more than 1,800 statistical series.

Handbook of Cyclical Indicators
(Washington, DC: U.S. Department of Commerce, U.S. Government Printing Office)
Monthly publication of indicators of business activity and economic conditions.

Index to International Business Publications
(Washington, DC: U.S. Domestic and International Business Administration, U.S. Government Printing Office)
Index to export market reports, foreign economic trends, global market surveys, and overseas business reports.

Index to Publications
(Washington, DC: U.S. Government Printing Office)
A quarterly publication of abstracts of congressional documents for all topics investigated by Congress.

Marketing Information Guide
(Washington, DC: U.S. Department of Commerce, U.S. Government Printing Office)
Monthly listing of current reports and statistics on marketing and distribution practices.

Measuring Markets: A Guide to the Use of Federal and State Statistical Data
(Washington, DC: U.S. Department of Commerce, U.S. Government Printing Office)
Guide to federal and state sources of statistical data.

Monthly Labor Review
(Washington, DC: U.S. Bureau of Labor Statistics, U.S. Government Printing Office)
Monthly listing of statistics on earnings, employment, hours worked, labor turnover, wholesale and retail prices, and work stoppages.

Standard Industrial Classification Manual
(Springfield, VA: U.S. Office of Management and Budget, U.S. Government Printing Office)
Manual containing the international classification of industrial products used by industry and government.

State and Metropolitan Area Databook
(Washington, DC: U.S. Department of Commerce, U.S. Government Printing Office)
Supplement to the *Statistical Abstract,* containing basic data on government, housing, manufacturing, population, retail and wholesale trade, and selected services aggregated by state and standard metropolitan statistical area.

Statistical Abstract of the United States
(Washington, DC: U.S. Bureau of the Census, U.S. Government Printing Office)
Annual compilation of over 1,400 statistical tables covering demographic, economic, political, and social topics.

Statistics of Income
(Washington, DC: Internal Revenue Service, U.S. Government Printing Office)
Series of publications prepared annually from federal income tax returns containing information on income, expenses, and assets. One publication for each tax category (corporations, sole proprietorships and partnerships, and individuals).

Survey of Current Business
(Washington, DC: U.S. Bureau of Economic Analysis, U.S. Government Printing Office)
Monthly publication of over 2,600 statistical series, covering business indicators, domestic trade, commodity prices, real estate, personal consumption expenditures by category, income, and employment.

United Nations Statistical Yearbook
(New York: United Nations)
Annual publication of statistics on economics, manufacturing, agriculture, and social indicators for U.N. member nations.

U.S. Industrial Outlook
(Washington, DC: Industrial Trade Administration, U.S. Department of Commerce, U.S. Government Printing Office)
Annual publication giving the recent trends and forecasts for over 350 manufacturing and service establishments.

World Almanac and Book of Facts
(New York: Newspaper Enterprise Association)
Annual collection of facts, including statistical tables on industrial, social, financial, and political variables.

Exploratory Research Design: Qualitative Research

The objective of qualitative research is to gain an understanding of the underlying reasons and motivations for people's attitudes, preferences, or behavior.

◆

OBJECTIVES

After reading this chapter, the student should be able to:

1. Explain the difference between qualitative and quantitative research in terms of the objectives, sampling, data collection and analysis, and outcomes.
2. Understand the various forms of qualitative research including direct procedures such as focus groups and depth interviews and indirect methods such as projective techniques.
3. Describe focus groups in detail, with emphasis on planning and conducting focus groups and on their advantages, disadvantages, and applications.
4. Describe depth interview techniques in detail, citing their advantages, disadvantages, and applications.
5. Explain projective techniques in detail and compare association, completion, construction, and expressive techniques.
6. Discuss the considerations involved in conducting qualitative research in an international setting.

7. Understand the ethical issues involved in conducting qualitative research.
8. Discuss the use of microcomputers and mainframes in obtaining and analyzing qualitative data.

OVERVIEW

Like secondary data analysis (see Chapter 4), qualitative research is a major methodology used in exploratory research (Chapter 3). Researchers undertake qualitative research to define the problem or to develop an approach (Chapter 2). In developing an approach, qualitative research is often used for generating hypotheses and identifying variables that should be included in the research. In cases where conclusive or quantitative research is not done, qualitative research and secondary data comprise the major part of the research project. In this chapter, we discuss the differences between qualitative and quantitative research and the role of each in the marketing research project. We present a classification of qualitative research and cover the major techniques—focus groups and depth interviews—in detail. We also consider the indirect procedures called projective techniques with emphasis on association, completion, construction, and expressive techniques. The considerations involved in conducting qualitative research when researching international markets are discussed. Several ethical issues that arise in qualitative research are identified. The chapter concludes with a discussion of the use of microcomputers in qualitative research. The following examples give a flavor of qualitative research and its applications in marketing research.

EXAMPLE
Focus on Big Business

Focus groups conducted by MCI revealed that consumers trusted the fact that businesses used MCI. Focus group participants evaluated services that were endorsed by big businesses as compared with those that were not (MCI's name was not mentioned). Even though people inherently distrust big business, they believe that something must be right if big businesses use a particular good or service; good businesses make good judgments. This discovery was the idea behind MCI's commercial entitled "Big Business." The commercial implied that MCI must be legitimate because more than 40,000 companies use it. The commercial first showed people in an office using MCI and stated, "Last year we saved big auto makers almost $2 million … all together 40,000 companies used us to cut their long-distance bills up to 50%." The commercial then showed people at home using MCI and stated how much MCI can save the home consumer. The commercial resulted in increased profits. Qualitative research, by providing insights into how consumers viewed long-distance calling, enabled MCI to design other successful advertising campaigns as well.[1] ◆

EXAMPLE
Spreckels Sugar Discovers a Sweet Packaging Idea

Recently, Spreckels Sugar Company began plans to reintroduce Spreckels as a consumer brand of granulated sugar after 20 years of refining and packaging sugar only for private-label grocery store brands on the West Coast. Faced with a commodity market,

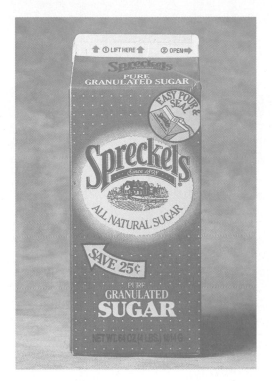

Vista Marketing Research of Oakland's RAM Group helped Spreckels conduct a series of depth interviews with light and heavy users of sugar. A team of three researchers sought to gain a better understanding of each consumer's attitudes and behaviors toward sugar. "If you are willing to take the time and energy to talk to thirty people for an hour each on a one-to-one basis, you get a complete understanding of the thought process of thirty consumers," Vista's managing director Tom McCarty said.

Spreckels's depth interviews uncovered subtle issues of packaged sugar's messiness, storage, and pourability. As a result, Spreckels found its market niche through new packaging, a stackable four-pound box with a top that pops into a gable-topped container like a milk carton. Spreckels sugar became the sugar that pours, seals, and stores easily.[2] ◆

Consumer needs discovered via depth interviews enabled Spreckles to develop a brand of sugar that pours, seals and stores easily. ◆ Churchill & Klehr.

EXAMPLE
I Heard It through the Grapevine

In a research project undertaken by Foote Cone and Belding, the advertising agency for the California Raisin Advisory Board, a major objective was to find out the personality of raisins. A projective technique was used, and the respondents were given a piece of paper that listed six snack foods: raisins, apples, granola bars, yogurt, cookies, and peanuts. They were asked to think of these six snack foods in terms of personality traits and people. The respondents were asked, "How would you describe these foods if they were people?" Raisin eaters described the raisin personality as powerful, special, up-to-date, good, old, and as a person who would have a lot of friends. Non–raisin eaters, on the other hand, described raisins as lonely, weak, boring, old, and ugly. Overall, both raisin eaters and non–raisin eaters described the fruit as healthy and energetic but also misunderstood. Both groups lacked an emotional attachment to raisins and said that raisins evoked negative imagery and connotations.

Foote Cone and Belding used the findings, after they were confirmed in subsequent research, to develop an advertising campaign for raisins. A clay animation technique called Claymation was used to create figures in the form of raisinlike human beings. To this was added the "I Heard It through the Grapevine" soundtrack. The campaign was very successful and resulted in an increase in raisin sales.[3] ◆

These examples illustrate the rich insights into the underlying behavior of consumers that can be obtained by using qualitative procedures.

PRIMARY DATA: QUALITATIVE VERSUS QUANTITATIVE RESEARCH

As explained in Chapter 4, primary data are originated by the researcher for the specific purpose of addressing the problem at hand. Primary data may be qualitative or quantitative in nature, as shown in Figure 5.1. The distinction between qualitative and quantitative research closely parallels the distinction between exploratory and conclusive research discussed in Chapter 3. The differences between the two research methodolo-

FIGURE 5.1

*A Classification
of Marketing
Research Data*

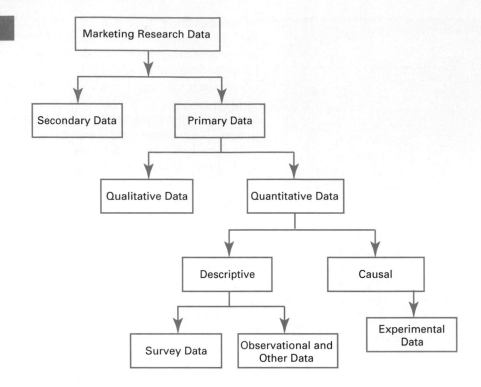

gies are summarized in Table 5.1.[4] **Qualitative research** provides insights and understanding of the problem setting, whereas **quantitative research** seeks to quantify the data and, typically, applies some form of statistical analysis. Whenever a new marketing research problem is being addressed, quantitative research must be preceded by appropriate qualitative research. Sometimes qualitative research is undertaken to explain the findings obtained from quantitative research. The findings of qualitative research are misused, however, when they are regarded as conclusive and are used to make generalizations to the population of interest.[5] It is a sound principle of marketing research to view qualitative and quantitative research as complementary, rather than in competition with each other.[6]

There is a story that Alfred Politz, a strong proponent of quantitative research, and Ernest Dichter, a strong proponent of qualitative research, were having their usual debate about the merits of the two methods. Politz stressed the importance of large-scale, projectable samples. Dichter answered, "But, Alfred, ten thousand times nothing is still

qualitative research An unstructured, exploratory research methodology based on small samples that provides insights and understanding of the problem setting.

quantitative research A research methodology that seeks to quantify the data and, typically, applies some form of statistical analysis.

TABLE 5.1

*Qualitative versus
Quantitative Research*

	Qualitative Research	Quantitative Research
Objective	To gain a qualitative understanding of the underlying reasons and motivations	To quantify the data and generalize the results from the sample to the population of interest
Sample	Small number of nonrepresentative cases	Large number of representative cases
Data collection	Unstructured	Structured
Data analysis	Nonstatistical	Statistical
Outcome	Develop an initial understanding	Recommend a final course of action

nothing!" As Dichter argued, mere quantification, when the underlying behavior of interest is not well understood, will not lead to meaningful results.[7]

RATIONALE FOR USING QUALITATIVE RESEARCH

There are several reasons to use qualitative research. It is not always possible, or desirable, to use fully structured or formal methods to obtain information from respondents (see Chapter 3). People may be unwilling or unable to answer certain questions. People are unwilling to give truthful answers to questions that invade their privacy, embarrass them, or have a negative impact on their ego or status. Examples of such sensitive questions include: "Have you recently purchased sanitary napkins? Drugs for nervous tension? Pills for anxiety?" Second, people may be unable to provide accurate answers to questions that tap their subconscious. The values, emotional drives, and motivations residing at the subconscious level are disguised from the outer world by rationalization and other ego defenses. For example, a person may have purchased an expensive sports car to overcome feelings of inferiority. But, if asked, "Why did you purchase this sports car?" he may say "I got a great deal," "My old car was falling apart," or "I need to impress my customers and clients." In such cases, the desired information can be best obtained through qualitative research by using one or more of the procedures described in the following section.[8]

A CLASSIFICATION OF QUALITATIVE RESEARCH PROCEDURES

direct approach One type of qualitative research in which the purposes of the project are disclosed to the respondent or are obvious given the nature of the interview.

A classification of qualitative research procedures is presented in Figure 5.2. These procedures are classified as either direct or indirect, based on whether the true purpose of the project is known to the respondents. A **direct approach** is not disguised. The purpose of the project is disclosed to the respondents or is otherwise obvious to them from the questions asked. Focus groups and depth interviews are the major direct techniques. In contrast, research that takes an **indirect approach** disguises the true purpose of the project. Projective techniques, the commonly used indirect techniques, consist of asso-

FIGURE 5.2

A Classification of Qualitative Research Procedures

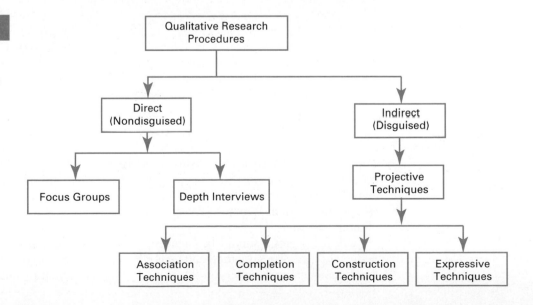

ciation, completion, construction, and expressive techniques. Each of these techniques is discussed in detail, beginning with focus groups.

FOCUS GROUP INTERVIEWS

indirect approach A type of qualitative research in which the purposes of the project are disguised from the respondents.

focus group An interview conducted by a trained moderator among a small group of respondents in an unstructured and natural manner.

A **focus group** is an interview conducted by a trained moderator in a nonstructured and natural manner with a small group of respondents. The moderator leads the discussion. The main purpose of focus groups is to gain insights by listening to a group of people from the appropriate target market talk about issues of interest to the researcher. The value of the technique lies in the unexpected findings often obtained from a free-flowing group discussion.

Focus groups are the most important qualitative research procedure. They are so popular that many marketing research practitioners consider this technique synonymous with qualitative research.[9] Several hundred facilities around the country now conduct focus groups several times a week, and as shown in Research in Practice 5.1, the typical focus group costs the client about $4,000. This adds up to more than $400 million a year.[10] Given their importance and popularity, we describe the salient characteristics of focus groups in detail.

A typical focus group session. ◆ Elrick and Lavidge.

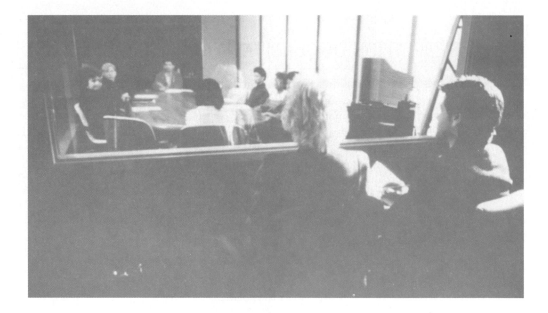

Characteristics

The major characteristics of a focus group are summarized in Table 5.2. A focus group generally includes eight to 12 members. Groups of fewer than eight are unlikely to generate the momentum and group dynamics necessary for a successful session. Likewise, groups of more than 12 may be too crowded and may not be conducive to a cohesive and natural discussion.[11]

A focus group should be homogeneous in terms of demographic and socioeconomic characteristics. Commonalty among group members avoids interactions and conflicts among group members on side issues.[12] Thus, a women's group should not combine

RESEARCH IN PRACTICE 5.1

Sample Costs of a Focus Group

Item	Cost
Developing outline and screening participants	$250
Moderator's fee	500
Facility rental, recruiting	800
Food	100
Respondent incentives ($30 × 10 people)	300
Analysis and report	500
	$2,450
Extras	
Videotaping	350
Travel costs for moderator and observers	1,200
Total	$4,000

married homemakers with small children, young unmarried working women, and elderly divorced or widowed women because their lifestyles are substantially different. Moreover, the participants should be carefully screened to meet certain criteria. The participants must have had adequate experience with the object or issue being discussed. People who have already participated in numerous focus groups should not be included. These so-called professional respondents are atypical, and their participation leads to serious validity problems.[13]

The physical setting for the focus group is also important. A relaxed, informal atmosphere encourages spontaneous comments. Light refreshments should be served before the session and made available throughout. Although a focus group may last from one to three hours, a duration of one and one-half to two hours is typical. This period is needed to establish rapport with the participants and to explore, in depth, their beliefs, feelings, ideas, attitudes and insights regarding the topics of concern. Focus group interviews are invariably recorded, often on videotape, for subsequent replay, transcription, and analysis. Videotaping has the advantage of recording facial expressions and body movements, but it can increase the costs significantly. Frequently, clients observe the session from an adjacent room using a one-way mirror. Video transmission technology enables the clients to observe focus group sessions live from a remote location.

The moderator plays a key role in the success of a focus group. The moderator must establish rapport with the participants, keep the discussion moving forward, and probe

TABLE 5.2 *Characteristics of Focus Groups*		
Group size	8–12	
Group composition	Homogeneous; respondents prescreened	
Physical setting	Relaxed, informal atmosphere	
Time duration	1–3 hours	
Recording	Use of audiocassettes and videotapes	
Moderator	Observational, interpersonal, and communication skills of the moderator	

the respondents to elicit insights. In addition, the moderator may have a central role in the analysis and interpretation of the data. Therefore, the moderator should possess skill, experience, knowledge of the discussion topic, and an understanding of the nature of group dynamics. The key qualifications of the moderator are summarized in Research in Practice 5.2.[14]

RESEARCH IN PRACTICE 5.2

Key Qualifications of Focus Group Moderators

1. *Kindness with firmness.* The moderator must combine a disciplined detachment with understanding empathy so as to generate the necessary interaction.
2. *Permissiveness.* The moderator must be permissive yet alert to signs that the group's cordiality or purpose is disintegrating.
3. *Involvement.* The moderator must encourage and stimulate intense personal involvement.
4. *Incomplete understanding.* The moderator must encourage respondents to be more specific about generalized comments by exhibiting incomplete understanding.
5. *Encouragement.* The moderator must encourage unresponsive members to participate.
6. *Flexibility.* The moderator must be able to improvise and alter the planned outline amid the distractions of the group process.
7. *Sensitivity.* The moderator must be sensitive enough to guide the group discussion at an intellectual as well as emotional level.

Planning and Conducting Focus Groups

The procedure for planning and conducting focus groups is described in Figure 5.3. Planning begins with an examination of the objectives of the marketing research project. In most instances, the problem has been defined by this stage, and if so, the general statement as well as the specific components of the problem should be carefully studied. Given the problem definition, the objectives of the qualitative research should be clearly specified, as illustrated by the department store patronage project.

DEPARTMENT STORE PATRONAGE PROJECT
Qualitative Research Objectives

In the department store study, the objectives of qualitative research were as follows:

1. Identify the relevant factors (choice criteria) used by households in selecting department stores.
2. Identify what consumers consider to be competing stores for specific product categories.
3. Identify the psychological characteristics of consumers likely to influence store patronage behavior.
4. Identify any other aspects of consumer choice behavior that may be relevant to store patronage. ◆

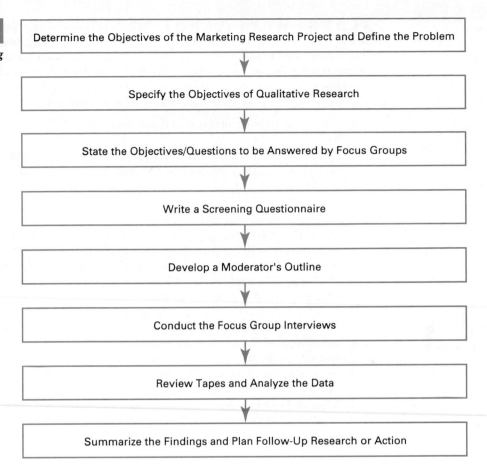

FIGURE 5.3

Procedure for Planning and Conducting Focus Groups

Determine the Objectives of the Marketing Research Project and Define the Problem

Specify the Objectives of Qualitative Research

State the Objectives/Questions to be Answered by Focus Groups

Write a Screening Questionnaire

Develop a Moderator's Outline

Conduct the Focus Group Interviews

Review Tapes and Analyze the Data

Summarize the Findings and Plan Follow-Up Research or Action

Note that these objectives are closely tied to the components of the department store problem defined in Chapter 2. The objectives must be specified before conducting any qualitative research, be it focus groups, depth interviews, or projective techniques.

The next step is to develop a detailed list of objectives for the focus group. This may take the form of a list of questions the researcher would like answered. Then a questionnaire to screen potential participants is prepared. Typical information obtained from the questionnaire includes product familiarity and knowledge, usage behavior, attitudes toward and participation in focus groups, and standard demographic characteristics.

A detailed moderator's outline for use during the focus group interview should be constructed. This involves extensive discussions among the researcher, client, and moderator. Because the moderator must be able to pursue important ideas when they are mentioned by participants, the moderator must understand the client's business, focus group objectives, and how the findings will be used. Use of a moderator's outline reduces some of the reliability problems inherent in focus groups, such as those caused by different moderators not covering the same content areas in comparable ways. Given its importance, we illustrate how a moderator's outline should be constructed using the department store example and the procedure developed by Arbor, Inc.[15]

DEPARTMENT STORE PATRONAGE PROJECT
The Moderator's Outline

Eighteen information requirements derived from attitude theory serve as the basis for developing the focus group moderator's guide. This example lists one of the several specific questions to be used for each information requirement.

1. Definition of significant classes of the attitude object. "What kinds of department stores are there?"
2. Brand awareness. "Which department stores are you familiar with?"
3. Evaluation of attitude objects. "Which department store is best, worst, and why?"
4. Situational contexts/relevant others. "How, when, and where do you shop for general merchandise?"
5. Weights of situational contexts/relevant others."When shopping in department stores for a gift, what is important?"
6. Evaluation of each attitude object in each situational context/relevant others. "Which department stores do you prefer when shopping for a gift, and why?"
7. Attributes of the attitude object for each situational context. "When you think about shopping, what features of the department store come to mind?"
8. Associations among attributes. "If a department store has liberal return policies, will it be more or less likely to offer high-quality products?"
9. Dimensions, level, and range of attributes. "When you say you want a high-quality product, what do you mean?"
10. Threshold of satisfaction. "What would be the features of a department store you consider satisfactory for shopping?"
11. Beliefs and opinions of brands on attributes, dimensions, and threshold of satisfaction. "Are discount department stores good enough for you to consider patronizing?"
12. Latitude of acceptance of beliefs and opinions. "Would you believe me if I said that the quality of the salespeople ultimately determines the image of a department store?"
13. Evaluation of attributes (salience). "For which of these things that you say you want in your department store would you be willing to pay more?"
14. Determination of values. "How would you characterize someone who is a good shopper?"
15. Hierarchy of values. "Would you rather be a good shopper or have more money to spend?"
16. Saliency of relationships between attributes and values. "You say you like a store that offers good value for money. What does that affect: your finances, your reputation as a shopper, or what?"
17. Attribute salience and latitude of acceptance as related to values. "How much do you think convenience of shopping can really affect your lifestyle?"
18. Category importance as related to value system. "How much time in an average month do you spend in department stores?" ◆

As can be seen, theory (Chapter 2) played an important role in developing the moderator's outline in the department store project. After a detailed outline is formulated, participants are recruited and the focus group interview conducted. During the interview, the moderator must (1) establish rapport with the group; (2) state the rules of group interaction; (3) set objectives; (4) probe the respondents and provoke intense discussion in the relevant areas; and (5) attempt to summarize the group's response to determine the extent of agreement.

Following the group discussion, either the moderator or an analyst reviews and analyzes the results. The analyst not only reports specific comments and findings but also looks for consistent responses, new ideas, concerns suggested by facial expressions and body language, and other hypotheses that may or may not have received confirmation from all the participants.

Because the number of participants is small, frequencies and percentages are not usually reported in a focus group summary. Instead, reports typically include expressions like "most participants thought" or "participants were divided on this issue." Meticulous documentation and interpretation of the session lay the groundwork for the final step: taking action. This usually means doing additional research.

The number of focus groups that should be conducted on a single subject depends on (1) the nature of the issue, (2) the number of distinct market segments, (3) the number of new ideas generated by each successive group, and (4) time and cost. Resources permitting, one should conduct additional discussion groups until the moderator can anticipate what will be said. This usually happens after three or four groups are conducted on the same topic.[16] It is recommended that at least two groups be conducted.[17] Properly conducted focus groups can generate important hypotheses that can serve as a basis for conducting quantitative research, as the following example indicates.

EXAMPLE

Automotive Association Assembles Hypotheses

The Automotive Parts and Accessories Association (APAA) set out to determine attitudes toward its member services by organizing a series of six focus groups, three in Chicago and three in Los Angeles. Each group represented a single segment of the membership: manufacturers, manufacturers' representatives, or retailers. Several hypotheses that came out of those focus groups struck APAA's leadership as particularly important. The following are some hypotheses of the focus groups. Hypotheses for association members are in parentheses.

- Focus group participants knew about the annual trade show but were ill-informed about other association benefits. (H1: The same would be true of association members.)
- The focus groups lambasted a proposal for new membership categories that association leadership had strongly approved. (H2: The same would be true of association members.)
- Participants said that they would get involved in legislative issues only when personally affected. (H3: The same would be true of association members.)
- The two focus groups made up of manufacturers' representatives complained that they were a "disenfranchised segment" of the association, receiving fewer special services than other occupational groups. (H4: The same would be true of other manufacturers' representatives.)

The focus group research became the basis of a mail questionnaire sent to a larger sample of members to test these hypotheses. Based on the results, programs were designed to educate the members about association benefits, and new services were offered. A special set of services was designed for the manufacturers' representatives.[18] ◆

Other Variations in Focus Groups

Focus groups can use several variations of the standard procedure. These include:

> *Two-way focus group.* This allows one target group to listen to and learn from a related group. In one application, physicians viewed a focus group of arthritis patients discussing the treatment they desired. A focus group of these physicians was then held to determine their reactions.[19]

> *Dual-moderator group.* This is a focus group interview conducted by two moderators. One moderator is responsible for the smooth flow of the session, and the other ensures that specific issues are discussed.

Dueling-moderator group. Here also there are two moderators, but they deliberately take opposite positions on the issues to be discussed. This allows the researcher to explore both sides of controversial issues.

Respondent-moderator group. In this type of focus group, the moderator asks selected participants to play the role of moderator temporarily to improve group dynamics.

Client-participant groups. Client personnel are identified and made part of the discussion group. Their primary role is to offer clarifications that will make the group process more effective.

Mini groups. These groups consist of a moderator and only four or five respondents. They are used when the issues of interest require more extensive probing than is possible in the standard group of 8 to 12.

Telesession groups. Focus group sessions by phone using conference calls.[20]

We conclude our section on focus groups with a discussion of the advantages and disadvantages.

Advantages and Disadvantages of Focus Groups

Focus groups offer several advantages over other data collection techniques. These may be summarized by the 10 Ss:[21]

1. *Synergism.* Putting a group of people together will produce a wider range of information, insight, and ideas than will individual responses secured privately.
2. *Snowballing.* A bandwagon effect often operates in a group interview in that one person's comment triggers a chain reaction from the other participants.
3. *Stimulation.* Usually after a brief introductory period, the respondents want to express their ideas and expose their feelings as the general level of excitement over the topic increases in the group.
4. *Security.* Because the participants' feelings are similar to those of other group members, they feel comfortable and are therefore willing to express their ideas and feelings.
5. *Spontaneity.* Because participants are not required to answer specific questions, their responses can be spontaneous and unconventional and should therefore provide an accurate idea of their views.
6. *Serendipity.* Ideas are more likely to arise out of the blue in a group than in an individual interview.
7. *Specialization.* Because a number of participants are involved simultaneously, use of a highly trained, but expensive, interviewer is justified.
8. *Scientific scrutiny.* The group interview allows close scrutiny of the data collection process in that observers can witness the session and it can be recorded for later analysis.
9. *Structure.* The group interview allows for flexibility in the topics covered and the depth with which they are treated.
10. *Speed.* Because a number of individuals are being interviewed at the same time, data collection and analysis proceed relatively quickly.

The disadvantages of focus groups may be summarized by the five Ms:

1. *Misuse.* Focus groups can be misused and abused by considering the results as conclusive rather than exploratory.
2. *Misjudge.* Focus group results can be more easily misjudged than the results of other data collection techniques. Focus groups are particularly susceptible to client and researcher biases.
3. *Moderation.* Focus groups are difficult to moderate. Moderators with all the desirable skills (see Research in Practice 5.2) are rare. The quality of the results depends heavily on the skills of the moderator.

4. *Messy.* The unstructured nature of the responses makes coding, analysis, and interpretation difficult. Focus group data tend to be messy.

5. *Misrepresentation.* Focus group results are not representative of the general population and are not projectable. Consequently, focus group results should not be the sole basis for decision making, as the following example illustrates.

EXAMPLE

Projecting the Unprojectable Projects Loss

A sophisticated insurance direct marketer conducted focus groups. The results were translated into clear-cut mail-order marketing strategies. Every single conclusion that grew out of the research, however, flopped. What happened? The insurance company made the mistake of trying to project the unprojectable.[22] ◆

This example illustrates a misuse and misrepresentation of focus groups. When properly conducted and used, however, focus groups have numerous applications.

Applications of Focus Groups

Focus groups can be used in almost any situation requiring some preliminary understanding and insights,[23] as illustrated in Research in Practice 5.3.[24] We will discuss some

RESEARCH IN PRACTICE 5.3

Use of Focus Groups at GM

The Buick division of General Motors used focus groups and survey research to help develop the Regal two-door, six-passenger coupe. Five years before the introduction, Buick held 20 focus groups across the country to determine what features customers wanted in a car. These focus groups told GM that customers wanted a legitimate back seat, at least 20 miles per gallon, and 0 to 60 miles per hour acceleration in 11 seconds or less. They wanted a stylish car, but they did not want it to look like it had landed from outer space.

Based on the focus group results, which were confirmed in subsequent research, Buick engineers then created clay models of the car and mock-ups of the interior. The company then went to another set of focus groups of target buyers. These respondents did not like the oversized bumpers and the severe slope of the hood, but liked the four-wheel disc brakes and independent suspension.

Focus groups also helped refine the advertising campaign for the Regal. Participants were asked which competing cars most resembled the Buick in image and features. The answer was Oldsmobile, a sister GM division. In an effort to differentiate the two, Buick was repositioned above Oldsmobile by focusing on comfort and luxury features.

Focus groups were shown four ad concepts in the form of prototype TV commercials and printed ad slicks and asked which were most effective. This led to the advertising theme "the new Buick Regal. There's nothing like it on the American Road."

substantive and methodological applications that represent the wide range of use of this technique.[25] Focus groups can be used to address substantive issues such as

1. Understanding consumers' perceptions, preferences, and behavior concerning a product category
2. Obtaining impressions of new product concepts
3. Generating new ideas about older products
4. Developing creative concepts and copy material for advertisements
5. Securing price impressions
6. Obtaining preliminary consumer reaction to specific marketing programs

The methodological applications of focus groups include:

1. Defining a problem more precisely
2. Generating alternative courses of action
3. Developing an approach to a problem
4. Obtaining information helpful in structuring consumer questionnaires
5. Generating hypotheses that can be tested quantitatively
6. Interpreting previously obtained quantitative results

DEPTH INTERVIEWS

depth interview An unstructured, direct, personal interview in which a single respondent is probed by a highly skilled interviewer to uncover underlying motivations, beliefs, attitudes, and feelings on a topic.

Depth interviews are another method of obtaining qualitative data. We describe the general procedure for conducting depth interviews and then illustrate some specific techniques. The advantages, disadvantages, and applications of depth interviews are also discussed.

Characteristics

Like focus groups, depth interviews are an unstructured and direct way of obtaining information, but unlike focus groups, depth interviews are conducted on a one-on-one basis. A depth interview is an unstructured, direct, personal interview in which a single respondent is probed by a highly skilled interviewer to uncover underlying motivations, beliefs, attitudes, and feelings on a topic.[26]

A depth interview may take from 30 minutes to more than one hour. To illustrate the technique in the context of the department store example, the interviewer begins by asking a general question such as, "How do you feel about shopping at department stores?" The interviewer then encourages the subject to talk freely about his or her attitudes toward department stores. After asking the initial question, the interviewer uses an unstructured format. The subsequent direction of the interview is determined by the respondent's initial reply, the interviewer's probes for elaboration, and the respondent's answers. Suppose that the respondent replies to the initial question by saying, "Shopping isn't fun anymore." The interviewer might then pose a question such as "Why isn't it fun anymore?" If the answer is not very revealing ("Fun has just disappeared from shopping"), the interviewer may ask a probing question, such as "Why was it fun before and what has changed?"

Although the interviewer attempts to follow a rough outline, the specific wording of the questions and the order in which they are asked is influenced by the subject's replies. Probing is of critical importance in obtaining meaningful responses and uncovering hidden issues. Probing is done by asking such questions as "Why do you say that?" "That's interesting, can you tell me more?" or "Would you like to add anything else?"[27] Probing is further discussed in Chapter 13 on field work. The value of information uncovered by probing is shown in the following example.

EXAMPLE
Probing for Intelligence

In a study designed to come up with new credit card features, when questioned in a structured way, respondents merely listed features of existing credit cards. Then depth interviews were employed to probe the respondents. For example, the interviewer asked respondents to ask themselves, "What is important to me? What problems do I have? How do I wish I could live?" As a result of this method, consumers relayed information they had previously been unaware of, and several new credit card features surfaced. The study uncovered the need for an "intelligent" credit card that could perform such tasks as keeping track of credit card and bank balances and emergency telephone numbers.[28] ◆

Qualitative research techniques such as depth interviews have played a major role in the design of credit card features. ◆ Chase Manhattan Bank.

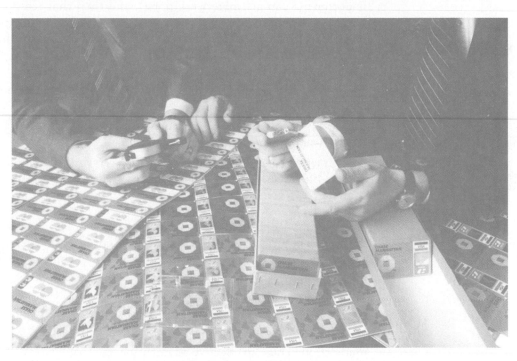

As this example indicates, probing is effective in uncovering underlying or hidden information. Probing is an integral part of depth interviews and is used in all depth interviewing techniques.

Techniques

laddering A technique for conducting depth interviews in which a line of questioning proceeds from product characteristics to user characteristics.

Three depth interviewing techniques that have recently gained popularity are laddering, hidden issue questioning, and symbolic analysis. In **laddering**, the line of questioning proceeds from product characteristics to user characteristics. This technique allows the

hidden issue questioning
A type of depth interview that attempts to locate personal sore spots related to deeply felt personal concerns.

symbolic analysis A technique for conducting depth interviews in which the symbolic meaning of objects is analyzed by comparing them with their opposites.

researcher to tap into the consumer's network of meanings. In **hidden issue questioning**, the focus is not on socially shared values but rather on personal "sore spots," not on general lifestyles but on deeply felt personal concerns. **Symbolic analysis** attempts to analyze the symbolic meaning of objects by comparing them with their opposites. To learn what something is, the researcher attempts to learn what it is not. The logical opposites of a product that are investigated are nonusage of the product, attributes of an imaginary "nonproduct," and opposite types of products. The three techniques are illustrated with the following example.

EXAMPLE
Hidden Issues and Hidden Dimensions in Air Travel

In this study, the researcher was investigating attitudes toward airlines among male middle-managers.

Laddering.

Each airline attribute, such as wide-body aircraft, was probed to determine why it was important (I can get more work done), and then that reason was probed (I accomplish more), and so on (I feel good about myself). Laddering indicated that managers preferred advance seat reservation, wide-body aircraft, and first-class cabin seating that resulted in greater physical comfort. This enabled them to get more work done while on the flight, leading to a sense of accomplishment and higher self-esteem. This technique showed that an advertising campaign, such as the old United Airlines campaign of "You're the Boss," that bolsters the self-esteem of the managers is worthy of consideration.

Hidden issue questioning.

Respondents were questioned about fantasies, work lives, and social lives to identify hidden life issues. The answers indicated that glamorous, historic, elite, "masculine-camaraderie," competitive activities—like Grand Prix car racing, fencing, and World War II airplane dog fighting—were of personal interest to the managers. These interests could be tapped with an advertising campaign like the one by Lufthansa German Airlines featuring a World War I–type "Red Baron" spokesperson. That campaign communicated the aggressiveness, high status, and competitive heritage of the airline.

Symbolic analysis.

Questions asked included "What would it be like if you could no longer use airplanes?" Responses like, "Without planes, I would have to rely on letters and long-distance calls" were received. This suggests that what airlines sell to the managers is face-to-face communication. Thus, an effective ad might be one that guarantees that the airline will do the same thing for a manager as FedEx does for a package.

Information revealed by these techniques can be used effectively to position an airline and to design appropriate advertising and communication strategies.[29] ◆

The interviewer's role is critical to the success of the depth interview. The interviewer should (1) avoid appearing superior and put the respondent at ease, (2) be detached and objective yet personable, (3) ask questions in an informative manner, (4) not accept brief yes or no answers, and (5) probe the respondent.

Advantages and Disadvantages of Depth Interviews

Depth interviews can uncover greater depth of insights than focus groups. Also, depth interviews attribute the responses directly to the respondent, unlike focus groups where it is often difficult to determine which respondent made a particular response. Depth interviews result in free exchange of information that may not be possible in focus groups because there is no social pressure to conform to group response.

Depth interviews suffer from many of the disadvantages of focus groups, and often to a greater extent. Skilled interviewers capable of conducting depth interviews are expensive and difficult to find. The lack of structure makes the results susceptible to the interviewer's influence, and the quality and completeness of the results depend heavily on the interviewer's skills. The data obtained are difficult to analyze and interpret, and the services of skilled psychologists are typically required for this purpose. The length of the interview combined with high costs means that the number of depth interviews in a project will be small. Despite these disadvantages, depth interviews do have some applications.

Applications of Depth Interviews

As with focus groups, the primary use of depth interviews is for exploratory research to gain insights and understanding. Unlike focus groups, however, depth interviews are used infrequently in marketing research. Nevertheless, depth interviews can be effectively employed in special problem situations, such as those requiring the following:[30]

1. Detailed probing of the respondent (automobile purchase)
2. Discussion of confidential, sensitive, or embarrassing topics (personal finances; loose dentures)
3. Situations where strong social norms exist and where the respondent may be easily swayed by group response (attitude of college students toward sports)
4. Detailed understanding of complicated behavior (department store shopping)
5. Interviews with professional people (industrial marketing research)
6. Interviews with competitors, who are unlikely to reveal the information in a group setting (travel agents' perceptions of airline package travel programs)
7. Situations where the product consumption experience is sensory in nature, affecting mood states and emotions (perfumes, bath soap)

The following example illustrates a case in which depth interviews were particularly helpful.

EXAMPLE
Soaps Look for a Fresh Way to Work Consumers into a Lather

In studies of bath soaps, respondents invariably say that a good soap makes them feel "clean and fresh" after a shower. They often have difficulty explaining what that means to them, however. Copywriters trying to find a new way to talk about freshness in their advertising do not find such data helpful. Hence, the respondents were probed via depth interviews about all the things "clean and fresh" meant to them: the times they felt this way, their mental pictures, the moods and feelings connected with it, what music and colors come to mind, and even what fantasies this term evoked.

Escape from ordinary life was one of the main themes that emerged from the depth interviews: getting away from the cramped, rushed city to being free, relaxed, unhindered, and surrounded by nature in the country. The words and images sparked by this theme offered new ideas for creative advertising, resulting in a successful campaign that was refreshingly different from competition.[31] ◆

This example illustrates the value of depth interviews in uncovering the hidden responses that underlie the clichés elicited in ordinary questioning.

PROJECTIVE TECHNIQUES

projective technique An unstructured and indirect form of questioning that encourages respondents to project their underlying motivations, beliefs, attitudes, or feelings regarding the issues of concern.

Both focus groups and depth interviews are direct approaches in which the true purpose of the research is disclosed to the respondents or is otherwise obvious to them. Projective techniques are different from these techniques in that they attempt to disguise the purpose of the research. A **projective technique** is an unstructured, indirect form of questioning that encourages respondents to project their underlying motivations, beliefs, attitudes, or feelings regarding the issues of concern.[32] In projective techniques, respondents are asked to interpret the behavior of others rather than to describe their own behavior. In interpreting the behavior of others, respondents indirectly project their own motivations, beliefs, attitudes, or feelings into the situation. Thus, the respondent's attitudes are uncovered by analyzing their responses to scenarios that are deliberately unstructured, vague, and ambiguous. The more ambiguous the situation, the more respondents project their emotions, needs, motives, attitudes, and values, as demonstrated by work in clinical psychology on which projective techniques are based.[33] As in psychology, these techniques are classified as association, completion, construction, and expressive. Each of these classifications is discussed.[34]

Association Techniques

association techniques A type of projective technique in which respondents are presented with a stimulus and are asked to respond with the first thing that comes to mind.

word association A projective technique in which respondents are presented with a list of words, one at a time. After each word, they are asked to give the first word that comes to mind.

In **association techniques**, an individual is presented with a stimulus and asked to respond with the first thing that comes to mind. **Word association** is the best known of these techniques. In word association, respondents are presented with a list of words, one at a time, and are asked to respond to each with the first word that comes to mind. The words of interest, called test words, are interspersed throughout the list, which also contains some neutral, or filler, words to disguise the purpose of the study. For example, in the department store study, some of the test words might be: *location, parking, shopping, quality,* and *price.* The subject's response to each word is recorded verbatim and responses are timed so that respondents who hesitate or reason out (defined as taking longer than three seconds to reply) can be identified. The interviewer, not the respondent, records the responses. This controls for the time required for the respondent to write the response.

The underlying assumption of this technique is that association allows respondents to reveal their inner feelings about the topic of interest. Responses are analyzed by calculating (1) the frequency with which any word is given as a response, (2) the amount of time that elapses before a response is given, and (3) the number of respondents who do not respond at all to a test word within a reasonable period of time. Those who do not respond at all are judged to have an emotional involvement so high that it blocks a response. It is often possible to classify the associations as favorable, unfavorable, or neutral. An individual's pattern of responses and the details of the response are used to determine the person's underlying attitudes or feelings on the topic of interest, as shown in the following example.

EXAMPLE

Dealing with Dirt

Word association was used to study women's attitudes toward detergents. Below is a list of stimulus words used and the responses of two women of similar age and household status. The set of responses are quite different, suggesting that the women differ in personality and in their attitudes toward housekeeping. Ms. M's associations suggest that she is resigned to dirt. She sees dirt as inevitable and does not do much about it. She does not do hard cleaning, nor does she get pleasure from her family. Ms. C sees dirt too, but is energetic, factual-minded, and less emotional. She is actively ready to combat dirt, and she uses soap and water as her weapons.[35]

STIMULUS	MS. M	MS. C
washday	everyday	ironing
fresh	and sweet	clean
pure	air	soiled
scrub	does not; husband does	clean
filth	this neighborhood	dirt
bubbles	bath	soap and water
family	squabbles	children
towels	dirty	wash

These findings suggest that the market for detergents could be segmented on the basis of attitudes. Firms (such as Procter & Gamble) that market several different brands of detergents (Tide, Cheer, Gain, Bold, etc.) could benefit from positioning different brands for different attitudinal segments. ◆

Procter & Gamble has positioned different detergent brands for different attitudinal segments. ◆ Teri Stratford.

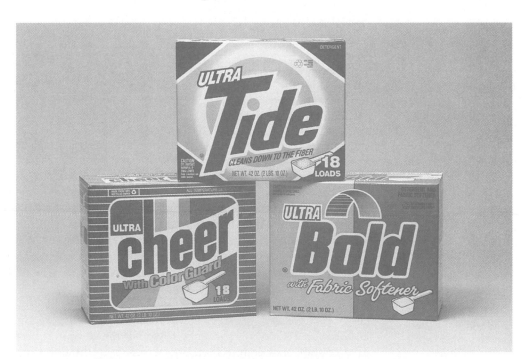

There are several variations to the standard word association procedure illustrated here. Respondents may be asked to give the first two, three, or four words that come to mind rather than only the first word. This technique can also be used in controlled tests, as contrasted with free association. In controlled tests, respondents might be asked, "What department stores come to mind first when I mention high-quality merchandise?" More detailed information can be obtained from completion techniques, which are a natural extension of association techniques.

Completion Techniques

completion technique A projective technique that requires respondents to complete an incomplete stimulus situation.

In **completion techniques**, respondents are asked to complete an incomplete stimulus situation. Common completion techniques in marketing research are sentence completion and story completion.

sentence completion A projective technique in which respondents are presented with a number of incomplete sentences and are asked to complete them.

Sentence Completion   **Sentence completion** is similar to word association. Respondents are given incomplete sentences and are asked to complete them. Generally, they are asked to use the first word or phrase that comes to mind, as illustrated in the department store patronage project.

DEPARTMENT STORE PATRONAGE PROJECT

Sentence Completion _____

In the context of the store patronage study, the following incomplete sentences may be used.

A person who shops at Sears is

_____

A person who receives a gift certificate good for Saks Fifth Avenue would be

_____

J.C. Penney is most liked by

_____

When I think of shopping in a department store, I

_____ ◆

This example illustrates one advantage of sentence completion over word association: Respondents can be provided with a more directed stimulus. Sentence completion may provide more information about the subjects' feelings than word association. Sentence completion is not as disguised as word association, however, and many respondents may be able to guess the purpose of the study. A variation of sentence completion is paragraph completion, in which the respondent completes a paragraph beginning with the stimulus phrase. A further expanded version of sentence completion and paragraph completion is story completion.

story completion A projective technique in which respondents are provided with part of a story and are required to give the conclusion in their own words.

Story Completion   In **story completion**, respondents are given part of a story, enough to direct attention to a particular topic but not to hint at the ending. They are required to give the conclusion in their own words, as in the following example.

DEPARTMENT STORE PATRONAGE PROJECT
Story Completion

A man was shopping for a business suit in his favorite department store. After spending 45 minutes trying on several suits, he finally picked one he liked. As he was proceeding to the checkout counter, he was approached by the salesclerk, who said, "Sir, at this time we have higher-quality suits on sale for the same price. Would you like to see them?"

What is the customer's response? Why? ◆

The respondent's completion of this story will reveal the relative value he or she places on the time spent selecting merchandise and the emotional investment he or she makes in the shopping.

Construction Techniques

construction technique A projective technique in which respondents are required to construct a response in the form of a story, dialogue, or description.

Construction techniques are closely related to completion techniques. Construction techniques require the respondents to construct a response in the form of a story, dialogue, or description. In a construction technique, the researcher provides less initial structure to the respondents than in a completion technique. The two main construction techniques are picture response techniques and cartoon tests.

picture response technique A projective technique in which respondents are shown a picture and are asked to tell a story describing it.

Picture Response Techniques   The roots of **picture response techniques** can be traced to the thematic apperception test (TAT), which consists of a series of pictures of ordinary as well as unusual events. In some of these pictures, the persons or objects are clearly depicted, while in others they are relatively vague. The respondent is asked to tell stories about these pictures. The respondent's interpretation of the pictures gives indications of that individual's personality. For example, an individual may be characterized as impulsive, creative, unimaginative, and so on. The term *thematic apperception test* is used because themes are elicited based on the subject's perceptual interpretation (apperception) of pictures.

In marketing research uses of picture response techniques, respondents are shown a picture and asked to tell a story describing it. The responses are used to evaluate attitudes toward the topic and describe the respondents, as illustrated by the following.

EXAMPLE
"Gimme a Double Shake and a Lard on White"

The light and healthy craze seems to be dying down for one segment of the population. In response to direct questioning, consumers are hesitant to say that they want food that is bad for them. This finding, however, emerged in a picture response test in which the respondents were asked to describe a picture depicting people consuming high-fat food rich in calories. A significant number of the respondents defended the behavior of the people in the picture by explaining that the increased stress in everyday life has caused people to turn from tasteless rice cakes to comfort foods, loaded with the ingredients that make life worth living.

Many marketers have capitalized upon this finding by introducing products that contain large amounts of salt, fat, and calories. Haagen-Dazs has recently introduced a

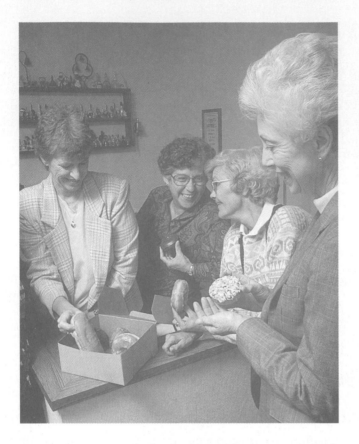

new line of deluxe ice creams called Extraas. The flavors include the new Triple Brownie Overload packed with fresh cream, sugar, chocolate liquor, butter, pecans, and egg yolks. The Extraas line has increased Haagen-Dazs's market share from 5.9 to 7.9%.

Another example of increased sales of "bad-for-you" food is the growth of the new Wendy's burgers packed with fried chicken, bacon, and loads of cheese. These burgers are outselling the more healthy, grilled chicken sandwiches by a margin of three to one.

Pepperidge Farm had recently introduced its own bid for the comfort food market, no-calories-barred soft-baked cookies with about 40% of the calories coming from fat. Recently launched, the new line is already the third biggest seller for the company.[36] ◆

Picture response techniques reveal that increased stress in everyday life has caused some people to turn to comfort foods, loaded with high fat and rich in calories. ◆ Tony Freeman/PhotoEdit.

Cartoon Tests   In **cartoon tests**, cartoon characters are shown in a specific situation related to the problem. Respondents are asked to indicate what one cartoon character might say in response to the comments of another character. The responses indicate the respondents' feelings, beliefs, and attitudes toward the situation. Cartoon tests are simpler to administer and analyze than picture response techniques. An example is shown in Figure 5.4.

FIGURE 5.4

A Cartoon Test

Expressive Techniques

cartoon tests Cartoon characters are shown in a specific situation related to the problem. Respondents are asked to indicate the dialogue that one cartoon character might make in response to the comment(s) of another character.

expressive techniques Projective techniques in which respondents are presented with a verbal or visual situation and are asked to relate the feelings and attitudes of other people to the situation.

role playing Respondents are asked to assume the behavior of someone else.

third-person technique A projective technique in which respondents are presented with a verbal or visual situation and are asked to relate the beliefs and attitudes of a third person to the situation.

In **expressive techniques**, respondents are presented with a verbal or visual situation and asked to relate the feelings and attitudes of other people to the situation. The respondents express not their own feelings or attitudes, but those of others. The two main expressive techniques are role playing and third-person technique.

Role Playing   In **role playing**, respondents are asked to play the role or to assume the behavior of someone else. The researcher assumes that the respondents will project their own feelings into the role. These can then be uncovered by analyzing the responses, as shown in the department store patronage project.[37]

DEPARTMENT STORE PATRONAGE PROJECT
Role Playing

Respondents are asked to play the role of a manager handling consumer complaints. How the role players handle the complaints reveals their feelings and attitudes toward shopping. Respondents who treat complaining customers with respect and courtesy indicate that they, as customers, expect these attitudes from the store management. ◆

Third-Person Technique   In the **third-person technique**, respondents are presented with a verbal or visual situation and are asked to relate the beliefs and attitudes of a third person rather than directly expressing personal beliefs and attitudes. This third person may be a friend, a neighbor, a colleague, or a "typical" person. Again, the researcher assumes that the respondents will reveal personal beliefs and attitudes while describing the reactions of a third party. Asking an individual to respond in the third person reduces the social pressure to give an acceptable answer, as the following example shows.

EXAMPLE
What Will the Neighbors Say?

A study was performed for a commercial airline to understand why some people do not fly. When the respondents were asked, "Are you afraid to fly?" very few people said yes. The major reasons given for not flying were cost, inconvenience, and delays caused by bad weather. It was suspected, however, that the answers were heavily influenced by the need to give socially desirable responses. Therefore, a follow-up study was done. In the second study, the respondents were asked, "Do you think your neighbor is afraid to fly?" The answers indicated that most of the neighbors who traveled by some other means of transportation were afraid to fly.[38] ◆

Note that asking the question in the first person ("Are you afraid to fly?") did not elicit the true response. Phrasing the same question in the third person ("Do you think your neighbor is afraid to fly?") lowered the respondent's defenses and resulted in truthful answers. In a popular version of the third-person technique the researcher presents the respondent with a description of a shopping list and asks for a characterization of the purchaser.[39]

We conclude our discussion of projective techniques by describing their advantages, disadvantages, and applications.

Advantages and Disadvantages of Projective Techniques

Projective techniques have a major advantage over the unstructured direct techniques (focus groups and depth interviews): they may elicit responses that subjects would be unwilling or unable to give if they knew the purpose of the study. At times, in direct questioning, the respondent may intentionally or unintentionally misunderstand, misinterpret, or mislead the researcher. In these cases, projective techniques can increase the validity of responses by disguising the purpose. This is particularly true when the issues to be addressed are personal, sensitive, or subject to strong social norms. Projective techniques are also helpful when underlying motivations, beliefs, and attitudes are operating at a subconscious level.[40]

Projective techniques suffer from many of the disadvantages of unstructured direct techniques, but to a greater extent. These techniques generally require personal interviews with highly trained interviewers. Skilled interpreters are also required to analyze the responses. Hence, they tend to be expensive. Furthermore, there is a serious risk of interpretation bias. With the exception of word association, all are open-ended techniques, making the analysis and interpretation difficult and subjective.

Some projective techniques such as role playing require respondents to engage in unusual behavior. In such cases, the researcher may assume that respondents who agree to participate are themselves unusual in some way. Therefore, they may not be representative of the population of interest. As a result, it is desirable to compare findings generated by projective techniques with the findings of the other techniques that permit a more representative sample. Table 5.3 gives a relative comparison of focus groups, depth interviews, and projective techniques.

Applications of Projective Techniques

Projective techniques are used less frequently than unstructured direct methods (focus groups and depth interviews). A possible exception may be word association, which is commonly used to test brand names and occasionally to measure attitudes about particular products, brands, packages, or advertisements. As the examples have shown, projective techniques can be used in a variety of situations. The usefulness of these techniques is enhanced when the following guidelines are observed.

1. Projective techniques should be used because the required information cannot be accurately obtained by direct methods.

TABLE 5.3

A Comparison of Focus Groups, Depth Interviews, and Projective Techniques

Criteria	Focus Groups	Depth Interviews	Projective Techniques
Degree of structure	Relatively high	Relatively medium	Relatively low
Probing of individual respondents	Low	High	Medium
Moderator bias	Relatively medium	Relatively high	Low to high
Interpretation bias	Relatively low	Relatively medium	Relatively high
Uncovering subconscious information	Low	Medium to high	High
Discovering innovative information	High	Medium	Low
Obtaining sensitive information	Low	Medium	High
Involve unusual behavior or questioning	No	To a limited extent	Yes
Overall usefulness	Highly Useful	Useful	Somewhat useful

2. Projective techniques should be used for exploratory research to gain initial insights and understanding.
3. Given their complexity, projective techniques should not be used naively.

Given these guidelines, projective techniques along with other qualitative techniques can yield valuable information.[41]

INTERNATIONAL MARKETING RESEARCH

Because the researcher is often not familiar with the foreign product market to be examined, qualitative research is crucial in international marketing research. In the initial stages of cross-national research, qualitative research can provide insights into the problem and help in developing an approach by generating relevant research questions and hypotheses, models, and characteristics that influence the research design. Thus, qualitative research may reveal the differences between the foreign and domestic markets. Focus groups can be used in many settings, particularly in industrialized countries. The moderator should not only be trained in focus group methodology but should also be familiar with the language, culture, and patterns of social interaction prevailing in that country. The focus group findings should be derived not only from the verbal contents but also from nonverbal cues such as voice intonations, inflections, expressions, and gestures.[42] In some countries, in the Middle East or Far East, people are hesitant to discuss their feelings in a group setting. In these cases, depth interviews should be used. The following example highlights the importance of cultural differences in qualitative research.

EXAMPLE
Bugs Bug British

Culture is a very important determinant of how qualitative research, such as focus groups, should be conducted. In focus group discussions in the United Kingdom, it is not easy to make a housewife admit that her house has cockroaches. To do this, the moderator must reassure her that everyone else also has that problem. In France, just the opposite occurs: the respondents start to chatter away about cockroaches within seconds of sitting down. Thus, to determine underlying attitudes toward cockroaches, depth interviews should be used in the United Kingdom and focus group in France. The cultural attitudes greatly influence which qualitative research techniques should be used and how they should be implemented.[43] ◆

The use of projective techniques in international marketing research should be carefully considered. Association techniques (word association), completion techniques (sentence completion, story completion), and expressive techniques (role playing, third-person technique) involve the use of verbal cues. Construction techniques (picture response and cartoon tests) employ nonverbal stimuli (pictures). Whether verbal or nonverbal stimuli are used, the equivalence of meaning across the cultures should be established. This can be a difficult task if the sociocultural environments in which the research is conducted vary greatly. Establishing the equivalence of pictures can be particularly problematic. Line drawings are subject to fewer problems of interpretation than photographs.[44] Techniques employing verbal cues, such as word association, however, can be applied with greater ease, as illustrated in the following.

EXAMPLE
What They Think of US

The theme of this study was to determine the attitude of Japanese consumers toward foreign countries. Respondents were asked to think any word or association that came to mind spontaneously. The foreign countries and states or cities were: America, California, Los Angeles, New York, and Canada. The following were the associated words and associated products.

America	California	Los Angeles	New York	Canada
		Associated Words		
Reagan, great, power, Statue of Liberty, large and wide	oranges, fruit sunshine, ocean	Disneyland, metropolis, skyscrapers, Olympics	skyscrapers Statue of Liberty, Manhattan metropolis	forests, nature, timber, mountains
		Associated Products		
cars, beef, oranges, wheat, corn	oranges, fruit, grapefruit, raisins, wine	cars, oranges, fruit, grapefruit, clothes	clothes, cars, accessories, fashion	lumber, salmon, furs, wheat, cardigan

Such product-related word associations helped American marketers better understand the Japanese consumer's perception toward foreign countries in general. Thus, the California Orange Growers Association can promote its fruits to the Japanese via commercials that feature ocean and beach scenes with plenty of sunshine. On the other hand, a marketer of fashion clothing in New York could enhance the product appeal by featuring skyscrapers of Manhattan or the Statue of Liberty. ◆

The usual limitations of qualitative techniques also apply in the international context, perhaps to a greater extent. It is often difficult to find trained moderators and interviewers overseas. The development of appropriate coding, analysis, and interpretation procedures poses additional difficulties.

ETHICS IN MARKETING RESEARCH

The researcher and the client must respect the respondents when conducting qualitative research. This should include protecting the anonymity of respondents, not misleading or deceiving them, conducting research in a way not to embarrass or harm the respondents, and using the research results in an ethical manner.[45]

Many client managers believe that because they are footing the bill, they should be able to sit in on and observe a focus group or depth interview. However, the respondents' participation may be biased if they are aware of the client's presence. Therefore, some qualitative researchers allow their clients to observe a group discussion by introducing them as colleagues helping with the project. This deception raises ethical concerns related to the preservation of the respondents' anonymity. Some researchers may believe that this deception is small and acceptable because the respondent will not find out. It has been shown, however, that when introduced in this way, many participants accurately conclude that the observer is in fact the client. The mistrust generated by this interaction hurts the integrity of marketing research. The Marketing Research Society's code reads, respondents "must be assured that no information which could be used to identify them will be made available without their agreement to anyone outside the agency responsible for conducting the research."[46]

Ethical questions also arise when videotaping sessions with the respondents. Some of the pertinent questions are how much to tell participants and when should the clients be allowed access. When videotaping groups, regardless of whether or not they were aware of the camera during the meeting, at the end of the meeting, participants should be asked to sign a written declaration conveying their permission to use the recording. This declaration should disclose the full purpose of the video, including who will be able to view it. If any respondent refuses, the tape should either be destroyed or edited to omit that respondent's identity and comments completely.

The researcher should be sensitive to the comfort level of the respondents and respect for the participants should warrant restraint. Sometimes respondents should be allowed to hold back during qualitative research and, especially, depth interviews. When a respondent feels uncomfortable and does not wish to go on, the researcher should not aggressively probe or confront any further. It has also been suggested that respondents should be allowed to reflect on all they have said at the end of the interview and should be given the opportunity to ask questions. This may help return the respondents to their pre-interview emotional state. A final issue relates to the ethics of using qualitative research results for questionable purposes, as in the Bush campaign profiled below.

EXAMPLE
Focus (Groups) on Mudslinging _____

The ethics of negative or "attack" ads have been debated for some time. The focus, however, has shifted from the ads themselves to the ethics of employing marketing research techniques to design the ad message. Nowhere is this phenomenon more prevalent than in political "mudslinging" campaigns. In particular, the Bush campaign against Dukakis in the 1988 U.S. presidential election has been cited. In designing negative ads about Dukakis, Bush campaign leaders tested negative information about Dukakis in focus groups. The idea was to develop some insight into how the American public would react if this negative information was released in the form of advertisements. Negative issues that elicited very negative emotions from the focus groups were chosen for Bush's political advertising. The result? After he was painted "as an ineffectual, weak, liberal, do-gooder lacking in common sense," Dukakis lost the election by a wide margin.[47] ◆

COMPUTER APPLICATIONS
_____

Microcomputers and mainframes can be used to select and screen respondents in qualitative research. A computerized system can maintain and manage respondent files, storing information on a large number of demographic and other characteristics for each respondent. Thus, respondents who meet stated criteria can be easily and quickly identified, and recruiting forms, confirmation letters, and sign-in sheets can be automatically generated. An example is Focus FMS, a focus group management system. This microcomputer software, developed by ECF Systems Development, has the following features:

1. It replaces respondent file cards with a completely menu-driven computer system.
2. It enables the researcher to search respondent files on 40 demographic criteria.
3. It identifies and eliminates professional respondents.
4. It eliminates the problem of respondents attending more than one group session for the same client.
5. The recruiting status of the group can be reviewed at a glance.
6. It automatically prints complete recruiting forms, confirmation letters, group sign-in sheets and job records.
7. It maintains information on clients and prepares complete histories of client activity.

Hence, this system can considerably improve the effectiveness and efficiency of managing a focus group.

A problem common to all qualitative research techniques is the coding and analysis of responses to open-ended questions. Microcomputers and mainframes are increasingly being used for this purpose. With an artificial intelligence program such as CATPAC from Terra Research and Computing of Royal Oak, Michigan, the difficulties of qualitative data analysis can be reduced dramatically.

CATPAC is designed to read and analyze text by identifying the patterns of similarity between important words. (Articles and prepositions normally omitted in content analysis of six different languages are contained in a special file.) CATPAC runs a "scanning window" through the text. The researcher can control the number of words that will appear in the window at any time, as well as how far ahead the window will "slide" with each sequential scan. Words that occur in any window become "active." As CATPAC moves through the document, the connections between simultaneously active words are strengthened. Then the program examines the connections among words throughout the entire text and attempts to find the underlying pattern.

CATPAC utilizes a self-organizing neural network (mimicking the structure of neurons linked by synapses in biological organisms) to account for complex interrelationships among the words in the text. Each word in the text is associated with a node in the neural network, and the relationships among the words are represented by the synaptic links among the nodes that represent the words. The synaptic connections among the nodes are strengthened or weakened in the neural network as more text is processed. Self-organizing neural networks do not require the analyst to determine the variables to be included before the analysis is run. Most CATPAC analyses are run with the default values specified in the program. Experienced users, however, can increase or decrease the rate at which synaptic connections are altered during the CATPAC analysis. In addition, the window size and scanning interval can be changed.

A depth interview about destinations for vacation trips in the last two years provides the text for an analysis using CATPAC. Exhibit 5.1 depicts a CATPAC report of word counts sorted by frequency and by alphabetical order. The left half of Exhibit 5.1 shows the words in descending frequency, with *city* being the most frequently used word (it was found nine times). The right half of Exhibit 5.1 shows the words in alphabetical order, with *big* being first and *you* being last.

Exhibit 5.2 depicts a spatial map of word associations. The results in this example indicate a three-group structure to the words in this consumer's depth interview. The group on the left relates to a West Coast city, San Diego (with words such as *San, Diego, sand, sun, surf, palm,* and *trees*). The group toward the center corresponds to a Great Lakes city, Detroit (with words such as *Detroit, exciting, fun,* and *big*). Finally, the group on the right concerns another Great Lakes city, Buffalo (with words such as *Buffalo, Niagara, friendly,* and *neighbors*).

EXHIBIT 5.1

A CATPAC Report of Word Counts

TITLE: test			
TOTAL WORDS	81	THRESHOLD	.000
TOTAL UNIQUE WORDS	10	RESTORING FORCE	.100
TOTAL WINDOWS	144	CYCLES	1
TOTAL LINES	23		
WINDOW SIZE	7	CLAMPING	YES
SLIDE SIZE	1		

DESCENDING FREQUENCY LIST

INDEX	FREQ.	PCENT.	WORD
1	9	11.11	CITY
2	8	9.88	BUFFALO
3	6	7.41	DETROIT
4	5	6.17	YOU
5	5	6.17	SAN
6	5	6.17	DIEGO
7	4	4.94	BIG
8	3	3.70	EXCITING
9	3	3.70	FUN
10	3	3.70	FRIENDLY
11	3	3.70	GOOD
12	3	3.70	NEIGHBORS
13	3	3.70	BROWN
14	3	3.70	WATER
15	3	3.70	PALM
16	3	3.70	TREES
17	3	3.70	SAND
18	3	3.70	SUN
19	3	3.70	SURF
20	3	3.70	NIAGARA

ALPHABETICALLY SORTED LIST

INDEX	FREQ.	PCENT.	WORD
7	4	4.94	BIG
13	3	3.70	BROWN
2	8	9.88	BUFFALO
1	9	11.11	CITY
3	6	7.41	DETROIT
6	5	6.17	DIEGO
8	3	3.70	EXCITING
10	3	3.70	FRIENDLY
9	3	3.70	FUN
11	3	3.70	GOOD
12	3	3.70	NEIGHBORS
20	3	3.70	NIAGARA
15	3	3.70	PALM
5	5	6.17	SAN
17	3	3.70	SAND
18	3	3.70	SUN
19	3	3.70	SURF
16	3	3.70	TREES
14	3	3.70	WATER
4	5	6.17	YOU

EXHIBIT 5.2

A Spatial Map of Word Associations

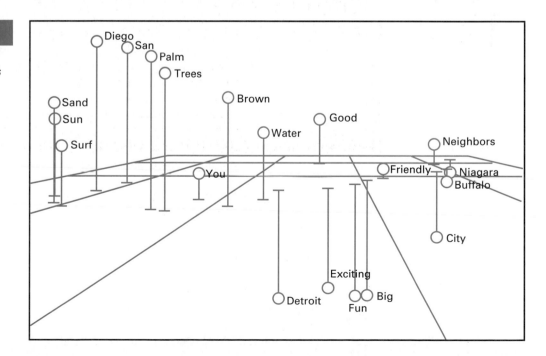

CATPAC also renders a weight input matrix (termed a "WIN" matrix) of numerical relationships among all he words it reads. This matrix can be used in other quantitative procedures. For example, the results from a number of individuals' depth interviews could be concatenated into one text. Then CATPAC could be used to produce a WIN matrix that could then be used as the input to more sophisticated quantitative procedures. These procedures could be used to discern an underlying or hidden structure in the responses of the individuals (e.g., in general, families not visiting relatives on vacations tend to go to beach destinations).

The final results of neural networks must be interpreted. Thus, CATPAC cannot preclude the introduction of some subjective bias by the researcher into an analysis. CATPAC can, however, be useful in expediting the arduous undertaking of qualitative analysis by quickly identifying patterns or by confirming relationships already identified by researchers.

SUMMARY

Qualitative and quantitative research should be viewed as complementary. Qualitative research methods may be direct or indirect. In direct methods respondents are able to discern the true purpose of the research, whereas indirect methods disguise the purpose of the research. The major direct methods are focus groups and depth interviews. Focus groups are conducted in a group setting, whereas depth interviews are one-on-one. Focus group interviews are the most widely used qualitative research technique.

The indirect techniques are called projective techniques because they aim to project the respondent's motivations, beliefs, attitudes, and feelings onto ambiguous situations. Projective techniques may be classified as association (word association), completion (sentence completion, story completion), construction (picture response, cartoon tests), and expressive (role playing, third person) techniques. Projective techniques are particularly useful when respondents are unwilling or unable to provide the required information by direct methods.

Qualitative research can reveal the salient differences between domestic and foreign markets. Whether focus groups or depth interviews should be conducted and how the findings should be interpreted depends heavily on the cultural differences. When conducting qualitative research, the researcher and the client must respect the respondents. This should include protecting the anonymity of respondents, honoring all statements and promises used to ensure participation, and conducting research in a way not to embarrass or harm the respondents. Microcomputers and mainframes can be used to select and screen respondents and in coding and analyzing qualitative data.[48]

ACRONYMS

The key characteristics of a focus group may be described by the acronym FOCUS GROUPS:

F   ocused (on a particular topic)
O   utline prepared for discussion
C   haracteristics of the moderator
U   nstructured
S   ize: 8–12 people
G   roup composition: homogeneous
R   ecorded: audiocassettes and videotapes
O   bservation: one-way mirror
U   ndisguised
P   hysical setting: relaxed
S   everal sessions needed: 1–3 hours each

The main features of a depth interview may be summarized by the acronym DEPTH:

D   epth of coverage
E   ach respondent individually interviewed
P   robe the respondent
T   alented interviewer required
H   idden motives may be uncovered

The main characteristics of projective techniques may be described by the acronym PROJECTIVE:

P   roject the underlying motivations, beliefs, attitudes
R   elationship: association techniques
O   vercome respondent's unwillingness or inability to answer
J   udgment required in interpretation of responses
E   xpressive techniques
C   onstruction, completion techniques
T   hematic: themes are elicited
I   ndirect
V   ague situations are used as stimuli
E   xploratory in nature

EXERCISES

QUESTIONS

1. What are the primary differences between qualitative and quantitative research techniques?
2. What is qualitative research and how is it conducted?
3. Differentiate between direct and indirect qualitative research. Give an example of each.
4. Why is the focus group the most popular qualitative research technique?
5. Why is the focus group moderator so important in obtaining quality results?
6. What are some key qualifications of focus group moderators?
7. Why should one safeguard against professional respondents?
8. Give two ways in which focus groups can be misused.
9. What is the difference between a dual moderator and a dueling moderator group?
10. What is the conference call technique? What are the advantages and disadvantages of this technique?
11. What is a depth interview? Under what circumstances is it preferable to focus groups?
12. What are the major advantages of depth interviews?
13. What are projective techniques? What are the four types of projective techniques?
14. Describe the word association technique. Give an example of a situation in which this technique is especially useful.
15. When should projective techniques be employed?

PROBLEMS

1. Following the methods outlined in the text, develop a plan for conducting a focus group to determine consumers' attitudes toward and preferences for imported automobiles. Specify the objectives of the focus group, write a screening questionnaire, and develop a moderator's outline.
2. Suppose that Baskin Robbins wants to know why some people do not eat ice cream regularly. Develop a cartoon test for this purpose.

COMPUTER EXERCISES

1. Construct a microcomputer- or mainframe-based word association test to determine consumers' underlying attitudes and feelings toward deodorants. Program the test using a database manager.

2. Could a depth interview be conducted successfully using microcomputers? The interviewer would sit in front of one microcomputer and the respondent in front of another. The two microcomputers would be linked together via a network. Both questions and answers would be typed into the computer. This would eliminate face-to-face, voice, and nonverbal (body language) communication. What are the advantages and disadvantages of this procedure over conventional depth interviews?

NOTES

1. Larry Kahaner, "When MCI Tested the Ad Waters," *Advertising Age* (March 17, 1987): 56.

2. Joseph Rydholm, "Regaining a Foothold," *Quirk's Marketing Research Review* 4 (10) (December 1990): 8–9, 50.

3. "Raisin Commercial Gets Nice Reviews," *Quirk's Marketing Research Review* (April 1987): 14–17.

4. For analysis and interpretation of qualitative data see, Susan Spiggle, "Analysis and Interpretation of Qualitative Data in Consumer Research," *Journal of Consumer Research* 21 (December 1994): 491–503; and Sue Robson, and Alan Hedges, "Analysis and Interpretation of Qualitative Findings. Report of the MRS Qualitative Interest Group," *Journal of the Market Research Society* 35 (January 1993): 63–76.

5. John Colwell, "Qualitative Market Research: A Conceptual Analysis and Review of Practitioner Criteria," *Journal of the Marketing Research Society* (UK) 32 (January 1990): 13–36; and Clive Gabriel, "The Validity of Qualitative Market Research," *Journal of the Market Research Society* (UK), 32 (October 1990): 507–19.

6. A positivist perspective on research is being adopted here. Positivism encompasses logical positivism, logical empiricism, and all forms of falsificationism. This is the dominant perspective in commercial marketing research. More recently, a relativist perspective has been offered. See, for example, Shelby D. Hunt, *Modern Marketing Theory* (Cincinnati: South-Western, 1991).

7. For assessing the reliability of qualitative data, see Roland T. Rust and Bruce Cooil, "Reliability Measures for Qualitative Data: Theory and Implications," *Journal of Marketing Research* 31 (February 1994): 1–14.

8. Catherine Marshall and Gretchen B. Rossman, *Designing Qualitative Research* (Beverly Hills: Sage Publications, 1989).

9. William T. Moran, "The Science of Qualitative Research," *Journal of Advertising Research*, 26 (June–July 1986): RC-16.

10. Betty Holcomb, "The Focus Groupie," *Madison Avenue* 27 (September 1985): 47.

11. The group size of eight to 12 is based on rules of thumb. For more discussion, see Edward F. Fern, "The Use of Focus Groups for Idea Generation: The Effects of Group Size, Acquaintanceship, and Moderator on Response Quantity and Quality," *Journal of Marketing Research* 19 (February 1982): 1–13.

12. James E. Nelson and Nancy Frontczak, "How Acquaintanceship and Analyst Can Influence Focus Group Results," *Journal of Advertising* 17 (1988): 41–48.

13. Hazel Kahn, "Professional Respondents Say They're Better for Research Than 'Virgins,' but They're Not," *Marketing News* (May 14, 1982): section 1, p. 22.

14. Adapted from Donald A. Chase, "The Intensive Group Interviewing in Marketing," *MRA Viewpoints* (1973).

15. Martin R. Lautman, and Andrew Mitchell, eds., "Focus Group: Theory and Method," *Advances in Consumer Research*, vol. 9 (Pittsburgh: Association for Consumer Research, 1982), p. 22.

16. David W. Stewart, and Prem N. Shamdasani, *Focus Groups: Theory and Practice* (Newbury Park, CA: Sage Publications, 1990).

17. Thomas L. Greenbaum, *The Practical Handbook and Guide to Focus Group Research* (Lexington, MA: D.C. Heath, 1988); and Joel L. Welch, "Researching Marketing Problems and Opportunities with Focus Groups," *Industrial Marketing Management* 14 (1985): 245–53.

18. Toni H. Lydecker, "Focus Group Dynamics," *Association Management* (March 1986): 73–78.

19. Michael Silverstein, "Two-Way Focus Groups Can Provide Startling Information," *Marketing News* (January 4, 1988): 31.

20. "Focus Groups Are a Phone Call Away," *Marketing News* (January 3, 1986): 22, 42.

21. John M. Hess and R. L. King, eds., "Group Interviewing," *New Science of Planning* (Chicago: American Marketing Association, 1968): 4.

22. Andrew J. Byrne, "Focus Groups: Valuable Data, but Not Basis of Sales Forecast," *Direct Marketing* (March 1984): 66, 71, 72.

23. See S. Ratneshwar and Allan D. Shocker, "Substitution in Use and the Role of Usage Context in Product Category Structures," *Journal of Marketing Research* 28 (August 1991): 281–95. Another useful reference for focus group applications is B. Higgenbotham and Keith K. Cox, eds., *Focus Group Interviews: A Reader* (Chicago: American Marketing Association, 1979).

24. From "Listening, the Old-Fashioned Way," *Forbes* (October 5, 1987): 202–4.

25. For other issues involved in focus groups, see W. A. Cook, and A. A. Mitchell, eds., "Turning Focus Groups Inside Out," *Advances in Consumer Research*, vol. 9 (Pittsburgh: Association for Consumer Research, 1982), pp. 52–56, 57–61, 62–64.

26. M. Z. Knox, "In-Depth Interviews Can Reveal 'What's in a Name,'" *Marketing News* 3 (January 1986): 4.

27. M. S. Payne, "Individual In-Depth Interviews Can Provide More Details than Groups," *Marketing Today* (Atlanta: Elrick and Lavidge, 1, 1982); and M. S. Payne, "Resurgence of In-Depth Interviewing Leads to Better Qualitative Research," *Marketing Today* (Elrick and Lavidge, 1, 1984).

28. Judith Langer, "'Story Time,' Is Alternative Research Technique," *Marketing News* (September 13, 1985): 19, 24.

29. This example is derived from Jeffrey F. Durgee, "Depth-Interview Techniques for Creative Advertising," *Journal of Advertising Research* 25 (December 1985–January 1986): 29–37.

30. H. Sokolow, "In-Depth Interviews Increasing in Importance," *Marketing News* (September 13, 1985): 26.

31. Langer, "'Story Time,'" p. 19, 24.

32. H. H. Kassarjian, "Projective Methods," in R. Ferber (ed.) *Handbook of Marketing Research* (New York: McGraw-Hill, 1974), pp. 3.85–3.100.

33. Sharon L. Hollander, "Projective Techniques Uncover Real Consumer Attitudes," *Marketing News* (January 4, 1988): 34.

34. G. Lindzey, "On the Classification of Projective Techniques," *Psychological Bulletin* (1959): 158–68.

35. "Interpretation Is the Essence of Projective Research Techniques," *Marketing News* (September 28, 1984): 20.

36. S. Bhargava, "Gimme a Double Shake and a Lard on White," *Business Week* (March 1, 1993): 59.

37. For issues involved in role playing, see Carol Suprenant, Gilbert A. Churchill, and Thomas C. Kinnear, eds., "Can Role Playing Be Substituted for Actual Consumption?" *Advances in Consumer Research* (Provo, UT: Association for Consumer Research, 1984), pp. 122–26.

38. Paul E. Green and Donald S. Tull, *Research for Marketing Decisions*, 4th ed. (Englewood Cliffs, NJ: Prentice Hall), p. 139.

39. Maison Haire, "Projective Techniques in Marketing Research," *Journal of Marketing* 14 (April 1950): 649–56; and G. S. Lane and G. L. Watson, "A Canadian Replication of Maison Haire's Shopping List Study," *Journal of the Academy of Marketing Science* 3 (Winter 1975): 48–59.

40. Robert K. Schnee, "Quality Research: Going Beyond the Obvious," *Journal of Advertising Research* 28 (February–March 1988): RC-9–RC-12; and Fred N. Kerlinger, *Foundations of Behavioral Research*, vol. 3 (New York: Holt, Rinehart and Winston, 1986), p. 471.

41. For more on projective techniques, see Virginia Valentine and Malcolm Evans, "The Dark Side of the Onion: Rethinking the Meaning of 'Rational' and 'Emotional' Responses," *Journal of the Market Research Society*, 35 (April 1993): 125–44.

42. For perceptions of focus groups in the United States, Germany, and Japan, see William J. McDonald, "Provider Perceptions of Focus Groups Research Use: A Multicountry Perspective," *Journal of the Academy of Marketing Science* 22 (Summer 1994): 265–73.

43. *Marketing* (April 2, 1987): 50.

44. Susan P. Douglas and C. Samuel Craig, *International Marketing Research* (Englewood Cliffs, NJ: Prentice Hall, 1983).

45. *MRS Code of Conduct* (The Market Research Society,).

46. S. Robson, "Ethics: Informed Consent or Misinformed Compliance?" *Journal of the Market Research Society*, 33 (1991): 19–28.

47. S. Banker, "The Ethics of Political Marketing Practices, the Rhetorical Perspective," *Journal of Business Ethics* 11 (1992): 843–48.

48. The assistance of James Agarwal with the international marketing research example, the assistance of Mark Leach and Gina Miller in writing the ethics section, and the assistance of Mark Peterson in writing the computer applications section is gratefully acknowledged.

CHAPTER SIX

Descriptive Research Design: Survey and Observation

No particular survey method is the best in all cases. Depending on the problem, none, one, two, or many methods may be appropriate.

OBJECTIVES

After reading this chapter, the student should be able to:

1. Discuss and classify survey methods available to marketing researchers and describe the various telephone, personal, and mail interviewing methods.
2. Identify the criteria for evaluating survey methods, compare the different methods, and evaluate which is best for a particular research project.
3. Explain and classify the different observation methods used by marketing researchers and describe personal observation, mechanical observation, audit, content analysis, and trace analysis.
4. Identify the criteria for evaluating observation methods, compare the different methods, and evaluate which, if any, is suited for a particular research project.
5. Describe the relative advantages and disadvantages of observational methods and compare them to survey methods.
6. Discuss the considerations involved in implementing surveys and observation methods in an international setting.
7. Understand the ethical issues involved in conducting survey and observation research.
8. Discuss the use of microcomputers and mainframes in surveys and observation methods.

OVERVIEW

In previous chapters, we explained that once the marketing research problem has been defined (step 1 of the marketing research process) and an appropriate approach developed (step 2), the researcher is in a position to formulate the research design (step 3). As discussed in Chapter 3, the major types of research designs are exploratory and conclusive. Exploratory designs employ secondary data analysis (Chapter 4) and qualitative research (Chapter 5) as the major methodologies. Conclusive research designs may be classified as causal or descriptive. Causal designs will be explained in Chapter 7.

In this chapter, we focus on the major methods employed in descriptive research designs: survey and observation. As explained in Chapter 3, descriptive research has as its major objective the description of something, usually market characteristics or functions. Survey, or communication, methods may be classified by mode of administration as traditional telephone interviews, computer-assisted telephone interviews, personal in-home interviews, mall-intercept interviews, computer-assisted personal interviews, mail interviews, and mail panels. We describe each of these methods and present a comparative evaluation of all the survey methods. Then we consider the major observational methods: personal observation, mechanical observation, audit, content analysis, and trace analysis. The relative advantages and disadvantages of observation over survey methods and the considerations involved in conducting survey and observation research when researching international markets are also discussed. Several ethical issues that arise in survey research and observation methods are identified. The chapter concludes with a discussion of the use of microcomputers and mainframes in survey and observation research. To begin our discussion, here are some examples of these methods.

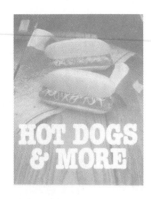

EXAMPLE
Mall Intercept, Frankly Speaking _____

Carousel Snack Bars of Minnesota, Inc., is a restaurant chain. Its 325 food outlets, also known as Hot Dogs & More, The Great Hot Dog Experience, The Great Hamburger Experience, Carousel Pizza, and Frankly Speaking, are located in major shopping malls nationwide. The chain's customers are 35% mall employees, 50% middle-age shoppers, and 15% teens and senior citizens. Carousel conducts mall-intercept interviews regularly to test new product introductions. Customers in shopping malls are questioned about their food preferences. The interviews help the restaurants find out what foods are appealing to customers and what new types of food they would like to see on the menu. These interviews also indicate how the consumers perceive the restaurants' service, responsiveness, cleanliness, menu variety, and price value. This research effort has paid rich dividends. The successful introduction of Carousel's International Sausages is but one example of the fruits of this research.[1] ◆

Mall-intercept interviews have helped Carousel Snack Bars to introduce many successful products such as International Sausages. ◆ Carousel Snack Bars of Minnesota, Inc.

EXAMPLE
Computer Interviewing Cuts through Soft Drink Fizz

Populus, a marketing research company, conducted a study of soft drink preferences. The study consisted of computer-assisted personal interviews that were completed by consumers at central locations. The questionnaire had 985 questions, and 1,200 interviews were completed on a nationwide sample within 18 days. Given the magnitude and complexity of the study, computer-assisted personal interviewing was the only realistic alternative; the questionnaire had extensive conditional branching and the computer interactive mode allowed randomization of items and response choices. Had this study been conducted by traditional methods, costs would have been 50 to 60% higher.[2] ◆

EXAMPLE
All Packages Are Not Created Equal

The NutraSweet Company, maker of Equal sugar substitute, wanted to reposition the product to compete with sugar and market it as a natural, more healthful replacement for use in foods. To achieve this objective, a new package was created for Equal. Nova Research, Inc., was commissioned to undertake research to test several new package designs. The study conducted involved a sample of 1,121 female heads of household between ages 21 and 59 who sweetened food and beverages on a regular basis.

Respondents participated in a standard tachistoscope (T-scope) shelf visibility test to measure speed of registration of the product category, brand identity, and key packaging elements for the Equal designs and competitive products within the array. The T-scope shelf visibility test uses an electronically timed shutter to control how long the respondents view a particular stimulus. In this case, respondents saw slides of grocery shelves stocked with variously arranged packages of Equal, competing sugar substitutes, and regular sugar.

A subsample of the total respondents also participated in eye-movement tracking research. These respondents were exposed to a series of slides that simulated a store walk-through. The slides included a mass display and a close-up of each Equal test package.

This research enabled Nova to select the best package for Equal. The package design that was selected was the one that scored fastest in speed of recognition. It also attained a high level of brand recognition and shelf visibility.[3] ◆

Mall-intercept interviews and computer-assisted personal interviews, as well as other survey methods, are becoming increasingly popular. Observation methods are employed less frequently, but they too have important uses in marketing research.

SURVEY METHODS

survey method A structured questionnaire given to a sample of a population and designed to elicit specific information from respondents.

The **survey method** of obtaining information is based on the questioning of respondents. Respondents are asked a variety of questions regarding their behavior, intentions, attitudes, awareness, motivations, and demographic and lifestyle characteristics. These questions may be asked verbally, in writing, or via computer, and the responses may be obtained in any of these forms. Typically, the questioning is structured. *Structured* here refers to the degree of standardization imposed on the data collection process. In **structured data collection**, a formal questionnaire is prepared and the questions are asked in a prearranged

structured data collection
Use of a formal questionnaire that presents questions in a prearranged order.

order; thus, the process is also direct. Whether research is classified as direct or indirect is based on whether the true purpose is known to the respondents. As explained in Chapter 5, a direct approach is nondisguised in that the purpose of the project is disclosed to the respondents or is otherwise obvious to them from the questions asked.

The structured direct survey, the most popular data collection method, involves administering a questionnaire. In a typical questionnaire, most questions are **fixed-response alternative questions** that require the respondent to select from a predetermined set of responses. Consider, for example, the following question designed to measure attitude toward department stores:

fixed-response alternative questions Questions that require respondents to choose from a set of predetermined answers.

	Disagree				Agree
Shopping in department stores is fun.	1	2	3	4	5

The survey method has several advantages. First, the questionnaire is simple to administer. Second, the data obtained are reliable because the responses are limited to the alternatives stated. The use of fixed-response questions reduces the variability in the results that may be caused by differences in interviewers. Finally, coding, analysis, and interpretation of data are relatively simple.[4]

Disadvantages are that respondents may be unable or unwilling to provide the desired information. For example, consider questions about motivational factors. Respondents may not be consciously aware of their motives for choosing specific brands or shopping at specific department stores. Therefore, they may be unable to provide accurate answers to questions about their motives. Respondents may be unwilling to respond if the information requested is sensitive or personal. Also, structured questions and fixed-response alternatives may result in loss of validity for certain types of data such as beliefs and feelings. Finally, wording questions properly is not easy (see Chapter 10 on questionnaire design). Despite these disadvantages, the survey approach is by far the most common method of primary data collection in marketing research. Research in Practice 6.1 illustrates this method.[5]

RESEARCH IN PRACTICE 6.1

Survey Research Is in the Cards for DEC

Digital Equipment Corporation (DEC) has made a conscious effort in the past years to shift from a product-driven focus to a more market- and consumer-driven focus. The product focus is not unusual in companies manufacturing high-tech products. There is a serious need for market research in these high-tech companies as they direct their products to the market. Still, market research in this arena is difficult. It is complicated by the rapid change of technology as well as the sheer size of the application market. Often the technology will be employed in many different industries. This holds true for the computer market where DEC is a key player. Computers are bought by individuals in every walk of life as well as by businesses in every market imaginable. The breadth of the market makes useful market research a formidable task.

(continued)

This task is being undertaken at DEC in their Corporate Marketing Services (CMS) Division, however. "Digital's Corporate Marketing Services Division has been a core element in the company's transition to a market-driven strategy." CMS is coordinating the company's strategy to redefine their product from simply computers to a broader view of business solutions. CMS has employed many research techniques to gain a better understanding of the "business solutions" market. Both primary and secondary research data are used. Primary data are obtained through the use of phone and mail surveys as well as seminars and focus groups. Phone surveys have been used to define customer needs better and to direct products to the customers better. Mail surveys have been used to study customer purchasing habits as well as future purchasing plans. Seminars are held to gain feedback on the long-term production plans at DEC. Finally, focus groups are used to determine whether the chosen strategy is good and one that will effectively manage and use the market's potential.

Without CMS and marketing research DEC would be facing the unknowns of their technology as well as the market. This combination of obstacles would have made the transition from a product-focused to a market- and consumer-focused company an impossibility.

Survey methods can be classified based on the mode used to administer the questionnaire. These classification schemes help distinguish among survey methods.

SURVEY METHODS CLASSIFIED BY MODE OF ADMINISTRATION

Survey questionnaires may be administered in three major modes: (1) telephone interviews, (2) personal interviews, and (3) mail interviews (see Figure 6.1). Telephone interviews may be further classified as traditional telephone interviews or computer-assisted telephone interviews. Personal interviews may be conducted in the home, as mall-intercept interviews, or as computer-assisted personal interviews. The third major method, mail interviews, takes the form of ordinary mail surveys or surveys conducted using mail panels. Of these methods, telephone interviews are the most popular, followed by personal interviews, and mail interviews are the least popular. We now describe each method.

TELEPHONE METHODS

As stated earlier, telephone interviews can be typed as traditional or computer-assisted.

Traditional Telephone Interviews

Traditional telephone interviews involve phoning a sample of respondents and asking them a series of questions. The interviewer uses a paper questionnaire and records the responses with a pencil. Low-priced WATS (wide-area telephone service) lines have made nationwide telephone interviewing from a central location practical. With the popularity of WATS lines, the use of local telephone interviewing has decreased in recent years.[6]

FIGURE 6.1

*A Classification
of Survey Methods*

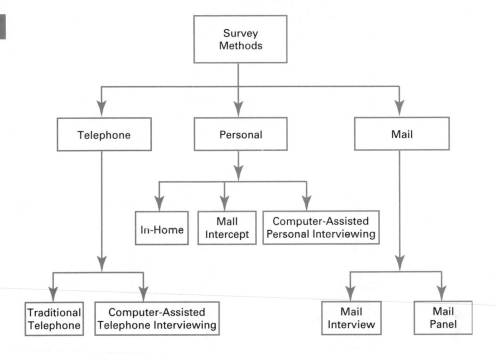

Computer-Assisted Telephone Interviews

Computer-assisted telephone interviewing from a central location is now more popular than the traditional telephone method. Computer-assisted telephone interviewing (CATI) uses a computerized questionnaire administered to respondents over the telephone. A computerized questionnaire may be generated using a mainframe computer, a minicomputer, or a personal computer. The interviewer sits in front of a cathode-ray tube (CRT) terminal and wears a small headset. The CRT replaces a paper-and-pencil questionnaire, and the headset substitutes for a telephone. Upon command, the computer dials the telephone number to be called. When contact is made, the interviewer reads questions posed on the CRT screen and records the respondent's answers directly into the computer memory bank.

In computer assisted telephone interviewing, the computer systematically guides the interviewer. ◆ Burke Marketing Research.

The computer systematically guides the interviewer. Only one question at a time appears on the CRT screen. The computer checks the responses for appropriateness and consistency. It uses the responses as they are obtained to personalize the questionnaire. The data collection flows naturally and smoothly. Interviewing time is reduced, data quality is enhanced, and the laborious steps in the data collection process—coding questionnaires and entering the data into the computer—are eliminated. Because the responses are entered directly into the computer, interim and update reports on data collection or results can be provided almost instantaneously. The following example shows how CATI helps ensure a representative sample.[7]

EXAMPLE

CASH Represents Dollars for Marketers

CASH, an acronym for continuing analysis of shopping habits, is a service of San Diego's leading newspaper, the *Union-Tribune*. CASH provides consumer buying information on a wide range of product categories. At the heart of CASH methods lies a yearly computer-assisted telephone interview with 3,300 adults living in San Diego County. Households are selected with a probability sampling scheme that ensures that each household in the county has an equal chance of being included in the survey, regardless of whether its phone number is listed.

To select the sample, the standard seven-digit telephone number is divided into two parts. The first group of three digits (for example, 454) occurs in the county with measurable frequency. In addition, the numerals in these three-digit groups are dependent on each other, on the location of the telephone within the county, and in some cases, on how the telephone is used. As a first step, a complete list of the valid three-digit numbers in the area and their frequency of occurrence is prepared. Then, the last four digits of every phone number are independently generated from a table of random numbers. This process ensures that unlisted phones or newly established phone numbers can be represented in the sample. The list of numbers so generated is reviewed and compared with valid listed numbers. Numbers that fall within obvious blocks of unused or commercial numbers are eliminated. The final list of numbers is used for three consecutive interview waves and then discarded. CASH provides a variety of information useful to marketers, including answers to questions such as what percentage of households in San Diego purchased cameras priced under $100 (7.3%) and what store garnered the largest share of shopper traffic (Target with 9.1%).[8] ◆

PERSONAL METHODS

Personal interviewing methods may be categorized as in-home, mall-intercept, or computer-assisted.

Personal In-Home Interviews

In personal in-home interviews, respondents are interviewed face to face in their homes. The interviewer's task is to contact the respondents, ask the questions, and record the responses. In recent years, the use of personal in-home interviews has declined due to its high cost. Nevertheless, they are still used, particularly by syndicated firms, such as the Roper Organization, which maintains omnibus panels (see Chapter 3).[9]

EXAMPLE
Limobus: A Limo or a Bus Ride into American Homes _____

The Roper Organization's omnibus panel, Limobus, conducts personal in-home interviews with 2,000 adult Americans every month and makes the results available four weeks after the survey. The sample size and composition of the panel for a specific project are tailored to the client's needs: all or some of the panel members may be asked questions of interest to a specific client. Limobus can be used for checking advertising and brand awareness; conducting pre- and postcampaign measurements; checking ad impact, recall, and communication; assessing brand penetration; testing new or altered packaging; evaluating new product performance; and other marketing research problems.[10] ◆

Despite their many applications, the use of personal in-home interviews is declining whereas mall-intercept interviews are becoming more frequent.

Mall-Intercept Personal Interviews

In mall-intercept personal interviews, respondents are intercepted while they are shopping in malls and are brought to test facilities in the malls. The interviewer then administers a questionnaire as in the in-home personal survey. The advantage of mall-intercept interviews is that it is more efficient for the respondent to come to the interviewer than for the interviewer to go to the respondent.[11] This method has become increasingly popular, and there are several hundred permanent mall research facilities. As the following example shows, mall-intercept interviews are especially appropriate when the respondents need to see, handle, or consume the product before they can provide meaningful information.

A mall-intercept interview in progress. ◆ Elrick and Lavidge.

EXAMPLE
Mall-Intercept Interviews Give Birth to Infant Apparel _____

Soft Care Apparel Inc., manufacturer of Curity children's wear, is the largest soft-goods manufacturer of infant apparel in the United States. Soft Care uses mall-intercept interviews to evaluate its new products. The company hires an independent research firm that tests the company's new designs against its current designs and the designs of its competition, simulating a marketplace situation. The company's product managers often go to test malls to receive firsthand feedback from potential customers. Several products, including printed crib sheets, comforters, and coordinated bedding, have been successfully designed and introduced using information obtained from mall-intercept interviews.[12] ◆

Computer-Assisted Personal Interviews

In computer-assisted personal interviewing (CAPI), the third form of personal interviewing, the respondent sits in front of a computer terminal and answers a questionnaire on the CRT screen by using the keyboard or a mouse. There are several user-friendly electronic packages that design questions that are easy for the respondent to understand. Help screens and courteous error messages are also provided. The colorful screens and on- and off-screen stimuli add to the respondent's interest and involvement in the task. This method has been classified as a personal interview technique because an interviewer is usually present to serve as a host or hostess and to guide the respondent as needed.

CAPI has been used to collect data at shopping malls, product clinics, conferences, and trade shows. You may wonder, however, how CAPI compares with the traditional method of conducting personal interviews, using paper-and-pencil questionnaires. The experience of the First National Bank of Chicago provides some insight.[13]

EXAMPLE
Banking on Computers Creates Interest _____

The First National Bank of Chicago compared CAPI with interviewer-assisted paper-and-pencil questionnaires. It was found that computer questionnaires took longer to complete, although the respondents underestimated the time they spent at the CRT. Respondents found the computer-assisted surveys more interesting than the other form and expressed more positive predispositions toward them. Greater variance and less-inhibited answers were obtained with CAPI. Computer-assisted interviews resulted, in certain instances, in 33 to 40% cost savings over interviewer-assisted paper-and-pencil questionnaires. Therefore, the First National Bank of Chicago has continued to use CAPI in many of its ongoing research programs.[14] ◆

MAIL METHODS

Mail interviews, the third major form of survey administration, can be conducted via ordinary mail or the mail panel.

Mail Interviews

In the traditional mail interview, questionnaires are mailed to preselected potential respondents. A typical mail interview package consists of the outgoing envelope, cover letter, ques-

PLEASE INDICATE YOUR SATISFACTION WITH:	PART II PLEASE CIRCLE YOUR RESPONSE.				
	VERY SATIS-FIED	SATIS-FIED	NEU-TRAL	DIS-SATIS-FIED	VERY DIS-SATIS-FIED
1. THE QUALITY OF YOUR EQUIPMENT	1	2	3	4	5
2. THE RESPONSE TIME TO YOUR CALL	1	2	3	4	5
3. THE QUALITY OF SERVICE PERFORMED	1	2	3	4	5
4. THE COURTESY OF MY SERVICE PERSON	1	2	3	4	5
5. MEETING OUR SERVICE COMMITMENTS TO YOU	1	2	3	4	5
6. MY OVERALL SERVICE	1	2	3	4	5

BUSINESS REPLY CARD
FIRST CLASS   PERMIT NO. 832   ATLANTA, GA
POSTAGE WILL BE PAID BY ADDRESSEE

ELRICK AND LAVIDGE, INC.
P.O. Box 4402
Atlanta, GA 30302

NO POSTAGE NECESSARY IF MAILED IN THE UNITED STATES

A mail questionnaire with return envelope. ◆ Elrick and Lavidge.

tionnaire, return envelope, and possibly an incentive.[15] The respondents complete and return the questionnaires. There is no verbal interaction between the researcher and the respondent.[16]

Before data collection can begin, however, the respondents need to be at least broadly identified. Therefore, an initial task is to obtain a valid mailing list. Mailing lists can be compiled from telephone directories, customer rosters, or association membership rolls or can be purchased from publication subscription lists or commercial mailing list companies.[17] Regardless of its source, a mailing list should be current and closely related to the population of interest. The researcher must also make decisions about the various elements of the mail interview package (see Table 6.1). Mail surveys are used for a variety of purposes including measurement of advertising effectiveness, as illustrated by the following example.

EXAMPLE
Advertising Outer Space Technology Is "Far Out"!

Aviation Week and Space Technology conducted research to determine the effectiveness of a series of advertisements for a satellite telecommunications company. Two direct mail surveys were conducted, one before the advertising campaign ran and the other after. Each survey was conducted among a sample of 750 *Aviation Week* subscribers in private industry,

TABLE 6.1 *Some Decisions Related to the Mail Interview Package*			
Outgoing Envelope			
Outgoing envelope: size, color, return address			
Postage	Method of addressing		
Cover Letter			
Sponsorship	Type of appeal	Postscript	
Personalization	Signature		
Questionnaire			
Length	Size	Layout	Format
Content	Reproduction	Color	Respondent anonymity
Return Envelope			
Type of envelope	Postage		
Incentives			
Monetary versus nonmonetary		Prepaid versus promised amount	

the government, and the military. A total of 257 returns (a 38% response rate) were received from the first survey and 330 (a 44% response rate) from the second.

Although most direct mail surveys include an incentive to help boost response rates, this one did not because government and military employees are not allowed to accept incentives. Instead, higher response rates were obtained by attempting to make the need for the survey appear legitimate. Compared with the first survey, the results from the second survey indicated that the ad campaign was successful. For example, 59% more respondents agreed with the statement that the telecommunications company "is technologically advanced." Other characteristics showed increases ranging from 31 to 59%. These findings convinced the satellite telecommunications company that its advertising dollars in *Aviation Week and Space Technology* were well spent.[18] ◆

Mail Panels

mail panels A large and nationally representative sample of households that have agreed to participate in periodical mail questionnaires, product tests, and telephone surveys.

Several magazines such as *Seventeen* maintain their own consumer panels. ◆ Paul Lange.

Mail panels were introduced in Chapters 3 and 4. A **mail panel** consists of a large, nationally representative sample of households that have agreed to participate in periodic mail questionnaires, product tests, and telephone surveys. The households are compensated with various incentives. Some marketing research organizations that maintain mail panels include National Family Opinion, Market Fact's Consumer Mail Panel, Marketing and Research Counselors' National Neighborhood Panel, and Home Testing Institute. Several magazines, such as *Seventeen*, maintain their own panels, as illustrated by the following example.[19]

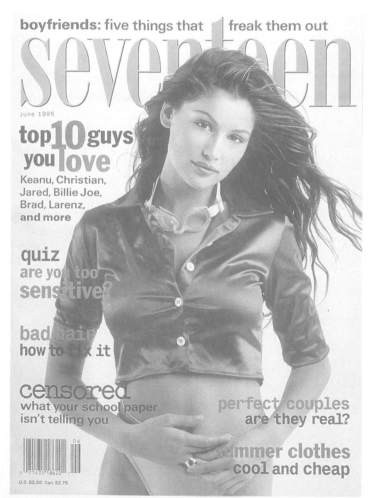

EXAMPLE
Mail Targets Female _____

Seventeen magazine conducted a study to determine the shopping habits of its readers. Questionnaires were mailed to 2,000 members of *Seventeen*'s Consumer Panel, representing a cross section of the female 13–21 market. Of these, 1,315 were returned, for a completion rate of 65.8%. The results were balanced by age and geographic area to census data so that they can reflect all females aged 13–21 in the United States. Some of the major findings were as follows:[20]

- Nine out of ten shopped at a large mall.
- Almost two-thirds shopped in a small shopping center.
- Over half shopped at a single standing store.

The magazine used these results to target advertisers and obtain higher advertising revenues. *Seventeen* magazine uses its mail panel to conduct periodic surveys. This helps it to stay in touch with its target market and keep abreast of changes. ◆

Mail panels can be used to obtain information from the same respondents repeatedly. Thus, they can be used to implement a longitudinal design. Remember, however, that not all survey methods are appropriate in a given situation. Therefore, the researcher should conduct a comparative evaluation to determine which methods are appropriate.

A COMPARATIVE EVALUATION OF SURVEY METHODS

Table 6.2 compares the different survey methods across a variety of factors. For any particular research project, the relative importance attached to these factors will vary. These factors consist of flexibility of data collection, diversity of questions, use of physical stimuli, sample control, control of the data collection environment, control of field force, quantity of data, response rate, perceived anonymity, social desirability, obtaining sensitive information, potential for interviewer bias, speed, and cost.

Flexibility of Data Collection

The personal interview, whether conducted as an in-home or a mall-intercept interview, allows the highest flexibility of data collection. Because the respondent and the interviewer meet face to face, the interviewer can administer complex questionnaires, explain and clarify difficult questions, and even use unstructured techniques.

By contrast, the traditional telephone interview allows only moderate flexibility because it is more difficult to use unstructured techniques, ask complex questions, or obtain in-depth answers to open-ended questions over the telephone. CATI and CAPI allow somewhat greater flexibility because the researcher can use various question formats, can personalize the questionnaire, and can handle complex skip patterns (directions for skipping questions in the questionnaire based on the subject's responses). Because the mail questionnaire allows for no interaction between the interviewer and the respondent, mail surveys and mail panels have low flexibility.

Diversity of Questions

A wide variety of questions can be asked in a personal interview because the interviewer is present to clarify ambiguities. Thus in-home interviews, mall-intercept interviews, and CAPI allow for diversity. In mail surveys and mail panels, less diversity is possible. In traditional telephone interviews and CATI, the respondent cannot see the questions while answering, and this limits the diversity of questions. For example, in a telephone interview or CATI, one could not ask respondents to rank 15 brands of automobiles in terms of preference.

Use of Physical Stimuli

Often it is helpful or necessary to use physical stimuli such as products, product prototypes, commercials, or promotional displays during the interview. For the most basic example, a taste test involves tasting the product. In other cases, photographs, maps, or other audiovisual cues are helpful. In these cases, personal interviews conducted at central locations (mall-intercept interviews and CAPI) are preferable to in-home interviews. Mail surveys and mail panels are moderate on this dimension, because sometimes it is possible to mail the facilitating aids or even product samples. The use of physical stimuli is limited in traditional telephone interviews and CATI.

TABLE 6.2

A Comparative Evaluation of Survey Methods

Criteria	Telephone Interviews	CATI	In-Home Interviews	Mall-Intercept Interviews	CAPI	Mail Surveys	Mail Panels
Flexibility of data collection	Moderate	Moderate to high	High	High	Moderate to high	Low	Low
Diversity of questions	Low	Low	High	High	High	Moderate	Moderate
Use of physical stimuli	Low	Low	Moderate to high	High	High	Moderate	Moderate
Sample control	Moderate to high	Moderate to high	Potentially high	Moderate	Moderate	Low	Moderate to high
Control of data collection environment	Moderate	Moderate	Moderate to high	High	High	Low	Low
Control of field force	Moderate	Moderate	Low	Moderate	Moderate	High	High
Quantity of data	Low	Low	High	Moderate	Moderate	Moderate	High
Response rate	Moderate	Moderate	High	High	High	Low	Moderate
Perceived anonymity of the respondent	Moderate	Moderate	Low	Low	Low	High	High
Social desirability	Moderate	Moderate	High	High	High	Low	Low
Obtaining sensitive information	High	High	Low	Low	Low to moderate	High	High
Potential for interviewer bias	Moderate	Moderate	High	High	Low	None	None
Speed	High	High	Moderate	Moderate to high	Moderate to high	Low	Low to moderate
Cost	Moderate	Moderate	High	Moderate to high	Moderate to high	Low	Low to moderate

Sample Control

sample control The ability of the survey mode to reach the units specified in the sample effectively and efficiently.

Sample control is the ability of the survey mode to reach the units specified in the sample effectively and efficiently.[21] At least in principle, in-home personal interviews offer the best sample control. It is possible to control which sampling units are interviewed, who is interviewed, the degree of participation of other members of the household, and many other aspects of data collection. In practice, to achieve a high degree of control, the researcher has to overcome several problems. It is difficult to find respondents at home during the day because many people work outside the home. Also, for safety reasons, interviewers are reluctant to venture into certain neighborhoods and people have become cautious of responding to strangers at their door.

Mall-intercept interviews allow only a moderate degree of sample control. Although the interviewer has control over which respondents to intercept, the choice is limited to mall shoppers, and frequent shoppers have a greater probability of being included. Also, potential respondents can intentionally avoid or initiate contact with the interviewer. Compared with mall-intercept interviews, CAPI offers slightly better control, as sampling quotas can be set and respondents randomized automatically.

sampling frame A representation of the elements of the target population that consists of a list or set of directions for identifying the target population.

Moderate to high sampling control can be achieved with traditional telephone interviews and CATI. Telephones offer access to geographically dispersed respondents and hard-to-reach areas. These procedures depend upon a **sampling frame**, a list of population units with their telephone numbers.[22] The sampling frames normally used are telephone directories, but telephone directories are limited in that (1) not everyone has a phone, (2) some people have unlisted phones, and (3) directories do not reflect new phones in service or recently disconnected phones. Although the telephone has achieved an almost total penetration of households, there are some variations by region and within regions. The percentage of households with unlisted numbers is about 31% and varies considerably by geographical region. In large metropolitan areas, it may be as high as 60%.[23] The total of unpublished numbers and new phones in service since a directory was published can account for as much as 40% of total telephone households in some metropolitan areas.[24]

random-digit dialing A technique used to overcome the bias of unpublished and recent telephone numbers by selecting all telephone number digits at random.

The **random-digit dialing** (RDD) technique is used to overcome the bias of unpublished and recent numbers. RDD consists of selecting all 10 (area code, prefix or exchange, suffix) digits of a telephone number at random. While this approach gives all households with telephones an approximately equal chance of being included in the sample, it suffers from limitations. It is costly and time consuming to implement, because not all possible telephone numbers are in service: although there are 10 billion possible telephone numbers, there are only about 90 million actual household telephone numbers. Also, RDD does not distinguish between telephone numbers that are of interest and those that are not (in a consumer survey, for example, business and government numbers are not of interest). There are several variations of RDD that reduce wasted effort. One variation randomly selects a working exchange and adds a block of four-digit random numbers. In **random-digit directory designs**, a sample of numbers is drawn from the directory. These numbers are modified to allow unpublished numbers a chance of being included in the sample. The popular approaches for modification of numbers include (1) adding a constant to the last digit, (2) randomizing the last r digits, and (3) a two-stage procedure. These procedures are described and illustrated in Figure 6.2. Of these three methods, adding a constant to the last digit, particularly plus-one sampling, results in high contact rates and representative samples.[25]

random-digit directory designs A research design for telephone surveys in which a sample of numbers is drawn from the telephone directory and modified to allow unpublished numbers a chance of being included in the sample.

Mail surveys require a list of addresses of individuals or households eligible for inclusion in the sample. Mail surveys can reach geographically dispersed respondents

FIGURE 6.2

Random-Digit Directory Designs

Adding a Constant to the Last Digit

An integer between 1 and 9 is added to the telephone number selected from the directory. In plus-one sampling the number added to the last digit is 1.

Number selected from directory: 953-3004 (exchange-block). Add one to the last digit to form 953-3005. This is the number to be included in the sample.

Randomizing the r Last Digits

Replace the r (r = 2, 3, or 4) last digits with an equal number of randomly selected digits.

Number selected from directory: 881-1124. Replace the last four digits of the block with randomly selected numbers 5, 2, 8, and 6 to form 881-5286.

Two-Stage Procedure

The first stage consists of selecting an exchange and telephone number from the directory. In the second stage, the last three digits of the selected number are replaced with a three-digit random number between 000 and 999.

Cluster 1

Selected exchange: 636
Selected number: 636-3230
Replace the last three digits (230) with randomly selected 389 to form 636-3389.
Repeat this process until the desired number of telephone numbers from this cluster is obtained.

and hard-to-reach areas.[26] Mailing lists are sometimes unavailable, outdated, or incomplete, however. Typically, telephone and street directories are used for a listing of the general population. Problems with these types of lists have been discussed already. As illustrated in Research in Practice 6.2, catalogs of mailing lists contain thousands of lists that can be purchased.[27]

RESEARCH IN PRACTICE 6.2

Sample Mailing Lists

List Title	Number on List	Price[a]
Advertising agencies' executives	3892	$45/M
Banks, main offices	11089	$85/M
Boat owners	4289601	$50/M
Chambers of Commerce	6559	$45/M
Personal computer owners	2218672	Inquire
Families	76000000	Inquire
Hardware wholesalers	7378	$45/M
Magazines, consumer	4119	$45/M
Photographic, portrait	33742	$45/M
Sales executives	190002	$55/M
Wives of professional men	1663614	$60/M
YMCA's	1036	$85

[a]Price shown is per 1,000 names (/M), except where noted.

Source: Best Mailing Lists, Inc., Catalog 1995 (800-692-2378)

Another factor outside the researcher's control is whether the questionnaire is answered and who answers it. Some subjects refuse to respond because of lack of interest or motivation; others cannot respond because they are illiterate.[28] For these reasons, the degree of sample control in mail surveys is low.[29]

Mail panels, on the other hand, provide moderate to high control over the sample. They provide samples matched to U.S. Bureau of the Census statistics on key demographic variables. It is also possible to identify specific user groups within a panel and to direct the survey to households with specific characteristics. Specific members of households in the panel can be questioned. Finally, low-incidence groups, groups that occur infrequently in the population, can be reached with panels, but there is a question of the extent to which a panel can be considered representative of the entire population.

Control of the Data Collection Environment

The degree of control a researcher has over the environment in which the respondent answers the questionnaire is another factor that differentiates the various survey modes. Personal interviews conducted at central locations (mall-intercept interviews and CAPI) offer the greatest degree of environmental control. For example, the researcher can set up a special facility for demonstrating the product. In-home personal interviews offer moderate to good control because the interviewer is present. Traditional telephone interviews and CATI offer moderate control. The interviewer cannot see the environment in which the interview is being conducted, but he or she can sense the background conditions and encourage the respondent to be attentive and involved. In mail panels and especially mail surveys, the researcher has little control over the environment.

Control of Field Force

field force Both the actual interviewers and the supervisors involved in data collection.

The **field force** consists of interviewers and supervisors involved in data collection. Because they require no such personnel, mail surveys and mail panels eliminate field force problems. Traditional telephone interviews, CATI, mall-intercept interviews, and CAPI all offer moderate degrees of control because the interviews are conducted at a central location, making supervision relatively simple. In-home personal interviews are problematic in this respect. Because many interviewers work in many different locations, continual supervision is impractical.[30]

Quantity of Data

In-home personal interviews allow the researcher to collect large amounts of data. The social relationship between the interviewer and the respondent, as well as the home environment, motivates the respondent to spend more time in the interview. Less effort is required of the respondent in a personal interview than in a telephone or mail interview. The interviewer records answers to open-ended questions and provides visual aids to help with lengthy and complex scales. Some personal interviews last for as long as 75 minutes. In contrast to in-home interviews, mall-intercept interviews and CAPI provide only moderate amounts of data. Because these interviews are conducted in shopping malls and other central locations, a respondent's time is more limited. Typically, the interview time is 30 minutes or less. For example, in recent mall-intercept interviews conducted by General Foods, the interview time was limited to 25 minutes.[31]

Mail surveys also yield moderate amounts of data. Fairly long questionnaires can be used because short questionnaires have not been shown to generate higher response rates than long ones. Mail panels, on the other hand, can generate large amounts of data because of the special relationship between the panel members and the sponsoring organization. For example, the author has used the Market Facts panel to administer a questionnaire that took two hours to complete.

Traditional telephone interviews and CATI result in the most limited quantities of data. They tend to be shorter than other surveys because respondents can easily terminate the telephone conversation at their own discretion. These interviews commonly last about 15 minutes, although longer interviews may be conducted when the subject matter is of interest to the respondents.[32] Studies indicate that respondents tend to underestimate the length of telephone interviews by as much as 50%. This suggests that telephone interviews may be conducted for a longer duration than is currently the practice.

Response Rate

response rate The percentage of the total attempted interviews that are completed.

Survey **response rate** is broadly defined as the percentage of the total attempted interviews that are completed. Personal, in-home, mall-intercept and computer-assisted interviews yield the highest response rate (typically more than 80%). Problems caused by not-at-homes can often be resolved by calling back at different times. Telephone interviews, traditional and CATI, yield response rates between 60 and 80%. These modes also suffer from not-at-homes or no-answers. Higher response rates are obtained by callbacks. Many telephone surveys attempt to call back at least three times.

nonresponse bias When actual respondents differ from those who refuse to participate.

Mail surveys have the poorest response rate. In a mail survey of randomly selected respondents, without any pre- or postmailing contact, the response rate is typically less than 15%. Such low response rate can lead to serious bias (nonresponse bias) because whether a person responds to a mail survey is related to his or her interest in the topic. The magnitude of **nonresponse bias** increases as the response rate decreases. The use of appropriate response-inducement procedures can increase the response rate in mail surveys to 80% or more, however. Response rates in mail panels are typically in the 70 to 80% range because of assured respondent cooperation.

A comprehensive review of the literature covering 497 response rates in 93 journal articles found weighted average response rates of 81.7%, 72.3%, and 47.3% for, respectively, personal, telephone, and mail surveys.[33] The same review also found that response rates increase with

- Either prepaid or promised monetary incentives
- An increase in the amount of monetary incentive
- Nonmonetary premiums and rewards (pens, pencils, books)
- Preliminary notification

critical request The target behavior being researched.

- Foot-in-the door techniques. These are multiple request strategies. The first request is relatively small, and all or most people agree to comply. The small request is followed by a larger request, called the **critical request**, which is actually the target behavior.
- Personalization (sending letters addressed to specific individuals)
- Follow-up letters

A further discussion of improving response rates is found in Chapter 12.

Perceived anonymity

perceived anonymity The respondent's perceptions that their identities will not be discerned by the interviewer or the researcher.

Perceived anonymity refers to the respondents' perceptions that their identities will not be discerned by the interviewer or the researcher. Perceived anonymity of the respondent is high in mail surveys and mail panels and low in personal interviews (in-home, mall-intercept, and computer-assisted). Traditional telephone interviews and CATI fall in the middle.

Social Desirability/Sensitive Information

social desirability The tendency of respondents to give answers that may not be accurate but that may be desirable from a social standpoint.

Social desirability is the tendency of respondents to give answers that are socially acceptable, whether or not they are true. As mail surveys and mail panels do not involve any social interaction between the interviewer and the respondent, they are least susceptible to social desirability. Evidence suggests that such methods are good for obtaining sensitive information such as that related to financial or personal behavior. Traditional telephone interviews and CATI are moderately good at avoiding socially desirable responses. They are also good for obtaining sensitive information.[34] Personal interviews—whether in-home, mall-intercept, or computer-assisted—are limited in this respect, although the problem is somewhat mitigated in the case of computer-assisted interviews.[35]

Potential for Interviewer Bias

An interviewer can bias the results of a survey by the manner in which he or she (1) selects respondents (interviewing somebody else when required to interview the male head of household), (2) asks research questions (omitting questions), and (3) records answers (recording an answer incorrectly or incompletely). The extent of the interviewer's role determines the potential for bias.[36] In-home and mall-intercept personal interviews are highly susceptible to interviewer bias. Traditional telephone interviews and CATI are less susceptible, although the potential is still there. For example, with inflection and tone of voice, interviewers can convey their own attitudes and thereby suggest answers. Computer-assisted interviews have a low potential for bias, and surveys and mail panels are free of it.

Speed

Traditional telephone interviews and CATI are the fastest ways of obtaining information. When a central telephone facility is used, several hundred telephone interviews can be done per day. Data for even large national surveys can be collected in two weeks or less. Next in speed are mall-intercept and computer-assisted interviews that reach potential respondents in central locations. In-home personal interviews are slower because there is dead time between interviews while the interviewer travels to the next respondent. To expedite data collection, interviews can be conducted in different markets or regions simultaneously. Mail surveys are typically the slowest. It usually takes several weeks to receive completed questionnaires; follow-up mailings take even longer. Mail panels are faster than mail surveys because little follow-up is required.

Cost

Personal interviews tend to be the most expensive mode of data collection per completed response, whereas mail surveys tend to be the least expensive. In general, mail surveys, mail panel, traditional telephone, CATI, CAPI, mall-intercept, and personal in-home interviews require progressively larger field staff and greater supervision and control. Hence, the cost increases in this order. Relative costs, however depend on the subject of inquiry and the procedures adopted.[37]

SELECTION OF SURVEY METHOD(S)

As is evident from Table 6.2 and the preceding discussion, no survey method is superior in all situations. Depending on such factors as information requirements, budgetary constraints (time and money), and respondent characteristics, none, one, two, or even all methods may be appropriate.[38] Remember that the various data collection modes are not mutually exclusive. Rather, they can be employed in a complementary fashion to build on each other's strengths and compensate for each other's weaknesses. The researcher can employ these methods in combination and develop creative methods. To illustrate, in a classic project, interviewers distributed the product, self-administered questionnaires, and return envelopes to respondents. Traditional telephone interviews were used for follow-up. Combining the data collection modes resulted in telephone cooperation from 97% of the respondents. Furthermore, 82% of the questionnaires were returned by mail.[39] The following examples illustrate the selection of survey modes.

DEPARTMENT STORE PATRONAGE PROJECT
Personal In-Home Interviews

In the department store project, personal in-home interviews were used for a number of reasons. Many diverse questions were asked. Some questions were complex and a relatively large amount of data had to be collected. The information obtained was not sensitive or threatening. Trained students were used as interviewers, thereby reducing the cost. Another critical consideration was that the personal interviews could be conducted without subcontracting the data collection to a field service organization.

Telephone methods were not chosen due to the complexity of the questions and amount of data needed. Mall-intercept interviews and CAPI were not appropriate either because so much data were needed. The use of a central location facility would have necessitated subcontracting with a field service organization. Mail surveys were ruled out due to low response rate and complexity of the information needed. Mail panels were inappropriate given the complexity of information needed; also, a self-administered questionnaire was not considered to be appropriate. ◆

EXAMPLE
New Product Development at Oscar Mayer Uses Old but Proven Methods

New Product Development at Oscar Mayer starts by using fact-based data and prior research to form questions such as

> Who is your target buyer?
> What product is this buyer currently using?
> What is this buyer's big problem with it?
> How will you solve this problem?

Once these questions are considered, a prototype of the new product idea is formed and tested in focus groups. The feedback from these groups allows the inventors to make adjustments to their products and in essence fine-tune the idea. Next, quantitative testing is used in the form of questionnaires mailed to households. Mail survey is used because it enables Oscar Mayer to collect the required quantity of data at a very low cost and elimi-

nates the potential for interviewer bias. The major drawback of low response rates is overcome by offering suitable incentives. Once information is received from these consumers, the data are compared with the normative database of prior research for evaluation. Once evaluated, the information is used to create options for the product in areas such as composition, packaging, size, or shape. These various designs are tested at the marketing research facility by bringing in approximately 200 target market consumers to give their opinions and to rate the product variations. Central location interviewing at the marketing research facility is chosen because the "use of physical stimuli" criterion dominates and it is necessary for the respondents to see, handle, and even taste the product. The information obtained at this stage is used to help choose between the possible product configurations.[40] ◆

Focus groups, mail surveys, and central location surveys have enabled Oscar Mayer to develop several successful products such as *Fat Free* Bologna. ◆ Klehr & Associates.

OBSERVATION METHODS

observation The recording of behavioral patterns of people, objects, and events in a systematic manner to obtain information about the phenomenon of interest.

Observation methods are the second type of methodology used in descriptive research. **Observation** involves recording the behavioral patterns of people, objects, and events in a systematic manner to obtain information about the phenomenon of interest. The observer does not question or communicate with the people being observed. Information may be recorded as the events occur or from records of past events. Observational methods may be structured or unstructured, direct or indirect. Furthermore, observation may be conducted in a natural or a contrived environment.[41]

Structured versus Unstructured Observation

structured observation Observation where the researcher clearly defines the behaviors to be observed and the methods by which they will be measured.

For **structured observation**, the researcher specifies in detail what is to be observed and how the measurements are to be recorded, such as when an auditor performs inventory analysis in a store. This reduces the potential for observer bias and enhances the reliability of the data. Structured observation is appropriate when the marketing research problem has been clearly defined and the information needed has been specified. In these circumstances, the details of the phenomenon to be observed can be clearly identified. Structured observation is suitable for use in conclusive research.

unstructured observation Observation that involves a researcher monitoring all relevant phenomena, without specifying the details in advance.

In **unstructured observation** the observer monitors all aspects of the phenomenon that seem relevant to the problem at hand, such as when observing children playing with new toys. This form of observation is appropriate when the problem has yet to be formulated precisely and when flexibility is needed in observation to identify key components of the problem and to develop hypotheses. In unstructured observation, potential for observer bias is high. For this reason, the observation findings should be treated as hypotheses to be tested rather than as conclusive findings. Thus, unstructured observation is most appropriate for exploratory research.

Disguised versus Undisguised Observation

In disguised observation, the respondents are unaware that they are being observed. Disguise enables respondents to behave naturally because people tend to behave differently when they know they are being observed. Disguise may be accomplished by using one-way mirrors, hidden cameras, or inconspicuous mechanical devices. Observers may be disguised as shoppers, sales clerks, or other appropriate roles.

In undisguised observation, the respondents are aware that they are under observation. For example, they may be aware of the presence of the observer. Researchers disagree on how much effect the presence of an observer has on behavior. One viewpoint is that the observer effect is minor and short-lived.[42] The other position is that the observer can seriously bias the behavior patterns.[43]

Natural versus Contrived Observation

natural observation
Observing behavior as it takes place in the environment.

contrived observation
Observing behavior in an artificial environment.

Natural observation involves observing behavior as it takes places in the environment. For example, one could observe the behavior of respondents eating fast food in Burger King. In **contrived observation**, respondents' behavior is observed in an artificial environment, such as a test kitchen.

The advantage of natural observation is that the observed phenomenon will more accurately reflect the true phenomenon. The disadvantages are the cost of waiting for the phenomenon to occur and the difficulty of measuring the phenomenon in a natural setting.

OBSERVATION METHODS CLASSIFIED BY MODE OF ADMINISTRATION

As shown in Figure 6.3, observation methods may be classified by mode of administration as personal observation, mechanical observation, audit, content analysis, and trace analysis.

Personal Observation

personal observation An observational research strategy in which human observers record the phenomenon being observed as it occurs.

In **personal observation**, a researcher observes actual behavior as it occurs. The observer does not attempt to control or manipulate the phenomenon being observed but merely records what takes place. For example, a researcher might record traffic counts and observe traffic flows in a department store. This information could aid in designing a store's layout and determining the location of individual departments, shelf locations, and merchandise displays. As another example, consider the following.

FIGURE 6.3

A Classification of Observation Methods

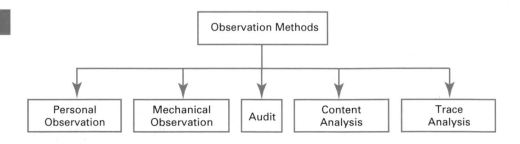

DEPARTMENT STORE PATRONAGE PROJECT
Personal Observation

In the department store project, license plate surveys could be used to establish the primary trading area of a shopping mall. These surveys help marketers determine where their customers live. In a license plate survey, observers record the license plate numbers of the automobiles in a parking lot. These numbers are fed into a computer and paired with automobile registration data. This results in a map of customers located by census tract or zip codes. Such a map, along with other demographic data, can help a department store chain determine new locations, decide on billboard space, and target direct marketing effort. License plate surveys cost less ($5,000 to $25,000) and are believed to be quicker and more reliable than direct communication methods such as interviews with shoppers.[44] ◆

Research in Practice 6.3 shows how one Japanese company used personal observation to make an important marketing decision.[45]

RESEARCH IN PRACTICE 6.3

Marketing Research: The Japanese Way

Japanese companies rely heavily on personal observation as means of obtaining information. When Canon Cameras was losing market share in the United States to Minolta, Canon decided that its distributor, Bell and Howell, was not giving adequate support. Canon, however, did not use data from a broad survey of consumers or retailers to make this decision. Instead, it sent three managers to the United States to look into the problem.

Canon's head of the team, Tatehiro Tsuruta, spent almost six weeks in America. On entering a camera store, he acted just like a customer. He noted how the cameras were displayed and how the clerks served customers. He observed that the dealers were not enthusiastic about Canon. He also observed that it would not be advantageous for Canon to use drugstores and other discount outlets. This led Canon to open its own sales subsidiary.

Mechanical Observation

mechanical observation
An observational research strategy in which mechanical devices, rather than human observers, record the phenomenon being observed.

In **mechanical observation**, mechanical devices, rather than human observers, record the phenomenon being observed. These devices may or may not require the respondents' direct participation. They are used for continuously recording ongoing behavior for later analysis.

Of the mechanical devices that do not require respondents' direct participation, the A. C. Nielsen audimeter is best known. The audimeter is attached to a television set to record continually the channel to which a set is tuned. Recently, people meters have been introduced. People meters attempt to measure not only the channels to which a set is tuned but also who is watching.[46] Other common examples include turnstiles that record the number of people entering or leaving a building and traffic counters placed across streets to determine the number of vehicles passing certain locations. On-site cameras (still, motion picture, or video) are increasingly used by retailers to assess package designs, counter space, floor displays, and traffic flow patterns.[47] Technological advances such as the universal product code (UPC) have made a major impact on mechanical observation. The UPC system together with optical scanners allow for mechanized information collection regarding consumer purchases by product category, brand, store type, price, and quantity (see Chapter 4). The following example shows how observation is used to monitor television viewing and related behaviors.

EXAMPLE
VCRs Used to View Home Video Market _____

VCRs are used an average of seven hours a week, according to a study by AGB Television Research. This result was obtained from the first VCR study using AGB's FingerPrinting technology. AGB attaches a small device to a VCR that automatically measures recording, playback, and playing of prerecorded tapes. This information is useful to firms like Blockbuster Video, which markets videos for home entertainment, education, and a variety of other purposes.[48] ◆

This study did not require direct involvement of the participants. In contrast, many mechanical observation devices do require such involvement. These mechanical devices may be classified into five groups: (1) eye-tracking monitors, (2) pupilometers, (3) psychogalvanometers, (4) voice pitch analyzers, and (5) devices measuring response latency. Eye-tracking equipment—such as oculometers, eye cameras, or eye view minuters—records the gaze movements of the eye. These devices can be used to determine how a respondent reads an advertisement or views a TV commercial and for how long the respondent looks at various parts of the stimulus. Such information is directly relevant to assessing advertising effectiveness. The pupilometer measures changes in the diameter of the pupils of the respondent's eyes. The respondent is asked to look at a screen on which an advertisement or other stimulus is projected. Image brightness and distance from the respondent's eyes are held constant. Changes in pupil size are interpreted as changes in cognitive (thinking) activity resulting from exposure to the stimulus. The underlying assumption is that increased pupil size reflects interest and positive attitudes toward the stimulus.[49]

The **psychogalvanometer** measures **galvanic skin response** (GSR) or changes in the electrical resistance of the skin.[50] The respondent is fitted with small electrodes that monitor electrical resistance and is shown stimuli such as advertisements, packages, and slogans. The theory behind this device is that physiological changes such as increased perspiration accompany emotional reactions. Excitement leads to increased perspiration, which increases the electrical resistance of the skin. From the strength of the response, the researcher infers the respondent's interest level and attitudes toward the stimuli.[51]

Voice pitch analysis measures emotional reactions through changes in the respondent's voice. Changes in the relative vibration frequency of the human voice that accompany emotional reaction are measured with audio-adapted computer equipment.[52]

Response latency is the time a respondent takes before answering a question. It is used as a measure of the relative preference for various alternatives.[53] Response time is thought to be directly related to uncertainty. Therefore, the longer a respondent takes to choose between two alternatives, the closer the alternatives are in terms of preference. On the other hand, if the respondent makes a quick decision, one alternative is

psychogalvanometer An instrument that measures a respondent's galvanic skin response.

galvanic skin response Changes in the electrical resistance of the skin that relate to a respondent's affective state.

voice pitch analysis Measurement of emotional reactions through changes in the respondent's voice.

response latency The amount of time it takes to respond.

clearly preferred. With the increased popularity of computer-assisted data collection, response latency can be recorded accurately and without the respondent's awareness.

Use of eye-tracking monitors, pupilometers, psychogalvanometers, and voice pitch analyzers assumes that physiological reactions are associated with specific cognitive and affective responses. This has yet to be clearly demonstrated.[54] Furthermore, calibration of these devices to measure physiological arousal is difficult, and they are expensive to use. Another limitation is that respondents are placed in an artificial environment and know that they are being observed.

Audit

In an audit, the researcher collects data by examining physical records or performing inventory analysis. Audits have two distinguishing features. First, data are collected personally by the researcher. Second, the data are based upon counts, usually of physical objects. Retail and wholesale audits conducted by marketing research suppliers were discussed in the context of secondary data (see Chapter 4). Here we focus on the role of audits in collecting primary data. In this respect, an important audit conducted at the consumer level, generally in conjunction with one of the survey methods, is the pantry audit. In a **pantry audit**, the researcher takes an inventory of brands, quantities, and package sizes in a consumer's home, perhaps in the course of a personal interview. Pantry audits greatly reduce the problem of untruthfulness or other forms of response bias. Obtaining permission to examine consumers' pantries can be difficult, however, and the field work is expensive. Furthermore, the brands in the pantry may not reflect the most preferred brands or the brands purchased most often. Moreover, similar data can be obtained from scanner panels more efficiently (Chapter 4). For these reasons, pantry audits are no longer commonly used, but audits are more common at the retail and wholesale level, as the following example illustrates.

pantry audit A type of audit where the researcher inventories the brands, quantities, and package sizes of products in a consumer's home.

EXAMPLE
The Product Pipeline

An important marketing research task is finding out where the product is in the long pipeline from manufacturer to consumer. This was a problem in the personal computer industry. No one was quite sure which computers people were actually buying and which were piling up in inventory. To remedy this situation, the A.C. Nielsen Company arranged with major computer chains to send in teams of auditors to take physical inventory and to determine what people were buying. The audit provided information on the retail sales of the various brands of personal computers and their movement in the distribution channels.[55] ◆

Content Analysis

Content analysis The objective, systematic, and quantitative description of the manifest content of a communication.

Content analysis is an appropriate method when the phenomenon to be observed is communication, rather than behavior or physical objects. It is defined as the objective, systematic, and quantitative description of the manifest content of a communication.[56] It includes observation as well as analysis. The unit of analysis may be words (different words or types of words in the message), characters (individuals or objects), themes (propositions), space and time measures (length or duration of the message), or topics (subject of the message). Analytical categories for classifying the units are developed, and the communication is broken down according to prescribed rules. Marketing research applications involve observing and analyzing the content or message of advertisements, newspaper articles, television and radio programs, and the like. For example, the frequency of appearance of blacks, women, and members of other minority groups in mass media has been studied using content analysis. In the department store patronage project, content analysis may be used to analyze magazine advertisements of the sponsoring and competing stores to compare their projected images. Content analysis has also been used in cross-cultural advertising research, as in the following example.

EXAMPLE
Cross-Cultural Content Makes Ad Agencies Content

Content analysis was used to compare the information content in American and Japanese magazine advertising. Six categories of magazines (general, women's, men's, professional, sports, and entertainment) were chosen from each country. All advertisements, except classifieds, from the May and June 1984 issues of each magazine were analyzed. This resulted in a total of 1,440 advertisements: 832 from American magazines and 608 from Japanese magazines. Three judges independently noted whether each advertisement was informative or uninformative, which criteria for information content were satisfied by the advertisement, the size of the ad, and the product category being advertised. Japanese magazine advertising was found to be consistently more informative than U.S. magazine advertising. For example, more than 85% of the Japanese ads analyzed satisfied at least one criterion for information content and thus were perceived to be informative, compared with only 75% of the American ads. Likewise, Japanese ads had an average of 1.7 information cues per ad, compared with 1.3 cues per ad for the U.S. ads. This information is useful for multinational companies and advertising agencies including Young and Rubicam, Saatchi and Saatchi Worldwide, Backer Spielvogel Bates Worldwide, McCann Erickson Worldwide, Ogilvy and Mather Worldwide, BBDO Worldwide and others with global operations conducting cross-cultural advertising campaigns.[57] ◆

Content analysis can involve tedious coding and analysis. Microcomputers and mainframes can be used to facilitate coding and analysis, however. The manifest content of the object can be computer coded. The observed frequencies of category codes can be aggregated and compared on the criteria of interest using computers. Although content analysis has not been widely used in marketing research, the technique offers great potential. For example, it could be profitably employed in the analysis of open-ended questions.

Trace Analysis

trace analysis An approach in which data collection is based on physical traces, or evidence, of past behavior.

An observation method that can be inexpensive if used creatively is trace analysis. In **trace analysis**, data collection is based on physical traces, or evidence, of past behavior. These traces may be left by the respondents intentionally or unintentionally. For example, in the context of the department store patronage project, store charge card slips are traces shoppers leave behind that can be analyzed to examine their store credit usage behavior. Several other innovative applications of trace analysis have been made in marketing research.[58]

- The selective erosion of tiles in a museum indexed by the replacement rate was used to determine the relative popularity of exhibits.

- The number of different fingerprints on a page was used to gauge the readership of various advertisements in a magazine.
- The position of the radio dials in cars brought in for service was used to estimate share of listening audience of various radio stations. Advertisers used the estimates to decide on which stations to advertise.
- The age and condition of cars in a parking lot were used to assess the affluence of customers.
- The magazines people donated to charity were used to determine people's favorite magazines.

As an additional example, consider the following.

EXAMPLE
One Man's Trash is a Marketer's Treasure

In a federally funded scientific project at the University of Arizona, researchers sifted through household refuse to determine what products and brands people consume and in what quantity. Their research revealed many interesting findings. For example, poor people eat meat as often as rich people and drink as much milk. As compared with the rich, the poor use more vitamins, household cleaners, and children's toys and books. Thus, many stereotypes about purchasing habits were found to be untrue.[59] ◆

In the Arizona project, trace analysis resulted in new insights into the consumption behavior of the rich and the poor. Although trace analysis has been creatively applied, it has limitations. Current evidence indicates that it should be used only when no other approach is possible.

A COMPARATIVE EVALUATION OF OBSERVATION METHODS

A comparative evaluation of the observation methods is given in Table 6.3. The different observation methods are evaluated in terms of the degree of structure, degree of disguise, ability to observe in a natural setting, observation bias, measurement and analysis bias, and additional general factors.

Structure relates to the specification of what is to be observed and how the measurements are to be recorded. As can be seen from Table 6.3, personal observation is low,

TABLE 6.3

A Comparative Evaluation of Observation Methods

Criteria	Personal Observation	Mechanical Observation	Audit	Content Analysis	Trace Analysis
Degree of structure	Low	Low to high	High	High	Medium
Degree of disguise	Medium	Low to high	Low	High	High
Ability to observe in natural setting	High	Low to high	High	Medium	Low
Observation bias	High	Low	Low	Medium	Medium
Analysis bias	High	Low to medium	Low	Low	Medium
General remarks	Most flexible	Can be intrusive	Expensive	Limited to communications	Method of last resort

trace analysis is medium, and audit and content analysis are high on the degree of structure. Mechanical observation can vary widely from low to high, depending on the methods used. Methods such as optical scanners are very structured in that the characteristics to be measured—for example, characteristics of items purchased scanned in supermarket checkouts—are precisely defined. Thus, these methods are high in the degree of structure. In contrast, mechanical methods such as use of hidden cameras to observe children at play with toys tend to be unstructured.

The degree of disguise is low in the case of audits as it is difficult to conceal the identity of auditors. Personal observation offers a medium degree of disguise because there are limitations on the extent to which the observer can be disguised as a shopper, sales clerk, employee, and so forth. Trace analysis and content analysis offer a high degree of disguise because the data are collected "after the fact," that is, after the phenomenon to be observed has taken place. Some mechanical observations such as hidden cameras offer excellent disguise, whereas others, such as the use of psychogalvanometers, are very difficult to disguise.

The ability to observe in a natural setting is low in trace analysis because the observation takes place after the behavior has occurred. It is medium in the case of content analysis because the communication being analyzed is only a limited representation of the natural phenomenon. Personal observation and audits are excellent on this score because human observers can observe people or objects in a variety of natural settings. Mechanical observation methods vary from low (e.g., use of psychogalvanometers) to high (e.g., use of turnstiles).

Observation bias is low in the case of mechanical observation because a human observer is not involved. It is also low for audits. Although the auditors are humans, the observation usually takes place on objects and the characteristics to be observed are well defined, leading to low observation bias. Observation bias is medium for trace analysis and content analysis. In both these methods, human observers are involved and the characteristics to be observed are not very well defined. The observers typically do not interact with human respondents during the observation process, however, thus lessening the degree of bias. It is high for personal observation due to the use of human observers who interact with the phenomenon being observed.

Data analysis bias is low for audits and content analysis because the variables are precisely defined, the data are quantitative, and statistical analysis is conducted. Trace analysis has a medium degree of bias as the definition of variables is not very precise. Mechanical observation methods can have a low (e.g., scanner data) to medium (e.g., hidden camera) degree of analysis bias, depending on the method. Unlike personal observation, the bias in mechanical observation is limited to the medium level due to improved measurement and classification because the phenomenon to be observed can be recorded continuously using mechanical devices.

In addition, personal observation is the most flexible because human observers can observe a wide variety of phenomenon in a wide variety of settings. Some mechanical observation methods, such as the use of psychogalvanometers, can be very intrusive, leading to artificiality and bias. Audits using human auditors tend to be expensive. Content analysis is well suited for and limited to the observation of communications. As mentioned earlier, trace analysis is a method of last resort. The application of these criteria will lead to the identification of an appropriate method, if observation is at all suitable in the given situation.

A COMPARISON OF SURVEY AND OBSERVATION METHODS

Other than the use of scanner data, few marketing research projects rely solely on observational methods to obtain primary data.[60] This implies that observational methods have some major disadvantages as compared with survey methods. Yet these methods offer some advantages that make their use in conjunction with survey methods quite fruitful.

Relative Advantages of Observation

The greatest advantage of observational methods is that they permit measurement of actual behavior rather than reports of intended or preferred behavior. There is no reporting bias, and potential bias caused by the interviewer and the interviewing process is eliminated or reduced. Certain types of data can be collected only by observation. These include behavior patterns of which the respondent is unaware or is unable to communicate. For example, information on babies' toy preferences is best obtained by observing babies at play, because they are unable to express themselves adequately. Moreover, if the observed phenomenon occurs frequently or is of short duration, observational methods may cost less and be faster than survey methods.

Relative Disadvantages of Observation

The most serious disadvantage of observation is that the reasons for the observed behavior may not be determined because little is known about the underlying motives, beliefs, attitudes, and preferences. For example, people observed buying a brand of cereal may or may not like it themselves; they may be purchasing that brand for someone else in the household. Another limitation of observation is that selective perception (bias in the researcher's perception) can bias the data. In addition, observational data is often time-consuming and expensive, and it is difficult to observe certain forms of behavior such as personal activities. Finally, in some cases, the use of observational methods may border on being unethical. The ethical issues involved in monitoring the behavior of people without their consent are still being debated.

To sum up, observation has the potential to provide valuable information when properly used. From a practical standpoint, it is best to view observation as a complement to survey methods, rather than as being in competition with them. The following example illustrates this point.

EXAMPLE
Stores Plan on Unplanned Purchases

Point-of-Purchase Advertising Institute, Inc. (POPAI) recently conducted a study to determine the purchasing behavior of grocery shoppers. Consumers were surveyed as they began their shopping trips and questioned on their intended purchases. At the checkout counter, their actual purchases were recorded with UPC scanners. These observational data were then compared with their intended purchases. It was found that 81% of all purchases were the result of in-store decisions, a substantial increase from 64.8% a decade ago. Unplanned purchases also were up; 60.4% of all items bought were classified as unplanned purchases. Shoppers are not committed to their shopping list when they enter the store. Moreover, brand decisions often are made at point-of-purchase. Thus, marketers of grocery products can greatly benefit from in-store advertising, point-of-purchase displays, and other in-store promotions.[61] ◆

The POPAI research combined a survey at the beginning of shopping with observational data at checkout to obtain rich insights into grocery shoppers' behavior.

INTERNATIONAL MARKETING RESEARCH

Selection of appropriate interviewing methods is much more difficult because of the challenges of conducting research in foreign countries. Given the differences in the economic, structural, informational and technological, and sociocultural environment, the feasibility and popularity of the different interviewing methods vary widely. In the United States and Canada, the telephone has achieved almost total penetration of households. As a result, telephone interviewing is the dominant mode of questionnaire administration. The same situation exists in some European countries, such as Sweden. In many other European countries, however, telephone penetration is still not complete. In developing countries, only very few households have telephones.

In-home personal interviews are the dominant mode of collecting survey data in many European countries such as Switzerland, newly industrialized countries, and developing countries. Although mall-intercept interviews are being conducted in some European countries, such as Sweden,[62] they are not popular in Europe or developing countries. In contrast, central location and street interviews constitute the dominant method of collecting survey data in France and the Netherlands.[63]

Because of low cost, mail interviews continue to be used in most developed countries where literacy is high and the postal system is well developed: the United States, Canada, Denmark, Finland, Iceland, Norway, Sweden, and the Netherlands, for example. In Africa, Asia, and South America, however, the use of mail surveys and mail panels is low because of illiteracy and the large proportion of population living in rural areas. Mail panels are extensively used only in a few countries outside the United States, such as Canada, the United Kingdom, France, Germany, and the Netherlands. The use of panels may increase with the advent of new technology, however. The different methods of survey administration are discussed in more detail in Chapter 23.

Selection of Survey Methods

No questionnaire administration method is superior in all situations. Table 6.4 presents a comparative evaluation of the major modes of collecting quantitative data in the context of international marketing research. In this table, the survey methods are discussed only under the broad headings of telephone, personal, and mail interviews. The use of CATI, CAPI, and mail panels depends heavily on the state of technological development in the country. Likewise, the use of mall-intercept interviewing is contingent upon the dominance of shopping malls in the retailing environment. The major methods of interviewing should be carefully evaluated on the criteria given in Table 6.4, as shown.

Another important consideration in selecting the methods of administering questionnaires is to ensure equivalence and comparability across countries. Different methods may have different reliabilities in different countries. In collecting data from different countries, it is desirable to use survey methods with equivalent levels of reliability, rather than the same method, as illustrated in the following example.

	Criteria	Telephone	Personal	Mail
TABLE 6.4 *A Comparative Evaluation of Survey Methods for International Marketing Research*	High sample control	+	+	−
	Difficulty in locating respondents at home	+	−	+
	Inaccessibility of homes	+	−	+
	Unavailability of a large pool of trained interviewers	+	−	+
	Large population in rural areas	−	+	−
	Unavailability of maps	+	−	+
	Unavailability of current telephone directory	−	+	−
	Unavailability of mailing lists	+	+	−
	Low penetration of telephones	−	+	+
	Lack of an efficient postal system	+	+	−
	Low level of literacy	−	+	−
	Face–to–face communication culture	−	+	−

Note: A + denotes an advantage, and a − denotes a disadvantage.

EXAMPLE
Using Dominant Survey Methods to Gain Dominant Market Share

Reebok International Ltd., with a 16% share of the athletic shoe market in the United States, is seeking to expand in Europe. Europe is a market with vast potential and sales of sneakers amounted to $5 billion in 1995. Rather than strictly compete with Nike, Adidas, and Puma in Europe for the athletic market, Reebok would like to institute strong marketing programs to sell street sneakers to the European masses. A survey of consumer preferences for sneakers is to be undertaken in three countries: Sweden, France, and Switzerland. Comparability of results can best be achieved by using the dominant mode of interviewing in each country: telephone interviews in Sweden, central location and street interviews in France, and in-home personal interviews in Switzerland.[64] ◆

As in the case of surveys, the selection of an appropriate observation method in international marketing research should also take into account the differences in the economic, structural, informational and technological, and sociocultural environment.

ETHICS IN MARKETING RESEARCH

The unethical use of survey research as a guise for targeting sales effort was discussed in Chapter 1. Respondents' anonymity, discussed in the context of qualitative research in Chapter 5, is salient in survey and observation research as well. Researchers are obligated to protect a respondent's identity and not disclose it to anyone outside the research organization including the client. The client is not entitled to the names of respondents. The only instance where respondents' identity can be revealed to the client is when respondents are notified in advance and their consent is obtained prior to administering the survey. Even in such situations, the researcher should have the assurance that the respondents' trust will be kept by the client and their identities will not be used in sales effort or misused in other ways.

The American Marketing Association's (AMA) code reads, "If respondents have been led to believe, directly or indirectly, that they are participating in a marketing research survey and that their anonymity will be protected, their names shall not be made known to any one outside the research organization or research department, or used for other than research purposes."[65] The International Code of Marketing and Social Research Practice, widely recognized in Europe, states, "the informant shall remain entirely anonymous. Special care must be taken to ensure that any record which contains a reference to the identity of an informant is securely and confidentially stored during any period before such reference is separated from that record and/or destroyed."[66] Ethical lapses in this respect by unscrupulous researchers and marketers have resulted in a serious back-lash for marketing research.

EXAMPLE
The Signal is Busy for Telephone Research _____

The Council for Marketing and Opinion Research (CMOR) recently identified the "major threats to research vitality." At the top of the list was telephone research due to concern over proposed legislation. About half of the states have introduced bills to regulate unsolicited telephone calls and the remaining are considering similar legislation. A California law, designed to limit eavesdropping, makes it illegal to listen in on an extension, and this might limit supervisory monitoring of telephone interviewers.

Another issue facing the marketing research industry is image, as the general public does not distinguish between telephone research and telemarketing. This identity crisis is exacerbated by the action of some firms to commit "sugging and frugging," industry terms for selling or fund-raising under the guise of a survey (discussed in Chapter 1).

All these barriers have raised the cost of telephone research and make it difficult for researchers to obtain representative samples. A study by Walker Research and Analysis revealed that the refusal rate in telephone interviews doubled in just ten years (15 % in 1982 compared to 31 % in 1992) due to annoyance with unsolicited calls and concern about privacy.

The CMOR is fighting back and has hired the Washington law firm of Covington and Burling to lobby Congress and coordinate state level lobbying. Another action under consideration is a "seal of approval" from the CMOR to raise the public's image perceptions of responsible research firms. The battle to save telephone research must be waged; all it takes is a phone call.[67] ◆

Although concerns for the respondents' psychological well being are mild in survey data collection when compared with either qualitative or experimental research, researchers should not place respondents in stressful situations. Disclaimers such as "there are no correct responses; we are only interested in your opinion" can relieve much of the stress innate to a survey.[68]

Observation of people's behavior without their consent is often done because informing the respondents may alter their behavior.[69] But this can compromise the privacy of the respondents. One guideline is that people should not be observed for research in situations where they would not expect to be observed by the public. Therefore, public places like a mall, or a grocery aisle are fair game. These are places where people observe other people routinely. However, notices should be posted in these areas stating that they are under observation by marketing researchers. After the data have been collected, the researcher should solicit the necessary permission from the respondents.[70]

COMPUTER APPLICATIONS

The use of microcomputers and mainframes has already been discussed in the context of CATI, CAPI, content analysis, and audits. Software for implementing these and other survey and observation methods is available. A handheld computer can replace paper questionnaires used in personal interviewing with the use of the SidePad utility and the ABase programming language from Advanced Data Research, Inc. (ADR) of Bloomfield Hills, Michigan. Using pen-based computing technology, this system uses the display memory as a software keypad. DOS-based PC survey software (such as Ci2, Ci3, or ACA being run simultaneously with the SidePad utility) accepts the touch of the screen as a keystroke on a keyboard.

The advantages of such a pen-based system include a reduction of entry errors over systems requiring the data entry person to look at a document instead of at the screen itself. In fact, with such a pen-based utility as SidePad, the need for a data entry person is eliminated entirely. The preinterviewing steps become less costly and less cumbersome by eliminating the typesetting, printing, collating, shipping, storing, and transport of questionnaires. The interviewing process is improved because skip patterns in the software bring accuracy by avoiding omissions of questions. Finally, the lengthy data entry process can be precluded using ADR's SidePad utility and ABase programming.

Pen-based computing can facilitate interviews at product clinics, drive tests, auto shows, mall intercepts, door-to-door surveys, and taste tests. The accompanying photograph shows a product clinic for the Dodge Minivan where three consumers simultaneously evaluate different features of this vehicle.

With the introduction of interactive graphics, pictures of potential products or automobile designs can be generated and presented to respondents. Such an extension of technology creates many possibilities for self-administered and customized surveys.

For open-ended questions, the VIEWER module can capture the handwriting of respondents or interviewers for later recall as a bit-mapped image. The interviewer or supervisor can sort these verbatim comments written to the handheld computer screen by the relevant question or demographic variable while on-site. For example, if the supervisor of the Dodge Minivan product clinic wanted to acquire an update on suggestions for minivan design, VIEWER would allow the handwritten comments from a demographic group to scroll across the screen of the interviewers' handheld computers. In Exhibit 6.1, the comments appear in order of respondent number (i.e., 1001–1003).

A variety of software is available for conducting mail surveys. MAIL IT! by Caddylak Systems Inc. eliminates list duplications, speeds up all mailing processes, and even helps users earn postal discounts. It can produce mailing labels, Rolodex cards, file cards, and postcards. CLEAN-A-LIST and ZIPLIST are two companion programs from DCC Data Service. CLEAN-A-LIST finds and fixes errors in mailing lists. ZIPLIST speeds data entry with a zip code data file directory for cities, counties, and states. CONQUEST DIRECT EXPRESS by Donnelley Marketing Information Services defines market areas and obtains counts and consumer lists for only those households or individuals in the block group or enumeration districts, census tracts, or zip codes in a desired area (geometric or geographic).

Mail questionnaires can also be administered electronically. Technological advances have made possible services like VIEWTEL by Viewfacts, which downloads

EXHIBIT 6.1

*Comments
of Respondents:
Viewer Module*

```
RESPONDENT: 1001

Age: 25-29              SEX: male          INCOME:$35,000-$39,999

If the designers and engineers were to make changes to MODEL X, what
would you tell them to CHANGE to better meet your needs?
The head supports are nonexistent. Please add them
```

> The head supports
> are nonexistent.
> Please add them.

```
RESPONDENT: 1002

Age: 25-29              SEX: male          INCOME: $50,000-<$59,999

If the designers and engineers were to make changes to MODEL X, what
would you tell them to CHANGE to better meet your needs?
Make the front end more aerodynamic
```

> Make the front end
> more aerodynamic

```
RESPONDENT: 1003

Age: 40-44              SEX: female        INCOME: $50,000-$59,999

If the designers and engineers were to make changes to MODEL X, what
would you tell them to CHANGE to better meet your needs?
More room in bed of truck. Makeup mirror on driver visor.
```

> more room in bed of
> Truck. Makeup mirror
> on Driver Visor.

Pen-based computing has facilitated interviewing at product clinics for the Dodge Minivan enabling continuous quality improvement (CQI). ◆ Dwight Cendrowski.

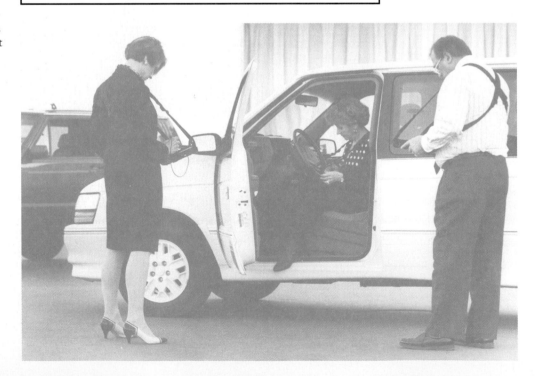

226

the questionnaire directly to consumers in their homes through their television sets. The questionnaire appears on the television screen and the respondents answer by using a handheld device provided by Viewfacts. Sample selection is limited to the Viewtel panel.

In addition to computerized audits (e.g., ELCAP discussed in Chapter 4), software can assist in conducting retail and wholesale audits. SPARTAC, by Spar Inc., is a real-time information collection and reporting system for use on in-store data collection by auditors. It has a proactive PC reporting system covering any in-store conditions, such as displays, out-of-stock, distribution, pricing, point-of-purchase, and promotion execution.

SUMMARY

The two basic means of obtaining primary quantitative data in descriptive research are survey and observation. Survey involves the direct questioning of respondents, while observation entails recording respondent behavior.

Surveys involve the administration of a questionnaire and may be classified, based on the method or mode of administration, as (1) traditional telephone interviews, (2) CATI, (3) in-home personal interviews, (4) mall-intercept interviews, (5) CAPI, (6) mail surveys, and (7) mail panels. Of these methods, traditional telephone interviews and CATI are the most popular. Each method has some general advantages and disadvantages, however. The various methods may be compared in terms of flexibility of data collection, diversity of questions, use of physical stimuli, sample control, control of the data collection environment, control of field force, quantity of data, social desirability, obtaining sensitive information, potential for interviewer bias, response rate, perceived anonymity, speed, and cost. Although these data collection methods are usually thought of as distinct and competitive, they should not be considered mutually exclusive. It is possible to employ them productively in combination.

Observational methods may be classified as structured or unstructured, disguised or undisguised, and natural or contrived. The major methods are personal observation, mechanical observation, audit, content analysis, and trace analysis. As compared with surveys, the relative advantages of observational methods are that (1) they permit measurement of actual behavior, (2) there is no reporting bias, and (3) there is less potential for interviewer bias. Also, certain types of data can best, or only, be obtained by observation. The relative disadvantages of observation are that: (1) very little can be inferred about motives, beliefs, attitudes, and preferences; (2) there is a potential for observer bias; (3) most methods are time-consuming and expensive; (4) it is difficult to observe some forms of behavior; and (5) there is a potential for being unethical. Observation is rarely used as the sole method of obtaining primary data, but it can be usefully employed in conjunction with survey methods.

In collecting data from different countries, it is desirable to use survey methods with equivalent levels of reliability rather than to use the same method. Respondents' anonymity should be protected, and their names should not be turned over to the clients. People should not be observed without consent for research in situations where they would not expect to be observed by the public. Microcomputers and mainframes are used extensively in survey research particularly in the context of CATI and CAPI. They also facilitate observation methods, particularly content analysis and audits.[71]

ACRONYMS

The classification of survey methods by mode of administration may be described by the acronym METHODS:

M   ail panels
E   lectronic/computer-assisted personal interviews
T   elephone interviews
H   ome (in-home personal) interviewing
O   n-site mall interviews
D   irect mail interviews
S   oftware for CATI

In using observational methods, you must WATCH the respondents' behavior. These methods may be described by the acronym WATCH:

W   alkie-talkie: mechanical observation
A   udit
T   race analysis
C   ontent analysis
H   uman (personal) observation

EXERCISES

QUESTIONS

1. Explain briefly how the topics covered in this chapter fit into the framework of the marketing research process.
2. What are the advantages and disadvantages of the structured direct survey method?
3. Name the major modes for obtaining information via a survey.
4. What are the relevant factors for evaluating which survey method is best suited to a particular research project?
5. What would be the most appropriate survey method for a project in which control of field force and cost are critical factors?
6. Name the types of mechanical observation and explain how they work.
7. Explain how content analysis could be employed in the analysis of open-ended questions. Comment on the relative advantages and disadvantages of using such a method.
8. Why is trace analysis used as a means of last resort?
9. What are the relative advantages and disadvantages of observation?

PROBLEMS

1. Describe a marketing research problem in which both survey and observation methods could be used for obtaining the information needed.
2. Collect 100 advertisements featuring women from recent issues of popular magazines. Do a content analysis of these ads to examine the different roles in which women are portrayed in advertising.
3. The campus food service would like to determine how many people eat in the student cafeteria. List the ways in which this information could be obtained. Which method is best?

COMPUTER EXERCISES

1. Ask your instructor or other faculty members if you could serve as a respondent in a computer-assisted personal interview. Then answer the same questionnaire in a pencil- and-paper format. Compare the two experiences.

2. Use simple spreadsheet software, such as Lotus 1-2-3 or Excel, or any appropriate microcomputer or mainframe program to conduct the content analysis described in problem 2.

NOTES

1. *Quirk's Marketing Research Review* (October–November 1987): 10, 36.

2. Nicolaos E. Synodinos and Jerry M. Brennan, "Computer Interactive Interviewing in Survey Research," *Psychology and Marketing* (Summer 1988): 117–37.

3. *Quirk's Marketing Research Review* (October–November 1987): 6–8.

4. Surveys are commonly used in marketing research. See, for example, Samaradasa Weerahandi and Soumyo Moitra, "Using Survey Data to Predict Adoption and Switching for Services," *Journal of Marketing Research* 32 (February 1995): 85–96; and Chan Su Park and V. Srinivasan, "A Survey-Based Method for Measuring and Understanding Brand Equity and Its Extendability," *Journal of Marketing Research* 31 (May 1994): 271–88.

5. "Digital Hears the Voice of the Market," *Marketing Research: A Magazine of Management and Applications* 4 (December 1992): 28–33.

6. James H. Frey, *Survey Research by Telephone* (Beverly Hills: Sage Publications, 1983).

7. Robert A. Groves and Nancy Mathiowetz, "Computer-Assisted Telephone Interviewing: Effects on Interviewers and Respondents," *Public Opinion Quarterly* 48 (Spring 1984): 356–59.

8. "Continuing Analysis of Shopping Habits in San Diego," *Quirk's Marketing Research Review* (April 1987): 6, 11, 12, 18, 24, 25.

9. *Consumer Market Research Technique Usage Patterns and Attitudes in 1983* (Chicago: Market Facts, Inc., 1983).

10. *Quirk's Marketing Research Review* (February 1988): 57.

11. A. J. Bush and J. F. Hair, Jr., "An Assessment of the Mall-intercept as a Data Collection Method," *Journal of Marketing Research* (May 1985): 158–67; and J. E. Rafael, "Self Administered CRT Interview: Benefits Far Outweigh the Problems," *Marketing News* (November 9, 1984): 16.

12. "Research Basic to Baby-Wear Business," *Marketing News* (February 13, 1987): 26.

13. John P. Liefeld, "Response Effects in Computer-Administered Questioning," *Journal of Marketing Research* 25 (November 1988): 405–9; and B. Whalen, "On-Site Computer Interviewing Yields Search Data Instantly," *Marketing News* (November 9, 1984): 1–17.

14. Nicolaos E. Synodinos and Jerry M. Brennan, "Computer Interactive Interviewing in Survey Research," *Psychology and Marketing* 5 (Summer 1988): 117–38.

15. Jeffrey S. Conant, Denise T. Smart, and Bruce J. Walker, "Mail Survey Facilitation Techniques: An Assessment and Proposal Regarding Reporting Practices," *Journal of Market Research Society* (UK) 32 (October 1990): 569–80; and Jeannine M. James and Richard Bolstein, "The Effect of Monetary Incentives and Follow-Up Mailings on the Response Rate and Response Quality in Mail Surveys," *Public Opinion Quarterly* 54 (Fall 1990): 346–61.

16. Mail surveys are common in institutional and industrial marketing research. See, for example, Shankar Ganesan, "Determinants of Long-Term Orientation in Buyer-Seller Relationships," *Journal of Marketing* 58 (April 1994): 1–19.

17. "Making a List, Selling It Twice," *Wall Street Journal* (May 20, 1985): 64–65.

18. *Quirk's Marketing Research Review* (February 1988): 6–8.

19. *Why Consumer Mail Panels Is the Superior Option* (Chicago: Market Facts, Inc., 1986).

20. *Seventeen*, retail survey, 1987.

21. Terry L. Childers and Steven J. Skinner, "Theoretical and Empirical Issues in the Identification of Survey Respondents," *Journal of the Market Research Society* 27 (January 1985): 39–53.

22. Ronald Czaja, Johnny Blair, and Jutta P. Sebestik, "Respondent Selection in a Telephone Survey: A Comparison of Three Techniques," *Journal of Marketing Research* (August 19, 1982): 381–85; and Diane O'Rourke and Johnny Blair, "Improving Random Respondent Selection in Telephone Interviews," *Journal of Marketing Research* 20 (November 1983): 428–32.

23. In 1994, Sacramento, California, was the top unlisted market with 68.3% of the phone households having unlisted numbers. Survey Sampling, Inc., "Sacramento Is Top Unlisted Market," *The Frame* (February 1995): 1.

24. Information provided by Survey Sampling, Inc., June 1, 1995. See also Tyzoon T. Tyebjee, "Telephone Survey Methods: The State of the Art," *Journal of Marketing* 43 (Summer 1979): 68–78; A. B. Blankenship, "Listed versus Unlisted Numbers in Telephone-Survey Samples," *Journal of Advertising Research* 17 (1977): 39–42; and Patricia E. Moberg, "Biases in Unlisted Phone Numbers," *Journal of Advertising Research*, 22 (August–September 1982): 51–55.

25. Johnny Blair and Ronald Czaja, "Locating a Special Population Using Random Digit Dialing," *Public Opinion Quarterly* 46 (Winter 1982): 585–90; and E. L. Landon, Jr., and S. K. Banks, "Relative Efficiency and Bias of Plus-One Telephone Sampling," *Journal of Marketing Research* 14 (August 1977): 294–99.

26. Paul M. Biner and Deborah L. Barton, "Justifying the Enclosure of Monetary Incentives in Mail Survey Cover Letters," *Psychology and Marketing* (Fall 1990): 153–62; and "Lists Make Targeting Easy," *Advertising Age* (July 9, 1984): 20.

27. Best Mailing Lists, Inc., *1995 Catalog of Mailing Lists*. (Tucson: Best Mailing Lists, 1995).

28. Jeffrey S. Conant, Denise T. Smart, and Bruce J. Walker, "Mail Survey Facilitation Techniques: An Assessment and Proposal Regarding Reporting Practices," *Journal of Market Research Society* (UK) 32 (October 1990): 569–80; and Chris Martell, "Illiteracy Hurts All, Author Says," *Wisconsin State Journal* (April 3, 1985): 1–2.

29. Raymond Hubbard and Eldon L. Little, "Promised Contributions to Charity and Mail Survey Responses: Replications with Extension," *Public Opinion Quarterly* 52 (Summer 1988): 223–30; Paul L. Erdos and Robert Ferber, eds., "Data Collection Methods: Mail Surveys," *Handbook of Marketing Research* (New York: McGraw-Hill, 1974), p. 102.

30. Pamela G. Guengel, Tracy R. Berchman, and Charles F. Cannell, *General Interviewing Techniques: A Self-Instructional Workbook for Telephone and Personal Interviewer Training* (Ann Arbor: Survey Research Center, University of Michigan, 1983).

31. Al Ossip, "Mall-Intercept Interviews," *Second Annual Advertising Research Foundation Research Quality Workshop* (New York: Advertising Research Foundation, 1984), p. 24.

32. Seymour Sudman, "Sample Surveys," *Annual Review of Sociology* (1976): 107–20.

33. Julie Yu, and Harris Cooper, "A Quantitative Review of Research Design Effects on Response Rates to Questionnaires," *Journal of Marketing Research* 20 (February 1983): 36–44. See also Jeannine M. James and Richard Bolstein, "The Effect of Monetary Incentives and Follow-Up Mailings on the Response Rate and Response Quality in Mail Surveys," *Public Opinion Quarterly* 54 (Fall 1990): 346–61.

34. C. S. Aneshensed, R. R. Frerichs, V. A. Clark, and P. A. Yokopenic, "Measuring Depression in the Community: A Comparison of Telephone and Personal Interviews," *Public Opinion Quarterly* (Spring 1982): 110–21.

35. J. Colombotos, "Personal vs. Telephone Interviews Effect Responses," *Public Health Report* (September 1969): 773–820.

36. Charles F. Cannell, Peter U. Miller, Lois Oksenberg, and Samuel Leinhardt, eds., "Research on Interviewing Techniques," *Sociological Methodology* (San Francisco: Jossey-Bass, 1981); Peter U. Miller, and Charles F. Cannell, "A Study of Experimental Techniques for Telephone Interviewing," *Public Opinion Quarterly* 46 (Summer 1982): 250–69.

37. For assessing the effectiveness of surveys, see Warren S. Martin, Robert E. Stanford, John E. Swan, Brent M. Wren, Thomas L. Powers, and W. Jack Duncan, *Journal of Business Research* 29 (January 1994): 39–45.

38. Hybrid methods that combine the features of these basic methods are also being employed. For example, the disk by mail (DBM) involves mailing the questionnaire on a disk to the respondents. This method is growing in popularity as it offers the benefits of both computer-assisted and mail surveys. "Disk-by-Mail Data Collection: A Researcher's Notes," *Sawtooth News* 10 (Winter 1994–95): 3–4.

39. Stanley L. Payne, "Combination of Survey Methods," *Journal of Marketing Research* (May 1964): 62.

40. Charlie Etmekjian and John Grede, "Marketing Research in a Team-Oriented Business: The Oscar Mayer Approach," *Marketing Research: A Magazine of Management and Applications* 2 (December 1990): 6–12.

41. Langbourne Rust, "How to Reach Children in Stores: Marketing Tactics Grounded in Observational Research," *Journal of Advertising Research* 33 (November–December 1993): 67–72.

42. Cliff Scott, David M. Klein, and Jennings Bryant, "Consumer Response to Humor in Advertising: A Series of Field Studies Using Behavioral Observation," *Journal of Consumer Research* 16 (March 1990): 498–501; and Fred N. Kerlinger, *Foundations of Behavioral Research*, 3rd ed. (New York: Holt, Rinehart and Winston, 1986), p. 538.

43. E. J. Webb, D. T. Campbell, K. D. Schwarts, and L. Sechrest, *Unobtrusive Measures: Nonreactive Research in the Social Sciences* (Chicago: Rand McNally, 1966): pp. 113–14.

44. Steve Raddock, "Follow That Car," *Marketing and Media Decisions* 16 (January 1981): 70–71, 103; and "License Plates Locate Customers," *Wall Street Journal* (February 5, 1981): 23.

45. Johnny K. Johansson and Ikujiro Nonaka, "Market Research the Japanese Way." *Harvard Business Review* (May–June 1987): 16–18.

46. Fred Gardner, "Acid Test for the People Meter," *Marketing and Media Decisions* (April 19, 1984): 74–75, 115.

47. R. Kurtz, "On-Site's Cameras Focus on the Retail Marketplace," *Marketing News* (November 9, 1984): 46.

48. "AGB's FingerPrinting Measures VCR Use," *Marketing News* (May 9, 1988): 13.

49. J. Edward Russo and France Leclerc, "An Eye-Fixation Analysis of Choice Processes for Consumer Nondurables," *Journal of Consumer Research* 21 (September 1994): 274–90.

50. For a recent application of GSR, see Piet Vanden Abeele and Douglas L. Maclachlan, "Process Tracing of Emotional Responses to TV Ads: Revisiting the Warmth Monitor," *Journal of Consumer Research* 20 (March 1994): 586-600.

51. "Psychogalvanometer Testing 'Most Predictive,'" *Marketing News* (June 16, 1981): 11.

52. Glen A. Buckman, "Uses of Voice-Pitch Analysis," *Journal of Advertising Research* 20 (April 1980): 69–73.

53. David A. Aaker, Richard P. Bagozzi, James M. Carman, and James M. MacLachlan, "On Using Response Latency to Measure Preference," *Journal of Marketing Research* 17 (May 1980): 237–44.

54. David W. Stewart, "Physiological Measurement of Advertising Effects," *Psychology and Marketing* (Spring 1984): 43–48; and David W. Stewart and David H. Furse, "Applying Psychological Measures to Marketing and Advertising Research Problems," in James H. Leigh and Claude R. Martin (eds.), *Current Issues in Advertising 1982* (Ann Arbor: University of Michigan Press, 1982), pp. 1–38.

55. Barry Stavro, "Rating Nielsen," *Forbes* (December 17, 1984): 100–05.

56. Richard H. Kolbe and Melissa S. Burnett, "Content-Analysis Research: An Examination of Applications with Directives for Improving Research Reliability and Objectivity," *Journal of Consumer Research* 18 (September 1991): 243–50; and Harold H. Kassarjian, "Social Values and the Sunday Comics: A Content Analysis," in Richard P. Bagozzi and Alice M. Tybout (eds.), *Advances in Consumer Research*, vol. 10 (Ann Arbor, MI: Association for Consumer Research, 1983): 434–38.

57. Charles S. Madden, Marjorie J. Caballero, and Shinya Matsukubo, "Analysis of Information Content in U.S. and Japanese Magazine Advertising," *Journal of Advertising* 15 (3), (1986): 38–45.

58. J. H. Bouchard, Jr., "Unobtrusive Measures: An Inventory of Uses," *Sociological Methods and Research* (February 1976): 267–301; and Lee Sechrest, *New Directions for Methodology of Behavior Science: Unobtrusive Measurement Today* (San Francisco: Jossey-Bass, 1979).

59. Joseph A. Cote, James McCullough, and Michael Reilly, "Effects of Unexpected Situations on Behavior-Intention Differences: A Garbology Analysis," *Journal of Consumer Research* 12 (September 1985): 188–94.

60. Michael L. Eay, *Unobtrusive Marketing Research Techniques* (Cambridge, MA: Marketing Science Institute, 1973), p. 13.

61. *Marketing News* (March 27, 1987): 38.

62. B. P. Kaiser, "Marketing Research in Sweden," *European Research* (February 1988): 64–70.

63. E. H. Demby, "ESOMAR Urges Changes in Reporting Demographics, Issues Worldwide Report," *Marketing News* 24(1) (January 8, 1990): 24–25.

64. Dori J. Yang, Micheal Oneal, Charles Hoots, and Robert Neff, "Can Nike Just Do It?" *Business Week* (April 18, 1994): 86–90.

65. As given in Appendix 3A of Gene R. Laczniak and Patrick E. Murphy, *Ethical Marketing Decisions: The Higher Road* (Needham Heights, MA: Allyn & Bacon, 1993), pp. 76-77.

66. R. M. Worcester and J. Downhan., eds., "ICC/ESOMAR International Code of Marketing and Social Research Practice," *Consumer Market Research Handbook* (Amsterdam: North-Holland, 1986), pp. 813–26.

67. Wade Leftwich, "How Researchers Can Win Friends and Influence Politicians," *American Demographics* (August 1993): 9.

68. A. M. Tybout and G. Zaltman, "Ethics in Marketing Research: Their Practical Relevance," *Journal of Marketing Research* 11 (November 1974): 357–68.

69. Marla Royne Stafford and Thomas F. Stafford, "Participant Observation and the Pursuit of Truth: Methodological and Ethical Considerations," *Journal of the Market Research Society* 35 (January 1993): 63–76.

70. C. N. Smith, and J. A. Quelch, *Ethics in Marketing* (Homewood, IL: Richard D. Irwin, 1993).

71. The assistance of James Agarwal with the international marketing research example, the assistance of Mark Leach and Gina Miller in writing the ethics section, and the assistance of Mark Peterson in writing the computer applications section is gratefully acknowledged.

CHAPTER SEVEN

Causal Research Design: Experimentation

We can never prove causality; in other words, we can never demonstrate it decisively. We can only infer a cause-and-effect relationship.

◆

OBJECTIVES

After reading this chapter, the student should be able to:

1. Explain the concept of causality as defined in marketing research and distinguish between the ordinary meaning and the scientific meaning of causality.
2. Define and differentiate the two types of validity: internal validity and external validity.
3. Discuss the various extraneous variables that can affect the validity of results obtained through experimentation and explain how the researcher can control extraneous variables.
4. Describe and evaluate experimental designs and the differences among preexperimental, true experimental, quasi-experimental, and statistical designs.
5. Compare and contrast the use of laboratory versus field experimentation and experimental versus nonexperimental designs in marketing research.
6. Describe test marketing and its various forms: standard test market, controlled test market, and simulated test market.
7. Understand why the internal and external validity of field experiments conducted overseas is generally lower than in the United States.
8. Describe the ethical issues involved in conducting causal research and the role of debriefing in addressing some of these issues.
9. Discuss the use of microcomputers and mainframes in causal research.

OVERVIEW

We introduced causal designs in Chapter 3, where we discussed their relationship to exploratory and descriptive designs and defined experimentation as the primary method employed in causal designs. This chapter explores the concept of causality further. We identify the necessary conditions for causality, examine the role of validity in experimentation, and consider the extraneous variables and procedures for controlling them. We present a classification of experimental designs and consider specific designs, along with the relative merits of laboratory and field experiments. An application in the area of test marketing is discussed in detail. The considerations involved in conducting experimental research when researching international markets are discussed. Several ethical issues which arise in experimentation are identified. The chapter concludes with a discussion of the use of microcomputers and mainframes in causal research. We begin with some examples.

EXAMPLE
It's in the Bag

LeSportsac, Inc., filed a suit against Kmart Corporation after Kmart introduced a "di Paris sac" line of bags, which LeSportsac claimed looked like its bags. According to LeSportsac, Kmart led consumers to believe that they were purchasing LeSportsac bags when they were not. To prove its point, LeSportsac undertook marketing research.

Two groups of women were selected in a field experiment. One group was shown two LeSportsac lightweight soft-sided bags from which all tags were removed and all words and designs were printed over within the distinctive LeSportsac ovals. The second group of women were shown two "di Paris sac" bags with the brand name visible and bearing the tags and labels these bags carry in Kmart stores. Information was obtained from both groups of women to learn whether or not these women perceive a single company or source or brand identification of masked bags, what identifications they make, if any, and the reasons they give for doing so.

The sample consisted of 200 women in each group selected by personal intercept interviews conducted in central locations in Chicago, Los Angeles, and New York. Rather than use a probability sample, the respondents were selected in accordance with age quotas.

The study indicated that many consumers could not distinguish the origin of the two makes of bags, supporting the position of LeSportsac. The field experiment helped LeSportsac convince the court of appeals to affirm the issuance of a preliminary injunction against Kmart. Kmart agreed to stop selling its "di Paris sac."[1] ◆

EXAMPLE
POP Buys

Eckerd Drug Company conducted an experiment to examine the effectiveness of in-store radio advertisements to induce point-of-purchase (POP) buys. Twenty statistically compatible stores were selected based on store size, geographical location, traffic flow count, and age. Half of these were randomly selected as test stores, and the other half served as control stores. The test stores aired the radio advertisements, whereas the control stores' POP radio systems were removed. Tracking data in the form of unit sales and

Drugstores such as Eckerd are increasingly experimenting with in-store advertising and other in-store promotions. ◆ Jack Eckerd Corporation.

dollar volume were obtained for three periods for seven days before the experiment, during the course of the four-week experiment, and seven days after the experiment. The products monitored varied from inexpensive items to small kitchen appliances. Results indicated that sales of the advertised products in the test stores at least doubled. Based on this evidence, Eckerd concluded that in-store radio advertising was highly effective in inducing POP buys, and they decided to continue it.[2] ◆

CONCEPT OF CAUSALITY

causality When the occurrence of X increases the probability of the occurrence of Y.

Experimentation is commonly used to infer causal relationships. The concept of **causality** requires some explanation. The scientific concept of causality is complex. "Causality" means something very different to the average person on the street than to a scientist.[3] A statement such as "X causes Y" will have the following meaning to an ordinary person and to a scientist.

Ordinary Meaning	*Scientific Meaning*
X is the only cause of Y.	X is only one of a number of possible causes of Y.
X must always lead to Y (X is a deterministic cause of Y).	The occurrence of X makes the occurrence of Y more probable (X is a probabilistic cause of Y).
It is possible to prove that X is a cause of Y.	We can never prove that X is a cause of Y. At best, we can infer that X is a cause of Y.

The scientific meaning of causality is more appropriate to marketing research than is the everyday meaning.[4] Marketing effects are caused by multiple variables and the relationship between cause and effect tends to be probabilistic. Moreover, we can never prove causality (i.e., demonstrate it conclusively); we can only infer a cause-and-effect relationship. In other words, it is possible that the true causal relation, if one exists, may not have been identified. We further clarify the concept of causality by discussing the conditions for causality.

CONDITIONS FOR CAUSALITY

Before making causal inferences, or assuming causality, three conditions must be satisfied: (1) concomitant variation, (2) time order of occurrence of variables, and (3) elimination of other possible causal factors. These conditions are necessary but not sufficient to demonstrate causality. No one of these three conditions, nor all three conditions combined, can demonstrate decisively that a causal relationship exists.[5] These conditions are explained in more detail in the following sections.

Concomitant Variation

concomitant variation A condition for inferring causality that requires that the extent to which a cause, X, and an effect, Y, occur together or vary together is predicted by the hypothesis under consideration.

Concomitant variation is the extent to which a cause, X, and an effect, Y, occur together or vary together in the way predicted by the hypothesis under consideration. Evidence pertaining to concomitant variation can be obtained in a qualitative or quantitative manner.

For example, in the qualitative case, the management of a department store believes that sales are highly dependent on the quality of in-store service. This hypothesis could be examined by assessing concomitant variation. Here, the causal factor X is in-store service and the effect factor Y is sales. A concomitant variation supporting the hypothesis would imply that stores with satisfactory in-store service would also have satisfactory sales. Likewise, stores with unsatisfactory service would exhibit unsatisfactory sales. If, on the other hand, the opposite pattern was found, we would conclude that the hypothesis was untenable.

For a quantitative example, consider a random survey of 1,000 respondents regarding purchase of fashion clothing from department stores. This survey yields the data in Table 7.1. The respondents have been classified into high- and low-education groups based on a median or even split. This table suggests that the purchase of fashion clothing is influenced by education level. Respondents with high education are likely to purchase more fashion clothing. Seventy-three percent of the respondents with high education have a high purchase level, whereas only 64% of those with low education have a high purchase level. Furthermore, this is based on a relatively large sample of 1,000 people.

Based on this evidence, can we conclude that high education causes high purchase of fashion clothing? Certainly not! All that can be said is that association makes

TABLE 7.1

Evidence of Concomitant Variation between Purchase of Fashion Clothing and Education

Purchase of Fashion Clothing, Y

Education, X	High	Low	
High	363 (73%)	137 (27%)	500 (100%)
Low	322 (64%)	178 (36%)	500 (100%)

the hypothesis more tenable; it does not prove it. What about the effect of other possible causal factors such as income? Fashion clothing is expensive, so people with higher incomes can buy more of it. Table 7.2 shows the relationship between purchase of fashion clothing and education for different income segments. This is equivalent to holding the effect of income constant. Here again, the sample has been split at the median to produce high- and low-income groups of equal size. Table 7.2 shows that the difference in purchase of fashion clothing between high- and low-education respondents has been reduced considerably. This suggests that the association indicated by Table 7.1 may be spurious.

We could give you similar examples to show why the absence of initial evidence of concomitant variation does not imply that there is no causation. It is possible that considering a third variable may crystallize an association that was originally obscure. The time order of the occurrence of variables provides additional insights into causality.

Time Order of Occurrence of Variables

The time order of occurrence condition states that the causing event must occur either before or simultaneously with the effect; it cannot occur afterwards. By definition, an effect cannot be produced by an event that occurs after the effect has taken place. It is possible, however, for each event in a relationship to be both a cause and an effect of the other event. In other words, a variable can be both a cause and an effect in the same causal relationship. To illustrate, customers who shop frequently in a department store are more likely to have the charge or credit card of that store. Also, customers who have the charge card for a department store are likely to shop there frequently.

Consider the in-store service and sales of a department store. If in-store service is the cause of sales, then improvements in service must be made before, or at least simultaneously with, an increase in sales. These improvements might consist of training or hiring more sales personnel. Then, in subsequent months, the sales of the department store should increase. Alternatively, sales might increase simultaneously with the training or hiring of additional sales personnel. Or, suppose that a store experienced an appreciable increase in sales and then decided to use some of that money to retrain its sales personnel, leading to an improvement in service. In this case, in-store service cannot be a cause of increased sales; rather, just the opposite hypothesis might be plausible.

TABLE 7.2

Purchase of Fashion Clothing by Income and Education

Low Income

Education	Purchase: High	Purchase: Low	Total
High	122 (61%)	78 (39%)	200 (100%)
Low	171 (57%)	129 (43%)	300 (100%)

High Income

Education	Purchase: High	Purchase: Low	Total
High	241 (80%)	59 (20%)	300
Low	151 (76%)	49 (24%)	200

Absence of Other Possible Causal Factors

The absence of other possible causal factors means that the factor or variable being investigated should be the only possible causal explanation. In-store service may be a cause of sales if we can be sure that changes in all other factors affecting sales, pricing, advertising, level of distribution, product quality, competition, and so forth, were held constant or were otherwise controlled.

In an after-the-fact examination of a situation, we can never confidently rule out all other causal factors. In contrast, with experimental designs it is possible to control for some of the other causal factors. It is also possible to balance the effects of some of the uncontrolled variables so that only random variations resulting from these uncontrolled variables will be measured. These aspects are discussed in more detail later in this chapter. The difficulty of establishing a causal relationship is illustrated by the following example.

EXAMPLE
Which Comes First?

Recent statistical data show that consumers increasingly make buying decisions in the store while they are shopping. Some studies indicate that as much as 80% of buying decisions are made at point-of-purchase (POP). POP buying decisions have increased concurrently with increased advertising efforts in the stores. These include radio advertisements, ads on shopping carts and grocery bags, ceiling signs, and shelf displays. It is difficult to ascertain from these data whether the increased POP decision making is the result of increased advertising efforts in the store or whether the increase in store advertising results from attempts to capture changing consumer attitudes toward purchasing and to capture sales from the increase in POP decision making. It is also possible that both variables may be both causes and effects in this relationship.[6] ◆

If, as the preceding example indicates, it is difficult to establish cause-and-effect relationships, what is the role of evidence obtained in experimentation?

Role of Evidence

Evidence of concomitant variation, time order of occurrence of variables, and elimination of other possible causal factors, even if combined, still do not demonstrate conclusively that a causal relationship exists. If all the evidence is strong and consistent, however, it may be reasonable to conclude that there is a causal relationship. Accumulated evidence from several investigations increases our confidence that a causal relationship exists. Confidence is further enhanced if the evidence is interpreted in light of intimate conceptual knowledge of the problem situation. Controlled experiments can provide strong evidence on all the three conditions.

DEFINITIONS AND CONCEPTS

In this section, we define some basic concepts and illustrate them using examples, including the LeSportsac and Eckerd examples given at the beginning of this chapter.

independent variables
Variables that are manipulated by the researcher and whose effects are measured and compared.

Independent Variables   **Independent variables** are variables or alternatives that are manipulated (i.e., the levels of these variables are changed by the researcher) and whose effects are measured and compared. These variables, also known as treatments, may include price levels, package designs, and advertising themes. In the two examples given at the beginning of this chapter, the treatments consisted of LeSportsac versus the "di Paris sac" bags in the first example and in-store radio advertising (present versus absent) in the second.

test units Individuals, organizations, or other entities whose response to independent variables or treatments is being studied.

Test Units   **Test units** are individuals, organizations, or other entities whose response to the independent variables or treatments is being examined. Test units may include consumers, stores, or geographic areas. The test units were women in the LeSportsac case and stores in the Eckerd example.

dependent variables Variables that measure the effect of the independent variables on the test units.

Dependent Variables   **Dependent variables** are the variables that measure the effect of the independent variables on the test units. These variables may include sales, profits, and market shares. The dependent variable was brand or source identification in the LeSportsac example and sales in the Eckerd example.

extraneous variables Variables, other than the independent variables, which influence the response of the test units.

Extraneous Variables   **Extraneous variables** are all variables other than the independent variables that affect the response of the test units. These variables can confound the dependent variable measures in a way that weakens or invalidates the results of the experiment. Extraneous variables include store size, store location, and competitive effort. In the Eckerd example, store size, geographical location, traffic flow count, and age of the stores were extraneous variables that had to be controlled.

experiment The process of manipulating one or more independent variables and measuring their effect on one or more dependent variables, while controlling for the extraneous variables.

Experiment   An **experiment** is formed when the researcher manipulates one or more independent variables and measures their effect on one or more dependent variables, while controlling for the effect of extraneous variables.[7] Both the LeSportsac and Eckerd research projects qualify as experiments based on this definition.

experimental design The set of experimental procedures specifying (1) the test units and sampling procedures, (2) the independent variables, (3) the dependent variables, and (4) how to control the extraneous variables.

Experimental Design   An **experimental design** is a set of procedures specifying (1) the test units and how these units are to be divided into homogeneous subsamples, (2) what independent variables or treatments are to be manipulated, (3) what dependent variables are to be measured, and (4) how the extraneous variables are to be controlled.[8]

As a further illustration of these definitions, consider the following example.

EXAMPLE
Taking Coupons at Face Value

An experiment was conducted to test the effects of the face value of coupons on the likelihood of coupon redemption, controlling for the frequency of brand usage. Personal interviews were conducted in greater New York with 280 shoppers who were entering or leaving a supermarket. Subjects were randomly assigned to two treatment groups. One offered 15¢ coupons and the other 50¢ coupons for four products: Tide detergent, Kellogg's corn flakes, Aim toothpaste, and Joy liquid detergent. During the interviews, the respondents answered questions about which brands they used and how likely they were to cash coupons of the given face value the next time they shopped. An interesting finding was that higher face-value coupons produced higher likelihood of redemption among infrequent or nonbuyers of the promoted brand but had little effect on regular buyers.[9] ◆

Marketers use coupons of varying face value to induce purchase. ◆ Irene Springer.

In the preceding experiment, the independent variable that was manipulated was the value of the coupon (15¢ versus 50¢). The dependent variable was the likelihood of cashing the coupon. The extraneous variable that was controlled was brand usage. The test units were individual shoppers. The experimental design required the random assignment of test units (shoppers) to treatment groups (15¢ coupon or 50¢ coupon).

DEFINITION OF SYMBOLS

To facilitate our discussion of extraneous variables and specific experimental designs, we define a set of symbols now commonly used in marketing research.[10]

X = the exposure of a group to an independent variable, treatment, or event, the effects of which are to be determined

O = the process of observation or measurement of the dependent variable on the test units or group of units

R = the random assignment of test units or groups to separate treatments

In addition, the following conventions are adopted:

- Movement from left to right indicates movement through time.
- Horizontal alignment of symbols implies that all those symbols refer to a specific treatment group.
- Vertical alignment of symbols implies that those symbols refer to activities or events that occur simultaneously.

For example, the symbolic arrangement

$$X \quad O_1 \quad O_2$$

means that a given group of test units was exposed to the treatment variable (X) and the response was measured at two different points in time O_1 and O_2.

Likewise, the symbolic arrangement

$$R \quad X_1 \quad O_1$$
$$R \quad X_2 \quad O_2$$

means that two groups of test units were randomly assigned to two different treatment groups at the same time, and the dependent variable was measured in the two groups simultaneously.

VALIDITY IN EXPERIMENTATION

When conducting an experiment, a researcher has two goals: (1) to draw valid conclusions about the effects of independent variables on the study group and (2) to make valid generalizations to a larger population of interest. The first goal concerns internal validity, the second, external validity.[11]

Internal Validity

internal validity A measure of accuracy of an experiment. It measures if the manipulation of the independent variables, or treatments, actually caused the effects on the dependent variable(s).

Internal validity refers to whether the manipulation of the independent variables or treatments actually caused the observed effects on the dependent variables. Thus, internal validity refers to whether the observed effects on the test units could have been caused by variables other than the treatment. If the observed effects are influenced or confounded by extraneous variables, it is difficult to draw valid inferences about the causal relationship between the independent and dependent variables. Internal validity is the basic minimum that must be present in an experiment before any conclusion about treatment effects can be made. Without internal validity, the experimental results are confounded. Control of extraneous variables is a necessary condition for establishing internal validity.

External Validity

external validity A determination of whether the cause-and-effect relationships found in the experiment can be generalized.

External validity refers to whether the cause-and-effect relationships found in the experiment can be generalized. In other words, can the results be generalized beyond the experimental situation, and if so, to what populations, settings, times, independent variables and dependent variables can the results be projected?[12] Threats to external validity arise when the specific set of experimental conditions do not realistically take into account the interactions of other relevant variables in the real world.

It is desirable to have an experimental design that has both internal and external validity, but in applied marketing research, we often have to trade one type of validity for another.[13] To control for extraneous variables, a researcher may conduct an experiment in an artificial environment. This enhances internal validity, but it may limit the generalizability of the results, thereby reducing external validity. For example, fast-food chains test customers' preferences for new formulations of menu items in test kitchens. Can the effects measured in this environment be generalized to fast-food outlets? (Further discussion on the influence of artificiality on external validity may be found in the section of this chapter on laboratory versus field experimentation.) Despite these deterrents to external validity, if an experiment lacks internal validity, it may not be meaningful to generalize the results. Factors that threaten internal validity may also threaten external validity, the most serious of these being extraneous variables.

EXTRANEOUS VARIABLES

The need to control extraneous variables to establish internal and external validity has already been discussed. In this section, we classify extraneous variables in the following categories: history, maturation, testing effects, instrumentation, statistical regression, selection bias, and mortality.

History

history Specific events that are external to the experiment but that occur at the same time as the experiment.

Contrary to what the name implies, **history** (H) does not refer to the occurrence of events before the experiment. Rather, history refers to specific events that are external to the experiment but that occur at the same time as the experiment. These events may affect the dependent variable. Consider the following experiment:

$$0_1 \qquad X_1 \qquad 0_2$$

where 0_1 and 0_2 are measures of sales of a department store chain in a specific region and X_1 represents a new promotional campaign. The difference $(0_2 - 0_1)$ is the treatment effect. Suppose that the experiment revealed that there was no difference between 0_2 and 0_1. Can we then conclude that the promotional campaign was ineffective? Certainly not! The promotional campaign (X_1) is not the only possible explanation of the difference between 0_2 and 0_1. The campaign might well have been effective. What if general economic conditions declined during the experiment and the local area was particularly hard hit by layoffs and plant closings (history)? Conversely, even if there was some difference between 0_2 and 0_1, it may be incorrect to conclude that the campaign was effective if history was not controlled, because the experimental effects might have been confounded by history. The longer the time interval between observations, the greater the possibility that history will confound an experiment of this type.[14]

Maturation

maturation An extraneous variable attributable to changes in the test units themselves that occur with the passage of time.

Maturation (MA) is similar to history except that it refers to changes in the test units themselves. These changes are not caused by the impact of independent variables or treatments but occur with the passage of time. In an experiment involving people, maturation takes place as people become older, more experienced, tired, bored, or uninterested. Tracking and market studies that span several months are vulnerable to maturation, since it is difficult to know how respondents are changing over time.

Maturation effects also extend to test units other than people. For example, consider the case in which the test units are department stores. Stores change over time in terms of physical layout, decor, traffic, and composition.

Testing Effects

Testing effects are caused by the process of experimentation. Typically, these are the effects on the experiment of taking a measure on the dependent variable before and after the presentation of the treatment. There are two kinds of testing effects: (1) main testing effect *(MT)* and (2) interactive testing effect *(IT)*.

main testing effect An effect of testing occurring when a prior observation affects a latter observation.

The **main testing effect** *(MT)* occurs when a prior observation affects a latter observation. Consider an experiment to measure the effect of advertising on attitudes toward a certain brand. The respondents are given a pretreatment questionnaire measuring background information and attitude toward the brand. They are then exposed to the test commercial embedded in an appropriate program. After viewing the commercial, the respondents again answer a questionnaire measuring, among other things, attitude toward the brand. Suppose that there is no difference between the pre- and posttreatment attitudes. Can we conclude that the commercial was ineffective? An alternative explanation might be that the respondents tried to maintain consistency between their pre- and posttreatment attitudes. As a result of the main testing effect, posttreatment attitudes were influenced more by pretreatment attitudes than by the treatment itself. The main testing effect may also be reactive, causing the respondents to change their attitudes simply because these attitudes have been measured. The main testing effect compromises the internal validity of the experiment.

interactive testing effect An effect in which a prior measurement affects the test unit's response to the independent variable.

In the **interactive testing effect** *(IT)*, a prior measurement affects the test unit's response to the independent variable. Continuing with our advertising experiment, when people are asked to indicate their attitudes toward a brand, they become aware of that brand: they are sensitized to that brand and become more likely to pay attention to the test commercial than people who were not included in the experiment. The measured effects are then not generalizable to the population; therefore, the interactive testing effects influence the experiment's external validity.

Instrumentation

instrumentation An extraneous variable involving changes in the measuring instrument, in the observers, or in the scores themselves.

Instrumentation *(I)* refers to changes in the measuring instrument, in the observers, or in the scores themselves. Sometimes measuring instruments are modified during the course of an experiment. In the advertising experiment, using a newly designed questionnaire to measure the posttreatment attitudes could lead to variations in the responses obtained. Consider an experiment in which dollar sales are measured before and after exposure to an in-store display (treatment). A nonexperimental price change between O_1 and O_2, results in a change in instrumentation because dollar sales will be measured using different unit prices. In this case, the treatment effect $(O_2 - O_1)$ could be attributed to a change in instrumentation.

As shown above, instrumentation effects are likely when interviewers make pre- and posttreatment measurements. The effectiveness of interviewers can be different at different times.

Statistical Regression

statistical regression An extraneous variable that occurs when test units with extreme scores move closer to the average score during the course of the experiment.

Statistical regression effects (SR) occur when test units with extreme scores move closer to the average score during the course of the experiment. In the advertising experiment, suppose that some respondents had either very favorable or very unfavorable attitudes. On posttreatment measurement, their attitudes might have moved toward the average. People's attitudes change continuously. People with extreme attitudes have more room for change, so variation is more likely. This has a confounding effect on the experimental results, because the observed effect (change in attitude) may be attributable to statistical regression rather than to the treatment (test commercial).

Selection Bias

selection bias An extraneous variable attributable to the improper assignment of test units to treatment conditions.

Selection bias (SB) refers to the improper assignment of test units to treatment conditions. This bias occurs when selection or assignment of test units results in treatment groups that differ on the dependent variable before the exposure to the treatment condition. If test units self-select their own groups or are assigned to groups on the basis of the researchers' judgment, selection bias is possible. For example, consider a merchandising experiment in which two different merchandising displays (old and new) are assigned to different department stores. The stores in the two groups may not be equivalent initially. They may vary with respect to a key characteristic, such as store size, which is likely to affect sales regardless of which merchandising display was assigned to a store.

Mortality

mortality An extraneous variable attributable to the loss of test units while the experiment is in progress.

Mortality (MO) refers to the loss of test units while the experiment is in progress. This happens for many reasons, such as test units refusing to continue in the experiment. Mortality confounds results because it is difficult to determine if the lost test units would respond in the same manner to the treatments as those that remain. Consider again the merchandising display experiment. Suppose that during the course of the experiment three stores in the new display treatment condition drop out. The researcher could not determine whether the average sales for the new display stores would have been higher or lower if these three stores had continued in the experiment.

The various categories of extraneous variables are not mutually exclusive, they can occur jointly and also interact with each other. To illustrate, testing—maturation—mortality refers to a situation where, because of pretreatment measurement, the respondents' beliefs and attitudes change over time and there is a differential loss of respondents from the various treatment groups.

CONTROLLING EXTRANEOUS VARIABLES

confounding variables Variables used to illustrate that extraneous variables can confound the results by influencing the dependent variable, synonymous with extraneous variables.

Extraneous variables represent alternative explanations of experimental results. They pose a serious threat to the internal and external validity of an experiment. Unless they are controlled for, they affect the dependent variable and thus confound the results. For this reason, they are also called **confounding variables**. There are four ways of controlling extraneous variables: randomization, matching, statistical control, and design control.

Randomization

randomization A method of controlling extraneous variables that involves randomly assigning test units to experimental groups by using random numbers. Treatment conditions are also randomly assigned to experimental groups.

Randomization refers to the random assignment of test units to experimental groups by using random numbers. Treatment conditions are also randomly assigned to experimental groups. For example, respondents are randomly assigned to one of three experimental groups. One of the three versions of a test commercial, selected at random, is administered to each group. As a result of random assignment, extraneous factors can be represented equally in each treatment condition. Randomization is the preferred procedure for ensuring the prior equality of experimental groups,[15] but it may not be effective when the sample size is small because it merely produces groups that are equal on average. It is possible, though, to check whether randomization has been effective by measuring the possible extraneous variables and comparing them across the experimental groups.

Matching

matching A method of controlling extraneous variables that involves matching test units on a set of key background variables before assigning them to the treatment conditions.

Matching involves comparing test units on a set of key background variables before assigning them to the treatment conditions. In the merchandising display experiment, stores could be matched on the basis of annual sales, size, or location. Then one store from each matched pair would be assigned to each experimental group.

Matching has two drawbacks. First, test units can be matched on only a few characteristics, so the test units may be similar on the variables selected but unequal on others. Second, if the matched characteristics are irrelevant to the dependent variable, then the matching effort has been futile.[16]

Statistical Control

statistical control A method of controlling extraneous variables by measuring the extraneous variables and adjusting for their effects through statistical methods.

Statistical control involves measuring the extraneous variables and adjusting for their effects through statistical analysis. This was illustrated in Table 7.2, which examined the relationship (association) between purchase of fashion clothing and education, controlling for the effect of income. More advanced statistical procedures, such as analysis of covariance (ANCOVA), are also available. In ANCOVA, the effects of the extraneous variable on the dependent variable are removed by an adjustment of the dependent variable's mean value within each treatment condition. ANCOVA is discussed in more detail in Chapter 16.

Design Control

design control A method of controlling extraneous variables that involves using specific experimental designs.

Design control involves the use of experiments designed to control specific extraneous variables. The types of controls possible by suitably designing the experiment are illustrated with the following example.

EXAMPLE
Experimenting with New Products

Controlled-distribution electronic test markets are used increasingly to conduct experimental research on new products. This method makes it possible to control for several extraneous factors that affect new product performance and manipulate the variables of interest. It is possible to ensure that a new product (1) obtains the right level of store acceptance and all commodity volume distribution, (2) is positioned in the correct aisle in each store, (3) receives the right number of facings on the shelf, (4) has the correct everyday price, (5) never has out-of-stock problems, and (6) obtains the planned level of trade promotion, display, and price features on the desired time schedule. Thus, a high degree of internal validity can be obtained.[17] ◆

Although test marketing is considered in more detail later in this chapter, the preceding example shows that controlled-distribution electronic test markets can be effective in controlling for specific extraneous variables. Extraneous variables can also be controlled by adopting specific experimental designs, as described in the next section.

A CLASSIFICATION OF EXPERIMENTAL DESIGNS

preexperimental designs Designs that do not control for extraneous factors by randomization.

Experimental designs may be classified as preexperimental, true experimental, quasi-experimental, and statistical designs (Figure 7.1). **Preexperimental designs** do not employ randomization procedures to control for extraneous factors. Examples of these

FIGURE 7.1

A Classification of Experimental Designs

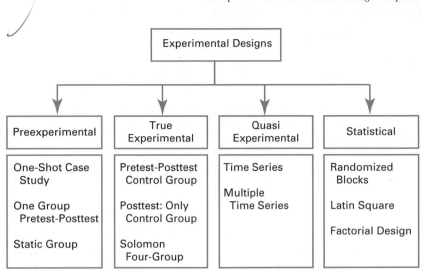

designs include the one-shot case study, the one-group pretest-posttest design, and the static-group. In **true experimental designs**, the researcher can randomly assign test units to experimental groups and treatments to experimental groups. Included in this category are the pretest-posttest control group design, the posttest-only control group design, and the Solomon four-group design. **Quasi-experimental designs** result when the researcher is unable to achieve full manipulation of scheduling or allocation of treatments to test units but can still apply part of the apparatus of true experimentation. Two such designs are time series and multiple time series designs. A **statistical design** is a series of basic experiments that allows for statistical control and analysis of external variables. The basic designs used in statistical designs include preexperimental, true experimental, and quasi-experimental. Statistical designs are classified on the basis of their characteristics and use. The important statistical designs include randomized block design, Latin square design, and factorial designs.[18]

We begin our discussion with the first type, preexperimental designs.

true experimental designs Experimental designs distinguished by the researcher randomly assigning test units to experimental groups and also randomly assigning treatments to experimental groups.

quasi-experimental designs Designs that apply part of the procedures of true experimentation yet lack full experimental control.

PREEXPERIMENTAL DESIGNS

statistical designs Designs that allow for the statistical control and analysis of external variables.

These designs are characterized by an absence of randomization. Three specific designs are described: the one-shot case study, the one-group pretest-posttest design, and the static group.

One-Shot Case Study

one-shot case study A preexperimental design in which a single group of test units is exposed to a treatment X, and then a single measurement on the dependent variable is taken.

Also known as the after-only design, the **one-shot case study** may be symbolically represented as

$$X \qquad O_1$$

A single group of test units is exposed to a treatment X, and then a single measurement on the dependent variable is taken (O_1). There is no random assignment of test units. Note that the symbol R is not used, because the test units are self-selected or selected arbitrarily by the researcher.

The danger of drawing valid conclusions from experiments of this type can be easily seen. It does not provide a basis of comparing the level of O_1 to what would happen when X was absent. Also, the level of 0_1 might be affected by many extraneous variables, including history, maturation, selection, and mortality. Lack of control for these extraneous variables undermines the internal validity. For these reasons, the one-shot case study is more appropriate for exploratory than for conclusive research.

One-Group Pretest-Posttest Design

one-group pretest-posttest design A preexperimental design in which a group of test units is measured twice.

The **one-group pretest-posttest design** may be symbolized as

$$0_1 \qquad X \qquad 0_2$$

In this design, a group of test units is measured twice. There is no control group. First a pretreatment measure is taken (0_1) then the group is exposed to the treatment (X). Finally, a posttreatment measure is taken (0_2). The treatment effect is computed as $0_2 - 0_1$, but the validity of this conclusion is questionable since extraneous variables are largely uncontrolled. History, maturation, testing (both main and interactive testing effects), instrumentation, selection, mortality, and regression could possibly be present. The following example shows how this design is used.

EXAMPLE
Theatrical Performance _____

Several marketing research services, such as the Advertising Research Service of Research Systems Corporation, employ the one-group pretest-posttest design to measure the effectiveness of test commercials. Respondents are recruited to central theater locations in different test cities. At the central location, respondents are first administered a personal interview to measure, among other things, attitudes toward the brand (0_1). Then they watch a TV program containing the test commercial (X). After viewing the TV program, the respondents are again administered a personal interview to measure attitudes toward the brand (0_2). The effectiveness of the test commercial is measured as $0_2 - 0_1$. ◆

Static Group Design

static group A preexperimental design in which there are two groups: the experimental group (EG), which is exposed to the treatment, and the control group (CG). Measurements on both groups are made only after the treatment, and test units are not assigned at random.

The **static group** is a two-group experimental design. One group, called the experimental group (EG), is exposed to the treatment, and the other, called the control group (CG), is not. Measurements on both groups are made only after the treatment, and test units are not assigned at random. This design may be symbolically described as

$$\begin{aligned} \text{EG:} \qquad & X \qquad 0_1 \\ \text{CG:} \qquad & \qquad 0_2 \end{aligned}$$

The treatment effect would be measured as $0_1 - 0_2$. Notice that this difference could also be attributed to at least two extraneous variables (selection and mortality). Because test units are not randomly assigned, the two groups (EG and CG) may differ before the treatment, and selection bias may be present. There may also be mortality effects, as more test units may withdraw from the experimental group than from the control group. This would be particularly likely to happen if the treatment were unpleasant.

In practice, a control group is sometimes defined as the group that receives current level of marketing activity, rather than a group that receives no treatment at all. The control group is defined this way because it is difficult to reduce current marketing activities such as advertising and personal selling to zero. We illustrate the static group and several other designs in the context of the department store patronage project.

DEPARTMENT STORE PATRONAGE PROJECT
Static Group

A static group comparison to measure the effectiveness of a test commercial for a department store would be conducted as follows. Two groups of respondents would be recruited on the basis of convenience. Only the experimental group would be exposed to the TV program containing the test commercial. Then, attitudes toward the department store of both the experimental and control group respondents would be measured. The effectiveness of the test commercial would be measured as O_1–O_2. ◆

TRUE EXPERIMENTAL DESIGNS

The distinguishing feature of the true experimental designs, as compared with preexperimental designs, is randomization. In true experimental designs, the researcher randomly assigns test units to experimental groups and treatments to experimental groups. True experimental designs include the pretest-posttest control group design, the posttest-only control group design, and the Solomon four-group design.

Pretest-Posttest Control Group Design

pretest-posttest control group design An experimental design in which the experimental group is exposed to the treatment but the control group is not. Pretest and posttest measures are taken on both groups.

In the **pretest-posttest control group design**, test units are randomly assigned to either the experimental or the control group and a pretreatment measure is taken on each group. This design is symbolized as

$$\text{EG:} \quad R \quad O_1 \quad X \quad O_2$$
$$\text{CG:} \quad R \quad O_3 \quad \quad O_4$$

The treatment effect (TE) is measured as

$$(O_2 - O_1) - (O_4 - O_3).$$

This design controls for most extraneous variables. Selection bias is eliminated by randomization. The other extraneous effects are controlled as follows:

$$O_2 - O_1 = TE + H + MA + MT + IT + I + SR + MO$$
$$O_4 - O_3 = H + MA + MT + I + SR + MO$$
$$= EV \text{ (extraneous variables)}$$

where the symbols for the extraneous variables are as defined previously. The experimental result is obtained by

$$(O_2 - O_1) - (O_4 - O_3) = TE + IT$$

Interactive testing effect is not controlled, because of the effect of the pretest measurement on the reaction of units in the experimental group to the treatment.

DEPARTMENT STORE PATRONAGE PROJECT
Pretest-Posttest Control Group

In the context of measuring the effectiveness of a test commercial for a department store, a pretest-posttest control group design would be implemented as follows. A sample of respondents would be selected at random. Half of these would be randomly assigned to the experimental group, and the other half would form the control group. Respondents in both groups would be administered a questionnaire to obtain a pretest measurement on attitudes toward the department store. Only the respondents in the experimental group would be exposed to the TV program containing the test commercial. Then, a questionnaire would be administered to respondents in both groups to obtain posttest measures on attitudes toward the store. ◆

As this example shows, the pretest-posttest control group design involves two groups and two measurements on each group. A simpler design is the posttest-only control group design.

Posttest-Only Control Group Design

posttest-only control group design
Experimental design in which the experimental group is exposed to the treatment but the control group is not and no pretest measure is taken.

The **posttest-only control group design** does not involve any premeasurement. It may be symbolized as

$$EG: \quad R \quad X \quad 0_1$$
$$CG: \quad R \quad \quad 0_2$$

The treatment effect is obtained by

$$TE = 0_1 - 0_2$$

This design is fairly simple to implement. Because there is no premeasurement, the testing effects are eliminated, but this design is sensitive to selection bias and mortality. It is assumed that the two groups are similar in terms of pretreatment measures on the dependent variable because of the random assignment of test units to groups. Because there is no pretreatment measurement, this assumption cannot be checked. This design is also sensitive to mortality. It is difficult to determine if those in the experimental group who discontinue the experiment are similar to their counterparts in the control group. Yet another limitation is that this design does not allow the researcher to examine changes in individual test units.

It is possible to control for selection bias and mortality through carefully designed experimental procedures. Examination of individual cases is often not of interest. On the other hand, this design possesses significant advantages in terms of time, cost, and sample size requirements. It involves only two groups and only one measurement per group. Because of its simplicity, the posttest-only control group design is probably the most popular design in marketing research.[19] Note that, except for premeasurement, the implementation of this design is very similar to that of the pretest-posttest control group design.

In this example, the researcher is not concerned with examining the changes in the attitudes of individual respondents. When this information is desired, the Solomon four-group design should be considered. The **Solomon four-group design** overcomes the limitations of the pretest-posttest control group and posttest-only control group designs in that it explicitly controls for interactive testing effect, in addition to controlling for

Solomon four-group design An experimental design that explicitly controls for interactive testing effects, in addition to controlling for all the other extraneous variables.

all the other extraneous variables (EV). But this design has practical limitations: it is expensive and time-consuming to implement. Hence, it is not considered further.[20]

In all true experimental designs, the researcher exercises a high degree of control. In particular, the researcher can control when the measurements are taken, on whom they are taken, and the scheduling of the treatments. Moreover, the researcher can randomly select the test units and randomly expose test units to the treatments. In some instances, the researcher cannot exercise this kind of control; then quasi-experimental designs should be considered.

QUASI-EXPERIMENTAL DESIGNS

A quasi-experimental design results when the researcher can control when measurements are taken and on whom they are taken but lacks control over the scheduling of the treatments and is also unable to expose test units to the treatments randomly. Quasi-experimental designs are useful because they can be used in cases when true experimentation cannot, and because they are quicker and less expensive. Because full experimental control is lacking, the researcher must consider the specific variables that are not controlled. Popular forms of quasi-experimental designs are time series and multiple time series designs.[21]

Time Series Design

time series design A quasi-experimental design that involves periodic measurements on the dependent variable for a group of test units. Then the treatment is administered by the researcher or occurs naturally. After the treatment, periodic measurements are continued to determine the treatment effect.

The **time series design** involves a series of periodic measurements on the dependent variable for a group of test units. The treatment is then administered by the researcher or occurs naturally. After the treatment, periodic measurements are continued to determine the treatment effect. A time-series experiment may be symbolized as

$$O_1 \quad O_2 \quad O_3 \quad O_4 \quad O_5 \quad X \quad O_6 \quad O_7 \quad O_8 \quad O_9 \quad O_{10}$$

This is a quasi experiment, because there is no randomization of test units to treatments, and the timing of treatment presentation, as well as which test units are exposed to the treatment, may not be within the researcher's control.

Taking a series of measurements before and after the treatment provides at least partial control for several extraneous variables. Maturation is at least partially controlled, because it would not affect O_5 and O_6 alone but would also influence other observations. By similar reasoning, main testing effect, and statistical regression are controlled as well. If the test units are selected randomly or by matching, selection bias can be reduced. Mortality may pose a problem, but it can be largely controlled by paying a premium or offering other incentives to respondents.

The major weakness of the time series design is the failure to control history. Another limitation is that the experiment may be affected by the interactive testing effect because multiple measurements are being made on the test units. Nevertheless, time series designs are useful, as illustrated by this example. The effectiveness of a test commercial (X) may be examined by broadcasting the commercial a predetermined number of times and examining the data from a preexisting test panel. Although the marketer can control the scheduling of the test commercial, it is uncertain when or whether the panel members are exposed to it. The panel members' purchases before, during, and after the campaign are examined to determine whether the test commercial has a short-term effect, a long-term effect, or no effect.

Multiple Time Series Design

multiple time series design A time series design that includes another group of test units to serve as a control group.

The **multiple time series design** is similar to the time series design except that another group of test units is added to serve as a control group. Symbolically, this design may be described as

$$\text{EG: } O_1 \quad O_2 \quad O_3 \quad O_4 \quad O_5 \quad X \quad O_6 \quad O_7 \quad O_8 \quad O_9 \quad O_{10}$$
$$\text{CG: } O_{11} \quad O_{12} \quad O_{13} \quad O_{14} \quad O_{15} \qquad O_{16} \quad O_{17} \quad O_{18} \quad O_{19} \quad O_{20}$$

If the control group is carefully selected, this design can be an improvement over the simple time series experiment. The improvement lies in the ability to test the treatment effect twice: against the pretreatment measurements in the experimental group and against the control group. To use the multiple time series design to assess the effectiveness of a commercial, the test panel example would be modified as follows. The test commercial would be shown in only a few of the test cities. Panel members in these cities would make up the experimental group. Panel members in cities where the commercial was not shown would constitute the control group. Another application of multiple time series design is the ADTEL split-cable TV advertising field experiment.

EXAMPLE
Splitting Commercials Shows Their Strength

A multiple time series design was used to examine the buildup effect of increased advertising. The data were obtained from Burke Marketing Services, Inc., from an ADTEL split-cable TV advertising field experiment. In the split-cable system, one group of households was assigned to the experimental panel and an equivalent group was assigned to the control panel. The two groups were matched on demographic variables. Data were collected for 76 weeks. Both panels received the same level of advertising for the first 52 weeks for the brand in question. For the next 24 weeks, the experimental panel was exposed to twice as much advertising as the control panel. The results indicated that the buildup effect of advertising was immediate with a duration of the order of the purchase cycle. Information of this type can be useful in selecting advertising timing patterns (allocating a set of advertising exposures over a specified period to obtain maximum impact).[22] ◆

In concluding our discussion of preexperimental, true experimental and quasi-experimental designs, we summarize in Table 7.3 the potential sources of invalidity that may affect each of these designs. It should be remembered that potential sources of invalidity are not the same as actual errors.

STATISTICAL DESIGNS

Statistical designs consist of a series of basic experiments that allow for statistical control and analysis of external variables. In other words, several basic experiments are conducted simultaneously. Thus, statistical designs are influenced by the same sources of invalidity that affect the basic designs being used. Statistical designs offer the following advantages:

TABLE 7.3

Potential Sources of Invalidity of Experimental Designs

Design	Source of invalidity — Internal							Source of invalidity — External
	History	Maturation	Testing	Instrumentation	Regression	Selection	Mortality	Interaction of testing and X
Preexperimental designs:								
One-shot case study X O	−	−				−	−	−
One-group pretest-posttest design O X O	−	−	−	−	?			
Static-group comparison X O O	+	?	+	+	+	−	−	
True experimental designs:								
Pretest-posttest control group R O X O R O O	+	+	+	+	+	+	+	−
Posttest-only control group design R X O R O	+	+	+	+	+	+	+	+
Quasi-experimental designs:								
Time series O O O X O O O	−	+	+	?	+	+	+	−
Multiple time series O O O X O O O O O O O O O	+	+	+	+	+	+	+	−

Note: A minus sign indicates a definite weakness, a plus sign indicates that the factor is controlled, a question mark denotes a possible source of concern, and a blank means that the factor is not relevant.

1. The effects of more than one independent variable can be measured.
2. Specific extraneous variables can be statistically controlled.
3. Economical designs can be formulated when each test unit is measured more than once.

The most common statistical designs are the randomized block design, the Latin square design, and the factorial design.

Randomized Block Design

randomized block design
A statistical design in which the test units are blocked on the basis of an external variable to ensure that the various experimental and control groups are matched closely on that variable.

A **randomized block design** is useful when there is only one major external variable—such as sales, store size, or income of the respondent—that might influence the dependent variable. The test units are blocked, or grouped, on the basis of the external variable. The researcher must be able to identify and measure the blocking variable. By blocking, the researcher ensures that the various experimental and control groups are matched closely on the external variable.

DEPARTMENT STORE PATRONAGE PROJECT
Randomized Block Design

Let us extend the department store test commercial example to measure the impact of humor on the effectiveness of advertising.[23] Three test commercials, A, B, and C, have, respectively, no humor, some humor, and high humor. Which of these would be the most effective? Management feels that the respondents' evaluation of the commercials will be influenced by the extent of their store patronage, so store patronage is identified as the blocking variable and the randomly selected respondents are classified into four blocks (heavy, medium, light, or nonpatrons of the department store). Respondents from each block are randomly assigned to the treatment groups (test commercials A, B, and C). The results reveal that the some humor commercial (B) was most effective overall (see Table 7.4). ◆

As this example illustrates, in most marketing research situations, external variables such as sales, store size, store type, location, income, occupation and social class of the respondent can influence the dependent variable. Therefore, randomized block designs are generally more useful than completely random designs. Their main limitation is that the researcher can control for only one external variable. When more than one variable must be controlled, the researcher must use Latin square or factorial designs.

Latin Square Design

Latin square design A statistical design that allows for the statistical control of two noninteracting external variables in addition to the manipulation of the independent variable.

A **Latin square design** allows the researcher to control statistically two noninteracting external variables as well as to manipulate the independent variable. Each external or

		Treatment Groups		
Block Number	Store Patronage	Commercial A	Commercial B	Commercial C
1	Heavy			
2	Medium			
3	Low			
4	None			

TABLE 7.4

An Example of a Randomized Block Design

blocking variable is divided into an equal number of blocks or levels. The independent variable is also divided into the same number of levels. A Latin square is conceptualized as a table (see Table 7.5), with the rows and the columns representing the blocks in the two external variables. The levels of the independent variable are then assigned to the cells in the table. The assignment rule is that each level of the independent variable should appear only once in each row and each column, as shown in Table 7.5.

DEPARTMENT STORE PATRONAGE PROJECT
Latin Square

To illustrate the Latin square design, suppose that in the previous example, in addition to controlling for store patronage, the researcher also wanted to control for interest in the store (defined as high, medium, or low). To implement a Latin square design, store patronage would also have to be blocked at three rather than four levels, (e.g., by combining the low and nonpatrons into a single block). Assignments of the three test commercials could then be made as shown in Table 7.5. Note that each commercial—A, B, or C—appears once, and only once, in each row and each column. ◆

Although Latin square designs are popular in marketing research, they are not without limitations. They require equal number of rows, columns, and treatment levels, which is sometimes problematic. Note that in the above example, the low and nonpatrons had to be combined to satisfy this requirement. Also, only two external variables can be controlled simultaneously. An additional variable can be controlled with an expansion of this design into a Greco-Latin square. Finally, Latin squares do not allow the researcher to examine interactions of the external variables with each other or with the independent variable. To examine interactions, factorial designs should be used.

Factorial Design

factorial design A statistical experimental design used to measure the effects of two or more independent variables at various levels and to allow for interactions between variables.

A **factorial design** is used to measure the effects of two or more independent variables at various levels. Unlike the randomized block design and the Latin square, factorial designs allow for interactions between variables.[24] An interaction is said to take place when the simultaneous effect of two or more variables is different from the sum of their separate effects. For example, an individual's favorite drink might be coffee and her favorite temperature level might be cold, but this individual might not prefer cold coffee, leading to an interaction.

A factorial design may also be conceptualized as a table. In a two-factor design, each level of one variable represents a row and each level of another variable represents a column. Multidimensional tables can be used for three or more factors. Factorial

TABLE 7.5
An Example of a Latin Square Design

	Interest in the Store		
Store Patronage	High	Medium	Low
Heavy			
High	B	A	C
Medium	C	B	A
Low and none	A	C	B

Note: A, B, and C denote the three test commercials, which have, respectively, no humor, some humor, and high humor.

designs involve a cell for every possible combination of treatment variables. Suppose that in the previous example, in addition to examining the effect of humor, the researcher was also interested in simultaneously examining the effect of amount of store information. Further, the amount of store information was also varied at three levels (high, medium and low). As shown in Table 7.6, this would require 3 × 3 = 9 cells. The respondents would be randomly selected and randomly assigned to the nine cells. Respondents in each cell would receive a specific treatment combination. For example, respondents in the upper left corner cell would view a commercial that had no humor and low store information. The results revealed a significant interaction between the two factors or variables. Respondents with low amount of store information preferred the high humor commercial (C). Those with high amount of store information, however, preferred the no humor commercial (A). Notice that although Table 7.6 may appear somewhat similar to Table 7.4, the random assignment of respondents and data analysis are very different for the randomized block design and the factorial design.[25]

Another example of a factorial design follows.

EXAMPLE
Price and Information Are for the Dogs

Burke Marketing Research, Inc., conducted an experiment to determine the effect of price and competitive set information on purchase intentions with respect to a new dog food. A two-factor design was used. Price was manipulated to have four levels: one discount ($1.07), two parity ($1.27, $1.47), and one premium ($1.67). Competitive set information was varied at two levels: whether or not information on competitive brands was provided. Approximately 240 respondents were randomly assigned to one of eight (4 × 2) treatment conditions. Respondents were asked to indicate their purchase intent for the new product on a five-point scale. The results indicated that neither price nor competitive set information had a significant effect on purchase intentions.[26] ◆

The main disadvantage of a factorial design is that the number of treatment combinations increases multiplicatively with an increase in the number of variables or levels. In the Burke Marketing Research example, if the price had been manipulated at six levels (e.g., $0.99, $1.07, $1.27, $1.47, $1.67, and $1.99) and competitive information at three levels (no information, partial information, and full information), the number of cells would have jumped from 8 to 18. All the treatment combinations are required if all the main effects and interactions are to be measured. If the researcher is interested in only a few of the interactions or main effects, fractional factorial designs may be used. As their name implies, these designs consist of only a fraction or portion of the corresponding full factorial design.

TABLE 7.6 *An Example of a Factorial Design*		Amount of Humor	
Amount of Store Information	No Humor	Medium Humor	High Humor
Low Medium High			

LABORATORY VERSUS FIELD EXPERIMENTS

field environment An experimental location set in actual market conditions.

laboratory environment An artificial setting for experimentation in which the researcher constructs the desired conditions.

Experiments may be conducted in laboratory or field environment. A laboratory environment is an artificial one that the researcher constructs with the desired conditions specific to the experiment. The term **field environment** is synonymous with actual market conditions. Our experiment to measure the effectiveness of a test commercial could be conducted in a **laboratory environment** by showing the test commercial embedded in a TV program to respondents in a test theater. The same experiment could also be conducted in a field environment by running the test commercial on actual TV stations. The differences between the two environments are summarized in Table 7.7.

Laboratory experiments have the following advantages over field experiments: the laboratory environment offers a high degree of control because it isolates the experiment in a carefully monitored environment. Therefore, the effects of history can be minimized. A laboratory experiment also tends to produce the same results if repeated with similar subjects, leading to high internal validity. Laboratory experiments tend to use a small number of test units, last for a shorter time, be more restricted geographically, and are easier to conduct than field experiments. Hence, they are generally less expensive as well.

demand artifacts Responses given because the respondents attempt to guess the purpose of the experiment and respond accordingly.

As compared with field experiments, laboratory experiments suffer from some main disadvantages. First, the artificiality of the environment may cause reactive error in that the respondents react to the situation itself rather than to the independent variable.[27] Also, the environment may cause **demand artifacts**, a phenomenon in which the respondents attempt to guess the purpose of the experiment and respond accordingly. For example, while viewing the test commercial, the respondents may recall pretreatment questions about the brand and guess that the commercial is trying to change their attitudes toward the brand.[28] Finally, laboratory experiments are likely to have lower external validity than field experiments. Because a laboratory experiment is conducted in an artificial environment, the ability to generalize the results to the real world may be diminished.

It has been argued that artificiality or lack of realism in a laboratory experiment need not lead to lower external validity. One must be aware of the aspects of the laboratory experiment that differ from the situation to which generalizations are to be made. External validity will be reduced only if these aspects interface with the independent variables explicitly manipulated in the experiment, as is often the case in applied marketing research. Another consideration, however, is that laboratory experiments allow

TABLE 7.7	Factor	Laboratory	Field
Laboratory versus Field Experiments	Environment	Artificial	Realistic
	Control	High	Low
	Reactive Error	High	Low
	Demand artifacts	High	Low
	Internal validity	High	Low
	External validity	Low	High
	Time	Short	Long
	Number of units	Small	Large
	Ease of implementtion	High	Low
	Cost	Low	High

for more complex designs than field experiments. Hence, the researcher can control for more factors or variables in the laboratory setting, which increases external validity.[29]

The researcher must consider all these factors when deciding whether to conduct laboratory or field experiments.[30] Field experiments are less common in marketing research than laboratory experiments, although laboratory and field experiments play complementary roles.[31]

EXPERIMENTAL VERSUS NONEXPERIMENTAL DESIGNS

In Chapter 3, we discussed three types of research designs: exploratory, descriptive, and causal. Of these, only causal designs are truly appropriate for inferring cause-and-effect relationships. Although descriptive survey data are often used to provide evidence of "causal" relationships, these studies do not meet all the conditions required for causality. For example, it is difficult in descriptive studies to establish the prior equivalence of the respondent groups with respect to both the independent and dependent variables. On the other hand, an experiment can establish this equivalence by random assignment of test units to groups. In descriptive research it is also difficult to establish time order of occurrence of variables. In an experiment, however, the researcher controls the timing of the measurements and the introduction of the treatment. Finally, descriptive research offers little control over other possible causal factors.

We do not wish to undermine the importance of descriptive research designs in marketing research. As mentioned in Chapter 3, descriptive research constitutes the most popular research design in marketing research, and we do not want to imply that it should never be used to examine causal relationships. Indeed, some authors have suggested procedures for drawing causal inferences from descriptive (nonexperimental) data.[32] Rather, our intent is to alert the reader to the limitations of descriptive research for examining causal relationships. Likewise, we also want to make the reader aware of the limitations of experimentation.[33]

LIMITATIONS OF EXPERIMENTATION

Experimentation is becoming increasingly important in marketing research, but there are limitations of time, cost, and administration of an experiment.

Time

Experiments can be time-consuming, particularly if the researcher is interested in measuring the long-term effects of the treatment, such as the effectiveness of an advertising campaign. Experiments should last long enough so that the posttreatment measurements include most or all the effects of the independent variables.

Cost

Experiments are often expensive. The requirements of experimental group, control group, and multiple measurements significantly add to the cost of research.

Administration

Experiments can be difficult to administer. It may be impossible to control for the effects of the extraneous variables, particularly in a field environment. Field experiments often interfere with a company's ongoing operations, and obtaining cooperation from the retailers, wholesalers, and others involved may be difficult. Finally, competitors may deliberately contaminate the results of a field experiment.

APPLICATION: TEST MARKETING

test marketing An application of a controlled experiment done in limited, but carefully selected, test markets. It involves a replication of the planned national marketing program for a product in test markets.

test markets A carefully selected part of the marketplace particularly suitable for test marketing.

standard test market A test market in which the product is sold through regular distribution channels. For example, no special considerations are given to products simply because they are being test-marketed.

Test marketing, also called market testing, is an application of a controlled experiment done in limited but carefully selected parts of the marketplace called **test markets**. It involves a replication of a planned national marketing program in test markets. Often, the marketing mix variables (independent variables) are varied in test marketing and the sales (dependent variable) are monitored so that an appropriate national marketing strategy can be identified. The two major objectives of test marketing are (1) to determine market acceptance of the product and (2) to test alternative levels of marketing mix variables. Test-marketing procedures may be classified as standard test markets, controlled and minimarket tests, and simulated test marketing.

Standard Test Market

In a **standard test market**, test markets are selected and the product is sold through regular distribution channels. Typically, the company's own sales force is responsible for distributing the product. Sales personnel stock the shelves, restock, and take inventory at regular intervals. One or more combinations of marketing mix variables (product, price, distribution, and promotional levels) are employed.

Designing a standard test market involves deciding what criteria are to be used for selecting test markets, how many test markets to use, and the duration of the test. Test markets must be carefully selected. The criteria for selection of test markets is described in Research in Practice 7.1. A list of commonly used test markets is given in Research in Practice 7.2.[34] In general, the more test markets that can be used, the better. If resources are limited, at least two test markets should be used for each program variation to be tested. Where external validity is important, however, at least four test markets should be used.

RESEARCH IN PRACTICE 7.1

Criteria for the Selection of Test Markets

Test markets should have the following qualities.
1. Be large enough to produce meaningful projections. They should contain at least 2% of the potential actual population.
2. Be representative demographically.
3. Be representative with respect to product consumption behavior.
4. Be representative with respect to media usage.
5. Be representative with respect to competition.
6. Be relatively isolated in terms of media and physical distribution.
7. Have normal historical development in the product class.
8. Have marketing research and auditing services available.
9. Not be overtested.

RESEARCH IN PRACTICE 7.2

Dancer Fitzgerald's Sample List of Recommended Test Markets

Albany–Schenectady-Troy, NY	Knoxville, TN
Boise, ID	Lexington, KY
Buffalo, NY	Little Rock, AR
Cedar Rapids–Waterloo, IA	Louisville, KY
Charlotte, NC	Minneapolis, MN
Cincinnati, OH	Nashville, TN
Cleveland, OH	Oklahoma City, OK
Colorado Springs–Pueblo, CO	Omaha, NE
Columbus, OH	Orlando–Daytona Beach, FL
Des Moines, IA	Phoenix, AZ
Erie, PA	Pittsburgh, PA
Evansville, IN	Portland, OR
Fargo, ND	Roanoke–Lynchburg, VA
Fort Wayne, IN	Rochester, NY
Green Bay, WI	Sacramento–Stockton, CA
Greensboro–High Point, NC	St. Louis, MO
Greenville–Spartanburg, SC	Salt Lake City, UT
Grand Rapids–Battle Creek, MI	Seattle–Tacoma, WA
Kansas City, MO	Wichita–Hutchinson, KA

The duration of the test depends on the repurchase cycle for the product, the probability of competitive response, cost considerations, the initial consumer response, and company philosophy. The test should last long enough for repurchase activity to be observed. This indicates the long-term impact of the product. If competitive reaction to the test is anticipated, the duration should be short. The cost of the test is also an important factor. The longer a test, the more it costs, and at some point the value of additional information is outweighed by its costs. Recent evidence suggests that tests of new brands should run for at least ten months. An empirical analysis found that the final test market share was reached in ten months 85% of the time and in 12 months 95% of the time.[35] Test marketing can be very beneficial to a product's successful introduction, as the following example demonstrates.

EXAMPLE
Product Introduction Mushrooms

Kraft leads the $550 million pourable dressings category, followed by Thomas J. Lipton's Wish-Bone brand, Clorox Company's Hidden Valley Ranch, and Anderson Clayton Food's Seven Seas. Recently, Kraft test-marketed two new dressings. Rancher's Choice, a creamy, ranch-style pourable dressing, was tested in Denver. Simultaneously, a two-item line of mushroom dressings was tested in selected southwestern cities. TV ads positioned Rancher's Choice directly against Hidden Valley's flagship ranch-style brand. The mushroom dressings received spot TV and freestanding newspaper inserts.[36] The test-marketing results were positive, leading to successful new product introductions. ◆

A standard test market, such as the Kraft example, constitutes a one-shot case study. In addition to the problems associated with this design, test marketing faces two unique problems. First, competitors often take actions such as increasing their promotional efforts to contaminate the test marketing program. When Procter & Gamble test-marketed its hand-and-body lotion Wondra, the market leader, Cheeseborough Ponds, started a competitive buy-one-get-one-free promotion for its flagship brand, Vaseline Intensive Care lotion. This encouraged consumers to stock up on Vaseline Intensive Care lotion and as a result, Wondra did poorly in the test market. Yet Procter & Gamble still launched the Wondra line nationally. Ponds again countered with the same promotional strategy. Today, Wondra has about 4% of the market, and Vaseline Intensive Care has 22%.[37]

Another problem is that while a firm's test marketing is in progress, competitors have an opportunity to beat it to the national market.[38] Hills Bros. High Yield Coffee was test-marketed and introduced nationally, but only after Procter & Gamble introduced Folger's Flakes. Procter & Gamble skipped test marketing Folger's Flakes and beat Hills Bros. to the national market. P & G also launched Ivory shampoo without test marketing.[39]

Sometimes it is not feasible to implement a standard test market using the company's personnel. Instead, the company must seek help from an outside supplier, in which case the controlled test market may be an attractive option.

Controlled Test Market

controlled test market A test-marketing program conducted by an outside research company in field experimentation. The research company guarantees distribution of the product in retail outlets that represent a predetermined percentage of the market.

In a **controlled test market**, the entire test-marketing program is conducted by an outside research company. The research company guarantees distribution of the product in retail outlets that represent a predetermined percentage of the market. It handles warehousing and field sales operations, such as stocking shelves, selling, and inventory control. The controlled test market includes both minimarket (or forced distribution) tests and the smaller controlled store panels. This service is provided by a number of research firms, including Audits and Surveys; Burgoyne, Inc.; Dancer, Fitzgerald, and Sample; and A. C. Nielsen.

Simulated Test Market

simulated test market A quasi test market in which respondents are preselected; they are then interviewed and observed on their purchases and attitudes toward the product.

Also called a laboratory test or test market simulation, a **simulated test market** yields mathematical estimates of market share based on initial reaction of consumers to a new product. The procedure works as follows. Typically, respondents are intercepted in high-traffic locations, such as shopping malls, and prescreened for product usage. The selected individuals are exposed to the proposed new product concept and given an opportunity to buy the new product in a real-life or laboratory environment. Those who purchase the new product are interviewed about their evaluation of the product and repeat purchase intentions. The trial and repeat-purchase estimates so generated are combined with data on proposed promotion and distribution levels to project a share of the market.[40]

Simulated test markets can be conducted in 16 weeks or less. The information they generate is confidential and the competition cannot obtain it. They are also relatively inexpensive. A standard test market can cost as much as $1 million, but simulated test markets cost less than 10% as much. The major firms supplying this service are Management Decision Systems, Elrick and Lavidge, Burke Marketing Services, and Yankelovich Partners Inc. Simulated test markets are becoming increasingly popular.[41]

DETERMINING A TEST-MARKETING STRATEGY

The first decision to be made is whether or not to test market the proposed new product, or whatever element of the marketing program that is under consideration. As shown in Figure 7.2, this decision must take into account the competitive environment; the sociocultural environment, particularly consumer preferences and past behaviors; the need to keep the firm's marketing efforts secret; and the overall marketing strategy of the firm. If the marketing research already undertaken to develop the new product provides compelling positive evidence, or if factors such as preempting competitive moves dominate, the new product may well be introduced nationally without test marketing. If the decision is to conduct test marketing, however, simulated test marketing may be conducted first, followed by controlled test marketing, then standard test marketing, and, if the results are positive, national introduction. Of course, very positive results at any stage may directly lead to national introduction, circumventing subsequent testing.

INTERNATIONAL MARKETING RESEARCH

If field experiments are difficult to conduct in the United States, the challenge they pose is greatly increased in the international arena. In many countries, the marketing, economic, structural, information and technological environment (see Chapter 23) is not

FIGURE 7.2

Selecting a Test-Marketing Strategy

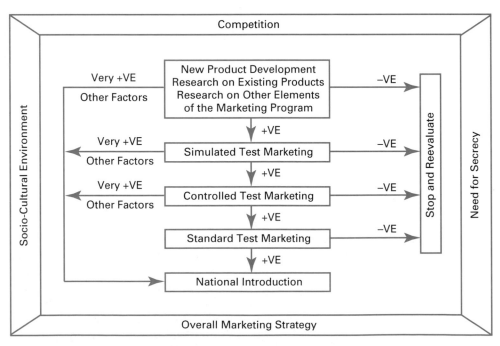

+VE = Positive   −VE = Negative

developed to the extent that it is in the United States. For example, in many countries, the TV stations are owned and operated by a government that may place severe restrictions on television advertising. This makes field experiments that manipulate advertising levels extremely difficult. Consider, for example, M & M/Mars, which has set up massive manufacturing facilities in Russia and advertises its candy bars on television. Yet, the sales potential has not been realized. Is Mars advertising too much, too little, or just enough? Although the answer could be determined by conducting a field experiment that manipulated the level of advertising, such causal research is not feasible given the tight control of the Russian government on television stations.

Likewise, the lack of major supermarkets in the Baltic states makes it difficult for P & G to conduct field experiments to determine the effect of in-store promotions on the sales of its detergents. In some countries in Asia, Africa, and South America, a majority of the population lives in small towns and villages. Yet basic infrastructures such as roads, transportation, and warehouse facilities are lacking, making it difficult to achieve desired levels of distribution. Even when experiments are designed, it is difficult to control for the time order of occurrence of variables and the absence of other possible causal factors, two of the necessary conditions for causality. Because the researcher has little control over the environment, control of extraneous variables is particularly problematic. Furthermore, it may not be possible to address this problem by adopting the most appropriate experimental design as environmental constraints may make that design infeasible.

Thus, the internal and external validity of field experiments conducted overseas is generally lower than in the United States. Although pointing to the difficulties of conducting field experiments in other countries, we do not wish to imply that such causal research cannot or should not be conducted. To the contrary, as the following example indicates, creatively designed field experiments can result in rich findings.

EXAMPLE
What You Hear Is What You Get

PepsiCo's strategy to fight archrival Coca-Cola in France was through increased ad spending through BBDO Worldwide. Part of their campaign was to use singers and celebrities such as Rod Stewart, Tina Turner, Gloria Estefan, and M. C. Hammer in their commercials as well as publicity tours. Marketing research, however, revealed that overplaying American celebrities may be detrimental in the French market. Pepsi thought that this was probably a weakness Coke had because Europeans considered Coca-Cola's marketing effort as "too American." Pepsi, therefore, decided to use taste as a competitive tool. The key was to highlight the product superiority, although not directly, as comparative advertising was prohibited in France. They came up with music as a means of communicating. How did this work?

Research showed that attitude toward the brand is influenced by attitude toward the ad, especially in low involvement products such as soft drinks. Sweet and melodious music played for Pepsi would transfer good feelings from the music to the brand Pepsi. Similarly, repugnant and undesirable music played for Coke would also transfer from the music to the brand Coke. This mechanism is called classical conditioning. To test these hypotheses, a two-factor experiment could be designed. The two factors would be type of music and the brand preferred, each varied at two levels as shown. A test commercial for each experimental condition would be run for a month, with each commercial being played in a different city. At the end of campaign, central location interviews would be used to examine the effect on brand.

Brand Type

The results of a similar experiment indicated positive effects for good music and negative effects for bad music. Pepsi designed its advertising based on these findings. Subsequently, retail sales in France increased although it still is in the second position, after Coke.[42] ◆

ETHICS IN MARKETING RESEARCH

As was explained in Chapter 6, many times it is believed that if the respondents are aware of the purpose of the research, they will give biased responses. In these situations, a deliberate attempt is made by the researcher to disguise the purpose of the research. This is often necessary with experimentation, where disguise is needed to produce valid results. Take, for example, a project conducted to determine the effectiveness of television commercials for Total cereal. The respondents are recruited and brought to a central facility. They are told that they will be watching a television program on nutrition and then will be asked some questions. Interspersed in the program is the commercial for Total cereal (test commercial) as well as commercials for some other products (filler commercials). After viewing the program and the commercials, the respondents are administered a questionnaire. The questionnaire obtains evaluations on the program content, the test commercial and some of the filler commercials. Note, the evaluations of the program content and the filler commercials are not of interest but are obtained to reinforce the nature of the disguise. If the respondents knew that the true purpose was to determine the effectiveness of the Total commercial, their responses might be biased. Disguising the purpose of the research should not, however, lead to deception.

Although this seems like a paradox, one solution is to disclose the possible existence of deception before the start of the experiment and allow the participants the right to redress at the conclusion of the experiment. The following four items should be conveyed: (1) inform respondents that in an experiment of this nature, a disguise of the purpose is often required for valid results; (2) inform them of the general nature of the experiment and what they will be asked to do; (3) make sure they know that they can leave the experiment at any time; and (4) inform them that the study will be fully explained after the data have been gathered and at that time, they may request that their information be withdrawn.

debriefing After the experiment, informing test subjects what the experiment was about and how the experimental manipulations were performed.

The procedure outlined in item (4) is called **debriefing**. It could be argued that disclosure in this way would also bias results. There is evidence, however, indicating that data collected from subjects informed of the possibility of deception and those not informed is similar.[43] Debriefing can alleviate the stress caused by the experiment and make the experiment a learning experience for the respondents. However, if not handled carefully, debriefing itself can be unsettling to subjects. In the Total cereal example, respondents may find it disheartening that they spent their time evaluating a cereal commercial. The researcher should anticipate and address this issue in the debriefing session.

One further ethical concern in experimentation involves using the appropriate experimental design to control errors caused by extraneous variables. It is the responsibility of the researcher to use the most applicable experimental design for the problem. As the following example illustrates, determining the most appropriate experimental design for the problem requires not only an initial evaluation but also continuous monitoring.

EXAMPLE

Correcting Errors Early: A Stitch in Time Saves Nine

A marketing research firm specializing in advertising research is examining the effectiveness of a television commercial for Nike athletic shoes. A one-group pretest-posttest design is used. Attitudes held by the respondents toward Nike athletic shoes are obtained prior to being exposed to a sports program and several commercials, including the one for Nike. Attitudes are again measured after viewing the program and the commercials. Initial evaluation based on a small sample found the one-group pretest-posttest design adopted in this study to be susceptible to demand artifacts: respondents attempt to guess the purpose of the experiment and respond accordingly. Because time and financial constraints make redesigning the study difficult at best, the research continues with correction. Continuing a research project after knowing errors were made in the early stages is not ethical behavior.[44] Experimental design problems should be disclosed immediately to the client. Decisions whether to re-design or accept the flaws should be made jointly. ◆

COMPUTER APPLICATIONS

Microcomputers and mainframes can be used in the design and analysis of experiments. The comprehensive statistical analysis software package MINITAB can be used to design experiments for the marketing researcher. Although similar in use to SPSS, SAS, or BMDP, Release 9 for Windows of MINITAB includes functions and documentation specifically for industrial-quality control work where factorial designs are encountered.

For example, researchers for a destination-type specialty retail outlet, such as Niketown, might want to investigate some of the interactions of independent variables, such as elements of store atmospherics in one section of their store. The dependent variable in this experiment would be the subjects' rating of the store section for browsing. Three factors would be included in this $2 \times 2 \times 2$ study. Assuming two lighting levels (i.e., low or medium), two sound types (i.e., outdoor stadium noise or indoor arena noise), and two olfactory stimuli (i.e., hot chocolate or hot popcorn smell), the best combinations of store atmospherics can be examined.

Exhibit 7.1 illustrates the commands used by MINITAB (written by Minitab, Inc. of State College, Pennsylvania) for its FFDESIGN procedure, along with the results of this procedure. The first row of commands directs MINITAB to name three columns a, b, or c. The second row of commands directs MINITAB to implement the FFDESIGN procedure with three factors (i.e., light, sound, and smell), and eight runs. Then, the two subcommands call for a randomized design and for a three-column printing of the matrix of treatment conditions.

The results of MINITAB's work begin with "full factorial design." Here, the data matrix uses a –1 or a 1 to show the levels of the factors to be used for each group of subjects to be run. The –1 designates the first option for each cell (e.g., low, when presented

EXHIBIT 7.1

*Using MINITAB
to Design Experiments*

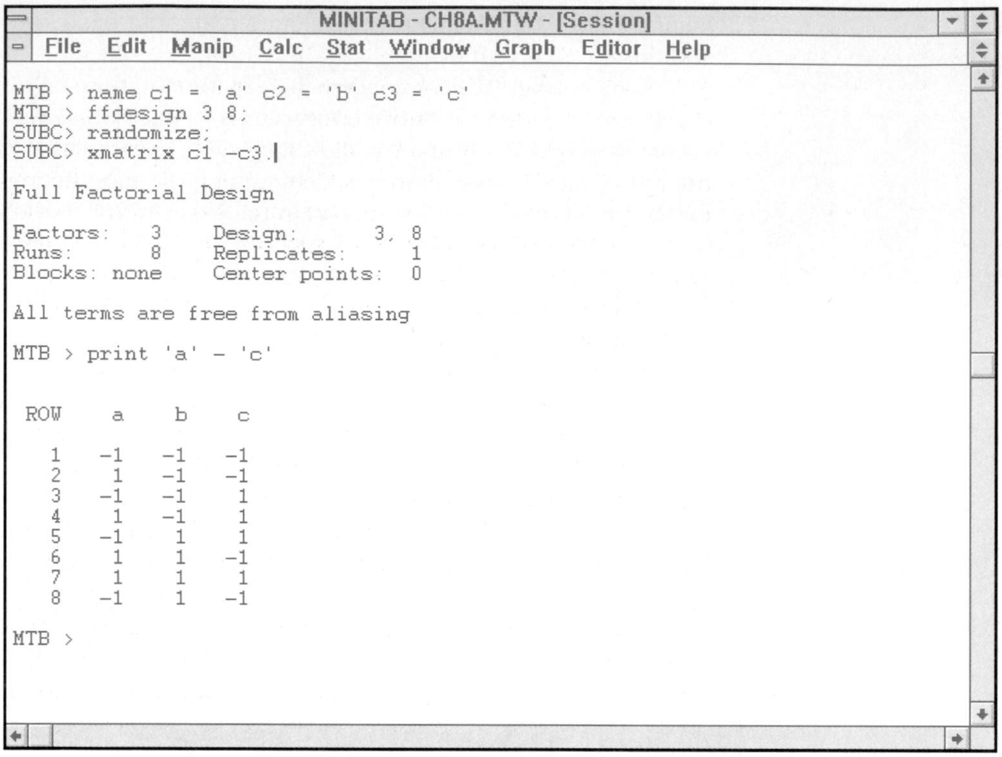

```
┌──────────────────────────────────────────────────────────────────────┐
│                    MINITAB - CH8A.MTW - [Session]              ▼  ▲    │
│ □   File   Edit   Manip   Calc   Stat   Window   Graph   Editor  Help ▲│
│                                                                      ▲ │
│ MTB > name c1 = 'a' c2 = 'b' c3 = 'c'                                  │
│ MTB > ffdesign 3 8;                                                    │
│ SUBC> randomize;                                                       │
│ SUBC> xmatrix c1 −c3.                                                  │
│                                                                        │
│ Full Factorial Design                                                  │
│                                                                        │
│ Factors:    3     Design:       3, 8                                   │
│ Runs:       8     Replicates:      1                                   │
│ Blocks: none      Center points:  0                                    │
│                                                                        │
│ All terms are free from aliasing                                       │
│                                                                        │
│ MTB > print 'a' − 'c'                                                  │
│                                                                        │
│   ROW    a    b    c                                                   │
│                                                                        │
│     1   −1   −1   −1                                                   │
│     2    1   −1   −1                                                   │
│     3   −1   −1    1                                                   │
│     4    1   −1    1                                                   │
│     5   −1    1    1                                                   │
│     6    1    1   −1                                                   │
│     7    1    1    1                                                   │
│     8   −1    1   −1                                                   │
│                                                                        │
│ MTB >                                                                  │
│                                                                      ▼ │
│ ◄                                                                  ► ▼ │
└──────────────────────────────────────────────────────────────────────┘
```

with low or medium levels of lighting). With all three factors being assigned a −1 for the first run of the experiment, the consumers to test this combination of atmospherics would be brought into a room with the following characteristics: low lighting level, outdoor stadium sound, and a hot chocolate aroma. The researcher can find the design of this example and similar ones in the catalog of designs section in the MINITAB documentation.

MINITAB offers the researcher a variety of other data analysis capabilities. The data entry format for MINITAB resembles that of a spreadsheet, so variables are referenced by column heading in command lines. Although MINITAB retains its old DOS-type command structure, Release 9 provides menus and dialog boxes for those who prefer not to type commands. Desired analyses can be selected by "pointing and clicking" on the menu bar. Dialog boxes can then expedite the completion of the DOS-type commands by offering the user the various options for the subcommands required to complete the desired analysis. More specialized software is also available.

Probe-PC by Concurrent Technologies is a time series and advanced time series package for analyzing data from quasi-experimental designs. It can be directly linked to public databases such as Citibase and Ipsharp. Market Matching by Management Science Associates has been designed for causal analysis. It selects matched test and control groups (geographical areas or stores) based on sales tracking data. It computes pretest-posttest net differences and corresponding significance levels. Pulse/Rsamp by Pulse Analytics generates complete and incomplete block-design random samples. It automatically balances for number, position, and pairs. GENFRIED is a program for analyzing unbalanced block data.[45] Finally, simulators like CHOISIM take the experimental results and make market share projections.[46]

SUMMARY

The scientific notion of causality implies that we can never prove that X causes Y. At best, we can only infer that X is one of the causes of Y in that it makes the occurrence of Y probable. Three conditions must be satisfied before causal inferences can be made: (1) concomitant variation, which implies that X and Y must vary together in a hypothesized way; (2) time order of occurrence of variables, which implies that X must precede Y; and (3) elimination of other possible causal factors, which implies that competing explanations must be ruled out. Experiments provide the most convincing evidence of all three conditions. An experiment is formed when one or more independent variables are manipulated or controlled by the researcher and their effect on one or more dependent variables is measured.

In designing an experiment, it is important to consider internal and external validity. Internal validity refers to whether the manipulation of the independent variables actually caused the effects on the dependent variables. External validity refers to the generalizability of experimental results. For the experiment to be valid, the researcher must control the threats imposed by extraneous variables, such as history, maturation, testing (main and interactive testing effects), instrumentation, statistical regression, selection bias, and mortality. There are four ways of controlling extraneous variables: randomization, matching, statistical control, and design control.

Experimental designs may be classified as preexperimental, true experimental, quasi-experimental, and statistical designs. An experiment may be conducted in a laboratory environment or under actual market conditions in a real-life setting. Only causal designs encompassing experimentation are appropriate for inferring cause-and-effect relationships.

Although experiments have limitations in terms of time, cost, and administration, they are becoming increasingly popular in marketing. Test marketing is an important application of experimental design.

The internal and external validity of field experiments conducted overseas is generally lower than in the United States. The level of development in many countries is lower and the researcher lacks control over many of the marketing variables. The ethical issues involved in conducting causal research include disguising the purpose of the experiment. Debriefing can be used to address some of these issues. Computers are very useful in the design and analysis of experiments.[47]

ACRONYMS

The extraneous factors that threaten the internal and external validity of the experiment may be described by the acronym THREATS:

T   esting
H   istory
R   egression
E   rrors in measurement: instrumentation
A   ging: maturation
T   ermination of test units: mortality
S   election bias

EXERCISES

QUESTIONS

1. What are the requirements for inferring a causal relationship between two variables?
2. Differentiate between internal and external validity.

3. List any five extraneous variables and give an example to show how each can reduce internal validity.

4. Describe the various methods for controlling extraneous sources of variation.

5. What is the key characteristic that distinguishes true experimental designs from preexperimental designs?

6. List the steps involved in implementing the posttest-only control group design. Describe the design symbolically.

7. What is a time series experiment? When is it used?

8. How is a multiple time series design different from a basic time series design?

9. What advantages do statistical designs have over basic designs?

10. What are the limitations of the Latin square design?

11. Compare laboratory and field experimentation.

12. Should descriptive research be used for investigating causal relationships? Why or why not?

13. What is test marketing? What are the three types of test marketing?

14. What is the main difference between a standard test market and a controlled test market?

15. Describe how simulated test marketing works.

PROBLEMS

1. A prolife group wanted to test the effectiveness of an antiabortion commercial. Two random samples, each of 250 respondents, were recruited in Atlanta. One group was shown the antiabortion commercial. Then, attitudes toward abortion were measured for respondents in both groups.

   a. Identify the independent and dependent variables in this experiment.

   b. What type of design was used?

   c. What are the potential threats to internal and external validity in this experiment?

2. In the experiment just described, suppose that the respondents had been selected by convenience rather than randomly. What type of design would result?

3. Consider the following table in which 500 respondents have been classified based on product use and income.

Product Use	High	Medium	Low
		Income	
High	40	30	40
Medium	35	70	60
Low	25	50	150

   a. Does this table indicate concomitant variation between product use and income?

   b. Describe the relationship between product use and income based on the above table.

4. State the type of experiment being conducted in the following situations. In each case, identify the potential threat to internal and external validity.

   a. A major distributor of office equipment is considering a new sales presentation program for its salespersons. The largest sales territory is selected, the new program is implemented, and the effect on sales is measured.

   b. Procter & Gamble wants to determine if a new package design for Tide is more effective than the current design. Twelve supermarkets are randomly selected in Chicago. In six of them, randomly selected, Tide is sold in the new packaging. In the other six, the detergent is sold in the old package. Sales for both groups of supermarkets are monitored for three months.

5. Describe a specific situation for which each of the following experimental designs is appropriate. Defend your reasoning.

a. One-group pretest-posttest design
b. Pretest-posttest control group design
c. Post-test-only control group design
d. Multiple time series design
e. Factorial design

COMPUTER EXERCISES

1. Survey the relevant literature and write a short paper on the role of the computer in controlled experiments in marketing research.

NOTES

1. "Surveys Help Settle Trade Dress Infringement Case," *Quirk's Marketing Research Review* (October–November 1987): 16, 17, 33.
2. "POP Radio Test Airs the Ads In-Store," *Marketing News* (October 24, 1986): 16.
3. David A. Kenny, *Correlation and Causality* (New York: Wiley, 1979), chapter 1.
4. For several references on the use of experiments in marketing, see David M. Gardner and Russell W. Belk, *A Basic Bibliography on Experimental Design in Marketing* (Chicago: American Marketing Association, 1980).
5. Claire Selltiz, Marie Jahoda, Morton Deutsch, and Stuart W. Cook, *Research Methods in Social Relations* (New York: Holt, Rinehart and Winston, 1959), pp. 83–88.
6. *Fortune* (November 23, 1987): 12.
7. Steven R. Brown, and Lawrence E. Melamed, *Experimental Design and Analysis* (Newbury Park, CA: Sage Publications, 1990).
8. A recent study employing experimental designs is Stephen J. Hoch, Xavier Dreze, and Mary E. Purk, "EDLP, Hi-Lo, and Margin Arithmetic," *Journal of Marketing* 58 (October 1994): 16–27.
9. Robert W. Shoemaker and Vikas Tibrewala, "Relating Coupon Redemption Rates to Past Purchasing of the Brand," *Journal of Advertising Research* 25 (October–November 1985): 40–47.
10. S. Banks, *Experimentation in Marketing* (New York: McGraw-Hill, 1965), pp. 168–79.
11. In addition to internal and external validity, there also exist construct and statistical conclusion validity. Construct validity addresses the question of what construct, or characteristic, is in fact being measured and is discussed in Chapter 9 on measurement and scaling. Statistical conclusion validity addresses the extent and statistical significance of the covariation that exists in the data and is discussed in the chapters on data analysis. See T. D. Cook and D. T. Campbell, *Quasi-Experimentation* (Chicago: Rand McNally, 1979), pp. 52–53; and, Donald T. Campbell and Julian C. Stanley, *Experimental and Quasi Experimental Designs for Research* (Chicago: Rand McNally, 1966).
12. John G. Lynch, Jr., "On the External Validity of Experiments in Consumer Research," *Journal of Consumer Research*, 9 (December 1982): 225–44.
13. J. G. Lynch, Jr., "The Role of External Validity in Theoretical Research," B. J. Calder, L. W. Phillips, and Alice Tybout, "Beyond External Validity," and J. E. McGrath and D. Brinberg, "External Validity and the Research Process," *Journal of Consumer Research* (June 1983): 109–11, 112–14, and 115–24.
14. C. O'Herlihy, "Why Ad Experiments Fail," *Journal of Advertising Research* (February 1980): 53–58.
15. T. D. Cook and D. T. Campbell, *Quasi-Experimentation* (Chicago: Rand McNally, 1979), pp. 52–53.
16. Steven R. Brown and Lawrence E. Melamed, *Experimental Design and Analysis* (Newbury Park, CA: Sage Publications, 1990).
17. Andrew M. Tarshis, "Natural Sell-in Avoids Pitfalls of Controlled Tests," *Marketing News* (October 24, 1986): 14.
18. Other experimental designs are also available. See R. S. Winer, "Analysis of Advertising Experiments," *Journal of Advertising Research* (June 1980): 25–31.
19. For some applications of this design, see Z. S. Demirdjian, "Sales Effectiveness of Comparative Advertising," *Journal of Consumer Research* (December 1983): 362–65; and C. P. Duncan, and J. E. Nelson, "Effects of Humor in a Radio Advertising Experiment," *Journal of Advertising* (1985): 33–40.
20. For an application of the Solomon four-group design, see Richard W. Mizerski, Neil K. Allison, and Stephen Calvert, "A Controlled Field Study of Corrective Advertising Using Multiple Exposures and a Commercial Medium," *Journal of Marketing Research* 17 (August 1980): 341–48.

21. S. Banks, *Experimentation in Marketing* (New York: McGraw-Hill, 1965), pp. 168–79.

22. Lakshman Krishnamurthi, Jack Narayan, and S. P. Raj, "Intervention Analysis of a Field Experiment to Assess the Buildup Effect of Advertising," *Journal of Marketing Research* 23 (November 1986): 337–45.

23. See, for example, Amitava Chattopadhyay and Kunal Basu, "Humor in Advertising: The Moderating Role of Prior Brand Evaluation," *Journal of Marketing Research* 27 (November 1990): 466–76.

24. For recent applications of factorial designs, see France Leclerc, Bernd H. Schmitt, and Laurette Dube, "Foreign Branding and Its Effects on Product Perceptions and Attitudes," *Journal of Marketing Research* 31 (May 1994): 263–70.

25. Albert C. Bemmaor and Dominique Mouchoux, "Measuring the Short-Term Effect of In-Store Promotion and Retail Advertising on Brand Sales: A Factorial Experiment," *Journal of Marketing Research* 28 (May 1991): 202–14.

26. James B. Miller, Norman T. Bruvold, and Jerome B. Kernan, "Does Competitive-Set Information Affect the Results of Concept Tests?" *Journal of Advertising Research* (April–May 1987): 16–23.

27. J. H. Barnes, Jr., and D. T. Seymour, "Experimenter Bias: Task, Tools, and Time," *Journal of the Academy of Marketing Science* (Winter 1980): 1–11.

28. J. Lim and J. O. Summers, "A Non-Experimental Investigation of Demand Artifacts in a Personal Selling Situation," *Journal of Marketing Research* (August 1984): 251–58.

29. John G. Lynch, Jr., "On the External Validity of Experiments in Consumer Research," *Journal of Consumer Research* 9 (December 1982): 225–44.

30. P. W. Farris and D. J. Reibstein, "Overcontrol in Advertising Experiments," *Journal of Advertising Research* (June–July 1984): 37–42.

31. M. J. Houston and M. L. Rothschild, "Policy-Related Experiments on Information Provision: A Normative Model and Explication," *Journal of Marketing Research* (November 1980): 432–49; and Alan G. Sawyer, Parker M. Worthing, and Paul E. Sendak, "The Role of Laboratory Experiments to Test Marketing Strategies," *Journal of Marketing*, 43 (Summer 1979): 60–67.

32. Hurbert M. Blalock, Jr., *Causal Inferences in Nonexperimental Research* (Chapel Hill: University of North Carolina Press, 1964); and T.D. Cook and D.T. Campbell, *Quasi-Experimentation* (Chicago: Rand McNally, 1979), chapter 7.

33. In some situations, surveys and experiments can complement each other and may both be used. For example, the results obtained in laboratory experiments may be further examined in a field survey. See Wesley J. Johnston and Keysuk Kim, "Performance, Attribution, and Expectancy Linkages in Personal Selling," *Journal of Marketing* 58 (October 1994): 68–81.

34. Reprinted with permission from *Marketing News* published by the American Marketing Association, Chicago, March 1, 1985, p. 15.

35. "Test Marketers on Target," *Sales and Marketing Management* (March 11, 1985): 81–116; and "The Time Test of Test Marketing Is Time," *Sales and Marketing Management* (March 14, 1983): 74.

36. Julie Franz, "Kraft Tests Dressings, Cheeses," *Advertising Age* (November 25, 1985): 43.

37. "How to Improve Your Chances for Test-Market Success," *Marketing News* (January 6, 1984): 12.

38. L. Adler, "Test Marketing—Its Pitfalls," *Sales and Marketing Management* (March 15, 1982): 78.

39. "Speeding Up Test Marketing," *Marketing Communications* (June 1985): 67–70.

40. For issues related to the validity of simulated test market, see Glen L. Urban and Gerald M. Katz, "Pre-Test-Market Models: Validation and Managerial Implications," *Journal of Marketing Research* 20 (August 1983): 221–34.

41. K. Higgins, "Simulated Test Marketing Winning Acceptance," *Marketing News* (March 1, 1985): 15.

42. Bruce Crumley, "French Cola Wars," *Advertising Age* (December 17, 1990): 22.

43. D. S. Holmes and D. H., Bennett, "Experiments to Answer Questions Raised by the Use of Deception in Psychological Research: I. Role Playing as an Alternative to Deception; II. Effectiveness of Debriefing after a Deception; III. Effect of Informed Consent on Deception." *Journal of Personality and Social Psychology* 29 (1974): 358–67.

44. O. C. Ferrell and S. J. Skinner, "Ethical Behavior and Bureaucratic Structure in Marketing Research Organizations," *Journal of Marketing Research* 25 (1988): 103–9.

45. Cindi G. Sarosky and Gary M. Mullet, "GENFRIED: A Program for the Analysis of Unbalanced Block Data," *Journal of Marketing Research* (November 1983): 444.

46. David R. Lambert, Kamlesh Mathur, and N. Mohan Reddy, "Choisim: A First-Choice Simulator for Conjoint Data," *Journal of Marketing Research* (May 1985): 219–21.

47. The assistance of James Agarwal with the international marketing research example, the assistance of Mark Leach and Gina Miller in writing the ethics section, and the assistance of Mark Peterson in writing the computer applications section is gratefully acknowledged.

Measurement and Scaling: Fundamentals and Comparative Scaling

"When you can measure what you are speaking about and express it in numbers, you know something about it."

Lord Kelvin

OBJECTIVES

After reading this chapter, the student should be able to:

1. Introduce the concepts of measurement and scaling and show how scaling may be considered an extension of measurement.

2. Discuss the primary scales of measurement and differentiate nominal, ordinal, interval, and ratio scales.

3. Classify and discuss scaling techniques as comparative and noncomparative and describe the comparative techniques of paired comparison, rank order, constant sum, and Q-sort scaling.

4. Explain the concept of verbal protocols and discuss how they could be employed to measure consumer response to advertising.

5. Discuss the considerations involved in implementing the primary scales of measurement in an international setting.

6. Understand the ethical issues involved in selecting scales of measurement.

7. Discuss the use of microcomputers and mainframes in implementing the primary scales of measurement.

OVERVIEW

Once the information to be obtained is specified and the type of research design has been determined (Chapters 3 through 7), the researcher can move to the next phase of the research design: deciding on measurement and scaling procedures. This chapter describes the concepts of scaling and measurement and discusses four primary scales of measurement: nominal, ordinal, interval, and ratio. We describe both comparative and noncomparative scaling techniques and explain comparative techniques in detail. Noncomparative techniques are covered in Chapter 9. The considerations involved in implementing the primary scales of measurement when researching international markets are discussed. Several ethical issues that arise in measurement and scaling are identified. The chapter concludes with a discussion of the use of microcomputers and mainframes in implementing the primary scales of measurement.

To begin, we give some examples of the uses of the primary scales of measurement.

EXAMPLE
Winning Votes with Marketing Research

Barna Research Group, based in Glendale, California, conducted a survey to identify the most important concerns facing the United States in the last decade of the twentieth century. According to the survey, the three most important issues, in order of importance, are (1) fighting substance abuse, (2) international politics, and (3) reducing the national debt. This order of importance reflects an ordinal scale. From a substantive viewpoint, these issues turned out to be crucial to the 1992 presidential election.[1] ◆

EXAMPLE
The Malling of America

According to a recent Maritz Ameri-Poll, visiting the local mall has become part of the American lifestyle. The results of this poll indicated that on average, 40% of adults shop at a mall one or two times per month. Another 20% shop three or four times per month, and 10% make five to eight trips. "Born to shop" describes the 7% of people who average eight or more trips each month. Information conveyed in this manner in the form of percentages is an illustration of a constant sum scale. This type of information can be useful to department store chains in planning the number of store locations in malls.[2] ◆

Visiting the local mall has become part of the American lifestyle. ◆ Bergen Mall, New Jersey.

Assigning importance rankings to issues of concern and percentages to specific categories of respondents are but two examples of the important role of measurement and scaling in marketing research.

MEASUREMENT AND SCALING

measurement The assignment of numbers or other symbols to characteristics of objects according to certain prespecified rules.

Measurement means assigning numbers or other symbols to characteristics of objects according to certain prespecified rules.[3] We measure not the object but some characteristic of it. Thus, we do not measure consumers, only their perceptions, attitudes, preferences, or other relevant characteristics. In marketing research, numbers are usually assigned for one of two reasons. First, numbers permit statistical analysis of the resulting data. Second, numbers facilitate the communication of measurement rules and results.

The most important aspect of measurement is the specification of rules for assigning numbers to the characteristics. The assignment process must be isomorphic: there must be one-to-one correspondence between the numbers and the characteristics being measured. For example, the same dollar figures are assigned to households with identical annual incomes. Only then can the numbers be associated with specific characteristics of the measured object, and vice versa. In addition, the rules for assigning numbers should be standardized and applied uniformly. They must not change over objects or time.

scaling The generation of a continuum upon which measured objects are located.

Scaling may be considered an extension of measurement. **Scaling** involves creating a continuum upon which measured objects are located. To illustrate, consider a scale for locating consumers according to the characteristic "attitude toward department stores." Each respondent is assigned a number indicating an unfavorable attitude (measured as 1), a neutral attitude (measured as 2), or a favorable attitude (measured as 3). Measurement is the actual assignment of 1, 2, or 3 to each respondent. Scaling is the process of placing the respondents on a continuum with respect to their attitude toward department stores. In our example, scaling is the process by which respondents would be classified as having an unfavorable, neutral, or positive attitude.

PRIMARY SCALES OF MEASUREMENT

There are four primary scales of measurement, nominal, ordinal, interval, and ratio.[4] These scales are illustrated in Figure 8.1, and their properties are summarized in Table 8.1 and discussed in the following sections.

Nominal Scale

nominal scale A scale whose numbers serve only as labels or tags for identifying and classifying objects with a strict one-to-one correspondence between the numbers and the objects.

A **nominal scale** is a figurative labeling scheme in which the numbers serve only as labels or tags for identifying and classifying objects. For example, the numbers assigned to the respondents in a study constitute a nominal scale. When a nominal scale is used for the purpose of identification, there is a strict one-to-one correspondence between the numbers and the objects. Each number is assigned to only one object, and each object has only one number assigned to it. Common examples include Social Security numbers and numbers assigned to football players. In marketing research, nominal scales are used for identifying respondents, brands, attributes, stores, and other objects.

When used for classification purposes, the nominally scaled numbers serve as labels for classes or categories. For example, you might classify the control group as group 1 and the experimental group as group 2. The classes are mutually exclusive and collectively exhaustive. The objects in each class are viewed as equivalent with respect to the characteristic represented by the nominal number. All objects in the same class have the same number, and no two classes have the same number.

The numbers in a nominal scale do not reflect the amount of the characteristic possessed by the objects. For example, a high Social Security number does not imply that

FIGURE 8.1

*An Illustration
of Primary Scales
of Management*

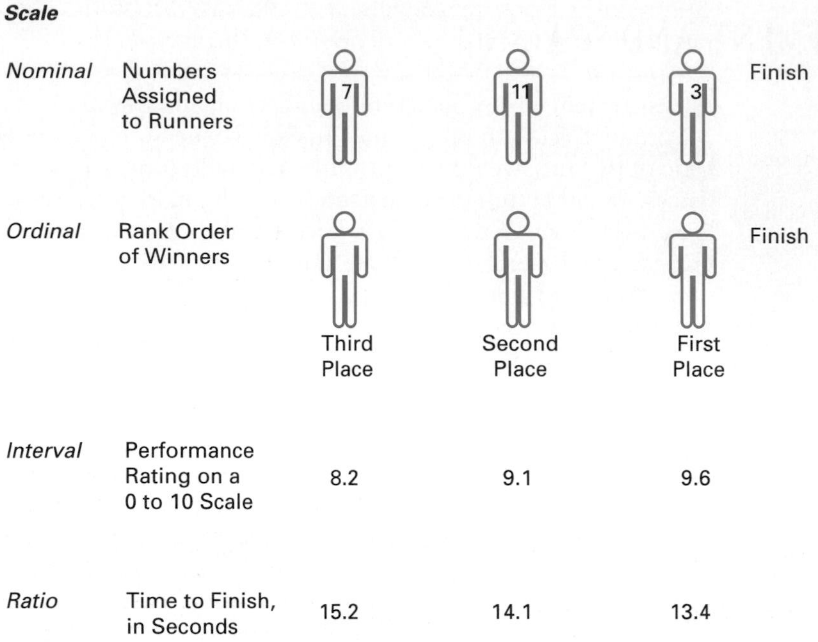

Scale

Nominal	Numbers Assigned to Runners

Finish

7   11   3

Ordinal	Rank Order of Winners

Finish

Third Place   Second Place   First Place

Interval	Performance Rating on a 0 to 10 Scale

8.2   9.1   9.6

Ratio	Time to Finish, in Seconds

15.2   14.1   13.4

the person is in some way superior to someone with a lower Social Security number, or vice versa. The same applies to numbers assigned to classes. The only permissible operation on the numbers in a nominal scale is counting. Only a limited number of statistics, all of which are based on frequency counts, are permissible. These include percent-

TABLE 8.1

Primary Scales of Measurement

Scale	Basic Characteristics	Common Examples	Marketing Examples	Permissible Statistics	
				Descriptive	Inferential
Nominal	Numbers identify and classify objects	Social Security numbers, numbering of football players	Brand numbers, store types, sex classification	Percentages, mode	Chi-square, binomial test
Ordinal	Numbers indicate the relative positions of the objects but not the magnitude of differences between them	Quality rankings, rankings of teams in a tournament	Preference rankings, market position, social class	Percentile, median	Rank-order correlation, Friedman ANOVA
Interval	Differences between objects can be compared; zero point is arbitrary	Temperature (Fahrenheit, Celsius)	Attitudes, opinions, index numbers	Range, mean, standard deviation	Product-moment correlations, t tests, ANOVA, regression, factor analysis
Ratio	Zero point is fixed; ratios of scale values can be computed	Length, weight	Age, income, costs, sales, market shares	Geometric mean, harmonic mean	Coefficient of variation

ages, mode, chi-square, and binomial tests (see Chapter 15). It is not meaningful to compute an average Social Security number, the average sex of the respondents in a survey, or the number assigned to an average department store, as in the following example.

DEPARTMENT STORE PATRONAGE PROJECT

Nominal Scale

In the department store project, the numbers 1 through 10 were assigned to the ten stores considered in the study (see Table 8.2). Thus, store 9 referred to Sears. It did not imply that Sears was in any way superior or inferior to Neiman Marcus; which was assigned the number 6. Any reassignment of the numbers, such as transposing the numbers assigned to Sears and Neiman Marcus, would have no effect on the numbering system, because the numerals did not reflect any characteristics of the stores. It is meaningful to make statements such as "75% of the respondents patronized Sears within the last month." Although the average of the assigned numbers is 5.5, it is not meaningful to state that the number of the average store is 5.5. ◆

A common and popular example of a nominal scale is numbers assigned to football players. ◆ Tony Stone Images.

Ordinal Scale

An **ordinal scale** is a ranking scale in which numbers are assigned to objects to indicate the relative extent to which the objects possess some characteristic. An ordinal scale allows you to determine whether an object has more or less of a characteristic than some

TABLE 8.2

Illustration of Primary Scales of Measurement

Nominal Scale		Ordinal Scale		Interval Scale		Ratio Scale
		Preference Rankings		Preference Ratings		Dollars Spent Last Two Months
No.	Store			1–7	11–17	
1	Lord & Taylor	7	79	5	15	0
2	Macy's	2	25	7	17	200
3	Kmart	8	82	7	17	0
4	Rich's	3	30	6	16	100
5	J.C. Penney	1	10	7	17	250
6	Neiman Marcus	5	53	5	15	35
7	Target	9	95	4	14	0
8	Saks Fifth Avenue	6	61	5	15	100
9	Sears	4	45	6	16	0
10	Woolworth	10	115	2	12	10

ordinal scale A ranking scale in which numbers are assigned to objects to indicate the relative extent to which some characteristic is possessed. Thus, it is possible to determine whether an object has more or less of a characteristic than some other object.

other object, but not how much more or less. Thus, an ordinal scale indicates relative position, not the magnitude of the differences between the objects. The object ranked first has more of the characteristic as compared with the object ranked second, but whether the object ranked second is a close second or a poor second is not known. Common examples of ordinal scales include quality rankings, rankings of teams in a tournament, socio-economic class, and occupational status. In marketing research, ordinal scales are used to measure relative attitudes, opinions, perceptions, and preferences. Measurements of this type include "greater than" or "less than" judgments from the respondents.

In an ordinal scale, as in a nominal scale, equivalent objects receive the same rank. Any series of numbers can be assigned that preserves the ordered relationships between the objects. For example, ordinal scales can be transformed in any way as long as the basic ordering of the objects is maintained.[5] In other words, any monotonic positive (order-preserving) transformation of the scale is permissible, since the differences in numbers are void of any meaning other than order (see the following example). For these reasons, in addition to the counting operation allowable for nominal scale data, ordinal scales permit the use of statistics based on centiles. It is meaningful to calculate percentile, quartile, median (Chapter 15), rank-order correlation (Chapter 17) or other summary statistics from ordinal data.

DEPARTMENT STORE PATRONAGE PROJECT
Ordinal Scale

Table 8.2 gives a particular respondent's preference rankings. Respondents ranked ten department stores in order of preference by assigning a rank 1 to the most preferred store, rank 2 to the second most preferred store, and so on. Note that J.C. Penney (ranked 1), is preferred to Macy's (ranked 2), but how much it is preferred we do not know. Also, it is not necessary that we assign numbers from 1 to 10 to obtain a preference ranking. The second ordinal scale, which assigns a number 10 to J.C. Penney, 25 to Macy's, 30 to Rich's, and so on, is an equivalent scale, as it was obtained by a monotonic positive transformation of the first scale. The two scales result in the same ordering of the stores according to preference. ◆

Interval Scale

interval scale A scale in which the numbers are used to rank objects such that numerically equal distances on the scale represent equal distances in the characteristic being measured.

In an **interval scale**, numerically equal distances on the scale represent equal values in the characteristic being measured. An interval scale contains all the information of an ordinal scale, but it also allows you to compare the differences between objects. The difference between any two scale values is identical to the difference between any other two adjacent values of an interval scale. There is a constant or equal interval between scale values. The difference between 1 and 2 is the same as the difference between 2 and 3, which is the same as the difference between 5 and 6. A common example in everyday life is a temperature scale. In marketing research, attitudinal data obtained from rating scales are often treated as interval data.[6]

In an interval scale, the location of the zero point is not fixed. Both the zero point and the units of measurement are arbitrary. Hence, any positive linear transformation of the form $y = a + bx$ will preserve the properties of the scale. Here, x is the original scale value, y is the transformed scale value, b is a positive constant, and a is any constant. Therefore, two interval scales that rate objects A, B, C, and D as 1, 2, 3, and 4 or as 22, 24, 26, and 28 are equivalent. Note that the latter scale can be derived from the former by using $a = 20$ and $b = 2$ in the transforming equation.

Because the zero point is not fixed, it is not meaningful to take ratios of scale values. As can be seen, the ratio of D to B values changes from 2:1 to 7:6 when the scale is transformed. Yet, ratios of differences between scale values are permissible. In this process, the constants a and b in the transforming equation drop out in the computations. The ratio of the difference between D and B to the difference between C and B is 2:1 in both the scales.

Statistical techniques that may be used on interval scale data include all those that can be applied to nominal and ordinal data in addition to the arithmetic mean, standard deviation (Chapter 15), product moment correlations (Chapter 17), and other statistics commonly used in marketing research. Certain specialized statistics such as geometric mean, harmonic mean, and coefficient of variation, however, are not meaningful on interval scale data. The department store example gives a further illustration of an interval scale.

DEPARTMENT STORE PATRONAGE PROJECT
Interval Scale

In Table 8.2, a respondent's preferences for the ten stores are expressed on a seven-point rating scale. We can see that although Sears received a preference rating of 6 and Woolworth a rating of 2, this does not mean that Sears is preferred three times as much as Woolworth. When the ratings are transformed to an equivalent 11 to 17 scale (next column), the ratings for these stores become 16 and 12, and the ratio is no longer 3:1. In contrast, the ratios of preference differences are identical on the two scales. The ratio of the preference difference between J.C. Penney and Woolworth to the preference difference between Neiman Marcus and Woolworth is 5:3 on both the scales. ◆

Ratio Scale

ratio scale The highest scale, this scale allows the researcher to identify or classify objects, rank order the objects, and compare intervals or differences. It is also meaningful to compute ratios of scale values.

A **ratio scale** possesses all the properties of the nominal, ordinal, and interval scales, and, in addition, an absolute zero point. Thus, in ratio scales we can identify or classify objects, rank the objects, and compare intervals or differences. It is also meaningful to compute ratios of scale values. Not only is the difference between 2 and 5 the same as the difference between 14 and 17, but also 14 is seven times as large as 2 in an absolute sense. Common examples of ratio scales include height, weight, age, and money. In marketing, sales, costs, market share, and number of customers are variables measured on a ratio scale.

Ratio scales allow only proportionate transformations of the form $y = bx$, where b is a positive constant. One cannot add an arbitrary constant, as in the case of an interval scale. An example of this transformation is provided by the conversion of yards to feet ($b = 3$). The comparisons between the objects are identical whether made in yards or feet.

All statistical techniques can be applied to ratio data. These include specialized statistics such as geometric mean, harmonic mean, and coefficient of variation. The ratio scale is further illustrated in the context of the department store example.

DEPARTMENT STORE PATRONAGE PROJECT
Ratio Scale

In the ratio scale illustrated in Table 8.2, a respondent is asked to indicate the dollar amounts spent in each of the ten stores during the last two months. Note that since this respondent spent $200 in Macy's and only $10 in Woolworth, this person spent 20 times as much in Macy's as at Woolworth's. Also, the zero point is fixed, since 0 means that the respondent did not spend anything at that store. Multiplying these numbers by 100 to convert dollars to cents results in an equivalent scale. ◆

The four primary scales (discussed here) do not exhaust the measurement level categories. It is possible to construct a nominal scale that provides partial information on order (the partially ordered scale). Likewise, an ordinal scale can convey partial information on distance, as in the case of an ordered metric scale. A discussion of these scales is beyond the scope of this text.[7]

A COMPARISON OF SCALING TECHNIQUES

comparative scales One of two types of scaling techniques in which there is direct comparison of stimulus objects with one another.

The scaling techniques commonly employed in marketing research can be classified into comparative and noncomparative scales (see Figure 8.2). **Comparative scales** involve the direct comparison of stimulus objects. For example, respondents might be asked whether they prefer Coke or Pepsi. Comparative scale data must be interpreted in relative terms and have only ordinal or rank order properties. For this reason, comparative scaling is also referred to as nonmetric scaling. As shown in Figure 8.2, comparative scales include paired comparisons, rank order, constant sum scales, Q-Sort, and other procedures.

The major benefit of comparative scaling is that small differences between stimulus objects can be detected. As they compare the stimulus objects, respondents are forced to choose between them. In addition, respondents approach the rating task from the same known reference points. Consequently, comparative scales are easily understood and can be applied easily. Other advantages of these scales are that they involve fewer theoretical assumptions, and they also tend to reduce halo or carryover effects from one judgment to another.[8] The major disadvantages of comparative scales include the ordinal nature of the

FIGURE 8.2

A Classification of Scaling Techniques

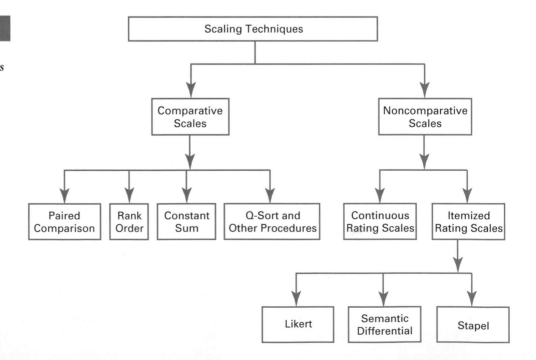

data and the inability to generalize beyond the stimulus objects scaled. For instance, to compare RC Cola to Coke and Pepsi the researcher would have to do a new study. These disadvantages are substantially overcome by the noncomparative scaling techniques.

In **noncomparative scales**, also referred to as monadic or metric scales, each object is scaled independently of the others in the stimulus set. The resulting data are generally assumed to be interval or ratio scaled.[9] For example, respondents may be asked to evaluate Coke on a 1 to 6 preference scale (1 = not all preferred, 6 = greatly preferred). Similar evaluations would be obtained for Pepsi and RC Cola. As can be seen in Figure 8.2, noncomparative scales can be continuous rating or itemized rating scales. The itemized rating scales can be further classified as Likert, semantic differential, or Stapel scales. Noncomparative scaling is the most widely used scaling technique in marketing research. Given its importance, Chapter 9 is devoted to noncomparative scaling. The rest of this chapter focuses on comparative scaling techniques.

noncomparative scales One of two types of scaling techniques in which each stimulus object is scaled independently of the other objects in the stimulus set.

COMPARATIVE SCALING TECHNIQUES

Paired Comparison Scaling

paired comparison scaling A comparative scaling technique in which a respondent is presented with two objects at a time and asked to select one object in the pair according to some criterion. The data obtained are ordinal in nature.

As its name implies, in **paired comparison scaling** a respondent is presented with two objects and asked to select one according to some criterion.[10] The data obtained are ordinal in nature. A respondent may state that she shops in J.C. Penney more than in Sears, likes Total cereal better than Kellogg's Product 19, or likes Crest more than Colgate. Paired comparison scales are frequently used when the stimulus objects are physical products. Coca-Cola is reported to have conducted more than 190,000 paired comparisons before introducing New Coke.[11] Paired comparison scaling is the most widely used comparative scaling technique.

Figure 8.3 shows paired comparison data obtained to assess a respondent's shampoo preferences. As can be seen, this respondent made ten comparisons to evaluate five

FIGURE 8.3

Obtaining Shampoo Preferences Using Paired Comparisons

Instructions
We are going to present you with ten pairs of shampo brands. For each pair, please indicate which one of the two brands of shampoo in the pair you would prefer for personal use.

Recording Form

	Jhirmack	Finesse	Vidal Sassoon	Head & Shoulders	Pert
Jhirmack		0	0	1	0
Finesse	1[a]		0	1	0
Vidal Sassoon	1	1		1	1
Head & Shoulders	0	0	0		0
Pert	1	1	0	1	
Number of Times Preferred[b]	3	2	0	4	1

[a]A 1 in a particular box means that the brand in that column was preferred over the brand in the corresponding row. A 0 means that the row brand was preferred over the column brand.
[b]The number of times a brand was preferred is obtained by summing the 1s in each column.

brands. In general, with *n* brands, $[n(n-1)/2]$ paired comparisons include all possible pairings of objects.[12]

Paired comparison data can be analyzed in several ways.[13] The researcher can calculate the percentage of respondents who prefer one stimulus over another by summing the matrices of Figure 8.3 for all the respondents, dividing the sum by the number of respondents, and multiplying by 100. Simultaneous evaluation of all the stimulus objects is also possible. Under the assumption of transitivity, it is possible to convert paired comparison data to a rank order. **Transitivity of preference** implies that if brand A is preferred to B, and brand B is preferred to C, then brand A is preferred to C. To arrive at a rank order, the researcher determines the number of times each brand is preferred by summing the column entries in Figure 8.3. Therefore, this respondent's order of preference, from most to the least preferred, is Head and Shoulders, Jhirmack, Finesse, Pert, and Vidal Sassoon. It is also possible to derive an interval scale from paired comparison data using the Thurstone case V procedure. Refer to the appropriate literature for a discussion of this procedure.[14]

Several modifications of the paired comparison technique have been suggested. One involves the inclusion of a neutral/no difference/no opinion response. Another

transitivity of preference
An assumption made to convert paired comparison data to rank order data. It implies that if brand A is preferred to brand B and brand B is preferred to brand C, then brand A is preferred to brand C.

RESEARCH IN PRACTICE 8.1

Paired Comparison Scaling

The most common method of taste testing is paired comparison. The consumer is asked to sample two different products and select the one with the most appealing taste. The test is done in private, either in homes or other predetermined sites. A minimum of 1,000 responses is considered an adequate sample.

A blind taste test for a soft drink, where imagery, self-perception and brand reputation are very important factors in the consumer's purchasing decision, may not be a good indicator of performance in the marketplace. The introduction of New Coke illustrates this point. New Coke was heavily favored in blind paired comparison taste tests, but its introduction was less than successful, because image plays a major role in the purchase of Coke.

A paired comparison taste test. ◆ Elrick and Lavidge.

extension is graded paired comparisons. In this method, respondents are asked which brand in the pair is preferred and how much it is preferred. The degree of preference may be expressed by how much more the respondent is willing to pay for the preferred brand. The resulting scale is a dollar metric scale. Another modification of paired comparison scaling is widely used in obtaining similarity judgments in multidimensional scaling (see Chapter 21).

Paired comparison scaling is useful when the number of brands is limited, since it requires direct comparison and overt choice. With a large number of brands, however, the number of comparisons becomes unwieldy. Other disadvantages are that violations of the assumption of transitivity may occur, and the order in which the objects are presented may bias the results.[15] Paired comparisons bear little resemblance to the marketplace situation, which involves selection from multiple alternatives. Also respondents may prefer one object over certain others, but they may not like it in an absolute sense. Research in Practice 8.1 provides further insights into paired comparison scaling.[16]

Rank Order Scaling

rank order scaling A comparative scaling technique in which respondents are presented with several objects simultaneously and asked to order or rank them according to some criterion.

After paired comparisons, the most popular comparative scaling technique is rank order scaling. In **rank order scaling** respondents are presented with several objects simultaneously and asked to order or rank them according to some criterion. For example, respondents may be asked to rank brands of toothpaste according to overall preference. As shown in Figure 8.4, these rankings are typically obtained by asking the respondents to assign a rank of 1 to the most preferred brand, 2 to the second most preferred, and so on, until a rank of *n* is assigned to the least preferred brand. Like paired comparison, this approach is also comparative in nature, and it is possible that the respondent may dislike the brand ranked 1 in an absolute sense. Furthermore, rank order scaling also results in ordinal data. See Table 8.2, which uses rank order scaling to derive an ordinal scale.

FIGURE 8.4

Preference for Toothpaste Brands Using Rank Order Scaling

Instructions

Rank the various brands of toothpaste in order of preference. Begin by picking out the one brand that you like most and assign it a number 1. Then find the second most preferred brand and assign it a number 2. Continue this procedure until you have ranked all the brands of toothpaste in order of preference. The least preferred brand should be assigned a rank of 10.

No two brands should receive the same rank number.

The criterion of preference is entirely up to you. There is no right or wrong answer. Just try to be consistent.

Brand	Rank Order
1. Crest	_____
2. Colgate	_____
3. Aim	_____
4. Gleem	_____
5. Macleans	_____
6. Ultra Brite	_____
7. Close Up	_____
8. Pepsodent	_____
9. Plus White	_____
10. Stripe	_____

Rank order scaling is commonly used to measure preferences for brands as well as attributes. Rank order data are frequently obtained from respondents in conjoint analysis (see Chapter 21), since rank order scaling forces the respondent to discriminate among the stimulus objects. Moreover, as compared with paired comparisons, this type of scaling process more closely resembles the shopping environment. It also takes less time and eliminates intransitive responses. If there are n stimulus objects, only $(n - 1)$ scaling decisions need be made in rank order scaling. However, in paired comparison scaling, $[n(n - 1)/2]$ decisions would be required. Another advantage is that most respondents easily understand the instructions for ranking. The major disadvantage is that this technique produces only ordinal data.

Finally, under the assumption of transitivity, rank order data can be converted to equivalent paired comparison data, and vice versa. This point was illustrated by Figure 8.3. Hence, it is possible to derive an interval scale from rankings using the Thurstone case V procedure. Other approaches for deriving interval scales from rankings have also been suggested.[17]

Constant Sum Scaling

constant sum scaling A comparative scaling technique in which respondents are required to allocate a constant sum of units such as points, dollars, chits, stickers, or chips among a set of stimulus objects with respect to some criterion.

In **constant sum scaling**, respondents allocate a constant sum of units, such as points, dollars, or chips, among a set of stimulus objects with respect to some criterion. As shown in Figure 8.5, respondents may be asked to allocate 100 points to attributes of a bathing soap in a way that reflects the importance they attach to each attribute. If an attribute is unimportant, the respondent assigns it zero points. If an attribute is twice as important as some other attribute, it receives twice as many points. The sum of all the points is 100. Hence, the name of the scale.

The attributes are scaled by counting the points assigned to each one by all the respondents and dividing by the number of respondents. These results are presented for three groups, or segments, of respondents in Figure 8.5. Segment I attaches overwhelming importance to price. Segment II considers basic cleaning power to be of prime impor-

FIGURE 8.5

Importance of Bathing Soap Attributes Using a Constant Sum Scale

Instructions
Below are eight attributes of bathing soaps. Please allocate 100 points among the attributes so that your allocation reflects the relative importance you attach to each attribute. The more points an attribute receives, the more important the attribute is. If an attribute is not at all important, assign it zero points. If an attribute is twice as important as some other attribute, it should receive twice as many points.

Form

AVERAGE RESPONSES OF THREE SEGMENTS

Attribute	Segment I	Segment II	Segment III
1. Mildness	8	2	4
2. Lather	2	4	17
3. Shrinkage	3	9	7
4. Price	53	17	9
5. Fragrance	9	0	19
6. Packaging	7	5	9
7. Moisturizing	5	3	20
8. Cleaning Power	13	60	15
Sum	100	100	100

Use of constant sum scaling to determine the relative importance of bathing soap attributes has enabled Irish Spring to develop a superior product. ◆ Colgate-Palmolive Company.

tance. Segment III values lather, fragrance, moisturizing, and cleaning power. Such information cannot be obtained from rank order data unless they are transformed into interval data. Note that the constant sum also has an absolute zero; 10 points are twice as many as 5 points, and the difference between 5 and 2 points is the same as the difference between 57 and 54 points. For this reason, constant sum scale data are sometimes treated as metric. Although this may be appropriate in the limited context of the stimuli scaled, these results are not generalizable to other stimuli not included in the study. Hence, strictly speaking, the constant sum should be considered an ordinal scale because of its comparative nature and the resulting lack of generalizability. It can be seen that the allocation of points in Figure 8.5 is influenced by the specific attributes included in the evaluation task.

The main advantage of the constant sum scale is that it allows for fine discrimination among stimulus objects without requiring too much time. It has two primary disadvantages, however. Respondents may allocate more or fewer units than those specified. For example, a respondent may allocate 108 or 94 points. The researcher must modify such data in some way or eliminate this respondent from analysis. Another potential problem is rounding error if too few units are used. On the other hand, the use of a large number of units may be too taxing on the respondent and cause confusion and fatigue.

Q-Sort and Other Procedures

q-sort scaling A comparative scaling technique that uses a rank order procedure to sort objects based on similarity with respect to some criterion.

Q-sort scaling was developed to discriminate among a relatively large number of objects quickly. This technique uses a rank order procedure in which objects are sorted into piles based on similarity with respect to some criterion. For example, respondents are given 100 attitude statements on individual cards and asked to place them into 11 piles, ranging from "most highly agreed with" to "least highly agreed with." The number of objects to be sorted should not be less than 60 nor more than 140; a reasonable range is 60 to 90 objects.[18] The number of objects to be placed in each pile is prespecified, often to result in a roughly normal distribution of objects over the whole set.

verbal protocol A technique used to understand respondents' cognitive responses or thought processes by having them think aloud while completing a task or making a decision.

Another comparative scaling technique is magnitude estimation.[19] In this technique, numbers are assigned to objects such that ratios between the assigned numbers reflect ratios on the specified criterion. For example, respondents may be asked to indicate whether they agree or disagree with each of a series of statements measuring attitude toward department stores. Then they assign a number between 0 to 100 to each statement to indicate the intensity of their agreement or disagreement. Providing this type of numbers imposes a cognitive burden on the respondents. Finally, mention must be made of Guttman scaling, or scalogram analysis, a procedure for determining whether a set of objects can be ordered into an internally consistent, unidimensional scale.

VERBAL PROTOCOLS

A particularly useful approach for measuring cognitive responses or thought processes consists of **verbal protocols**. Respondents are asked to "think out loud" and verbalize anything going through their heads while making a decision or performing a task.[20] The researcher says, "If you think anything, say it aloud, no matter how trivial the thought may be." Even with such explicit instruction, the respondent may be silent. At these times, the researcher will say, "Remember to say aloud everything you are thinking." Everything that the respondent says is tape recorded. This record of the respondent's verbalized thought processes is referred to as a protocol.[21]

Protocols have been used to measure consumers' cognitive responses in actual shopping trips as well as in simulated shopping environments. An interviewer accompanies the respondent and holds a microphone into which the respondent talks. Protocols, thus collected, have been used to determine the attributes and cues used in making purchase decisions, product usage behavior, and the impact of the shopping environment on consumer decisions. Protocol analysis has also been employed to measure consumer response to advertising. Immediately after seeing an ad, the respondent is asked to list all the thoughts that came to mind while watching the ad. The respondent is given a limited amount of time to list the thoughts so as to minimize the probability of collecting thoughts generated after, rather than during, the message. After the protocol has been collected, the individual's thoughts or cognitive responses are coded into three categories.[22]

Category	Definition	Example
Support argument	Support the claim made by the message	"Diet Coke tastes great."
Counterargument	Refute the claim made by the message	"Diet Coke has an aftertaste."
Source derogation	Negative opinion about the source of the message	"Coca-Cola is not an honest company."

Protocols are, typically, incomplete. The respondent has many thoughts that she or he cannot or will not verbalize. The researcher must take the incomplete record and infer from it a measure of the underlying cognitive response.

INTERNATIONAL MARKETING RESEARCH

In the four primary scales, the level of measurement increases from nominal to ordinal to interval to ratio scale. This increase in measurement level is obtained at the cost of complexity. From the viewpoint of the respondents, nominal scales are the simplest to use whereas the ratio scales are the most complex. Respondents in many developed countries, due to higher education and consumer sophistication levels, are quite used to providing responses on interval and ratio scales. It has been argued that opinion formation may not be well crystallized in some developing countries, however. Hence, these respondents experience difficulty in expressing the gradation required by interval and ratio scales. Preferences can, therefore, be best measured by using ordinal scales. In particular, the use of binary scales (e.g., preferred/not preferred), the simplest type of ordinal scale, has been recommended.[23] For example, while measuring preferences for jeans in the United States, Levi Strauss and Company could ask consumers to rate their preferences for wearing jeans on specified occasions using a seven point interval scale. Consumers in Papua New Guinea, however, could be shown a pair of jeans and simply asked whether or not they would prefer to wear them for a specific occasion (e.g., when shopping, working, relaxing on a holiday). The advantage of selecting the primary scales to match the profile of the target respondents is well illustrated by the Japanese survey of automobile preferences in Europe.

EXAMPLE
Car War——Japan Making A Spearhead

For the first time, European journalists had given their car-of-the-year award to a Japanese model, Nissan's new British-made Micra, a $10,000 subcompact. This came as big blow to the European automakers who have been trying to keep the Japanese onslaught at bay. "They will change the competitive balance," warns Bruce Blythe, Ford of Europe Inc.'s head of business strategy. How did the Japanese do it?

Nissan conducted a survey of European consumers' preferences for automobiles using interval scales to capture the magnitude of the preference differences. The use of interval scales enabled Nissan to compare the differences between automobile features and determine which features were preferred. The findings revealed distinct consumer preferences. So the Japanese made inroads by transplants in production and building technical centers in Europe to customize to local styling tastes and preferences. By 1995 the Japanese were producing 775,000 cars a year in Europe, 75% of them in Britain. The Japanese are taking away share from Renault in the French, Italian, and Spanish market. The European automakers need to be on guard against such fierce competition.[24] ◆

It should also be noted that comparative scales, except for paired comparisons, require comparisons of multiple stimulus objects and are, therefore, taxing on the respondents. In contrast, in noncomparative scales, each object is scaled independently of others in the stimulus set, that is, objects are scaled one at a time. Hence, noncomparative scales are simpler to administer and more appropriate in cultures where the respondents are less educated or are unfamiliar with marketing research.

ETHICS IN MARKETING RESEARCH

The researcher has the responsibility to use the appropriate type of scales to get the data needed to answer the research questions and test the hypotheses. Take, for example, a newspaper like *The Wall Street Journal* wanting information on the personality profiles of its readers and nonreaders. Information on the personality characteristics might best be obtained by giving respondents (readers and nonreaders) several velcro nameplates, each listing one personality characteristic. Respondents are also given a felt board on which to arrange the nameplates. The researcher then instructs the respondents to rank-order the personality characteristics, listing, in order, those they believe describe their personality best first, and those which do not describe themselves last. This results in ordinal data. Although it will provide rich insight into the personality characteristics by allowing respondents to compare personality characteristics, shuffle them, compare again, and reshuffle, these data cannot be easily used in multivariate analysis. To examine differences in the personality characteristics of readers and nonreaders and relate them to other consumer behavior variables, interval scale data are needed. It is the obligation of the researcher to obtain the data that are most appropriate given the research questions, as the following example illustrates.

EXAMPLE
Scaling Ethical Dilemmas

In a study designed to measure ethical judgments of marketing researchers, scale items from a previously developed and tested scale were used. After a pretest was conducted on a convenience sample of 65 marketing professionals, however, it became apparent that some original scale items were worded in a way that did not reflect current usage. Therefore, these items were updated. For example, an item that was gender specific, such as, "He pointed out that..." was altered to read "The project manager pointed out that..." Respondents were requested to show their approval or disapproval of the stated action (item) of a marketing research director with regard to specific scenarios. Realizing that a binary or dichotomous scale would be too restrictive, approval or disapproval was indicated by having respondents supply interval level data via five point scales with descriptive anchors of 1 = disapprove, 2 = disapprove somewhat, 3 = neither approve or disapprove, 4 = approve somewhat, and 5 = approve. In this way, scaling dilemmans were resolved.[25] ◆

After the data have been collected, they should be analyzed correctly. If nominal scaled data are gathered then statistics permissible for nominal scaled data must be used. Likewise, when ordinal scale data are collected, statistical procedures developed for use with interval or ratio data should not be used. Conclusions based on the misuse of statistics are misleading. In *The Wall Street Journal* example, ordinal data would be collected. If after collection the client wishes to know how the readers and the nonreaders differed, the researcher should treat these data correctly and use nonmetric techniques for analysis (discussed in Chapter 15). When the researcher lacks the expertise or the computer software to compute these statistics, ethical dilemmas arise. Researchers know that they should admit to their shortcomings and should see to it that correct statistics are computed. Either an outside statistician should be hired or the relevant software should be obtained. Admitting your shortcomings, however, is rarely easy.

COMPUTER APPLICATIONS

Database managers allow researchers to develop and test several different scales to determine their appropriateness for a particular application. For example, the author has developed and tested ordinal, interval, and ratio scale configurations using dBASE IV. Database managers are also available for mainframes, which handle larger amounts of data faster. Several off-the-shelf packages are also available.

QUIK-POLL by Touch Base Computing of Rome, Georgia enables the user to create questionnaires, enter responses, and then tabulate and analyze results. In the module for questionnaire creation, the type of scale for each question can be selected, so that the data for each question can be correctly analyzed later using QUIK-POLL. Although the four principal types of scales (i.e., nominal, ordinal, interval, and ratio scales) can be implemented in these surveys using QUIK-POLL, examples of only two types (i.e., nominal, and interval) follow.

In Exhibit 8.1, the question creation screen for a marital status question in a consumer survey about breakfast preferences can be seen. Here, six options to the marital status variable are to be offered to the respondents. The type of question is marked S, indicating a single response is needed, while the numbering method is marked A, indicating each of the six options would have a distinguishing letter of the alphabet (i.e., response a, response b, etc.). Because this question has a nominal scale, only a distinct label is needed to record the single response given. As a result, a single character can be used. These characters imply no scale for ordering the responses.

Exhibit 8.2 shows the question creation screen for a question asking for ratings of breakfast drinks. Here, the type of question is marked R, indicating a rating question. Each breakfast drink could be rated from 1 to 5 with 1 being best and 5 being worst. This is an

EXHIBIT 8.1

*Measuring Marital
Status Using
QUIK-POLL*

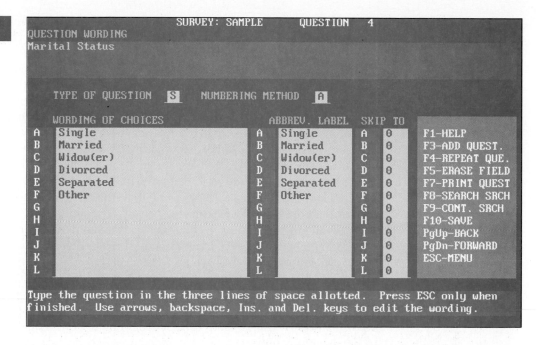

```
                          SURVEY: SAMPLE        QUESTION    4
QUESTION WORDING
Marital Status



     TYPE OF QUESTION   S    NUMBERING METHOD   A

     WORDING OF CHOICES            ABBREV. LABEL   SKIP TO
 A   Single                    A   Single         A   0     F1-HELP
 B   Married                   B   Married        B   0     F3-ADD QUEST.
 C   Widow(er)                 C   Widow(er)      C   0     F4-REPEAT QUE.
 D   Divorced                  D   Divorced       D   0     F5-ERASE FIELD
 E   Separated                 E   Separated      E   0     F7-PRINT QUEST
 F   Other                     F   Other          F   0     F8-SEARCH SRCH
 G                             G                  G   0     F9-CONT. SRCH
 H                             H                  H   0     F10-SAVE
 I                             I                  I   0     PgUp-BACK
 J                             J                  J   0     PgDn-FORWARD
 K                             K                  K   0     ESC-MENU
 L                             L                  L   0

Type the question in the three lines of space allotted.  Press ESC only when
finished.  Use arrows, backspace, Ins. and Del. keys to edit the wording.
```

example of a question with an interval scale. For this question, QUIK-POLL will tabulate the counts for each breakfast drink and will display or print a table showing the quantity and percentage of each breakfast drink's rating on each level of the scale from 1 to 5.

Microcomputers have been used to administer paired comparison scales in taste tests. Several programs are available for designing and administering paired comparison scales. EZPAIR by Barry Cohen can design paired comparison scales and paired comparison product tests using statistical quality-control techniques. It allows testing to end early, without compromising test reliability, if one product is clearly winning.

EXHIBIT 8.2

*Ratings of Breakfast
Drinks Using
QUIK-POLL*

```
                          SURVEY: SAMPLE        QUESTION   11
QUESTION WORDING
Rate the following breakfast drinks from 1 to 5, with 1 being best and five
being worst.


     TYPE OF QUESTION   R    NUMBERING METHOD   A

     WORDING OF CHOICES            ABBREV. LABEL   MAX NO.
 A   Orange Juice              A   Orange Juic    A   5     F1-HELP
 B   Coffee                    B   Coffee                   F3-ADD QUEST.
 C   Tang                      C   Tang                     F4-REPEAT QUE.
 D   Tea                       D   Tea                      F5-ERASE FIELD
 E   Milk                      E   Milk                     F7-PRINT QUEST
 F   Prune Juice               F   Prune Juice              F8-SEARCH SRCH
 G   Tomato Juice              G   Tomato Juic              F9-CONT. SRCH
 H   Grapefruit Juice          H   Grapefruit               F10-SAVE
 I   Water                     I   Water                    PgUp-BACK
 J   Other                     J   Other                    PgDn-FORWARD
 K                             K                            ESC-MENU
 L                             L

Type the question in the three lines of space allotted.  Press ESC only when
finished.  Use arrows, backspace, Ins. and Del. keys to edit the wording.
```

SUMMARY

Measurement is the assignment of numbers or other symbols to characteristics of objects according to set rules. Scaling involves the generation of a continuum upon which measured objects are located. The four primary scales of measurement are nominal, ordinal, interval, and ratio. Of these, the nominal scale is the most basic in that the numbers are used only for identifying or classifying objects. In the ordinal scale, the next higher-level scale, the numbers indicate the relative position of the objects but not the magnitude of difference between them. The interval scale permits a comparison of the differences between the objects. Because it has an arbitrary zero point, however, it is not meaningful to calculate ratios of scale values on an interval scale. The highest level of measurement is represented by the ratio scale in which the zero point is fixed. The researcher can compute ratios of scale values using this scale. The ratio scale incorporates all the properties of the lower-level scales.

Scaling techniques can be classified as comparative or noncomparative. Comparative scaling involves a direct comparison of stimulus objects. Comparative scales include paired comparisons, rank order, constant sum, and the Q-sort. The data obtained by these procedures have only ordinal properties. Verbal protocols, where the respondent is instructed to think out loud, can be used for measuring cognitive responses.

Respondents in many developed countries, due to higher education and consumer sophistication levels, are quite used to providing responses on interval and ratio scales. In developing countries, however, preferences can be best measured by using ordinal scales. Ethical considerations require that appropriate type of scales be used to get the data needed to answer the research questions and test the hypotheses. Database managers, as well as several specialized computer programs, are available to implement the different types of scales.[26]

ACRONYMS

The four primary types of scales may be described by the acronym FOUR:

F   igurative: nominal scale
O   rdinal scale
U   nconstrained zero point: interval scale
R   atio scale

The different comparative and noncomparative scales may be represented by the acronym SCALES:

S   emantic differential scale
C   onstant sum scale
A   rranged in order: rank order scale
L   ikert scale
E   ngaged: paired comparison scale
S   tapel scale

EXERCISES

QUESTIONS

1. What is measurement?
2. What are the primary scales of measurement?
3. Describe the differences between a nominal and an ordinal scale.
4. What are the implications of having an arbitrary zero point in an interval scale?

5. What are the advantages of a ratio scale over an interval scale? Are these advantages significant?

6. What is a comparative rating scale?

7. What is a paired comparison?

8. What are the advantages and disadvantages of paired comparison scaling?

9. Describe the constant sum scale. How is it different from the other comparative rating scales?

10. Describe the Q-sort methodology.

11. What is a verbal protocol? How are verbal protocols used?

PROBLEMS

1. Identify the type of scale (nominal, ordinal, interval, or ratio) being used in each of the following. Please explain your reasoning.

   a. I like to solve cross-word puzzles.

Disagree				Agree
1	2	3	4	5

   b. How old are you? _____

   c. Please rank the following activities in terms of your preference by assigning ranks 1 to 5.

   i. Reading magazines   _____

   ii. Watching television   _____

   iii. Dating   _____

   iv. Shopping   _____

   v. Eating out   _____

   d. What is your Social Security number? _____

   e. On an average weekday, how much time do you spend doing your homework and class assignments?

   i. Less than 15 minutes   _____

   ii. 15 to 30 minutes   _____

   iii. 31 to 60 minutes   _____

   iv. 61 to 120 minutes   _____

   v. More than 120 minutes   _____

   f. How much money did you spend last month on entertainment? _____

2. Suppose that each question a through f above was administered to 100 respondents. Identify the kind of analysis that should be done for each question to summarize the results.

COMPUTER EXERCISES

1. Using a database manager such as dBASE IV, develop ordinal, interval, and ratio scale configurations for measuring attitudes toward the programs run by your student center on the campus.

NOTES

1. "Americans Rate Nation's Woes," *Quirk's Marketing Research Review* (May 1990): 14.

2. "The Malling of America," *Quirk's Marketing Research Review* (May 1990): 15.

3. William R. Doucette and Joseph B. Wiederholt, "Measuring Product Meaning for Prescribed Medication Using a Means-End Model," *Journal of Health Care Marketing* 12 (March 1992): 48–54; and Jum C. Nunnally, *Psychometric Theory*, 2nd ed. (New York: McGraw-Hill, 1978), p. 3.

4. Stanley S. Stevens, "Mathematics, Measurement and Psychophysics," in Stanley S. Steven (ed.), *Handbook of Experimental Psychology* (New York: Wiley, 1951).

5. Neil R. Barnard and Andrew S. C. Ehrenberg, "Robust Measures of Consumer Brand Beliefs," *Journal of Marketing Research* 27 (November 1990): 477–84; and William D. Perreault, Jr., and Forrest W. Young, "Alternating Least Squares Optimal Scaling: Analysis of Nonmetric Data in Marketing Research," *Journal of Marketing Research* 17 (February 1980): 1–13.

6. G. Albaum, R. Best, and D. I. Hawkins, "Measurement Properties of Semantic Scale Data," *Journal of the Market Research Society* (January 1977): 21–28; and Mark Taylor, "Ordinal and Interval Scaling," *Journal of the Market Research Society* 25(4): 297–303.

7. For a discussion of these scales, refer to C. H. Coombs, "Theory and Methods of Social Measurement," in L. Festinger and D. Katz (eds.), *Research Methods in the Behavioral Sciences* (New York: Holt, Rinehart and Winston, 1953).

8. Richard R. Bastell and Yoram Wind, "Product Development: Current Methods and Needed Developments," *Journal of the Market Research Society* 8 (1980): 122–26.

9. There is, however, some controversy regarding this issue. See Gary M. Mullet, "Itemized Rating Scales: Ordinal or Interval?" *European Research* (April 1983): 49–52.

10. Kim P. Corfman, "Comparability and Comparison Levels Used in Choices among Consumer Products," *Journal of Marketing Research* 28 (August 1991): 368–74; B. S. Buchanan and D. G. Morrison, "Taste Tests," *Psychology and Marketing* (Spring 1984): 69–91.

11. "Coke's Flip-Flop Underscores Risks of Consumer Taste Tests," *Wall Street Journal* (July 18, 1985): 25.

12. It is not necessary to evaluate all possible pairs of objects, however. Procedures such as cyclic designs can significantly reduce the number of pairs evaluated. A treatment of such procedures may be found in Naresh K. Malhotra, Arun K. Jain, and Christian Pinson, "The Robustness of MDS Configurations in the Case of Incomplete Data," *Journal of Marketing Research* 25 (February 1988): 95–102.

13. For an advanced application involving paired comparison data, see William R. Dillon, Ajith Kumar, and Melinda S. de Borrero, "Capturing Individual Differences in Paired Comparisons: An Extended BTL Model Incorporating Descriptor Variables," *Journal of Marketing Research* 30 (February 1993): 42–51.

14. L. L. Thurstone, *The Measurement of Values* (Chicago: University of Chicago Press, 1959). For an application of the case V procedure, see Malhotra, N. K., "Marketing Linen Services to Hospitals: A Conceptual Framework and an Empirical Investigation Using Thurstone's Case V Analysis," *Journal of Health Care Marketing* 6 (March 1986): 43–50.

15. P. Daniles and J. Lawford, "The Effect of Order in the Presentation of Samples in Paired Comparison Tests," *Journal of the Market Research Society* 16 (April 1974): 127–33.

16. Tim Davis, "Taste Tests: Are the Blind Leading the Blind?" *Beverage World* (April 1987): 43–48, 85.

17. William L. Hays, *Quantification in Psychology* (Belmont, CA: Brooks/Cole, 1967), pp. 35–39.

18. Fred Kerlinger, *Foundations of Behavioral Research*, 3rd. ed. (New York: Holt, Rinehart and Winston, 1973), pp. 583–92.

19. H. R. Moskowitz, B. Jacobs, and N. Firtle, "Discrimination Testing and Product Decisions," *Journal of Marketing Research* (February 1980): 84–90.

20. John R. Hayes, "Issues in Protocol Analysis," in G. R. Ungson and D. N. Braunste (eds.), *Decision Making: An Interdisciplinary Inquiry* (Boston: Kent Publishing, 1982), pp. 61–77.

21. For a recent application of verbal protocols, see S. F. Gardial, D. S. Clemons, R. B. Woodruff, D. W. Schumann, and M. J. Burns, "Comparing Consumers' Recall of Prepurchase and Postpurchase Product Evaluation Experiences," *Journal of Consumer Research* 20 (March 1994): 548–60.

22. David Glen Mick, "Levels of Subjective Comprehension in Advertising Processing and Their Relations to Ad Perceptions, Attitudes, and Memory," *Journal of Consumer Research* 18 (March 1992): 411–24; Peter L. Wright, "Cognitive Processes Mediating Acceptance of Advertising," *Journal of Marketing Research* 10 (February 1973): 53–62; and Peter L. Wright, "Cognitive Responses to Mass Media Advocacy and Cognitive Choice Processes," in R. Petty, T. Ostrum, and T. Brock (eds.), *Cognitive Responses to Persuasion* (New York: McGraw-Hill, 1978).

23. N. K. Malhotra, "A Methodology for Measuring Consumer Preferences in Developing Countries," *International Marketing Review* 5 (Autumn 1988): 52–66.

24. *Business Week*, (December 14, 1992).

25. I. P. Akaah, "Differences in Research Ethics Judgments Between Male and Female Marketing Professionals," *Journal of Business Ethics* 8 (1989) 375–81.

26. The assistance of James Agarwal with the international marketing research example, the assistance of Mark Leach and Gina Miller in writing the ethics section, and the assistance of Mark Peterson in writing the computer applications section is gratefully acknowledged.

CHAPTER NINE

Measurement and Scaling: Noncomparative Scaling Techniques

Scales should be evaluated by examining reliability and validity.

◆

OBJECTIVES

After reading this chapter, the student should be able to:

1. Describe the noncomparative scaling techniques, distinguish between continuous and itemized rating scales, and explain Likert, semantic differential, and Stapel scales.
2. Discuss the decisions involved in constructing itemized rating scales with respect to the number of scale categories, balanced versus unbalanced scales, odd or even number of categories, forced versus nonforced choice, degree of verbal description, and the physical form of the scale.
3. Discuss the criteria used for scale evaluation and explain how to assess reliability, validity, and generalizability.
4. Discuss the considerations involved in implementing noncomparative scales in an international setting.
5. Understand the ethical issues involved in developing noncomparative scales.
6. Discuss the use of microcomputers and mainframes in implementing continuous and itemized rating scales.

OVERVIEW

As discussed in Chapter 8, scaling techniques are classified as comparative or noncomparative. The comparative techniques—consisting of paired comparison, rank order, constant sum, and Q-sort scaling—were discussed in the last chapter. The subject of this chapter is noncomparative techniques, which are composed of continuous and itemized rating scales. We discuss the popular itemized rating scales—the Likert, semantic differential, and Stapel scales—as well as the construction of multiitem rating scales. We show how scaling techniques should be evaluated in terms of reliability and validity and consider how the researcher selects a particular scaling technique. Mathematically derived scales are also presented. The considerations involved in implementing noncomparative scales when researching international markets are discussed. Several ethical issues that arise in rating scale construction are identified. The chapter concludes with a discussion of the use of microcomputers and mainframes in developing continuous and itemized rating scales. We begin with some examples of noncomparative scaling techniques.

EXAMPLE
Scaling Emotional Peaks _____

PEAC Media Research, a Toronto-based company, has developed a Program Evaluation Analysis Computer to aid in recording the emotions of focus group members. This computer is a handheld device with a row of buttons or a dial that registers responses ranging from negative to neutral to positive. Respondents press the appropriate buttons as they watch a commercial. This device allows for continuous and unbiased recording of emotional responses by the members of the focus group. It was recently used to measure response to a series of commercials for McDonald's, and the researchers found that daughters and their mothers responded differently to different images in the commercials. Since McDonald's attempts to design "slice of life" commercials that appeal to all segments, the researchers used PEAC to determine which aspects of the commercials appealed to which segments. Commercials with the greatest emotional appeal across segments were selected for the campaign.[1] ◆

EXAMPLE
Super Markets _____

In a survey of the services industry conducted by the Gallup Organization, participants were asked to rate services on a ten-point Likert-type scale, with 1 signifying low quality and 10 signifying very high quality. Over half the respondents gave supermarkets a rating of 8 or better. Restaurants and banks were also well regarded. Hotels, department stores, insurance companies, auto repair companies, and airlines ended up in the middle. Toward the bottom of the scale were local government, public transportation, and real estate. Therefore, to engender public goodwill and patronage, local governments, public transportation authorities, and real estate agencies need to improve their services and communicate the improvements to their constituents and customers.[2] ◆

The PEAC example illustrated a continuous rating scale used to measure emotion, and the Gallup survey used an itemized rating scale to measure perceptions. Both are examples of noncomparative scaling techniques.

It is not a matter of luck. Rather, superior products and services designed to meet customer needs have enabled supermarkets like Lucky to score high quality ratings. ◆ Lucky Stores.

NONCOMPARATIVE SCALING TECHNIQUES

noncomparative scales
One of two types of scaling techniques in which each stimulus object is scaled independently of the other objects in the stimulus set.

Respondents using a **noncomparative scale** employ whatever rating standard seems appropriate to them. They do not compare the object being rated either with another object or to some specified standard, such as "your ideal brand." They evaluate only one object at a time; thus, noncomparative scales are often referred to as monadic scales. Noncomparative techniques consist of continuous and itemized rating scales, which are described in Table 9.1 and discussed in the following sections.

Continuous Rating Scale

In a **continuous rating scale**, also referred to as a graphic rating scale, respondents rate the objects by placing a mark at the appropriate position on a line that runs from one extreme of the criterion variable to the other. Thus, the respondents are not restricted to selecting

TABLE 9.1

Basic Noncomparative Scales

Scale	Basic Characteristics	Examples	Advantages	Disadvantages
Continuous rating scale	Place a mark on a continuous line	Reaction to TV commercials	Easy to construct	Scoring can be cumbersome unless computerized
Itemized Rating Scales				
Likert scale	Degree of agreement on a 1 (strongly disagree) to 5 (strongly agree) scale	Measurement of attitudes	Easy to construct, administer, and understand	More time-consuming
Semantic differential	Seven-point scale with bipolar labels	Brand, product, and company images	Versatile	Controversy as to whether the data are interval
Stapel scale	Unipolar ten-point scale, −5 to +5, without a neutral point (zero)	Measurement of attitudes and images	Easy to construct, administered over telephone	Confusing and difficult to apply

continuous rating scale
A measurement scale that has respondents rate the objects by placing a mark at the appropriate position on a line that runs from one extreme of the criterion variable to the other. The form may vary considerably. Also referred to as graphic rating scale.

from marks previously set by the researcher. The form of the continuous scale may vary considerably. For example, the line may be vertical or horizontal; scale points, in the form of numbers or brief descriptions, may be provided; and if provided, the scale points may be few or many. Three versions of a continuous rating scale are illustrated below.

DEPARTMENT STORE PATRONAGE PROJECT

Continuous Rating Scales

How would you rate Sears as a department store?

Version 1

Probably the worst - - - - - - - - I - Probably the best

Version 2

Probably the worst - - - - - - - I - Probably the best

    0   10   20   30   40   50   60   70   80   90   100

Version 3

                   Very bad   Neither good   Very good
                                         nor bad

Probably the worst - - - - - - - I - Probably the best

    0   10   20   30   40   50   60   70   80   90   100 ◆

Once the respondent has provided the ratings, the researcher divides the line into as many categories as desired and assigns scores based on the categories into which the ratings fall.[3] In the department store project example, the respondent exhibits an unfavorable attitude toward Sears. These scores are typically treated as interval data.

The advantage of continuous scales is that they are easy to construct, however, scoring is cumbersome and unreliable.[4] Moreover, continuous scales provide little new information. Hence, their use in marketing research has been limited. Recently, however, with the increased popularity of computer-assisted personal interviewing and other technologies, their use is becoming more frequent,[5] as illustrated by Research in Practice 9.1.[6]

ITEMIZED RATING SCALES

itemized rating scale A measurement scale having numbers or brief descriptions associated with each category. The categories are ordered in terms of scale position.

In an **itemized rating scale**, respondents are provided with a scale that has a number or brief description associated with each category. The categories are ordered in terms of scale position; and the respondents are required to select the specified category that best describes the object being rated. Itemized rating scales are widely used in marketing research and form the basic components of more complex scales, such as multiitem rating scales. We first describe the commonly used itemized rating scales—the Likert, semantic differential, and Stapel scales—and then examine the major issues surrounding the use of itemized rating scales.

Likert Scale

Named after its developer, Rensis Likert, the **Likert scale** is a widely used rating scale that requires the respondents to indicate a degree of agreement or disagreement with each of a series of statements about the stimulus objects.[7] Typically, each scale item has five response categories, ranging from "strongly disagree" to "strongly agree." We illus-

RESEARCH IN PRACTICE 9.1

RATE: Rapid Analysis and Testing Environment

A relatively new research tool, the perception analyzer, provides continuous measurement of "gut reaction." A group of up to 400 respondents is presented with TV or radio spots or advertising copy. The measuring device consists of a dial that contains a 100-point range. Each participant is given a dial and is instructed to continuously record his or her reaction to the material being tested. As the respondents turn the dials, the information is fed to a computer, which tabulates second-by-second response profiles. As the results are recorded by the computer, they are superimposed on a video screen, enabling the researcher to view the respondents' scores immediately. The responses are also stored in a permanent data file for use in further analysis. The response scores can be broken down by categories, such as age, income, sex, or product usage.

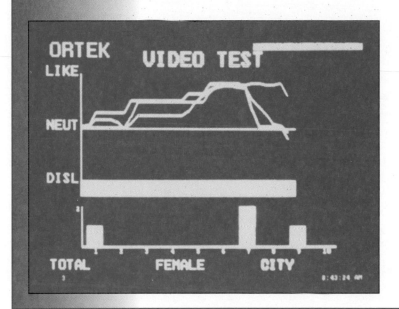

Systems such as RATE from ORTEK enable the continuous measurement of reactions to a company video, commercial, or any audio/visual material. ◆ ORTEK Data Systems, Inc.

Likert scale A measurement scale with five response categories ranging from "strongly disagree" to "strongly agree" that requires respondents to indicate a degree of agreement or disagreement with each of a series of statements related to the stimulus objects.

trate with a Likert scale for evaluating attitudes toward Sears in the context of the Department Store Patronage Project.

To conduct the analysis, each statement is assigned a numerical score, ranging either from −2 to +2 or 1 to 5. The analysis can be conducted on an item-by-item basis (profile analysis), or a total (summated) score can be calculated for each respondent by summing across items. Suppose that the Likert scale in the department store example was used to measure attitudes toward Sears as well as J.C. Penney. Profile analysis would involve comparing the two stores in terms of the average respondent ratings for each item, such as quality of merchandise, in-store service, and brand mix. The summated approach is most frequently used, and as a result, the Likert scale is also referred to as a summated scale.[8] When using this approach to determine the total score for each respondent on each store, it is important to use a consistent scoring procedure so that a high (or low) score consistently reflects a favorable response. This requires that the categories assigned to the negative statements by the respondents be scored by reversing the scale. Note that for a negative statement, an agreement reflects an unfavorable response, whereas for a positive statement, agreement represents a favorable response. Accordingly, a "strongly agree" response to a favorable statement and a "strongly disagree" response to an unfavorable statement would both receive scores of five.[9] In the scale shown above, if a higher score is to denote a more favorable attitude, the scoring of items 2, 4, 5, and 7 will be reversed. The respondent in the department store project example has an attitude score of 22. Each respondent's total score for each store is calculated. A respondent will have the most favorable attitude toward the store with the highest score. The procedure for developing summated Likert scales is described later in the section on multiitem scales.

DEPARTMENT STORE PATRONAGE PROJECT
Likert Scale

Instructions

Listed below are different opinions about Sears. Please indicate how strongly you agree or disagree with each by putting an X next to your choice on the following scale:

1 = Strongly disagree   4 = Agree
2 = Disagree   5 = Strongly agree
3 = Neither agree nor disagree

	Strongly disagree	Disagree	Neither agree nor disagree	Agree	Strongly agree
1. Sears sells high quality merchandise.	1	2X	3	4	5
2. Sears has poor in-store service.	1	2X	3	4	5
3. I like to shop at Sears.	1	2	3X	4	5
4. Sears does not offer a good mix of different brands within a product category.	1	2	3	4X	5
5. The credit policies at Sears are terrible.	1	2	3	4X	5
6. Sears is where America shops.	1X	2	3	4	5
7. I do not like the advertising done by Sears.	1	2	3	4X	5
8. Sears sells a wide variety of merchandise.	1	2	3	4X	5
9. Sears charges fair prices.	1	2X	3	4	5 ◆

The Likert scale has several advantages. It is easy to construct and administer, and respondents readily understand how to use the scale, making it suitable for mail, telephone, or personal interviews. The major disadvantage of the Likert scale is that it takes longer to complete than other itemized rating scales because respondents have to read each statement. The following example shows another use of a Likert scale in marketing research.

EXAMPLE
Job Satisfaction——Intrinsic or Extrinsic?

A study investigated the hypothesis that salespeople's intrinsic job satisfaction (IJS) is related positively to the length of time they will stay in a company. Intrinsic job satisfaction was measured using the standard Likert scale.[10] One of the items used to measure IJS is as follows:

	Strongly disagree	Disagree	Neutral	Agree	Strongly agree
I get a feeling of accomplishment from the work I am doing.	1	2	3	4	5

Empirical data provided support for the hypothesis. The study concluded that sales managers should spend more effort on recruiting, training, and supporting salespeople so as to increase intrinsic job satisfaction and thereby reduce sales force turnover. ◆

To reduce sales force turnover, it is very important to increase intrinsic job satisfaction. ◆ Rhoda Sidney.

Semantic Differential Scale

semantic differential A seven-point rating scale with end points associated with bipolar labels that have semantic meaning.

The **semantic differential** is a seven-point rating scale with end points associated with bipolar labels that have semantic meaning. In a typical application, respondents rate objects on a number of itemized, seven-point rating scales bounded at each end by one of two bipolar adjectives, such as "cold" and "warm."[11] We illustrate this scale by presenting a respondent's evaluation of Sears on five attributes.

DEPARTMENT STORE PATRONAGE PROJECT
Semantic Differential Scale

Instructions

This part of the study measures what certain department stores mean to you by having you judge them on a series of descriptive scales bounded at each end by one of two bipolar adjectives. Please mark (X) the blank that best indicates how accurately one or the other adjective describes what the store means to you.

Please be sure to mark every scale; do not omit any scale.

Form

SEARS IS:

Powerful :—:—:—:—:-X-:—:—: Weak
Unreliable :—:—:—:—:—:-X-:—: Reliable
Modern :—:—:—:—:—:—:-X-: Old-fashioned
Cold :—:—:—:—:—:-X-:—: Warm
Careful :—:-X-:—:—:—:—:—: Careless ◆

The respondents mark the blank that best indicates how they would describe the object being rated.[12] Thus, in our example, Sears is evaluated as somewhat weak, reliable, very old fashioned, warm, and careful. The negative adjective or phrase sometimes appears at the left side of the scale and sometimes at the right. This controls the tendency of some respondents, particularly those with very positive or very negative attitudes, to mark the right- or left-hand sides without reading the labels. The methods for selecting the scale labels and constructing a semantic differential scale have been described elsewhere, where a general semantic differential scale for measuring self-concepts, person concepts, and product concepts has been developed,[13] as illustrated in Research in Practice 9.2.

Individual items on a semantic differential scale may be scored on either a −3 to +3 or a 1 to 7 scale. The resulting data are commonly analyzed through profile analysis.

RESEARCH IN PRACTICE 9.2

A Semantic Differential Scale for Measuring Self-Concepts, Person Concepts, and Product Concepts

1. Rugged:—:—:—:—:—:—:Delicate
2. Excitable:—:—:—:—:—:—:Calm
3. Uncomfortable:—:—:—:—:—:—:Comfortable
4. Dominating:—:—:—:—:—:—:Submissive
5. Thrifty:—:—:—:—:—:—:Indulgent
6. Pleasant:—:—:—:—:—:—:Unpleasant
7. Contemporary:—:—:—:—:—:—:Noncontemporary
8. Organized:—:—:—:—:—:—:Unorganized
9. Rational:—:—:—:—:—:—:Emotional
10. Youthful:—:—:—:—:—:—:Mature
11. Formal:—:—:—:—:—:—:Informal
12. Orthodox:—:—:—:—:—:—:Liberal
13. Complex:—:—:—:—:—:—:Simple
14. Colorless:—:—:—:—:—:—:Colorful
15. Modest:—:—:—:—:—:—:Vain

In profile analysis, means or median values on each rating scale are calculated and compared by plotting or statistical analysis. This helps determine the overall differences and similarities among the objects. To assess differences across segments of respondents, the researcher can compare mean responses of different segments. Although the mean is most often used as a summary statistic, there is some controversy as to whether the data obtained should be treated as an interval scale.[14] On the other hand, in cases when the researcher requires an overall comparison of objects, such as to determine store preference, the individual item scores are summed to arrive at a total score.

Its versatility makes the semantic differential a popular rating scale in marketing research. It has been widely used in comparing brand, product, and company images. It has also been used to develop advertising and promotion strategies and in new product development studies.[15] Several modifications of the basic scale have been proposed.[16]

Stapel Scale

Stapel scale A scale for measuring attitudes that consists of a single adjective in the middle of an even-numbered range of values.

The **Stapel scale**, named after its developer, Jan Stapel, is a unipolar rating scale with ten categories numbered from –5 to +5, without a neutral point (zero).[17] This scale is usually presented vertically. Respondents are asked to indicate by selecting an appropriate numerical response category how accurately or inaccurately each term describes the object. The higher the number, the more accurately the term describes the object, as shown in the Department Store Patronage Project.[18] In this example, Sears is evaluated as not having high-quality merchandise and having somewhat poor service.

DEPARTMENT STORE PATRONAGE PROJECT
Stapel Scale

Instructions

Please evaluate how accurately each word or phrase describes each of the department stores. Select a plus number for the phrases you think describe the store accurately. The more accurately you think the phrase describes the store, the larger the plus number you should choose. You should select a minus number for phrases you think do not describe it accurately. The less accurately you think the phrase describes the store, the larger the minus number you should choose. You can select any number, from +5 for phrases you think are very accurate, to –5 for phrases you think are very inaccurate.

Form

Sears

+5	+5
+4	+4
+3	+3
+2	+2X
+1	+1
High Quality	Poor Service
–1	–1
–2	–2
–3	–3
–4X	–4
–5	–5 ◆

The data obtained by using a Stapel scale can be analyzed in the same way as semantic differential data. The Stapel scale produces results similar to the semantic differential.[19] The Stapel scale's advantages are that it does not require a pretest of the adjectives or phrases to ensure true bipolarity and that it can be administered over the telephone. Some researchers, however, believe the Stapel scale is confusing and difficult to apply. Of the three itemized rating scales considered, the Stapel scale is used least.[20] Nonetheless, this scale merits more attention than it has received.

NONCOMPARATIVE ITEMIZED RATING SCALE DECISIONS

As is evident from the discussion so far, noncomparative itemized rating scales need not be used as originally proposed but can take many different forms. The researcher must make six major decisions when constructing any of these scales.

1. The number of scale categories to use
2. Balanced versus unbalanced scale
3. Odd or even number of categories
4. Forced versus nonforced choice
5. The nature and degree of the verbal description
6. The physical form of the scale

Number of Scale Categories

Two conflicting considerations are involved in deciding the number of scale categories or response options. The greater the number of scale categories, the finer the discrimination among stimulus objects that is possible. On the other hand, most respondents cannot handle more than a few categories. Traditional guidelines suggest that the appropriate number of categories should be seven plus or minus two: between five and nine.[21] Yet there is no single optimal number of categories. Several factors should be taken into account in deciding on the number of categories.

If the respondents are interested in the scaling task and are knowledgeable about the objects, many categories may be employed. On the other hand, if the respondents are not very knowledgeable or involved with the task, fewer categories should be used. Likewise, the nature of the objects is also relevant. Some objects do not lend themselves to fine discrimination, so a small number of categories is sufficient. Another important factor is the mode of data collection. If telephone interviews are involved, many categories may confuse the respondents. Likewise, space limitations may restrict the number of categories in mail questionnaires.

How the data are to be analyzed and used should also influence the number of categories. In situations where several scale items are added together to produce a single score for each respondent, five categories are sufficient. The same is true if the researcher wishes to make broad generalizations or group comparisons. If, however, individual responses are of interest or if the data will be analyzed by sophisticated statistical techniques, seven or more categories may be required. The size of the correlation coefficient, a common measure of relationship between variables (Chapter 17), is influenced by the number of scale categories. The correlation coefficient decreases with a reduction in the number of categories. This, in turn, has an impact on all statistical analysis based on the correlation coefficient.[22]

Balanced versus Unbalanced Scale

balanced scale A scale with an equal number of favorable and unfavorable categories.

In a **balanced scale**, the number of favorable and unfavorable categories is equal; in an unbalanced scale, the categories are unequal in number.[23] Examples of balanced and unbalanced scales are given in Figure 9.1. In general, in order to obtain objective data, the scale should be balanced. If the distribution of responses is likely to be skewed, however, either positively or negatively, an unbalanced scale with more categories in the direction of skewness may be appropriate. If an unbalanced scale is used, the nature and degree of unbalance in the scale should be taken into account in data analysis.

Odd or Even Number of Categories

With an odd number of categories, the middle scale position is generally designated as neutral or impartial.[24] The presence, position, and labeling of a neutral category can have a significant influence on the response.[25] The Likert scale is a balanced rating scale with an odd number of categories and a neutral point.

The decision to use an odd or even number of categories depends on whether some of the respondents may be neutral on the response being measured. If a neutral or indifferent response is possible from at least some of the respondents, an odd number of categories should be used. If, on the other hand, the researcher wants to force a response or believes that no neutral or indifferent response exists, a rating scale with an even number of categories should be used. A related issue is whether the choice should be forced or nonforced.

Forced versus Nonforced Choice

forced rating scale A rating scale that forces respondents to express an opinion because a "no opinion" or "no knowledge" option is not provided.

On **forced rating scales** the respondents are forced to express an opinion because a "no opinion" option is not provided. In such a case, respondents without an opinion may mark the middle scale position. If a sufficient proportion of the respondents do not have opinions on the topic, marking the middle position will distort measures of central tendency and variance. In situations where the respondents are expected to have no opinion, as opposed to simply being reluctant to disclose it, the accuracy of data may be improved by a nonforced scale that includes a "no opinion" category.[26]

Nature and Degree of Verbal Description

The nature and degree of verbal description associated with scale categories varies considerably and can have an effect on the responses.[27] Scale categories may have verbal,

---

FIGURE 9.1

Balanced and Unbalanced Scales

Balanced Scale		Unbalanced Scale	
JOVAN MUSK FOR MEN IS		*JOVAN MUSK FOR MEN IS*	
Extremely good	_____	Extremely good	_____
Very good	_____	Very good	_____
Good	_____	Good	_____
Bad	_____	Somewhat good	_____
Very bad	_____	Bad	_____
Extremely bad	_____	Very bad	_____

numerical, or even pictorial descriptions. Furthermore, the researcher must decide whether to label every scale category, some scale categories, or only extreme scale categories. Surprisingly, providing a verbal description for each category may not improve the accuracy or reliability of the data. Yet an argument can be made for labeling all or many scale categories to reduce scale ambiguity. The category descriptions should be located as close to the response categories as possible.[28]

The strength of the adjectives used to anchor the scale may influence the distribution of the responses. With strong anchors (1 = completely disagree, 7 = completely agree), respondents are less likely to use the extreme scale categories. This results in less variable and more peaked response distributions. Weak anchors (1 = generally disagree, 7 = generally agree), in contrast, produce uniform or flat distributions. Procedures have been developed to assign values to category descriptors so as to result in balanced or equal interval scales.[29]

Physical Form of the Scale

A number of options are available with respect to scale form or configuration. Scales can be presented vertically or horizontally. Categories can be expressed by boxes, discrete lines, or units on a continuum and may or may not have numbers assigned to them. If numerical values are used, they may be positive, negative, or both. Several possible configurations are presented in Figure 9.2.

Two unique rating scale configurations used in marketing research are the thermometer scale and the smiling face scale. For the thermometer scale, the higher the tem-

FIGURE 9.2

Rating Scale Configurations

A variety of scale configurations may be employed to measure the gentleness of Cheer detergent. Some examples include:

Cheer detergent is:

1. Very harsh — — — — — — — Very gentle

2. Very harsh 1 2 3 4 5 6 7 Very gentle

3. • Very harsh
   •
   •
   • Neither harsh nor gentle
   •
   •
   • Very gentle

4. —— —— —— —— —— —— ——
   Very harsh   Harsh   Somewhat harsh   Neither harsh nor gentle   Somewhat gentle   Gentle   Very gentle

   [−3] [−2] [−1] [0] [+1] [+2] [+3]

5. Very harsh   Neither harsh nor gentle   Very gentle

perature, the more favorable the evaluation. Likewise, happier faces indicate more favorable evaluations. These scales are especially useful for children.[30] Examples of these scales are shown in Figure 9.3. Table 9.2 summarizes the six decisions in designing rating scales.

Thermometer Scale

Instructions

   Please indicate how much you like McDonald's hamburgers by coloring in the thermometer with your blue pen. Start at the bottom and color up to the temperature level that best indicates how strong your preference is for McDonald's hamburgers.

Form

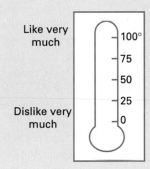

Smiling Face Scale

Instructions

   Please tell me how much you like the Barbie Doll by pointing to the face that best shows how much you like it. If you did not like the Barbie Doll at all, you would point to Face 1. If you liked it very much, you would point to Face 5. Now tell me, how much did you like the Barbie Doll?

Form

1. Number of categories	Although there is no single, optimal number, traditional guidelines suggest that there should be between five and nine categories.
2. Balanced versus unbalanced	In general, the scale should be balanced to obtain objective data.
3. Odd or even number of categories	If a neutral or indifferent scale response is possible from at least some of the respondents, an odd number of categories should be used.
4. Forced versus nonforced	In situations where the respondents are expected to have no opinion, the accuracy of data may be improved by a nonforced scale.
5. Verbal description	An argument can be made for labeling all or many scale categories. The category descriptions should be located as close to the response categories as possible.
6. Physical form	A number of options should be tried and the best one selected.

MULTIITEM SCALES

The development of multiitem rating scales requires considerable technical expertise.[31] Figure 9.4 is a paradigm for constructing multiitem scales. The characteristic to be measured is frequently called a construct. Scale development begins with an underlying theory of the construct being measured. A theory is necessary not only for constructing the scale but also for interpreting the resulting scores. The next step is to generate an initial pool of scale items. Typically, this is based on theory, analysis of secondary data, and qualitative research. From this pool, a reduced set of potential scale items is generated by the judgment of the researcher and other knowledgeable individuals. Some qualitative criterion is adopted to aid their judgment. The reduced set of items is still too large to constitute a scale. Thus, further reduction is achieved in a quantitative manner.

Data are collected on the reduced set of potential scale items from a large pretest sample of respondents. The data are analyzed using techniques such as correlations, factor analysis, cluster analysis, discriminant analysis, and statistical tests discussed later in this book. As a result of these statistical analyses, several more items are eliminated, resulting in a purified scale. The purified scale is evaluated for reliability and validity by collecting more data from a different sample (see the following section). On the basis of these assessments, a final set of scale items is selected. As can be seen from Figure 9.4, the scale development process is an iterative one with several feedback loops.[32]

An example of a scale developed for use in industrial marketing research is given on page 303.

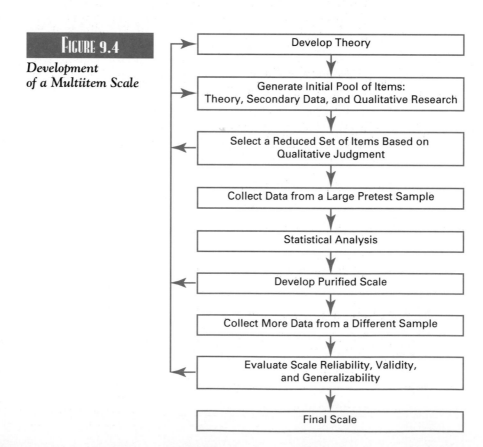

FIGURE 9.4

Development of a Multiitem Scale

Develop Theory

Generate Initial Pool of Items: Theory, Secondary Data, and Qualitative Research

Select a Reduced Set of Items Based on Qualitative Judgment

Collect Data from a Large Pretest Sample

Statistical Analysis

Develop Purified Scale

Collect More Data from a Different Sample

Evaluate Scale Reliability, Validity, and Generalizability

Final Scale

EXAMPLE

Measuring Technical Sophistication with a Technically Sophisticated Scale ___

The following multiitem scale measures the technical sophistication of a product line.[33]

1. Technical	1	2	3	4	5	6	7	Nontechnical
2. Low engineering content	1	2	3	4	5	6	7	High engineering content
3. Fast changing	1	2	3	4	5	6	7	Slowly changing
4. Unsophisticated	1	2	3	4	5	6	7	Sophisticated
5. Commodity	1	2	3	4	5	6	7	Customized
6. Unique	1	2	3	4	5	6	7	Common
7. Complex	1	2	3	4	5	6	7	Simple

Items 1, 3, 6, and 7 are reversed while scoring. This scale can be used in industrial marketing to measure the technical sophistication of a customer's product line and to suggest changes to improve technical quality. ◆

SCALE EVALUATION

A multiitem scale should be evaluated for accuracy and applicability.[34] As shown in Figure 9.5, this involves an assessment of reliability, validity, and generalizability of the scale. Approaches to assessing reliability include test-retest reliability, alternative-forms reliability, and internal consistency reliability. Validity can be assessed by examining content validity, criterion validity, and construct validity.

Before we can examine reliability and validity we need an understanding of measurement accuracy; it is fundamental to scale evaluation.

Measurement Accuracy

measurement error The variation in the information sought by the researcher and the information generated by the measurement process employed.

As mentioned in Chapter 8, a measurement is a number that reflects some characteristic of an object. A measurement is not the true value of the characteristic of interest but rather an observation of it. A variety of factors can cause **measurement error**, which results in the measurement or observed score being different from the true score of the

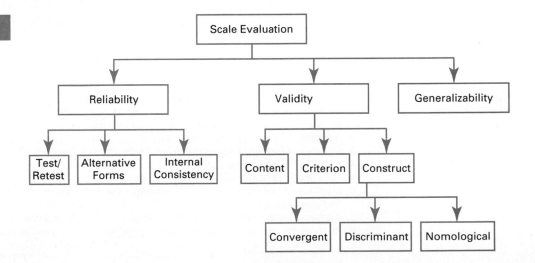

true score model A mathematical model that provides a framework for understanding the accuracy of measurement.

characteristic being measured (see Figure 9.6). The **true score model** provides a framework for understanding the accuracy of measurement.[35] According to this model,

$$X_O = X_T + X_S + X_R$$

where

X_O = the observed score or measurement
X_T = the true score of the characteristic
X_S = systematic error
X_R = random error

systematic error An error that affects the measurement in a constant way and represents stable factors that affect the observed score in the same way each time the measurement is made.

random error An error that arises from random changes or differences in respondents or measurement situations.

reliability The extent to which a scale produces consistent results if repeated measurements are made on the characteristic.

test-retest reliability An approach for assessing reliability in which respondents are administered identical sets of scale items at two different times under as nearly equivalent conditions as possible.

Note that the total measurement error includes the systematic error, X_S, and the random error, X_R. **Systematic error** affects the measurement in a constant way. It represents stable factors that affect the observed score in the same way each time the measurement is made, such as mechanical factors (see Figure 9.6). **Random error**, on the other hand, is not constant. It represents transient factors that affect the observed score in different ways each time the measurement is made, such as transient personal or situational factors. The distinction between systematic and random error is crucial to our understanding of reliability and validity.

Reliability

Reliability refers to the extent to which a scale produces consistent results if repeated measurements are made.[36] Systematic sources of error do not have an adverse impact on reliability, because they affect the measurement in a constant way and do not lead to inconsistency. In contrast, random error produces inconsistency, leading to lower reliability. Reliability can be defined as the extent to which measures are free from random error, X_R. If $X_R = 0$, the measure is perfectly reliable.

Reliability is assessed by determining the proportion of systematic variation in a scale. This is done by determining the association between scores obtained from different administrations of the scale. If the association is high, the scale yields consistent results and is therefore reliable. Approaches for assessing reliability include the test-retest, alternative-forms, and internal consistency methods.

Test-retest reliability   In **test-retest reliability**, respondents are administered identical sets of scale items at two different times under as nearly equivalent conditions as possible. The time interval between tests or administrations is typically two to four weeks. The degree of similarity between the two measurements is determined by computing a

FIGURE 9.6

Potential Sources of Error in Measurement

1. Other relatively stable characteristics of the individual that influence the test score, such as intelligence, social desirability, and education.
2. Short-term or transient personal factors, such as health, emotions, fatigue.
3. Situational factors, such as the presence of other people, noise, and distractions.
4. Sampling of items included in the scale: addition, deletion, or changes in the scale items.
5. Lack of clarity of the scale, including the instructions or the items themselves.
6. Mechanical factors, such as poor printing, overcrowding items in the questionnaire, and poor design.
7. Administration of the scale, such as differences among interviewers.
8. Analysis factors, such as differences in scoring and statistical analysis.

correlation coefficient (see Chapter 17). The higher the correlation coefficient, the greater the reliability.

Several problems are associated with the test-retest approach to determining reliability. First, it is sensitive to the time interval between testing. Other things being equal, the longer the time interval, the lower the reliability. Second, the initial measurement may alter the characteristic being measured. For example, measuring respondents' attitude toward low-fat milk may cause them to become more health conscious and to develop a more positive attitude toward low-fat milk. Third, it may be impossible to make repeated measurements (for example, the research topic may be respondent's initial reaction to a new product). Fourth, the first measurement may have a carryover effect to the second or subsequent measurements. Respondents may attempt to remember answers they gave the first time. Fifth, the characteristic being measured may change between measurements. For example, favorable information about an object between measurements may make a respondent's attitude more positive. Finally, the test-retest reliability coefficient can be inflated by the correlation of each item with itself. These correlations tend to be higher than correlations between different scale items across administrations. Hence, it is possible to have high test-retest correlations because of the high correlations between the same scale items measured at different times even though the correlations between different scale items are quite low. Because of these problems, a test-retest approach is best applied in conjunction with other approaches, such as alternative-forms reliability.

Alternative-forms reliability   In **alternative-forms reliability**, two equivalent forms of the scale are constructed. The same respondents are measured at two different times, usually two to four weeks apart. The scores from the administrations of the alternative scale forms are correlated to assess reliability.[37]

There are two major problems with this approach. First, it is time-consuming and expensive to construct an equivalent form of the scale. Second, it is difficult to construct two equivalent forms of a scale. The two forms should be equivalent with respect to content. In a strict sense, this requires that the alternative sets of scale items should have the same means, variances, and intercorrelations. Even if these conditions are satisfied, the two forms may not be equivalent in content. Thus, a low correlation may reflect either an unreliable scale or nonequivalent forms.

Internal consistency reliability   **Internal consistency reliability** is used to assess the reliability of a summated scale where several items are summed to form a total score. In a scale of this type, each item measures some aspect of the construct measured by the entire scale, and the items should be consistent in what they indicate about the characteristic. This measure of reliability focuses on the internal consistency of the set of items forming the scale.

The simplest measure of internal consistency is **split-half reliability**. The items on the scale are divided into two halves and the resulting half scores are correlated. High correlations between the halves indicate high internal consistency. The scale items can be split into halves based on odd- and even-numbered items or randomly. The problem is that the results will depend on how the scale items are split. A popular approach to overcoming this problem is to use the coefficient alpha.

The **coefficient alpha**, or Cronbach's alpha, is the average of all possible split-half coefficients resulting from different ways of splitting the scale items.[38] This coefficient varies from 0 to 1, and a value of 0.6 or less generally indicates unsatisfactory internal consistency reliability. An important property of coefficient alpha is that its value tends

alternative-forms reliability An approach for assessing reliability that requires two equivalent forms of the scale to be constructed and then the same respondents to be measured at two different times.

internal consistency reliability An approach for assessing the internal consistency of the set of items by summing the individual consistencies for the items in the set to form a total score for the scale.

split-half reliability A form of internal consistency reliability in which the items constituting the scale are divided into two halves and the resulting half scores are correlated.

coefficient alpha A measure of internal consistency reliability that is the average of all possible split-half coefficients resulting from different splittings of the scale items.

to increase with an increase in the number of scale items. Therefore, coefficient alpha may be artificially, and inappropriately, inflated by including several redundant scale items.[39] Another coefficient that can be employed in conjunction with coefficient alpha is coefficient beta. Coefficient beta assists in determining whether the averaging process used in calculating coefficient alpha is masking any inconsistent items.

Some multiitem scales include several sets of items designed to measure different aspects of a multidimensional construct. For example, store image is a multidimensional construct that includes quality of merchandise, variety and assortment of merchandise, returns and adjustment policy, service of store personnel, prices, convenience of location, layout of the store, and credit and billing policies. Hence, a scale designed to measure store image would contain items measuring each of these dimensions. Because these dimensions are somewhat independent, a measure of internal consistency computed across dimensions would be inappropriate. If several items are used to measure each dimension, however, internal consistency reliability can be computed for each dimension, as in the Beaumont Emotion Battery.

EXAMPLE
Emotionally Charged Battery

The Beaumont Emotion Battery has been developed by the Beaumont Organization, Ltd., to measure emotional response to advertising. Respondents rate the advertisement or commercial to which they are exposed across a battery of items that tap eight primary emotions: acceptance, fear, surprise, sadness, disgust, anger, anticipation, and joy. The internal consistency reliability of this battery, measured in terms of Cronbach's alpha, has been determined for each primary emotion. For the emotions listed, these reliability coefficients are 0.73, 0.66, 0.63, 0.75, 0.72, 0.81, 0.79, and 0.85. These results indicate satisfactory internal consistency reliability for the Beaumont emotion battery.[40] ◆

Validity

validity The extent to which differences in observed scale scores reflect true differences among objects on the characteristic being measured, rather than systematic or random errors.

The **validity** of a scale may be defined as the extent to which differences in observed scale scores reflect true differences among objects on the characteristic being measured, rather than systematic or random error. Perfect validity requires that there be no measurement error ($X_O = X_T$, $X_R = 0$, $X_S = 0$). Researchers may assess content validity, criterion validity, or construct validity.[41]

content validity A type of validity, sometimes called face validity, that consists of a subjective but systematic evaluation of the representativeness of the content of a scale for the measuring task at hand.

Content validity   Content validity, sometimes called face validity, is a subjective but systematic evaluation of how well the content of a scale represents the measurement task at hand. The researcher or someone else examines whether the scale items adequately cover the entire domain of the construct being measured. Thus, a scale designed to measure store image would be considered inadequate if it omitted any of the major dimensions (quality, variety and assortment of merchandise, etc.). Given its subjective nature, content validity alone is not a sufficient measure of the validity of a scale, yet it aids in a common-sense interpretation of the scale scores. A more formal evaluation can be obtained by examining criterion validity.

criterion validity A type of validity that examines whether the measurement scale performs as expected in relation to other variables selected as meaningful criteria.

Criterion validity   Criterion validity reflects whether a scale performs as expected in relation to other variables selected (criterion variables) as meaningful criteria. Criterion variables may include demographic and psychographic characteristics, attitudinal and behav-

construct validity A type of validity that addresses the question of what construct or characteristic the scale is measuring. An attempt is made to answer theoretical questions of why a scale works and what deductions can be made concerning the theory underlying the scale.

convergent validity A measure of construct validity that measures the extent to which the scale correlates positively with other measures of the same construct.

discriminant validity A type of construct validity that assesses the extent to which a measure does not correlate with other constructs from which it is supposed to differ.

nomological validity A type of validity that assesses the relationship between theoretical constructs. It seeks to confirm significant correlations between the constructs as predicted by a theory.

ioral measures, or scores obtained from other scales. Based on the time period involved, criterion validity can take two forms, concurrent validity and predictive validity.

Concurrent validity is assessed when the data on the scale being evaluated and on the criterion variables are collected at the same time. To assess concurrent validity, a researcher may develop short forms of standard personality instruments, such as Beaumont Emotion Battery. The original instruments and the short versions would be administered simultaneously to a group of respondents and the results compared. To assess predictive validity, the researcher collects data on the scale at one point in time and data on the criterion variables at a future time. For example, attitudes toward cereal brands could be used to predict future purchases of cereals by members of a scanner panel. Attitudinal data are obtained from the panel members, and then their future purchases are tracked with scanner data. The predicted and actual purchases are compared to assess the predictive validity of the attitudinal scale.

Construct validity Construct validity addresses the question of what construct or characteristic the scale is, in fact, measuring. When assessing construct validity, the researcher attempts to answer theoretical questions about why the scale works and what deductions can be made concerning the underlying theory. Thus, construct validity requires a sound theory of the nature of the construct being measured and how it relates to other constructs. Construct validity is the most sophisticated and difficult type of validity to establish. As Figure 9.5 shows, construct validity includes convergent, discriminant, and nomological validity.

Convergent validity is the extent to which the scale correlates positively with other measures of the same construct. It is not necessary that all these measures be obtained by using conventional scaling techniques. **Discriminant validity** is the extent to which a measure does not correlate with other constructs from which it is supposed to differ. It involves demonstrating a lack of correlation among differing constructs. **Nomological validity** is the extent to which the scale correlates in theoretically predicted ways with measures of different but related constructs. A theoretical model is formulated that leads to further deductions, tests, and inferences. Gradually, a nomological net is built in which several constructs are systematically interrelated. We illustrate construct validity in the context of a multiitem scale designed to measure self-concept.[42]

EXAMPLE
To Thine Own Self Be True

The following findings would provide evidence of construct validity for a multiitem scale to measure self-concept:

- High correlations with other scales designed to measure self-concepts and with reported classifications by friends (convergent validity)
- Low correlations with unrelated constructs of brand loyalty and variety seeking (discriminant validity)
- Brands that are congruent with the individual's self-concept are more preferred, as postulated by the theory (nomological validity)
- A high level of reliability ◆

Notice that a high level of reliability was included as an evidence of construct validity in this example. This illustrates the relationship between reliability and validity.

Relationship between Reliability and Validity

The relationship between reliability and validity can be understood in terms of the true score model. If a measure is perfectly valid, it is also perfectly reliable. In this case, $X_O = X_T$, $X_R = 0$, and $X_S = 0$. Thus, perfect validity implies perfect reliability. If a measure is unreliable, it cannot be perfectly valid, since at a minimum $X_O = X_T + X_R$. Furthermore, systematic error may also be present, that is, $X_S \neq 0$. Thus, unreliability implies invalidity. If a measure is perfectly reliable, it may or may not be perfectly valid, because systematic error may still be present ($X_O = X_T + X_S$). Although lack of reliability constitutes negative evidence for validity, reliability does not in itself imply validity. Reliability is a necessary, but not sufficient, condition for validity.

Generalizability

generalizability The degree to which a study based on a sample applies to the population as a whole.

Generalizability refers to the extent to which one can generalize from the observations at hand to a universe of generalizations. The set of all conditions of measurement over which the investigator wishes to generalize is the universe of generalization. These conditions may include items, interviewers, and situations of observation. A researcher may wish to generalize a scale developed for use in personal interviews to other modes of data collection, such as mail and telephone interviews. Likewise, one may wish to generalize from a sample of items to the universe of items, from a sample of times of measurement to the universe of times of measurement, from a sample of observers to a universe of observers, and so on.[43]

In generalizability studies, measurement procedures are designed to investigate each universe of interest by sampling conditions of measurement from each. For each universe of interest, an aspect of measurement called a facet is included in the study. Traditional reliability methods can be viewed as single-facet generalizability studies. A test-retest correlation is concerned with whether scores obtained from a measurement scale are generalizable to the universe scores across all times of possible measurement. Even if the test-retest correlation is high, nothing can be said about the generalizability of the scale to other universes. To generalize to other universes, generalizability theory procedures must be employed.

CHOOSING A SCALING TECHNIQUE

In addition to theoretical considerations and evaluation of reliability and validity, certain practical factors should be considered in selecting scaling techniques for a particular marketing research problem.[44] These include the level of information (nominal, ordinal, interval, or ratio) desired, the capabilities of the respondents, the characteristics of the stimulus objects, the method of administration, the context, and cost.

As a general rule, using the scaling technique that will yield the highest level of information feasible in a given situation will permit using the greatest variety of statistical analyses. Also, regardless of the type of scale used, whenever feasible, several scale items should measure the characteristic of interest. This provides more accurate measurement than a single-item scale. In many situations, it is desirable to use more than one scaling technique or to obtain additional measures using mathematically derived scales.

MATHEMATICALLY DERIVED SCALES

All the scaling techniques discussed in this chapter require the respondents to evaluate directly various characteristics of the stimulus objects. In contrast, mathematical scaling techniques allow researchers to infer respondents' evaluations of characteristics of stimulus objects. These evaluations are inferred from the respondents' overall judgments of the objects. Two popular mathematically derived scaling techniques are multidimensional scaling and conjoint analysis, which are discussed in detail in Chapter 21.

INTERNATIONAL MARKETING RESEARCH

In designing the scale or response format, respondents' educational or literacy levels should be taken into account.[45] One approach is to develop scales that are pan-cultural, or free of cultural biases. Of the scaling techniques we have considered, the semantic differential scale may be said to be pan-cultural. It has been tested in a number of countries and has consistently produced similar results.

EXAMPLE
Copying the Name Xerox

Xerox was a name well received in the former Soviet Union since the late 1960s. In fact, the act of copying documents was called Xeroxing, a term coined after the name of the company. It was a brand name people equated with quality. With the disintegration of Soviet Union into the Commonwealth of Independent States, however, Xerox's sales started to fall. The management initially considered this problem to be the intense competition with strong competitors such as Canon, Ricoh Company, Mitsubishi Electric Corporation, and Minolta Camera Company. First attempts of making the product more competitive did not help. Subsequently, marketing research was undertaken to measure the image of Xerox and its competitors. Semantic differential scales were used as this type of scale is considered pan-cultural. The bipolar labels used were carefully tested to ensure that they had the intended semantic meaning in the Russian context.

The results of the study revealed that the real problem was a growing negative perception of Russian customers toward Xerox products. What could have gone wrong? The problem was not with Xerox, but with several independent producers of copying machines that had illegally infringed on Xerox trademark rights. With the disintegration of Soviet Union, the protection of these trademarks was unclear and trademark infringement kept growing. As a result, customers developed a misconception toward Xerox selling low-quality products. Among other courses of action, Xerox ran a corporate campaign on the national Russian TV and radio networks as well as in local print media. The campaign emphasized Xerox's leadership position in the commonwealth countries where quality demands were very high. This was a definite step in removing some misconceptions of Russian consumers toward Xerox. Xerox also registered its trademark separately in each republic.[46] ◆

Although the semantic differential worked well in the Russian context, an alternative approach is to develop scales that use a self-defined cultural norm as a base referent. For example, respondents may be required to indicate their own anchor point and position relative to a culture-specific stimulus set. This approach is useful for measuring attitudes that are defined relative to cultural norms (e.g., attitude toward marital roles). In developing response formats, verbal rating scales appear to be the most suitable. Even less educated respondents can readily understand and respond to verbal scales. Special attention should be devoted to determining equivalent verbal descriptors in different languages and cultures. The end points of the scale are particularly prone to different interpretations. In some cultures, 1 may be interpreted as best, whereas in others it may be interpreted as worst, regardless of how it is scaled. It is important that the scale end points and the verbal descriptors be employed in a manner consistent with the culture.

Finally, in international marketing research, it is critical to establish the equivalence of scales and measures used to obtain data from different countries. This topic is complex and is discussed in some detail in Chapter 23.

ETHICS IN MARKETING RESEARCH

Ethical issues can arise in the construction of noncomparative scales. Consider, for example, the use of scale descriptors. The descriptors used to frame a scale can be manipulated to bias results in any direction. They can be manipulated to generate a positive view of the client's brand or a negative view of a competitor's brand. A researcher who wants to project the client's brand favorably can ask respondents to indicate their opinion of the brand on several attributes using seven-point scales framed by the descriptors extremely poor to good. Using a strongly negative descriptor with only a mildly positive one has an interesting effect. As long as the product is not the worst, respondents will be reluctant to rate the product extremely poorly. In fact, respondents who believe the product to be only mediocre will end up responding favorably. Try this yourself. How would you rate BMW automobiles on the following attributes?

Reliability:	Horrible	1	2	3	4	5	6	7	Good
Performance:	Very poor	1	2	3	4	5	6	7	Good
Quality:	One of the worst	1	2	3	4	5	6	7	Good
Prestige:	Very low	1	2	3	4	5	6	7	Good

Did you find yourself rating BMW cars positively? Using this same technique, a researcher can negatively bias evaluations of competitors' products by providing mildly negative descriptors against strong positive descriptors.

Thus we see how important it is to use balanced scales with comparable positive and negative descriptors. When this guide is not practiced, responses are biased and should be interpreted accordingly. This concern also underscores the need to adequately establish the reliability, validity, and generalizability of scales before using them in a research project. Scales that are either invalid, unreliable, or not generalizable to the target market provide the client with flawed results and misleading findings, thus raising serious ethical issues. The researcher has a responsibility to both the client and respondents to ensure the applicability and usefulness of the scale, as we see in the following example.

EXAMPLE
An Ethical Scale for Measuring Ethics _____

Although everyone knows ethics are important, how do you go about measuring ethical evaluations of marketing activities? To answer this question, one set of researchers turned to concepts of moral philosophy (see Chapter 24) to develop a scale for measuring ethical evaluations. Twenty-nine seven-point bipolar scales, developed from moral philosophy and ranging from fair to unfair and efficient to inefficient resulted. Tests of these scales, through their use in evaluating various ethical scenarios, indicated that the reliabilities for these scales (measured via Cronbach's alpha) were high, and validity measures indicated a strong degree of construct validity. Accordingly, this scale has been useful in a variety of contexts for investigating ethical issues in marketing.[47] ◆

COMPUTER APPLICATIONS

Microcomputers are useful for developing and testing continuous and itemized rating scales, particularly multiitem scales. EZWRITER, a module of the computer-assisted telephone interviewing system C-SURVENT, uses a series of menu-driven screens to guide the market researcher through the scale development process. EZWRITER by Computers for Marketing Corporation (CfMC) of San Francisco can customize scales for printed questionnaires or for use by telephone interviewers at computer screens in a fraction of the time it would take without automation.

For each new scale, the researcher would be presented a screen asking for information about the intended scale. For example, if the question is a noncomparatively scaled question, then the researcher would indicate that a "number" response is sought. The researcher would then indicate the valid range of the numbers.

After this, a second screen would allow formatting of the scale on the screen as interviewers would see it during data collection. Exhibit 9.1 depicts a balanced scale for the

---

EXHIBIT 9.1

Constructing a Balanced Scale

```
On a scale from one to five where one is very unpleasant and
five is very tasty, how would you rate Calorisimo's flavor?

      Very Unpleasant        Neutral          Very Tasty
     1............2...........3...........4............5

 5 Very tasty
 4 Somewhat tasty
 3 Neutral/not very tasty
 2 Unpleasant tasting, or
 1 Very Unpleasant
—>5




                                              [TASTES]*PRACTICE
```

variable of "taste" with five response categories in two forms. In the first form, the scale for taste appears horizontally with labels for the anchors (i.e., very unpleasant, and very tasty), as well as for the midpoint (i.e., neutral). In the second form, the scale for taste appears vertically with a label for each response category. Both forms of this scale can be saved for later use. The scale developer would need only one form for a question in a questionnaire and could choose the desired form when matching the scale to the specific question.

EZWRITER includes a feature called a "dictionary" where previously written scales can be stored for later retrieval. The researcher can then write template scales so that only one or two items need be inserted by the researcher to acquire a finished scale. For example, the scale in Exhibit 9.1 receives the name "TASTE5." Each scale receives a name prior to being saved in the dictionary. If the researcher wanted a similar scale for "smell," "TASTE5" could be recalled and modified by swapping the word "aromatic" for the word "tasty." In fact, blocks of scales can be rapidly produced like this and saved for later recall. In this way, multiitem scale development becomes speedier and more efficient. In addition, last-minute changes can be made with ease.

The two menu-driven screens just discussed handle all the specification writing and programming work. In addition, a "help" key can be used at any point in the writing of a scale to receive an explanation of the options provided by an EZWRITER menu. The program checks for scale completeness, accuracy, and format problems as the scale develops. For example, an invalid range for answers to a noncomparatively scaled question would cause EZWRITER to give a warning to the researcher.

Other specialized programs are also available for constructing itemized rating scales. Attitude Scales by Persimmon Software constructs a variety of rating scales for measuring attitudes in marketing and opinion research. Several of the questionnaire design packages discussed in Chapter 10 can construct comparative and noncomparative scales.

SUMMARY

In noncomparative scaling, each object is scaled independently of the other objects in the stimulus set. The resulting data are generally assumed to be interval or ratio scaled. Noncomparative rating scales can be either continuous or itemized. The itemized rating scales are further classified as Likert, semantic differential, or Stapel scales. When using noncomparative itemized rating scales, the researcher must decide on the number of scale categories, balanced versus unbalanced scales, odd or even number of categories, forced versus nonforced choices, nature and degree of verbal description, and the physical form or configuration.

Multiitem scales consist of a number of rating scale items. These scales should be evaluated in terms of reliability and validity. Reliability refers to the extent to which a scale produces consistent results if repeated measurements are made. Approaches to assessing reliability include test-retest, alternative-forms, and internal consistency. Validity, or accuracy of measurement, may be assessed by evaluating content validity, criterion validity, and construct validity.

The choice of particular scaling techniques in a given situation should be based on theoretical and practical considerations. As a general rule, the scaling technique used should be the one that will yield the highest level of information feasible. Also, multiple measures should be obtained.

In international marketing research, special attention should be devoted to determining equivalent verbal descriptors in different languages and cultures. The misuse of scale descriptors also raises serious ethical concerns. The researcher has a responsibility to both the client and respondents to ensure the applicability and usefulness of the scales. Computers are useful for developing and testing continuous and itemized rating scales, particularly multiitem scales.[48]

ACRONYMS

The rating scale decisions may be described by the acronym RATING:

R esponse option: forced versus nonforced
A ttractive versus unattractive number of categories: balanced versus unbalanced
T otal number of categories
I mpartial or neutral category: odd versus even number of categories
N ature and degree of verbal description
G raphics: physical form and configuration

EXERCISES

QUESTIONS

1. What is a semantic differential scale? For what purpose is this scale used?
2. Describe the Likert scale.
3. What are the differences between the Stapel scale and the semantic differential? Which scale is more popular?
4. What are the major decisions involved in constructing an itemized rating scale?
5. How many scale categories should be used in an itemized rating scale? Why?
6. What is the difference between balanced and unbalanced scales?
7. Should an odd or even number of categories be used in an itemized rating scale?
8. What is the difference between forced and nonforced scales?
9. How does the nature and degree of verbal description affect the response to itemized rating scales?
10. What are multiitem scales?
11. Describe the true score model.
12. What is reliability?
13. What are the differences between test-retest and alternative-forms reliability?
14. Describe the notion of internal consistency reliability.
15. What is validity?
16. What is criterion validity? How is it assessed?
17. How would you assess the construct validity of a multiitem scale?
18. What is the relationship between reliability and validity?
19. How would you select a particular scaling technique?

PROBLEMS

1. Develop a Likert, semantic differential, and a Stapel scale for measuring store loyalty.
2. Develop a multiitem scale to measure students' attitudes toward internationalization of the management curriculum. How would you assess the reliability and validity of this scale?

COMPUTER EXERCISES

1. Using a database manager such as dBASE IV, develop several different rating scale configurations for measuring attitudes toward health fitness centers.

Notes

1. R. Edel, "New Technologies Add Dimensions to Copy Testing," *Advertising Age* (November 24, 1986).

2. "Americans Voice Opinions on the Services Industry," *Marketing News* (November 20, 1987): 18.

3. C. L. Narayana, "Graphic Positioning Scale: An Economical Instrument for Surveys," *Journal of Marketing Research* 14 (February 1977): 118–22.

4. A. O. Gregg, "Some Problems Concerning the Use of Rating Scales for Visual Assessment," *Journal of the Market Research Society* 8 (January 1980): 29–43.

5. For arguments in favor of graphic rating scales, see S. I. Lampert, "The Attitude Pollimeter: A New Attitude Scaling Device," *Journal of Marketing Research* (November 1979): 578–82; and D. S. Tillinghast, "Direct Magnitude Scales in Public Opinion Surveys," *Public Opinion Quarterly* (Fall 1980): 377–84.

6. ORTEK Data Systems, Inc.

7. Rensis Likert, "A Technique for the Measurement of Attitudes," *Archives of Psychology* 140 (1932). For a recent application, see Rajshekhar Javalgi and W. Benoy Joseph, "Physicians' Attitudes and Behaviors toward Home Health Care Services," *Journal of Health Care Marketing* (December 1991): 14–21.

8. Allen M. Weiss and Erin Anderson, "Converting from Independent to Employee Salesforces: The Role of Perceived Switching Costs," *Journal of Marketing Research* 29 (February 1992): 101–15.

9. Delia A. Sumrall, Nermin Eyuboglu, and Sucheta S. Ahlawat, "Developing a Scale to Measure Hospital Sales Orientation," *Journal of Health Care Marketing* (December 1991): 39–50.

10. George H. Lucas, Jr., A. Parasuraman, Robert A. Davis, and Ben M. Enis, "An Empirical Study of Salesforce Turnover," *Journal of Marketing* 51 (July 1987): 34–59.

11. John Dickson and Gerald Albaum, "A Method for Developing Tailor-Made Semantic Differentials for Specific Marketing Content Areas," *Journal of Marketing Research* 14 (February 1977): 87–91.

12. Eugene D. Jaffe and Israel D. Nebenzahl, "Alternative Questionnaire Formats for Country Image Studies," *Journal of Marketing Research* 21 (November 1984): 463–71.

13. Naresh K. Malhotra, "A Scale to Measure Self-Concepts, Person Concepts and Product Concepts," *Journal of Marketing Research* 18 (November 1981): 456–64.

14. There is little difference in the results based on whether the data are ordinal or interval, however. See John Gaiton, "Measurement Scales and Statistics: Resurgence of an Old Misconception," *Psychological Bulletin* 87 (1980): 564–67.

15. S. Malhotra, S. Van Auken, and S. C. Lonial, "Adjective Profiles in Television Copy Testing," *Journal of Advertising Research* (August 1981): 21–25.

16. R. H. Evans, "The Upgraded Semantic Differential: A Further Test," *Journal of the Market Research Society* 2 (1980): 143–47; and J. E. Swan and C. M. Futrell, "Increasing the Efficiency of the Retailer's Image Study," *Journal of the Academy of Marketing Science* (Winter 1980): 51–57.

17. Jan Stapel, "About 35 Years of Market Research in the Netherlands," *Markonderzock Kwartaalschrift* 2 (1969): 3–7.

18. Michael J. Etzel, Terrell G. Williams, John C. Rogers, and Douglas J. Lincoln, "The Comparability of Three Stapel Scale Forms in a Marketing Setting," in Ronald F. Bush and Shelby D. Hunt (eds.), *Marketing Theory: Philosophy of Science Perspectives* (Chicago: American Marketing Association, 1982), pp. 303–6.

19. Del I. Hawkins, Gerald Albaum, and Roger Best, "Stapel Scale or Semantic Differential in Marketing Research?" *Journal of Marketing Research* 11 (August 1974): 318–322; and Dennis Menezes and Norbert F. Elbert, "Alternative Semantic Scaling Formats for Measuring Store Image: An Evaluation," *Journal of Marketing Research* 16 (February 1979): 80–87.

20. Gregory D. Upah and Steven C. Cosmas, "The Use of Telephone Dials as Attitude Scales," *Journal of the Academy of Marketing Science* (Fall 1980): 416–26.

21. Eli P. Cox III, "The Optimal Number of Response Alternatives for a Scale: A Review," *Journal of Marketing Research* 17 (November 1980): 407–22; and F. D. Reynolds and J. Neter, "How Many Categories for Respondent Classification," *Journal of the Market Research Society* (October 1982): 345–46; and R. J. Lawrence, "Reply," *Journal of the Market Research Society* (October 1982): 346–48.

22. M. M. Givon and Z. Shapira, "Response to Rating Scales: A Theoretical Model and Its Application to the Number of Categories Problem," *Journal of Marketing Research* (November 1984): 410–19; and D. E. Stem, Jr., and S. Noazin, "The Effects of Number of Objects and Scale Positions on Graphic Position Scale Reliability," in R. F. Lusch et al., *1985 AMA Educators' Proceedings* (Chicago: American Marketing Association, 1985), pp. 370–72.

23. H. Schuman and S. Presser, *Questions and Answers in Attitude Surveys* (New York: Academic Press, 1981), pp. 179–201.

24. G. J. Spagna, "Questionnaires: Which Approach Do You Use?" *Journal of Advertising Research* (February–March 1984): 67–70.

25. E. A. Holdaway, "Different Response Categories and Questionnaire Response Patterns," *Journal of Experimental Education* (Winter 1971): 59.

26. G. F. Bishop, R. W. Oldendick, and A. J. Tuchfarber, "Effects of Filter Questions in Public Opinion Surveys," *Public Opinion Quarterly* (Winter 1983): 528–46; D. I. Hawkins and K. A. Coney, "Uninformed Response Error in Survey Research," *Journal of Marketing Research* (August 1981): 370–74; and K. C. Schneider, "Uninformed Response Rate in Survey Research," *Journal of Business Research* (April 1985): 153–62.

27. H. H. Friedman and J. R. Leefer, "Label versus Position in Rating Scales," *Journal of the Academy of Marketing Science* (Spring 1981): 88–92; and R. I. Haley and P. B. Case, "Testing Thirteen Attitude Scales for Agreement and Brand Discrimination," *Journal of Marketing* (Fall 1979): 20–32; and A. R. Wildt and M. B. Mazis, "Determinants of Scale Response: Label versus Position," *Journal of Marketing Research* (May 1978): 261–67.

28. F. M. Andrews, "Construct Validity and Error Components of Survey Measures," *Public Opinion Quarterly* (Summer 1984): 432; Gilbert A. Churchill, Jr., and J. P. Peter, "Research Design Effects on the Reliability of Rating Scales," *Journal of Marketing Research* (November 1984): 365–66; and D. E. Stem, Jr., C. W. Lamb Jr., and D. L. MacLachlan, "Remote versus Adjacent Scale Questionnaire Designs," *Journal of the Market Research Society* (January 1978): 3–13.

29. A. Schofield, "Adverbial Qualifiers for Adjectival Scales," *Journal of the Market Research Society* (July 1975): 204–07; and P. Bartram and D. Yelding, "Reply," *Journal of the Market Research Society* (July 1975): 207–8.

30. M. E. Goldberg, G. J. Gorn, and W. Gibson, "TV Messages for Snack and Breakfast Foods: Do They Influence Children's Preferences?" *Journal of Consumer Research* 5 (September 1978): 73–81.

31. For a recent construction of a multiitem scale, see Ajay K. Kohli, Bernard J. Jaworski, and Ajith Kumar, "MARKOR: A Measure of Market Orientation," *Journal of Marketing Research* 31 (November 1993): 467–77. A recent application may be found in Judy A. Siguaw, Gene Brown, and Robert E. Widing II, "The Influence of the Market Orientation of the Firm on Sales Force Behavior and Attitude," *Journal of Marketing Research* 31 (February 1994): 106–16.

32. For example, see Naresh K. Malhotra, "A Scale to Measure Self Concepts, Person Concepts, and Product Concepts," *Journal of Marketing Research* 18 (November 1981): 456–64.

33. Erin Anderson, Wujin Chu, and Barton Weitz, "Industrial Purchasing: An Empirical Exploration of the Buyclass Framework," *Journal of Marketing* 51 (July 1987): 71–86.

34. Eric A. Greenleaf, "Improving Rating Scale Measures by Detecting and Correcting Bias Components in Some Response Styles," *Journal of Marketing Research* 29 (May 1992): 176–88.

35. The true score model is not the only theory of measurement. See F. M. Lord and M. R. Novick, *Statistical Theories of Mental Test-Scores* (Reading, MA : Addison-Wesley, 1968).

36. William D. Perreault, Jr. and Laurence E. Leigh, "Reliability of Nominal Data Based on Qualitative Judgments," *Journal of Marketing Research* 25 (May 1989): 135–48; and J. Paul Peter, "Reliability: A Review of Psychometric Basics and Recent Marketing Practices," *Journal of Marketing Research* 16 (February 1979): 6–17.

37. M. N. Segal, "Alternate Form Conjoint Reliability," *Journal of Advertising Research* 4 (1984): 31–38.

38. L. J. Cronbach, "Coefficient Alpha and the Internal Structure of Tests," *Psychometrika* 16 (1951): 297–334.

39. Robert A. Peterson, "A Meta-Analysis of Cronbach's Coefficient Alpha," *Journal of Consumer Research* 21 (September 1994): 381–91.

40. David M. Zeitlin and Richard A. Westwood, "Measuring Emotional Response," *Journal of Advertising Research* (October–November 1986): 34–44.

41. Jagdip Singh and Gary K. Rhoads, "Boundary Role Ambiguity in Marketing-Oriented Positions: A Multidimensional, Multifaceted Operationalization," *Journal of Marketing Research* 28 (August 1991): 328–38; and J. Paul Peter, "Construct Validity: A Review of Basic Issues and Marketing Practices," *Journal of Marketing Research* 18 (May 1981): 133–45.

42. For further details on validity, see Rosann L. Spiro and Barton A. Weitz, "Adaptive Selling: Conceptualization, Measurement, and Nomological Validity," *Journal of Marketing Research* 27 (February 1990): 61–69; and N. Schmitt and D. M. Stults, "Methodology Review: Analysis of Multitrait-Multimethod Matrices," *Applied Psychological Measurement* 10 (1986): 1–22.

43. For a discussion of the generalizability theory and its applications in marketing research, see Joseph O. Rentz, "Generalizability Theory: A Comprehensive Method for Assessing and Improving the Dependability of Marketing Measures," *Journal of Marketing Research* 24 (February 1987), 19–28; and J. Paul Peter, "Reliability, Generalizability, and Consumer Research," in W. D. Perreault, Jr. (ed.). *Advances in Consumer Research*, vol. 4, Atlanta: Association for Consumer Research, 1977: pp. 394–400; and J. Paul Peter, "Reliability: A Review of Psychometric Basis and Recent Marketing Practices," *Journal of Marketing Research* 16 (February 1979), 6–17.

44. Del I. Hawkins, Gerald Albaum, and Roger Best, "Stapel Scale or Semantic Differential in Marketing Research?" *Journal of Marketing Research* 11 (August 1974): 318–22; and R. I. Haley and P. B. Case, "Testing

Thirteen Attitude Scales for Agreement and Brand Discrimination," *Journal of Marketing* (Fall 1979): 20–32; S. I. Lampert, "The Attitude Pollimeter: A New Attitude Scaling Device," *Journal of Marketing Research* (November 1979): 578–82; and Dennis Menezes and Norbert F. Elbert, "Alternative Semantic Scaling Formats for Measuring Store Image: An Evaluation," *Journal of Marketing Research* 16 (February 1979): 80–87.

45. Ingrid M. Martin and Sevgin Eroglu, "Measuring a Multidimensional Construct: Country Image," *Journal of Business Research* 28 (November 1993): 191–210.

46. Betsy Mckay, "Xerox Fights Trademark Battle," *Advertising Age International* (April 27, 1992): I-39.

47. R. E. Reidenbach and Donald P. Robin, "Some Initial Steps toward Improving the Measurement of Ethical Evaluations of Marketing Activities," *Journal of Business Ethics* 7 (1988): 871–79; and R. Eric Reidenbach and Donald P. Robin, "A Response to 'On Measuring Ethical Judgments,'" *Journal of Business Ethics* 14 (February 1995): 159–62.

48. The assistance of James Agarwal with the international marketing research example, the assistance of Mark Leach and Gina Miller in writing the ethics section, and the assistance of Mark Peterson in writing the computer applications section is gratefully acknowledged.

Questionnaire and Form Design

The questionnaire must motivate the respondent to cooperate, become involved, and provide complete and accurate answers.

◆

OBJECTIVES

After reading this chapter, the student should be able to:

1. Explain the purpose of a questionnaire and its objectives of asking questions that respondents can and will answer, encouraging respondents, and minimizing response error.
2. Describe the process of designing a questionnaire, the steps involved, and guidelines that must be followed at each step.
3. Discuss the observational form of data collection and specify the who, what, when, where, why, and way of behavior to be observed.
4. Discuss the considerations involved in designing questionnaires for international marketing research.
5. Understand the ethical issues involved in questionnaire design.
6. Discuss the use of microcomputers and mainframes in designing questionnaires.

OVERVIEW

Questionnaire or form design is an important step in formulating a research design. Once the researcher has specified the nature of research design (Chapters 3 through 7) and determined the scaling procedures (Chapters 8 and 9), he or she can develop a questionnaire or an observational form. This chapter discusses the importance of questionnaires and observational forms. Next, we describe the objectives of a questionnaire and the steps involved in designing questionnaires. We provide several guidelines for developing sound questionnaires. We also consider the design of observation forms. The considerations involved in designing questionnaires when conducting international marketing research are discussed. Several ethical issues that arise in questionnaire design are identified. The chapter concludes with a discussion of the use of microcomputers and mainframes in designing questionnaires.

We begin with an example to introduce questionnaire design and show the types of information that can be obtained from a questionnaire.

EXAMPLE
Driving at *Seventeen*

Seventeen magazine carefully designed a self-administered questionnaire to obtain information on the driving habits of females aged 15 to 21. Questions were asked about driver's license status, number of miles driven in the past week, reasons for using a car, specific car driven, how the car was acquired, cost of a new car, method of new car purchase, most important reasons for selecting a new car, make of car owned, information sources most important in new car selection, reasons for preferring an American- or foreign-made car, and degree of interest in seeing car ads in *Seventeen*. Different question formats and scaling techniques were employed. The questionnaire was mailed to 2,150 members of *Seventeen*'s Consumer Panel. The total of 1,143 returns received represented a response rate of 53.2%. Some of the major findings of the survey were the following:

- The average amount driven in the past week was 123 miles.
- The most important reasons for selecting a new car were styling and features, price, and gas mileage.
- Among drivers who owned their own cars, two-thirds owned a domestic model. One-fifth owned a Chevrolet; almost one-fifth owned a Ford.

Seventeen used this information to solicit advertising from major automobile companies and to plan articles that would appeal to readers.[1] ◆

QUESTIONNAIRES AND OBSERVATION FORMS

As discussed in Chapter 5, survey and observation are the two basic methods for obtaining quantitative primary data in descriptive research. Both methods require some procedure for standardizing the data collection process so that the data obtained are internally consistent and can be analyzed in a uniform and coherent manner. If 40 different interviewers conduct personal interviews or make observations in different parts of the country, the data they collect will not be comparable unless they follow specific guidelines and ask questions and record answers in a standard way. A standardized questionnaire or form will ensure comparability of the data, increase speed and accuracy of recording, and facilitate data processing.

Questionnaire Definition

questionnaire A structured technique for data collection consisting of a series of questions, written or verbal, that a respondent answers.

A **questionnaire**, whether it is called a schedule, interview form, or measuring instrument, is a formalized set of questions for obtaining information from respondents. Typically, a questionnaire is only one element of a data collection package that might also include (1) field work procedures, such as instructions for selecting, approaching, and questioning respondents (see Chapter 13); (2) some reward, gift, or payment offered to respondents; and (3) communication aids, such as maps, pictures, advertisements, and products (as in personal interviews) and return envelopes (in mail surveys). Regardless of the form of administration, a questionnaire is characterized by some specific objectives.

Objectives of a Questionnaire

Any questionnaire has three specific objectives. First, it must translate the information needed into a set of specific questions that the respondents can and will answer. Developing questions that respondents can and will answer and that will yield the desired information is difficult. Two apparently similar ways of posing a question may yield different information. Hence, this objective is a challenge.

Second, a questionnaire must uplift, motivate, and encourage the respondent to become involved in the interview, to cooperate, and to complete the interview. Incomplete interviews have limited usefulness at best. In designing a questionnaire, the researcher should strive to minimize respondent fatigue, boredom, and effort to minimize incompleteness and nonresponse.

Third, a questionnaire should minimize response error. The potential sources of error in research designs were discussed in Chapter 3, where response error was defined as the error that arises when respondents give inaccurate answers or when their answers are misrecorded or misanalyzed. A questionnaire can be a major source of response error. Minimizing this error is an important objective of questionnaire design. Research in Practice 10.1 illustrates how questionnaires can be designed to achieve these objectives.[2]

RESEARCH IN PRACTICE 10.1

Youth Research Achieves Questionnaire Objectives

Youth Research (YR) of Brookfield, Connecticut, conducts an omnibus survey of children every quarter. Typically, YR interviews 150 boys and girls between ages 6 and 8, along with 150 boys and girls between ages 9 and 12. YR uses mall intercepts of mothers in malls to recruit for its one-on-one interviews, which last eight minutes. The study obtains children's views on favorite snack foods, television shows, commercials, radio, magazines, buzzwords, and movies.

YR intentionally keeps its questionnaire to eight minutes because of attention span limits of children. YR President Karen Forcade notes that some clients attempt to meet all their research objectives with one study, instead of iteratively surveying, fine-tuning objectives, and resurveying. In doing so, these clients overlook attention limits of young respondents when developing questionnaires. "The questionnaires keep going through the approval process and people keep adding questions, 'Well let's ask this question, let's add that question, and why don't we talk about this also,' " Forcade said. "And so you end up keeping children 25 minutes in a central location study and they get kind of itchy." The response error increases and the quality of data suffers.

Forcade notes other lessons from interviewing children. When asking questions, interviewers should define the context to which the question refers. "It involves getting

(continued)

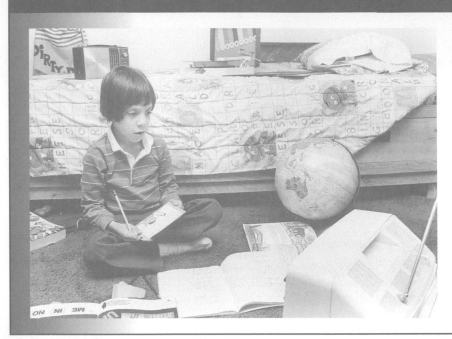

them to focus on things, putting them in a situation so that they can identify with it," Forcade said. "For example, when asking about their radio listening habits we said, 'What about when you're in Mom's car, do you listen to radio?' rather than, 'How often do you listen to radio? More than once a day, once a day, more than once a week?' Those are kind of big questions for little children."

Questionnaires designed by Youth Research to obtain children's views on favorite snack foods, television shows, commercials, radio, magazines, buzzwords, and movies attempt to minimize response error. ◆ Michael Weisbrot/Stock Boston.

QUESTIONNAIRE DESIGN PROCESS

The great weakness of questionnaire design is lack of theory. Because there are no scientific principles that guarantee an optimal or ideal questionnaire, questionnaire design is a skill acquired through experience. It is an art rather than a science. Stanley Payne's *The Art of Asking Questions*, published in 1951, is still a basic work in the field.[3] This section presents guidelines useful to beginning researchers in designing questionnaires. Although these rules can help you avoid major mistakes, the fine-tuning of a questionnaire comes from the creativity of a skilled researcher.

Questionnaire design will be presented as a series of steps, as shown in Figure 10.1, and we will present guidelines for each step. In practice the steps are interrelated and the development of a questionnaire will involve some iteration and looping. For example, the researcher may discover that respondents misunderstand all the possible wordings of a question. This may require a loop back to the earlier step of deciding on the question structure.[4]

SPECIFY THE INFORMATION NEEDED

The first step in questionnaire design is to specify the information needed. This is also the first step in the research design process. Note that as the research project progresses, the information needed becomes more and more clearly defined. It is helpful to review

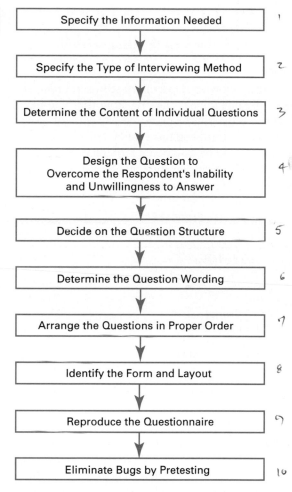

FIGURE 10.1

Questionnaire Design Process

the components of the problem and the approach, particularly the research questions, hypotheses, and characteristics that influence the research design. To further ensure that the information obtained fully addresses all the components of the problem, the researcher should prepare a set of dummy tables. A dummy table is a blank table used to catalog data. It describes how the analysis will be structured once the data have been collected.

It is also important to have a clear idea of the target population. The characteristics of the respondent group have a great influence on questionnaire design. Questions that are appropriate for college students may not be appropriate for housewives. Understanding is related to respondent socioeconomic characteristics.[5] Furthermore, poor understanding is associated with a high incidence of uncertain or no opinion responses. The more diversified the respondent group, the more difficult it is to design a single questionnaire appropriate for the entire group.

TYPE OF INTERVIEWING METHOD

An appreciation of how the type of interviewing method influences questionnaire design can be obtained by considering how the questionnaire is administered under each method (see Chapter 6). In personal interviews, respondents see the questionnaire and interact face to face with the interviewer. Thus, lengthy, complex, and varied questions can be asked. In telephone interviews the respondents interact with the interviewer, but they do not see the questionnaire. This limits the type of questions that can be asked to short and simple ones (see the department store patronage project). Mail questionnaires are self-administered, so the questions must be simple and detailed instructions must be provided. In computer-assisted interviewing (CAPI and CATI), complex skip patterns and randomization of questions to eliminate order bias can be easily accommodated. Questionnaires designed for personal and telephone interviews should be written in a conversational style.

DEPARTMENT STORE PATRONAGE PROJECT
Effect of Interviewing Method on Questionnaire Design

Mail Questionnaire

Please rank order the following department stores in order of your preference to shop at these stores. Begin by picking out the one store that you like most and assign it a number 1. Then find the second most preferred department store and assign it a number 2. Continue this procedure until you have ranked all the stores in order of preference. The least preferred store should be assigned a rank of 10.

No two stores should receive the same rank number.

The criterion of preference is entirely up to you. There is no right or wrong answer. Just try to be consistent.

Store	Rank Order
1. Lord & Taylor	_____
2. Macy's	_____
3. Kmart	_____
4. Rich's	_____
5. J.C. Penney	_____
6. Neiman Marcus	_____
7. Target	_____
8. Saks Fifth Avenue	_____
9. Sears	_____
10. Woolworth	_____

Telephone Questionnaire

I will read to you the names of some department stores. Please rate them in terms of your preference to shop at these stores. Use a six-point scale, where 1 denotes not so preferred and 6 denotes greatly preferred. Numbers between 1 and 6 reflect intermediate degrees of preference. Again, please remember that the higher the number, the greater the degree of preference. Now, please tell me your preference to shop at ... (**Read One Store at a Time.**)

Store	Not So Preferred					Greatly Preferred
1. Lord & Taylor	1	2	3	4	5	6
2. Macy's	1	2	3	4	5	6
3. Kmart	1	2	3	4	5	6
4. Rich's	1	2	3	4	5	6
5. J.C. Penney	1	2	3	4	5	6
6. Neiman Marcus	1	2	3	4	5	6
7. Target	1	2	3	4	5	6
8. Saks Fifth Avenue	1	2	3	4	5	6
9. Sears	1	2	3	4	5	6
10. Woolworth	1	2	3	4	5	6

Personal Questionnaire

(**Hand Department Store Cards to the Respondent.**) Here is a set of department store names, each written on a separate card. Please examine these cards carefully. (**Give**

Respondent Time.) Now, please examine these cards again and pull out that card with the name of the store you like the most, that is, your most preferred store for shopping. **(Record the Store Name and Keep this Card with You.)** Now, please examine the remaining nine cards. Of these remaining nine stores, what is your most preferred store for shopping? **(Repeat This Procedure Sequentially until the Respondent Has Only One Card Left.)**

	Store Rank	Name of Store
1.	1	
2.	2	
3.	3	
4.	4	
5.	5	
6.	6	
7.	7	
8.	8	
9.	9	
10.	10	◆

In the department store project example, ranking ten stores is too complex a task to be administered over the telephone. Instead, the simpler rating task, where the stores are rated one at a time, is selected to measure preferences. Note the use of cards to facilitate the ranking task in the personal interview. Interviewer instructions (typed in bold letters) are much more extensive in the personal interview. Another difference is that whereas the respondent records the ranks in the mail survey, the interviewer records the store names in the personal interview. The type of interviewing method also influences the content of individual questions.

INDIVIDUAL QUESTION CONTENT

Once the information needed is specified and the type of interviewing method decided, the next step is to determine individual question content: what to include in individual questions.[6]

Is the Question Necessary?

Every question in a questionnaire should contribute to the information needed or serve some specific purpose. If there is no satisfactory use for the data resulting from a question, that question should be eliminated.

In certain situations, however, questions may be asked that are not directly related to the needed information. It is useful to ask some neutral questions at the beginning of the questionnaire to establish involvement and rapport, particularly when the topic of the questionnaire is sensitive or controversial. Sometimes filler questions are asked to disguise the purpose or sponsorship of the project. For example, rather than limiting the questions to the brand of interest, questions about competing brands may also be included to disguise the sponsorship. Questions unrelated to the immediate problem may sometimes be included to generate client support for the project. At times, certain questions may be duplicated for the purpose of assessing reliability or validity.[7]

Are Several Questions Needed Instead of One?

Once we have ascertained that a question is necessary, we must make sure that it is sufficient to get the desired information. Sometimes several questions are needed to obtain the required information in an unambiguous manner. Consider the question, "Do you think Coca-Cola is a tasty and refreshing soft drink?" A yes answer will presumably be clear, but what if the answer is no? Does this mean that the respondent thinks that Coca-Cola is not tasty, that it is not refreshing, or that it is neither tasty nor refreshing? Such a question is called a **double-barreled question**, because two or more questions are combined into one. To obtain the required information, two distinct questions should be asked: "Do you think Coca-Cola is a tasty soft drink?" and "Do you think Coca-Cola is a refreshing soft drink?"

Another example of multiple questions embedded in a single question is the why question. In the context of the department store study, consider the question, "Why do you shop at Nike Town?" The possible answers may include: "to buy athletic shoes," "it is more conveniently located than other stores," and "it was recommended by my best friend." Each answer relates to a different question embedded in the why question. The first tells why the respondent shops in the athletic merchandise store, the second reveals what the respondent likes about Nike Town compared with other stores, and the third tells how the respondent learned about Nike Town. The three answers are not comparable and any one answer may not be sufficient. Complete information may be obtained by asking two separate questions: "What do you like about Nike Town compared with other stores?" and "How did you first happen to shop in Nike Town?" Most why questions about the use of a product or choice alternative involve two aspects: (1) attributes of the product and (2) influences leading to knowledge of it.[8]

double-barreled question
A single question that attempts to cover two issues. Such questions can be confusing to respondents and result in ambiguous responses.

A question such as "What do you like about Nike Town as compared to other stores?" will reveal several positive features of Nike Town. ◆ Steve Hall/Hedrick Blessing/Nike Town.

OVERCOMING INABILITY TO ANSWER

Researchers should not assume that respondents can provide accurate or reasonable answers to all questions. The researcher should attempt to overcome the respondents' inability to answer. Certain factors limit the respondents' ability to provide the desired information. The respondents may not be informed, may not remember, or may be unable to articulate certain types of responses.

Is the Respondent Informed?

Respondents are often asked about topics on which they are not informed. A husband may not be informed about monthly expenses for groceries and department store purchases, if it is the wife who makes these purchases, or vice versa. Research has shown that respondents will often answer questions even though they are uninformed, as the following example shows.

EXAMPLE
Unknown Answers

In one study, respondents were asked to express their degree of agreement or disagreement with the following statement: "The National Bureau of Consumer Complaints provides an effective means for consumers who have purchased a defective product to obtain relief." As many as 96.1% of the lawyers and 95% of the general public who responded expressed an opinion. Even with a "don't know" option in the response set, 51.9% of the lawyers and 75.0% of the general public still expressed an opinion about the National Bureau of Consumer Complaints. Why should these high response rates be problematic? Because there is no such entity as the National Bureau of Consumer Complaints![9] ◆

filter question An initial question in a questionnaire that screens potential respondents to ensure they meet the requirements of the sample.

In situations where not all respondents are likely to be informed about the topic of interest, **filter questions** that measure familiarity, product use, and past experience should be asked before questions about the topics themselves.[10] Filter questions enable the researcher to filter out respondents who are not adequately informed.

The department store questionnaire included questions related to ten different department stores, ranging from prestigious stores to discount stores. It was likely that many respondents would not be sufficiently informed about all the stores, so information on familiarity and frequency of patronage was obtained for each store. This allowed for separate analysis of data on stores about which the respondents were not informed. A "don't know" option appears to reduce uninformed responses without reducing the overall response rate or the response rate for questions about which the respondents have information. Hence, this option should be provided unless there are explicit reasons for not doing so.[11]

Can the Respondent Remember?

Many things that we might expect everyone to know are remembered by only a few. Test this on yourself. Can you remember the brand name of the shirt you are wearing, what you had for lunch a week ago, or what you were doing a month ago today? Further, do you know how many gallons of soft drinks you consumed during the last four weeks? Evidence indicates that consumers are particularly poor at remembering quantities of products consumed. In situations where factual data were available for comparison, it was found that consumer reports of product usage exceeded actual usage by 100% or more.[12]

telescoping A psychological phenomenon that takes place when an individual telescopes or compresses time by remembering an event as occurring more recently than it actually occurred.

The inability to remember leads to errors of omission, telescoping and creation. *Omission* is the inability to recall an event that actually took place. **Telescoping** takes place when an individual telescopes or compresses time by remembering an event as occurring more recently than it actually occurred.[13] For example, a respondent reports three trips to the supermarket in the last two weeks when, in fact, one of these trips was made 18 days ago. *Creation* error takes place when a respondent "remembers" an event that did not actually occur.

The ability to remember an event is influenced by (1) the event itself, (2) the time elapsed since the event, and (3) the presence or absence of events that would aid memory. We tend to remember events that are important or unusual or that occur frequently. People remember their wedding anniversary and birthday. Likewise, more recent events are remembered better. A grocery shopper is more likely to remember what he purchased on his last shopping trip as compared with what he bought three shopping trips ago.

Research indicates that questions that do not provide the respondent with cues to the event, and that rely on unaided recall, can underestimate the actual occurrence of an event. For example, unaided recall of soft drink commercials could be measured by questions like, "What brands of soft drinks do you remember being advertised last night on TV?" The aided recall approach attempts to stimulate the respondent's memory by providing cues related to the event of interest. The aided recall approach would list a number of soft drink brands and then ask, "Which of these brands were advertised last night on TV?" In presenting cues, the researcher must guard against biasing the responses by employing several successive levels of stimulation. The influence of stimulation on responses can then be analyzed to select an appropriate level of stimulation.

Can the Respondent Articulate?

Respondents may be unable to articulate certain types of responses. For example, if asked to describe the atmosphere of the department store they would prefer to patronize, most respondents may be unable to phrase their answers. On the other hand, if the respondents are provided with alternative descriptions of store atmosphere, they will be able to indicate the one they like the best. If the respondents are unable to articulate their responses to a question, they are likely to ignore that question and refuse to respond to the rest of the questionnaire. Thus, respondents should be given aids such as pictures, maps, and descriptions to help them articulate their responses.

OVERCOMING UNWILLINGNESS TO ANSWER

Even if respondents are able to answer a particular question, they may be unwilling to do so, either because too much effort is required, the situation or context may not seem appropriate for disclosure, no legitimate purpose or need for the information requested is apparent, or the information requested is sensitive.

Effort Required of the Respondents

Most respondents are unwilling to devote much effort to provide information. Suppose that the researcher is interested in determining from which departments in a store respondents purchased merchandise on their most recent shopping trip. This information can be obtained in at least two ways. The researcher could ask the respondent to list all the items purchased on her most recent shopping trip, or the researcher could provide a list of departments and ask the respondent to check the applicable ones. The second option is preferable, because it requires less effort from respondents.

Context

Some questions may seem appropriate in certain contexts but not in others. For example, questions about personal hygiene habits may be appropriate when asked in a survey sponsored by the American Medical Association but not in one sponsored by a cereal manufacturer. Respondents are unwilling to respond to questions they consider to be inappropriate for the given context. Sometimes, the researcher can manipulate the context in which the questions are asked so that the questions seem appropriate.

Legitimate Purpose

Respondents are also unwilling to divulge information that they do not see as serving a legitimate purpose. Why should a firm marketing cereals want to know their age, income, and occupation? Explaining why the data are needed can make the request for the information seem legitimate and may increase the respondents' willingness to answer. A statement such as, "To determine how the consumption of cereal and preferences for cereal brands vary among people of different ages, incomes and occupations, we need information on…" can make the request for information seem legitimate.

Sensitive Information

Respondents may be unwilling to disclose, at least accurately, sensitive information because this may cause embarrassment or threaten the respondent's prestige or self-image, or be seen as too personal and an invasion of privacy. If pressed for the answer, respondents may give biased responses, especially during personal interviews[14] (see Table 6.2). Sensitive topics include money, family life, political and religious beliefs, and involvement in accidents or crimes. The techniques described in the following section can be adopted to increase the likelihood of obtaining information that respondents are unwilling to give.

Increasing the Willingness of Respondents

Respondents may be encouraged to provide information which they are unwilling to give by the following techniques.[15]

1. Place sensitive topics at the end of the questionnaire. By then, initial mistrust has been overcome, rapport has been created, legitimacy of the project has been established, and respondents are more willing to give information.
2. Preface the question with a statement that the behavior of interest is common. For example, before requesting information on credit card debt, say "Recent studies show that most

Americans are in debt." This technique, called the use of counterbiasing statements, is further illustrated by the following example.

EXAMPLE
Public versus Private _____

A recent poll conducted by the Roper Organization for *U.S. News & World Report* sought to obtain information on whether personal information about political candidates or ordinary citizens should be disclosed to the public. This question was prefaced with the following statement: "The question of where to draw the line on the matter of privacy has been much debated, with some saying that the standards should be different for candidates for important public office than for ordinary citizens." This statement increased the willingness of the people to respond. ◆

3. Ask the question using the third-person technique (see Chapter 5): phrase the question as if it referred to other people.

4. Hide the question in a group of other questions that respondents are willing to answer. The entire list of questions can then be asked quickly.

5. Provide response categories rather than asking for specific figures.[16] Do not ask, "What is your household's annual income?" Instead, ask the respondent to check the appropriate income category: under $25,000, $25,001–$50,000, $50,001–$75,000 or over $75,000. In personal interviews, give the respondents cards that list the numbered choices. The respondents then indicate their responses by number.

6. Use randomized techniques. In these techniques, respondents are presented with two questions, one sensitive and the other a neutral question with a known probability of yes responses (e.g., "Is your birthday in March?"). They are asked to select one question randomly by flipping a coin, for example. The respondent then answers the selected question yes or no, without telling the researcher which question is being answered.[17] Given the overall probability of a yes response, the probability of selecting the sensitive question, and the probability of a yes response to the neutral question, the researcher can determine the probability of yes response to the sensitive question using the law of probability. The researcher cannot, however, determine which respondents have answered yes to the sensitive question.[18]

CHOOSING QUESTION STRUCTURE

A question may be unstructured or structured. In the following sections, we define unstructured questions and discuss their relative advantages and disadvantages and then consider the major types of structured questions: multiple-choice, dichotomous, and scales.[19]

Unstructured Questions

unstructured questions
Open-ended questions that respondents answer in their own words.

Unstructured questions are open-ended questions that respondents answer in their own words. They are also referred to as free-response or free-answer questions. The following are some examples:

- What is your occupation?
- What do you think of people who patronize discount department stores?
- Who is your favorite political figure?

Open-ended questions are good first questions on a topic. They enable the respondents to express general attitudes and opinions that can help the researcher interpret their responses to structured questions. Unstructured questions have a much less biasing influence on response than structured questions. Respondents are free to express any views. Their comments and explanations can provide the researcher with rich insights. Hence, unstructured questions are useful in exploratory research.

A principal disadvantage is that potential for interviewer bias is high. Whether the interviewers record the answers verbatim or write down only the main points, the data depend on the skills of the interviewers. Tape recorders should be used if verbatim reporting is important.

Another major disadvantage of unstructured questions is that the coding of responses is costly and time-consuming.[20] The coding procedures required to summarize responses in a format useful for data analysis and interpretation can be extensive. Implicitly, unstructured or open-ended questions give extra weight to respondents who are more articulate. Also, unstructured questions are not very suitable for self-administered questionnaires (mail and CAPI), because respondents tend to be briefer in writing than in speaking.

Precoding can overcome some of the disadvantages of unstructured questions. Expected responses are recorded in multiple-choice format, although the question is presented to the respondents as an open-ended question. Based on the respondent's reply, the interviewer selects the appropriate response category. Because the response alternatives are limited, this approach may be satisfactory when the respondent can easily formulate the response and when it is easy to develop precoded categories. For example, this approach may be used to obtain information on ownership of appliances. It has also been used successfully in business surveys, as shown by the following example.

EXAMPLE

Assessing Access Attitudes

A major telecommunications firm conducted a national telephone survey to determine the attitudes of businesses toward equal access. One of the questions was asked as an open-ended question with precoded responses.[21]

Which company or companies is your business presently using for long-distance telephone service? If more than one, please indicate the names of all the companies. **(Ask as an open-ended question. Allow for multiple responses and score as follows:)**

1. ____ MCI
2. ____ US SPRINT
3. ____ CONTEL
4. ____ AT&T
5. ____ Regional Bell operating company (insert name)
6. ____ Other (specify)
7. ____ Don't know/no answer ◆

In general, open-ended questions are useful in exploratory research and as opening questions. Otherwise, their disadvantages outweigh their advantages in a large survey.[22]

Structured Questions

Structured questions specify the set of response alternatives and the response format. A structured question may be multiple-choice, dichotomous, or a scale.

Multiple-Choice Questions   In multiple-choice questions, the researcher provides a choice of answers and respondents are asked to select one or more of the alternatives given. Consider the following question: Which of the following items have you purchased from a department store in the last two months? Please check as many as apply.

1. Women's dresses   ____
2. Men's apparel   ____
3. Children's apparel   ____
4. Cosmetics   ____
   .
   .
   .
16. Jewelry   ____
17. Other (please specify)   ____

Several of the issues discussed in Chapter 9 with respect to itemized rating scales also apply to multiple-choice answers. Two additional concerns in designing multiple-choice questions are the number of alternatives that should be included and order or position bias.

The response alternatives should include the set of all possible choices. The general guideline is to list all alternatives that may be of importance and to include an alternative labeled "other (please specify)," as shown above. The response alternatives should be mutually exclusive. Respondents should also be able to identify one, and only one, alternative, unless the researcher specifically allows two or more choices (for example, "Please indicate all the brands of soft drinks that you have consumed in the past week"). If the response alternatives are numerous, consider using more than one question to reduce the information processing demands on the respondents.

Order or **position bias** is the respondents' tendency to check an alternative merely because it occupies a certain position or is listed in a certain order. Respondents tend to check the first or the last statement in a list, particularly the first.[23] For a list of numbers (quantities or prices), there is a bias toward the central value on the list. To control for order bias, several forms of the questionnaire should be prepared with the order in which the alternatives are listed varied from form to form. Each alternative should appear once in each of the extreme positions, once in the middle, and once somewhere in between.[24]

Multiple-choice questions overcome many of the disadvantages of open-ended questions because interviewer bias is reduced and these questions are administered quickly. Also, coding and processing of data are much less costly and time-consuming. In self-administered questionnaires, respondent cooperation is improved if the majority of the questions are structured.

Multiple-choice questions are not without disadvantages. Considerable effort is required to design effective multiple-choice questions. Exploratory research using open-ended questions may be required to determine the appropriate response alternatives. It is difficult to obtain information on alternatives not listed. Even if an "other (please specify)" category is included, respondents tend to choose among the listed alternatives. In addition, showing respondents the list of possible answers produces biased responses.[25] There is also the potential for order bias.

dichotomous question
A structured question with only two response alternatives, such as yes and no.

Dichotomous Questions   A **dichotomous question** has only two response alternatives, such as yes or no, or agree or disagree. Often, the two alternatives of interest are supplemented by a neutral alternative, such as "no opinion," "don't know," "both," or "none," as in this example.[26]

Do you intend to buy a new automobile within the next six months?
_____ Yes
_____ No
_____ Don't know

Note that this question could also be framed as a multiple-choice question using response alternatives "Definitely will buy," "Probably will buy," "Probably will not buy," and so forth. The decision to use a dichotomous question should be guided by whether the respondents approach the issue as a yes-or-no question. Although decisions are often characterized as series of binary or dichotomous choices, the underlying decision-making process may reflect uncertainty that can best be captured by multiple-choice responses. For example, two individuals may be equally likely to buy a new automobile within the next six months if the economic conditions remain favorable. One individual, who is being optimistic about the economy, will answer yes, however, while the other, feeling pessimistic, will answer no.

Another issue in the design of dichotomous questions is whether to include a neutral response alternative. If it is not included, respondents are forced to choose between yes and no even if they feel indifferent. On the other hand, if a neutral alternative is included, respondents can avoid taking a position on the issue, thereby biasing the results. We offer the following guidelines. If a substantial proportion of the respondents can be expected to be neutral, include a neutral alternative. If the proportion of neutral respondents is expected to be small, avoid the neutral alternative.[27]

The general advantages and disadvantages of dichotomous questions are very similar to those of multiple-choice questions. Dichotomous questions are the easiest type of questions to code and analyze, but they have one acute problem. The response can be influenced by the wording of the question. To illustrate, the statement "Individuals are more to blame than social conditions for crime and lawlessness in this country," produced agreement from 59.6% of the respondents. On a matched sample that responded to the opposite statement, "Social conditions are more to blame than individuals for crime and lawlessness in this country," however, 43.2% (as opposed to 40.4%) agreed.[28] To overcome this problem, the question should be framed in one way on one-half of the questionnaires and in the opposite way on the other half. This is referred to as the split ballot technique.

Scales   Scales were discussed in detail in Chapters 8 and 9. To illustrate the difference between scales and other kinds of structural questions, consider the question about intentions to buy a new automobile. One way of framing this using a scale is as follows:

Do you intend to buy a new automobile within the next six months?				
Definitely will not buy	Probably will not buy	Undecided	Probably will buy	Definitely will buy
1	2	3	4	5

This is only one of several scales that could be used to ask this question (see Chapters 8 and 9).

CHOOSING QUESTION WORDING

Question wording is the translation of the desired question content and structure into words that respondents can clearly and easily understand. Deciding on question wording is perhaps the most critical and difficult task in developing a questionnaire. If a question is worded poorly, respondents may refuse to answer it or answer it incorrectly. The first condition, known as item nonresponse, can increase the complexity of data analysis.[29] The second condition leads to response error, discussed earlier. Unless the respondents and the researcher assign exactly the same meaning to the question, the results will be seriously biased.[30]

To avoid these problems, we offer the following guidelines: (1) Define the issue, (2) Use ordinary words, (3) Use unambiguous words, (4) Avoid leading questions, (5) Avoid implicit alternatives, (6) Avoid implicit assumptions, (7) Avoid generalizations and estimates, and (8) Use positive and negative statements.

Define the Issue

A question should clearly define the issue being addressed. Beginning journalists are admonished to define the issue in terms of who, what, when, where, why, and way (the six Ws).[31] These can also serve as guidelines for defining the issue in a question. (See Chapter 3 for an application of these guidelines to descriptive research.) Consider the following question:

> Which brand of shampoo do you use?

On the surface, this may seem to be a well-defined question, but we may reach a different conclusion when we examine it under the microscope of who, what, when, and where. "Who" in this question refers to the respondent. It is not clear, though, whether the researcher is referring to the brand the respondent uses personally or the brand used by the household. "What" is the brand of shampoo. But what if more than one brand of shampoo is being used? Should the respondent mention the most preferred brand, the brand used most often, the brand used most recently, or the brand that comes to mind first? "When" is not clear; does the researcher mean last time, last week, last month, last year, or ever? As for "where," it is implied that the shampoo is used at home, but this is not stated clearly. A better wording for this question would be:

A well-defined question is needed to determine which brand of shampoo a person uses. ◆ Bob Daemmrich/Image Works.

> Which brand or brands of shampoo have you personally used at home during the last one month? In case of more than one brand, please list all the brands that apply.

Use Ordinary Words

Ordinary words should be used in a questionnaire, and they should match the vocabulary level of the respondents.[32] When choosing words, keep in mind that the average person in the United States has a high school, not a college, education. For certain respondent groups, the education level is even lower. For example, the author did a project for a major telecommunications firm which operates primarily in rural areas. The average educational level in these areas is less than high school, and many respondents had only fourth- to sixth-grade education. Technical jargon should also be avoided. Most respondents do

Assessing the distribution of soft drinks requires the use of words as ordinary and commonplace as soft drinks themselves. ◆ C. J. Allen/Stock, Boston.

not understand technical marketing words. For example, instead of asking, "Do you think the distribution of soft drinks is adequate?" ask, "Do you think soft drinks are readily available when you want to buy them?"

Use Unambiguous Words

The words used in a questionnaire should have a single meaning that is known to the respondents.[33] A number of words that appear unambiguous have different meanings to different people.[34] These include "usually," "normally," "frequently," "often," "regularly," "occasionally," and "sometimes." Consider the following question:

In a typical month, how often do you shop in department stores?

_____ Never

_____ Occasionally

_____ Sometimes

_____ Often

_____ Regularly

The answers to this question are fraught with response bias, because the words used to describe category labels have different meanings for different respondents. Three respondents who shop once a month may check three different categories: occasionally, sometimes, and often. A much better wording for this question would be the following:

In a typical month, how often do you shop in department stores?

_____ Less than once

_____ 1 or 2 times

_____ 3 or 4 times

_____ More than 4 times

Note that this question provides a consistent frame of reference for all respondents. Response categories have been objectively defined, and respondents are no longer free to interpret them in their own way.

In deciding on the choice of words, researchers should consult a dictionary and thesaurus and ask the following questions of each word used:

1. Does it mean what we intended?
2. Does it have any other meanings?
3. If so, does the context make the intended meaning clear?
4. Does the word have more than one pronunciation?
5. Is there any word of similar pronunciation that might be confused with this word?
6. Is a simpler word or phrase suggested?

Avoid Leading or Biasing Questions

leading question A question that gives the respondent a clue as to what the answer should be.

A **leading question** is one that clues the respondent to what the answer should be, as in the following:

Do you think that patriotic Americans should buy imported
automobiles when that would put American labor out of work?

_____ Yes

_____ No

_____ Don't know

This question would lead respondents to a "No" answer. After all, how can patriotic Americans put American labor out of work? Therefore, this question would not help determine the preferences of Americans for imported versus domestic automobiles.

Bias may also arise when respondents are given clues about the sponsor of the project. Respondents tend to respond favorably toward the sponsor. The question, "Is Colgate your favorite toothpaste?" is likely to bias the responses in favor of Colgate. A more unbiased way of obtaining this information would be to ask, "What is your favorite toothpaste brand?" Likewise, the mention of a prestigious or nonprestigious name can bias the response; as in, "Do you agree with the American Dental Association that Colgate is effective in preventing cavities?"[35]

Avoid Implicit Alternatives

implicit alternative An alternative that is not explicitly expressed.

An alternative that is not explicitly expressed in the options is an **implicit alternative**. Making an implied alternative explicit may increase the percentage of people selecting that alternative, as in the two following questions.

1. Do you like to fly when traveling short distances?
2. Do you like to fly when traveling short distances, or would you rather drive?

In the first question, the alternative of driving is only implicit, but in the second question, it is explicit. The first question is likely to yield a greater preference for flying than the second question.

Questions with implicit alternatives should be avoided unless there are specific reasons for including them.[36] When the alternatives are close in preference or large in number, the alternatives at the end of the list have a greater chance of being selected. To overcome this bias, the split ballot technique should be used to rotate the order in which the alternatives appear.

Avoid Implicit Assumptions

Questions should not be worded so that the answer is dependent on implicit assumptions about what will happen as a consequence. Implicit assumptions are assumptions that are not stated in the question, as in the following example.[37]

1. Are you in favor of a balanced budget?
2. Are you in favor of a balanced budget if it would result in an increase in the personal income tax?

Implicit in question 1 are the consequences that will arise as a result of a balanced budget. There might be a cut in defense expenditures, an increase in personal income tax, a cut in social programs, and so on. Question 2 is a better way to word this question. Question 1's failure to make its assumptions explicit would result in overestimating the respondents' support for a balanced budget.

Avoid Generalizations and Estimates

Questions should be specific, not general. Moreover, questions should be worded so that the respondent does not have to make generalizations or compute estimates. Suppose that we were interested in households' annual per capita expenditure on groceries. If we asked respondents the question, "What is the annual per capita expenditure on groceries in your household?" they would first have to determine the annual expenditure on groceries by multiplying the monthly expenditure on groceries by 12 or the weekly expenditure by 52. Then they would have to divide the annual amount by the number of persons in the household. Most respondents would be unwilling or unable to perform these calculations. A better way of obtaining the required information would be to ask the respondents two simple questions: "What is the monthly (or weekly) expenditure on groceries in your household?" and "How many members are there in your household?" The researcher can then perform the necessary calculations.

Use Positive and Negative Statements

Many questions, particularly those measuring attitudes and lifestyles, are worded as statements to which respondents indicate their degree of agreement or disagreement. Evidence indicates that the response obtained is influenced by the directionality of the statements: whether they are stated positively or negatively. In these cases, it is better to use dual statements, some of which are positive and others are negative. Two different questionnaires could be prepared. One questionnaire would contain half negative and half positive statements in an interspersed way. The direction of these statements would be reversed in the other questionnaire. An example of dual statements was provided in the summated Likert scale in Chapter 9 designed to measure attitudes toward Sears.

DETERMINING THE ORDER OF QUESTIONS

Opening Questions

The opening questions can be crucial in gaining the confidence and cooperation of respondents. They should be interesting, simple, and nonthreatening. Questions that ask respondents for their opinions can be good opening questions, because most people like to express their opinions. Sometimes such questions are asked even though they are unrelated to the research problem and their responses are not analyzed.[38] The American Chicle Youth Poll is a good example.

EXAMPLE

Opening Opinion Question Opens the Door to Cooperation _____

The American Chicle Youth Poll was commissioned by the American Chicle Group, Warner-Lambert Company, and conducted by the Roper Organization, Inc. A nationwide cross section of 1,000 American young people, aged 8 to 17 and attending school, was interviewed. The questionnaire contained a simple opening question asking opinion about living in the local town or city.[39]

To begin with, I'd like to know, how much do you like living in this (town/city)? Would you say you like it a lot, a little, or not too much?

A lot   _____
A little   _____
Not too much   _____
Don't know   _____ ◆

In some instances, it is necessary to qualify the respondents, or determine whether the respondent is eligible to participate in the interview. In these cases, the qualifying questions serve as the opening questions.

DEPARTMENT STORE PATRONAGE PROJECT

Opening Question _____

In the department store project, the questionnaire was to be answered by the male or female head of household who did most of the shopping in department stores. The first question asked was, "Who in your household does most of the shopping in department stores?" Thus, the opening question helped identify the eligible respondents. It also gained cooperation because of its simple and nonthreatening nature. ◆

Type of Information

classification information Socioeconomic and demographic characteristics used to classify respondents.

identification information A type of information obtained in a questionnaire that includes name, address and phone number.

The type of information obtained in a questionnaire may be classified as (1) basic information, (2) classification information, and (3) identification information. Basic information relates directly to the research problem. **Classification information**, consisting of socioeconomic and demographic characteristics, is used to classify the respondents and understand the results. **Identification information** includes name, address, and telephone number. Identification information may be obtained for a variety of purposes, including verifying that the respondents listed were actually interviewed and remitting promised incentives. As a general guideline, basic information should be obtained first, followed by classification, and finally identification information. The basic information is of greatest importance to the research project and should be obtained first, before we risk alienating the respondents by asking a series of personal questions.

Difficult Questions

Difficult questions or questions that are sensitive, embarrassing, complex, or dull should be placed late in the sequence. After rapport has been established and the respondents become involved, they are less likely to object to these questions. Thus, in the department store patronage project, information about credit card debt was asked at the end of the section on basic information. Likewise, income should be the last question in the classification section, and telephone number should be the final item in the identification section.

Effect on Subsequent Questions

Questions asked early in a sequence can influence the responses to subsequent questions. As a rule of thumb, general questions should precede the specific questions. This prevents specific questions from biasing responses to the general questions. Consider the following sequence of questions:

Q1: "What considerations are important to you in selecting a department store?"

Q2: "In selecting a department store, how important is convenience of location?"

Note that the first question is general whereas the second is specific. If these questions were asked in the reverse order, respondents would be clued about convenience of location and would be more likely to give this response to the general question.

funnel approach A strategy for ordering questions in a questionnaire in which the sequence starts with the general questions, which are followed by progressively specific questions, to prevent specific questions from biasing general questions.

Going from general to specific is called the **funnel approach**. The funnel approach is particularly useful when information has to be obtained about respondents' general choice behavior and their evaluations of specific products.[40] Sometimes the inverted-funnel approach may be useful. In this approach, questioning starts with specific questions and concludes with the general questions. The respondents are compelled to provide specific information before making general evaluations. This approach is useful when respondents have no strong feelings or have not formulated a point of view.

Logical Order

Questions should be asked in a logical order. All questions that deal with a particular topic should be asked before beginning a new topic. When switching topics, brief transitional phrases should be used to help respondents switch their train of thought.

branching question A question used to guide an interviewer through a survey by directing the interviewer to different spots on the questionnaire depending on the answers given.

Branching questions should be designed carefully.[41] **Branching questions** direct respondents to different places in the questionnaire based on how they respond to the question at hand. These questions ensure that all possible contingencies are covered. They also help reduce interviewer and respondent error and encourage complete responses. Skip patterns based on the branching questions can become quite complex. A simple way to account for all contingencies is to prepare a flowchart of the logical possibilities and then develop branching questions and instructions based on it. A flowchart used to assess the use of credit in store purchases is shown in Figure 10.2.

Placement of branching questions is important and the following guidelines should be followed: (1) the question being branched (the one to which the respondent is being directed) should be placed as close as possible to the question causing the branching, and (2) the branching questions should be ordered so that the respondents cannot anticipate what additional information will be required. Otherwise, the respondents may discover that they can avoid detailed questions by giving certain answers to branching questions. For example, the respondents should first be asked if they have seen any of the listed commercials before they are asked to evaluate commercials. Otherwise, the respondents will quickly discover that stating that they have seen a commercial leads to detailed questions about that commercial and that they can avoid detailed questions by stating that they have not seen the commercial.

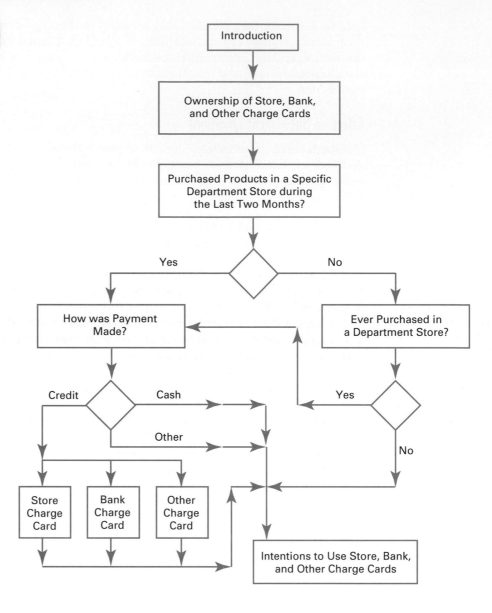

FIGURE 10.2

*Flowchart
for Questionnaire
Design*

FORM AND LAYOUT

The format, spacing, and positioning of questions can have a significant effect on the results,[42] particularly self-administered questionnaires. Experiments on mail questionnaires for the 1980 U.S. census revealed that questions at the top of the page received more attention than those at the bottom. Instructions printed in red made little difference except that they made the questionnaire appear more complicated to the respondents.[43]

It is a good practice to divide a questionnaire into several parts. Several parts may be needed for questions pertaining to the basic information.

DEPARTMENT STORE PATRONAGE PROJECT
Form and Layout

In the department store project, the questionnaire was divided into several parts. Part A contained the qualifying question, information on familiarity, frequency of shopping, evaluation of the ten stores on each of the eight factors of the choice criteria, and preference ratings for the ten stores. Part B contained questions on the relative importance attached to each factor of the choice criteria and the preference rankings of the ten stores. Part C obtained information on lifestyles. Finally, part D obtained standard demographic and identification information. Identification information was obtained along with classification information, rather than in a separate part, so as to minimize its prominence. Dividing the questionnaire into parts in this manner provided natural transitions. It also alerted the interviewer and the respondent that, as each part began, a different kind of information was being solicited. ◆

precoding In questionnaire design, assigning a code to every conceivable response before data collection.

The questions in each part should be numbered, particularly when branching questions are used. Numbering of questions also makes the coding of responses easier. In addition, the questionnaires should preferably be precoded. In **precoding**, the codes to enter in the computer are printed on the questionnaire. Typically, the code identifies the line number and the column numbers in which a particular response will be entered. Research in Practice 10.2 gives an example of a precoded questionnaire. To conserve space, only part of the questionnaire is reproduced.[44] Note that when CATI or CAPI are used, the precoding is built into the software. Coding of questionnaires is explained in more detail in Chapter 14 on data preparation.

The questionnaires themselves should be numbered serially. This facilitates the control of questionnaires in the field as well as the coding and analysis. Numbering makes it easy to account for the questionnaires and to determine if any have been lost. A possible exception to this rule is mail questionnaires. If these are numbered, respondents assume that a given number identifies a particular respondent. Some respondents may refuse to participate or answer differently under these conditions. Recent research suggests, however, that this loss of anonymity has little, if any, influence on the results.

REPRODUCTION OF THE QUESTIONNAIRE

How a questionnaire is reproduced for administration can influence the results. For example, if the questionnaire is reproduced on poor-quality paper or is otherwise shabby in appearance, the respondents will think that the project is unimportant and the quality of response will be adversely affected. Therefore, the questionnaire should be reproduced on good-quality paper and have a professional appearance.

When a printed questionnaire runs to several pages, it should take the form of a booklet rather than a number of sheets of paper clipped or stapled together. Booklets are easier for the interviewer and the respondents to handle and do not easily come apart with use. They allow the use of a double-page format for questions and look more professional.

Each question should be reproduced on a single page (or double-page spread). A researcher should avoid splitting a question, including its response categories. Split questions can mislead the interviewer or the respondent into thinking that the question has ended at the end of a page. This will result in answers based on incomplete questions.

RESEARCH IN PRACTICE 10.2

Example of a Precoded Survey

THE AMERICAN LAWYER
A Confidential Survey of Our Subscribers

(5-1)

(Please ignore the numbers alongside the answers. They are only to help us in data processing.)

1. Considering all the times you pick it up, about how much time, in total, do you spend in reading or looking through a typical issue of THE AMERICAN LAWYER?

(6)

Less than 30 minutes . . . .❏-1	1½ hours to 1 hour 59 minutes . . . .❏-4
30 to 59 minutes . . . .❏-2	2 hours to 2 hours 59 minutes . . . .❏-5
1 hour to 1 hour 29 minutes. . . .❏-3	3 hours or more . . . .❏-6

2. After you have finished reading an issue of THE AMERICAN LAWYER, what do you usually do with it?

(7)

Save entire issue for firm library . . . .❏-1	Place in a waiting room/
Save entire issue for home use . . . . .❏-2	public area . . . .❏-5
Pass it along (route it) to others	Discard it . . . .❏-6
in my company . . . .❏-3	
Clip and save items of interest. . . . . .❏-4	Other_____
	(Please specify) ❏-7

3. Not including yourself, how many other people, on the average, would you estimate read or look through your personal copy (not the office copy) of THE AMERICAN LAWYER?

(7)

Number of additional readers per copy:

One . . . .❏-1	Two . . . .❏-2	Three . . . .❏-3
Four . . . .❏-4	Five . . . .❏-5	Six . . . .❏-6
Seven . . . . . .❏-7	8–9 . . . .❏-8	10–14 . . . .❏-9
15 or more . . .❏-x	None . . . .❏-0	

Vertical response columns should be used for individual questions. It is easier for interviewers and respondents to read down a single column rather than sideways across several columns. Sideways formatting and splitting, done frequently to conserve space, should be avoided. Consider the following example.

What was the approximate gross income of your household from all sources, before taxes, in the past year?

__ Under $10,100	__$25,000 to $29,999	__ $45,000 to $49,999
__ $10,000 to $14,999	__$30,000 to $34,999	__ $50,000 to $54,999
__ $15,000 to $19,999	__$35,000 to $39,999	__ $55,000 to $59,999
__ $20,000 to $24,999	__$40,000 to $44,999	__ Over $60,000

These response categories should be listed in a single column, rather than in three columns as shown. Grids are useful when there are a number of related questions that use the same set of response categories.[45]

The tendency to crowd questions together to make the questionnaire look shorter should be avoided. Overcrowded questions with little blank space between them can lead to errors in data collection and yield shorter and less informative replies. Moreover, they give the impression that the questionnaire is complex and can result in lower cooperation and completion rates. Although shorter questionnaires are more desirable than longer ones, the reduction in size should not be obtained at the expense of crowding.[46]

Directions or instructions for individual questions should be placed as close to the questions as possible. Instructions relating to how the question should be administered or answered by the respondent should be placed just before the question. Instructions concerning how the answer should be recorded or how the probing should be done should be placed after the question (for more information on probing and other interviewing procedures, see Chapter 13). It is a common practice to distinguish instructions from questions by using distinctive type (such as capital or boldfaced letters).

Although color does not influence response rates to questionnaires, it can be employed advantageously in some respects. Color coding is useful for branching questions. The next question to which the respondent is directed is printed in a color that matches the space in which the answer to the branching question was recorded. Surveys directed at different respondent groups can be reproduced on paper of a different color. In a mail survey conducted for a major telecommunications firm, the business questionnaire was printed on white paper and the household questionnaire was printed on yellow paper.

The questionnaire should be reproduced in such a way that it is easy to read and answer. The type should be large and clear. Reading the questionnaire should not impose a strain.

Several technologies allow researchers to obtain better print quality and simultaneously reduce costs. One effort along these lines resulted in a lowering of printing costs from $1,150 to $214.[47]

PRETESTING

pretesting Testing the questionnaire on a small sample of respondents for the purpose of improving the questionnaire by identifying and eliminating potential problems.

Pretesting refers to testing the questionnaire on a small sample of respondents to identify and eliminate potential problems.[48] Even the best questionnaire can be improved by pretesting. As a general rule, a questionnaire should not be used in the field survey without adequate pretesting.[49] A pretest should be extensive. All aspects of the questionnaire should be tested, including question content, wording, sequence, form and layout, question difficulty, and instructions. The respondents in the pretest should be similar to those who will be included in the actual survey in terms of background characteristics, familiarity with the topic, and attitudes and behaviors of interest.[50] In other words, respondents for the pretest and for the actual survey should be drawn from the same population.

Pretests are best done by personal interviews, even if the actual survey is to be conducted by mail or telephone, because interviewers can observe respondents' reactions and attitudes. After the necessary changes have been made, another pretest could be conducted by mail or telephone if those methods are to be used in the actual survey. The latter pretests should reveal problems peculiar to the interviewing method. To the extent possible, a pretest should involve administering the questionnaire in an environment and context similar to that of the actual survey.

A variety of interviewers should be used for pretests. The project director, the researcher who developed the questionnaire, and other key members of the research team should conduct some pretest interviews. This will give them a good feel for potential problems and the nature of the expected data. Most of the pretest interviews, however, should be conducted by regular interviewers. It is good practice to employ both experienced and new interviewers. Experienced interviewers can easily perceive uneasiness, confusion, and resistance in the respondents, and new interviewers can help the researcher identify interviewer-related problems. Ordinarily the pretest sample size is small, varying from 15 to 30 respondents for the initial testing, depending on the heterogeneity of the target population. The sample size can increase substantially if the pretesting involves several stages.

Protocol analysis and debriefing are two commonly used procedures in pretesting. In protocol analysis, the respondent is asked to "think aloud" while answering the questionnaire, as explained in Chapter 8. Typically, the respondent's remarks are tape-recorded and analyzed to determine the reactions invoked by different parts of the questionnaire. Debriefing occurs after the questionnaire has been completed. Respondents are told that the questionnaire they just completed was a pretest and the objectives of pretesting are described to them. They are then asked to describe the meaning of each question, to explain their answers, and to state any problems they encountered while answering the questionnaire.

Editing involves correcting the questionnaire for the problems identified during pretesting. After each significant revision of the questionnaire, another pretest should be conducted, using a different sample of respondents. Sound pretesting involves several stages. One pretest is a bare minimum. Pretesting should be continued until no further changes are needed.

Finally, the responses obtained from the pretest should be coded and analyzed. The analysis of pretest responses can serve as a check on the adequacy of the problem definition and the data and analysis required to obtain the necessary information. The dummy tables prepared before developing the questionnaire will point to the need for the various sets of data. If the response to a question cannot be related to one of the preplanned dummy tables, either those data are superfluous or some relevant analysis has not been foreseen. If part of a dummy table remains empty, a necessary question may have been omitted. Analysis of pretest data helps to ensure that all data collected will be utilized and that the questionnaire will obtain all the necessary data.[51]

Table 10.1 summarizes the questionnaire design process in the form of a checklist.

OBSERVATIONAL FORMS

Forms for recording observational data are easier to construct than questionnaires. The researcher need not be concerned with the psychological impact of the questions and the way they are asked. Instead, the researcher need only develop a form that identifies the required information clearly, makes it easy for the field worker to record the information accurately, and simplifies the coding, entry, and analysis of data.

Observational forms should specify the who, what, when, where, why, and way of behavior to be observed. In the department store patronage project, an observational form for the study of purchases would include space for all the following information.

DEPARTMENT STORE PATRONAGE PROJECT
Observation

Who: Purchasers, browsers, males, females, parents with children, children alone.

What: Products and brands considered, products and brands purchased, size, price of package inspected, influence of children or other family members.

TABLE 10.1	*Questionnaire Design Checklist*

Step 1   Specify The Information Needed

1. Ensure that the information obtained fully addresses all the components of the problem. Review components of the problem and the approach, particularly the research questions, hypotheses, and characteristics that influence the research design.
2. Prepare a set of dummy tables.
3. Have a clear idea of the target population.

Step 2   Type of Interviewing Method

1. Review the type of interviewing method determined based on considerations discussed in Chapter 6.

Step 3   Individual Question Content

1. Is the question necessary?
2. Are several questions needed instead of one to obtain the required information in an unambiguous manner?
3. Do not use double-barreled questions.

Step 4   Overcome Inability and Unwillingness to Answer

1. Is the respondent informed?
2. If the respondent is not likely to be informed, filter questions that measure familiarity, product use, and past experience should be asked before questions about the topics themselves.
3. Can the respondent remember?
4. Avoid errors of omission, telescoping, and creation.
5. Questions that do not provide the respondent with cues can underestimate the actual occurrence of an event.
6. Can the respondent articulate?
7. Minimize the effort required of the respondent.
8. Is the context in which the questions are asked appropriate?
9. Make the request for information seem legitimate.
10. If the information is sensitive:
    a. Place sensitive topics at the end of the questionnaire.
    b. Preface the question with a statement that the behavior of interest is common.
    c. Ask the question using the third-person technique.
    d. Hide the question in a group of other questions that respondents are willing to answer.
    e. Provide response categories rather than asking for specific figures.
    f. Use randomized techniques, if appropriate.

Step 5   Choose Question Structure

1. Open-ended questions are useful in exploratory research and as opening questions.
2. Use structured questions whenever possible.
3. In multiple-choice questions, the response alternatives should include the set of all possible choices and should be mutually exclusive.
4. In a dichotomous question, if a substantial proportion of the respondents can be expected to be neutral, include a neutral alternative.
5. Consider the use of the split ballot technique to reduce order bias in dichotomous and multiple-choice questions.
6. If the response alternatives are numerous, consider using more than one question to reduce the information processing demands on the respondents.

Step 6   Choose Question Wording

1. Define the issue in terms of who, what, when, where, why, and way (the six Ws).
2. Use ordinary words. Words should match the vocabulary level of the respondents.
3. Avoid ambiguous words: usually, normally, frequently, often, regularly, occasionally, sometimes, etc.
4. Avoid leading questions that clue the respondent to what the answer should be.
5. Avoid implicit alternatives that are not explicitly expressed in the options.
6. Avoid implicit assumptions.

(continued)

TABLE 10.1   *(continued)*

7. Respondent should not have to make generalizations or compute estimates.
8. Use positive and negative statements.

Step 7   Determine the Order of Questions
1. The opening questions should be interesting, simple, and nonthreatening.
2. Qualifying questions should serve as the opening questions.
3. Basic information should be obtained first, followed by classification and finally identification information.
4. Difficult, sensitive, or complex questions should be placed late in the sequence.
5. General questions should precede the specific questions.
6. Questions should be asked in a logical order.
7. Branching questions should be designed carefully to cover all possible contingencies.
8. The question being branched should be placed as close as possible to the question causing the branching, and (2) the branching questions should be ordered so that the respondents cannot anticipate what additional information will be required.

Step 8   Form and Layout
1. Divide a questionnaire into several parts.
2. Questions in each part should be numbered.
3. The questionnaire should be precoded.
4. The questionnaires themselves should be numbered serially.

Step 9   Reproduce the Questionnaire
1. The questionnaire should have a professional appearance.
2. A booklet format should be used for long questionnaires.
3. Each question should be reproduced on a single page (or double-page spread).
4. Vertical response columns should be used.
5. Grids are useful when there are a number of related questions that use the same set of response categories.
6. The tendency to crowd questions to make the questionnaire look shorter should be avoided.
7. Directions or instructions for individual questions should be placed as close to the questions as possible.

Step 10   Pretest
1. Pretesting should always be done.
2. All aspects of the questionnaire should be tested, including question content, wording, sequence, form and layout, question difficulty, and instructions.
3. The respondents in the pretest should be similar to those who will be included in the actual survey.
4. Begin the pretest by using personal interviews.
5. The pretest should also be conducted by mail or telephone if those methods are to be used in the actual survey.
6. A variety of interviewers should be used for pretests.
7. The pretest sample size is small, varying from 15 to 30 respondents for the initial testing.
8. Use protocol analysis and debriefing to identify problems.
9. After each significant revision of the questionnaire, another pretest should be conducted, using a different sample of respondents.
10. The responses obtained from the pretest should be coded and analyzed.

When: Day, hour, date of observation.
Where: Inside the store, at the checkout counter, in a particular department within the store.
Why: Influence of price, brand name, package size, promotion, family members on the purchase.
Way: Personal observer disguised as sales clerk, undisguised personal observer, hidden camera, obtrusive mechanical device. ◆

The form and layout as well as the reproduction of observational forms should follow the same guidelines discussed for questionnaires. A well-designed form permits field workers to record individual observations but not to summarize observations, as that would lead to error. Finally, like questionnaires, observational forms also require adequate pretesting.

INTERNATIONAL MARKETING RESEARCH

The questionnaire or research instrument should be adapted to the specific cultural environment and should not be biased in terms of any one culture. This requires careful attention to each step of the questionnaire design process. The information needed should be clearly specified. It is important to take into account any differences in underlying consumer behavior, decision-making processes, psychographics, lifestyles, and demographic variables. In the context of demographic characteristics, information on marital status, education, household size, occupation, income, and dwelling unit may have to be specified differently for different countries, as these variables may not be directly comparable across countries. For example, household definition and size varies greatly, given the extended family structure in some countries and the practice of two or even three families living under the same roof.

Although personal interviewing is the dominant survey method in international marketing research, different interviewing methods may be used in different countries. Hence, the questionnaire may have to be suitable for administration by more than one method. For ease of comprehension and translation, it is desirable to have two or more simple questions rather than a single complex question. In overcoming the inability to answer, the variability in the extent to which respondents in different cultures are informed about the subject matter of the survey should be taken into account. Respondents in some parts of the world—for example, in the Far East or the former Soviet Union—may not be as well-informed as people in the United States.

The use of unstructured or open-ended questions may be desirable if the researcher lacks knowledge about the determinants of response in other countries. Because they do not impose any response alternatives, unstructured questions also reduce cultural bias, but they are more affected by differences in educational levels than structured questions. They should be used with caution in countries with high illiteracy rates. When appropriately used, unstructured questions can provide rich insights, as in the research S. C. Johnson and Company conducted in Japan.

EXAMPLE
Johnson Solidifies the Japanese Oil Solidifier Market _____

S. C. Johnson has succeeded in cracking the market in Japan despite rumors of difficulties in working with the Japanese. Johnson derives about 60% of its $3 billion–plus worldwide sales from overseas. Asia-Pacific is the fastest growing region, and Japanese sales grew to over $300 million in 1994. The secret behind this success is that Johnson directed efforts studying the market and conducted extensive consumer research.

In a questionnaire designed to investigate tempura oil, several unstructured or open-ended questions were used. The use of open-ended questions was justified because

(1) the response options to these questions could not be easily predetermined, (2) Japanese women are educated and would therefore have no difficulty in responding, and (3) the questionnaire would be administered by the interviewers during in-home interviews. The kind of unstructured questions in the questionnaire included "What problems do you experience in using oil for cooking tempura in the home?" and "What can manufacturers do to address these problems?"

The unstructured questions resulted in several useful findings. For example, it was identified that disposing of hot oil used for tempura was a problem for Japanese households. It not only clogged the plumbing but also polluted Japan's rivers and streams. Furthermore, disposing tempura oil as a solid waste would be greatly preferred by the Japanese. Based on the findings, the company developed a new product, tempura oil solidifier, which has the capability to dispose oil as a solid waste.

By following a similar process, Johnson also developed a special formula of grout cleaner to remove mildew. Both these products are being launched in other countries as well. Japan offers a conducive environment for new products because Japanese consumers are very innovative and always willing to try something new. "Japan is probably a close second [to the United States] in developing our products," says Mr. Carpenter, President and CEO of S. C. Johnson.[52] ◆

As in the preceding example, the questionnaire may have to be translated for administration in different cultures. The researcher must ensure that the questionnaires in different languages are equivalent. The special procedures designed for this purpose are discussed in Chapter 23.

Pretesting the questionnaire is complicated in international research because linguistic equivalence must be pretested. Two sets of pretests are recommended. The translated questionnaire should be pretested on monolingual subjects in their native language, and the original and translated versions should also be administered to bilingual subjects. The pretest data from administration of the questionnaire in different countries or cultures should be analyzed and the pattern of responses compared to detect any cultural biases.

ETHICS IN MARKETING RESEARCH

The researcher must be mindful of the demands placed on the respondents when designing questionnaires and observation forms. Because the administration of the questionnaire is a substantial intrusion by the researcher, several ethical concerns arise pertaining to the researcher-respondent relationship. Ethical issues impinging on the researcher-client relationship may also have to be addressed.

In consideration of the respondents, exceedingly long questionnaires should be avoided. According to the Professional Marketing Research Society of Canada, "an overly long questionnaire may vary in length of time depending on variables, such as subject matter, the number of open-ended questions, and the frequency of use of complex scales. As a general guideline, the following are generally considered 'overly long': a personal interview in-home over 60 minutes, a telephone interview over 30 minutes, a mall-intercept interview over 30 minutes."[53] Overly long questionnaires are burdensome on the respondents and adversely affect the quality of responses. Similarly, questions that are confusing, exceed the respondents' ability, are difficult, or otherwise improperly worded, should be avoided.

Overly sensitive questions deserve special attention. A real ethical dilemma exists for researchers investigating social problems such as poverty, drug use, and sexually transmitted diseases like AIDS, or conducting studies of highly personal products like feminine hygiene products or financial products.[54] Candid and truthful responses are needed to generate meaningful results. But how do we obtain such data without asking sensitive questions that invade respondents' privacy? When asking sensitive questions, researchers should attempt to minimize the discomfort of the respondents. It should be made clear at the beginning of the questionnaire that respondents are not obligated to answer any question that makes them uncomfortable.[55]

One researcher-client issue worth mentioning is piggybacking, which occurs when a questionnaire contains questions pertaining to more than one client. One client's questions take up a part of the questionnaire, while a second client's study takes up the rest. Although there is some risk that one study will contaminate the other or that the questionnaire may not be very coherent, piggybacking can substantially reduce the cost. Thus, it can be a good way for clients with limited research budgets to collect primary data they would not be able to afford otherwise. In these cases all clients must be aware of and consent to the arrangement. Unfortunately, piggybacking is sometimes used without disclosure to the clients for the sole purpose of increasing the researcher's profit. This is unethical.

Finally, the researcher has the ethical responsibility of designing the questionnaire so as to obtain the required information in an unbiased manner. Deliberately biasing the questionnaire in a desired direction—for example, by asking leading questions—cannot be condoned. In deciding the question structure, the most appropriate rather than the most convenient option should be adopted, as illustrated by the next example. Also, the questionnaire should be thoroughly pretested before field-work begins, or an ethical breach has occurred.

EXAMPLE
Questioning International Marketing Ethics

In designing a questionnaire, open-ended questions may be most appropriate if the response categories are not known. In a study designed to identify ethical problems in international marketing, series of open-ended questions were used. The objective of the survey was to elicit the three most frequently encountered ethical problems, in order of priority, to Australian firms that engage in international marketing activities. After reviewing the results, the researcher tabulated and categorized them into ten categories that occurred most often: traditional small-scale bribery; large-scale bribery; gifts, favors, and entertainment; pricing; inappropriate products or technology; tax evasion practices; illegal or immoral activities; questionable commissions to channel members; cultural differences, and involvement in political affairs. The sheer number of categories indicates that international marketing ethics should probably be questioned more closely! The use of structured questions in this case, although more convenient, would have been inappropriate, raising ethical concerns.[56] ◆

COMPUTER APPLICATIONS

Commercial software packages enable researchers to design and administer questionnaires using microcomputers and mainframes.[57] This eliminates the nightmare of index cards, complicated skip routines, and tedious repetitive tasks involved in developing questionnaires by hand. Electronic questionnaire design allows researchers to use any type of question format and eliminates the data entry and verification tasks. Furthermore, the output is automatically recorded and can be directly imported to most statistical packages for analysis.

Many questionnaire design packages are available, especially for microcomputers. Some well-known packages are the Ci2 and Ci3 systems. Another recent release, SURVEYOR, by Computers for Marketing Corporation, can also create, test, and prepare questionnaires and pass the completed questionnaires to compatible interviewing systems for field work. SURVEYPRO by Apian Software of Menlo Park, California, brings ease-of-use and desktop publishing capabilities to printed questionnaire design. SurveyPro comes in two editions: the standard edition for small or occasional surveys and the advanced edition for surveys of any size and complexity. During data entry following the data collection phase of a study, SURVEYPRO can automatically generate data entry screens from the questionnaire (which link data entry keystrokes to correct column locations in the data matrix being formed). During the data analysis phase of a study, SURVEYPRO can provide basic statistical analysis of the researcher's data set.

Better customization of the printed questionnaire results from SurveyPro's ability to import PCX and TIFF files (containing non-text images from draw or paint software programs). Company logos, product images, and other graphic files can now appear on questionnaires and reports. In the accompanying figure (Exhibit 10.1), the "ABC Corporation" logo was generated in a type generating software program, such as ADOBE TYPE MANAGER, and then copied into the SurveyPro document. The accompanying figure's header (including the ABC Corporation logo, and "Annual Customer Survey") demonstrate the lines and boxes special effects which extend the desktop publishing capabilities of SURVEYPRO. In designing the appearance of the survey form, a full-page editor enables the researcher to view both the content and form of other questions.

Some of the possible question response formats can be seen in Exhibit 10.1. These include: check boxes, free-form text, and Likert type scale response formats (four check boxes corresponding to the categories of "Very Important," "Somewhat Important," "Little Importance," and "Not Needed"). In addition to these, other possible response formats include Yes/No/Uncertain, range rulers, numbers, or dates.

Exhibit 10.2 illustrates how a question about the level of customer service could be added to CMC International's customer survey. Here, the response format chosen for the service question features check boxes with four levels (excellent, good, O.K., and poor). Under "Layout," the questionnaire designer can designate the form and position of the next question. This service question will be placed below the previous question, with the scale to the right of the service question. In addition, the check boxes will be placed below those words.

SURVEYPRO's desktop publishing enhancements make it a powerful and flexible tool for the researcher. As a result of its use, the researcher can more effectively present survey questions to respondents for accurate responses and can more quickly complete the data entry and basic statistical analysis of survey work.

EXHIBIT 10.1

*Constructing
a Questionnaire
Using SurveyPro* ◆
Apian Software, Menlo
Park, CA.

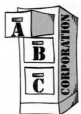

Annual Customer Survey

Thank you for being an ABC customer over the past year. We would appreciate your feedback so we can continue to improve our products and better serve you. Please take 5 minutes to fill out this questionnaire and return it by January 31 in the enclosed postage-paid envelope, or Fax it to (408) 555-1234.

What products did you order last year?

❑ XC407 4-dr, legal file cabinet   ❑ BZ800 Desk hutch   ❑ QQ201 Deluxe lit. rack
❑ XC357 4-dr, letter file cabinet   ❑ CZ902 Copier stand   ❑ KL300 Ergonomic chair
❑ XC286 2-dr, letter file cabinet   ❑ QQ200 Literature rack   ❑ DF309 Monitor stand
❑ Other: _____

Would you like to see any changes in the above products? (Attach pages as needed.)

_____

_____

Please rate the following items, both on their importance to you, and on our performance over the past year.

	Very Important	Somewhat Important	Little Importance	Not Needed	Performance			
					Excellent	Good	Fair	Poor
Credit policies	❑	❑	❑	❑	❑	❑	❑	❑
Delivery time	❑	❑	❑	❑	❑	❑	❑	❑
Customer service	❑	❑	❑	❑	❑	❑	❑	❑
Price	❑	❑	❑	❑	❑	❑	❑	❑
Product quality	❑	❑	❑	❑	❑	❑	❑	❑
Product features	❑	❑	❑	❑	❑	❑	❑	❑
Special orders	❑	❑	❑	❑	❑	❑	❑	❑
Repair services	❑	❑	❑	❑	❑	❑	❑	❑

Please explain any performance ratings of Fair or Poor. (Attach pages as needed.)

_____

_____

Approximately how much was your average monthly order last year?

❑ $0-99   ❑ $100-199   ❑ $200-399   ❑ $400-599   ❑ $600-799   ❑ $800+

What size is your business?

❑ Small (Under 100 employees)   ❑ Medium (100-1000 employees)   ❑ Large (Over 1000 employees)

Optional information:

Name: _____   Company: _____

Thank you for your time!

Sample Printout from Apian Software's Survey Pro™ for Windows

EXHIBIT 10.2

Adding a Question
Using SurveyPro

```
HELP F1            EDIT SCALE F2        SETUP PAGE      CANCEL Esc        DONE F10

QUESTION:  Service




SCALE:      Written answer into box
            Yes or No
            Yes, Uncertain, or No
            *Excellence - 4 levels
            *Excellence - 6 levels
            0 to 10, box for answers
            Circle number 0 to 10

LAYOUT:     Place this QUESTION (*) below, or ( ) to right of previous question.
            Place this SCALE ( ) below, or (*) to right of this question.
            Place checkoff boxes (*) below, or ( ) to left of the words.
            Print into [    ] inch width (leave blank to use what's available)
            Indent Left [    ], First [    ]              (blanks automatic)
```

SUMMARY

To collect quantitative primary data, a researcher must design a questionnaire or an observation form. A questionnaire has three objectives. It must translate the information needed into a set of specific questions the respondents can and will answer. It must motivate respondents to complete the interview. It must also minimize response error.

Designing a questionnaire is an art rather than a science. The process begins by specifying (1) the information needed and (2) the type of interviewing method. The next step (3) is to decide on the content of individual questions.

The question should overcome the respondents' inability to answer (4). Respondents may be unable to answer if they are not informed, cannot remember, or cannot articulate the response. The unwillingness of the respondents to answer must also be overcome. Respondents may be unwilling to answer if the question requires too much effort, is asked in a situation or context deemed inappropriate, does not serve a legitimate purpose, or solicits sensitive information. Then comes the decision regarding the question structure (5). Questions can be unstructured (open-ended) or structured, to varying degrees. Structured questions include multiple-choice, dichotomous questions, and scales.

Determining the wording of each question (6) involves defining the issue, using ordinary words, using unambiguous words, and using dual statements. The researcher should avoid leading questions, implicit alternatives, implicit assumptions, and generalizations and estimates. Once the questions have been worded, the order in which they will appear in the questionnaire must be decided (7). Special consideration should be given to opening questions, type of information, difficult questions, and the effect on subsequent questions. The questions should be arranged in a logical order.

The stage is now set for determining the form and layout of the questions (8). Several factors are important in reproducing the questionnaire (9). These include appearance, use of booklets, fitting entire question on a page, response category format, avoiding overcrowding, placement of directions, color coding, easy-to-read format, and cost. Last but not least is pretesting (10). Important issues are the extent of pretesting, nature of respondents, type of interviewing method, type of interviewers, sample size, protocol analysis and debriefing, and editing and analysis.

The design of observational forms requires explicit decisions about what is to be observed and how that behavior is to be recorded. It is useful to specify the who, what, when, where, why, and way of the behavior to be observed. Microcomputer software can greatly assist the researcher in designing sound questionnaires and observational forms.

The questionnaire or research instrument should be adapted to the specific cultural environment and should not be biased in terms of any one culture. Also, the questionnaire may have to be suitable for administration by more than one method because different interviewing methods may be used in different countries. For ease of comprehension and translation, it is desirable to have simple, rather than complex, questions. Several commercial software packages are available for designing and administering questionnaires using microcomputers and mainframes.[58]

ACRONYMS

The objectives and steps involved in developing a questionnaire may be defined by the acronym QUESTIONNAIRE:

Objectives	Q	uestions that respondents can answer
	U	plift the respondent
	E	rror elimination
Steps	S	pecify the information needed
	T	ype of interviewing method
	I	ndividual question content
	O	vercoming inability and unwillingness to answer
	N	onstructured versus structured questions
	N	onbiased question wording
	A	rrange the questions in proper order
	I	dentify form and layout
	R	eproduction of the questionnaire
	E	liminate bugs by pretesting

The guidelines for question wording may be summarized by the acronym WORDING:

W ho, what, when, where, why, and way
O rdinary words
R egularly, normally, usually, and so forth should be avoided
D ual statements (positive and negative)
I mplicit alternatives and assumptions should be avoided
N onleading and nonbiasing questions
G eneralizations and estimates should be avoided

The guidelines for deciding on the order of questions may be summarized by the acronym ORDER:

O pening questions: simple
R udimentary or basic information should be obtained first
D ifficult questions toward the end
E xamine the influence on subsequent questions
R eview the sequence to ensure a logical order

The guidelines for reproducing a questionnaire may be summarized by the acronym REPRODUCE:

R   esponse category format
E   ntire question on a page
P   rofessional appearance
R   educe costs
O   vercrowding should be avoided
D   irections or instructions
U   se of booklets
C   olor coding
E   asy to read

The guidelines for pretesting a questionnaire may be summarized by the acronym PRETEST:

P   rotocol analysis and debriefing
R   espondents from the same population
E   xtent: extensive
T   ype of interviewing method
E   diting and analysis
S   ample size: 15 to 30 per iteration
T   ype of interviewers

EXERCISES

QUESTIONS

1. What is the purpose of questionnaires and observation forms?
2. Explain how the mode of administration affects questionnaire design.
3. How would you determine whether a specific question should be included in a questionnaire?
4. What is a double-barreled question?
5. What are the reasons that respondents may be unable to answer the question asked?
6. Explain the errors of omission, telescoping, and creation. What can be done to reduce such errors?
7. Explain the concepts of aided and unaided recall.
8. What are the reasons that respondents may be unwilling to answer specific questions?
9. What can a researcher do to make the request for information seem legitimate?
10. Explain the use of randomized techniques in obtaining sensitive information.
11. What are the advantages and disadvantages of unstructured questions?
12. What are the issues involved in designing multiple-choice questions?
13. What are the guidelines available for deciding on question wording?
14. What is a leading question? Give an example.
15. What is the proper order for questions intended to obtain basic, classification, and identification information?
16. What guidelines are available for deciding on the form and layout of a questionnaire?
17. Describe the issues involved in pretesting a questionnaire.
18. What are the major decisions involved in designing observational forms?

PROBLEMS

1. Develop three double-barreled questions related to flying and passengers' airline preferences. Also develop corrected versions of each question.
2. List at least ten ambiguous words that should not be used in framing questions.

3. Do the following questions define the issue? Why or why not?
   a. What is your favorite brand of toothpaste?
   b. How often do you go on a vacation?
   c. Do you consume orange juice?
      1. Yes   2. No
4. Design an open-ended question to determine whether households engage in gardening. Also develop a multiple-choice and a dichotomous question to obtain the same information. Which form is the most desirable?
5. Formulate five questions that ask respondents to provide generalizations or estimates.
6. Develop a series of questions for determining the proportion of households with children under age ten where child abuse takes place. Use the randomized response technique.
7. A new graduate hired by the marketing research department of a major telephone company is asked to prepare a questionnaire to determine household preferences for telephone calling cards. The questionnaire is to be administered in mall-intercept interviews. Using the principles of questionnaire design, critically evaluate this questionnaire.

Household Telephone Calling Card Survey

1. Your name? _____
2. Age _____
3. Marital status _____
4. Income _____ _____
5. Which, if any of the following telephone calling cards do you have?
   1. ____ AT&T   2. ____ MCI
   3. ____US Sprint   4. ____ Others
6. How frequently do you use a telephone calling card?

Infrequently   Very Frequently
         1   2   3   4   5   6   7
7. What do you think of the telephone calling card offered by AT&T?

_____

8. Suppose that your household were to select a telephone calling card. Please rate the importance of the following factors in selecting a card.

	Not important			Very important	
a. Cost per call	1	2	3	4	5
b. Easy of use	1	2	3	4	5
c. Local and long-distance charges included in the same bill	1	2	3	4	5
d. Rebates and discounts on calls	1	2	3	4	5
e. Quality of telephone service	1	2	3	4	5
f. Quality of customer service	1	2	3	4	5

9. How important is it for a telephone company to offer a calling card?

Not important   Very important
         1   2   3   4   5   6   7
10. Do you have children living at home? _____

Thank You for Your Help.

COMPUTER EXERCISES

1. Develop the questionnaire for measuring preferences for sneakers using an electronic questionnaire design package such as the Ci3 System. Administer this questionnaire using a microcomputer to ten students.
2. Redesign the questionnaire for problem 7 using an electronic questionnaire design package. Compare your experiences in designing this questionnaire electronically and manually.

NOTES

1. *Seventeen Research, Automotive Survey*, 1987.
2. Joseph Rydholm, "Omnibus Study Talks to Kids," *Quirk's Marketing Research Review* 5 (6) (June–July 1991): 42.
3. S. L. Payne, *The Art of Asking Questions* (Princeton, NJ: Princeton University Press, 1951), p. 141.
4. These guidelines are drawn from several books on questionnaire design: C. H. Backstrom and G. Hursh-Csar, *Survey Research* (Cambridge, MA: Wiley, 1981); Douglas R. Berdie and John F. Anderson, *Questionnaires: Design and Use* (Metuchen, NJ: Scarecrow Press, 1974); A. B. Blankenship, *Professional Telephone Surveys* (New York: McGraw-Hill, 1977), pp. 94–95; D. Dillman, *Mail and Telephone Surveys: The Total Design Method* (New York: Wiley, 1978); Paul L. Erdos, *Professional Mail Surveys* (Malabar, FL: Robert E. Krieger, 1983); Arthur Korhauser and Paul B. Sheatsley, "Questionnaire Construction and Interview Procedure," in Claire Selltiz, Lawrence S. Wrightsman, and Stuart W. Cook, *Research Methods in Social Relations*, 3rd ed. (New York: Holt, Rinehart and Winston, 1976), pp. 541–73; P. Labau, *Advanced Questionnaire Design* (Orlando, FL: Abt Books, 1981); Herbert Schuman and Stanley Presser, *Questions and Answers in Attitude Surveys* (Orlando, FL: Academic Press, 1981); and Seymour Sudman and Norman M. Bradburn, *Asking Questions* (San Francisco: Jossey-Bass, 1983). For earlier references on questionnaire design, see Wayne G. Daniel, *Questionnaire Design: A Selected Bibliography for the Survey Researcher* (Monticello, IL: Vance Bibliographics, 1979).
5. Jagdip Singh, Roy D. Howell, and Gary K. Rhoads, "Adaptive Designs for Likert-Type Data: An Approach for Implementing Marketing Surveys," *Journal of Marketing Research* 27 (August 1990): 304–21; and R. A. Peterson and R. A. Kerin, and M. Sabertehrani, "Question Understanding in Self-Report Data," in B. J. Walker et al., *An Assessment of Marketing Thought and Practice* (Chicago: American Marketing Association, 1982), pp. 426–29.
6. Ilene K. Kleinsorge and Harold F. Koenig, "The Silent Customers: Measuring Customer Satisfaction in Nursing Homes," *Journal of Health Care Marketing* (December 1991): 2–13.
7. Paul Hague, "Good and Bad in Questionnaire Design," *Industrial Marketing Digest* (UK), 12 (Third Quarter 1987): 161–70.
8. Harper W. Boyd, Jr., Ralph Westfall, and Stanley F. Stasch, *Marketing Research: Text and Cases*, 7th ed. (Homewood, IL: Richard D. Irwin, 1989), p. 277.
9. See D. I. Hawkins and K. A. Coney, "Uninformed Response Error in Survey Research," *Journal of Marketing Research* (August 1981): 373. Similar examples of opinions on fictitious issues are provided by George F. Bishop, Alfred J. Tuchfarber, and Robert W. Oldendick, "Opinions on Fictitious Issues: The Pressure to Answer Survey Questions," *Public Opinion Quarterly* (Summer 1986): 240–50; and K. C. Schneider, "Uninformed Response Rates in Survey Research," *Journal of Business Research* (April 1985): 153–62.
10. George F. Bishop, Robert W. Oldendick, and Alfred J. Tuchfarber, "Effects of Filter Questions in Public Opinion Surveys," *Public Opinion Quarterly* 46 (Spring 1982): 66–85.
11. D. I. Hawkins and K. A. Coney, "Uninformed Response Error in Survey Research," *Journal of Marketing Research* (August 1981): 373.
12. Terry Haller, *Danger: Marketing Researcher at Work* (Westport, CT: Quorum Books, 1983), p. 149.
13. William A. Cook, "Telescoping and Memory's Other Tricks," *Journal of Advertising Research* (February–March 1987): 5–8; and Seymour Sudman, A. Finn, and L. Lannom, "The Use of Bounded Recall Procedures in Single Interviews," *Public Opinion Quarterly* (Summer 1984): 520–24.
14. J. H. Malrin and J. M. Moskowitz, "Anonymous versus Identifiable Self-Reports," *Public Opinion Quarterly* (Winter 1983): 557–66.
15. Kent H. Marquis, M. Susan Marquis, and Michael J. Polich, "Response Bias and Reliability in Sensitive Topic Surveys," *Journal of the American Statistical Association* (June 1986): 381–89; Thomas W. Mangione, Ralph Hingson, and Jane Barrett, "Collecting Sensitive Data: A Comparison of Three Survey Strategies," *Sociological Methods and Research* 10 (February 1982): 337–46; and Kent H. Marquis, et al., *Response Errors in Sensitive Topic Survey: Estimates, Effects, and Correction Options* (Santa Monica, CA: Rand Corporation, 1981).

16. R. A. Peterson, "Asking the Age Question: A Research Note," *Public Opinion Quarterly* (Spring 1984): 379–83; and J. N. Sheth, A. LeClaire, Jr., and D. Wachsprass, "Impact of Asking Race Information in Mail Surveys," *Journal of Marketing* (Winter 1980): 67–70.

17. For a recent application, see Brian K. Burton and Janet P. Near, "Estimating the Incidence of Wrongdoing and Whistle-blowing: Results of a Study Using Randomized Response Technique," *Journal of Business Ethics* 14 (January 1995): 17–30.

18. M. D. Geurtz, "Using a Randomized Response Research Design to Eliminate Non-Response and Response Biases in Business Research," *Journal of the Academy of Marketing Science* (Spring 1980): 83–91; D. E. Stem, Jr., W. T. Chao, and R. K. Steinhorst, "A Randomization Dance for Mail Survey Applications of the Randomized Response Model," in R. P. Bagozzi et al., *Marketing in the 80's* (Chicago: American Marketing Association, 1980), pp. 320–23; D. E. Stem, Jr., and R. K. Steinhorst, "Telephone Interview and Mail Questionnaire Applications of the Randomized Response Model," *Journal of the American Statistical Association* (September 1984): 555–64; and Paul E. Tracy and James Alan Fox, "The Validity of Randomized Response for Sensitive Measurements," *American Sociological Review* 46 (April 1981): 187–200.

19. S. Seiberling, S. Taylor, and M. Ursic, "Open-Ended Question vs. Rating Scale," in John C. Rogers III (ed.), *Developments in Marketing Science: Proceedings of the Seventh Annual Conference of the Academy of Marketing Science*, vol. 6 (Ann Arbor, MI: Books on Demand, 1983), pp. 440–45; and Gregory J. Spagna, "Questionnaires: Which Approach Do You Use?" *Journal of Advertising Research* 24 (February–March 1984): 67–70.

20. S. Jones, "Listening to Complexity," *Journal of the Market Research Society* (January 1981): 26–39; and C. McDonald, "Coding Open-Ended Answers with the Help of a Computer," *Journal of the Market Research Society* (January 1982): 9–27.

21. Based on a marketing research project conducted by the author.

22. S. L. Payne, "Are Open-Ended Questions Worth the Effort?" *Journal of Marketing Research* 2 (November 1965): 417–18.

23. Jon A. Krosnick and Duane F. Alwin, "An Evaluation of a Cognitive Theory of Response-Order Effects in Survey Measurement," *Public Opinion Quarterly* (Summer 1987): 201–19; and S. L. Payne, *The Art of Asking Questions* (Princeton, NJ: Princeton University Press, 1951), p. 141.

24. Niels J. Blunch, "Position Bias in Multiple-Choice Questions," *Journal of Marketing Research* 21 (May 1984): 216–20, has argued that position bias in multiple-choice questions cannot be eliminated by rotating the order of the alternatives. This viewpoint is contrary to the common practice.

25. George F. Bishop, "Experiments with the Middle Response Alternative in Survey Questions," *Public Opinion Quarterly* (Summer 1987): 220–32; and Herbert Schuman and Stanley Presser, *Questions and Answers in Attitude Surveys* (Orlando, FL: Academic Press, 1981).

26. George F. Bishop, Robert W. Oldendick, and Alfred J. Tuchfarber, "What Must My Interest in Politics Be If I Told You I Don't Know," *Public Opinion Quarterly* (Summer 1984): 510–19; and R. W. Mizerski, J. B. Freiden, and R. C. Green, Jr., "The Effect of the 'Don't Know' Option on TV Ad Claim Recognition Tests," in *Advances in Consumer Research* (Association for Consumer Research 10, 1983), pp. 283–87.

27. Graham Kalton and Howard Schuman, "The Effect of the Question on Survey Responses: A Review," *Journal of the Royal Statistical Society*, Series A, 145 (Part 1, 1982): 44–45.

28. Herbert Schuman and Stanley Presser, "Question Wording as an Independent Variable in Survey Analysis," *Sociological Methods and Research* (November 1977): 155.

29. G. S. Omura, "Correlates of Item Nonresponse," *Journal of the Market Research Society* (October 1983): 321–30; and S. Presser, "Is Inaccuracy on Factual Survey Items Item-Specific or Respondent-Specific?" *Public Opinion Quarterly* (Spring 1984): 344–55.

30. Fred W. Morgan, "Judicial Standards for Survey Research: An Update and Guidelines," *Journal of Marketing* 54 (January 1990): 59–70; and R. A. Peterson and R. A. Kerin, "The Quality of Self-Report Data: Review and Synthesis," in Ben Enis and Kenneth Roering (eds.), *Annual Review of Marketing 1981* (Chicago: American Marketing Association, 1981), pp. 5–20.

31. Harper W. Boyd, Jr., Ralph Westfall, and Stanley F. Stasch, *Marketing Research: Text and Cases*, 7th ed. (Homewood, IL: Richard D. Irwin, 1989), p. 286.

32. John O'Brien, "How Do Market Researchers Ask Questions?" *Journal of the Market Research Society* 26 (April 1984): 93–107; O. D. Duncan and H. Schuman, "Effects of Question Wording and Context," *Journal of the American Statistical Association* (June 1980): 269–75; T. W. Smith, "Qualifications to Generalized Absolutes," *Public Opinion Quarterly* (Summer 1981): 224–30; and N. Webb, "Levels of Adult Numeracy," *Journal of the Market Research Society* (April 1984): 129–39; and P. Shepherd, "Literacy and Numeracy and Their Implication for Survey Research," *Journal of the Market Research Society* (April 1984): 147–58.

33. Tom W. Smith, "That Which We Call Welfare by Any Other Name Would Smell Sweeter. An Analysis of the Impact of Question Wording on Response Patterns," *Public Opinion Quarterly* (Spring 1987): 75–83.

34. P. Billins, "Research or Research"; and P. Robinson, "Language in Data Collection," both in *Journal of the Market Research Society* (Spring 1982): 69–85.

35. Herbert Schuman and Stanley Presser, "Question Wording as an Independent Variable in Survey Analysis," *Sociological Methods and Research* (November 1977): 155.

36. George F. Bishop, Robert W. Oldendick, and Alfred J. Tuchfarber, "Effects of Presenting One Versus Two Sides of an Issue in Survey Questions," *Public Opinion Quarterly* 46 (Spring 1982): 66–85; and E. Noelle-Neumann and B. Worcester, "International Opinion Research," *European Research* (July 1984): 124–31.

37. F. M. Andrews, "Construct Validity and Error Components of Survey Measures," *Public Opinion Quarterly* (Summer 1984): 409–42; and E. D. Jaffe and I. D. Nebenzahl, "Alternative Questionnaire Formats for Country Image Studies," *Journal of Marketing Research* (November 1984): 463–71.

38. Jon A. Krosnick and Duane F. Alwin, "An Evaluation of a Cognitive Theory of Response-Order Effects in Survey Measurement," *Public Opinion Quarterly* (Summer 1987): 201–19; I. Crespi and D. Morris, "Question Order Effect," *Public Opinion Quarterly* (Fall 1984): 578–91; and H. Schuman, G. Kalton, and J. Ludwig, "Context and Contiguity in Survey Questionnaires," *Public Opinion Quarterly* (Spring 1983): 112–15.

39. Warner-Lambert Company, *The American Chicle Youth Poll*, 1987.

40. Rating a brand on specific attributes early in a survey may affect responses to a later overall brand evaluation. For example, see Barbara A. Bickart, "Carryover and Backfire Effects in Marketing Research," *Journal of Marketing Research* 30 (February 1993): 52–62.

41. Donald J. Messmer and Daniel J. Seymour, "The Effects of Branching on Item Nonresponse," *Public Opinion Quarterly* 46 (Summer 1982): 270–77.

42. Charles S. Mayer and Cindy Piper, "A Note on the Importance of Layout in Self-Administered Questionnaires," *Journal of Marketing Research* 19 (August 1982): 390–91.

43. N. D. Rothwell and A. M. Rustemeyer, "Studies of Census Mail Questionnaires," *Journal of Marketing Research* (August 1975): 405.

44. Erdos and Morgan, Inc., *The American Lawyer Subscriber Study*, 1987.

45. Illustration of grids may be found in the Warner-Lambert Company, *The American Chicle Youth Poll*, 1987.

46. J. R. Dickinson and E. Kirzner, "Questionnaire Item Omission as a Function of Within-Group Question Position," *Journal of Business Research* (February 1985): 71–75; and A. Regula Herzog and Jerald G. Bachman, "Effects of Questionnaire Length on Response Quality," *Public Opinion Quarterly* 45 (Winter 1981): 549–59.

47. David F. Wolfe, "A New Questionnaire Design," *Journal of Marketing* 21 (October 1956): 186–90.

48. Shelby D. Hunt, Richard D. Sparkman, Jr., and James Wilcox, "The Pretest in Survey Research: Issues and Preliminary Findings," *Journal of Marketing Research* (May 1982): 269–73.

49. R. N. Zelnio and J. P. Gagnon, "The Construction and Testing of an Image Questionnaire," *Journal of the Academy of Marketing Science* (Summer 1981): 288–99.

50. A. Diamantopoulos, Bodo B. Schlegelmilch, and Nina Reynolds, "Pretesting in Questionnaire Design: The Impact of Respondent Characteristics on Error Detection," *Journal of the Market Research Society* 36 (October 1994): 295–314.

51. Nina Reynolds, A. Diamantopoulos and Bodo B. Schlegelmilch, "Pretesting in Questionnaire Design: A Review of the Literature and Suggestions for Further Research," *Journal of the Market Research Society* 35 (April 1993): 171–82.

52. Julie Skur Hill, "Japan Hatches New Brands for Johnson," in *Advertising Age* (September 2, 1991): 36.

53. Rules of Conduct and Good Practice of the Professional Marketing Research Society of Canada (1984).

54. G. R. Laczniak and P. E. Murphy, *Ethical Marketing Decisions the Higher Road*, (Needhan Heights, MA: Allyn and Bacon, 1993).

55. A. M. Tybout and G. Zaltman, "Ethics in Marketing Research: Their Practical Relevance," *Journal of Marketing Research* 11 (1974): 357–68.

56. R. W. Armstrong, "An Empirical Investigation of International Marketing Ethics: Problems Encountered by Australian Firms," *Journal of Business Ethics* 11 (1992): 161–71.

57. Naresh K. Malhotra, Armen Tashchian, and Essam Mahmoud, "The Integration of Microcomputers in Marketing Research and Decision Making," *Journal of the Academy of Marketing Science* 15 (Summer 1987): 69–82.

58. The assistance of James Agarwal with the international marketing research example, the assistance of Mark Leach and Gina Miller in writing the ethics section, and the assistance of Mark Peterson in writing the computer applications section is gratefully acknowledged.

CHAPTER ELEVEN

Sampling: Design and Procedures

When determining the characteristics of a population, it is often advantageous to examine a part of the population (a sample) rather than the whole (a census).

◆

OBJECTIVES

After reading this chapter, the student should be able to:

1. Differentiate a sample from a census and identify the conditions that favor the use of a sample versus a census.
2. Discuss the sampling design process: definition of the target population, determination of the sampling frame, selection of sampling technique(s), determination of sample size, and execution of the sampling process.
3. Classify sampling techniques as nonprobability and probability sampling techniques.
4. Describe the nonprobability sampling techniques of convenience, judgmental, quota, and snowball sampling.
5. Describe the probability sampling techniques of simple random, systematic, stratified, and cluster sampling.
6. Identify the conditions that favor the use of nonprobability sampling versus probability sampling.
7. Understand the sampling design process and the use of sampling techniques in international marketing research.
8. Identify the ethical issues related to the sampling design process and the use of appropriate sampling techniques.
9. Explain the use of microcomputers and mainframes in sampling design.

OVERVIEW

Sampling is one component of a research design. The formulation of the research design is the third step of the marketing research process. At this stage, the information needed to address the marketing research problem has been identified and the nature of the research design (exploratory, descriptive, or causal) has been determined (Chapters 3 through 7). Furthermore, the scaling and measurement procedures have been specified (Chapters 8 and 9), and the questionnaire has been designed (Chapter 10). The next step is to design suitable sampling procedures. Sampling design involves several basic questions: (1) Should a sample be taken? (2) If so, what process should be followed? (3) What kind of sample should be taken? (4) How large should it be? and (5) What can be done to control and adjust for nonresponse errors?

This chapter introduces the fundamental concepts of sampling and the qualitative considerations necessary to answer these questions. We address the question of whether or not to sample and describe the steps involved in sampling. Next, we present non-probability and probability sampling techniques. We discuss the use of sampling techniques in international marketing research and identify the relevant ethical issues. Statistical determination of sample size, and the causes for, control of, and adjustments for nonresponse error are discussed in Chapter 12.

We begin with the following example, which illustrates the usefulness of sampling.

EXAMPLE

A Sampler on Sampling

The American Chicle Youth Poll, conducted by the Roper Organization for the American Chicle Group of Warner-Lambert Company, is the most comprehensive and systematic study of children and teens: their hopes and worries, their families and schools, and their opinions on a broad range of issues.

The survey consisted of personal in-home interviews with a nationwide cross section of 1,000 American young people aged 8 to 17 who were attending school. The sample was representative of the population of 8- to 17-year-olds attending school in the continental United States. A three-stage, stratified probability sampling technique was used to select interviewing locations:

1. After all the counties in the nation had been stratified by population size within each geographic region, 100 counties were selected at random, proportionate to the general population.
2. Cities and towns within the sample counties were drawn at random, proportionate to the general population.
3. Where census tract statistics within cities and towns were available, tracts were selected at random, proportionate to the general population. Where no statistics were available, rural route segments were drawn at random.

Interviewers were then given starting points within the census tract or rural route segment. Quotas were imposed for sex and age levels of respondents to ensure proper representation of each group in the sample. The assigned quotas resulted in the correct number of males and females aged 8 to 12 and 13 to 17, but small imbalances were found when the sample was examined more minutely. For example, there were too few 8- to 10-year-olds and too many 11- and 12-year-olds. To overcome this imbalance, the sample was weighted to achieve the correct proportions of males and females in each age category (8–10, 11 and 12, 13 and 14, and 15–17).[1] ◆

This example illustrates the various aspects of sampling design: defining the target population (American young people aged 8 to 17 who are attending school), determining the sampling frame (list of all the counties in the United States and cities and towns within counties), selecting a sampling technique (three-stage, stratified probability sampling), determining sample size (1,000), and executing the sampling process (steps 1, 2, and 3 and interviewer instructions). Before we discuss these aspects of sampling in detail, we address the question of whether the researcher should sample or take a census.

SAMPLE OR CENSUS

population The aggregate of all the elements, sharing some common set of characteristics, that comprise the universe for the purpose of the marketing research problem.

census A complete enumeration of the elements of a population or study objects.

sample A subgroup of the elements of the population selected for participation in the study.

The objective of most marketing research projects is to obtain information about the characteristics or parameters of a population. A **population** is the aggregate of all the elements that share some common set of characteristics and that comprise the universe for the purpose of the marketing research problem. The population parameters are typically numbers, such as the proportion of consumers who are loyal to a particular brand of toothpaste. Information about population parameters may be obtained by taking a census or a sample. A **census** involves a complete enumeration of the elements of a population. The population parameters can be calculated directly in a straightforward way after the census is enumerated. A **sample**, on the other hand, is a subgroup of the population selected for participation in the study. Sample characteristics, called statistics, are then used to make inferences about the population parameters. The inferences that link sample characteristics and population parameters are estimation procedures and tests of hypotheses. These inference procedures are considered in Chapters 15 to 21.

Table 11.1 summarizes the conditions favoring the use of a sample versus a census. Budget and time limits are obvious constraints favoring the use of a sample. A census is both costly and time-consuming to conduct. A census is unrealistic if the population is large, as it is for most consumer products. In the case of many industrial products, however, the population is small making a census feasible as well as desirable. For example, in investigating the use of certain machine tools by U.S. automobile manufacturers, a census would be preferred to a sample. Another reason for preferring a census in this case is that variance in the characteristic of interest is large. For example, machine tool usage of Ford will vary greatly from the usage of Honda. Small population sizes as well as high variance in the characteristic to be measured favor a census.

If the cost of sampling errors is high (e.g., if the sample omitted a major manufacturer like Ford, the results could be misleading), a census, which eliminates such errors, is desirable. High cost of nonsampling errors, on the other hand, would favor sampling.

TABLE 11.1 *Sample versus Census*		Conditions Favoring the Use of	
		Sample	Census
	1. Budget	Small	Large
	2. Time available	Short	Long
	3. Population size	Large	Small
	4. Variance in the characteristic	Small	Large
	5. Cost of sampling errors	Low	High
	6. Cost of nonsampling errors	High	Low
	7. Nature of measurement	Destructive	Nondestructive
	8. Attention to individual cases	Yes	No

A census can greatly increase nonsampling error to the point that these errors exceed the sampling errors of a sample. Nonsampling errors are found to be the major contributor to total error, whereas random sampling errors have been relatively small in magnitude (see Chapter 3).[2] Hence, in most cases, accuracy considerations would favor a sample over a census. This is one reason that the U.S. Bureau of the Census checks the accuracy of various censuses by conducting sample surveys.[3] It is not always possible to reduce nonsampling error sufficiently to compensate for sampling error, however, as in the case of a study involving U.S. automobile manufacturers.

A sample may be preferred if the measurement process results in the destruction or contamination of the elements sampled. For example, product usage tests result in the consumption of the product. Therefore, taking a census in a study that requires households to use a new brand of photographic film would not be feasible. Sampling may also be necessary to focus attention on individual cases, as in the case of depth interviews. Finally, other pragmatic considerations, such as the need to keep the study secret, may favor a sample over a census.

THE SAMPLING DESIGN PROCESS

The sampling design process includes five steps, which are shown sequentially in Figure 11.1. These steps are closely interrelated and relevant to all aspects of the marketing research project, from problem definition to the presentation of the results. Therefore, sample design decisions should be integrated with all other decisions in a research project.[4]

Define the Target Population

target population The collection of elements or objects that possess the information sought by the researcher and about which inferences are to be made.

Sampling design begins by specifying the **target population**. The target population is the collection of elements or objects that possess the information sought by the researcher and about which inferences are to be made. The target population must be defined precisely. Imprecise definition of the target population will result in research that is ineffective at best and misleading at worst. Defining the target population involves translating the problem definition into a precise statement of who should and should not be included in the sample.

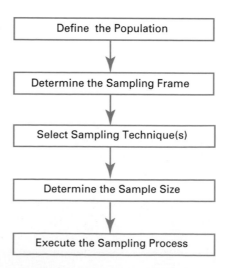

FIGURE 11.1

The Sampling Design Process

Define the Population

↓

Determine the Sampling Frame

↓

Select Sampling Technique(s)

↓

Determine the Sample Size

↓

Execute the Sampling Process

The target population should be defined in terms of elements, sampling units, extent, and time. An **element** is the object about which or from which the information is desired. In survey research, the element is usually the respondent. A **sampling unit** is an element, or a unit containing the element, that is available for selection at some stage of the sampling process. Suppose that Revlon wanted to assess consumer response to a new line of lipsticks and wanted to sample females over 18 years of age. It may be possible to sample females over 18 directly, in which case a sampling unit would be the same as an element. Alternatively, the sampling unit might be households. In the latter case, households would be sampled and all females over 18 in each selected household would be interviewed. Here, the sampling unit and the population element are different. Extent refers to the geographical boundaries, and the time factor is the period under consideration. We use the department store patronage project to illustrate.

element An object that possesses the information sought by the researcher and about which inferences are to be made.

sampling unit The basic unit containing the elements of the population to be sampled.

DEPARTMENT STORE PATRONAGE PROJECT
Target Population

The target population for the department store patronage project was defined as follows:

> Elements: male or female head of the household responsible for most of the shopping at department stores
> Sampling units: households
> Extent: metropolitan Atlanta
> Time: 1994 ◆

Defining the target population may not be as easy as it was in this example. Consider a marketing research project assessing consumer response to a new brand of men's cologne. Who should be included in the target population? All men? Men who have used a cologne during the last month? Men 17 or older? Should females be included, because some women buy colognes for men that they know? These and similar questions must be resolved before the target population can be appropriately defined.[5]

Determine the Sampling Frame

sampling frame A representation of the elements of the target population that consists of a list or set of directions for identifying the target population.

A **sampling frame** is a representation of the elements of the target population. It consists of a list or set of directions for identifying the target population. Examples of a sampling frame include the telephone book, an association directory listing the firms in an industry, a mailing list purchased from a commercial organization, a city directory, or a map.[6] If a list cannot be compiled, then at least some directions for identifying the target population should be specified such as random-digit dialing procedures in telephone surveys (see Chapter 6).

Often it is possible to compile or obtain a list of population elements, but the list may omit some elements of the population or may include other elements that do not belong. Therefore, the use of a list will lead to sampling frame error, which was discussed in Chapter 3.[7]

In some instances, the discrepancy between the population and the sampling frame is small enough to ignore. In most cases, however, the researcher should recognize and treat the sampling frame error. This can be done in at least three ways. One approach is to redefine the population in terms of the sampling frame. If the telephone book is used as a sampling frame, the population of households could be redefined as those with a correct listing in the telephone book in a given area. Although this approach is simplistic, it does prevent the researcher from being misled about the actual population being investigated.[8]

Another way is to account for sampling frame error by screening the respondents in the data collection phase. The respondents could be screened with respect to demographic characteristics, familiarity, product usage, and other characteristics to ensure that they satisfy the criteria for the target population. Screening can eliminate inappropriate elements contained in the sampling frame, but it cannot account for elements that have been omitted.

Yet another approach is to adjust the data collected by a weighting scheme to counterbalance the sampling frame error. This is discussed in Chapter 12 and also in Chapter 14. Regardless of which approach is adopted, it is important to recognize any sampling frame error that exists so that inappropriate population inferences can be avoided.

Select a Sampling Technique

Selecting a sampling technique involves several decisions of a broader nature. The researcher must decide whether to use a Bayesian or traditional sampling approach, to sample with or without replacement, and to use nonprobability or probability sampling.

Bayesian approach A selection method where the elements are selected sequentially. The Bayesian approach explicitly incorporates prior information about population parameters as well as the costs and probabilities associated with making wrong decisions.

In the **Bayesian approach**, the elements are selected sequentially. After each element is added to the sample, the data are collected, sample statistics computed, and sampling costs determined. The Bayesian approach explicitly incorporates prior information about population parameters as well as the costs and probabilities associated with making wrong decisions. This approach is theoretically appealing. Yet it is not used widely in marketing research because much of the required information on costs and probabilities is not available. In the traditional sampling approach, the entire sample is selected before data collection begins. Because the traditional approach is the most common approach used, it is assumed in the following sections.

sampling with replacement A sampling technique in which an element can be included in the sample more than once.

In **sampling with replacement**, an element is selected from the sampling frame and appropriate data are obtained. Then the element is placed back in the sampling frame. As a result, it is possible for an element to be included in the sample more than once. In **sampling without replacement**, once an element is selected for inclusion in the sample, it is removed from the sampling frame and therefore cannot be selected again. The calculation of statistics is done somewhat differently for the two approaches, but statistical inference is not very different if the sampling frame is large relative to the ultimate sample size. Thus, the distinction is important only when the sampling frame is small compared with the sample size.

sampling without replacement A sampling technique in which an element cannot be included in the sample more than once.

The most important decision about the choice of sampling technique is whether to use probability or nonprobability sampling. Given its importance, the issues involved in this decision are discussed in great detail in this chapter.

If the sampling unit is different from the element, it is necessary to specify precisely how the elements within the sampling unit should be selected. With in-home personal interviews and telephone interviews, merely specifying the address or the telephone number may not be sufficient. For example, should the person answering the doorbell or the telephone be interviewed, or someone else in the household? Often, more than one person in a household may qualify. For example, both the male and female head of household may be eligible to participate in a study examining family leisure-time activities. When a probability sampling technique is being employed, a random selection must be made from all the eligible persons in each household. A simple procedure for random selection is the next birthday method. The interviewer asks which of the eligible persons in the household has the next birthday and includes that person in the sample.

Determine the Sample Size

sample size The number
of units to be included in
a study.

Sample size refers to the number of elements to be included in the study. Determining the sample size is complex and involves several qualitative and quantitative considerations. The qualitative factors are discussed in this section, and the quantitative factors are considered in Chapter 12. Important qualitative factors to be considered in determining the sample size include (1) the importance of the decision, (2) the nature of the research, (3) the number of variables, (4) the nature of the analysis, (5) sample sizes used in similar studies, (6) incidence rates, (7) completion rates, and (8) resource constraints.

In general, for more important decisions, more information is necessary, and that information should be obtained very precisely. This calls for larger samples, but as the sample size increases, each unit of information is obtained at greater cost. The degree of precision may be measured in terms of the standard deviation of the mean. The standard deviation of the mean is inversely proportional to the square root of the sample size. The larger the sample, the smaller the gain in precision by increasing the sample size by one unit.

The nature of the research also has an impact on the sample size. For exploratory research designs, such as those using qualitative research, the sample size is typically small. For conclusive research, such as descriptive surveys, larger samples are required. Likewise, if data are being collected on a large number of variables, larger samples are required. The cumulative effects of sampling error across variables are reduced in a large sample.

If sophisticated analysis of the data using multivariate techniques is required, the sample size should be large. The same applies if the data are to be analyzed in great detail. Thus, a larger sample would be required if the data are being analyzed at the subgroup or segment level than if the analysis is limited to the aggregate or total sample.

Sample size is influenced by the average size of samples in similar studies. Table 11.2 gives an idea of sample sizes used in different marketing research studies. These sample sizes have been determined based on experience and can serve as rough guidelines, particularly when nonprobability sampling techniques are used.

Finally, the sample size decision should be guided by a consideration of the resource constraints. In any marketing research project, money and time are limited. Other constraints include the availability of qualified personnel for data collection. The sample size required should be adjusted for the incidence of eligible respondents and the completion rate, as explained in the next chapter.

Execute the Sampling Process

Execution of the sampling process requires a detailed specification of how the sampling design decisions with respect to the population, sampling frame, sampling unit, sampling technique, and sample size are to be implemented. If households are the sampling unit,

TABLE 11.2 *Sample Sizes Used in Marketing Research Studies*	Type of Study	Minimum Size	Typical Range
	Problem identification research (e.g., market potential)	500	1,000–2,500
	Problem-solving research (e.g., pricing)	200	300–500
	Product tests	200	300–500
	Test marketing studies	200	300–500
	TV, radio, or print advertising (per commercial or ad tested)	150	200–300
	Test-market audits	10 stores	10–20 stores
	Focus groups	2 groups	4–12 groups

an operational definition of a household is needed. Procedures should be specified for vacant housing units and for callbacks in case no one is at home. Detailed information must be provided for all sampling design decisions. We illustrate with a survey done for the Florida Department of Tourism.

EXAMPLE
Tourism Department Telephones Birthday Boys and Girls

A telephone survey was conducted for the Florida Department of Tourism to gain an understanding of the travel behavior of in-state residents. The households were stratified by north, central, and south Florida regions. A computerized random-digit sample was used to reach these households. Households were screened to locate family members who met four qualifications:

1. Age 25 or older
2. Live in Florida at least seven months of the year
3. Have lived in Florida for at least two years
4. Have a Florida driver's license

To obtain a representative sample of qualified individuals, a random method was used to select the respondent from within a household. All household members meeting the four qualifications were listed and the person with the next birthday was selected. Repeated callbacks were made to reach that person. The steps in the sampling design process were as follows.

1. *Target population*: adults meeting the four qualifications (element) in a household with a working telephone number (sampling unit) in the state of Florida (extent) during the survey period (time).
2. *Sampling frame*: computer program for generating random telephone numbers.
3. *Sampling unit*: working telephone numbers.
4. *Sampling technique*: stratified sampling. The target population was geographically stratified into three regions: north, central, and south Florida.
5. *Sample size*: 868.
6. *Execution*: allocate the sample among strata; use computerized random-digit dialing; list all the members in the household who meet the four qualifications; select one member of the household using the next birthday method.[9] ◆

Surveys based on sound sampling designs have helped the Florida Department of Tourism market the state to in-state as well as out-of-state customers. ◆ Vision Impact.

A CLASSIFICATION OF SAMPLING TECHNIQUES

Sampling techniques may be broadly classified as nonprobability and probability (see Figure 11.2). **Nonprobability sampling** relies on the personal judgment of the researcher rather than on chance to select sample elements. The researcher can arbitrarily or con-

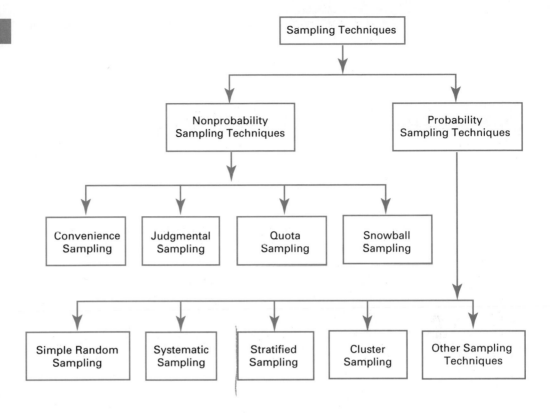

FIGURE 11.2

*A Classification
of Sampling
Techniques*

nonprobability sampling
Sampling techniques that
do not use chance selec-
tion procedures but rather
rely on the personal judgment of the researcher.

sciously decide what elements to include in the sample. Nonprobability samples may
yield good estimates of the population characteristics, but they do not allow for objective evaluation of the precision of the sample results. Because there is no way of determining the probability of selecting any particular element for inclusion in the sample,
the estimates obtained are not statistically projectable to the population. Commonly
used nonprobability sampling techniques include convenience sampling, judgmental
sampling, quota sampling, and snowball sampling (see the next section).

probability sampling A
sampling procedure in
which each element of
the population has a fixed
probabilistic chance of
being selected for the
sample.

In **probability sampling,** sampling units are selected by chance. It is possible to
prespecify every potential sample of a given size that could be drawn from the population, as well as the probability of selecting each sample. Every potential sample need
not have the same probability of selection, but it is possible to specify the probability
of selecting any particular sample of a given size. This requires not only a precise definition of the target population but also a general specification of the sampling frame.
Because sample elements are selected by chance, it is possible to determine the precision of the sample estimates of the characteristics of interest. Confidence intervals,
which contain the true population value with a given level of certainty, can be calculated. This permits the researcher to make inferences or projections about the target
population from which the sample was drawn. Classification of probability sampling
techniques is classified based on

- Element versus cluster sampling
- Equal unit probability versus unequal probabilities
- Unstratified versus stratified selection
- Random versus systematic selection
- Single-stage versus multistage techniques

All possible combinations of these five aspects result in 32 different probability sampling techniques. Of these techniques, we consider simple random sampling, systematic sampling, stratified sampling, and cluster sampling in depth and briefly touch on some others. First, however, we discuss nonprobability sampling techniques.

NONPROBABILITY SAMPLING TECHNIQUES

Convenience Sampling

convenience sampling A nonprobability sampling technique that attempts to obtain a sample of convenient elements. The selection of sampling units is left primarily to the interviewer.

Convenience sampling attempts to obtain a sample of convenient elements. The selection of sampling units is left primarily to the interviewer. Often, respondents are selected because they happen to be in the right place at the right time. Examples of convenience sampling include: (1) use of students, church groups, and members of social organizations, (2) mall intercept interviews without qualifying the respondents, (3) department stores using charge account lists, (4) tear-out questionnaires included in a magazine, and (5) "people on the street" interviews.[10]

Convenience sampling is the least expensive and least time-consuming of all sampling techniques. The sampling units are accessible, easy to measure, and cooperative. Despite these advantages, this form of sampling has serious limitations. Many potential sources of selection bias are present, including respondent self-selection. Convenience samples are not representative of any definable population. Hence, it is not theoretically meaningful to generalize to any population from a convenience sample, and convenience samples are not appropriate for marketing research projects involving population inferences. Convenience samples are not recommended for descriptive or causal research, but they can be used in exploratory research for generating ideas, insights, or hypotheses. Convenience samples can be used for focus groups, pretesting questionnaires, or pilot studies. Even in these cases, caution should be exercised in interpreting the results. Nevertheless, this technique is sometimes used even in large surveys, as in the example that follows.

EXAMPLE
Money Drops in Value

A survey was conducted involving a convenience sample of 1,300 of the 1,700 student leaders from the 50 states, Washington, D.C., and Puerto Rico who attended the 51st annual national conference of the National Association of Student Councils. The survey, with 39 questions on current topics, trends, and values, found the things students considered most desirable are, in order of importance, a successful career, a good first marriage, being better parents, and making contributions to society. Making more money was ranked in fifth place.[11] ◆

judgmental sampling A form of convenience sampling in which the population elements are purposely selected based on the judgment of the researcher.

Judgmental Sampling

Judgmental sampling is a form of convenience sampling in which the population elements are selected based on the judgment of the researcher. The researcher, exercising judgment or expertise, chooses the elements to be included in the sample because he or she believes that they are representative of the population of interest or are otherwise appropriate. Common examples of judgmental sampling include: (1) test markets selected to determine the potential of a new product, (2) purchase engineers selected in industrial marketing research because they are considered to be representative of the company, (3) bellwether precincts selected in voting behavior research, (4) expert witnesses used in court, and (5) department stores selected to test a new merchandising display system. The use of this technique is illustrated in the context of the department store patronage project.

DEPARTMENT STORE PATRONAGE PROJECT
Sampling Technique

In the department store study, 20 census tracts in the metropolitan area were selected based on judgment. Tracts with very poor people and those with undesirable (high crime-rate) areas were excluded. In each tract, blocks judged to be representative or typical were selected. Finally, households located ten houses apart from each other were selected within each block. The interviewer instructions were as follows.

"Start at the southeast corner of the designated block. Go around the entire block in a clockwise manner. After completing an interview, skip ten households to select the next one. Go to the next dwelling unit, however, if you encounter any of following situations: respondent not at home, respondent refuses to cooperate, or no qualified respondent available. After completing a block, go to the next assigned block and follow the same procedure until you reach your quota." ◆

In this example, judgment was used to select specific tracts, blocks, and households. Judgmental sampling is inexpensive, convenient, and quick, yet it does not allow direct generalizations to a specific population, usually because the population is not defined explicitly. Judgmental sampling is subjective and its value depends entirely on the researcher's judgment, expertise, and creativity. It may be useful if broad population inferences are not required. As in the department store example, judgment samples are frequently used in commercial marketing research projects. An extension of this technique involves the use of quotas.

Quota Sampling

quota sampling A non-probability sampling technique that is a two-stage restricted judgmental sampling. The first stage consists of developing control categories or quotas of population elements. In the second stage, sample elements are selected based on convenience or judgment.

Quota sampling may be viewed as two-stage restricted judgmental sampling. The first stage consists of developing control categories, or quotas, of population elements. To develop these quotas, the researcher lists relevant control characteristics and determines the distribution of these characteristics in the target population. The relevant control characteristics, which may include sex, age, and race, are identified on the basis of judgment. Often, the quotas are assigned so that the proportion of the sample elements possessing the control characteristics is the same as the proportion of population elements with these characteristics. In other words, the quotas ensure that the composition of the sample is the same as the composition of the population with respect to the characteristics of interest. In the second stage, sample elements are selected based on convenience or judgment. Once the quotas have been assigned, there is considerable freedom in selecting the elements to be included in the sample. The only requirement is that the elements selected fit the control characteristics. This technique is illustrated with the following example.[12]

EXAMPLE
Does Metropolitan Magazine Readership Measure Up? _____

A study is undertaken to determine the readership of certain magazines by the adult population of a metropolitan area with a population of 350,000. A quota sample of 1,000 adults is selected. The control characteristics are sex, age, and race. Based on the composition of the adult population of the community, the quotas are assigned as follows:

	Population Composition	Sample Composition	
Control Characteristic	Percentage	Percentage	Number
Sex			
Male	48	48	480
Female	52	52	520
	100	100	1,000
Age			
18–30	27	27	270
31–45	39	39	390
46–60	16	16	160
Over 60	18	18	180
	100	100	1,000
Race			
White	59	59	590
Black	35	35	350
Other	6	6	60
	100	100	1,000 ◆

Quota sampling can be highly effective in determining magazine readership. ◆ Margot Granitsas/Photo Researchers, Inc.

In this example, quotas are assigned such that the composition of the sample is the same as that of the population. In certain situations, however, it is desirable either to under- or oversample elements with certain characteristics. To illustrate, it may be desirable to oversample heavy users of a product so that their behavior can be examined in detail. Although this type of sample is not representative, it may nevertheless be very relevant.

Even if the sample composition mirrors that of the population with respect to the control characteristics, there is no assurance that the sample is representative. If a characteristic that is relevant to the problem is overlooked, the quota sample will not be representative. Relevant control characteristics are often omitted because there are practical difficulties associated with including many control characteristics. Because the elements within each quota are selected based on convenience or judgment, many sources of selection bias are potentially present. The interviewers may go to selected areas where eligible respondents are more likely to be found. Likewise, they may avoid people who look unfriendly or are not well dressed or those who live in undesirable locations. Quota sampling does not permit assessment of sampling error.[13]

Quota sampling attempts to obtain representative samples at a relatively low cost. Its advantages are the lower costs and greater convenience to the interviewers in selecting elements for each quota. Recently, tighter controls have been imposed on interviewers and interviewing procedures that tend to reduce selection bias, and guidelines have been suggested for improving the quality of mall-intercept quota samples.[14] Under certain conditions, quota sampling obtains results close to those for conventional probability sampling.[15]

Snowball Sampling

snowball sampling A nonprobability sampling technique in which an initial group of respondents is selected randomly. Subsequent respondents are selected based on the referrals or information provided by the initial respondents. By obtaining referrals from referrals, this process may be carried out in waves.

In **snowball sampling**, an initial group of respondents is selected, usually at random. After being interviewed, these respondents are asked to identify others who belong to the target population of interest. Subsequent respondents are selected based on the referrals. By obtaining referrals from referrals, this process may be carried out in waves, thus leading to a snowballing effect. Even though probability sampling is used to select the initial respondents, the final sample is a nonprobability sample. The referrals will have demographic and psychographic characteristics more similar to the persons referring them than would occur by chance.[16]

A major objective of snowball sampling is to estimate characteristics that are rare in the population. Examples include users of particular government or social services, such as food stamps, whose names cannot be revealed; special census groups, such as widowed males under 35; and members of a scattered minority population. Snowball sampling is used in industrial buyer-seller research to identify buyer-seller pairs. The major advantage of snowball sampling is that it substantially increases the likelihood of locating the desired characteristic in the population. It also results in relatively low sampling variance and costs. Snowball sampling is illustrated by the following example.[17]

EXAMPLE
Survey Snowball

To study the demographic profile of marketing research interviewers in Ohio, a sample of interviewers was generated using a variation of snowball sampling. Initial contact with interviewers was made by placing classified advertisements in newspapers in seven major metropolitan areas. These notices asked experienced marketing research interviewers willing to answer 25 questions about their job to write to the author. These responses were increased through a referral system: each interviewer was asked for the names and addresses of other interviewers. Eventually this process identified interviewers from many communities throughout the state who had not seen the original newspaper notices. Only 27% of returned questionnaires resulted from the classified notices; the remainder could be traced to referrals and referrals from referrals.[18] ◆

In this example, note the nonrandom selection of the initial group of respondents through classified advertisements. This procedure was more efficient than random selection. In other cases, random selection of respondents through probability sampling techniques is more appropriate.

PROBABILITY SAMPLING TECHNIQUES

Probability sampling techniques vary in terms of sampling efficiency. Sampling efficiency is a concept that reflects a tradeoff between sampling cost and precision. Precision refers to the level of uncertainty about the characteristic being measured. Precision is inversely related to sampling errors but positively related to cost. The greater the precision, the greater the cost, and most studies require a tradeoff. The researcher should strive for the most efficient sampling design, subject to the budget allocated. The efficiency of a probability sampling technique may be assessed by comparing it with that of simple random sampling.

Simple Random Sampling

simple random sampling A probability sampling technique in which each element in the population has a known and equal probability of selection. Every element is selected independently of every other element, and the sample is drawn by a random procedure from a sampling frame.

In **simple random sampling** (SRS), each element in the population has a known and equal probability of selection. Furthermore, each possible sample of a given size (n) has a known and equal probability of being the sample actually selected. This implies that every element is selected independently of every other element. The sample is drawn by a random procedure from a sampling frame. This method is equivalent to a lottery system in which names are placed in a container, the container is shaken and the names of the winners are then drawn out in an unbiased manner.

To draw a simple random sample, the researcher first compiles a sampling frame in which each element is assigned a unique identification number. Then random numbers are generated to determine which elements to include in the sample. The random numbers may be generated with a computer routine or a table (see Table 1 shown in the Appendix of Statistical Tables). Suppose that a sample of size ten is to be selected from a sampling frame containing 800 elements. This could be done by starting with row 1 and column 1 of Table 1, considering the three right-most digits, and going down the column until ten numbers between 1 and 800 have been selected. Numbers outside this range are ignored. The elements corresponding to the random numbers generated constitute the sample. Thus, in our example, elements 480, 368, 130, 167, 570, 562, 301, 579, 475, and 553 would be selected. Note that the last three digits of row 6 (921) and row 11 (918) were ignored, because they were out of range.

SRS has many desirable features. It is easily understood, the sample results may be projected to the target population, and most approaches to statistical inference assume that the data have been collected by simple random sampling. SRS suffers from at least four significant limitations, however. First, it is often difficult to construct a sampling frame that will permit a simple random sample to be drawn. Second, SRS can result in samples that are very large or spread over large geographic areas, thus increasing the time and cost of data collection. Third, SRS often results in lower precision with larger standard errors than other probability sampling techniques. Fourth, SRS may or may not result in a representative sample. Although samples drawn will represent the population well on average, a given simple random sample may grossly misrepresent the target population. This is more likely if the size of the sample is small. For these reasons, SRS is not widely used in marketing research. Procedures such as systematic sampling are more popular.

Systematic Sampling

systematic sampling A probability sampling technique in which the sample is chosen by selecting a random starting point and then picking every ith element in succession from the sampling frame.

In **systematic sampling**, the sample is chosen by selecting a random starting point and then picking every ith element in succession from the sampling frame. The sampling interval, i, is determined by dividing the population size N by the sample size n and rounding to the nearest integer. For example, there are 100,000 elements in the population and a sample of 1,000 is desired. In this case, the sampling interval, i, is 100. A random number between 1 and 100 is selected. If, for example, this number is 23, the sample consists of elements 23, 123, 223, 323, 423, 523, and so on.[19]

Systematic sampling is similar to SRS in that each population element has a known and equal probability of selection. It is different from SRS, however, in that only the permissible samples of size *n* that can be drawn have a known and equal probability of selection. The remaining samples of size *n* have a zero probability of being selected.

For systematic sampling, the researcher assumes that the population elements are ordered in some respect. In some cases, the ordering (for example, alphabetic listing in a telephone book) is unrelated to the characteristic of interest. In other instances, the ordering is directly related to the characteristic under investigation. For example, credit card customers may be listed in order of outstanding balance, or firms in a given industry may be ordered according to annual sales. If the population elements are arranged in a manner unrelated to the characteristic of interest, systematic sampling will yield results quite similar to SRS.

On the other hand, when the ordering of the elements is related to the characteristic of interest, systematic sampling increases the representativeness of the sample. If firms in an industry are arranged in increasing order of annual sales, a systematic sample will include some small and some large firms. A simple random sample may be unrepresentative because it may contain, for example, only small firms or a disproportionate number of small firms. If the ordering of the elements produces a cyclical pattern, systematic sampling may decrease the representativeness of the sample. To illustrate, consider the use of systematic sampling to generate a sample of monthly department store sales from a sampling frame containing monthly sales for the last 60 years. If a sampling interval of 12 is chosen, the resulting sample would not reflect the month-to-month variation in sales.[20]

Systematic sampling is less costly and easier than SRS because random selection is done only once. Moreover, the random numbers do not have to be matched with individual elements as in SRS. Because some lists contain millions of elements, considerable time can be saved, which reduces the costs of sampling. If information related to the characteristic of interest is available for the population, systematic sampling can be used to obtain a more representative and reliable (lower sampling error) sample than SRS. Another relative advantage is that systematic sampling can even be used without knowledge of the composition (elements) of the sampling frame. For example, every *i*th person leaving a department store or mall can be intercepted. For these reasons, systematic sampling is often employed in consumer mail, telephone, and mall-intercept interviews, as illustrated by the following example.

EXAMPLE

Tennis's Systematic Sampling Returns a Smash

Tennis magazine conducted a mail survey of its subscribers to gain a better understanding of its market. Systematic sampling was employed to select a sample of 1,472 subscribers from the publication's domestic circulation list. If we assume that the subscriber list had 1,472,000 names, the sampling interval would be 1,000 (1,472,000/1,472). A number from 1 to 1,000 was drawn at random. Beginning with that number, every 1,000th was selected.

A brand-new dollar bill was included with the questionnaire as an incentive to respondents. An alert postcard was mailed one week before the survey. A second, follow-up, questionnaire was sent to the whole sample ten days after the initial questionnaire. There were 76 post office returns, so the net effective mailing was 1,396. Six weeks after the first mailing, 778 completed questionnaires were returned, yielding a response rate of 56%.[21] ◆

Stratified Sampling

stratified sampling A probability sampling technique that uses a two-step process to partition the population into subpopulations, or strata. Elements are selected from each stratum by a random procedure.

Stratified sampling is a two-step process in which the population is partitioned into subpopulations, or strata. The strata should be mutually exclusive and collectively exhaustive in that every population element should be assigned to one and only one stratum and no population elements should be omitted. Next, elements are selected from each stratum by a random procedure, usually SRS. Technically, only SRS should be employed in selecting the elements from each stratum. In practice, sometimes systematic sampling and other probability sampling procedures are employed. Stratified sampling differs from quota sampling in that the sample elements are selected probabilistically rather than based on convenience or judgment. A major objective of stratified sampling is to increase precision without increasing cost.[22]

The variables used to partition the population into strata are referred to as stratification variables. The criteria for the selection of these variables consist of homogeneity, heterogeneity, relatedness, and cost. The elements within a stratum should be as homogeneous as possible, but the elements in different strata should be as heterogeneous as possible. The stratification variables should also be closely related to the characteristic of interest. The more closely these criteria are met, the greater the effectiveness in controlling extraneous sampling variation. Finally, the variables should decrease the cost of the stratification process by being easy to measure and apply. Variables commonly used for stratification include demographic characteristics (as illustrated in the example for quota sampling), type of customer (credit card versus non–credit card), size of firm, or type of industry. It is possible to use more than one variable for stratification, although more than two are seldom used because of pragmatic and cost considerations. Although the number of strata to use is a matter of judgment, experience suggests the use of no more than six. Beyond six strata, any gain in precision is more than offset by the increased cost of stratification and sampling. The selection of stratification variables is illustrated with an example from the American Express National Travel Forecast survey.

EXAMPLE
Tracking Travel By Telephone

The American Express National Travel Forecast survey was conducted by R. H. Bruskin and Associates, through OmniTel, a weekly telephone omnibus survey. A total of 1,030 people (525 women, 505 men) was interviewed. The variables used for stratification were sex, age, income, and census region. The survey found that Americans in the age group of 25 to 49 years, who are most likely to have children at home, were most interested in visiting Orlando, Florida. With the elderly (65 or older), Washington, D.C., was particularly popular. Younger Americans aged 18 to 34 were most likely to rank vacations as a top priority. Because travel preferences varied with age, age was indeed a useful stratification variable. The other stratification variables—namely sex, income, and census region—did not have a significant effect on travel preferences. Hence, sampling costs could have been decreased without decreasing precision by stratifying on the basis of age alone.[23] ◆

Another important decision involves the use of proportionate or disproportionate sampling (see Figure 11.2). In proportionate stratified sampling, the size of the sample drawn from each stratum is proportionate to the relative size of that stratum in the total population. In disproportionate stratified sampling, the size of the sample from each stra-

The American Express Travel Service is positioned to appeal to the different demographic segments of the travel market. ◆ American Express Travel Services.

tum is proportionate to the relative size of that stratum and to the standard deviation of the distribution of the characteristic of interest among all the elements in that stratum. The logic behind disproportionate sampling is simple. First, strata with larger relative sizes arc more influential in determining the population mean, and these strata should also exert a greater influence in deriving the sample estimates. Consequently, more elements should be drawn from strata of larger relative size. Second, to increase precision, more elements should be drawn from strata with larger standard deviations and fewer elements should be drawn from strata with smaller standard deviations. (If all the elements in a stratum arc identical, a sample size of one will result in perfect information.) Note that the two methods are identical if the characteristic of interest has the same standard deviation within each stratum.

Disproportionate sampling requires that some estimate of the relative variation, or standard deviation of the distribution of the characteristic of interest, within strata be known. As this information is not always available, the researcher may have to rely on intuition and logic to determine sample sizes for each stratum. For example, large retail stores might be expected to have greater variation in the sales of some products as compared with small stores. Hence, the size of large stores in a sample may be disproportionately large. When the researcher is primarily interested in examining differences between strata, a common sampling strategy is to select the same sample size from each stratum.

Stratified sampling can ensure that all the important subpopulations are represented in the sample. This is particularly important if the distribution of the characteristic of interest in the population is skewed. For example, because most households have annual incomes of less than $50,000, the distribution of household incomes is skewed. Very few households have annual incomes of $125,000 or more. If a simple random sample is taken, households with incomes of $125,000 or more may not be adequately represented. Stratified sampling would guarantee that the sample contains a certain number of these households. Stratified sampling combines the simplicity of SRS with potential gains in precision. Therefore, it is a popular sampling technique.

Cluster Sampling

cluster sampling A two-step probability sampling technique where the target population is first divided into mutually exclusive and collectively exhaustive subpopulations called clusters and then, a random sample of clusters is selected based on a probability sampling technique such as simple random sampling. For each selected cluster, either all the elements are included in the sample or a sample of elements is drawn probabilistically.

In **cluster sampling**, the target population is first divided into mutually exclusive and collectively exhaustive subpopulations, or clusters. Then, a random sample of clusters is selected, based on a probability sampling technique such as SRS. For each selected cluster, either all the elements are included in the sample or a sample of elements is drawn probabilistically. If all the elements in each selected cluster are included in the sample, the procedure is called one-stage cluster sampling. If a sample of elements is drawn probabilistically from each selected cluster, the procedure is two-stage cluster sampling. As shown in Figure 11.3, two-stage cluster sampling can be either simple two-stage cluster sampling involving SRS or probability proportionate to size (PPS) sampling. Furthermore, a cluster sample can have multiple (more than two) stages, as in multistage cluster sampling.

The key distinction between cluster sampling and stratified sampling is that in cluster sampling only a sample of subpopulations (clusters) is chosen, whereas in stratified sampling all the subpopulations (strata) are selected for further sampling. The objectives of the two methods are also different. The objective of cluster sampling is to increase sampling efficiency by decreasing costs, but the objective of stratified sampling is to increase precision. With respect to homogeneity and heterogeneity, the criteria for forming clusters are just the opposite of that for strata. Elements within a cluster should be as heterogeneous as possible, but clusters themselves should be as homogeneous as possible. Ideally, each cluster should be a small-scale representation of the population. In cluster sampling, a sampling frame is needed only for those clusters selected for the sample.

area sampling A common form of cluster sampling in which the clusters consist of geographic areas such as counties, housing tracts, blocks, or other area descriptions.

A common form of cluster sampling is **area sampling**, in which the clusters consist of geographic areas, such as counties, housing tracts, or blocks. If only one level of sampling takes place in selecting the basic elements (for example, if the researcher samples blocks and then all the households within the selected blocks are included in the sample), the design is called single-stage area sampling. If two (or more) levels of sampling take place before the basic elements are selected (if the researcher samples blocks and then samples households within selected blocks), the design is called two-stage (or multistage) area sampling. The distinguishing feature of one-stage area sample is that all the households in the selected blocks (or geographic areas) are included in the sample.

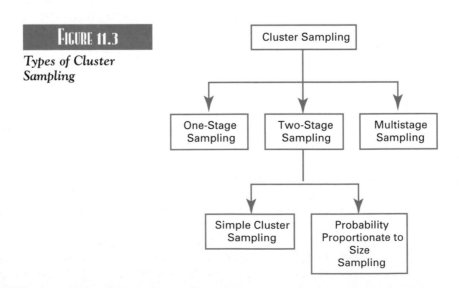

FIGURE 11.3

Types of Cluster Sampling

There are two types of two-stage designs, as shown in Figure 11.3. One type involves SRS at the first stage (e.g., sampling blocks) as well as the second stage (e.g., sampling households within blocks). This design is called simple two-stage cluster sampling. In this design the fraction of elements (e.g., households) selected at the second stage is the same for each sample cluster (e.g., selected blocks). The following example illustrates two-stage area sampling.

EXAMPLE
Blocks with Bucks

A marketing research project investigated the behavior of affluent consumers. A simple random sample of 800 block groups was selected from a listing of neighborhoods with average incomes exceeding $50,000 in the states ranked in the top half by income according to census data. Commercial list organizations supplied head-of-household names and addresses for approximately 95% of the census-tabulated homes in these 800 block groups. From the 213,000 enumerated households, 9,000 were selected by simple random sampling.[24] ◆

Two-stage area sampling has been used to select affluent households. ◆ Gary Russ/The Image Bank.

probability proportionate to size A selection method where the probability of selecting a sampling unit in a selected cluster varies inversely with the size of the cluster. Therefore, the size of all the resulting clusters is approximately equal.

This design is appropriate when the clusters are equal in size, that is, when the clusters contain approximately the same number of sampling units. If they differ greatly in size, however, simple two-stage cluster sampling can lead to biased estimates. Sometimes the clusters can be made of equal size by combining clusters. When this option is not feasible, probability proportionate to size (PPS) sampling can be used.

In **probability proportionate to size** (PPS) sampling, the clusters are sampled with probability proportional to size. The size of a cluster is defined in terms of the number of sampling units within that cluster. Thus, in the first stage, large clusters are more likely to be included than small clusters. In the second stage, the probability of selecting a sampling unit in a selected cluster varies inversely with the size of the cluster. Thus, the probability that any particular sampling unit will be included in the sample is equal for all units, because the unequal first stage probabilities are balanced by the unequal second stage probabilities. The numbers of sampling units included from the selected clusters are approximately equal.

Cluster sampling has two major advantages: feasibility and low cost. In many situations the only sampling frames readily available for the target population are clusters, not population elements. It is often impossible to compile a list of all consumers in a population, given the resources and constraints. Lists of geographical areas, telephone exchanges and other clusters of consumers, however, can be constructed relatively easily. Cluster sampling is the most cost-effective probability sampling technique. This advantage must be weighed against several limitations. Cluster sampling results in relatively imprecise samples, and it is difficult to form heterogeneous clusters, because, for example, households in a block tend to be similar rather than dissimilar.[25] It can be difficult to compute and interpret statistics based on clusters. The strengths and weaknesses of cluster sampling and the other basic sampling techniques are summarized in Table 11.3. Figure 11.4 describes the procedures for drawing probability samples.

Other Probability Sampling Techniques

In addition to the four basic probability sampling techniques, there are a variety of other sampling techniques. Most of these may be viewed as extensions of the basic techniques and were developed to address complex sampling problems. Two techniques with some relevance to marketing research are sequential sampling and double sampling.

TABLE 11.3 *Strengths and Weaknesses of Basic Sampling Techniques*	Technique	Strengths	Weaknesses
	Nonprobability Sampling		
	Convenience sampling	Least expensive, least time-consuming, most convenient	Selection bias, sample not representative, not recommended for descriptive or causal research
	Judgmental sampling	Low cost, convenient, not time-consuming	Does not allow generalization, subjective
	Quota sampling	Sample can be controlled for certain characteristics	Selection bias, no assurance of representativeness
	Snowball sampling	Can estimate rare characteristics	Time-consuming
	Probability Sampling		
	Simple random sampling (SRS)	Easily understood, results projectable	Difficult to construct sampling frame, expensive, lower precision, no assurance of representativeness
	Systematic sampling	Can increase representativeness, easier to implement than SRS, sampling frame not necessary	Can decrease representativeness
	Stratified sampling	Includes all important subpopulations, precision	Difficult to select relevant stratification variables, not feasible to stratify on many variables, expensive
	Cluster sampling	Easy to implement, cost effective	Imprecise, difficult to compute and interpret results

FIGURE 11.4

*Procedures
for Drawing
Probability Samples*

Simple Random Sampling

1. Select a suitable sampling frame.
2. Each element is assigned a number from 1 to N (population size).
3. Generate n (sample size) different random numbers between 1 and N using a micro-computer or mainframe software package or using a table of simple random numbers (Table 1 in the Appendix of Statistical Tables). To use Table 1, select the appropriate number of digits (e.g., if $N = 900$, select three digits). Arbitrarily select a beginning number. Then proceed either up or down until n different numbers between 1 and N have been selected. Discard 0, duplicate numbers, and numbers greater than N.
4. The numbers generated denote the elements that should be included in the sample.

Systematic Sampling

1. Select a suitable sampling frame.
2. Each element is assigned a number from 1 to N (population size).
3. Determine the sampling interval, i: $i = N/n$. If i is a fraction, round to the nearest integer.
4. Select a random number, r, between 1 and i, as explained in simple random sampling.
5. The elements with the following numbers will comprise the systematic random sample: $r, r + i, r + 2i, r + 3i, r + 4i, ..., r + (n - 1)i$.

Stratified Sampling

1. Select a suitable sampling frame.
2. Select the stratification variable(s) and the number of strata, H.
3. Divide the entire population into H strata. Based on the classification variable, each element of the population is assigned to one of the H strata.
4. In each stratum, number the elements from 1 to N_h (the population size of stratum h).
5. Determine the sample size of each stratum, n_h, based on proportionate or disproportionate stratified sampling, where $\sum_{h=1}^{H} n_h = n$.
6. In each stratum, select a simple random sample of size n_h.

Cluster Sampling

We describe the procedure for selecting a two-stage PPS sample, because this represents the most commonly used general case.

1. Assign a number from 1 to N to each element in the population.
2. Divide the population into C clusters of which c will be included in the sample.
3. Calculate the sampling interval, i, $i = N/c$. If i is a fraction, round to the nearest integer.
4. Select a random number, r, between 1 and i, as explained in simple random sampling.
5. Identify elements with the following numbers: $r, r + i, r + 2i, r + 3i, ..., r + (c - 1)i$.
6. Select the clusters that contain the identified elements.
7. Select sampling units within each selected cluster based on SRS or systematic sampling. The number of sampling units selected from each sample cluster is approximately the same and equal to n/c.
8. If the population of a cluster exceeds the sampling interval i, that cluster is selected with certainty. That cluster is removed from further consideration. Calculate the new population size, N^*, the number of clusters to be selected c^* ($= c - 1$), and the new sampling interval i_*. Repeat this process until each of the remaining clusters has a population less than the relevant sampling interval. If b clusters have been selected with certainty, select the remaining $c - b$ clusters according to steps 1 through 7. The fraction of units to be sampled from each cluster selected with certainty is the overall sampling fraction $= n/N$. Thus, for clusters selected with certainty, we would select $n_s = n/N(N_1 + N_2 + ... + N_b)$ units. The units selected from clusters selected under PPS sampling will therefore be $n^* = n - n_s$.

sequential sampling A probability sampling technique in which the population elements are sampled sequentially, data collection and analysis are done at each stage, and a decision is made as to whether additional population elements should be sampled.

In **sequential sampling**, the population elements are sampled sequentially, data collection and analysis are done at each stage, and a decision is made as to whether additional population elements should be sampled. The sample size is not known in advance, but a decision rule is stated before sampling begins. At each stage, this rule indicates whether sampling should be continued or whether enough information has been obtained. Sequential sampling has been used to determine preferences for two competing alternatives. In one study, respondents were asked which of two alternatives they preferred, and sampling was terminated when sufficient evidence was accumulated to validate a preference. It has also been used to establish the price differential between a standard model and a deluxe model of a consumer durable.[26]

double sampling A sampling technique in which certain population elements are sampled twice.

In **double sampling**, also called two-phase sampling, certain population elements are sampled twice. In the first phase, a sample is selected and some information is collected from all the elements in the sample. In the second phase, a subsample is drawn from the original sample and additional information is obtained from the elements in the subsample. The process may be extended to three or more phases, and the different phases may take place simultaneously or at different times. Double sampling can be useful when no sampling frame is readily available for selecting final sampling units but when the elements of the frame are known to be contained within a broader sampling frame. For example, a researcher wants to select households in a given city that consume apple juice. The households of interest are contained within the set of all households, but the researcher does not know which ones they are. In applying double sampling, the researcher would obtain a sampling frame of all households in the first phase. This would be constructed from the city directory or purchased. Then a sample of households would be drawn, using systematic random sampling to determine the amount of apple juice consumed. In the second phase, households that consume apple juice would be selected and stratified according to the amount of apple juice consumed. Then a stratified random sample would be drawn and detailed questions regarding apple juice consumption asked.[27]

CHOOSING NONPROBABILITY VERSUS PROBABILITY SAMPLING

The choice between nonprobability and probability samples should be based on considerations such as the nature of the research, relative magnitude of nonsampling versus sampling errors, and variability in the population, as well as statistical and operational considerations (see Table 11.4). For example, in exploratory research, the findings are treated as preliminary and the use of probability sampling may not be warranted. On the other hand, in conclusive research where the researcher wishes to use the results to estimate overall market shares or the size of the total market, probability sampling is favored. Probability samples allow statistical projection of the results to a target population.

For some research problems, highly accurate estimates of population characteristics are required. In these situations, the elimination of selection bias and the ability to calculate sampling error make probability sampling desirable. Probability sampling will not always result in more accurate results, however. If nonsampling errors are likely to be an important factor, then nonprobability sampling may be preferable because the use of judgment may allow greater control over the sampling process.

Another consideration is the homogeneity of the population with respect to the variables of interest. A heterogeneous population would favor probability sampling because it would be more important to secure a representative sample. Probability sampling is preferable from a statistical viewpoint, as it is the basis of most common statistical techniques.

TABLE 11.4		Conditions Favoring the Use of	
Choosing Nonprobability vs. Probability Sampling	Factors	Nonprobability Sampling	Probability Sampling
	Nature of research	Exploratory	Conclusive
	Relative magnitude of sampling and nonsampling errors	Nonsampling errors are larger	Sampling errors are larger
	Variability in the population	Homogeneous (low)	Heterogeneous (high)
	Statistical considerations	Unfavorable	Favorable
	Operational considerations	Favorable	Unfavorable

Probability sampling is sophisticated and requires statistically trained researchers, however. It generally costs more and takes longer than nonprobability sampling. In many marketing research projects, it is difficult to justify the additional time and expense. Therefore, in practice, the objectives of the study dictate which sampling method will be used.

USES OF NONPROBABILITY AND PROBABILITY SAMPLING

Nonprobability sampling is used in concept tests, package tests, name tests, and copy tests where projections to the populations are usually not needed. In such studies, interest centers on the proportion of the sample that gives various responses or expresses various attitudes. Samples for these studies can be drawn using methods such as mall-intercept quota sampling. On the other hand, probability sampling is used when there is a need for highly accurate estimates of market share or sales volume for the entire market. National market tracking studies, which provide information on product category and brand usage rates as well as psychographic and demographic profiles of users, use probability sampling. Studies that use probability sampling generally employ telephone interviews. Stratified and systematic sampling are combined with some form of random-digit dialing to select the respondents.

INTERNATIONAL MARKETING RESEARCH

Implementing the sampling design process in international marketing research is seldom easy. Several factors should be considered in defining the target population. The relevant element (respondent) may differ from country to country. In the United States, children play an important role in the purchase of children's cereals. In countries with authoritarian child-rearing practices, however, the mother may be the relevant element. Women play a key role in the purchase of automobiles and other durables in the United States, but in male-dominated societies, such as in the Middle East, such decisions are made by men. Accessibility also varies across countries. In Mexico, houses cannot be entered by strangers because of boundary walls and servants. Additionally, dwelling units may be unnumbered and streets unidentified, making it difficult to locate designated households.[28]

Developing an appropriate sampling frame is a difficult task. In many countries, particularly in developing countries, reliable information about the target population may not be available from secondary sources. Government data may be unavailable or highly biased. Population lists may not be available commercially. The time and money required to compile these lists may be prohibitive. For example, in Saudi Arabia, there is no officially recognized census of population, no elections and hence no voter registration records, and no accurate maps of population centers. In this situation, the interviewers could be instructed to begin at specified starting points and to sample every nth dwelling until the specified number of units has been sampled.

Given the lack of suitable sampling frames, the inaccessibility of certain respondents, such as women in some cultures, and the dominance of personal interviewing, probability sampling techniques are uncommon in international marketing research. Quota sampling has been used widely in the developed and developing countries in both consumer and industrial surveys. Snowball sampling is also appealing when the characteristic of interest is rare in the target population or when respondents are hard to reach. For example, it has been suggested that in Saudi Arabia graduate students be employed to hand-deliver questionnaires to relatives and friends.[29] These initial respondents can be asked for referrals to other potential respondents and so on. This approach would result in a large sample size and a high response rate.

Sampling techniques and procedures vary in accuracy, reliability, and cost from country to country. If the same sampling procedures are used in each country, the results may not be comparable.[30] To achieve comparability in sample composition and representativeness, it may be desirable to use different sampling techniques in different countries, as the following example illustrates.

EXAMPLE
Achieving Sample Comparability through Diversity

Research in the United States has shown that most consumers feel that a purchase is accompanied by a degree of risk when they choose among alternative brands. A study was conducted to compare the U.S. results with those from Mexico, Thailand, and Saudi Arabia. The targeted respondent in each culture was an upper-middle-income woman residing in a major city. Differences in sampling occurred across the countries, however. In the United States, random sampling from the telephone directory was used. In Mexico, judgmental sampling was used by having experts identify neighborhoods where the target respondent lived; homes were then randomly selected for personal interviews. In Thailand, judgmental sampling was also used, but the survey took place in major urban centers and a store-intercept technique was used to select respondents. And in Saudi Arabia, convenience sampling employing the snowball procedure was used because there were no lists from which sampling frames could be drawn and because social customs prohibited spontaneous personal interviews. Thus, comparability in sample composition and representativeness was achieved by using different sampling procedures in different countries.[31] ◆

ETHICS IN MARKETING RESEARCH

The researcher has several ethical responsibilities to both the client and the respondents pertaining to sampling. With regards to the client, the researcher must develop a sampling design that best fits the project in an effort to minimize the sampling and nonsampling errors (see Chapter 3). When probability sampling can be used it should be.

When nonprobability or convenience sampling is used, effort should be made to obtain a representative sample. It is unethical and misleading to treat nonprobability samples as probability samples and to project the results to a target population. As the following example demonstrates, appropriate definition of the population and the sampling frame, and application of the correct sampling techniques are essential if the research is to be conducted and the findings used ethically.

EXAMPLE

Systematic Sampling Reveals Systematic Gender Differences in Ethical Judgments

In an attempt to explore differences in research ethical judgments between male and female marketing professionals, data were obtained from 420 respondents. The population was defined as marketing professionals, and the sampling frame was the American Marketing Association directory. The respondents were selected based on a systematic sampling plan from the directory. Attempts were made to overcome nonresponse by not only mailing a cover letter and a stamped, preaddressed return envelope along with the questionnaire, but also by promising to provide each respondent with a copy of the research study results. Results of the survey showed that female marketing professionals, in general, demonstrated higher levels of research ethical judgments than their male counterparts.[32] ◆

Researchers must be extremely sensitive to preserving the anonymity of the respondents when conducting business to business research with small populations, particularly when reporting the findings to the client. When the population size is small, it is easier to discern the identities of the respondents than when the samples are drawn from a large population. Special care must be taken when sample details are too revealing and when using verbatim quotations in reports to the client. This problem is acute in areas such as employee research. Here a breech of a respondent's anonymity can cost the respondent a raise, a promotion, or, at worst, employment. In such situations, a special effort should be made to protect the identities of the respondents.

COMPUTER APPLICATIONS

Microcomputers and mainframes can make the sampling design process more effective and efficient than other methods. Because they can handle lists of population elements as well as geographical maps, computers can be used for specifying the sampling frame. Microcomputers and mainframes may be employed to select the sample needed, using either nonprobability or probability techniques. Once the sampling frame has been determined, simulations can be used to generate random numbers and select the sample directly from the database. Software such as SPSS, SAS, or BMDP (microcomputer and mainframe packages) or Lotus 1-2-3 can be used for this purpose.[33]

Microcomputers are particularly suited for sample generation and control in telephone interviewing. For example, GENESYS sampling systems provide the market researcher the power to compose an accurate random-digit dialing (RDD) sample while avoiding the waste of dialing nonproductive numbers during surveys. In this way, GENESYS systems by Marketing Systems Group of Philadelphia bring the power to compose a sample frame efficiently and then to perform simple random sampling.

According to Michael McDonald, sampling services manager at Sophisticated Data Research (SDR) in Atlanta, the key advantage to the GENESYS system is that it provides the user with the capability to generate RDD samples with the greatest efficiency possible. An example from the sampling of potential customers for a cable TV system illustrates this point. Although a cable TV franchise has strict physical and legal boundaries, the phone exchanges within its boundaries include many phone numbers not in the franchise area. The researcher must screen the population of households for these telephone exchanges to determine a more accurate sampling frame.

In Exhibit 11.1, the Zip Code Coverage Report is presented for a cable TV franchise in Anniston, Alabama. The first column of numbers represents the Anniston telephone exchanges (telephone numbers in an exchange share the same first three digits) with their preceding 205 area code. The second column represents numbers of households (HH). The row designated Total shows that just 61% of the numbers in the 12 telephone exchanges associated with the zip codes of the franchise area include telephone numbers actually in the cable TV system's franchise area. As can be seen, the sampling frame can be accurately identified using GENESYS. Here, 12,290 (39%) of the households with telephone exchanges associated with the zip codes of the cable system franchise area can be eliminated from the sampling frame.

Because the RDD samples are randomly generated from a base of known residential exchanges, they include both listed and unlisted households within the sampling frame, providing the best overall representation and projectability of the population. Still, a typical RDD sample will contain about 10% business numbers. To address this inefficiency, GENESYS-Plus provides additional screening by purging numbers for Yellow Page–listed businesses from the sample frame. As a result, the percentage of businesses within the sample frame can be reduced to approximately 5%. (Unfortunately, many businesses choose not to be listed in the Yellow Pages or have secondary phone lines not listed in the Yellow Pages.)

To accomplish this additional screening, GENESYS-Plus is updated twice annually to reflect the most current residential exchanges as well as the most recent update to the national file of Yellow Page–listed businesses. In addition, the GENESYS-Plus

EXHIBIT 11.1

Zip Code Coverage Report

```
ZIP Code Coverage Report

Exchange File: SYS$SYSDEVICE:[GENESYS.BID.MEM]ZIP.EXC;1
```

Exchange	HH	AREA 1 HH	%	%	AREA 2 HH	%	%	NON-COVERAGE HH	%	%
Total	31404	19114	61	100	0	0	100	12290	39	100
205235	136	136	100	1	0	0	0	0	0	0
205231	46	46	100	1	0	0	0	0	0	0
205236	4600	4457	97	24	0	0	0	143	3	1
205237	4713	4533	96	48	0	0	0	180	4	3
205238	1572	1497	95	56	0	0	0	75	5	3
205835	1515	1378	91	63	0	0	0	137	9	4
205831	5180	4641	90	87	0	0	0	539	10	9
205848	77	38	49	88	0	0	0	39	51	9
205820	4616	2156	47	99	0	0	0	2460	3	29
205435	4785	200	4	100	0	0	0	4585	96	66
205892	1586	21	1	100	0	0	0	1565	99	79
205447	2578	11	0	100	0	0	0	2567	100	100

process compares the data file of 14 million businesses against the file of 70 million listed residential phone numbers. This minimizes the sampling error that would be normally associated with purging the nearly 800,000 residences that share a business phone number.

The GENESYS-ID system offers further increases in efficiency by identifying and purging nonworking and disconnected numbers through a nonringing verification feature. This process can identify up to 50% of the nonworking numbers within a sample. The base rate for GENESYS' RDD sampling is 10¢ per resulting telephone number in the sample. The cost for a GENESYS Plus alone would bring the cost to 11.5¢ per element in the sample, while adding GENESYS-ID would bring the total cost to 14¢ per number.

Firms like Survey Sampling Inc., SDR Sampling Services, and Maritz Sampling System have developed proprietary sampling software to generate samples using a variety of sampling techniques. For example, Survey Sampling Inc. has developed software for a range of random-digit dialing samples, clustered samples, and directory listed samples. They have also developed software to screen and predetermine nonworking telephone numbers. This greatly increases the efficiency of the sample and saves time and money.

SUMMARY

Information about the characteristics of a population may be obtained by conducting either a sample or a census. Budget and time limits, large population size, and small variance in the characteristic of interest favor the use of a sample. Sampling is also preferred when the cost of sampling error is low, the cost of nonsampling error is high, the nature of measurement is destructive, and attention must be focused on individual cases. The opposite set of conditions favors the use of a census.

Sampling design begins by defining the target population in terms of elements, sampling units, extent, and time. Then the sampling frame should be determined. A sampling frame is a representation of the elements of the target population. It consists of a list of directions for identifying the target population. At this stage, it is important to recognize any sampling frame errors that may exist. The next step involves selecting a sampling technique and determining the sample size. In addition to quantitative analysis, several qualitative considerations should be taken into account in determining the sample size. Finally, execution of the sampling process requires detailed specifications for each step in the sampling process.

Sampling techniques may be classified as nonprobability and probability techniques. Nonprobability sampling techniques rely on the researcher's judgment. Consequently, they do not permit an objective evaluation of the precision of the sample results, and the estimates obtained are not statistically projectable to the population. The commonly used nonprobability sampling techniques include convenience sampling, judgmental sampling, quota sampling, and snowball sampling.

In probability sampling techniques, sampling units are selected by chance. Each sampling unit has a nonzero chance of being selected, and the researcher can prespecify every potential sample of a given size that could be drawn from the population as well as the probability of selecting each sample. It is also possible to determine the precision of the sample estimates and inferences and make projections to the target population. Probability sampling techniques include simple random sampling, systematic sampling, stratified sampling, cluster sampling, sequential sampling, and double sampling. The choice between probability and nonprobability sampling should be based on the nature of the research, degree of error tolerance, relative magnitude of sampling and nonsampling errors, variability in the population, and statistical and operational considerations.

When conducting international marketing research, it is desirable to achieve comparability in sample composition and representativeness even though this may require the use of different sampling techniques in different countries. It is unethical and misleading to treat nonprobability samples as probability samples and to project the results to a target population. Computers can be used to make the sampling design process more effective and efficient.[34]

ACRONYMS

The sampling design process and the steps involved may be represented by the acronym SAMPLE:

S   ampling design process
A   mount: sample size determination
M   ethod: sampling technique selection
P   opulation definition
L   ist: sampling frame determination
E   xecution of the sampling process

EXERCISES

QUESTIONS

1. What is the major difference between a sample and a census?
2. Under what conditions would a sample be preferable to a census? A census preferable to a sample?
3. Describe the sampling design process.
4. How should the target population be defined?
5. What is a sampling unit? How is it different from the population element?
6. What qualitative factors should be considered in determining the sample size?
7. How do probability sampling techniques differ from nonprobability sampling techniques?
8. What is the least expensive and least time-consuming of all sampling techniques? What are the major limitations of this technique?
9. What is the major difference between judgmental and convenience sampling?
10. What is the relationship between quota sampling and judgmental sampling?
11. What are the distinguishing features of simple random sampling?
12. Describe the procedure for selecting a systematic random sample.
13. Describe stratified sampling. What are the criteria for the selection of stratification variables?
14. What are the differences between proportionate and disproportionate stratified sampling?
15. Describe the cluster sampling procedure. What is the key distinction between cluster sampling and stratified sampling?
16. What factors should be considered in choosing between probability and nonprobability sampling?

PROBLEMS

1. Define the appropriate target population and the sampling frame in each of the following situations:
   a. The manufacturer of a new cereal brand wants to conduct in-home product usage tests in Chicago.
   b. A national chain store wants to determine the shopping behavior of customers who have its store charge card.

    c. A local TV station wants to determine households' viewing habits and programming preferences.

    d. The local chapter of the American Marketing Association wants to test the effectiveness of its new member drive in Atlanta.

2. A manufacturer would like to survey users to determine the demand potential for a new power press. The new press has a capacity of 500 tons and costs $225,000. It is used for forming products from lightweight and heavyweight steel and can be used by automobile, construction equipment, and major appliance manufacturers.

    a. Identify the population and sampling frame that could be used.

    b. Describe how a simple random sample can be drawn using the identified sampling frame.

    c. Could a stratified sample be used? If so, how?

    d. Could a cluster sample be used? If so, how?

    e. Which sampling technique would you recommend? Why?

COMPUTER EXERCISES

1. Using software such as GENESYS, generate a random-digit telephone sample of 1,000 people in your metropolitan area.

2 Using a microcomputer or mainframe program, generate a set of 1,000 random numbers for selecting a simple random sample.

NOTES

1. The Warner-Lambert Company, *The American Chicle Youth Poll*, 1987.

2. H. Assael and J. Keon, "Nonsampling vs. Sampling Errors in Sampling Research," *Journal of Marketing* (Spring 1982): 114–23.

3. "Just a Traditional Census," *U.S. News & World Report* (July 29, 1991): 10.

4. This discussion is based on: Rena Bartos, "Alfred Politz: Sampling Innovator," *Journal of Advertising Research* 26 (February–March 1986): 26–29.; Martin R. Frankel, "Sampling Theory," in Peter H. Rossi, James D. Wright, and Andy B. Anderson (eds.), *Handbook of Survey Research* (Orlando, FL: Academic Press, 1983), pp. 21–67; R. M. Jaeger, *Sampling in Education and the Social Sciences* (New York: Longman, 1984): pp. 28–29; and Graham Kalton, *Introduction to Survey Sampling* (Beverly Hills: Sage Publications, 1982).

5. Seymour Sudman, "Applied Sampling," in Peter H. Rossi, James D. Wright, and Andy B. Anderson (eds.), *Handbook of Survey Research* (Orlando, FL: Academic Press, 1983), pp. 145–94.

6. Edward Blair, "Sampling Issues in Trade Area Maps Drawn from Shopper Surveys," *Journal of Marketing* 47 (Winter 1983): 98–106.

7. For a comparison of directory-based sampling with random-digit dialing, see R. Czaja, J. Blair, and J. P. Sebestik, "Respondent Selection in a Telephone Survey: A Comparison of Three Techniques," *Journal of Marketing Research* (August 1982); P. Ellison, "Phone Directory Samples Just as Balanced as Samples from Computer Random Digit Dialing," *Marketing News* (January 11, 1980): 8; and P. E. Moberg, "Biases in Unlisted Phone Numbers," *Journal of Advertising Research* (August–September 1982): 51–55.

8. For the effect of sample frame error on research results, see Kelly E. Fish, James H. Barnes, and Benjamin F. Banahan III, "Convenience or Calamity," *Journal of Health Care Marketing* 14 (Spring 1994): 45–49.

9. "Florida Travel Habits Subject of Phone Survey," *Quirk's Marketing Research Review* (May 1987): 10, 11, 31, 56, 60.

10. For a recent application of convenience sampling, see Banwari Mittal, "An Integrated Framework for Relating Diverse Consumer Characteristics to Supermarket Coupon Redemption," *Journal of Marketing Research* 31 (November 1994): 533–45.

11. "Students Seek Good Careers, Successful Marriages," *Quirk's Marketing Research Review* (June–July 1988): 26.

12. Catherine Marsh and E. Scarbrough, "Testing Nine Hypotheses about Quota Sampling," *Journal of Market Research Society* (UK) 32 (October 1990): 485–506; and Leslie Kish, *Survey Sampling* (New York: Wiley, 1965), p. 552.

13. R. M. Jaeger, *Sampling in Education and the Social Sciences* (New York: Longman, 1984).

14. Seymour Sudman, "Improving the Quality of Shopping Center Sampling," *Journal of Marketing Research* 17 (November 1980): 423–31.

15. Graham Kalton, *Introduction to Survey Sampling* (Beverly Hills: Sage Publications, 1982).

16. For a recent application of snowball sampling, see Gary L. Frankwick, James C. Ward, Michael D. Hutt, and Peter H. Reingen, "Evolving Patterns of Organizational Beliefs in the Formation of Strategy," *Journal of Marketing* 58 (April 1994): 96–110.

17. If certain procedures for listing members of the rare population are followed strictly, the snowball sample can be treated as a probability sample. See Graham Kalton and Dallas W. Anderson, "Sampling Rare Populations," *Journal of the Royal Statistical Association* (1986): 65–82; Patrick Biernacki and Dan Waldorf, "Snowball Sampling: Problems and Techniques of Chain Referred Sampling," *Sociological Methods and Research* 10 (November 1981): 141–63; and George S. Rothbart, Michelle Fine, and Seymour Sudman, "On Finding and Interviewing the Needles in the Haystack: The Use of Multiplicity Sampling," *Public Opinion Quarterly* 46 (Fall 1982): 408–21.

18. Raymond F. Barker, "A Demographic Profile of Marketing Research Interviewers," *Journal of the Market Research Society* (July 1987): 279–92.

19. When the sampling interval, *i*, is not a whole number, the easiest solution is to use as the interval the nearest whole number below or above *i*. If rounding has too great an effect on the sample size, add or delete the extra cases.

20. For a recent application of systematic random sampling, see Goutam Chakraborty, Richard Ettenson, and Gary Gaeth, "How Consumers Choose Health Insurance," *Journal of Health Care Marketing* 14 (Spring 1994): 21–33.

21. "Readership Survey Serves *Tennis* Magazine's Marketing Needs," *Quirk's Marketing Research Review* (May 1988): 75–76.

22. For a recent application of stratified random sampling, see Samaradasa Weerahandi and Soumyo Moitra, "Using Survey Data to Predict Adoption and Switching for Services," *Journal of Marketing Research* 32 (February 1995): 85–96.

23. "Vacations High Priority Among Americans, Survey Shows," *Quirk's Marketing Research Review* (May 1988): 16–19.

24. Thomas J. Stanley and Murphy A. Sewall, "The Response of Affluent Consumers to Mail Surveys," *Journal of Advertising Research* (June–July 1986): 55–58.

25. Geographic clustering of rare populations, however, can be an advantage. See Seymour Sudman, "Efficient Screening Methods for the Sampling of Geographically Clustered Special Populations," *Journal of Marketing Research* 22 (February 1985): 20–29.

26. E. J. Anderson, K. Gorton, and R. Tudor, "The Application of Sequential Analysis in Market Research," *Journal of Marketing Research* 17 (February 1980): 97–105.

27. For more discussion of double sampling, see Martin R. Frankel and Lester R. Frankel, "Probability Sampling," in Robert Ferber (ed.) *Handbook of Marketing Research* (New York: McGraw-Hill, 1974): pp. 2-230–2-246.

28. For the use of different nonprobability and probability sampling techniques in cross-cultural research, see Samiee Saeed and Insik Jeong, "Cross-Cultural Research in Advertising: An Assessment of Methodologies," *Journal of the Academy of Marketing Science* 22 (Summer 1994): 205–15.

29. S. Tuncalp, "The Marketing Research Scene in Saudi Arabia," *European Journal of Marketing* 22(5) (1988): 15–22.

30. Lucy Webster, "Comparability in Multi-Country Surveys," *Journal of Advertising Research* 6 (December 1966): 14–18.

31. B. J. Verhage, U. Yavas, R. T. Green, and E. Borak, "The Perceived Risk Brand Loyalty Relationship: An International Perspective," *Journal of Global Marketing* 3(3) (1990): 7–22.

32. I. P. Akaah, "Differences in Research Ethics Judgments Between Male and Female Marketing Professionals," *Journal of Business Ethics* 8(1989): 375–81.

33. Naresh K. Malhotra, Armen Tashchian, and Essam Mahmoud, "The Integration of Microcomputers in Marketing Research and Decision Making," *Journal of the Academy of Marketing Science* 15 (Summer 1987): 69–82.

34. The assistance of James Agarwal with the international marketing research example, the assistance of Mark Leach and Gina Miller in writing the ethics section, and the assistance of Mark Peterson in writing the computer applications section is gratefully acknowledged.

Sampling: Final and Initial Sample Size Determination

Statistical approaches to determining sample size are based on estimating the unknown population values of parameters by means of sample statistics.

◆

OBJECTIVES

After reading this chapter, the student should be able to:

1. Define key concepts and symbols pertinent to sampling.
2. Understand the concepts of the sampling distribution, statistical inference, and standard error.
3. Discuss the statistical approach to determining sample size based on simple random sampling and the construction of confidence intervals.
4. Derive the formulas to determine statistically the sample size for estimating means and proportions.
5. Discuss the nonresponse issues in sampling and the procedures for improving response rates and adjusting for nonresponse.
6. Understand the difficulty of statistically determining the sample size in international marketing research.
7. Identify the ethical issues related to sample size determination, particularly the estimation of population variance.
8. Explain the use of microcomputers and mainframes in statistically determining the sample size.

OVERVIEW

In Chapter 11, we considered the role of sampling in research design formulation, described the sampling process, and presented the various nonprobability and probability sampling techniques.

This chapter focuses on the determination of sample size in simple random sampling. We define various concepts and symbols and discuss the properties of the sampling distribution. Additionally, we describe statistical approaches to sample size determination based on confidence intervals. We present the formulas for calculating the sample size with these approaches and illustrate their use. We briefly discuss the extension to determining sample size in other probability sampling designs. The sample size determined statistically is the final or net sample size; that is, it represents the completed number of interviews or observations. To obtain this final sample size, however, a much larger number of potential respondents have to be contacted initially. We describe the adjustments that need to be made to the statistically determined sample size to account for incidence and completion rates and calculate the initial sample size. We also cover the nonresponse issues in sampling, with a focus on improving response rates and adjusting for nonresponse. We discuss the difficulty of statistically determining the sample size in international marketing research, identify the relevant ethical issues, and explain the role of microcomputers and mainframes.

Statistical determination of sample size requires knowledge of the normal distribution and the use of normal probability tables. The normal distribution is bell-shaped and symmetrical. Its mean, median, and mode are identical (see Chapter 15). Information on the normal distribution and the use of normal probability tables is presented in Appendix 12A. The following example illustrates the statistical aspects of sampling.

EXAMPLE

Bicycling Reduces Accidents Due to Error

The sample size in *Bicycling* magazine's survey of U.S. retail bicycle stores was influenced by statistical considerations. The allowance for sampling error was limited to 5 percentage points.

The table that follows was used to determine the allowances that should be made for sampling error. The computed confidence intervals took into account the effect of the sample design on sampling error. These intervals indicate the range (plus or minus the figure shown) within which the results of repeated samplings in the same time period could be expected to vary, 95% of the time, assuming that the sample procedure, survey execution, and questionnaire used were the same.[1]

Recommended Allowance for Sampling Error of a Percentage

In Percentage Points (at .95 Confidence Level for a Sample Size of 456)

Percentage near 10	3
Percentage near 20	4
Percentage near 30	4
Percentage near 40	5
Percentage near 50	5
Percentage near 60	5
Percentage near 70	4
Percentage near 80	4
Percentage near 90	3

Like the cyclists who read it, *Bicycling* attempted to limit the sampling error due to chance factors. ◆ Jean-Claude LeJeune/Stock, Boston.

The table should be used as follows: If a reported percentage is 43, look at the row labeled "percentages near 40." The number in this row is 5, the 43% obtained in the sample is subject to a sampling error of ±5 percentage points. Another way of saying this is that very probably (95 times out of 100) the average of repeated samplings would be somewhere between 38% and 48%, with the most likely figure being 43%. ◆

This example illustrates the importance of calculating confidence intervals to estimate the effect of sampling errors.

DEFINITIONS AND SYMBOLS

Confidence intervals and other statistical concepts that play a central role in sample size determination are defined in the following list.

Parameter. A parameter is a summary description of a fixed characteristic or measure of the target population. A parameter denotes the true value that would be obtained if a census rather than a sample was undertaken.

Statistic. A statistic is a summary description of a characteristic or measure of the sample. The sample statistic is used as an estimate of the population parameter.

Finite Population Correction. The finite population correction (fpc) is a correction for overestimation of the variance of a population parameter—for example, a mean or proportion—when the sample size is 10% or more of the population size.

Precision level. When estimating a population parameter by using a sample statistic, the precision level is the desired size of the estimating interval. This is the maximum permissible difference between the sample statistic and the population parameter.

Confidence interval. The confidence interval is the range into which the true population parameter will fall, assuming a given level of confidence.

Confidence level. The confidence level is the probability that a confidence interval will include the population parameter.

TABLE 12.1	Variable	Population	Sample
Symbols for Population and Sample Variables	Mean	μ	$\overline{X}$
	Proportion	π	p
	Variance	σ^2	s^2
	Standard deviation	σ	s
	Size	N	n
	Standard error of the mean	$\sigma_{\overline{x}}$	$S_{\overline{x}}$
	Standard error of the proportion	σ_p	S_p
	Standardized variate (z)	$\dfrac{X-\mu}{\sigma}$	$\dfrac{X-\overline{X}}{S}$
	Coefficient of variation (C)	$\dfrac{\sigma}{\mu}$	$\dfrac{S}{\overline{X}}$

The symbols used in statistical notation for describing population and sample characteristics are summarized in Table 12.1.

THE SAMPLING DISTRIBUTION

sampling distribution
The distribution of the values of a sample statistic computed for each possible sample that could be drawn from the target population under a specified sampling plan.

The **sampling distribution** is the distribution of the values of a sample statistic computed for each possible sample that could be drawn from the target population under a specified sampling plan.[2] Suppose that a simple random sample of five hospitals is to be drawn from a population of 20 hospitals. There are $(20 \times 19 \times 18 \times 17 \times 16)/(1 \times 2 \times 3 \times 4 \times 5)$, or 15,504 different samples of size 5 that can be drawn. The relative frequency distribution of the values of the mean of these 15,504 different samples would specify the sampling distribution of the mean.

An important task in marketing research is to calculate statistics, such as the sample mean and sample proportion, and use them to estimate the corresponding true population values. This process of generalizing the sample results to the population results is referred to as **statistical inference**. In practice, a single sample of predetermined size is selected, and the sample statistics (such as mean and proportion) are computed. Hypothetically, to estimate the population parameter from the sample statistic, every possible sample that could have been drawn should be examined. If all possible samples were actually to be drawn, the distribution of the statistic would be the sampling distribution. Although in practice only one sample is actually drawn, the concept of a sampling distribution is still relevant. It enables us to use probability theory to make inferences about the population values.

statistical inference The process of generalizing the sample results to the population results.

The important properties of the sampling distribution of the mean, and the corresponding properties for the proportion, for large samples (30 or more) are as follows:

1. The sampling distribution of the mean is a normal distribution (see Appendix 12A). Strictly speaking, the sampling distribution of a proportion is a binomial. For large samples (n = 30 or more), however, it can be approximated by the normal distribution.

2. The mean of the sampling distribution of the mean $\left(\overline{X} = \left(\displaystyle\sum_{i=1}^{n} X_i \right) \Big/ n \right)$ or of the proportion

(p) equals the corresponding population parameter value, μ or π, respectively.

standard error The standard deviation of the sampling distribution of the mean or proportion.

3. The standard deviation is called the **standard error** of the mean or the proportion to indicate that it refers to a sampling distribution of the mean or the proportion and not to a sample or a population. The formulas are

Mean   Proportion

$$\sigma_{\bar{x}} = \frac{\sigma}{\sqrt{n}} \qquad\qquad \sigma_p = \sqrt{\frac{\pi\,(1-\pi)}{n}}$$

4. Often the population standard deviation, σ, is not known. In these cases, it can be estimated from the sample by using the following formula:

$$s = \sqrt{\frac{\sum_{i=1}^{n}(X_i - \bar{X})^2}{n-1}} \quad \text{or} \quad s = \sqrt{\frac{\sum_{i=1}^{n}X_i^2 - \frac{\left(\sum_{i=1}^{n}X_i\right)^2}{n}}{n-1}}$$

In cases where σ is estimated by s, the standard error of the mean becomes

$$\text{est. } \sigma_{\bar{X}} = \frac{s}{\sqrt{n}}$$

where "est." denotes that s has been used as an estimate of σ.

 Assuming no measurement error, the reliability of an estimate of a population parameter can be assessed in terms of its standard error.

5. Likewise, the standard error of the proportion can be estimated by using the sample proportion p as an estimator of the population proportion, π, as

$$\text{est. } s_p = \sqrt{\frac{p\,(1-p)}{n}}$$

z value The number of standard errors a point is away from the mean.

6. The area under the sampling distribution between any two points can be calculated in terms of **z values**. The z value for a point is the number of standard errors a point is away from the mean. The z values may be computed as follows:

$$z = \frac{\bar{X} - \mu}{\sigma_{\bar{X}}}$$

For example, the areas under one side of the curve between the mean and points that have z values of 1.0, 2.0, and 3.0 are, respectively, .3413, .4772, and .4986. (See Table 2 in the Appendix of Statistical Tables.) In the case of proportion, the computation of z values is similar.

7. When the sample size is 10% or more of the population size, the standard error formulas will overestimate the standard deviation of the population mean or proportion. Hence, these should be adjusted by a finite population correction factor defined by

$$\sqrt{\frac{N-n}{N-1}}$$

In this case,

$$\sigma_{\bar{X}} = \frac{\sigma}{\sqrt{n}} \sqrt{\frac{N-n}{N-1}}$$

STATISTICAL APPROACH TO DETERMINING SAMPLE SIZE

Several qualitative factors should also be taken into consideration when determining the sample size (see Chapter 11). These include the importance of the decision, the nature of the research, the number of variables, the nature of the analysis, sample sizes used in similar studies, incidence rates, completion rates, and resource constraints. The statistically determined sample size is the net or final sample size: the sample remaining after eliminating potential respondents who do not qualify or who do not complete the interview. Depending on incidence and completion rates, the size of the initial sample may have to be much larger. In commercial marketing research, limits on time, money, and expert resources can exert an overriding influence on sample size determination. In the department store patronage project, the sample size was determined based on these considerations.

The statistical approach to determining sample size that we consider is based on traditional statistical inference.[3] In this approach the precision level is specified in advance. This approach is based on the construction of confidence intervals around sample means or proportions.

THE CONFIDENCE INTERVAL APPROACH

The confidence interval approach to sample size determination is based on the construction of confidence intervals around the sample means or proportions using the standard error formula. As an example, suppose that a researcher has taken a simple random sample of 300 households to estimate the monthly expenses on department store shopping and found that the mean household monthly expense for the sample is $182. Past studies indicate that the population standard deviation σ can be assumed to be $55.

We want to find an interval within which a fixed proportion of the sample means would fall. Suppose that we want to determine an interval around the population mean that will include 95% of the sample means, based on samples of 300 households. The 95% could be divided into two equal parts, half below and half above the mean, as shown in Figure 12.1. Calculation of the confidence interval involves determining a distance below ($\overline{X}_L$) and above ($\overline{X}_U$) the population mean ($\overline{X}$), which contains a specified area of the normal curve.

The z values corresponding to $\overline{X}_L$ and $\overline{X}_U$ may be calculated as

$$z_L = \frac{\overline{X}_L - \mu}{\sigma_{\bar{x}}}$$

FIGURE 12.1

95% Confidence Interval

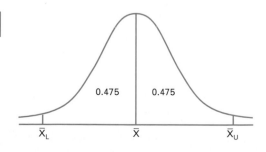

$$z_U = \frac{\overline{X}_U - \mu}{\sigma_{\overline{x}}}$$

where $z_L = -z$ and $z_U = +z$. Therefore, the lower value of $\overline{X}$ is

$$\overline{X}_L = \mu - z\sigma_{\overline{x}}$$

and the upper value of $\overline{X}$ is

$$\overline{X}_U = \mu - z\sigma_{\overline{x}}$$

Note that μ is estimated by $\overline{X}$. The confidence interval is given by

$$\overline{X} \pm z\sigma_{\overline{x}}$$

We can now set a 95% confidence interval around the sample mean of $182. As a first step, we compute the standard error of the mean:

$$\sigma_{\overline{x}} = \frac{\sigma}{\sqrt{n}} = \frac{55}{\sqrt{300}} = 3.18$$

From Table 2 in the Appendix of Statistical Tables, it can be seen that the central 95% of the normal distribution lies within ±1.96 z values. The 95% confidence interval is given by

$$\overline{X} \pm 1.96\ \sigma_{\overline{x}}$$
$$= 182.00 \pm 1.96\ (3.18)$$
$$= 182.00 \pm 6.23$$

Thus, the 95% confidence interval ranges from $175.77 to $188.23. The probability of finding the true population mean to be within $175.77 and $188.23 is 95%.

Sample Size Determination: Means

The approach used here to construct a confidence interval can be adapted to determine the sample size that will result in a desired confidence interval.[4] Suppose that the researcher wants to estimate the monthly household expense on department store shopping more precisely so that the estimate will be within ± $5.00 of the true population value. What should be the size of the sample? The following steps, summarized in Table 12.2, will lead to an answer.

1. Specify the level of precision. This is the maximum permissible difference (D) between the sample mean and the population mean. In our example, $D = \pm$ $5.00.
2. Specify the level of confidence. Suppose that a 95% confidence level is desired.
3. Determine the z value associated with the confidence level using Table 2 in the Appendix of Statistical Tables. For a 95% confidence level, the probability that the population mean will fall outside one end of the interval is .025 (.05/2). The associated z value is 1.96.
4. Determine the standard deviation of the population. The standard deviation of the population may be known from secondary sources. If not, it might be estimated by conducting a pilot study. Alternatively, it might be estimated on the basis of the researcher's judgment. For example, the range of a normally distributed variable is approximately equal to plus or

Estimating monthly household expenses on department store shopping can be done only with a certain degree of confidence. ◆ New York Convention and Visitors Bureau.

TABLE 12.2

Sample Size Determination for Means and Proportions

Steps	Means	Proportions
1. Specify the level of precision.	$D = \pm\$5.00$	$D = p - \pi = \pm.05$
2. Specify the confidence level (CL).	$CL = 95\%$	$CL = 95\%$
3. Determine the z value associated with the CL.	z value is 1.96	z value is 1.96.
4. Determine the standard deviation of the population.	Estimate σ: $\sigma = 55$	Estimate π: $\pi = 0.64$
5. Determine the sample size using the formula for the standard error.	$n = \dfrac{\sigma^2 z^2}{D^2}$ $n = \dfrac{55^2(1.96)^2}{5^2}$ $= 465$	$n = \dfrac{\pi(1-\pi)z^2}{D^2}$ $n = \dfrac{0.64(1-.64)(1.96)^2}{(.05)^2}$ $= 355$
6. If the sample size represents 10% of the population, apply the finite population correction (fpc).	$n_c = \dfrac{nN}{N+n-1}$	$n_c = \dfrac{nN}{N+n-1}$
7. If necessary, reestimate the confidence interval by employing s to estimate σ.	$= \overline{X} \pm z s_{\overline{x}}$	$p \pm z s_p$
8. If precision is specified in relative rather than absolute terms, determine the sample size by substituting for D.	$D = R\mu$ $n = \dfrac{C^2 z^2}{R^2}$	$D = R\pi$ $n = \dfrac{z^2(1-\pi)}{R^2\pi}$

minus three standard deviations, and one can thus estimate the standard deviation by dividing the range by six. The researcher can often estimate the range based on knowledge of the phenomenon.

5. Determine the sample size using the formula for the standard error of the mean.

$$z = \frac{\overline{X} - \mu}{\sigma_{\overline{x}}}$$

$$= \frac{D}{\sigma_{\overline{x}}}$$

or

$$\sigma_{\overline{x}} = \frac{D}{z}$$

or

$$\frac{\sigma}{\sqrt{n}} = \frac{D}{z}$$

or

$$n = \frac{\sigma^2 z^2}{D^2}$$

In our example,

$$n = \frac{55^2 (1.96)^2}{5^2}$$

$$= 464.83$$

$$= 465 \text{ (rounded to the next highest integer)}$$

It can be seen from the formula for sample size that sample size increases with an increase in the population variability, degree of confidence, and the precision level required of the estimate.

6. If the resulting sample size represents 10% or more of the population, the finite population correction (fpc) should be applied. The required sample size should then be calculated from the formula

$$n_c = \frac{nN}{N + n - 1}$$

where

$$n = \text{sample size without fpc}$$
$$n_c = \text{sample size with fpc}$$

7. If the population standard deviation, σ, is unknown and an estimate is used, it should be re-estimated once the sample has been drawn. The sample standard deviation, s, is used as an estimate of σ. A revised confidence interval should then be calculated to determine the precision level actually obtained.

Suppose that the value of 55.00 used for was an estimate because the true value was unknown. A sample of $n = 465$ is drawn, and these observations generate a mean $\overline{X}$ of 180.00 and a sample standard deviation s of 50.00. The revised confidence interval is then

$$\overline{X} \pm z s_{\overline{x}} = 180.00 \pm 1.96 \frac{50.0}{\sqrt{465}}$$

$$= 180.00 \pm 4.55$$

or

$$175.45 \leq \mu \leq 184.55$$

Note that the confidence interval obtained is narrower ($\overline{X} \pm 4.55$) than planned ($\overline{X} \pm 5.00$), because the population standard deviation was overestimated, as judged by the sample standard deviation.

8. In some cases, precision is specified in relative rather than absolute terms. In other words, it may be specified that the estimate be within plus or minus R percentage points of the mean. Symbolically,

$$D = R\mu$$

In these cases, the sample size may be determined by

$$n = \frac{\sigma^2 z^2}{D^2}$$

$$= \frac{C^2 z^2}{R^2}$$

where the coefficient of variation $C = \sigma/\mu$ would have to be estimated.

The population size, N, does not directly affect the size of the sample, except when the finite population correction factor has to be applied. Although this may be counterintuitive, upon reflection it makes sense. For example, if all the population elements are identical on the characteristics of interest, then a sample size of one will be sufficient to estimate the mean perfectly. This is true whether there are 50, 500, 5,000, or 50,000 elements in the population. What directly affects the sample size is the variability of the characteristic in the population. This variability enters into the sample size calculation by way of population variance σ^2 or sample variance s^2.

Sample Size Determination: Proportions

If the statistic of interest is a proportion rather than a mean, the approach to sample size determination is similar. Suppose that the researcher is interested in estimating the proportion of households possessing a department store credit card. The following steps should be followed.[5]

1. Specify the level of precision. Suppose that the desired precision is such that the allowable interval is set as $D = p - \pi = \pm.05$.
2. Specify the level of confidence. Suppose that a 95% confidence level is desired.
3. Determine the z value associated with the confidence level. As explained in the case of estimating the mean, this will be $z = 1.96$.
4. Estimate the population proportion π. As explained earlier, the population proportion may be estimated from secondary sources, from a pilot study, or based on the judgment of the researcher. Suppose that based on secondary data the researcher estimates that 64% of the households in the target population possess a department store credit card. Hence, $\pi = .64$.
5. Determine the sample size using the formula for the standard error of the proportion.

$$\sigma_p = \frac{p - \pi}{z}$$

$$= \frac{D}{z}$$

$$= \sqrt{\frac{\pi(1-\pi)}{n}}$$

or
$$n = \frac{\pi(1-\pi)z^2}{D^2}$$

In our example,

$$n = \frac{.64\ (1-.64)(1.96)^2}{(.05)^2}$$

$$= 354.04$$

$$= 355 \text{ (rounded to the next highest integer)}$$

6. If the resulting sample size represents 10% or more of the population, the finite population correction (fpc) should be applied. The required sample size should then be calculated from the formula

$$n_c = \frac{nN}{N+n-1}$$

where

$$n = \text{sample size without fpc}$$

$$n_c = \text{sample size with fpc}$$

7. If the estimate of π turns out to be poor, the confidence interval will be more or less precise than desired. Suppose that after the sample has been taken, the proportion p is calculated to have a value of .55. The confidence interval is then reestimated by employing s_p to estimate the unknown σ_p as

$$p \pm z s_p$$

where

$$s_p = \sqrt{\frac{p(1-p)}{n}}$$

In our example,

$$s_p = \sqrt{\frac{.55\ (1-.55)}{355}}$$

$$= .0264$$

The confidence interval, then, is

$$.55 \pm 1.96(.0264) = .55 \pm .052$$

which is wider than that specified. This is because the sample standard deviation based on $p = .55$ was larger than the estimate of the population standard deviation based on $\pi = .64$.

If a wider interval than specified is unacceptable, the sample size can be determined to reflect the maximum possible variation in the population. This occurs when the product $\pi(1 - \pi)$ is the greatest, which happens when π is set at .5. This result can also be seen intuitively. Since one-half the population has one value of the characteristic and the other half the other value, more evidence would be required to obtain a valid inference than if the situation was more clear-cut and the majority had one particular value. In our example, this leads to a sample size of

$$n = \frac{.5\ (.5)(1.96)^2}{(.05)^2}$$

$$= 384.16$$

$$= 385 \quad \text{rounded to the next higher integer.}$$

8. Sometimes, precision is specified in relative rather than absolute terms. In other words, it may be specified that the estimate be within plus or minus R percentage points of the population proportion. Symbolically,

$$D = R\pi$$

In such a case, the sample size may be determined by

$$n = \frac{z^2(1-\pi)}{R^2\pi}$$

MULTIPLE CHARACTERISTICS AND PARAMETERS

In the preceding examples, we focused on the estimation of a single parameter. In commercial marketing research, several characteristics, not just one, are of interest in any project. The researcher is required to estimate several parameters, not just one. The calculation of sample size in these cases should be based on a consideration of all the parameters that must be estimated, as illustrated in the department store example.

DEPARTMENT STORE PATRONAGE PROJECT
Sample Size Estimation

Suppose that in addition to the mean household monthly expenses on department store shopping, it was decided to estimate the mean household monthly expense on clothes and on gifts. The sample sizes needed to estimate each of the three mean monthly expenses are given in Table 12.3 and are 465 for department store shopping, 246 for clothes, and 217 for gifts. If all the three variables were equally important, the most conservative approach would be to select the largest value of $n = 465$ to determine the sample size. This will lead to each variable being estimated at least as precisely as specified. If the researcher was most concerned with the mean household monthly expense on clothes, however, a sample size of $n = 246$ could be selected. ◆

TABLE 12.3

Sample Size for Estimating Multiple Parameters

	Variable Mean Household Monthly Expense on		
	Department Store Shopping	Clothes	Gifts
Confidence level	95%	95%	95%
z value	1.96	1.96	1.96
Precision level (D)	$5	$5	$4
Standard deviation of the population (σ)	$55	$40	$30
Required sample size (n)	465	246	217

So far, the discussion of sample size determination has been based on the methods of traditional statistical inference and has assumed simple random sampling. Next, we discuss the determination of sample size when other sampling techniques are used.

OTHER PROBABILITY SAMPLING TECHNIQUES

The determination of sample size for other probability sampling techniques is based on the same underlying principles. The researcher must specify the level of precision and the degree of confidence and estimate the sampling distribution of the test statistic.

In simple random sampling, cost does not enter directly into the calculation of sample size. In the case of stratified or cluster sampling, however, cost has an important influence. The cost per observation varies by strata or cluster, and the researcher needs some initial estimates of these costs.[6] In addition, the researcher must take into account within-strata variability or within- and between-cluster variability. Once the overall sample size is determined, the sample is apportioned among strata or clusters. This increases the complexity of the sample size formulas. The interested reader is referred to standard works on sampling theory for more information.[7] In general, to provide the same reliability as simple random sampling, sample sizes are the same for systematic sampling, smaller for stratified sampling, and larger for cluster sampling.

ADJUSTING THE STATISTICALLY DETERMINED SAMPLE SIZE

The sample size determined statistically represents the final or net sample size that must be achieved to ensure that the parameters are estimated with the desired degree of precision and the given level of confidence. In surveys, this represents the number of interviews that must be completed. To achieve this final sample size, a much greater number of potential respondents have to be contacted. In other words, the initial sample size has to be much larger because typically the incidence rates and completion rates are less than 100%.[8]

incidence rate The rate of occurrence of persons eligible to participate in the study expressed as a percentage.

Incidence rate refers to the rate of occurrence or the percentage of persons eligible to participate in the study. Incidence rate determines how many contacts need to be screened for a given sample size requirement.[9] Suppose that a study of floor cleaners calls for a sample of female heads of households aged 25 to 55. Of the women between the ages of 20 and 60 who might reasonably be approached to see if they qualify, approximately 75% are heads of households aged 25 to 55. This means that, on average, 1.33 women would be approached to obtain one qualified respondent. Additional criteria for qualifying respondents (for example, product usage behavior) will further increase the number of contacts. Suppose that an added eligibility requirement is that the women should have used a floor cleaner during the last two months. It is estimated that 60% of the women contacted would meet this criteria. Then the incidence rate is .75 X .60 = .45. Thus the finial sample size will have to be increased by a factor of (1/0.45) or 2.22.

completion rate The percentage of qualified respondents who complete the interview. It enables researchers to take into account anticipated refusals by people who qualify.

Similarly, the determination of sample size must take into account anticipated refusals by people who qualify. The **completion rate** denotes the percentage of qualified respondents who complete the interview. If, for example, the researcher expects an interview completion rate of 80% of eligible respondents, the number of contacts should be increased by a factor of 1.25. The incidence rate and the completion rate together imply that the number of potential respondents contacted—that is, the initial sample size—should be 2.22 X 1.25 or 2.77 times the sample size required. In general, if there are c qualifying factors with an incidence of $Q_1, Q_2, Q_3,..., Q_c$, each expressed as a proportion, the following are true:

$$\text{Incidence rate} = Q_1 \times Q_2 \times Q_3 \text{K } Q_c$$

$$\text{Initial sample size} = \frac{\text{final sample size}}{\text{incidence rate} \times \text{completion rate}}$$

The number of units that will have to be sampled will be determined by the initial sample size. Often, as in the example below, a number of variables are used for qualifying potential respondents, thereby decreasing the incidence rate.

EXAMPLE
Tuning Up a Symphony Sample _____

A telephone survey was conducted to determine the consumer's awareness of and attitudes toward the Jacksonville Symphony Orchestra. The screening qualifications for a respondent included in the survey were: (1) lives in the Jacksonville area for more than one year, (2) 25 years old or older, (3) listens to classical or pop music, and (4) attends live performances of classical or pop music. These qualifying criteria decreased the incidence rate to less than 15% leading to a substantial increase in the number of contacts. Although having four qualifying factors resulted in a highly targeted or tuned sample, it also made the interviewing process inefficient.[10] ◆

The Jacksonville Symphony Orchestra tuned up the right sample by appropriately screening the respondents. ◆ Jacksonville Symphony Orchestra.

Completion rates are affected by nonresponse. Hence, nonresponse issues deserve attention.

NONRESPONSE ISSUES IN SAMPLING

The two major nonresponse issues in sampling are improving response rates and adjusting for nonresponse. Nonresponse error arises when some of the potential respondents included in the sample do not respond (see Chapter 3). This is one of the most significant problems in survey research. Nonrespondents differ from respondents in terms of demographic, psychographic, personality, attitudinal, motivational, and behavioral variables.[11] For a given study, if the nonrespondents differ from the respondents on the characteristics of interest, the sample estimates will be seriously biased. Higher response rates, in general, imply lower rates of nonresponse bias, yet response rate may not be an adequate indicator of nonresponse bias. Response rates themselves do not indicate whether the respondents are representative of the original sample.[12] Increasing the response rate may not reduce nonresponse bias if the additional respondents are not different from those who have already responded but do differ from those who still do not respond. As low response rates increase the probability of nonresponse bias, an attempt should be made to improve the response rate.[13]

Improving the Response Rates

The primary causes of low response rates are refusals and not-at-homes, as shown in Figure 12.2.

Refusals   Refusals, which result from the unwillingness or inability of people included in the sample to participate, result in lower response rates and increased potential for nonresponse bias. Refusal rates, the percentage of contacted respondents who refuse to participate, range from 0 to 50% in telephone surveys. Refusal rates for mall-intercept

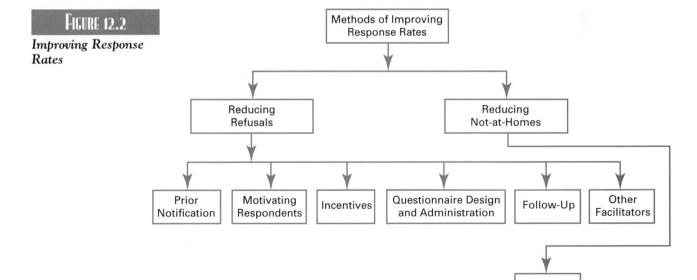

FIGURE 12.2

Improving Response Rates

interviews are even higher, and they are highest of all for mail surveys. Most refusals occur immediately after the interviewer's opening remarks or when the potential respondent first opens the mail package. In a national telephone survey, 40% of those contacted refused at the introduction stage, but only 6% refused during the interview. The following example gives further information on refusals, terminations, and completed interviews.

EXAMPLE
Reasons for Refusal _____

In a study investigating the refusal problem in telephone surveys, telephone interviews were conducted with responders and nonresponders to a previous survey, using quotas of 100 for each subsample. The results are presented in the following table.[14]

Refusals, Terminations, and Completed Interviews

Property	Total Sample	Responders	Nonresponders
Number of refusals (1)	224	31	193
Number of terminations (2)	100	33	67
Number of completed interviews (3)	203	102	101
Total number of contacts $(1 + 2 + 3)$[a]	527	166	361
Refusal rate $(1/[1 + 2 + 3])$[b]	42.5%	18.7%	53.5%
Termination rate $(2/[1 + 2 + 3])$	19.0%	19.9%	18.5%
Completion rate $(3/[1 + 2 + 3])$[b]	38.5%	61.4%	28.0%

[a] A total of 1,388 attempts was required to make these contacts. The 166 responder contacts required 406 attempts (with one callback per respondent), and the 361 nonresponder contacts required 982 attempts (with two callbacks per respondent). The sampling frame contained 965 phone numbers (313 responders and 652 nonresponders).

[b] Responder/nonresponder differences were significant at $\alpha = .05$ (two-tail test).

The study found that people who are likely to participate in a telephone survey (responders) differ from those who are likely to refuse (nonresponders) in the following ways: (1) confidence in survey research, (2) confidence in the research organization, (3) demographic characteristics, and (4) beliefs and attitudes about telephone surveys. ◆

Given the differences between responders and nonresponders that this study demonstrated, researchers should attempt to lower refusal rates. This can be done by prior notification, motivating the respondents, incentives, good questionnaire design and administration, and follow-up.

Prior notification. In prior notification, potential respondents are sent a letter notifying them of the imminent mail, telephone, or personal survey. Prior notification increases response rates for samples of the general public because it reduces surprise and uncertainty and creates a more cooperative atmosphere.[15]

Motivating the respondents. Potential respondents can be motivated to participate in the survey by increasing their interest and involvement. Two of the ways this can be done are the foot-in-the-door and door-in-the-face strategies. Both strategies attempt to obtain participation through the use of sequential requests. As explained briefly in Chapter 6, in the foot-in-the-door strategy, the interviewer starts with a relatively small request, such as "Will you please take five minutes to answer five questions," to which a large majority of people will comply. The small request is followed by a larger request, the critical request, that solicits participation in the survey or experiment. The rationale is that compliance with an initial request should increase the chances of compliance with the subsequent request. The door-in-the-face is the reverse strategy. The initial request is relatively large and a majority of people refuse to comply. The large request is followed by a smaller request, the critical request, soliciting participation in the survey. The underlying reasoning is that the concession offered by the subsequent critical request should increase the chances of compliance. Foot-in-the-door is more effective than door-in-the-face.[16]

Incentives. Response rates can be increased by offering monetary as well as nonmonetary incentives to potential respondents. Monetary incentives can be prepaid or promised. The prepaid incentive is included with the survey or questionnaire. The promised incentive is sent to only those respondents who complete the survey. The most commonly used nonmonetary incentives are premiums and rewards, such as pens, pencils, books, and offers of survey results. Prepaid incentives have been shown to increase response rates to a greater extent than promised incentives. The amount of incentive can vary from 10¢ to $50 or more. The amount of incentive has a positive relationship with response rate, but the cost of large monetary incentives may outweigh the value of additional information obtained.

Questionnaire design and administration. A well-designed questionnaire can decrease the overall refusal rate as well as refusals to specific questions (see Chapter 10). Likewise, the skill used to administer the questionnaire in telephone and personal interviews can increase the response rate. Trained interviewers are skilled in refusal conversion or persuasion. They do not accept a no response without an additional plea. The additional plea might emphasize the brevity of the questionnaire or importance of the respondent's opinion. Skilled interviewers can decrease refusals by about 7% on average. Interviewing procedures are discussed in more detail in Chapter 13.

Follow-up. Follow-up, or contacting the nonrespondents periodically after the initial contact, is particularly effective in decreasing refusals in mail surveys. The researcher might send a postcard or letter to remind nonrespondents to complete and return the questionnaire. Two or three mailings are needed in addition to the original one. With proper follow-up, the response rate in mail surveys can be increased to 80% or more. Follow-ups can also be done by telephone, telegraph or personal contacts.

Other facilitators. Personalization, or sending letters addressed to specific individuals, is effective in increasing response rates.[17] Research in Practice 12.1 illustrates the procedure employed by *Bicycling* magazine to increase its response rate.[18]

RESEARCH IN PRACTICE 12.1

Bicycling *Magazine's Procedure for Increasing Response to Mail Surveys*

Bicycling magazine conducts a semiannual survey of individual bicycle dealers throughout the United States. The following procedure is used to increase the response to the survey:

1. An "alert" letter is sent to advise the respondent that a questionnaire is coming.
2. A questionnaire package is mailed five days after the "alert" letter. The package contains a cover letter, a five-page questionnaire, a new $1 bill, and a stamped return envelope.
3. A second package containing a reminder letter, a questionnaire, and a stamped return envelope is mailed five days after the first package.
4. A follow-up postcard is mailed a week after the second package.
5. A second follow-up postcard is mailed a week after the first.

In a recent survey, 1,000 questionnaires were mailed to bicycle dealers, and 68% of these were returned. This represents a good response rate in a mail survey.

Not-at-Homes   The second major cause of low response rates is not-at-homes. In telephone and in-home personal interviews, low response rates can result if the potential respondents are not at home when contact is attempted. A study analyzing 182 commercial telephone surveys involving a total sample of over one million consumers revealed that a large percentage of potential respondents was never contacted. The median noncontact rate was 40%. In nearly 40% of the surveys, only a single attempt was made to contact potential respondents. The results of 259,088 first-call attempts using the sophisticated random-digit dialing M/A/R/C Telno System shows that less than 10% of the calls resulted in completed interviews, and 14.3% of those contacted refused to participate.[19]

The likelihood that potential respondents will not be at home varies with several factors. People with small children are more likely to be at home. Consumers are more likely to be at home on weekends than on weekdays and in the evening as opposed to during the afternoon. Prenotification and appointments increase the likelihood that the respondent will be at home when contact is attempted.

The percentage of not-at-homes can be substantially reduced by employing a series of callbacks, or periodic follow-up attempts to contact nonrespondents. The decision about the number of callbacks should weigh the benefits of reducing nonresponse bias against the additional costs. As callbacks are completed, the callback respondents should be compared with those who have already responded to determine the usefulness of making further callbacks. In most consumer surveys, three to four callbacks may be desirable. Although the first call yields the most responses, the second and third calls have higher response per call. It is important that callbacks be made and controlled according to a prescribed plan.

Adjusting for Nonresponse

High response rates decrease the probability that nonresponse bias is substantial. Nonresponse rates should always be reported, and whenever possible, the effects of nonresponse should be estimated. This can be done by linking the nonresponse rate to estimated differences between respondents and nonrespondents. Information on differences between the two groups may be obtained from the sample itself. For example, differences found through callbacks could be extrapolated, or a concentrated follow-up could be conducted on a subsample of the nonrespondents. Alternatively, it may be possible to estimate these differences from other sources.[20] To illustrate, in a survey of owners of major appliances, demographic and other information may be obtained for respondents and nonrespondents from the warranty cards. For a mail panel, a wide variety of information is available for both groups from syndicate organizations. If the sample is supposed to be representative of the general population, then comparisons can be made with census figures. Even if it is not feasible to estimate the effects of nonresponse, some adjustments should still be made during data analysis and interpretation.[21] The strategies available to adjust for nonresponse error include subsampling of nonrespondents, replacement, substitution, subjective estimates, trend analysis, simple weighting, and imputation.

Subsampling of Nonrespondents   Subsampling of nonrespondents, particularly in the case of mail surveys, can be effective in adjusting for nonresponse bias. In this technique, the researcher contacts a subsample of the nonrespondents, usually by means of telephone or personal interviews. This often results in a high response rate within that subsample. The values obtained for the subsample are then projected to all the nonrespondents, and the survey results are adjusted to account for nonresponse. This method can estimate the effect of nonresponse on the characteristic of interest.

Replacement   In replacement, the nonrespondents in the current survey are replaced with nonrespondents from an earlier, similar survey. The researcher attempts to contact these nonrespondents from the earlier survey and administer the current survey questionnaire to them, possibly by offering a suitable incentive. It is important that the nature of nonresponse in the current survey be similar to that of the earlier survey. The two surveys should use similar kinds of respondents, and the time interval between them should be short. As an example, if the department store survey is being repeated one year later, the nonrespondents in the present survey may be replaced by the nonrespondents in the original survey.

substitution A procedure that substitutes for nonrespondents other elements from the sampling frame who are expected to respond.

Substitution   In **substitution**, the researcher substitutes for nonrespondents other elements from the sampling frame who are expected to respond. The sampling frame is divided into subgroups that are internally homogeneous in terms of respondent characteristics but heterogeneous in terms of response rates. These subgroups are then used to identify substitutes who are similar to particular nonrespondents but dissimilar to respondents already in the sample. Note that this approach would not reduce nonresponse bias if the substitutes are similar to respondents already in the sample. Research in Practice 12.2 illustrates the use of this method.[22]

RESEARCH IN PRACTICE 12.2

Exit Polling of Voters

Warren Mitofsky, executive director of Voter Research and Surveys (VRS), states that planning exit interviews for a presidential election begins two years before the big day. The New York City–based staff of 22 grows to 60 during an election year; on election day, it blossoms to 6,000 workers who conduct exit interviews at 1,500 polling places.

VRS workers give voters a list of about 25 questions. Certain issues are well-known determinants of a voter's choice, whereas other questions deal with last-minute events such as political scandals. The questions are written at the last possible moment. The questionnaire is designed to determine not only for whom people voted but on what basis.

Uncooperative pollsters are a problem among exit polling. VRS workers are told to record a basic demographic profile for noncompliers. From this demographic data, a voter profile is developed to replace the uncooperative pollster using the method of substitution. Age, sex, race, and residence are strong indicators of how Americans vote. For example, younger voters are more likely to be swayed by moral issues whereas older voters are more likely to consider a candidate's personal qualities. Thus, VRS substitutes for nonrespondents other potential respondents who are similar in age, sex, race, and residence. The broad coverage of exit interviews and the substitution technique for noncompliant pollsters allow VRS to obtain margins of error close to 3 to 4%.

Subjective Estimates   When it is no longer feasible to increase the response rate by subsampling, replacement, or substitution, it may be possible to arrive at subjective estimates of the nature and effect of nonresponse bias. This involves evaluating the likely effects of nonresponse based on experience and available information. For example, married adults with young children are more likely to be at home than single or divorced adults or than married adults with no children. This information provides a basis for evaluating the effects of nonresponse due to not-at-homes in personal or telephone surveys.

trend analysis A method of adjusting for nonresponse in which the researcher tries to discern a trend between early and late respondents. This trend is projected to nonrespondents to estimate their characteristic of interest.

Trend Analysis   **Trend analysis** is an attempt to discern a trend between early and late respondents. This trend is projected to nonrespondents to estimate where they stand on the characteristic of interest. For example, Table 12.4 presents the results of several waves of a mail survey. The characteristic of interest is dollars spent on shopping in department stores during the last two months. The known value of the characteristic for the total sample is given at the bottom of the table. The value for each successive wave of respondents becomes closer to the value for nonrespondents. For example, those responding to the second mailing spent 79% of the amount spent by those who responded to the first mailing. Those responding to the third mailing spent 85% of the amount spent by those who responded to the second mailing. Continuing this trend, one might estimate that those who did not respond spent 91% [85 + (85 − 79)] of the amount spent by those who responded to the third mailing. This results in an estimate of $252 (277 × .91) spent by nonrespondents and an estimate of $288 for the average amount spent in shopping at department stores during the last two months for the overall sample. Note that the actual amount spent by the respondents was $230 rather than the $252 and that the actual sample average was $275 rather than the $288 estimated by trend analysis. Although the trend estimates are wrong, the error is smaller than the error that would have resulted from ignoring the nonrespondents. Had the nonrespondents been ignored, the average amount spent would have been estimated at $335 for the sample.

weighting A statistical procedure that attempts to account for nonresponse by assigning differential weights to the data depending on the response rates.

Weighting   **Weighting** attempts to account for nonresponse by assigning differential weights to the data depending on the response rates.[23] For example, in a survey on personal computers, the sample was stratified according to income. The response rates were 85%, 70%, and 40%, respectively, for the high-, medium-, and low-income groups. In analyzing the data, these subgroups are assigned weights inversely proportional to their response rates. That is, the weights assigned would be 100/85, 100/70, and 100/40, respectively, for the high-, medium-, and low-income groups. Although weighting can correct for the differential effects of nonresponse, it destroys the self-weighting nature of

TABLE 12.4 *Use of Trend Analysis in Adjusting for Nonresponse*	Percentage Response	Average Dollar Expenditure	Percentage of Previous Wave's Response
First mailing	12	412	—
Second mailing	18	325	79
Third mailing	13	277	85
Nonresponse	(57)	(230)	91
Total	100	275	

the sampling design and can introduce complications. Weighting is further discussed in Chapter 14 on data preparation.

imputation A method to adjust for nonresponse by assigning the characteristic of interest to the nonrespondents based on the similarity of the variables available for both nonrespondents and respondents.

Imputation   **Imputation** involves imputing, or assigning, the characteristic of interest to the nonrespondents based on the similarity of the variables available for both nonrespondents and respondents.[24] For example, a respondent who does not report brand usage may be imputing the usage of a respondent with similar demographic characteristics. Often there is a high correlation between the characteristic of interest and some other variables. In such cases, this correlation can be used to predict the value of the characteristic for the nonrespondents (see Chapter 17).

INTERNATIONAL MARKETING RESEARCH

When conducting marketing research in foreign countries, statistical estimation of sample size may be difficult because estimates of the population variance may be unavailable. Hence, the sample size is often determined by qualitative considerations, as discussed in Chapter 11: (1) the importance of the decision, (2) the nature of the research, (3) the number of variables, (4) the nature of the analysis, (5) sample sizes used in similar studies, (6) incidence rates, (7) completion rates, and (8) resource constraints. If statistical estimation of sample size is at all attempted, it should be realized that the estimates of the population variance may vary from country to country. For example, in measuring consumer preferences, a greater degree of heterogeneity may be encountered in countries where consumer preferences are not that well developed. Thus, it may be a mistake to assume that the population variance is the same or to use the same sample size in different countries.

EXAMPLE
The Chinese Take to the Sky

The airline industry seems to have a strong and promising market potential in the People's Republic of China. The airline market in China is growing rapidly. With billions of dollars spent, China is trying to satisfy surging demand and to catch up with the rest of the world. The domestic airline traffic is growing at a rate of up to 30% a year. Strong economic growth, surging foreign trade, and a revival in tourism as the memory of the massacre in Tiananmen Square recedes have helped to fuel the boom. China is making rapid progress in increasing its fleet and training pilots. In 1984, the country had only 15 commercial aircraft, mostly outdated Soviet-made models. The fleet is now more than 20 times as large with aircraft from Boeing, McDonnell Douglas, and Airbus. The Civil Aviation Administration of China (which used to be known as "Chinese Airlines Always Cancel") has granted much flexibility to the individual airlines. Yet for millions of Chinese, air travel is a relatively new experience and many more millions have never flown. Hence, Chinese preferences for air travel are likely to exhibit much more variability compared with Americans. In a survey by Delta Airlines to compare the attitude toward air travel in China and the United States, the sample size of the Chinese survey would have to be larger than the American survey in order for the two survey estimates to have comparable precision.[25] ◆

For millions of Chinese, travel is a relatively new experience and Chinese preferences for air travel are likely to exhibit much more variability as compared with preferences of Americans. ◆ ChromoSohm/Sohm/Unicorn Stock Photos.

ETHICS IN MARKETING RESEARCH

As discussed in this chapter, statistical methods can be used to determine the sample size and, therefore, have an impact on the cost of the project. While this is usually an objective way of determining the sample size, it is, nonetheless, susceptible to fraud. The sample size is heavily dependent on the standard deviation of the variable and there is no way of knowing the standard deviation until the data have been collected. To resolve this paradox, the computation of the sample size must be performed using an estimate of the standard deviation. This estimate is derived based on secondary data, judgment, or a small pilot study. By inflating the standard deviation, it is possible to increase the sample size and thus the project revenue. Using the sample size formula it can be seen that increasing the standard deviation by 20%, for example, will increase the sample size by 44%. But this is clearly unethical.

Ethical dilemmas can arise even when the standard deviation is estimated honestly. It is possible, indeed common, that the standard deviation in the actual study is different from that estimated initially. When the standard deviation is larger than initially estimated, the confidence interval will also be larger than desired. When such a situation arises, the researcher has the responsibility to disclose this to the client and jointly decide on a course of action. The ethical ramifications of miscommunicating the confidence intervals of survey estimates based on statistical samples are underscored in political polling.

EXAMPLE
Surveys Serve Up Elections _____

The dissemination of some survey results has been strongly criticized as manipulative and unethical. In particular, the ethics of releasing political poll results before and during the election have been questioned. Opponents of such surveys claim that the general public is misled by these results. First, before the election, voters are influenced by whom the polls predict will win. If they see that the candidate they favor is trailing, they may decide not to vote; they assume that there is no way their candidate can win. The attempt to predict the election results while the election is in progress has come under even harsher criticism. Opponents of this practice feel that this predisposes voters to vote for the projected winner for their state or that it may even discourage voters from voting, even though the polls have not closed in their state, because the media projects that there is already a winner. Furthermore, not only are the effects of these projections questionable, but frequently the accuracy of the projections is questionable as well. Although voters may be told a candidate has a certain percentage of the votes within ±1%, the confidence interval may be much larger, depending on the sample size. ◆

Researchers also have the ethical responsibility to investigate the possibility of nonresponse bias. The methodology adopted and the extent of nonresponse bias found should be clearly communicated.

COMPUTER APPLICATIONS

Microcomputers and mainframes can determine the sample size for various sampling techniques. For simple applications, appropriate sample size formulas can be entered using spreadsheet programs. The researcher specifies the desired precision level, confidence level, and population variance, and the program determines the appropriate sample size for the study. By incorporating the cost of each sampling unit, the sample size can be adjusted based on budget considerations. Standard Error by Bardsley and Haslacher, Inc., uses spreadsheets to calculate mean standard errors and 95% confidence intervals and can be used for computing sample sizes. Statchek by Detail Technologies, Inc., calculates confidence intervals and can be used to determine sample sizes. Several marketing research firms supply sample design software and services including statistical determination of sample sizes and estimation of sample statistics. Survey Sampling, Inc., has a line of sampling products. Their Contact and Cooperation Rate Adjustment software statistically adjusts sample sizes by taking into account the expected incidence and completion rates.

EzPair by Barry Cohen of Brooklyn, New York, can enable a researcher to truncate a paired comparison study when the outcome meets prespecified statistical criteria. Such early terminations can save time as well as money. EzPair avoids a mistake made by researchers in stopping a series of paired comparisons with only a significance test to test for a type I error (i.e., rejecting the null hypothesis and declaring the test product as the winner or preferred brand when it should not be the winner). EzPair also accounts for the statistical power required to avoid a type II error (i.e., *not* rejecting the null hypothesis and so not declaring the test product as the preferred brand when it should be declared as the winner).

Exhibit 12.1 depicts the input for the EzPair program. The first "maximum probability" corresponds to type I error acceptable in the study, while the second "maximum probability" corresponds to type II error designated as tolerable by the researcher.

The second accompanying figure (Exhibit 12.2) details the output for an EzPair paired comparison study. Rows with entries for both "acceptance number" and "rejection number" indicate that the study can be terminated if the results match those for the row's acceptances and rejections. For example, if a blind taste test of two colas—brand J (Coca-Cola) and brand K (President's Club)—has used 15 respondents and 13 of these

EXHIBIT 12.1

Input for the EzPair Program

```
┌─────────────────────────────────────────────────────────────────────┐
│  ┌─────────────────────────────────────────────────────────────────┐ │
│  │        SEQUENTIAL PAIRED COMPARISON TEST SPECIFICATIONS          │ │
│  └─────────────────────────────────────────────────────────────────┘ │
│  ┌─────────────────────────────────────────────────────────────────┐ │
│  │                                                                   │ │
│  │  Maximum number of interviews to be conducted:  50                │ │
│  │                                                                   │ │
│  │  Level of Confidence........................:   90%               │ │
│  │                                                                   │ │
│  │  Maximum probability of falsely concluding                        │ │
│  │  that the test product IS preferred.........:   0.010             │ │
│  │                                                                   │ │
│  │  Maximum probability of falsely concluding                        │ │
│  │  that the test product is NOT preferred......:  0.010             │ │
│  │                                                                   │ │
│  │                                                                   │ │
│  │  ┌─ <F2> = Accept edited specifications.  <Esc> = Use/Restore defaults. ─┐ │
│  │                                                                   │ │
│  │                                                                   │ │
│  │                                                         NUM  INS  │ │
│  └─────────────────────────────────────────────────────────────────┘ │
└─────────────────────────────────────────────────────────────────────┘
```

respondents preferred brand K, then brand K can be declared as the winner of the paired comparison test with 90% confidence. No more respondents would need to be presented the brands. The column listed as "number of violations observed" can be used as a score sheet to track the cumulative total of rejections made (the number of times the test brand Coke was not preferred) by respondents.

SUMMARY

The statistical approaches to determining sample size are based on confidence intervals. These approaches may involve the estimation of the mean or proportion. When estimating the mean, determination of sample size using the confidence interval approach requires the specification of precision level, confidence level, and population standard deviation. In the case of proportion, the precision level, confidence level, and an estimate of the population proportion must be specified. The sample size determined statistically represents the final or net sample size that must be achieved. To achieve this final sample size, a much greater number of potential respondents have to be contacted to account for reduction in response due to incidence rates and completion rates.

Nonresponse error arises when some of the potential respondents included in the sample do not respond. The primary causes of low response rates are refusals and not-at-homes. Refusal rates may be reduced by prior notification, motivating the respondents, incentives, proper questionnaire design and administration, and follow-up. The percentage of not-at-homes can be substantially reduced by callbacks. Adjustments for nonresponse can be made by subsampling nonrespondents, replacement, substitution, subjective estimates, trend analysis, simple weighting, and imputation.

The statistical estimation of sample size is even more complicated in international marketing research because the population variance may differ from one country to the next. The preliminary estimation of population variance for the purpose of determining the sample size also has ethical ramifications. Microcomputers and mainframes can assist in determining the sample size and adjusting it to account for expected incidence and completion rates.[26]

EXHIBIT 12.2

Output for an EzPair Paired Comparison Study

SAMPLE SEQUENTIAL PRODUCT TEST SCHEDULE

Level of Confidence = 90%
Acceptance Proportion = 0.38
Rejection Proportion = 0.62

Maximum Sample Size = 50
p (false test product WIN) = 0.010
p (false test product LOSS) = 0.010

Number of Respondents Tested	Acceptance Number	Number of Violations Observed	Rejection Number
1		——	
2		——	
3		——	
4		——	
5		——	
6		——	
7		——	
8		——	
9		——	
10	0	——	10
11	0	——	11
12	1	——	11
13	1	——	12
14	2	——	12
15	2	——	13
16	3	——	13
17	3	——	14
18	4	——	14
19	4	——	15
20	5	——	15
21	5	——	16
22	6	——	16
23	6	——	17
24	7	——	17
25	7	——	18
26	8	——	18
27	8	——	19
28	9	——	19
29	9	——	20
30	10	——	20
31	10	——	21
32	11	——	21
33	11	——	22
34	12	——	22
35	12	——	23
36	13	——	23
37	13	——	24
38	14	——	24
39	14	——	25
40	15	——	25
41	15	——	26
42	16	——	26
43	16	——	27
44	17	——	27
45	17	——	28
46	18	——	28
47	18	——	29
48	19	——	29
49	19	——	30
50	20	——	30

NOTE: Rows in which either the acceptance or rejection number is blank should be ignored; that is, testing must continue until a row with two non blank entries is reached.

ACRONYMS

The statistical considerations involved in determining the sample size may be summarized by the acronym SIZE:

S   ampling distribution
I   nterval (confidence)
Z   value
E   stimation of population standard deviation

EXERCISES

QUESTIONS

1. Define the sampling distribution.
2. What is the standard error of the mean?
3. Define finite population correction.
4. Define a confidence interval.
5. What is the procedure for constructing a confidence interval around a mean?
6. Describe the difference between absolute precision and relative precision when estimating a population mean.
7. How do the degree of confidence and the degree of precision differ?
8. Describe the procedure for determining the sample size necessary to estimate a population mean, given the degree of precision and confidence and a known population variance. After the sample is selected, how is the confidence interval generated?
9. Describe the procedure for determining the sample size necessary to estimate a population mean, given the degree of precision and confidence but the population variance is unknown. After the sample is selected, how is the confidence interval generated?
10. How is the sample size affected when the absolute precision with which a population mean is estimated is doubled?
11. How is the sample size affected when the degree of confidence with which a population mean is estimated is increased from 95 to 99%?
12. Define what is meant by absolute precision and relative precision when estimating a population proportion.
13. Describe the procedure for determining the sample size necessary to estimate a population proportion given the degree of precision and confidence. After the sample is selected, how is the confidence interval generated?
14. How can the researcher ensure that the generated confidence interval will be no larger than the desired interval when estimating a population proportion?
15. When several parameters are being estimated, what is the procedure for determining the sample size?
16. Define incidence rate and completion rate. How do these rates affect the determination of the final sample size?
17. What strategies are available for adjusting for nonresponse?

PROBLEMS

1. Using Table 2 of the Appendix of Statistical Tables, calculate the probability that
   a. z is less than 1.48
   b. z is greater than 1.90
   c. z is between 1.48 and 1.90
   d. z is between −1.48 and 1.90

2. What is the value of z if

   a. 60% of all values of z are larger

   b. 10% of all values of z are larger

   c. 68.26% of all possible z values (symmetrically distributed around the mean) are to be contained in this interval

3. The management of a local restaurant wants to determine the average monthly amount spent by households in fancy restaurants. Some households do not spend anything at all, whereas other households spend as much as $300 per month. Management wants to be 95% confident of the findings and does not want the error to exceed ±$5.

   a. What sample size should be used to determine the average monthly household expenditure?

   b. After the survey was conducted, the average expenditure was found to be $90.30 and the standard deviation was $45. Construct a 95% confidence interval. What can be said about the level of precision?

4. To determine the effectiveness of the advertising campaign for a new VCR, management would like to know what percentage of the households are aware of the new brand. The advertising agency thinks that this figure is as high as 70%. The management would like a 95% confidence interval and a margin of error no greater than ±2%.

   a. What sample size should be used for this study?

   b. Suppose that management wanted to be 99% confident but could tolerate an error of ±3%. How would the sample size change?

5. Assuming that $n = 100$, $N = 1,000$, and $\sigma = 5$, compute the standard error of the mean with and without the finite population correction factor.

COMPUTER EXERCISES

1. Using a spreadsheet (Lotus 1-2-3 or Excel) or a database manager such as dBASE IV, program the formulas for determining the sample size under the various approaches.

2. Solve problems 1 through 4 using the programs that you have developed.

NOTES

1. *Bicycling Magazine's 1987 Semiannual Study of U.S. Retail Bicycle Stores*, September 1987.

2. A discussion of the sampling distribution may be found in any basic statistics textbook. For example, see Mark L. Berenson and David M. Levine, *Basic Business Statistics: Concepts and Applications*, 5th ed. (Englewood Cliffs, NJ: Prentice Hall, 1992).

3. Other statistical approaches are also available. A discussion of these is beyond the scope of this book, however. The interested reader is referred to Clifford Nowell and Linda R. Stanley, "Length-Biased Sampling in Mall Intercept Surveys," *Journal of Marketing Research* 28 (November 1991): 475–479; Raphael Gillett, "Confidence Interval Construction by Stein's Method: A Practical and Economical Approach to Sample Size Determination," *Journal of Marketing Research* 26 (May 1989): 237; Martin Frankel, "Sampling Theory," in Peter H. Rossi, James D. Wright, and Andy B. Anderson (eds.), *Handbook of Survey Research* (New York: Academic Press, 1983), pp. 21–67; L. Kish, *Survey Sampling* (New York: Wiley, 1965), p. 102; and Seymour Sudman, *Applied Sampling* (New York: Academic Press, 1976), pp. 85–105.

4. Helena Chmura Kraemer and Sue Thiemann, *How Many Subjects?* (Newbury Park, CA: Sage Publications, 1988).

5. Martin Frankel, "Sampling Theory," in Peter H. Rossi, James D. Wright, and Andy B. Anderson (eds.), *Handbook of Survey Research* (New York: Academic Press, 1983), pp. 21–67.

6. For a discussion of estimating sample costs, see L. Kish, *Survey Sampling* (New York: Wiley, 1965); and Seymour Sudman, *Applied Sampling* (New York: Academic Press, 1976).

7. See, for example, Seymour Sudman, "Applied Sampling," in Peter H. Rossi, James D. Wright, and Andy B. Anderson (eds.), *Handbook of Survey Research* (Orlando, FL: Academic Press, 1983), pp. 145–194.

8. Adjusting for incidence and completion rates is discussed in Louis G. Pol and Sukgoo Pak, "The Use of Two-Stage Survey Design in Collecting Data from Those Who Have Attended Periodic or Special Events," *Journal of the Market Research Society*, 36 (October 1994): 315–26.

9. K. G. Lee, "Incidence Is a Key Element," *Marketing News* (September 13, 1985): 50.

10. "Sales Makes Sweet Music," *Quirk's Marketing Research Review* (May 1988): 10–12.

11. Charles Martin, "The Impact of Topic Interest on Mail Survey Response Behaviour," *Journal of the Market Research Society*, 36 (October 1994): 327–38.

12. Stephen W. McDaniel, Charles S. Madden, and Perry Verille, "Do Topic Differences Affect Survey Nonresponse?" *Journal of the Market Research Society* (January 1987): 55–66; and L. Leslie, "Are High Response Rates Essential to Valid Surveys?" *Social Science Research* (September 1971): 332–34.

13. For minimizing the incidence of nonresponse and adjusting for its effects, see Michael Brown, "What Price Response?" *Journal of the Market Research Society* 36 (July 1994): 9227–44.

14. Jolene M. Struebbe, Jerome B. Kernan, and Thomas J. Grogan, "The Refusal Problem in Telephone Surveys," *Journal of Advertising Research* (June-July 1986): 29–38.

15. J. Scott Armstrong and Edward J. Lusk, "Return Postage in Mail Surveys: A Meta-Analysis," *Public Opinion Quarterly* (Summer 1987): 233–48; and Julie Yu and Harris Cooper, "A Quantitative Review of Research Design Effects on Response Rates to Questionnaires," *Journal of Marketing Research* 20 (February 1983): 36–44.

16. Edward F. Fern, Kent B. Monroe, and Ramon A. Avila, "Effectiveness of Multiple Request Strategies: A Synthesis of Research Results," *Journal of Marketing Research*, 23 (May 1986): 144–53.

17. Thomas V. Greer and Ritu Lohtia, "Effects of Source and Paper Color on Response Rates in Mail Surveys," *Industrial Marketing Management*, 23 (February 1994): 47–54.

18. *Bicycling Magazine's 1987 Semiannual Study of U.S. Retail Bicycle Stores*, September 1987.

19. R. A. Kerin and R. A. Peterson, "Scheduling Telephone Interviews," *Journal of Advertising Research* (May 1983): 44.

20. D. A. Dillman, *Mail and Telephone Surveys: The Total Design Method* (New York: Wiley, 1978), p. 53.

21. Dennis K. Pearl and David Fairley, "Testing for the Potential for Nonresponse Bias in Sample Surveys," *Public Opinion Quarterly* 49 (Winter 1985): 553–60.

22. John Maines, "Taking the Pulse of the Voter," *American Demographics* (November 1992): 20.

23. James C. Ward, Bertram Russick, and William Rudelius, "A Test of Reducing Callbacks and Not-at-Home Bias in Personal Interviews by Weighting At-Home Respondents," *Journal of Marketing Research* 2 (February 1985): 66–73.

24. D. W. Chapman, "Survey of Nonresponse Imputation Procedures," *Proceedings of the Social Statistics Section, American Statistical Association*, Part 1 (Washington, DC: American Statistical Association, 1976), pp. 245–51.

25. *The Economist*, "Another Chinese Take-Off," (December 19, 1992).

26. The assistance of James Agarwal with the international marketing research example, the assistance of Mark Leach and Gina Miller in writing the ethics section, and the assistance of Mark Peterson in writing the computer applications section is gratefully acknowledged.

APPENDIX 12A

THE NORMAL DISTRIBUTION

In this appendix, we provide a brief overview of the normal distribution and the use of the normal distribution table. The normal distribution is used in calculating the sample size, and it serves as the basis for classical statistical inference. Many continuous phenomena follow the normal distribution or can be approximated by it. The normal distribution can, likewise, be used to approximate many discrete probability distributions.[1]

normal distribution A basis for classical statistical inference that is bell-shaped and symmetrical in appearance. Its measures of central tendency are all identical.

The **normal distribution** has some important theoretical properties. It is bell-shaped and symmetrical in appearance. Its measures of central tendency (mean, median, and mode) are all identical. Its associated random variable has an infinite range $(-\infty < x < +\infty)$.

The normal distribution is defined by the population mean μ and population standard deviation σ. Since an infinite number of combination of μ and σ exist, an infinite number of normal distributions exist and an infinite number of tables would be required. By standardizing the data, however, we need only one table, such as Table 2 in the Appendix of Statistical Tables. Any normal random variable X can be converted to a standardized normal random variable z by the formula

$$z = \frac{X - \mu}{\sigma}$$

Note that the random variable z is always normally distributed with a mean of 0 and a standard deviation of 1. The normal probability tables are generally used for two purposes: (1) finding probabilities corresponding to known values of X or z and (2) finding values of X or z corresponding to known probabilities. Each of these uses is discussed.

FINDING PROBABILITIES CORRESPONDING TO KNOWN VALUES

Suppose that Figure 12A.1 represents the distribution of the number of engineering contracts received per year by an engineering firm. Because the data span the entire history of the firm, Figure 12A.1 represents the population. Therefore, the probabilities or proportion of area under the curve must add up to 1.0. The vice-president of marketing wishes to determine the probability that the number of contracts received next year will be between 50 and 55. The answer can be determined by using Table 2 of the Appendix of Statistical Tables.

Table 2 gives the probability or area under the standardized normal curve from the mean (zero) to the standardized value of interest, z. Only positive entries of z are listed in the table. For a symmetrical distribution with zero mean, the area from the mean to $+z$ (i.e., z standard deviations above the mean) is identical to the area from the mean to $-z$ (z standard deviations below the mean).

Note that the difference between 50 and 55 corresponds to a z value of 1.00. Note that to use Table 2, all z values must be recorded to two decimal places. To read the probability or area under the curve from the mean to $z = +1.00$, scan down the z column of Table 2 until the z value of interest (in tenths) is located. In this case, stop in the row $z = 1.00$. Then, read across this row until you intersect the column containing the hun-

[1]This material is drawn from Mark L. Berenson and David M. Levine, *Basic Business Statistics: Concepts and Applications*, 5th ed. (Englewood Cliffs, NJ: Prentice Hall, 1992).

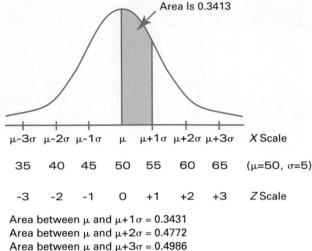

FIGURE 12A.1

Finding Probability Corresponding to a Known Value

Area between μ and μ+1σ = 0.3431
Area between μ and μ+2σ = 0.4772
Area between μ and μ+3σ = 0.4986

dredths place of the z value. Thus, in Table 2, the tabulated probability for z = 1.00 corresponds to the intersection of the row z = 1.0 with the column z = .00. This probability is .3413. As shown in Figure 12A.1, the probability is .3413 that the number of contracts received by the firm next year will be between 50 and 55. It can also be concluded that the probability is .6826 (2 × .3413) that the number of contracts received next year will be between 45 and 55.

This result could be generalized to show that for any normal distribution, the probability is .6826 that a randomly selected item will fall within ±1 standard deviations above or below the mean. Also, it can be verified from Table 2 that there is a .9544 probability that any randomly selected normally distributed observation will fall within ±2 standard deviations above or below the mean and a .9973 probability that the observation will fall within ±3 standard deviations above or below the mean.

FINDING VALUES CORRESPONDING TO KNOWN PROPERTIES

Suppose that the vice president of marketing wishes to determine how many contracts must come in so that 5% of the contracts for the year have come in. If 5% of the contracts have come in, 95% of the contracts have yet to come. As shown in Figure 12A.2, this 95% can be broken down into two parts: contracts above the mean (i.e., 50%) and

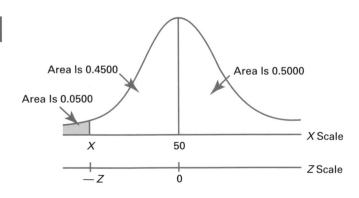

FIGURE 12A.2

Finding Values Corresponding to Known Probabilities

Area Is 0.4500
Area Is 0.5000
Area Is 0.0500

contracts between the mean and the desired z value (i.e., 45%). The desired z value can be determined from Table 2, since the area under the normal curve from the standardized mean, 0, to this z must be .4500. From Table 2, we search for the area or probability .4500. The closest value is .4495 or .4505. For .4495, we see that the z value corresponding to the particular z row (1.6) and z column (.04) is 1.64. The z value, however, must be recorded as negative (i.e., $z = -1.64$), since it is below the standardized mean of 0. Similarly, the z value corresponding to the area of .4505 is -1.65. Since .4500 is midway between .4495 and .4505, the appropriate z value could be midway between the two z values and estimated as -1.645. The corresponding X value can then be calculated from the standardization formula, as follows:

$$X = \mu + z\sigma$$
$$= 50 + (-1.645)5$$
$$= 41.775$$

Suppose that the vice-president wanted to determine the interval in which 95% of the contracts for next year are expected to lie. As can be seen from Figure 12A.3, the corresponding z values are ± 1.96. This corresponds to X values of 50 $\pm$ (1.96)5, or 40.2 and 59.8. This range represents the 95% confidence interval.

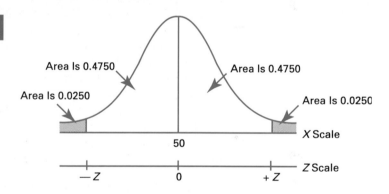

FIGURE 12A.3

Finding Values Corresponding oto Known Probabilities: Confidence Interval

Area Is 0.4750

Area Is 0.4750

Area Is 0.0250

Area Is 0.0250

X Scale

50

Z Scale

$-Z$ 0 $+Z$

PROFESSIONAL PERSPECTIVES

Focus Groups and Qualitative Research

Twenty years ago focus groups were conducted in living rooms or rec rooms of "typical" suburban homes. Participants were generally homemakers who were invited to discuss any one of a multitude of consumer products: diapers, cleansers, bread, or coffee. Today, focus groups are conducted in advanced focus group facilities and participants have varied backgrounds, such as management-level engineers discussing the implementation of new telecommunications technology.

The qualitative industry has evolved in two primary areas. First, marketers and advertising people have been drawn more deeply into the research process. No longer do they sit quietly and invisibly in the corner of a living room. Instead, they may watch the group discussion via closed circuit television or from behind a one-way mirror. Second, moderators have grown in experience and methodology as they are drawn more deeply into the marketing process from the client's point of view. They must understand the product, be it baby diapers, telecommunication links, or corporate financial planning. Moderator analysis must be marketing-oriented with an actionable plan of recommendations, generally providing input into the quantitative phase of the project.

It is no longer acceptable for brand managers or account planners to brainstorm ideas about what customers need. Concepts can no longer be developed with only their associates' approval. All levels of employees must leave their ivory towers to uncover the real motivations behind customer actions. Engineers, sales personnel, research and design employees, and support personnel are beginning to listen to their customers firsthand. Group discussions are conducted among chief financial officers, cardiologists, real estate developers, and environmentalists as well as direc-

Susan C. Lowe

As supervisor of qualitative research, Susan Lowe is involved in all phases of the qualitative research projects conducted by Burke Marketing Research, Inc. Her responsibilities include study design, implementation, and analysis. Working closely with the qualitative research group, Ms. Lowe ensures the smooth transition of a study into the quantitative phase. Her product category experience ranges from consumer packaged goods to business services and technologies. Burke Marketing Research conducts over 400 focus groups and 450 in-depth interviews each year, the largest percentage of qualitative research conducted by one firm in the United States.

tors of management information systems, frequent business travelers, and carriers of incurable diseases. Exchanges of information between users and makers in virtually all industries has resulted in the sharing of common experience-based outlooks. This valuable experience base may be used to improve the product or service.

The second primary change in the qualitative industry involves the role of the moderator. Moderators, like physicians, have become more specialized. No longer do they diagnose general marketing ailments. Moderators have become critical to understanding and evaluating qualitative research. Because of the high-tech boom of the past decade, the facilitator must be conversant with a variety of high-tech topics, such as protocol converters, local area networks, integrated workstations, and digital transmission terminals. Qualitative research flourishes in a variety of nontraditional research industries, such as financial services, health care, shipping and transportation, and nonprofit organizations. This growth in qualitative research applications demands a moderator who understands not only the product or service but the industry as a whole. Hence, the moderator's tools have been developed for specific applications. These tools now include techniques requiring in-depth psychological evaluation. Laddering, idea generation, projective techniques, and psychographic analysis are only a few techniques that have been used to uncover buyer perceptions and motivations.

In addition to understanding the client's world, moderators must also facilitate the exchange of information from buyer to seller. The moderator's role is to bring the client beyond the point of just listening to the point of listening critically and analytically. Additionally, the moderator must piece together multiple fragments of information, both what is said and what is unsaid, to provide a constructive overview with an actionable recommendation. The moderator has become a research consultant.

The future of qualitative research portends additional growth and development. Manufacturing-driven sales are increasingly being replaced by customer demands and satisfaction. This is currently reflected in the enormous increase of customer satisfaction programs. Additionally, the rapid increase of offshore competition and the world of mergers and acquisitions are forcing corporations to tighten their belts as internal resources shrink. In this increasingly competitive society, corporations can no longer risk the expense of an unsuccessful product launch. Customer input must be sought in the early stages of product development via qualitative research.

Computer-Assisted Personal Interviewing

Traditionally in marketing research, data have been collected in person directly on a paper copy of a questionnaire. For many years, this was the norm for most interviewing methods including door-to-door interviewing, central location testing, and mall-intercept interviewing. Even when telephones became popular as a method of respondent contact, telephone interviewers continued to record their responses on paper.

Although there are inherent problems and biases with all methods of data collection, this is especially true of paper-and-pencil data collection. The interviewer must translate what is heard from the respondent and record an answer. Since interviewer judgment is required, biases in interpretation and in recording can occur. Once the data have been collected, they must be entered into a database before they can be analyzed. Again, data entry staff must interpret the interviewer's writing, and biases in interpretation and in entering responses can occur. A substantial amount of time is required to enter the data from every respondent twice (once by the interviewer and once by data entry staff) before it is ready to be analyzed.

Another bias from paper-and-pencil data collection is based on response demand characteristics. This type of bias is evident in two distinct forms. First, the way interviewers ask questions may, consciously or subconsciously, bias a respondent's answers. Second, respondents may consciously or subconsciously try to provide socially desirable responses.

Nancy L. Messinger

Nancy L. Messinger is a senior research analyst at Burke Marketing Research, Inc. She is responsible for designing studies to address specific client problems, analyzing and interpreting the data collected, and assimilating results in the form of written reports or verbal presentations. More recently, Ms. Messinger has concentrated her efforts in computer-assisted personal interviewing. She has played an active role in improving the cost effectiveness of this increasingly popular method of data collection.

With the evolution of data collection techniques in marketing research, the computer has been adopted in an attempt to improve data collection efficiencies and minimize some of the inherent problems and biases in paper-and-pencil techniques. Over the past ten years, computer-assisted personal interviewing (CAPI) has been replacing paper-and-pencil data collection. In this method, respondents sit in front of the computer and input their own responses. An interviewer, in the role of a host or hostess, is present, but the respondent interacts directly with the computer. Having respondents input their own data minimizes response biases, eliminates biases caused by interviewer interpretation of the data, and reduces recording errors. Once a respondent has completed the interview, the data file is stored in a form that is ready for analysis.

Software packages have been designed specifically for use on personal computers (PCs). These packages are menu-driven and easy to program. Because of the user-friendly programming, these packages are rapidly gaining in popularity not only with marketing research firms but also with advertising agencies, service organizations, manufacturers of consumer and industrial products, and universities.

CAPI is also popular because data can be collected from respondents in so many different locations. Once an interview has been programmed, the interview is copied on to field disks that are designed to collect the data from the interviews directly onto the interviewing diskette. These diskettes can be mailed to mall facilities for use with their own PCs, mailed to respondents such as physicians to answer on their own computers, or loaded onto portable PCs to collect data from people who are difficult to reach. The full potential of field disks is still being realized.

Although many of the biases and problems of traditional paper-and-pencil methods of data collection have been overcome with CAPI, there are, unfortunately, many disadvantages to this method of data collection, including:

- The cost of some software for PC interviewing
- The time to initially learn to program the software
- Programming limitations: premade software never addresses all the demands of custom research
- Cost of disks and mailing
- Problems with damaging or losing disks in the mail
- Logistical complexities of some field work
- The variety of computer types, disk drive sizes, and DOS versions currently in use
- Field interviewer personnel who are unfamiliar with computers
- Respondents pressing the wrong keys and entering wrong responses
- Open-ended responses are difficult for most respondents to answer, so these questions often receive short answers or are left blank

Though there are many disadvantages of CAPI, some of these are slowly beginning to disappear as interviewers in field locations gain experience with computers. With the increased demand for CAPI, field interviewers have learned how to operate PCs and handle diskettes. Also, software is being adapted to handle more of the common programming problems. Though it is difficult to develop software to meet all the programming needs for custom marketing research, the software is continually being improved to address common questionnaire design problems. Finally, many field agencies are purchasing modems for data transfer. It may no longer be necessary to mail disks and risk damaged disks or lost data.

Over the past several years, CAPI has rapidly increased in popularity. The greatest advantage is the improved time efficiency in getting a clean data set that is ready for analysis. In the future, the use of modems may further improve the speed with which data are available for analysis. After data are collected, the field locations will be able to modem the data back to the company conducting the study. With the use of modems, data could be available for analysis almost as soon as a respondent finishes an interview. CAPI will continue to grow and develop as a popular method of data collection.

Using a Cash Incentive to Heighten Mail Survey Response

Market Facts, Inc.

There are many reasons why mail surveys continue to be a popular form of data collection. Apart from the pragmatic matter of expense, there are several technical considerations that favor mail surveys: the ease of obtaining a geographically dispersed sample, the ability to get to difficult-to-reach respondents (e.g., soldiers, business executives, those away from a telephone), freedom from worries of interviewer bias, greater privacy, the opportunity for respondents to answer thoughtfully and, when necessary, time to access difficult-to-locate information needed for the response.

The most compelling argument against mailed questionnaires, however, has been the typically unsatisfactory response rates often achieved, which can run as low as 10 to 20% in many general public/consumer surveys.[1] Given the need to make inferences from the sample to some population, low response rates necessarily raise suspicions about possible nonresponse bias and, thus, any inferences made.

Cash incentives may be one way to boost mail response, whether sent along with the questionnaire or made conditional upon the respondent's first completing and returning it. The size of the incentives tested has tended to be modest, mostly 25¢; very few researchers have experimented with incentives as high as $1.00.

For some, even incentives of 25¢ might seem a strain on the research budget, and are rejected as a result. Cash incentives might not be as expensive as they first appear, however. Higher response rates are attainable, in certain cases, at little or no additional cost per respondent.

[1]Response rates using samples selected from ongoing panels recruited to be regular survey respondents tend to be much higher. Surveys using Market Facts' Consumer Mail Panel typically achieve response rates of 60 to 80%.

AN EXPERIMENT USING A CASH INCENTIVE

As part of a larger study, Market Facts recently directed a survey among Canadian Jews about travel to Israel. Most of the questions concerned past travel experiences or attitudes toward possible future trips. The sample ($n = 600$) was drawn from the telephone directories of four Canadian cities—Toronto, Montreal, Vancouver, and Winnipeg—using a procedure known as "distinctive Jewish name sampling."

The object of the experiment was to assess the effectiveness of a $1.00 cash incentive in encouraging mail survey recipients to complete and return a rather lengthy (8-page legal size) questionnaire. A dollar bill (U.S.) was included in 300 (half) of the randomly selected mailings ("test group"), while no incentive was sent with the other 300 questionnaires ("control group"). All the packages contained a stamped return envelope and a cover letter to describe the purpose of the study, explain the sample selection process, and request cooperation. The letter sent to the test sample also referred to the enclosed incentive. A follow-up, reminder postcard was mailed to all respondents approximately eight days later, and a second questionnaire was mailed to remaining nonresponders about two weeks later.

RESULTS OF THE EXPERIMENT

Table I presents the outcome of the experiment, showing the effect of the incentive on response. The cash incentive cell has a 34% response rate, twice that of the non-cash cell. The difference is statistically significant with at least 99% confidence.

There is little reason to doubt that increases in response rates could also be achieved in a wide variety of other mail surveys. But how much of an incentive should be used? The answer, of course, depends in part on the level of response desired as well as on available resources. Some research suggests that, in general, $1.00 may be more than is needed to achieve a marked increase in returns (compared with using no incentive). In fact, for some surveys, 25¢ or 50¢ might do just as nicely. The answer also likely depends on the length of the questionnaire, the composition of the sample, the salience of the survey topic, the number of follow-up attempts, and other factors.

An equally important issue related to the technical quality of the research is the possibility of self-selection bias: Does a monetary incentive disproportionately elicit responses from certain types of individuals, causing the obtained sample to be unrepresentative?

To test the self-selection hypothesis in the present experiment, the incentive and nonincentive groups were compared on a series of personal attributes and behavioral measures to determine if any significant differences exist. No differences between the groups were observed on these items, which included past travel to Israel, intent to travel in the future, religious beliefs, and others.

RELATIVE COST

How much greater, if at all, is the expected cost per completed questionnaire (CPQ) for a sample sent an incentive, compared with a sample *not* sent an incentive? For the test sample mailed the incentive, the sum of the direct cost of the labor in preparing the mailing, the nonpostage direct expense (paper, envelopes, printing), outgoing and incoming postage, and the $1.00 incentive came to $726. This amount divided by 95 (the number of completed questionnaires received) equals $7.64 *per returned questionnaire*. In order to elicit the same number of completed questionnaires *without the incentive* would have require mailing to about 559 recipients, assuming a 17% response rate ($0.17 \times 559 = 95$). The sum of the labor, postage, and nonpostage expenses for this size mailing would have been $727. Dividing this by 95 equals $7.65 *per completed questionnaire*—virtually the same CPQ as in the test sample.[2] The $1.00 incentive turns out to fully pay for itself. In this case, the heightened rate of response represents a technical improvement in the research, at no additional cost.

APPENDIX

BUSINESS REPLY CARD

In the study described above, it was not feasible to use a business reply envelope so that incoming postage would only be charged for returned questionnaires. Rather, returned postage had to be paid on all mailings. The difference has a dramatic effect on the relative cost comparison. Were the same design applied to a survey in the

---

[2]Excluding the cost of the incentive in this comparison, the *cost per mailed-out questionnaire* would be $1.50 for the test group and $1.30 for the control group. The difference is due to being able to spread the fixed costs—those unrelated to the size of the mailing—among a larger number of mailings in the no-incentive group (559) than in the group that would receive the incentive (300).

TABLE 1

The Results of Market Facts' Mail Survey Response Incentive Experiment

	$1.00 Incentive	No Incentive
Questionnaires mailed	300	300
Envelopes undeliverable (returned because of "bad address")	24	26
Completed questionnaires received (from first mailing and reminder card)	95	46
Response rate	95/276 = 34%	46/274 = 17%

United States (where a business reply envelope could be used, thereby incurring postage costs only for returned questionnaires), the total cost for the group of 300 receiving the incentive would have been $632, or a CPQ of $6.65. The control group sample mailing to 559 would have cost $514, or a CPQ of $5.41. (The same response rates were assumed in this hypothetical scenario.) Under these conditions, simply increasing the size of the mailout and using no incentive would have been more efficient.

In such instances, the decision about whether to mail a monetary incentive is not as easy. Here, the improved response rate produced by the incentive needs to be balanced against the additional cost required to obtain the same number of replies. The actual cost differential of generating returned questionnaires in a given study will depend, among other factors, upon the desired final sample size (and, thus, the number of questionnaires which need to be mailed). Researchers will have to judge the cost-quality tradeoff in the context of their research needs and priorities.

This material is reproduced in an abridged form from Research on Research, Report No. 39, by Market Facts, Inc. with permission of the company. A complete copy of this report may be obtained from the company.

Dialing Selection Techniques: Random Digit versus Directory

Market Facts, Inc.

BACKGROUND

There is a growing tendency for researchers to conduct telephone surveys using a random- or systematic-digit selection technique rather than telephone numbers listed in directories. Because a large number of telephone numbers are not listed in directories, a more representative sample of listed and unlisted numbers is expected when the random-digit selection technique is used.

The methodology of the random-digit selection technique has many variations. Theoretically, the method consists of a computerized generation of randomly selected telephone numbers. As a practical matter, many randomly selected ten digit numbers are nonworking telephone numbers.

The raised integer method is a variation of the random-digit selection technique that tends to minimize the frequency of nonworking numbers. An arbitrary but small constant value—say 1 to 9—is selected. The constant value is added to the last digit of a working and nonbusiness telephone number that is systematically selected from a directory. Even with this procedure, at least 10 to 15% of the resultant telephone numbers are business or nonworking. Consequently, interviewing costs are higher for the random-digit selection process than for a sample limited to listed numbers only.

Briefly then, a random-digit selection technique is theoretically more desirable than restricting the dialing attempts to numbers listed in the telephone directory. But does the random-digit selection technique produce significantly different results than directory selection techniques? Is the additional cost justified? These questions are addressed in the following report.

RESEARCH METHOD

Market Facts, Inc. conducted a national study that selected telephone numbers by using a systematic-digit

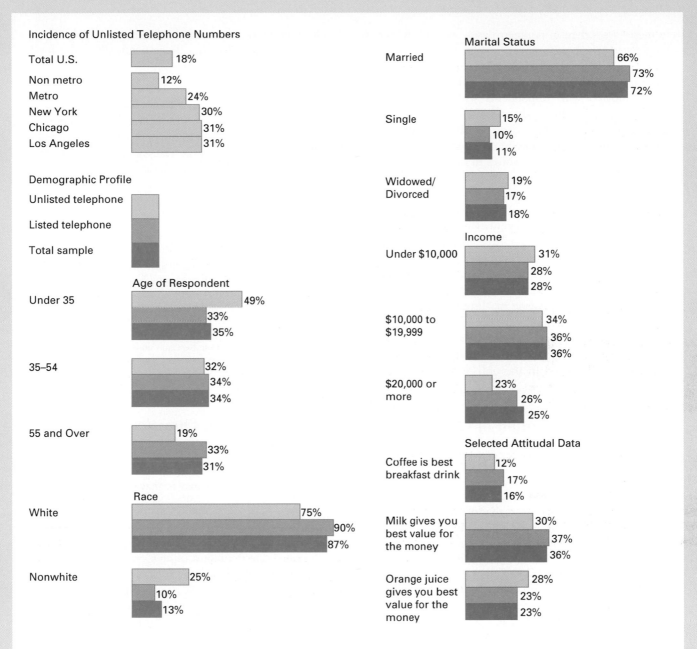

Incidence of Unlisted Telephone Numbers

Total U.S.	18%
Non metro	12%
Metro	24%
New York	30%
Chicago	31%
Los Angeles	31%

Demographic Profile

Unlisted telephone

Listed telephone

Total sample

Age of Respondent

Under 35	49% / 33% / 35%
35–54	32% / 34% / 34%
55 and Over	19% / 33% / 31%

Race

White	75% / 90% / 87%
Nonwhite	25% / 10% / 13%

Marital Status

Married	66% / 73% / 72%
Single	15% / 10% / 11%
Widowed/Divorced	19% / 17% / 18%

Income

Under $10,000	31% / 28% / 28%
$10,000 to $19,999	34% / 36% / 36%
$20,000 or more	23% / 26% / 25%

Selected Attitudal Data

Coffee is best breakfast drink	12% / 17% / 16%
Milk gives you best value for the money	30% / 37% / 36%
Orange juice gives you best value for the money	28% / 23% / 23%

selection technique. The raised integer method was employed to complete approximately 3,000 interviews. The interviewing was conducted primarily during evening hours and on weekends, with no callbacks.

The objective of the study was to determine attitudes and awareness of drinks and beverages among female heads of households. At the conclusion of the interview, the interviewer asked, "Is your telephone number listed or unlisted?"

RESULTS

Eighteen percent of the respondents reported that their telephone number was not listed in the local telephone directory. This figure includes requests for unpublished numbers and new or changed numbers that missed the publication date of the directory.

The incidence of unlisted telephone numbers varied by region and population density. Twice as many respondents in metro areas than in nonmetro areas were likely to have an unlisted telephone number. In fact, in the three largest metro areas in the United States, more than 30% of the respondents claimed to have an unlisted telephone number.

Compared with respondents with listed telephone numbers, respondents with unlisted telephone numbers were significantly younger, more likely to be single, and have a somewhat lower income. Nonwhites were two and one-half times as likely as whites in claiming to have an unlisted telephone number. Attitudinal differences were clearly shown by the two groups.

Thus, the data show that there are significant demographic and attitudinal differences between respondents whose telephone numbers are listed and those respondents having unlisted telephone numbers. Nevertheless, the data reveal that there is *no significant difference on any demographic or attitudinal measure included in this study*, when a comparison is made of "listed" respondents and total respondents (including listed and unlisted numbers).

Since unlisted telephone numbers comprise less than 20% of the total telephone owning households, the differences that were noted in the unlisted telephone households occurred in only one-fifth of the total sample. Their influence therefore does not dramatically affect the total results of this study.

CONCLUSIONS

The data suggest judgment and a careful examination of objectives and cost differences are appropriate before making the decision regarding the sampling technique. Specifically, a random- or systematic-digit selection technique would likely be appropriate if an analysis of metro areas—especially large metro areas—is being made.

On the other hand, a directory selection technique may be appropriate for an analysis of a universe known to have an average to low incidence of unlisted telephone numbers. This lower-cost technique would probably produce results comparable with the higher cost random-digit selection technique.

This material is reproduced from Research on Research Report No. 10, by Market Facts, Inc. with permission of the company. A copy of this report may be obtained from the company.

An Examination of Order Bias (On Self-Administered Questionnaires)
Market Facts, Inc.

THE PROBLEM

A dilemma that often confronts marketing researchers in the design of questionnaires is that of eliminating or averaging bias to the greatest extent possible. The wording of the questions, the sequence of questioning, and the ordering of structured responses to certain questions—whether asked by an interviewer or presented to the respondent on an exhibit card or self-administered questionnaire—can all influence the respondent's answers. This discussion focuses on one of these potential sources of bias: the order of structured responses on self-administered questionnaires.

The most commonly used method of averaging order bias in structured responses is to rotate the order of presentation of the stimulus; for example, a frequency of use scale might range from high to low for half the respondents and low to high for the other half. Often rotation is not employed for a number of reasons. Two of the major reasons are (1) the extra cost and trouble associated with developing various versions of the questionnaire and (2) the additional data processing effort, time, and cost required to reassemble each version into a common format for analysis. Depending on the scope of the research these may or may not be valid reasons.

RESEARCH METHOD

Market Facts, Inc. investigated the issue of order bias in self-administered questionnaires using Consumer Mail Panels, its controlled mail panel research facility. Responses to five questions, directed to female heads of households in two balanced panels of Consumer Mail Panels members, were analyzed for bias. One panel received questionnaires with the structured responses in one order and the order was reversed for the other panel. The number of respondents in each panel exceeded 760.

The five questions covered a variety of topics—presidential performance, the weather, television viewing, restaurant patronage, and home repairs.

RESULTS

Statistical analysis of the data obtained from the two panels reveals that significant levels of order bias exist in three of

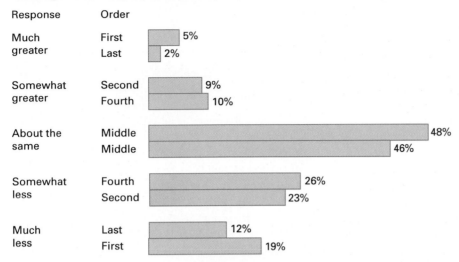

(Compared with a year ago) the amount of time spent watching televistion by my household is ...

Response	Order		
Much greater	First		5%
	Last		2%
Somewhat greater	Second		9%
	Fourth		10%
About the same	Middle		48%
	Middle		46%
Somewhat less	Fourth		26%
	Second		23%
Much less	Last		12%
	First		19%

the five questions: those relating to television viewing, restaurant patronage, and home repairs. The reason that order bias was not detected in two questions could be a function of the simplicity of the response or the scales used. Because a significant level of order bias was detected in a self-administered, mail panel questionnaire, a research medium where order bias is least likely to occur, it can be assumed that the bias will be much greater in telephone surveys or interviews in which the structured response is read to respondents.

Clearly, the issue of order bias deserves serious consideration and the rotation of structured responses to permit averaging of the data should be employed whenever feasible.

DISCUSSION OF THE DATA

Examination of "top-box" scores for frequency of television viewing reveals that respondents are more likely to admit to greater television viewing when this response option is presented in the first position. The difference in the "top-box" response is significantly different at the 95% confidence level. To test for bias in the complete distribution, further analysis was performed and differences, significant at the 95% level of confidence, were detected.

This material is reproduced in an abridged form from Research on Research, Report No. 1, by Market Facts, Inc. with permission of the company. A complete copy of this report may be obtained from the company.

When the frozen-foods industry realized that it was losing sales to other departments in supermarkets and to the restaurant industry, it sent out a call for innovative product ideas, better shelf management, and directed marketing. The crisis was further heightened when its number one unit seller, concentrated orange juice, lost out to chilled orange juice.

Proof of this crisis was evident in statistics that showed that food purchases, which totaled $500 billion in 1995, accounted for about 20% of consumer expenditure, and that approximately 58% of these sales were at supermarkets. This is in sharp contrast to figures from approximately 30 years previously, when 75% of food purchases were made at supermarkets. A study revealed that consumers on the average spend $30 a week for food consumed at locations other than their homes. Furthermore, 11.3% of the respondents in the study planned to eat out even more in the following year.

The results of the above market research study emphasized that these consumers had to be encouraged to go back to making purchases at the supermarket. The research firm felt that precision target marketing and broad-scale advertising, carrying crisp messages, would increase consumer awareness of price, variety, and type. Additionally, scanners at checkout counters could be used to provide information about the consumers that the industry was trying to target. Psychographic and demographic information could be obtained through surveys at the retail level or through direct mail. Coupons, if effectively used, could help to increase the sales of frozen foods. For example, scanner panel data could identify purchasers of dry macaroni and cheese. These consumers could then be given coupons for frozen macaroni and cheese.

The demographic information these techniques provide would be an immensely beneficial resource to the frozen-foods industry. Also, studies of the market could yield similar information. For example, one study provided the following information. First, the exact demographics of frozen-foods consumers were not known; it was known, however, that a wide range of consumers comprised the frozen-foods market and that three factors—smaller households, less free time, and less affluent consumers—described most of the consumers that used frozen-food products. Smaller households and less free time for consumers were growing trends in the marketplace, whereas less affluent consumers resulted more from America's changing society.

Smaller households, consisting of one or two persons, accounted for as much as three-fourths of total frozen-foods sales. Smaller households included single adults, couples with no children, and senior citizens. A general reason that these groups used frozen foods was the relative difficulty of preparing fresh foods in small quantities. In this instance, frozen foods became both cost and time effective. Single meals and entrees especially offered smaller households an alternative to eating out, without elaborate preparation, and were very popular in this market segment. Senior citizens often did not have the income or ability to eat out or to prepare many fresh foods. Therefore, as the U.S. population has aged, this market segment has continued to grow in importance as major consumers of frozen foods.

The second factor was less free time. This market segment was essentially made up of working women. With well over half of American women working, wives and mothers have less time to prepare meals. Frozen foods' appeal to this group is its time- and labor-saving aspect. This aspect became especially important when the industry realized that insulated lunch bags containing entrees could be a good marketing idea for consumers interested in a quality lunch that could be warmed up in an office microwave oven. Another promising opportunity was nutritionally oriented frozen meals. ConAgra's Healthy Choice frozen dinners, Stouffer's Right Course frozen entrees, and Kraft's Eating Right entrees have proven to be successful in this arena.

Less affluent consumers constituted the third most important frozen-foods market segment. Less affluent consumers used frozen foods not only for budgetary reasons but for convenience as well. This segment was characterized by smaller families or families in which both parents worked. Frequently, these consumers, like senior citizens, were unable to dine out. Also, some products, such as meats and seafood, were prohibitively expensive in their fresh forms, but frozen products were available at a substantially reduced cost.

Because frozen entrees were popular across many segments, a wide array of new entries came into the market. In 1991, Clorox introduced its Hidden Valley frozen-foods line, and Jeno's frozen pizza introduced Italian entrees named after the founder's mother, Michelina. Industry analysts did not feel that these two lines had much of a chance for success because most of the growth in the market for frozen entrees was in reduced-calorie, -fat, and -cholesterol offerings, although they comprised only 25% of the market, not the full-calorie segment (75% market share) targeted by Hidden Valley and Michelina.

Early 1992 to late 1993 was characterized by intense price and promotion wars in the frozen-foods market. The new introduction by Jeno's, the Michelina line of pasta dishes, has made inroads in the tough market by competing on price. Pasta is less expensive to produce than many of the more mainstay frozen entrees, and Michelina entrees are usually priced at less than $2 a dinner. Other members of the frozen-foods market such as Weight Watchers Food Company, Stouffer, and Campbell Soup Company are moving to reduce the focus on price. Marketing in 1995 was drastically cut for many of the big names as they cut corners to better compete in the price war. The current trend is to cut product lines that are clearly not making a profit and concentrate on new product introductions and marketing support.

It has also often been pointed out that retailers should put as much effort into merchandising frozen foods as they do into their service departments. For example, when consumers buy something from the deli, they should be encouraged to purchase something frozen for the next night. Furthermore, Pillsbury suggested giving frozen-food departments names like "The Menu Planning Center." Fish and entrees should also be stocked in the area where juice is traditionally stocked so that products that could be used to make up a meal are visually grouped. In this way, marketers have planned to entice consumers back into the stores, to result in an "unfreezing" of frozen-foods sales.

QUESTIONS

1. What kind of information related to frozen foods could be obtained using scanner volume tracking data?

2. What kind of information could be obtained using a scanner panel?

3. Identify other potential sources of secondary data related to the frozen-foods industry.

4. According to the Pillsbury Company, the frozen-foods industry should develop new packaging and new product concepts. Discuss the role of qualitative research in identifying such concepts. Which qualitative research techniques should be used?

5. If a survey were to be conducted to determine consumer preferences for frozen foods, which interviewing method would you recommend? Why?

6. Can observation methods be used to determine consumer preferences for frozen foods? If so, which observational methods would you use? Why?

REFERENCES

1. "The Conquest of Convenience." *Supermarket News* (January 1, 1990): 20–30.

2. Harris, John. "Jeno's Next Course." *Forbes* (May 27, 1991): 358.

3. Johnson, Bradley. "Clorox Joins Frozen Fray." *Advertising Age* (March 18, 1991): 17.

4. DeNitto, Emily. "Frozen-Food Results Chill Top 100." *Advertising Age* (September 29, 1993): 28.

CASE 2.2

Who Is the Host with the Most?

The once traditionally complacent hotel industry had to learn to market its services due to the increase in the number of hotels and the accompanying drop in occupancy rates. The many marketing ploys that have been pursued have resulted in some successes, some failures, and many "wait-and-sees." Some techniques that have been used include concentrated direct mail, television and print advertising, aggressive expansion into new markets, and giveaways of airline tickets.

Perhaps the most troublesome problem the industry has faced is the lack of customer loyalty. Most hoteliers provide similar facilities, and most customers do not travel enough to recognize distinctions between them. For this reason, many companies opted to differentiate their hotels through multiple branding or through moving into different market segments. In an attempt to draw more customers, some hoteliers have used costly consumer research before beginning new advertising and promotional campaigns for their hotels. Unfortunately, a company's marketing efforts are often copied by its competitors. And since the industry has slim profit margins, the tendency is to spend only approximately 1 to 2% of revenues on advertising. One campaign employed by hoteliers was Ramada Inns' "true hotel stories" campaign, which portrayed a businessman beset with problems during a hotel stay. This ad, however, received both praise and criticism that the hotel was overpromising. The company changed the campaign to more positive commercials.

On the other hand, Marriott reduced its advertising and put all its emphasis on its Honored Guest bonus program, which was analogous to the airlines' frequent flyer programs. The program received internal criticisms, but the company was confident that it would generate new business. The program allowed the company to gather detailed information about its frequent customers, and based on this information, Marriott could offer, through direct mail, incentives to shop in Marriott's stores, eat in its restaurants, and stay in its hotels with lagging occupancy. Furthermore, from the information it gathered, Marriott conceived the idea for Courtyard Hotels.

In early 1990, Marriott began to offer hotel rooms designed to meet the needs of corporate travelers. Marriott felt that it could enter the moderately priced market by targeting corporate travelers with the Courtyard Hotel concept. To market the idea, Marriott recreated a Courtyard room inside a 48-by-8-foot truck. The truck visited approximately 20 cities, inviting local corporate travel department executives to view the facility, in the hopes that the chain could garner these corporations' future travel business.

Holiday Inn offered its Crowne Plaza and Embassy Suites chains, which were geared toward the upscale business traveler, to compete with Courtyard Hotels. The company used the name Holiday Inn for its middle-class image hotels and the name Hampton Inn to compete with such economy chains as Motel 6, Red Roof, Days Inn, Super 8, and Econo Lodge. Holiday Inn still experienced difficulties in differentiating its various brands, however, especially when more than one was located in the same city.

Additionally, Holiday Inn was not as successful with its marketing programs as its competitors, even though it was the first hotel chain to offer a bonus program like the ones copied by Marriott and Ramada. The program was unsuccessful because, although it generated more business than estimated, the program itself cost more than was budgeted.

Although one can feel the riches that a Ritz-Carlton hotel has to offer, it is sad that the owners cannot reap the same riches that the guests can. Out of the 30 Ritz hotels that opened in 1993, only 12 are believed to be "in the black." This is probably due to today's environment in which travelers are trying to cut their hotel costs. Some contend that Ritz is more concerned with enhancing its brand image than with enhancing its shareholders' investment. For example, in one year, a hotel might spend $200,000 for flowers. Lately, the Ritz chain has bypassed conventional wisdom and placed its hotels in three-star markets such as Phoenix and Kansas City. The managers of these hotels have had to sell rooms and services that did not meet costs so as to subsidize its guests. Furthermore, other Ritz hotels have begun to define luxury downward by closing some of the fine dining rooms as general-use restaurants and making them only open for private parties. It was revealed that Ritz needed to charge at least $185 per night to cover its costs.

More recently, the hotel industry has shifted its focus away from cost and pricing concerns and has put more emphasis on special promotions and special offers. The hope of the players in the industry is that the special promotions will serve to differentiate the individuals from the pack. Marriott recently introduced a new program offering frequent flyer miles or free rooms when travelers stay at their hotels. Hilton wasted no time criticizing Marriott's move by pointing out that their hotel offers both airline miles and free rooms for frequent visitors.

Marriott's leaders often attribute their financial success to their unique database marketing system. Touted as the largest database for marketing purposes, the database contains preferences of repeat customers that help Marriott provide the best possible airline and hotel accommodations for each customer. The driving reason behind this database is Marriott's emphasis on customer sensitivity to other promotional offers and discounts. By offering the best possible service, Marriott hopes to counteract the effect of many of the competitive offers made to snare travelers. This just goes to show that for a hotel to be successful in attracting customers, it must be the "host with the most."

1. Identify some possible sources of secondary data for the hotel industry.

2. The hotel industry has faced the troublesome problem of differentiation. Hampton Inns would like to undertake marketing research to determine how it can differentiate itself from its competitors. What research design would you recommend?

3. What information is needed for Hampton Inns to develop a program to differentiate itself from its competition?

4. Design a questionnaire to obtain the relevant information.

REFERENCES

1. "Marriott Bets on Price Slashing to Build Brand Awareness for Its Budget Motels." *Wall Street Journal* (May 5, 1989): A9.

2. "Frequent Flyer Mile for Stay." *Wall Street Journal* (April 14, 1993): A8.

3. Hirsch, James S. "Of Luxury and Losses: Many Ritz Hotels Are in the Red." *Wall Street Journal* (April 22, 1994): B1, B3.

CASE 2.3

Candy Is Dandy for Hershey

The battle was on! Hershey and Mars, the two candy giants, dueling over the number one spot in the $7-billion-a-year candy industry. Hershey lost its throne in the early 1970s, and it took the company time to get back into the competitive arena. By 1985, however, Mars and Hershey were the manufacturers of the top ten candy bars, and together they shared 70% of the market. Cadbury held about 9% of the market and Nestlé only 6%. Then in 1988, Hershey acquired Cadbury and its share jumped from 36% to 44% of the candy market. The addition of brands such as Cadbury Dairy Milk Chocolate, Peter Paul Mounds, Almond Joy, and York Peppermint Pattie enabled Hershey to regain its throne in the candy market. The late 1980s and early 1990s produced the introduction of such products as Hershey's Kisses with Almonds, Hugs, Hugs with Almonds, Amazin' Fruit gummy bears, and the Cookies 'n' Mint Chocolate bar. In 1994, Hershey Food Corporation celebrated its 100th year in business. The decisions over the past 100 years have been both diverse and profitable (see Tables 1 and 2).

One of the factors that was in Hershey's favor in their battle with M&M/Mars was its excellent marketing research department. Hershey's research showed that the typical consumer viewed candy as a luxury good or as a self-indulgence. Because of these attitudes and beliefs, 70% of all candy sales were attributed to impulse buying. Candy customers also tended to be fickle, rarely purchasing the same candy bar twice in a row. A consumer's age was also shown to influence buying habits. Surveys indicated that of consumers in the 18 to 34 age group, 60% indulged themselves at least once a week, and 55% of all the candy items sold were consumed by people over 18. Of consumers in the 35 to 64 age group, however, only 6% indulged themselves at least once a week.

Market research also informed Hershey that the population was getting older. In the 1970s and early 1980s, young people from age 13 to their late 20s was the dominant age group. In the 1990s, it is becoming the 35 to 50 age group. For this reason, the candy industry decided to move upscale to attract baby-boom adults. By the year 2000, the median age for Americans will be 40. The National Confectioners Association believes that as Americans get older, they tend to favor the better things in life. Among these better things are quality confections. A multiple cross-sectional analysis of consumption patterns revealed that adults were consuming an ever-increasing percentage of candy (Table 3). The adult market has therefore proven to be increasingly lucrative.

TABLE 1

Hershey's Timeline

1895	First Hershey's Chocolate Bar is sold.
1907	Hershey's Kisses are introduced.
1908	Hershey's Milk Chocolate Bar with Almonds is introduced.
1911	Sales reach $5 million.
1925	Mr. Goodbar chocolate bar is introduced.
1938	The Hershey's Krackel bar is introduced.
1939	Hershey's Miniatures are introduced.
1945	Milton Hershey dies at the age of 88.
1963	Reese Candy Company, producer of Reeses peanut butter cups, is purchased.
1966	Hershey purchases San Giorgio Macaroni Company.
1968	Hershey Chocolate Corporation changes its name to Hershey Food Corporation.
1977	Y & S Candies Inc., manufacturer of licorice and licorice-type products such as Twizzlers and Nibs, is purchased.
1986	Luden's and 5th Avenue trademarks are added through acquisition of the Dietrich Corporations confectionery operations.
1988	Hershey Foods Corporation acquires Peter Paul/Cadbury U.S. confectionery operations. Brands acquired include Peter Paul Mounds and Almond Joy bars and York Peppermint Patties.
1990	Hershey's Kisses with Almonds are introduced.
1991	Fluid milk plant used to produce a chocolate drink is purchased.
1992	Hershey's Cookies 'n' Mint bar and Amazin' Fruit gummy bears are introduced.
1993	Hershey's Hugs and Hershey's Hugs with Almonds are introduced.
1994	Hershey's Nuggets chocolates and Reese's Peanut Butter Puffs brand cereal are introduced.

TABLE 2

Top 20 Chocolate Brands for the 12 Months Ended September 1992

Rank	Brand	1992	1991
1	Snickers	10.20%	9.55%
2	Reese's	9.33	9.40
3	M&M Peanut	6.31	7.43
4	M&M Plain	5.26	6.04
5	Kit Kat	4.97	4.68
6	Butterfinger	4.71	3.96
7	Hershey Almond	3.39	3.40
8	Crunch	3.33	2.88
9	Milky Way	3.25	3.04
10	Hershey Milk	2.91	2.68
11	Baby Ruth	2.53	2.36
12	York Mint	2.40	2.24
13	3 Musketeers	2.27	2.15
14	Almond Joy	2.21	2.18
15	Twix Caramel	1.78	1.95
16	Mounds	1.54	1.53
17	Mr. Goodbar	1.43	1.28
18	Fifth Avenue	1.41	1.28
19	Rolo	1.28	1.26
20	Milky Way Dark	1.21	1.53

TABLE 3

Candy Consumption by Age Group

Age Group	1980	1985	1990	1995 (Est.)
0–17 yrs	46%	42%	38%	35%
18–34 yrs	22%	22%	23%	23%
35–45 yrs	20%	22%	24%	26%
46+ yrs	12%	14%	15%	16%

Hershey successfully launched its adult-oriented Golden chocolate line and subsequently introduced Grand Slam, a combination of caramel, peanuts, and crisp rice that was targeted at the 18 to 34 age group. Hershey's Solitaire and Life Saver's Fruit Juice flavors had also increased in popularity in the adult market. In 1989, Hershey introduced Solitaire, a premium chocolate bar with almonds and toffee chips. It was Hershey's first new milk chocolate bar since the classic Hershey's milk chocolate bar nearly a century ago.

Additionally, to gain market share, Hershey decided to become a fearless product innovator. For adults, Hershey introduced Skor, a chocolate-covered toffee bar, and Five, a chocolate-covered wafer and peanut-cream bar, which did well in the test market. Bar None, introduced in 1988, exceeded expectations. Golden Almond Nuggets and Symphony also were released nationally. Earlier, Hershey had introduced its 2.2 ounce bars, followed by Big Blocks, which were 50% larger than ordinary Hershey bars. This trend continued with the launching of 3.2 ounce premium bars such as Golden Almond and Golden Pecan. In 1990, Hershey was again successful with the introduction of Kisses with Almonds. In 1993, the Kisses line extension continued with Hugs and Hugs with Almonds. Hugs were supposed to be chocolate Kisses that had been "hugged" by white chocolate. It was a natural brand extension for the company. As the sales of small and regular-sized candy bars declined, Hugs rang up sales of approximately $5.4 million in the supermarkets during the same quarter. In April 1994, Hershey's Hugs won one of Marketing News' Edison Best New Products Awards. The candy's success was attributed to creative advertising, publicity, consumer and trade programs, and Hershey's strong brand name.

Hershey has claimed that brand recognition is the key to the success of new product entries and that new products are the lifeblood of the industry due to the consumer's fickleness. With an aggressive advertising campaign designed to increase brand awareness, and the goal of one new product per year, Hershey has no plans to allow its market to decay. In fact, in the early 1990s, spending for promotion and advertising jumped more than 40%, and Hershey planned to spend even more in the future (see Table 4).

A more recent assessment of the sales versus the growth rate of the industry shows that the candy industry has grown only a modest 3% for the measured period in Table 5. This compares with a growth rate of 7.5% during the 52-week period that ended on the same date as the table data.

TABLE 4

Advertising, Sales, and Market Share of Candy Industry

	Advertising	Sales	Market Share
Hershey			
1991	$56.8 million	$1.77 billion	26.6%
1992	$57.3 million	$1.87 billion	27.0%
M & M/Mars			
1991	$74.1 million	$1.66 billion	25.0%
1992	$87.5 million	$1.66 billion	23.4%

TABLE 5

Candy Sales (in Millions) in Supermarkets, Drugstores and Mass Merchandisers During the 12 Weeks Ended May 23, 1993

Manufacturer	Sales	Change from Previous Year	Share of Category
Hershey Chocolate USA	$349.4	3.2%	26.2%
M & M/Mars	231.9	−5.6	17.4
Russell Stover Candies	87.8	14.4	6.6
E. J. Brach	86.5	−1.2	6.5
Nestlé	61.1	−10.4	4.6

For many reasons, Hershey, like its competitors, has been looking toward the snack industry with the insight that sweets do not just consist of candy. Today's more sophisticated consumers look at ice cream bars, cookies, and chocolate-covered granola bars when they crave something sweet. Hershey has already entered the granola market with New Trail granola bars. They have also entered the nonchocolate candy market with their acquisition of Y & S Candies, which produces Twizzlers and Nibs. Hershey's current entries in the nonchocolate market are doing well. For the 12 months ended September 1992, Twizzlers were down in percent share of wholesale distributor shipments from the previous 12 months by a margin of nearly 0.8% (1992 = 3.15% and 1991 = 3.94%). This earned them the sixth place designation among nonchocolate candies. Reeses Pieces were also ranked for the above time period. They took 12th place with 2.28% share in 1992, down from 2.61% in 1991. Finally, Y & S Nibs ranked 16th in the top 20 nonchocolate candies with a 1.30% for 1992, down from 1.72% in 1991. As far as snacks are concerned, Hershey has no plans to stop here, especially with the shrewd realization that candy bars alone may not give the company its sweetest bottom line.

QUESTIONS

1. Describe the kind of market research that could have led to the introduction of Skor. Discuss the kind of research design that would be appropriate.
2. Describe the target audience for Skor. What kind of information about their preferences, purchase intentions, behaviors, lifestyles, psychographics, and demographics had to be obtained?
3. Discuss the scaling techniques that should be used to measure preferences, purchase intentions, lifestyles,

attitudes, and knowledge about candy. What is the nature (nominal, ordinal, interval or ratio) of information obtained from each of these scales?

4. Design part of a questionnaire that could be used to obtain this information.

5. What would be the best way to administer the questionnaire? Which interviewing method should be used? Why?

6. Recommend an appropriate sampling technique for this survey. How should the sample size be determined?

7. Could the observation method be used to determine consumer preferences for different kinds of candy bars? If so, which observation method would you use? Why?

REFERENCES

1. "Hershey's Next Century." *U.S. Distribution Journal* (September 15, 1993): 43–45.

2. "Hershey Widens Lead over Mars." *Advertising Age* (February 15, 1993): 4.

3. "Candy Market in Down Period." *U.S. Distribution Journal* (August 15, 1993): 6.

4. "Candy by the Numbers." *U.S. Distribution Journal* (February 15, 1993): 24.

5. "1993 Edison Best New Products Awards Winners." *Marketing News* (April 25, 1994): E7.

6. Deveny, Kathleen. "Chocolate Bar Sales Fell Sharply in Quarter." *Wall Street Journal* (December 21, 1993): B5.

7. Fisher, Christy. "Ad Flurry Pushes Hershey Ahead in Candy." *Advertising Age* (September 29, 1993): 28.

CASE 2.4 Fragrances Are Sweet, but Competition Is Bitter

The mature fragrance industry had become a marketing war zone. Every manufacturer is battling for its piece of market share. In the 1970s, fragrances ranked in the top 20s among items with the highest dollar expenditures; by the early 1990s, however, they had dropped to the top 50s. As a result, manufacturers relied heavily on new product introductions to stimulate consumer interest, sometimes at the price of older brands. The number of new product introductions shot up from 20 to 25 per year in the early 1980s to 30 to 40 in the early 1990s. New product introductions failed to increase total bottle sales, however. Since 1981, purchases of women's fragrances in the United States have tumbled by about 34% in total bottle sales. Total dollar sales increased, but only because of higher prices. Information Resources Inc.'s InfoScan service showed 1993 sales of $3 billion were down by 9% in the fourth quarter for supermarkets, drugstores, and mass merchandisers, which account for approximately two-thirds of all fragrance sales.

A major theme in perfume advertising is sex. The reduced fourth quarter sales in 1993 suggest that the sex angle did not have as much appeal as some fragrance makers had hoped (see Table 1). The one hit of the 1993 Christmas season was Coty's new Vanilla Fields. These ads were much more tame than previous ads and featured a single hummingbird in a field of flowers.

The rising costs of selling perfume, combined with the slowdown in bottle sales and the consolidation trend, forced many smaller manufacturers out of the industry. In 1981, 54.1% of the market belonged to small manufacturers. In 1990, the number had dropped to 29.3% (see Table 2).

The competitive nature of the industry forced several manufacturers to explore new markets. One of these was the drugstore market. Consolidation among department stores reduced the number of distribution outlets for fragrances. Research indicated that drugstore consumers were purchasing more nondrug items, such as makeup and fragrances. Consumers between the ages of 30 and 60 were found to go to the drugstore for prescriptions more often than younger consumers. Women in their twenties and thirties who had small children also made frequent trips to drugstores. Women under age 25, who accounted for 8 to 9% of fragrance purchases, preferred shopping for fragrances in drugstores over department stores. Thirty-three percent of fragrances were purchased by women who were

TABLE 1

Top 10 Mass Market Women's Fragrances (1993)

Brand	Marketer	Sales (in millions of dollars)	Percent Change From Year Earlier	Percent Share of Category
Vanderbilt	Cosmair (of L'Oreal)	15.2	− 5.6	5.2
Exclamation	Coty	13.7	−15.5	4.7
Navy	Procter & Gamble	11.8	0.8	4.0
Vanilla Fields	Coty	10.4	—	3.5
Charlie	Revlon	10.0	−16.3	3.4
Lady Stetson	Coty	8.5	−38.8	2.9
Jovan Musk	Coty	7.2	5.8	2.5
Tabu	Les Parfums de Dana	6.7	−10.5	2.3
Sand & Sable	Coty	6.5	− 4.5	2.2
Windsong	Parfums de Coeur	6.2	−20.5	2.1

TABLE 2

U.S. Women's Fragrance Market Shares

	1981	1988	1990
Avon	15.8%	19.5%	15.4%
Revlon	12.8%	11.6%	14.0%
Unilever	N/A	12.4%	15.0%
Estée Lauder	12.3%	12.5%	12.4%
Chanel	5.0%	6.0%	6.2%
Cosmair	N/A	5.6%	7.7%
Small companies	54.1%	32.4	29.3%
Total Sales	$2.3 billion	$2.6 billion	$2.24 billion

TABLE 3

Minority Markets

	Male Fragrance Users	Popular Male Fragrances	Popular Female Fragrances
Black	73%	Old Spice, Brut	Tatiana, Giorgio
Hispanic	62%	Eau Savage	Jean Naté

45 and over, had high incomes, and had discretionary buying power, and these women generally bought from department stores. Apparel specialty stores had also gained attention because their total overall sales increased at twice the rate compared with the increase in department and discount department store sales.

Minorities represented another potential market segment. The spending of blacks, Hispanics, and Asian Americans on perfumes is expected to grow at a much faster rate than the rest of the population. Table 3 shows fragrance preferences of black and Hispanic males and females. The male segment is predicted to gain a stronger focus. Because the 1980s was the era of developing a positive image for the female, it is believed that the 1990s will be the era of developing a positive image for the male.

Another segment that perfume manufacturers cannot afford to overlook is the older American. By the year 2000, one-third of the population will be over 50. In the past, advertisers have tended to gear their products toward 18 to 49-year-olds. Venetia Hands of Ogilvy and Mather

has suggested that the older segment should be broken into two more segments: the Luckies, 50–64, and the Savvies, 64 and up. The Luckies were children during the Depression and were able to reap the benefits of the post–World War II economy. The Savvies were adults during the Depression and tend to be price conscious.

A relatively new area of research, aromachology, is the use of fragrances to relax or stay alert. Research has revealed that CAT scan patients feel more relaxed when scents are released into the testing room. In Japan, the error rate of keypunch operators decreased 50% after they were exposed to a lemon scent and nearly 80% after they were exposed to a lavender scent. Avon has released a relaxing scent called Tranquil Moments; in Japan, the Shimizu Corporation has already developed a computer system for releasing scents in the workplace. Perhaps the cultivation of the aromachology market, along with other equally promising market segments, will provide a way for fragrance marketers to mask the bitter taste of competition with the sweet smell of success.

EXHIBIT 1

New Fragrance
Survey

Please fill out the following survey, answering the questions as accurately as possible.

PART I

1. What is your sex?
_____Male   _____Female

2. What age group are you in?
_____18–24   _____25–29   _____30–34   _____35–44   _____45 and over

3. What category of income do you fit into?
_____0–$15,000   _____$15,000–$25,000   _____$25,000–$35,000   _____$35,000–$45,000   _____$45,000 and above

4. What is your marital status?
_____Married   _____Single

5. If you are married, how many children do you have?
_____One   _____Two   _____Three   _____Four or more

6. How often do you go to the mall?
_____Once a week (or more)   _____Once a month   _____Once every 6 months   _____Once a year

7. If you shop at department stores, which one do you frequent?
_____Macy's   _____J.C. Penney   _____Sears   _____Sak's Fifth Avenue/Neiman-Marcus

PART II

8. I usually buy my fragrances in a department store.

1	2	3	4	5
Strongly agree	Agree	Don't know	Disagree	Strongly disagree

9. I usually buy my fragrances in a drugstore.

1	2	3	4	5
Strongly agree	Agree	Don't know	Disagree	Strongly disagree

10. I only buy one brand of fragrance.

1	2	3	4	5
Strongly agree	Agree	Don't know	Disagree	Strongly disagree

11. Department store fragrances are worth the extra cost.

1	2	3	4	5
Strongly agree	Agree	Don't know	Disagree	Strongly disagree

12. Free gift packages are a definite incentive to buy a fragrance product.

1	2	3	4	5
Strongly agree	Agree	Don't know	Disagree	Strongly disagree

13. Celebrity endorsement of a fragrance gives it more appeal.

1	2	3	4	5
Strongly agree	Agree	Don't know	Disagree	Strongly disagree

14. Fragrances endorsed by celebrities are higher in quality.

1	2	3	4	5
Strongly agree	Agree	Don't know	Disagree	Strongly disagree

15. I would be interested in a new fragrance.

1	2	3	4	5
Strongly agree	Agree	Don't know	Disagree	Strongly disagree

16. I frequently try new fragrances.

1	2	3	4	5
Strongly agree	Agree	Don't know	Disagree	Strongly disagree

PART III

17. How often do you buy fragrances?

_____

18. What is your favorite fragrance?

_____

19. What are the qualities you look for in a fragrance?

_____

20. Are you happy with the fragrances currently on the market?

_____

Thank you for your time. Your assistance will help us in better meeting your fragrance needs.

QUESTIONS

1. Identify some possible sources of secondary data for the fragrance industry.

2. Discuss the kind of market research fragrance manufacturers could conduct to determine if there is a demand for a new fragrance.

3. Once an audience for a new fragrance has been targeted, what kind of information is needed about their attitudes, preferences, purchase intentions, behaviors, motivations, psychographics, and demographics?

4. Which techniques would you recommend for collecting the information needed above? Discuss.

5. Design appropriate scales for obtaining the information identified above.

6. For a marketing research project aimed at assessing the demand for a new fragrance, a junior analyst designed the questionnaire shown in Exhibit 1. Is this a well-designed questionnaire? If not, how could it be improved?

REFERENCES

1. Van Meter, J. "Fashion, Fragrance, and Bottled Fantasy." *Vogue* (September 1990): 342–44.

2. Braun, Harvey D. "Consumer Reports Expose the Fallacy in Minority Profiles." *Consumer Market Intelligence* (Deloitte and Touche 1991): 1–7.

3. "Revlon Deal to Shake Up Industry." *Chain Drug Review* (March 25, 1991): 1–2.

4. "Holiday Fragrance Sales Slumped." *Wall Street Journal* (January 25, 1994): B1.

CASE 2.5

Is Super Bowl Advertising Super Effective?

Advertising time during the Super Bowl is limited and priced at a premium. The fight for the prime spots starts months in advance of the actual air time. Large companies with the most money to spend jockey to obtain the most highly visible air times. In 1992, the most highly coveted time slots went for $800,000 per 30 seconds. In 1993, however, that number had jumped to $850,000 for the same 30 seconds. This figure exceeded $1 million in 1996.

There is some speculation on which times are the best. In the later quarters of the football game, viewership usually falls somewhat. This, of course, is not the case when the score of the game is close, but that has been rare in the recent past. Therefore, the most highly coveted time spots are in the first quarter of the game. In the 1993 Super Bowl, Pepsi assured its commercials good positioning by purchasing four minutes of airtime at a cost of $6.8 million (Table 1). For their money, Pepsi bought the first commercial slot, in which they had planned to introduce their new Crystal Pepsi brand, as well as the guarantee that no other soft drinks would be advertised during the quarters in which they had purchased airtime.

Faced with the inability to match such huge outlays of cash, smaller advertisers such as 7-Up and Purina Cat Chow had to make use of other options. 7-Up purchased several spots in the fourth quarter of the game where air time was not at such a premium. Many advertisers would not even consider purchasing time during the later quarter due to the drop in viewership. 7-Up, however, likes this option, believing that they achieve a coup if the game is close and viewers stay tuned until the final outcome. Even if the game is not close, 7-Up does not believe that the average drop of 4.2 rating points makes their investment unprofitable.

Some advertisers like Purina Cat Chow are taking a slightly different approach by purchasing airtime on the show directly following the Super Bowl. They obtain airtime at one-sixth of the cost during the game, and they believe that they retain approximately 40% of the audience.

TABLE 1

Media Plans of Key Super Bowl Sponsors, 1993

Client	Airtime (in minutes)	Cost (in millions of dollars)
Pepsi	4.0	6.8
Anheuser-Busch	4.0	6.8
Reebok	2.0	3.4
7-Up	1.5	2.5
Nike	1.5	2.5
Coopers and Lybrand	1.0	1.7

Which advertiser is getting the biggest bang for the bucks, Pepsi, 7-Up, or Purina Cat Chow? Without systematic marketing research aimed at measuring Super Bowl advertising effectiveness, questions such as these beg answers.

QUESTIONS

1. What kind of research design would you recommend for determining the effectiveness of PepsiCo's advertising during the first quarter of the Super Bowl?
2. If the research design involves a survey of households, which survey method would you recommend and why?
3. What kind of measures and scales will you employ in your survey?
4. Can the observation method be used to determine the effectiveness of PepsiCo's advertising during the first quarter of the Super Bowl? If so, which observation method would you recommend and why?
5. Which syndicated services discussed in the book can provide useful information?

REFERENCES

1. Landler, M. "Super Bowl '93: The Bodies Are Already Piled Up." *Business Week* (January 25, 1993): 65.

CASE 2.6
Taste the Arby's Difference

At a time when the fast-food market was soft, intensely competitive, and experiencing a decline in customer traffic, Arby's was one of the few chains to experience rapid growth. The 2,675-unit Arby's chain was the world's largest roast beef sandwich chain, with outlets in the United States, Canada, Asia, the Middle East, and the Caribbean. Arby's total system sales in 1993 were $1.5 billion, a 5% increase from 1992. Innovative marketing has been one of the keys to Arby's success.

Vastly outspent by the hamburger chains that dominate the industry, Arby's has managed to post significant gains. The "Taste the Arby's Difference" theme successfully carved a niche for Arby's. Arby's was successful in positioning the roast beef chain as the nationwide alternative to hamburgers. Arby's recognized that the key factors to success in the fast-food industry were:

1. Creative advertising and promotions that further defined the Arby's difference
2. Interesting new product lines that focused on wholesome food and emerging consumer tastes
3. Implementation of technological advances that enhanced the dining experience and expedited service

With the fierce competition in the industry, battles for market share led to heavy discounting and couponing.

Arby's launched several successful promotional programs. These, combined with couponing, have proved successful in luring customers to Arby's.

In the hope of securing further successes, in 1990, Arby's targeted a promotional campaign to children. Arby's children's Adventure Meal series featured Babar, King of the Elephants. Besides being a worldwide favorite, Babar was also the mascot for former First Lady Barbara Bush's literacy campaign. In conjunction with this program, Arby's helped sponsor a poster for Literacy Volunteers of America that was used for local recruitment. This campaign was expected to lead to an additional increase in market share.

In addition to promotional campaigns, Arby's, like other fast-food chains, planned to continue expanding its product line to accommodate consumer's tastes better. In 1989, Arby's added the Roast Chicken Club, the Chicken Cordon Bleu, and the Sub Deluxe sandwiches to its menu. Along with being a leader in new products and aggressive promotions, Arby's has proven to be a technological leader in the fast-food industry. Arby's was the first fast-food chain to accept MasterCard and Visa credit cards. It found that credit card usage reduced payment transactions by 10 to 20 seconds.

Arby's continued to remain innovative by developing the Touch 2000 system, introduced in selected markets in 1990. This computerized system allows customers to order food via a touch-sensitive display screen. Once touched on the screen, the selection is processed through an IBM PC and displayed on monitors in the food preparation area. The machine automatically keeps a running tab on the order, and some machines offer bilingual services so that customers can order in English or Spanish. Interestingly enough, the system was developed to increase the personal touch. The system allows fewer employees to wait on more customers and to focus on those customers without being distracted by taking orders. Touch 2000 also increases the speed of service; order-taking time is reduced from 100 seconds to 45 seconds.

Touch 2000 offers many benefits to Arby's because it helps increase sales by suggesting other menu items. With Touch 2000, the average check increased by 4%. Furthermore, by reducing labor requirements, the system has helped Arby's to circumvent the labor shortage that plagues the fast-food industry. Research conducted by Arby's also indicated that 77% of its customers preferred ordering through Touch 2000, 90% said that it was easy to use, and 54% said that using the computer was faster.

Arby's has put more stress on profitability and cost concerns in 1994 and 1995. Arby's has traditionally been a higher priced fast-food restaurant, with 90% of their products priced above $2. Higher prices have been fueled by menu items that are of higher quality ingredients (more expensive) and require more labor to prepare. Arby's is now looking into using more preprocessed food in their restaurants, which would cut food costs and reduce labor time for preparation.

Arby's is also considering trying a 99¢ value menu because this has proven to be successful for other firms such as Wendy's. In addition to the 99¢ menu, Arby's is planning to price approximately 20 items between $1.00 and $1.50 to provide a second price strata for customers to choose from. These price strategies are aimed at improving per unit profits by improving traffic in the stores. The average per unit volume for Arby's was approximately $700,000 in 1994.

Another possibility for improving the traffic and thus raising profitability is to integrate two or more different stores to broaden the product choice for the consumer. One Arby's franchise in California has teamed with a Green Burrito franchise to provide both menus under one roof. The result has been improved sales and a larger client base.

Marketing research at Arby's yielded the older slogan "Taste the Arby's Difference" as well as the more recent one, "Different Is Good." Through the use of focus groups conducted in 1992 and 1993, which included over 120 people, Arby's has found that when people think about Arby's food they actually "crave" it. Upon this discovery, Arby's used the "Crave" concept in marketing in 25 test markets. This helped boost sales significantly.

In the test market, Arby's attempted to appeal to the crave concept by focusing heavily on the product. The commercials have shots that linger on the food to help induce that craving for an Arby's sandwich. The main idea is to focus on quality and taste. This is not the typical focus of fast-food establishments.

In the 1990s, Arby's also hoped to integrate its credit card acceptance program into Touch 2000. This would mean that Visa and MasterCard, and possibly Discover, would be accepted for payment on the system. The integration of credit into Touch 2000 is predicted to further increase sales, as credit card use stimulates add-on purchases, resulting in an average $5 to $6 order total for credit as opposed to an average $2.80 total for cash transactions. This may mean that customers can "Taste the Arby's Difference" by using credit as well as cash.

QUESTIONS

1. Suggest a research design suitable for determining the image of Arby's relative to that of McDonald's, Burger King, and Wendy's.
2. Discuss the role of exploratory research in this image study.
3. If a survey is to be conducted, what would be the best means of administering the questionnaire?
4. Which scaling technique would you recommend for measuring the image of Arby's relative to McDonald's, Burger King, and Wendy's? Defend your reasoning.
5. How would you select the respondents for this survey? Discuss your sampling design process.

REFERENCES

1. "Arby's New Leaders Position for 'Crave Reviews.'" *Nation's Restaurant News* (June 14, 1993): 24.
2. "Nontraditional Thrusts by Industry Point the Way to Food Service Future." *Nation's Restaurant News* (May 3, 1993): 37.
3. Howard, Theresa. "Arby's: Profit, Value Are Top Priorities." *Nation's Restaurant News* (September 20, 1993): 7.
4. Goldman, Kevin. "Arby's Goes Western to Corral More Sales." *Wall Street Journal* (August 12, 1994): B8.

CASE 2.7

Can Independent Carriers Go the Distance?

The breakup of the Bell System in 1984 resulted in the emergence of many long-distance telephone companies, each trying to establish itself as the nation's premiere carrier in a market that continues to grow steadily. In 1994, the $216-billion-a-year long-distance market was dominated by AT&T, MCI and Sprint. Together, these carriers account for nearly 90% of the revenues attributed to long-distance carriers.

Just after the breakup and before deregulation, the long-distance business was practically a no-lose proposition. MCI, Sprint, and many other independent carriers leased lines from AT&T and resold the capacity to companies and individuals. Independents could profitably undercut AT&T's prices, because the Federal Communications Commission (FCC) gave them a hefty break (up to 70%) on charges long-distance carriers paid to link up to local phone lines at both ends of a call.

With deregulation and equal access, however, the independent carriers had to pay the same high prices as AT&T to link up to local phone lines. And, with equal access features, a customer was faced with having to decide on a long-distance company from a half a dozen or more candidates. If customers failed to make choices, they might be assigned to a company they did not want.

Hence, equal access led to an increase in expenses for the independent carriers. In fact, industry analysts said that these extra expenses for providing equal access accounted for 40 to 50% of the total cost incurred by each carrier, and these expenses were expected to zoom higher. Equal access had caused many a carrier to report losses or deteriorating earnings. For MCI, access charges jumped from 17.6% of revenues in the quarter that ended September 30, 1983, to 26.3% in the same period a year later. MCI finished 1986 with a $498 million loss. The company was forced to lay off 15% of its employees. MCI's cofounder and chairman, William McGowan, suffered a near-fatal heart attack and soon afterward underwent a heart transplant. MCI's future looked so bleak that even top executives considered putting it up for sale.

In the late 1980s, MCI made a tremendous comeback. Instead of selling the company in 1986, top executives agreed to mount an all-out offensive against AT&T. Their planned attack included advances in high technology and new services. MCI switched from its out-of-date microwave transmitters to fiber-optic lines that could carry 100,000 calls per route instead of only 8,000. MCI developed a private line discount system (Vnet), a FAX network, and call tracing. The company soon set out to capture the lucrative corporate market, whereas they had formerly concentrated on residential and small business accounts. Since 1987, MCI has captured former AT&T customers like Chrysler, United Airlines, Westinghouse, Merrill Lynch, and Procter & Gamble. Therefore, although AT&T still managed to hold 86% of the big business market in 1987, MCI has proved to be a serious threat to AT&T.

MCI was successful in the consumer segment also. In 1989 and into 1990, MCI was the fastest-growing long-distance company in the consumer segment, adding 70,000 customers per week. In 1988, MCI offered its first pay-phone service, a flat rate discount program (Prime Time), and a charging system. MCI has since turned into a profit machine. Earnings in 1989 were $626, a 76% increase over the year before. In 1990, sales rose to $7.68 billion with a profit of $666 million. MCI's success proved that deregulation had achieved a more competitive environment. Industry analysts believed that eventually MCI would rival AT&T in size.

More recently, MCI has been making huge gains in the consumer and toll-free 800 market as well as inroads into the local service market. The attacks on the local service market have been initiated to help cut access charges that can cost MCI up to 45¢ on every revenue dollar they make. MCI is planning to build fiber-optic systems initially in 20 U.S. cities. This would allow them to compete directly with the Baby Bells, which now have a stranglehold on local markets.

MCI reported fourth quarter earnings in 1993 of $107 million, a drop of 33% from a year earlier. This number also included a write-off of $150 million for restructuring the company, however. This restructuring consolidated the facilities and streamlined the workforce. Had the cost of restructuring not been included, the net income from 1992 to 1993 would have grown more than 24%, to $199

FIGURE 1

Long-Distance Market

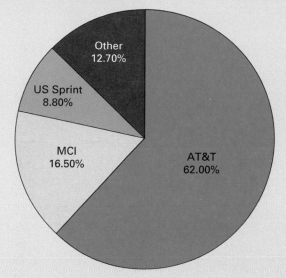

Source: Standard and Poor's Industry Surveys, Telecommunications (April 1, 1993): T-24.

million. Meanwhile, AT&T reported second quarter 1993 earnings of $1.04 billion, and Sprint reported second quarter 1993 earnings of $165 million.

In March 1994, Sprint, the nation's third largest long-distance company, announced its plans to invest $350 million over the next three years to install an advanced form of fiber-optic transmission equipment in its advanced, 23,000 mile network. The purpose of this latest move by Sprint is aimed at assuring Sprint's customers of uninterrupted long-distance service when a problem exists within the lines and to give the customers the ability to transmit video and data traffic over its network at speeds approximately two times faster than those speeds currently available.

Furthermore, for MCI and other independent carriers to increase their market share and company profits, they had to find out exactly what their customers wanted. After equal access they were no longer able to harp on discount prices. As a result, companies began to market their services feverishly, offering gifts, trips, and donations to environmental organizations, if consumers would choose their company. Moreover, they turned to marketing research. When MCI first came into the market, it used focus groups to build its knowledge of customer wants. Focus groups revealed answers to the following questions: How do you present a palatable product to the public? How much do you charge? What are they willing to pay? What kind of billing

are they interested in? MCI found out that businesses were willing to pay a minimum fee of $75 to use Execunet, but residential customers were willing to pay a flat fee of up to only $10. They further learned that customers did not blame the phone company for charging them higher prices but instead blamed themselves for talking longer.

In the 1990s, long-distance carriers realized that new markets for the industry were available. The international long-distance market was one of the fastest growing segments of the industry, with over one billion calls made in 1990. All three carriers introduced new international services and cut international rates. An even larger market, however, was in the 800-number service, where demand was extremely high, especially from corporations. Toll-free 800 numbers send the message that a company cares about its customers. With 800 numbers, consumers can compare prices on products from suppliers, get information from customer service and consumer hot lines, and make travel arrangements. The market was expected to continue to grow as it was realized that consumers preferred 800 numbers not only over regular long-distance numbers but also over local numbers.

With equal access, the independent carriers will be able to compete on the same playing field as AT&T. But the question of whether they will be able to go the distance or be disconnected from the long-distance market remains unanswered.

QUESTIONS

1. Describe the kinds of qualitative and quantitative market research companies like MCI and Sprint could conduct to determine what consumers want.

2. Do you think that the focus groups conducted by MCI were effective? Which other qualitative research techniques could MCI have used?

3. Suppose that a survey is to be conducted to determine consumer perceptions of and preferences for telephone calling cards. How should the questionnaire be administered? Discuss the advantages and disadvantages of the various survey methods.

4. What kind of information should be obtained from the respondents? Why?

5. A novice marketing researcher designed a questionnaire for determining calling card preferences (see Exhibit 1). Evaluate this questionnaire critically. Design an improved questionnaire for use in the survey.

6. What kind of rating scales would be best suited for obtaining information on preferences for long-distance companies? Justify your recommendation.

7. Which sampling plan would you recommend for selecting respondents? Explain your reasoning.

EXHIBIT 1

*Calling Card
Preference Survey*

Household Calling Card Survey

Please answer ALL the questions, whether or not your household currently has a calling card.

1 Your sex
1. _____ Male   2. _____ Female

2 Marital status
1. _____ Married   2. _____ Never married   3. _____ Divorced/separated/widowed

3 Your age: _____

4 Your formal education
1. Less than high school _____   2. High school graduate _____
3. Some college _____   4. College graduate _____

5 What is the approximate combined annual income of your household before taxes?
1. $10,000 or less _____   2. $10,000 to $20,000 _____   3. $20,000 to 30,000 _____
4. $30,000 to $40,000 _____   5. $40,000 to $60,000 _____   6. $60,000 and over _____

6 Which, if any, of the following telephone calling cards does your household have? Please check as many as apply.
1. _____ AT&T   2. _____ MCI   3. _____ US Sprint
4. _____ Others (specify)   5. _____ Do not have a calling card

7 How frequently does your household use a telephone calling card?

Do Not Use				Use Very Frequently	
1	2	3	4	5	6

8 Has your household ever charged any of the following types of calls to a telephone card or a credit card? Please circle 0 if not charged or 1 if charged.

Type of Call	Telephone Card	Credit Card
Local calls	0 or 1	0 or 1
Long-distance calls	0 or 1	0 or 1
International calls	0 or 1	0 or 1

9 Suppose that your household were to select a telephone calling card. Please rate the relative importance of the factors you would consider in selecting a card.

	Not So Important				Very Important	
a. Cost per call compared witho other cards	1	2	3	4	5	6
b. Easy to use	1	2	3	4	5	6
c. Local charges and long -distance calls included on the same bill	1	2	3	4	5	6
d. Credit points offered toward the purchase of other products	1	2	3	4	5	6
e. Quality of telephone service	1	2	3	4	5	6
f. The firm offering the card is my local telephone company	1	2	3	4	5	6

10. How important is it to you that a long-distance company offers a calling card so that making calls is convenient to you?

Not So Important				Very Important	
1	2	3	4	5	6

11. How likely is your household to request a telephone calling card (or additional card, if you already have one or more) in the future?

Not So Likely				Very Likely	
1	2	3	4	5	6

12. Do you think it is desirable to have and use a telephone calling card? Why or why not?

_____

_____

13. Which of the following telephone companies' services does your household use? Please check as many as apply
1. _____ AT&T
2. _____ MCI
3. _____ Contel
4. _____ US Sprint
5. _____ Others (specify)

Thank you for your participation.

REFERENCES

1. Sussman, Vic. "Long-Distance Calls Minus the Confusion." *U.S. News & World Report* (May 6, 1991): 71.

2. "AT&T's Earnings Are Flat, Nynex Profits Slip, US West Inches Up." *New York Times* (January 25, 1991): D1–D2.

3. "Sprint Plans $350 Million for Upgrading Its Network." *Wall Street Journal* (March 14, 1994): A8.

4. Standard and Poor's Industry Survey. *Telecommunications* (April 1, 1993): T-24.

PART III

Data Collection

Chapter 13   *Field Work*
PROFESSIONAL PERSPECTIVES FOR PART III
CASES FOR PART III

◆

This part presents a practical and managerial-oriented discussion of field work, the fourth step in the marketing research process. It describes how field workers make contact with the respondents, administer questionnaires and observation forms, record the data, and turn in completed forms for processing. In addition to describing the field work process and the management of field work, we offer several guidelines for interviewer training, supervision, and conducting interviews.

Field Work

The key to field work is investing in the selection, training, supervision, and evaluation of field workers.

OBJECTIVES

After reading this chapter, the student should be able to:

1. Describe the field work process and explain the selecting, training, and supervising field workers, validating field work, and evaluating field workers.
2. Discuss the training of field workers in making the initial contact, asking the questions, probing, recording the answers, and terminating the interview.
3. Discuss supervising field workers in terms of quality control and editing, sampling control, control of cheating, and central office control.
4. Describe evaluating field workers in areas of cost and time, response rates, quality of interviewing, and the quality of data.
5. Explain the issues related to field work when conducting international marketing research.
6. Discuss the ethical aspect of field work.
7. Illustrate the use of microcomputers and mainframes in field work.

OVERVIEW

Field work is the fourth step in the marketing research process. It follows problem definition and development of the approach (Chapter 2) and formulation of the research design (Chapters 3 through 12). During this phase, the field workers make contact with the respondents, administer the questionnaires or observation forms, record the data, and turn in the completed forms for processing. A personal interviewer administering questionnaires door to door, an interviewer intercepting shoppers in a mall, a telephone interviewer calling from a central location, a worker mailing questionnaires from an office, an observer counting customers in a particular section of a store, and others involved in data collection and supervision of the process are all field workers.

This chapter describes the nature of field work and the general field work/data collection process. This process involves selecting, training, and supervising field workers, validating field work, and evaluating field workers. We briefly discuss field work in the context of international marketing research, identify the relevant ethical issues, and explain the role of microcomputers and mainframes. To begin, we present brief examples that highlight the nature of field work.

DEPARTMENT STORE PATRONAGE PROJECT
Field Work

In the department store patronage project, in-home personal interviews were conducted by interviewers who were graduate and undergraduate students enrolled in marketing research courses taught by the author. The field workers' training included having each interviewer (1) act as a respondent and self-administer the questionnaire and (2) administer the questionnaire to a few other students not involved in the project (dummy respondents). Detailed guidelines for interviewing were developed and provided to each interviewer. The supervision of interviewers was carried out by graduate students who monitored the field work activities on a day-to-day basis. All the respondents were called back to verify that the interviewer had actually administered the questionnaire to them and to thank them for participating in the survey. A 100% validation check was performed. All the field workers, interviewers and supervisors, were evaluated by the author. ◆

EXAMPLE
Narrowing the Field of Refusals

Recently, the "Your Opinion Counts™" (YOC) National Steering Committee conducted a benchmark study to determine the level and nature of respondent refusal rates in consumer surveys. The overall refusal rate was found to be 38%. Initial refusal amounted to almost 90% of total refusals. Several guidelines offered by the YOC Committee for reducing refusal rates relate to field work:

- Interviewer training programs should be routinely administered so that field workers will be effective at their jobs.
- Courtesy should be exercised when deciding what hours of the day to call respondents. YOC recommends calling between 9 A.M. and 9 P.M.
- If mall respondents indicate that the time is not convenient, an appointment should be made to conduct the interview later.
- The subject matter should be disclosed to the respondents if this can be done without biasing the data. The more information people are given, the less reason they have to be suspicious.
- Field workers should make the interviews as pleasant and appealing as possible.[1] ◆

Efforts by the Your Opinion Counts™ Committee aimed at reducing refusal rates are really making the opinions of people count. ◆ Reprinted with permission from the Marketing Research Association, Inc., Rocky Hill, CT. Copyright © 1994, 1995.

THE NATURE OF FIELD WORK

Marketing research data are rarely collected by the persons who design the research. Researchers have two major options for collecting their data: they can develop their own organizations or they can contract with a field work agency. In either case, data collection involves the use of some kind of field force. The field force may operate either in the field (personal in-home, mall-intercept, computer-assisted personal interviewing, and observation) or from an office (telephone and mail surveys). The field workers who collect the data typically have little research background or training. Ethical concerns are particularly germane to field work. Although there is ample opportunity for violation of ethical standards, clients need not be overly concerned when dealing with reputable field work agencies. Michael Redington, senior vice-president for corporate development at Marketing and Research Counselors, is an aggressive advocate of field quality. His evaluation of the quality of field work in the marketing research industry is as follows: "I was very pleased to help shoot down the myth that data collection is characterized by a bunch of people out there attempting to bend the rules, to rip you off and to cheat on interviews. There are a lot of people on the client side who believe just that. Quite frankly, we were out trying to find it, but we didn't. That was a revelation to us. We were afraid that there were more unethical practices in the field than there really were."[2] The quality of field work is high because the field work and data collection process is streamlined and well controlled, as discussed in the following section.

FIELD WORK AND DATA COLLECTION PROCESS

All field work involves selecting, training, and supervising persons who collect data.[3] The validation of field work and the evaluation of field workers are also parts of the process. Figure 13.1 represents a general framework for the field work and data collection process. Even though we describe a general process, it should be recognized that the nature of field work varies with the mode of data collection and that the relative emphasis on the different steps will be different for telephone, personal, and mail interviews.

SELECTING FIELD WORKERS

The first step in the field work process is the selection of field workers. The researcher should (1) develop job specifications for the project, taking into account the mode of data collection; (2) decide what characteristics the field workers should have; and (3) recruit appropriate individuals.[4] Interviewers' background characteristics, opinions, perceptions, expectations, and attitudes can affect the responses they elicit.[5]

For example, the social acceptability of a field worker to the respondent may affect the quality of data obtained, especially in personal interviewing. Researchers generally agree that the more characteristics the interviewer and the respondent have in common, the greater the probability of a successful interview, as illustrated in the following example.

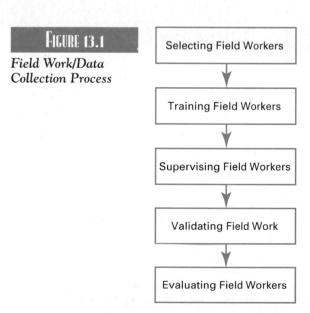

FIGURE 13.1

Field Work/Data Collection Process

EXAMPLE
Searching for Common Ground _____

In a survey dealing with emotional well-being and mental health, older interviewers got better cooperation from older respondents than younger interviewers, and this performance appeared to be independent of years of experience. When the interviewer and the respondent were of the same race the cooperation rate was higher than when there was a mismatch on race.[6] ◆

Thus, to the extent possible, interviewers should be selected to match respondents' characteristics. The job requirements will also vary with the nature of the problem and the type of data collection method. But there are some general qualifications of field workers

- *Healthy.* Field work can be strenuous, and workers must have the stamina required to do the job.
- *Outgoing.* Interviewers should be able to establish rapport with respondents. They should be able to relate to strangers.
- *Communicative.* Effective speaking and listening skills are a great asset.
- *Pleasant appearance.* If a field worker's physical appearance is unpleasant or unusual, the data collected may be biased.
- *Educated.* Interviewers must have good reading and writing skills. A majority of field work agencies require a high school education, and many prefer some college education.
- *Experienced.* Experienced interviewers are likely to do a better job in following instructions, obtaining respondent cooperation, and conducting the interview, as illustrated in the following example.

EXAMPLE
Your Experience Counts _____

Research has found the following effects of interviewer experience on the interviewing process.

- Inexperienced interviewers are more likely to commit coding errors, to misrecord responses, and to fail to probe.
- Inexperienced interviewers have a particularly difficult time filling quotas of respondents.
- Inexperienced interviewers have larger refusal rates. They also accept more "don't know" responses and refusals to answer individual questions.[7] ◆

Field workers are generally paid an hourly rate or on a per interview basis. The typical interviewer is a married woman aged 35 to 54, with an above-average education and an above-average household income.[8] The following example illustrates a psychographic breakdown of interviewers.

EXAMPLE
The Four Faces of Interviewers _____

Interviewers can be segmented into four distinct psychographic groups based on an analysis made by M/A/R/C for Marketing Research Association.

Dedicated Debbie: To the Dedicated Debbie, interviewing is not just a job but something much more important. She interviews because she enjoys it.

Independent Inez: Independent Inez interviews because of the independence it gives her. Interviewing gives her freedom to choose when she wants to work and some freedom on the job as well.

Social Sara: This interviewer enjoys interviewing almost as much as Dedicated Debbie, but she does not feel that interviewing is important. The thing that really turns her on is the chance to socialize, to meet interesting people, to interact.

Professional Pat: This is the career-oriented interviewer. She sees the job not only as a means to earn her living, but as a market research career opportunity. Professional Pat considers that the two most important attributes of an interviewer are a detailed mind and exceptional intelligence.

Professional Pat at work.

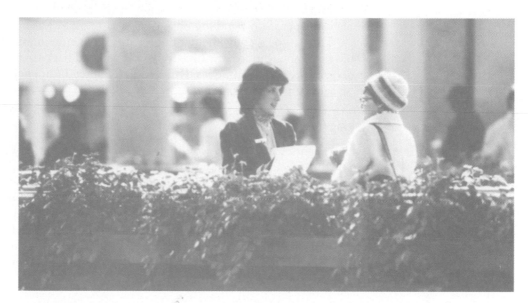

Such an understanding of the psychographic profile of interviewers along with their demographic characteristics can greatly assist in the identification and selection of the right interviewers.[9] ◆

TRAINING FIELD WORKERS

Training field workers is critical to the quality of data collected. Training may be conducted in person at a central location, or if the interviewers are geographically dispersed, by mail. Training ensures that all interviewers administer the questionnaire in the same manner so that the data can be collected uniformly. Training should cover making the initial contact, asking the questions, probing, recording the answers, and terminating the interview.[10]

Making the Initial Contact

The initial contact can result in cooperation or the loss of potential respondents.[11] Interviewers should be trained to make opening remarks that will convince potential respondents that their participation is important. This is illustrated in the context of the department store patronage project.

DEPARTMENT STORE PATRONAGE PROJECT

Initial Contact Statement _____

Hello, my name is _____. I represent the Marketing Department of Georgia Tech. We are conducting a survey about household preferences for department stores. You are one of the select group of respondents who have been scientifically selected to participate in this survey. We highly value your opinion and would like to ask you a few questions.[12] ◆

Notice that the interviewer did not specifically ask the respondent's permission. Questions that directly ask permission, such as "May I have some of your valuable time?" or "Would you like to answer a few questions?" should be avoided. Interviewers should be also instructed on handling objections and refusals. For example, if the respondent says, "This is not a convenient time for me," the interviewer should respond, "What would be a more convenient time for you? I will call back then." If the foot-in-the-door or door-in-the-face techniques discussed in Chapter 12 are being employed, interviewers should be trained accordingly.

Asking the Questions

Even a slight change in the wording, sequence, or manner in which a question is asked can distort its meaning and bias the response.[13] Asking questions is an art. Training in asking questions can yield high dividends in eliminating potential sources of bias. Changing the phrasing or order of questions during the interview can make significant differences in the response obtained. "While we could be faulted for not writing as perfect a questionnaire as we possibly could, still it must be asked in the exact way it was written. It's a challenge for us to try to get the interviewers more conversational, but despite this the field force absolutely must ask questions as they are written."[14] The following are guidelines for asking questions:[15]

1. Be thoroughly familiar with the questionnaire.
2. Ask the questions in the order in which they appear in the questionnaire.
3. Use the exact wording given in the questionnaire.
4. Read each question slowly.
5. Repeat questions that are not understood.
6. Ask every applicable question.
7. Follow instructions, skip patterns, probing carefully.

Probing

probing A motivational technique used when asking survey questions to induce the respondents to enlarge on, clarify, or explain their answers and to help the respondents focus on the specific content of the interview.

Probing is intended to motivate respondents to enlarge on, clarify, or explain their answers. Probing also helps respondents focus on the specific content of the interview and provide only relevant information. Probing should not introduce any bias. Listed below are some commonly used probing techniques.[16]

1. *Repeating the question*. Repeating the question in the same words can be effective in eliciting a response.
2. *Repeating the respondent's reply*. Respondents can be stimulated to provide further comments by repeating verbatim their replies. This can be done as the interviewer records the replies.

3. *Using a pause or silent probe.* A silent probe, or an expectant pause or look, can cue the respondent to provide a more complete response. The silence should not become embarrassing, however.

4. *Boosting or reassuring the respondent.* If the respondent hesitates, the interviewer should reassure the respondent with comments: "There are no right or wrong answers. We are just trying to get your opinions." If the respondent needs an explanation of a word or phrase, the interviewer should not offer an interpretation, unless written instructions to do so have been provided. Rather, the responsibility for the interpretation should be returned to the respondent. This can be done with a comment such as, "Just whatever it means to you."

5. *Eliciting clarification.* The respondent's motivation to cooperate with the interviewer and provide complete answers can be aroused with a question: "I don't quite understand what you mean by that. Could you please tell me a little more?"

6. *Using objective or neutral questions or comments.* Research in Practice 13.1 provides several examples of the common questions or comments used as probes.[17] Corresponding abbreviations are also provided. The interviewer should record the abbreviations on the questionnaire in parentheses next to the question asked.

Recording the Answers

Although recording respondent answers seems simple, several mistakes are common.[18] All interviewers should use the same format and conventions to record the interviews and edit completed interviews. Although the rules for recording answers to structured questions vary with each specific questionnaire, the general rule is to check the box that reflects the respondent's answer. The general rule for recording answers to unstructured questions is to record the responses verbatim. The Interviewer's Manual of the Survey Research Center provides the following specific guidelines for recording answers to unstructured questions.

1. Record responses during the interview.
2. Use the respondent's own words.
3. Do not summarize or paraphrase the respondent's answers.
4. Include everything that pertains to the question objectives.

RESEARCH IN PRACTICE 13.1

Commonly Used Probes and Abbreviations

Standard Interviewer's Probe	Abbreviation
Any other reason?	(AO?)
Any others?	(Other?)
Anything else?	(AE or Else?)
Could you tell me more about your thinking on that?	(Tell more)
How do you mean?	(How mean?)
Repeat question	(RQ)
What do you mean?	(What mean?)
Which would be closer to the way you feel?	(Which closer?)
Why do you feel that way?	(Why?)
Would you tell me what you have in mind?	(What in mind?)

5. Include all probes and comments.
6. Repeat the response as it is written down.

Terminating the Interview

The interview should not be closed before all the information is obtained. Any sponta-neous comments the respondent offers after all the formal questions have been asked should be recorded. The interviewer should answer the respondent's questions about the project. The respondent should be left with a positive feeling about the interview. It is important to thank the respondent and express appreciation.

The Council of American Survey Research Organizations' guidelines on inter-viewer training are given in Research in Practice 13.2.

RESEARCH IN PRACTICE 13.2

Guidelines on Interviewer Training: The Council of American Survey Research Organizations

Training should be conducted under the direction of supervisory personnel and should cover the following:

1. The research process: how a study is developed, implemented and reported
2. The importance of the interviewers to this process; the need for honesty, objectivity, organizational skills, and professionalism
3. Confidentiality of the respondent and client
4. Familiarity with market research terminology
5. The importance of following the exact wording and recording responses verbatim
6. The purpose and use of probing and clarifying techniques
7. The reason for and use of classification and respondent information questions
8. A review of samples of instructions and questionnaires
9. The importance of the respondent's positive feelings about survey research

No person is to work as an interviewer unless that person has been trained in the general interviewing techniques as outlined above.

SUPERVISING FIELD WORKERS

Supervising field workers means making sure that they are following the procedures and techniques in which they were trained. Supervision involves quality control and editing, sampling control, control of cheating, and central office control.[19]

Quality Control and Editing

Quality control of field workers requires checking to see if the field procedures are being properly implemented.[20] If any problems are detected, the supervisor should discuss them with the field workers and provide additional training if necessary. To understand the interviewers' problems, the supervisors should also do some interviewing. Supervisors should collect questionnaires and other forms and edit them daily. They should examine the questionnaires to make sure all appropriate questions have been completed, that unsatisfactory or incomplete answers have not been accepted, and that the writing is legible.

Supervisors should also keep a record of hours worked and expenses. This will allow a determination of the cost per completed interview, whether the job is moving on schedule, and if any interviewers are having problems.

Sampling Control

sampling control An aspect of supervising that ensures that the interviewers strictly follow the sampling plan rather than select sampling units based on convenience or accessibility.

An important aspect of supervision is **sampling control**, which attempts to ensure that the interviewers are strictly following the sampling plan rather than selecting sampling units based on convenience or accessibility.[21] Interviewers tend to avoid dwellings or sampling units that they perceive as difficult or undesirable. If the sampling unit is not at home, interviewers may be tempted to substitute the next available unit rather than call back. Interviewers sometimes stretch the requirements of quota samples. For example, a 58-year-old person may be placed in the 46-to-55 category and interviewed to fulfill quota requirements.

To control these problems, supervisors should keep daily records of the number of calls made, the number of not-at-homes, the number of refusals, the number of completed interviews for each interviewer, and the total for all interviewers under their control.

Control of Cheating

Cheating involves falsifying part of a question or the entire questionnaire. An interviewer may falsify part of an answer to make it acceptable or may fake answers. The most blatant form of cheating occurs when the interviewer falsifies the entire questionnaire, merely filling in fake answers without contacting the respondent. Cheating can be minimized through proper training, supervision, and validation of field work.[22]

Central Office Control

Supervisors provide quality and cost-control information to the central office so that a total progress report can be maintained. In addition to the controls initiated in the field, other controls may be added at the central office to identify potential problems. Central office control includes tabulation of quota variables, important demographic characteristics, and answers to key variables. Research in Practice 13.3 provides guidelines for supervision from the Council of American Survey Research Organizations.

VALIDATING FIELD WORK

Validating field work means verifying that the field workers are submitting authentic interviews. To validate the study, the supervisors call 10 to 25% of the respondents to inquire whether the field workers actually conducted the interviews. The supervisors ask about the length and quality of the interview, reaction to the interviewer, and basic demographic data. The demographic information is cross-checked against the information reported by the interviewers on the questionnaires.

RESEARCH IN PRACTICE 13.3

Guidelines on Supervision: The Council of American Survey Research Organizations

All research projects should be properly supervised. It is the responsibility of the data collection agency to:

1. Properly supervise interviewers
2. See that an agreed-upon proportion of interviewers' telephone calls are monitored
3. Be available to report on the status of the project daily to the project director, unless otherwise instructed
4. Keep all studies, materials, and findings confidential
5. Notify concerned parties if the anticipated schedule is not likely to be met
6. Attend all interviewer briefings
7. Keep current and accurate records of the interviewing progress
8. Make sure interviewers have all materials in time
9. Edit each questionnaire
10. Provide consistent and positive feedback to interviewers
11. Not falsify any work

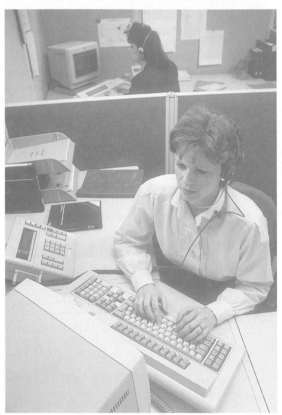

CATI Systems enable on-line supervisors to monitor the screen as well as the conversation. ◆ Ed Wheeler/The Stock Market.

EVALUATING FIELD WORKERS

It is important to evaluate field workers to provide them with feedback on their performance as well as to identify the better field workers and build a better, high-quality field force. The evaluation criteria should be clearly communicated to the field workers during their training. The evaluation of field workers should be based on the criteria of cost and time, response rates, quality of interviewing, and quality of data.[23]

Cost and Time

The interviewers can be compared in terms of the total cost (salary and expenses) per completed interview. If the costs differ by city size, comparisons should be made only among field workers working in comparable cities. The field workers should also be evaluated on how they spend their time. Time should be broken down into categories such as actual interviewing, travel, and administration.

Response Rates

It is important to monitor response rates on a timely basis so that corrective action can be taken if these rates are too low.[24] Supervisors can help interviewers with an inordinate number of refusals by listening to the introductions they use and providing immediate feedback. When all the interviews are over, different field workers' percentage of refusals can be compared to identify the better workers.

Quality of Interviewing

To evaluate interviewers on the quality of interviewing, the supervisor must directly observe the interviewing process. The supervisor can do this in person or the field worker can record the interview on tape. The quality of interviewing should be evaluated in terms of (1) the appropriateness of the introduction, (2) the precision with which the field worker asks questions, (3) the ability to probe in an unbiased manner, (4) the ability to ask sensitive questions, (5) interpersonal skills displayed during the interview, and (6) the manner in which the interview is terminated.

Quality of Data

The completed questionnaires of each interviewer should be evaluated for the quality of data. Some indicators of quality data are that (1) the recorded data are legible; (2) all instructions, including skip patterns, are followed; (3) the answers to unstructured questions are recorded verbatim; (4) the answers to unstructured questions are meaningful and complete enough to be coded; and (5) item nonresponse occurs infrequently.

Guidelines on interviewing from the Council of American Survey Research Organizations are given in Research in Practice 13.4.

INTERNATIONAL MARKETING RESEARCH

The selection, training, supervision, and evaluation of field workers is critical in international marketing research. Local field work agencies are unavailable in many countries. Therefore, it may be necessary to recruit and train local field workers or import trained foreign workers. The use of local field workers is desirable, because they are familiar with the local language and culture. They can create an appropriate climate for the interview and sensitivity to the concerns of the respondents. Extensive training may be required and close supervision may be necessary. As observed in many countries, interviewers tend to help the respondent with the answers and select household or sampling units based on personal considerations rather than the sampling plan. Finally,

RESEARCH IN PRACTICE 13.4

Guidelines on Interviewing: The Council of American Survey Research Organizations

Each interviewer is to follow these techniques for good interviewing:

1. Provide his or her full name, if asked by the respondent, as well as a phone number for the research firm.
2. Read each question exactly as written. Report any problems to the supervisor as soon as possible.
3. Read the questions in the order indicated on the questionnaire, following the proper skip sequences.
4. Clarify any question by the respondent in a neutral way.
5. Not mislead respondents as to the length of the interview.
6. Not reveal the identity of the ultimate client unless instructed to do so.
7. Keep a tally on each terminated interview and the reason for each termination.
8. Remain neutral in interviewing. Do not indicate agreement or disagreement with the respondent.
9. Speak slowly and distinctly so that words will be understood.
10. Record all replies verbatim, not paraphrased.
11. Avoid unnecessary conversations with the respondent.
12. Probe and clarify for additional comments on all open-ended questions, unless otherwise instructed. Probe and clarify in a neutral way.
13. Write neatly and legibly.
14. Check all work for thoroughness before turning it in to the supervisor.
15. When terminating a respondent, do so in a neutral way such as, "Thank you," or "Our quota has already been filled in this area, but thank you anyway."
16. Keep all studies, materials, and findings confidential.
17. Not falsify any interviews or any answers to any question.
18. Thank the respondent for participating in the study.

interviewer cheating may be more of a problem in many foreign countries than in the United States. Validation of field work is critical. Proper application of field work procedures can greatly reduce these difficulties and result in consistent and useful findings, as the following example demonstrates.

EXAMPLE

Americanism Unites Europeans

An image study conducted by Research International, a U.K. market research company, showed that despite unification of the European market, European consumers still increasingly favor U.S. products. It is expected that Americanism will unite the consumers in Europe. The survey was conducted in Germany, the United Kingdom, Italy and the Netherlands. In each country, local interviewers and supervisors were used because it was felt they would be able to identify better with the respondents. The field workers, however, were trained extensively and supervised closely to ensure quality results and to minimize the variability in country-to-country results due to differences in interviewing procedures.

A total of 6,724 personal interviews were conducted. Some of the findings were that Europeans gave U.S. products high marks for being innovative and some countries also regarded them as fashionable and of high quality. Interestingly, France, usually considered anti-American, also emerged as pro-American. Among the 1,034 French consumers surveyed, 40% considered U.S. products fashionable and 38% believed that they were innovative, whereas 15% said U.S. products were of high quality. In addition, when asked what nationality they preferred for a new company in their area, a U.S. company was the first choice. These findings were comparable and consistent across the four countries. A key to the discovery of these findings was the use of local field workers and extensive training and supervision which resulted in high-quality data.

This study is very useful for marketers to drum up and overplay the American brand name in European market. "Rather than trying to hide the fact that they are American, we think companies ought to stress or try to exploit their American heritage," says Eric Salama, director of European operations for the Henley Center, the U.K. economic forecasting consultancy.[25] ◆

ETHICS IN MARKETING RESEARCH

The data, whether collected by the internal marketing research department or by an external field work agency, should be obtained by following high ethical standards. The researchers and field workers should make the respondents feel comfortable by addressing their apprehensions. One way in which the comfort level of the respondents can be increased is by providing them with adequate information about the project, addressing their questions, and clearly stating the responsibilities and expectations of the field workers and the respondents. If this is not done, the respondents may be unsure about how their answers will be used and they may not respond candidly. Moreover, the "respondents typically receive nothing in return for their voluntary participation in research studies, so there is strong obligation on the part of the researchers to respect respondents' time, feelings, dignity, and right to self-determination."[26]

The researchers and the field work agencies are also responsible to the clients for following the accepted procedures for the selection, training, supervision, validation, and evaluation of field workers.[27] The field work procedures should be carefully documented and made available to the clients. The American Marketing Association's code of ethics states, "Evidence that fieldwork has been completed according to specifications will, upon request, be made available to buyers of research."[28] Appropriate actions by researchers and field work agencies can go a long way in addressing ethical concerns associated with field work, as illustrated by the following example.

EXAMPLE
Sophisticated Data Research is Sophisticated in its Field Work _____

Information provided while responding to an 800 number, using a credit card, or purchasing a product is often used to compile lists of customers and potential customers. These lists are rarely sold to telemarketing and direct marketing organizations. The public perception is different, however, and many people feel that marketers and marketing researchers misuse the information they collect. This misperception is giving marketing research a negative image.

In an effort to fight back, many marketing researchers and field work agencies are addressing these issues directly at the start of the interview. For example, when contacting potential respondents, Sophisticated Data Research (SDR) of Atlanta provides them with information about the firm (SDR) and the marketing research project. The respondents are assured that SDR operates within a code of ethics. Some marketing research firms and field work agencies provide potential respondents with toll-free numbers which they can call to obtain more information or verify the information given by the field workers. Such actions make the respondents more comfortable and informed, and result in higher quality data for the clients.[29] ◆

COMPUTER APPLICATIONS

Microcomputers and mainframes, like the Ci3 System by Sawtooth Software, Inc., can be used in field work for respondent selection, interviewer planning, and supervision and control. Ci3 CATI's ability to guide the interview process makes it a valuable asset in marketing research. Exhibit 13.1 shows the screen presented to the telephone interviewer for U.S. Surveys during the first callback attempt to interview Sue Smith of Chicago about her use of toothpaste. This screen would be presented during the automatic dialing of Smith's residence. As can be seen, the opening script for the interviewer is included in this screen. After reading the opening script, the interviewer could begin the interview by pressing the "1" key. By doing this, screens with the survey questions would appear in proper sequence to the interviewer.

In a typical use situation, Ci3 CATI would be installed on a local area network (LAN) with up to 60 interview stations. Simultaneous supervision of the interviews

EXHIBIT 13.1

A Ci3 CATI Screen

```
Study 100                          CALL HISTORY                   Record   1047
Phone Number      (312) 555 - 1110           Callback Time

Contact Name      Sue Smith                  Callback Date
Firm Name                                    Open
Message
Primary Cell
Secondary Cell                               Resp #

Attempt Number    2                          Start Time        10:29 AM
Last Disposition  No Answer                   Time Last Call     7:48 PM
Interviewer       310                         Date Last Call     5/11
   Call Status :   Definite Appointments = 2   Callbacks = 1   Busys = 1

  Hello, my name is _____.    I'm calling from U.S. Surveys.  May
  I speak to   Sue Smith    . (INTERVIEWER: IF CONTACT PERSON ANSWERS,
  CONTINUE WITH:) I'd like to ask you a few questions about the brand of
  toothpaste you use.  This will take about 5 minutes.

     INTERVIEWER : PRESS  1  TO START INTERVIEW
                          2  IF SOMEONE OTHER THAN CONTACT PERSON ANSWERS
                             BUT CONTACT PERSON IS AVAILABLE
                          3  IF NO ANSWER, BUSY, OR TO SCHEDULE CALLBACK
                          4  TO VIEW CALLS WAITING
```

call disposition Call disposition records the outcome of an interview call.

could occur in the telephone room or remotely from an office. For the supervisor, Ci3 CATI offers call disposition, quota control, and marginal tabulation of responses to each question in the survey. **Call disposition** records the outcome of a call: no answer/not at home, immediate refusal, failed to qualify, callback, complete, and so forth. Exhibit 13.2 shows the report for call dispositions. Here, the fourth entry in the last column shows that almost 10% (9.9) of all calls result in completed toothpaste surveys.

Should quota sampling be used, Ci3 CATI enables the supervisor to prioritize categories of respondents that would be filled first by Ci3 CATI as interviews proceeded. This feature avoids oversampling to fill harder-to-find categories in studies.

For peeking at survey results, the marginal tabulation capability of Ci3 CATI permits market researchers to access response summaries of each question while the interviewing is in progress. In Exhibit 13.3, the supervisor can quickly examine the tabulation of responses to the question regarding family size. Here, the supervisor observes that almost half of those completing the survey (49.29%) indicate having some children, with a family size from 3 to 5.

The Interviewer Productivity Report of Ci3 CATI not only allows monitoring of interviewer performance, but also comparing the productivity of each individual interviewer with other interviewers assigned to the project. The report shows the number of dialings made by the interviewer, the disposition of calls made (e.g., no answer, answering machine, busy, did not qualify, quota cell full, or completed interviews). In addition to these reports for the supervisor, Ci3 CATI also provides the interviewer with callback control, random-digit dialing from a list of potential respondents (a sample frame), autodialing, and on-line progress reports. With such benefits to both the interviewer and the supervisor, Ci3 CATI is an indispensable tool in conducting effective telephone surveys.

Computers can also be used to manage mailing lists. For example, the mailing lists can be sorted according to zip codes, geographical regions, or other prespecified characteristics. Computers can also electronically monitor mail survey nonresponse.

EXHIBIT 13.2

A Report of Call Dispositions

```
                              DISPOSITIONS

            Attempt:   1st    2nd    3rd    4th   5th+   Total   Pct

  1  No Answer         1262   1121   945    19     4     3351   45.3
  2  Busy              138    123    86     1      1     349    4.7
  .
  .
 11  Didn't Qualify Q#5 117   102    72     4      0     295    4.0
  .
  .
 40  Complete          278    256    178    14     3     729    9.9

          Incidence (Pct)  15    17     14     18     2      16
          Total Dialings  2681  2332  2092   55     8    7168  100.0



        Press PgUp for previous page, ESC to return to menu.
```

EXHIBIT 13.3

*A Tabulation
of Responses*

```
                          MARGINAL TABULATION

This is a marginal tabulation for the Ci3 question FAMSIZE.  FAMSIZE
asked respondents for the size of their family.
_____

Tabulation of specified categories for FAMSIZE

                        MIN    MAX      COUNT      PERCENT
              1          1      1         89        25.36
              2          2      2         64        18.23
          3 - 5          3      5        173        49.29
         6 - 20          6     20         25         7.12

SUMMARY STATISTICS
   Number of responses =         351
              Average  =           4.23
   Standard Deviation  =           1.70
        Minimum Value  =           1
        Maximum Value  =          11
_____


                                    Press ESC to return to menu.
```

Computers can generate accurate and timely reports for supervision and control purposes. These include quota reports, call disposition reports, incidence reports, top-line reports of respondent data, and interviewer productivity reports. Automatic reporting enhances supervision and control and increases the overall quality of data collection. Because less time is spent compiling reports, more time can be spent on data interpretation and on supervision.

SUMMARY

Researchers have two major options for collecting data: developing their own organizations or contracting with field work agencies. In either case, data collection involves the use of a field force. Field workers should be healthy, outgoing, communicative, pleasant, educated, and experienced. They should be trained in important aspects of field work, including making the initial contact, asking the questions, probing, recording the answers, and terminating the interview. Supervising field workers involves quality control and editing, sampling control, control of cheating, and central office control. Validating field work can be accomplished by calling 10 to 25% of those who have been identified as interviewees and inquiring whether the interviews took place. Field workers should be evaluated on the basis of cost and time, response rates, quality of interviewing, and quality of data collection.

Selecting, training, supervising, and evaluating field workers is even more critical in international marketing research because local field work agencies are not available in many countries. Ethical issues include making the respondents feel comfortable in the data collection process so that their experience is positive. Every effort must be undertaken to ensure that the data are of high quality. Microcomputer and mainframe software, like the Ci3 System, can greatly facilitate and improve the quality of field work.[30]

ACRONYMS

In the field work/data collection process, the organization VESTS in the field workers:

V   alidating field work
E   valuating field workers
S   electing field workers
T   raining field workers
S   upervising field workers

The areas in which field workers should be trained may be summarized by the acronym TRAIN:

T   erminating the interview
R   ecording the answers
A   sking the questions
I   nitial contact development
N   osy behavior: probing

EXERCISES

QUESTIONS

1. What options are available to researchers for collecting data?
2. Describe the field work/data collection process.
3. What qualifications should field workers possess?
4. What are the guidelines for asking questions?
5. What is probing?
6. How should the answers to unstructured questions be recorded?
7. How should the field worker terminate the interview?
8. What aspects are involved in the supervision of field workers?
9. How can respondent selection problems be controlled?
10. What is validation of field work? How is this done?
11. Describe the criteria that should be used for evaluating field workers.
12. Describe the major sources of error related to field work.

PROBLEMS

1. Write some interviewer instructions for in-home personal interviews to be conducted by students.
2. Comment on the following field situations, making recommendations for corrective action.
   a. One of the interviewers has an excessive rate of refusals in in-home personal interviewing.
   b. In a CATI situation, many phone numbers are giving a busy signal during the first dialing attempt.
   c. An interviewer reports that at the end of the interviews, many respondents asked if they had answered the questions correctly.
   d. While validating the field work, a respondent reports that she cannot remember being interviewed over the telephone, but the interviewer insists that the interview was conducted.

COMPUTER EXERCISES

1. Using PERT/CPM software such as MacProject, Timeline, Harvard Project Manager, Microsoft Project, or Category PERTmaster, develop a field work schedule for conducting a national survey of consumer preferences for fast foods involving 2,500 mall-intercept interviews in Los Angeles, Salt Lake City, Dallas, St. Louis, Milwaukee, New Orleans, Cincinnati, Orlando, Atlanta, New York City, and Boston.

2. Use Ci3 or other CATI software to conduct a brief survey to determine whether people in your area like the local newspaper. Call ten numbers selected from the telephone book but modified by using the one plus technique (see Chapter 6).

NOTES

1. "Study Tracks Trends in Refusal Rates," *Quirk's Marketing Research Review* (August–September 1989): 16–18, 42–43.

2. "JDC Interviews Michael Redington," *Journal of Data Collection* 25 (Spring 1985): 2–6.

3. F. J. Fowler, Jr., and T. W. Mangione, "The Role of Interviewer Training and Supervision in Reducing Effects on Survey Data," in *Proceedings of the American Statistical Association Meetings*, Survey Research Methods Section (Washington, DC: American Statistical Association, 1983): pp. 124–28; and Lee Andrews, "Interviewers: Recruiting, Selecting, Training, and Supervising," in Robert Farber (ed.), *Handbook of Marketing Research* (New York: McGraw-Hill, 1974), pp. 124–32.

4. Robert M. Groves and Lou J. Magilavy, "Measuring and Explaining Interviewer Effects in Centralized Telephone Surveys," *Public Opinion Quarterly* 50 (Summer 1986): 251–66.

5. Philip B. Coulter, "Race of Interviewer Effects on Telephone Interviews," *Public Opinion Quarterly* 46 (Summer 1982): 278–84; and Eleanor Singer, Martin R. Frankel, and Marc B. Glassman, "The Effect of Interviewer Characteristics and Expectations on Response," *Public Opinion Quarterly* 47 (Spring 1983): 68–83.

6. Raymond F. Barker, "A Demographic Profile of Marketing Research Interviewers," *Journal of the Market Research Society* (UK) (July 29, 1987): 279–92.

7. Martin Collins and Bob Butcher, "Interviewer and Clustering Effects in an Attitude Survey," *Journal of the Market Research Society* (UK) 25 (January 1983): 39–58; and R. F. Q. Johnson, "Pitfalls in Research: The Interview as an Illustrative Model," *Psychological Reports* 38 (1976): 3–17.

8. Raymond F. Barker, "A Demographic Profile of Marketing Research Interviewers," *Journal of the Market Research Society* (UK) (July 29, 1987): 279–92.

9. Bud Phillips, "The Four Faces of Interviewers," *Journal of Data Collection* 23 (Winter 1983): 35–40.

10. P. J. Guenzel, T. R. Berkmans, and C. F. Cannell, *General Interviewing Techniques* (Ann Arbor, MI: Institute for Social Research, 1983).

11. Peter V. Miller and Charles F. Cannell, "A Study of Experimental Techniques for Telephone Interviewing," *Public Opinion Quarterly* (Summer 1982): 250–67. The following discussion draws on this source.

12. This procedure is similar to that followed by Elrick and Lavidge, Atlanta.

13. Norman M. Bradburn and Seymour Sudman, *Improving Interview Method and Questionnaire Design* (San Francisco: Jossey-Bass, 1979), p. 26.

14. "JDC Interviews Michael Redington," *Journal of Data Collection* 25 (Spring 1985): 2–6.

15. This section follows closely the material in *Interviewer's Manual*, rev. ed. (Ann Arbor: Survey Research Center, Institute for Social Research, University of Michigan, 1976); and P. J. Guenzel, T. R. Berkmans, and C. F. Cannell, *General Interviewing Techniques* (Ann Arbor, MI: Institute for Social Research, 1983).

16. For an extensive treatment of probing, see *Interviewer's Manual*, rev. ed. (Ann Arbor: Survey Research Center, Institute for Social Research, University of Michigan, 1976), pp. 15–19.

17. *Interviewer's Manual*, rev. ed. (Ann Arbor: Survey Research Center, Institute for Social Research, University of Michigan, 1976), p. 16. Reprinted by permission of the Institute for Social Research.

18. Jean Morton-Williams and Wendy Sykes, "The Use of Interaction Coding and Follow-Up Interviews to Investigate Comprehension of Survey Questions," *Journal of the Market Research Society* 26 (April 1984): 109–27.

19. F. J. Fowler, Jr., and T. W. Mangione, "The Role of Interviewer Training and Supervision in Reducing Effects on Survey Data," in *Proceedings of the American Statistical Association Meetings*, Survey Research Methods Section (Washington, DC: American Statistical Association, 1983), pp. 124–28.

20. Martin Collins and Bob Butcher, "Interviewer and Clustering Effects in an Attitude Survey," *Journal of the Market Research Society* (UK) 25 (January 1983): 39–58.

21. R. Czaja, J. Blair, and J. P. Sebestik, "Respondent Selection in Telephone Survey: A Comparison of Three Techniques," *Journal of Marketing Research* (August 1982): 381–85.

22. Donald S. Tull and Larry E. Richards, "What Can Be Done about Interviewer Bias," in Jagdish Sheth (ed.), *Research in Marketing* (Greenwich, CT: JAI Press, 1980); pp. 143–62.

23. Two useful general sources are: Ronald Anderson, Judith Kasper, and Martin R. Frankel, *Total Survey Error* (San Francisco: Jossey-Bass, 1979); and J. Rothman, "Acceptance Checks for Ensuring Quality in Research," *Journal of the Market Research Society* (UK) 22 (July 1980): 192–204.

24. "On the Definition of Response Rates," *CASRO Special Report* (Port Jefferson, NY: Council of American Survey Research Organizations, 1982). The following discussion draws on this source.

25. Laurel Wentz, "Poll: Europe Favors U.S. Products," *Advertising Age* (September 23, 1991).

26. C. N. Smith and J. A. Quelch, *Ethics in Marketing* (Homewood, IL: Richard D. Irwin, 1993).

27. "Rules of Conduct and Good Practice of the Professional Marketing Research Society of Canada (1984)" in C. N. Smith and J. A. Quelch, *Ethics in Marketing* (Homewood, IL: Richard D. Irwin, 1993).

28. As given in Appendix 3A of Gene R. Laczniak and Patrick E. Murphy, *Ethical Marketing Decisions: The Higher Road* (Needham Heights, MA: Allyn & Bacon, 1993), pp. 76-77.

29. Howard Schlossberg, "Right to Privacy Issue Pits Consumers against Marketers, Researchers," *Marketing News* (Oct. 23, 1989).

30. The assistance of James Agarwal with the international marketing research example, the assistance of Mark Leach and Gina Miller in writing the ethics section, and the assistance of Mark Peterson in writing the computer applications section is gratefully acknowledged.

PROFESSIONAL PERSPECTIVES

Field Work

Several types of marketing research companies conduct field work. This paper briefly describes each type and then elaborates on how the field department operates at Burke Marketing Research, a national full-service marketing research firm.

TYPES OF DATA COLLECTION FIRMS

Within the marketing research industry, firms that conduct field work tend to specialize by data collection method. Companies operating at shopping mall locations are typically small, family-owned firms. Their field work consists of intercepting and interviewing respondents, either in the mall or in a secure room off the main mall area. Generally, the sample frame is composed of mall traffic; however, these firms can prerecruit respondents from various sources to participate in a variety of central location testing. Personal computers and laptops are making inroads as data collection tools in malls, as the need for ever faster methods of data collection extends to this type of research. There are several networks of mall operators that link field facilities in numerous locations.

Some companies specialize in telephone field work. Most of the large telephone centers are equipped with CATI and will soon have predictive dialing capabilities. Whereas the computer controls skip patterns within the interview, controls sampling, and provides management reports, the predictive dialer dials the number and disposes of calls not resulting in a contact, thus substantially increasing productivity and reducing boredom on the part of the interviewer. Most telephone centers are independently owned and operated, and networking is not as prevalent as in the mall business.

A third type of company maintains a mail panel for collecting data. These firms invest large sums of money to

Joe Ottaviani

Joe Ottaviani has spent nearly 20 years at Burke Marketing Research. His responsibilities have ranged from salesman to sales office manager to senior vice-president, data collection. He has been a guest lecturer at Indiana University, Miami University, University of Cincinnati, Xavier University, and Northern Kentucky University.

build and maintain panels that are balanced by demographic, usage, and geographic variables. Panels provide an economical means of obtaining large amounts of usage and attitudinal data. Economy is achieved in two ways. Since the demographic and usage characteristics of each member are known, it is relatively inexpensive to identify target respondents, especially low-incidence respondents. Also, since data are collected via self-administered questionnaires, the cost of the interviewer is eliminated. The rather large investment required to start a panel serves as an effective barrier to entry; therefore, only a few companies compete in this arena.

Most national full-service marketing research firms have either a department or division that maintains a group of field workers. These departments or divisions are organized to collect data, as well as to monitor and control the various activities that occur in the field.

FUNCTIONS OF FIELD DEPARTMENT

The field department at Burke performs two main functions: it collects data, and it monitors and controls the data collection function. The primary means of data collection at Burke is the telephone. Our telephone centers are responsible for data collection, and the home office is responsible for monitoring and control. However, as described below, both of these functions are often performed in both parts of the organization.

DATA COLLECTION

In terms of size, the part of the department responsible for collecting data is by far the largest, numbering in the hundreds. Most of our interviewing staff, works between 17½ and 20 hours per week.

The proper selection, training, and retention of these interviewers is of extreme importance to the success of our organization. We pay a slightly higher hourly rate than other data collection firms in the areas where we are located. We also expect more of our people. We look for people who are tractable, can be motivated, and have had work experience requiring personal contact with consumers. Our five-day paid training program is unique in the industry. All training is geared to our field standard operating procedures (SOPs), and the trainee is introduced to the telephone on the very first day of training. Full-time trainers are assigned to each of our data collection facilities. After we invest in the selection and training of data collectors, it makes good business sense to take measures to retain them. One of the best means of developing interviewer retention programs is the focus group. This qualitative technique is extremely powerful in determining what interviewer's needs and concerns are. The fact that we are occasionally surprised by interviewers' input makes it all the more important to consider it in developing a retention program.

Field workers are evaluated on several dimensions. Since the supervisors know the budget for each study, they can set a production goal and compare it with each interviewer's production. (At the end of a study, each interviewer's expected production rate is computed, based on average interview length, incidence of locating qualified respondents, etc., and compared with actual production.) Supervisors work with those who perform significantly below the goal. Also, in an effort to produce high-quality work, each interviewer is listened to at least once daily. Supervisors randomly listen to and evaluate the work of interviewers in an inconspicuous manner using specially designed monitoring equipment. Interviewers are evaluated on their ability to screen qualified respondents (especially important when interviewing professionals such as doctors or when interviewing a client's customers) to ask questions as written, to record answers accurately, and to probe incomplete or ambiguous answers. Several reports, generated by our CATI system, track the interviewer's ability to handle various types of questions in the interview. Problems with ratings questions (high number of "don't know's"), on volunteered brands questions (low number of brands volunteered per respondent), or on open-ended questions (skips over open-ended questions, making interviews shorter) can be identified daily and addressed immediately. Compiling and analyzing this information for each interviewer serves two important functions: it helps us identify potential training needs and provides data that assist in the more efficient scheduling of interviewers.

While interviewers are the life's blood of a data collection firm, supervisors provide the backbone. Without good supervision, it is nearly impossible to do quality work. To become a good supervisor, one must be able to manage people as well as to take overall responsibility for the project. Since these skills are not acquired overnight, our field workers progress through three levels of supervision, with a new skill being taught at each level. At the first level, supervisors are trained to manage a study from a technical standpoint: for example, they learn how to employ the SOPs to a study. At the second level, they acquire people-managing skills and have interviewers reporting to them for the first time. At the final level, they assume the entire administration of a study, from scheduling interviewers to managing the time and cost budgets. We strongly believe that supervisors must be knowledgeable about the project's purpose, as well as cost and timing, to do a quality job.

MONITORING AND CONTROL

A much smaller but no less important part of the department monitors and controls the data collection process. Responsibilities here include preplanning and design input, managing cost and time estimates, problem solving, and maintaining a liaison with other functional departments in the company as well as with outside suppliers. The functions performed by this group include pretesting questionnaires, checking interview programs written for the CATI system, attending job meetings with interviewers at the start of a study, tracking daily production, answering technical questions from the interviewers, and facilitating the smooth transition of a study from the field to other departments within the company (coding, report processing, etc.).

Monitoring and controlling is also provided on those occasions when data collection resources are secured from outside suppliers, either because additional telephone capacity is required or because the study design requires a data collection method not provided internally (e.g., mall interviewing). A database containing information about various mall facilities and telephone centers enables us to locate qualified data collection facilities in various parts of the country as the need arises.

Another important monitoring and controlling function is the purchase and handling of samples. This includes keeping track of millions of sampling units annually and prescribing the correct dialing method for each telephone study.

The computer plays a significant role in the data collection process of any major telephone interviewing facility. It increases the quality of interviewing by reducing the chance for interviewer error, significantly speeds up the tabulation process, and provides management with a variety of reports designed to control both quality and productivity.

CLOSING COMMENTS

There are many other important functions performed by many dedicated workers both in and out of our field that make the entire marketing research process possible. First, within the field, the contributions of our systems support group should not go unmentioned. This group, which is on call up to 14 hours a day, seven days a week, literally keeps us in business whenever hardware or programming problems arise. Outside of the field, the support from those in our systems, telecommunications, human resources, and accounting departments is greatly appreciated.

Gerber Outgrows Its Slogan

Gerber has become synonymous with baby food, having captured 70 to 72% of the baby food market in 1993 with sales of nearly $803 million, and it is known for its slogan, "Babies are our business, our only business." The company did not feel, however, that the Gerber label was restricted to baby food alone. For this reason, Gerber tried to implement a growth strategy that involved diversifying into other baby products. Gerber considered its entry into nonfoods a necessary move, because with the decrease in birth rate, Gerber could no longer rely on increased baby-food volumes to maintain its leadership in the baby products industry.

In carrying out its growth strategy, Gerber changed some product offerings to stay abreast of current trends. Items such as microwave feeding bowls and computer software to monitor a baby's diet and physical growth were introduced. Gerber also acquired several baby product companies and operated each as a separate profit center. Gerber's acquisitions included the Buster Brown apparel company and Weather Tamer, makers of outerwear for children. Other acquisitions were Reliance Products (makers of Nuk brand bottle nipples and pacifiers), Century Products (car seats, highchairs, and walkers), Bilt-Rite Juvenile Products (playpens, carriages, and furniture), Okla Homer Smith Furniture Manufacturing Company (baby wear), Wooltex International (soft sculptures), Palo Alto Educational System (day-care centers), Bates Nitewear Company, Hankscraft (vaporizers and humidifiers), and Nursery Originals (lamps, mobiles, and toys). Gerber's rationale for dedicating itself to the children's market was, "It's what we know best."

This diversification strategy failed, even though Gerber's marketing research revealed growth opportunities in the baby product industry. Research had determined that parents and grandparents tend to spend ten times as much on the first baby as on subsequent ones and that 40% of babies are first-time births. Findings also indicated that young professional parents spent more on their children than their parents had spent on them. Gerber's 89 day-care centers (Gerber Children's Centers) were a further attempt to reach these young professional parents. But Gerber soon realized that this information, although accurate, did not represent a large market, because less than 5% of U.S. households have babies.

A different growth strategy was mapped out for Gerber when David Johnson became CEO in 1987. His job was to achieve a turnaround. Gerber began to seek ways to expand its baby-food franchise into the adult market, and $13 million was budgeted for research and development of this new line. This was Gerber's second effort to move into this market, and this time the company exercised caution in its pursuit of the older consumer. Its earlier attempt to capture a share of the adult market with its Singles line (dinners that catered to the adult palate) failed because they were packaged in what looked like baby-food jars. Older consumers were too embarrassed to buy or even try the product.

Their second foray into this market was more successful. Gerber introduced a line of applesauce-based fruit cups and tested bottled water and a shelf-stable homogenized milk, with the precaution of putting the Gerber name on the label in very small print to prevent the consumer from feeling reluctant to purchase a "baby" product. This attempt was successful.

Another recent growth strategy undertaken by Gerber concerns its mainstay baby-food line. Facing a decline in annual baby-food consumption from 66 dozen jars in 1972 to 53 dozen jars in 1991, Gerber launched a new line of "Gerber Graduates." The new food line offers food for children aged 10 to 30 months. This new line addresses the loss in enthusiasm of today's mothers in traditional strained baby foods. According to Gerber, the marketing strategy is to "feed an infant sooner, more, and longer." A spokesperson for Gerber, Steve Poole, stated "by producing a line of toddler foods, we have more than doubled our potential market."

Gerber also felt that because of its large market share in the baby-food industry in the United States, it should turn its attention to the European market. In 1991, Gerber began taking over the European marketing of the Gerber brand from licensee CPC International. Gerber felt that it could increase sales and market share in Europe and become a dominant brand if it marketed more aggressively. Furthermore, Gerber announced its intentions of taking over the marketing rights of its brand from other licensees in its overseas markets. The recent venture in exporting baby food to Poland as well as the agreement to license a plant in Egypt to produce Gerber cereals were further indications of the seriousness of Gerber's intentions to conquer the overseas market.

In their 1993 annual report, Gerber stated that extending sales into the international arena was their most important thrust for the future. Latin America, Western Europe and the Mediterranean, Central Europe, Asia, and Pacific Rim are targeted areas for Gerber. A Mexican joint venture is also producing excellent returns for Gerber. The strong Puerto Rican business will be used to launch future Caribbean growth. In 1993, Gerber entered a joint venture in Venezuela. In 1994, Gerber established businesses in both Argentina and Chile.

These aggressive measures, however, were not really surprising, considering that Gerber is a big believer in marketing. The company spends an estimated $50 million on marketing annually in the United States, including direct mail, couponing, and other promotional efforts. These U.S. marketing figures should serve as a warning to overseas competitors, especially because Gerber has added gobbling up the overseas market to its menu.

QUESTIONS

1. To continue its expansion into the adult market, Gerber would like to determine the preferences of adult consumers for prepared dinners. It plans to conduct a survey using mall-intercept interviews. Describe the field work process that should take place.

2. Develop appropriate guidelines for interviewer training.

3. Develop appropriate guidelines for conducting the interviews.

4. Discuss the role of supervision of field workers in this survey.

5. How should the field workers be evaluated?

REFERENCES

1. Strand, Patricia. "Gerber to Grow in Europe." *Advertising Age* (March 18, 1991): 17.

2. "Miscellaneous Grocery (The 1991 Supermarket Sales Manual)." *Progressive Grocer* (July 1991): 59–62.

3. "Baby Food Is Growing Up." *American Demographics* (May 1993): 20–22.

4. Gerber Products Company. 1993 annual report.

CASE 3.2

Revlon's Channels Open the Door to Innovation

Revlon Inc. and its subsidiaries manufacture and distribute cosmetics and fragrances as well as beauty care and treatment products. In 1993, Revlon's corporate sales were $1.6 billion, down from $3.14 billion in 1990, reflecting how the cosmetics market has become more competitive in recent years. Growth in sales dropped to only 3 to 4% per year in the late 1980s and early 1990s, down sharply from 10 to 11% per year in the early 1980s. Furthermore, the market is expected to expand by only 4 to 5% per year over the next few years. The 1994 third quarter earnings of Revlon showed a marked improvement over previous year's third quarter earnings: $1 million net income from $476.9 million in sales versus a $29.6 million loss from sales of $412.2 million.

Revlon has traditionally competed in both the department store and drugstore cosmetic markets. In the department store market, Revlon's major competitors include Estée Lauder, Unilever, and Cosmair. Major competitors in the drugstore market include Maybelline, Noxell (owned by Procter & Gamble), and L'Oreal. Although drugstores have opened the way for innovations, particularly in packaging, for Revlon the competition is fierce. Maybelline and P & G have recently begun to market aggressively to Revlon's target market: women over 35.

In direct contrast to its department store business, Revlon's drugstore business was booming. A 1989 survey report showed that Revlon had recently dramatically improved its standing in drugstores. Some 75% of the buyers surveyed said that Revlon's products were either excellent or above average, compared with only 35% three years previously. Revlon's drugstore avenue of distribution opened the way for innovation at Revlon. New products were developed and introduced to the market at a much faster rate than previously.

In hope of capturing more market share, Revlon used innovative packaging to introduce its Clean & Clear line, which was designed to rival such brands as Neutrogena, Oil of Olay, and Finesse. The new packaging was the first design to use noncontact coding as part of the primary package labeling. The coding was molded into the clear plastic package and was virtually invisible. The coding allowed the product to shine through without being hidden by four different inventory labels on the back.

With such innovations, Revlon's management believed that there was big money to be made through drugstores and supermarkets. But Revlon's classic middle-market pricing hurt the company in an era of market segmentation, when growth was occurring at the high and low ends. Revlon was also hurt by its heavy-handed attitude toward drugstore retailers. Since the 1980s, Revlon managers had fulfilled their sales quota by trade loading: oversupplying retailers through discounts and other means. The situation changed with the advent of bar code technology, the consolidation of retailers, and sluggish consumer demand: retailers fought back and refused to allow Revlon to dictate buying decisions. Retailers' past acceptance of trade loading, however, allowed Revlon to conduct business on shaky ground. For example, Revlon would flood stores with new products without conducting much-needed market research. Inevitably, some products failed; those would be ignored while the successful products were supported. Additionally, marketing programs for new products were virtually neglected. As a result, 1992 sales of $1.63 billion fell short of projections by $100 million.

Marketing plans subsequently were vigorously supported by Revlon. It increased its marketing budget by 40% in 1994, contributing to the success of products such as Colorstay lipstick and Age Defying makeup whose spokesmodel is actress Melanie Griffith. In addition, to make the best use of its marketing budget, Revlon introduced only four new products in 1994 and 1995, compared with 15 in 1992 and 1993.

Perhaps the greatest change in Revlon has been the brands under its company umbrella. In 1991, Revlon, in heavy debt, agreed to sell its Max Factor cosmetics firm and Betrix, a German makeup and fragrance manufacturer, to Procter & Gamble for $1.14 billion in cash. This placed Revlon in a more difficult position to compete with P & G in the industry, especially because P & G had already acquired Richardson-Vicks (maker of Oil of Olay), and Noxell (Cover Girl and Clarion lines).

In 1993, the Revlon Consumer Products Corporation became the first large cosmetics company to sell lipsticks and mascara over the airwaves through the use of infomercials. The company introduced a line of cosmetics named after and sold by singer and actress Dolly Parton. Furthermore, Parton hosted the 30-minute infomercials. The cosmetics were sold in packages that include lipstick, mascara, and other products, ranging in price from $80 to $100. The first infomercials were followed by others that introduced a Dolly fragrance and a Dolly skin treatment line.

Revlon's theory behind the infomercial is "that there is an untapped market of women who do not use makeup because they are put off by sophisticated beauty advisers behind makeup counters in department stores, are baffled by wall displays that feature 80 different colors of lipstick, or are tired of making mistakes in buying shades of eye shadow, foundation, or other cosmetics." The company feels that its best customer will be the educated consumer. The infomercial was designed to educate the consumer by introducing a relatively simple kit that was explained by Parton. The company hopes that home shopping will continue to grow. An added benefit to the company will be that these infomercials will allow the company to go after new business without cannibalizing its sales of its existing products. Finally, some believe that selling cosmetics on television may be a cushion against "pitched battles being fought by Revlon and its competitors to gain shelf space in mass merchandise and discount stores, where sales of cosmetics continue to increase."

Traditionally, cosmetic manufacturers have marketed their products almost exclusively to Caucasian women. One study indicated that as much as 95% of all makeup on the market is manufactured for white women who have pink undertones in their skin color. This study also indicated that approximately 75% of the women in population need a makeup that is made for women with yellow and darker undertones. The current population includes approximately 33 million African-American, Hispanic, and Asian-American women. This number is expected to rise to approximately 40 million by the year 2000. To meet the needs of these changing faces of America, Revlon as well as other major manufacturers plan to do a "makeover" on their product lines and will introduce a line of makeup specifically formulated for the needs of minority women. Revlon plans to offer a line of makeup and a fragrance that is specifically for African-American women. The makeup will be called ColorStyle and will be endorsed by model Veronica Webb. This is a different marketing strategy for Revlon because it has used mostly white models for its makeup advertisements. In addition, Revlon plans to use a Hispanic spokesperson to target the Hispanic market. Retail sales for ethnic cosmetics is expected to reach $300 million by 1997.

Despite these moves, one has to wonder if Revlon can reopen the door to innovation and high market share in the cosmetics industry or whether it is locked out for good.

QUESTIONS

1. To determine consumers' attitudes toward and preferences for cosmetics sold over the airwaves through the use of infomercials, Revlon would like to conduct a telephone survey using CATI. Describe the field work process that must take place.

2. In what areas should the field workers be trained?

3. Develop appropriate guidelines for the supervision of field workers.

4. Would interviewer cheating be a problem in this case? Discuss.

5. How should the validation of field work be conducted in this survey?

REFERENCES

1. Strom, Stephanie. "With Help from Dolly Parton, Revlon Will Try Direct TV Marketing." *New York Times* (September 20, 1993): C8.

2. Omelia, Johanna. "Cosmetic Marketers Target Women of Color." *Drug & Cosmetic Industry* (November 1993): 24–27.

3. Miller, Cyndee. "Cosmetics Firms Finally Discover the Ethnic Market." *Marketing News* (August 30, 1993): 2.

4. Stern, Gabriella. "P & G Hopes Kaplan Can Bring Some Zip to Its Cosmetics and Perfume Business." *Wall Street Journal* (March 25, 1994): B1, B12.

5. Hwang, Suein L. "Revlon Inc. Says It's on the Mend after Ruinous 1993." *Wall Street Journal* (October 28, 1994): B4.

PART IV

Data Preparation and Analysis

◆

When the field work is complete, the researcher moves on to data preparation and analysis, the fifth step of the marketing research process. In this part, we emphasize the importance and discuss the process of preparing data to make them suitable for analysis. We then describe various data analysis techniques. We cover not only the basic techniques of frequency distribution, cross-tabulation, and hypothesis testing, but also the commonly used multivariate techniques of analysis of variance and regression. Finally, we describe more advanced techniques: discriminant, factor, and cluster analysis as well as multidimensional scaling and conjoint analysis. In the discussion of each statistical technique, the emphasis is on explaining the procedure, interpreting the results, and explaining the managerial implications, rather than focusing on statistical elegance. Three of the cases with statistical data sets provide ample opportunities to practice these techniques. Four additional cases with data sets are found in the supplement entitled *Exercises in Marketing Research*.

CHAPTER FOURTEEN

Data Preparation

Care exercised at the data preparation stage can substantially enhance the quality of the statistical results.

OBJECTIVES

After reading this chapter, the student should be able to:

1. Discuss the nature and scope of data preparation and the data preparation process.
2. Explain questionnaire checking and editing and the treatment of unsatisfactory responses by returning to the field, assigning missing values, and discarding unsatisfactory responses.
3. Describe the guidelines for coding questionnaires including the coding of structured and unstructured questions.
4. Discuss the data cleaning process and the methods used to treat missing responses: substitution of a neutral value, imputed response, casewise deletion, and pairwise deletion.
5. State the reasons for and methods of statistically adjusting data: weighting, variable respecification, and scale transformation.
6. Describe the procedure for selecting a data analysis strategy and the factors influencing the process.
7. Classify statistical techniques and give a detailed classification of univariate techniques as well as a classification of multivariate techniques.
8. Understand the intracultural, pan-cultural, and cross-cultural approaches to data analysis in international marketing research.
9. Identify the ethical issues related to data processing, particularly discarding of unsatisfactory responses, violation of the assumptions under-

lying the data analysis techniques, and evaluation and interpretation of results.

10. Explain the use of microcomputers and mainframes in data preparation and analysis.

OVERVIEW

After the research problem has been defined and a suitable approach developed (Chapter 2), an appropriate research design formulated (Chapters 3 through 12) and the field work conducted (Chapter 13), the researcher can move to data preparation and analysis, the fifth step of the marketing research process. Before the raw data contained in the questionnaires can be subjected to statistical analysis, they must be converted into a form suitable for analysis. The quality of statistical results depends on the care exercised in the data preparation phase. Paying inadequate attention to data preparation can seriously compromise statistical results, leading to biased findings and incorrect interpretation.

This chapter describes the data collection process, which begins with checking the questionnaires for completeness. Then, we discuss the editing of data and provide guidelines for handling illegible, incomplete, inconsistent, ambiguous, or otherwise unsatisfactory responses. We also describe coding, transcribing, and data cleaning, emphasizing the treatment of missing responses and statistical adjustment of data. We discuss the selection of a data analysis strategy and classify statistical techniques. The intracultural, pan-cultural, and cross-cultural approaches to data analysis in international marketing research are explained. The ethical issues related to data processing are identified with emphasis on discarding of unsatisfactory responses, violation of the assumptions underlying the data analysis techniques, and evaluation and interpretation of results. Finally, we explain the use of microcomputers and mainframes in data preparation and analysis.

We begin with some examples of data preparation.

DEPARTMENT STORE PATRONAGE PROJECT
Data Preparation

In the department store patronage project, the data were obtained by in-home personal interviews. The questionnaires were edited by the supervisors as they were being turned in by the interviewers. The questionnaires were checked for incomplete, inconsistent and ambiguous responses. Questionnaires with unsatisfactory responses were returned to the field, and the interviewers were asked to recontact the respondents to obtain the required information. Nine questionnaires were discarded because the proportion of unsatisfactory responses was large. This resulted in a final sample size of 271.

A codebook was developed for coding the questionnaires. Coding was relatively simple because there were no open-ended questions. The data were transcribed onto a computer tape via keypunching. About 25% of the data were verified for keypunching errors. The data were cleaned by identifying out-of-range and logically inconsistent responses. Most of the rating information was obtained using six-point scales, so responses of 0, 7, and 8 were considered out-of-range and a code of 9 was assigned to missing responses.

Any missing responses were treated by casewise deletion in which respondents with any missing values were dropped from the analysis. Casewise deletion was selected because the number of cases (respondents) with missing values was small and the sample size was sufficiently large. In statistically adjusting the data, dummy variables were created for the categorical variables. New variables that were composites of original variables were also created. For example, the familiarity ratings of the ten department stores were summed to create a familiarity index. Finally, a data analysis strategy was developed. ◆

EXAMPLE
Custom Cleaning

According to Joann Harristhal of Custom Research, Inc., completed questionnaires from the field often have many small errors because of the inconsistent quality of interviewing. For example, qualifying responses are not circled or skip patterns are not followed accurately.

These small errors can be costly. When responses from such questionnaires are put into a computer, Custom Research runs a cleaning program that checks for completeness and logic. Discrepancies are identified on a computer printout, which is checked by the tabulation supervisors. Once errors are identified, appropriate corrective action is taken before data analysis is carried out. Custom Research has found that this procedure substantially increases the quality of statistical results.[1] ◆

The department store example describes the various phases of the data preparation process. Note that the process is initiated while the field work is still in progress. The Custom Research example describes the importance of cleaning data and of identifying and correcting errors before the data are analyzed. A systematic description of the data preparation process follows.

THE DATA PREPARATION PROCESS

The data preparation process is shown in Figure 14.1. The entire process is guided by the preliminary plan of data analysis that was formulated in the research design phase (Chapter 3). The first step is to check for acceptable questionnaires. This is followed by editing, coding, and transcribing the data. The data are cleaned and a treatment for missing responses prescribed. Often, statistical adjustment of the data may be necessary to make them representative of the population of interest. The researcher should then select an appropriate data analysis strategy. The final data analysis strategy differs from the preliminary plan of data analysis due to the information and insights gained since the preliminary plan was formulated. Data preparation should begin as soon as the first batch of questionnaires is received from the field, while the field work is still going on. Thus, if any problems are detected, the field work can be modified to incorporate corrective action.

QUESTIONNAIRE CHECKING

The initial step in questionnaire checking involves reviewing all questionnaires for completeness and interviewing quality. Often these checks are made while field work is still under way. If the field work was contracted to a data collection agency, the researcher should make an independent check after it is over. A questionnaire returned from the field may be unacceptable for several reasons:

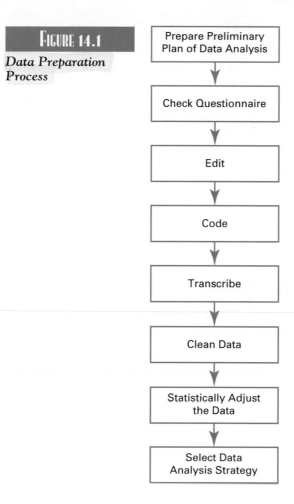

FIGURE 14.1

Data Preparation Process

Prepare Preliminary Plan of Data Analysis

Check Questionnaire

Edit

Code

Transcribe

Clean Data

Statistically Adjust the Data

Select Data Analysis Strategy

1. Parts of the questionnaire may be incomplete.
2. The pattern of responses may indicate that the respondent did not understand or follow the instructions. For example, skip patterns may not have been followed.
3. The responses show little variance. For example, a respondent has checked only 4s on a series of seven-point rating scales.
4. The returned questionnaire is physically incomplete: one or more pages is missing.
5. The questionnaire is received after the preestablished cutoff date.
6. The questionnaire is answered by someone who does not qualify for participation.

If quotas or cell group sizes have been imposed, the acceptable questionnaires should be classified and counted accordingly. Any problems in meeting the sampling requirements should be identified, and corrective action, such as conducting additional interviews in the underrepresented cells, should be taken before the data are edited.

EDITING

Editing is the review of the questionnaires with the objective of increasing accuracy and precision. It consists of screening questionnaires to identify illegible, incomplete, inconsistent, or ambiguous responses.

editing A review of the questionnaires with the objective of increasing accuracy and precision.

Responses may be illegible if they have been poorly recorded. This is particularly common in questionnaires with a large number of unstructured questions. The data must be legible if they are to be properly coded. Likewise, questionnaires may be incomplete to varying degrees. A few or many questions may be unanswered.

At this stage, the researcher makes a preliminary check for consistency. Certain obvious inconsistencies can be easily detected. For example, a respondent reports an annual income of less than $20,000 yet indicates frequent shopping at prestigious department stores like Saks Fifth Avenue and Neiman Marcus.

Responses to unstructured questions may be ambiguous and difficult to interpret clearly. The answer may be abbreviated, or some ambiguous words may have been used. For structured questions, more than one response may be marked for a question designed to elicit a single response. Suppose that a respondent circles 2 and 3 on a five-point rating scale. Does this mean that 2.5 was intended? To complicate matters further, the coding procedure may allow for only a single-digit response.

Treatment of Unsatisfactory Responses

Unsatisfactory responses are commonly handled by returning to the field to get better data, assigning missing values, and discarding unsatisfactory respondents.

Returning to the Field Questionnaires with unsatisfactory responses may be returned to the field, where the interviewers recontact the respondents. This approach is particularly attractive for business and industrial marketing surveys, where the sample sizes are small and the respondents are easily identifiable. The data obtained the second time, however, may be different from those obtained during the original survey. These differences may be attributed to changes over time or differences in the mode of questionnaire administration (e.g., telephone versus in-person interview).

Assigning Missing Values If returning the questionnaires to the field is not feasible, the editor may assign missing values to unsatisfactory responses. This approach may be desirable if (1) the number of respondents with unsatisfactory responses is small, (2) the proportion of unsatisfactory responses for each of these respondents is small, or (3) the variables with unsatisfactory responses are not the key variables.

Discarding Unsatisfactory Respondents In another approach, the respondents with unsatisfactory responses are simply discarded. This approach may have merit when (1) the proportion of unsatisfactory respondents is small (less than 10%); (2) the sample size is large; (3) the unsatisfactory respondents do not differ from satisfactory respondents in obvious ways (e.g., demographics, product usage characteristics); (4) the proportion of unsatisfactory responses for each of these respondents is large; or (5) responses on key variables are missing. Unsatisfactory respondents may differ from satisfactory respondents in systematic ways, however, and the decision to designate a respondent as unsatisfactory may be subjective. Both these factors bias the results. If the researcher decides to discard unsatisfactory respondents, the procedure adopted to identify these respondents and their number should be reported, as in the following example.

EXAMPLE

Declaring Discards

In a cross-cultural survey of marketing managers from English-speaking African countries, questionnaires were mailed to 565 firms. A total of 192 completed questionnaires was returned, of which four were discarded because respondents suggested that they were not in charge of overall marketing decisions. The decision to discard the four questionnaires was based on the consideration that the sample size was sufficiently large and the proportion of unsatisfactory respondents was small.[2] ◆

CODING

coding Assigning a code to represent a specific response to a specific question along with the data record and column position that the code will occupy.

Coding means assigning a code, usually a number, to each possible response to each question. The code includes an indication of the column position (field) and data record it will occupy. For example, sex of respondents may be coded as 1 for females and 2 for males. A field represents a single item of data, such as sex of the respondent. A record consists of related fields, such as sex, marital status, age, household size, or occupation. All the demographic and personality characteristics of a respondent may be contained in a single record. Normally, each record has 80 columns, although this is not a requirement. A number of records may be used for each respondent.

The data (all the records) for all the respondents are stored in a computer file, as illustrated in Table 14.1. In this table, the columns represent the fields and the rows represent the records. Table 14.1 presents coded data for part of the first record for respondents in the department store patronage project. These data have been coded according to the coding scheme specified in Figure 14.2. Columns 1 through 3 represent a single field and contain the respondent numbers coded 001 to 271. Column 4 contains the record number. This column has a value of 1 for all the rows because only the first record of the respondents is displayed. Columns 5 and 6 contain the project code which is 31. The next two columns, 7 and 8, display the interviewer code which varies from 01 to 55 for respondent number 271. Columns 26 to 35, each representing one field, contain familiarity ratings for the ten stores, with values ranging from 1 to 6. Finally, column 77 represents the rating of store 10 on prices. Note that columns 78 to 80 are blank. There are ten records for each respondent. There are 2710 rows, indicating that data for 271 respondents are stored in this file.

If the questionnaire contains only structured questions or very few unstructured questions, it is precoded. This means that codes are assigned before field work is con-

	TABLE 14.1								
Illustrative Computer File: Department Store Patronage Project				Fields Column Numbers					
	Records	1–3	4	5–6	7–8	…	26 … 35	77	
	Record 1	001	1	31	01		6544234553	5	
	Record 11	002	1	31	01		5564435433	4	
	Record 21	003	1	31	01		4655243324	4	
	Record 31	004	1	31	01		5463244645	6	
	Record 2701	271	1	31	55		6652354435	5	

FIGURE 14.2

Codebook Excerpt Showing Information for the First Record: Department Store Patronage Project

Column Number	Variable Number	Variable Name	Question Number	Coding Instructions
1–3	1	Respondent ID		001 to 890 add leading zeros as necessary
4	2	Record number		1 (same for all respondents)
5–6	3	Project code		31 (same for all respondents)
7–8	4	Interview code		As coded on the questionnaire
9–14	5	Date code		As coded on the questionnaire
15–20	6	Time code		As coded on the questionnaire
21–22	7	Validation code		As coded on the questionnaire
23–24		Blank		Leave these columns blank
25	8	Who shops	I	Male head = 1
				Female head = 2
				Other = 3
				Punch the Number Circled
				Missing values = 9
26	9	Familiarity with store 1	IIa	For question II parts a through **j**
				Punch the Number Circled
27	10	Familiarity with store 2	IIb	Not so familiar = 1
				Very familiar = 6
				Missing values = 9
28	11	Familiarity with store 3	IIc	
35	18	Familiarity with store 10	IIj	
36	19	Frequency : Store 1	IIIa	For question III parts a through **j**
				Punch the Number Circled
37	20	Frequence : Store 2	IIIb	Not at all = 1
				Very frequently = 6
				Missing values = 9
45	28	Frequency : Store 10	IIIj	
46–47		Blank		Leave these columns blank
48	29	Rating of store 1 on quality	IVa	For store IV through XI, **Punch the Number Circled**
57	38	Rating of store 10 on quality	IVa	
58	39	Rating of store 1 on variety	IVb	
67	48	Rating of store 10 on variety	IVb	
68	49	Rating of store 1 on prices	IVc	
77	58	Rating of store 10 on prices	IVc	
78–80		Blank		Leave these columns blank

ducted. If the questionnaire contains unstructured questions, codes are assigned after the questionnaires have been returned from the field (postcoding).[3] Precoding was briefly discussed in Chapter 10 on questionnaire design; further guidelines are provided below.[4]

Coding Questions

fixed field code A code in which the number of records for each respondent is the same and the same data appear in the same columns for all respondents.

The respondent code and the record number should appear on each record in the data. The following additional codes should be included for each respondent: project code, interviewer code, date and time codes, and validation code. **Fixed field codes**, which mean that the number of records for each respondent is the same and that the same data appear in the same column(s) for all respondents, are highly desirable. If possible, standard codes should be used for missing data. For example, a code of 9 could be used for a single column variable, 99 for a double-column variable, and so on. The missing value codes should be distinct from the codes assigned to the legitimate responses.

Coding of structured questions is relatively simple, because the response options are predetermined. The researcher assigns a code for each response to each question and specifies the appropriate record and columns in which the response codes are to appear. For example,

Do you have a currently valid passport?
1. Yes   2. No (2/54)

For this question, a yes response is coded 1 and a no response 2. The numbers in parentheses indicate that the code assigned will appear on the second record for this respondent in column 54. Because only one response is allowed and there are only two possible responses (1 or 2), a single column is sufficient.[5] In general, a single column is sufficient to code a structured question with a single response if there are fewer than 9 possible responses.

In questions that permit a large number of responses, each possible response option should be assigned a separate column. Such questions include those about brand ownership or usage, magazine readership, and television viewing. For example,

Which accounts do you <u>now</u> have at this bank? ("X" as many as apply)		
		Record #9
Regular savings account	❑	(62)
Regular checking account	❑	(63)
Mortgage	❑	(64)
Now account	❑	(65)
Club account (Christmas, etc.)	❑	(66)
Line of credit	❑	(67)
Term savings account (time deposits, etc.)	❑	(68)
Savings bank life insurance	❑	(69)
Home improvement loan	❑	(70)
Auto loan	❑	(71)
Other services	❑	(72)

In this example, suppose that a respondent checked regular savings, regular checking, and term savings accounts. On record 9, a 1 will be entered in the column numbers 62, 63, and 68. All the other columns (64, 65, 66, 67, 69, 70, 71, and 72) will receive a 0.

The coding of unstructured or open-ended questions is more complex. Respondents' verbatim responses are recorded on the questionnaire. Codes are then developed and assigned to these responses. Sometimes, based on previous projects or theoretical considerations, the researcher can develop the codes before beginning field work. Usually, this must wait until the completed questionnaires are received. Then the researcher lists 50 to 100 responses to an unstructured question to identify the categories suitable for coding. Once codes are developed, the coders should be trained to assign the correct codes to the verbatim responses. The following guidelines are suggested for coding unstructured questions and questionnaires in general.[6]

Category codes should be mutually exclusive and collectively exhaustive. Categories are mutually exclusive if each response fits into one and only one category code. Categories should not overlap. Categories are collectively exhaustive if every response fits into one of the assigned category codes. This can be achieved by adding an additional category code of "other" or "none of the above." Only a few (10% or less) of the responses, however, should fall into this category; the vast majority of the responses should be classified into meaningful categories.

Category codes should be assigned for critical issues even if no one has mentioned them. It may be important to know that no one has mentioned a particular response. For example, the management of a major consumer goods company was concerned about the packaging for a new brand of toilet soap. Hence, packaging was included as a separate category in coding responses to the question, "What do you like least about this bar soap?"

Data should be coded to retain as much detail as possible. For example, if data on the exact number of trips made on commercial airlines by business travelers have been obtained, they should be coded as such rather than grouped into two category codes of "infrequent flyers" and "frequent flyers." Obtaining information on the exact number of trips allows the researcher to later define categories of business travelers in several different ways. If the categories were predefined, the subsequent analysis of data would be limited by those categories.[7]

Codebook

codebook A book containing coding instructions and the necessary information about variables in the data set.

A **codebook** contains coding instructions and the necessary information about variables in the data set. A codebook guides the coders in their work and helps the researcher identify and locate the variables properly. Even if the questionnaire has been precoded, it is helpful to prepare a formal codebook. A codebook generally contains the following information: (1) column number, (2) record number, (3) variable number, (4) variable name, (5) question number, and (6) instructions for coding. Figure 14.2 is an excerpt from a coding book developed for the department store patronage project.

Coding Questionnaires

Figure 14.3 is an example of questionnaire coding, showing the coding of part of the questionnaire used in the department store patronage project. This questionnaire was precoded. The respondent code and the record number appear on each record in the data. The first record contains the additional codes: project code, interviewer code, date and time codes, and validation code. It is a good practice to insert blanks between parts. Sometimes, instead of writing the codes on the questionnaire, the codes are written on special 80-column paper called coding sheets.

TRANSCRIBING

Transcribing data involves transferring the coded data from the questionnaires or coding sheets onto disks or magnetic tapes or directly into computers by keypunching. If the data have been collected via CATI or CAPI, this step is unnecessary because the data are entered directly into the computer as they are collected. Besides keypunching, the data can be transferred by using mark sense forms, optical scanning, or computerized sensory analysis (see Figure 14.4). Mark sense forms require responses to be recorded with a special pencil in a predesignated area coded for that response, and the data can then be read by a machine. Optical scanning involves direct machine reading of the codes and simultaneous transcription. A familiar example of optical scanning is the transcription of universal product code (UPC) data at supermarket checkout counters. Technological advances have resulted in computerized sensory analysis systems, which automate the data collection process. The questions appear on a computerized gridpad, and responses are recorded directly into the computer using a sensing device.

If keypunching is used, errors can occur, and it is necessary to verify the data set, or at least a portion of it, for keypunching errors. A verifier machine and a second oper-

FIGURE 14.3

Example of Questionnaire Coding Showing Coding of Demographic Data

Finally, in this part of the questionnaire we would like to ask you some background information for classification purposes.

PART D Record #7

1. This questionnaire was answered by   (29)
    1. _____ Primarily the male head of household
    2. _____ Primarily the female head of household
    3. _____ Jointly by the male and female heads of household

2. Marital Status   (30)
    1. _____ Married
    2. _____ Never married
    3. _____ Divorced/separated/widowed

3. What is the total number of family members living at home? _____   (31–32)

4. Number of children living at home:
    a. Under six years _____   (33)
    b. Over six years _____   (34)

5. Number of children not living at home: _____   (35)

6. Number of years of formal education which you (and your spouse, if applicable) have completed (please circle)

		College		
	High School	Undergraduate	Graduate	
a. You	8 or less 9 10 11 12	13 14 15 16	17 18 19 20 21 22 or more	(36–37)
b. Spouse	8 or less 9 10 11 12	13 14 15 16	17 18 19 20 21 22 or more	(38–39)

7. **a.** Your age: _____   (40–41)
     b. Age of spouse (if applicable): _____   (42–43)

8. If employed, please indicate your household's occupations by checking the appropriate category.

	(44) Male Head	(45) Female Head
1. Professional and technical	_____	_____
2. Managers and administrators	_____	_____
3. Sales workers	_____	_____
4. Clerical and kindred workers	_____	_____
5. Craftsman/operative/laborers	_____	_____
6. Homemakers	_____	_____
7. Others (please specify)	_____	_____
8. Not applicable	_____	_____

9. Is your place of residence presently owned by household?   (46)
    1. Owned _____
    2. Rented _____

10. How many years have you been residing in the greater Atlanta area?
    _____ years.   (47–48)

11. What is the appropriate combined annual income of your household before taxes?
Please check.   (49–50)

01. less than $10,000	_____	**08.** $40,000 to $44,999	_____
02. $10,000 to $14,999	_____	**09.** $45,000 to $49,999	_____
03. $15,000 to $19,999	_____	**10.** $50,000 to $54,999	_____
04. $20,000 to $24,999	_____	**11.** $55,000 to $59,999	_____
05. $25,000 to $29,999	_____	**12.** $60,000 to $69,999	_____
06. $30,000 to $34,999	_____	**13.** $70,000 to $89,999	_____
07. $35,000 to $39,999	_____	**14.** $90,000 and over	_____

Note: Columns 1–3 of this record contain the respondent ID, column 4 the record number (7), columns 5 and 6 are blank. Columns 7 through 27 contain information from part C, and column 28 is blank. Thus, information on Part D is coded beginning with column number 29.

FIGURE 14.4

Data Transcription

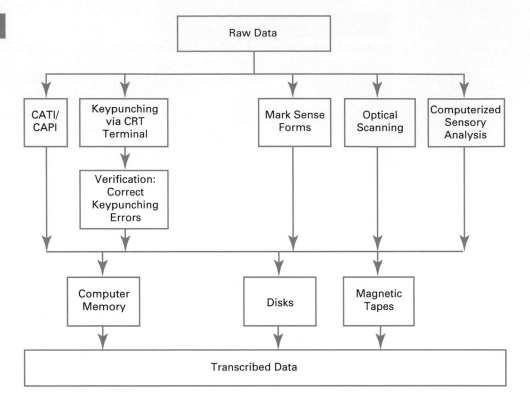

ator are used for data verification. The second operator repunches the data from the coded questionnaires. The transcribed data from the two operators are compared record by record. Any discrepancy between the two sets of transcribed data is investigated to identify and correct for keypunching errors. Verification of the entire data set will double the time and cost of data transcription. Given the time and cost constraints, and that experienced keypunch operators are quite accurate, it is sufficient to verify only 25 to 50% of the data.

When CATI or CAPI are employed, data are verified as they are collected. In the case of inadmissible responses, the computer will prompt the interviewer or respondent. In case of admissible responses, the interviewer or the respondent can see the recorded response on the screen and verify it before proceeding.

The selection of a data transcription method is guided by the type of interviewing method used and the availability of equipment. If CATI or CAPI are used, the data are entered directly into the computer. Keypunching via CRT terminal is most frequently used for ordinary telephone, in-home, mall-intercept, and mail interviews. The use of computerized sensory analysis systems in personal interviews is increasing with the increasing use of gridpads and handheld computers, however. Optical scanning can be used in structured and repetitive surveys, and mark sense forms are used in special cases.

DATA CLEANING

Data cleaning includes consistency checks and treatment of missing responses. Even though preliminary consistency checks have been made during editing, the checks at this stage are more thorough and extensive, because they are made by computer.

Consistency Checks

data cleaning Thorough and extensive checks for consistency and treatment of missing responses.

consistency checks A part of the data cleaning process that identifies data that are out of range, logically inconsistent, or have extreme values. Data with values not defined by the coding scheme are inadmissible.

Consistency checks identify data that are out of range, logically inconsistent, or have extreme values. Out-of-range data values are inadmissible and must be corrected. For example, respondents have been asked to express their degree of agreement with a series of lifestyle statements on a 1 to 5 scale. Assuming that 9 has been designated for missing values, data values of 0, 6, 7, and 8 are out of range. Computer packages like SPSS, SAS, and BMDP can be programmed to identify out-of-range values for each variable and to print out the respondent code, variable code, variable name, record number, column number, and out-of-range value.[8] This makes it is easy to check each variable systematically for out-of-range values. The correct responses can be determined by going back to the edited and coded questionnaire.

Responses can be logically inconsistent in various ways. For example, a respondent may indicate that she charges long-distance calls to a calling card, although she does not have one. Or a respondent reports both unfamiliarity with and frequent usage of the same product. The necessary information (respondent code, variable code, variable name, record number, column number, and inconsistent values) can be printed to locate these responses and to take corrective action.

Finally, extreme values should be closely examined. Not all extreme values result from errors, but they may point to problems with the data. For example, an extremely low evaluation of a brand may be the result of the respondent indiscriminately circling 1s (on a 1 to 7 rating scale) on all attributes of this brand.

Treatment of Missing Responses

missing responses Values of a variable that are unknown because these respondents provided ambiguous answers to the question.

Missing responses represent values of a variable that are unknown either because respondents provided ambiguous answers or because their answers were not properly recorded. Treatment of missing responses poses problems, particularly if the proportion

Consistency checks are extremely valuable in identifying data that are out of range, are logically inconsistent, or have extreme values.

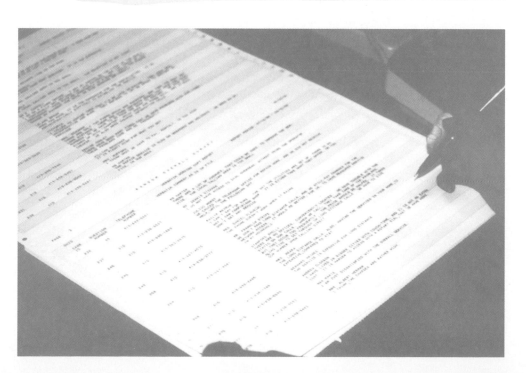

of missing responses is more than 10%. The following options are available for the treatment of missing responses.[9]

Substitute a Neutral Value   A neutral value, typically the mean response to the variable, is substituted for the missing responses. Thus, the mean of the variable remains unchanged, and other statistics such as correlations are not affected much. Although this approach has some merit, the logic of substituting a mean value (say 4) for respondents who, if they had answered, might have used either high ratings (6 or 7) or low ratings (1 or 2) is questionable.[10]

Substitute an Imputed Response   The respondents' pattern of responses to other questions are used to impute or calculate a suitable response to the missing questions. The researcher attempts to infer from the available data the responses the individuals would have given if they had answered the questions. This can be done statistically by determining the relationship of the variable in question to other variables based on the available data. For example, product usage could be related to household size for respondents who have provided data on both variables. Given that respondent's household size, the missing product usage response for a respondent could then be calculated. This approach, however, requires considerable effort and can introduce serious bias. Sophisticated statistical procedures have been developed to calculate imputed values for missing responses.[11]

casewise deletion A method for handling missing responses in which cases or respondents with any missing responses are discarded from the analysis.

Casewise Deletion   In **casewise deletion**, cases or respondents with any missing responses are discarded from the analysis. Because many respondents may have some missing responses, this approach could result in a small sample. Throwing away large amounts of data is undesirable because it is costly and time-consuming to collect data. Furthermore, respondents with missing responses could differ from respondents with complete responses in systematic ways. If so, casewise deletion could seriously bias the results.

pairwise deletion A method of handling missing values in which all cases or respondents with any missing values are not automatically discarded; rather, for each calculation, only the cases or respondents with complete responses are considered.

Pairwise Deletion   In **pairwise deletion**, instead of discarding all cases with any missing values, the researcher uses only the cases or respondents with complete responses for each calculation. As a result, different calculations in an analysis may be based on different sample sizes. This procedure may be appropriate when (1) the sample size is large, (2) there are few missing responses, and (3) the variables are not highly related. Yet this procedure can produce unappealing or even infeasible results.

The different procedures for the treatment of missing responses may yield different results, particularly when the responses are not missing at random and the variables are related. Hence, missing responses should be kept to a minimum. The researcher should carefully consider the implications of the various procedures before selecting a particular method for the treatment of nonresponse.

STATISTICALLY ADJUSTING THE DATA

Procedures for statistically adjusting the data consist of weighting, variable respecification, and scale transformations. These adjustments are not always necessary but can enhance the quality of data analysis.

Weighting

In **weighting**, each case or respondent in the database is assigned a weight to reflect its importance relative to other cases or respondents. The value 1.0 represents the unweighted case. The effect of weighting is to increase or decrease the number of cases in the sample that possess certain characteristics. (See Chapter 12, which discussed the use of weighting to adjust for nonresponse.)

Weighting is most widely used to make the sample data more representative of a target population on specific characteristics. For example, it may be used to give greater importance to cases or respondents with higher-quality data. Yet another use of weighting is to adjust the sample so that greater importance is attached to respondents with certain characteristics. If a study is conducted to determine what modifications should be made to an existing product, the researcher might want to attach greater weight to the opinions of heavy users of the product. This could be accomplished by assigning weights of 3.0 to heavy users, 2.0 to medium users, and 1.0 to light users and nonusers. Because it destroys the self-weighting nature of the sample design, weighting should be applied with caution. If used, the weighting procedure should be documented and made a part of the project report.[12]

EXAMPLE
Determining the Weight of Fast-Food Customers

A mail survey was conducted in the Los Angeles–Long Beach area to determine consumer patronage of fast-food restaurants. The resulting sample composition differed in educational level from the area population distribution as compiled from recent census data. Therefore, the sample was weighted to make it representative in terms of educational level. The weights applied were determined by dividing the population percentage by the corresponding sample percentage. The distribution of education for the sample and population, as well as the weights applied, are given in the following table.

Use of Weighting for Representativeness

Years of Education	Sample Percentage	Population Percentage	Weight
Elementary School			
0 to 7 years	2.49	4.23	1.70
8 years	1.26	2.19	1.74
High School			
1 to 3 years	6.39	8.65	1.35
4 years	25.39	29.24	1.15
College			
1 to 3 years	22.33	29.42	1.32
4 years	15.02	12.01	0.80
5 to 6 years	14.94	7.36	0.49
7 years or more	12.18	6.90	0.57
Totals	100.00	100.00	

Categories underrepresented in the sample received higher weights whereas overrepresented categories received lower weights. Thus, the data for a respondent with 1 to

The patronage of fast-food restaurants is influenced by demographic characteristics such as education. ◆ Laimute E. Druskis.

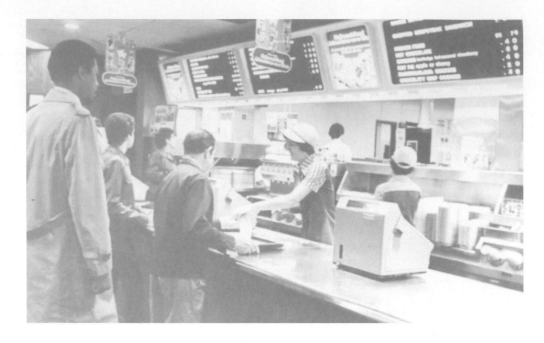

3 years of college education would be overweighted by multiplying with 1.32 whereas the data for a respondent with 7 or more years of college education would be underweighted by multiplying by 0.57. ◆

Variable Respecification

variable respecification The transformation of data to create new variables or the modification of existing variables so that they are more consistent with the objectives of the study.

Variable respecification involves the transformation of data to create new variables or to modify existing variables. The purpose of respecification is to create variables that are consistent with the objectives of the study. For example, suppose that the original variable was product usage, with ten response categories. These might be collapsed into four categories: heavy, medium, light, and nonuser. Or, the researcher may create new variables that are composites of several other variables. For example, the researcher may create an Index of Information Search (IIS), which is the sum of information customers seek from dealers, promotional materials, and independent sources. Likewise, one may take the ratio of variables. If the amount of purchases at department stores (X_1) and the amount of purchases charged (X_2) have been measured, the proportion of purchases charged can be a new variable created by taking the ratio of the two (X_2/X_1). Other respecifications of variables include square root and log transformations, which are often applied to improve the fit of the model being estimated.

dummy variables A respecification procedure using variables that take on only two values, usually 0 or 1.

An important respecification procedure involves the use of dummy variables for respecifying categorical variables. **Dummy variables** are also called *binary, dichotomous, instrumental,* or *qualitative* variables. They are variables that may take on only two values, such as 0 or 1. The general rule is that to respecify a categorical variable with K categories, $K - 1$ dummy variables are needed. The reason for having $K - 1$, rather than K, dummy variables is that only $K - 1$ categories are independent. Given the sample data, information about the Kth category can be derived from information about the other $K - 1$ categories. Consider sex, a variable having two categories. Only one dummy variable is needed. Information on the number or percentage of males in the sample can be readily derived from the number or percentage of females. The following example further illustrates the concept of dummy variables.

EXAMPLE
"Frozen" Consumers Treated as Dummies
In a study of consumer preferences for frozen foods, the respondents were classified as heavy users, medium users, light users, and nonusers, and they were originally assigned codes of 4, 3, 2, and 1, respectively. This coding was not meaningful for several statistical analyses. To conduct these analyses, product usage was represented by three dummy variables, X_1, X_2, and X_3, as shown.

Product Usage Category	Original Variable Code	Dummy Variable Code X_1	X_2	X_3
Nonusers	1	1	0	0
Light users	2	0	1	0
Medium users	3	0	0	1
Heavy users	4	0	0	0

Note that $X_1 = 1$ for nonusers and 0 for all others. Likewise, $X_2 = 1$ for light users and 0 for all others, and $X_3 = 1$ for medium users and 0 for all others. In analyzing the data, X_1, X_2, and X_3 are used to represent all user/nonuser groups. ◆

Dummy variable coding is frequently used to classify consumers of frozen foods.
◆ Barbara Rios/Photo Researchers, Inc.

scale transformation A manipulation of scale values to ensure comparability with other scales or otherwise to make the data suitable for analysis.

Scale Transformation

Scale transformation involves a manipulation of scale values to ensure comparability with other scales or otherwise to make the data suitable for analysis. Frequently, different scales are employed for measuring different variables. For example, image variables may be measured on a seven-point semantic differential scale, attitude variables on a continuous rating scale, and lifestyle variables on a five-point Likert scale. Therefore, it would not be meaningful to make comparisons across the measurement scales for any respondent. To compare attitudinal scores with lifestyle or image scores, it would be necessary to transform the various scales. Even if the same scale is employed for all the variables, different respondents may use the scale differently. For example, some respondents consistently use the upper end of a rating scale whereas others consistently use the lower end. These differences can be corrected by appropriately transforming the data.

EXAMPLE
Health Care Services: Transforming Consumers _____

In a study examining preference segmentation of health care services, respondents were asked to rate the importance of 18 factors affecting preferences for hospitals on a three-point scale (very, somewhat, or not important). Before analyzing the data, each individual's ratings were transformed. For each individual, preference responses were averaged across all 18 items. Then this mean was subtracted from each item rating, and a constant was added to the difference. Thus, the transformed data, X_t, were obtained by

$$X_t = X_i - \overline{X} + C$$

Subtraction of the mean value corrected for uneven use of the importance scale. The constant C was added to make all the transformed values positive, since negative importance ratings are not meaningful conceptually. This transformation was desirable because some respondents, especially those with low incomes, had rated almost all the preference items as very important. Others, high-income respondents in particular, had assigned the very important rating to only a few preference items. Thus, subtraction of the mean value provided a more accurate idea of the relative importance of the factors.[13] ◆

standardization The process of correcting data to reduce them to the same scale by subtracting the sample mean and dividing by the standard deviation.

In this example, the scale transformation is corrected only for the mean response. A more common transformation procedure is **standardization**. To standardize a scale X_i, we first subtract the mean, $\overline{X}$, from each score and then divide by the standard deviation, s_x. Thus, the standardized scale will have a mean of zero and a standard deviation of 1. This is essentially the same as the calculation of z scores (see Chapter 12). Standardization allows the researcher to compare variables that have been measured using different types of scales.[14] Mathematically, standardized scores, z_i, may be obtained as

$$z_i = \frac{(X_i - \overline{X})}{s_x}$$

SELECTING A DATA ANALYSIS STRATEGY

The process of selecting a data analysis strategy is described in Figure 14.5. The selection of a data analysis strategy should be based on the earlier steps of the marketing research process, known characteristics of the data, properties of statistical techniques, and the background and philosophy of the researcher.

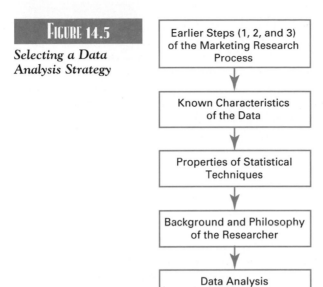

FIGURE 14.5

Selecting a Data Analysis Strategy

Earlier Steps (1, 2, and 3) of the Marketing Research Process

↓

Known Characteristics of the Data

↓

Properties of Statistical Techniques

↓

Background and Philosophy of the Researcher

↓

Data Analysis Strategy

Data analysis is not an end in itself. Its purpose is to produce information that will help address the problem at hand. The selection of a data analysis strategy must begin with a consideration of the earlier steps in the process: problem definition (step 1), development of an approach (step 2), and research design (step 3). The preliminary plan of data analysis prepared as part of the research design should be used as a springboard. Changes may be necessary in light of additional information generated in subsequent stages of the research process.

The next step is to consider the known characteristics of the data. The measurement scales used exert a strong influence on the choice of statistical techniques (see Chapter 8). In addition, the research design may favor certain techniques. For example, analysis of variance (see Chapter 16) is suited for analyzing experimental data from causal designs. The insights into the data obtained during data preparation can be valuable for selecting a strategy for analysis.

It is also important to take into account the properties of the statistical techniques, particularly their purpose and underlying assumptions. Some statistical techniques are appropriate for examining differences in variables, others for assessing the magnitudes of the relationships between variables, and still others for making predictions. The techniques also involve different assumptions, and some techniques can withstand violations of the underlying assumptions better than others. A classification of statistical techniques is presented in the next section.

Finally, the researcher's background and philosophy affect the choice of a data analysis strategy. The experienced, statistically trained researcher will employ a range of techniques, including advanced statistical methods. Researchers differ in their willingness to make assumptions about the variables and their underlying populations. Researchers who are conservative about making assumptions will limit their choice of techniques to distribution-free methods. In general, several techniques may be appropriate for analyzing the data from a given project. We use the department store patronage project for illustration.

DEPARTMENT STORE PATRONAGE PROJECT
Data Analysis Strategy

As part of the analysis conducted in the department store project, store choice was modeled in terms of store image characteristics or the factors influencing the choice criteria. The sample was split into halves. The respondents in each half were clustered on the basis of the importance attached to the store image characteristics. Statistical tests for clusters were conducted, and four segments were identified. Store preference was modeled in terms of the evaluations of the stores on the image variables. The model was estimated separately for each segment. Differences between segment preference functions were statistically tested. Finally, model verification and cross-validation were conducted for each segment. The data analysis strategy adopted is depicted in the following.[15] ◆

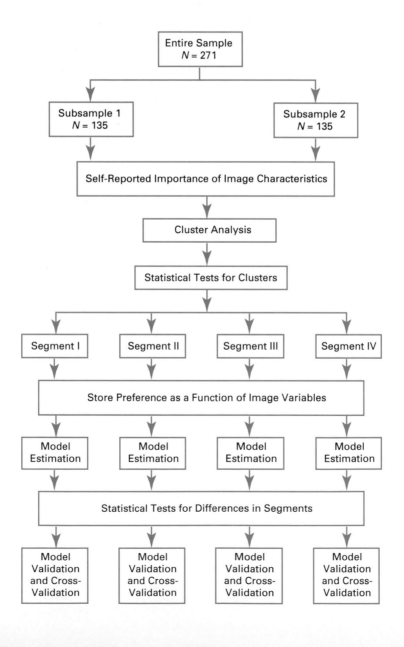

A CLASSIFICATION OF STATISTICAL TECHNIQUES

univariate techniques
Statistical techniques appropriate for analyzing data when there is a single measurement of each element in the sample, or, if there are several measurements on each element, when each variable is analyzed in isolation.

multivariate techniques
Statistical techniques suitable for analyzing data when there are two or more measurements on each element and the variables are analyzed simultaneously. Multivariate techniques are concerned with the simultaneous relationships among two or more phenomena.

metric data Data that are interval or ratio in nature.

nonmetric data Data derived from a nominal or ordinal scale.

Statistical techniques can be classified as univariate or multivariate. **Univariate techniques** are appropriate when there is a single measurement of each element in the sample or when there are several measurements of each element but each variable is analyzed in isolation. **Multivariate techniques**, on the other hand, are suitable for analyzing data when there are two or more measurements of each element and the variables are analyzed simultaneously. Multivariate techniques are concerned with the simultaneous relationships among two or more phenomena. Multivariate techniques differ from univariate techniques in that they shift the focus away from the levels (averages) and distributions (variances) of the phenomena, concentrating instead on the degree of relationships (correlations or covariances) among these phenomena.[16] The univariate and multivariate techniques are described in detail in subsequent chapters, but here we show how the various techniques relate to each other in an overall scheme of classification.

Univariate techniques can be further classified based on whether the data are metric or nonmetric. **Metric data** are measured on an interval or ratio scale, whereas **nonmetric data** are measured on a nominal or ordinal scale. For metric data, when there is only one sample, the z test and the t test can be used. When there are two or more independent samples, the z test and t test can be used for two samples, and one-way analysis of variance (one-way ANOVA) can be used for more than two samples. In the case of two or more related samples, the paired t test can be used. For nonmetric data involving a single sample, frequency distribution, chi-square, Kolmogorov-Smirnov (K-S), runs, and binomial tests can be used. For two independent samples with nonmetric data, the chi-square, Mann-Whitney, Median, K-S, and Kruskal-Wallis one-way analysis of variance (K-W ANOVA) can be used. In contrast, when there are two or more related samples, the sign, McNemar, and Wilcoxon tests should be used. (See Figure 14.6.)

FIGURE 14.6

A Classification of Univariate Techniques

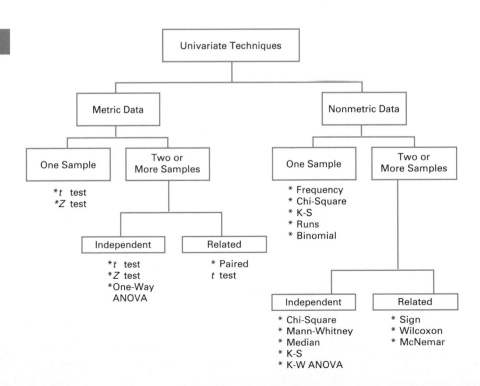

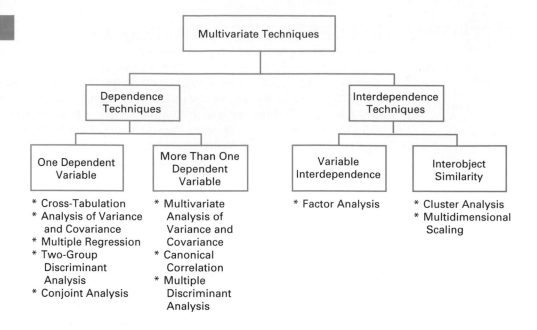

FIGURE 14.7

A Classification of Multivariate Techniques

dependence techniques
Multivariate techniques appropriate when one or more of the variables can be identified as dependent variables and the remaining as independent variables.

Multivariate statistical techniques can be classified as dependence techniques or interdependence techniques (see Figure 14.7). **Dependence techniques** are appropriate when one or more variables can be identified as dependent variables and the remaining as independent variables. When there is only one dependent variable, cross-tabulation, analysis of variance and covariance, regression, two-group discriminant analysis, and conjoint analysis can be used. If there is more than one dependent variable, however, the appropriate techniques are multivariate analysis of variance and covariance, canonical correlation, and multiple discriminant analysis. In **interdependence techniques**, the variables are not classified as dependent or independent; rather, the whole set of interdependent relationships is examined. These techniques focus on either variable interdependence or interobject similarity. The major technique for examining variable interdependence is factor analysis. Analysis of interobject similarity can be conducted by cluster analysis and multidimensional scaling.[17]

INTERNATIONAL MARKETING RESEARCH

interdependence techniques Multivariate statistical techniques that attempt to group data based on underlying similarity and thus allow for interpretation of the data structures. No distinction is made as to which variables are dependent and which are independent.

Before analyzing the data, the researcher should ensure that the units of measurement are comparable across countries or cultural units. For example, the data may have to be adjusted to establish currency equivalents or metric equivalents. Furthermore, standardization or normalization of the data may be necessary to make meaningful comparisons and achieve consistent results.

EXAMPLE
A Worldwide Scream for Ice Cream

Haagen-Dazs, the hyperrich U.S. ice cream, is the latest hot U.S. export. Its sales in Asia doubled to $120 million since 1989 and zoomed to $30 million from $2 million in just two years in Britain, France, and Germany. By 1995, consumers worldwide were licking up

$1 billion worth of Haagen-Dazs products annually. Over half the sales were coming from the international market. How did this come about? The strategy for whetting foreign appetites is simple. Marketing research conducted in several European countries (e.g., Britain, France, and Germany) and several Asian countries (e.g., Japan, Singapore, and Taiwan) revealed that consumers were hungry for a high-quality ice cream with premium image and were willing to pay a premium price for it. These consistent findings emerged after the price of ice cream in each country was standardized to have a mean of zero and a standard deviation of unity. Standardization was desirable because the prices were specified in different local currencies and a common basis was needed for comparison across countries. Also, in each country, the premium price had to be defined in relation to the prices of competing brands. Standardization accomplished both these objectives.

Based on these findings, Haagen-Dazs first introduced the brand at a few high-end retailers; it then built company-owned stores in high-traffic areas; and finally it rolled into convenience stores and supermarkets. It maintained the premium quality brand name by starting first with few high-end retailers. It also supplied free freezers to retailers. Hungry for quality product, Britishers shelled out $5 a pint, double or triple the price of home brands. "It is easily the largest selling ice cream shop in the world under a trademark name," says John Riccitiello, senior vice-president for international sales. Back home in the United States, Haagen-Dazs remains popular, although faced with intense competition and a health-conscious market. This added to the impetus to enter the foreign markets.[18] ◆

Appropriate transformation and analysis of data collected in several countries have enabled Haagen-Dazs to effectively market its products worldwide. ◆ Jesper Westley Jorgensen/ Haagen-Dazs.

Data analysis could be conducted at three levels: (1) individual, (2) within country or cultural unit, and (3) across countries or cultural units. Individual level analysis requires that the data from each respondent be analyzed separately. For example, one might compute a correlation coefficient or run a regression analysis for each respondent. This means that enough data must be obtained from each individual to allow analysis at the individual level, which is often not feasible. Yet it has been argued that in international marketing or cross-cultural research, the researcher should possess a sound knowledge of the consumer in each culture. This can best be accomplished by individual level analysis.[19]

In within-country or cultural unit analysis, the data are analyzed separately for each country or cultural unit. This is also referred to as **intracultural analysis**. This level of analysis is quite similar to that conducted in domestic marketing research. The objective is to gain an understanding of the relationships and patterns existing in each country or cultural unit. In across-countries analysis, the data of all the countries are analyzed simultaneously. Two approaches to this method are possible. The data for all respondents from all the countries can be pooled and analyzed. This is referred to as **pan-cultural analysis**. Alternatively, the data can be aggregated for each country, and then these aggregate statistics can be analyzed. For example, one could compute means of variables for each country, and then compute correlations on these means. This is referred to as **cross-cultural analysis**. The objective of this level of analysis is to assess the comparability of findings from one country to another. The similarities as well as the differences between countries should be investigated. When examining differences, not only differences in means but also differences in variance and distribution should be assessed. All the statistical techniques that have been discussed in this book can be applied to within-country or across-country analysis and, subject to the amount of data available, to individual-level analysis as well.[20]

intracultural analysis
Within-country analysis of international data.

pan-cultural analysis
Across-countries analysis in which the data for all respondents from all the countries are pooled and analyzed.

cross-cultural analysis A type of across countries analysis in which the data could be aggregated for each country and then these aggregate statistics could be analyzed.

ETHICS IN MARKETING RESEARCH

New ethical issues can arise during the data preparation and analysis step of the marketing research process. While checking, editing, coding, transcribing, and cleaning, researchers can get some idea about the quality of the data. Sometimes it is easy to identify respondents who did not take the questionnaire seriously or who otherwise provided data of questionable quality. Consider, for example, a respondent who checks the "neither agree nor disagree" response to all the 20 items measuring attitude toward spectator sports. Decisions whether such respondents should be discarded—not included in the analysis—can raise ethical concerns. A good rule of thumb is to make such decisions during the data preparation phase before conducting any analysis.

In contrast, suppose that the researcher conducted the analysis without first attempting to identify unsatisfactory responses. The analysis, however, does not reveal the expected relationship; the analysis does not show that attitude toward spectator sports influences attendance of spectator sports. The researcher then decides to examine the quality of data obtained. In checking the questionnaires, a few respondents with unsatisfactory data are identified. These respondents are eliminated and the reduced data set analyzed to obtain the expected results. Discarding respondents after analyzing the data raises ethical concerns, particularly if the report does not state that the initial analysis was inconclusive. Moreover, the procedure used to identify unsatisfactory respondents and the number of respondents discarded should be clearly disclosed, as in the following example.

EXAMPLE
Elimination of Decision Makers Unwilling to be Ethical
In a study of MBA's responses to marketing ethics dilemmas, respondents were required to respond to fourteen questions regarding ethically ambiguous scenarios by writing a

simple sentence regarding what action they would take if they were the manager. The responses were then analyzed to determine if the respondent's response was indicative of ethical behavior. However, in the data preparation phase, six respondents out of the 561 total respondents were eliminated from further analysis because their responses indicated that they did not follow the directions which told them to state clearly their choice of action. This is an example of ethical editing of the data. The criterion for unsatisfactory responses is clearly stated, the unsatisfactory respondents are identified before the analysis, and the number of respondents eliminated is disclosed.[21] ◆

While analyzing the data, the researcher may also have to deal with ethical issues. The assumptions underlying the statistical techniques used to analyze the data must be satisfied to obtain meaningful results. For example, the error terms in bivariate regression must be normally distributed about zero, with a constant variance, and be uncorrelated (Chapter 17). The researcher has the responsibility to test these assumptions and take appropriate corrective actions if necessary. The appropriateness of the statistical techniques used for analysis should be discussed when presenting the results. When this is not done, ethical questions can be raised. The American Marketing Association's code of ethics clearly states, "There will be no intentional or deliberate misrepresentation of research methods or results."[22]

The last ethical concern relates to interpretation of the results, drawing conclusions, and making recommendations. "There are few fields of scientific activity that are as susceptible to fraud as some aspects of consumer research. In many cases, what is really being paid for by a client is an interpretation of detailed data; the temptations that beset the researcher in such a situation are very real."[23] While interpretations, conclusions, and recommendations necessarily involve the subjective judgment of the researcher, this judgment must be exercised honestly, free from personal biases or agendas of the researcher or the client.

COMPUTER APPLICATIONS

Several microcomputer and mainframe programs are available to assist in data preparation. For example, PCPUNCH by Pros and Cons, Inc. of Bethesda, Maryland, is a data preparation program for the IBM PC that permits data entry, consistency checks, assignment of missing values, statistical adjustments to the data, and basic data analysis. Out-of-range checks and logical-inconsistency checks can be preprogrammed. Hence, these types of errors can be detected while the data are being keypunched. This not only reduces keypunching errors but also facilitates corrective action.

PCPUNCH facilitates the data entry process by presenting "fill-in-the-blank" screens to data entry personnel. It includes a programming logic so that certain responses to designated blanks will result in a branching to additional screens for data entry. In addition, it provides supervisors with work summaries for data entry employees. The project organizer prepares for data entry by using the menus of PCPUNCH to enter the specifications for the data matrix. As in the use of database programs, "fields" correspond to question responses and "records" correspond to subjects or questionnaires. To set up the project, the organizer designates field type (e.g., alphanumeric, numeric), field width (i.e., number of digits), value ranges, and any logic required during field specification.

For ease of data entry, PCPUNCH moves the cursor on the data entry screen to the next entry blank after each keystroke. During data entry, PCPUNCH also checks for out-of-range values and improper field types. The program alerts the operator of these errors. The project organizer can program the automatic save feature of PCPUNCH to save work after every second or after intervals spanning minutes or hours. PCPUNCH can also save after each record (questionnaire) is entered or after many records are entered (i.e., 99).

To check the accuracy of the data entered, PCPUNCH provides a verify records option. This feature allows another operator to reenter the data to verify that each field has been correctly entered. If the second operator's entries do not match those of the first, the program signals a discrepancy to the second operator. The second operator could then make sure of the correct entry and could continue until completing an accurate data matrix.

After checking accuracy, PCPUNCH allows the organizer to select certain records, to view the order of data fields, and then to change the order of the data. This permits the rapid manipulation of a data set where some subjects received a different ordering of certain questions. Researchers would induce such alternative ordering to counter the emergence of "order effects" occurring when the brand first presented to subjects might be suspected of receiving more favorable ratings.

Exhibit 14.1 shows the view operator statistics (VOS) screen, which presents the supervisor with the productivity of data entry operators in keystrokes per hour. Here, the job or batch total indicates that the individual operator is making many mistakes at the outset of data entry. In fact, the operator makes more keystrokes in correcting or editing (391), than in adding data to the file (358).

If an operator left the keyboard for more than three minutes, the keyboard time-out feature engages and deducts the lost time from the entry time. PCPUNCH also can present an aggregation of all operators' statistics so as to manage resources for project completion. This "total" function of the VOS brings valuable information to the supervisor and to the organizer for judging if the project requires more workers for timely com-

EXHIBIT 14.1

Viewer Operator Statistics

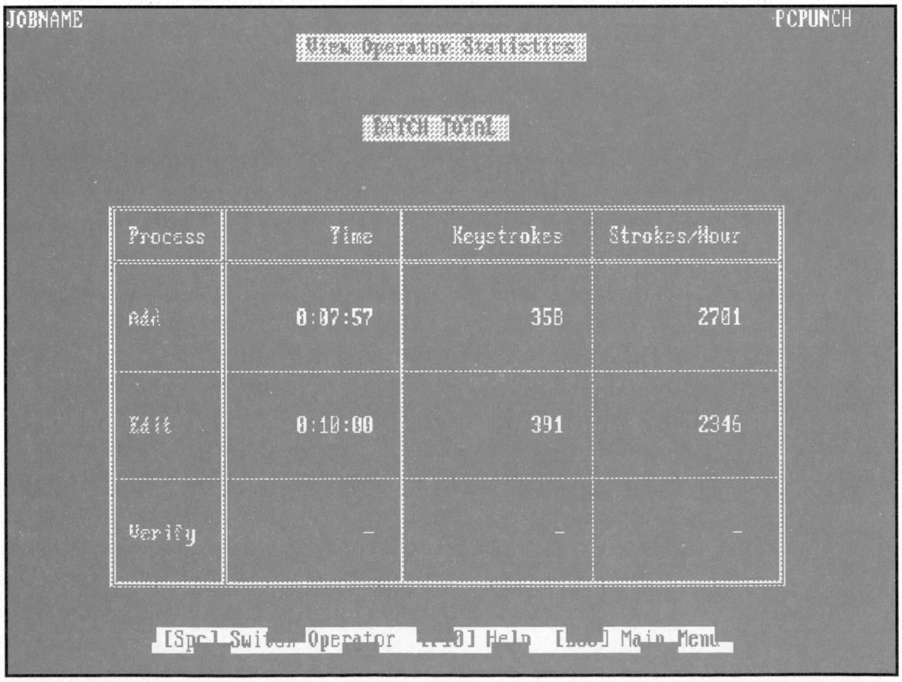

Process	Time	Keystrokes	Strokes/Hour
Add	0:07:57	358	2701
Edit	0:10:00	391	2346
Verify	–	–	–

[Spc] Switch Operator   [..0] Help   [...] Main Menu

pletion. All these features make PCPUNCH a success in automating a formidable labor undertaking in the marketing research process.

Exhibit 14.2 details the use of SPSS, SAS, and BMDP to make consistency checks. These packages also contain options for handling missing responses and for statistically adjusting the data.

SUMMARY

Data preparation begins with a preliminary check of all questionnaires for completeness and interviewing quality. Then more thorough editing takes place. Editing consists of screening questionnaires to identify illegible, incomplete, inconsistent, or ambiguous responses. Such responses may be handled by returning questionnaires to the field, assigning missing values, or discarding the unsatisfactory respondents.

The next step is coding. A numeric or alphanumeric code is assigned to represent a specific response to a specific question along with the column position that code will occupy. It is often helpful to prepare a codebook containing the coding instructions and the necessary information about the variables in the data set. The coded data are transcribed onto disks or magnetic tapes or entered into computers via keypunching. Mark sense forms, optical scanning, or computerized sensory analysis may also be used.[24]

EXHIBIT 14.2

Computer Programs for Data Preparation

Similar programs are available in the mainframe as well as the microcomputer versions of the three packages listed below. Hence, the mainframe versus microcomputer distinction will not be made.

SPSS

Out-of-range values can be selected using the SELECT IF or PROCESS IF statements. These cases, with the identifying information (subject identification, record number, variable name, variable value) can then be printed using the PRINT or WRITE commands. As a further check, the LIST command can be used to display the values of variables for each case. SPSS Data Entry II simplifies the process of entering new data files. It facilitates data cleaning and checking for logical inconsistencies.

SAS

The IF, IF-THEN, and IF-THEN/ELSE statements can be used to select cases with missing or out-of-range values. The select statement executes one of several statements or groups of statements. The LIST statement is useful for printing suspicious input lines. The LOSTCARD statement can be used to identify missing records in the data. The PRINT and PRINTTO procedures can be used to identify cases and to print variable names and variable values. In addition, the OUTPUT and PUT statements can be used to write the values of variables.

BMDP

The TRANSFORM paragraph can be used to select out-of-range cases. The transformation word USE and several functions and logical operators provide powerful selection capabilities. Several programs have special capabilities for listing data. For example, ID can print only cases with missing or out-of-range values, but it can list all the data in such a way that each column contains all the values of one variable. Alternatively, all the variables for one case can be printed before those of the next case. AM can print the positions of the missing and out-of-range values, and 4D can print the data in a compact card image form or print only cases that contain nonnumeric symbols.

Cleaning the data requires consistency checks and treatment of missing responses. Options available for treating missing responses include substitution of a neutral value such as the mean, substitution of an imputed response, casewise deletion, and pairwise deletion. Statistical adjustments such as weighting, variable respecification, and scale transformations often enhance the quality of data analysis. The selection of a data analysis strategy should be based on the earlier steps of the marketing research process, known characteristics of the data, properties of statistical techniques, and the background and philosophy of the researcher. Statistical techniques may be classified as univariate or multivariate.

Before analyzing the data in international marketing research, the researcher should ensure that the units of measurement are comparable across countries or cultural units. The data analysis could be conducted at three levels: (1) individual, (2) within country or cultural unit (intracultural analysis), and (3) across countries or cultural units: pancultural or cross-cultural analysis. Several ethical issues are related to data processing, particularly the discarding of unsatisfactory responses, violation of the assumptions underlying the data analysis techniques, and evaluation and interpretation of results. Microcomputers and mainframes play a significant role in data preparation and analysis.

ACRONYMS

The data preparation process may be summarized by the acronym DATA PREP:

D   ata cleaning
A   djusting the data statistically
T   ranscribing
A   nalysis strategy
P   ost field work questionnaire checking
R   ecording numeric or alphanumeric values: coding
E   diting
P   reliminary plan of data analysis

EXERCISES

QUESTIONS

1. Describe the data preparation process.
2. What activities are involved in the preliminary checking of questionnaires that have been returned from the field?
3. What is meant by editing a questionnaire?
4. How are unsatisfactory responses that are discovered in editing treated?
5. What is the difference between precoding and postcoding?
6. Describe the guidelines for the coding of unstructured questions.
7. What does transcribing the data involve?
8. What kinds of consistency checks are made in cleaning the data?
9. What options are available for the treatment of missing data?
10. What kinds of statistical adjustments are sometimes made to the data?
11. Describe the weighting process. What are the reasons for weighting?
12. What are dummy variables? Why are such variables created?
13. Explain why scale transformations are made.
14. Which scale transformation procedure is most commonly used? Briefly describe this procedure.
15. What considerations are involved in selecting a data analysis strategy?

PROBLEMS

1. Develop dummy variable coding schemes for the following variables.

   • Sex
   • Marital status consisting of the following four categories: never married, now married, divorced, other (separated, widowed, etc.)
   • Frequency of international travel, measured as:

     1. Do not travel abroad
     2. Travel abroad one or two times a year
     3. Travel abroad three to five times a year
     4. Travel abroad six to eight times a year
     5. Travel abroad more than eight times a year

2. Shown below is part of a questionnaire used to determine consumer preferences for cameras. Set up a coding scheme for these three questions.

---

9. Please rate the importance of the following features you would consider when shopping for a new camera.

	Not so important				Very important
a. DX film speed setting	1	2	3	4	5
b. Auto film advance	1	2	3	4	5
c. Autofocus	1	2	3	4	5
d. Autoloading	1	2	3	4	5

10. If you were to buy a new camera, which of the following outlets would you visit? Please check as many as apply.

   a. ____   Drugstore
   b. ____   Camera store
   c. ____   Discount/mass merchandiser
   d. ____   Supermarket
   e. ____   Other

11. Where do you get most of your photo processing done? Please check only one option.

   a. ____   Drugstore
   b. ____   Minilabs
   c. ____   Camera stores
   d. ____   Discount/mass merchandiser
   e. ____   Supermarkets
   f. ____   Mail order
   g. ____   Kiosk/other

COMPUTER EXERCISES

1. Using either SPSS, SAS, or BMDP, write a program to make consistency checks for the questionnaire given in problem 2.
2. Use an electronic questionnaire design and administration package such as Ci3 to program the camera preference questionnaire given in problem 2. Add one or two questions of your

own. Administer the questionnaire to five students and prepare the data for analysis. Does computer administration of the questionnaire facilitate data preparation?

NOTES

1. Joann Harristhal, "Interviewer Tips," *Applied Marketing Research*, 28 (Fall 1988): 42–45.
2. Kofi Q. Dadzie, "Demarketing Strategy in Shortage Marketing Environment," *Journal of the Academy of Marketing Science* (Spring 1989): 157–65.
3. For a detailed discussion of coding, see Philip S. Sidel, "Coding," in Robert Ferber (ed.), *Handbook of Marketing Research* (New York: McGraw-Hill, 1974), pp. 2-178–2-199.
4. Pamela L. Alreck and Robert B. Settle, *The Survey Research Handbook* (Homewood, IL: Richard D. Irwin, 1985), pp. 254–86.
5. The American Lawyer, *The American Lawyer Subscriber Study*, 1987.
6. J. Pope, *Practical Marketing Research* (New York: AMACOM, 1981), pp. 89–90.
7. The American Lawyer, *The American Lawyer Subscriber Study*, 1987.
8. For mainframe packages, see:

   SPSS Base Systems User's Guide (Englewood Cliffs, NJ: Prentice Hall, 1994).

   SAS Language and Procedure: Usage, V 6 (Cary, NC: SAS Institute, 1989).

   SAS Language and Procedure: Usage 2, V 6 (Cary, NC: SAS Institute, 1991).

   SAS Procedures Guide, V 6, 3rd ed. (Cary, NC: SAS Institute, 1990).

   SAS Language: Reference, V 6 (Cary, NC: SAS Institute, 1990).

   BMDP Statistical Software Manual, vols. 1 and 2 (Berkeley: University of California Press, 1990).

   For microcomputer packages, see:

   SPSS/PC+™ V 4.0 BASE MANUAL (Englewood Cliffs, NJ: Prentice Hall, 1990).

   SPSS/PC+ Advanced Statistics™, V 4.0 (Englewood Cliffs, NJ: Prentice Hall, 1990).

   SAS/STAT™ User Guide, V 6, 4th ed., vols. 1 and 2 (Cary, NC: SAS Institute, 1990).

   The BMDP manual for microcomputers is the same as that for the mainframe.
9. Naresh K. Malhotra, "Analyzing Marketing Research Data with Incomplete Information on the Dependent Variable," *Journal of Marketing Research* 24 (February 1987): 74–84.
10. A meaningful and practical value should be imputed. The value imputed should be a legitimate response code. For example, a mean of 3.86 may not be practical if only single-digit response codes have been developed. In such cases, the mean should be rounded to the nearest integer.
11. Naresh K. Malhotra, "Analyzing Marketing Research Data with Incomplete Information on the Dependent Variable," *Journal of Marketing Research* 4 (February 1987): 74–84.
12. Some weighting procedures require adjustments in subsequent data analysis techniques. See Trevor Sharot, "Weighting Survey Results," *Journal of the Market Research Society* (UK) 28 (July 1986): 269–84; and Martin R. Frankel, *Inference from Survey Samples* (Ann Arbor: Institute for Social Research, University of Michigan, 1971).
13. Arch G. Woodside, Robert L. Nielsen, Fred Walters, and Gale D. Muller, "Preference Segmentation of Health Care Services: The Old-Fashioneds, Value Conscious, Affluents, and Professional Want-It-Alls," *Journal of Health Care Marketing* (June 1988): 14–24.
14. See Ronald E. Frank, "Use of Transformations," *Journal of Marketing Research* (August 1966): 247–53, for specific transformations frequently used in marketing research.
15. For a similar data analysis strategy, see Naresh K. Malhotra, "Modeling Store Choice Based on Censored Preference Data," *Journal of Retailing* (Summer 1986): 128–44.
16. Bivariate techniques have been included here with multivariate techniques. Although bivariate techniques are concerned with pairwise relationships, multivariate techniques examine more complex simultaneous relationships among phenomena. See Jagdish N. Sheth, "What Is Multivariate Analysis?" in Jagdish N. Sheth (ed.), *Multivariate Methods for Market and Survey Research* (Chicago: American Marketing Association, 1977).
17. Paul E. Green, *Analyzing Multivariate Data* (Hinsdale, IL: Dryden Press, 1978).
18. Mark Maremont, "They're All Screaming for Haagen-Dazs," *Business Week* (October 14, 1991).
19. C. T. Tan, J. McCullough, and J. Teoh, "An Individual Analysis Approach to Cross-Cultural Research," in Melanie Wallendorf and Paul Anderson (eds.), *Advances in Consumer Research*, vol. 14 (Provo, UT: Association for Consumer Research, 1987): 394–97.

20. See, for example, Lisa D. Spiller and Alexander J. Campbell, "The Use of International Direct Marketing by Small Businesses in Canada, Mexico, and the United States: A Comparative Analysis," *Journal of Direct Marketing* 8 (Winter 1994): 7–16; and Meee-Kau Nyaw and Ignace Ng, "A Comparative Analysis of Ethical Beliefs: A Four Country Study," *Journal of Business Ethics*, 13 (July 1994): 543–56.

21. G. M. Zinkhan, M. Bisesi, and M. J. Saxton, "MBAs' Changing Attitudes toward Marketing Dilemmas: 1981–1987," *Journal of Business Ethics* 8 (1989): 963–74.

22. As given in Appendix 3A of Gene R. Laczniak and Patrick E. Murphy, *Ethical Marketing Decisions: The Higher Road* (Needham Heights, MA: Allyn & Bacon, 1993), pp. 76-7.

23. R. L. Day, "A Comment on Ethics in Marketing Research," *Journal of Marketing Research* 12 (1974): 232–33.

24. The assistance of James Agarwal with the international marketing research example, the assistance of Mark Leach and Gina Miller in writing the ethics section, and the assistance of Mark Peterson in writing the computer applications section is gratefully acknowledged.

CHAPTER FIFTEEN

Frequency Distribution, Cross-Tabulation, and Hypothesis Testing

Frequency distribution, cross-tabulation, and hypothesis testing provide valuable insights into the data and guide the rest of the data analysis as well as the interpretation of the results.

OBJECTIVES

At the end of this chapter, the student should be able to:

1. Describe the significance of preliminary data analysis and the insights that can be obtained from such an analysis.
2. Discuss data analysis associated with frequencies including measures of location, measures of variability, and measures of shape.
3. Explain data analysis associated with cross-tabulations and the associated statistics: chi-square, phi coefficient, contingency coefficient, Cramer's V, and lambda coefficient.
4. Describe data analysis associated with parametric hypothesis testing for one sample, two independent samples, and paired samples.
5. Understand data analysis associated with nonparametric hypothesis testing for one sample, two independent samples, and paired samples.

OVERVIEW

Once the data have been prepared for analysis (Chapter 14), the researcher should conduct some basic analysis. This chapter describes basic data analysis including frequency distribution, cross-tabulation, and hypothesis testing. First, we describe the frequency distribution and explain how it provides both an indication of the number of out-of-range, missing, or extreme values as well as insights into the central tendency, variability, and shape of the underlying distribution. Next, we introduce hypothesis testing by describing the general procedure. Hypothesis testing procedures are classified as tests of associations or tests of differences. We consider the use of cross-tabulation for understanding the associations between variables taken two or three at a time. Although the nature of the association can be observed from tables, statistics are available for examining the significance and strength of the association. Finally, we present tests for examining hypotheses related to differences based on one or two samples.

Many commercial marketing research projects do not go beyond basic data analysis. These findings are often displayed using tables and graphs, as discussed further in Chapter 22. Although the findings of basic analysis are valuable in their own right, they also provide guidance for conducting multivariate analysis. The insights gained from the basic analysis are also invaluable in interpreting the results obtained from more sophisticated statistical techniques. To provide the reader with a flavor of these techniques, we illustrate the use of cross-tabulation, chi-square analysis, and hypothesis testing.

DEPARTMENT STORE PATRONAGE PROJECT
Basic Data Analysis

In the department store patronage project, basic data analysis formed the foundation for conducting subsequent multivariate analysis. Data analysis began by obtaining a frequency distribution and descriptive statistics for each variable. In addition to identifying possible problems with the data (see Chapter 14), this information provided a good idea of the data and insights into how specific variables should be treated in subsequent analyses. For example, should some variables be treated as categorical, and if so, how many categories should there be? Several two- and three-variable cross-tabulations were also conducted to identify associations in the data. The effects of variables with two categories on the metric dependent variables of interest were examined by means of *t* tests and other hypotheses testing procedures. ◆

EXAMPLE
Commercial Battle of the Sexes

A comparison of television advertising in Australia, Mexico, and the United States focused on the analysis of sex roles in advertising. Results showed differences in the portrayal of the sexes in different countries. Australian advertisements revealed somewhat fewer, and Mexican advertisements slightly more, sex-role differences than U.S. advertisements. Cross-tabulation and chi-square analysis provided the following information for Mexico.

Product Advertised Used by	Persons Appearing in the Ad (%):	
	Women	Men
Females	25.0	4.0
Males	6.8	11.8
Either	68.2	84.2
	$\chi^2 = 19.73, p \leq .001$	

In the United States, men appear in commercials for products used by either sex. ◆ PepsiCo Inc.

These results indicate that in Mexican commercials, women appeared in commercials for products used by women or by either sex but rarely in commercials for men's products. Men appeared in commercials for products used by either sex. These differences were also found in the U.S. ads, although to a lesser extent, but were not found in Australian ads.[1] ◆

EXAMPLE
Catalogs Are Risky Business

Twelve product categories were examined to compare catalog with store shopping. The hypothesis that there is no significant difference in the overall amount of risk perceived when buying products by catalog compared with buying the same products in a retail store was rejected. The hypothesis was tested by computing 12 (one for each product) paired-observations *t* tests. Mean scores for overall perceived risk for some of the products in both buying situations are presented in the following table, with higher scores indicating greater risk.

Mean Scores of Overall Perceived Risk for Products by Purchase Mode

Product	OVERALL PERCEIVED RISK	
	Catalog	Retail Store
Stereo hi-fi	48.89	41.98[a]
Record albums	32.65	28.74[a]
Dress shoes	58.60	50.80[a]
13-inch color TV	48.53	40.91[a]
Athletic socks	35.22	30.22[a]
Pocket calculator	49.62	42.00[a]
35-mm camera	48.13	39.52[a]
Perfume	34.85	29.79[a]

[a] Significant at .01 level.

Despite the risk involved, the popularity of catalog shopping is increasing due to convenience and time savings. ◆ Teri Stratford.

As can be seen, a significantly ($p < .01$) higher overall amount of perceived risk was attached to products purchased by catalog as compared with those purchased from a retail store.[2] ◆

The department store example illustrates the role of basic data analysis used in conjunction with multivariate procedures, whereas the other two examples show how such analysis can be useful in its own right. The cross-tabulation and chi-square analysis in the international television advertising example and the paired t tests in the catalog shopping example enabled us to draw specific conclusions from the data. Before these types of conclusions are drawn, it is useful to examine the frequency distributions of the relevant variables.

FREQUENCY DISTRIBUTION

Marketing researchers often need to answer questions about a single variable. For example:

- How many users of the brand may be characterized as brand loyal?
- What percentage of the market consists of heavy users, medium users, light users, and nonusers?
- How many customers are very familiar with a new product offering? How many are familiar, somewhat familiar, or unfamiliar with the brand? What is the mean familiarity rating? Is there much variance in the extent to which customers are familiar with the new product?
- What is the income distribution of brand users? Is this distribution skewed toward low-income brackets?

frequency distribution
A mathematical distribution whose objective is to obtain a count of the number of responses associated with different values of one variable and to express these counts in percentage terms.

The answers to these kinds of questions can be determined by examining frequency distributions. In a **frequency distribution**, one variable is considered at a time.

The objective is to obtain a count of the number of responses associated with different values of the variable. The relative occurrence, or frequency, of different values of the variable is expressed in percentages. A frequency distribution for a variable produces a table of frequency counts, percentages, and cumulative percentages for all the values associated with that variable.

Table 15.1 gives the frequency distribution of familiarity with a national department store chain based on data obtained in the department store study. These data were collected using a six-point Likert type scale (1 = not so familiar, 6 = very familiar). In the table, the first column contains the labels assigned to the different categories of the variable and the second column indicates the codes assigned to each value. Note that a code of 9 has been assigned to missing values. The third column gives the number of respondents checking each value. For example, 62 respondents checked value 6, indicating that they were very familiar with this store. The fourth column displays the percentage of respondents checking each value. The next column shows percentages calculated by excluding the cases with missing values. If there are no missing values, columns 4 and 5 are identical. The last column represents cumulative percentages after adjusting for missing cases. As can be seen, of the 271 respondents who participated in the survey, 19.2% checked value 3. If the one respondent with a missing value is excluded, this percentage changes to 19.3. The cumulative percentage corresponding to the value of 3 is 47.8. In other words, 47.8% of the respondents with valid responses indicated a value of 3 or less.

A frequency distribution helps determine the extent of item nonresponse (1 respondent out of 271 in Table 15.1). It also indicates the extent of illegitimate responses. Values of 0, 7, and 8 would be illegitimate responses, or errors. The cases with these values could be identified and corrective action could be taken. The presence of outliers or cases with extreme values can also be detected. In the case of a frequency distribution of household size, a few isolated families with household sizes of 9 or more might be considered outliers. A frequency distribution also indicates the shape of the empirical distribution of the variable. The frequency data may be used to construct a histogram, or a vertical bar chart in which the values of the variable are portrayed along the x axis and the absolute or relative frequencies of the values are placed along the y axis. Figure 15.1 is a histogram of the frequency data in Table 15.1. From the histogram, one could examine whether the observed distribution is consistent with an expected or assumed distribution. For further illustration, consider the following example.

TABLE 15.1 *Frequency Distribution of Familiarity with a National Department Store Chain*	Value Label	Value	Frequency (N)	Percentage	Valid Percentage	Cumulative Percentage
	Not so familiar	1	36	13.3	13.3	13.3
		2	41	15.1	15.2	28.5
		3	52	19.2	19.3	47.8
		4	43	15.9	15.9	63.7
		5	36	13.3	13.3	77.0
	Very familiar	6	62	22.9	23.0	100.0
		9	1	0.4	MISSING	
		TOTAL	271	100.1	100.0	

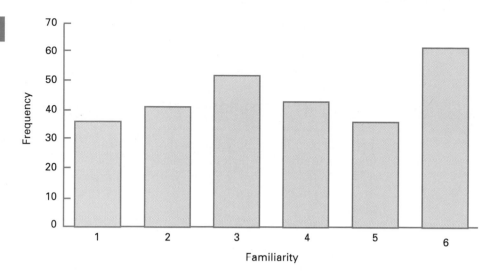

FIGURE 15.1

*Frequency
of Familiarity
with a National
Department Store
Chain*

EXAMPLE
Advertising's Ethical Dilemmas

In a survey of ethical issues, advertising executives were asked to describe the most difficult ethical or moral problem confronting them in their daily work. A frequency distribution indicated that the most often reported ethical problem was (1) treating our clients fairly, followed by (2) creating honest, nonmisleading, socially desirable advertisements; (3) representing clients whose product or services are unhealthy, unneeded, useless, or unethical; (4) treating suppliers, vendors, and media fairly; (5) treating employees and managers fairly; and (6) treating other agencies fairly.[3]

Ethical Problems of Advertising Agency Executives

Problem	Responses No	Percent
1. Treating clients fairly	80	28
2. Creating honest, nonmisleading, socially desirable advertisements	66	24
3. Representing clients whose products or services are unhealthy, unneeded, useless, or unethical	34	12
4. Treating suppliers, vendors, and media fairly	25	9
5. Treating employees and managers fairly	15	5
6. Treating other agencies fairly	7	3
7. Other	11	4
8. None	43	15
TOTAL	281	100%

The most frequently reported ethical problem facing advertising executives is treating clients fairly.◆ Matt Meadows.

The numbers and percentages in the preceding example indicate the extent of the various ethical problems. Because numbers are involved, a frequency distribution can be used to calculate descriptive or summary statistics. We discuss some of the statistics associated with frequency distribution in the next section.

STATISTICS ASSOCIATED WITH FREQUENCY DISTRIBUTION

As illustrated in the previous section, a frequency distribution is a convenient way of looking at different values of a variable. A frequency table is easy to read and provides basic information, but sometimes this information may be too detailed and the researcher must summarize it by the use of descriptive statistics.[4] The most commonly used statistics associated with frequencies are measures of location (mean, mode, and median), measures of variability (range, interquartile range, standard deviation, and coefficient of variation), and measures of shape (skewness and kurtosis).[5]

Measures of Location

measures of location A statistic that describes a location within a data set. Measures of central tendency describe the center of the distribution.

mean The average; that value obtained by summing all elements in a set and dividing by the number of elements.

The **measures of location** that we discuss are measures of central tendency because they tend to describe the center of the distribution. If the entire sample is changed by adding a fixed constant to each observation, then the mean, mode, and median change by the same fixed amount.

Mean   The **mean**, or average value, is the most commonly used measure of central tendency. It is used to estimate the mean when the data have been collected using an interval or ratio scale. The data should display some central tendency, with most of the responses distributed around the mean.

The mean, $\overline{X}$, is given by

$$\overline{X} = \frac{\sum_{i=1}^{n} X_i}{n}$$

where

$$X_i = \text{observed values of the variable X}$$
$$n = \text{number of observations (sample size)}$$

Generally, the mean is a robust measure and does not change markedly as data values are added or deleted. For the frequencies given in Table 15.1, the mean value is calculated as follows:

$$\overline{X} = \frac{36 \times 1 + 41 \times 2 + 52 \times 3 + 43 \times 4 + 36 \times 5 + 62 \times 6}{270}$$

$$= \frac{36 + 82 + 156 + 172 + 180 + 372}{270}$$

$$= \frac{998}{270}$$

$$= 3.696$$

Mode   The **mode** is the value that occurs most frequently. It represents the highest peak of the distribution. The mode is a good measure of location when the variable is inherently categorical or has otherwise been grouped into categories. The mode in Table 15.1 is 6.000.

Median   The **median** of a sample is the middle value when the data are arranged in ascending or descending order. If the number of data points is even, the median is usually estimated as the midpoint between the two middle values by adding the two middle values and dividing their sum by 2. The median is the 50th percentile. The median is an appropriate measure of central tendency for ordinal data. In Table 15.1, the two middle values are both 4.000, so the median is 4.000.

As can be seen from Table 15.1, the three measures of central tendency for this distribution are different (mean = 3.696, mode = 6.000, median = 4.000). This is not surprising, since each measure defines central tendency in a different way. So which measure should be used? If the variable is measured on a nominal scale, the mode should be used. If the variable is measured on an ordinal scale, the median is appropriate. If the variable is measured on an interval or ratio scale, the mode is a poor measure of central tendency. This can be seen from Table 15.1. Although the modal value of 6.000 has the highest frequency, it represents only 23% of the sample. In general, for interval or ratio data, the median is a better measure of central tendency, although it too ignores available information about the variable. The actual values of the variable above and below the median are ignored. The mean is the most appropriate measure of central tendency for interval or ratio data. The mean makes use of all the information available since all of the values are used in computing it. The mean, however, is sensitive to extremely small or extremely large values (outliers). When there are outliers in the data, the mean is not a good measure of central tendency, and it is useful to consider both the mean and the median.

Measures of Variability

The **measures of variability**, which are calculated on interval or ratio data, include the range, interquartile range, variance or standard deviation, and coefficient of variation.

Range   The **range** measures the spread of the data. It is simply the difference between the largest and smallest values in the sample

$$range = X_{largest} - X_{smallest}$$

As such, the range is directly affected by outliers. If all the values in the data are multiplied by a constant, the range is multiplied by the same constant. The range in Table 15.1 is 6 − 1 = 5.000.

Interquartile Range   The **interquartile range** is the difference between the 75th and 25th percentile. For a set of data points arranged in order of magnitude, the pth percentile is the value that has $p\%$ of the data points below it and $(100 - p)\%$ above it. If all the data points are multiplied by a constant, the interquartile range is multiplied by the same constant. The interquartile range in Table 15.1 is 5 − 2 = 3.000.

Variance and Standard Deviation   The difference between the mean and an observed value is called the deviation from the mean. The **variance** is the mean squared deviation

mode A measure of central tendency given as the value that occurs the most in a sample distribution.

median A measure of central tendency given as the value above which half of the values fall and below which half of the values fall.

measures of variability A statistic that indicates the distribution's dispersion.

range The difference between the smallest and largest values of a distribution.

interquartile range The range of a distribution encompassing the middle 50% of the observations.

variance The mean squared deviation of all the values from the mean.

from the mean. The variance can never be negative. When the data points are clustered around the mean, the variance is small. When the data points are scattered, the variance is large. If all the data values are multiplied by a constant, the variance is multiplied by the square of the constant. The **standard deviation** is the square root of the variance. Thus, the standard deviation is expressed in the same units as the data, rather than in squared units.

standard deviation The square root of the variance.

The standard deviation of a sample, s_x, is calculated as

$$s_x = \sqrt{\sum_{i=1}^{n} \frac{(X_i - \overline{X})^2}{n-1}}$$

We divide by $n - 1$ instead of n because the sample is drawn from a population and we are trying to determine how much the responses vary from the mean of the entire population. The population mean is unknown, however; therefore, the sample mean is used instead. The use of the sample mean makes the sample seem less variable than it really is. By dividing by $n - 1$ instead of by n, we compensate for the smaller variability observed in the sample. For the data given in Table 15.1, the variance is calculated as follows:

$$
\begin{aligned}
s_x^2 &= \frac{\{36 \times (1 - 3.696)^2 + 41 \times (2 - 3.696)^2 + 52 \times (3 - 3.696)^2 + 43 \times (4 - 3.696)^2 + 36 \times (5 - 3.696)^2 + 62 \times (6 - 3.696)^2\}}{269} \\
&= \frac{261.663 + 117.933 + 25.190 + 3.974 + 61.215 + 329.12}{269} \\
&= \frac{799.097}{269} \\
&= 2.971
\end{aligned}
$$

The standard deviation, therefore, is calculated as

$$
\begin{aligned}
s_x &= \sqrt{2.971} \\
&= 1.724
\end{aligned}
$$

coefficient of variation A useful expression in sampling theory for the standard deviation as a percentage of the mean.

Coefficient of Variation   The **coefficient of variation** is the ratio of the standard deviation to the mean expressed as a percentage, and it is a unitless measure of relative variability. The coefficient of variation, CV, is expressed as

$$CV = \frac{s_x}{\overline{X}}$$

The coefficient of variation is meaningful only if the variable is measured on a ratio scale. It remains unchanged if all the data values are multiplied by a constant. Since the data in Table 15.1 are not measured on a ratio scale, it is not meaningful to calculate the coefficient of variation.

Measures of Shape

In addition to measures of variability, measures of shape are also useful in understanding the nature of the distribution. The shape of a distribution is assessed by examining skewness and kurtosis.

Skewness   Distributions can be either symmetric or skewed. In a symmetric distribution, the values on either side of the center of the distribution are the same, and the mean, mode, and median are equal. The positive and corresponding negative deviations from the mean are also equal. In a skewed distribution, the positive and negative deviations from the mean are unequal. **Skewness** is the tendency of the deviations from the mean to be larger in one direction than in the other. It can be thought of as the tendency for one tail of the distribution to be heavier than the other (see Figure 15.2). The skewness value for the data of Table 15.1 is –0.062, indicating a slight negative skew.

skewness A characteristic of a distribution that assesses its symmetry about the mean.

Kurtosis   **Kurtosis** is a measure of the relative peakedness or flatness of the curve defined by the frequency distribution. The kurtosis of a normal distribution is zero. If the kurtosis is positive, then the distribution is more peaked than a normal distribution. A negative value means that the distribution is flatter than a normal distribution. The value of this statistic for Table 15.1 is –1.265, indicating that the distribution is flatter than a normal distribution.

kurtosis A measure of the relative peakedness of the curve defined by the frequency distribution.

INTRODUCTION TO HYPOTHESIS TESTING

This section provides an introduction to hypothesis testing. Basic analysis invariably involves some hypothesis testing. Examples of hypotheses generated in marketing research abound:

- A department store is being patronized by more than 10% of the households.
- The heavy and light users of a brand differ in terms of psychographic characteristics.
- One hotel has a more upscale image than its close competitor.
- Familiarity with a restaurant results in greater preference for that restaurant.

FIGURE 15.2

Skewness of a Distribution

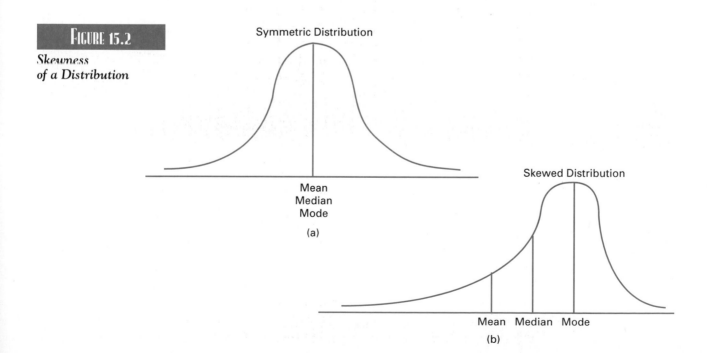

Chapter 12 covered the concepts of the sampling distribution, standard error of the mean or the proportion, and the confidence interval.[6] All these concepts are relevant to hypothesis testing and should be reviewed. We now describe a general procedure for hypothesis testing that can be applied to test hypotheses about a wide range of parameters.

A GENERAL PROCEDURE FOR HYPOTHESIS TESTING

The following steps are involved in hypothesis testing (Figure 15.3).

1. Formulate the null hypothesis H_0 and the alternative hypothesis H_1.
2. Select an appropriate statistical technique and the corresponding test statistic.
3. Choose the level of significance, α.
4. Determine the sample size and collect the data. Calculate the value of the test statistic.
5. Determine the probability associated with the test statistic under the null hypothesis, using the sampling distribution of the test statistic. Alternatively, determine the critical values associated with the test statistic that divide the rejection and nonrejection region.

FIGURE 15.3

A General Procedure for Hypothesis Testing

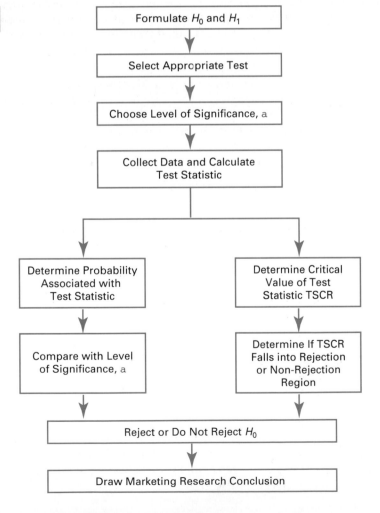

6. Compare the probability associated with the test statistic with the level of significance specified. Alternatively, determine whether the test statistic has fallen into the rejection or the nonrejection region.
7. Make the statistical decision to reject or not reject the null hypothesis.
8. Express the statistical decision in terms of the marketing research problem.

Step 1: Formulating the Hypothesis

null hypothesis A statement in which no difference or effect is expected. If the null hypothesis is not rejected, no changes will be made.

alternative hypothesis A statement that some difference or effect is expected. Accepting the alternative hypothesis will lead to changes in opinions or actions.

The first step is to formulate the null and alternative hypothesis. A **null hypothesis** is a statement of the status quo, one of no difference or no effect. If the null hypothesis is not rejected, no changes will be made. An **alternative hypothesis** is one in which some difference or effect is expected. Accepting the alternative hypothesis will lead to changes in opinions or actions. Thus, the alternative hypothesis is the opposite of the null hypothesis.

The null hypothesis is always the hypothesis that is tested. The null hypothesis refers to a specified value of the population parameter (e.g., μ, σ, π), not a sample statistic (e.g., $\overline{X}$). A null hypothesis may be rejected, but it can never be accepted based on a single test. A statistical test can have one of two outcomes: that the null hypothesis is rejected and the alternative hypothesis accepted or that the null hypothesis is not rejected based on the evidence. It would be incorrect, however, to conclude that since the null hypothesis is not rejected, it can be accepted as valid. In classical hypothesis testing, there is no way to determine whether the null hypothesis is true.

In marketing research, the null hypothesis is formulated in such a way that its rejection leads to the acceptance of the desired conclusion. The alternative hypothesis represents the conclusion for which evidence is sought. For example, an industrial marketing firm is considering the introduction of a new servicing plan for hydraulic parts. The plan will be introduced if it is preferred by more than 40% of the customers. The appropriate way to formulate the hypotheses is

$$H_0: \pi \leq 0.40$$
$$H_1: \pi > 0.4$$

If the null hypothesis H_0 is rejected, then the alternative hypothesis H_1 will be accepted and the new service plan introduced. On the other hand, if H_0 is not rejected, then the new service plan should not be introduced unless additional evidence is obtained.

one-tailed test A test of the null hypothesis where the alternative hypothesis is expressed directionally.

two-tailed test A test of the null hypothesis where the alternative hypothesis is not expressed directionally.

The test of the null hypothesis is a **one-tailed test** because the alternative hypothesis is expressed directionally: the proportion of customers who express a preference is greater than 0.40. On the other hand, suppose that the researcher wanted to determine whether the new service plan is different (superior or inferior) from the current plan, which is preferred by 40% of the customers. Then a **two-tailed test** would be required, and the hypotheses would be expressed as

$$H_0: \pi = 0.400$$
$$H_1: \pi \neq 0.40$$

In commercial marketing research, the one-tailed test is used more often than a two-tailed test. Typically, there is some preferred direction for the conclusion for which evidence is sought. For example, the higher the profits, sales, and product quality, the better. The one-tailed test is more powerful than the two-tailed test. The power of a statistical test is discussed further in step 3.

Step 2: Selecting an Appropriate Test

To test the null hypothesis, it is necessary to select an appropriate statistical technique. The researcher should take into consideration how the test statistic is computed and the sampling distribution that the sample statistic (e.g., the mean) follows. The **test statistic** measures how close the sample has come to the null hypothesis. The test statistic often follows a well-known distribution, such as the normal, t, or chi-square distribution. Guidelines for selecting an appropriate test or statistical technique are discussed later in this chapter. In our example, the z statistic, which follows the standard normal distribution, would be appropriate. This statistic would be computed as follows:

where

$$z = \frac{p - \pi}{\sigma_p}$$

$$\sigma_p = \sqrt{\frac{\pi(1-\pi)}{n}}$$

test statistic A measure of how close the sample has come to the null hypothesis. It often follows a well-known distribution, such as the normal, t, or chi-square distribution.

Step 3: Choosing Level of Significance

Whenever we draw inferences about a population, there is a risk that an incorrect conclusion will be reached. Two types of error can occur.

type I error An error that occurs when the sample results lead to the rejection of a null hypothesis that is in fact true. Also known as alpha error.

Type I Error   Type I error occurs when the sample results lead to the rejection of the null hypothesis when it is in fact true. In our example, a type I error would occur if we concluded, based on sample data, that the proportion of customers preferring the new service plan was greater than 0.40, when in fact it was less than or equal to 0.40. The probability of type I error (α) is also called the **level of significance**. The type I error is controlled by establishing the tolerable level of risk of rejecting a true null hypothesis. The selection of a particular risk level should depend on the cost of making a type I error.

level of significance The probability of making a type I error.

type II error An error that occurs when the sample results lead to acceptance of a null hypothesis that is in fact false. Also known as beta error.

Type II Error   Type II error occurs when, based on the sample results, the null hypothesis is not rejected when it is in fact false. In our example, the type II error would occur if we concluded, based on sample data, that the proportion of customers preferring the new service plan was less than or equal to 0.40 when in fact it was greater than 0.40. The probability of type II error is denoted by β. Unlike α, which is specified by the researcher, the magnitude of β depends on the actual value of the population parameter (proportion). The probability of type I error (α) and the probability of type II error (β) are shown in Figure 15.4. The complement ($1 - \beta$) of the probability of a type II error is called the power of a statistical test.

power of a test The probability of rejecting the null hypothesis when it is in fact false and should be rejected.

Power of a Test   The **power of a test** is the probability ($1 - \beta$) of rejecting the null hypothesis when it is false and should be rejected. Although β is unknown, it is related to α. An extremely low value of α (e.g., = .001) will result in intolerably high β errors. So it is necessary to balance the two types of errors. As a compromise, α is often set at .05; sometimes it is .01; other values of α are rare. The level of α along with the sample size will determine the level of β for a particular research design. The risk of both α and β can be controlled by increasing the sample size. For a given level of α, increasing the sample size will decrease β, thereby increasing the power of the test.

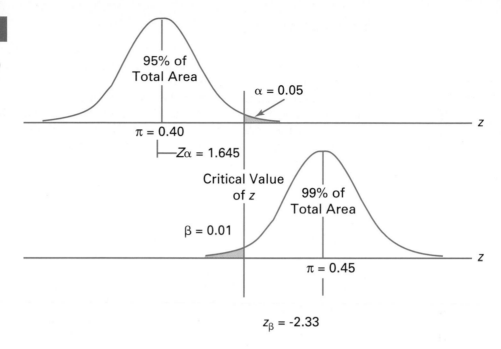

FIGURE 15.4

Type I Error (α) and Type II Error (β)

Step 4: Data Collection

Sample size is determined after taking into account the desired α and β errors and other qualitative considerations, such as budget constraints. Then the required data are collected and the value of the test statistic computed. Suppose, in our example, that 500 customers were surveyed and 220 expressed a preference for the new service plan. Thus the value of the sample proportion is $\hat{p} = 220/500 = 0.44$.

The value of σ_p can be determined as follows:

$$\sigma_{\hat{p}} = \sqrt{\frac{\pi(1-\pi)}{n}}$$

$$= \sqrt{\frac{(.40)(.6)}{500}}$$

$$= .0219$$

The test statistic z can be calculated as follows:

$$z = \frac{\hat{p} - \pi}{\sigma_{\hat{p}}}$$

$$= \frac{.44 - .40}{.0219}$$

$$= 1.83$$

Step 5: Determining the Probability (Critical Value)

Using standard normal tables (Table 2 of the Statistical Appendix), the probability of obtaining a z value of 1.83 can be calculated (see Figure 15.5). The shaded area between $-\infty$ and 1.83 is .9664. Therefore, the area to the right of $z = 1.83$ is $1.0000 - .9664 = .0336$. Alternatively, the critical value of z, which will give an area to the right side of the critical value of 0.05, is between 1.64 and 1.65 and equals 1.645. Note that in determining the critical value of the test statistic, the area to the right of the critical value is either α or $\alpha/2$. It is α for a one-tail test and $\alpha/2$ for a two-tail test.

Steps 6 and 7: Comparing the Probability (Critical Value) and Making the Decision

The probability associated with the calculated or observed value of the test statistic is .0336. This is probability of getting a p value of .44 when $\pi = .40$. This is less than the level of significance of .05. Hence, the null hypothesis is rejected. Alternatively, the calculated value of the test statistic $z = 1.83$ lies in the rejection region, beyond the value of 1.645. Again, the same conclusion to reject the null hypothesis is reached. Note that the two ways of testing the null hypothesis are equivalent but mathematically opposite in the direction of comparison. If the probability associated with the calculated or observed value of the test statistic (TS_{CAL}) is *less than* the level of significance (α), the null hypothesis is rejected. If the calculated value of the test statistic is *greater than* the critical value of the test statistic (TS_{CR}), however, the null hypothesis is rejected. The reason for this sign shift is that the larger the value of TS_{CAL}, the smaller the probability of obtaining a more extreme value of the test statistic under the null hypothesis. This sign shift can be easily seen:

$$\text{if probability of } TS_{CAL} < \text{ significance level } (\alpha), \text{ then reject } H_0$$

but

$$\text{if } TS_{CAL} > TS_{CR}, \text{ then reject } H_0$$

Step 8: Marketing Research Conclusion

The conclusion reached by hypothesis testing must be expressed in terms of the marketing research problem. In our example, we conclude that there is evidence that the proportion of customers preferring the new service plan is significantly greater than .40. Hence, the recommendation would be to introduce the new service plan.

As can be seen from Figure 15.6, hypotheses testing can be related to either an examination of associations or an examination of differences. In tests of associations the null hypothesis is that there is no association between the variables (H_0: . . . is NOT related to . . .). In tests of differences the null hypothesis is that there is no difference (H_0: ... is NOT different than . . .). Tests of differences could relate to distributions, means, proportions, or medians or rankings. First, we discuss hypotheses related to associations in the context of cross-tabulations.

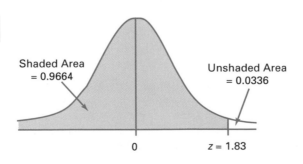

FIGURE 15.5

Probability of z with a One-Tailed Test

Shaded Area = 0.9664

Unshaded Area = 0.0336

0          $z = 1.83$

FIGURE 15.6

A Broad Classification of Hypothesis Testing Procedures

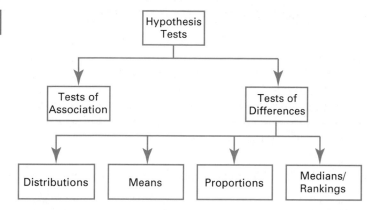

CROSS-TABULATIONS

Although answers to questions related to a single variable are interesting, they often raise additional questions about how to link that variable to other variables. To introduce the frequency distribution, we posed several representative marketing research questions. For each of these, a researcher might pose additional questions to relate these variables to other variables. For example:

- How many brand loyal users are males?
- Is product use (measured in terms of heavy users, medium users, light users, and nonusers) related to interest in outdoor activities (high, medium, and low)?
- Is familiarity with a new product related to age and education levels?
- Is product ownership related to income (high, medium, and low)?

cross-tabulation A statistical technique that describes two or more variables simultaneously and results in tables that reflect the joint distribution of two or more variables that have a limited number of categories or distinct values.

The answers to such questions can be determined by examining cross-tabulations. A frequency distribution describes one variable at a time, but a **cross-tabulation** describes two or more variables simultaneously. Cross-tabulation results in tables that reflect the joint distribution of two or more variables with a limited number of categories or distinct values. The categories of one variable are cross-classified with the categories of one or more other variables. Thus, the frequency distribution of one variable is subdivided according to the values or categories of the other variables.

Suppose that a researcher was interested in determining whether length of residence in a metropolitan area was associated with the degree of familiarity with local department stores. In the department store patronage project, respondents' familiarity with each of the ten stores was summed to arrive at an overall familiarity variable. The respondents were divided into two categories, unfamiliar or familiar, based on a rough median split of the overall familiarity variable. In other words, those in the lower half of the distribution were classified as unfamiliar and those in the upper half as familiar. The length of residence in the area was classified into three categories: less than 13 years, 13 to 30 years, and more than 30 years.

The cross-tabulation is shown in Table 15.2. A cross-tabulation includes a cell for every combination of the categories of the two variables. The number in each cell shows how many respondents gave that combination of responses. In Table 15.2, 45 respondents had lived in the area less than 13 years and were unfamiliar with the department

TABLE 15.2		Length of Residence			
Length of Residence and Familiarity with Department Stores	Familiarity	Less than 13 years	13 to 30 years	More than 30 years	Row Total
	Unfamiliar	45	34	55	134
	Familiar	52	53	27	132
	Column total	97	87	82	266

Number of missing observations = 5.

contingency table A cross-tabulation table. It contains a cell for every combination of categories of the two variables.

stores. The marginal totals in this table indicate that of the 266 respondents with valid responses on both the variables, 134 were unfamiliar and 132 were familiar. Based on length of residence, 97 respondents had lived in the area less than 13 years, 87 for 13 to 30 years, and 82 more than 30 years. Note that this information could have been obtained from a separate frequency distribution for each variable. In general, the margins of a cross-tabulation show the same information as the frequency tables for each of the variables. Cross-tabulation tables are also called **contingency tables**. The data are considered to be qualitative or categorical data, because each variable is assumed to have only a nominal scale.[7]

Cross-tabulation is widely used in commercial marketing research because (1) cross-tabulation analysis and results can be easily interpreted and understood by managers who are not statistically oriented; (2) the clarity of interpretation provides a stronger link between research results and managerial action; (3) a series of cross-tabulations may provide greater insights into a complex phenomenon than a single multivariate analysis; (4) cross-tabulation may alleviate the problem of sparse cells, which could be serious in discrete multivariate analysis; and (5) cross-tabulation analysis is simple to conduct and appealing to less-sophisticated researchers.[8] We will discuss cross-tabulation for two and three variables.

Two Variables

Cross-tabulation with two variables is also known as bivariate cross-tabulation. Consider again the cross-classification of length of residence and familiarity with department stores given in Table 15.2. Is familiarity related to length of residence? It appears to be from Table 15.2. We see that disproportionately more of the respondents who have lived in the area for either less than 13 years or 13 to 30 years are familiar with the stores, compared with those who have lived there for more than 30 years. Computation of percentages can provide more insights.

Because two variables have been cross-classified, percentages could be computed either columnwise, based on column totals (Table 15.3), or rowwise, based on row totals (Table 15.4). Which table is more useful? The answer depends on which variable will be

TABLE 15.3		Length of Residence		
Familiarity with Department Stores by Length of Residence	Familiarity	Less than 13 Years	13 to 30 Years	More than 30 Years
	Unfamiliar	46.4%	39.1%	67.1%
	Familiar	53.6%	60.9%	32.9%
	Column total	100.0%	100.0%	100.0%

	Length of Residence			
Familiarity	Less than 13 years	13 to 30 years	More than 30 years	Row Total
Unfamiliar	33.6%	25.4%	41.0%	100.0%
Familiar	39.4%	40.1%	20.5%	100.0%

TABLE 15.4

Length of Residence by Familiarity with Department Stores

considered as the independent variable and which as the dependent variable.[9] The general rule is to compute the percentages in the direction of the independent variable, across the dependent variable. In our analysis, length of residence may be considered as the independent variable and familiarity as the dependent variable, and the correct way of calculating percentages is shown in Table 15.3. Note that while 53.6% of those residing less than 13 years and 60.9% of those residing for 13 to 30 years are familiar with the department stores, only 32.9% of those residing more than 30 years are familiar. This seems to indicate that people who live in the same area for long periods are less familiar with the shopping environment. This finding seems plausible, because people who stay in an area for a long time may be less dynamic in general and therefore less informed about department stores.

Note that computing percentages in the direction of the dependent variable across the independent variable, as shown in Table 15.4, is not meaningful in this case. Table 15.4 implies that unfamiliarity with local department stores influences people to live in the area for longer periods. This latter finding seems implausible. It is possible, however, that the association between length of residence and familiarity is mediated by a third variable, such as age. Is it possible that people who have lived in the area for more than 30 years tend to be older and that older people are less familiar with department stores than younger people? Although an analysis of the data indicated that age was not a factor in this case, this kind of possibility points to the need to examine the effect of a third variable.

Three Variables

Often the introduction of a third variable clarifies the initial association (or lack of it) observed between two variables. As shown in Figure 15.7, the introduction of a third variable can result in four possibilities:

1. It can refine the association observed between the two original variables.
2. It can indicate no association between the two variables, although an association was initially observed. In other words, the third variable indicates that the initial association between the two variables was spurious.
3. It can reveal some association between the two variables, although no association was initially observed. In this case, the third variable reveals a suppressed association between the first two variables.
4. It can indicate no change in the initial association.[10]

These cases are explained with examples based on a sample of 1,000 respondents. Although these examples are contrived to illustrate specific cases, such cases are not uncommon in commercial marketing research.

Refine an Initial Relationship   An examination of the relationship between the purchase of fashion clothing and marital status resulted in the data reported in Table 15.5. The respondents were classified into either high or low categories based on their pur-

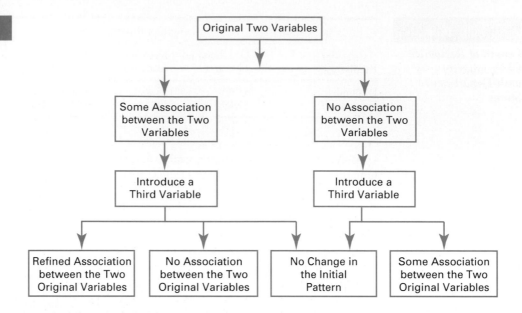

FIGURE 15.7

*The Introduction
of a Third Variable
in Cross-Tabulation*

chase of fashion clothing. Marital status was also measured in terms of two categories: currently married or unmarried. As can be seen from Table 15.5, 52% of unmarried respondents fell in the high-purchase category as opposed to 31% of the married respondents. Before concluding that unmarried respondents purchase more fashion clothing than those who are married, a third variable, the buyer's sex, was introduced into the analysis.

The buyer's sex was selected as the third variable based on past research. The relationship between purchase of fashion clothing and marital status was reexamined in light of the third variable, as shown in Table 15.6. In the case of females, 60% of the unmarried respondents fall in the high-purchase category compared with 25% of those who are married. On the other hand, the percentages are much closer for males, with 40% of the unmarried respondents and 35% of the married respondents falling in the high-purchase category. Hence, the introduction of sex (third variable) has refined the relationship between marital status and purchase of fashion clothing (original variables). Unmarried respondents are more likely to fall into the high-purchase category than married ones, and this effect is much more pronounced for females than for males.

Initial Relationship Was Spurious   A researcher working for an advertising agency promoting a line of automobiles costing more than $30,000 was attempting to explain the ownership of expensive automobiles (see Table 15.7). The table shows that 32% of

TABLE 15.5

*Purchase of Fashion
Clothing by Marital
Status*

Purchase of Fashion Clothing	Current Marital Status	
	Married	Not Married
High	31%	52%
Low	69%	48%
Column	100%	100%
Number of respondents	700	300

TABLE 15.6

Purchase of Fashion Clothing by Marital Status and Sex

Purchase of Fashion Clothing	Male Marital Status		Female Marital Status	
	Married	Not Married	Married	Not Married
High	35%	40%	25%	60%
Low	65%	60%	75%	40%
Column totals	100%	100%	100%	100%
Number of cases	400	120	300	180

those with college degrees own an expensive (more than $30,000) automobile compared with 21% of those without college degrees. The researcher was tempted to conclude that education influenced ownership of expensive automobiles. Realizing that income may also be a factor, the researcher decided to reexamine the relationship between education and ownership of expensive automobiles in light of income level. This resulted in Table 15.8. Note that the percentages of those with and without college degrees who own expensive automobiles are the same for each income group. When the data for the high-income and low-income groups are examined separately, the association between education and ownership of expensive automobiles disappears, indicating that the initial relationship observed between these two variables was spurious.

Reveal Suppressed Association   A researcher suspected desire to travel abroad may be influenced by age. A cross-tabulation of the two variables produced the results in Table 15.9, however, indicating no association. When sex was introduced as the third variable, Table 15.10 was obtained. Among men, 60% of those under 45 indicated a desire to travel abroad compared with 40% of those 45 or older. The pattern was reversed for women, where 35% of those under 45 indicated a desire to travel abroad as opposed to 65% of those 45 or older. Since the association between desire to travel abroad and age runs in the opposite direction for males and females, the relationship between these two variables is masked when the data are aggregated across sex as in Table 15.9. But when

TABLE 15.7

Ownership of Expensive Automobiles by Education Level

Own Expensive Automobile	Education	
	College Degree	No College Degree
Yes	32%	21%
No	68%	79%
Column total	100%	100%
Number of cases	250	750

TABLE 15.8

Ownership of Expensive Automobiles by Education and Income Levels

Own Expensive Automobile	Low Income Education		High Income Education	
	College Degree	No College Degree	College Degree	No College Degree
Yes	20%	20%	40%	40%
No	80%	80%	60%	60%
Column totals	100%	100%	100%	100%
Number of respondents	100	700	150	50

TABLE 15.9	Desire to Travel Abroad	Age	
		Under 45	45 or older
Desire to Travel Abroad by Age	Yes	50%	50%
	No	50%	50%
	Column total	100%	100%
	Number of respondents	500	500

the effect of sex is controlled, as in Table 15.10, the suppressed association between preference and age is revealed for the separate categories of males and females.

No Change in Initial Relationship   In some cases, the introduction of the third variable does not change the initial relationship observed, regardless of whether the original variables were associated. This suggests that the third variable does not influence the relationship between the first two. Consider the cross-tabulation of family size and the tendency to eat in fast-food restaurants frequently as shown in Table 15.11. The respondents' families were classified into small- and large-size categories based on a median split of the distribution, with 500 respondents in each category. No association is observed. The respondents were further classified into high- or low-income groups based on a median split. When income was introduced as a third variable in the analysis, Table 15.12 was obtained. Again, no association was observed.

General Comments on Cross-Tabulation

Even though more than three variables can be cross-tabulated, the interpretation is quite complex. Also, because the number of cells increases multiplicatively, maintaining an adequate number of respondents or cases in each cell can be problematic. As a general rule, there should be at least five expected observations in each cell for the computed statistics to be reliable. Thus, cross-tabulation is an inefficient way of examining

TABLE 15.10	Desire to Travel Abroad	Sex			
		Male Age		Female Age	
Desire to Travel Abroad by Age and Sex		Under 45	45 or older	Under 45	45 or Older
	Yes	60%	40%	35%	65%
	No	40%	60%	65%	35%
	Column total	100%	100%	100%	100%
	Number of cases	300	300	200	200

TABLE 15.11	Eat Frequently in Fast-Food Restaurants	Family Size	
		Small	Large
Eating Frequently in Fast-Food Restaurants by Family Size	Yes	65%	65%
	No	35%	35%
	Column total	100%	100%
	Number of cases	500	500

TABLE 15.12	Income			
	Low Income		High Income	
	Family Size		Family Size	
Eating Frequently in Fast-Food Restaurants by Family Size and Income / Eat Frequently in Fast-Food Restaurants	Small	Large	Small	Large
Yes	65%	65%	65%	65%
No	35%	35%	35%	35%
Column total	100%	100%	100%	100%
Number of respondents	250	250	250	250

relationships when there are several variables. Note that cross-tabulation examines association between variables, not causation. To examine causation, the causal research design framework should be adopted (see Chapter 7).

STATISTICS ASSOCIATED WITH CROSS-TABULATION

We now discuss the statistics commonly used for assessing the statistical significance and strength of association of cross-tabulated variables. The statistical significance of the observed association is commonly measured by the chi-square statistic. The strength of association, or degree of association, is important from a practical or substantive perspective. Generally, the strength of association is of interest only if the association is statistically significant. The strength of the association can be measured by the phi correlation coefficient, the contingency coefficient, Cramer's V, and the lambda coefficient. These statistics are described in detail.

Chi-Square

chi-square statistic The statistic used to test the statistical significance of the observed association in a cross-tabulation. It assists us in determining whether a systematic association exists between the two variables.

The **chi-square statistic** (χ^2) is used to test the statistical significance of the observed association in a cross-tabulation. It assists us in determining whether a systematic association exists between the two variables. The null hypothesis, H_0, is that there is no association between the variables. The test is conducted by computing the cell frequencies that would be expected if no association were present between the variables, given the existing row and column totals. These expected cell frequencies, denoted f_e, are then compared with the actual observed frequencies, f_o, found in the cross-tabulation to calculate the chi-square statistic. The greater the discrepancies between the expected and actual frequencies, the larger the value of the statistic. Assume that a cross-tabulation has r rows and c columns and a random sample of n observations. Then the expected frequency for each cell can be calculated by using a simple formula:

$$f_e = \frac{n_r n_c}{n}$$

where

n_r = total number in the row

n_c = total number in the column

n = total sample size

For the data in Table 15.2, the expected frequencies for the cells going from left to right and from top to bottom, are

$$\frac{134 \times 97}{266} = 48.87 \qquad \frac{134 \times 87}{266} = 43.83 \qquad \frac{134 \times 82}{266} = 41.31$$

$$\frac{132 \times 97}{266} = 48.14 \qquad \frac{132 \times 87}{266} = 43.17 \qquad \frac{132 \times 82}{266} = 40.69$$

Then the value of χ^2 is calculated as follows:

$$\chi^2 = \sum_{\text{all cells}} \frac{(f_0 - f_e)^2}{f_e}$$

For the data in Table 15.2, the value of χ^2 is calculated as

$$\chi^2 = \frac{(45 - 48.87)^2}{48.87} + \frac{(34 - 43.83)^2}{43.83} + \frac{(55 - 41.31)^2}{41.31}$$

$$+ \frac{(52 - 48.14)^2}{48.14} + \frac{(53 - 43.17)^2}{43.17} + \frac{(27 - 40.69)^2}{40.69}$$

$$= 0.306 + 2.204 + 4.537 + 0.310 + 2.238 + 4.606$$

$$= 14.201$$

To determine whether a systematic association exists, the probability of obtaining a value of chi-square as large or larger than the one calculated from the cross-tabulation is estimated. An important characteristic of the chi-square statistic is the number of degrees of freedom (df) associated with it. In general, the number of degrees of freedom is equal to the number of observations less the number of constraints needed to calculate a statistical term. In the case of a chi-square statistic associated with a cross-tabulation, the number of degrees of freedom is equal to the product of number of rows (r) less one and the number of columns (c) less one. That is, df = $(r - 1) \times (c - 1)$.[11] The null hypothesis (H_0) of no association between the two variables will be rejected only when the calculated value of the test statistic is greater than the critical value of the chi-square distribution with the appropriate degrees of freedom, as shown in Figure 15.8.

chi-square distribution A skewed distribution whose shape depends solely on the number of degrees of freedom. As the number of degrees of freedom increases, the chi-square distribution becomes more symmetrical.

The **chi-square distribution** is a skewed distribution whose shape depends solely on the number of degrees of freedom.[12] As the number of degrees of freedom increases, the chi-square distribution becomes more symmetrical. Table 3 in the Statistical Appendix contains upper-tail areas of the chi-square distribution for different degrees of freedom. In this table, the value at the top of each column indicates the area in the upper portion (the right side, as shown in Figure 15.8) of the chi-square distribution. To illustrate, for 2 degrees of freedom, the value for an upper-tail area of .05 is 5.991. This

FIGURE 15.8

Chi-Square Test of Association

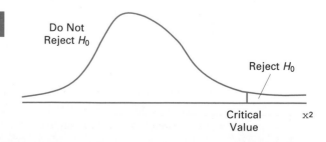

Do Not Reject H_0

Reject H_0

Critical Value

x2

indicates that for 2 degrees of freedom the probability of exceeding a chi-square value of 5.991 is .05. In other words, at the .05 level of significance with 2 degrees of freedom, the critical value of the chi-square statistic is 5.991.

For the cross-tabulation given in Table 15.2, there are $(2 - 1) \times (3 - 1) = 2$ degrees of freedom. The calculated chi-square statistic had a value of 14.201. Since this exceeds the critical value of 5.991, the null hypothesis of no association can be rejected, indicating that the association is statistically significant at the .05 level.

The chi-square statistic can also be used in goodness-of-fit tests to determine whether certain models fit the observed data. These tests are conducted by calculating the significance of sample deviations from assumed theoretical (expected) distributions and can be performed on cross-tabulations as well as on frequencies (one-way tabulations). The calculation of the chi-square statistic and the determination of its significance is the same as illustrated above.

The chi-square statistic should be estimated only on counts of data. When the data are in percentage form, they should first be converted to absolute counts or numbers. In addition, an underlying assumption of the chi-square test is that the observations are drawn independently. As a general rule, chi-square analysis should not be conducted when the expected or theoretical frequencies in any of the cells is less than five. If the number of observations in any cell is less than ten, or if the table has two rows and two columns (a 2×2 table), a correction factor should be applied.[13] In the case of a 2×2 table, the chi-square is related to the phi coefficient.

Phi Coefficient

phi coefficient A measure of the strength of association in the special case of a table with two rows and two columns (a 2×2 table).

The **phi coefficient** (ϕ) is used as a measure of the strength of association in the special case of a table with two rows and two columns (a 2×2 table). The phi coefficient is proportional to the square root of the chi-square statistic. For a sample of size n, this statistic is calculated as

$$\phi = \sqrt{\frac{\chi^2}{n}}$$

It takes the value of 0 when there is no association, which would be indicated by a chi-square value of 0 as well. When the variables are perfectly associated, phi assumes the value of 1 and all the observations fall just on the main or minor diagonal. (In some computer programs, phi assumes a value of -1 rather than $+1$ when there is perfect negative association.) In the more general case involving a table of any size, the strength of association can be assessed by using the contingency coefficient.

Contingency Coefficient

contingency coefficient A measure of the strength of association in a table of any size.

Although the phi coefficient is specific to a 2×2 table, the **contingency coefficient** (C) can be used to assess the strength of association in a table of any size. This index is also related to chi-square, as follows:

$$C = \sqrt{\frac{\chi^2}{\chi^2 + n}}$$

The contingency coefficient varies between 0 and 1. The 0 value occurs in the case of no association (i.e., the variables are statistically independent), but the maximum value of 1 is never achieved. Rather, the maximum value of the contingency coefficient depends on the size of the table (number of rows and number of columns). For this reason, it should be used only to compare tables of the same size. The value of the contingency coefficient for Table 15.2 is

$$C = \sqrt{\frac{14.201}{14.201 + 266}}$$

$$= \sqrt{\frac{14.201}{280.201}}$$

$$= 0.2251$$

This value of C indicates that the association is not very strong.

Another statistic that can be calculated for any table is Cramer's V.

Cramer's V

Cramer's V A measure of the strength of association used in tables larger than 2 × 2.

Cramer's V is a modified version of the phi correlation coefficient, ϕ, and is used in tables larger than 2 × 2. When phi is calculated for a table larger than 2 × 2, it has no upper limit. Cramer's V is obtained by adjusting phi for either the number of rows or the number of columns in the table based on which of the two is smaller. The adjustment is such that V will range from 0 to 1. A large value of V merely indicates a high degree of association. It does not indicate how the variables are associated. For a table with r rows and c columns, the relationship between Cramer's V and the phi correlation coefficient is expressed as

$$V = \sqrt{\frac{\phi^2}{\min (r-1),\ (c-1)}} \quad \text{or} \quad V = \sqrt{\frac{\chi^2/n}{\min (r-1),\ (c-1)}}$$

The value of Cramer's V for Table 15.2 is

$$V = \sqrt{\frac{14.201/266}{1}}$$

$$= 0.2310$$

asymmetric lambda A measure of the percentage improvement in predicting the value of the dependent variable given the value of the independent variable in contingency table analysis. Lambda also varies between 0 and 1.

Thus, the association is not very strong.

Another statistic commonly estimated is the lambda coefficient.

Lambda Coefficient

The lambda coefficient assumes that the variables are measured on a nominal scale. **Asymmetric lambda** measures the percentage improvement in predicting the value of the dependent variable, given the value of the independent variable. The lambda coefficient also varies between 0 and 1. A value of 0 means no improvement in prediction. A value of 1 indicates that the prediction can be made without error. This happens when each independent variable category is associated with a single category of the dependent variable.

symmetric lambda The symmetric lambda does not make an assumption about which variable is dependent. It measures the overall improvement when prediction is done in both directions.

Asymmetric lambda is computed for each of the variables (treating it as the dependent variable). The two asymmetric lambdas are likely to be different since the marginal distributions are not usually the same. A **symmetric lambda**, a kind of average of the two asymmetric values, is also computed. The symmetric lambda does not make an assumption about which variable is dependent. It measures the overall improvement when prediction is done in both directions.[14] The value of asymmetric lambda in Table 15.2, with familiarity as the dependent variable, is .1970. This indicates that knowledge of length of residence increases our predictive ability by the proportion of .1970, that is, a 19.7% improvement. The value of lambda with length of residence as the dependent variable is .0651. The symmetric lambda is .1229.

Other Statistics

tau *b* A test statistic that measures the association between two ordinal-level variables. It makes an adjustment for ties and is most appropriate when the table of variables is square.

tau *c* A test statistic that measures the association between two ordinal-level variables. It makes an adjustment for ties and is most appropriate when the table of variables is not square but a rectangle.

gamma A test statistic that measures the association between two ordinal-level variables. It does not makes an adjustment for ties.

Other statistics like tau *b*, tau *c*, and gamma are available to measure association between two ordinal-level variables. All these statistics use information about the ordering of categories of variables by considering every possible pair of cases in the table. Each pair is examined to determine if its relative ordering on the first variable is the same as its relative ordering on the second variable (concordant), if the ordering is reversed (discordant), or if the pair is tied. The manner in which the ties are treated is the basic difference between these statistics. Both tau *b* and tau *c* adjust for ties. **Tau *b*** is the most appropriate with square tables in which the number of rows and the number of columns are equal. Its value varies between +1 and −1. For a rectangular table in which the number of rows is different than the number of columns, **tau *c*** should be used. **Gamma** does not make an adjustment for either ties or table size. Gamma also varies between +1 and −1 and generally has a higher numerical value than tau *b* or tau *c*. For the data in Table 15.2, the value of tau *c* is −0.1710 and gamma is −0.2508. Both these statistics indicate that the association is significant but not very strong. All these statistics can be estimated by using the appropriate computer programs for cross-tabulation. Other statistics for measuring the strength of association, namely product moment correlation, and nonmetric correlation are discussed in Chapter 17.

CROSS-TABULATION IN PRACTICE

While conducting cross-tabulation analysis in practice, it is useful to proceed along the following steps.

1. Test the null hypothesis that there is no association between the variables using the chi-square statistic. If you fail to reject the null hypothesis, then there is no relationship.
2. If H_0 is rejected, then determine the strength of the association using an appropriate statistic (phi coefficient, contingency coefficient, Cramer's V, lambda coefficient, or other statistics), as discussed earlier.
3. If H_0 is rejected, interpret the pattern of the relationship by computing the percentages in the direction of the independent variable, across the dependent variable.

HYPOTHESES TESTING RELATED TO DIFFERENCES

parametric tests ypothesis testing procedures that assume that the variables of interest are measured on at least an interval scale.

The previous section considered hypotheses testing related to associations. We now focus on hypotheses testing related to differences. A classification of hypothesis testing procedures for examining differences is presented in Figure 15.9. Note that this figure is consistent with the classification of univariate techniques presented in Figure 14.6. Hypothesis testing procedures can be broadly classified as parametric or nonparametric, based on the measurement scale of the variables involved. **Parametric tests** assume that the variables of interest are measured on at least an interval scale. The most popular

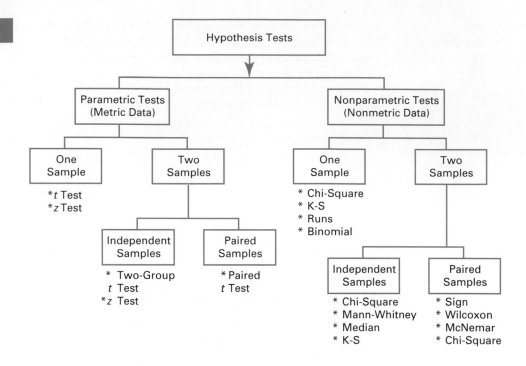

FIGURE 15.9

Hypothesis Testing Procedures

parametric test is the *t* test conducted for examining hypotheses about means. The *t* test could be conducted on the mean of one sample or two samples of observations. In the case of two samples, the samples could be independent or paired.

nonparametric tests
Hypothesis testing procedures that assume that the variables are measured on a nominal or ordinal scale.

     Nonparametric tests assume that the variables are measured on a nominal or ordinal scale. Nonparametric tests based on observations drawn from one sample include the Kolmogorov-Smirnov test, the chi-square test, the runs test, and the binomial test. In case of two independent samples, the Mann-Whitney *U* test, the median test, and the Kolmogorov-Smirnov two sample test are used for examining hypotheses about location. These tests are nonparametric counterparts of the two group *t* test. For paired samples, nonparametric tests include the Wilcoxon matched-pairs signed-ranks test and the sign test. These tests are the counterparts of the paired *t* test. Parametric as well as nonparametric tests are also available for evaluating hypotheses relating to more than two samples. These tests are considered in later chapters.

PARAMETRIC TESTS

t test A univariate hypothesis test using the *t* distribution, which is used when the standard deviation is unknown and the sample size is small.

Parametric tests provide inferences for making statements about the means of parent populations. A **t test** is commonly used for this purpose. This test is based on the Student's *t* statistic. The **t statistic** assumes that the variable is normally distributed and the mean is known (or assumed to be known) and the population variance is estimated from the sample. Assume that the random variable *X* is normally distributed, with mean μ and unknown population variance σ^2, which is estimated by the sample variance s^2. Recall that the standard deviation of the sample mean, $\overline{X}$, is estimated as $s_{\overline{x}} = s/\sqrt{n}$. Then, $t = (\overline{X} - \mu)/s_{\overline{x}}$ is *t* distributed with $n - 1$ degrees of freedom.

     The **t distribution** is similar to the normal distribution in appearance. Both distributions are bell-shaped and symmetric. Compared with the normal distribution, however, the *t* distribution has more area in the tails and less in the center. This is because

t statistic A statistic that assumes that the variable has a symmetric bell-shaped distribution, that the mean is known (or assumed to be known), and that the population variance is estimated from the sample.

t distribution A symmetric bell-shaped distribution that is useful for small sample (n< 30) testing.

population variance σ^2 is unknown and is estimated by the sample variance s^2. Given the uncertainty in the value of s^2, the observed values of t are more variable than those of z. Thus, we must go a larger number of standard deviations from zero to encompass a certain percentage of values from the t distribution than is the case with the normal distribution. Yet, as the number of degrees of freedom increases, the t distribution approaches the normal distribution. In fact, for large samples of 120 or more, the t distribution and the normal distribution are virtually indistinguishable. Table 4 in the Statistical Appendix shows selected percentiles of the t distribution. Although normality is assumed, the t test is quite robust to departures from normality.

The procedure for hypothesis testing, for the special case when the t statistic is used, is as follows.

1. Formulate the null (H_0) and the alternative (H_1) hypotheses.
2. Select the appropriate formula for the t statistic.
3. Select a significance level, α, for testing H_0. Typically, the .05 level is selected.[15]
4. Take one or two samples and compute the mean and standard deviation for each sample. Calculate the t statistic assuming that H_0 is true.
5. Calculate the degrees of freedom and estimate the probability of getting a more extreme value of the statistic from Table 4. (Alternatively, calculate the critical value of the t statistic.)
6. If the probability computed in step 5 is smaller than the significance level selected in step 3, reject H_0. If the probability is larger, do not reject H_0. (Alternatively, if the value of the calculated t statistic in step 4 is larger than the critical value determined in step 5, reject H_0. If the calculated value is smaller than the critical value, do not reject H_0.) Failure to reject H_0 does not necessarily imply that H_0 is true. It only means that the true state is not significantly different than that assumed by H_0.[16]
7. Express the conclusion reached by the t test in terms of the marketing research problem.

We illustrate the general procedure for conducting t tests in the following sections, beginning with the one-sample case.

One Sample

In marketing research, the researcher is often interested in making statements about a single variable against a known or given standard. Examples of such statements include the market share for a new product will exceed 15%, at least 65% of customers will like a new package design, and 80% of dealers will prefer the new pricing policy. These statements can be translated to null hypotheses that can be tested using a one-sample test, such as the t test or the z test. In the case of a t test for a single mean, the researcher is interested in testing whether the population mean conforms to a given hypothesis (H_0). Suppose that a new machine attachment would be introduced if it receives a mean of at least 7 on a ten-point scale. A sample of 20 purchase engineers is shown the attachment and asked to evaluate it. The results indicate a mean rating of 7.9 with a standard deviation of 1.6. A significance level of α = .05 is selected. Should the part be introduced?

$$H_0 = \mu \leq 7.0$$
$$H_1 = \mu > 7.0$$

$$t = \frac{(\bar{X} - \mu)}{s_{\bar{x}}}$$

$$s_{\bar{x}} = \frac{s}{\sqrt{n}}$$

$$s_{\bar{x}} = \frac{1.6}{\sqrt{20}} = \frac{1.6}{4.472} = 0.358$$

$$t = \frac{(7.9 - 7.0)}{0.358} = \frac{0.9}{0.358} = 2.514$$

The degrees of freedom for the t statistic to test hypothesis about one mean are $n - 1$. In this case, $n - 1 = 20 - 1$, or 19. From Table 4 in the Statistical Appendix, the probability of getting a more extreme value than 2.514 is less than .05. (Alternatively, the critical t value for 19 degrees of freedom and a significance level of .05 is 1.7291, which is less than the calculated value.) Hence, the null hypothesis is rejected, favoring the introduction of the part.

z test A univariate hypothesis test using the standard normal distribution.

Note that if the population standard deviation was assumed to be known as 1.5, rather than estimated from the sample, a **z test** would be appropriate. In this case, the value of the z statistic would be

$$z = \frac{\bar{X} - \mu}{\sigma_{\bar{x}}}$$

where

$$\sigma_{\bar{x}} = \frac{1.5}{\sqrt{20}} = \frac{1.5}{4.472} = 0.335$$

and

$$z = \frac{7.9 - 7.0}{0.358} = \frac{0.9}{0.358} = 2.514$$

From Table 2 in the Statistical Appendix, the probability of getting a more extreme value of z than 2.514 is less than .05. (Alternatively, the critical z value for a one-tailed test and a significance level of .05 is 1.645, which is less than the calculated value.) Therefore, the null hypothesis is rejected, reaching the same conclusion arrived at earlier by the t test.

The procedure for testing a null hypothesis with respect to a proportion was illustrated earlier in this chapter when we introduced hypothesis testing.

Two Independent Samples

Several hypotheses in marketing relate to parameters from two different populations: for example, the users and nonusers of a brand differ in terms of their perceptions of the brand, the high-income consumers spend more on entertainment than low-income consumers, or the proportion of brand loyal users in segment I is more than the proportion in segment II. Samples drawn randomly from different populations are termed **independent samples**. As in the case for one sample, the hypotheses could relate to means or proportions.

independent samples Two samples that are not experimentally related. The measurement of one sample has no effect on the values of the second sample.

Means   In the case of means for two independent samples, the hypotheses take the following form:

$$H_0: \mu_1 = \mu_2$$
$$H_1: \mu_1 \neq \mu_2$$

The two populations are sampled and the means and variances are computed based on samples of sizes n_1 and n_2. If both populations are found to have the same variance, a pooled variance estimate is computed from the two sample variances as follows:

$$s^2 = \frac{\sum_{i=1}^{n_1}(X_{n_1} - \overline{X}_1)^2 + \sum_{i=1}^{n_2}(X_{n_2} - \overline{X}_2)^2}{n_1 + n_2 - 2}$$

The standard deviation of the test statistic can be estimated as

$$s_{\overline{X}_1 - \overline{X}_2} = \sqrt{s^2\left(\frac{1}{n_1} + \frac{1}{n_2}\right)}$$

The appropriate value of t can be calculated as

$$t = \frac{(\overline{X}_1 - \overline{X}_2) - (\mu_1 - \mu_2)}{s_{\overline{X}_1 - \overline{X}_2}}$$

The degrees of freedom in this case are $(n_1 + n_2 - 2)$.

If the two populations have unequal variances, an exact t cannot be computed for the difference in sample means. Instead, an approximation to t is computed. The number of degrees of freedom in this case is usually not an integer, but a reasonably accurate probability can be obtained by rounding to the nearest integer.[17]

F test A statistical test of the equality of the variances of two populations.

An **F test** of sample variance may be performed if it is not known whether the two populations have equal variance. In this case the hypotheses are

$$H_0: \sigma_1^2 = \sigma_2^2$$
$$H_1: \sigma_1^2 \neq \sigma_2^2$$

F statistic The ratio of two sample variances.

The **F statistic** is computed from the sample variances as follows:

$$F_{(n_1 - 1),\ (n_2 - 1)} = \frac{s_1^2}{s_2^2}$$

where

$$n_1 = \text{size of sample 1}$$
$$n_2 = \text{size of sample 2}$$
$$n_1 - 1 = \text{degrees of freedom for sample 1}$$
$$n_2 - 1 = \text{degrees of freedom for sample 2}$$
$$s_1^2 = \text{sample variance for sample 1}$$
$$s_2^2 = \text{sample variance for sample 2}$$

F distribution A frequency distribution that depends upon two sets of degrees of freedom: the degrees of freedom in the numerator and the degrees of freedom in the denominator.

As can be seen, the critical value of the **F distribution** depends on two sets of degrees of freedom: those in the numerator and those in the denominator. The critical values of F for various degrees of freedom for the numerator and denominator are given in Table 5 of the Statistical Appendix. If the probability of F is greater than the significance level α, H_0 is not rejected and t based on the pooled variance estimate can be used. On the other hand, if the probability of F is less than or equal to α, H_0 is rejected and t based on a separate variance estimate is used.

Using the department store patronage example, suppose that the researcher wanted to determine whether respondents who are familiar with the department stores attach different importance to store credit and billing policies than those who are unfamiliar with the store. As before, respondents were divided into two familiarity groups based on a median split. A two independent samples *t* test was conducted, and the results are presented in Table 15.13. Note that the *F* test of sample variances has a probability that exceeds .05. Accordingly, H_0 cannot be rejected, and the *t* test based on the pooled variance estimate should be used. The *t* value is –1.99, and with 265 degrees of freedom, this gives a probability of .048, which is less than the significance level of .05. Therefore, the null hypothesis of equal means is rejected. Since the mean importance for the unfamiliar group is 3.9778 and that for the familiar group is 4.3712, those who are familiar attach significantly greater importance to store credit and billing policies when selecting a department store than those who are not familiar. We also show the *t* test using separate variance estimate since most computer programs automatically conduct the *t* test both ways. As an application of *t* test, consider the following example.

EXAMPLE
Stores Seek to Suit Elderly to a "*t*"

A study based on a national sample of 789 respondents who were 65 or older attempted to determine the effect of lack of mobility on patronage behavior. A major research question related to the differences in the physical requirements of dependent and self-reliant elderly persons. That is, did the two groups require different things to get to the store or after they arrived at the store? A more detailed analysis of the physical requirements conducted by two independent samples *t* tests (shown in the table) indicated that dependent elderly persons are more likely to look for stores that offer home delivery and phone orders and for stores to which they have accessible transportation. They are also more likely to look for a variety of stores located close together.[18]

Differences in Physical Requirements between Dependent and Self-Reliant Elderly

Physical Requirement Items	MEAN[a]		*t* test Probability
	Self-Reliant	Dependent	
Delivery to home	1.787	2.000	.023
Phone in order	2.030	2.335	.003
Transportation to store	2.188	3.098	.000
Convenient parking	4.001	4.095	.305
Location close to home	3.177	3.325	.137
Variety of stores close together	3.456	3.681	.023

[a]Measured on a five-point scale from not important (1) to very important (5). ◆

In this example, we tested the difference between means. A similar test is available for testing the difference between proportions for two independent samples.

Proportions   A case involving proportions for two independent samples is illustrated in Table 15.14, which gives the number of users and nonusers of jeans in the United States and Hong Kong. Is the proportion of users the same in the United States and Hong Kong samples? The null and alternative hypotheses are:

$$H_0: \pi_1 = \pi_2$$
$$H_1: \pi_1 \neq \pi_2$$

A *z* test is used as in testing the proportion for one sample. In this case, however, the test statistic is given by

TABLE 15.13	Summary Statistics		
Two Independent Samples t Test	Number of Cases	Mean	Standard Deviation
Unfamiliar Group	135	3.9778	1.604
Familiar Group	132	4.3712	1.627

F Test for Equality of Variances	
F value	Two-tail probability
1.03	.871

t Test					
Pooled Variance Estimate			Separate Variance Estimate		
t value	Degrees of freedom	Two-tail probability	t value	Degrees of freedom	Two-tail probability
−1.99	265	.048	−1.99	264.65	.048

$$z = \frac{P_1 - P_2}{S_{\bar{P}_1 - \bar{P}_2}}$$

In the test statistic, the numerator is the difference between the proportions in the two samples, P_1 and P_2. The denominator is the standard error of the difference in the two proportions and is given by

$$S_{\bar{P}_1 - \bar{P}_2} = \sqrt{P(1-P)\left(\frac{1}{n_1} + \frac{1}{n_2}\right)}$$

where

$$P = \frac{n_1 P_1 + n_2 P_2}{n_1 + n_2}$$

A significance level of $\alpha = .05$ is selected. Given the data of Table 15.14, the test statistic can be calculated as

$$P_1 - P_2 = .8 - .6 = .20$$

$$P = \frac{200 \times 0.8 + 200 \times 0.6}{200 + 200} = 0.7$$

$$S_{\bar{P}_1 - \bar{P}_2} = \sqrt{0.7 \times 0.3 \left(\frac{1}{200} + \frac{1}{200}\right)} = 0.04583$$

$$z = \frac{.2}{.04583} = 4.36$$

Given a two-tail test, the area to the right of the critical value is $\alpha/2$, or .025. Hence, the critical value of the test statistic is 1.96. Since the calculated value exceeds the crit-

TABLE 15.14	Usage of Jeans		
	Sample	Users	Nonusers	Row Totals
Comparing the Proportions of Jeans Users for the United States and Hong Kong	United States	160	40	200
	Hong Kong	120	80	200
	Column Totals	280	120	

ical value, the null hypothesis is rejected. Thus, the proportion of users (.80 for the United States, and .60 for Hong Kong) is significantly different for the two samples.

Paired Samples

paired samples In hypothesis testing, the observations are paired so that the two sets of observations relate to the same respondents.

paired samples t test A test for differences in the means of paired samples.

In many marketing research applications, the observations for the two groups are not selected from independent samples. Rather, the observations relate to **paired samples** in that the two sets of observations relate to the same respondents. A sample of respondents may rate two competing brands, may indicate the relative importance of two attributes of a product, or may evaluate a brand at two different times. The difference in these cases is examined by a **paired samples t test**. To compute t for paired samples, the paired difference variable, denoted by D, is formed and its mean and variance calculated. Then the t statistic is computed. The degrees of freedom are $n - 1$, where n is the number of pairs. The relevant formulas are

$$H_0: \mu_D = 0$$
$$H_1: \mu_D \neq 0$$

$$t_{n-1} = \frac{\overline{D} - \mu_D}{\frac{s_D}{\sqrt{n}}}$$

where,

$$\overline{D} = \frac{\sum_{i=1}^{n} D_i}{n}$$

$$s_D = \sqrt{\frac{\sum_{i=1}^{n} (D_i - \overline{D})^2}{n-1}}$$

In the store patronage project, a paired t test could be used to determine if the respondents attached more importance to the quality of merchandise than to store credit and billing policies. The resulting output is shown in Table 15.15. The mean difference between the variables is 1.4391, with a standard deviation of 1.6087 and a standard error

TABLE 15.15							
Paired Samples t Test							

Variable	Number of Cases	Mean	Standard Deviation	Standard Error
Quality	271	5.6273	0.670	.041
Store credit	271	4.1882	1.619	.098

(Difference) Mean	Standard Deviation	Standard Error	Correlation	Two-tail Probability	t value	Degrees of Freedom	Two-tail Probability
1.4391	1.6087	.0977	.222	.000	14.73	270	.000

of .0977. This results in a *t* value of (1.4391/.0977) = 14.73, with 271 − 1 = 270 degrees of freedom and a probability of less than 0.001. Therefore, the quality of merchandise is more important than store credit and billing policies in selecting a department store. Another application is provided in the context of determining the relative effectiveness of 15-second versus 30-second television commercials.

EXAMPLE

Seconds Count

A survey of 83 media directors of the largest Canadian advertising agencies was conducted to determine the relative effectiveness of 15-second versus 30-second commercial advertisements. By use of a five-point rating scale (1 being excellent and 5 being poor), 15- and 30-second commercials were rated by each respondent for brand awareness, main idea recall, persuasion, and ability to tell an emotional story. The table indicates that 30-second commercials were rated more favorably on all the dimensions. Paired *t* tests indicated that these differences were significant, and the 15-second commercials were evaluated as less effective.[19]

Mean Rating of 15- and 30-Second Commercials on the Four Communication Variables

Brand Awareness		Main Idea Recall		Persuasion		Ability to Tell Emotional Story	
15	30	15	30	15	30	15	30
2.5	1.9	2.7	2.0	3.7	2.1	4.3	1.9 ◆

The difference in proportions for paired samples can be tested by using the McNemar test or the chi-square test, as explained in the following section on nonparametric tests.

NONPARAMETRIC TESTS

Nonparametric tests are used when the variables are nonmetric. Like parametric tests, nonparametric tests are available for testing variables from one sample, two independent samples, or two related samples.

One Sample

Sometimes the researcher wants to test whether the observations for a particular variable could reasonably have come from a particular distribution, such as the normal, uniform, or Poisson distribution. Knowledge of the distribution is necessary for finding probabilities corresponding to known values of the variable or variable values corresponding to known probabilities (see Appendix 12A). The **Kolmogorov-Smirnov (K-S) one-sample test** is one such goodness-of-fit test. The K-S compares the cumulative distribution function for a variable with a specified distribution. A_i denotes the cumulative relative frequency for each category of the theoretical (assumed) distribution, and O_i denotes the comparable value of the sample frequency. The K-S test is based on the maximum value of the absolute difference between A_i and O_i. The test statistic is

$$K = \text{Max} |A_i - O_i|$$

The decision to reject the null hypothesis is based on the value of K. The larger K is, the more confidence we have that H_0 is false. Note that this is one-tailed test, since the value of K is always positive, and we reject H_0 for large values of K. For $\alpha = .05$, the critical value of K for large samples (over 35) is given by $1.36/n$.[20] Alternatively, K can be transformed into a normally distributed z statistic and its associated probability determined.

In the context of the store patronage project, suppose that one wanted to test whether the distribution of the importance attached to the store credit and billing policies was normal. A K-S one-sample test is conducted, yielding the data shown in Table 15.16. The largest absolute difference between the observed and normal distribution was $K = 0.1975$. The critical value for K is $1.36/271 = 0.005$. Since the calculated value of K is larger than the critical value, the null hypothesis is rejected. Alternatively, Table 15.16 indicates that the probability of observing a K value of 0.1975, as determined by the normalized z statistic, is less than .001. Since this is less than the significance level of .05, the null hypothesis is rejected, leading to the same conclusion. Hence, the distribution of the importance attached to store credit and billing policies variable deviates significantly from the normal distribution.

As mentioned earlier, the chi-square test can also be performed on a single variable from one sample. In this context, the chi-square serves as a goodness-of-fit test. It tests whether a significant difference exists between the observed number of cases in each category and the expected number. Other one-sample nonparametric tests include the runs test and the binomial test. The **runs test** is a test of randomness for the dichotomous variables. This test is conducted by determining whether the order or sequence in which observations are obtained is random. The **binomial test** is also a goodness-of-fit test for dichotomous variables. It tests the goodness of fit of the observed number of

Kolmogorov-Smirnov one-sample test A one-sample nonparametric goodness-of-fit test that compares the cumulative distribution function for a variable with a specified distribution.

runs test A test of randomness for a dichotomous variable.

binomial test A goodness-of-fit statistical test for dichotomous variables. It tests the goodness of fit of the observed number of observations in each category to the number expected under a specified binomial distribution.

TABLE 15.16 *K-S One-Sample Test for Normality*	Test Distribution, Normal				
Mean:	4.19				
Standard Deviation:	1.62				
Cases:	271				

	Most Extreme Differences				
Absolute	Positve	Negative	K-S z	Two-Tailed p	
0.19754	0.13150	−0.19754	3.252	.000	

observations in each category to the number expected under a specified binomial distribution. For more information on these tests, refer to standard statistical literature.[21]

Two Independent Samples

Mann-Whitney U test A statistical test for a variable measured on an ordinal scale comparing the difference in the location of two populations based on observations from two independent samples.

When the difference in the location of two populations is to be compared based on observations from two independent samples and the variable is measured on an ordinal scale, the **Mann-Whitney U test** can be used.[22] This test corresponds to the two independent sample *t* test, for interval scale variables, when the variances of the two populations are assumed equal.

In the Mann-Whitney *U* test, the two samples are combined and the cases are ranked in order of increasing size. The test statistic, *U*, is computed as the number of times a score from sample or group 1 precedes a score from group 2. If the samples are from the same population, the distribution of scores from the two groups in the rank list should be random. An extreme value of *U* would indicate a nonrandom pattern pointing to the inequality of the two groups. For samples of less than 30, the exact significance level for *U* is computed. For larger samples, *U* is transformed into a normally distributed *z* statistic. This *z* can be corrected for ties within ranks.

Since the distribution of importance attached to the store credit and billing policies was determined to be nonnormal, it is appropriate to examine again whether respondents who are familiar with the department stores attach different importance to store credit and billing policies than those who are unfamiliar. This time, though, the Mann-Whitney *U* test is used. The results are given in Table 15.17. Again, a significant difference is found between the two groups, corroborating the results of the two independent samples *t* test reported earlier. Since the ranks are assigned from the smallest observation to the largest, the higher mean rank (144.39) of respondents with greater familiarity indicates that they attach greater importance to store credit and billing policies than those who are less familiar (mean rank = 123.84).

Researchers often wish to test for a significant difference in proportions obtained from two independent samples. In this case, as an alternative to the parametric *z* test considered earlier, one could also use the cross-tabulation procedure to conduct a chi-square test.[23] In this case, we will have a 2 × 2 table. One variable will be used to denote the sample and will assume the value 1 for sample 1 and the value of 2 for sample 2. The other variable will be the binary variable of interest.

two-sample median test Nonparametric test statistic that determines whether two groups are drawn from populations with the same median. This test is not as powerful as the Mann-Whitney U.

Two other independent-samples nonparametric tests are the median test and Kolmogorov-Smirnov test. The **two-sample median test** determines whether the two groups are drawn from populations with the same median. It is not as powerful as the

TABLE 15.17	Mean Rank	Cases		
Mann-Whitney U Test	123.84	135 Familiarity = 1.00		
	144.39	132 Familiarity = 2.00		
Mann-Whitney U-Wilcoxon Rank Sum W Test, Store Credit by Familiarity		267 Total		
	U	W	*z*	Corrected for ties, Two-tailed *p*
	7538.00	19060.00	−2.2219	.0263

Note: *U* = Mann-Whitney test statistic, *W* = Wilcoxon *W* statistic, *z* = *U* transformed into a normally distributed *z* statistic.

Kolmogorov-Smirnov two-sample test
Nonparametric test statistic that determines whether two distributions are the same. It takes into account any differences in the two distributions, including median, dispersion, and skewness.

Mann-Whitney U test because it merely uses the location of each observation relative to the median, and not the rank, of each observation. The **Kolmogorov-Smirnov two-sample test** examines whether the two distributions are the same. It takes into account any differences between the two distributions, including the median, dispersion, and skewness, as illustrated by the following example.

EXAMPLE
Directors Change Direction

How do marketing research directors and users in Fortune 500 manufacturing firms perceive the role of marketing research in initiating changes in marketing strategy formulation? It was found that the marketing research directors were more strongly in favor of initiating changes in strategy and less in favor of holding back than were users of marketing research. Using the Kolmogorov-Smirnov test, these differences of role definition were statistically significant at the .05 level, as shown below.[24]

The Role of Marketing Research in Strategy Formulation

Stage/item Strategy formulation	Sample	n	Absolutely Must	Preferably Should	May or May Not	Preferably Should Not	Absolutely Must Not	Kolmogorov-Smirnov test Significance
"Initiate change in the marketing strategy of the firm whenever possible."	D[a]	77	7	26	43	19	5	
	U[a]	68	2	15	32	35	16	.05

[a]D = directors, U = users

In this example, the marketing research directors and users comprised two independent samples. The samples, however, are not always independent. In the case of paired samples, a different set of tests should be used.

Paired Samples

Wilcoxon matched-pairs signed-ranks test A nonparametric test that analyzes the differences between the paired observations, taking into account the magnitude of the differences.

An important nonparametric test for examining differences in the location of two populations based on paired observations is the **Wilcoxon matched-pairs signed-ranks test**. This test analyzes the differences between the paired observations, taking into account the magnitude of the differences. It computes the differences between the pairs of variables and ranks the absolute differences. The next step is to sum the positive and negative ranks. The test statistic, z, is computed from the positive and negative rank sums. Under the null hypothesis of no difference, z is a standard normal variate with mean 0 and variance 1 for large samples. This test corresponds to the paired t test considered earlier.[25]

The example considered for the paired t test, whether the respondents attached more importance to the quality of merchandise or to store credit and billing policies, is considered again. Suppose that we assume that both these variables are measured on ordinal rather than interval scales. Accordingly, we use the Wilcoxon test. The results are shown in Table 15.18. Again, a significant difference is found in the variables, and the results are in accordance with the conclusion reached by the paired t test. There are 177 negative differences (importance attached to store credit and billing policies is less than that attached to quality of merchandise). The mean rank of these negative differences is 99.89. On the other hand, there are only 14 positive differences (the importance

TABLE 15.18	Mean Rank	Quality with Store Credit	
Wilcoxon Matched-Pairs Signed-Ranks Test		Cases	(Store Credit Quality)
	99.88	177	− Ranks
	46.89	14	+ Ranks
		80	Ties
		<u>271</u>	Total
	$z = -11.1262$		2-tailed $p = .0000$

sign test A nonparametric test for examining differences in the location of two populations, based on paired observations, that only compares the signs of the differences between pairs of variables without taking into account the magnitude of the differences.

attached to store credit exceeds that of quality). The mean rank of these differences is 46.89. There are 80 ties, or observations with the same value for both variables. These numbers indicate that quality of merchandise is more important than store credit and billing policies. Furthermore, the probability associated with the z statistic is less than .05, indicating that the difference is indeed significant.

Another paired sample nonparametric test is the **sign test**.[26] This test is not as powerful as the Wilcoxon matched-pairs signed-ranks test because it only compares the signs of the differences between pairs of variables without taking into account the magnitude of the differences. In the special case of a binary variable where the researcher wishes to test differences in proportions, the McNemar test can be used. Alternatively, the chi-square test can also be used for binary variables. The various parametric and nonparametric tests are summarized in Table 15.19. Research in Practice 15.1 illustrates the

TABLE 15.19

A Summary of Hypothesis Testing

Sample	Application	Level of Scaling	Test/Comments
One Sample			
One Sample	Distributions	Nonmetric	K-S and chi-square for goodness of fit Runs test for randomness Binomial test for goodness of fit for dichotomous variables
One sample	Means	Metric	t test, if variance is unknown z test, if variance is known
One sample	Proportions	Metric	z test
Two Independent Samples			
Two independent samples	Distributions	Nonmetric	K-S two-sample test for examining the equivalence of two distributions
Two independent samples	Means	Metric	Two-group t test F test for equality of variances
Two independent samples	Proportions	Metric Nonmetric	z test Chi-square test
Two independent samples	Rankings/medians	Nonmetric	Mann-Whitney U test is more powerful than the median test
Paired Samples			
Paired samples	Means	Metric	Paired t test
Paired samples	Proportions	Nonmetric	McNemar test for binary variables Chi-square test
Paired samples	Rankings/medians	Nonmetric	Wilcoxon matched-pairs ranked-signs test is more powerful than the sign test

use of hypothesis testing in international branding strategy,[27] whereas Research in Practice 15.2 cites the use of descriptive statistics in research on ethics.[28]

RESEARCH IN PRACTICE 15.1

International Brand Equity: The Name of the Game

In the 1990s, the trend is toward global marketing. How can marketers market a brand abroad where diverse historical and cultural differences exist? According to Bob Kroll, former president of Del Monte International, uniform packaging may be an asset, yet catering to individual countries' culinary taste preferences is more important. One recent survey on international product marketing makes this clear. Marketing executives now believe that it is best to think globally but act locally. Respondents included 100 brand and product managers and marketing people from some of the nation's largest food, pharmaceutical, and personal product companies. Of these respondents, 39% said that it would not be a good idea to use uniform packaging in foreign markets whereas 38% were in favor of it. Those in favor of regionally targeted packaging, however, mentioned the desirability of maintaining as much brand equity and package consistency as possible from market to market. But they also believed that it was necessary to tailor the package to fit the linguistic and regulatory needs of different markets. Thus, a suitable research question can be: Do consumers in different countries prefer to buy global name brands with different packaging customized to suit their local needs? Based on this research question, one can frame a hypothesis that other things being constant, standardized branding with customized packaging for a well-established name brand will result in greater market share. The hypotheses may be formulated as follows:

H_0:   Standardized branding with customized packaging for a well-established name brand will not lead to greater market share in the international market.

H_1:   Other factors remaining equal, standardized branding with customized packaging for a well-established name brand will lead to greater market share in the international market.

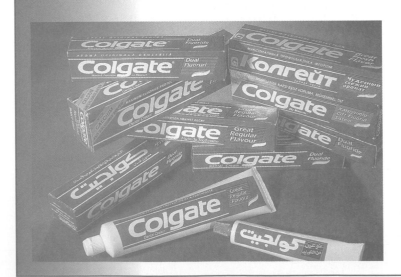

To test the null hypothesis, a well-established brand like Colgate toothpaste that has followed a mixed strategy can be selected. The market share in countries with standardized branding and standardized packaging can be compared with market share in countries with standardized branding and customized packaging, after controlling for the effect of other factors. A two independent samples *t* test can be used.

Colgate toothpaste has followed a mixed strategy of standardized branding with customized packaging in some foreign markets to increase its share of the global market. ◆

RESEARCH IN PRACTICE 15.2

Statistics Describe Distrust

Descriptive statistics indicate that the public perception of ethics in business, and thus ethics in marketing, are poor. In a poll conducted by *Business Week*, 46% of those surveyed said that the ethical standards of business executives are only fair. A *Time* magazine survey revealed that 76% of Americans felt that business managers (and thus researchers) lacked ethics and that this lack contributes to the decline of moral standards in the United States. The general public is not alone in its disparagement of business ethics, however. In a Touche Ross survey of businesspersons, results showed that the general feeling was that ethics were a serious concern and that media portrayal of the lack of ethics in business has not been exaggerated.

COMPUTER APPLICATIONS

All three standard statistical packages (SPSS, SAS, and BMDP) have similar programs in their microcomputer and mainframe versions for computing frequency distributions, cross-tabulations, and testing hypotheses. The major programs for frequency distribution are FREQUENCIES (SPSS), UNIVARIATE (SAS), and 2D (BMDP). Other programs provide only the frequency distribution (FREQ in SAS, 4D in BMDP) or only some of the associated statistics, as described in Exhibit 15.1. A summary comparison of these programs is presented in Table 15.20.[29]

EXHIBIT 15.1

Computer Programs for Frequency

SPSS

The main program in SPSS is FREQUENCIES. It produces a table of frequency counts, percentages, and cumulative percentages for the values of each variable. It gives all the associated statistics except for the coefficient of variation. If the data are interval scaled and only the summary statistics are desired, the DESCRIPTIVES procedure can be used. All the statistics computed by DESCRIPTIVES are available in FREQUENCIES. DESCRIPTIVES is more efficient, however, because it does not sort values into a frequency table. An additional program, MEANS, computes means and standard deviations for a dependent variable over subgroups of cases defined by independent variables.

SAS

The main program in SAS is UNIVARIATE. In addition to providing a frequency table, this program provides all of the associated statistics. Another procedure available is FREQ. For one-way frequency distribution, FREQ does not provide any associated statistics. If only summary statistics are desired, procedures such as MEANS, SUMMARY, and TABULATE can be used. It should be noted that FREQ is not available as an independent program in the microcomputer version.

BMDP

The main procedure in BMDP is 2D, which gives the frequency distribution and all the associated statistics except for the coefficient of variation. 1D provides the summary statistics for interval data but does not give the frequency distribution. 4D gives a frequency distribution for numeric and nonnumeric data but does not compute the summary statistics.

TABLE 15.20

Computer Programs for Frequencies and Summary Statistics

	SPSS			SAS				BMDP		
	Frequencies	Descriptives	Means	Univariate	Summary	Tabulate	Freq	P1D	P2D	P4D
Frequency distribution	X			X			X		X	X
Location										
Mean	X	X	X	X	X	X		X	X	
Mode	X			X					X	
Median	X			X					X	
Variability										
Range	X	X	X	X	X	X		X	X	
Variance	X	X	X	X	X	X		X	X	
Coefficient of variation			X	X	X	X		X		
Interquartile range	X			X					X	
Shape										
Skewness	X	X		X					X	
Kurtosis	X	X		X					X	

The major cross-tabulation programs are CROSSTABS (SPSS), FREQ (SAS), and 4F (BMDP). All these programs will display the cross-classification tables and provide cell counts, row and column percentages, the chi-square test for significance, and all the measures of the strength of the association that have been discussed. In addition, the TABULATE (SAS) program can be used for obtaining cell counts and row and column percentages, although it does not provide any of the associated statistics.

The major program for conducting t tests in SPSS is T-TEST. This program can be used to conduct t tests on independent as well as paired samples. All the nonparametric tests that we have discussed can be conducted by using the NPAR TESTS program. In SAS, the program TTEST can be used. The nonparametric tests may be conducted by using NPAR1WAY. This program will conduct the two independent samples tests (Mann-Whitney, median, and K-S) as well as the Wilcoxon test for paired samples. The parametric t tests in BMDP may be conducted by using the 3D program and the nonparametric tests by using 3S.

SUMMARY

Basic data analysis provides valuable insights and guides the rest of the data analysis as well as the interpretation of the results. A frequency distribution should be obtained for each variable in the data. This analysis produces a table of frequency counts, percentages, and cumulative percentages for all the values associated with that variable. It indicates the extent of out-of-range, missing, or extreme values. The mean, mode, and median of a frequency distribution are measures of central tendency. The variability of the distribution is described by the range, the variance or standard deviation, coefficient of variation, and interquartile range. Skewness and kurtosis provide an idea of the shape of the distribution.

Cross-tabulations are tables that reflect the joint distribution of two or more variables. In cross-tabulation, the percentages can be computed either by column, based on column totals, or by row, based on row totals. The general rule is to compute the percentages in the direction of the independent variable, across the dependent variable. Often the introduction of a third variable can provide additional insights. The chi-square statistic provides a test of the statistical significance of the observed association in a cross-tabulation. The phi coefficient, contingency coefficient, Cramer's V, and lambda coefficient provide measures of the strength of association between the variables.

Parametric and nonparametric tests are available for testing hypotheses related to differences. In the parametric case, the t test is used to examine hypotheses related to the population mean. Different forms of the t test are suitable for testing hypotheses based on one sample, two independent samples, or paired samples. In the nonparametric case, popular one-sample tests include the Kolmogorov-Smirnov, chi-square, runs, and binomial tests. For two independent nonparametric samples, the Mann-Whitney U test, median test, and the Kolmogorov-Smirnov test can be used. For paired samples, the Wilcoxon matched-pairs signed-ranks test and the sign test are useful for examining hypotheses related to measures of location.[30]

ACRONYMS

The statistics associated with frequencies may be summarized by the acronym Frequencies:

F   latness or peakedness: kurtosis
R   ange
E   stimate of location: mean
Q   uotients: percentages
U   ndulation: variance
E   stimate of location: mode
N   umbers or counts
C   oefficient of variation
I   nterquartile range
E   stimate of location: median
S   kewness

The salient characteristics of cross-tabulations may be summarized by the acronym C Tabulations:

C   ube: chi-square, contingency coefficient, and Cramer's V

T   wo by two table statistic: phi coefficient
A   dditional insights or refinements provided by third variable
B   ased on cell count of at least five
U   nchanged association with third variable introduction
L   ambda coefficient
A   ssociation and not causation is measured
T   wo- and three-variable cases
I   nitial relationship may be spurious
O   ver three variables poses problems
N   umbers and percentages
S   uppressed association may be revealed

EXERCISES

QUESTIONS

1. Describe the procedure for computing frequencies.
2. What measures of location are commonly computed?

3. Define the interquartile range. What does it measure?
4. What is meant by the coefficient of variation?
5. How is the relative flatness or peakedness of a distribution measured?
6. What is a skewed distribution? What does it mean?
7. What is the major difference between cross-tabulation and frequency distribution?
8. What is the general rule for computing percentages in cross-tabulation?
9. Define a spurious correlation.
10. What is meant by a suppressed association? How is it revealed?
11. Discuss the reasons for the frequent use of cross-tabulations. What are some of the limitations?
12. Present a classification of hypothesis testing procedures.
13. Describe the general procedure for conducting a *t* test.
14. What is the major difference between parametric and nonparametric tests?
15. Which nonparametric tests are the counterparts of the two independent samples *t* test for parametric data?
16. Which nonparametric tests are the counterparts of the paired samples *t* test for parametric data?

PROBLEMS

1. In each of the following situations, indicate the statistical analysis you would conduct and the appropriate test or test statistic that should be used.
   a. Consumer preferences for Camay bath soap were obtained on an 11-point Likert scale. The same consumers were then shown a commercial about Camay. After the commercial, preferences for Camay were again measured. Has the commercial been successful in inducing a change in preferences?
   b. Does the preference for Camay bath soap follow a normal distribution?
   c. Respondents in a survey of 1,000 households were classified as heavy users, medium users, light users, or nonusers of ice cream. They were also classified as being in high-, medium, or low-income categories. Is the consumption of ice cream related to income level?
   d. In a survey using a representative sample of 2,000 households from the Market Facts consumer mail panel, the respondents were asked to rank ten department stores, including Sears, in order of preference. The sample was divided into small and large households based on a median split of the household size. Does preference for shopping in Sears vary by household size?
2. The current advertising campaign for a major soft drink would be changed if less than 30% of the consumers like it.
   a. Formulate the null and alternative hypotheses.
   b. Discuss the type I and type II errors that could occur in hypothesis testing.
   c. Which statistical test would you use? Why?
   d. A random sample of 300 consumers was surveyed, and 84 respondents indicated that they liked the campaign. Should the campaign be changed? Why?
3. A major department store chain is having an end-of-season sale on refrigerators. The number of refrigerators sold during this sale at a sample of ten stores was:

$$80 \quad 110 \quad 0 \quad 40 \quad 70 \quad 80 \quad 100 \quad 50 \quad 80 \quad 30$$

   a. Is there evidence that an average of more than 50 refrigerators per store was sold during this sale? Use $\alpha = .05$.
   b. What assumption is necessary to perform this test?

COMPUTER EXERCISES

1. Use one of the mainframe statistical packages (SPSS, SAS, or BMDP) or the corresponding microcomputer version to conduct one statistical test for Problem 3.

NOTES

1. Mary C. Gilly, "Sex Roles in Advertising: A Comparison of Television Advertisements in Australia, Mexico, and the United States," *Journal of Marketing* 52 (April 1988): 75–85.

2. Troy A. Festervand, Don R. Snyder, and John D. Tsalikis, "Influence of Catalog vs. Store Shopping and Prior Satisfaction on Perceived Risk," *Journal of the Academy of Marketing Science* (Winter 1986): 28–36.

3. Shelby D. Hunt and Lawrence B. Chonko, "Ethical Problems of Advertising Agency Executives," *Journal of Advertising* 16 (Fall, 1987): 16–24.

4. For an application of frequencies and descriptive statistics, see Mary Jo Bitner, Bernard H. Booms, and Lois A. Mohr, "Critical Service Encounters: The Employee's Viewpoint," *Journal of Marketing* 58 (October 1994): 95–106.

5. See any introductory statistics book for a more detailed description of these statistics; for example, see Mark L. Berenson and David M. Levine, *Basic Business Statistics: Concepts and Applications*, 5th ed. (Englewood Cliffs, NJ: Prentice Hall, 1992).

6. For our purposes, no distinction will be made between formal hypothesis testing and statistical inference by means of confidence intervals.

7. Excellent discussions of ways to analyze cross-tabulations can be found in O. Hellevik, *Introduction to Causal Analysis: Exploring Survey Data by Crosstabulation* (Beverly Hills: Sage Publications, 1984).

8. Lawrence F. Feick, "Analyzing Marketing Research Data with Association Models," *Journal of Marketing Research* 21 (November 1984): 376–86. For a recent application, see Boris W. Becker and Dennis O. Kaldenberg, "Determination of Fees by Professionals: An Exploratory Investigation of Dentists," *Journal of Health Care Marketing* (September 1991): 28–35.

9. See the classic book by Hans Zeisel, *Say It with Figures*, 5th ed. (New York: Harper and Row, 1968).

10. See, for example, O. Hellevik, *Introduction to Causal Analysis: Exploring Survey Data by Crosstabulation* (Beverly Hills: Sage Publications, 1984); and J. G. Upton Graham, *The Analysis of Cross-Tabulated Data* (Chichester, England: Wiley, 1978).

11. See H. O. Lancaster, *The Chi Squared Distribution* (New York: Wiley, 1969), or any basic statistics book.

12. Mark L. Berenson and David M. Levine, *Basic Business Statistics: Concepts and Applications*, 5th ed. (Englewood Cliffs, NJ: Prentice Hall, 1992).

13. Some statisticians, however, disagree. They feel that a correction should not be applied. See, for example, John E. Overall, "Power of Chi-Square Tests for 2 x 2 Contingency Tables with Small Expected Frequencies," *Psychological Bulletin* (January 1980): 132–35.

14. Significance tests and confidence intervals are also available for either lambda asymmetric or lambda symmetric. See L. A. Goodman and W. H. Kruskal, "Measures of Association for Cross Classification: Appropriate Sampling Theory," *Journal of the American Statistical Association* 88 (June 1963): 310–64.

15. Michael Cowles and Caroline Davis, "On the Origins of the .05 Level of Statistical Significance," *American Psychologist* (May 1982): 553–58. See also Masaaki Kotabe, Dale F. Duhan, David K. Smith, Jr., and R. Dale Wilson, "The Perceived Veracity of PIMS Strategy Principles in Japan: An Empirical Inquiry," *Journal of Marketing* 55 (January 1991): 26–41.

16. Technically, a null hypothesis cannot be accepted. It can be either rejected or not rejected. This distinction, however, is inconsequential in applied research.

17. The condition when the variances cannot be assumed to be equal is known as the Behrens-Fisher problem. There is some controversy over the best procedure in this case.

18. James R. Lumpkin and James B. Hunt, "Mobility as an Influence on Retail Patronage Behavior of the Elderly: Testing Conventional Wisdom," *Journal of the Academy of Marketing Science* (Winter 1989): 1–12.

19. Jerry A. Rosenblatt and Janet Mainprize, "The History and Future of 15-Second Commercials: An Empirical Investigation of the Perception of Ad Agency Media Directors," in William Lazer, Eric Shaw, and Chow-Hou Wee (eds.), *World Marketing Congress, International Conference Series*, vol. 4 (Boca Raton, FL: Academy of Marketing Science, 1989), pp. 169–77.

20. Donald L. Harnett, *Statistical Methods*, 3rd ed. (Reading, MA: Addison-Wesley, 1982).

21. W. J. Conover, *Practical Nonparametric Statistics*, 2nd ed. (New York: Wiley, 1980).

22. There is some controversy over whether nonparametric statistical techniques should be used to make inferences about population parameters.

23. The t test in this case is equivalent to a chi-square test for independence in a 2×2 contingency table. The relationship is

$$\chi^2_{.95(1)} = t^2_{.05(n_1 + n_2 - 2)}$$

For large samples, the t distribution approaches the normal distrbution and so the t test and the z test are equivalent.

24. James R. Krum, Pradeep A. Rau, and Stephen K. Keiser, "The Marketing Research Process: Role Perceptions of Researchers And Users," *Journal of Advertising Research* (December–January 1988): 9–21.

25. For a recent application of Wilcoxon matched-pairs signed ranks test, see Manohar U. Kalwani and Narakesari Narayandas, "Long-Term Manufacturer-Supplier Relationships: Do They Pay Off for Supplier Firms?" *Journal of Marketing* 59 (January 1995): 1–16.

26. Wayne W. Daniel and James C. Terrell, *Business Statistics*, 6th ed. (Boston: Houghton Mifflin 1992); and J. G. Field, "The World's Simplest Test of Significance," *Journal of the Market Research Society* (July 1971): 170–72.

27. John Blyth, "U.S. Firms Are Becoming More Realistic About Global Marketing,"

28. G. R. Laczniak and P. E. Murphy, "Fostering Ethical Marketing Decisions," *Journal of Business Ethics* 10 (1991): 259–71.

29. For mainframe packages, see:

   SPSS Base Systems User's Guide (Englewood Cliffs, NJ: Prentice Hall, 1994).

   SAS Language and Procedure: Usage, V 6 (Cary, NC: SAS Institute, 1989).

   SAS Language and Procedure: Usage 2, V 6 (Cary, NC: SAS Institute, 1991).

   SAS Procedures Guide, V 6, 3rd ed. (Cary, NC: SAS Institute, 1990).

   SAS Language: Reference, V 6 (Cary, NC: SAS Institute, 1990).

   BMDP Statistical Software Manual, vols. 1 and 2 (Berkeley: University of California Press, 1990).

   For microcomputer packages, see:

   SPSS/PC+™ V 4.0 BASE MANUAL (Englewood Cliffs, NJ: Prentice Hall, 1990).

   SPSS/PC+ Advanced Statistics™, V 4.0 (Englewood Cliffs, NJ: Prentice Hall, 1990).

   SAS/STAT™ User Guide, V 6, 4th ed., vols. 1, 2 (Cary, NC: SAS Institute, 1990).

   The BMDP manual for microcomputers is the same as that for the mainframe.

30. The assistance of James Agarwal with the international marketing research example, the assistance of Mark Leach and Gina Miller in writing the ethics section, and the assistance of Mark Peterson in writing the computer applications section is gratefully acknowledged.

Analysis of Variance and Covariance

Analysis of variance and analysis of covariance must have a dependent variable that has been measured using an interval or ratio scale; there must also be one or more independent variables that are all categorical or are combinations of categorical and interval or ratio variables.

◆

OBJECTIVES

After reading this chapter, the student should be able to:

1. Discuss the scope of the analysis of variance (ANOVA) technique and its relationship to *t* test, and regression.
2. Describe one-way analysis of variance including decomposition of the total variation, measurement of effects, significance testing, and interpretation of results.
3. Describe *n*-way analysis of variance and the testing of the significance of the overall effect, the interaction effect, and the main effect of each factor.
4. Describe analysis of covariance and show how it accounts for the influence of uncontrolled independent variables.
5. Explain key factors pertaining to the interpretation of results with emphasis on interactions, relative importance of factors, and multiple comparisons.
6. Discuss specialized ANOVA techniques applicable to marketing such as repeated measures ANOVA, nonmetric analysis of variance, and multivariate analysis of variance (MANOVA).

OVERVIEW

In Chapter 15, we examined tests of differences between two means or two medians. In this chapter, we discuss procedures for examining differences between more than two means or medians. These procedures are called analysis of variance and analysis of covariance. These procedures have traditionally been used for analyzing experimental data, but they are also used for analyzing survey or observational data.

We describe the analysis of variance and covariance procedures and discuss their relationship to other techniques. Then we describe one-way analysis of variance, the simplest of these procedures, followed by *n*-way analysis of variance and analysis of covariance. Special attention is given to issues in interpretation of results as they relate to interactions, relative importance of factors, and multiple comparisons. Some specialized topics such as repeated measures analysis of variance, nonmetric analysis of variance, and multivariate analysis of variance are briefly discussed. We begin with some examples illustrating the applications of analysis of variance.

DEPARTMENT STORE PATRONAGE PROJECT
Analysis of Variance

In the department store patronage project, several independent variables were examined as categorical variables having more than two categories. For example, familiarity with the department stores considered was respecified as high, medium, or low. The effects of these independent variables on metric dependent variables were examined using analysis of variance procedures. Several useful insights were obtained that guided subsequent data analysis and interpretation. For example, a three-category respecification of familiarity produced results that were not significant, whereas treating familiarity as a binary variable (high or low) produced significant results. This, along with the frequency distribution, indicated that treating familiarity as having only two categories was most appropriate. ◆

EXAMPLE
Electronic Shopping Risks

Analysis of variance was used to test differences in preferences for electronic shopping for products with different economic and social risks. In a 2 × 2 design, economic risk and social risk were varied at two levels each (high, low). Preference for electronic shopping served as the dependent variable. The results indicated a significant interaction of social risk with economic risk. Electronic shopping was not perceived favorably for high-social-risk products, regardless of the level of economic product risk, but it was preferred for low-economic-risk products over high-economic-risk products when the level of social risk was low.[1] ◆

EXAMPLE
Antacids are Treatments for ANOVA

The role of verbal content and relative newness of a brand in determining the effectiveness of a comparative advertising format for over-the-counter antacids was investigated. The measure of attitude toward the sponsoring brand was the dependent variable. Three factors, advertising format (AF), verbal content (VC), and relative newness

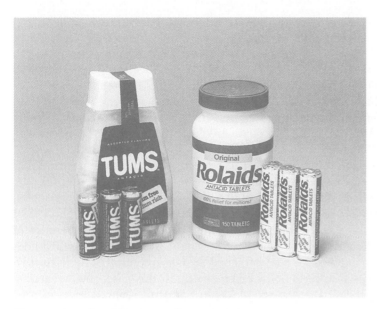

Comparative advertising emphasizing factual information is best suited for launching a new brand of antacids. ◆ Teri Stratford.

(RN), each manipulated at two levels, were the independent variables.

Advertising format was either noncomparative or comparative. In the comparative format, well-known national brands (Rolaids and Tums) were used for comparison. Relative newness was manipulated by changing the brand's sponsor. Alka-Seltzer was the sponsor in the well-established brand treatment, whereas Acid-Off was the sponsor in the new-brand condition. The name "Acid-Off" was chosen based on a pretest. Verbal content was manipulated to reflect factual or evaluative content in an ad.

The subjects were recruited at a shopping mall and randomly assigned to the treatment by an interviewer who was blind to the purpose of the study. A total of 207 responses was collected, 200 of which were usable. Twenty-five subjects were assigned to each of the eight ($2 \times 2 \times 2$) treatments.

A three-way analysis of variance was performed, with attitude as the dependent variable. The overall results were significant. The three-way interaction was also significant. The only two-way interaction that was significant was between ad format and relative newness. A major conclusion from these results was that a comparative format that emphasized factual information was best suited for launching a new brand.[2] ◆

In the department store example, when familiarity had three categories, the *t* test was not appropriate to examine the overall difference in category means, so analysis of variance was used instead. The electronic shopping study involved a comparison of means when there were two factors (independent variables), each of which was varied at two levels. The more complex comparative advertising study involved three factors, each with two levels. In the latter two examples, *t* tests were not appropriate, since the effect of each factor was not independent of the effect of other factors (in other words, interactions were significant). Analysis of variance provided meaningful conclusions in these studies. The relationship of analysis of variance to the *t* test and other techniques is considered in the next section.

RELATIONSHIP AMONG TECHNIQUES

analysis of variance (ANOVA) A statistical technique for examining the differences among means for two or more populations.

Analysis of variance and analysis of covariance are used for examining the differences in the mean values of the dependent variable associated with the effect of the controlled independent variables, after taking into account the influence of the uncontrolled independent variables. Essentially, **analysis of variance (ANOVA)** is used as a test of means for two or more populations. The null hypothesis, typically, is that all means are equal. For example, suppose that the researcher was interested in examining whether heavy users, medium users, light users, and nonusers of yogurt differed in their preference for Dannon yogurt, measured on a nine-point Likert scale. The null hypothesis that the four groups were not different in preference for Dannon could be tested using analysis of variance.

In its simplest form, analysis of variance must have a dependent variable (preference for Dannon yogurt) that is metric (measured using an interval or ratio scale). There must also be one or more independent variables (product use: heavy, medium, light, and nonusers). The independent variables must be all categorical (nonmetric). Categorical independent variables are also called **factors**. A particular combination of factor levels, or categories, is called a **treatment**. **One-way analysis of variance** (ANOVA) involves only one categorical variable, or a single factor. The differences in preference of heavy users, medium users, light users, and nonusers would be examined by one-way ANOVA. In one-way analysis of variance, a treatment is the same as a factor level (medium users constitute a treatment). If two or more factors are involved, the analysis is termed **n-way analysis of variance**. (If, in addition to product use, the researcher also wanted to examine the preference for Dannon yogurt of customers who are loyal and those who are not, an n-way analysis of variance would be conducted.)

If the set of independent variables consists of both categorical and metric variables, the technique is called **analysis of covariance (ANCOVA)**. For example, analysis of covariance would be required if the researcher wanted to examine the preference of product use groups and loyalty groups, taking into account the respondents' attitudes toward nutrition and the importance they attached to dairy products. The latter two variables would be measured on nine-point Likert scales. In this case, the categorical independent variables (product use and brand loyalty) are still referred to as factors, whereas the metric-independent variables (attitude toward nutrition and importance attached to dairy products) are referred to as **covariates**.

The relationship of analysis of variance to t tests and other techniques, such as regression (see Chapter 17), is shown in Figure 16.1. These techniques all involve a met-

factors Categorical independent variables. The independent variables must be all categorical (nonmetric) to use ANOVA.

treatment In ANOVA, a particular combination of factor levels or categories.

one-way analysis of variance An ANOVA technique in which there is only one factor.

n-way analysis of variance An ANOVA model where two or more factors are involved.

FIGURE 16.1

Relationship between t Test, Analysis of Variance, Analysis of Covariance, and Regression

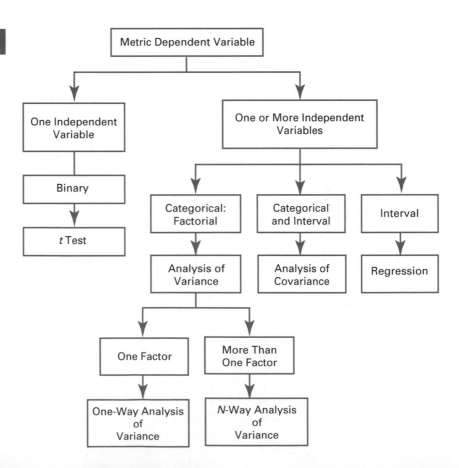

analysis of covariance (ANCOVA) An advanced analysis of variance procedure in which the effects of one or more metric-scaled extraneous variables are removed from the dependent variable before conducting the ANOVA.

covariate A metric-independent variable used in ANCOVA.

ric-dependent variable. ANOVA and ANCOVA can include more than one independent variable (product use, brand loyalty, attitude, importance). Furthermore, at least one of the independent variables must be categorical, and the categorical variables may have more than two categories (in our example, product use has four categories). A *t* test, on the other hand, involves a single, binary independent variable. For example, the difference in the preferences of loyal and nonloyal respondents could be tested by conducting a *t* test. Regression analysis, like ANOVA and ANCOVA, can also involve more than one independent variable. All the independent variables, however, are generally interval scaled, although binary or categorical variables can be accommodated using dummy variables. For example, the relationship between preference for Dannon yogurt, attitude toward nutrition, and importance attached to dairy products could be examined via regression analysis.

ONE-WAY ANALYSIS OF VARIANCE

Marketing researchers are often interested in examining the differences in the mean values of the dependent variable for several categories of a single independent variable or factor. For example:

- Do the various segments differ in terms of their volume of product consumption?
- Do the brand evaluations of groups exposed to different commercials vary?
- Do retailers, wholesalers, and agents differ in their attitudes toward the firm's distribution policies?
- How do consumers' intentions to buy the brand vary with different price levels?
- What is the effect of consumers' familiarity with the store (measured as high, medium, and low) on preference for the store?

The answer to these and similar questions can be determined by conducting one-way analysis of variance. Before describing the procedure, we define the important statistics associated with one-way analysis of variance.[3]

STATISTICS ASSOCIATED WITH ONE-WAY ANALYSIS OF VARIANCE

eta^2 (η^2). The strength of the effects of X (independent variable or factor) on Y (dependent variable) are measured by *eta^2* (η^2). The value of η^2 varies between 0 and 1.

F statistic. The null hypothesis that the category means are equal in the population is tested by an *F statistic* based on the ratio of mean square related to X and mean square related to error.

Mean square. This is the sum of squares divided by the appropriate degrees of freedom.

SS$_{between}$. Also denoted as SS_x, this is the variation in Y related to the variation in the means of the categories of X. This represents variation between the categories of X or the portion of the sum of squares in Y related to X.

SS$_{within}$. Also referred to as SS_{error}, this is the variation in Y due to the variation within each of the categories of X. This variation is not accounted for by X.

SSy. This is the total variation in Y.

Conducting One-Way Analysis of Variance

The procedure for conducting one-way analysis of variance is described in Figure 16.2. It involves identifying the dependent and independent variables, decomposing the total variation, measuring effects, significance testing, and interpreting results. We consider these steps in detail and illustrate them with some applications.

Identifying the Dependent and Independent Variables

The dependent variable is denoted by Y and the independent variable by X, and X is a categorical variable having c categories. There are n observations on Y for each category of X, as shown in Table 16.1. As can be seen, the sample size in each category of X is n, and the total sample size $N = n \times c$. Although the sample sizes in the categories of X (the group sizes) are assumed to be equal for the sake of simplicity, this is not a requirement.

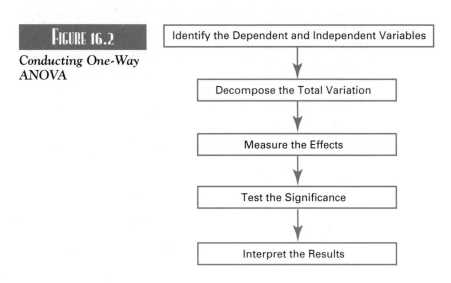

FIGURE 16.2

Conducting One-Way ANOVA

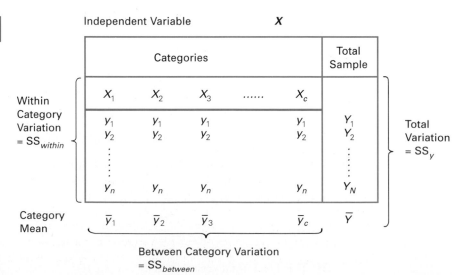

TABLE 16.1

Decomposition of the Total Variation: One-Way ANOVA

Decomposing the Total Variation

In examining the differences among means, one-way analysis of variance involves the **decomposition of the total variation** observed in the dependent variable. This variation is measured by the sums of squares corrected for the mean (SS). Analysis of variance is so named because it examines the variability or variation in the sample (dependent variable) and, based on the variability, determines whether there is reason to believe that the population means differ.

The total variation in Y, denoted by SS_y, can be decomposed into two components:

$$SS_y = SS_{between} + SS_{within}$$

where the subscripts *between* and *within* refer to the categories of X.[4] $SS_{between}$ is the variation in Y related to the variation in the means of the categories of X. It represents variation between the categories of X. In other words, $SS_{between}$ is the portion of the sum of squares in Y related to the independent variable or factor X. For this reason, $SS_{between}$ is also denoted as SS_x. SS_{within} is the variation in Y related to the variation within each category of X. SS_{within} is not accounted for by X. Therefore, it is referred to as SS_{error}. The total variation in Y may be decomposed as

$$SS_y = SS_x + SS_{error}$$

where

$$SS_y = \sum_{i=1}^{N} (Y_i - \overline{Y})^2$$

$$SS_x = \sum_{j=1}^{c} n(\overline{Y}_j - \overline{Y})^2$$

$$SS_{error} = \sum_{j}^{c} \sum_{i}^{n} (Y_{ij} - \overline{Y}_j)^2$$

Y_i = individual observation

$\overline{Y}_j$ = mean for category j

$\overline{Y}$ = mean over the whole sample, or grand mean

Y_{ij} = ith observation in the jth category

The logic of decomposing the total variation in Y, SS_y, into $SS_{between}$ and SS_{within} to examine differences in group means can be intuitively understood. Recall from Chapter 15 that if the variation of the variable in the population was known or estimated, one could estimate how much the sample mean should vary because of random variation alone. In analysis of variance, there are several different groups (e.g., heavy, medium, and light users, and nonusers). If the null hypothesis is true and all the groups have the same mean in the population, one can estimate how much the sample means should vary because of sampling (random) variations alone. If the observed variation in the sample means is more than what would be expected by sampling variation, it is reasonable to conclude that this extra variability is related to differences in group means in the population.

In analysis of variance, we estimate two measures of variation: within groups (SS_{within}) and between groups ($SS_{between}$). Within-group variation is a measure of how much the observations, Y values, within a group vary. This is used to estimate the variance within a group in the population. It is assumed that all the groups have the same variation in the population. But because it is not known that all the groups have the same mean, we cannot calculate the variance of all the observations together. The variance for each of the groups must be calculated individually, and these are combined into an "average" or "overall" variance. Likewise, another estimate of the variance of the Y values may be obtained by examining the variation between the means. (This process is the reverse of determining the variation in the means, given the population variance σ.) If the population mean is the same in all the groups, then the variation in the sample means and the sizes of the sample groups can be used to estimate the variance of Y. The reasonableness of this estimate of the Y variance depends on whether the null hypothesis is true. If the null hypothesis is true and the population means are equal, the variance estimate based on between-group variation is correct. On the other hand, if the groups have different means in the population, the variance estimate based on between-group variation will be too large. Thus, by comparing the Y variance estimates based on between-group and within-group variation, we can test the null hypothesis.[5] Decomposition of the total variation in this manner also enables us to measure the effects of X on Y.

Measuring Effects

The effects of X on Y are measured by SS_x. Since SS_x is related to the variation in the means of the categories of X, the relative magnitude of SS_x increases as the differences among the means of Y in the categories of X increase. The relative magnitude of SS_x also increases as the variations in Y within the categories of X decrease. The strength of the effects of X on Y are measured as follows:

$$\eta^2 = \frac{SS_x}{SS_y} = \frac{SS_y - SS_{error}}{SS_y}$$

The value of η^2 varies between 0 and 1. It assumes a value of 0 when all the category means are equal, indicating that X has no effect on Y. The value of η^2 will be 1 when there is no variability within each category of X but there is some variability between categories. Thus, η^2 is a measure of the variation in Y that is explained by the independent variable X. Not only can we measure the effects of X on Y, but we can also test for their significance.

Significance Testing

In one-way analysis of variance, the interest lies in testing the null hypothesis that the category means are equal in the population.[6] In other words,

$$H_0: \mu_1 = \mu_2 = \mu_3 = \cdots = \mu_c$$

Under the null hypothesis, SS_x and SS_{error} come from the same source of variation. In such a case, the estimate of the population variance of Y can be based on either between category variation or within category variation. In other words, the estimate of the population variance of Y,

$$S_y^2 = \frac{SS_x}{c-1}$$
$$= \text{mean square due to X}$$
$$= MS_x$$

or

$$S_y^2 = \frac{SS_{error}}{N-c}$$

$$= \text{mean square due to error}$$

$$= MS_{error}$$

The null hypothesis may be tested by the F statistic based on the ratio between these two estimates:

$$F = \frac{SS_x/(c-1)}{SS_{error}/(N-c)} = \frac{MS_x}{MS_{error}}$$

This statistic follows the F distribution, with $(c-1)$ and $(N-c)$ degrees of freedom (df). A table of the F distribution is given as Table 5 in the Statistical Appendix at the end of the book. As mentioned in Chapter 15, the F distribution is a probability distribution of the ratios of sample variances. It is characterized by degrees of freedom for the numerator and degrees of freedom for the denominator.[7]

Interpreting Results

If the null hypothesis of equal category means is not rejected, then the independent variable does not have a significant effect on the dependent variable. On the other hand, if the null hypothesis is rejected, then the effect of the independent variable is significant. In other words, the mean value of the dependent variable will be different for different categories of the independent variable. A comparison of the category mean values will indicate the nature of the effect of the independent variable. Other salient issues in the interpretation of results, such as examination of differences among specific means, are discussed later. In the next section, we illustrate the application of the ANOVA technique.

ILLUSTRATIVE APPLICATIONS OF ONE-WAY ANALYSIS OF VARIANCE

We illustrate the concepts of ANOVA first with an example showing calculations done by hand and then by computer analysis. Suppose that a major department store is attempting to determine the effect of in-store promotion (X) on sales (Y). In-store promotion is varied at three levels: high, medium, and low. Fifteen stores are randomly selected, and five stores are randomly assigned to each treatment condition. The experiment lasts for four weeks. Sales are monitored, normalized to account for extraneous factors (store size, traffic, etc.) and converted to a 0-to-10 scale. The data obtained (Y_{ij}) are reported in Table 16.2. The null hypothesis is that the category means are equal: $H_0: \mu_1 = \mu_2 = \mu_3$.

To test the null hypothesis, the various sums of squares are computed as follows:

$$\begin{aligned} SS_y &= (10-6)^2 + (9-6)^2 + (10-6)^2 + (8-6)^2 + (8-6)^2 + (6-6)^2 + (4-6)^2 + \\ &\quad (7-6)^2 + (3-6)^2 + (5-6)^2 + (5-6)^2 + (6-6)^2 + (5-6)^2 + (2-6)^2 + (2-6)^2 \\ &= 16 + 9 + 16 + 4 + 4 + 0 + 4 + 1 + 9 + 1 + 1 + 0 + 1 + 16 + 16 \\ &= 98 \end{aligned}$$

$$\begin{aligned} SS_x &= 5(9-6)^2 + 5(5-6)^2 + 5(4-6)^2 \\ &= 45 + 5 + 20 \\ &= 70 \end{aligned}$$

| | | Normalized Sales | |
| | | Level of In-Store Promotion | |
Store Number	High	Medium	Low
1	10	6	5
2	9	4	6
3	10	7	5
4	8	3	2
5	8	5	2

TABLE 16.2

Effect of In-Store Promotion on Sales

Category means: $\overline{Y}_j$ $\dfrac{45}{5}$ $\dfrac{25}{5}$ $\dfrac{20}{5}$

$= 9$ $= 5$ $= 4$

Grand mean, $\overline{Y}$ $= \dfrac{45 + 25 + 20}{15} = 6$

$$
\begin{aligned}
SS_{error} &= (10-9)^2 + (9-9)^2 + (10-9)^2 + (8-9)^2 + (8-9)^2 + (6-5)^2 + (4-5)^2 + \\
&\quad (7-5)^2 + (3-5)^2 + (5-5)^2 + (5-4)^2 + (6-4)^2 + (5-4)^2 + (2-4)^2 + (2-4)^2 \\
&= 1 + 0 + 1 + 1 + 1 + 1 + 1 + 4 + 4 + 0 + 1 + 4 + 1 + 4 + 4 \\
&= 28
\end{aligned}
$$

It can be verified that

$$ SS_y = SS_x + SS_{error} $$

as follows:

$$ 98 = 70 + 28 $$

The strength of the effects of X on Y are measured as follows:

$$
\begin{aligned}
\eta^2 &= \frac{SS_x}{SS_y} \\
&= \frac{70}{98} \\
&= .714
\end{aligned}
$$

In other words, 71.4% of the variation in sales (Y) is accounted for by in-store promotion (X), indicating a strong effect. The null hypothesis may now be tested.

$$ F = \frac{SS_x/(c-1)}{SS_{error}/(N-c)} = \frac{MS_x}{MS_{error}} $$

$$ F = \frac{70/(3-1)}{28/(15-3)} $$

$$ = 15.0 $$

From Table 5 in the Statistical Appendix we see that for 2 and 12 degrees of freedom, the critical value of F is 6.93. Because the calculated value of F is greater than the critical value, we reject the null hypothesis. We conclude that the population means for the three levels of in-store promotion are indeed different. The relative magnitudes of the means for the three categories indicate that a high level of in-store promotion leads to significantly higher sales.

We now illustrate the analysis of variance procedure using a computer program. In Chapter 15, in the context of the department store project, we examined whether respondents who are familiar with the stores attach differential importance to store credit and billing policies. Let us examine the same question again, this time forming three familiarity groups (high, medium, and low familiarity) rather than two. The null hypothesis is

$$H_0: \mu_1 = \mu_2 = \mu_3$$

The results of conducting a one-way analysis of variance are presented in Table 16.3. The value of SS_x denoted by between-group sums of squares is 6.4123 with two df; that of SS_{error} (within group sums of squares) is 695.6626 with 264 df. Therefore, MS_x = 6.4123/2 = 3.2062 and MS_{error} = 695.6626/264 = 2.6351. The value of F = 3.2062/2.6351 = 1.2167 with 2 and 264 degrees of freedom, resulting in a probability of .2979. Since the associated probability is larger than the significance level of .05, the null hypothesis of equal population means cannot be rejected. Alternatively, it can be seen from Table 5 in the Statistical Appendix that the critical value of F for 2 and 264 (∞) degrees of freedom is 4.61. Since the calculated value of F (1.2167) is less than the critical value, the null hypothesis cannot be rejected. As can be seen from Table 16.3, the sample means—with values of 4.0217, 4.1209, and 4.3929—are quite close to each other. In Chapter 15, when the respondents were divided into two familiarity groups, a significant difference was observed in the importance attached to the store credit and billing policy variable. When the sample is divided into three groups, however, no significant differences are observed. This illustrates the importance of carefully categorizing interval scaled variables.

The procedure for conducting one-way analysis of variance and the illustrative applications help us understand the assumptions involved.

ASSUMPTIONS IN ANALYSIS OF VARIANCE

The salient assumptions in analysis of variance can be summarized as follows.

1. Ordinarily, the categories of the independent variable are assumed to be fixed. Inferences are made only to the specific categories considered. This is referred to as the *fixed-effects model*. Other models are also available. In the *random-effects model*, the categories or treatments are considered to be random samples from a universe of treatments. Inferences are made to other categories not examined in the analysis. A *mixed-effects model* results if some treatments are considered fixed and others random.[8]

TABLE 16.3

One-Way ANOVA: Effect of Familiarity on Importance Attached to Credit Policies

Source	df	Sum of Squares	Mean square	F ratio	F probability
Between groups	2	6.4123	3.2062	1.2167	.2979
Within groups	264	695.6626	2.6351		
Total	266	702.0749			

Group	Count	Mean	Standard Deviation	Standard Error
Group 1	92	4.0217	1.6440	.1714
Group 2	91	4.1209	1.5765	.1653
Group 3	84	4.3929	1.6502	.1801
Total	267	4.1723	1.6246	.0994

2. The error term is normally distributed, with a zero mean and a constant variance. The error is not related to any of the categories of X. Modest departures from these assumptions do not seriously affect the validity of the analysis. Furthermore, the data can be transformed to satisfy the assumption of normality or equal variances.

3. The error terms are uncorrelated. If the error terms are correlated (i.e., the observations are not independent), the F ratio can be seriously distorted.

In many data analysis situations, these assumptions are reasonably met. Analysis of variance is therefore a common procedure, as illustrated by the following example.

EXAMPLE

Videologs Put Marketers in the Picture

Although the videolog, a shop-at-home video catalog, is still in its infancy, many direct marketers have shown an interest in its use. Companies like Spiegel, Neiman Marcus, and Sears either plan to or already have offered video catalogs to consumers.

A study was designed to investigate the effectiveness of videolog retailing as a form of direct marketing. Subjects were randomly assigned to one of three treatments: (a) videolog only; (b) both videolog and catalog; or (c) catalog only. The dependent variables of interest, consisting of attitudes and opinions, were (1) assessments of product (clothing) attributes; (2) assessments of the videolog or catalog sponsoring company; (3) assessments of price information; and (4) intentions to purchase.

One-way analysis of variance was conducted separately for each dependent variable. The results showed that respondents exposed to the videolog or to the videolog and catalog perceived the clothing more positively than did those exposed only to the catalog. Although the videolog-only treatment enhanced perceptions of the sponsoring company, the results were not as striking as were those for clothing perceptions. No significant differences were found in price perceptions and intentions to purchase. Yet the mean number of items respondents said they were likely to purchase was greater for those viewing both the videolog and catalog than those seeing just the videolog or the catalog.

Although this study was an exploratory effort, the positive results found in assessments of clothing seen in the videolog suggest that this is an area that may have potential for direct marketers.[9] ◆

The videolog and catalog are complementary sales tools aimed at the shop-at-home market.
◆ Teri Stratford.

N-WAY ANALYSIS OF VARIANCE

In marketing research, one is often concerned with the effect of more than one factor simultaneously.[10] For example:

- How do the consumers' intentions to buy a brand vary with different levels of price and different levels of distribution?
- How do advertising levels (high, medium, and low) interact with price levels (high, medium, and low) to influence a brand's sale?
- Do educational levels (less than high school, high school graduate, some college, and college graduate) and age (younger than 35, 35–55, older than 55) effect consumption of a brand?
- What is the effect of consumers' familiarity with a department store (high, medium, and low) and store image (positive, neutral, and negative) on preference for the store?

interaction When assessing the relationship between two variables, an interaction occurs if the effect of X_1 depends on the level of X_2, and vice versa.

In determining such effects, n-way analysis of variance can be used. A major advantage of this technique is that it enables the researcher to examine interactions between the factors. **Interactions** occur when the effects of one factor on the dependent variable depend on the level (category) of the other factors. The procedure for conducting n-way analysis of variance is similar to that for one-way analysis of variance. The statistics associated with n-way analysis of variance are also defined similarly. Consider the simple case of two factors X_1 and X_2 having categories c_1 and c_2. The total variation in this case is partitioned as follows:

$$SS_{total} = SS \text{ due to } X_1 + SS \text{ due to } X_2 + SS \text{ due to interaction of } X_1 \text{ and } X_2 + SS_{within}$$

or

$$SS_y = SS_{x_1} + SS_{x_2} + SS_{x_1 x_2} + SS_{error}$$

A larger effect of X_1 will be reflected in a greater mean difference in the levels of X_1 and a larger SS_{x_1}. The same is true for the effect of X_2. The larger the interaction between X_1 and X_2, the larger $SS_{x_1 x_2}$ will be. On the other hand, if X_1 and X_2 are independent, the value of $SS_{x_1 x_2}$ will be close to zero.[11]

multiple η^2 The strength of the joint effect of two (or more) factors, or the overall effect.

The strength of the joint effect of two factors, called the overall effect, or **multiple η^2**, is measured as follows:

$$\text{multiple } \eta^2 = (SS_{x_1} + SS_{x_2} + SS_{x_1 x_2})/SS_y$$

significance of the overall effect A test that some differences exist between some of the treatment groups.

The **significance of the overall effect** may be tested by an F test, as follows:

$$F = \frac{(SS_{x_1} + SS_{x_2} + SS_{x_1 x_2})/df_n}{SS_{error}/df_d}$$

$$= \frac{SS_{x_1, x_2, x_1 x_2}/df_n}{SS_{error}/df_d}$$

$$= \frac{MS_{x_1, x_2, x_1 x_2}}{MS_{error}}$$

where

$$\begin{aligned} df_n &= \text{degrees of freedom for the numerator} \\ &= (c_1 - 1) + (c_2 - 1) + (c_1 - 1)(c_2 - 1) \\ &= c_1 c_2 - 1 \end{aligned}$$

$$df_d = \text{degrees of freedom for the denominator}$$
$$= N - c_1 c_2$$
$$MS = \text{mean square}$$

If the overall effect is significant, the next step is to examine the **significance of the interaction effect**. Under the null hypothesis of no interaction, the appropriate F test is

$$F = \frac{SS_{x_1 x_2} / df_n}{SS_{error} / df_d}$$

$$= \frac{MS_{x_1 x_2}}{MS_{error}}$$

where

$$df_n = (c_1 - 1)(c_2 - 1)$$
$$df_d = N - c_1 c_2$$

If the interaction effect is found to be significant, then the effect of X_1 depends on the level of X_2, and vice versa. Since the effect of one factor is not uniform but varies with the level of the other factor, it is not generally meaningful to test the significance of the main effects. It is meaningful to test the significance of each main effect of each factor, however, if the interaction effect is not significant.[12]

The **significance of the main effect** of each factor may be tested as follows for X_1:

$$F = \frac{SS_{x_1} / df_n}{SS_{error} / df_d}$$

$$= \frac{MS_{x_1}}{MS_{error}}$$

where

$$df_n = c_1 - 1$$
$$df_d = N - c_1 c_2$$

The foregoing analysis assumes that the design was orthogonal, or balanced (the number of cases in each cell was the same). If the cell size varies, the analysis becomes more complex. The following application illustrates n-way analysis of variance.

An experiment was conducted to determine the effect of type of game and feedback on the amount of information sought while playing a promotional game.[13] Type of game was varied at two levels: whether the game required skill or was based on chance. The feedback factor was also varied at two levels: whether feedback on performance was provided or not. The subjects were 84 students who were randomly assigned to the different experimental conditions. The overall effect was significant (see Table 16.4). As

	TABLE 16.4						
Two-Way Analysis of Variance	Source of Variation	Sum of Squares	df	Mean Square	F	Sig. of F	ω^2
	Type of game	390.01	1	390.01	6.62	.012	.06
	Feedback	121.44	1	121.44	2.06	.155	.01
	Two-way interaction	131.25	1	131.25	2.23	.140	.01
	Residual	4714.29	80	58.93			

can be seen, the interaction effect was not significant. Hence, the main effects can be evaluated. The main effect of type of game was significant, whereas the main effect of feedback was not. Subjects sought more information when playing a game of skill than when playing a game of chance.

The following example illustrates the use of *n*-way analysis.

EXAMPLE

Country Affects TV Reception

A study examined the impact of country affiliation on the credibility of product-attribute claims for TVs. The dependent variables were the following product-attribute claims: good sound, reliability, crisp-clear picture, and stylish design. The independent variables which were manipulated consisted of price, country affiliation, and store distribution. A 2 × 2 × 2 between-subjects design was used. Two levels of price, $349.95 (low) and $449.95 (high), two levels of country affiliation, South Korea and the United States, and two levels of store distribution, Hudson's and without Hudson's, were specified.

Data were collected from two suburban malls in a large midwestern city. Thirty respondents were randomly assigned to each of the eight treatment cells for a total of 240 subjects. Table 1 presents the results for manipulations that had significant effects on each of the dependent variables.

TABLE 1

Analyses for Significant Manipulations

Effect	Dependent Variable	Univariate F	df	p
Country × price	Good sound	7.57	1,232	.006
Country × price	Reliability	6.57	1,232	.011
Country × distribution	Crisp-clear picture	6.17	1,232	.014
Country × distribution	Reliability	6.57	1,232	.011
Country × distribution	Stylish design	10.31	1,232	.002

The directions of country-by-distribution interaction effects for the three dependent variables are shown in Table 2. Although the credibility ratings for the crisp-clear picture, reliability, and stylish design claims are improved by distributing the Korean-made TV set through Hudson's rather than some other distributor, the same is not true of a U.S.-made set. Similarly, the directions of country-by-price interaction effects for the two dependent variables are shown in Table 3. At $449.95, the credibility ratings for the "good sound" and "reliability" claims are higher for the U.S.-made TV set than for its Korean counterpart, but there is little difference related to country affiliation when the product is priced at $349.95.

This study demonstrates that credibility of attribute claims, for products traditionally exported to the United States by a company in a newly industrialized country, can be significantly improved if the same company distributes the product through a prestigious U.S. retailer and considers making manufacturing investments in the United States. Specifically, three product attribute claims (crisp-clear picture, reliability, and stylish design) are perceived as more credible when the TVs are made in South Korea if they are also distributed through a prestigious U.S. retailer. Also, the "good sound" and

Attribute claims for TVs are perceived to be more credible for U.S.-made sets sold at a higher price ◆ RCA Electronics.

TABLE 2

Country by Distribution Interaction Means

Country × distribution	Crisp-Clear Picture	Reliability	Stylish Design
South Korea			
Hudson's	3.67	3.42	3.82
Without Hudson's	3.18	2.88	3.15
United States			
Hudson's	3.60	3.47	3.53
Without Hudson's	3.77	3.65	3.75

TABLE 3

Country by Price Interaction Means

Country × price	Good Sound	Reliability
$349.95		
South Korea	3.75	3.40
United States	3.53	3.45
$449.95		
South Korea	3.15	2.90
United States	3.73	3.67

"reliability" claims for TVs are perceived to be more credible for a U.S.-made set sold at a higher price, possibly offsetting the potential disadvantage of higher manufacturing costs in the United States.[14] ◆

ANALYSIS OF COVARIANCE

When examining the differences in the mean values of the dependent variable related to the effect of the controlled independent variables, it is often necessary to take into account the influence of uncontrolled independent variables. For example:

- In determining how consumers' intentions to buy a brand vary with different levels of price, attitude toward the brand may have to be taken into consideration.
- In determining how different groups exposed to different commercials evaluate a brand, it may be necessary to control for prior knowledge.
- In determining how different price levels will affect a household's cereal consumption, it may be essential to take household size into account.

In such cases, analysis of covariance should be used. Analysis of covariance includes at least one categorical independent variable and at least one interval or metric-independent variable. The categorical independent variable is called a *factor*, whereas the metric-independent variable is called a *covariate*. The most common use of the covariate is to remove extraneous variation from the dependent variable, because the effects of the factors are of major concern. The variation in the dependent variable due to the covariates is removed by an adjustment of the dependent variable's mean value within each treatment condition.

An analysis of variance is then performed on the adjusted scores.[15] The significance of the combined effect of the covariates, as well as the effect of each covariate, is tested by using the appropriate F tests. The coefficients for the covariates provide insights into the effect that the covariates exert on the dependent variable. Analysis of covariance is most useful when the covariate is linearly related to the dependent variable and is not related to the factors.[16]

Here we use the effect of familiarity on the importance attached to store credit and billing policies, as discussed in Chapter 15 using a t test, to illustrate covariance. Suppose that the researcher feels that respondents' age and educational levels would influence the dependent variable. Both these variables are measured on a ratio scale: age in years and educational level in number of years of formal education. As with a t test, respondents are divided into two groups based on a rough median split of the familiarity variables, and an analysis of covariance is performed. The dependent variable consists of the importance attached to store credit and billing policies. The factor of familiarity has two levels (familiar and unfamiliar), and age and educational level are the two covariates. The results are shown in Table 16.5. As can be seen, the effect of the two covariates combined, as well as the effect of each covariate, is significant. The main effect of familiarity continues to be significant. The signs of the covariate coefficients indicate that the older people, as well as the less educated, attach greater importance to store credit and billing policies.

TABLE 16.5 *Analysis of Covariance*	Source of Variation	Sum of Squares	df	Mean Square	F	Sig. of F
	Covariates	47.387	2	23.693	9.678	.000
	Age	18.944	1	18.944	7.738	.006
	Education	20.222	1	20.222	8.260	.004
	Main effects	9.608	1	9.608	3.925	.049
	Familiarity	9.608	1	9.608	3.925	.049
	Explained	56.995	3	18.998	7.761	.000
	Residual	638.945	261	2.448		
	Total		695.940	264	2.636		

Covariate	Raw Coefficient
Age	0.019
Educational level	−0.104

ISSUES IN INTERPRETATION

Important issues involved in the interpretation of ANOVA results include interactions, relative importance of factors, and multiple comparisons.

Interactions

The different interactions that can arise when conducting ANOVA on two or more factors are shown in Figure 16.3. One outcome is that ANOVA may indicate that there are no interactions (the interaction effects are not found to be significant). The other

**A Classification
of Interaction Effects**

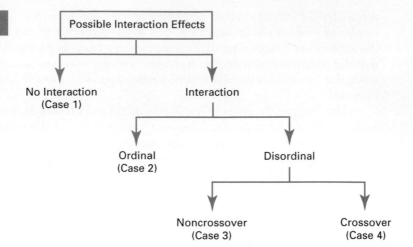

ordinal interaction An interaction where the rank order of the effects attributable to one factor does not change across the levels of the second factor.

disordinal interaction The change in the rank order of the effects of one factor across the levels of another.

possibility is that the interaction is significant. An *interaction effect* occurs when the effect of an independent variable on a dependent variable is different for different categories or levels of another independent variable. The interaction may be ordinal or disordinal. In **ordinal interaction**, the rank order of the effects related to one factor does not change across the levels of the second factor. **Disordinal interaction**, on the other hand, involves a change in the rank order of the effects of one factor across the levels of another. If the interaction is disordinal, it could be of a noncrossover or crossover type.[17]

These interaction cases are displayed in Figure 16.4, which assumes that there are two factors, X_1 with three levels (X_{11}, X_{12}, and X_{13}) and X_2 with two levels (X_{21} and X_{22}). Case 1 depicts no interaction. The effects of X_1 on Y are parallel over the two levels of X_2. Although there is some departure from parallelism, this is not beyond what might be expected from chance. Parallelism implies that the net effect of X_{22} over X_{21} is the same across the three levels of X_1. In the absence of interaction, the joint effect of X_1 and X_2 is simply the sum of their individual main effects.

Case 2 depicts an ordinal interaction. The line segments depicting the effects of X_1 and X_2 are not parallel. The difference between X_{22} and X_{21} increases as we move from X_{11} to X_{12} and from X_{12} to X_{13}, but the rank order of the effects of X_1 is the same over the two levels of X_2. This rank order, in ascending order, is X_{11}, X_{12}, X_{13}, and it remains the same for X_{21} and X_{22}.

Disordinal interaction of a noncrossover type is displayed by case 3. The lowest effect of X_1 at level X_{21} occurs at X_{11}, and the rank order of effects is X_{11}, X_{12}, and X_{13}. At level X_{22}, however, the lowest effect of X_1 occurs at X_{12}, and the rank order is changed to X_{12}, X_{11}, X_{13}. Because it involves a change in rank order, disordinal interaction is stronger than ordinal interaction.

In disordinal interactions of a crossover type, the line segments cross each other, as shown by case 4 in Figure 16.4. In this case, the relative effect of the levels of one factor changes with the levels of the other. Note that X_{22} has a greater effect than X_{21} when the levels of X_1 are X_{11} and X_{12}. When the level of X_1 is X_{13}, the situation is reversed, and X_{21} has a greater effect than X_{22}. (Note that in cases 1, 2, and 3, X_{22} had a greater impact than X_{21} across all three levels of X_1.) Hence, disordinal interactions of a crossover type represent the strongest interactions.[18]

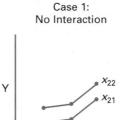

FIGURE 16.4

Patterns of Interaction

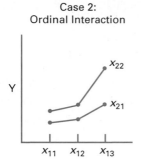

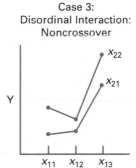

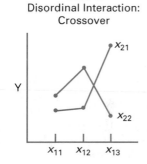

Relative Importance of Factors

Experimental designs are usually balanced in that each cell contains the same number of respondents. This results in an orthogonal design in which the factors are uncorrelated. Hence, it is possible to determine unambiguously the relative importance of each factor in explaining the variation in the dependent variable.[19] The most commonly used measure in ANOVA is **omega squared, ω^2**. This measure indicates what proportion of the variation in the dependent variable is related to a particular independent variable or factor. The relative contribution of a factor X is calculated as follows:[20]

omega squared (ω^2) A measure indicating the proportion of the variation in the dependent variable explained by a particular independent variable or factor.

$$\omega_x^2 = \frac{SS_x - (df_x \times MS_{error})}{SS_{total} + MS_{error}}$$

Normally, ω^2 is interpreted only for statistically significant effects.[21] In Table 16.4, ω^2 associated with type of game is calculated as follows:

$$\omega_x^2 = \frac{390.01 - (1 \times 58.93)}{5356.99 + 58.93}$$

$$= \frac{331.08}{5415.92}$$

$$= 0.06$$

In Table 16.4, note that

$$SS_{total} = 390.01 + 121.44 + 131.25 + 4714.29$$
$$= 5356.99$$

As a guide to interpreting ω^2, a large experimental effect produces an ω^2 of .15 or greater, a medium effect produces an index of around .06, and a small effect produces an index of .01.[22] In Table 16.4, the effect produced by type of game is medium.

Multiple Comparisons

contrasts In ANOVA, a method of examining differences among two or more means of the treatment groups.

The ANOVA F test examines only the overall difference in means. If the null hypothesis of equal means is rejected, we can only conclude that not all the group means are equal. Only some of the means may be statistically different, however, and we may wish to examine differences among specific means. This can be done by specifying appropriate **contrasts**, or comparisons used to determine which of the means are statistically different. Contrasts may be a priori or a posteriori. **A priori contrasts** are determined before conducting the analysis, based on the researcher's theoretical framework. Generally, a priori contrasts are used in lieu of the ANOVA F test. The contrasts selected are orthogonal (they are independent in a statistical sense).

a priori contrasts Contrasts that are determined before conducting the analysis, based on the researcher's theoretical framework.

A posteriori contrasts are made after the analysis. These are generally **multiple comparison tests**. They enable the researcher to construct generalized confidence intervals that can be used to make pairwise comparisons of all treatment means. These tests, listed in order of decreasing power, include least significant difference, Duncan's multiple range, Student-Newman-Keuls, Tukey's alternate procedure, honestly significant difference, modified least significant difference, and Scheffe's tests. Of these, least significant difference is the most powerful and Scheffe's the most conservative. For further discussion on a priori and a posteriori contrasts, refer to the literature.[23]

a posteriori contrasts Contrasts made after the analysis. These are generally multiple comparison tests.

Our discussion so far has assumed that each subject is exposed to only one treatment or experimental condition. Sometimes subjects are exposed to more than one experimental condition, in which case repeated measures ANOVA should be used.

REPEATED MEASURES ANOVA

multiple comparison tests A posteriori contrasts that enable the researcher to construct generalized confidence intervals that can be used to make pairwise comparisons of all treatment means.

In marketing research, there are often large differences in the background and individual characteristics of respondents. If this source of variability can be separated from treatment effects (effects of the independent variable) and experimental error, then the sensitivity of the experiment can be enhanced. One way of controlling the differences between subjects is by observing each subject under each experimental condition (see Table 16.6). In this sense, each subject serves as its own control. For example, in a survey attempting to determine differences in evaluations of various airlines, each respondent evaluates all the major competing airlines. In a study examining the differences among heavy users, medium users, light users, and nonusers of a brand, each respondent provides ratings on the relative importance of each attribute. Because repeated measurements are obtained from each respondent, this design is referred to as within-subjects design or **repeated measures analysis of variance**. This differs from the assumption we made in our earlier discussion that each respondent is exposed to only one treatment condition, also referred to as between-subjects design.[24] Repeated measures analysis of variance may be thought of as an extension of the paired-samples t test to the case of more than two related samples.

repeated measures analysis of variance An ANOVA technique used when respondents are exposed to more than one treatment condition and repeated measurements are obtained.

In the case of a single factor with repeated measures, the total variation, with $nc - 1$ degrees of freedom, may be split into between-people variation and within-people variation.

$$SS_{total} = SS_{between\ people} + SS_{within\ people}$$

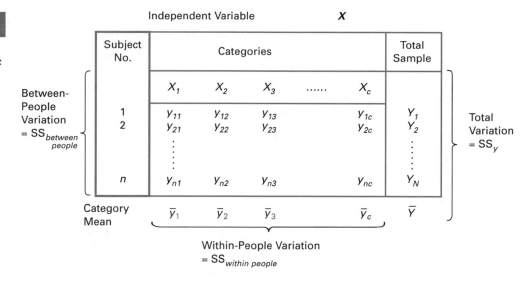

TABLE 16.6

Decomposition of the Total Variation: Repeated Measures ANOVA

The between-people variation, which is related to the differences between the means of people, has $n - 1$ degrees of freedom. The within-people variation has $n(c - 1)$ degrees of freedom. The within-people variation may, in turn, be divided into two different sources of variation. One source is related to the differences between treatment means, and the second consists of residual or error variation. The degrees of freedom corresponding to the treatment variation are $c - 1$ and that corresponding to residual variation are $(c - 1)(n - 1)$. Thus,

$$SS_{within\ people} = SS_x + SS_{error}$$

A test of the null hypothesis of equal means may now be constructed in the usual way:

$$F = \frac{SS_x/(c-1)}{SS_{error}/(n-1)(c-1)} = \frac{MS_x}{MS_{error}}$$

So far we have assumed that the dependent variable is measured on an interval or ratio scale. If the dependent variable is nonmetric, however, a different procedure should be used.

NONMETRIC ANALYSIS OF VARIANCE

nonmetric analysis of variance An ANOVA technique for examining the difference in the central tendencies of more than two groups when the dependent variable is measured on an ordinal scale.

K-sample median test A nonparametric test used to examine differences among groups when the dependent variable is measured on an ordinal scale.

Nonmetric analysis of variance examines the difference in the central tendencies of more than two groups when the dependent variable is measured on an ordinal scale. One such procedure is the **k-sample median test**. As its name implies, this is an extension of the median test for two groups, which was considered in Chapter 15. The null hypothesis is that the medians of the k populations are equal. The test involves the computation of a common median over the k samples. Then, a $2 \times k$ table of cell counts based on cases above or below the common median is generated. A chi-square statistic is computed. The significance of the chi-square implies a rejection of the null hypothesis.

A more powerful test is the **Kruskal-Wallis one-way analysis of variance**. This is an extension of the Mann-Whitney test (Chapter 15). This test also examines the difference in medians. The null hypothesis is the same as in the k-sample median test, but the testing procedure is different. All cases from the k groups are ordered in a single ranking. If the k populations are the same, the groups should be similar in terms of ranks

Kruskal-Wallis one-way analysis of variance A nonmetric ANOVA test that uses the rank value of each case, not merely its location relative to the median.

within each group. The rank sum is calculated for each group. From these, the Kruskal-Wallis H statistic, which has a chi-square distribution, is computed.

The Kruskal-Wallis test is more powerful than the k-sample median test because it uses the rank value of each case, not merely its location relative to the median. If there are a large number of tied rankings in the data, however, the k-sample median test may be a better choice.

Nonmetric analysis of variance is not popular in commercial marketing research. Another procedure that is also only rarely used is multivariate analysis of variance.

MULTIVARIATE ANALYSIS OF VARIANCE

multivariate analysis of variance (MANOVA) An ANOVA technique using two or more metric dependent variables.

Multivariate analysis of variance (MANOVA) is similar to analysis of variance (ANOVA) except that instead of one metric-dependent variable we have two or more. The objective is the same, since MANOVA is also concerned with examining differences between groups. Although ANOVA examines group differences on a single dependent variable, MANOVA examines group differences across multiple dependent variables simultaneously. In ANOVA, the null hypothesis is that the means of the dependent variable are equal across the groups. In MANOVA, the null hypothesis is that the vector of means on multiple dependent variables are equal across groups. Multivariate analysis of variance is appropriate when there are two or more dependent variables that are correlated. If there are multiple dependent variables that are uncorrelated or orthogonal, ANOVA on each of the dependent variables is more appropriate than MANOVA.[25]

As an example, suppose that four groups, each consisting of 100 randomly selected individuals, were exposed to four different commercials about Tide detergent. After seeing the commercial, each individual provided ratings on preference for Tide, preference for Procter & Gamble (the company marketing Tide), and preference for the commercial itself. Because these three preference variables are correlated, multivariate analysis of variance should be conducted to determine which commercial is the most effective (produced the highest preference across the three preference variables). Research in Practice 16.1 illus-

RESEARCH IN PRACTICE 16.1

The Commonality of Unethical Research Practices Worldwide

A study examined marketing professionals' perceptions of the commonality of unethical marketing research practices on a cross-national basis. The sample of marketing professionals was drawn from Australia, Canada, Great Britain, and the United States.

Respondents' evaluations were analyzed using computer programs for MANOVA and ANOVA. Country of respondent comprised the predictor variable in the analysis, and 15 commonality evaluations served as the criterion variables. The F values from the ANOVA analyses indicated that only two of the 15 commonality evaluations achieved significance ($p < .05$ or better). Further, the MANOVA F value was not statistically significant, implying the lack of overall differences in commonality evaluations across respondents of the four countries. Therefore, it was concluded that marketing professionals in the four countries evince similar perceptions of the commonality of unethical research practices. This finding is not surprising, given research evidence that organizations in the four countries reflect similar corporate cultures.

trates the application of ANOVA and MANOVA in international marketing research,[26] whereas Research in Practice 16.2 shows an application of these techniques in examining ethics in marketing research.[27]

RESEARCH IN PRACTICE 16.2

"MAN"OVA Demonstrates That Man Is Different from Woman

To investigate differences between research ethics judgments in men and women, the statistical techniques of MANOVA and ANOVA were used. Respondents were asked to indicate their degree of approval with regard to series of scenarios involving decisions of an ethical nature. These evaluations served as the dependent variable in the analysis, while sex of the respondent served as the independent variable. MANOVA was used for multivariate analysis and its resultant F value was significant at the $p < .001$ level, indicating that there was an "overall" difference between males and females in research ethics judgments. Univariate analysis was conducted via ANOVA, and F values indicated that three items were the greatest contributors to the overall gender difference in ethical evaluations: the use of ultraviolet ink to precode a mail questionnaire, the use of an ad that encourages consumer misuse of a product, and unwillingness by researcher to offer data help to an inner city advisory group.

COMPUTER APPLICATIONS

All three computer packages considered in this book (SPSS, SAS, and BMDP) have programs for conducting analysis of variance and covariance available for the microcomputer and mainframe versions. In addition to the basic analysis we have considered, these programs can also perform more complex analysis. Exhibit 16.1 on page 568 contains a description of the relevant programs. Refer to the user manuals for these packages for more details.[28]

SUMMARY

In ANOVA and ANCOVA, the dependent variable is metric and the independent variables are all categorical or are combinations of categorical and metric variables. One-way ANOVA involves a single independent categorical variable. Interest lies in testing the null hypothesis that the category means are equal in the population. The total variation in the dependent variable is decomposed into two components: variation related to the independent variable and variation related to error. The variation is measured in terms of the sums of squares corrected for the mean (SS). The mean square is obtained by dividing the SS by the corresponding degrees of freedom (df). The null hypothesis of equal means is tested by an F statistic, which is the ratio of the mean square related to the independent variable to the mean square related to error.

N-way analysis of variance involves the simultaneous examination of two or more categorical independent variables. A major advantage is that the interactions between

EXHIBIT 16.1

*Computer Programs
for ANOVA
and ANCOVA*

Given the importance of analysis of variance and covariance, several programs are available in each package. These programs are available in the microcomputer and mainframe versions of these packages.

SPSS

One-way ANOVA can be efficiently performed using the program ONEWAY. This program also allows the user to test a priori and a posteriori contrasts, which cannot be done in other SPSS programs. For performing *n*-way analysis of variance, the program Anova can be used. Although covariates can be specified, Anova does not perform a full analysis of covariance. For comprehensive analysis of variance or analysis of covariance, including repeated measures and multiple dependent measures, the MANOVA procedure is recommended. For nonmetric analysis of variance, including the *k*-sample median test and Kruskal-Wallis one-way analysis of variance, the program NPAR TESTS should be used.

SAS

The main program for performing analysis of variance in the case of a balanced design is ANOVA. This program can handle data from a wide variety of experimental designs, including multivariate analysis of variance and repeated measures. Both a priori and a posteriori contrasts can be tested. For unbalanced designs, the more general GLM procedure can be used. This program performs analysis of variance, analysis of covariance, repeated measures analysis of variance, and multivariate analysis of variance. It also allows the testing of a priori and a posteriori contrasts. Although GLM can also be used for analyzing balanced designs, it is not as efficient as ANOVA for such models. The VARCOMP procedure computes variance components. For nonmetric analysis of variance, the NPAR1WAY procedure can be used. For constructing designs and randomized plans, the PLAN procedure can be used.

BMDP

For one-way analysis of variance, the program P1V can be used. It also performs analysis of covariance and can test user-specified contrasts of group means. The more general model, however, is P2V, which performs analysis of variance and covariance for a wide variety of fixed-effects models. It can handle repeated measures and balanced as well as unbalanced designs. P4V, a more advanced program, can perform multivariate analysis of variance and covariance, including analysis of complex experimental designs. Another specialized program is P3V, which uses the maximum-likelihood approach for analyzing fixed- and random-coefficient models. It allows for balanced as well as unbalanced designs. P8V is a general model that performs an analysis of variance for any complete design with equal cell sizes, including some complex designs. Nonparametric analysis of variance can be performed using P3S. Finally, P7D, in addition to providing histograms, can perform a one-way analysis of variance.

the independent variables can be examined. The significance of the overall effect, interaction terms, and main effects of individual factors is examined by appropriate F tests. It is meaningful to test the significance of main effects only if the corresponding interaction terms are not significant.

ANCOVA includes at least one categorical independent variable and at least one interval or metric-independent variable. The metric-independent variable, or covariate, is commonly used to remove extraneous variation from the dependent variable.

When analysis of variance is conducted on two or more factors, interactions can arise. An interaction occurs when the effect of an independent variable on a dependent variable is different for different categories or levels of another independent variable. If the interaction is significant, it may be ordinal or disordinal. Disordinal interaction may be of a noncrossover or crossover type. In balanced designs, the relative importance of factors in explaining the variation in the dependent variable is measured by omega squared (ω^2). Multiple comparisons in the form of a priori or a posteriori contrasts can be used for examining differences among specific means.

In repeated measures analysis of variance, observations on each subject are obtained under each treatment condition. This design is useful for controlling for the differences in subjects that exist prior to the experiment. Nonmetric analysis of variance involves examining the differences in the central tendencies of two or more groups when the dependent variable is measured on an ordinal scale. Multivariate analysis of variance (MANOVA) involves two or more metric-dependent variables.[29]

ACRONYMS

The major characteristics of analysis of variance may be described by the acronym ANOVA:

A   nalysis of total variation
N   ormally distributed errors that are uncorrelated
O   ne or more categorical independent variables with fixed categories
V   ariance is assumed to be constant
A   single dependent variable that is metric

The major characteristics of analysis of covariance may be summarized by the acronym ANCOVA:

A   nalysis of total variation
N   ormally distributed errors that are uncorrelated
C   ovariates: one or more metric independent variables
O   ne or more categorical independent variables with fixed categories
V   ariance is assumed to be constant
A   single dependent variable that is metric

EXERCISES

QUESTIONS

1. Discuss the similarities and differences between analysis of variance and analysis of covariance.
2. What is the relationship between analysis of variance and the *t* test?
3. What is total variation? How is it decomposed in a one-way analysis of variance?
4. What is the null hypothesis in one-way ANOVA? What basic statistic is used to test the null hypothesis in one-way ANOVA? How is this statistic computed?
5. How does *n*-way analysis of variance differ from the one-way procedure?
6. How is the total variation decomposed in *n*-way analysis of variance?
7. What is the most common use of the covariate in ANCOVA?
8. Define an interaction.
9. What is the difference between ordinal and disordinal interaction?
10. How is the relative importance of factors measured in a balanced design?
11. What is an a priori contrast?
12. What is the most powerful test for making a posteriori contrasts? Which test is the most conservative?
13. What is meant by repeated measures ANOVA? Describe the decomposition of variation in repeated measures ANOVA.
14. What are the differences between metric and nonmetric analyses of variance?
15. Describe two tests used for examining differences in central tendencies in nonmetric ANOVA.
16. What is multivariate analysis of variance? When is it appropriate?

PROBLEMS

1. After receiving some complaints from readers, your campus newspaper decides to redesign its front page. Two new formats, B and C, were developed and tested against the current format, A. A total of 75 students was randomly selected, and 25 students were randomly assigned to each of three format conditions. The students were asked to evaluate the effectiveness of the format on a 11-point scale (1 = poor, 11 = excellent).

   a. State the null hypothesis.

   b. What statistical test should you use?

   c. What are the degrees of freedom associated with the test statistic?

2. A marketing researcher wants to test the hypothesis that, in the population, there is no difference in the importance attached to shopping by consumers living in the northern, southern, eastern, and western United States. A study is conducted and analysis of variance is used to analyze the data. The results obtained are presented in the following table.

Source	df	Sum of Squares	Mean F Squares	F Ratio	Probability
Between groups	3	70.212	23.404	1.12	.3
Within groups	996	20812.416	20.896		

   a. Is there sufficient evidence to reject the null hypothesis?

   b. What conclusion can be drawn from the table?

   c. If the average importance was computed for each group, would you expect the sample means to be similar or different?

   d. What was the total sample size in this study?

3. In a pilot study examining the effectiveness of three commercials (A, B, and C), ten consumers were assigned to view each commercial and rate it on a nine-point Likert scale. The data obtained are shown in the table.

	Commercial	
A	B	C
4	7	8
5	4	7
3	6	7
4	5	6
3	4	8
4	6	7
4	5	8
3	5	8
5	4	5
5	4	6

   a. Calculate the category means and the grand mean.

   b. Calculate SS_y, SS_x, and SS_{error}.

   c. Calculate η^2.

   d. Calculate the value of F.

   e. Are the three commercials equally effective?

4. An experiment tested the effects of package design and shelf display on the likelihood of purchase of Product 19 cereal. Package design and shelf display were varied at two levels each, resulting in a 2 × 2 design. Purchase likelihood was measured on a seven-point scale. The results are partially described in the following table.

Source of Variation	Sum of Squares	df	Mean Square	F	Significance of F	ω^2
Package design	68.76	1				
Shelf display	320.19	1				
Two-way interaction	55.05	1				
Residual error	176.00	40				

a. Complete the table by calculating the mean square, F, significance of F, and ω^2 values.

b. How should the main effects be interpreted?

COMPUTER EXERCISES

1. Using the appropriate microcomputer and mainframe programs in the package of your choice (SPSS, SAS, or BMDP), analyze the data of problem 3.

NOTES

1. Pradeep Korgaonkar and George P. Moschis, "The Effects of Perceived Risk and Social Class on Consumer Preferences for Distribution Outlets," in Paul Bloom, Russ Winer, Harold H. Kassarjian, Debra L. Scammon, Bart Weitz, Robert Spekman, Vijay Mahajan, and Michael Levy (eds.), *Enhancing Knowledge Development in Marketing*, series no. 55 (Chicago: American Marketing Association, 1989), pp. 39–43.

2. Easwar S. Iyer, "The Influence of Verbal Content and Relative Newness on the Effectiveness of Comparative Advertising," *Journal of Advertising* 17 (1988): 15–21.

3. For recent applications of ANOVA, see Rohit Deshpande and Douglas M. Stayman, "A Tale of Two Cities: Distinctiveness Theory and Advertising Effectiveness," *Journal of Marketing Research* 31 (February 1994): 57–64.

4. See, for instance, Geoffrey Keppel, *Design and Analysis: A Researcher's Handbook*, 2nd ed. (Englewood Cliffs, NJ: Prentice Hall, 1982).

5. M. J. Norusis, *The SPSS Guide to Data Analysis for SPSS/PC+* (Chicago: SPSS Inc., 1988).

6. Richard K. Burdick, "Statement of Hypotheses in the Analysis of Variance," *Journal of Marketing Research* (August 1983): 320–24.

7. The F test is a generalized form of the t test. If a random variable is t distributed with N degrees of freedom, then t^2 is F distributed with 1 and N degrees of freedom. Where there are two factor levels or treatments, ANOVA is equivalent to the two-sided t test.

8. Although computations for the fixed-effects and random-effects models are similar, interpretations of results differ. A comparison of these approaches is found in J. Neter, W. Wasserman, and M. Kutner, *Applied Linear Statistical Models*, 2nd ed. (Homewood, IL: Richard D. Irwin, 1985).

9. Denise T. Smart, James E. Zemanek, Jr., and Jeffrey S. Conant, "Videolog Retailing: How Effective Is This New Form of Direct Mail Marketing?" in Paul Bloom, Russ Winer, Harold H. Kassarjian, Debra L. Scammon, Bart Weitz, Robert Spekman, Vijay Mahajan, and Michael Levy (eds.), *Enhancing Knowledge Development in Marketing*, series no. 55 (Chicago: American Marketing Association, 1989), p. 85.

10. We consider only the full factorial designs, which incorporate all possible combinations of factor levels. For example, see William B. Dodds, Kent B. Monroe, and Dhruv Grewal, "Effects of Price, Brand, and Store Information on Buyers' Product Evaluations," *Journal of Marketing Research* 28 (August 1991): 307–19.

11. Jerome L. Mayers, *Fundamentals of Experimental Design*, 3rd ed. (Boston: Allyn and Bacon, 1979). See also H. Rao Unnava and Robert E. Burnkrant, "An Imagery-Processing View of the Role of Pictures in Print Advertisements," *Journal of Marketing Research* 28 (May 1991): 226–31.

12. Wayne W. Daniel and James C. Terrell, *Business Statistics*, 6th ed. (Boston: Houghton Mifflin, 1992).

13. Paul R. Hill and James C. Ward, "Mood Manipulation in Marketing Research: An Examination of Potential Confounding Effects," *Journal of Marketing Research* 27 (February 1989): 97–104.

14. Paul Chao, "The Impact of Country Affiliation on the Credibility of Product Attribute Claims," *Journal of Advertising Research* (April–May 1989): 35–41.

15. Although this is the most common way in which analysis of covariance is performed, other situations are also possible. For example, covariate and factor effects may be of equal interest, or the set of covariates may

be of major concern. For a recent application, see Kevin Lane Keller and David A. Aaker, "The Effects of Sequential Introduction of Brand Extensions," *Journal of Marketing Research* 29 (February 1992): 35–50.

16. For a more detailed discussion, see A. R. Wildt and O. T. Ahtola, *Analysis of Covariance* (Beverly Hills: Sage Publications, 1978).

17. See C. Whan Park, Sandra Milberg, and Robert Lawson, "Evaluation of Brand Extensions: The Role of Product Feature Similarity and Brand Concept Consistency," *Journal of Consumer Research* 18 (September 1991): 185–93; and J. H. Leigh and T. C. Kinnear, "On Interaction Classification," *Educational and Psychological Measurement* 40 (Winter 1980): 841–43.

18. For an examination of interactions using an ANOVA framework see Brian Wansink, "Advertising's Impact on Category Substitution," *Journal of Marketing Research* 31 (November 1994): 505–15; and Laura A. Peracchio and Joan Meyers-Levy, "How Ambiguous Cropped Objects in Ad Photos Can Affect Product Evaluations," *Journal of Consumer Research* 21 (June 1994): 190–204.

19. A. Sawyer and J. P. Peter, "The Significance of Statistical Significance Tests in Marketing Research," *Journal of Marketing Research* 20 (May 1983): 125; and R. F. Beltramini, "A Meta-Analysis of Effect Sizes in Consumer Behavior Experiments," *Journal of Consumer Research* 12 (June 1985): 97–103.

20. This formula does not hold if repeated measurements are made on the dependent variable. See David H. Dodd and Roger F. Schultz, Jr., "Computational Procedures for Estimating Magnitude of Effect for Some Analysis of Variance Designs," *Psychological Bulletin* (June 1973): 391–95.

21. The ω^2 formula is attributed to Hays. See W. L. Hays, *Statistics for Psychologists* (New York: Holt, Rinehart and Winston, 1963). For a recent application, see S. Ratneshwar and Shelly Chaiken, "Comprehension's Role in Persuasion: The Case of Its Moderating Effect on the Persuasive Impact of Source Cues," *Journal of Consumer Research* 18 (June 1991): 52–62.

22. Jacob Cohen, *Statistical Power Analysis for the Behavioral Sciences* (New York: Academic Press, 1969).

23. B. J. Winer, *Statistical Principles in Experimental Design*, 2nd ed. (New York: McGraw-Hill, 1971).

24. It is possible to combine between-subjects and within-subjects factors in a single design. See, for example, Susan M. Broniarczyk and Joseph W. Alba, "The Importance of the Brand in Brand Extension," *Journal of Marketing Research* 31 (May 1994): 214–28; Aradhna Krishna, "The Effect of Deal Knowledge on Consumer Purchase Behavior," *Journal of Marketing Research* 31 (February 1994): 76–91.

25. See J. H. Bray and S. E. Maxwell, *Multivariate Analysis of Variance* (Beverly Hills: Sage Publications, 1985). For an application of MANOVA, see Eric M. Olson, Orville C. Walker, Jr., and Robert W. Ruekert, "Organizing for Effective New Product Development: The Moderating Role of Product Innovativeness," *Journal of Marketing* 59 (January 1995): 48–62.

26. Ishmael P. Akaah, "A Cross-National Analysis of the Perceived Commonality of Unethical Practices in Marketing Research," in William Lazer, Eric Shaw, and Chow-Hou Wee (eds.), *World Marketing Congress*, International Conference Series, vol. 4 (Boca Raton, FL: Academy of Marketing Science, 1989), pp. 2–9.

27. Ishmael P. Akaah, "Differences in Research Ethics Judgments Between Male and Female Marketing Professionals," *Journal of Business Ethics* 8 (1989): 375–81.

28. For mainframe packages, see:

    SPSS Base Systems User's Guide (Englewood Cliffs, NJ: Prentice Hall, 1994).

    SAS Language and Procedure: Usage, V 6 (Cary, NC: SAS Institute, 1989).

    SAS Language and Procedure: Usage 2, V 6 (Cary, NC: SAS Institute, 1991).

    SAS Procedures Guide, V 6 3rd ed. (Cary, NC: SAS Institute, 1990).

    SAS Language: Reference, V 6 (Cary, NC: SAS Institute, 1990).

    BMDP Statistical Software Manual, vols. 1 and 2 (Berkeley: University of California Press, 1990).

    For microcomputer packages, see:

    SPSS/PC+™ V 4.0 BASE MANUAL (Englewood Cliffs, NJ: Prentice Hall, 1990).

    SPSS/PC+ Advanced Statistics™, V 4.0 (Englewood Cliffs, NJ: Prentice Hall, 1990).

    SAS/STAT™ User Guide, V 6, 4th ed., vols. 1 and 2 (Cary, NC: SAS Institute, 1990).

    The BMDP manual for microcomputers is the same as that for the mainframe.

29. The assistance of James Agarwal with the international marketing research example, the assistance of Mark Leach and Gina Miller in writing the ethics section, and the assistance of Mark Peterson in writing the computer applications section is gratefully acknowledged.

CHAPTER SEVENTEEN

Correlation and Regression

The product moment correlation is the most widely used statistic for summarizing the strength of association between two metric variables. Regression analysis is a powerful and flexible procedure for analyzing associative relationships between a metric-dependent variable and one or more independent variables.

◆

OBJECTIVES

After reading this chapter, the student should be able to:

1. Discuss the concepts of product moment correlation, partial correlation, and part correlation and show how they provide a foundation for regression analysis.
2. Discuss nonmetric correlation and measures such as Spearman's rho and Kendall's tau.
3. Explain the nature and methods of bivariate regression analysis and describe the general model, estimation of parameters, standardized regression coefficient, significance testing, prediction accuracy, residual analysis, and model cross-validation.
4. Explain the nature and methods of multiple regression analysis and the meaning of partial regression coefficients.
5. Describe specialized techniques used in multiple regression analysis, particularly stepwise regression, regression with dummy variables, and analysis of variance and covariance with regression.

OVERVIEW

Chapter 16 examined the relationship among the *t* test, analysis of variance and covariance, and regression. This chapter describes regression analysis, which is widely used for explaining variation in market share, sales, brand preference and other marketing results in terms of marketing management variables such as advertising, price, distribution, and product quality. Before discussing regression, however, we describe the concepts of product moment correlation and partial correlation coefficient, which lay the conceptual foundation for regression analysis.

In introducing regression analysis, we discuss the simple bivariate case first. We describe estimation, standardization of the regression coefficients, and testing and examination of the strength and significance of association between variables, prediction accuracy, and the assumptions underlying the regression model. Next, we discuss the multiple regression model, emphasizing the interpretation of parameters, strength of association, significance tests, and examination of residuals.

We then cover topics of special interest in regression analysis, such as stepwise regression, multicollinearity, relative importance of predictor variables, and cross-validation. We describe regression with dummy variables and the use of this procedure to conduct analysis of variance and covariance. We begin with some examples illustrating applications of regression analysis.

DEPARTMENT STORE PATRONAGE PROJECT
Multiple Regression

In the department store patronage project, multiple regression analysis was used to develop a model that explained store preference in terms of respondents' evaluations of the store on the eight-choice criteria. The dependent variable was the preference for each store. The independent variables were the evaluations of each store on quality of merchandise, variety and assortment of merchandise, returns and adjustment policy, service of store personnel, prices, convenience of location, layout of store, and credit and billing policies. The results indicated that all the factors of the choice criteria, except service of store personnel, were significant in explaining store preference. The coefficients of all the variables were positive, indicating that higher evaluations on each of the significant factors led to higher preference for that store. The model had a good fit and good ability to predict store preference. ◆

EXAMPLE
Retailing Revolution

Many retailing experts suggest that electronic shopping will be the next revolution in retailing. A research project investigating this trend looked for correlates of consumers' preferences for electronic shopping services via home videotex (computerized in-home shopping services). The explanation of consumers' preferences was sought in psychographic, demographic, and communication variables suggested in the literature. The study was conducted in southern Florida where Viewtron, a videotex service, has been offered since 1983. Viewtron, a subsidiary of Knight-Ridder Corporation, spent more than $1 million on advertising in the area. All the respondents were familiar with the concept of computerized shopping from home.

Multiple regression was used to analyze the data. The overall multiple regression model was significant at .05 level. Univariate *t* tests indicated that the following variables in the model were significant at .05 level or better: price orientation, sex, age, occupation, ethnicity, and education. None of the three communication variables (mass media, word-of-mouth, and publicity) was significantly related to consumer preference, the dependent variable.

The results suggest that electronic shopping is preferred by white females who are older, are better educated, price-oriented shoppers who work in supervisory or higher level occupations. Information of this type is valuable in targeting marketing effort to electronic shoppers.[1] ◆

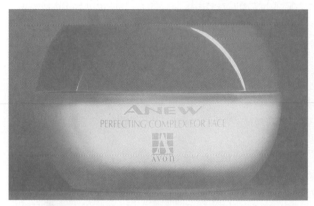

Good products, well-trained sales reps, and sophisticated regression models have opened the doors for Avon, enabling it to penetrate the cosmetics market. ◆ Avon Products, Inc.

EXAMPLE
Regression Rings the Right Bell for Avon _____

Avon Products, Inc., was having significant problems with the sales staff. The company's business, dependent on sales representatives, was facing a shortage of sales reps without much hope of getting new ones. Regression models, operating on IBM PCs, were developed to reveal the possible variables that were fueling this situation. The models revealed that the most significant variable was the level of the appointment fee that reps pay for materials. With data to back up its actions, the company lowered the fee. This resulted in an improvement in the recruitment and retention of sales reps.[2] ◆

These examples illustrate some of the uses of regression analysis in determining which independent variables explain a significant variation in the dependent variable of interest, the structure and form of the relationship, the strength of the relationship, and predicted values of the dependent variable. Fundamental to regression analysis is an understanding of the product moment correlation.

PRODUCT MOMENT CORRELATION

In marketing research, we are often interested in summarizing the strength of association between two metric variables, as in the following situations:

- How strongly are sales related to advertising expenditures?
- Is there an association between market share and size of the sales force?
- Are consumers' perceptions of quality related to their perceptions of prices?

product moment correlation (r) A statistic summarizing the strength of association between two metric variables.

In situations like these, the **product moment correlation**, *r*, is the most widely used statistic, summarizing the strength of association between two metric (interval or ratio scaled) variables, say X and Y. It is an index used to determine whether a linear or straight line relationship exists between X and Y. It indicates the degree to which the variation in one variable, X, is related to the variation in another variable, Y. Because it was originally proposed by Karl Pearson, it is also known as the *Pearson correlation coef-*

ficient and also referred to as *simple correlation, bivariate correlation,* or merely the *correlation coefficient.* From a sample of n observations, X and Y, the product moment correlation, r, can be calculated as

$$r = \frac{\sum_{i=1}^{n}(X_i - \overline{X})(Y_i - \overline{Y})}{\sqrt{\sum_{i=1}^{n}(X_i - \overline{X})^2 \sum_{i=1}^{n}(Y_i - \overline{Y})^2}}$$

Division of the numerator and denominatory by n − 1 gives

$$r = \frac{\sum_{i=1}^{n}\dfrac{(X_i - \overline{X})(Y_i - \overline{Y})}{n-1}}{\sqrt{\sum_{i=1}^{n}\dfrac{(X_i - \overline{X})^2}{n-1} \sum_{i=1}^{n}\dfrac{(Y_i - \overline{Y})^2}{n-1}}}$$

$$= \frac{COV_{xy}}{S_x S_y}$$

covariance A systematic relationship between two variables in which a change in one implies a corresponding change in the other (COV_{xy}).

In these equations, $\overline{X}$ and $\overline{Y}$ denote the sample means and S_x and S_y the standard deviations. COV_{xy}, the **covariance** between X and Y, measures the extent to which X and Y are related. The covariance may be either positive or negative. Division by $S_x S_y$ achieves standardization so that r varies between −1.0 and +1.0. Note that the correlation coefficient is an absolute number and is not expressed in any unit of measurement. The correlation coefficient between two variables will be the same regardless of their underlying units of measurement.

As an example, suppose that a researcher wants to explain attitudes toward a respondent's city of residence in terms of duration of residence in the city. The attitude is measured on an 11-point scale (1 = do not like the city, 11 = very much like the city), and the duration of residence is measured in terms of the number of years the respondent has lived in the city. In a pretest of 12 respondents, the data shown in Table 17.1 are obtained.

The correlation coefficient may be calculated as follows:

$$\overline{X} = (10 + 12 + 12 + 4 + 12 + 6 + 8 + 2 + 18 + 9 + 17 + 2)/12$$
$$= 9.333$$

$$\overline{Y} = (6 + 9 + 8 + 3 + 10 + 4 + 5 + 2 + 11 + 9 + 10 + 2)/12$$
$$= 6.583$$

$$\sum_{i=1}^{n}(X_i - \overline{X})(Y_i - \overline{Y}) = (10 - 9.33)(6 - 6.58) + (12 - 9.33)(9 - 6.58)$$
$$+ (12 - 9.33)(8 - 6.58) + (4 - 9.33)(3 - 6.58)$$
$$+ (12 - 9.33)(10 - 6.58) + (6 - 9.33)(4 - 6.58)$$
$$+ (8 - 9.33)(5 - 6.58) + (2 - 9.33)(2 - 6.58)$$
$$+ (18 - 9.33)(11 - 6.58) + (9 - 9.33)(9 - 6.58)$$
$$+ (17 - 9.33)(10 - 6.58) + (2 - 9.33)(2 - 6.58)$$

$$= -0.3886 + 6.4614 + 3.7914 + 19.0814 + 9.1314 + 8.5914$$
$$+ 2.1014 + 33.5714 + 38.3214 - 0.7986 + 26.2314 + 33.5714$$

$$= 179.6668$$

	Respondent Number	Attitude toward the City	Duration of Residence	Importance Attached to Weather
TABLE 17.1	1	6	10	3
	2	9	12	11
Explaining Attitude	3	8	12	4
Toward the City	4	3	4	1
of Residence	5	10	12	11
	6	4	6	1
	7	5	8	7
	8	2	2	4
	9	11	18	8
	10	9	9	10
	11	10	17	8
	12	2	2	5

$$\sum_{i=1}^{n}(X_i - \overline{X})^2 = (10 - 9.33)^2 + (12 - 9.33)^2 + (12 - 9.33)^2 + (4 - 9.33)^2$$
$$+ (12 - 9.33)^2 + (6 - 9.33)^2 + (8 - 9.33)^2 + (2 - 9.33)^2$$
$$+ (18 - 9.33)^2 + (9 - 9.33)^2 + (17 - 9.33)^2 + (2 - 9.33)^2$$

$$= 0.4489 + 7.1289 + 7.1289 + 28.4089 + 7.1289 + 11.0889 + 1.7689$$
$$+ 53.7289 + 75.1689 + 0.1089 + 58.8289 + 53.7289$$

$$= 304.6668$$

$$\sum_{i=1}^{n}(Y_i - \overline{Y})^2 = (6 - 6.58)^2 + (9 - 6.58)^2 + (8 - 6.58)^2 + (3 - 6.58)^2$$
$$+ (10 - 6.58)^2 + (4 - 6.58)^2 + (5 - 6.58)^2 + (2 - 6.58)^2$$
$$+ (11 - 6.58)^2 + (9 - 6.58)^2 + (10 - 6.58)^2 + (2 - 6.58)^2$$

$$= 0.3364 + 5.8564 + 2.0164 + 12.8164 + 11.6964 + 6.6564 + 2.4964$$
$$+ 20.9764 + 19.5364 + 5.8564 + 11.6964 + 20.9764$$

$$= 120.9168$$

Thus,

$$r = \frac{179.6668}{\sqrt{(304.6668)(120.9168)}}$$

$$= 0.9361$$

In this example, $r = 0.9361$, a value close to 1.0. This means that respondents' duration of residence in the city is strongly associated with their attitude toward the city. Furthermore, the positive sign of r implies a positive relationship; the longer the duration of residence, the more favorable the attitude and vice versa.

Since r indicates the degree to which variation in one variable is related to variation in another, it can also be expressed in terms of the decomposition of the total variation (see Chapter 16). In other words,

$$r^2 = \frac{\text{explained variation}}{\text{total variation}}$$

$$= \frac{SS_x}{SS_y}$$

$$= \frac{\text{total variation} - \text{error variation}}{\text{total variation}}$$

$$= \frac{SS_y - SS_{error}}{SS_y}$$

Hence, r^2 measures the proportion of variation in one variable that is explained by the other. Both r and r^2 are symmetric measures of association. In other words, the correlation of X with Y is the same as the correlation of Y with X. It does not matter which variable is considered to be the dependent variable and which the independent. The product moment coefficient measures the strength of the linear relationship and is not designed to measure nonlinear relationships. Thus $r = 0$ merely indicates that there is no linear relationship between X and Y. It does not mean that X and Y are unrelated. There could well be a nonlinear relationship between them, which would not be captured by r (see Figure 17.1).

When computed for a population rather than a sample, the product moment correlation is denoted by the Greek letter rho, ρ. The coefficient r is an estimator of ρ. Note that the calculation of r assumes that X and Y are metric variables whose distributions have the same shape. If these assumptions are not met, r is deflated and underestimates ρ. In marketing research, data obtained by using rating scales with a small number of categories may not be strictly interval. This tends to deflate r, resulting in an underestimation of ρ.[3]

The statistical significance of the relationship between two variables measured by using r can be conveniently tested. The hypotheses are

$$H_0\colon \rho = 0$$
$$H_1\colon \rho \neq 0$$

The test statistic is

$$t = r\left[\frac{n-2}{1-r^2}\right]^{1/2}$$

which has a t distribution with $n-2$ degrees of freedom.[4] For the correlation coefficient calculated based on the data given in Table 17.1,

$$t = 0.9361\left[\frac{12-2}{1-(0.9361)^2}\right]^{1/2}$$

$$= 8.414$$

and the degrees of freedom = $12 - 2 = 10$. From the t distribution table (Table 4 in the Statistical Appendix), the critical value of t for a two-tailed test and $\alpha = .05$ is 2.228.

FIGURE 17.1

A Nonlinear Relationship for Which $r = 0$

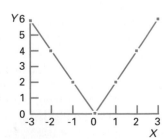

Hence, the null hypothesis of no relationship between X and Y is rejected. This, along with the positive sign of r, indicates that attitude toward the city is positively related to the duration of residence in the city. Moreover, the high value of r indicates that this relationship is strong.

In conducting multivariate data analysis, it is often useful to examine the simple correlation between each pair of variables. These results are presented in the form of a correlation matrix, which indicates the coefficient of correlation between each pair of variables. Usually, only the lower triangular portion of the matrix is considered. The diagonal elements all equal 1.00, since a variable correlates perfectly with itself. The upper triangular portion of the matrix is a mirror image of the lower triangular portion, since r is a symmetric measure of association. The form of a correlation matrix for five variables, V_1 through V_5, is as follows:

	V_1	V_2	V_3	V_4	V_5
V_1					
V_2	0.5				
V_3	0.3	0.4			
V_4	0.1	0.3	0.6		
V_5	0.2	0.5	0.3	0.7	

Although a matrix of simple correlations provides insights into pairwise associations, sometimes researchers want to examine the association between two variables after controlling for one or more other variables. In the latter case, partial correlation should be estimated.

PARTIAL CORRELATION

partial correlation coefficient A measure of the association between two variables after controlling or adjusting for the effects of one or more additional variables.

Whereas the product moment or simple correlation is a measure of association describing the linear association between two variables, a **partial correlation coefficient** measures the association between two variables after controlling for or adjusting for the effects of one or more additional variables. This statistic is used to answer the following questions:

- How strongly are sales related to advertising expenditures when the effect of price is controlled?
- Is there an association between market share and size of the sales force after adjusting for the effect of sales promotion?
- Are consumers' perceptions of quality related to their perceptions of prices when the effect of brand image is controlled?

As in these situations, suppose that a researcher wanted to calculate the association between X and Y after controlling for a third variable, Z. Conceptually, one would first remove the effect of Z from X. To do this, one would predict the values of X based on a knowledge of Z by using the product moment correlation between X and Z, r_{xz}. The predicted value of X is then subtracted from the actual value of X to construct an adjusted value of X. In a similar manner, the values of Y are adjusted to remove the effects of Z. The product moment correlation between the adjusted values of X and the adjusted values of Y is the partial correlation coefficient between X and Y, after controlling for the effect of Z, and is denoted by $r_{xy.z}$. Statistically, since the simple correlation between two variables completely describes the linear relationship between them, the partial correlation coefficient can be calculated by a knowledge of the simple correlations alone, without using individual observations.

$$r_{xy.z} = \frac{r_{xy} - (r_{xz})(r_{yz})}{\sqrt{1 - r_{xz}^2}\sqrt{1 - r_{yz}^2}}$$

To continue our example, suppose that the researcher wanted to calculate the association between attitude toward the city, Y, and duration of residence, X_1, after controlling for a third variable, importance attached to weather, X_2. These data are presented in Table 17.1. The simple correlations between the variables are

$$r_{yx_1} = .9361 \qquad r_{yx_2} = .7334 \qquad r_{x_1 x_2} = .5495$$

The required partial correlation be calculated as follows:

$$r_{yx_1.x_2} = \frac{.9361 - (.5495)(.7334)}{\sqrt{1 - (.5495)^2}\sqrt{1 - (.7334)^2}}$$

$$= .9386$$

As can be seen, controlling for the effect of importance attached to weather has little effect on the association between attitude toward the city and duration of residence.

Partial correlations have an *order* associated with them that indicates how many variables are being adjusted or controlled for. The simple correlation coefficient, r, has a zero order, because it does not control for any additional variables while measuring the association between two variables. The coefficient $r_{xy.z}$ is a first-order partial correlation coefficient, because it controls for the effect of one additional variable, Z. A second-order partial correlation coefficient controls for the effects of two variables, a third-order for the effects of three variables, and so on. The higher order partial correlations are calculated similarly. The $(n + 1)$th-order partial coefficient may be calculated by replacing the simple correlation coefficients on the right side of the preceding equation with the nth-order partial coefficients.

Partial correlations can be helpful for detecting spurious relationships (see Chapter 15). The relationship between X and Y is spurious if it is solely because X is associated with Z, which is indeed the true predictor of Y. In this case, the correlation between X and Y disappears when the effect of Z is controlled. Consider a case in which consumption of a cereal brand (C) is positively associated with income (I), with r_{ci} = 0.28. Because this brand was popularly priced, income was not expected to be a significant factor. Therefore, the researcher suspected that this relationship was spurious. The sample results also indicated that income is positively associated with household size (H), r_{hi} = 0.48, and that household size is associated with cereal consumption, r_{ch} = 0.56. These figures seem to indicate that the real predictor of cereal consumption is not income but household size. To test this assertion, the first-order partial correlation between cereal consumption and income is calculated, controlling for the effect of household size. The reader can verify that this partial correlation, $r_{ci.h}$, is 0.02, and the initial correlation between cereal consumption and income vanishes when the household size is controlled. Therefore, the correlation between income and cereal consumption is spurious. The special case when a partial correlation is larger than its respective zero-order correlation involves a suppressor effect (see Chapter 15).[5]

Another correlation coefficient of interest is the **part correlation coefficient**. This coefficient represents the correlation between Y and X when the linear effects of the other independent variables have been removed from X but not from Y. The part correlation coefficient, $r_{y(x.z)}$ is calculated as follows:

part correlation coefficient A measure of the correlation between Y and X when the linear effects of the other independent variables have been removed from X (but not from Y).

$$r_{y(x.z)} = \frac{r_{xy} - r_{yz}\,r_{xz}}{\sqrt{1 - r_{xz}^2}}$$

The part correlation between attitude toward the city and the duration of residence, when the linear effects of the importance attached to weather have been removed from the duration of residence, can be calculated as

$$r_{y(x_1.x_2)} = \frac{.9361 - (.5495)(.7334)}{\sqrt{1 - (.5495)^2}}$$

$$= .63806$$

The partial correlation coefficient is generally viewed as more important than the part correlation coefficient. The product moment correlation, partial correlation, and the part correlation coefficient all assume that the data are interval or ratio scaled. If the data do not meet these requirements, the researcher should consider the use of non-metric correlation.

EXAMPLE
Selling Ads to Home Shoppers

Advertisements play a very important role in forming attitudes and preferences for brands. In general, it has been found that for low-involvement products, attitude toward the advertisement mediates brand cognition (beliefs about the brand) and attitude toward the brand. What would happen to the effect of this mediating variable when products are purchased through a home shopping network? Home Shopping Budapest in Hungary conducted research to assess the impact of advertisements toward purchase. A survey was conducted where several measures—such as attitude toward the product, attitude toward the brand, attitude toward the ad characteristics, brand cognitions, and so on—were taken. It was hypothesized that in a home shopping network, advertisements largely determined attitude toward the brand. To find the degree of association of attitude toward the ad with both attitude toward the brand and brand cognition, a partial correlation coefficient could be computed. The partial correlation would be calculated between attitude toward the brand and brand cognitions after controlling for the effects of attitude toward the ad on the two variables. If attitude toward the ad is significantly high, then the partial correlation coefficient should be significantly less than the product moment correlation between brand cognition and attitude toward the brand. Research was conducted which supported this hypothesis. Then, Saatchi and Saatchi designed the ads aired on Home Shopping Budapest to generate positive attitude toward the advertising and this turned out to be a major competitive weapon for the network.[6] ◆

NONMETRIC CORRELATION

nonmetric correlation A correlation measure for two nonmetric variables that relies on rankings to compute the correlation.

At times the researcher may have to compute the correlation coefficient between two variables that are nonmetric. It may be recalled that nonmetric variables do not have interval or ratio scale properties and do not assume a normal distribution. If the nonmetric variables are ordinal and numeric, Spearman's rho, ρ_s, and Kendall's tau, τ, are two measures of **nonmetric correlation** which can be used to examine the correlation between them. Both these measures use rankings rather than the absolute values of the variables, and the basic concepts underlying them are quite similar. Both vary from −1.0 to +1.0.

In the absence of ties, Spearman's ρ_s yields a closer approximation to the Pearson product moment correlation coefficient, r, than does Kendall's τ. In these cases, the absolute magnitude of τ tends to be smaller than Pearson's r. On the other hand, when the data contain a large number of tied ranks, Kendall's τ seems more appropriate. As a rule of thumb, Kendall's τ is to be preferred when a large number of cases fall into a relatively small number of categories (thereby leading to a large number of ties). Conversely, the use of Spearman's ρ_s is preferable when we have a relatively larger number of categories (thereby having fewer ties).[7]

The product moment as well as the partial and part correlation coefficients provide a conceptual foundation for bivariate as well as multiple regression analysis.

REGRESSION ANALYSIS

regression analysis A statistical procedure for analyzing associative relationships between a metric-dependent variable and one or more independent variables.

Regression analysis is a powerful and flexible procedure for analyzing associative relationships between a metric-dependent variable and one or more independent variables. It can be used in the following ways:

1. To determine whether the independent variables explain a significant variation in the dependent variable: whether a relationship exists
2. To determine how much of the variation in the dependent variable can be explained by the independent variables: strength of the relationship
3. To determine the structure or form of the relationship: the mathematical equation relating the independent and dependent variables
4. To predict the values of the dependent variable
5. To control for other independent variables when evaluating the contributions of a specific variable or set of variables

Although the independent variables may explain the variation in the dependent variable, this does not necessarily imply causation. The use of the terms *dependent* or *criterion* variables and *independent* or *predictor* variables in regression analysis arises from the mathematical relationship between the variables. These terms do not imply that the criterion variable is dependent on the independent variables in a causal sense. Regression analysis is concerned with the nature and degree of association between variables and does not imply or assume any causality. Bivariate regression is discussed first, followed by multiple regression.

BIVARIATE REGRESSION

bivariate regression A procedure for deriving a mathematical relationship, in the form of an equation, between a single metric-dependent variable and a single metric-independent variable.

Bivariate regression is a procedure for deriving a mathematical relationship, in the form of an equation, between a single metric-dependent or criterion variable and a single metric independent or predictor variable. The analysis is similar in many ways to determining the simple correlation between two variables. Since an equation has to be derived, however, one variable must be identified as the dependent variable and the other as the independent variable. The examples given earlier in the context of simple correlation can be translated into the regression context.

- Can variation in sales be explained in terms of variation in advertising expenditures? What is the structure and form of this relationship, and can it be modeled mathematically by an equation describing a straight line?
- Can the variation in market share be accounted for by the size of the sales force?
- Are consumers' perceptions of quality determined by their perceptions of price?

Before discussing the procedure for conducting bivariate regression, we define some important statistics.

STATISTICS ASSOCIATED WITH BIVARIATE REGRESSION ANALYSIS

The following statistics and statistical terms are associated with bivariate regression analysis.

Bivariate regression model.   The basic regression equation is $Y_i = \beta_0 + \beta_1 X_i + e_i$, where Y = dependent or criterion variable, X = independent or predictor variable, β_0 = intercept of the line, β_1 = slope of the line, and e_i is the error term associated with the *i*th observation.

Coefficient of determination.   The strength of association is measured by the coefficient of determination, r^2. It varies between 0 and 1 and signifies the proportion of the total variation in Y that is accounted for by the variation in X.

estimated or predicted value The value $\hat{Y}_i = a + b_x$, where *a* and *b* are, respectively, estimators of β_0 and β_1, the corresponding population parameters.

Estimated or predicted value.   The **estimated or predicted value** of Y_i is $\hat{Y}_i = a + bx$, where $\hat{Y}_i$ is the predicted value of Y_i, and *a* and *b* are estimators of β_0 and β_1, respectively.

Regression coefficient.   The estimated parameter *b* is usually referred to as the nonstandardized regression coefficient.

Scattergram.   A scatter diagram, or scattergram, is a plot of the values of two variables for all the cases or observations.

Standard error of estimate.   This statistic, the SEE, is the standard deviation of the actual Y values from the predicted $\hat{Y}$ values.

Standard error.   The standard deviation of *b*, SE_b, is called the standard error.

Standardized regression coefficient.   Also termed the beta coefficient or beta weight, this is the slope obtained by the regression of Y on X when the data are standardized.

Sum of squared errors.   The distances of all the points from the regression line are squared and added together to arrive at the sum of squared errors, which is a measure of total error, $\sum e_j^2$.

t statistic.   A *t* statistic with $n - 2$ degrees of freedom can be used to test the null hypothesis that no linear relationship exists between X and Y, or $H_0: \beta_1 = 0$, where

$$t = \frac{b}{SE_b}.$$

CONDUCTING BIVARIATE REGRESSION ANALYSIS

The steps involved in conducting bivariate regression analysis are described in Figure 17.2. Suppose that the researcher wants to explain attitudes toward the city of residence in terms of the duration of residence (see Table 17.1). In deriving such relationships, it is often useful to first examine a scatter diagram.

Scatter Diagram

A scatter diagram, or scattergram, is a plot of the values of two variables for all the cases or observations. It is customary to plot the dependent variable on the vertical axis and the independent variable on the horizontal axis. A scatter diagram is useful for determining the form of the relationship between the variables. A plot can alert the researcher to patterns in the data or to possible problems. Any unusual combinations of the two variables can be easily identified. A plot of Y (attitude toward the city) against X (duration of residence) is given in Figure 17.3. The points seem to be arranged in a band running from the bottom left to the top right. One can see the pattern: as one variable increases, so does the other. It appears from this scattergram that the relationship between X and Y is linear and could be well described by a straight line. How should the straight line be fitted to best describe the data?

FIGURE 17.2

Conducting Bivariate Regression Analysis

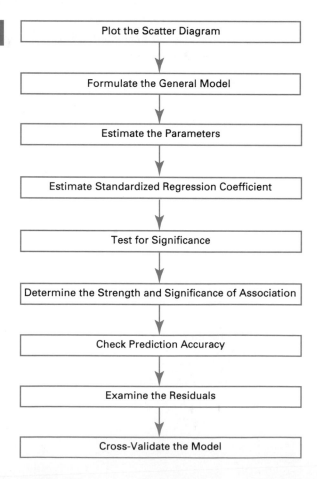

Plot the Scatter Diagram

Formulate the General Model

Estimate the Parameters

Estimate Standardized Regression Coefficient

Test for Significance

Determine the Strength and Significance of Association

Check Prediction Accuracy

Examine the Residuals

Cross-Validate the Model

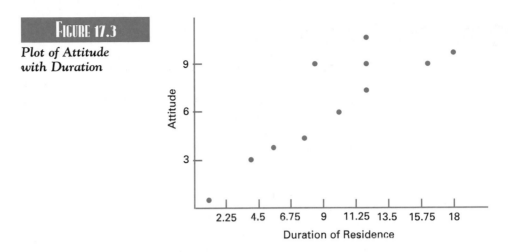

FIGURE 17.3

Plot of Attitude with Duration

The most commonly used technique for fitting a straight line to a scattergram is the **least squares procedure**. This technique determines the best-fitting line by minimizing the vertical distances of all the points from the line. The best-fitting line is called the *regression line*. Any point that does not fall on the regression line is not fully accounted for. The vertical distance from the point to the line is the error, e_j (see Figure 17.4). The distances of all the points from the line are squared and added together to arrive at the sum of squared errors, which is a measure of total error, $\sum e_j^2$.

In fitting the line, the least squares procedure minimizes the sum of squared errors. If Y is plotted on the vertical axis and X on the horizontal axis, as in Figure 17.4, the best-fitting line is called the regression of Y on X, since the vertical distances are minimized. The scatter diagram indicates whether the relationship between Y and X can be modeled as a straight line and, consequently, whether the bivariate regression model is appropriate.

least squares procedure
A technique for fitting a straight line to a scattergram by minimizing the vertical distances of all the points from the line.

FIGURE 17.4

Bivariate Regression

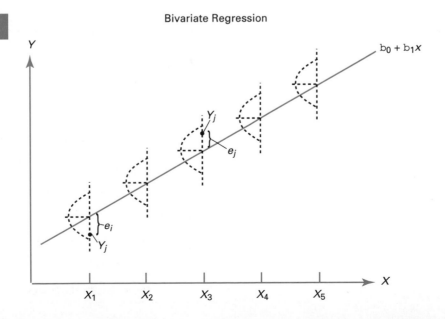

BIVARIATE REGRESSION MODEL

In the bivariate regression model, the general form of a straight line is

$$Y = \beta_0 + \beta_1 X$$

where

Y = dependent or criterion variable

X = independent or predictor variable

β_0 = intercept of the line

β_1 = slope of the line

This model implies a deterministic relationship in that Y is completely determined by X. The value of Y can be perfectly predicted if β_0 and β_1 are known. In marketing research, however, very few relationships are deterministic. Thus, the regression procedure adds an error term to account for the probabilistic or stochastic nature of the relationship. The basic regression equation becomes

$$Y_i = \beta_0 + \beta_1 X_i + e_i$$

where e_i is the error term associated with the ith observation.[8] Estimation of the regression parameters, β_0 and β_1, is relatively simple.

Estimation of Parameters

In most cases, β_0 and β_1 are unknown and are estimated from the sample observations using the equation

$$\hat{Y}_i = a + bx_i$$

where $\hat{Y}_i$ is the estimated or predicted value of Y_i, and a and b are estimators of β_0 and β_1, respectively. The constant b is usually referred to as the nonstandardized regression coefficient. It is the slope of the regression line, and it indicates the expected change in Y when X is changed by one unit. The formulas for calculating a and b are simple.[9] The slope, b, may be computed in terms of the covariance between X and Y (COV_{xy}) and the variance of X as

$$b = \frac{COV_{xy}}{S_x^2}$$

$$= \frac{\sum_{i=1}^{n}(X_i - \overline{X})(Y_i - \overline{Y})}{\sum_{i=1}^{n}(X_i - \overline{X})^2}$$

$$= \frac{\sum_{i=1}^{n}X_i Y_i - n\overline{XY}}{\sum_{i=1}^{n}X_i^2 - n\overline{X}^2}$$

The intercept, *a*, may then be calculated using

$$a = \overline{Y} - b\overline{X}$$

For the data in Table 17.1, the estimation of parameters may be illustrated as follows:

$$\sum_{i=1}^{12} X_i Y_i = (10)(6) + (12)(9) + (12)(8) + (4)(3) + (12)(10) + (6)(4) + (8)(5)$$
$$+ (2)(2) + (18)(11) + (9)(9) + (17)(10) + (2)(2)$$
$$= 917$$

$$\sum_{i=1}^{12} X_i^2 = 10^2 + 12^2 + 12^2 + 4^2 + 12^2 + 6^2 + 8^2 + 2^2 + 18^2 + 9^2 + 17^2 + 2^2$$
$$= 1350$$

It may be recalled from earlier calculations of the simple correlation that

$$\overline{X} = 9.333$$
$$\overline{Y} = 6.583$$

Given *n* = 12, *b* can be calculated as

$$b = \frac{917 - (12)(9.333)(6.583)}{1350 - (12)(9.333)^2}$$
$$= 0.5897$$

$$a = \overline{Y} - b\overline{X}$$
$$= 6.583 - (0.5897)(9.333)$$
$$= 1.0793$$

Note that these coefficients have been estimated on the raw (untransformed) data. Should standardization of the data be considered desirable, the calculation of the standardized coefficients is also straightforward.

Standardized Regression Coefficient

Standardization is the process by which the raw data are transformed into new variables that have a mean of 0 and a variance of 1 (Chapter 14). When the data are standardized, the intercept assumes a value of 0. The term *beta coefficient* or *beta weight* is used to denote the standardized regression coefficient. In this case, the slope obtained by the regression of Y on X, B_{yx}, is the same as the slope obtained by the regression of X on Y, B_{xy}. Moreover, each of these regression coefficients is equal to the simple correlation between X and Y

$$B_{yx} = B_{xy} = r_{xy}$$

There is a simple relationship between the standardized and nonstandardized regression coefficients

$$B_{yx} = b_{yx}\left(\frac{S_x}{S_y}\right)$$

For the regression results given in Table 17.2, the value of the beta coefficient is estimated as 0.9361.

Once the parameters have been estimated, they can be tested for significance.

TABLE 17.2					
Bivariate Regression					

Multiple R	0.93608
R^2	0.87624
Adjusted R^2	0.86387
Standard Error	1.22329

		Analysis of Variance	
	df	Sum of Squares	Mean Square
Regression	1	105.95222	105.95222
Residual	10	14.96444	1.49644
$F = 70.80266$	Significance of F = 0.0000		

			Variables in the Equation		
Variable	b	SE_b	Beta (β)	T	Significance of T
DURATION	0.58972	0.07008	0.93608	8.414	.0000
(Constant)	1.07932	0.74335		1.452	.1772

Significance Testing

The statistical significance of the linear relationship between X and Y may be tested by examining the hypotheses

$$H_0: \ \beta_1 = 0$$
$$H_1: \ \beta_1 \neq 0$$

The null hypothesis implies that there is no linear relationship between X and Y. The alternative hypothesis is that there is a relationship, positive or negative, between X and Y. Typically, a two-tailed test is done. A t statistic with $n - 2$ degrees of freedom can be used, where

$$t \ = \ \frac{b}{SE_b}$$

and SE_b denotes the standard deviation of b, called the *standard error*.[10] The t distribution was discussed in Chapter 15.

Using a computer program, the regression of attitude on duration of residence, using the data shown in Table 17.1, yielded the results shown in Table 17.2. The intercept, a, equals 1.0793, and the slope, b, equals 0.5897. Therefore, the estimated equation is

$$\text{attitude } (\hat{Y}) \ = \ 1.0793 + 0.5897 \text{ (duration of residence)}$$

The standard error or standard deviation of b is estimated as 0.07008, and the value of the t statistic, $t = 0.5897/0.0700 = 8.414$, with $n - 2 = 10$ degrees of freedom. From Table 4 in the Statistical Appendix, we see that the critical value of t with 10 degrees of freedom and $\alpha = .05$ is 2.228 for a two-tailed test. Since the calculated value of t is larger than the critical value, the null hypothesis is rejected. Hence, there is a significant linear relationship between attitude toward the city and duration of residence in the city. The positive sign of the slope coefficient indicates that this relationship is positive. In other words, those who have resided in the city for a longer time have more positive attitudes toward the city.

Strength and Significance of Association

A related inference involves determining the strength and significance of the association between Y and X. The strength of association is measured by the coefficient of determination, r^2. In bivariate regression, r^2 is the square of the simple correlation coefficient obtained by correlating the two variables. The coefficient r^2 varies between 0 and 1. It signifies the proportion of the total variation in Y that is accounted for by the variation in X. The decomposition of the total variation in Y is similar to that for analysis of variance (Chapter 16). As shown in Figure 17.5, the total variation, SS_y, may be decomposed into the variation accounted for by the regression line, SS_{reg}, and the error or residual variation, SS_{error} or SS_{res}, as follows:

$$SS_y = SS_{reg} + SS_{res}$$

where

$$SS_y = \sum_{i=1}^{n}(Y_i - \overline{Y})^2$$

$$SS_{reg} = \sum_{i=1}^{n}(\hat{Y}_i - \overline{Y})^2$$

$$SS_{res} = \sum_{i=1}^{n}(Y_i - \hat{Y}_i)^2$$

The strength of association may then be calculated as follows:

$$r^2 = \frac{SS_{reg}}{SS_y}$$

$$= \frac{SS_y - SS_{res}}{SS_y}$$

To illustrate the calculations of r^2, let us consider again the effect of attitude toward the city on the duration of residence. It may be recalled from earlier calculations of the simple correlation coefficient that

$$SS_y = \sum_{i=1}^{n}(Y_i - \overline{Y})^2$$

$$= 120.9168$$

The predicted values ($\hat{Y}$) can be calculated using the regression equation

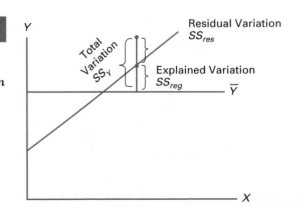

FIGURE 17.5

*Decomposition
of the Total Variation
in Bivariate Regression*

attitude $(\hat{Y})$ = 1.0793 + 0.5897 (duration of residence)

For the first observation in Table 17.1, this value is

$$(\hat{Y}) = 1.0793 + 0.5897 \times 10 = 6.9763$$

For each successive observation, the predicted values are, in order, 8.1557, 8.1557, 3.4381, 8.1557, 4.6175, 5.7969, 2.2587, 11.6939, 6.3866, 11.1042, 2.2587. Therefore,

$$
\begin{aligned}
SS_{reg} = \sum_{i=1}^{n}(\hat{Y}_i - \overline{Y})^2 &= (6.9763 - 6.5833)^2 + (8.1557 - 6.5833)^2 + (8.1557 - 6.5833)^2 \\
&\quad + (3.4381 - 6.5833)^2 + (8.1557 - 6.5833)^2 + (4.6175 - 6.5833)^2 \\
&\quad + (5.7969 - 6.5833)^2 + (2.2587 - 6.5833)^2 + (11.6939 - 6.5833)^2 \\
&\quad + (6.3866 - 6.5833)^2 + (11.1042 - 6.5833)^2 + (2.2587 - 6.5833)^2 \\
&= 0.1544 + 2.4724 + 2.4724 + 9.8922 + 2.4724 + 3.8643 + 0.6184 \\
&\quad + 18.7021 + 26.1182 + 0.0387 + 20.4385 + 18.7021 \\
&= 105.9524
\end{aligned}
$$

$$
\begin{aligned}
SS_{res} = \sum_{i=1}^{n}(Y_i - \hat{Y}_i)^2 &= (6 - 6.9763)^2 + (9 - 8.1557)^2 + (8 - 8.1557)^2 + (3 - 3.4381)^2 \\
&\quad + (10 - 8.1557)^2 + (4 - 4.6175)^2 + (5 - 5.7969)^2 + (2 - 2.2587)^2 \\
&\quad + (11 - 11.6939)^2 + (9 - 6.3866)^2 + (10 - 11.1042)^2 \\
&\quad + (2 - 2.2587)^2 \\
&= 14.9644
\end{aligned}
$$

It can be seen that $SS_y = SS_{reg} + SS_{res}$. Furthermore,

$$
\begin{aligned}
r^2 &= \frac{SS_{reg}}{SS_y} \\
&= \frac{105.9524}{120.9168} \\
&= 0.8762
\end{aligned}
$$

Another equivalent test for examining the significance of the linear relationship between X and Y (significance of b) is the test for the significance of the coefficient of determination. The hypotheses in this case are

$$H_0: \; R^2_{pop} = 0$$

$$H_1: \; R^2_{pop} > 0$$

The appropriate test statistic is the F statistic

$$F = \frac{SS_{reg}}{SS_{res}/(n-2)}$$

which has an F distribution with 1 and $n-2$ degrees of freedom. The F test is a generalized form of the t test (see Chapter 15). If a random variable is t distributed with n degrees of freedom, then t^2 is F distributed with 1 and n degrees of freedom. Hence, the F test for testing the significance of the coefficient of determination is equivalent to testing the following hypotheses:

$$H_0: \; \beta_1 = 0$$

$$H_1: \; \beta_1 \neq 0$$

or

$$H_0: \rho = 0$$
$$H_1: \rho \neq 0$$

From Table 17.2, it can be seen that

$$r^2 = \frac{105.9522}{105.9522 + 14.9644}$$

$$= 0.8762$$

which is the same as the value calculated earlier. The value of the F statistic is

$$F = \frac{105.9522}{14.9644/10}$$

$$= 70.8027$$

with 1 and 10 degrees of freedom. The calculated F statistic exceeds the critical value of 4.96 determined from Table 5 in the Statistical Appendix. Therefore, the relationship is significant at $\alpha = .05$, corroborating the results of the t test. If the relationship between X and Y is significant, it is meaningful to predict the values of Y based on the values of X and to estimate prediction accuracy.

Prediction Accuracy

To estimate the accuracy of predicted values, $\hat{Y}$, it is useful to calculate the standard error of estimate, SEE. This statistic is the standard deviation of the actual Y values from the predicted $\hat{Y}$ values.

$$SEE = \sqrt{\frac{\sum_{i=1}^{n}(Y_i - \hat{Y})^2}{n-2}}$$

$$SEE = \sqrt{\frac{SS_{res}}{n-2}}$$

or, more generally, if there are k independent variables,

$$SEE = \sqrt{\frac{SS_{res}}{n-k-1}}$$

SEE may be interpreted as a kind of average residual or average error in predicting Y from the regression equation.[11]

Two cases of prediction may arise. The researcher may want to predict the mean value of Y for all the cases with a given value of X, say X_0, or predict the value of Y for a single case. In both situations, the predicted value is the same and is given by $\hat{Y}$, where

$$\hat{Y} = a + bX_0$$

But the standard error is different in the two situations, although in both situations it is a function of SEE. For large samples, the standard error for predicting mean value of Y is $SEE/\sqrt{n}$, and for predicting individual Y values it is SEE. Hence, the construction of confidence intervals (see Chapter 12) for the predicted value varies, depending upon whether the mean value or the value for a single observation is being predicted.

For the data given in Table 17.2, the SEE is estimated as follows:

$$SEE = \sqrt{\frac{14.9644}{12-2}}$$

$$= 1.22329$$

The final two steps in conducting bivariate regression, namely examination of residuals and model cross-validation, are considered later, and we now turn to the assumptions underlying the regression model.

Assumptions

The regression model makes a number of assumptions in estimating the parameters and in significance testing, as shown in Figure 17.4:

1. The error term is normally distributed. For each fixed value of X, the distribution of Y is normal.[12]
2. The means of all these normal distributions of Y, given X, lie on a straight line with slope *b*.
3. The mean of the error term is 0.
4. The variance of the error term is constant. This variance does not depend on the values assumed by X.
5. The error terms are uncorrelated. In other words, the observations have been drawn independently.

Insights into the extent to which these assumptions have been met can be gained by an examination of residuals, which is covered in the next section on multiple regression.[13]

MULTIPLE REGRESSION

multiple regression A statistical technique that simultaneously develops a mathematical relationship between two or more independent variables and an interval-scaled dependent variable.

Multiple regression involves a single dependent variable and two or more independent variables. The questions raised in the context of bivariate regression can also be answered via multiple regression by considering additional independent variables:

- Can variation in sales be explained in terms of variation in advertising expenditures, prices, and level of distribution?
- Can variation in market shares be accounted for by the size of the sales force, advertising expenditures, and sales promotion budgets?
- Are consumers' perceptions of quality determined by their perceptions of prices, brand image, and brand attributes?

Additional questions can also be answered by multiple regression:

- How much of the variation in sales can be explained by advertising expenditures, prices, and level of distribution?
- What is the contribution of advertising expenditures in explaining the variation in sales when the levels of prices and distribution are controlled?
- What levels of sales may be expected given the levels of advertising expenditures, prices, and level of distribution?

EXAMPLE
Global Brands, Local Ads

Europeans welcome brands from other countries, but when it comes to advertising, they prefer the home-grown variety. A survey done by Yankelovich and Partners and its affiliates finds that most European consumers' favorite commercials are for local brands even though they are more than likely to buy foreign brands. Respondents in France, Germany, and the United Kingdom named Coca-Cola as the most often purchased soft drink. The French, however, selected the famous award winning spot for France's Perrier bottled water as their favorite commercial. Similarly, in Germany, the favorite advertising was for a German brand of nonalcoholic beer, Clausthaler. In the United Kingdom, though, Coca-Cola was the favorite soft drink and also the favorite advertising. In the light of such findings, the important question is, Does advertising help? Does it help increase the purchase probability of the brand or does it merely maintain the brand recognition rate high? One way of finding out is by running a regression where the dependent variable is the likelihood of brand purchase and the independent variables are brand attribute evaluations and advertising evaluations. Separate models with and without advertising can be run to assess any significant difference in the contribution. Individual t tests could also be examined to find out the significant contribution of both the brand attributes and advertising. The results will indicate the degree to which advertising plays an important part on brand purchase decisions.[14] ◆

multiple regression model An equation used to explain the results of multiple regression analysis.

The general form of the **multiple regression model** is as follows:

$$Y = \beta_0 + \beta_1 X_1 + \beta_2 X_2 + \beta_3 X_3 + \cdots + \beta_k X_k + e$$

which is estimated by the following equation:

$$\hat{Y} = a + b_1 X_1 + b_2 X_2 + b_3 X_3 + \cdots + b_k X_k$$

As before, the coefficient a represents the intercept, but the b's are now the partial regression coefficients. The least squares criterion estimates the parameters in such a way as to minimize the total error, SS_{res}. This process also maximizes the correlation between the actual values of Y and the predicted values $\hat{Y}$. All the assumptions made in bivariate regression also apply in multiple regression. We define some associated statistics and then describe the procedure for multiple regression analysis.[15]

STATISTICS ASSOCIATED WITH MULTIPLE REGRESSION

Most of the statistics and statistical terms described under bivariate regression also apply to multiple regression. In addition, the following statistics are used:

Adjusted R^2. R^2, coefficient of multiple determination, is adjusted for the number of independent variables and the sample size to account for the diminishing returns. After the first few variables, the additional independent variables do not make much contribution.

Coefficient of multiple determination.   The strength of association in multiple regression is measured by the square of the multiple correlation coefficient, R^2, which is also called the coefficient of multiple determination.

F test.   The F test is used to test the null hypothesis that the coefficient of multiple determination in the population, R^2_{pop}, is zero. This is equivalent to testing the null hypothesis H_0: $\beta_1 = \beta_2 = \beta_3 = \cdots = \beta_k = 0$. The test statistic has an F distribution with k and $(n - k - 1)$ degrees of freedom.

Partial F test.   The significance of a partial regression coefficient, β_i, of X_i may be tested using an incremental F statistic. The incremental F statistic is based on the increment in the explained sum of squares resulting from the addition of the independent variable X_i to the regression equation after all the other independent variables have been included.

Partial regression coefficient.   The partial regression coefficient, b_1, denotes the change in the predicted value, $\hat{Y}$, per unit change in X_1 when the other independent variables, X_2 to X_k, are held constant.

CONDUCTING MULTIPLE REGRESSION ANALYSIS

The steps involved in conducting multiple regression analysis are similar to those for bivariate regression analysis. The discussion focuses on partial regression coefficients, strength of association, significance testing, and examination of residuals.

Partial Regression Coefficients

To understand the meaning of a partial regression coefficient, let us consider a case in which there are two independent variables, so that

$$\hat{Y} = a + b_1 X_1 + b_2 X_2$$

First, note that the relative magnitude of the partial regression coefficient of an independent variable is, in general, different from that of its bivariate regression coefficient. In other words, the partial regression coefficient, b_1, will be different from the regression coefficient, b, obtained by regressing Y on only X_1. This happens because X_1 and X_2 are usually correlated. In bivariate regression, X_2 was not considered, and any variation in Y that was shared by X_1 and X_2 was attributed to X_1. In the case of multiple independent variables, however, this is no longer true.

The interpretation of the partial regression coefficient, b_1, is that it represents the expected change in Y when X_1 is changed by one unit but X_2 is held constant or otherwise controlled. Likewise, b_2 represents the expected change in Y for a unit change in X_2, when X_1 is held constant. Thus, calling b_1 and b_2 partial regression coefficients is appropriate. It can also be seen that the combined effects of X_1 and X_2 on Y are additive. In other words, if X_1 and X_2 are each changed by one unit, the expected change in Y would be $(b_1 + b_2)$.

Conceptually, the relationship between the bivariate regression coefficient and the partial regression coefficient can be illustrated as follows. Suppose that one was to remove the effect of X_2 from X_1. This could be done by running a regression of X_1 on X_2. In other words, one would estimate the equation $\hat{X}_1 = a + bX_2$ and calculate the residual $X_r = (X_1 - \hat{X}_1)$. The partial regression coefficient, b_1, is then equal to the bivariate regression coefficient, b, obtained from the equation $\hat{Y} = a + bX_r$. In other words, the partial regression coefficient, b_1, is equal to the regression coefficient, b, between Y and the residuals of X_1 from which the effect of X_2 has been removed. The partial coefficient, b_2, can also be interpreted along similar lines.

Extension to the case of k variables is straightforward. The partial regression coefficient, b_1, represents the expected change in Y when X_1 is changed by one unit and X_2 through X_k are held constant. It can also be interpreted as the bivariate regression coefficient, b, for the regression of Y on the residuals of X_1, when the effect of X_2 through X_k has been removed from X_1.

The beta coefficients are the partial regression coefficients obtained when all the variables (Y, X_1, X_2, ..., X_k) have been standardized to a mean of 0 and a variance of 1 before estimating the regression equation. The relationship of the standardized to the nonstandardized coefficients remains the same as before:

$$B_1 = b_1 \frac{S_{x1}}{S_y}$$

$$\mathrm{M}$$

$$B_k = b_k \frac{S_{xk}}{S_y}$$

The intercept and the partial regression coefficients are estimated by solving a system of simultaneous equations derived by differentiating and equating the partial derivatives to 0. Since these coefficients are automatically estimated by the various computer programs, we will not present the details. Yet it is worth noting that the equations cannot be solved if (1) the sample size, n, is smaller than or equal to the number of independent variables, k, or (2) one independent variable is perfectly correlated with another.

Suppose that in explaining the attitude toward the city, we now introduce a second variable, importance attached to the weather. The data for the 12 pretest respondents on attitude toward the city, duration of residence, and importance attached to the weather are given in Table 17.1. The results of multiple regression analysis are depicted in Table 17.3. The partial regression coefficient for duration (X_1) is now 0.4811, different from what it was in the bivariate case. The corresponding beta coefficient is 0.7636.

TABLE 17.3						
Multiple Regression	Multiple R	.97210				
	R^2	.94498				
	Adjusted R^2	.93276				
	Standard error	.85974				

		Analysis of Variance			
	df		Sum of Squares		Mean Square
Regression	2		114.26425		57.13213
Residual	9		6.65241		0.73916
$F = 77.29364$	Significance of F = .0000				

			Variables in the Equation			
Variable	b	SEb	Beta (B)	T	Significance of T
Importance	0.28865	0.08608	0.31382	3.353	.0085
Duration	0.48108	0.05895	0.76363	8.160	.0000
(Constant)	0.33732	0.56736		0.595	.5668

The partial regression coefficient for importance attached to weather (X_2) is 0.2887, with a beta coefficient of 0.3138. The estimated regression equation is

$$(\hat{Y}) = 0.33732 + 0.48108X_1 + 0.28865X_2$$

or

$$\text{attitude} = 0.33732 + 0.48108 \text{ (duration)} + 0.28865 \text{ (importance)}$$

This equation can be used for a variety of purposes, including predicting attitudes toward the city, given a knowledge of the respondents' duration of residence in the city and the importance they attach to weather.

Strength of Association

The strength of the relationship stipulated by the regression equation can be determined by using appropriate measures of association. The total variation is decomposed as in the bivariate case

$$SS_y = SS_{reg} + SS_{res}$$

where

$$SS_y = \sum_{i=1}^{n}(Y_i - \overline{Y})^2$$

$$SS_{reg} = \sum_{i=1}^{n}(\hat{Y}_i - \overline{Y})^2$$

$$SS_{res} = \sum_{i=1}^{n}(Y_i - \hat{Y}_i)^2$$

The strength of association is measured by the square of the multiple correlation coefficient, R^2, which is also called the coefficient of multiple determination

$$R^2 = \frac{SS_{reg}}{SS_y}$$

The multiple correlation coefficient, R, can also be viewed as the simple correlation coefficient, r, between Y and $\hat{Y}$. Several points about the characteristics of R^2 are worth noting. The coefficient of multiple determination, R^2, cannot be less than the highest bivariate, r^2, of any individual independent variable with the dependent variable. R^2 will be larger when the correlations between the independent variables are low. If the independent variables are statistically independent (uncorrelated), then R^2 will be the sum of bivariate r^2 of each independent variable with the dependent variable. R^2 cannot decrease as more independent variables are added to the regression equation. Yet diminishing returns set in, so that after the first few variables, the additional independent variables do not make much of a contribution.[16] For this reason, R^2 is adjusted for the number of independent variables and the sample size by using the following formula:

$$\text{adjusted } R^2 = R^2 - \frac{k(1-R^2)}{n-k-1}$$

For the regression results given in Table 17.3, the value of R^2 is

$$R^2 = \frac{114.2643}{114.2643 + 6.6524}$$

$$= .9450$$

This is higher than the r^2 value of .8762 obtained in the bivariate case. The r^2 in the bivariate case is the square of the simple (product moment) correlation between attitude toward the city and duration of residence. The R^2 obtained in multiple regression is also higher than the square of the simple correlation between attitude and importance attached to weather (which can be estimated as .5379). The adjusted R^2 is estimated as

$$\text{adjusted } R^2 = \frac{.9450 - 2(1.0 - .9450)}{12 - 2 - 1}$$

$$= .9328$$

Note that the value of adjusted R^2 is close to R^2 and both are higher than r^2 for the bivariate case. This suggests that the addition of the second independent variable, importance attached to weather, makes a contribution in explaining the variation in attitude toward the city.

Significance Testing

Significance testing involves testing the significance of the overall regression equation as well as specific partial regression coefficients. The null hypothesis for the overall test is that the coefficient of multiple determination in the population, R^2_{pop}, is zero

$$H_0 : R^2_{pop} = 0$$

This is equivalent to the following null hypothesis:

$$H_0: \beta_1 = \beta_2 = \beta_3 = \cdots = \beta_k = 0$$

The overall test can be conducted by using an F statistic

$$F = \frac{SS_{reg}/k}{SS_{res}/(n-k-1)}$$

$$= \frac{R^2/k}{(1-R^2)/(n-k-1)}$$

which has an F distribution with k and $n - k - 1$ degrees of freedom.[17] For the multiple regression results given in Table 17.3,

$$F = \frac{114.2643/2}{6.6524/9} = 77.2936$$

which is significant at $\alpha = .05$.

If the overall null hypothesis is rejected, one or more population partial regression coefficients have a value different from 0. To determine which specific coefficients (β_i's) are nonzero, additional tests are necessary. Testing for the significance of the β_i's can be done in a manner similar to that in the bivariate case by using t tests. The significance of the partial coefficient for importance attached to weather may be tested by the following equation:

$$t = \frac{b}{SE_b}$$

$$= \frac{0.2887}{0.08608}$$

$$= 3.353$$

which has a t distribution with $n - k - 1$ degrees of freedom. This coefficient is significant at $\alpha = .05$. The significance of the coefficient for duration of residence is tested in a similar way and found to be significant. Therefore, both the duration of residence and importance attached to weather are important in explaining attitude toward the city.

Some computer programs provide an equivalent F test, often called the partial F test, which involves a decomposition of the total regression sum of squares, SS_{reg}, into components related to each independent variable. In the standard approach, this is done by assuming that each independent variable has been added to the regression equation after all the other independent variables have been included. The increment in the explained sum of squares, resulting from the addition of an independent variable, X_i, is the component of the variation attributed to that variable and is denoted SS_{xi}.[18] The significance of the partial regression coefficient for this variable, β_i, is tested using an incremental F statistic

$$F = \frac{SS_{xi}/1}{SS_{res}/(n-k-1)}$$

which has an F distribution with 1 and $(n - k - 1)$ degrees of freedom.

While high R^2 and significant partial regression coefficients are comforting, the efficacy of the regression model should be evaluated further by an examination of the residuals.

Examination of Residuals

residual The difference between the observed value of Y_i and the value predicted by the regression equation $\hat{Y}_i$.

A **residual** is the difference between the observed value of Y_i and the value predicted by the regression equation $\hat{Y}_i$. Residuals are used in the calculation of several statistics associated with regression. In addition, scattergrams of the residuals—in which the residuals are plotted against the predicted values, $\hat{Y}_i$, time, or predictor variables—provide useful insights in examining the appropriateness of the underlying assumptions and regression model fitted.[19]

The assumption of a normally distributed error term can be examined by constructing a histogram of the residuals. A visual check reveals whether the distribution is normal. Additional evidence can be obtained by determining the percentages of residuals falling within ±1 SE or ±2 SE. These percentages can be compared with what would be expected under the normal distribution (68% and 95%, respectively). More formal assessment can be made by running the K-S one-sample test.

The assumption of constant variance of the error term can be examined by plotting the residuals against the predicted values of the dependent variable, $\hat{Y}_i$. If the pattern is not random, the variance of the error term is not constant. Figure 17.6 shows a pattern whose variance is dependent on the $\hat{Y}_i$ values.

A plot of residuals against time, or the sequence of observations, will throw some light on the assumption that the error terms are uncorrelated. A random pattern should

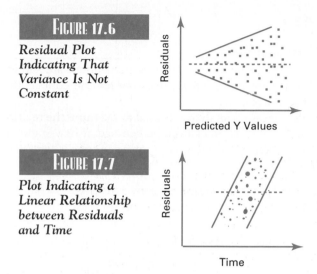

FIGURE 17.6

Residual Plot Indicating That Variance Is Not Constant

Predicted Y Values

FIGURE 17.7

Plot Indicating a Linear Relationship between Residuals and Time

Time

be seen if this assumption is true. A plot like the one in Figure 17.7 indicates a linear relationship between residuals and time. A more formal procedure for examining the correlations between the error terms is the Durbin-Watson test.[20]

Plotting the residuals against the independent variables provides evidence of the appropriateness or inappropriateness of using a linear model. Again, the plot should result in a random pattern. The residuals should fall randomly, with relatively equal distribution dispersion about 0. They should not display any tendency to be either positive or negative.

To examine whether any additional variables should be included in the regression equation, one could run a regression of the residuals on the proposed variables. If any variable explains a significant proportion of the residual variation, it should be considered for inclusion. Inclusion of variables in the regression equation should be strongly guided by the researcher's theory. Thus, an examination of the residuals provides valuable insights into the appropriateness of the underlying assumptions and the model that is fitted. Figure 17.8 shows a plot that indicates that the underlying assumptions are met and that the linear model is appropriate. If an examination of the residuals indicates that the assumptions underlying linear regression are not met, the researcher can transform the variables in an attempt to satisfy the assumptions. Transformations, such as taking logs, square roots, or reciprocals, can stabilize the variance, make the distribution normal, or make the relationship linear. We further illustrate the application of multiple regression with an example.

FIGURE 17.8

Plot of Residuals Indicating That a Fitted Model Is Appropriate

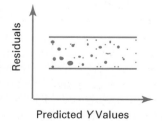

Predicted *Y* Values

EXAMPLE
At No "Ad"ditional Cost

It is widely believed that consumer magazines' prices are subsidized by the advertising carried within the magazines. A study examined the contribution of advertising to the price per copy of magazines.

Multiple regression analysis was used to examine the relationships among price per copy and editorial pages, circulation, percentage of newsstand circulation, promotional expenditures, percentage of color pages, and per copy advertising revenues. The form of the analysis was

$$PPC = b_0 + b_1(\text{ed. pages}) + b_2(\text{circ.}) + b_3(\text{\% news circ.}) + b_4(\text{PE}) + b_5(\text{\% color}) + b_6(\text{ad revs.})$$

where

PPC	=	price per copy (in dollars)
ed. pages	=	editorial pages per average issue
circ.	=	the log of average paid circulation (in thousands)
% news circ.	=	percentage newsstand circulation
PE	=	promotional expenditures (in dollars)
% color	=	percentage of pages printed in color
ad revs.	=	per copy advertising revenues (in dollars)

Table 1 shows the zero-order Pearson product moment correlations among the variables. The correlations provide directional support for the predicted relationships and show that collinearity among the independent variables is sufficiently low so as not to affect the stability of the regression analysis. The highest correlation among the independent variables was between promotional expenditures and circulation ($r = .42$).

TABLE 1

Zero-Order Correlation Matrix of Variables in Analyses

	Price per copy	Price per edit. page	Circulation	Editorial pages	Promotion expenditures	% color pages	% newsstand circ.
Price per edit. page	.60[a]						
Circulation	−.21[a]	−.42[a]					
Editorial pages	.52[a]	−.30[a]	.29[a]				
Promotion expenditures	−.22[a]	−.06	.42[a]	−.19			
% color pages	.01	−.15	.33[a]	.19	−.15		
% newsstand circ.	.46[a]	.17	.09	.31[a]	.26[a]	.02	
Ad revenues per copy	.29[a]	−.04	−.25[a]	.30[a]	−.14	.15	.08

[a]$p < .05$.

The results of the regression analysis using price per copy as the dependent variable are given in Table 2. Of the six independent variables, three were significant ($p < .05$): the number of editorial pages, average circulation, and percentage newsstand circulation. The three variables accounted for virtually all of the explained variance ($R^2 = .51$; adjusted $R^2 = .48$). The direction of the coefficients was consistent with prior expectations: the number of editorial pages was positive, circulation was negative, and percentage newsstand circulation was positive. This was expected, given the structure of the magazine publishing industry, and confirmed the hypothesized relationship.

Promotional expenditures, use of color, and per copy advertising revenues were found to have no relationship with price per copy, after the effects of circulation, percentage newsstand circulation, and editorial pages were controlled in the regression analysis.

Because the effect of per copy advertising revenue was not significant, no support was found for the contention that advertising decreases the price per editorial page or the price per copy of consumer magazines. It was concluded that advertising in magazines is provided free to consumers but does not subsidize prices.[21]

TABLE 2

Regression Analysis Using Price per Copy as Dependent Variable

	b	SE	F
Dependent variable: Price per copy			
Independent variables:			
Editorial pages	0.0084	0.0017	23.04[a]
Circulation	−0.4180	0.1372	9.29[a]
Percentage newsstand circulation	0.0067	0.0016	18.46[a]
Promotional expenditures	0.13 – 04[b]	0.0000	0.59
Percentage color pages	0.0227	0.0092	0.01
Per copy ad revenues	0.1070	0.0412	0.07
Overall R^2 = 0.51	df = 6,93		Overall F = 16.19[a] ◆

[a]$p < .05$.

[b]Decimal moved in by four zeros.

Advertising in magazines is provided free to consumers but does not subsidize prices. ◆ Teri Stratford.

In the preceeding example, promotional expenditures, percentage of color pages, and per copy advertising revenues were not found to be significantly related to the price per copy of magazines. Some of independent variables considered in a study often turn out to be nonsignificant. When there are a large number of independent variables and the researcher suspects that not all of them are significant, stepwise regression should be used.

Stepwise Regression

stepwise regression A regression procedure in which the predictor variables enter or leave the regression equation one at a time.

The purpose of **stepwise regression** is to select, from a large number of predictor variables, a small subset of variables that account for most of the variation in the dependent or criterion variable. In this procedure, the predictor variables enter or are removed from the regression equation one at a time.[22] There are several approaches to stepwise regression.

1. *Forward inclusion.* Initially, there are no predictor variables in the regression equation. Predictor variables are entered one at a time, only if they meet certain criteria specified in terms of F ratio. The order in which the variables are included is based on the contribution to the explained variance.
2. *Backward elimination.* Initially, all the predictor variables are included in the regression equation. Predictors are then removed one at a time based on the F ratio for removal.
3. *Stepwise solution.* Forward inclusion is combined with the removal of predictors that no longer meet the specified criterion at each step.

Stepwise procedures do not result in regression equations which are optimal, in the sense of producing the largest R^2, for a given number of predictors.[23] Because of the correlations between predictors, an important variable may never be included or less important variables may enter the equation. To identify an optimal regression equation, one would have to compute combinatorial solutions in which all possible combinations are examined. Nevertheless, stepwise regression can be useful when the sample size is large in relation to the number of predictors, as shown in the following example.

EXAMPLE
Stepping Out...To the Mall

A profile of browsers in regional shopping malls was constructed using three sets of independent variables: demographics, shopping behavior, and psychological and attitudinal variables. The dependent variable consisted of a browsing index. In a stepwise regression including all three sets of variables, demographics were found to be the most powerful predictors of browsing behavior. The final regression equation, which contained 20 of the possible 36 variables, included all the demographics. The table presents the regression coefficients, standard errors of the coefficients, and their significance levels.

In interpreting the coefficients, it should be recalled that the smaller the browsing index (the dependent variable), the greater the tendency to exhibit behaviors associated with browsing. The two predictors with the largest coefficients are sex and employment status. Browsers are more likely to be employed females. They also tend to be somewhat downscale, compared with other mall patrons, exhibiting lower levels of education and income, after accounting for the effects of sex and employment status. Although browsers tend to be somewhat younger than nonbrowsers, they are not necessarily single; those who reported larger family sizes tended to be associated with smaller values of the browsing index.

Regression of Browsing Index on Descriptive and Attitudinal Variables by Order of Entry into Stepwise Regression

Variable Description	Coefficient	SE	Significance
Sex (0 = male, 1 = female)	−0.485	0.164	.001
Employment status (0 = employed)	0.391	0.182	.003
Self-confidence	−0.152	0.128	.234
Education	0.079	0.072	.271
Brand intention	−0.063	0.028	.024
Watch daytime TV? (0 = yes)	0.232	0.144	.107
Tension	−0.182	0.069	.008
Income	0.089	0.061	.144
Frequency of mall visits	−0.130	0.059	.028
Fewer friends than most	0.162	0.084	.054
Good shopper	−0.122	0.090	.174
Others' opinions important	−0.147	0.065	.024
Control over life	−0.069	0.069	.317
Family size	−0.086	0.062	.165
Enthusiastic person	−0.143	0.099	.150
Age	0.036	0.069	.603
Number purchases made	−0.068	0.043	.150
Purchases per store	0.209	0.152	.167
Shop on tight budget	−0.055	0.067	.412
Excellent judge of quality	−0.070	0.089	.435
Constant	3.250		
Overall R^2 = .477			

The downscale profile of browsers relative to other mall patrons indicates that specialty stores in malls should emphasize moderately priced products. This may explain the historically low rate of failure in malls among such stores and the tendency of high-priced specialty shops to be located in only the prestigious malls or upscale nonenclosed shopping centers.[24] ◆

Browsers are more likely to be employed females and are somewhat younger and exhibit lower levels of education and income. ◆ Laimute E. Druskis.

MULTICOLLINEARITY

multicollinearity A state of high intercorrelations among independent variables.

Stepwise regression and multiple regression are complicated by the presence of multi-collinearity. Virtually all multiple regression analyses done in marketing research involve predictors or independent variables that are related. **Multicollinearity**, however, arises when intercorrelations among the predictors are very high.[25] Multicollinearity can result in several problems, including the following:

1. The partial regression coefficients may not be estimated precisely. The standard errors are likely to be high.
2. The magnitudes as well as the signs of the partial regression coefficients may change from sample to sample.
3. It becomes difficult to assess the relative importance of the independent variables in explaining the variation in the dependent variable.
4. Predictor variables may be incorrectly included or removed in stepwise regression.

What constitutes serious multicollinearity is not always clear, although several rules of thumb and procedures have been suggested in the literature. Procedures of varying complexity have also been suggested to cope with multicollinearity.[26] A simple procedure consists of using only one of the variables in a highly correlated set of variables. Alternatively, the set of independent variables can be transformed into a new set of predictors that are mutually independent by using techniques such as principal components analysis (see Chapter 19). More specialized techniques, such as ridge regression and latent root regression, can also be used.[27]

RELATIVE IMPORTANCE OF PREDICTORS

When multicollinearity is present, special care is required in assessing the relative importance of independent variables. In applied marketing research, it is valuable to determine the *relative importance of the predictors*. In other words, how important are the independent variables in accounting for the variation in the criterion or dependent variable?[28] Unfortunately, because the predictors are correlated, there is no unambiguous measure of relative importance of the predictors in regression analysis.[29] Several approaches, however, are commonly used to assess the relative importance of predictor variables.

1. *Statistical significance.* If the partial regression coefficient of a variable is not significant, as determined by an incremental F test, that variable is judged to be unimportant. An exception to this rule is made if there are strong theoretical reasons for believing that the variable is important.
2. *Square of the simple correlation coefficient.* This measure, r^2, represents the proportion of the variation in the dependent variable explained by the independent variable in a bivariate relationship.
3. *Square of the partial correlation coefficient.* This measure, $R^2_{yx_i.x_jx_k}$, is the coefficient of determination between the dependent variable and the independent variable, controlling for the effects of the other independent variables.
4. *Square of the part correlation coefficient.* This coefficient represents an increase in R^2 when a variable is entered into a regression equation that already contains the other independent variables.
5. *Measures based on standardized coefficients or beta weights.* The most commonly used measures are the absolute values of the beta weights, $|\beta_i|$, or the squared values, β_i^2. Because they

are partial coefficients, beta weights take into account the effect of the other independent variables. These measures become increasingly unreliable as the correlations among the predictor variables increase (multicollinearity increases).

6. *Stepwise regression.* The order in which the predictors enter or are removed from the regression equation is used to infer their relative importance.

Given that the predictors are correlated, at least to some extent, in virtually all regression situations, none of these measures is satisfactory. It is also possible that the different measures may indicate a different order of importance of the predictors.[30] Yet if all the measures are examined collectively, useful insights may be obtained into the relative importance of the predictors.

CROSS-VALIDATION

cross-validation A test of validity that examines whether a model holds on comparable data not used in the original estimation.

Before assessing the relative importance of the predictors or drawing any other inferences, it is necessary to cross-validate the regression model. Regression and other multivariate procedures tend to capitalize on chance variations in the data. This could result in a regression model or equation that is unduly sensitive to the specific data used to estimate the model. One approach for evaluating the model for this and other problems associated with regression is cross-validation. **Cross-validation** examines whether the regression model continues to hold on comparable data not used in the estimation. The typical cross-validation procedure used in marketing research is as follows:

1. The regression model is estimated using the entire data set.
2. The available data are split into two parts, the *estimation sample* and the *validation sample*. The estimation sample generally contains 50 to 90% of the total sample.
3. The regression model is estimated using the data from the estimation sample only. This model is compared with the model estimated on the entire sample to determine the agreement in terms of the signs and magnitudes of the partial regression coefficients.
4. The estimated model is applied to the data in the validation sample to predict the values of the dependent variable, $\hat{Y}_i$, for the observations in the validation sample.
5. The observed values, Y_i, and the predicted values, $\hat{Y}_i$, in the validation sample are correlated to determine the simple r^2. This measure, r^2, is compared with R^2 for the total sample and with R^2 for the estimation sample to assess the degree of shrinkage.

double cross-validation A special form of validation in which the sample is split into halves. One half serves as the estimation sample and the other as a validation sample. The roles of the estimation and validation halves are then reversed and the cross-validation process repeated.

A special form of validation is called double cross-validation. In **double cross-validation** the sample is split into halves. One half serves as the estimation sample, and the other is used as a validation sample in conducting cross-validation. The roles of the estimation and validation halves are then reversed, and the cross-validation is repeated.[31]

REGRESSION WITH DUMMY VARIABLES

Cross-validation is a general procedure that can be applied even in some special applications of regression, such as regression with dummy variables. Nominal or categorical variables may be used as predictors or independent variables by coding them as dummy variables. The concept of dummy variables was introduced in Chapter 14. In that chapter, we explained how a categorical variable with four categories (heavy users, medium users, light users, and nonusers) can be coded in terms of three dummy variables, $D_1, D_2,$ and D_3, as shown.

Product Usage Category	Original Variable Code	Dummy Variable Code		
		D_1	D_2	D_3
Nonusers	1	1	0	0
Light users	2	0	1	0
Medium users	3	0	0	1
Heavy users	4	0	0	0

Suppose that the researcher was interested in running a regression analysis of the effect of attitude toward the brand on product use. The dummy variables D_1, D_2, and D_3 would be used as predictors. *Regression with dummy variables* would be modeled as

$$\hat{Y}_i = a + b_1 D_1 + b_2 D_2 + b_3 D_3$$

In this case, heavy users has been selected as a reference category and has not been directly included in the regression equation. Note that for heavy users, D_1, D_2, and D_3 assume a value of 0, and the regression equation becomes

$$\hat{Y}_i = a$$

For nonusers, D_1 = 1, and D_2 = D_3 = 0, and the regression equation becomes

$$\hat{Y}_i = a + b_1$$

Thus, the coefficient b_1 is the difference in predicted Y_i for nonusers, as compared with heavy users. The coefficients b_2 and b_3 have similar interpretations. Although heavy users was selected as a reference category, any of the other three categories could have been selected for this purpose.[32]

ANALYSIS OF VARIANCE AND COVARIANCE WITH REGRESSION

Regression with dummy variables provides a framework for understanding the analysis of variance and covariance. Although multiple regression with dummy variables provides a general procedure for the analysis of variance and covariance, we show only the equivalence of regression with dummy variables to one-way analysis of variance. In regression with dummy variables, the predicted $\hat{Y}$ for each category is the mean of Y for each category. To illustrate using the dummy variable coding of product use we just considered, the predicted $\hat{Y}$ and mean values for each category are as follows:

Product Usage Category	Predicted Value $\hat{Y}$	Mean Value $\overline{Y}$
Nonusers	$a + b_1$	$a + b_1$
Light users	$a + b_2$	$a + b_2$
Medium users	$a + b_3$	$a + b_3$
Heavy users	a	a

Given this equivalence, it is easy to see further relationships between dummy variable regression and one-way ANOVA.[33]

Dummy Variable Regression	One-Way ANOVA
$SS_{res} = \sum_{i=1}^{n}(Y_i - \hat{Y}_i)^2$	$= SS_{within}$
$SS_{reg} = \sum_{i=1}^{n}(\hat{Y}_i - \overline{Y})^2$	$= SS_{between}$
R^2	$= \eta^2$
Overall F test	$= F$ test

Thus, we see that regression in which the single independent variable with c categories has been recoded into $c - 1$ dummy variables is equivalent to one-way analysis of variance. Using similar correspondences, one can also illustrate how n-way analysis of variance and analysis of covariance can be performed using regression with dummy variables.

Regression analysis, in its various forms, is a widely used technique. Research in Practice 17.1 illustrates an application in the context of international marketing research,[34] and Research in Practice 17.2 shows how regression can be used in investigating ethics in marketing research.[35]

RESEARCH IN PRACTICE 17.1

Frequent Flyers: Fly From the Clouds to the Clear

Airline companies in Asia faced uncertainty and tough competition from U.S. carriers for a long time. Asian Airlines, hit by global recession and preemptive competitive deals, awakened to the realization of banding together to increase air patronage.

(continued)

Frequent flyer programs are critical in influencing passengers' choice of airlines. ◆ Singapore Airlines.

RESEARCH IN PRACTICE 17.1 (CONTINUED)

Secondary data revealed that the important factors leading to airline selection by consumers included price, on-time schedules, destinations, deals available, kitchen and food service, and on-flight service. Asian airlines offered these services at par if not better than U.S. carriers. In fact, research showed that in-flight and kitchen services may have been even better. So, why were they feeling the competitive pressure? Qualitative research in the form of focus groups revealed that the frequent flyer program was a critical factor for a broad segment in general and the business segment in particular. A survey of international passengers was conducted, and multiple regression analyses was used to analyze the data. The likelihood of flying and other choice measures served as the dependent variable, and the set of service factors, including the frequent flyer program, were the independent variables. The results indicated that frequent flyer program, indeed, had a significant effect on the choice of an airline. Based on these findings, Cathay Pacific, Singapore International Airlines, and Malaysian Airline systems introduced a cooperative frequent flyer program called Passages available to all travelers. The program was the first time the Asian carriers offered free travel in return for regular patronage. A multimillion-dollar marketing and advertising campaign was started in 1993 to promote Passages. Frequent flyers thus flew from the clouds to the clear, and the Asian airlines experienced increased passenger traffic.

RESEARCH IN PRACTICE 17.2

Reasons for Researchers Regressing to Unethical Behavior

Marketing research has been targeted as a major source of ethical problems within the discipline of marketing. In particular, marketing researchers have been charged with engaging in deception, conflict of interest, violation of anonymity, invasion of privacy, data falsifications, dissemination of faulty research findings, and the use of research as a guise to sell merchandise. It has been speculated that when a researcher chooses to participate in unethical activities, that decision may be influenced by organizational factors. Therefore, a study using multiple regression analysis was designed to examine organizational factors as determinants of the incidence of unethical research practices. Six organizational variables were used as the independent variables: extent of ethical problems within the organization, top management actions on ethics, code of ethics, organizational rank, industry category, and organizational role. The respondent's evaluation of the incidence of unethical research practices served as the dependent variable. Regression analysis of the data suggested that four of the six organization variables influenced the extent of unethical research practice: extent of ethical problems within the organization, top management actions on ethics, organizational role, and industry category.

COMPUTER APPLICATIONS

The computer programs available for conducting correlation analysis are described in Exhibit 17.1. In SPSS, CORRELATIONS can be used for computing Pearson product moment correlations, PARTIAL CORR for partial correlations, and NONPAR CORR for Spearman's ρ and Kendall's τ. The SAS program CORR can be used for calculating Pearson, Spearman's, Kendall's, and partial correlations. In BMDP, P8D computes Pearson product moment correlations, P3S Spearman's and Kendall's correlations, and P6R computes partial correlations.

As described in Exhibit 17.2, the microcomputer and mainframe packages contain several programs for performing regression analysis, calculating the associated statistics, performing tests for significance, and plotting the residuals. In SPSS, the main program is REGRESSION. In SAS, the most general program is REG. Other specialized programs such as RSREG, ORTHOREG, GLM, and NLIN are also available, but readers not familiar with the intricate aspects of regression analysis are advised to stick to REG when using SAS. In BMDP, P1R is the main program for performing bivariate and multiple regression, and P2R for stepwise regression. P9R and P4R are more specialized in their orientation. These programs are available in mainframe and microcomputer versions.[36]

SUMMARY

The product moment correlation coefficient, r, measures the linear association between two metric (interval or ratio scaled) variables. Its square, r^2, measures the proportion of variation in one variable explained by the other. The partial correlation coefficient measures the association between two variables after controlling, or adjusting for, the

---

EXHIBIT 17.1

Computer Programs for Correlations

SPSS

The CORRELATIONS program computes Pearson product moment correlations with significance levels. Univariate statistics, covariance, and cross-product deviations may also be requested. PARTIAL CORR computes partial correlations. The effects of one or more confounding variables can be controlled while describing the relationship between two variables. NONPAR CORR can be used for computing nonmetric correlations.

SAS

CORR produces metric and nonmetric correlations between variables, including Pearson's product moment correlation. It also computes partial correlations.

BMDP

P8D can be used to compute Pearson product moment correlations among a set of variables. A matrix of correlations is printed. Procedures are available for handling incomplete data. P3S is the primary nonparametric analysis program in BMDP. P6R computes partial correlations between two variables, after adjusting for the effects of a second set of variables.

Microcomputer Packages

The microcomputer versions of SAS and BMDP are equivalent to their mainframe counterparts. For the SPSS package, the microcomputer version, SPSS/PC+, does not contain PARTIAL CORR.

EXHIBIT 17.2

Computer Programs
for Regression

The mainframe and microcomputer packages contain the same programs.

SPSS

REGRESSION calculates bivariate and multiple regression equations, associated statistics, and plots. It allows for an easy examination of residuals. Stepwise regression can also be conducted. Regression statistics can be requested with PLOT, which produces simple scattergrams and some other types of plots.

SAS

REG is a general-purpose regression procedure that fits bivariate and multiple regression models using the least squares procedure. All the associated statistics are computed, and residuals can be plotted. Stepwise methods can be implemented. RSREG, a more specialized procedure that fits a quadratic response surface model using least squares regression, is useful for determining factor levels that optimize a response. The ORTHOREG procedure is recommended for regression when the data are ill-conditioned. GLM uses the method of least squares to fit general linear models and can also be used for regression analysis. NLIN computes the parameters of a nonlinear model using least squares or weighted least squares procedures.

BMDP

P1R estimates bivariate and multiple linear regressions. The associated statistics and plots of residuals can be obtained. P2R is a stepwise regression program providing various approaches. The order of entry or removal of variables can be predetermined, partially specified, or determined only by the criteria for entry and removal of variables. P9R performs all possible subsets regression. It identifies "best" subsets of predictors or can be used for multiple regression without selecting subsets. P4R computes regression analysis on a set of principal components obtained from the independent variables.

effects of one or more additional variables. The order of a partial correlation indicates how many variables are being adjusted or controlled. Partial correlations can be very helpful for detecting spurious relationships.

Bivariate regression derives a mathematical equation between a single metric criterion variable and a single metric predictor variable. The equation is derived in the form of a straight line by using the least squares procedure. When the regression is run on standardized data, the intercept assumes a value of 0, and the regression coefficients are called beta weights. The strength of association is measured by the coefficient of determination, r^2, which is obtained by computing a ratio of SS_{reg} to SS_y. The standard error of estimate is used to assess the accuracy of prediction and may be interpreted as a kind of average error made in predicting Y from the regression equation.

Multiple regression involves a single dependent variable and two or more independent variables. The partial regression coefficient, b_1, represents the expected change in Y when X_1 is changed by one unit and X_2 through X_k are held constant. The strength of association is measured by the coefficient of multiple determination, R^2. The significance of the overall regression equation may be tested by the overall F test. Individual partial regression coefficients may be tested for significance using the incremental F test. Scattergrams of the residuals, in which the residuals are plotted against the predicted values, $\hat{Y}_i$, time, or predictor variables, are useful for examining the appropriateness of the underlying assumptions and the regression model fitted.

In stepwise regression, the predictor variables are entered or removed from the regression equation one at a time for the purpose of selecting a smaller subset of predictors that account for most of the variation in the criterion variable. Multicollinearity, or very high intercorrelations among the predictor variables, can result in several problems. Because the predictors are correlated, regression analysis provides no unambiguous measure of relative importance of the predictors. Cross-validation examines whether the regression model continues to hold true for comparable data not used in estimation. It is a useful procedure for evaluating the regression model.

Nominal or categorical variables may be used as predictors by coding them as dummy variables. Multiple regression with dummy variables provides a general procedure for the analysis of variance and covariance.[37]

ACRONYMS

The main features of regression analysis may be summarized by the acronym REGRESSION:

R   esidual analysis is useful
E   stimation of parameters: solution of simultaneous equations
G   eneral model is linear
R^2 strength of association
E   rror terms are independent and $N(0, \sigma2)$
S   tandardized regression coefficients
S   tandard error of estimate: prediction accuracy
I   ndividual coefficients and overall F tests
O   ptimal: minimizes total error
N   on standardized regression coefficients

EXERCISES

QUESTIONS

1. What is the product moment correlation coefficient? Does a product moment correlation of 0 between two variables imply that the variables are not related to each other?
2. What is a partial correlation coefficient?
3. What are the main uses of regression analysis?
4. What is the least squares procedure?
5. Explain the meaning of standardized regression coefficients.
6. How is the strength of association measured in bivariate regression? In multiple regression?
7. What is meant by prediction accuracy?
8. What is the standard error of estimate?
9. What assumptions underlie bivariate regression?
10. What is multiple regression? How is it different from bivariate regression?
11. Explain the meaning of a partial regression coefficient. Why is it called that?
12. State the null hypothesis in testing the significance of the overall multiple regression equation. How is this null hypothesis tested?
13. What is gained by an examination of residuals?
14. Explain the stepwise regression approach. What is its purpose?
15. What is multicollinearity? What problems can arise because of multicollinearity?
16. What are some of the measures used to assess the relative importance of predictors in multiple regression?

17. Describe the cross-validation procedure. Describe the double cross-validation procedure.
18. Demonstrate the equivalence of regression with dummy variables to one-way ANOVA.

PROBLEMS

1. A major supermarket chain wants to determine the effect of promotion on relative competitiveness. Data were obtained from 15 states on the promotional expenses relative to a major competitor (competitor expenses = 100) and on sales relative to this competitor (competitor sales = 100).

State Number	Relative Promotional Expense	Relative Sales
1	95	98
2	92	94
3	103	110
4	115	125
5	77	82
6	79	84
7	105	112
8	94	99
9	85	93
10	101	107
11	106	114
12	120	132
13	118	129
14	75	79
15	99	105

You are assigned the task of telling the manager whether there is any relationship between relative promotional expense and relative sales.

a. Plot the relative sales (y axis) against the relative promotional expense (x axis), and interpret this diagram.

b. Which measure would you use to determine whether there is a relationship between the two variables? Why?

c. Run a bivariate regression analysis of relative sales on relative promotional expense.

d. Interpret the regression coefficients.

e. Is the regression relationship significant?

f. If the company matched the competitor in terms of promotional expense (if the relative promotional expense was 100), what would the company's relative sales be?

g. Interpret the resulting r^2.

2. To understand the role of quality and price in influencing the patronage of drugstores, 14 major stores in a large metropolitan area were rated in terms of preference to shop, quality of merchandise, and fair pricing. All the ratings were obtained on an 11-point scale, with higher numbers indicating more positive ratings.

Store Number	Preference	Quality	Price
1	6	5	3
2	9	6	11
3	8	6	4
4	3	2	1
5	10	6	11
6	4	3	1
7	5	4	7
8	2	1	4

9	11	9	8
10	9	5	10
11	10	8	8
12	2	1	5
13	9	8	5
14	5	3	2

a. Run a multiple regression analysis explaining store preference in terms of quality of merchandise and pricing.

b. Interpret the partial regression coefficients.

c. Determine the significance of the overall regression.

d. Determine the significance of the partial regression coefficients.

e. Do you think that multicollinearity is a problem in this case? Why or why not?

3. You come across a magazine article reporting the following relationship between annual expenditure on prepared dinners (*PD*) and annual income (*INC*)

$$PD = 23.4 + 0.003INC$$

The coefficient of the *INC* variable is reported as significant.

a. Does this relationship seem plausible? Is it possible to have a coefficient that is small in magnitude and yet significant?

b. From the information given, can you tell how good the estimated model is?

c. What are the expected expenditures on prepared dinners of a family earning $30,000?

d. If a family earning $40,000 spent $130 annually on prepared dinners, what is the residual?

e. What is the meaning of a negative residual?

COMPUTER EXERCISES

1. Use an appropriate microcomputer or mainframe program (SPSS, SAS, or BMDP) to analyze the data for
   a. Problem 1
   b. Problem 2

NOTES

1. Pradeep K. Korgaonkar and Allen E. Smith, "Shopping Orientation, Demographic and Media Preference Correlates of Electronic Shopping," in Kenneth D. Bahn (ed.), *Developments in Marketing Science*, vol. 11 (Blacksburg, VA: Academy of Marketing Science, 1988), pp. 52–55.

2. Cyndee Miller, "Computer Modeling Rings the Right Bell for Avon," *Marketing News* (May 9, 1988): 14.

3. W. S. Martin, "Effects of Scaling on the Correlation Coefficient: Additional Considerations," *Journal of Marketing Research*, 15 (May 1978): 304–8; and K. A. Bollen and K. H. Barb, "Pearson's R and Coarsely Categorized Measures," *American Sociological Review* 46 (1981): 232–39.

4. John Neter, William Wasserman, and Michael J. Kutner, *Applied Linear Statistical Methods*, 2nd ed. (Homewood, IL: Richard D. Irwin, 1985), pp. 501–3.

5. Although the topic is not discussed here, partial correlations can also be helpful in locating intervening variables and making certain types of causal inferences. See Hubert M. Blalock, *Causal Inference in Nonexperimental Research* (Chapel Hill: University of North Carolina Press, 1964).

6. Ken Kasriel, "Hungary's Million-Dollar Slap," *Advertising Age* (June 8, 1992).

7. Another advantage to τ is that it can be generalized to a partial correlation coefficient. See S. Siegel, *Nonparametric Statistics for the Behavioral Sciences* (New York: McGraw-Hill, 1957), pp. 213–29.

8. In a strict sense, the regression model requires that errors of measurement be associated only with the criterion variable and that the predictor variables be measured without error.

9. See any text on regression, such as John Neter, William Wasserman, and Michael H. Kutner, *Applied Linear Regression Models* (Homewood, IL: Richard D. Irwin, 1983).

10. Technically, the numerator is $b - \beta$. Since it has been hypothesized that $\beta = 0.0$, however, it can be omitted from the formula.

11. The larger the SEE, the poorer the fit of the regression.

12. The assumption of fixed levels of predictors applies to the "classical" regression model. It is possible, if certain conditions are met, for the predictors to be random variables. Their distribution is not allowed to depend on the parameters of the regression equation, however. See John Neter, William Wasserman, and Michael H. Kutner, *Applied Linear Regression Models* (Homewood, IL: Richard D. Irwin, 1983) pp. 83–84; and Thomas H. Wonnacott and Ronald J. Wonnacott, *Regression: A Second Course in Statistics* (New York: Wiley, 1981), pp. 49–50.

13. For an approach to handling the violations of these assumptions, see S. K. Reddy, Susan L. Holak, and Subodh Bhat, "To Extend or Not to Extend: Success Determinants of Line Extensions," *Journal of Marketing Research* 31 (May 1994): 243–62.

14. Nancy Giges, "Europeans Buy Outside Goods, But Like Local Ads," *Advertising Age International* (April 27, 1992).

15. For other recent applications of multiple regression see Nirmalya Kumar, Lisa K. Scheer, and Jan-Benedict E. M. Steenkamp, "The Effects of Supplier Fairness on Vulnerable Resellers," *Journal of Marketing Research* 32 (February 1995): 54–65; and Gregory T. Gundlach and Ernest R. Cadotte, "Exchange Interdependence and Interfirm Interaction: Research in a Simulated Channel Setting," *Journal of Marketing Research* 31 (November 1994): 516–32.

16. Yet another reason for adjusting R^2 is that as a result of the optimizing properties of the least squares approach it is a maximum. Thus, to some extent, R^2 always overestimates the magnitude of a relationship. For recent applications of adjusted R^2 see David Glen Mick, "Levels of Subjective Comprehension in Advertising Processing and Their Relations to Ad Perceptions, Attitudes, and Memory," *Journal of Consumer Research* 18 (March 1992): 411–24; and Lauranne Buchanan, "Vertical Trade Relationships: The Role of Dependence and Symmetry in Attaining Organizational Goals," *Journal of Marketing Research* 29 (February 1992): 65–75.

17. If R^2_{pop} is zero, then the sample R^2 reflects only sampling error, and the F ratio will tend to be equal to unity.

18. Another approach is the hierarchical method, in which the variables are added to the regression equation in an order specified by the researcher. For a recent application of multiple regression, see Kim P. Corfman, "Perceptions of Relative Influence: Formation and Measurement," *Journal of Marketing Research* 28 (May 1991): 125–36.

19. D. Belsley, E. Kuh, and R. E. Walsh, *Regression Diagnostics* (New York: Wiley, 1980).

20. The Durbin-Watson test is discussed in virtually all regression textbooks. See, for example, N. R. Draper and H. Smith, *Applied Regression Analysis* (New York: Wiley, 1981).

21. Lawrence Soley and R. Krishnan, "Does Advertising Subsidize Consumer Magazine Prices?" *Journal of Advertising* 16 (Spring, 1987): 4–9.

22. Shelby H. McIntyre, David B. Montgomery, V. Srinivasan, and Barton A. Weitz, "Evaluating the Statistical Significance of Models Developed by Stepwise Regression," *Journal of Marketing Research* 20 (February 1983): 1–11.

23. For a recent application of stepwise regression, see Michael Laroche and Robert Sadokierski, "Role of Confidence in a Multi-Brand Model of Intentions for a High-Involvement Service," *Journal of Business Research* 29 (January 1994): 1–12.

24. Glen R. Jarboe and Carl D. McDaniel, "A Profile of Browsers in Regional Shopping Malls," *Journal of the Academy of Marketing Science* (Spring 1987): 46–53.

25. Chezy Ofir and Andre Khuri, "Multicollinearity in Marketing Models: Diagnostics and Remedial Measures," *International Journal of Research in Marketing* 3 (1986): 181–205.

26. Possible procedures are given in Charlotte H. Mason and William D. Perreault, Jr., "Collinearity, Power, and Interpretation of Multiple Regression Analysis," *Journal of Marketing Research* 28 (August 1991): 268–80; R. R. Hocking, "Developments in Linear Regression Methodology: 1959–1982," *Technometrics* 25 (August 1983): 219–30, and Ronald D. Snee, "Discussion," *Technometrics* 25 (August 1983): 230–37.

27. Albert R. Wildt, "Equity Estimation and Assessing Market Response," *Journal of Marketing Research* 31 (February 1994): 437–51; and Subhash Sharma and William L. James, "Latent Root Regression: An Alternative Procedure for Estimating Parameters in the Presence of Multicollinearity," *Journal of Marketing Research* (May 1981): 154–61.

28. Only relative importance can be determined, since the importance of an independent variable depends upon all the independent variables in the regression model.

29. Paul E. Green, J. Douglas Carroll, and Wayne S. DeSarbo, "A New Measure of Predictor Variable Importance in Multiple Regression," *Journal of Marketing Research* (August 1978): 356–60; and Barbara Bund Jackson, "Comment on 'A New Measure of Predictor Variable Importance in Multiple Regression,'" *Journal of Marketing Research* (February 1980): 116–18.

30. In the rare situation in which all the predictors are uncorrelated, simple correlations = partial correlations = part correlations = betas. Hence, the squares of these measures will yield the same rank order of the relative importance of the variables.

31. For more on cross-validation, see Bruce Cooil, Russell S. Winer, and David L. Rados, "Cross-Validation for Prediction," *Journal of Marketing Research* (August 1987): 271–79.

32. For a recent application of dummy variable regression, see Aradhna Krishna, "Effect of Dealing Patterns on Consumer Perceptions of Deal Frequency and Willingness to Pay," *Journal of Marketing Research* 28 (November 1991): 441–51. For further discussion on dummy variable coding, see Jacob Cohen and Patricia Cohen, *Applied Multiple Regression Correlation Analysis for the Behavioral Sciences*, 2nd ed. (Hillsdale, NJ: Lawrence Erlbaum Associates, 1983), pp. 181–222.

33. For an application of regression analysis to conduct analysis of covariance, see Peter A. Dancin and Daniel C. Smith, "The Effect of Brand Portfolio Characteristics on Consumer Evaluations of Brand Extensions," *Journal of Marketing Research* 31 (May 1994): 229–42.

34. Andrew Geddes, "Asian Airlines Try Loyalty Offers," *Advertising Age* (December 14, 1992).

35. I. P. Akaah and E. A. Riordan, "The Incidence of Unethical Practices in Marketing Research: An Empirical Investigation," *Journal of the Academy of Marketing Science* 18 (1990): 143–52.

36. For mainframe packages see:

    SPSS Base Systems User's Guide (Englewood Cliffs, NJ: Prentice Hall, 1994).

    SAS Language and Procedure: Usage, V 6 (Cary, NC: SAS Institute, 1989).

    SAS Language and Procedure: Usage 2, V 6 (Cary, NC: SAS Institute, 1991).

    SAS Procedures Guide, V 6, 3rd ed. (Cary, NC: SAS Institute, 1990).

    SAS Language: Reference, V 6 (Cary, NC: SAS Institute, 1990).

    BMDP Statistical Software Manual, vols. 1 and 2 (Berkeley: University of California Press, 1990).

    For microcomputer packages see:

    SPSS/PC+™ V 4.0 BASE MANUAL (Englewood Cliffs, NJ: Prentice Hall, 1990).

    SPSS/PC+ Advanced Statistics™, V 4.0 (Englewood Cliffs, NJ: Prentice Hall, 1990).

    SAS/STAT™ User Guide, V 6, 4th ed., vols. 1 and 2 (Cary, NC: SAS Institute, 1990).

    The BMDP manual for microcomputers is the same as that for the mainframe.

37. The assistance of James Agarwal with the international marketing research example, the assistance of Mark Leach and Gina Miller in writing the ethics section, and the assistance of Mark Peterson in writing the computer applications section is gratefully acknowledged.

CHAPTER EIGHTEEN

Discriminant Analysis

Discriminant analysis is used for discriminating among groups by analyzing data with a categorical dependent variable and interval scaled independent variables.

OBJECTIVES

After reading this chapter, the student should be able to:

1. Describe the concept of discriminant analysis, its objectives, and its applications in marketing research.
2. Outline the procedures for conducting discriminant analysis including the formulation of the problem, estimation of the discriminant function coefficients, determination of significance, interpretation, and validation.
3. Discuss multiple discriminant analysis and the distinction between two-group and multiple discriminant analysis.
4. Explain stepwise discriminant analysis and describe the Mahalanobis procedure.

OVERVIEW

This chapter discusses the technique of discriminant analysis. We begin by examining the relationship of this procedure to regression analysis (Chapter 17) and analysis of variance (Chapter 16). We present a model and describe the general procedure for conducting discriminant analysis, with an emphasis on formulation, estimation, determination of significance, interpretation, and validation of the results. The procedure is illustrated with an example of two-group discriminant analysis, followed by an example of multiple (three-group) discriminant analysis. The stepwise discriminant analysis procedure is also covered.

We begin with examples illustrating the applications of two-group and multiple discriminant analysis.

DEPARTMENT STORE PATRONAGE PROJECT
Two-Group Discriminant Analysis

In the store patronage project, two-group discriminant analysis was used to examine if respondents who were familiar with the stores, versus those who were unfamiliar, attached different relative importance to the eight factors of the choice criteria. The dependent variable was the two familiarity groups, and the independent variables were the importance attached to the eight factors of the choice criteria. The overall discriminant function was significant, indicating significant differences between the two groups. The results indicated that compared with the unfamiliar respondents, the familiar respondents attached greater relative importance to quality of merchandise, return and adjustment policy, service of store personnel, and credit and billing policies. ◆

EXAMPLE
Rebate Redeemers

A study of 294 consumers was undertaken to determine the correlates of rebate proneness, or the characteristics of consumers who respond favorably to rebate promotions. The predictor variables were four factors related to household shopping attitudes and behaviors and to selected demographic characteristics (sex, age, and income). The dependent variable was the respondent's degree of rebate proneness, of which three levels were identified. Respondents who reported no rebate-triggered purchases during the past 12 months were classified as nonusers, those who reported one or two such purchases as light users, and those with more than two purchases as frequent users of rebates. Multiple discriminant analysis was used to analyze the data.

Two primary findings emerged. First, consumers' perception of the effort/value relationship was the most effective variable in discriminating among frequent users, light users, and nonusers of rebate offers. Clearly, rebate-sensitive consumers associate less effort with fulfilling the requirements of the rebate purchase, and they are willing to accept a relatively smaller refund, than other customers. Second, consumers who are aware of the regular prices of products, so that they recognize bargains, are more likely than others to respond to rebate offers.[1] ◆

BusinessWeek
SUBSCRIBER REBATE
worth $2.50

Subscribe to Business Week and you'll be credited for the $2.50 cover price of one issue. You'll get 28 issues for only $22.45 instead of the regular basic rate of $24.95. That's only 80¢ per issue. You save 10% off the basic rate and 68% off the $2.50 cover price.

Mr. Ms.   Name (please print)   Title

Company   ☐ Manufacturer
                                           ☐ Non-Manufacturer

Product or Service

Please send Business Week to   Payment enclosed ☐
☐ home   ☐ business address noted below.   Bill me ☐

Street

City   State   Zip

Please allow 4-6 weeks for shipment of first issue. Offer good in U.S. and possessions. In Canada: 28 weeks C$35.95 price includes GST. Newsstand rate: 28 issues for $70.00. Prices and Terms are subject to change.   CSC9126

Rebate-sensitive consumers associate less effort with fulfilling the requirements of the rebate purchase and they are willing to accept a relatively smaller refund than other customers.

In the department store example, there were two groups of respondents (familiar and unfamiliar), whereas the rebate proneness example examined three groups (nonusers, light users, and frequent users of rebates). In both studies, significant intergroup differences were found using multiple predictor variables. An examination of differences across groups lies at the heart of the basic concept of discriminant analysis.

BASIC CONCEPT

discriminant analysis A technique for analyzing marketing research data when the criterion or dependent variable is categorical and the predictor or independent variables are interval in nature.

discriminant function The linear combination of independent variables developed by discriminant analysis that will best discriminate between the categories of the dependent variable.

Discriminant analysis is a technique for analyzing data when the criterion or dependent variable is categorical and the predictor or independent variables are interval in nature.[2] For example, the dependent variable may be the choice of a brand of personal computer (A, B, or C) and the independent variables may be ratings of attributes of PCs on a seven-point Likert scale. The objectives of discriminant analysis are as follows:

1. Development of **discriminant functions**, or linear combinations of the predictor or independent variables, that best discriminate between the categories of the criterion or dependent variable (groups).
2. Examination of whether significant differences exist among the groups, in terms of the predictor variables.
3. Determination of which predictor variables contribute to most of the intergroup differences.
4. Classification of cases to one of the groups based on the values of the predictor variables.
5. Evaluation of the accuracy of classification.

two-group discriminant analysis Discriminant analysis technique where the criterion variable has two categories.

multiple discriminant analysis Discriminant analysis technique where the criterion variable involves three or more categories.

Discriminant analysis techniques are described by the number of categories possessed by the criterion variable. When the criterion variable has two categories, the technique is known as **two-group discriminant analysis**. When three or more categories are involved, the technique is referred to as **multiple discriminant analysis**. The main distinction is that in the two-group case, it is possible to derive only one discriminant function, but in multiple discriminant analysis, more than one function may be computed.[3]

Examples of discriminant analysis abound in marketing research. This technique can be used to answer questions such as the following:[4]

- In terms of demographic characteristics, how do customers who exhibit store loyalty differ from those who do not?
- Do heavy users, medium users, and light users of soft drinks differ in terms of their consumption of frozen foods?
- What psychographic characteristics help differentiate between price-sensitive and non–price-sensitive buyers of groceries?
- Do the various market segments differ in their media consumption habits?
- In terms of lifestyles, what are the differences between heavy patrons of regional department store chains and patrons of national chains?
- What are the distinguishing characteristics of consumers who respond to direct mail solicitations?

RELATIONSHIP TO REGRESSION AND ANOVA

The relationship among discriminant analysis, analysis of variance (ANOVA), and regression analysis is shown in Table 18.1. We explain this relationship with an example in which the researcher is attempting to explain the amount of life insurance purchased in terms of age and income. All three procedures involve a single criterion or

	ANOVA	Regression	Discriminant Analysis
Similarities			
Number of dependent variable	One	One	One
Number of independent variables	Multiple	Multiple	Multiple
Differences			
Nature of the dependent variable	Metric	Metric	Categorical
Nature of the independent variables	Categorical	Metric	Metric

TABLE 18.1

Similarities and Differences Among ANOVA, Regression, and Discriminant Analysis

dependent variable and multiple predictor or independent variables. The nature of these variables differ, however. In analysis of variance and regression analysis, the dependent variable is metric or interval scaled (amount of life insurance purchased in dollars), whereas in discriminant analysis, it is categorical (amount of life insurance purchased classified as high, medium, or low). The independent variables are categorical in the case of analysis of variance (age and income are each classified as high, medium, or low) but metric in the case of regression and discriminant analysis (age in years and income in dollars, i.e., both measured on a ratio scale).

Two-group discriminant analysis, in which the dependent variable has only two categories, is closely related to multiple regression analysis. In this case, multiple regression, in which the dependent variable is coded as a 0 or 1 dummy variable, results in partial regression coefficients that are proportional to discriminant function coefficients (see the following section on the discriminant analysis model).

DISCRIMINANT ANALYSIS MODEL

discriminant analysis model The statistical model on which discriminant analysis is based.

The **discriminant analysis model** involves linear combinations of the following form:

$$D = b_0 + b_1X_1 + b_2X_2 + b_3X_3 + \cdots + b_kX_k$$

where

D = discriminant score

b = discriminant coefficients or weights

X = predictor or independent variable

The coefficients or weights (b) are estimated so that the groups differ as much as possible on the values of the discriminant function. This occurs when the ratio of between-group sum of squares to within-group sum of squares for the discriminant scores is at a maximum. Any other linear combination of the predictors will result in a smaller ratio. The technical details of estimation are described in Appendix 18A. Several statistics are associated with discriminant analysis.

STATISTICS ASSOCIATED WITH DISCRIMINANT ANALYSIS

The following are important statistics associated with discriminant analysis.

Canonical correlation. Canonical correlation measures the extent of association between the discriminant scores and the groups. It is a measure of association between the single discriminant function and the set of dummy variables that define the group membership.

Centroid. The centroid is the mean values for the discriminant scores for a particular group. There are as many centroids as there are groups, as there is one for each group. The means for a group on all the functions are the *group centroids*.

Classification matrix. Sometimes also called *confusion* or *prediction matrix*, the classification matrix contains the number of correctly classified and misclassified cases. The correctly classified cases appear on the diagonal, because the predicted and actual groups are the same. The off-diagonal elements represent cases that have been incorrectly classified. The sum of the diagonal elements divided by the total number of cases represents the *hit ratio*.

Discriminant function coefficients. The discriminant function coefficients (unstandardized) are the multipliers of variables, when the variables are in the original units of measurement.

Discriminant scores. The unstandardized coefficients are multiplied by the values of the variables. These products are summed and added to the constant term to obtain the discriminant scores.

Eigenvalue. For each discriminant function, the eigenvalue is the ratio of between-group to within-group sums of squares. Large eigenvalues imply superior functions.

F values and their significance. F values are calculated from a one-way ANOVA, with the grouping variable serving as the categorical independent variable. Each predictor, in turn, serves as the metric-dependent variable in the ANOVA.

Group means and group standard deviations. Group means and group standard deviations are computed for each predictor for each group.

Pooled within-group correlation matrix. The pooled within-group correlation matrix is computed by averaging the separate covariance matrices for all the groups.

Standardized discriminant function coefficients. The standardized discriminant function coefficients are the discriminant function coefficients and are used as the multipliers when the variables have been standardized to a mean of 0 and a variance of 1.

Structure correlations. Also referred to as *discriminant loadings*, the structure correlations represent the simple correlations between the predictors and the discriminant function.

Total correlation matrix. If the cases are treated as if they were from a single sample and the correlations are computed, a total correlation matrix is obtained.

Wilks' λ. Sometimes also called the *U statistic*, Wilks' λ for each predictor is the ratio of the within-group sum of squares to the total sum of squares. Its value varies between 0 and 1. Large values of λ (near 1) indicate that group means do not seem to be different. Small values of λ (near 0) indicate that the group means seem to be different.

The assumptions in discriminant analysis are that each of the groups is a sample from a multivariate normal population and that all the populations have the same covariance matrix. The role of these assumptions and the statistics just described can be better understood by examining the procedure for conducting discriminant analysis.

CONDUCTING DISCRIMINANT ANALYSIS

The steps involved in conducting discriminant analysis consist of formulation, estimation, determination of significance, interpretation, and validation (see Figure 18.1). These steps are discussed and illustrated within the context of two-group discriminant analysis. Discriminant analysis with more than two groups is discussed later in this chapter.

Formulation

The first step in discriminant analysis is to formulate the problem by identifying the objectives, the criterion variable, and the independent variables. The criterion variable must consist of two or more mutually exclusive and collectively exhaustive categories. When the dependent variable is interval or ratio scaled, it must first be converted into categories. For example, attitude toward the brand, measured on a six-point scale, could be categorized as unfavorable (1, 2, 3), or favorable (4, 5, 6). Alternatively, one could plot the distribution of the dependent variable and form groups of equal size by determining the appropriate cutoff points for each category. The predictor variables should be selected based on a theoretical

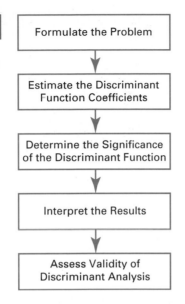

FIGURE 18.1

Conducting Discriminant Analysis

Formulate the Problem

↓

Estimate the Discriminant Function Coefficients

↓

Determine the Significance of the Discriminant Function

↓

Interpret the Results

↓

Assess Validity of Discriminant Analysis

validation sample That part of the total sample used to check the results of the estimation sample.

model or previous research, or in the case of exploratory research, the experience of the researcher should guide their selection.

The next step is to divide the sample into two parts. One part of the sample, called the estimation or *analysis sample*, is used for estimation of the discriminant function. The other part, called the *holdout* or **validation sample**, is reserved for validating the discriminant function. When the sample is large enough, it can be split in half. One half serves as the analysis sample, and the other is used for validation. The role of the halves is then interchanged and the analysis is repeated. This is called double cross-validation and is similar to the procedure discussed in regression analysis (Chapter 17).

Often, the distribution of the number of cases in the analysis and validation samples follows the distribution in the total sample. For instance, if the total sample contained 50% loyal and 50% nonloyal consumers, then the analysis and validation samples would each contain 50% loyal and 50% nonloyal consumers. On the other hand, if the sample contained 25% loyal and 75% nonloyal consumers, the analysis and validation samples would be selected to reflect the same distribution (25% vs. 75%).

Finally, it has been suggested that the validation of the discriminant function should be conducted repeatedly. Each time, the sample should be split into different analysis and validation parts. The discriminant function should be estimated and the validation analysis carried out. Thus, the validation assessment is based on a number of trials. More rigorous methods have also been suggested.[5]

To illustrate two-group discriminant analysis better, let us look at an example. Suppose that we want to determine the salient characteristics of families that have visited a vacation resort during the last two years. Data were obtained from a pretest sample of 42 households. Of these, 30 households, shown in Table 18.2, were included in the

Two-group discriminant analysis can be used to determine the salient characteristics of families that have visited a vacation resort. ◆ The Stock Market.

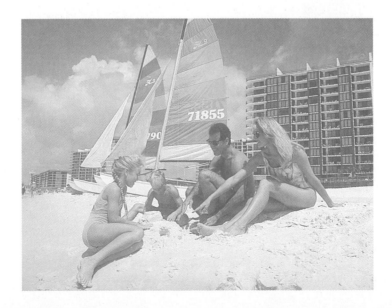

TABLE 18.2

Information on Resort Visits: Analysis Sample

Number	Resort Visit	Annual Family Income (in thousands of dollars)	Attitude toward Travel	Importance Attached to Family Vacation	Household Size	Age of Head of Household	Amount Spent on Family Vacation
1	1	50.2	5	8	3	43	M (2)
2	1	70.3	6	7	4	61	H (3)
3	1	62.9	7	5	6	52	H (3)
4	1	48.5	7	5	5	36	L (1)
5	1	52.7	6	6	4	55	H (3)
6	1	75.0	8	7	5	68	H (3)
7	1	46.2	5	3	3	62	M (2)
8	1	57.0	2	4	6	51	M (2)
9	1	64.1	7	5	4	57	H (3)
10	1	68.1	7	6	5	45	H (3)
11	1	73.4	6	7	5	44	H (3)
12	1	71.9	5	8	4	64	H (3)
13	1	56.2	1	8	6	54	M (2)
14	1	49.3	4	2	3	56	H (3)
15	1	62.0	5	6	2	58	H (3)
16	2	32.1	5	4	3	58	L (1)
17	2	36.2	4	3	2	55	L (1)
18	2	43.2	2	5	2	57	M (2)
19	2	50.4	5	2	4	37	M (2)
20	2	44.1	6	6	3	42	M (2)
21	2	38.3	6	6	2	45	L (1)
22	2	55.0	1	2	2	57	M (2)
23	2	46.1	3	5	3	51	L (1)
24	2	35.0	6	4	5	64	L (1)
25	2	37.3	2	7	4	54	L (1)
26	2	41.8	5	1	3	56	M (2)
27	2	57.0	8	3	2	36	M (2)
28	2	33.4	6	8	2	50	L (1)
29	2	37.5	3	2	3	48	L (1)
30	2	41.3	3	3	2	42	L (1)

TABLE 18.3

Information on Resort Visits: Holdout Sample

Number	Resort Visit	Annual Family Income (in thousands of dollars)	Attitude toward Travel	Importance Attached to Family Vacation	Household Size	Age of Head of Household	Amount Spent on Family Vacation
1	1	50.8	4	7	3	45	M (2)
2	1	63.6	7	4	7	55	H (3)
3	1	54.0	6	7	4	58	M (2)
4	1	45.0	5	4	3	60	M (2)
5	1	68.0	6	6	6	46	H (3)
6	1	62.1	5	6	3	56	H (3)
7	2	35.0	4	3	4	54	L (1)
8	2	49.6	5	3	5	39	L (1)
9	2	39.4	6	5	3	44	H (3)
10	2	37.0	2	6	5	51	L (1)
11	2	54.5	7	3	3	37	M (2)
12	2	38.2	2	2	3	49	L (1)

analysis sample and the remaining 12, shown in Table 18.3, were part of the validation sample. The households that visited a resort during the last two years are coded as 1; those that did not, as 2 (visit). Both the analysis and validation samples were balanced in terms of visit. As can be seen, the analysis sample contains 15 households in each category whereas the validation sample has six in each category. Data were also obtained on annual family income (income), attitude toward travel (travel, measured on a nine-point scale), importance attached to family vacation (vacation, measured on a nine-point scale), household size (hsize), and age of the head of the household (age).

Estimation

direct method An approach to discriminant analysis that involves estimating the discriminant function so that all the predictors are included simultaneously.

stepwise discriminant analysis Discriminant analysis in which the predictors are entered sequentially based on their ability to discriminate between the groups.

Once the analysis sample has been identified, as in Table 18.2, we can estimate the discriminant function coefficients. Two broad approaches are available. The **direct method** involves estimating the discriminant function so that all the predictors are included simultaneously. In this case, each independent variable is included, regardless of its discriminating power. This method is appropriate when, based on previous research or a theoretical model, the researcher wants the discrimination to be based on all the predictors. An alternative approach is the stepwise method. In **stepwise discriminant analysis**, the predictor variables are entered sequentially, based on their ability to discriminate among groups. This method, described in more detail later, is appropriate when the researcher wants to select a subset of the predictors for inclusion in the discriminant function.

The results of running two-group discriminant analysis on the data of Table 18.2 using a popular computer program are presented in Table 18.4. Some intuitive feel for the results may be obtained by examining the group means and standard deviations. It appears that the two groups are more widely separated in terms of income than other variables, and there appears to be more of a separation on the importance attached to the family vacation than on attitude toward travel. The difference between the two groups on age of the head of the household is small, and the standard deviation of this variable is large.

The pooled within-groups correlation matrix indicates low correlations between the predictors. Multicollinearity is unlikely to be a problem. The significance of the univariate F ratios indicates that when the predictors are considered individually, only income, importance of vacation, and household size significantly differentiate between those who visited a resort and those who did not.

Because there are two groups, only one discriminant function is estimated. The eigenvalue associated with this function is 1.7862, and it accounts for 100% of the explained variance. The canonical correlation associated with this function is .8007. The square of this correlation, $(.8007)^2 = .64$, indicates that 64% of the variance in the dependent variable (visit) is explained or accounted for by this model. The next step is determination of significance.

Determination of Significance

It would not be meaningful to interpret the analysis if the discriminant functions estimated were not statistically significant. The null hypothesis that, in the population, the means of all discriminant functions in all groups are equal can be statistically tested. In SPSS, this test is based on Wilks' λ. If several functions are tested simultaneously (as in the case of multiple discriminant analysis), the Wilks' λ statistic is the product of the univariate λ for each function. The significance level is estimated based

TABLE 18.4

Results of Two-Group Discriminant Analysis

Group Means

Visit	Income	Travel	Vacation	Hsize	Age
1	60.52000	5.40000	5.80000	4.33333	53.73333
2	41.91333	4.33333	4.06667	2.80000	50.13333
Total	51.21667	4.86667	4.93333	3.56667	51.93333

Group Standard Deviations

	Income	Travel	Vacation	Hsize	Age
1	9.83065	1.91982	1.82052	1.23443	8.77062
2	7.55115	1.95180	2.05171	.94112	8.27101
Total	12.79523	1.97804	2.09981	1.33089	8.57395

Pooled Within-Groups Correlation Matrix

	Income	Travel	Vacation	Hsize	Age
Income	1.00000				
Travel	.19745	1.00000			
Vacation	.09148	.08434	1.00000		
Hsize	.08887	–.01681	.07046	1.00000	
Age	–.01431	–.19709	.01742	–.04301	1.00000

Wilks' λ (U statistic) and univariate F ratio with 1 and 28 degrees of freedom

Variable	Wilks' λ	F	Significance
Income	.45310	33.80	.0000
Travel	.92479	2.277	.1425
Vacation	.82377	5.990	.0209
Hsize	.65672	14.64	.0007
Age	.95441	1.338	.2572

Canonical Discriminant Functions

Function	Eigenvalue	Percent of Variance	Cumulative Percentage	Canonical Correlation	After Function	Wilks' λ	Chi-Square	df	Significance
					: 0	.3589	26.130	5	.0001
1*	1.7862	100.00	100.00	.8007	:				

* Marks the 1 canonical discriminant function remaining in the analysis.

Standard Canonical Discriminant Function Coefficients

	Func 1
Income	.74301
Travel	.09611
Vacation	.23329
Hsize	.46911
Age	.20922

Structure Matrix:
Pooled within-groups correlations between discriminating variables and canonical discriminant functions (variables ordered by size of correlation within function)

	Func 1
Income	.82202
Hsize	.54096
Vacation	.34607
Travel	.21337
Age	.16354

(continued)

TABLE 18.4
(continued)

Unstandardized canonical discriminant function coefficients

	Func 1
Income	.8476710E-01
Travel	.4964455E-01
Vacation	.1202813
Hsize	.4273893
Age	.2454380E-01
(constant)	−7.975476

Canonical discriminant functions evaluated at group means (group centroids)

Group	Func 1
1	1.29118
2	−1.29118

Classification results for cases selected for use in analysis

			Predicted Group Membership	
Actual Group		No. of Cases	1	2
Group	1	15	12	3
			80.0%	20.0%
Group	2	15	0	15
			.0%	100.0%

Percent of grouped cases correctly classified: 90.00%

Classification results for cases not selected for use in the analysis (holdout sample)

			Predicted Group Membership	
Actual Group		No. of Cases	1	2
Group	1	6	4	2
			66.7%	33.3%
Group	2	6	0	6
			.0%	100.0%

Percent of grouped cases correctly classified: 83.33%.

on a chi-square transformation of the statistic. In testing for significance in the vacation resort example (see Table 18.4), it may be noted that the Wilks' λ associated with the function is .3589, which transforms to a chi-square of 26.13 with 5 degrees of freedom. This is significant beyond the .05 level. In SAS, an approximate F statistic, based on an approximation to the distribution of the likelihood ratio, is calculated. In BMDP, the test of the null hypothesis is based on an F transformation of Wilks' λ . If the null hypothesis is rejected, indicating significant discrimination, one can proceed to interpret the results.[6]

Interpretation

The interpretation of the discriminant weights, or coefficients, is similar to that in multiple regression analysis. The value of the coefficient for a particular predictor depends on the other predictors included in the discriminant function. The signs of the coefficients are arbitrary, but they indicate which variable values result in large and small function values and associate them with particular groups.

Given the multicollinearity in the predictor variables, there is no unambiguous measure of the relative importance of the predictors in discriminating between the groups.[7] With this caveat in mind, we can obtain some idea of the relative importance of the variables by examining the absolute magnitude of the standardized discriminant function coefficients. Generally, predictors with relatively large standardized coefficients contribute more to the discriminating power of the function, as compared with predictors with smaller coefficients.

Some idea of the relative importance of the predictors can also be obtained by examining the **structure correlations**, also called *canonical loadings* or *discriminant loadings*. These simple correlations between each predictor and the discriminant function represent the variance that the predictor shares with the function. Like the standardized coefficients, these correlations must also be interpreted with caution.

An examination of the standardized discriminant function coefficients for the vacation resort example is instructive. Given the low intercorrelations between the predictors, one might cautiously use the magnitudes of the standardized coefficients to suggest that income is the most important predictor in discriminating between the groups, followed by household size and importance attached to the family vacation. The same observation is obtained from examination of the structure correlations. These simple correlations between the predictors and the discriminant function are listed in order of magnitude.

The unstandardized discriminant function coefficients are also given. These can be applied to the raw values of the variables in the holdout set for classification purposes. The group centroids, giving the value of the discriminant function evaluated at the group means, are also shown. Group 1, those who have visited a resort, has a positive value, whereas Group 2 has an equal negative value. The signs of the coefficients associated with all the predictors are positive, which suggests that higher family income, household size, importance attached to family vacation, attitude toward travel, and age are more likely to result in the family visiting the resort. It would be reasonable to develop a profile of the two groups in terms of the three predictors that seem to be the most important: income, household size, and importance of vacation. The values of these three variables for the two groups are given at the beginning of Table 18.4.

The determination of relative importance of the predictors is further illustrated by the following example.

EXAMPLE
Satisfied Salespeople Stay

Discriminant analysis was used to determine what factors explained the differences between salespeople who left a large computer manufacturing company and those who stayed. The independent variables were company rating, job security, seven job-satisfaction dimensions, four role-conflict dimensions, four role-ambiguity dimensions, and nine measures of sales performance. The dependent variable was the dichotomy between those who stayed and those who left. The canonical correlation, an index of discrimination ($R = .4572$), was significant (Wilks' $\lambda = .7909$, $F(26,173) = 1.7588$, $p = 0.0180$). This result indicated that the variables discriminated between those who left and those who stayed.

The results from simultaneously entering all variables in discriminant analysis are presented in the table. The rank order of importance, as determined by the relative magnitude of the canonical loadings, is presented in the first column. Satisfaction with the job and promotional opportunities were the two most important discriminators, followed by job security. Those who stayed in the company found the job to be more exciting, satisfying, challenging, and interesting than those who left.[8]

Discriminant Analysis Results

Variable	Coefficients	Standardized Coefficients	Canonical Loadings
1. Work[a]	0.0903	0.3910	.5446
2. Promotion[a]	0.0288	0.1515	.5044
3. Job security	0.1567	0.1384	.4958
4. Customer relations[b]	0.0086	0.1751	.4906
5. Company rating	0.4059	0.3240	.4824
6. Working with others[b]	0.0018	0.0365	.4651
7. Overall performance[b]	−0.0148	−0.3252	.4518
8. Time-territory management[b]	0.0126	0.2899	.4496
9. Sales produced[b]	0.0059	0.1404	.4484
10. Presentation skill[b]	0.0118	0.2526	.4387
11. Technical information[b]	0.0003	0.0065	.4173
12. Pay-benefits[a]	0.0600	0.1843	.3788
13. Quota achieved[b]	0.0035	0.2915	.3780
14. Management[a]	0.0014	0.0138	.3571
15. Information collection[b]	−0.0146	−0.3327	.3326
16. Family[c]	−0.0684	−0.3408	−.3221
17. Sales manager[a]	−0.0121	−0.1102	.2909
18. Coworker[a]	0.0225	0.0893	.2671
19. Customer[c]	−0.0625	−0.2797	−.2602
20. Family[d]	0.0473	0.1970	.2180
21. Job[d]	0.1378	0.5312	.2119
22. Job[c]	0.0410	0.5475	−.1029
23. Customer[d]	−0.0060	−0.0255	.1004
24. Sales manager[c]	−0.0365	−0.2406	−.0499
25. Sales manager[d]	−0.0606	−0.3333	.0467
26. Customer[a]	−0.0338	−0.1488	.0192

Note: Rank order of importance is based on the magnitude of the canonical loadings:
[a]Satisfaction
[b]Performance
[c]Ambiguity
[d]Conflict

In this example, promotion was identified as the second most important variable based on the canonical loadings. It is not the second most important variable based on the absolute magnitude of the standardized discriminant function coefficients, however. This anomaly results from multicollinearity.

Another aid to interpreting discriminant analysis results is to develop a **characteristic profile** for each group by describing each group in terms of the group means for the predictor variables. If the important predictors have been identified, then a comparison of the group means on these variables can assist in understanding the intergroup differences. Before any findings can be interpreted with confidence, however, it is necessary to validate the results.

characteristic profile An aid to interpreting discriminant analysis results by describing each group in terms of the group means for the predictor variables.

Validation

As explained earlier, the data are randomly divided into two subsamples. One, the analysis sample, is used for estimating the discriminant function, and the validation sample is used for developing the classification matrix. The discriminant weights, estimated by using the analysis sample, are multiplied by the values of the predictor variables in the holdout sample to generate discriminant scores for the cases in the holdout sample. The cases are then

hit ratio The percentage of cases correctly classified by the discriminant analysis.

assigned to groups based on their discriminant scores and an appropriate decision rule. For example, in two-group discriminant analysis, a case will be assigned to the group whose centroid is the closest. The **hit ratio**, or the percentage of cases correctly classified, can then be determined by summing the diagonal elements and dividing by the total number of cases.[9]

It is helpful to compare the percentage of cases correctly classified by discriminant analysis to the percentage that would be obtained by chance. When the groups are equal in size, the percentage of chance classification is 1 divided by the number of groups. How much improvement should be expected over chance? No general guidelines are available, although some authors have suggested that classification accuracy achieved by discriminant analysis should be at least 25% greater than that obtained by chance.[10]

Most discriminant analysis programs also estimate a classification matrix based on the analysis sample. Because they capitalize on chance variation in the data, such results are invariably better than the classification obtained on the holdout sample.[11]

Table 18.4, of the vacation resort example, also shows the classification results based on the analysis sample. The hit ratio, or the percentage of cases correctly classified, is (12 + 15)/30 = 0.90, or 90%. One might suspect that this hit ratio is artificially inflated, as the data used for estimation were also used for validation. Conducting classification analysis on an independent holdout set of data results in the classification matrix with a slightly lower hit ratio of (4 + 6)/12 = 0.833, or 83.3% (see Table 18.4). Given two groups of equal size, by chance one would expect a hit ratio of 1/2 = 0.50, or 50%. Hence, the improvement over chance is more than 25%, and the validity of the discriminant analysis is judged as satisfactory.

Another application of two-group discriminant analysis is provided by the following example.

EXAMPLE
Home Bodies and Couch Potatoes _____

Two-group discriminant analysis was used to assess the strength of each of five dimensions used in classifying individuals as TV users or nonusers. The discriminant-analysis procedure was appropriate for this use because of the nature of the predefined categorical groups (users and nonusers) and the interval scales used to generate individual factor scores.

Two equal groups of 185 elderly consumers, users and nonusers (total n = 370), were created. The discriminant equation for the analysis was estimated by using a subsample of 142 respondents from the sample of 370. Of the remaining respondents, 198 were used as a validation subsample in a cross-validation of the equation. Thirty respondents were excluded from the analysis because of missing discriminant values.

The canonical correlation for the discriminant function was .4291, significant at the p < .0001 level. The eigenvalue was 0.2257. The table summarizes the standardized canonical discriminant coefficients. A substantial portion of the variance is explained by the discriminant function. In addition, as the table shows, the home-orientation dimension made a fairly strong contribution to classifying individuals as users or nonusers of television. Morale, security and health, and respect also contributed significantly. The social factor appeared to make little contribution.

The cross-validation procedure using the discriminant function from the analysis sample gave support to the contention that the dimensions aided researchers in discriminating between users and nonusers of television. As the table shows, the discriminant function was successful in classifying 75.76% of the cases. This suggests that consideration of the identified dimensions will help marketers understand the elderly market.[12]

Summary of Discriminant Analysis

Standard Canonical Discriminant Function Coefficients

Morale	0.27798
Security & health	0.39850
Home orientation	0.77496
Respect	0.32069
Social	−0.01996

Classification Results for Cases Selected for Use in the Analysis

Actual Group	Number of Cases	Predicted Group Membership Nonusers	Users
TV nonusers	77	56	21
		72.7%	27.3%
TV users	65	24	41
		36.9%	63.1%

Percent of grouped cases correctly classified: 68.31%

Classification Results for Cases Used for Cross Validation

Actual Group	Number of Cases	Predicted Group Membership Nonusers	Users
TV nonusers	108	85	23
		78.7%	21.3%
TV users	90	25	65
		27.8%	72.2%

Percent of grouped cases correctly classified: 75.76%   ◆

The extension from two-group discriminant analysis to multiple discriminant analysis involves similar steps and is illustrated with an application.

MULTIPLE DISCRIMINANT ANALYSIS

Formulation

The data presented in Tables 18.2 and 18.3 can also be used to illustrate three-group discriminant analysis. In the last column of these tables, the households are classified into three categories, based on the amount spent on family vacation (high, medium, or low). Ten households fall in each category. The question of interest is whether the households that spend high, medium, or low amounts on their vacations (amount) can be differentiated in terms of annual family income (income), attitude toward travel (travel), importance attached to family vacation (vacation), household size (hsize), and age of the head of household (age).[13]

Estimation

Table 18.5 presents the results of estimating three-group discriminant analysis. An examination of group means indicates that income appears to separate the groups more widely than any other variable. There is some separation on travel and vacation. Groups 1 and 2 are very close in terms of household size and age. Age has a large standard devi-

TABLE 18.5

Results of Three-Group Discriminant Analysis

Group Means

Amount	Income	Travel	Vacation	Hsize	Age
1	38.57000	4.50000	4.70000	3.10000	50.30000
2	50.11000	4.00000	4.20000	3.40000	49.50000
3	64.97000	6.10000	5.90000	4.20000	56.00000
Total	51.21667	4.86667	4.93333	3.56667	51.93333

Group Standard Deviations

1	5.29718	1.71594	1.88856	1.19722	8.09732
2	6.00231	2.35702	2.48551	1.50555	9.25263
3	8.61434	1.19722	1.66333	1.13529	7.60117
Total	12.79523	1.97804	2.09981	1.33089	8.57395

Pooled Within-Groups Correlation Matrix

	Income	Travel	Vacation	Hsize	Age
Income	1.00000				
Travel	.05120	1.00000			
Vacation	.30681	.03588	1.00000		
Hsize	.38050	.00474	.22080	1.00000	
Age	−.20939	−.34022	−.01326	−.02512	1.00000

Wilks' λ (U statistic) and univariate F ratio with 2 and 27 degrees of freedom

Variable	Wilks' λ	F	Significance
Income	.26215	38.00	.0000
Travel	.78790	3.634	.0400
Vacation	.88060	1.830	.1797
Hsize	.87411	1.944	.1626
Age	.88214	1.804	.1840

Canonical Discriminant Functions

Function	Eigenvalue	Percent of Variance	Cumulative Percentage	Canonical Correlation	After Function	Wilks' λ	Chi-Square	df	Significance
					: 0	.1664	44.831	10	.00
1*	3.8190	93.93	93.93	.8902	: 1	.8020	5.517	4	.24
2*	.2469	6.07	100.00	.4450	:				

* Marks the two canonical discriminant functions remaining in the analysis.

Standard Canonical Discriminant Function Coefficients

	Func 1	Func 2
Income	1.04740	−.42076
Travel	.33991	.76851
Vacation	−.14198	.53354
Hsize	−.16317	.12932
Age	.49474	.52447

Structure Matrix:
Pooled within-groups correlations between discriminating variables and canonical discriminant functions (variables ordered by size of correlation within function)

	Func 1	Func 2
Income	.85556*	−.27833
Hsize	.19319*	.07749
Vacation	.21935	.58829*
Travel	.14899	.45362*
Age	.16576	.34079*

(continued)

	TABLE 18.5
	(continued)

Unstandardized canonical discriminant function coefficients

	Func 1	Func 2
Income	.1542658	–.6197148E-01
Travel	.1867977	.4223430
Vacation	–.6952264E-01	.2612652
Hsize	–.1265334	.1002796
Age	.5928055E-01	.6284206E-01
(constant)	–11.09442	–3.791600

Canonical discriminant functions evaluated at group means (group centroids)

Group	Func 1	Func 1
1	–2.04100	.41847
2	–.40479	–.65867
3	2.44578	.24020

Classification results:

	Actual Group	No. of Cases	Predicted Group Membership 1	2	3
Group	1	10	9 90.0%	1 10.0%	0 .0%
Group	2	10	1 10.0%	9 90.0%	0 .0%
Group	3	10	0 .0%	2 20.0%	8 80.0%

Percent of grouped cases correctly classified: 86.67%

Classification results for cases not selected for use in the analysis

	Actual Group	No. of Cases	Predicted Group Membership 1	2	3
Group	1	4	3 75.0%	1 25.0%	0 .0%
Group	2	4	0 .0%	3 75.0%	1 25.0%
Group	3	4	1 25.0%	0 .0%	3 75.0%

Percent of grouped cases correctly classified: 75.00%

ation relative to the separation between the groups. The pooled within-groups correlation matrix indicates some correlation of vacation and household size with income. Age has some negative correlation with travel. Yet these correlations are on the lower side indicating that although multicollinearity may be of some concern, it is not likely to be a serious problem. The significance attached to the univariate F ratios indicates that when the predictors are considered individually, only income and travel are significant in differentiating between the two groups.

In multiple discriminant analysis, if there are G groups, $G - 1$ discriminant functions can be estimated if the number of predictors is larger than this quantity. In general, with G groups and k predictors, it is possible to estimate up to the smaller of $G - 1$, or k, discriminant functions. The first function has the highest ratio of between-groups to within-groups sum of squares. The second function, uncorrelated with the first, has the second highest ratio, and so on. Not all the functions may be statistically significant, however.

Because there are three groups, a maximum of two functions can be extracted. The eigenvalue associated with the first function is 3.8190, and this function accounts for

93.93% of variance in the data. The eigenvalue is large, so the first function is likely to be superior. The second function has a small eigenvalue of 0.2469 and accounts for only 6.07% of the variance.

Determination of Significance

To test the null hypothesis of equal group centroids, both the functions must be considered simultaneously. It is possible to test the means of the functions successively by first testing all means simultaneously. Then one function is excluded at a time, and the means of the remaining functions are tested at each step. In Table 18.5, the 0 below "After Function" indicates that no functions have been removed. The value of Wilks' λ is .1644. This transforms to a chi-square of 44.831, with 10 degrees of freedom, which is significant beyond the .05 level. Thus, the two functions together significantly discriminate among the three groups. When the first function is removed, however, the Wilks' λ associated with the second function is .8020, which is not significant at the .05 level. Therefore, the second function does not contribute significantly to group differences.

Interpretation

The interpretation of the results is aided by an examination of the standardized discriminant function coefficients, the structure correlations, and certain plots. The standardized coefficients indicate a large coefficient for income on function 1; whereas function 2 has relatively larger coefficients for travel, vacation, and age. A similar conclusion is reached by an examination of the structure matrix (see Table 18.5). To help interpret the functions, variables with large coefficients for a particular function are grouped together. These groupings are shown with asterisks. Thus income and household size have asterisks for function 1 because these variables have coefficients which are larger for function 1 than for function 2. These variables are associated primarily with function 1. On the other hand, travel, vacation, and age are predominantly associated with function 2, as indicated by the asterisks.

Figure 18.2 is a scattergram plot of all the groups on function 1 and function 2. It can be seen that group 3 has the highest value on function 1, group 1 the lowest. Because function 1 is primarily associated with income and household size, one would expect the three groups to be ordered on these two variables. Those with higher incomes and higher household size are likely to spend large amounts of money on vacations. Conversely, those with low incomes and smaller household size are likely to spend small amounts on vacations. This interpretation is further strengthened by an examination of group means on income and household size.

Figure 18.2 further indicates that function 2 tends to separate group 1 (highest value) and group 2 (lowest value). This function is primarily associated with travel, vacation, and age. Given the positive correlations of these variables with function 2 in the structure matrix, we expect to find group 1 to be higher than group 2 in terms of travel, vacation, and age. This is indeed true for travel and vacation, as indicated by the group means of these variables. If families in group 1 have more favorable attitudes toward travel and attach more importance to family vacation than group 2, why do they spend less? Perhaps they would like to spend more on vacations but cannot afford it because they have low incomes.

A similar interpretation is obtained by examining a **territorial map**, as shown in Figure 18.3. In a territorial map, each group centroid is indicated by an asterisk. The group boundaries are shown by numbers corresponding to the groups. Thus, group 1 centroid is bounded by 1's; group 2, centroid by 2's; and group 3, centroid by 3's.

territorial map A tool for assessing discriminant analysis results that plots the group membership of each case on a graph.

FIGURE 18.2

*All-Groups
Scattergram*

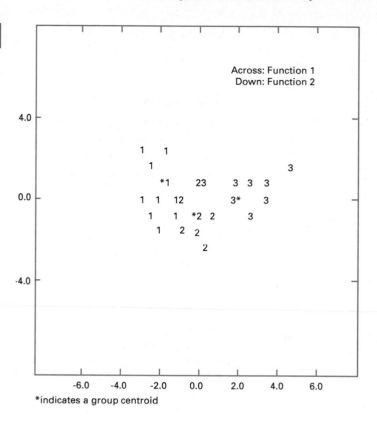

*indicates a group centroid

FIGURE 18.3

Territorial Map

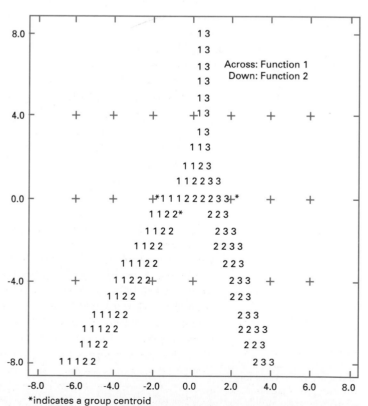

*indicates a group centroid

Validation

The classification results based on the analysis sample indicate that (9 + 9 + 8)/30 = 86.67% of the cases are correctly classified. When the classification analysis is conducted on the independent holdout sample of Table 18.3, a slightly lower hit ratio of 83.3% is obtained. Given three groups of equal size, by chance alone one would expect a hit ratio of 1/3 = 0.333 or 33.3%. The improvement over chance is more than 25%, indicating at least satisfactory validity.[14]

Further illustration of multiple group discriminant analysis is provided by the following example.

EXAMPLE
The Home Is Where the Patient's Heart Is _____

Consumers were surveyed to determine their attitudes toward four systems of health care delivery (home health care, hospitals, nursing homes, and outpatient clinics) along ten attributes. A total of 102 responses were obtained, and the results were analyzed using multiple discriminant analysis (Table 1). Three discriminant functions were identified. Chi-square tests performed on the results indicated that all three discriminant functions were significant at the .01 level. The first function accounted for 63% of the total discriminative power, and the remaining two functions contributed 29.4% and 7.6%, respectively.

Table 1 gives the standardized discriminant function coefficients of the ten variables in the discriminant equations. Coefficients ranged in value from –1 to +1. In determining the ability of each attribute to classify the delivery system, absolute values were used. In the first discriminant function, the two variables with the largest coefficients were comfort (0.53) and privacy (0.40). Because both related to personal attention and care, the first dimension was labeled "personalized care." In the second function, the two variables with the largest coefficients were quality of medical care (0.67) and likelihood of faster recovery (0.32). Hence, this dimension was labeled "quality of medical care." In the third discriminant function, the most significant attributes were sanitation (–0.70) and expense (0.52). Because these two attributes represent value and price, the third discriminant function was labeled "value."

The four group centroids are shown in Table 2. This table shows that home health care was evaluated most favorably along the dimension of personalized care, and hospitals were evaluated least favorably. Along the dimension of quality of medical care, there were a substantial separation between nursing homes and the other three systems. Also, home health care received higher evaluations on the quality of medical care than did outpatient clinics. Outpatient clinics, on the other hand, were judged to offer the best value.

Classification analysis of the 102 responses, reported in Table 3, showed correct classifications ranging from 86% for hospitals to 68% for outpatient clinics. The misclassifications for hospitals were 6% each to nursing homes and outpatient clinics, and 2% to home health care. Nursing homes showed misclassifications of 9% to hospitals, 10% to outpatient clinics, and 3% to home health care. For outpatient clinics, 9% misclassifications were made to hospitals, 13% to nursing homes, and 10% to home health care. For home health care, the misclassifications were 5% to hospitals, 4% to nursing homes, and 13% to outpatient clinics. The results demonstrated that the discriminant functions were fairly accurate in predicting group membership.[15]

TABLE 1

Standardized Discriminant Function Coefficients

Variable	Discriminant Function 1	2	3
Safe	−0.20	−0.04	0.15
Convenient	0.08	0.08	0.07
Chance of medical complications[a]	−0.27	0.10	0.16
Expensive[a]	0.30	−0.28	0.52
Comfortable	0.53	0.27	−0.19
Sanitary	−0.27	−0.14	−0.70
Best medical care	−0.25	0.67	−0.10
Privacy	0.40	0.08	0.49
Faster recovery	0.30	0.32	−0.15
Staffed with best medical personnel	−0.17	−0.03	0.18
Percentage of explained variance	63.0	29.4	7.6
Chi-square	663.3[b]	289.2[b]	70.1[b]

[a]These two items were worded negatively on the questionnaire. They were reverse coded for purposes of data analysis.

[b]$p < .01$

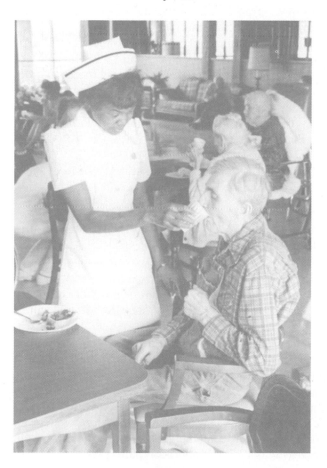

TABLE 2

Centroids of Health Care Systems in Discriminant Space

System	Discriminant Function 1	2	3
Hospital	−1.66	0.97	−0.08
Nursing home	−0.60	−1.36	−0.27
Outpatient clinic	0.54	−0.13	0.77
Home health care	1.77	0.50	−0.39

TABLE 3

Classification Table

System	Classification (%) Hospital	Nursing Home	Outpatient Clinic	Home Health Care
Hospital	86	6	6	2
Nursing home	9	78	10	3
Outpatient clinic	9	13	68	10
Home health care	5	4	13	78

Nursing homes are perceived unfavorably on the dimensions of personalized care, quality of medical care, and value. ◆ Peter Menzel/Stock, Boston.

STEPWISE DISCRIMINANT ANALYSIS

Stepwise discriminant analysis is analogous to stepwise multiple regression (see Chapter 17) in that the predictors are entered sequentially based on their ability to discriminate between the groups. An F ratio is calculated for each predictor by conducting a univariate analysis of variance in which the groups are treated as the categorical variable and the predictor as the criterion variable. The predictor with the highest F ratio is the first to be selected for inclusion in the discriminant function, if it meets certain significance and tolerance criteria. A second predictor is added based on the highest adjusted or partial F ratio, taking into account the predictor already selected.

Each predictor selected is tested for retention based on its association with other predictors selected. The process of selection and retention is continued until all predictors meeting the significance criteria for inclusion and retention have been entered in the discriminant function. Several statistics are computed at each stage. In addition, at the conclusion, a summary of the predictors entered or removed is provided. The standard output associated with the direct method is also available from the stepwise procedure.

Mahalanobis procedure
A stepwise procedure used in discriminant analysis to maximize a generalized measure of the distance between the two closest groups.

The selection of the stepwise procedure is based on the optimizing criterion adopted. The **Mahalanobis procedure** is based on maximizing a generalized measure of the distance between the two closest groups. This procedure allows marketing researchers to make maximal use of the available information.[16]

The Mahalanobis method was used to conduct a two-group stepwise discriminant analysis on the data pertaining to the visit variable in Tables 18.2 and 18.3. The first predictor variable to be selected was income, followed by household size and then vacation. The order in which the variables were selected also indicates their importance in discriminating between the groups. This was further corroborated by an examination of the standardized discriminant function coefficients and the structure correlation coefficients. Note that the findings of the stepwise analysis agree with the conclusions reported earlier by the direct method.

Research in Practice 18.1 gives an application of discriminant analysis in international marketing research,[17] whereas Research in Practice 18.2 presents an application in ethics.[18]

COMPUTER APPLICATIONS

In the mainframe version of SPSS, the DISCRIMINANT procedure is used for conducting discriminant analysis. This is a general program that can be used for two-group or multiple discriminant analysis. Furthermore, the direct or the stepwise method can be adopted. A similar program, DSCRIMINANT, is available in SPSS/PC+.

In SAS, the DISCRIM procedure can be used for performing two-group or multiple discriminant analysis. If the assumption of a multivariate normal distribution cannot be met, the NEIGHBOR procedure can be used. In this procedure, a nonparametric nearest neighbor rule is used for classifying the observations. CANDISC performs canonical discriminant analysis and is related to principal component analysis and canonical correlation. The STEPDISC procedure can be used for performing stepwise discriminant analysis. The mainframe and microcomputer versions are similar, except that the program NEIGHBOR is not available on the microcomputer version.

RESEARCH IN PRACTICE 18.1

Satisfactory Results of Satisfaction Programs in Europe

These days, more and more computer companies are emphasizing customer service programs rather than their erstwhile emphasis on computer features and capabilities. Hewlett-Packard learned this lesson while doing business in Europe. Research conducted on the European market revealed that there was a difference in emphasis on service requirements across age segments. Focus groups revealed that customers above 40 years of age had a hard time with the technical aspects of the computer and greatly required the customer service programs. On the other hand, young customers appreciated the technical aspects of the product that added to their satisfaction. To uncover the factors leading to differences in the two segments, further research in the form of a large single cross-sectional survey was done. A two-group discriminant analysis was conducted with satisfied and dissatisfied customers as the two groups and several independent variables such as technical information, ease of operation, variety and scope of customer service programs, etc. Results confirmed the fact that the variety and scope of customer satisfaction programs was indeed a strong differentiating factor. This was a crucial finding because Hewlett-Packard could better handle dissatisfied customers by focusing more on customer services than on technical details. Consequently, Hewlett-Packard successfully started three programs on customer satisfaction: customer feedback, customer satisfaction surveys, and total quality control. This effort resulted in increased customer satisfaction.

RESEARCH IN PRACTICE 18.2

Discriminant Analysis Discriminates Ethical and Unethical Firms

How do you distinguish ethical firms from unethical firms? Prior research suggested that the distinguishing variables are attitudes, leadership, the presence or absence of ethical codes of conduct, and the organization's size. Discriminant analysis was used to determine which of these variables are the best predictors of ethical behavior.

In a recent survey of 149 firms, the respondents were asked to indicate how their firms operated in 18 different ethical situations, nine of which related to marketing activities. These situations included using misleading sales presentations, accepting gifts for preferential treatment, and pricing below out-of-pocket expenses. Based on the responses to these situations, the respondent firms were classified into two groups: never practice and practice unethical marketing. A two-group analysis was conducted and the variables that influenced classification examined. It was found that attitudes and company size were the best predictors of ethical behavior. Smaller firms demonstrated more ethical marketing behavior than larger firms.

In BMDP, the P7M program can be used to perform stepwise discriminant analysis. It does not print the standardized discriminant function coefficients. The program P7M is available in both mainframe and microcomputer versions.[19]

SUMMARY

Discriminant analysis is useful for analyzing data when the criterion or dependent variable is categorical and the predictor or independent variables are interval scaled. When the criterion variable has two categories, the technique is known as two-group discriminant analysis. Multiple discriminant analysis refers to the case when three or more categories are involved.

Conducting discriminant analysis is a five-step procedure. First, formulating the discriminant problem requires identification of the objectives and the criterion and predictor variables. The sample is divided into two parts. One part, the analysis sample, is used to estimate the discriminant function. The other part, the holdout sample, is reserved for validation. Estimation, the second step, involves developing a linear combination of the predictors, called discriminant functions, so that the groups differ as much as possible on the predictor values.

Determination of statistical significance is the third step. It involves testing the null hypothesis that, in the population, the means of all discriminant functions in all groups are equal. If the null hypothesis is rejected, it is meaningful to interpret the results.

The fourth step, the interpretation of discriminant weights or coefficients, is similar to that in multiple regression analysis. Given the multicollinearity in the predictor variables, there is no unambiguous measure of the relative importance of the predictors in discriminating between the groups. Some idea of the relative importance of the variables, however, may be obtained by examining the absolute magnitude of the standardized discriminant function coefficients and by examining the structure correlations or discriminant loadings. These simple correlations between each predictor and the discriminant function represent the variance that the predictor shares with the function. Another aid to interpreting discriminant analysis results is to develop a characteristic profile for each group, based on the group means for the predictor variables.

Validation, the fifth step, involves developing the classification matrix. The discriminant weights estimated by using the analysis sample are multiplied by the values of the predictor variables in the holdout sample to generate discriminant scores for the cases in the holdout sample. The cases are then assigned to groups based on their discriminant scores and an appropriate decision rule. The percentage of cases correctly classified is determined and compared with the rate that would be expected by chance classification.

Two broad approaches are available for estimating the coefficients. The direct method involves estimating the discriminant function so that all the predictors are included simultaneously. An alternative is the stepwise method in which the predictor variables are entered sequentially, based on their ability to discriminate among groups.

In multiple discriminant analysis, if there are G groups and k predictors, it is possible to estimate up to the smaller of $G - 1$, or k, discriminant functions. The first function has the highest ratio of between-group to within-group sums of squares; the second function, uncorrelated with the first, has the second highest ratio; and so on.[20]

ACRONYMS

The steps involved and some key concepts in discriminant analysis may be summarized by the acronym DISCRIMINANT:

D ependent variable: categorical
I ndependent variable: metric
S tructure correlations or discriminant loadings
C alculation of the discriminant function
R elative importance of predictors: ambiguous
I nterpretation: scattergram and territorial map
M eans and standard deviations for groups
I nference: determination of significance
N umber of functions possible: minimum $(G - 1, k)$
A ssociation: canonical correlation
N umber 1 function has highest eigenvalue
T esting for validity: classification analysis

EXERCISES

QUESTIONS

1. What are the objectives of discriminant analysis?
2. What is the main distinction between two-group and multiple discriminant analysis?
3. Describe the relationship of discriminant analysis to regression and ANOVA.
4. What are the steps involved in conducting discriminant analysis?
5. How should the total sample be split for estimation and validation purposes?
6. What is Wilks' λ? For what purpose is it used?
7. Define discriminant scores.
8. Explain what is meant by an eigenvalue.
9. What is a classification matrix?
10. Explain the concept of structure correlations.
11. How is the statistical significance of discriminant analysis determined?
12. Describe a common procedure for determining the validity of discriminant analysis.
13. When the groups are of equal size, how is the accuracy of chance classification determined?
14. How does the stepwise discriminant procedure differ from the direct method?

PROBLEMS

1. In investigating the differences between heavy and light users or nonusers of frozen foods, it was found that the two largest standardized discriminant function coefficients were 0.97 for convenience orientation and 0.61 for income. Is it correct to conclude that convenience orientation is more important than income when each variable is considered by itself?
2. Given the following information, calculate the discriminant score for each respondent. The value of the constant is 2.04.

Unstandardized Discriminant Function Coefficients

Age	0.38
Income	0.44
Risk taking	−0.39
Optimistic	1.26

Respondent ID	Age	Income	Risk Taking	Optimistic
0246	36	43.7	21	65
1337	44	62.5	28	56
2375	57	33.5	25	40
2454	63	38.7	16	36

COMPUTER EXERCISES

1. Conduct a two-group discriminant analysis on the data given in Tables 18.2 and 18.3 using the SPSS, SAS, and BMDP packages (microcomputer or mainframe). Compare the output from all three packages. Discuss the similarities and differences.

2. Conduct a three-group stepwise discriminant analysis on the data given in Tables 18.2 and 18.3 using the SPSS, SAS, or BMDP package. Compare the results with those given in Table 18.5 for three-group discriminant analysis.

NOTES

1. Marvin A. Jolson, Joshua L. Wiener, and Richard B. Rosecky, "Correlates of Rebate Proneness," *Journal of Advertising Research* (February–March 1987): 33–43.

2. A detailed discussion of discriminant analysis may be found in P. A. Lachenbruch, *Discriminant Analysis* (New York: Hafner Press, 1975). For a recent application, see Chris T. Allen, Karen A. Machleit, and Susan Schultz Kleine, "A Comparison of Attitudes and Emotions as Predictors of Behavior at Diverse Levels of Behavioral Experience," *Journal of Consumer Research* 18 (March 1992): 493–504.

3. See W. R. Klecka, *Discriminant Analysis* (Beverly Hills: Sage, 1980). See also Steven A. Sinclair and Edward C. Stalling, "How to Identify Differences between Market Segments With Attribute Analysis," *Industrial Marketing Management* 19 (February 1990): 31–40.

4. For a recent application, see J. K. Sager and Ajay Menon, "The Role of Behavioral Intentions in Turnover of Salespeople," *Journal of Business Research* 29 (March 1994): 179–88; and Valerie Kijewski, Eunsang Yoon, and Gary Young, "How Exhibitors Select Trade Shows," *Industrial Marketing Management* 22 (November 1993): 287–98.

5. M. R. Crask and W. D. Perreault, Jr., "Validation of Discriminant Analysis in Marketing Research," *Journal of Marketing Research* 14 (February 1977): 60–68.

6. Strictly speaking, before testing for the equality of group means, the equality of group covariance matrices should be tested. Box's M test can be used for this purpose. If the equality of group covariance matrices is rejected, the results of discriminant analysis should be interpreted with caution. In this case, the power of the test for the equality of group means decreases.

7. See D. G. Morrison, "On the Interpretation of Discriminant Analysis," *Journal of Marketing Research* 6 (May 1969): 156–63. For use of other techniques in conjunction with discriminant analysis to aid interpretation, see Rajiv P. Dant, James R. Lumpkin and Robert P. Bush, "Private Physicians or Walk-In Clinics: Do the Patients Differ?," *Journal of Health Care Marketing* (June 1990): 23–35.

8. Edward F. Fern, Ramon A. Avila, and Dhruv Grewal, "Salesforce Turnover: Those Who Left and Those Who Stayed," *Industrial Marketing Management* (1989): 1–9. For another example in determining the relative importance of predictors, see Ronald B. Marks and Jeff W. Totten, "The Effects of Mortality Cues on Consumers' Ratings of Hospital Attributes," *Journal of Health Care Marketing* (September 1990): 4–12.

9. For the validation of discriminant analysis, see Robert P. Bush, David J. Ortinau, and Alan J. Bush, "Personal Value Structures and AIDS Prevention," *Journal of Health Care Marketing* 14 (Spring 1994): 12–20.

10. Joseph F. Hair, Jr., Ralph E. Anderson, Ronald L. Tatham, and William C. Black, *Multivariate Data Analysis with Readings*, 4th ed. (Englewood Cliffs, NJ: Prentice Hall, 1995), pp. 178–255.

11. See G. Albaum and K. Baker, "The Sampling Problem in Validation of Multiple Discriminant Analysis," *Journal of the Market Research Society* 18 (July 1976).

12. Don R. Rahtz, M. Joseph Sirgy, and Rustan Kosenko, "Using Demographics and Psychographic Dimensions to Discriminate between Mature Heavy and Light Television Users: An Exploratory Analysis," in Kenneth D. Bahn (ed.), *Developments in Marketing Science*, Vol. 11 (Blacksburg, VA: Academy of Marketing Science, 1988), pp. 2–7.

13. For advanced discussion of multiple discriminant analysis, see R. A. Johnson and D. W. Wichern, *Applied Multivariate Statistical Analysis* (Englewood Cliffs, NJ: Prentice Hall, 1982). For a recent application, see Rajiv P. Dant and Patrick L. Schul, "Conflict Resolution Processes in Contractual Channels of Distribution," *Journal of Marketing* 56 (January 1992): 38–54.

14. For a recent application of multiple discriminant analysis, see Stephen J. O'Connor, Richard M. Shewchuk and Lynn W. Carney, "The Great Gap," *Journal of Health Care Marketing* 14 (Summer 1994): 32–39.

15. Jeen-Su Lim and Ron Zallocco, "Determinant Attributes in Formulation of Attitudes Toward Four Health Care Systems," *Journal of Health Care Marketing* (June 1988): 25–30.

16. Joseph F. Hair, Jr., Ralph E. Anderson, Ronald L. Tatham, and William C. Black, *Multivariate Data Analysis with Readings*, 4th ed. (Englewood Cliffs, NJ: Prentice Hall, 1995), chapter 4.

17. Charlotte Klopp and John Sterlicchi, "Customer Satisfaction Just Catching on in Europe," *Marketing News* (May 28, 1990).

18. Paul R. Murphy, Jonathan E. Smith, and James M. Daley, "Executive Attitudes, Organizational Size and Ethical Issues: Perspectives on a Service Industry," *Journal of Business Ethics* 11 (1992): 11–19.

19. For mainframe packages, see:
SPSS Base Systems User's Guide (Englewood Cliffs, NJ: Prentice Hall, 1994).
SAS Language and Procedure: Usage, V 6 (Cary, NC: SAS Institute, 1989).
SAS Language and Procedure: Usage 2, V 6 (Cary, NC: SAS Institute, 1991).
SAS Procedures Guide, V 6, 3rd ed. (Cary, NC: SAS Institute, 1990).
SAS Language: Reference, V 6 (Cary, NC: SAS Institute, 1990).
BMDP Statistical Software Manual, vols. 1 and 2 (Berkeley: University of California Press, 1990).

For microcomputer packages, see:
SPSS/PC+™ V 4.0 BASE MANUAL (Englewood Cliffs, NJ: Prentice Hall, 1990).
SPSS/PC+ Advanced Statistics™ V 4.0 (Englewood Cliffs, NJ: Prentice Hall, 1990).
SAS/STAT™ User Guide, V 6, 4th ed., vols. 1 and 2 (Cary, NC: SAS Institute, 1990).
The BMDP manual for microcomputers is the same as that for the mainframe.

20. The assistance of James Agarwal with the international marketing research example, the assistance of Mark Leach and Gina Miller in writing the ethics section, and the assistance of Mark Peterson in writing the computer applications section is gratefully acknowledged.

APPENDIX 18A

ESTIMATION OF DISCRIMINANT FUNCTION COEFFICIENTS

Suppose that there are G groups, $i = 1, 2, 3, \ldots, G$, each containing n_i observations on K independent variables, $X_1 \, X_2, \ldots, X_k$. The following notations are used:

$$N = \text{Total sample size}$$

$$= \sum_{i=1}^{G} n_i$$

W_i = matrix of mean corrected sum of squares and cross products for the ith group

W = matrix of pooled within groups mean corrected sum of squares and cross products

B = matrix of between groups mean corrected sum of squares and cross products

T = matrix of total mean corrected sum of squares and cross products for all the N observations (= $W + B$)

$\overline{X}_i$ = vector of means of observations in the ith group

$\overline{X}$ = vector of grand means for all the N observations

λ = ratio of between groups to within-group sums of squares

b = vector of discriminant coefficients or weights

Then,

$$T = \sum_{i=1}^{G} \sum_{j=1}^{n_j} (X_{ij} - \overline{X})(X_{ij} - \overline{X})'$$

$$W_i = \sum_{j=1}^{n_j} (X_{ij} - \overline{X}_i)(X_{ij} - \overline{X}_i)'$$

$$W = W_1 + W_2 + W_3 + L + W_G$$

$$B' = T - W$$

Define the linear composite $D = b_i'X$. Then, with reference to D, the between-groups and within-groups sums of squares are, $b_i'Bb$ and $b_i'Wb$, respectively. To maximally discriminate the groups, the discriminant functions are estimated to maximize the between-group variability. The coefficients b are calculated to maximize λ, by solving

$$\text{Max } \lambda = \frac{b'Bb}{b'Wb}$$

Taking the partial derivative with respect to λ and setting it equal to zero, with some simplification, yields

$$(B - \lambda W)b = 0$$

To solve for b, it is more convenient to premultiply by W^{-1} and solve the following characteristic equation:

$$(W^{-1}B - \lambda I)b = 0$$

The maximum value of λ is the largest eigenvalue of the matrix $W^{-1}B$, and b is the associated eigenvector. The elements of b are the discriminant coefficients, or weights, associated with the first discriminant function. In general, it is possible to estimate up to the smaller of $G - 1$ or k discriminant functions, each with its associated eigenvalue. The discriminant functions are estimated sequentially. In other words, the first discriminant function exhausts most of the between-group variability, the second function maximizes the between-group variation that was not explained by the first one, and so on.

Factor Analysis

In factor analysis, there is no distinction between dependent and independent variables; rather, the whole set of interdependent relationships between variables is examined to identify underlying dimensions or factors.

◆

OBJECTIVES

After reading this chapter, the student should be able to:

1. Describe the concept of factor analysis and explain how it is different from analysis of variance, multiple regression, and discriminant analysis.
2. Discuss the procedure for conducting factor analysis including problem formulation, construction of the correlation matrix, selection of an appropriate method, determination of the number of factors, rotation and interpretation of factors.
3. Understand the distinction between principal component factor analysis and common factor analysis methods.
4. Explain the selection of surrogate variables and their application with emphasis on their use in subsequent analysis.
5. Describe the procedure for determining the fit of a factor analysis model using the observed and the reproduced correlations.

OVERVIEW

In analysis of variance (Chapter 16), regression (Chapter 17), and discriminant analysis (Chapter 18), one of the variables is clearly identified as the dependent variable. We now turn to a procedure, factor analysis, in which variables are not classified as independent or dependent. Instead, the whole set of interdependent relationships among variables is examined. This chapter discusses the basic concept of factor analysis and gives an exposition of the factor model. We describe the steps in factor analysis and illustrate them in the context of principal components analysis. Next, we present an application of common factor analysis. To begin, we provide some examples to illustrate the usefulness of factor analysis.

DEPARTMENT STORE PATRONAGE PROJECT
Factor Analysis

In the department store patronage project, the respondents' ratings of 21 lifestyle statements were factor analyzed to determine the underlying lifestyle factors. Seven factors emerged: bank card versus store card preference, credit proneness, credit avoidance, leisure time orientation, credit card favorableness, credit convenience, and credit card cost consciousness. These factors, along with the demographic characteristics, were used to profile the segments formed as a result of clustering. ◆

EXAMPLE
Factor Analysis Earns Interest at Banks

How do consumers evaluate banks? Respondents in a survey were asked to rate the importance of 15 bank attributes. A five-point scale ranging from not important to very important was employed. These data were analyzed via principal components analysis.

A four-factor solution resulted, with the factors being labeled as traditional services, convenience, visibility, and competence. Traditional services included interest rates on loans, reputation in the community, low rates for checking, friendly and personalized serv-

Consumers evaluate banks using the four basic factors of traditional service, convenience, visibility, and competence. ◆ Richard G. Winburn/ Manufacturers Hanover Trust.

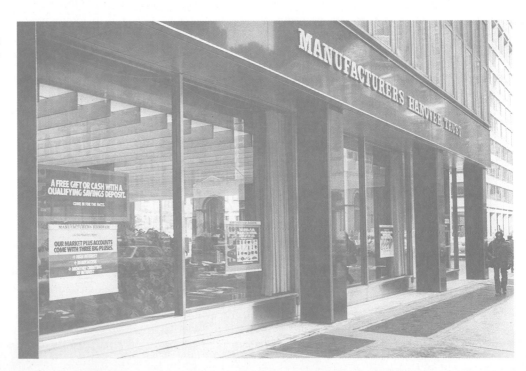

ice, easy-to-read monthly statements, and obtainability of loans. Convenience was composed of convenient branch location, convenient ATM locations, speed of service, and convenient banking hours. The visibility factor included recommendations from friends and relatives, attractiveness of the physical structure, community involvement, and obtainability of loans. Competence consisted of employee competence and availability of auxiliary banking services. It was concluded that consumers evaluated banks using the four basic factors of traditional services, convenience, visibility, and competence.[1] ◆

BASIC CONCEPT

factor analysis A class of procedures primarily used for data reduction and summarization.

Factor analysis is a general name denoting a class of procedures primarily used for data reduction and summarization. In marketing research, there may be a large number of variables, most of which are correlated and which must be reduced to a manageable level. Relationships among sets of many interrelated variables are examined and represented in terms of a few underlying factors. For example, store image may be measured by asking respondents to evaluate stores on a series of items on a semantic differential scale. These item evaluations may then be analyzed to determine the factors underlying store image.

In analysis of variance, multiple regression, and discriminant analysis, one variable is considered the dependent or criterion variable, and the others independent or predictor variables. But no such distinction is made in factor analysis. Rather, factor analysis is an **interdependence technique** in that an entire set of interdependent relationships is examined.[2]

interdependence techniques A multivariate statistical technique in which the whole set of interdependent relationships is examined.

factor An underlying dimension that explains the correlations among a set of variables.

Factor analysis is used in the following circumstances:

1. To identify underlying dimensions, or **factors**, that explain the correlations among a set of variables. For example, a set of lifestyle statements may be used to measure the psychographic profiles of consumers. These statements may then be factor analyzed to identify the underlying psychographic factors, as illustrated in the department store example.[3]
2. To identify a new, smaller, set of uncorrelated variables to replace the original set of correlated variables in subsequent multivariate analysis (regression or discriminant analysis). For example, the psychographic factors identified may be used as independent variables in explaining the differences between loyal and nonloyal consumers.
3. To identify a smaller set of salient variables from a larger set for use in subsequent multivariate analysis. For example, a few of the original lifestyle statements that correlate highly with the identified factors may be used as independent variables to explain the differences between the loyal and nonloyal users.

Factor analysis has numerous applications in marketing research. For example:

- Factor analysis can be used in market segmentation for identifying the underlying variables on which to group the customers. New car buyers might be grouped based on the relative emphasis they place on economy, convenience, performance, comfort, and luxury. This might result in five segments: economy seekers, convenience seekers, performance seekers, comfort seekers, and luxury seekers.
- In product research, factor analysis can be employed to determine the brand attributes that influence consumer choice. Toothpaste brands might be evaluated in terms of protection against cavities, whiteness of teeth, taste, fresh breath, and price.
- In advertising studies, factor analysis can be used to understand the media consumption habits of the target market. The users of frozen foods may be heavy viewers of cable TV, see a lot of movies, and listen to country music.
- In pricing studies, factor analysis can be used to identify the characteristics of price-sensitive consumers. For example, these consumers might be methodical, economy minded, and home centered.

FACTOR ANALYSIS MODEL

Mathematically, factor analysis is somewhat similar to multiple regression analysis in that each variable is expressed as a linear combination of underlying factors. The amount of variance a variable shares with all other variables included in the analysis is referred to as *communality*. The covariation among the variables is described in terms of a small number of common factors plus a unique factor for each variable. These factors are not overtly observed. If the variables are standardized, the factor model may be represented as

$$X_i = A_{i1}F_1 + A_{i2}F_2 + A_{i3}F_3 + \dots + A_{im}F_m + V_iU_i$$

where

X_i = *i*th standardized variable

A_{ij} = standardized multiple regression coefficient of variable *i* on common factor *j*

F = common factor

V_i = standardized regression coefficient of variable *i* on unique factor *i*

U_i = the unique factor for variable *i*

m = number of common factors

The unique factors are correlated with each other and with the common factors.[4] The common factors themselves can be expressed as linear combinations of the observed variables

$$F_i = W_{i1}X_1 + W_{i2}X_2 + W_{i3}X_3 + \dots + W_{ik}X_k$$

where

F_i = estimate of *i*th factor

W_i = weight or factor score coefficient

k = number of variables

It is possible to select weights or factor score coefficients so that the first factor explains the largest portion of the total variance. Then a second set of weights can be selected so that the second factor accounts for most of the residual variance, subject to being uncorrelated with the first factor. This same principle could be applied to selecting additional weights for the additional factors. Thus, the factors can be estimated so that their factor scores, unlike the values of the original variables, are not correlated. Furthermore, the first factor accounts for the highest variance in the data, the second factor the second highest, and so on. A technical treatment of the factor analysis model is presented in Appendix 19A. Several statistics are associated with factor analysis.

STATISTICS ASSOCIATED WITH FACTOR ANALYSIS

The key statistics associated with factor analysis are as follows:

> *Bartlett's test of sphericity.* Bartlett's test of sphericity is a test statistic used to examine the hypothesis that the variables are uncorrelated in the population. In other words, the population correlation matrix is an identify matrix; each variable correlates perfectly with itself ($r = 1$) but has no correlation with the other variables ($r = 0$).

Correlation matrix. A correlation matrix is a lower triangle matrix showing the simple correlations, r, between all possible pairs of variables included in the analysis. The diagonal elements, which are all 1, are usually omitted.

Communality. Communality is the amount of variance a variable shares with all the other variables being considered. This is also the proportion of variance explained by the common factors.

Eigenvalue. The eigenvalue represents the total variance explained by each factor.

Factor loadings. Factor loadings are simple correlations between the variables and the factors.

Factor loading plot. A factor loading plot is a plot of the original variables using the factor loadings as coordinates.

Factor matrix. A factor matrix contains the factor loadings of all the variables on all the factors extracted.

Factor scores. Factor scores are composite scores estimated for each respondent on the derived factors.

Kaiser-Meyer-Olkin (KMO) measure of sampling adequacy. The Kaiser-Meyer-Olkin (KMO) measure of sampling adequacy is an index used to examine the appropriateness of factor analysis. High values (between .5 and 1.0) indicate that factor analysis is appropriate. Values below .5 imply that factor analysis may not be appropriate.

Percentage of variance. The percent of the total variance attributed to each factor.

Residuals. Residuals are the differences between the observed correlations, as given in the input correlation matrix, and the reproduced correlations, as estimated from the factor matrix.

Scree plot. A scree plot is a plot of the eigenvalues against the number of factors in order of extraction.

We describe the uses of these statistics in the next section, in the context of the procedure for conducting factor analysis.

CONDUCTING FACTOR ANALYSIS

The steps involved in conducting factor analysis are illustrated in Figure 19.1. The first step is to define the factor analysis problem and identify the variables to be factor analyzed. Then a correlation matrix of these variables is constructed and a method of factor analysis is selected. The researcher decides on the number of factors to be extracted and the method of rotation. Next, the rotated factors should be interpreted. Depending on the objectives, the factor scores may be calculated, or surrogate variables selected, to represent the factors in subsequent multivariate analysis. Finally, the fit of the factor analysis model is determined. We discuss these steps in more detail in the following sections.[5]

Problem Formulation

Problem formulation includes several tasks. First, the objectives of factor analysis should be identified. The variables to be included in the factor analysis should be specified based on past research, theory, and judgment of the researcher. It is important that the variables be appropriately measured on an interval or ratio scale. An appropriate sample size should be used. As a rough guideline, there should be at least four or five times as many observations (sample size) as there are variables.[6] In many marketing research situations, the sample size is small, and this ratio is considerably lower. In these cases, the results should be interpreted cautiously.

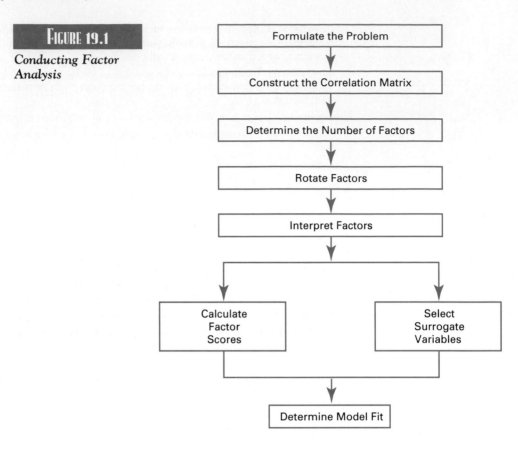

FIGURE 19.1

Conducting Factor Analysis

Formulate the Problem

Construct the Correlation Matrix

Determine the Number of Factors

Rotate Factors

Interpret Factors

Calculate Factor Scores

Select Surrogate Variables

Determine Model Fit

To illustrate factor analysis, suppose that the researcher wants to determine the underlying benefits consumers seek from the purchase of a toothpaste. A sample of 237 respondents was interviewed using mall-intercept interviewing. The respondents were asked to indicate their degree of agreement with the following statements using a seven-point scale (1 = strongly disagree, 7 = strongly agree):

V_1 It is important to buy a toothpaste that prevents cavities.
V_2 I like a toothpaste that gives shiny teeth.
V_3 A toothpaste should strengthen your gums.
V_4 I prefer a toothpaste that freshens breath.
V_5 Prevention of tooth decay should be an important benefit offered by a toothpaste.
V_6 The most important consideration in buying a toothpaste is attractive teeth.
V_7 A toothpaste should give you strong teeth.

A correlation matrix was constructed based on these ratings data. This construction process is discussed in the next section.

Construction of the Correlation Matrix

The analytical process is based on a matrix of correlations between the variables. Valuable insights can be gained from an examination of this matrix. For factor analysis to be appropriate, the variables must be correlated. In practice, this is usually the case. If the correlations between all the variables are small, factor analysis may not be appropriate. We would also expect that variables that are highly correlated with each other would also highly correlate with the same factor or factors.

Formal statistics are available for testing the appropriateness of the factor model. Bartlett's test of sphericity can be used to test the null hypothesis that the variables are uncorrelated in the population; in other words, the population correlation matrix is an identity matrix. In an identity matrix, all the diagonal terms are 1, and all off-diagonal terms are 0. The test statistic for sphericity is based on a chi-square transformation of the determinant of the correlation matrix. A large value of the test statistic will favor the rejection of the null hypothesis. If this hypothesis cannot be rejected, then the appropriateness of factor analysis should be questioned. Another useful statistic is the Kaiser-Meyer-Olkin (KMO) measure of sampling adequacy. This index compares the magnitudes of the observed correlation coefficients with the magnitudes of the partial correlation coefficients. Small values of the KMO statistic indicate that the correlations between pairs of variables cannot be explained by other variables and that factor analysis may not be appropriate.

The correlation matrix, constructed from the data obtained to understand toothpaste benefits, is shown in Table 19.1. There are relatively high correlations among V_1 (prevention of cavities), V_3 (strong gums), V_5 (prevention of tooth decay), and V_7 (strong teeth). We would expect these variable to correlate with the same set of factors. Likewise, there are relatively high correlations among V_2 (shiny teeth), V_4 (fresh breath), and V_6 (attractive teeth). These variables may also be expected to correlate with the same factors.[7]

The results of factor analysis are given in Table 19.2. The null hypothesis—that the population correlation matrix is an identity matrix—is rejected by Bartlett's test of sphericity. The value of the KMO statistic (.61724) is also large (> .5). Thus factor analysis may be considered an appropriate technique for analyzing the correlation matrix of Table 19.1

Method of Factor Analysis

Once it has been determined that factor analysis is an appropriate technique for analyzing the data, an appropriate method must be selected. The approach used to derive the weights or factor score coefficients differentiates the various methods of factor analysis. The two basic approaches are principal components analysis and common factor analysis. In **principal components analysis**, the total variance in the data is considered. The diagonal of the correlation matrix consists of unities, and full variance is brought into the factor matrix. Principal components analysis is recommended when the primary concern is to determine the minimum number of factors that will account for maximum variance in the data for use in subsequent multivariate analysis. The factors are called *principal components*.

principal components analysis An approach to factor analysis that considers the total variance in the data.

TABLE 19.1	Variables	V_1	V_2	V_3	V_4	V_5	V_6	V_7
Correlation Matrix	V_1	1.00						
	V_2	.13	1.00					
	V_3	.67	.21	1.00				
	V_4	.17	.71	.19	1.00			
	V_5	.70	.15	.49	.13	1.00		
	V_6	.13	.69	.16	.69	.21	1.00	
	V_7	.56	.22	.73	.27	.72	.31	1.00

TABLE 19.2

Results of Principal Components Analysis

Bartlett test of sphericity = 1009.2719, significance = .00000

Kaiser-Meyer-Olkin measure of sampling adequacy = .61724

Initial statistics:

Variable	Communality	*	Factor	Eigenvalue	Percent of Variance	Cumulative Percentage
V_1	1.00000	*	1	3.38111	48.3	48.3
V_2	1.00000	*	2	1.96150	28.0	76.3
V_3	1.00000	*	3	.52851	7.6	83.9
V_4	1.00000	*	4	.44928	6.4	90.3
V_5	1.00000	*	5	.30112	4.3	94.6
V_6	1.00000	*	6	.27965	4.0	98.6
V_7	1.00000	*	7	.09883	1.4	100.0

Final statistics:

Variable	Communality	*	Factor	Eigenvalue	Percent of Variance	Cumulative Percentage
V_1	.73961	*	1	3.38111	48.3	48.3
V_2	.80066	*	2	1.96150	28.0	76.3
V_3	.70680	*				
V_4	.80169	*				
V_5	.72541	*				
V_6	.78882	*				
V_7	.77962	*				

Factor matrix:

	Factor 1	Factor 2
V_1	.73011	−.45448
V_2	.58106	.68046
V_3	.75017	−.37952
V_4	.59422	.66977
V_5	.74088	−.42013
V_6	.60364	.65149
V_7	.82538	−.31362

Rotated factor matrix:

	Factor 1	Factor 2
V_1	.85906	.04039
V_2	.09201	.89005
V_3	.83302	.11348
V_4	.10890	.88872
V_5	.84842	.07478
V_6	.12705	.87902
V_7	.85752	.21043

Factor score coefficient matrix:

	Factor 1	Factor 2
V_1	.30931	−.06814
V_2	−.05548	.38315
V_3	.29250	−.03331
V_4	−.04918	.38087
V_5	.30199	−.05191
V_6	−.04160	.37478
V_7	.29173	.00697

(continued)

TABLE 19.2

(continued)

Reproduced correlation matrix:

	V_1	V_2	V_3	V_4	V_5	V_6	V_7
V_1	.73961*	.01501	−.05020	.04055	−.03186	−.01464	−.18516
V_2	.11499	.80066*	.03235	−.09103	.00538	−.10407	−.04620
V_3	.72020	.17765	.70680*	−.00157	−.22524	−.04559	−.00821
V_4	.12945	.80103	.19157	.80169*	−.02885	−.10504	−.01040
V_5	.73186	.14462	.71524	.15885	.72541*	.03648	−.02327
V_6	.14464	.79407	.20559	.79504	.17352	.78882*	.01608
V_7	.74516	.26620	.73821	.28040	.74327	.29392	.077962*

The lower left triangle contains the reproduced correlation matrix; the diagonal, the communalities; and the upper right triangle, the residuals between the observed correlations and the reproduced correlations.

common factor analysis
An approach to factor analysis that estimates the factors based only on the common variance.

In **common factor analysis**, the factors are estimated based only on the common variance. Communalities are inserted in the diagonal of the correlation matrix. This method is appropriate when the primary concern is to identify the underlying dimensions and the common variance is of interest. This method is also known as *principal axis factoring*.

Other approaches for estimating the common factors are also available. These include the methods of unweighted least squares, generalized least squares, maximum likelihood, alpha method, and image factoring. These methods are complex and are not recommended for inexperienced users.[8]

Table 19.2 shows the application of principal components analysis to the toothpaste example. Under initial statistics, it can be seen that the communality for each variable, V_1 to V_7, is 1.0 as unities were inserted in the diagonal of the correlation matrix. The eigenvalues for the factors are, as expected, in decreasing order of magnitude as we go from factor 1 to factor 7. The eigenvalue for a factor indicates the total variance attributed to that factor. The total variance accounted for by all the seven factors is 7.00, which is equal to the number of variables. Factor 1 accounts for a variance of 3.38111, which is (3.38111/7) or 48.3% of the total variance. Likewise, the second factor accounts for (1.96150/7) or 28.0% of the total variance, and the first two factors combined account for 76.3% of the total variance. Several considerations are involved in determining the number of factors that should be used in the analysis.

Number of Factors

It is possible to compute as many principal components as there are variables, but in doing so, no parsimony is gained. To summarize the information contained in the original variables, a smaller number of factors should be extracted. The question is, how many? Several procedures have been suggested for determining the number of factors. These included a priori determination and approaches based on eigenvalues, scree plot, percentage of variance accounted for, split-half reliability, and significance tests.

A Priori Determination Sometimes, because of prior knowledge, the researcher knows how many factors to expect and thus can specify the number of factors to be extracted beforehand. The extraction of factor ceases when the desired number of factors have been extracted. Most computer programs allow the user to specify the number of factors, allowing for an easy implementation of this approach.

Determination Based on Eigenvalues   In this approach, only factors with eigenvalues greater than 1.0 are retained; the other factors are not included in the model. An eigenvalue represents the amount of variance associated with the factor. Hence, only factors with a variance greater than 1.0 are included. Factors with variance less than 1.0 are no better than a single variable because, due to standardization, each variable has a variance of 1.0. If the number of variables is less than 20, this approach will result in a conservative number of factors.

Determination Based on Scree Plot   A *scree plot* is a plot of the eigenvalues against the number of factors in order of extraction. The shape of the plot is used to determine the number of factors. Typically, the plot has a distinct break between the steep slope of factors, with large eigenvalues and a gradual trailing off associated with the rest of the factors. This gradual trailing off is referred to as the *scree*. Experimental evidence indicates that the point at which the scree begins denotes the true number of factors. Generally, the number of factors determined by a scree plot will be one or a few more than that determined by the eigenvalue criterion.

Determination Based on Percentage of Variance   In this approach, the number of factors extracted is determined so that the cumulative percentage of variance extracted by the factors reaches a satisfactory level. What level of variance is satisfactory depends upon the problem. It is recommended that the factors extracted should account for at least 60% of the variance, however.

Determination Based on Split-Half Reliability   The sample is split in half, and factor analysis is performed on each half. Only factors with high correspondence of factor loadings across the two subsamples are retained.

Determination Based on Significance Tests   It is possible to determine the statistical significance of the separate eigenvalues and retain only those factors that are statistically significant. A drawback is that with large samples (size greater than 200), many factors are likely to be statistically significant, although from a practical viewpoint many of these account for only a small proportion of the total variance.

In Table 19.2, we see that the eigenvalue greater than 1.0 (default option) results in two factors being extracted. Our a priori knowledge tells us that toothpaste is bought for two major reasons. The scree plot associated with this analysis is given in Figure 19.2. From the scree plot, a distinct break occurs at three factors. Finally, from the cumulative percentage of variance accounted for, we see that the first two factors account for 76.3% of the variance and that the gain achieved in going to three factors is marginal. Furthermore, split-half reliability also indicates that two factors are appropriate. Given the large sample size, statistical tests are not very useful. Thus, two factors appear to be reasonable in this situation.

The section labeled "final statistics" in Table 19.2 gives relevant information after the desired number of factors have been extracted. It shows the communalities for the variables, along with the variance accounted for by each factor that is retained. The factor statistics are the same under the "initial statistics" and "final statistics" headings. This is always the case in principal components analysis, but the communalities for the variables are different because all the variances associated with the variables are not explained unless all the factors are retained. Interpretation of the solution is often enhanced by a rotation of the factors.

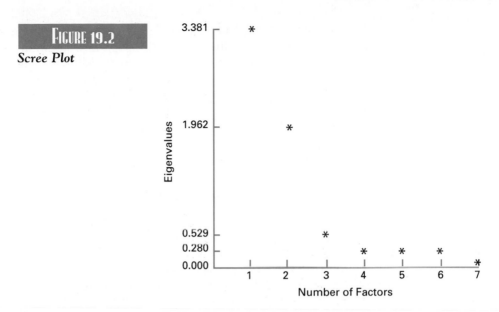

FIGURE 19.2

Scree Plot

Rotation of Factors

An important output from factor analysis is the factor matrix, also called the *factor pattern matrix*. The factor matrix contains the coefficients used to express the standardized variables in terms of the factors. These coefficients, the *factor loadings*, represent the correlations between the factors and the variables. A coefficient with a large absolute value indicates that the factor and the variable are closely related. The coefficients of the factor matrix can be used to interpret the factors.

Although the initial or unrotated factor matrix indicates the relationship between the factors and individual variables, it seldom results in factors that can be interpreted, because the factors are correlated with many variables. For example, in Table 19.2, factor 1 is highly correlated with all seven variables. How should this factor be interpreted? In such a complex matrix, it is difficult to interpret the factors. Therefore, through rotation, the factor matrix is transformed into a simpler one that is easier to interpret.

In rotating the factors, we would like each factor to have nonzero, or significant, loadings or coefficients for only some of the variables. Likewise, we would like each variable to have nonzero or significant loadings with only a few factors, and if possible, with only one. If several factors have high loadings with the same variable, it is difficult to interpret them. Rotation does not affect the communalities and the percentage of total variance explained. The percentage of variance accounted for by each factor does change, however. The variance explained by the individual factors is redistributed by rotation. Hence, different methods of rotation may result in the identification of different factors.

The rotation is called **orthogonal rotation** if the axes are maintained at right angles. The most commonly used method for rotation is the **varimax procedure**. This is an orthogonal method of rotation that minimizes the number of variables with high loadings on a factor, thereby enhancing the interpretability of the factors.[9] Orthogonal rotation results in factors that are uncorrelated. The rotation is called **oblique rotation** when the axes are not maintained at right angles, and the factors are correlated. Sometimes, allowing for correlations among factors can simplify the factor pattern matrix. Oblique rotation should be used when factors in the population are likely to be strongly correlated.

orthogonal rotation Rotation of factors in which the axes are maintained at right angles.

varimax procedure An orthogonal method of factor rotation that minimizes the number of variables with high loadings on a factor, thereby enhancing the interpretability of the factors.

oblique rotation Rotation of factors when the axes are not maintained at right angles.

In Table 19.2, by comparing the varimax rotated factor matrix with the unrotated matrix (entitled factor matrix), we can see how rotation achieves simplicity and enhances interpretability. Although all seven variables correlated highly with factor 1 in the unrotated matrix, only variables V_1, V_3, V_5, and V_7 correlate highly with factor 1 after rotation. The remaining variables—V_2, V_4, and V_6—correlate highly with factor 2. Furthermore, no variable correlates highly with both the factors. The rotated factor matrix forms the basis for interpretation of the factors.

Interpretation of Factors

Interpretation is facilitated by identifying the variables that have large loadings on the same factor. That factor can then be interpreted in terms of the variables that load high on it. Another useful aid in interpretation is to plot the variables, using the factor loadings as coordinates. Variables at the end of an axis are those that have high loadings on only that factor and hence describe the factor. Variables near the origin have small loadings on both the factors. Variables that are not near any of the axes are related to both the factors. If a factor cannot be clearly defined in terms of the original variables, it should be labeled as an undefined or a general factor.

In the rotated factor matrix of Table 19.2, factor 1 has high coefficients for variables V_1 (prevention of cavities), V_3 (strong gums), V_5 (prevention of tooth decay), and V_7 (strong teeth). Therefore, this factor may be labeled a health benefit factor. Factor 2 is highly related with variables V_2 (shiny teeth), V_4 (fresh breath), and V_6 (attractive teeth). Thus factor 2 may be labeled a social benefit factor. A plot of the factor loadings, given in Figure 19.3, confirms this interpretation. Variables V_1, V_5, and V_7 (denoted 1, 3, 5, and 7, respectively) are at the end of the horizontal axis (factor 1), whereas variables V_2, V_4, and V_6 (denoted 2, 4, and 6) are at the end of the vertical axis (factor 2). One could summarize the data by stating that consumers appear to seek two major kinds of benefits from a toothpaste: health benefits and social benefits.

Factor Scores

Following interpretation, factor scores can be calculated, if necessary. Factor analysis has its own stand-alone value. If the goal of factor analysis is to reduce the original set of

FIGURE 19.3

Factor Loading Plot

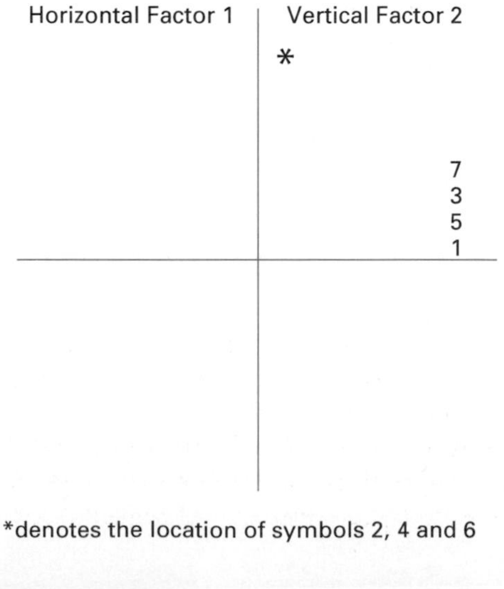

Horizontal Factor 1	Vertical Factor 2	Symbol	Variable	Coordinates	
	*	1	V_1	0.859	0.040
		2	V_2	0.092	0.890
		3	V_3	0.833	0.113
	7	4	V_4	0.109	0.889
	3	5	V_5	0.848	0.075
	5	6	V_6	0.127	0.879
	1	7	V_7	0.858	0.210

*denotes the location of symbols 2, 4 and 6

variables to a smaller set of composite variables (factors) for use in subsequent multivariate analysis, however, it is useful to compute factor scores for each respondent. A factor is simply a linear combination of the original variables. The **factor scores** for the ith factor may be estimated as follows:

$$F_i = W_{i1}X_1 + W_{i2}X_2 + W_{i3}X_3 + \cdots + W_{ik}X_k$$

where the symbols are as defined earlier in the chapter.

The weights or factor score coefficients used to combine the standardized variables are obtained from the factor score coefficient matrix. Most computer programs allow you to request factor scores. Only in the case of principal components analysis is it possible to compute exact factor scores. Moreover, in principal component analysis, these scores are uncorrelated. In common factor analysis, estimates of these scores are obtained, and there is no guarantee that the factors will be uncorrelated with each other. Factor scores can be used instead of the original variables in subsequent multivariate analysis. For example, using the factor score coefficient matrix in Table 19.2, one could compute two factor scores for each respondent. The standardized variable values would be multiplied by the corresponding factor score coefficients to obtain the factor scores.

Selection of Surrogate Variables

Sometimes, instead of computing factor scores, the researcher wishes to select surrogate variables. Selection of substitute or *surrogate variables* involves singling out some of the original variables for use in subsequent analysis. This allows the researcher to conduct subsequent analysis and to interpret the results in terms of original variables rather than factor scores. By examining the factor matrix, one could select for each factor the variables rather than factor scores. By examining the factor matrix, one could select for each factor the variable with the highest loading on that factor. That variable could then be used as a surrogate variable for the associated factor. This process works well if one factor loading for a variable is clearly higher than all other factor loadings. The choice is not as easy, however, if two or more variables have similarly high loadings. In such a case, the choice between these variables should be based on theoretical and measurement considerations. For example, theory may suggest that a variable with a slightly lower loading is more important than one with a slightly higher loading. Likewise, if a variable has a slightly lower loading but has been measured more precisely, it should be selected as the surrogate variable. In Table 19.2, the variables V_1, V_3, V_5, and V_7 all have high loadings on factor 1, and all are fairly close in magnitude. If prior knowledge suggests that prevention of tooth decay is a very important benefit, V_5 would be selected as the surrogate for factor 1. Also, the choice of a surrogate for factor 2 is not straightforward. Variables V_2, V_4, and V_6 all have comparable high loadings on this factor. If prior knowledge suggests that shiny teeth is the most important social benefit sought from a toothpaste, the researcher would select V_2.

Model Fit

The final step in factor analysis involves the determination of model fit. A basic assumption underlying factor analysis is that the observed correlation between variables can be attributed to common factors. Hence, the correlations between the variables can be deduced or reproduced from the estimated correlations between the variables and the factors. The differences between the observed correlations (as given in the input correlation matrix) and the reproduced correlations (as estimated from the factor matrix) can be examined to determine model fit. These differences are called *residuals*. If there are many large residuals, the factor model does not provide a good fit to the data and the model should be reconsidered. In Table 19.2, we see that only four residuals are larger than .1, and six are larger than .05, indicating an acceptable model fit.

The following example further illustrates principal components factoring in the context of trade promotion.

EXAMPLE
Manufacturing Promotion Components

The objective of this study was to develop a rather comprehensive inventory of manufacturer-controlled trade promotion variables and to demonstrate that an association exists between these variables and the retailer's promotion support decision. Retailer or trade support was defined operationally as the trade buyer's attitude toward the promotion.

Factor analysis was performed on the explanatory variables with the primary goal of data reduction. The principal components method, using varimax rotation, reduced the 30 explanatory variables to eight factors having eigenvalues greater than 1.0. For the purpose of interpretation, each factor was composed of variables that loaded .40 or higher on that factor. In two instances, where variables loaded .40 or above on two factors, each variable was assigned to the factor where it had the highest loading. Only one variable, ease of handling/stocking at retail, did not load at least .40 on any factor. In all, the eight factors explained 62% of the total variance. Interpretation of the factor-loading matrix was straightforward. Table 1 lists the factors in the order in which they were extracted.

Item importance and item profitability are the most important factors influencing the retailer's promotion support decision. ◆ BIC Pen Corporation.

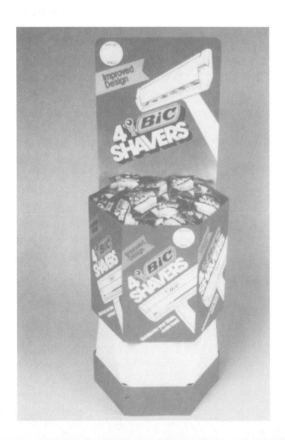

TABLE 1

Factors Influencing Trade Promotional Support

Factor	Factor Interpretation (% variance explained)	Loading	Variables Included in the Factor
F_1	Item importance (16.3%)	.77	Item is significant enough to warrant promotion
		.75	Category responds well to promotion
		.66	Closest trade competitor is likely to promote item
		.64	Importance of promoted product category
		.59	Item regular (nondeal) sales volume
		.57	Deal meshes with trade promotional requirements
			Buyer's estimate of sales increase on the basis of:
F_2	Promotion elasticity (9.3%)	.86	Price reduction and display
		.82	Display only
		.80	Price reduction only
		.70	Price reduction, display, and advertising
F_3	Manufacturer brand support (8.2%)		Manufacturer's brand support in form of:
		.85	Coupons
		.81	Radio and television advertising
		.80	Newspaper advertising
		.75	Point-of-purchase promotion (e.g., display)
F_4	Manufacturer reputation (7.3%)	.72	Manufacturer's overall reputation
		.72	Manufacturer cooperates in meeting trade's promotional needs
		.64	Manufacturer cooperates on emergency orders, backhaul, and so forth
		.55	Quality of sales presentation
		.51	Manufacturer's overall product quality
F_5	Promotion wearout (6.4%)	.93	Product category is overpromoted
		.93	Item is overpromoted
F_6	Sales velocity (5.4%)	−.81	Brand market share rank[a]
		.69	Item regular sales volume[a]
		.46	Item regular sales volume
F_7	Item profitability (4.5%)	.79	Item regular gross margin
		.72	Item regular gross margin[a]
		.49	Reasonableness of deal performance requirements
F_8	Incentive amount (4.2%)	.83	Absolute amount of deal allowances
		.81	Deal allowances as percent of regular trade cost[a]
		.49	Absolute amount of deal allowances[a]

[a]Denotes objectives (archival) measure.

Stepwise discriminant analysis was conducted to determine which, if any, of the eight factors predicted trade support to a statistically significant degree. The factor scores for the eight factors were the explanatory variables. The dependent variable consisted of the retail buyer's overall rating of the deal (rating), which was collapsed into a three-group (low, medium, and high) measure of trade support. The results of the discriminant analyses are shown in Table 2. All eight entered the discriminant functions. Goodness-of-fit measures indicated that, as a group, the eight factors discriminated between high, medium, and low levels of trade support. Multivariate F ratios, indicating the degree of discrimination between each pair of groups, were significant at $p < .001$. Correct classification into high, medium, and low categories was achieved for 65% of the cases. The order of entry into discriminant analysis was used to determine the relative importance of factors as trade support influencers, as shown in Table 3.[10]

TABLE 2

Discriminant Analysis Results: Analysis on Rating and Perform (n = 564)

		Standardized discriminant coefficients Analysis of Rating	
Factor		Function 1	Function 2
F_1	Item importance	0.861	−0.253
F_2	Promotion elasticity	0.081	0.398
F_3	Manufacturer brand support	0.127	−0.036
F_4	Manufacturer reputation	0.394	0.014
F_5	Promotion wearout	−0.207	0.380
F_6	Sales velocity	0.033	−0.665
F_7	Item profitability	0.614	0.357
F_8	Incentive amount	0.461	0.254
	Wilks' λ (for each factor)	All significant at $p < .001$	
	Multivariate F ratios	All significant at $p < .001$	
	Percentage of cases correctly classified	65% correct ($t = 14.4, p < .001$)	

TABLE 3

Relative Importance of Trade Support Influencers (as indicated by order of entry into the discriminant analysis)

	Analysis of Rating
Order of entry	Factor name
1	Item importance
2	Item profitability
3	Incentive amount
4	Manufacturer reputation
5	Promotion wearout
6	Sales velocity
7	Promotion elasticity
8	Manufacturer brand support ◆

In the next section, we describe common factor analysis and provide applications of this method.

APPLICATIONS OF COMMON FACTOR ANALYSIS

The correlation matrix shown in Table 19.1 was analyzed using the common factor analysis model. Instead of using unities in the diagonal, the communalities were inserted. The output, shown in Table 19.3, is similar to the output from principal components analysis presented in Table 19.2 The initial statistics table is the same as in Table 19.2 except that the communalities for the variables are no longer 1.0. Based on the eigenvalue criterion, again two factors are extracted. The final statistics, after extracting the factors, are different from the initial statistics. The first factor accounts for 43.6% of the variance, whereas the second accounts for 23.4%, in each case a little less than what was observed in principal components analysis.

TABLE 19.3

Results of Common Factor Analysis

Bartlett test of sphericity = 1009.2719, significance = .00000
Kaiser-Meyer-Olkin measure of sampling adequacy = .61724

Initial statistics:

Variable	Communality	*	Factor	Eigenvalue	Percent of Variance	Cumulative Percentage
V_1	.68263	*	1	3.38111	48.3	48.3
V_2	.60376	*	2	1.96150	28.0	76.3
V_3	.71310	*	3	0.52851	7.6	83.9
V_4	.60594	*	4	0.44928	6.4	90.3
V_5	.72173	*	5	0.30112	4.3	94.6
V_6	.58597	*	6	0.27965	4.0	98.6
V_7	.76372	*	7	0.09883	1.4	100.0

Final statistics:

Variable	Communality	*	Factor	Eigenvalue	Percent of Variance	Cumulative Percentage
V_1	.63867	*	1	3.04960	43.6	43.6
V_2	.70338	*	2	1.64092	23.4	67.0
V_3	.60090	*				
V_4	.70795	*				
V_5	.62793	*				
V_6	.67873	*				
V_7	.73295	*				

Factor matrix:

	Factor 1	Factor 2
V_1	.68096	−.41829
V_2	.56493	.61987
V_3	.69355	−.34625
V_4	.57868	.61080
V_5	.69067	−.38846
V_6	.58235	.58275
V_7	.79668	−.31346

Rotated factor matrix:

	Factor 1	Factor 2
V_1	.79724	.05541
V_2	.09943	.83276
V_3	.76562	.12135
V_4	.11589	.83338
V_5	.78782	.08533
V_6	.13518	.81268
V_7	.83048	.20797

Factor score coefficient matrix:

	Factor 1	Factor 2
V_1	.34295	−.05898
V_2	−.02312	.36321
V_3	.15844	−.02150
V_4	−.06357	.36945
V_5	.18444	−.03433
V_6	−.04586	.32517
V_7	.42645	.00095

(continued)

	TABLE 19.3
	(continued)

Reproduced correlation matrix:

	V_1	V_2	V_3	V_4	V_5	V_6	V_7
V_1	.63867*	.00459	−.05289	.03143	.06719	−.02280	−.11362
V_2	.12541	.70338*	.03282	.00447	.00061	−.00022	−.03576
V_3	.61711	.17718	.60090*	.00015	−.12352	−.04212	.06893
V_4	.13857	.70553	.18985	.70795*	−.03241	−.00294	.00044
V_5	.63281	.14939	.61352	.16241	.62793*	.03416	.04799
V_6	.15280	.69022	.20212	.69294	.17584	.67873*	.02872
V_7	.67362	.25576	.66107	.26956	.67201	.28128	.73295*

The lower left triangle contains the reproduced correlation matrix; the diagonal, the communalities; and the upper right triangle, the residuals between the observed correlations and the reproduced correlations.

The values in the unrotated factor pattern matrix of Table 19.3 are a little different than those in Table 19.2, although the pattern of the coefficient is similar. Sometimes, however, the pattern of loadings for common factor analysis is different than that for principal components analysis, with some variables loading on different factors. The rotated factors matrix has the same pattern as that in Table 19.2, leading to a similar interpretation of the factors.

We end with another application of common factor analysis, in the context of consumer perception of rebates.

EXAMPLE
"Common" Rebate Perceptions

Rebates are effective in obtaining new users, brand switching, and repeat purchases among current users. A study was undertaken to determine the factors underlying consumer perception of rebates. A set of 24 items measuring consumer perceptions of rebates was constructed. Respondents were asked to express their degree of agreement with these items on five-point Likert scales. The data were collected by a one-stage area telephone survey conducted in the Memphis metropolitan area. A total of 303 usable questionnaires was obtained.

The 24 items measuring perceptions of rebates were analyzed using common factor analysis. The initial factor solution did not reveal a simple structure of underlying rebate perceptions. Therefore, items that had low loadings were deleted from the scale, and the factor analysis was performed on the remaining items. This second solution yielded three interpretable factors. The factor loadings and the reliability coefficients are presented in the table below. The three factors contained four, four, and three items, respectively. Factor 1 seemed to capture the consumers' perceptions of the efforts and difficulties associated with rebate redemption (efforts). Factor 2 was defined as a representation of consumers' faith in the rebate system (faith). Factor 3 represented consumers' perceptions of the manufacturers' motives for offering rebates (motives). The loadings of items on their respective factor ranged from 0.527 to 0.744.[11]

Factor Analysis of Perceptions of Rebates

	Factor loading		
Scale Items[a]	Factor 1	Factor 2	Factor 3
Manufacturers make the rebate process too complicated	.194	.671	−.127
Mail-in rebates are not worth the trouble involved	−.031	.612	.352
It takes too long to receive the rebate check from the manufacturer	.013	.718	.051
Manufacturers could do more to make rebates easier to use	.205	.616	.173

Manufacturers offer rebates because consumers want them[b]	.660	.172	.101
Today's manufacturers take real interest in consumer welfare[b]	.569	.203	.334
Consumer benefit is usually the primary consideration in rebate offers[b]	.660	.002	.318
In general, manufacturers are sincere in their rebate offers to consumers[b]	.716	.047	−.033
Manufacturers offer rebates to get consumers to buy something they do not really need	.099	.156	.744
Manufacturers use rebate offers to induce consumers to buy slow-moving items	.090	.027	.702
Rebate offers require you to buy more of a product than you need	.230	.066	.527
Eigenvalues	2.030	1.344	1.062
Percentage of explained variance	27.500	12.2	9.700

[a]The response categories for all items were strongly agree (1), agree (2), neither agree nor disagree (3), disagree (4), strongly disagree (5), and don't know (6). "Don't know" responses were excluded from data analysis.

[b]The scores of these items were reversed.   ◆

Three factors characterizing consumers' perceptions of rebates are faith in the rebate system, efforts associated with rebate redemption, and manufacturers' motives for offering rebates. ◆ Copyright 1991 by the Drakett Company. Reprinted by permission.

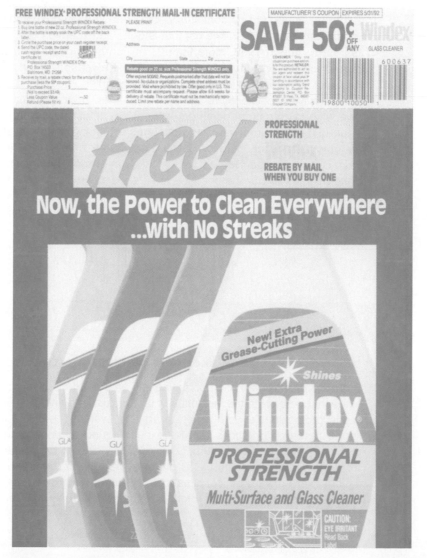

In this example, when the initial factor solution was not interpretable, items which had low loadings were deleted and the factor analysis was performed on the remaining items. If the number of variables is large (greater than 15), principal components analysis and common factor analysis result in similar solutions. Principal components analysis is less prone to misinterpretation, however, and is recommended for the nonexpert. Research in Practice 19.1 illustrates an application of principal components analysis in international marketing research,[12] whereas Research in Practice 19.2 presents an application in the area of ethics.[13]

RESEARCH IN PRACTICE 19.1

Driving Nuts for Beetles

Generally, with time, consumer needs and tastes change. Consumer preferences for automobiles need to be continually tracked to identify changing demands and specifications. There is, however, one car that is quite an exception, the Volkswagen Beetle. Since its introduction in 1938, more than 21 million have been built. Surveys have been conducted in different countries to determine the reasons why people purchase Beetles. Principal components analyses of the variables measuring the reasons for owning Beetles have consistently revealed one dominant factor, fanatic loyalty. The company has long wished its natural death but without any effect. This noisy and cramped "bug" has inspired devotion in drivers. Now old bugs are being sought everywhere. "The Japanese are going absolutely nuts for Beetles," says Jack Finn, a recycler of old Beetles in West Palm Beach, Florida. Beetles are still made in Mexico, but they cannot be exported to the United States or Europe because of safety and emission standards. Because of faithful loyalty for the bug, VW has repositioned the beetle as a new shiny VW Passat, a premium-quality car that gives an image of sophistication and class as opposed to the old one that symbolized a low-priced brand.

RESEARCH IN PRACTICE 19.2

Factors Predicting Unethical Marketing Research Practices

A survey of 420 marketing professionals was conducted to identify organizational variables that determine the incidence of unethical marketing research practices. These marketing professionals were asked to provide evaluations of the incidence of fifteen marketing research practices that have been found to pose ethical problems. They also provided responses on several other scales, including an 11-item scale pertaining to the extent to which ethical problems plagued the organization, and what top management's actions were toward ethical situations. The commonly used method of principal components analysis with varimax rotation indicated that these 11-items could be represented by two factors.

(continued)

Factor Analysis of Ethical Problems and Top Management Action Scales

	Extent of Ethical Problems within the Organization (factor 1)	Top Management Actions on Ethics (factor 2)
1. Successful executives in my company make rivals look bad in the eyes of important people in my company.	.66	
2. Peer executives in my company often engage in behaviors that I consider to be unethical.	.68	
3. There are many opportunities for peer executives in my company to engage in unethical behaviors.	.43	
4. Successful executives in my company take credit for the ideas and accomplishments of others.	.81	
5. To succeed in my company, it is often necessary to compromise one's ethics.	.66	
6. Successful executives in my company are generally more unethical than unsuccessful executives.	.64	
7. Successful executives in my company look for a "scapegoat" when they feel they may be associated with failure.	.78	
8. Successful executives in my company withhold information that is detrimental to their self-interest.	.68	
9. Top management in my company has let it be known in no uncertain terms that unethical behaviors will not be tolerated.		.73
10. If an executive in my company is discovered to have engaged in unethical behavior that results primarily in person gain (rather than corporate gain), he or she will be promptly reprimanded.		.80
11. If an executive in my company is discovered to have engaged in an unethical behavior that results primarily in corporate gain (rather than personal gain), he or she will be promptly reprimanded.		.78
Eigenvalue	5.06	1.17
Percentage of Variance Explained	46%	11%

Note: To simplify the table, only varimax-rotated loadings of .40 or greater are reported. Each was rated on a five-point scale with 1 = strongly agree and 5 = strongly disagree.

The first factor could be interpreted as the incidence of unethical practices, while the second factor denotes top management actions related to unethical practices. The two factors together account for more than half the variation in the data with the first factor being dominant. These two factors along with four other variables were then used as predictors in a multiple regression. The results indicated that they were the two best predictors of unethical marketing research practices.

COMPUTER APPLICATIONS

Computer programs are available to implement both the approaches: principal components analysis and common factor analysis. The mainframe and microcomputer programs are similar for SPSS, SAS, and BMDP. In the SPSS packages, the program FAC-

TOR may be used for principal components analysis as well as for common factor analysis. Some other methods of factor analysis are also available and factor scores are calculated.

In the SAS system, the program PRINCOMP performs principal components analysis and calculates principal component scores. To perform common factor analysis, the program FACTOR can be used. The FACTOR program also performs principal components analysis. In the BMDP package, principal components analysis and common factor analysis can be performed with the 4M program.[14]

SUMMARY

Factor analysis is a class of procedures used for reducing and summarizing data. Each variable is expressed as a linear combination of the underlying factors. Likewise, the factors themselves can be expressed as linear combinations of the observed variables. The factors are extracted in such a way that the first factor accounts for the highest variance in the data, the second the next highest, and so on. Additionally, it is possible to extract the factors so that the factors are uncorrelated, as in principal components analysis.

In formulating the factor analysis problem, the variables to be included in the analysis should be specified based on past research, theory, and the judgment of the researcher. These variables should be measured on an interval or ratio scale. Factor analysis is based on a matrix of correlation between the variables. The appropriateness of the correlation matrix for factor analysis can be statistically tested.

The two basic approaches to factor analysis are principal components analysis and common factor analysis. In principal components analysis, the total variance in the data is considered. Principal components analysis is recommended when the researcher's primary concern is to determine the minimum number of factors that will account for maximum variance in the data for use in subsequent multivariate analysis. In common factor analysis, the factors are estimated based only on the common variance. This method is appropriate when the primary concern is to identify the underlying dimensions and when the common variance is of interest. This method is also known as principal axis factoring.

The number of factors that should be extracted can be determined a priori or based on eigenvalues, scree plots, percentage of variance, split-half reliability, or significance tests. Although the initial or unrotated factor matrix indicates the relationships between the factors and individual variables, it seldom results in factors that can be interpreted because the factors are correlated with many variables. Therefore, rotation is used to transform the factor matrix into a simpler one that is easier to interpret. The most commonly used method of rotation is the varimax procedure, which results in orthogonal factors. If the factors are highly correlated in the population, oblique rotation can be used. The rotated factor matrix forms the basis for interpreting the factors.

Factor scores can be computed for each respondent. Alternatively, surrogate variables may be selected by examining the factor matrix and selecting a variable with the highest or near highest loading for each factor. The differences between the observed correlations and the reproduced correlations, as estimated from the factor matrix, can be examined to determine model fit.[15]

ACRONYMS

The steps involved in conducting factor analysis may be summarized by the acronym FACTOR STEP:

F   ormulate the problem
A   priori or otherwise determine the number of factors
C   orrelation matrix
T   est for the appropriateness of factor analysis
O   bserve the rotated factor matrix; interpretation of factors
R   otation

S   urrogate variable
T   esting for model fit
E   stimate the factor scores
P   rincipal components or common factor analysis

EXERCISES

QUESTIONS

1. How is factor analysis different from multiple regression and discriminant analysis?
2. What are the major uses of factor analysis?
3. Describe the factor analysis model.
4. What hypothesis is examined by Bartlett's test of sphericity? For what purpose is this test used?
5. What is meant by the term communality of a variable?
6. Briefly define the following: eigenvalue, factor loadings, factor matrix, and factor scores.
7. For what purpose is the Kaiser-Meyer-Olkin measure of sampling adequacy used?
8. What is the major difference between principal components analysis and common factor analysis?
9. Explain how eigenvalues are used to determine the number of factors.
10. What is a scree plot? For what purpose is it used?
11. Why is it useful to rotate the factors? Which is the most common method of rotation?
12. What guidelines are available for interpreting the factors?
13. When is it useful to calculate factor scores?
14. What are surrogate variables? How are they determined?
15. How is the fit of the factor analysis model examined?

PROBLEMS

1. Complete the following portion of an output from principal component analysis:

Variable	Communality	Factor	Eigenvalue	Percentage of Variance
V_1	1.0	1	3.25	
V_2	1.0	2	1.78	
V_3	1.0	3	1.23	
V_4	1.0	4	0.78	
V_5	1.0	5	0.35	
V_6	1.0	6	0.30	
V_7	1.0	7	0.19	
V_8	1.0	8	0.12	

2. Draw a scree plot based on the data given in problem 1.
3. How many factors should be extracted in problem 1? Explain your reasoning.

COMPUTER EXERCISES

1. In a study of the relationship between household behavior and shopping behavior, data on the following lifestyle statements were obtained on a seven-point scale (1 = disagree, 7 = agree):

V_1 I would rather spend a quiet evening at home that go out to a party.
V_2 I always check prices, even on small items.
V_3 Magazines are more interesting than movies.
V_4 I won't buy products advertised on billboards.
V_5 I am a homebody.
V_6 I save and cash coupons.
V_7 Companies waste a lot of money advertising.

The data obtained from a pretest sample of 25 respondents are given below:

Number	V_1	V_2	V_3	V_4	V_5	V_6	V_7
1	6	2	7	6	5	3	5
2	5	7	5	6	6	6	4
3	5	3	4	5	6	6	7
4	3	2	2	5	1	3	2
5	4	2	3	2	2	1	3
6	2	6	2	4	3	7	5
7	1	3	3	6	2	5	7
8	3	5	1	4	2	5	6
9	7	3	6	3	5	2	4
10	6	3	3	4	4	6	5
11	6	6	2	6	4	4	7
12	3	2	2	7	6	1	6
13	5	7	6	2	2	6	1
14	6	3	5	5	7	2	3
15	3	2	4	3	2	6	5
16	2	7	5	1	4	5	2
17	3	2	2	7	2	4	6
18	6	4	5	4	7	3	3
19	7	2	6	2	5	2	1
20	5	6	6	3	4	5	3
21	2	3	3	2	1	2	6
22	3	4	2	1	4	3	6
23	2	6	3	2	1	5	3
24	6	5	7	4	5	7	2
25	7	6	5	4	6	5	3

a. Analyze these data using principal components analysis, using the varimax rotation procedure.
b. Interpret the factors extracted.
c. Calculate factor scores for each respondent.
d. If surrogate variables were to be selected, which ones would you select?
e. Examine the model fit.
f. Analyze the data using common factor analysis and answer questions b through e.

NOTES

1. James M. Sinukula and Leanna Lawtor, "Positioning in the Financial Services Industry: A Look at the Decomposition of Image," in Jon M. Hawes and George B. Glisan (eds.), *Developments in Marketing Science*, vol. 10 (Akron, OH: Academy of Marketing Science, 1987), pp. 439–42.

2. For a detailed discussion of factor analysis, see George H. Dunteman, *Principal Components Analysis* (Newbury Park, CA: Sage Publications, 1989). For recent applications, see Lisa K. Scheer and Louis W. Stern, "The Effect of Influence Type and Performance Outcomes on Attitude toward the Influencer," *Journal of Marketing Research* 29 (February 1992): 128–42; and Thomas R. Wotruba and Pradeep K. Tyagi, "Met Expectations and Turnover in Direct Selling," *Journal of Marketing* 55 (July 1991): 24–35.

3. See, for example, Shirley Taylor, "Waiting for Service: The Relationship between Delays and Evaluations of Service," *Journal of Marketing* 58 (April 1994): 56–69.

4. See John L. Lastovicka and Kanchana Thamodaran, "Common Factor Score Estimates in Multiple Regression Problems," *Journal of Marketing Research* 28 (February 1991): 105–12; and W. R. Dillon and M. Goldstein, *Multivariate Analysis: Methods and Applications* (New York: Wiley, 1984), pp. 23–99.

5. For a recent application of factor analysis, see Shankar Ganesan, "Negotiation Strategies and the Nature of Channel Relationships," *Journal of Marketing Research* 30 (May 1993): 183–203.

6. Joseph F. Hair, Jr., Ralph E. Anderson, Ronald L. Tatham, and William C. Black, *Multivariate Data Analysis with Readings*, 4th ed. (Englewood Cliffs: Prentice Hall, 1995), pp. 364–419.

7. Factor analysis is influenced by the relative size of the correlations rather than the absolute size.

8. See Sangit Chatterjee, Linda Jamieson, and Frederick Wiseman, "Identifying Most Influential Observations in Factor Analysis," *Marketing Science* (Spring 1991): 145–60; and Frank Acito and Ronald D. Anderson, "A Monté Carlo Comparison of Factor Analytic Methods," *Journal of Marketing Research* 17 (May 1980): 228–36.

9. Other methods of orthogonal rotation are also available. The quartimax method minimizes the number of factors needed to explain a variable. The equimax method is a combination of varimax and quartimax.

10. Ronald C. Curhan and Robert J. Kopp, "Obtaining Retailer Support for Trade Deals: Key Success Factors," *Journal of Advertising Research* (December 1987–January 1988): 51–60.

11. Peter Tat, William A. Cunningham III, and Emin Babakus, "Consumer Perceptions of Rebates," *Journal of Advertising Research* (August–September 1988): 45–50.

12. "The Car That Just Won't Die," *The Economist* (May 23, 1992).

13. Ishmael P. Akaah and Edward A. Riordan, "The Incidence of Unethical Practices in Marketing Research: An Empirical Investigation," *Journal of the Academy of Marketing Science* 18 (1990): 143–52.

14. For mainframe packages, see:
SPSS Base Systems User's Guide (Englewood Cliffs, NJ: Prentice Hall, 1994).
SAS Language and Procedure: Usage, V 6 (Cary, NC: SAS Institute, 1989).
SAS Language and Procedure: Usage 2, V 6 (Cary, NC: SAS Institute, 1991).
SAS Procedures Guide, V 6, 3rd ed. (Cary, NC: SAS Institute, 1990).
SAS Language: Reerence, V 6 (Cary, NC: SAS Institute, 1990).
BMDP Statistical Software Manual, vols. 1 and 2 (Berkeley: University of California Press, 1990).
For microcomputer packages, see:
SPSS/PC+™ V 4.0 BASE MANUAL (Englewood Cliffs, NJ: Prentice Hall, 1990).
SPSS/PC+ Advanced Statistics™, V 4.0 (Englewood Cliffs, NJ: Prentice Hall, 1990).
SAS/STAT™ User Guide, V 6, 4th ed. vols. 1 and 2 (Cary, NC: SAS Institute, 1990).
The BMDP manual for microcomputers is the same as that for the mainframe.

15. The assistance of James Agarwal with the international marketing research example, the assistance of Mark Leach and Gina Miller in writing the ethics section, and the assistance of Mark Peterson in writing the computer applications section is gratefully acknowledged.

APPENDIX 19A

FUNDAMENTAL EQUATIONS OF FACTOR ANALYSIS

In the factor analysis model, hypothetical components are derived that account for the linear relationship between observed variables.[1] The factor analysis model requires that the relationships between observed variables be linear and that the variables have nonzero correlations between them. The derived hypothetical components have the following properties:

1. They form a linearly independent set of variables. No hypothetical component is derivable from the other hypothetical components as a linear combination of them.

2. The hypothetical components' variables can be divided into two basic kinds of components: common factors and unique factors. These two components can be distinguished in terms of the patterns of weights in the linear equations that derive the observed variables from the hypothetical components' variables. A common factor has more than one variable with a nonzero weight or factor loading associated with the factor. A unique factor has only one variable with a nonzero weight associated with the factor. Hence, only one variable depends on a unique factor.

3. Common factors are always assumed to be uncorrelated with the unique factors. Unique factors are also usually assumed to be mutually uncorrelated, but common factors may or may not be correlated with each other.

4. Generally, it is assumed that there are fewer common factors than observed variables. The number of unique factors is usually assumed to be equal to the number of observed variables, however.

The following notations are used.

$$\mathbf{X} = \text{an } n \times 1 \text{ random vector of observed random variables } X_1, X_2, X_3, \ldots, X_n$$

It is assumed that

$$E(\mathbf{X}) = 0$$

$$E(\mathbf{X}\mathbf{X}') = \mathbf{R}_{xx}, \text{ a correlation matrix with unities in the main diagonal}$$

$$\mathbf{F} = \text{an } m \times 1 \text{ vector of } m \text{ common factors } F_1, F_2, \ldots, F_m$$

It is assumed that

$$E(\mathbf{F}) = 0$$

$$E(\mathbf{F}\mathbf{F}') = \mathbf{R}_{ff}, \text{ a correlation matrix}$$

$$\mathbf{U} = \text{an } n \times 1 \text{ random vector of the } n \text{ unique factors variables, } U_1, U_2, \ldots, U_n$$

It is assumed that

$$E(\mathbf{U}) = 0$$

$$E(\mathbf{U}\mathbf{U}') = \mathbf{I}$$

The unique factors are normalized to have unit variances and are mutually uncorrelated.

$$\mathbf{A} = \text{an } n \times m \text{ matrix of coefficients called the factor pattern matrix}$$

$$\mathbf{V} = \text{an } n \times n \text{ diagonal matrix of coefficients for the unique factors}$$

---

[1]The material in this appendix has been drawn from Stanley A. Muliak, *The Foundations of Factor Analysis* (New York: McGraw-Hill, 1972).

The observed variables, which are the coordinates of $\mathbf{X}$, are weighted combinations of the common factors and the unique factors. The fundamental equation of factor analysis can then be written as

$$\mathbf{X} = \mathbf{AF} + \mathbf{VU}$$

The correlations between variables in terms of the factors may be derived as follows:

$$
\begin{aligned}
R_{xx} &= E(\mathbf{XX'}) \\
&= E\{(\mathbf{AF} + \mathbf{VU})(\mathbf{AF} + \mathbf{VU'})\} \\
&= E\{(\mathbf{AF} + \mathbf{VU})(\mathbf{F'A'} + \mathbf{U'V'})\} \\
&= E(\mathbf{AFF'A'} + \mathbf{AFU'V'} + \mathbf{VUF'A'} + \mathbf{VUU'V'}) \\
&= \mathbf{AR}_{ff}\mathbf{A'} + \mathbf{AR}_{fu}\mathbf{V'} + \mathbf{VR}_{uf}\mathbf{A'} + \mathbf{V}^2
\end{aligned}
$$

Given that the common factors are uncorrelated with the unique factors, we have

$$\mathbf{R}_{fu} = \mathbf{R}_{uf}{}' = 0$$

Hence,

$$\mathbf{R}_{xx} = \mathbf{AR}_{ff}\mathbf{A'} + \mathbf{V}^2$$

Suppose that we subtract the matrix of unique factor variance, $\mathbf{V}^2$, from both sides. We then obtain

$$\mathbf{R}_{xx} - \mathbf{V}^2 = \mathbf{AR}_{ff}\mathbf{A'}$$

$\mathbf{R}_{xx}$ is dependent only on the common factor variables, and the correlations among the variables are related only to the common factors. Let $\mathbf{R}_c = \mathbf{R}_{xx} - \mathbf{V}^2$ be the reduced correlation matrix.

We have already defined the factor pattern matrix $\mathbf{A}$. The coefficients of the factor pattern matrix are weights assigned to the common factors when the observed variables are expressed as linear combinations of the common and unique factors. We now define the factor structure matrix. The coefficients of the factor structure matrix are the covariances between the observed variables and the factors. The factor structure matrix is helpful in the interpretation of factors as it shows which variables are similar to a common factor variable. The factor structure matrix, $\mathbf{A}_s$, is defined as

$$
\begin{aligned}
\mathbf{A}_s &= E(\mathbf{XF'}) \\
&= E[(\mathbf{AF} + \mathbf{VUF'})] \\
&= \mathbf{AR}_{ff} + \mathbf{VR}_{uf} \\
&= \mathbf{AR}_{ff}
\end{aligned}
$$

Thus, the factor structure matrix is equivalent to the factor pattern matrix $\mathbf{A}$ multiplied by the matrix of covariances among the factors $\mathbf{R}_{ff}$. Substituting $\mathbf{A}_s$ for $\mathbf{AR}_{ff}$, the reduced correlation matrix becomes the product of factor structure and the factor pattern matrix.

$$
\begin{aligned}
\mathbf{R}_c &= \mathbf{AR}_{ff}\mathbf{A'} \\
&= \mathbf{A}_s\mathbf{A'}
\end{aligned}
$$

Cluster Analysis

Like birds of a feather, consumers, stores, brands, and other objects in the marketing environment that are similar in terms of key variables often flock (cluster) together, and such clusters are discovered via cluster analysis.

◆

OBJECTIVES

After reading this chapter, the student should be able to:

1. Describe the basic concept and scope of cluster analysis and its importance in marketing research.
2. Discuss the statistics associated with cluster analysis.
3. Explain the procedure for conducting cluster analysis including formulating the problem, selecting a distance measure, selecting a clustering procedure, deciding on the number of clusters, interpreting clusters, and profiling clusters.
4. Describe the purpose and methods for evaluating the quality of clustering results and assessing reliability and validity.
5. Discuss the applications of nonhierarchical clustering and clustering of variables.

OVERVIEW

Like factor analysis (Chapter 19), cluster analysis examines an entire set of interdependent relationships. Cluster analysis makes no distinction between dependent and independent variables. Rather, interdependent relationships between the whole set of variables are examined. The primary objective of cluster analysis is to classify objects into relatively homogeneous groups based on the set of variables considered. Objects in a group are relatively similar in terms of these variables and different from objects in other groups. When used in this manner, cluster analysis is the obverse of factor analysis in that it reduces the number of objects, not the number of variables, by grouping them into a much smaller number of clusters.

This chapter describes the basic concept of cluster analysis. The steps involved in conducting cluster analysis are discussed and illustrated in the context of hierarchical clustering by using a popular computer program. Then an application of nonhierarchical clustering is presented, followed by a discussion of clustering of variables. We begin with two examples.

DEPARTMENT STORE PATRONAGE PROJECT
Cluster Analysis

In the department store project, respondents were clustered on the basis of self-reported importance attached to each factor of the choice criteria used in selecting a department store. The results indicated that respondents could be clustered into four segments. Differences among the segments were statistically tested. Thus, each segment contained respondents who were relatively homogeneous with respect to their choice criteria. The store choice model was then estimated separately for each segment. This procedure resulted in choice models that better represented the underlying choice process of respondents in specific segments. ◆

Haagen-Dazs increased its penetration by identifying geodemographic clusters offering potential for increased ice cream sales.
◆ Robert Frerck/Tony Stone Images.

EXAMPLE
Ice Cream Shops for "Hot" Regions

Haagen-Dazs Shoppe Company, with more than 300 retail ice cream shops throughout the United States, was interested in expanding its customer base. The objective was to identify potential consumer segments that could generate additional sales. Geodemography—a method of clustering consumers based on geographic, demographic, and lifestyle characteristics—was employed for this purpose. Primary research was conducted to develop demographic and psychographic profiles of Haagen-Dazs Shoppe users, including frequency of purchase, time of the day they came in, day of the week, and other product use variables. The addresses and zip codes of the respondents were also obtained. The respondents were then assigned to 40 geodemographic clusters based on the clustering procedure developed by Claritas. For each geodemographic cluster, the profile of Haagen-Dazs customers was compared with the cluster profile to determine the degree of penetration. Using this information, Haagen-Dazs was also able to identify several potential customer groups from which to attract traffic.[1] ◆

The Haagen-Dazs example illustrates the use of clustering to arrive at homogeneous segments for the purpose of formulating specific marketing strategies. In the department store example, clustering was used to group respondents for subsequent multivariate analysis.

BASIC CONCEPT

Cluster analysis is a class of techniques used to classify objects or cases into relatively homogeneous groups called *clusters*. Objects in each cluster tend to be similar to each other and dissimilar to objects in the other clusters. Cluster analysis is also called *classification analysis* or *numerical taxonomy*.[2] We are concerned with clustering procedures that assign each object to one and only one cluster.[3] Figure 20.1 shows an ideal clustering situation in which the clusters are distinctly separated on two variables: quality consciousness (variable 1) and price sensitivity (variable 2). Note that each consumer falls into one cluster and there are no overlapping areas. Figure 20.2, on the other hand, presents a clustering situation more likely to be encountered in practice. In Figure 20.2, the boundaries for some of the clusters are not clear-cut, and the classification of some consumers is not obvious, because many of them could be grouped into one cluster or another.

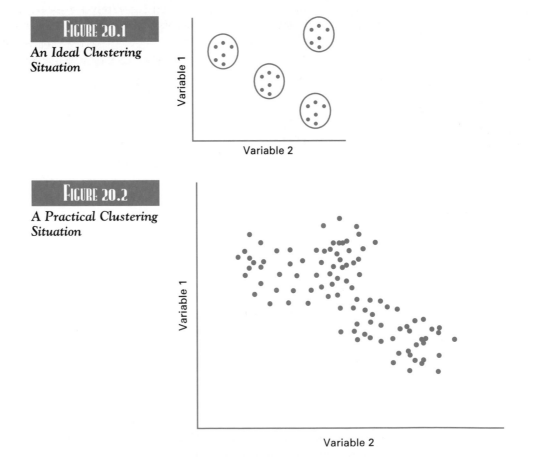

FIGURE 20.1

An Ideal Clustering Situation

FIGURE 20.2

A Practical Clustering Situation

Both cluster analysis and discriminant analysis are concerned with classification. Discriminant analysis, however, requires prior knowledge of the cluster or group membership for each object or case included, to develop the classification rule. In contrast, in cluster analysis there is no a priori information about the group or cluster membership for any of the objects. Groups or clusters are suggested by the data, not defined a priori.[4]

Cluster analysis has been used in marketing for a variety of purposes, including the following:[5]

- *Segmenting the market.* For example, consumers may be clustered on the basis of benefits sought from the purchase of a product. Each cluster would consist of consumers who are relatively homogeneous in terms of the benefits they seek.[6] This approach is called *benefit segmentation*. We illustrate it with the following example.

EXAMPLE

The Vacationing Demanders, Educationalists, and Escapists _____

In a study examining decision-making patterns among international vacationers, 260 respondents provided information on six psychographic orientations: psychological, educational, social, relaxational, physiological, and aesthetic. Cluster analysis was used to group respondents into psychographic segments. The results suggested that there were three meaningful segments based on these lifestyles. The first segment (53%) consisted of individuals who were high on nearly all lifestyle scales; this group was called the "demanders." The second group (20%) was high on the educational scale and was named the "educationalists." The last group (26%) was high on relaxation and low on social scales and was named the "escapists." Specific marketing strategies were formulated to attract vacationers in each segment.[7] ◆

Cluster analysis has revealed distinct market segments of international vacationers. ◆ Tony Stone Images.

- *Understanding buyer behaviors*. Cluster analysis can be used to identify homogeneous groups of buyers. Then the buying behavior of each group may be examined separately, as in the department store patronage project, where respondents were clustered on the basis of self-reported importance attached to each factor of the choice criteria used in selecting a department store. Cluster analysis has also been used to identify the kinds of strategies automobile purchasers use to obtain external information.
- *Identifying new product opportunities*. By clustering brands and products, competitive sets within the market can be determined. Brands in the same cluster compete more fiercely with each other than with brands in other clusters. A firm can examine its current offerings compared with those of its competitors to identify potential new product opportunities.
- *Selecting test markets*. By grouping cities into homogeneous clusters, it is possible to select comparable cities to test various marketing strategies.
- *Reducing data*. Cluster analysis can be used as a general data reduction tool to develop clusters or subgroups of data that are more manageable than individual observations. Subsequent multivariate analysis is conducted on the clusters rather than on the individual observations. For example, to describe differences in consumers' product usage behavior, the consumers may first be clustered into groups. The differences among the groups may then be examined using multiple discriminant analysis.

STATISTICS ASSOCIATED WITH CLUSTER ANALYSIS

Before discussing the statistics associated with cluster analysis, it should be mentioned that most clustering methods are relatively simple procedures that are not supported by an extensive body of statistical reasoning. Rather, most clustering methods are heuristics, which are based on algorithms. Thus, cluster analysis contrasts sharply with analysis of variance, regression, discriminant analysis, and factor analysis, which are based upon an extensive body of statistical reasoning. Although many clustering methods have important statistical properties, the fundamental simplicity of these methods needs to be recognized.[8] The following statistics and concepts are associated with cluster analysis.

Agglomeration schedule. An agglomeration schedule gives information on the objects or cases being combined at each stage of a hierarchical clustering process.

Cluster centroid. The cluster centroid is the mean values of the variables for all the cases or objects in a particular cluster.

Cluster centers. The cluster centers are the initial starting points in nonhierarchical clustering. Clusters are built around these centers or *seeds*.

Cluster membership. Cluster membership indicates the cluster to which each object or case belongs.

Dendrogram. A dendrogram, or *tree graph*, is a graphical device for displaying clustering results. Vertical lines represent clusters that are joined together. The position of the line on the scale indicates the distances at which clusters were joined. The dendrogram is read from left to right. Figure 20.8 is a dendrogram.

Distances between cluster centers. These distances indicate how separated the individual pairs of clusters are. Clusters that are widely separated are distinct and therefore desirable.

Icicle diagram. An icicle diagram is a graphical display of clustering results, so called because it resembles a row of icicles hanging from the eaves of a house. The columns correspond to the objects being clustered, and the rows correspond to the number of clusters. An icicle diagram is read from bottom to top. Figure 20.7 is an icicle diagram.

Similarity/distance coefficient matrix. A similarity/distance coefficient matrix is a lower-triangle matrix containing pairwise distances between objects or cases.

CONDUCTING CLUSTER ANALYSIS

The steps involved in conducting cluster analysis are listed in Figure 20.3. The first step is to formulate the clustering problem by defining the variables on which the clustering will be based. Then, an appropriate distance measure must be selected. The distance measure determines how similar or dissimilar the objects being clustered are. Several clustering procedures have been developed, and the researcher should select one that is appropriate for the problem at hand. Deciding on the number of clusters requires judgment on the part of the researcher. The derived clusters should be interpreted in terms of the variables used to cluster them and profiled in terms of additional salient variables. Finally, the researcher must assess the validity of the clustering process.

Formulating the Problem

Perhaps the most important part of formulating the clustering problem is selecting the variables on which the clustering is based. Inclusion of even one or two irrelevant variables may distort an otherwise useful clustering solution. Basically, the set of variables selected should describe the similarity between objects in terms that are relevant to the marketing research problem. The variables should be selected based on past research, theory, or a consideration of the hypotheses being tested. In exploratory research, the researcher should exercise judgment and intuition.

To illustrate, we consider a clustering of consumers based on attitudes toward shopping. Based on past research, six attitudinal variables were identified. Consumers were asked to express their degree of agreement with the following statements on a seven-point scale (1 = disagree, 7 = agree):

V1 Shopping is fun.
V2 Shopping is bad for your budget.
V3 I combine shopping with eating out.
V4 I try to get the best buys while shopping.

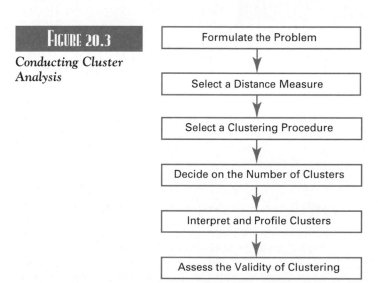

FIGURE 20.3

Conducting Cluster Analysis

V5   I don't care about shopping.

V6   You can save a lot of money by comparing prices.

Data obtained from a pretest sample of 20 respondents are shown in Table 20.1. Note that, in practice, clustering is done on much larger samples of 100 or more. A small sample size has been used to illustrate the clustering process.

Selecting a Distance or Similarity Measure

Because the objective of clustering is to group similar objects together, some measure is needed to assess how similar or different the objects are. The most common approach is to measure similarity in terms of distance between pairs of objects. Objects with smaller distances between them are more similar to each other than are those at larger distances. There are several ways to compute the distance between two objects.[9]

euclidean distance The square root of the sum of the squared differences in values for each variable.

The most commonly used measure of similarity is the euclidean distance or its square.[10] The **euclidean distance** is the square root of the sum of the squared differences in values for each variable. Other distance measures are also available. The *city-block* or *Manhattan distance* between two objects is the sum of the absolute differences in values for each variable. The *Chebychev distance* between two objects is the maximum absolute difference in values for any variable. For our example, we use the squared euclidean distance.

If the variables are measured in vastly different units, the clustering solution will be influenced by the units of measurement. In a supermarket shopping study, attitudinal variables may be measured on a nine-point Likert type scale; patronage, in terms of frequency of visits per month and the dollar amount spent; and brand loyalty, in terms of percentage of grocery shopping expenditure allocated to the favorite supermarket. In these cases, before clustering respondents, we must standardize the data by rescaling each variable to have a mean of zero and a standard deviation of unity. Although standardization can remove the influence of the unit of measurement, it can also reduce the dif-

	Case Number	V_1	V_2	V_3	V_4	V_5	V_6
TABLE 20.1							
Attitudinal Data for Clustering	1	6	4	7	3	2	3
	2	2	3	1	4	5	4
	3	7	2	6	4	1	3
	4	4	6	4	5	3	6
	5	1	3	2	2	6	4
	6	6	4	6	3	3	4
	7	5	3	6	3	3	4
	8	7	3	7	4	1	4
	9	2	4	3	3	6	3
	10	3	5	3	6	4	6
	11	1	3	2	3	5	3
	12	5	4	5	4	2	4
	13	2	2	1	5	4	4
	14	4	6	4	6	4	7
	15	6	5	4	2	1	4
	16	3	5	4	6	4	7
	17	4	4	7	2	2	5
	18	3	7	2	6	4	3
	19	4	6	3	7	2	7
	20	2	3	2	4	7	2

ferences between groups on variables that may best discriminate groups or clusters. It is also desirable to eliminate outliers (cases with atypical values).[11]

Use of different distance measures may lead to different clustering results. Hence, it is advisable to use different measures and to compare the results. Having selected a distance or similarity measure, we can next select a clustering procedure.

Selecting a Clustering Procedure

Figure 20.4 is a classification of clustering procedures. Clustering procedures can be hierarchical or nonhierarchical. **Hierarchical clustering** is characterized by the development of a hierarchy or treelike structure. Hierarchical methods can be agglomerative or divisive. **Agglomerative clustering** starts with each object in a separate cluster. Clusters are formed by grouping objects into bigger and bigger clusters. This process is continued until all objects are members of a single cluster. **Divisive clustering** starts with all the objects grouped in a single cluster. Clusters are divided or split until each object is in a separate cluster.

hierarchical clustering
A clustering procedure characterized by the development of a hierarchy or treelike structure.

agglomerative clustering
A hierarchical clustering procedure where each object starts out in a separate cluster. Clusters are formed by grouping objects into bigger and bigger clusters.

FIGURE 20.4

A Classification of Clustering Procedures

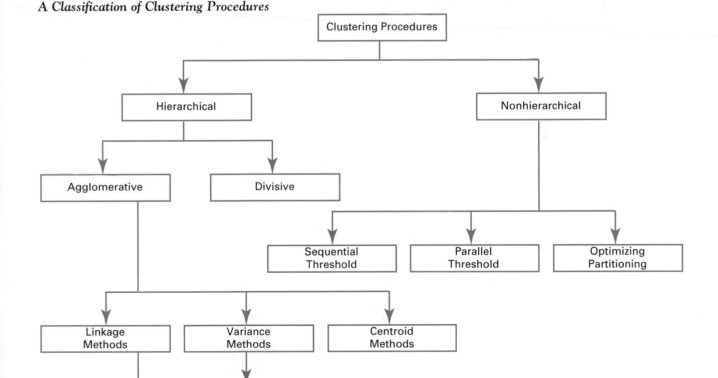

divisive clustering A hierarchical clustering procedure where all objects start out in one giant cluster. Clusters are formed by dividing this cluster into smaller and smaller clusters.

linkage methods Agglomerative methods of hierarchical clustering that cluster objects based on a computation of the distance between them.

single linkage A linkage method based on minimum distance or the nearest neighbor rule.

complete linkage A linkage method that is based on maximum distance or the farthest neighbor approach.

Agglomerative methods are commonly used in marketing research. They consist of linkage methods, error sums of squares or variance methods, and centroid methods. **Linkage methods** include single linkage, complete linkage, and average linkage. The **single linkage** method is based on minimum distance or the nearest neighbor rule. The first two objects clustered are those that have the smallest distance between them. The next shortest distance is identified, and either the third object is clustered with the first two or a new two-object cluster is formed. At every stage, the distance between two clusters is the distance between their two closest points (see Figure 20.5). Two clusters are merged at any stage by the single shortest link between them. This process is continued until all objects are in one cluster. The single linkage method does not work well when the clusters are poorly defined. The **complete linkage** method is similar to single linkage, except that it is based on the maximum distance or the farthest neighbor approach. In complete linkage, the distance between two clusters is calculated as the distance between their two farthest points. The *average linkage* method works similarly. In this method, however, the distance between two clusters is defined as the average of the distances between all pairs of objects, where one member of the pair is from each of the clusters (Figure 20.5). As can be seen, the average linkage method uses information on all pairs of distances, not merely the minimum or maximum distances. For this reason, it is usually preferred to the single and complete linkage methods.

The **variance methods** attempt to generate clusters to minimize the within-cluster variance. A commonly used variance method is **Ward's procedure**. For each cluster, the means for all the variables are computed. Then, for each object, the squared euclidean distance to the cluster means is calculated (Figure 20.6); and these distances are summed for all the objects. At each stage, the two clusters with the smallest increase in the overall sum of squares within cluster distances are combined. In the **centroid method**, the

FIGURE 20.5

Linkage Methods of Clustering

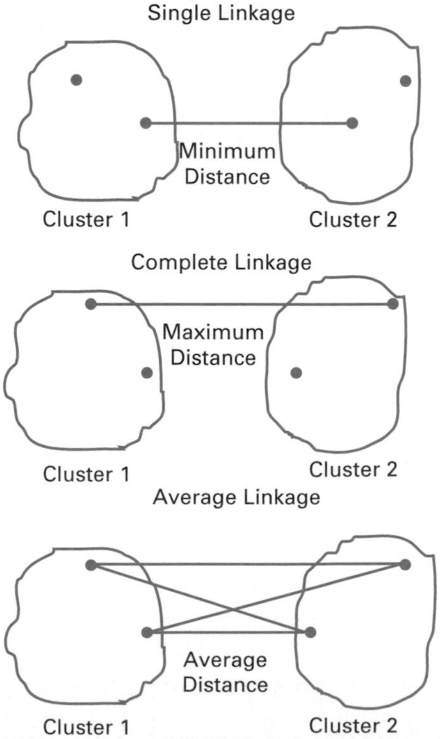

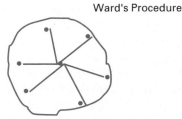
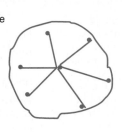

FIGURE 20.6

Other Agglomerative Clustering Methods

Ward's Procedure

Centroid Method

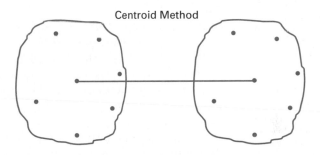

variance method An agglomerative method of hierarchical clustering in which clusters are generated to minimize the within-cluster variance.

Ward's procedure A variance method in which the squared euclidean distance to the cluster means is minimized.

centroid method A variance method of hierarchical clustering in which the distance between two clusters is the distance between their centroids (means for all the variables).

nonhierarchical clustering A procedure that first assigns or determines a cluster center and then groups all objects within a prespecified threshold value from the center.

distance between two clusters is the distance between their centroids (means for all the variables), as shown in Figure 20.6. Every time objects are grouped, a new centroid is computed. Of the hierarchical methods, the average linkage method and Ward's procedure have been shown to perform better than the other procedures.[12]

The second type of clustering procedures, the **nonhierarchical clustering** methods, are frequently referred to as *k*-means clustering. These methods include sequential threshold, parallel threshold, and optimizing partitioning. In the *sequential threshold method*, a cluster center is selected and all objects within a prespecified threshold value from the center are grouped together. A new cluster center or seed is then selected, and the process is repeated for the unclustered points. Once an object is clustered with a seed, it is no longer considered for clustering with subsequent seeds. The **parallel threshold method** operates similarly except that several cluster centers are selected simultaneously and objects within the threshold level are grouped with the nearest center. The **optimizing partitioning method** differs from the two threshold procedures in that objects can later be reassigned to clusters to optimize an overall criterion, such as average within-cluster distance for a given number of clusters.

Two major disadvantages of the nonhierarchical procedures are that the number of clusters must be prespecified and that the selection of cluster centers is arbitrary. Furthermore, the clustering results may depend on how the centers are selected. Many nonhierarchical programs select the first *k* (*k* = number of clusters) cases without missing values as initial cluster centers. Thus, the clustering results may depend on the order of observations in the data. Yet nonhierarchical clustering is faster than hierarchical methods and has merit when the number of objects or observations is large. It has been suggested that the hierarchical and nonhierarchical methods be used in tandem. First, an initial clustering solution is obtained using a hierarchical procedure, such as average linkage or Ward's. The number of clusters and cluster centroids so obtained are used as inputs to the optimizing partitioning method.[13]

parallel threshold method A nonhierarchical clustering method that specifies several cluster centers at once. All objects that are within a prespecified threshold value from the center are grouped together.

optimizing partitioning method A nonhierarchical clustering method that allows for later reassignment of objects to clusters to optimize an overall criterion.

Choice of a clustering method and choice of a distance measure are interrelated. For example, squared euclidean distances should be used with the Ward's and centroid methods. Several nonhierarchical procedures also use squared euclidean distances.

We will use Ward's procedure to illustrate hierarchical clustering. The output obtained by clustering the data of Table 20.1 is given in Table 20.2. Useful information is contained in the agglomeration schedule, which shows the number of cases or clusters being combined at each stage. The first line represents stage 1, with 19 clusters. Respondents 14 and 16 are combined at this stage, as shown in the columns labeled "clusters combined." The squared euclidean distance between these two respondents is given under the column labeled "coefficient." The column entitled "stage cluster first appears" indicates the stage at which a cluster is first formed. To illustrate, an entry of 1 at stage 7 indicates that respondent 14 was first grouped at stage 1. The last column, "next stage," indicates the stage at which another case (respondent) or cluster is combined with this one. Because the number in the first line of the last column is 7, we see that at stage 7, respondent 10 is combined with 14 and 16 to form a single cluster. Similarly, the second line represents stage 2 with 18 clusters. In stage 2, respondents 2 and 13 are grouped together.

Another important part of the output is contained in the icicle plot given in Figure 20.7. The columns correspond to the objects being clustered; in this case, they are the respondents labeled 1 through 20. The rows correspond to the number of clusters. This figure is read from bottom to top. At first, all cases are considered as individual clusters. Since there are 20 respondents, there are 20 initial clusters. At the first step, the two closest objects are combined, resulting in 19 clusters. The last line of Figure 20.7 shows

FIGURE 20.7

Vertical Icicle Plot Using Ward's Procedure

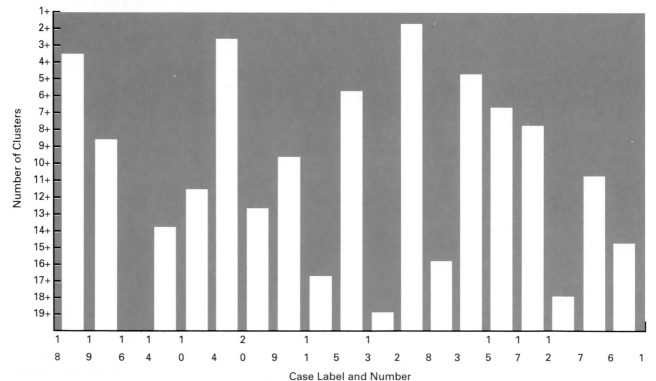

TABLE 20.2	

Results of Hierarchical Clustering

Agglomeration Schedule using Ward's Procedure

	CLUSTERS COMBINED			STAGE CLUSTER FIRST APPEARS		Next
Stage	Cluster 1	Cluster 2	Coefficient	Cluster 1	Cluster 2	Stage
1	14	16	1.000000	0	0	7
2	2	13	2.500000	0	0	15
3	7	12	4.000000	0	0	10
4	5	11	5.500000	0	0	11
5	3	8	7.000000	0	0	16
6	1	6	8.500000	0	0	10
7	10	14	10.166667	0	1	9
8	9	20	12.666667	0	0	11
9	4	10	15.250000	0	7	12
10	1	7	18.250000	6	3	13
11	5	9	22.750000	4	8	15
12	4	19	27.500000	9	0	17
13	1	17	32.700001	10	0	14
14	1	15	40.500000	13	0	16
15	2	5	51.000000	2	11	18
16	1	3	63.125000	14	5	19
17	4	18	78.291664	12	0	18
18	2	4	171.291656	15	17	19
19	1	2	330.450012	16	18	0

Cluster Membership of Cases Using Ward's Procedure

	NUMBER OF CLUSTERS		
Label Case	4	3	2
1	1	1	1
2	2	2	2
3	1	1	1
4	3	3	2
5	2	2	2
6	1	1	1
7	1	1	1
8	1	1	1
9	2	2	2
10	3	3	2
11	2	2	2
12	1	1	1
13	2	2	2
14	3	3	2
15	1	1	1
16	3	3	2
17	1	1	1
18	4	3	2
19	3	3	2
20	2	2	2

these 19 clusters. The two cases, respondents 14 and 16, that have been combined at this stage have no blank (white) space separating them. Row number 18 corresponds to the next stage, with 18 clusters. At this stage, respondents 2 and 13 are grouped together. Thus, at this stage there are 18 clusters; 16 of them consist of individual respondents, and two contain two respondents each. Each subsequent step leads to the formation of a new cluster in one of three ways: (1) two individual cases are grouped together, (2) a case is joined to an already existing cluster, or (3) two clusters are grouped together.

Another graphic device that is useful in displaying clustering results is the dendrogram (see Figure 20.8). The dendrogram is read from left to right. Vertical lines represent clusters that are joined together. The position of the line on the scale indicates the distances at which clusters were joined. Because many distances in the early stages are of similar magnitude, it is difficult to tell the sequence in which some of the early clusters are formed. It is clear, however, that in the last two stages, the distances at which the clusters are being combined are large. This information is useful in deciding on the number of clusters (see the next section).

It is also possible to obtain information on cluster membership of cases if the number of clusters is specified. Although this information can be discerned from the icicle plot, a tabular display is helpful. Table 20.2 contains the cluster membership for the cases, depending on whether the final solution contains two, three, or four clusters. Information of this type can be obtained for any number of clusters and is useful for deciding on the number of clusters.

Deciding on the Number of Clusters

A major issue in cluster analysis is deciding on the number of clusters. Although there are no hard and fast rules, some guidelines are available.

1. Theoretical, conceptual, or practical considerations may suggest a certain number of clusters. For example, if the purpose of clustering is to identify market segments, management may want a particular number of clusters.
2. In hierarchical clustering, the distances at which clusters are combined can be used as criteria. This information can be obtained from the agglomeration schedule or from the dendrogram. In our case, we see from the agglomeration schedule in Table 20.2 that the value in the "coefficient" column suddenly more than doubles between stages 17 and 18.

FIGURE 20.8

Dendrogram Using Ward's Procedure

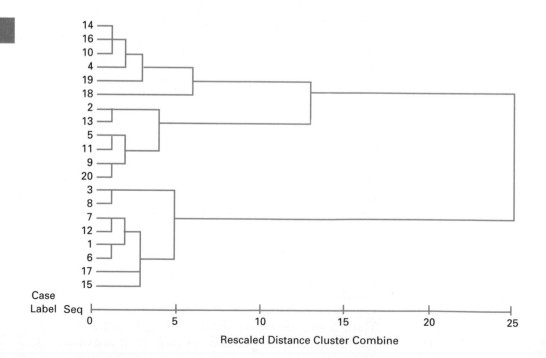

Case
Label Seq

Rescaled Distance Cluster Combine

Likewise, at the last two stages of the dendrogram in Figure 20.8, the clusters are being combined at large distances. Therefore, it appears that a three-cluster solution is appropriate.

3. In nonhierarchical clustering, the ratio of total within-group variance to between-group variance can be plotted against the number of clusters. The point at which an elbow or a sharp bend occurs indicates an appropriate number of clusters. Increasing the number of clusters beyond this point is usually not worthwhile.

4. The relative sizes of the clusters should be meaningful. In Table 20.2, by making a simple frequency count of cluster membership, we see that a three-cluster solution results in clusters with eight, six, and six elements. If we go to a four-cluster solution, however, the sizes of the clusters are eight, six, five, and one. It is not meaningful to have a cluster with only one case, so a three-cluster solution is preferable in this situation.

Interpreting and Profiling the Clusters

Interpreting and profiling clusters involves examining the cluster centroids. The centroids represent the mean values of the objects contained in the cluster on each of the variables. The centroids enable us to describe each cluster by assigning it a name or label. If the clustering program does not print this information, it may be obtained through discriminant analysis. Table 20.3 gives the centroids or mean values for each cluster in our example. Cluster 1 has relatively high values on variables V_1 (Shopping is fun) and V_3 (I combine shopping with eating out). It also has a low value on V_5 (I don't care about shopping). Hence cluster 1 could be labeled "fun-loving and concerned shoppers." This cluster consists of cases 1, 3, 6, 7, 8, 12, 15, and 17. Cluster 2 is just the opposite, with low values on V_1 and V_3 and a high value on V_5, and this cluster could be labeled "apathetic shoppers." Members of cluster 2 are cases 2, 5, 9, 11, 13, and 20. Cluster 3 has high values on V_2 (Shopping upsets my budget), V_4 (I try to get the best buys while shopping), and V_6 (You can save a lot of money by comparing prices). Thus, this cluster could be labeled "economical shoppers." Cluster 3 is composed of cases 4, 10, 14, 16, 18, and 19.

It is often helpful to profile the clusters in terms of variables that were not used for clustering, such as demographic, psychographic, product usage, media usage, or other variables. For example, the clusters may have been derived based on benefits sought. Further profiling may be done in terms of demographic and psychographic variables to target marketing efforts for each cluster. The variables that significantly differentiate between clusters can be identified via discriminant analysis and one-way analysis of variance.

Assessing Reliability and Validity

Given the several judgments entailed in cluster analysis, no clustering solution should be accepted without some assessment of its reliability and validity. Formal procedures for assessing the reliability and validity of clustering solutions are complex and not fully defensible.[14] Hence, we omit them here. The following procedures, however, provide adequate checks on the quality of clustering results.

TABLE 20.3 *Cluster Centroids*	Cluster Number	Means of Variables					
		V_1	V_2	V_3	V_4	V_5	V_6
	1	5.750	3.625	6.000	3.125	1.750	3.875
	2	1.667	3.000	1.833	3.500	5.500	3.333
	3	3.500	5.833	3.333	6.000	3.500	6.000

1. Perform cluster analysis on the same data using different distance measures. Compare the results across measures to determine the stability of the solutions.
2. Use different methods of clustering and compare the results.
3. Split the data randomly into halves. Perform clustering separately on each half. Compare cluster centroids across the two subsamples.
4. Delete variables randomly. Perform clustering based on the reduced set of variables. Compare the results with those obtained by clustering based on the entire set of variables.
5. In nonhierarchical clustering, the solution may depend on the order of cases in the data set. Make multiple runs using different order of cases until the solution stabilizes.

We further illustrate hierarchical clustering with a study of differences in marketing strategy among U.S., Japanese, and British firms.

EXAMPLE
It Is a Small World

Data for a study of U.S., Japanese, and British competitors were obtained from detailed personal interviews with chief executives and top marketing decision makers for defined product groups in 90 companies. To control for market differences, the methodology was based upon matching 30 British companies with their major American and Japanese competitors in the British market. The study involved 30 triads of companies, each composed of a British, U.S., and Japanese business that competed directly with one another.

Most of the data on the characteristics of the companies' performance, strategy, and organization were collected on five-point semantic differential scales. The first stage of the analysis involved factor analysis of variables describing the firms' strategies and marketing activities. The factor scores were used to identify groups of similar companies using Ward's hierarchical clustering routine. A six-cluster solution was developed.

Strategic Clusters

CLUSTER	I	II	III	IV	V	VI
Name	Innovators	Quality Marketeers	Price Promoters	Product Marketeers	Mature Marketeers	Aggressive Pushers
Size	22	11	14	13	13	17
Successful (%)	55	100	36	38	77	41
Nationality (%):						
Japanese	59	46	22	31	15	18
American	18	36	14	31	54	53
British	23	18	64	38	31	29

Membership in the six clusters was then interpreted against the original performance, strategy, and organizational variables. All the clusters contained some successful companies, although some contained significantly more than others. The clusters lent support to the hypothesis that successful companies were similar irrespective of nationality, since U.S., British, and Japanese companies were found in all the clusters. There was, however, a preponderance of Japanese companies in the more successful clusters and a predominance of British companies in the two least successful clusters. Apparently, Japanese companies do not deploy strategies that are unique to them; rather, more of them pursue strategies that work effectively in the British market.

The findings indicate that there are generic strategies that describe successful companies irrespective of their industry. Three successful strategies can be identified. The first is the quality marketeers' strategy. These companies have strengths in marketing and research and development. They concentrate their technical developments on achieving high quality rather than pure innovation. These companies are characterized by entrepreneurial organizations, long-range planning, and well-communicated sense of mission. The second generic strategy is that of the innovators, who are weaker on advanced R & D but are entrepreneurial and driven by a quest for innovation. The last successful group is the mature marketeers, who are highly profit-oriented and have in-depth marketing skills. All three appear to consist of highly marketing-oriented businesses.[15] ◆

APPLICATIONS OF NONHIERARCHICAL CLUSTERING

We illustrate the nonhierarchical procedure using the data in Table 20.1 and an optimizing partitioning method. Based on the results of hierarchical clustering, a three-cluster solution was prespecified. The results are presented in Table 20.4. The initial cluster centers are the values of the first three cases. The classification cluster centers are interim centers used for the assignment of cases. Each case is assigned to the nearest classification cluster center. The classification centers are updated until the stopping criteria are reached. The final cluster centers represent the variable means for the cases in the final clusters.

Table 20.4 also displays cluster membership and the distance between each case and its classification center. Note that the cluster memberships given in Table 20.2 (hierarchical clustering) and Table 20.4 (nonhierarchical clustering) are identical. (Cluster 1 of Table 20.2 is labeled cluster 3 in Table 20.4, and cluster 3 of Table 20.2

TABLE 20.4				
Results of Nonhierarchical Clustering				

Initial Cluster Centers

Cluster	V_1	V_2	V_3	V_4
1	4.0000	6.0000	3.0000	7.0000
2	2.0000	3.0000	2.0000	4.0000
3	7.0000	2.0000	6.0000	4.0000

Cluster	V_5	V_6
1	2.0000	7.0000
2	7.0000	2.0000
3	1.0000	3.0000

Classification Cluster Centers

Cluster	V_1	V_2	V_3	V_4
1	3.8135	5.8992	3.2522	6.4891
2	1.8507	3.0234	1.8327	3.7864
3	6.3558	2.8356	6.1576	3.6736

Cluster	V_5	V_6
1	2.5149	6.6957
2	6.4436	2.5056
3	1.3047	3.2010

(continued)

TABLE 20.4
(continued)

Case Listing of Cluster Membership

Case ID	Cluster	Distance
1	3	1.780
2	2	2.254
3	3	1.174
4	1	1.882
5	2	2.525
6	3	2.340
7	3	1.862
8	3	1.410
9	2	1.843
10	1	2.112
11	2	1.923
12	3	2.400
13	2	3.382
14	1	1.772
15	3	3.605
16	1	2.137
17	3	3.760
18	1	4.421
19	1	0.853
20	2	0.813

Final Cluster Centers

Cluster	V_1	V_2	V_3	V_4
1	3.5000	5.8333	3.3333	6.0000
2	1.6667	3.0000	1.8333	3.5000
3	5.7500	3.6250	6.0000	3.1250

Cluster	V_5	V_6
1	3.5000	6.0000
2	5.5000	3.3333
3	1.7500	3.8750

Distances between Final Cluster Centers

Cluster	1	2	3
1	0.0000		
2	5.5678	0.0000	
3	5.7353	6.9944	0.0000

Analysis of Variance

Variable	Cluster MS	df	Error MS	df	F	p
V_1	29.1083	2	0.6078	17.0	47.8879	.000
V_2	13.5458	2	0.6299	17.0	21.5047	.000
V_3	31.3917	2	0.8333	17.0	37.6700	.000
V_4	15.7125	2	0.7279	17.0	21.5848	.000
V_5	24.1500	2	0.7353	17.0	32.8440	.000
V_6	12.1708	2	1.0711	17.0	11.3632	.001

Number of Cases in each Cluster

Cluster	Unweighted Cases	Weighted Cases
1	6.0	6.0
2	6.0	6.0
3	8.0	8.0
Missing	0.0	
Total	20.0	20.0

is labeled cluster 1 in Table 20.4.) The distances between the final cluster centers indicate that the pairs of clusters are well separated. The univariate F test for each clustering variable is presented. These F tests are only descriptive. Because the cases or objects are systematically assigned to clusters to maximize differences on the clustering variables, the resulting probabilities should not be interpreted as testing the null hypothesis of no differences among clusters.

The following example of hospital choice further illustrates nonhierarchical clustering.

EXAMPLE

Segmentation with Surgical Precision _____

Cluster analysis was used to classify respondents who preferred hospitals for inpatient care to identify hospital preference segments. The clustering was based on the reasons respondents gave for preferring a hospital. The demographic profiles of the grouped respondents were compared to learn whether the segments could be identified efficiently.

Quick Cluster (SPSS), a minimum variance clustering method, was used for grouping the respondents based on their answers to the hospital preference items. The squared euclidean distances between all clustering variables were minimized. Because different individuals perceive scales of importance differently, each individual's ratings were normalized before clustering. The results indicated that the respondents could be best classified into four clusters. The cross-validation procedure for cluster analysis was run twice, on halves of the total sample.

As expected, the four groups differed substantially by their distributions and average responses to the reasons for their hospital preferences. The names assigned to the four groups reflected the demographic characteristics and reasons for hospital preferences: old-fashioned, affluent, value conscious, and professional want-it-alls.[16] ◆

Cluster analysis was used to classify consumers who preferred hospitals for inpatient care as old-fashioned, affluent, value conscious, or professional want-it-alls. ◆ Cathy Cheney/Stock, Boston.

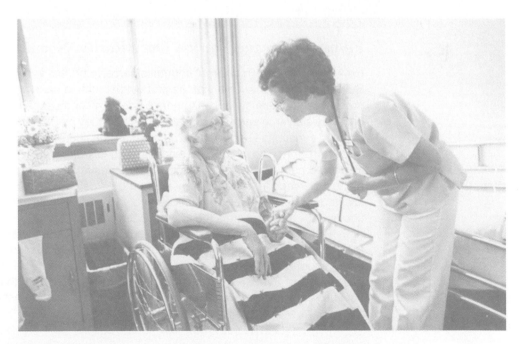

CLUSTERING VARIABLES

Sometimes cluster analysis is also used for clustering variables to identify homogeneous groups. In this instance, the units used for analysis are the variables, and the distance measures are computed for all pairs of variables. For example, the correlation coefficient, either the absolute value or with the sign, can be used as a measure of similarity (the opposite of distance) between variables.

Hierarchical clustering of variables can aid in the identification of unique variables, or variables that make a unique contribution to the data. Clustering can also be used to reduce the number of variables. Associated with each cluster is a linear combination of the variables in the cluster, called the *cluster component*. A large set of variables can often be replaced by the set of cluster components with little loss of information. A given number of cluster components does not generally explain as much variance as the same number of principal components, however. Why, then, should the clustering of variables be used? Cluster components are usually easier to interpret than the principal components, even if the latter are rotated.[17] We illustrate the clustering of variables with an example from advertising research. A study was conducted to identify feelings that are precipitated by advertising. A total of 655 feelings were reduced to a set of 180 that were judged by respondents to be most likely to be stimulated by advertising. This group was clustered on the basis of judgments of similarity between feelings resulting in 31 feeling clusters. These were divided into 16 positive and 15 negative clusters.[18]

Cluster analysis, particularly clustering of objects, is also frequently used in international marketing research (Research in Practice 20.1[19]) and could also be useful in researching ethical evaluations (Research in Practice 20.2[20]).

RESEARCH IN PRACTICE 20.1

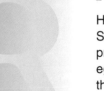

Perceived Product Parity: Once Rarity, Now Reality

How do consumers in different countries perceive brands in different product categories? Surprisingly, the answer is that the product perception parity rate is quite high. Perceived product parity means that consumers perceive all or most of the brands in a product category as similar to each other or at par. A new study by BBDO Worldwide shows that two-thirds of consumers surveyed in 28 countries considered brands in 13 product categories to be at parity. The product categories ranged from airlines to credit cards to coffee. Perceived parity averaged 63% for all categories in all countries. The Japanese have the highest perception of parity across all product categories at 99% and Colombians the lowest at 28%. Viewed by product category, credit cards have the highest parity perception at 76% and cigarettes the lowest at 52%.

BBDO clustered the countries based on product parity perceptions to arrive at clusters that exhibited similar levels and patterns of parity perceptions. The highest perception parity figure came from the Asia/Pacific region (83%), which included Australia, Japan, Malaysia, and South Korea, and also France. It is no surprise that France was in this list because for most products, French consumers use highly emotional, visual advertising

(continued)

that is feelings-oriented. The next cluster was U.S.-influenced markets (65%), which included Argentina, Canada, Hong Kong, Kuwait, Mexico, Singapore, and the United States. The third cluster, primarily European countries (60%) included Austria, Belgium, Denmark, Italy, the Netherlands, South Africa, Spain, the United Kingdom, and Germany.

What all this means is that to differentiate the product or brand, advertising can not just focus on product performance but must also relate the product to the person's life in an important way. Also, a much greater marketing effort will be required in the Asia/Pacific region and in France to differentiate the brand from competition and to establish a unique image. A big factor in this growing parity is, of course, the emergence of the global market.

RESEARCH IN PRACTICE 20.2

Clustering Marketing Professionals Based on Ethical Evaluations

Cluster analysis can be used to explain the differences in ethical perceptions by using a multiitem, multidimensional scale developed to evaluate different ethical situations. One such scale, consisting of 29 items which tap five dimensions, was developed by Reidenbach and Robin. In responding to this scale, a respondent will read about certain ethical situations (for example, a marketing researcher who provided proprietary information related to one client to a second client) and evaluate them on the 29-item ethics scale. The scale is a semantic differential with bi-polar items such as just versus unjust, violates versus does not violate an unwritten contract.

Two important questions should be investigated by clustering respondents based on these 29 items. First, how do the clusters differ with respect to the five ethical dimensions that comprise the scale: justice, relativist, egoism, utilitarianism, and deontology (see Chapter 24). Second, what types of firms comprise each cluster? The clusters could be described in terms of industry classification (SIC), firm size, firm sales, market share, and marketing orientation. This type of analysis should indicate the nature of firms that use specific dimensions to evaluate ethical situations. For instance, does the cluster high on utilitarianism contain more firms with high sales than firms with low sales?

COMPUTER APPLICATIONS

The mainframe and microcomputer clustering programs are similar for SPSS, SAS, and BMDP. In SPSS, the main program for hierarchical clustering of objects or cases is CLUSTER. Different distance measures can be computed, and all the hierarchical clustering procedures discussed here are available. For nonhierarchical clustering, the QUICK CLUSTER program can be used. This program is particularly helpful for clustering a large number of cases. All the default options will result in a k-means clustering. To cluster variables, the distance measures should be computed across variables using the PROXIMITIES program. This proximity matrix can be read into CLUSTER to obtain a grouping of the variables.

In SAS, the CLUSTER program can be used for the hierarchical clustering of cases or objects. All the clustering procedures discussed here are available, as well as some additional ones. Nonhierarchical clustering of cases or objects can be accomplished using FASTCLUS. For clustering of variables, the VARCLUS program can be used. Dendrograms are not automatically computed but can be obtained using the TREE program.

In the BMDP package, the main program for the clustering of cases using the hierarchical procedures is 2M. Although this program allows the use of several distance measures, it permits the use of only single linkage, centroid, or k nearest-neighbor clustering procedures. For nonhierarchical clustering, the KM program can be used for performing k-means clustering of cases. Clustering of variables can be done using the 1M program. It permits the use of single linkage, complete linkage, and average linkage procedures. A special program, 3M, is available for constructing block clusters for categorical data. Subsets of cases are grouped into clusters that are alike for subsets of variables.[21]

SUMMARY

Cluster analysis is used for classifying objects or cases, and sometimes variables, into relatively homogeneous groups. The groups or clusters are suggested by the data and are not defined a priori.

The variables on which the clustering is based should be selected based on past research, theory, the hypotheses being tested, or the judgment of the researcher. An appropriate measure of distance or similarity should be selected. The most commonly used measure is the euclidean distance or its square.

Clustering procedures may be hierarchical or nonhierarchical. Hierarchical clustering is characterized by the development of a hierarchy or treelike structure. Hierarchical methods can be agglomerative or divisive. Agglomerative methods consist of linkage methods, variance methods, and centroid methods. Linkage methods are composed of single linkage, complete linkage, and average linkage. A commonly used variance method is the Ward's procedure. The nonhierarchical methods are frequently referred to as k-means clustering. These methods can be classified as sequential threshold, parallel threshold, and optimizing partitioning. Hierarchical and nonhierarchical methods can be used in tandem. The choice of a clustering procedure and the choice of a distance measure are interrelated.

The number of clusters may be based on theoretical, conceptual, or practical considerations. In hierarchical clustering, the distances at which the clusters are being combined is an important criterion. The relative sizes of the clusters should be meaningful. The clusters should be interpreted in terms of cluster centroids. It is often helpful to profile the clusters in terms of variables that were not used for clustering. The reliability and validity of the clustering solutions may be assessed in different ways.[22]

ACRONYMS

The steps involved and the salient concepts in clustering may be summarized by the acronym CLUSTERING:

C   entroid methods
L   inkage methods
U   nderlying problem: selection of clustering variables
S   imilarity or distance measures
T   ype of clustering method: hierarchical versus nonhierarchical
E   rror sums of squares or variance methods
R   eliability and validity assessment
I   nterpreting and profiling clusters
N   umber of clusters
G   raphical aids: dendrogram and icicle plot

EXERCISES

QUESTIONS

1. Discuss the similarity and difference between cluster analysis and discriminant analysis.
2. What are some of the uses of cluster analysis in marketing?
3. Briefly define the following terms: dendrogram, icicle plot, agglomeration schedule, and cluster membership.
4. What is the most commonly used measure of similarity in cluster analysis?
5. Present a classification of clustering procedures.
6. Why is the average linkage method usually preferred to single linkage and complete linkage?
7. What are the two major disadvantages of nonhierarchical clustering procedures?
8. What guidelines are available for deciding the number of clusters?
9. What is involved in the interpretation of clusters?
10. What are some of the additional variables used for profiling the clusters?
11. Describe some procedures available for assessing the quality of clustering solutions.
12. How is cluster analysis used to group variables?

PROBLEMS

1. Are the following statements true or false?
   a. Hierarchical and nonhierarchical clustering methods always produce different results.
   b. One should always standardize data before performing cluster analysis.
   c. Small distance coefficients in the agglomeration schedule imply that dissimilar cases are being merged.
   d. It does not matter which distance measure you use; the clustering solutions are essentially similar.
   e. It is advisable to analyze the same data set using different clustering procedures.

COMPUTER EXERCISES

1. Analyze the data in Table 20.1 using the following methods: (a) single linkage, (b) complete linkage, and (c) method of centroid. Use SPSS or SAS. Compare your results with those given in Table 20.2.

NOTES

1. Dwight J. Shelton, "Birds of a Geodemographic Feather Flock Together," *Marketing News* (August 28, 1987): 13.

2. For a recent application of cluster analysis, see George S. Day and Prakash Nedungadi, "Managerial Representation of Competitive Advantage," *Journal of Marketing* 58 (April 1994): 31–44.

3. Overlapping clustering methods that permit an object to be grouped into more than one cluster are also available. See P. Arabie, J. D. Carroll, W. DeSarbo, and J. Wind, "Overlapping Clustering: A New Method for Product Positioning," *Journal of Marketing Research* 18 (August 1981): 310–17; and P. Arabie and J. D. Carroll, "MAPCLUS: A Hierarchical Programming Approach to Fitting the ADCLUS Model," *Psychometrika* (June 1980): 211–35.

4. Excellent discussions on the various aspects of cluster analysis may be found in M. S. Aldenderfer and R. K. Blashfield, *Cluster Analysis* (Beverly Hills: Sage Publications, 1984); B. Everitt, *Cluster Analysis*, 2nd ed. (New York: Halsted Press, 1980); and H. C. Romsburg, *Cluster Analysis for Researchers* (Belmont, CA: Lifetime Learning Publications, 1984).

5. These applications of cluster analysis in marketing have been identified by G. Punj and D. Stewart, "Cluster Analysis in Marketing Research: Review and Suggestions for Application," *Journal of Marketing Research* 20 (May 1983): 134–48.

6. For use of cluster analysis for segmentation, see "Using Cluster Analysis for Segmentation," *Sawtooth News* 10 (Winter 1994–95): 6–7.

7. George P. Moschis and Daniel C. Bello, "Decision-Making Patterns among International Vacationers: A Cross-Cultural Perspective," *Psychology & Marketing* (Spring 1987): 75–89.

8. M. S. Aldenderfer and R. K. Blashfield, *Cluster Analysis* (Beverly Hills: Sage Publications, 1984), pp. 7–16.

9. For a detailed discussion on the different measures of similarity, and formulas for computing them, see H. C. Romsburg, *Cluster Analysis for Researchers* (Belmont, CA: Lifetime Learning Publications, 1984).

10. Joseph F. Hair, Jr., Ralph E. Anderson, Ronald L. Tatham, and William C. Black, *Multivariate Data Analysis with Readings*, 4th ed. (Englewood Cliffs, NJ: Prentice Hall, 1995), pp. 420–83; and Marija J. Normors, *SPSS-X Advanced Statistics Guide* (Chicago: SPSS Inc., 1988); and Marija J. Normors, *SPSS Guide to Data Analysis for Release 4.0* (Chicago: SPSS Inc., 1990).

11. For further discussion of the issues involved in standardization, see H. C. Romsburg, *Cluster Analysis for Researchers* (Belmont, CA: Lifelong Learning Publications, 1984), pp. 77–91.

12. G. Milligan, "An Examination of the Effect of Six Types of Error Perturbation on Fifteen Clustering Algorithms," *Psychometrika* 45 (September 1980): 325–42.

13. G. Punj and D. Stewart, "Cluster Analysis in Marketing Research: Reviews and Suggestions for Application," *Journal of Marketing Research* 20 (May 1983): 134–48.

14. For a formal discussion of reliability, validity, and significance testing in cluster analysis, see G. Ray Funkhouser, "A Note on the Reliability of Certain Clustering Algorithms," *Journal of Marketing Research* 30 (February 1983): 99–102; T. D. Klastorin, "Assessing Cluster Analysis Results," *Journal of Marketing Research* 20 (February 1983): 92–98; and S. J. Arnold, "A Test for Clusters," *Journal of Marketing Research* 16 (November 1979): 545–51.

15. Peter Doyle, John Saunders, and Veronica Wong, "International Marketing Strategies and Organizations: A Study of U.S., Japanese, and British Competitors," in Paul Bloom, Russ Winer, Harold H. Kassarjian, Debra L. Scammon, Bart Weitz, Robert E. Spekman, Vijay Mahajan, and Michael Levy (eds.), *Enhancing Knowledge Development in Marketing*, series no. 55 (Chicago: American Marketing Association, 1989), pp. 100–104.

16. Arch G. Woodside, Robert L. Nielsen, Fred Walters, and Gale D. Muller, "Preference Segmentation of Health Care Services: The Old-Fashioneds, Value Conscious, Affluents, and Professional Want-It-Alls," *Journal of Health Care Marketing* (June 1988): 14–24.

17. *SAS User's Guide: Statistics*, 5th ed. (Cary, NC: SAS Institute, 1985); and *SAS Procedures*, V 6.06 (Cary, NC: SAS Institute, 1990).

18. David A. Aaker, Douglas M. Stayman, and Richard Vezina, "Identifying Feelings Elicited by Advertising," *Psychology & Marketing* (Spring 1988): 1–16.

19. Nancy Giges, "World's Product Parity Perception High," *Advertising Age* (June 20, 1988).

20. R. E. Reidenbach and D. P. Robin, "Some Initial Steps toward Improving the Measurement of Ethical Evaluations of Marketing Activities," *Journal of Business Ethics* 7 (1988): 871–79.

21. For a review of other programs for cluster analysis, see R. K. Blashfield and L. Morey, "Cluster Analysis Software," in P. Krishnaiah and L. Kanal (eds.), *Handbook of Statistics*, vol. 2 (Amsterdam: New Holland, 1982), pp. 245–66.

22. The assistance of James Agarwal with the international marketing research example, the assistance of Mark Leach and Gina Miller in writing the ethics section, and the assistance of Mark Peterson in writing the computer applications section is gratefully acknowledged.

CHAPTER TWENTY-ONE

Multidimensional Scaling and Conjoint Analysis

Multidimensional scaling represents the perceptions and preferences of respondents geometrically in a spatial map. Conjoint analysis determines the relative importance consumers attach to salient attributes and the utilities they attach to the levels of attributes.

OBJECTIVES

After reading this chapter, the student should be able to:

1. Discuss the basic concept and scope of multidimensional scaling (MDS) in marketing research and describe its various applications.

2. Describe the steps involved in multidimensional scaling of perception data including formulating the problem, obtaining input data, selecting an MDS procedure, deciding on the number of dimensions, labeling the dimensions and interpreting the configuration, and assessing reliability and validity.

3. Explain the multidimensional scaling of preference data and distinguish between internal and external analysis of preferences.

4. Explain correspondence analysis and discuss its advantages and disadvantages.

5. Understand the relationship between MDS, discriminant analysis, and factor analysis.

6. Discuss the basic concepts of conjoint analysis, contrast it with MDS, and discuss its various applications.

7. Describe the procedure for conducting conjoint analysis including formulating the problem, constructing the stimuli, deciding the form of input data, selecting a conjoint analysis procedure, interpreting the results, and assessing reliability and validity.

8. Define the concept of hybrid conjoint analysis and explain how it simplifies the data collection task.

OVERVIEW

This final chapter on data analysis presents two related techniques for analyzing consumer perceptions and preferences: multidimensional scaling (MDS) and conjoint analysis. We outline and illustrate the steps involved in conducting MDS and discuss the relationships among MDS, factor analysis, and discriminant analysis. Then we describe conjoint analysis and present a step-by-step procedure for conducting it. We also provide brief coverage of hybrid conjoint models.

We begin with examples illustrating MDS and conjoint analysis.

DEPARTMENT STORE PATRONAGE PROJECT
Multidimensional Scaling

In the department store project, respondents' evaluations of the ten stores on each of the eight factors of the choice criteria were used to derive similarity measures between the stores. Euclidean distances were calculated between each pair of stores. These data were analyzed using multidimensional scaling to obtain spatial maps that represented the respondents' perceptions of the ten stores. In one such map, the dimensions were identified as prestigious versus discount stores, and local versus national store chains. Stores that competed directly with each other (e.g., Saks Fifth Avenue and Neiman Marcus) were located close together in the perceptual space. These perceptual maps were used to gain insights into the competitive positioning of the ten department stores. ◆

EXAMPLE
Colas Collide

In a survey, respondents were asked to rank-order all the possible pairs of ten brands of soft drinks in terms of their similarity. These data were analyzed via multidimensional scaling and resulted in the spatial representation of soft drinks on page 695.

From other information obtained in the questionnaire, the horizontal axis was labeled "cola flavor." Tab was perceived to be the most cola-flavored and 7-Up the least cola-flavored. The vertical axis was labeled "dietness," with Tab being perceived to be the most dietetic and Dr. Pepper the least dietetic. Note that Coke, Pepsi, and Coke Classic were perceived to be very similar as indicated by their closeness in the perceptual map. Close similarity was also perceived between 7-Up and Slice, Diet 7-Up and Diet Slice, and Tab and Diet Pepsi. Notice that Dr. Pepper is perceived to be relatively dissimilar to the other brands. Such MDS maps are very useful in understanding the competitive structure of the soft drink market.[1] ◆

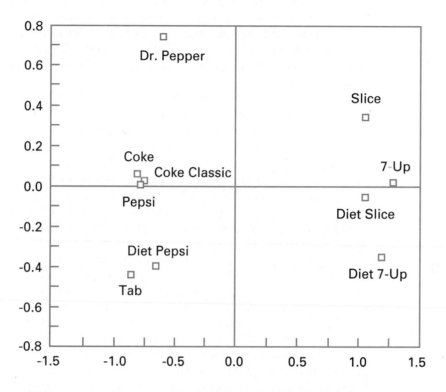

MDS has been used to understand consumers' perceptions of soft drinks and the competitive structure of the soft drink market. ◆ Teri Stratford.

EXAMPLE
Complete Credit Card Features Identified by Conjoint Analysis

The Complete MasterCard—a "cobranded" card with Ameritech, one of the seven regional Bell telephone companies—resulted from the adroit use of focus group research and conjoint analysis research. The Complete MasterCard became available to Ameritech's ten million residential customers in Illinois, Indiana, Michigan, Ohio, and Wisconsin recently.

"With the increased competition in the calling card market, we needed to offer our customers the convenience of a multipurpose card in order to meet their expectations," Rich Bialek, director of Ameritech's credit card services, said. "We wanted market research to help us determine what mix of features would make our card most appealing to customers."

In the first round of eight focus group sessions with users of both credit cards and calling cards, Kennedy Research Inc., of Grand Rapids, Michigan focused on the acceptance and expectations for the concept of a credit card with a calling card feature. In the second round of focus groups, Kennedy researchers probed to identify a new card's features to be studied in the subsequent conjoint analysis phase.

During the conjoint analysis study, Kennedy recruited 500 Ameritech customers—about 100 in each of the five states served—to participate in a self-administered, computerized questionnaire taking 30 minutes. Kennedy included 15 features of a credit and calling card, such as annual fee (four options), interest rate (three options), and card name (seven options). All questions gave the respondents two choices. For example, "What is more important, a card with no annual fee or a card that offers a variable interest rate?"

"By the time participants went through a series of 50 or so questions, they weren't sure what they wanted, " Jamal Din, Kennedy's conjoint designer said. "The computer was able to assign relative values to the various features, based on each individual's answers, and then design the one card that would most likely be irresistible to that individual."

As a result of the study, the card received the name "Ameritech Complete MasterCard." The card featured no annual fee and an annual automatic rebate of 10%—paid by the sponsoring bank—on most local and long-distance calls made with the card. In addition, the card included a tiered interest rate with a 25-day grace period. The usefulness of conjoint analysis in designing the Ameritech Complete MasterCard is demonstrated by the gratifying customer response to the card.[2] ◆

The first two examples illustrate the derivation and use of perceptual maps, which lie at the heart of MDS. The Ameritech Complete MasterCard example involves tradeoffs respondents make while evaluating alternatives. The conjoint analysis procedure is based on these tradeoffs.

BASIC CONCEPTS IN MULTIDIMENSIONAL SCALING (MDS)

multidimensional scaling (MDS) A class of procedures for representing perceptions and preferences of respondents spatially by means of a visual display.

Multidimensional scaling (MDS) is a class of procedures for representing perceptions and preferences of respondents spatially by means of a visual display. Perceived or psychological relationships among stimuli are represented as geometric relationships among points in a multidimensional space. These geometric representations are often called spatial maps. The axes of the spatial map are assumed to denote the psychological bases or underlying dimensions respondents use to form perceptions and preferences for stimuli.[3] MDS has been used in marketing to identify the following:

1. The number and nature of dimensions consumers use to perceive different brands in the marketplace
2. The positioning of current brands on these dimensions
3. The positioning of consumers' ideal brand on these dimensions

Information provided by MDS has been used for a variety of marketing applications, including:

- *Image measurement.* The customers' and noncustomers' perceptions of the firm with the firm's perceptions of itself can be compared.
- *Market segmentation.* Brands and consumers can be positioned in the same space and thus groups of consumers with relatively homogeneous perceptions can be identified.
- *New product development.* Gaps in a spatial map indicate potential opportunities for positioning new products. MDS can be used to evaluate new product concepts and existing brands on a test basis to determine how consumers perceive the new concepts. The proportion of preferences for each new product is one indicator of its success.
- *Assessing advertising effectiveness.* Spatial maps can be used to determine whether advertising has been successful in achieving the desired brand positioning.
- *Pricing analysis.* Spatial maps developed with and without pricing information can be compared to determine the impact of pricing.
- *Channel decisions.* Judgments on compatibility of brands with different retail outlets could lead to spatial maps useful for making channel decisions.
- *Attitude scale construction.* MDS techniques can be used to develop the appropriate dimensionality and configuration of the attitude space.

STATISTICS AND TERMS ASSOCIATED WITH MULTIDIMENSIONAL SCALING

The important statistics and terms associated with MDS include the following:

Similarity judgments. Similarity judgments are ratings on all possible pairs of brands or other stimuli in terms of their similarity using a Likert-type scale.

Preference rankings. Preference rankings are rank orderings of the brands or other stimuli from the most preferred to the least preferred. They are normally obtained from the respondents.

Stress. Stress is a lack-of-fit measure; higher values of stress indicate poorer fits.

R-square. R-square is a squared correlation index that indicates the proportion of variance of the optimally scaled data that can be accounted for by the MDS procedure.

Spatial map. Perceived relationships among brands or other stimuli are represented as geometric relationships among points in a multidimensional space called a spatial map.

Coordinates. Coordinates indicate the positioning of a brand or a stimulus in a spatial map.

Unfolding. The representation of both brands and respondents as points in the same space is referred to as unfolding.

CONDUCTING MULTIDIMENSIONAL SCALING

Figure 21.1 shows the steps in MDS. The researcher must formulate the MDS problem carefully because a variety of data may be used as input into MDS. The researcher must also determine an appropriate form in which data should be obtained and select an MDS procedure for analyzing the data. An important aspect of the solution involves determining the number of dimensions for the spatial map. Also, the axes of the map should be labeled and the derived configuration interpreted. Finally, the researcher must assess

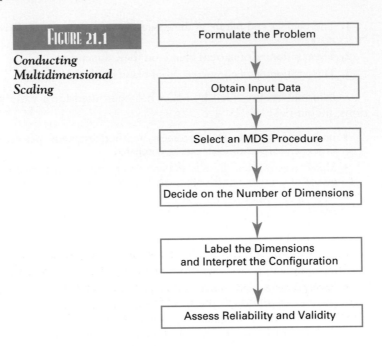

FIGURE 21.1

Conducting Multidimensional Scaling

the quality of the results obtained.[4] We describe each of these steps, beginning with problem formulation.

Formulating the Problem

Formulating the problem requires that the researcher specify the purpose for which the MDS results would be used and select the brands or other stimuli to be included in the analysis. The number of brands or stimuli selected and the specific brands included determine the nature of the resulting dimensions and configurations. At a minimum, eight brands or stimuli should be included to obtain a well-defined spatial map. Including more than 25 brands is likely to be cumbersome and may result in respondent fatigue.

The decision regarding which specific brands or stimuli to include should be made carefully. Suppose that a researcher is interested in obtaining consumer perceptions of automobiles. If luxury automobiles are not included in the stimulus set, this dimension may not emerge in the results. The choice of the number and specific brands or stimuli to be included should be based on the statement of the marketing research problem, theory, and the judgment of the researcher.

Multidimensional scaling will be illustrated in the context of obtaining a spatial map for ten toothpaste brands. These brands are Aqua-Fresh, Crest, Colgate, Aim, Gleem, Macleans, Ultra Brite, Close Up, Pepsodent, and Dentagard. Given the list of brands, the next question, then, is, How should we obtain data on these ten brands?

Obtaining Input Data

As shown in Figure 21.2, input data obtained from the respondents may be related to perceptions or preferences. Perception data, which may be direct or derived, is discussed first.

Perception Data: Direct Approaches   In direct approaches to gathering perception data, respondents are asked to judge how similar or dissimilar various brands or stimuli are, using their own criteria. Respondents are often required to rate all possible pairs of

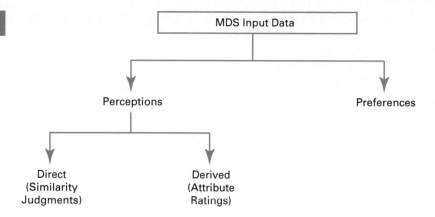

FIGURE 21.2

*Input Data
for Multidimensional
Scaling*

brands or stimuli in terms of similarity on a Likert scale. These data are referred to as similarity judgments. For example, similarity judgments on all the possible pairs of toothpaste brands may be obtained in the following manner:

	Very Dissimilar						Very Similar
Crest versus Colgate	1	2	3	4	5	6	7
Aqua-Fresh versus Crest	1	2	3	4	5	6	7
Crest versus Aim	1	2	3	4	5	6	7
.							
Colgate versus Aqua-Fresh	1	2	3	4	5	6	7

The number of pairs to be evaluated is $n(n-1)/2$, where n is the number of stimuli. Other procedures are also available. Respondents could be asked to rank-order all the possible pairs from the most similar to the least similar. In another method, the respondent rank-orders the brands in terms of their similarity to an anchor brand. Each brand, in turn, serves as the anchor.

In our example, the direct approach was adopted. Subjects were asked to provide similarity judgments for all 45 ($10 \times 9/2$) pairs of toothpaste brands, using a seven-point scale. The data obtained from one respondent are given in Table 21.1.

TABLE 21.1

Similarity Ratings of Toothpaste Brands

	Aqua-Fresh	Crest	Colgate	Aim	Gleem	Macleans	UltraBrite	Close Up	Pepsodent	Dentagard
Aqua-Fresh										
Crest	5									
Colgate	6	7								
Aim	4	6	6							
Gleem	2	3	4	5						
Macleans	3	3	4	4	5					
Ultra Brite	2	2	2	3	5	5				
Close Up	2	2	2	2	6	5	6			
Pepsodent	2	2	2	2	6	6	7	6		
Dentagard	1	2	4	2	4	3	3	4	3	

derived approaches In MDS, attribute-based approaches to collecting perception data requiring respondents to rate the stimuli on the identified attributes using semantic differential or Likert scales.

Perception Data: Derived Approaches   **Derived approaches** to collecting perception data are attribute-based approaches requiring the respondents to rate the brands or stimuli on the identified attributes using semantic differential or Likert scales.[5] For example, the different brands of toothpaste may be rated on attributes like these:

Whitens teeth	__ __ __ __ __ __ __ __ __ __ __	Does not whiten teeth
Prevents tooth decay	__ __ __ __ __ __ __ __ __ __ __	Does not prevent tooth decay
. . Pleasant tasting	__ __ __ __ __ __ __ __ __ __ __	Unpleasant tasting

Sometimes an ideal brand is also included in the stimulus set. The respondents are asked to evaluate their hypothetical ideal brand on the same set of attributes. If attribute ratings are obtained, a similarity measure (such as euclidean distance) is derived for each pair of brands.

Direct versus Derived Approaches   Direct approaches have the advantage that the researcher does not have to identify a set of salient attributes. Respondents make similarity judgments using their own criteria, as they would under normal circumstances. The disadvantages are that the criteria are influenced by the brands or stimuli being evaluated. If the various brands of automobiles being evaluated are in the same price range, then price will not emerge as an important factor. It may be difficult to determine before analysis if and how the individual respondent's judgments should be combined. Furthermore, it may be difficult to label the dimensions of the spatial map.

The advantage of the attribute-based approach is that it is easy to identify respondents with homogeneous perceptions. The respondents can be clustered based on the attribute ratings. It is also easier to label the dimensions. A disadvantage is that the researcher must identify all the salient attributes, a difficult task. The spatial map obtained depends on the attributes identified.

The direct approaches are more frequently used than the attribute-based approaches. It may, however, be best to use both these approaches in a complementary way. Direct similarity judgments may be used for obtaining the spatial map, and attribute ratings may be used as an aid to interpreting the dimensions of the perceptual map. Similar procedures are used for preference data.

Preference Data   Preference data order the brands or stimuli in terms of respondents' preference for some property. A common way in which such data are obtained is preference rankings. Respondents are required to rank the brands from the most preferred to the least preferred. Alternatively, respondents may be required to make paired comparisons and indicate which brand in a pair they prefer. Another method is to obtain preference ratings for the various brands. (The rank-order, paired comparison, and rating scales were discussed in Chapters 8 and 9 on scaling techniques.) When spatial maps are based on preference data, distance implies differences in preference. The configuration derived from preference data may differ greatly from that obtained from similarity data. Two brands may be perceived as different in a similarity map yet similar in a preference map, and vice versa. For example, Crest and Pepsodent may be perceived by a group of respondents as very different brands and thus appear far apart on a perception map. But these two brands may be about equally preferred and may appear close together on a preference map. We will continue using the perception data obtained in the toothpaste example to illustrate the MDS procedure and then consider the scaling of preference data.

Selecting an MDS Procedure

nonmetric MDS A type of multidimensional scaling which assumes that the input data are ordinal.

metric MDS A multidimensional scaling method that assumes that input data are metric.

Selecting a specific MDS procedure depends on whether perception or preference data are being scaled or whether the analysis requires both kinds of data. The nature of the input data is also a determining factor. **Nonmetric MDS** procedures assume that the input data are ordinal, but they result in metric output. The distances in the resulting spatial map may be assumed to be interval scaled. These procedures find, in a given dimensionality, a spatial map whose rank orders of estimated distances between brands or stimuli best preserve or reproduce the input rank orders. In contrast, **metric MDS** methods assume that input data are metric. Since the output is also metric, a stronger relationship between the output and input data is maintained, and the metric (interval or ratio) qualities of the input data are preserved. The metric and nonmetric methods produce similar results.[6]

Another factor influencing the selection of a procedure is whether the MDS analysis will be conducted at the individual respondent level or at an aggregate level. In individual-level analysis, the data are analyzed separately for each respondent, resulting in a spatial map for each respondent. Although individual-level analysis is useful from a research perspective, it is not appealing from a managerial standpoint. Marketing strategies are typically formulated at the segment or aggregate level, rather than at the individual level. If aggregate-level analysis is conducted, some assumptions must be made in aggregating individual data. Typically, it is assumed that all respondents use the same dimensions to evaluate the brands or stimuli, but that different respondents weight these common dimensions differentially.

The data of Table 21.1 were treated as rank ordered and scaled using a nonmetric procedure. Because these data were provided by one respondent, an individual-level analysis was conducted. Spatial maps were obtained in one to four dimensions, and then a decision on an appropriate number of dimensions was made. This decision is central to all MDS analyses; therefore, it is explored in greater detail in the following section.

Deciding on the Number of Dimensions

The objective in MDS is to obtain a spatial map that best fits the input data in the smallest number of dimensions. Spatial maps are computed in such a way that the fit improves as the number of dimensions increases, however. Therefore, a compromise has to be made. The fit of an MDS solution is commonly assessed by the stress measure. Stress is a lack-of-fit measure; higher values of stress indicate poorer fits. The following guidelines are suggested for determining the number of dimensions.

elbow criterion A plot of stress versus dimensionality used in MDS. The point at which an elbow or a sharp bend occurs indicates an appropriate dimensionality.

1. *A priori knowledge.* Theory or past research may suggest a particular number of dimensions.
2. *Interpretability of the spatial map.* Generally, it is difficult to interpret configurations or maps derived in more than three dimensions.
3. *Elbow criterion.* A plot of stress versus dimensionality should be examined. The points in this plot usually form a convex pattern, as shown in Figure 21.3. The point at which an elbow or a sharp bend occurs indicates an appropriate number of dimensions. Increasing the number of dimensions beyond this point is usually not worth the improvement in fit. This criterion for determining the number of dimensions is called the **elbow criterion**.

FIGURE 21.3

*Plot of Stress versus
Dimensionality*

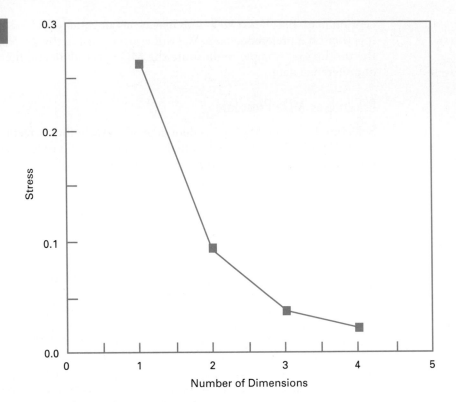

4. *Ease of use*. It is generally easier to work with two-dimensional maps or configurations than with those involving more dimensions.

5. *Statistical approaches*. For the sophisticated user, statistical approaches are also available for determining the dimensionality.[7]

Based on the plot of stress versus dimensionality (Figure 21.3), interpretability of the spatial map, and ease of use criteria, it was decided to retain a two-dimensional solution. This is shown in Figure 21.4.

Labeling the Dimensions and Interpreting the Configuration

Once a spatial map is developed, the dimensions must be labeled and the configuration interpreted. Labeling the dimensions requires subjective judgment on the part of the researcher. The following guidelines can assist in this task:

1. Even if direct similarity judgments are obtained, ratings of the brands on researcher-supplied attributes may still be collected. Using statistical methods such as regression, these attribute vectors may be fitted in the spatial map (see Figure 21.5). The axes may then be labeled for the attributes with which they are most closely aligned.

2. After providing direct similarity or preference data, the respondents may be asked to indicate the criteria they used in making their evaluations. These criteria may then be subjectively related to the spatial map to label the dimensions.

3. If possible, the respondents can be shown their spatial maps and asked to label the dimensions by inspecting the configurations.

4. If objective characteristics of the brands are available (e.g., horsepower or miles per gallon for automobiles), these could be used as an aid in interpreting the subjective dimensions of the spatial maps.

FIGURE 21.4

A Spatial Map of Toothpaste Brands

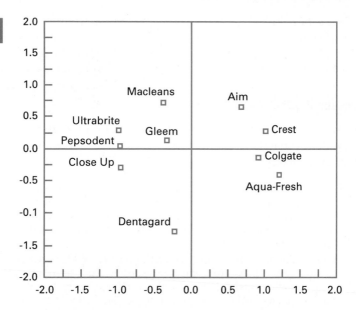

Often, the dimensions represent more than one attribute. The configuration or the spatial map may be interpreted by examining the coordinates and relative positions of the brands. For example, brands located near each other compete more fiercely than brands far apart. An isolated brand has a unique image. Brands that are farther along in the direction of a descriptor are stronger on that characteristic than others. Thus, the strengths and weaknesses of each product can be understood. Gaps in the spatial map may indicate potential opportunities for introducing new products.

In Figure 21.5, the horizontal axis might be labeled as cavity-fighting protection versus whiteness of teeth. Brands with high positive values on this axis include Aqua-Fresh, Crest, Colgate, and Aim (high cavity-fighting protection). Brands with large negative values on this dimension include Ultra Brite, Close Up, and Pepsodent (high

FIGURE 21.5

Using Attribute Vectors to Label Dimensions

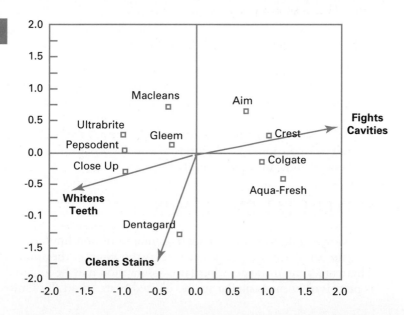

whiteness of teeth). The vertical axis may be interpreted as poor stain removal versus good stain removal. Note that Dentagard, known for its stain-removing ability, loads negatively on the vertical axis. The gaps in the spatial map indicate potential opportunities for a brand that could offer high cavity protection as well as high stain removal.

Assessing Reliability and Validity

The input data, and consequently the MDS solutions, are invariably subject to substantial random variability. Hence, it is necessary that some assessment be made of the reliability and validity of MDS solutions. The following guidelines are suggested.

1. The index of fit, or *R*-square, should be examined. This is a squared correlation index that indicates the proportion of variance of the optimally scaled data that can be accounted for by the MDS procedure. Thus, it indicates how well the MDS model fits the input data. Although higher values of *R*-square are desirable, values of .60 or better are considered acceptable.
2. Stress values are also indicative of the quality of MDS solutions. Whereas *R*-square is a measure of goodness-of-fit, stress measures badness-of-fit, or the proportion of variance of the optimally scaled data that is not accounted for by the MDS model. Stress values vary with the type of MDS procedure and the data being analyzed. For Kruskal's stress formula 1, the recommendations for evaluating stress values are as follows.[8]

Stress (Percent)	Goodness of Fit
20	Poor
10	Fair
5	Good
2.5	Excellent
0	Perfect

3. If an aggregate-level analysis has been done, the original data should be split into two or more parts. MDS analysis should be conducted separately on each part and the results compared.
4. Stimuli can be selectively eliminated from the input data and the solutions determined for the remaining stimuli.
5. A random error term could be added to the input data. The resulting data are subjected to MDS analysis and the solutions compared.
6. The input data could be collected at two different points in time and the test-retest reliability determined.

Formal procedures are available for assessing the validity of MDS.[9] In the case of our illustrative example, the stress value of .095 indicates a fair fit. One brand, namely Dentagard, is different from the others. Would the elimination of Dentagard from the stimulus set appreciably alter the relative configuration of the other brands? The spatial map obtained by deleting Dentagard is shown in Figure 21.6. There is some change in the relative positions of the brands, particularly Gleem and Macleans. Yet the changes are modest, indicating fair stability.[10]

ASSUMPTIONS AND LIMITATIONS OF MDS

It is worthwhile to point out some assumptions and limitations of MDS. It is assumed that the similarity of stimulus A to B is the same as the similarity of stimulus B to A. There are some instances where this assumption may be violated. For example, Mexico is perceived as more similar to the United States than the United States is to Mexico.

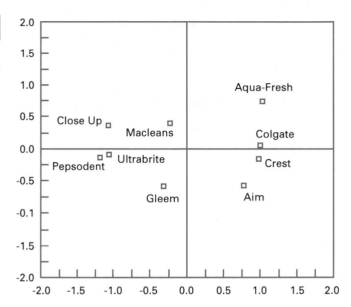

FIGURE 21.6

Assessment of Stability by Deleting One Brand

MDS assumes that the distance (similarity) between two stimuli is some function of their partial similarities on each of several perceptual dimensions. Not much research has been done to test this assumption. When a spatial map is obtained, it is assumed that interpoint distances are ratio scaled and that the axes of the map are multidimensional interval scaled. A limitation of MDS is that dimension interpretation relating physical changes in brands or stimuli to changes in the perceptual map is difficult at best. These limitations also apply to the scaling of preference data.

SCALING PREFERENCE DATA

internal analysis of preferences A method of configuring a spatial map such that the spatial map represents both brands or stimuli and respondent points or vectors and is derived solely from the preference data.

external analysis of preferences A method of configuring a spatial map such that the ideal points or vectors based on preference data are fitted in a spatial map derived from perception data.

Analysis of preference data can be internal or external. In **internal analysis of preferences**, a spatial map representing both brands or stimuli and respondent points or vectors is derived solely from the preference data. Thus, by collecting preference data, both brands and respondents can be represented in the same spatial map. In **external analysis of preferences**, the ideal points or vectors based on preference data are fitted in a spatial map derived from perception (e.g., similarities) data. To perform external analysis, both preference and perception data must be obtained. The representation of both brands and respondents as points in the same space, by using internal or external analysis, is referred to as *unfolding*.

External analysis is preferred in most situations.[11] In internal analysis, the differences in perceptions are confounded with differences in preferences. It is possible that the nature and relative importance of dimensions may vary between the perceptual space and the preference space. Two brands may be perceived to be similar (located closely to each other in the perceptual space), yet one brand may be distinctly preferred over the other (i.e., the brands may be located apart in the preference space). These situations cannot be accounted for in internal analysis. In addition, internal analysis procedures are beset with computational difficulties.[12]

We illustrate external analysis by scaling the preferences of our respondent into his spatial map. The respondent ranked the brands in the following order of preference (most preferred first): Colgate, Crest, Aim, Aqua-Fresh, Gleem, Pepsodent, Ultra Brite, Macleans, Close Up, and Dentagard. These preference rankings, along with the coordinates of the spatial map (Figure 21.5), were used as input into a preference scaling program to derive Figure 21.7. Notice the location of the ideal point. It is close to Colgate, Crest, Aim and Aqua-Fresh, the four most preferred brands, and far from Close Up and Dentagard, the two least preferred brands. If a new brand were to be located in this space, its distance from the ideal point, relative to the distances of other brands from the ideal point, would determine the degree of preference for this brand. Another application is provided by the following example.

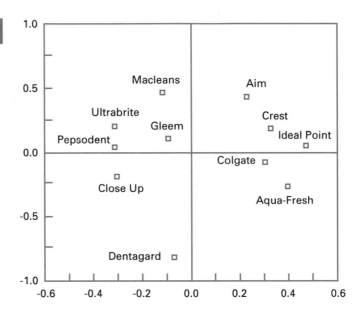

FIGURE 21.7

External Analysis of Preference Data

EXAMPLE

Respondents Park in Different Spaces

An illustrative MDS map of selected automobile brands derived from similarity data is shown. In this spatial representation, each brand is identified by its distance from the other brands. The closer two brands are (e.g., Volkswagen and Dart), the more similar they are perceived to be. The farther apart two brands are (e.g., Volkswagen and Mercedes), the less similar they are perceived to be. Small distance (i.e., similarity) may also indicate competition. To illustrate, Capri competes closely with Vega, Monté Carlo, Chevrolet, and Camaro, but not with Buick or Corvette. The dimensions can be interpreted as economy or prestige versus sportiness or nonsportiness, and the position of each car on these dimensions can be determined.

The preference data consisted of a simple rank order of the brands according to consumers' preferences. Respondents' ideal points are also located in the same spatial representation. Each ideal point represents the locus of preference of a particular respondent. Thus, respondent 1 (denoted I1) prefers the sporty cars: Camaro, Firebird, and Capri. Respondent 2 (denoted I2) on the other hand, prefers luxury cars: Continental, Mercedes, and Cadillac.

*Joint Space
Configuration
of Automobiles Brands
and Consumer
Preferences
(Illustrative Output)*

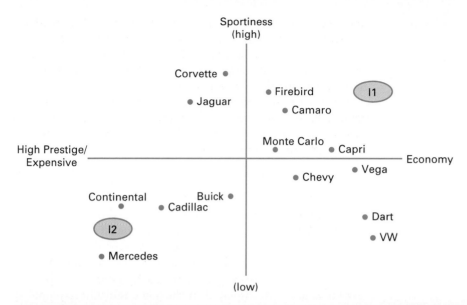

MDS has been used to identify consumers who prefer sporty cars, like Corvettes. ◆ Courtesy of General Motors.

Such analysis can be done at the individual respondent level, enabling the researcher to segment the market according to similarities in the respondents' ideal points. Alternatively, the respondents can be clustered based on their similarity with respect to the original preference ranking and ideal points established for each segment.[13] ◆

Although we have considered only quantitative data so far, qualitative data can also be mapped using procedures such as correspondence analysis.

CORRESPONDENCE ANALYSIS

Correspondence analysis is an MDS technique for scaling qualitative data in marketing research. The input data are in the form of a contingency table indicating a qualitative association between the rows and columns. Correspondence analysis scales the rows and

correspondence analysis
An MDS technique for scaling qualitative data that scales the rows and columns of the input contingency table in corresponding units so that each can be displayed in the same low-dimensional space.

columns in corresponding units so that each can be displayed graphically in the same low-dimensional space. These spatial maps provide insights into (1) similarities and differences within the rows with respect to a given column category, (2) similarities and differences within the column categories with respect to a given row category, and (3) relationship among the rows and columns.[14]

The interpretation of results in correspondence analysis is similar to that in principal components analysis (Chapter 19), given the similarity of the algorithms. Correspondence analysis results in the grouping of categories (activities, brands, or other stimuli) found within the contingency table, just as principal components analysis involves the grouping of the independent variables. The results are interpreted in terms of proximities among the rows and columns of the contingency table. Categories that are closer together than others are more similar in underlying structure.[15]

Compared with other multidimensional scaling techniques, the advantage of correspondence analysis is that it reduces the data collection demands imposed on the respondents, since only binary or categorical data are obtained. The respondents are merely asked to check which attributes apply to each of several brands. The input data are the number of yes responses for each brand on each attribute. The brands and the attributes are then displayed in the same multidimensional space. The disadvantage is that between-set (i.e., between column and row) distances cannot be meaningfully interpreted. Correspondence analysis is an exploratory data analysis technique that is not suitable for hypothesis testing.[16]

MDS, including correspondence analysis, is not the only procedure available for obtaining perceptual maps. Two other techniques that we have discussed before, discriminant analysis (Chapter 18) and factor analysis (Chapter 19), can also be used for this purpose.

RELATIONSHIP AMONG MDS, FACTOR ANALYSIS, AND DISCRIMINANT ANALYSIS

If the attribute-based approaches are used to obtain input data, spatial maps can also be obtained by using factor or discriminant analysis. In this approach, each respondent rates *n* brands on *m* attributes. By factor analyzing the data, one could derive for each respondent *n* factor scores for each factor, one for each brand. By plotting brand scores on the factors, a spatial map could be obtained for each respondent. If an aggregate map is desired, the factor score for each brand for each factor can be averaged across respondents. The dimensions would be labeled by examining the factor loadings, which are estimates of the correlations between attribute ratings and underlying factors.[17]

The goal of discriminant analysis is to select the linear combinations of attributes that best discriminate between the brands or stimuli. To develop spatial maps by means of discriminant analysis, the dependent variable is the brand rated and the independent or predictor variables are the attribute ratings. A spatial map can be obtained by plotting the discriminant scores for the brands. The discriminant scores are the ratings on the perceptual dimensions, based on the attributes which best distinguish the brands. The dimensions can be labeled by examining the discriminant weights, or the weightings of attributes that make up a discriminant function or dimension.[18]

BASIC CONCEPTS IN CONJOINT ANALYSIS

conjoint analysis A technique that attempts to determine the relative importance consumers attach to salient attributes and the utilities they attach to the levels of attributes.

Conjoint analysis attempts to determine the relative importance consumers attach to salient attributes and the utilities they attach to the levels of attributes.[19] This information is derived from consumers' evaluations of brands or from brand profiles composed of these attributes and their levels. The respondents are presented with stimuli that consist of combinations of attribute levels. They are asked to evaluate these stimuli in terms of their desirability. Conjoint procedures attempt to assign values to the levels of each attribute so that the resulting values or utilities attached to the stimuli match, as closely as possible, the input evaluations provided by the respondents. The underlying assumption is that any set of stimuli—such as products, brands, or stores—is evaluated as a bundle of attributes.[20]

Like multidimensional scaling, conjoint analysis relies on respondents' subjective evaluations. In MDS, however, the stimuli are products or brands. In conjoint analysis, the stimuli are combinations of attribute levels determined by the researcher. The goal in MDS is to develop a spatial map depicting the stimuli in a multidimensional perceptual or preference space. Conjoint analysis, on the other hand, seeks to develop the part-worth or utility functions describing the utility consumers attach to the levels of each attribute. The two techniques are complementary.[21]

Conjoint analysis has been used in marketing for a variety of purposes, including the following:

Determining the relative importance of attributes in the consumer choice process. A standard output from conjoint analysis consists of derived relative importance weights for all the attributes used to construct the stimuli used in the evaluation task. The relative importance weights indicate which attributes are important in influencing consumer choice.

Estimating market share of brands that differ in attribute levels. The utilities derived from conjoint analysis can be used as input into a choice simulator to determine the share of choices, and hence the market share, of different brands.

Determining the composition of the most preferred brand. The brand features can be varied in terms of attribute levels and the corresponding utilities determined. The brand features that yield the highest utility indicate the composition of the most preferred brand.

Segmenting the market based on similarity of preferences for attribute levels. The part-worth functions derived for the attributes may be used as a basis for clustering respondents to arrive at homogeneous preference segments.[22]

Applications of conjoint analysis have been made in consumer goods, industrial goods, and financial and other services. Moreover, these applications have spanned all areas of marketing. A recent survey of conjoint analysis reported applications in the areas of new product and concept identification, competitive analysis, pricing, market segmentation, advertising, and distribution.[23]

STATISTICS AND TERMS ASSOCIATED WITH CONJOINT ANALYSIS

The important statistics and terms associated with conjoint analysis include the following:

Part-worth functions. The part-worth or *utility functions* describe the utility consumers attach to the levels of each attribute.

Relative importance weights. The relative importance weights are estimated and indicate which attributes are important in influencing consumer choice.

Attribute levels. The attribute levels denote the values assumed by the attributes.

Full profiles. Full profiles or complete profiles of brands are constructed in terms of all the attributes by using the attribute levels specified by the design.

Pairwise tables. In pairwise tables, the respondents evaluate two attributes at a time until all the required pairs of attributes have been evaluated.

Cyclical designs. Cyclical designs are designs employed to reduce the number of paired comparisons.

Fractional factorial designs. Fractional factorial designs are designs employed to reduce the number of stimulus profiles to be evaluated in the full-profile approach.

Orthogonal arrays. Orthogonal arrays are a special class of fractional designs that enable the efficient estimation of all main effects.

Internal validity. Internal validity involves correlations of the predicted evaluations for the holdout or validation stimuli with those obtained from the respondents.

CONDUCTING CONJOINT ANALYSIS

Figure 21.8 lists the steps in conjoint analysis. Formulating the problem involves identifying the salient attributes and their levels. These attributes and levels are used for constructing the stimuli to be used in a conjoint evaluation task. The respondents rate or rank the stimuli using a suitable scale, and the data obtained are analyzed. The results are interpreted and their reliability and validity assessed. We now describe each of the steps of conjoint analysis in detail.

Formulating the Problem

In formulating the conjoint analysis problem, the researcher must identify the attributes and attribute levels to be used in constructing the stimuli. Attribute levels denote the values assumed by the attributes. From a theoretical standpoint, the attributes selected should be salient in influencing consumer preference and choice. For example, in the

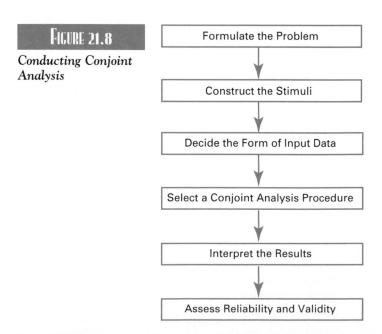

FIGURE 21.8

Conducting Conjoint Analysis

Formulate the Problem

Construct the Stimuli

Decide the Form of Input Data

Select a Conjoint Analysis Procedure

Interpret the Results

Assess Reliability and Validity

choice of an automobile brand, price, gas mileage, interior space, and so forth should be included. From a managerial perspective, the attributes and their levels should be actionable. To tell a manager that consumers prefer a sporty car to one that is conservative looking is not helpful, unless sportiness and conservativeness are defined in terms of attributes over which a manager has control. The attributes can be identified through discussions with management and industry experts, analysis of secondary data, qualitative research, and pilot surveys. A typical conjoint analysis study involves six or seven attributes.

Once the salient attributes have been identified, their appropriate levels should be selected. The number of attribute levels determines the number of parameters that will be estimated and also influences the number of stimuli that will be evaluated by the respondents. To minimize the respondent evaluation task and yet estimate the parameters with reasonable accuracy, it is desirable to restrict the number of attribute levels. The utility or part-worth function for the levels of an attribute may be nonlinear. For example, a consumer may prefer a medium-sized car to either a small or a large one. Likewise, the utility for price may be nonlinear. The loss of utility in going from a low price to a medium price may be much smaller than the loss in utility in going from a medium price to a high price. In these cases, at least three levels should be used. Some attributes, though, may naturally occur in binary form (two levels): a car does or does not have a sunroof.

The attribute levels selected will affect the consumer evaluations. If the price of an automobile brand is varied at $10,000, $12,000 and $14,000, price will be relatively unimportant. On the other hand, if the price is varied at $10,000, $20,000 and $30,000, it will be an important factor. Hence, the researcher should take into account the attribute levels prevalent in the marketplace and the objectives of the study. Using attribute levels that are beyond the range reflected in the marketplace will decrease the believability of the evaluation task, but it will increase the accuracy with which the parameters are estimated. The general guideline is to select attribute levels so that the ranges are somewhat greater than those prevalent in the marketplace but not so large as to impact the believability of the evaluation task adversely.

We illustrate the conjoint methodology by considering the problem of how students evaluate sneakers. Qualitative research identified three attributes as salient: the sole, the upper, and the price.[24] Each was defined in terms of three levels, as shown in Table 21.2. These attributes and their levels were used for constructing the conjoint analysis stimuli. It has been argued that pictorial stimuli should be used when consumers' marketplace choices are strongly guided by the product's styling, such that the choices are heavily based on an inspection of actual products or pictures of products.[25]

		Level	
TABLE 21.2	Attribute	Number	Description
Sneaker Attributes and Levels	Sole	3	Rubber
		2	Polyurethane
		1	Plastic
	Upper	3	Leather
		2	Canvas
		1	Nylon
	Price	3	$15.00
		2	$30.00
		1	$45.00

Constructing the Stimuli

Two broad approaches are available for constructing conjoint analysis stimuli: the pairwise approach and the full-profile procedure. In the pairwise approach, also called *two-factor evaluations*, respondents evaluate two attributes at a time until all the possible pairs of attributes have been evaluated. This approach is illustrated in the context of the sneaker example in Figure 21.9. For each pair, respondents evaluate all the combinations of levels of both the attributes, which are presented in a matrix. In the full-profile approach, also called *multiple-factor evaluations*, full or complete profiles of brands are constructed for all the attributes. Typically, each profile is described on a separate index card. This approach is illustrated in the context of the sneaker example in Table 21.3.

It is not necessary to evaluate all the possible combinations, nor is it feasible in all cases. In the pairwise approach, it is possible to reduce the number of paired comparisons by using cyclical designs. Likewise, in the full-profile approach, the number of stimulus profiles can be greatly reduced by means of fractional factorial designs. A special class of fractional designs, *orthogonal arrays*, allow for the efficient estimation of all

FIGURE 21.9

Pairwise Approach to Collecting Conjoint Data

You will be presented with information on sneakers in terms of pairs of features described in the form of a matrix. For each matrix, please rank the nine feature combinations in terms of your preference. A rank of 1 should be assigned to the most preferred combination and 9 to the least preferred.

	Sole		
Upper	Rubber	Polyurethane	Plastic
Leather			
Canvas			
Nylon			

	Sole		
Price	Rubber	Polyurethane	Plastic
$15.00			
$30.00			
$45.00			

	Price		
Upper	$15.00	$30.00	$45.00
Leather			
Canvas			
Nylon			

TABLE 21.3	Example of a Sneaker Product Profile	
Full-Profile Approach to Collecting Conjoint Data	Sole	Made of rubber
	Upper	Made of nylon
	Price	$15.00

main effects. Orthogonal arrays permit the measurement of all main effects of interest on an uncorrelated basis. These designs assume that all interactions are negligible. Orthogonal arrays are constructed from basic full factorial designs by substituting a new factor for selected interaction effects that are presumed to be negligible.[26] Generally, two sets of data are obtained. One, the *estimation set*, is used to calculate the part-worth functions for the attribute levels. The other, the *holdout set*, is used to assess reliability and validity.

The advantage of the pairwise approach is that it is easier for the respondents to provide these judgments. Its relative disadvantage, however, is that it requires more evaluations than the full-profile approach. Also, the evaluation task may be unrealistic when only two attributes are being evaluated simultaneously. Studies comparing the two approaches indicate that both methods yield comparable utilities, yet the full-profile approach is more commonly used.

The sneaker example follows the full-profile approach. Given three attributes, defined at three levels each, a total of $3 \times 3 \times 3 = 27$ profiles can be constructed. To reduce the respondent evaluation task, a fractional factorial design was employed and a set of nine profiles was constructed to constitute the estimation stimuli set (see Table 21.4). Another set of nine stimuli was constructed for validation purposes. Input data were obtained for both the estimation and validation stimuli. Before the data could be obtained, however, it was necessary to decide on the form of the input data.[27]

Deciding on the Form of Input Data

As in the case of MDS, conjoint analysis input data can be either nonmetric or metric. For nonmetric data, respondents are typically required to provide rank-order evaluations. For the pairwise approach, respondents rank all the cells of each matrix in terms

Sneaker manufacturers like Reebok have made use of conjoint analysis to develop sneakers with appealing features. ◆ Reebok.

		Attribute Levels[a]			
Profile Number	Sole	Upper	Price	Preference Rating	
1	1	1	1	9	
2	1	2	2	7	
3	1	3	3	5	
4	2	1	2	6	
5	2	2	3	5	
6	2	3	1	6	
7	3	1	3	5	
8	3	2	1	7	
9	3	3	2	6	

TABLE 21.4

Sneaker Profiles and Their Ratings

[a]The attribute levels correspond to those in Table 21.2.

of their desirability. For the full-profile approach, they rank all the stimulus profiles. Rankings involve relative evaluations of the attribute levels. Proponents of ranking data believe that such data accurately reflect the behavior of consumers in the marketplace.

In the metric form, respondents provide ratings, rather than rankings. In this case, the judgments are typically made independently. Advocates of rating data believe that they are more convenient for the respondents and easier to analyze than rankings. In recent years, the use of ratings has become increasingly common.

In conjoint analysis, the dependent variable is usually preference or intention to buy. In other words, respondents provide ratings or rankings in terms of their preference or intentions to buy. The conjoint methodology, however, is flexible and can accommodate a range of other dependent variables, including actual purchase or choice.

In evaluating sneaker profiles, respondents were required to provide preference ratings for the sneakers described by the nine profiles in the estimation set. These ratings were obtained using a nine-point Likert scale (1 = not preferred, 9 = greatly preferred). Ratings obtained from one respondent are shown in Table 21.4.

Selecting a Conjoint Analysis Procedure

conjoint analysis model
The mathematical model expressing the fundamental relationship between attributes and utility in conjoint analysis.

The basic **conjoint analysis model** may be represented by the following formula:[28]

$$U(X) = \sum_{i=1}^{m} \sum_{j=1}^{k_i} \alpha_{ij} x_{ij}$$

where

$U(X)$ = overall utility of an alternative

$\quad$ = the part-worth contribution or utility associated with the jth level ($j, j = 1, 2, ..., k_i$) of the ith attribute ($i, i = 1, 2, ..., m$)

k_i = number of levels of attribute i

m = number of attributes

The importance of an attribute, I_i, is defined in terms of the range of the part-worths, α_{ij}, across the levels of that attribute:

$$I_i = \{\text{Max}(\alpha_{ij}) - \text{Min}(\alpha_{ij})\} \quad \text{for each } i$$

The attribute's importance is normalized to ascertain its importance relative to other attributes, W_i:

$$W_i = \frac{I_i}{\sum_{i=1}^{m} I_i}$$

so that

$$\sum_{i=1}^{m} W_i = 1$$

Several different procedures are available for estimating the basic model. The simplest, and one which is gaining in popularity, is dummy variable regression (see Chapter 17). In this case, the predictor variables consist of dummy variables for the attribute levels. If an attribute has k_i levels, it is coded in terms of $k_i - 1$ dummy variables. If metric data are obtained, the ratings, assumed to be interval scaled, form the dependent variable. If the data are nonmetric, the rankings may be converted to 0 or 1 by making paired comparisons between brands. In this case, the predictor variables represent the differences in the attribute levels of the brands being compared. Other procedures that are appropriate for nonmetric data include LINMAP, MONANOVA, and the LOGIT model.[29]

The researcher must also decide whether the data will be analyzed at the individual respondent or the aggregate level. At the individual level, the data of each respondent are analyzed separately. If an aggregate-level analysis is to be conducted, some procedure for grouping the respondents must be devised. One common approach is to estimate individual-level part-worth or utility functions first. Respondents are then clustered on the basis of the similarity of their part-worth functions. Aggregate analysis is then conducted for each cluster.[30] An appropriate model for estimating the parameters should be specified.[31]

The data reported in Table 21.4 were analyzed using ordinary least squares (OLS) regression with dummy variables. The dependent variable was the preference ratings. The independent variables or predictors were six dummy variables, two for each variable. The transformed data are shown in Table 21.5. Since the data pertain to a single respondent, an individual-level analysis was conducted. The part-worth or utility functions estimated for each attribute, as well the relative importance of the attributes, are given in Table 21.6.[32]

The model estimated may be represented as

$$U = b_0 + b_1 X_1 + b_2 X_2 + b_3 X_3 + b_4 X_4 + b_5 X_5 + b_6 X_6$$

TABLE 21.5 *Sneaker Data Coded for Dummy Variable Regression*	Preference Ratings Y	Attributes					
		Sole X_1	X_2	Upper X_3	X_4	Price X_5	X_6
	9	1	0	1	0	1	0
	7	1	0	0	1	0	1
	5	1	0	0	0	0	0
	6	0	1	1	0	0	1
	5	0	1	0	1	0	0
	6	0	1	0	0	1	0
	5	0	0	1	0	0	0
	7	0	0	0	1	1	0
	6	0	0	0	0	0	1

TABLE 21.6			Level		
Results of Conjoint Analysis	Attribute	Number	Description	Utility	Importance
	Sole	3	Rubber	0.778	
		2	Polyurethane	−0.556	
		1	Plastic	−0.222	0.286
	Upper	3	Leather	0.445	
		2	Canvas	0.111	
		1	Nylon	−0.556	0.214
	Price	3	$15.00	1.111	
		2	$30.00	0.111	
		1	$45.00	−1.222	0.500

where

$$X_1, X_2 = \text{dummy variables representing sole}$$
$$X_3, X_4 = \text{dummy variables representing upper}$$
$$X_5, X_6 = \text{dummy variables representing price}$$

For sole, the attribute levels were coded as follows:

	X_1	X_2
Level 1	1	0
Level 2	0	1
Level 3	0	0

The levels of the other attributes were coded similarly. The parameters were estimated as follows:

$$b_0 = 4.222$$
$$b_1 = 1.000$$
$$b_2 = -0.333$$
$$b_3 = 1.000$$
$$b_4 = 0.667$$
$$b_5 = 2.333$$
$$b_6 = 1.333$$

Given the dummy variable coding, in which level 3 is the base level, the coefficients may be related to the part-worths. As explained in Chapter 17, each dummy variable coefficient represents the difference in the part-worth for that level minus the part-worth for the base level. For sole, we have the following:

$$\alpha_{11} - \alpha_{13} = b_1$$
$$\alpha_{12} - \alpha_{13} = b_2$$

To solve for the part-worths, an additional constraint is necessary. The part-worths are estimated on an interval scale, so the origin is arbitrary. Therefore, the additional constraint imposed is of the form

$$\alpha_{11} + \alpha_{12} + \alpha_{13} = 0$$

These equations for the first attribute, sole, are

$$\alpha_{11} - \alpha_{13} = 1.000$$
$$\alpha_{12} - \alpha_{13} = -0.333$$
$$\alpha_{11} + \alpha_{12} + \alpha_{13} = 0$$

Solving these equations, we get

$$\alpha_{11} = 0.778$$
$$\alpha_{12} = -0.556$$
$$\alpha_{13} = -0.222$$

The part-worths for other attributes reported in Table 21.6 can be estimated similarly. For upper, we have

$$\alpha_{21} - \alpha_{23} = b_3$$
$$\alpha_{22} - \alpha_{23} = b_4$$
$$\alpha_{21} + \alpha_{22} + \alpha_{23} = 0$$

For the third attribute, price, we have

$$\alpha_{31} - \alpha_{33} = b_5$$
$$\alpha_{32} - \alpha_{33} = b_6$$
$$\alpha_{31} + \alpha_{32} + \alpha_{33} = 0$$

The relative importance weights were calculated based on ranges of part-worths, as follows:

$$\text{Sum of ranges of part-worths} = [0.778 - (-0.556)] + [0.445 - (-0.556)]$$
$$+ [1.111 - (-1.222)]$$
$$= 4.668$$

$$\text{Relative importance of sole} = \frac{1.334}{4.668} = 0.286$$

$$\text{Relative importance of upper} = \frac{1.001}{4.668} = 0.214$$

$$\text{Relative importance of price} = \frac{2.333}{4.668} = 0.500$$

The estimation of the part-worths and the relative importance weights provides the basis for interpreting the results.

INTERPRETING THE RESULTS

For interpreting the results, it is helpful to plot the part-worth functions. The part-worth function values for each attribute given in Table 21.6 are graphed in Figure 21.10. As can be seen from Table 21.6 and Figure 21.10, this respondent has the greatest preference for a rubber sole when evaluating sneakers. Second preference is for a plastic sole, and a polyurethane sole is least preferred. A leather upper is most preferred, followed by canvas and nylon. As

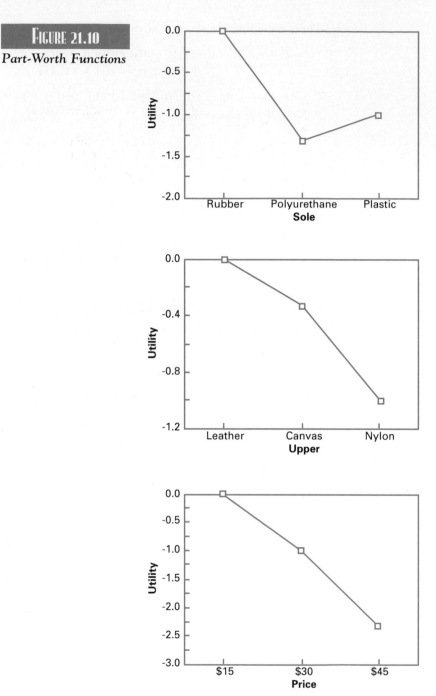

FIGURE 21.10

Part-Worth Functions

expected, a price of $15.00 has the highest utility and a price of $45.00 the lowest. The utility values reported in Table 21.6 have only interval scale properties, and their origin is arbitrary. In terms of relative importance of the attributes, we see that price is number one. Second most important is sole, followed closely by upper. Because price is by far the most important attribute for this respondent, this person could be labeled as price sensitive.

Assessing Reliability and Validity

Several procedures are available for assessing the reliability and validity of conjoint analysis results.[33]

1. The goodness of fit of the estimated model should be evaluated. For example, if dummy variable regression is used, the value of R^2 will indicate the extent to which the model fits the data. Models with poor fit are suspect.

2. Test-retest reliability can be assessed by obtaining a few replicated judgments later in data collection. In other words, at a later stage in the interview, the respondents are asked to evaluate certain selected stimuli again. The two values of these stimuli are then correlated to assess test-retest reliability.

3. The evaluations for the holdout or validation stimuli can be predicted by the estimated part-worth functions. The predicted evaluations can then be correlated with those obtained from the respondents to determine internal validity.

4. If an aggregate-level analysis has been conducted, the estimation sample can be split in several ways and conjoint analysis conducted on each subsample. The results can be compared across subsamples to assess the stability of conjoint analysis solutions.

In running a regression analysis on the data of Table 21.5, an R^2 of .934 was obtained, indicating a good fit. The preference ratings for the nine validation profiles were predicted from the utilities reported in Table 21.6. These were correlated with the input ratings for these profiles obtained from the respondent. The correlation coefficient was .95, indicating a good predictive ability. This correlation coefficient is significant at $\alpha = .05$.

The following example further illustrates the conjoint analysis procedure.

EXAMPLE

Examining Microcomputer Tradeoffs Microscopically _____

Conjoint analysis was used to determine how consumers make tradeoffs between various attributes when selecting microcomputers. Four attributes were chosen as salient. These attributes and their levels are as follows:

Input mode	Screen size
• Keyboard	• 13 inch
• Mouse	• 9 inch
Display monitor	Price level
• Black and white	• $1,000
• Color	• $1,500
	• $2,000

All possible combinations of these attribute levels result in 24 ($2 \times 2 \times 2 \times 3$) profiles of microcomputers. One such profile is as follows:

Input mode:	Mouse
Display monitor:	Color
Screen size:	13 inch
Price level:	$1,500

Respondents rank-ordered these profiles in terms of preferences. The data for each respondent can be used to develop preference functions. The preference functions for one individual are illustrated.

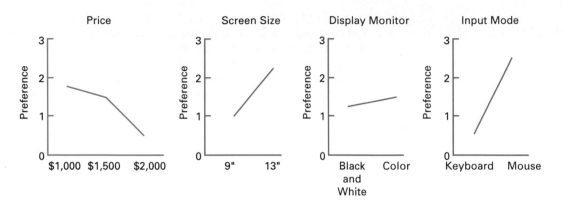

Based on the derived part-worth or preference functions, the relative importance of the various attributes in determining these consumer preferences can be estimated by comparing part-worth functions as follows:

Relative importance

Evaluative Criteria	Importance
Input mode	45%
Display monitor	5%
Screen size	25%
Price level	25%

For this consumer, input mode is the most important feature and the mouse is the preferred option. Although price and screen size are also important, price becomes a factor only between $1,500 and $2,000. As expected, a screen size of 13″ is preferred. Whether the display monitor is black and white or color does not matter much. Information provided by the part-worth functions and relative importance weights can be used to cluster respondents to determine benefit segments for micro-computers.[34] ◆

Consumers make tradeoffs between various attributes when buying microcomputers. ◆ IBM.

ASSUMPTIONS AND LIMITATIONS OF CONJOINT ANALYSIS

Although conjoint analysis is a popular technique, like MDS, it carries a number of assumptions and limitations. Conjoint analysis assumes that the important attributes of a product can be identified. Furthermore, it assumes that consumers evaluate the choice alternatives in terms of these attributes and make tradeoffs. In situations where image or brand name is important, however, consumers may not evaluate the brands or alternatives in terms of attributes. Even if consumers consider product attributes, the tradeoff model may not be a good representation of the choice process. Another limitation is that data collection may be complex, particularly if a large number of attributes are involved and the model must be estimated at the individual level. This problem has been mitigated to some extent by procedures such as interactive or adaptive conjoint analysis and hybrid conjoint analysis. It should also be noted that the part-worth functions are not unique. For more technical issues, and for the limitations of conjoint analysis, refer to the literature.[35]

HYBRID CONJOINT ANALYSIS

hybrid conjoint analysis
A form of conjoint analysis that can simplify the data collection task and estimate selected interactions as well as all main effects.

Hybrid conjoint analysis is an attempt to simplify the burdensome data collection task required in traditional conjoint analysis. Each respondent evaluates a large number of profiles, yet usually only simple part-worth functions, without any interaction effects, are estimated. In the simple part-worths or main effects model, the value of a combination is simply the sum of the separate main effects (simple part-worths). In actual practice, two attributes may interact in the sense that the respondent may value the combination more than the average contribution of the separate parts. Hybrid models have been developed to serve two main purposes: (1) to simplify the data collection task by imposing less of a burden on each respondent and (2) to permit the estimation of selected interactions (at the subgroup level) as well as all main (or simple) effects at the individual level.

In the hybrid approach, the respondents evaluate a limited number, generally no more than nine, conjoint stimuli, such as full profiles. These profiles are drawn from a large master design and different respondents evaluate different sets of profiles so that over a group of respondents, all the profiles of interest are evaluated. In addition, respondents directly evaluate the relative importance of each attribute and desirability of the levels of each attribute. By combining the direct evaluations with those derived from the evaluations of the conjoint stimuli, it is possible to estimate a model at the aggregate level and still retain some individual differences.[36]

MDS and conjoint analysis are complementary techniques and may be used in combination, as the following example shows.

EXAMPLE
Weeding Out the Competition

ICI Americas Agricultural Products did not know whether it should lower the price of Fusilade, its herbicide. It knew that it had developed a potent herbicide, but it was not sure that the weed killer would survive in a price-conscious market. So a survey was designed to assess the relative importance of different attributes in selecting herbicides and measure and map perceptions of major herbicides on the same attributes. Personal interviews were conducted with 601 soybean and cotton farmers who had at least 200 acres dedicated to growing these crops and who had used herbicides during the past growing season. First, conjoint analysis was used to determine the relative importance of attributes farmers use when selecting herbicides. Then multidimensional scaling was used to map farmers' perceptions of herbicides. The study showed that price greatly influenced herbicide selections, and respondents were particularly sensitive when costs were more than $18 an acre. But price was not the only determinant. Farmers also considered how much weed control the herbicide provided. They were willing to pay higher prices to keep weeds off their land. The study showed that herbicides that failed to control even one of the four most common weeds would have to be very inexpensive to attain a reasonable market share. Fusilade promised good weed control. Furthermore, multidimensional scaling indicated that one of Fusilade's competitors was considered to be expensive. Hence, ICI kept its original pricing plan and did not lower the price of Fusilade.[37] ◆

Both MDS and conjoint analysis are useful in conducting international marketing research as illustrated by Research in Practice 21.1[38] and 21.2.[39] Research in Practice 21.3 presents an application of MDS in researching ethical perceptions.[40]

RESEARCH IN PRACTICE 21.1

Herit-Age or Merit-Age in Europe?

European car manufacturers are increasingly focusing on an attribute that competitors will not be able to buy or build, heritage. For BMW, it is superior engineering. A. B. Volvo of Sweden has a reputation for safe cars. Italian Alfa Romeo rides on the laurels of engines that won numerous races. The French Renault has savoir faire. On the other hand, Japanese cars are advanced technologically but do not have class or heritage. For example, Lexus and Infiniti are high-performance cars, but they lack class. Philip Gamba, vice-president of marketing at Renault, believes that Japanese brands lack the "French touch" of that automaker's design and credibility. These days, Renault is building a car with a focus on comfort. BMW is trying to emphasize not the prestige of owning a luxury automobile but the "inner value" of its cars. To communicate value in cars is of growing importance. BMW has the edge of German heritage.

Because performance and heritage are important attributes or dimensions in automobile preferences of Europeans, the positioning of different European cars on these two dimensions is shown. Notice that BMW has attained the best positioning on both these dimensions. Typical of most U.S. and Japanese cars in the 1980s has been the emphasis on quality, reliability, and efficiency. To compete in the European market in the 1990s, however, Americans and Japanese are faced with the challenge of an added dimension, heritage. This calls for new marketing strategies by U.S. and Japanese automakers.

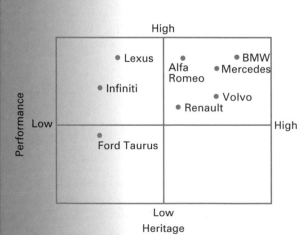

RESEARCH IN PRACTICE 21.2

Fab's Fabulous Foamy Fight

Competition in the detergent market was brewing in Thailand. Superconcentrate detergent is fast becoming the prototype, with a market share of over 26% in the detergent category by the end of 1995. Market potential research in Thailand indicated that superconcentrates would grow by about 40% a year. In addition, this category had already dominated other Asian markets such as Taiwan, Hong Kong, and Singapore. Consequently, Colgate entered this new line of competition with Fab Power Plus with the objective of capturing 4% market share. The main players in the market were Kao Corporation's Attack (14.6%), Lever Brothers' Breeze Ultra (2.8%), Lion Corporation's Pao M. Wash (1.1%), and Lever's Omo (0.4%). Based on qualitative research and secondary data, Colgate assessed the critical factors for the success of superconcentrates. Some of these factors were environmental appeal, hand-wash and machine-wash convenience, superior cleaning abilities, optimum level of suds for hand wash, and brand name. Market research also revealed that no brand had both hand-wash and machine-wash capabilities. Pao Hand Force was formulated as the hand-washing brand, and Pao M. Wash was the machine-wash version. Lever's Breezematic was targeted for machine use. Therefore, a formula that had both hand- and machine-wash capabilities was desirable. A conjoint study was designed, and these factors varied at either two or three levels. Preference ratings were gathered from respondents, and part-worth functions for the factors were estimated both at the individual and the group level. Results showed that the factor on hand-machine capability had a substantial contribution supporting earlier claims. Based on these findings, Fab Power Plus was successfully introduced as a brand with both hand- and machine-wash capabilities.

COMPUTER APPLICATIONS

Over the years, several computer programs have been developed for conducting MDS analysis using microcomputers and mainframes.[41] The ALSCAL program, available in the mainframe versions of both SPSS and SAS, incorporates several different MDS models and can be used for conducting individual or aggregate level analysis. Other MDS programs are easily available and widely used. Most are available in both microcomputer and mainframe versions.

- MDSCAL 5M derives a spatial map of brands in a specified number of dimensions. Similarity data are used. A variety of input data formats and distance measures can be accommodated.
- KYST performs metric and nonmetric scaling and unfolding using similarity data.
- INDSCAL, denoting individual differences scaling, is useful for conducting MDS at the aggregate-level. Similarity data are used as input.
- MDPREF performs internal analysis of preference data. The program develops vector directions for preferences and the configuration of brands or stimuli in a common space.
- PREFMAP performs external analysis of preference data. This program uses a known spatial map of brands or stimuli to portray an individual's preference data. PREFMAP2 performs both internal and external analysis.

RESEARCH IN PRACTICE 21.3

Ethical Perceptions of Marketing Research Firms

Two of the factors which have been shown to have acceptable reliability and validity in measuring the degree to which a certain situation is ethical are a broad-based moral equity dimension (factor 1), and a relativistic dimension (factor 2). These two dimensions should emerge in a multidimensional scaling analysis of the perceived ethicalness of marketing research firms. Such an MDS plot might look like the following.

While this example is hypothetical, some interesting observations can be made. Internal marketing research departments have the highest ethical perceptions on both dimensions. Full service firms are perceived to be more ethical as compared to the limited service firms on both the dimensions. Large marketing research firms are perceived to be more ethical on the relativistic dimension, whereas small firms are more ethical on the moral equity factor. The same is true of international marketing research firms compared with domestic firms.

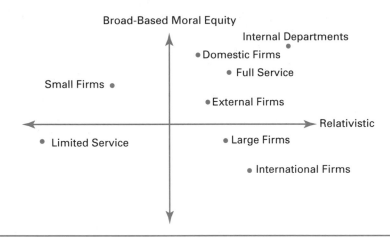

- PC-MDS contains a variety of multidimensional scaling algorithms, including factor analysis, discriminant analysis, and some other multivariate procedures. It is available for the IBM PC and compatibles.
- APM (adaptive perceptual mapping) is an adaptive scaling program, available for the microcomputer, that can handle up to 30 brands and 50 attributes. There is no limit on the number of respondents per study or the number of computers that can be used to collect the data.
- MAPWISE by Market Action Research Software, Inc., is perceptual mapping software for conducting correspondence analysis. CORRESPONDENCE ANALYSIS by the Beaumont Organization Ltd. conducts correspondence analysis, what-if simulations, and ideal product analysis. Another program for correspondence analysis is SIMCA by Greenacre.

If Ordinary Least Squares regression is used as the estimation procedure in conjoint analysis, these programs are universally available. In particular, the microcomputer and mainframe versions of SAS, SPSS, and BMDP have several regression programs that were discussed in Chapter 17. Several specialized programs are also available for conjoint analysis. MONANOVA (monotone analysis of variance) is a nonmetric procedure that uses full-profile data. For pairwise data, the TRADEOFF procedure can be used. TRADE-OFF is also a nonmetric procedure that uses the rank ordering of preferences for attribute-level pairs. Both MONANOVA and TRADEOFF are available for the mainframe and microcomputers. Other popular programs include LINMAP and ACA (adaptive conjoint analysis). PC-MDS also contains a program for conjoint analysis. Other useful programs include software by Bretton-Clark, including CONJOINT DESIGNER, CONJOINT ANALYZER, CONJOINT LINMAP, SIMGRAF, and BRIDGER. POSSE (Product Optimization and Selected Segmentation Evaluation) by Robinson Associates, Inc., is a generalized system for optimizing product and service designs using hybrid conjoint analysis and experimental design methods. It uses consumer choice simulators, response surface modeling, and optimization procedures to develop optimal product configurations.

SUMMARY

Multidimensional scaling is used for obtaining spatial representations of respondents' perceptions and preferences. Perceived or psychological relationships among stimuli are represented as geometric relationships among points in a multidimensional space. Formulating the MDS problem requires a specification of the brands or stimuli to be included. The number and nature of brands selected influences the resulting solution. Input data obtained from the respondents can be related to perceptions or preferences. Perception data can be direct or derived. The direct approaches are more common in marketing research.

The selection of an MDS procedure depends on the nature (metric or nonmetric) of the input data and whether perceptions or preferences are being scaled. Another determining factor is whether the analysis will be conducted at the individual or aggregate level. The decision about the number of dimensions in which to obtain a solution should be based on theory, interpretability, elbow criterion, and ease of use considerations. Labeling of the dimensions is a difficult task that requires subjective judgment. Several guidelines are available for assessing the reliability and validity of MDS solutions. Preference data can be subjected to either internal or external analysis. If the input data are of a qualitative nature, they can be analyzed via correspondence analysis. If the attribute-based approaches are used to obtain input data, spatial maps can also be obtained by means of factor or discriminant analysis.

Conjoint analysis is based on the notion that the relative importance that consumers attach to salient attributes, and the utilities they attach to the levels of attributes can be determined when consumers evaluate brand profiles that are constructed using these attributes and their levels. Formulating the problem requires an identification of the salient attributes and their levels. The pairwise and the full-profile approaches are commonly employed for constructing the stimuli. Statistical designs are available for reducing the number of stimuli in the evaluation task. The input data can be either nonmetric (rankings) or metric (ratings). Typically, the dependent variable is preference or intention to buy.

Although other procedures are available for analyzing conjoint analysis data, regression using dummy variables is becoming increasingly important. Interpreting the results requires an examination of the part-worth functions and relative importance weights. Several procedures are available for assessing the reliability and validity of conjoint analysis results.[42]

ACRONYMS

The steps involved in conducting multidimensional scaling may be represented by the acronym SCALING:

S   timuli selection: problem formulation
C   hoice of an MDS procedure
A   ssessing reliability and validity
L   abeling dimensions
I   nput data: metric or nonmetric
N   umber of dimensions
G   eometric representation and interpretation

The steps involved in conducting conjoint analysis may be represented by the acronym ANALYSIS:

A   ssessing reliability and validity
N   umber and levels of attributes: problem formulation
A   ttribute importance determination
L   evel of analysis: individual versus aggregate
Y   axis: utility values for attribute levels
S   timuli construction: full profile versus pairwise
I   nput data: metric or nonmetric
S   election of a conjoint procedure

EXERCISES

QUESTIONS

1. For what purposes are MDS procedures used?
2. What is meant by a spatial map?
3. Describe the steps involved in conducting MDS.
4. Describe the direct and derived approaches to obtaining MDS input data.
5. What factors influence the choice of an MDS procedure?
6. What guidelines are used for deciding on the number of dimensions in which to obtain an MDS solution?
7. Describe the ways in which the reliability and validity of MDS solutions can be assessed.
8. What is the difference between internal and external analysis of preference data?
9. Briefly describe correspondence analysis.
10. What is involved in formulating a conjoint analysis problem?
11. Describe the full profile approach to constructing stimuli in conjoint analysis.
12. Describe the pairwise approach to constructing stimuli in conjoint analysis.
13. How can regression analysis be used for analyzing conjoint data?
14. Graphically illustrate what is meant by part-worth functions.
15. What procedures are available for assessing the reliability and validity of conjoint analysis results?
16. Briefly describe hybrid conjoint analysis.

PROBLEMS

1. Identify two marketing research problems where MDS could be applied. Explain how you would apply MDS in these situations.
2. Identify two marketing research problems where conjoint analysis could be applied. Explain how you would apply conjoint analysis in these situations.

COMPUTER EXERCISES

1. Analyze the data of Table 21.1 using an appropriate MDS procedure. Compare your results with those given in the text.

2. Consider the following 12 brands of bar soap: Jergens, Dove, Zest, Dial, Camay, Ivory, Palmolive, Irish Spring, Lux, Safeguard, Tone, and Monchel. Form all the possible 66 pairs of these brands. Rate these pairs of brands in terms of similarity using a seven-point scale. Analyze the similarity judgments that you provided for the 12 bar soap brands. Use an appropriate MDS procedure, such as ALSCAL or KYST. Label the dimensions and interpret your own spatial map.

3. Construct the nine sneaker profiles given in Table 21.4. Rate these nine profiles in terms of your preference using a nine-point rating scale. Use OLS regression to develop part-worth functions for the three sneaker attributes, using the data you provided. How do your results compare with those reported in the text?

NOTES

1. Paul E. Green, Frank J. Carmone, Jr., and Scott M. Smith, *Multidimensional Scaling: Concepts and Applications* (Boston: Allyn and Bacon, 1989), pp. 16–17.

2. Mary Tonnenberger, "In Search of the Perfect Plastic," *Quirk's Marketing Research Review* 5 (May 1992): 6–7, 37.

3. For a review of MDS studies in marketing, see Lee G. Cooper, "A Review of Multidimensional Scaling in Marketing Research," *Applied Psychological Measurement* 7 (Fall 1983): 427–50.

4. An excellent discussion of the various aspects of MDS may be found in M. L. Davison, *Multidimensional Scaling* (New York: Wiley-Interscience, 1983); S. S. Schiffman, M. L. Reynolds, and F. W. Young, *Introduction to Multidimensional Scaling: Theory, Methods, and Applications* (New York: Academic Press, 1981); and J. B. Kruskal and M. Wish, *Multidimensional Scaling* (Beverly Hills, CA: Sage Publications, 1978).

5. Paul E. Green, Frank J. Carmone, Jr., and Scott M. Smith, *Multidimensional Scaling: Concepts and Applications* (Boston: Allyn and Bacon, 1989); and Joel Huber and Morris B. Holbrook, "Using Attribute Ratings for Product Positioning: Some Distinctions among Compositional Approaches," *Journal of Marketing Research* 16 (November 1979): 507–16.

6. See Naresh K. Malhotra, Arun K. Jain, and Christian Pinson, "The Robustness of MDS Configurations in the Case of Incomplete Data," *Journal of Marketing Research* 25 (February 1988): 95–102; P. E. Green, "On the Robustness of Multidimensional Scaling Techniques," *Journal of Marketing Research* 12 (1975): 73–81; and D. G. Weeks and P. M. Bentler, "A Comparison of Linear and Monotone Multidimensional Scaling Models," *Psychological Bulletin* 86 (1979): 349–54.

7. See J. B. Kruskal and M. Wish, *Multidimensional Scaling* (Beverly Hill: Sage Publications, 1978), pp. 89–92.

8. Kruskal's stress is probably the most commonly used measure for lack of fit. See J. B. Kruskal, "Multidimensional Scaling by Optimizing Goodness of Fit to a Nonmetric Hypothesis," *Psychometrika* 29 (March 1964): 1–27.

9. See Naresh K. Malhotra, "Validity and Structural Reliability of Multidimensional Scaling," *Journal of Marketing Research* 24 (May 1987): 164–73.

10. For a recent examination of the reliability and validity of MDS solutions, see Jan-Benedict E. M. Steenkamp, Hans C. M. Van Trijp, and Jos M. F. Ten Berge, "Perceptual Mapping Based on Idiosyncratic Sets of Attributes," *Journal of Marketing Research* 31 (February 1994): 15–27.

11. Joseph F. Hair, Jr., Ralph E. Anderson, Ronald L. Tatham, and William C. Black, *Multivariate Data Analysis with Readings*, 4th ed. (Englewood Cliffs: Prentice Hall, Inc., 1995), pp. 484–555.

12. See, for example, Wayne S. DeSarbo and D. Hoffman, "Constructing MDS Joint Spaces From Binary Choice Data: A New Multidimensional Unfolding Threshold Model for Marketing Research," *Journal of Marketing Research* 24 (February 1987): 40–54.

13. Yoram J. Wind, *Product Policy: Concepts, Methods, and Strategy* (Reading, MA: Addison-Wesley, 1982), pp. 83–88.

14. For a recent application of correspondence analysis see Paul E. Green and Abba M. Krieger, "A Simple Approach to Target Market Advertising Strategy," *Journal of the Market Research Society* 35 (April 1993): 161–70.

15. Paul F. Green, Frank J. Carmone, Jr., and Scott M. Smith, *Multidimensional Scaling: Concepts and Applications* (Boston: Allyn and Bacon, 1989), pp. 16–17.

16. See Michael J. Greenacre, "The Carroll-Green-Schaffer Scaling in Correspondence Analysis: A Theoretical and Empirical Appraisal," *Journal of Marketing Research* 26 (August 1989): 358–65; Michael J. Greenacre, *Theory and Applications of Correspondence Analyses* (New York: Academic Press, 1984); and D. L. Hoffman and G. R. Franke, "Correspondence Analysis: Graphical Representation of Categorical Data in Marketing Research," *Journal of Marketing Research* 23 (August 1986): 213–27.

17. For the use of factor analysis in constructing spatial maps, see Larry Hasson, "Monitoring Social Change," *Journal of the Market Research Society* 37 (January 1995): 69–80.

18. John R. Hauser and Frank S. Koppelman, "Alternative Perceptual Mapping Techniques: Relative Accuracy and Usefulness," *Journal of Marketing Research* 16 (November 1979): 495–506. Hauser and Koppelman conclude that factor analysis is superior to discriminant analysis.

19. For recent applications and issues in conjoint analysis, see Rajeev Kohli and Vijay Mahajan, "A Reservation-Price Model for Optimal Pricing of Multiattribute Products in Conjoint Analysis," *Journal of Marketing Research* 28 (August 1991): 347–54; Paul E. Green, Abba M. Krieger, and Manoj K. Agarwal, "Adaptive Conjoint Analysis: Some Caveats and Suggestions," *Journal of Marketing Research* 28 (May 1991): 215–22; and Paul E. Green and Abba M. Krieger, "Segmenting Markets With Conjoint Analysis," *Journal of Marketing* 55 (October 1991): 20–31.

20. For a managerial overview of conjoint analysis, see Paul E. Green and Yoram Wind, "New Way to Measure Consumers' Judgments," *Harvard Business Review* (July–August 1975): 107–17.

21. For an overview of conjoint analysis in marketing, see Paul E. Green and V. Srinivasan, "Conjoint Analysis in Marketing: New Developments with Implications for Research and Practice," *Journal of Marketing* 54 (October 1990): 3–19; and P. E. Green and V. Srinivasan, "Conjoint Analysis in Consumer Research: Issues and Outlook," *Journal of Consumer Research* 5 (September 1978): 102–23.

22. The various applications of conjoint analysis have been described in Philippe Cattin and Dick R. Wittink, "Commercial Use of Conjoint Analysis: A Survey," *Journal of Marketing* 46 (Summer 1982): 44–53.

23. Dick R. Wittink and Philippe Cattin, "Commercial Use of Conjoint Analysis: An Update," *Journal of Marketing* 53 (July 1989): 91–97. For using conjoint analysis to measure price sensitivity, see "Multi-Stage Conjoint Methods to Measure Price Sensitivity," *Sawtooth News* 10 (Winter 1994–1995): 5–6.

24. These three attributes are a subset of five attributes used by Michael Etgar and Naresh K. Malhotra, in "Determinants of Price Dependency: Personal and Perceptual Factors," *Journal of Consumer Research* 8 (September 1981): 217–22.

25. Gerard H. Loosschilder, Edward Rosbergen, Marco Vriens, and Dick R. Wittink, "Pictorial Stimuli in Conjoint Analysis-to Support Product Styling Decisions," *Journal of the Market Research Society* 37 (January 1995): 17–34.

26. See Sidney Addleman, "Orthogonal Main-Effect Plans for Asymmetrical Factorial Experiments," *Technometrics* 4 (February 1962): 21–36; Paul E. Green, "On the Design of Choice Experiments Involving Multifactor Alternatives," *Journal of Consumer Research* 1 (September 1974): 61–68; and Warren F. Kuhfeld, Randall D. Tobias, and Mark Garratt, "Efficient Experimental Designs with Marketing Applications," *Journal of Marketing Research* 31 (November 1994): 545–57.

27. More complex conjoint designs are also possible. See Harmen Oppewal, Jordan J. Louviere, and Harry J. P. Timmermans, "Modeling Hierarchical Conjoint Processes with Integrated Choice Experiments," *Journal of Marketing Research* 31 (February 1994): 15–27.

28. Arun K. Jain, Franklin Acito, Naresh K. Malhotra, and Vijay Mahajan, "A Comparison of the Internal Validity of Alternative Parameter Estimation Methods in Decompositional Multiattribute Preference Models," *Journal of Marketing Research* (August 1979): 313–22.

29. Arun K. Jain, Franklin Acito, Naresh K. Malhotra, and Vijay Mahajan, "A Comparison of the Internal Validity of Alternative Parameter Estimation Methods in Decompositional Multiattribute Preference Models," *Journal of Marketing Research* (August 1979): 313–22; and Dick R. Wittink and Philippe Cattin, "Alternative Estimation Methods for Conjoint Analysis: A Monté Carlo Study," *Journal of Marketing Research* 18 (February 1981): 101–6.

30. William L. Moore, "Levels of Aggregation in Conjoint Analysis: An Empirical Comparison," *Journal of Marketing Research* 17 (November 1980): 516–23.

31. F. J. Carmone and P. E. Green, "Model Misspecification in Multiattribute Parameter Estimation," *Journal of Marketing Research* 18 (February 1981): 87–93.

32. For a recent application of conjoint analysis using OLS regression see Amy Ostrom and Dawn Iacobucci, "Consumer Trade-Offs and the Evaluation of Services," *Journal of Marketing* 59 (January 1995): 17–28.

33. Naresh K. Malhotra, "Structural Reliability and Stability of Nonmetric Conjoint Analysis," *Journal of Marketing Research* 19 (May 1982): 199–207; Thomas W. Leigh, David B. MacKay, and John O. Summers, "Reliability and Validity of Conjoint Analysis and Self-Explicated Weights: A Comparison," *Journal of Marketing Research* 21 (November 1984): 456–62; and Madhav N. Segal, "Reliability of Conjoint Analysis: Contrasting Data Collection Procedures," *Journal of Marketing Research* 19 (February 1982): 139–43.

34. Del I. Hawkins, Roger J. Best, and Kenneth A. Coney, *Consumer Behavior Implications for Marketing Strategy* 5th ed. (Homewood, IL: Richard D. Irwin, 1992), pp. 503–5.

35. Paul E. Green and V. Srinivasan, "Conjoint Analysis in Consumer Research: Issues and Outlook," *Journal of Consumer Research* (September 1978): 103–23.

36. For an exposition of hybrid models, see Paul E. Green, "Hybrid Models for Conjoint Analysis: An Expository Review," *Journal of Marketing Research* 21 (May 1984): 155–69.

37. Diane Schneidman, "Research Method Designed to Determine Price for New Products, Line Extensions," *Marketing News* (October 23, 1987): 11.

38. Diana T. Kurylko, "In Europe, Image Is Key."

39. David Butler, "Thai Superconcentrates Foam," *Advertising Age* (January 18, 1993).

40. R. E. Reidenbach and D. P. Robin, "Toward the Development of a Multidimensional Scale for Improving Evaluations of Business Ethics," *Journal of Business Ethics* 9 (1990): 639–53.

41. A. P. M. Coxon, *The User's Guide to Multidimensional Scaling* (London: Heinemann, 1982).

42. The assistance of James Agarwal with the international marketing research example, the assistance of Mark Leach and Gina Miller in writing the ethics section, and the assistance of Mark Peterson in writing the computer applications section is gratefully acknowledged.

PROFESSIONAL PERSPECTIVES

The Logic of Statistical Significance Tests
Market Facts, Inc.

INTRODUCTION

Statistical significance testing, or "hypothesis testing," plays an important role in marketing research. Significance tests are routinely carried out on sample means, proportions or percentages, correlation coefficients, differences between means or proportions, etc. When used appropriately, such tests allow the user to control the risks of drawing erroneous conclusions or inferences about characteristics of the population based on data obtained from a representative sample.

This report describes the logic underlying tests of statistical significance. Understanding this logic is crucial for interpreting statistical test results correctly and for drawing valid inferences from these results.

OVERVIEW AND EXAMPLE

The basic logic involved in a statistical significance test can best be understood in the context of an example. Every significance test begins with a question or hypothesis about some characteristic of the population. For example, a researcher may be interested in whether the true average tread life of a particular type of tire is 40,000 miles, as claimed by the manufacturer. In this case, the population of interest is all tires of the specified type produced by that manufacturer, and the hypothesis to be "tested" is that the true average tread life is 40,000 miles.

The decision of whether or not to reject this hypothesis will be based on results obtained from a random sample of such tires. In this example, the sample size is 100 tires. If the sample yields an average tread life "near" 40,000 miles, then there is little reason to doubt the validity of the manufacturer's claim. (A numeric definition of "near" necessarily depends on the risks the researcher is willing to tolerate of reaching a wrong conclusion, either rejecting the claim if it is actually true, or not rejecting the claim if it is false. These risks are discussed in more detail later.) On the other hand, if the sample average differs substantially from 40,000 miles—an improbable result if the claim is true—then one is led to believe the claim is false, and the hypothesis that the true average tread life is

40,000 miles is rejected. In this case, the researcher would conclude that the true average is either less than or greater than 40,000 miles, depending on the results observed in the sample.

This example will be used throughout this report to illustrate specific points concerning the logic involved in significance tests. Although this example pertains to an hypothesis about a population mean, similar logic applies to all other situations as well, such as tests concerning proportions, correlations, differences between means, and so forth.

THE NULL AND ALTERNATIVE HYPOTHESES

As the preceding example illustrates, the problem addressed by a significance test is one of choosing between two competing hypotheses about the population value in question. The hypothesis actually tested is often referred to as the "null hypothesis" and is denoted H_0. (The term *null* is customarily used because the hypothesis states that the population mean, proportion, correlation, difference, etc., does *not* differ from the stated value.) In the example, the null hypothesis is $H_0: \mu = 40,000$ (or $H_0: \mu - 40,000 = 0$), where μ denotes the population average. This hypothesis is *assumed to be true* for the purpose of the test.

The alternative hypothesis, denoted H_A, is the one to be accepted if the null hypothesis is rejected. The alternative hypothesis can be either nondirectional (e.g., $H_A: \mu \neq 40,000$) or directional (e.g., $H_A: \mu < 40,000$), depending on the nature of the question to be answered. It is important to note that the alternative hypothesis *must* be specified *before* looking at the sample data in order for the prespecified risks of drawing an erroneous conclusion to be valid.

A nondirectional alternative allows the user to reject the null hypothesis if the sample outcome differs from the hypothesized value in either direction. In the example, a sample mean that is substantially less than or greater than 40,000 can lead to rejection of H_0.

When a directional alternative is specified, the null hypothesis can be rejected *only* if the sample result is in the direction specified by H_A. In the example, if the manufacturer's claim was that the tires last *at least* 40,000 miles, then it would be appropriate to specify the alternative hypothesis as H_A: $\mu < 40{,}000$. (In this case, the null hypothesis could be stated as H_0: $\mu \geq 40{,}000$.) Note that the null hypothesis in this situation cannot be rejected if the sample average exceeds 40,000, *regardless* of the magnitude of the difference. That is, the researcher is forced to ignore any difference in the unanticipated direction, regardless of size. If the sample mean in the example turned out to be 67,400 miles, many researchers would find it difficult to resist concluding that the true average exceeds 40,000 miles, even though this conclusion is unwarranted if the alternative hypothesis is H_A: $\mu < 40{,}000$. The issue of directional versus nondirectional hypothesis tests is discussed further at the end of this paper.

TYPES OF DECISION ERRORS

Since the null hypothesis is a statement about a characteristic of the population, one will never know, based on sample results, whether it is true or false. Therefore, one runs a risk of rejecting the null hypothesis if it is true or failing to reject it if it is false. It will not be known if an error has been made, but the risk of doing so can be controlled; the purpose of a significance test is to control this risk.

The possible outcomes of a statistical significance test are displayed in Exhibit 1. If the null hypothesis is *true* and the sample yields a value that differs substantially from the value assumed under H_0 (i.e., a result which is improbable if H_0 is true), then H_0 is rejected and a type I error is made. The risk of making this type of error is called the *significance level* of the test and is denoted α. The *maximum* tolerable risk of committing this type of error is set by the researcher. After the significance test calculations have been carried out, the researcher can also ascertain the *actual* risk of committing a type I error. As the actual type I error risk becomes smaller, the researcher becomes more confident that H_0 should be rejected. If the actual risk is less than the prespecified maximum risk, then H_0 is rejected; otherwise, it is not. In the example, if the researcher adopted a maximum risk level of $\alpha = .05$, there would be at most a 5% risk of obtaining a sample average that would lead to rejecting H_0: $\mu = 40{,}000$ if H_0 is, in fact, true. In other words, H_0 would be rejected only if the obtained sample average is among the 5% most extreme expected if H_0 is true.

If the null hypothesis is *true* and a sample result is obtained which is "close" to the value specified by H_0, then H_0 is not rejected—a correct decision. The probability of this happening is the probability of *not* committing a type I error, or $1 - \alpha$. In the example, the probability is .95 that H_0: $\mu = 40{,}000$ would not be rejected if it is true.

When the null hypothesis is *false* but the sample value does not differ substantially from the assumed value, then H_0 is not rejected—a type II error. The actual probability of committing this type of error (denoted β) depends on the size of the difference between the *true* population value and the value assumed under the null hypothesis. This difference is called the *effect size*.[1] The larger the effect size, the smaller the risk of a type II error (i.e., failing to detect the difference). In the example, the researcher is less likely to obtain a sample mean close to 40,000 if the true average is 50,000 than if it is 41,000. Note that since the true population value is unknown, the actual probability of committing a type II error is also unknown, although it can be calculated for various specified effect sizes. In the example, one could compute the risk of a type II error assuming the effect size is 1,000 miles, 2,000 miles, and so forth.

Finally, if the null hypothesis is false and it is rejected, then a correct decision is made. The *power* of the test represents the probability of detecting a difference when a true difference exists. This is the probability of *not* committing a type II error, or $1 - \beta$. Since the true probability of a type II error is unknown, the true power is unknown as well, although it can be computed for various effect sizes.

MAKING A DECISION

The decision of whether or not to reject the null hypothesis is based on the probability of obtaining a sample result at least as extreme as the result actually obtained, under the assumption that the null hypothesis is true. In the example, if the mean tread life for the sample of 100 tires is 41,200 miles, then (assuming a nondirectional test) the question becomes, "What is the probability of obtaining a sample average that differs from 40,000 by at least 1,200 miles, given that no difference is expected?" Stated another way, "What is the probability of obtaining a sample average < 38,800 or > 41,200 if the true average is 40,000?" If the obtained sample average is among the 5% most extreme that would be expected assuming H_0 is true, then H_0 will be rejected.

---

[1]An "effect size" is often defined in terms of standard deviation units rather than in the original scale (miles, in the example). For the purposes of this report, however, the distinction is not important.

EXHIBIT 1

Possible Outcomes of a Significance Test

		DECISION	
		Reject H_0	Do Not Reject H_0
True Situation	H_0 is true	Type I error Probability = α (Significance level)	Correct decision Probability = $1 - \alpha$
	H_0 is false	Correct decision Probability = $1 - \beta$ (Power of the test)	Type II error Probability = β

To answer this question, one must determine the distribution of means of random samples of size 100 under the assumption that H_0 is true. In this case, statistical theory indicates that the distribution of sample means is approximately normal with a mean of 40,000 and a standard deviation equal to the population standard deviation (σ) divided by the square root of the sample size. This quantity, $\sigma / \sqrt{n}$, is called the standard error of the mean. (The standard error is a measure of the "uncertainty" one has about the true population value; the larger the sample size, the less uncertainty one has.) When the population standard deviation is unknown, the sample standard deviation(s) can be used as an estimate. If the sample standard deviation is 5,000 miles, then the standard error of the mean (i.e., the estimated standard deviation of means of samples of size 100) is $5,000 / \sqrt{100} = 500$.

Given the mean and standard error of the distribution of sample means (40,000 and 500, respectively), a t distribution with $n - 1$ degrees of freedom can be used to determine the probability associated with the sample outcome. In this case, if H_0 is true, then 95% of the sample means will fall between $40,000 \pm 1.98$ standard errors, that is, between $40,000 \pm 1.98 \times 500 = 40,000 \pm 990$ miles, where 1.98 is the t-value for 99 degrees of freedom. So, given a maximum type I error risk of 5%, any sample mean < 39,010 or > 40,990 would lead to rejection of the null hypothesis. (This rejection region is illustrated in Exhibit 2.) Since the obtained sample mean is among these, H_0 can be rejected. In this instance, the actual sample mean lies $1,200/500 = 2.4$ standard errors above 40,000. From a t distribution table, one can ascertain that a sample mean this extreme would

occur with a probability of about .018, or 18 times in 1,000 samples, if H_0 is true. Hence, the actual risk of a type I error (rejecting H_0 if it is true) is .018. The conclusion that H_0 should be rejected would typically be stated by saying that the difference between the sample mean and the hypothesized mean is significant "at the .018 level," or "with at least 98.2 percent confidence." In general, the confidence level is $100 \times (1 - \text{type I error risk})$.

It should be noted that there is a direct correspondence between statistical significance tests and confidence intervals. A confidence interval specifies a range, drawn around a sample value, within which the true population value is expected to lie with some chosen degree of confidence. Specifically, if a difference is statistically significant at the α level (using a nondirectional test), then a 100 $(1 - \alpha)$ percent confidence interval drawn around the sam-

EXHIBIT 2

Null Hypothesis is True

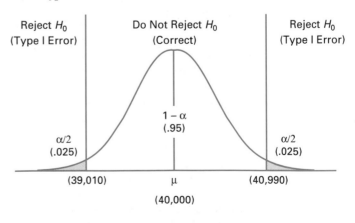

ple value will not contain the hypothesized population value. In the tire example, the difference between the sample mean of 41,200 and the hypothesized mean of 40,000 is significant at the .05 level, so a 95 percent confidence interval drawn around 41,200 will not include 40,000. A 95% confidence interval for the example would extend from (41,200 – 990) to (41,200 + 990), or from 40,210 to 42,190 miles.

When the null hypothesis concerns a population characteristic other than a mean (such as a population proportion or correlation), the approach is similar. The appropriate sample statistic is calculated and statistical theory is relied upon to determine the nature of the distribution of that statistic in repeated random samples, assuming that H_0 is true.

GRAPHIC ILLUSTRATION OF A SIGNIFICANCE TEST

All the concepts involved in a significance test (error risks, power, etc.) are illustrated in Exhibits 2 and 3. These figures apply specifically to the problem of testing the null hypothesis that the population mean is equal to some specified value, as in the example considered. However, analogous pictures could be drawn to illustrate tests concerning correlations, proportions, variances, differences between means, and so forth. Exhibit 2 depicts the situation in which the null hypothesis is true and Exhibit 3 the situation in which it is false. The rejection regions shown in these figures apply to the case in which a nondirectional

alternative hypothesis is specified. The numbers in parentheses pertain specifically to the tire tread life example.

In Exhibit 2, the null hypothesis is true, so the hypothesized sampling distribution of means and the true sampling distribution are the same. As indicated earlier this distribution is normal, with mean = μ and standard deviation = $\sigma/\sqrt{n}$. For a type I error risk of α = .05, the rejection region (shaded) would include the 5% most extreme sample means. Note that with a nondirectional test, the total type I error risk is divided between the two tails (usually equally, with $\alpha/2$ in each tail, as shown). If a more stringent type I error risk were specified (e.g., α = .01), the decision lines would be further from μ; the total shaded area would be .01 (with .005 in each tail).

In Exhibit 3, the null hypothesis is false, so there are actually two sampling distributions to be considered. The hypothesized distribution of sample means is centered at the hypothesized mean, μ (40,000 in the example), but the *true* (actual) sampling distribution is centered at the true population mean, μ_{True}. In practice, this value is unknown, so the true power and type II error risk are unknown as well, as indicated earlier. For the purpose of this example, it will be assumed that the true average tread life for the type of tire in question is 41,100 miles, as shown in the figure. Hence, the *true* effect size in this case is 41,100 – 40,000 = 1,100 miles.

The decision lines in Exhibit 3 are the same as those in Exhibit 2, since they are determined assuming that the null hypothesis is *true*. However, when H_0 is false, *more*

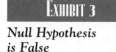

Null Hypothesis is False

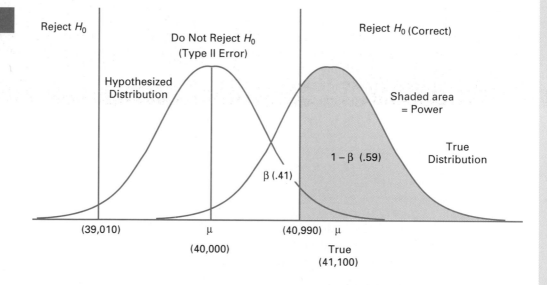

733

than 5% of the samples one could draw would have means lying in the rejection region. The true probability of rejecting the null hypothesis—that is, the power of the test—is the proportion of the *true* sampling distribution that lies in the rejection region. This is the shaded area in Exhibit 3. For the example data, the true power of the test is the proportion of the true distribution that lies to the right of 40,990 miles (plus the negligible proportion that lies to the left of 39,010 miles). The value, 40,990, is .22 standard errors below the true mean of 41,100; using a *t* distribution table, one can determine that 59% of the true distribution lies to the right of this value. Hence, the true power is .59. If the population means is 41,100 miles and the standard deviation is 5,000 miles, the chances are about 6 in 10 that one would obtain a sample mean that differs significantly from 40,000. The true type II error risk is 1 − .59 = .41. This is the actual probability of failing to reject the null hypothesis when it should be rejected.

TYPE I VERSUS TYPE II ERRORS

For a given sample size, there is a tradeoff between the risks of committing a type I and a type II error. Specifically, adopting a lower type I error risk causes the type II error risk to rise, and vice versa. In Exhibits 2 and 3, reducing the type I error risk amounts to moving the decision lines further from 40,000, making the rejection regions (and thus power) smaller. Conversely, allowing a greater risk of a type I error moves the decision lines closer to 40,000, thus increasing the size of the rejection region (and power) and reducing the risk of a type II error.

There *is* a way to reduce the risk of a type II error without increasing the risk of a type I error: increase the sample size. The effect of increasing the sample size is to reduce the uncertainty one has about the population value. As noted earlier, a measure of this uncertainty is provided by the standard error, which determines the width of the distributions in Exhibits 2 and 3. Hence, in these displays, the distributions become narrower as the sample size increases.

If the sample size in the example was increased from 100 to 400, the standard error of the mean would be cut in half—from 500 to 250—without affecting the risk of a type I error. With a sample size of 400, the *t* value corresponding to a type I error risk of 5% is 1.96. Hence, the rejection region consists of all values that lie at least 1.96 standard errors, or 1.96 × 250 = 490 miles, away from 40,000; that is, all values below 39,510 and above 40,490 miles. The power of the test would be the proportion of

the *true* sampling distribution lying in this range, which is approximately .99, so the risk of committing a type II error would be reduced from .41 to .01.

Since power is affected by sample size, it is wise to consider power when deciding on the sample size to be used. Although the *true* power will be unknown, one can determine the sample size necessary to achieve some desired degree of power for the smallest effect size that is considered to be of any practical importance. A sample that is too small will have insufficient power to detect an effect size of interest, whereas a sample that is too large can lead to trivial effects being deemed statistically significant with high degrees of confidence.

DIRECTIONAL VERSUS NONDIRECTIONAL TESTS

In the tire example, a directional hypothesis is reasonable if the manufacturer claims that the tires are designed to last *at least* 40,000 miles, and this claim is based on physical attributes of the tire (rubber composition, tread depth, etc.). However, in most marketing research situations, it is difficult to predict the direction of a difference prior to collecting the sample data. This is because the data typically constitute respondents' attitudes and *perceptions* of products, rather than physical characteristics of the products themselves. For example, in product preference tests, consumers are not constrained to favor one product over the other, even if one is an "improved" version of the other. One user of the data, who wants to switch to the "new" product only if it can be shown to be more preferred, might specify the alternative hypothesis that preference for the improved product exceeds preference for the original product. However, another user of the data may want to go with the new product unless it is less preferred than the original product, which corresponds to the alternative hypothesis that preference for the original product is greater. The only way to statistically address both questions is to specify the nondirectional hypothesis that the products are not equally preferred. In most situations, nondirectional tests are recommended, since they allow the user more flexibility in terms of the inferences that can be drawn.

STATISTICAL SIGNIFICANCE VERSUS PRACTICAL IMPORTANCE

It is important to recognize that the "*statistical* significance" of an effect has *nothing* to do with its "*practical* significance" or "importance." Statistical significance is based solely on laws of probability; a statistically significant effect is simply one which is "rare" if the null hypothesis is true. As the comments in the preceding section indicate, the statistical significance of an effect is largely a function of sample size; given a large enough sample, *any* difference regardless of size, can be declared "statistically significant." The size of a "practically important" difference must be determined without recourse to statistical considerations, and the answer may vary from one researcher to another. However, once the size of a "practically important" difference has been defined, one can use this definition to determine a sample size that will ensure adequate power to detect real differences of that size or larger.

Balancing Confidence and Power for Decision Making
Market Facts, Inc.

INTRODUCTION

Tests of consumer preference are performed to reduce risk to the manufacturer. A new product formulation may be compared with an existing product using this type of testing with the intent of "improving" the product line. Improvement may come from increased profits from existing share or from increased share. Inherent in any product change is the chance that the product modification is to the detriment of the manufacturer. The manufacturer risks loss in sales if the new product is worse than the current one. Conversely, there is the risk of losing the chance to increase profits by not producing a cheaper, yet equally preferable, product. Unfortunately, statistical analyses performed on product test data rarely take these risks into account. This paper presents an example of a product test, relating monetary risks to levels of significance and power of the test of product preference.

EXAMPLE

Consider a manufacturer that is planning to test consumer preference for two products: A, currently on the market, and B, a cheaper variation of A. If management can produce product B without disrupting the $100 million franchise built on sales of product A, $1 million per year in production costs will be saved. The objective of the preference test is to determine whether product B is at least as preferable as product A; management will produce product B if it is at least equal in preference to A.

A test among consumers will be performed to assess this difference in preference. Consumers will taste both products and then be asked to state their preference for either product A or B. (For simplicity of exposition, a response of "no preference" would not be allowed.) The proportion of respondents preferring each are to be compared.

OUTCOMES

A comparison of the preference proportions yields three possible outcomes: B is worse than A, B is better than A, or the two products are equally preferred. However, the manufacturer has decided to introduce product B if the test either indicates that product B is more preferred than A or there is no difference in preference. Therefore, future production for the manufacturer can be determined by combining these outcomes such that only two competing results need to be considered when performing statistical significance testing: (1) B is worse than A versus (2) B is equal to or better than A. In statistical theory, these are referred to as the alternative hypothesis and null hypothesis, respectively. Further, the outcomes to be tested correspond to a one-tail test of significance. These hypotheses can be taken as conjectures about how the products truly compare among all members of the population to whom inference about the product test is to be made. These population situations are cross-referenced by possible sample outcomes in Table 1. Note that the effect of sampling variability may lead the manufacturer to a conclusion different than that which should be made.

DECISION ERRORS

Since the manufacturer's decision of whether to replace product A with B will be based on data obtained from a sample, there are elements of risk, or error, associated with interpreting the test results. Specifically, there are two errors that can be made, type I and type II, as indicated in the table.

TABLE 1

Population Situation	Sample Outcome	
	B is Worse Than A (Manufacturer Stays with A)	B is Better Than or Equal to A (Manufacturer Introduces B)
B is better than or equal to A	Miss opportunity to save $1 million per year (type I error)	Save $1 million per year (correct decision)
B is worse than A	Protected from introducing less preferred product (correct decision)	Save $1 million per year at risk of eroding franchise (type II error)

A type I error is made if the test results indicate that product A is more preferred than B but in reality either product B is more preferred or both products are preferred equally. The cost to the manufacturer of making this type of error is the lost opportunity of saving $1 million per year in production costs.

Consider next that product A is truly better than B in the population. If the test results either indicate that product B is more preferred or there is no difference in preference (i.e., product B is considered to be at least equally preferable to product A), then a type II error has been committed. The cost of this type of error may be more serious. Here management will save $1 million per year in production costs, sales may drop with the introduction of the less preferred product. For example, if the manufacturer experienced a 4% drop in sales, the loss would be approximately $4 million based on the $100 million franchise. In this situation, a type II error is more costly than a type I error.

Unfortunately, many researchers do not consider the losses associated with type I and type II errors. Typically, a manufacturer will perform a product test and apply a 95% confidence level decision rule for interpreting the test results. This high level of confidence limits the risk of type I error to 5%. However, no consideration is given to making a type II error, which may, as in this case, be more costly.

EXAMPLE, REVISITED

Suppose that the manufacturer has a budget that allows for a sample of 200 consumers for the product test. Further, management is willing to consider A and B as being roughly equal in preference even if preference for B is 10 percentage points lower than A. If 55% of the consumers prefer product A, then 45% must prefer product B (assuming a response of "no preference" is not allowed).

With a given sample size, there is a trade-off between the risks of committing a type I and type II error. Specifically, for type II error risk to fall, the type I error risk must rise, and vice versa. For a given difference of interest, the only way to reduce the risk of type II error without affecting type I error is to increase the sample size. However, in this situation (as well as in many research studies) limited research dollars prevent the manufacturer from affording this luxury.

Given these constraints, the power of the test can be statistically determined for various confidence levels through the use of power tables found in many statistical texts. Returning to the example, if management chooses the typical confidence level of 95%, the power of the test is only 42%. That is, if the true population proportions for A and B are .55 and .45, respectively (for a difference of 10 percentage points), and 95% confidence is used, the difference would be detected and considered significant only 42% of the time in repeated sampling and testing with 200 consumers from the same population. In other words, the odds are stacked against management detecting a real difference of .10. Considering the large dollar risk associated with a type II error, it is in management's interests to increase power. (Note that a difference between product preference proportions of .10, as conjectured here, is far larger than typically desired by most researchers. Yet power, the ability to detect a difference of this magnitude, is still poor.)

POWER

As previously mentioned, for a given difference and confidence level, power can be increased (risk of type II error decreased) by increasing the sample size. However, in this instance, the sample size is constrained by the budget. Consequently, the power of the test can only be increased

TABLE 2

Confidence Level (1 – type I error)	Power[a] (1 – type II error)
95%	42%
90%	53%
80%	72%
60%	88%

[a]Based on $N = 200$, difference $= .10$

by decreasing the confidence level. To illustrate this, Table 2 lists the power associated with various confidence levels (given the constraints discussed above).

In reviewing this table, the tradeoff between the two probabilities becomes evident confidence is sacrificed as power increases. For management to increase the power of the test to 88%, a 60% confidence level must be used in testing the difference between preference proportions. This level of confidence is substantially lower than the typical 95% rule. However, the higher power associated with this confidence level will protect the manufacturer from risking sales by introducing an "equally or more preferable" product that is in fact less preferable. Specifically, with this choice of confidence and power, management would consider product A as preferable if the proportion preferring product A was greater than that for product B and the difference was significant with at least 60% confidence.

This material is reproduced from Research on Research, Report No. 43 by Market Facts, Inc. with permission of the company. A copy of this report may be obtained from the company.

An Alternative to the Mean

Market Facts, Inc.

INTRODUCTION

Information on a population of interest is typically gathered by drawing a sample from that population. The distribution of sample responses on a variable of interest is used as an approximation of the population distribution. Usually the sample mean, or average response, is calculated and serves as an estimate of the actual population mean. This statistic is, then, viewed as the value that typifies, or characterizes, the population of interest. Although this practice of relying upon the sample mean to represent the population is generally sound, there are instances when the mean should *not* be relied upon. This paper discusses the use of an alternative statistic, the sample median, in such instances.

BEVERAGE CONSUMPTION EXAMPLE

A sample of drinkers of a certain type of beverage was drawn from Market Facts' Consumer Mail Panel to examine the amount of beverage consumed. Respondents were asked, "How many drinks or glasses of beverage have you drunk, both at home or away from home, in the past, seven days?" The average consumption per seven days, in the sample, was 11.6 drinks or glasses. The distribution of the 682 responses obtained is displayed in Figure 1. This serves as an approximation of the distribution of consumption for the entire population of beverage drinkers.

The frequency distribution is asymmetric. The tail of the distribution on the right-hand side of the plot is drawn out, or somewhat pronounced, in comparison to the left-hand tail. This is termed a *skewed* distribution, in this case *skewed to the right*, or *positively skewed*, in that the pronounced tail is on the right, or extends in the direction of larger positive values. Essentially, there are a few extremely large observations, not matched by a corresponding number of extremely small observations, which cause this skewness.

THE MEAN—TYPICAL VALUE?

A histogram of the sample frequency distribution (such as the one presented in Figure 1) can be viewed as a "complete" summary of the information obtained from the sample on the variable of interest. The sample mean is a descriptive statistic that commonly can provide a more concise, or convenient, summary; the sample mean serves as an estimate or measure of location of the population center. As such, the mean is typically viewed as that value that best typifies, or summarizes, the values of all respondents in the population (and, more immediately, of the sample) on that variable. The mean may also serve as an "expected value": given no other information about a

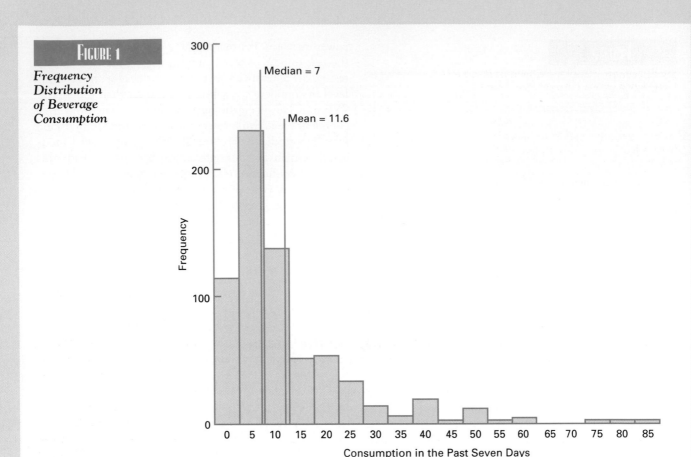

FIGURE 1

Frequency Distribution of Beverage Consumption

Median = 7

Mean = 11.6

Frequency

300

200

100

0

0   5   10   15   20   25   30   35   40   45   50   55   60   65   70   75   80   85

Consumption in the Past Seven Days

member of the population of interest, the mean may be the researcher's best guess as to that member's actual value.[1]

As mentioned, the mean represents the center of the observations in the sample or population. To illustrate, a histogram of the frequency distribution balances when supported at the mean. If the distribution is *normal* (symmetric and bell-shaped), or just symmetric and unimodal, the mean of the observations is found in the middle of the distribution, at the heaviest concentration of observations, and so legitimately can be viewed as the typical value. More often than not, the sample mean is useful as a typical or representative value, since the distributions dealt with in practice frequently do not differ greatly from bell-shaped.

However, certain types of data collected by market researchers tend to have a pronounced tail to the right or left. Such skewed distributions are commonly encountered when dealing with questions of consumption (gen-

erally with a few respondents consuming relatively large quantities of the product of interest), frequency of product usage, income, and so forth. In general, any variable with either a fixed lower or upper bound will tend to have skewed distribution. If a unimodal distribution is grossly skewed, the mean becomes of declining utility, that is, the mean no longer serves as the most reasonable summary or typical value.[2]

To illustrate this, first consider a very small sample (n = 5) of beverage drinkers, for which the consumption data are presented in Table 1. Mean consumption was 16.4 drinks or glasses. Note, though, that exclusion of the fifth respondent would dramatically lower the mean to a value of 5.5 per seven days, a value much closer to, and thus more representative of, the majority of the observations. The mean is very sensitive to the extreme consumption rate

---

[1]The mean is the best guess if the researcher chooses to minimize squared errors (see Table 1), such as the sample variance (s^2).

[2]The mean may also be of questionable utility if the distribution is multimodal. However, further exposition and an alternative in such cases is beyond the scope of this paper.

TABLE 1

Small Sample Beverage Consumption Data

Respondent	Past Seven Days Consumption	ABSOLUTE DIFFERENCE FROM		SQUARED DIFFERENCE FROM	
		Mean (16.4)	Median (7)	Mean (16.4)	Median (7)
1	0	16.4	7	268.96	49
2	5	11.4	2	129.96	4
3	7	9.4	0	88.36	0
4	10	6.4	3	40.96	9
5	60	43.6	53	1900.96	2809
		87.2	65	2429.20	2871

reported by the fifth respondent, making the mean a higher, unrepresentative value. In general, the mean is very sensitive to extreme, or outlying observations.

Returning to the original example, the pronounced right-hand tail (skewness) of the distribution has the same effect on the mean as the extreme rate of consumption reported by the fifth respondent in the small sample just discussed (Table 1). The mean is very sensitive to the presence of data in such far flung tails and is shifted (pulled) in the direction of the extreme values, compromising the mean's customary role of a typical value. In this case, as always with positively skewed distributions, the mean is a higher value than that which would be viewed as typical, or an accurate summary, of the majority of the data. Thus, use of the sample mean as an estimate of the "representative," or typical, value in such cases is ill-advised.

AN ALTERNATIVE—THE MEDIAN

The median is another descriptive statistic that can provide a concise summary of location for a sample and population. The median is defined as that value (in an ordered list) that has an equal number of responses on either side of it or as the value associated with the respondent in the "middle" (50th percentile) of the distribution. Thus, the median divides a frequency distribution into two halves and for this reason has intuitive appeal as a descriptor of location.

The median is much less influenced than the mean by extreme values by virtue of its definition. The sample values are initially ranked, with the middle-ranked observation defined as the median. The pronounced tail of a skewed distribution corresponds to the highest (or lowest)

few ranked observations, which largely ignores that these observations are extreme. Since the ranks give no indication as to the size of differences among data values, the few extreme observations have little effect on the median.

Returning to the example, the median consumption from the sample of beverage drinkers was 7 drinks or glasses. The two reference lines contained in Figure 1 depict the median consumption along with the mean, or average, reported beverage consumption (11.6 per seven days) for the sample. Note that the median is, indeed, closer to the heaviest concentration of data in the distribution. This is a direct result of the infrequent high rates of consumption (those in the pronounced right-hand tail) exerting much greater influence on the mean than on the median. Thus, the median is more representative of the majority of the data than the mean in this case.

To further demonstrate that the median is not overly influenced by extreme observations, recall the small sample of beverage drinkers presented earlier (Table 1), which contained one extreme observation (reported consumption of 60 drinks or glasses per seven days). While the mean shifted dramatically depending on whether this value was included or not (16.4 and 5.5, respectively), the median consumption is 7 for the entire sample and 6 when the extreme observation is excluded, a small shift.

In summary, the median is a more representative summary statistic than the mean in cases where the data are unimodal yet markedly skewed and thus should be preferred to the mean in such cases. As demonstrated, the mean is affected by extreme observations (either high, as is the case in the consumption example, or low), but the median is not.

QUANTIFYING "TYPICAL"

To this point, the mean and median have been described as typical values when they are effective summaries. Typical has been portrayed in a rather qualitative sense, as simply at or near the middle of a distribution of data. A quantification of what is meant by typical will yield a less subjective evaluation of the goodness of the mean and median as summary statistics. The statistic that is most typical would be considered the best summary.

Defining a measure of closeness of each observation to the mean or median is, perhaps, the simplest approach in assessing how "typical" each of these statistics may be. An intuitively reasonable measure is the difference, regardless of direction, of each value from the mean or median. The sum of these absolute differences across the sample then gives an overall assessment. Clearly, the statistic yielding the smallest sum of absolute differences is most "typical."

Returning first to the small sample of beverage drinkers ($n = 5$), the sums found in Table 1 reveal that the median yields the smallest sum of absolute differences (65, versus 87.2 for the mean) and therefore is considered the better "typical" value. The same is true for the original example (682 beverage drinkers); the sum of absolute differences from the mean and median are 5,906.5 and 5,476, respectively. In general, when comparing the mean and median on this basis, the median will always yield a value smaller than, or at most equal to, that for the mean.

As mentioned, the sum of absolute differences can be equal for the mean and median. This occurs when the distribution of the data collected is unimodal and symmetric, because, importantly, the mean and median are equal in such cases. In such cases, the mean is generally preferred because it possesses some other desirable statistical characteristics (for instance, subsample means can be combined to obtain a total-sample mean). (In fact, because of such characteristics and especially for analytic purposes, the mean is generally preferred unless the sum of absolute differences for the mean greatly exceeds that for the median. This will not occur with distributions that are reasonably close to bell-shaped, but will for grossly skewed distributions.)

SUMMARY

The sample mean is commonly relied upon as an estimate of the value that accurately typifies, or represents, the population on the variable of interest. However, variables having a skewed distribution are cases where application of a median over the mean is preferred. The mean is markedly affected by the observations in the pronounced tail of a skewed distribution, shifting the mean toward the extreme value(s), making the mean an unrepresentative value. Thus, use of the mean as an estimate of the typical value in such cases is ill-advised. On the other hand, the median is little affected by such observations and therefore yields a more representative measure than the mean in such cases.

This material is adapted in an abridged form from Research on Research, Report No. 48 by Market Facts, Inc. with permission from the company. A complete copy of this report may be obtained from the company.

Interpretation of t Test Results
Market Facts, Inc.

AN EXAMPLE

A study was conducted to determine the potential market acceptance of two variations of peanut butters. The products, as concepts, were presented for evaluation to two samples of 150 respondents each. Degree of believability was measured in addition to purchase intent and overall appeal.

A seven-point scale (1 representing totally unbelievable and 7 being totally believable) was used for measuring believability. Table 1 contains descriptive statistics summarizing responses.

TABLE 1

Descriptive Statistics for Believability

	Mean	Variance	Sample Size
Concept one	5.7	2.81	150
Concept two	4.9	2.94	150
Pooled variance: 2.875			

Statistical Analysis

A t test used to test the significance of the difference between the means yielded a t value of 4.09, statistically significant with at least 99% confidence; concept one was judged to be more believable.

It was also of interest to study the relationship or strength of association between believability and purchase intent (likelihood to purchase). A correlation coefficient of .23 was obtained. Although this correlation is statistically significantly greater than zero (again, with at least 99% confidence) it was dismissed as being too small to be of practical utility; no real relationship was felt to exist.

Discussion of Analysis

An interpretive "double standard" appears when comparing decision rules for evaluating the significance of t statistics from tests of mean differences and correlation coefficients. Statistical significance and the practical importance of a difference between two means are often considered synonymous. Indeed, some researchers may conclude marketing actions should be undertaken when two means differ with at least 95% confidence. Often, little regard is given to absolute magnitude of the difference.

Correlation coefficients, on the other hand, are evaluated quite differently. The size of the correlation, not statistical significance, forms the basis for assessing practical importance. Researchers frequently assume that the correlations are statistically significant (or they completely ignore the statistical test). Then they move to a second interpretive stage of evaluating the *size* of the correlation. As such, correlations below .4, although they may be statistically significant, are usually interpreted as indicating no "meaningful" relationship. Herein lies the double standard: researchers typically do not go to this second interpretive stage of examining size of mean differences when evaluating t statistics from tests of mean differences.

A valuable rule for evaluating mean differences beyond usual significance tests can be obtained by exploiting this double standard: combining the statistical/probabilistic advantages of significance testing and the realistic interpretive advantages of taking the magnitude of mean differences into account. This combination is possible through the use and understanding of the mathematical relationship between t statistics and correlation coefficients.

A t statistic can be expressed as a correlation. As such, t statistics can be interpreted in the perhaps more easily understood correlation scale of -1 to $+1$. While examining this mathematical relationship, it will be of interest to show that correlations that result from reexpressing statistically significant t statistics can be quite small. A change in perspective about interpreting t statistics or correlations may be warranted.

The Relationship Between the t Statistic and the Correlation Coefficient

The t statistic is by far the most popular form of standardizing the difference between two means. The relationship between the t statistic (t) and the correlation coefficient (r) can be shown by exploiting the idea of a standardized difference. (Standardization in this sense means dividing some statistics by a measure of its variability, typically its standard error.) The t statistic is of the form

$$ t = \frac{\overline{X}_1 - \overline{X}_2}{\sqrt{\hat{\sigma}_p^2 \left(\frac{1}{n_1} + \frac{1}{n_2} \right)}} $$

where the denominator is the standard error of the difference between the means using a pooled estimate of variability, $\hat{\sigma}_p^2$.

A second form of standardization of the mean difference is the point biserial correlation, a special correlation coefficient:

$$ r_{pb} = \frac{\overline{X}_1 - \overline{X}_2}{\sqrt{\frac{\sum (X_{ij} - \overline{X})^2}{(N)(P_1)(P_2)}}} $$

where

r_{pb} is called the point biserial correlation

N is the total sample size

P_1 and P_2 are the proportions of respondents in groups one and two, respectively

$\overline{X}_1$ and $\overline{X}_2$ are the two group means

$\sum (X_{ij} - \overline{X})^2$ is the sum of squared deviations of all scores (X_{ij}) from the grand mean

Although mean differences can be expressed as a correlation using r_{pb}, it is only one step toward showing the relationship between the t statistic and the correlation coefficient. The second step is taken by noting that the significance of the difference of any correlation coefficient from zero can be tested by the use of a t statistic. Using the point biserial correlation as a specific instance, the formula is

$$t = \frac{r_{pb}}{\sqrt{\dfrac{1 - r_{pb}^2}{df}}}$$

where df represents the number of degrees of freedom associated with the standard error of the correlation.

Reexpressing the above formula to solve for r_{pb} yields[1]

$$r_{pb} = \sqrt{\frac{t^2}{t^2 + df}}$$

As such, given a t statistic computed from a test of mean differences and its associated degrees of freedom it is possible to express that t statistic as a correlation coefficient.

Note: The point biserial correlation can also be calculated using the usual Pearson product moment correlation formula. A second variable consisting of ones and zeroes is constructed and correlated with the variable containing the quantities of interest. This one/zero variable, called a dummy variable, would be created by arbitrarily assigning a score of one to one of the two groups of respondents. The second group would receive zero values. The absolute value of the correlation obtained by the method will match the absolute point biserial correlation value. The sign of the correlation may differ depending on which group receives what code.

RECONSIDERATION OF EARLIER EXAMPLE

Reconsider the example and data supplied earlier. The t statistic is

$$t = \frac{(5.7 - 4.9)}{\sqrt{2.875\left(\dfrac{1}{150} + \dfrac{1}{150}\right)}}$$

$$= 4.09$$

with 298 degrees of freedom.

Next, the mean difference of .8, $(5.7 - 4.9)$, can be standardized to give the point biserial correlation:

[1] r_{pb} takes the original sign (+ or −) assumed by the t statistic prior to squaring.

$$r_{pb} = \frac{(5.7 - 4.9)}{\sqrt{\dfrac{904.75}{(300)(.5)(.5)}}}$$

$$= .23$$

The relationship between the t statistic and the correlation can be shown in two ways. The t statistic can be reexpressed as a correlation:

$$r = \sqrt{\frac{(4.09)^2}{(4.09)^2 + 298}}$$

$$= .23$$

matching the point biserial result. Or, the significance of the point biserial correlation of .23 from zero can be tested:

$$t = \frac{.23033}{\sqrt{\dfrac{1 - .0531}{298}}}$$

$$= 4.09$$

matching the t test results (more decimal points are used to reduce round-off error). In both instances, the results are consistent.

INTERPRETATION

Along with expressing mean differences and their associated t statistics as correlations come the usual interpretive trappings. Correlations in this context retain their ease of interpretation. Specifically, the correlation measures the degree of systematic change in response, as indicated by group means, from one group to the other. The degree of change is represented by the absolute magnitude of the correlation; a large difference relative to its error variability would yield a large correlation. The larger the difference, the closer the correlation would be to ±1, depending on the direction of the difference. Conversely, zero correlation would indicate no systematic change: the means are equal.

Further, the square of the correlation retains the meaning of "proportion of variability accounted for." Tailored slightly to fit this context, r^2 indicates the percentage of total variability of the measured quantity ("believability" in the preceding example) due to the systematic change in average response from group to group. If

TABLE 2

Correlation Coefficients for Various Sample Sizes

n	r	n	r
50	0.277350	550	0.085126
100	0.158030	600	0.081514
150	0.162221	650	0.078326
200	0.140720	700	0.075485
250	0.125988	750	0.072932
300	0.115087	800	0.070622
350	0.106600	850	0.068519
400	0.099751	900	0.066593
450	0.094072	950	0.064820
500	0.089264	1000	0.063182

this percentage is small then, again, the difference between means is also small (relative to the total variability).

t-STATISTIC/CORRELATION COEFFICIENT RELATIONSHIP CONTINUED

Consider the size of correlations corresponding to a *t* value of 2.00 for various sample sizes (*n*) displayed in Table 2. The use of 2.00 is selected because it closely represents a statistical result being significant with 95% confidence with a sample size of at least 50. Although the mean differences are large enough to be considered statistically significant, the corresponding correlations are quite small suggesting limited practical importance. Clearly, statistically significant *t* statistics will not always correspond to correlations of an "acceptable" magnitude. As such, incorporating correlations into the realm of tests of mean differences shows that larger *t* statistics may be desired.

EVALUATING *t* STATISTICS: A RULE OF THUMB

A researcher can judge the *t* statistic/correlation coefficient relationship in one of two ways: discount statistically significant *t* statistics that correspond to small cor-

relations or have more respect for small correlations. The first of these alternatives may be more useful than the second because it can identify statistically significant mean differences that are also large enough to be of practical importance. Although there are no hard and fast rules for determining a small correlation (or when a correlation stops being small), experience with correlational techniques (regression and factor analysis) suggests a value of .4 to be on the border line. A rule of thumb can be developed by substituting .4 into the significance test formula for correlations:

$$t = \frac{r_{pb}}{\sqrt{\dfrac{1 - r_{pb}^2}{df}}}$$

Setting r_{pb} = .4 and rearranging terms shows that the absolute value of the *t* statistic equals $(.4364)\sqrt{df}$. As such, a *t* statistic would be considered as reflecting a practically useful mean difference if it were statistically significant with a reasonable level of confidence *and* roughly greater, in absolute size, than .4 times the square root of the number of degrees of freedom associated with the statistic.

From the example cited earlier, with 298 degrees of freedom, the *t* statistic would need to exceed 7.53 to be considered a statistically significant and practically useful mean difference.

SUMMARY

Having a statistically significant *t* statistic *may not* be enough to warrant a conclusion of "meaningful difference" or "practical importance." The magnitude of the mean difference should also be taken into account. Linking correlations with *t* statistics is a simple way of providing some guidance.

CASE 4.1 Danger! Celebrity in Use

Businesses have traditionally paid hefty prices to celebrities for endorsing their products, and for this reason they are entitled to more than just a pretty face or someone who simply reads a script. When celebrities sign up for campaigns, they must understand the goals of the business and not be content with just memorizing the words in the script. A campaign frequently involves not only broadcast and print advertising but also appearances at sales meetings and conventions. Hence, the celebrities may have to mingle with the distributors of the product and make them feel that they care about the product and are out there to help the client.

One Hollywood team that has successfully matched celebrities with products is Heldfond and Rix. They matched James Garner with Polaroid, Judd Hirsch with Yoplait yogurt, and Karen Grassle with a cookie product. Heldfond and Rix prefer that the celebrities be familiar with the products they endorse so that they better understand the company goals. For example, Mariette Hartley drank Celestial Seasonings, a product she endorsed, in her home. But not all agencies share this view. Some examples of matches made by such agencies were the ill-fated Pepsi/Madonna team and the alliance of Cybill Shepherd with the beef industry.

Pepsi signed Madonna for several million dollars to feature her in their Pepsi campaign. The controversy over the religious imagery in Madonna's "Prayer" video led to the threat of a consumer boycott, and Pepsi lost $10 million. Cybill Shepherd's ad for the beef industry flopped when she publicly admitted that she rarely ate red meat. These examples are only a few of the problems with celebrity endorsements. Unfortunately, there have always been hidden dangers when using celebrities, as exemplified by the use of O. J. Simpson in Hertz advertising.

In 1987, the celebrity approval rating by consumers was only 17%. Since then, the ratings have been on the rebound and were at 27% in 1992, and in 1993, celebrity ratings reached 28%. But 1994 celebrity ratings declined. It was reported that the 1992 and 1993 rises in approval ratings were due to marketers becoming more discerning at handling celebrity "snafus" and continuing to demand that the stars who endorse their products actually like those products. In addition, companies such as NutraSweet, represented by Cher and more recently actress Lauren Hutton, have moved away from scripted advertising and toward taping certain segments of an interview to advertise its products. The trend in early 1993 was to move toward those celebrities whose images were not tarnished with tabloid events. With this inclination, companies began to move toward athletes such as Bo Jackson and women sponsors such as Candice Bergen for Sprint. Nancy Kerrigan, the U.S. silver medalist in ice skating in the 1994 Winter Olympics, signed multimillion dollar deals to endorse Disney World, Revlon, Campbell's, Seiko, Ray-Ban, and Reebok. Most of the contracts that were issued did contain morality clauses given the potential dangers of using celebrities. These dangers may have caused the 1994 overall celebrity ratings to decline. Says David Vehedra, president of Video Storyboard Tests, a New York research firm, "One has to wonder whether this (decline) has anything to do with celebrities like O. J. Simpson and Michael Jackson."

In 1994, only three celebrities carried over from the 1993 top 10 list: Cindy Crawford, Candice Bergen, and Bill Cosby (Table 1). All three changed positions on the list. Cindy Crawford moved to first place from fourth; Candice Bergen dropped to second from first place; and Bill Cosby came in third, down from second place the year before. Thus, celebrity popularity is very sensitive to change.

If so many dangers abound, why use celebrities? Many advertisers feel that celebrities make an advertisement more effective. PepsiCo's Pepsi cola and Revlon, for example, have boosted their products' images and sales by using Cindy Crawford in commercials. The use of celebrities has been demonstrated to lead to higher recall of an advertisement. Further evidence supporting the use of celebrities includes research showing that for attractiveness-related products, physically attractive celebrities elicit high credibility and attitude ratings for an ad.

One researcher, Michael Kamins, employed marketing research techniques to explore the uses of celebrities in advertising more scientifically. Kamins states that three processes of social influence determine whether an individual will adopt the attitude an advertiser is trying to

TABLE 1

Top TV Endorsers Ranked by Consumer Appeal

Rank 1994	1993	Name	Endorsements
1	4	Cindy Crawford	Pepsi-Cola, Revlon
2	1	Candice Bergen	Sprint
3	2	Bill Cosby	Jell-O
4	–	Elizabeth Taylor	White Diamonds Perfume
5	–	Jerry Seinfeld	American Express
6	–	Whitney Houston	AT&T
7	–	Shari Belafonte	Ultra Slim-Fast
8	–	June Allyson	Depend
9	–	Chevy Chase	Doritos
10	–	Cybill Shepherd	L'Oreal

convey: compliance, identification, and internalization. Although the first of these factors is not relevant to Kamins's study, the last two hold considerable implications for celebrity advertising. Identification, where individuals try to imitate another person because they want to be like that person, is the most important factor determining a celebrity's influence in an advertisement. Internalization occurs when individuals imitate another because they perceive the other person to be sincere and to have values similar to their own. But this factor is not usually associated with celebrities.

Kamins inferred, however, that if both identification and internalization could be achieved, the effectiveness of advertising would be increased. Therefore, he studied whether celebrities could increase the effectiveness of advertising through the identification component, and whether so-called truth in advertising (operationalized as two-sided advertising, or advertising that included both positive and negative aspects about a product) could increase effectiveness through internalization. Furthermore, he wondered whether combining these two approaches resulted in even greater effectiveness.

To research this, a 2×2 factorial design was adopted. Sidedness (one-sided versus two-sided) and type of spokesperson (celebrity versus noncelebrity) were the two factors. Seventy-seven executives enrolled in an executive M.B.A. program were randomly assigned to four groups: one-sided/noncelebrity, one-sided/celebrity, two-sided/noncelebrity, and two-sided/celebrity. Four ads corresponding to these criteria were made up, and each member of each group evaluated the appropriate ad on the basis of four variables: expectancy-value brand attitude (A), global brand attitude (B), global attitude toward the ad (C), and purchase intention (D). Expectancy-value brand attitude represented the degree to which the subject believed that the product possessed an attribute the ad claimed it had. Global brand attitude was a measure of how appealing the subjects found the product in the ad to be. Global attitude toward the ad was an evaluation of the ad's effectiveness. Purchase intention indicated how likely a subject was to purchase the product when an opportunity to do so came about.

Table 2 shows the mean ($\bar{x}$) and standard deviation values (sd), along with the number of subjects (n), for each variable across each of the groups in Kamins's study. Note that the results from related groups can be combined to yield information on each of the four group characteristics (one-sided, two-sided, noncelebrity, and celebrity) separately. Table 3 contains the ANOVA results for the effect of the independent variables of sidedness (E) and type of spokesperson (F). These results provide valuable information about the effectiveness of celebrity spokespersons in advertisements.

Although the above research results are useful, they are also very specific. Celebrity advertising can be researched in other ways. For example, dead celebrities have been shown to be hip, hot, and safe. They are not cheap (advertisers do have to pay licensing fees to the celebrities' estates), but they are safe, because they cannot do anything unpredictable that might jeopardize a product's image or embarrass the sponsor. Abbott and Costello have been used to sell bran cereal, Humphrey Bogart to lend flair to cellular phones and Diet Coke, and Charlie Chaplin to push IBM personal computers. This just goes to show that although the celebrities themselves may be dead, their use as advertising spokespersons has a long life.

TABLE 2

Means, Standard Deviations, and Number of Subjects

Experimental Condition		Expectancy-Value Brand Attitude (A)	Global Brand Attitude (B)	Global Attitude toward the Ad (C)	Purchase Intention (D)
	$(\bar{x})$	7.97	3.47	3.4	2.22
	(sd)	3.92	1.47	1.52	1.4
One-sided	(n)	38	40	40	40
	$(\bar{x})$	8.33	4.22	3.65	2.92
	(sd)	5.32	1.6	1.62	1.44
Two-sided	(n)	36	37	37	37
	$(\bar{x})$	8.04	3.5	3.65	2.55
	(sd)	4.73	1.55	1.46	1.38
Noncelebrity	(n)	38	40	40	40
	$(\bar{x})$	8.26	4.19	3.38	2.57
	(sd)	4.58	1.52	1.67	1.56
Celebrity	(n)	36	37	37	37
	$(\bar{x})$	7.89	3.45	3.55	2.4
	(sd)	4.48	1.57	1.39	1.5
One-sided noncelebrity	(n)	19	20	20	20
	$(\bar{x})$	8.04	3.5	3.25	2.05
	(sd)	3.4	1.4	1.65	1.32
One-sided celebrity	(n)	19	20	20	20
	$(\bar{x})$	8.18	3.55	3.75	2.7
	(sd)	5.09	1.57	1.55	1.26
Two-sided noncelebrity	(n)	19	20	20	20
	$(\bar{x})$	8.5	5	3.53	3.18
	(sd)	5.72	1.27	1.74	1.63
Two-sided celebrity	(n)	17	17	17	17

TABLE 3

ANOVA Results for the Dependent Measures

Variable	Main Effect for Sidedness (E)	Main Effect for Spokesperson (F)	Interaction (E × F)
Expectancy-value brand attitude (A)	F = 0.013	F = 0.035	F = 0.003
Global brand attitude (B)	F = 10.876[a]	F = 4.355[a]	F = 4.233[a]
Global attitude toward the ad (C)	F = 0.209	F = 0.276	F = 0.001
Purchase intention (D)	F = 4.845[a]	F = 0.050	F = 1.868

[a]Indicates significance at $p \leq .05$.

QUESTIONS

1. What kind of marketing research could businesses conduct to determine if their products would perform better with celebrity endorsements?

2. Discuss the role of multidimensional scaling in the matching of a celebrity to the right product.

3. Could conjoint analysis be used to determine whether celebrities should be used, and if so, which celebrity should be selected? How could conjoint analysis be used?

4. What kinds of precautions or pretesting should the researcher engage in to ensure that the celebrities and

two-sided ads used in the experiment were appropriate? What complications or contaminations might be present in the experimental results if these precautions were not taken?

5. Based on the results presented, do two-sided ads have an advantage over one-sided ads? Celebrity ads over noncelebrity ads?

6. Which type of ad is the most effective? The least effective? (Hint: Look at the ANOVA results.)

7. Is analysis of variance an appropriate technique to use to analyze the data obtained in this study? Why or why not?

8. Could regression analysis be used to analyze the data obtained in this research? If so, how?

REFERENCES

1. Kamins, Michael A. "Celebrity and Noncelebrity Advertising in a Two-Sided Context." *Journal of Advertising Research* (June–July 1989): 34–42.

2. Kamins, Michael. "An Investigation into the 'Match-Up' Hypothesis in Celebrity Advertising: When Beauty May Be Only Skin Deep." *Journal of Advertising* 19(1), (1990): 4–13.

3. Kamins, M., M. Brand, S. Hoeke, and J. Moe. "Two-Sided Versus One-Sided Celebrity Endorsements: The Impact on Advertising Effectiveness and Credibility." *Journal of Advertising* 18(2), (1989): 4–10.

4. Renker, Greg. "A Marketing Marriage: Celebs and Infomercials." *Advertising Age* (January 25, 1993): M8.

5. Vadehra, Dave. "My, How TV Spots Have Changed!" *Advertising Age* (August 16, 1993): 16.

6. Miller, Cyndee. "Celebrities Hot Despite Scandals." *Marketing News* (March 28,1994): 1–2, 5.

7. Miller, Cyndee. "Well-Known Winners Will Reap More Olympic Gold." *Marketing News* (March 28, 1994): 2.

8. Goldman, Kevin. "Catch a Falling Star: Big Names Plummet From List of Top 10 Celebrity Endorsers." *Wall Street Journal* (October 19, 1994): B1.

CASE 4.2

The Demographic Discovery of the Decade

Statistics for the 1990s indicate that by the year 2010, 75 million people, or about 26% of the U.S. population, will be 55 or older, and one in seven people will be 65 or older. This segment is projected to be in possession of approximately 70% of the nation's discretionary income as well as 80% of all financial assets of savings and loan institutions and 65% of all money market assets.

The mature market is divisible into four segments. There are the so-called older adults ranging from 55 to 64 years of age. This group is looking seriously at retirement. In 1991, there was an estimated 22 million people in this segment. The second market segment, the elderly, is made up of those aged 65 to 74. They numbered 18 million in 1991. The aged, those from 75 to 84, totaled 10 million, and the very old, those age 85 and over, totaled approximately 3 million.

In the coming years, the very old group will grow most rapidly, increasing to 4 million in 1995. The aged will grow to 12 million and the elderly to 20 million. The older population will shrink about 6%, although it will still make up the largest segment of the mature market, or 37% of the total. The mature market would grow from the 53 million of 1991 to 56 million in 1995 and will therefore make up one-fifth of the American population.

A closer look at the older group reveals that they are interested in maintaining a youthful appearance and are major targets for exercise equipment, health programs, diets, cosmetics, cosmetic surgery, sports clothing, designer wear, and a wide array of personal services that improve appearance. Leading active lives and participating in leisure endeavors such as tennis, golf, cycling, fishing, boating, camping, jogging, and swimming, they represent a market for travel and spectator activities. Additionally, they tend to work to live, rather than live to work. As a result, increasing numbers of older adults opt for early retirement or move into new careers and part-time jobs.

The elderly group is composed of those who have been retired for some time. They tend to take a keen interest in health and nutrition and to be concerned with diet, salt intake, cholesterol, fried foods, and calories. They often drink less alcohol than the younger population and are a good market for skin-care products, prescriptions, vitamins and minerals, health and beauty aids, and medicines that ease pain and promote the performance of everyday activities. This group also engaged in exercise, although less rigorously than the older group.

The aged group often has health and mobility problems and hence requires health care services and special care facilities. The very old need help in their day-to-day tasks. They find it difficult to get around and need regular medical and hospital care. Again, they represent a large market for health care facilities.

Although the classification of the mature market into these four segments has been useful, another classification, and perhaps a better one for advertising purposes, is based on attitudes toward advertising. These segments could then be profiled in terms of psychographic variables. A major concern of advertisers targeting the aged consumer has been the way in which the older population uses and evaluates information from advertising to make purchasing decisions. One recent study by Davis and French explored aged consumers' use of advertising as a primary source of information in purchase decisions. The respondents were clustered based on attitudes toward advertising. Psychographic profiles were developed for each of the derived segments.

A database of annual lifestyle surveys was used to obtain a sample of 217 married female respondents aged 60 and over who were not employed outside the home. Respondents were asked to rate their degree of agreement with each of the 200 AIO (activities, interests, opinions) statements on the survey. Respondents were also asked to rate four attitudinal statements measuring information usage and beliefs about advertising as well as the credibility of the source of advertising. Identical information obtained from a previous study was used for replication purposes by Davis and French.

The data on the four statements (shown in Table 1) measuring attitudes toward advertising were analyzed using Ward's procedure of clustering. Three clusters—engaged, autonomous, and receptive consumers—were identified. Mean scores for each cluster are presented in Table 1. To test stability, replication of the cluster analysis was undertaken using the data obtained in the previous study. Ward's procedure was used to analyze the data from the previous study. Again, three clusters were obtained. Cluster means on each of the clustering variables for the replication sample (previous study) obtained by Davis and French are also shown in Table 1.

To determine the psychographic differences among the three clusters, two additional steps were taken. First, one-way ANOVA was carried out to determine the discriminating variables. The three segments formed the grouping or the independent variable, and each psychographic statement served as a dependent variable. Forty-one of the original 200 psychographic statements were

TABLE 1

Cluster Variable Scores by Segment

Cluster Variable	Segment	Means	
		Study Sample	Replication
Advertising insults my intelligence.	Engaged	5.24 (agree)	4.35 (agree)
	Autonomous	4.86 (agree)	5.01 (agree)
	Receptive	2.20 (disagree)	2.10 (disagree)
Information from advertising helps me make better buying decisions.	Engaged	4.69 (agree)	4.88 (agree)
	Autonomous	3.65 (agree)	3.30 (disagree)[a]
	Receptive	4.78 (agree)	4.18 (agree)
I often seek out the advice of friends regarding brands and products.	Engaged	4.55 (agree)	4.21 (agree)
	Autonomous	2.16 (disagree)	1.87 (disagree)
	Receptive	2.99 (disagree)	3.02 (disagree)
I don't believe a company's ad when it claims that test results show its product to be better than competitive products.	Engaged	4.78 (agree)	4.25 (agree)
	Autonomous	4.85 (agree)	5.00 (agree)
	Receptive	4.12 (agree)	4.94 (agree)

[a] 3.5 is the neutral point.

found to be statistically significant. With the realization that some of these significant variables were probably measuring the same characteristics, a principal components factor analysis was carried out, with four factors (accounting for 60.3% of the variance) extracted in a varimax rotation. Factor scores were computed for each of the three segments by Davis and French, and Table 2 shows these scores, along with the variables that loaded highly on these factors and the variable means. This information can be used to provide psychographic profiles for each of the three segments identified in cluster analysis.

TABLE 2

Study Sample Mean Factor Scores by Cluster

Factor		Engaged	Autonomous	Receptive
Factor 1		0.45	−0.11	−0.21
I am interested in the cultures of other countries.	(loading = .58966)	4.41	3.92	3.87
I get personal satisfaction from using cosmetics.	(loading = .48283)	4.29	3.74	3.45
I enjoy looking through fashion magazines.	(loading = .41592)	4.89	4.31	4.55
Factor 2		0.29	−0.32	0.17
I like to bake.	(loading = .70466)	5.49	4.75	5.19
I like to cook.	(loading = .60793)	5.28	4.63	5.01
I always bake from scratch.	(loading = .54404)	3.76	3.15	3.62
Factor 3		0.28	−0.26	0.10
I try to select foods that are fortified with vitamins and minerals.	(loading = .49480)	4.89	4.36	4.59
I try to buy a company's products if they support educational TV.	(loading = .43730)	4.13	3.53	3.72
I am usually among the first to try new products.	(loading = .42521)	3.47	2.81	3.19
Factor 4		0.26	0.14	−0.36
Generally, manufacturers' warranties are not worth the paper they are printed on.	(loading = .50313)	3.31	3.47	2.82
Most big companies are just out for themselves.	(loading = .47638)	4.25	4.50	3.93
TV advertising is condescending toward women.	(loading = .41031)	4.25	4.24	3.55

The results of this research and similar studies help marketers target the elderly, an especially promising group in light of the financial assets that they possess. A look at the financial assets of U.S. households showed that Americans over age 50 are the richest consumer group, controlling half the country's discretionary income and about 70% of its assets. By 2025, some 113 million Americans—about 40% of the population—will be over age 50. Hence, the discovery of the mature market represents a golden opportunity for marketers to target an old segment in a new way.

QUESTIONS

1. Studies have found that the older, elderly, aged and the very old segments of the mature market need good supporting health services and facilities. Describe in detail how health maintenance organizations (HMOs) can effectively determine the differences in the health care needs of these segments. What kind of information should be obtained? Which statistical techniques should be used to analyze the data?

2. Do you think that the data analysis strategy adopted in the study reported in this case was appropriate? Why or why not?

3. Qualitatively describe each of the three clusters, based on the information in Table 1.

4. Interpret each factor in Table 2.

5. Do you think that the study reported in the case should have used discriminant analysis? If so, how?

6. Suggest an alternative data analysis strategy for the study reported.

REFERENCES

1. Davis, B. and W. French. "Exploring Advertising Usage Segments among the Aged." *Journal of Advertising Research* (February–March 1989): 26.

2. Rager, Les. "The Future Grows Older." *Nation's Business* (March 1991): 48–49.

3. Hartman, C. R. "Diet Dishes to Go." *D&B Reports* (May–June 1991): 62–63.

4. Lunt, Penny. "The New Demographics." *ABA Banking Journal* (January, 1994): 34–38.

5. Maty, Joe. "Shifts in Population Signal End of the 'Youth Sells' Era." *American Paint & Coatings Journal* (October 27, 1993): 5–7.

CASE 4.3

The Magic Wand of PepsiCo

What has made PepsiCo so dynamic and different? The answer: PepsiCo's magic wand, which brought together two basic concepts: marketing research techniques and good old-fashioned gut feelings.

Known to many as the producer of Pepsi, the cola that took on Coca-Cola in the Pepsi Challenge, PepsiCo also owns Pizza Hut, KFC (formerly Kentucky Fried Chicken), and Taco Bell as well as Frito-Lay snack foods. Table 1 defines the financial and competitive position of PepsiCo at the end of 1992. Recent information revealed that PepsiCo's Pepsi Division obtained $2483.5 million in sales during 1993. The success story of PepsiCo is briefly described here by major product divisions (beverages, restaurants, and snack foods).

Beverages

First, consider soft drinks. Marketing research by PepsiCo demonstrated that there was a market for a diet cola made with 100% NutraSweet and also revealed that

TABLE 1

Net Sales and Operating Profit (in millions of dollars)

Division	Sales	Percentage of Total	Operating Profit	Percentage of Total
Beverages	$7,606	35%	$799	32%
Restaurants	$8,232	37%	$719	29%
Snack foods	$6,132	28%	$985	39%
Total	$21,970	100%	$2,503	100%

teenagers were the largest consumers of sugared soft drinks. In November 1984, Pepsi sneaked its Diet Pepsi with 100% NutraSweet into the market without even test marketing the product so as to avoid tipping off Coca-Cola. Gut feeling and qualitative marketing research told Pepsi that the time was ripe to launch this NutraSweet product. Although taste tests indicated that consumers could not taste the difference between a saccharin/aspartame blend and pure aspartame, consumers overwhelmingly preferred the 100% NutraSweet product when told about the difference. Furthermore, tests indicated that they preferred it so strongly that they were willing to pay more for a diet cola with 100% NutraSweet. Not surprisingly, Diet Pepsi with NutraSweet took the market by storm, and within two years, sales of Diet Pepsi exceeded $1 billion.

To capture the teenage market, Pepsi ads highlighted superstars Michael Jackson and Lionel Ritchie with the theme, "Choice of a New Generation." Other "New Generation" stars featured in Pepsi ads included Don Johnson (of *Miami Vice* fame), Michael J. Fox (star of *Back to the Future*), and comedian Billy Crystal. A copromotion for the 1989 Christmas season with Nintendo was another attempt to capture the teenage market. These methods effectively strengthened the image of Pepsi. More recently, the "You've Got The Right One Baby, Uh Huh!" campaign for Diet Pepsi has been highly successful for Pepsi. The campaign's star singer was Ray Charles. The most recent, regular Pepsi campaign introduced the "Gotta Have It" theme for their soft drink. The company distributed "Gotta Have It" cards that provided holders with discounts on a range of consumer products to consumers. Table 2 lists both profits and sales for the beverages division ending 1992.

One type of promotion that Pepsi has frequently used is television advertising. One way to examine the effect of advertising on Pepsi sales is through split-cable TV advertising. Household-level multidimensional scaling (MDS) joint spaces can be generated to show how households cluster to form segments that are homogeneous with respect to ideal points. In other words, several market segments can be identified, and their ideal points, before and after advertising, can be plotted on a two-dimensional map. Then product positions, before and after advertising, can be mapped on the same plot. One plot is prepared for the control group and one for the experimental group. The movement of the points from their before-advertising positions to their after-advertising positions can be examined for each plot, and the two plots can be compared to get an idea about the effectiveness of the advertising.

An MDS plot for an experimental group's movement from the before-advertising (pretest condition) to the after-advertising (posttest condition) is shown in Figure 1. In this experiment by Winer and Moore, marketing mix information was known only for the Pepsi brand, and the advertising on the split-cable was for Pepsi. Therefore, if a brand moved closer to Pepsi, more joint purchasing was occurring. If Pepsi moved closer to a segment (ideal point), then the probability of someone in that segment picking Pepsi had increased.

Figure 1 shows how advertising can affect product sales. Increased product sales might arise through other means, however, especially new product introductions. For example, Pepsi was able to create a totally new market segment with the introduction of its Slice product line. When Slice was initially subject to taste tests, Pepsi had consumers rate Slice against other lemon-lime soft drinks. Slice repeatedly failed the taste tests. Finally, the researchers decided to tell the subjects that Slice, unlike other lemon-lime soft drinks, contained real fruit juice. A new market segment and a new highly successful product were born.

Pepsi has since capitalized on Slice by extending the product line to such varieties as Orange Mandarin, Apple, and Cherry Cola Slice. But the company was really able to benefit from the juice added benefit from an unexpected quarter, the diet cola market. The juice angle allowed Pepsi to garner diet Slice sales that represented about 50% of the total Slice product sales, instead of the usual 35% of parent brand sales that diet products bring in.

Pepsi had also entered several new beverage venues by 1992. Pepsi entered the new and lucrative market for canned or bottled ice tea by forming a partnership with Thomas J. Lipton Company. In September 1992, they launched two new iced tea flavors, raspberry and peach. With the recent surging popularity of bottled water, Pepsi

TABLE 2

Sales and Profits for the Beverages Division: 1992 (in millions of dollars)

	Domestic	International	Total
Sales	$5,485	$2,121	$7,606
Percent change	+6%	+22%	+10%
Profits	$687	$112	$799
Percent change	−8%	−4%	−7%

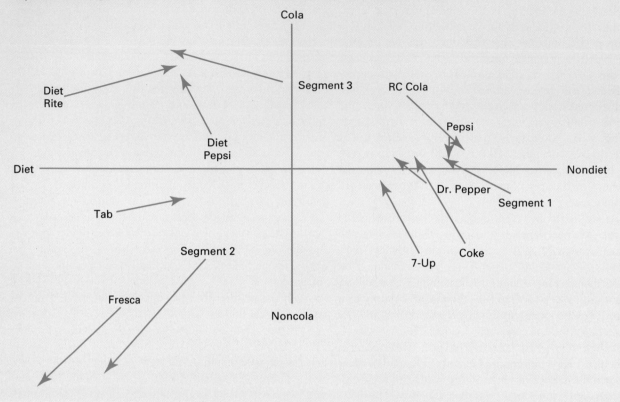

FIGURE 1

Soft Drinks: Experimental Group's Movement from Pretest to Posttest Period

is now selling H₂Oh! a new bottled water. Sales have been increasing since inception of the project.

In 1993, Pepsi introduced Crystal Pepsi, its stab at the clear cola market. But this time Pepsi had the wrong one. In fact, Pepsi had the wrong name, wrong packaging, wrong advertising and wrong taste. Pepsi is resilient, however, and has decided not to call it quits on Crystal Pepsi just yet. Pepsi plans to relaunch the product with the new advertising, packaging, and most important, a new taste. In addition, Crystal Pepsi will just be called Crystal. Pepsi will relaunch this product as a citrus cola to take on its rivals, Sprite and 7-Up.

Restaurants

PepsiCo also owns several restaurant chains. Research showed that the Pizza Hut chain needed not superstar endorsers, in its ads, but endorsers with whom its customers could relate. So, Pizza Hut ads featured endorsers such as comedian Martin Mull and boxer Marvelous Marvin Hagler.

New product ideas have been consistently tested at Pizza Hut through marketing research. In 1983, Pepsi introduced the Personal Pan pizza, which reduced waiting time to less than five minutes. The product boosted Pizza Hut's revenues by 50% in the first year. Pizza Hut also went into the home delivery business in a big way. Its marketing research showed that the take-out market was growing fast. Several hundred outlets that were devoted exclusively to home delivery were added. More recently, many of the Pizza Hut restaurants introduced the popular lunch buffet as well as the Big Foot pizza. The Big Foot was designed to compete against the two pizza offers made by the Little Caesar's pizza chain. Between 1991 and 1992, Pizza Hut's worldwide sales increased $345 million, up 11% to $3.6 billion.

PepsiCo also owns the Taco Bell chain. When Taco Bell became a PepsiCo division, a survey showed that its customers viewed these restaurants as cheap-looking stands and were offended by the company logo, a Mexican dozing under a large sombrero. So Pepsi committed $200 million to a makeover and expansion drive. Part of this makeover involved price cuts and special promotions, such as Tacos-to-Go. The makeover appeared to pay off, since Taco Bell became the fastest-growing restaurant chain in the country. In 1992, Taco Bell's worldwide sales were up 21% from 1991. Taco Bell's commitment to low prices has boosted their sales in individual stores by approximately 6%. PepsiCo has also been expanding the Taco Bell influence into Mexico City by introducing several kiosk's within the city, bringing Taco Bell's unique Mexican-style food to Mexico itself.

The final restaurant owned by PepsiCo is KFC. The KFC franchise has been in a refurbishing mode for most of 1992. New restaurants were added and old ones were improved. New products have dominated KFC's bid to win new customers. Items such as Oriental Chicken Wings, Popcorn Chicken, and Honey BBQ Chicken have made short-running appearances at selected KFC's to improve customer satisfaction and to offer a wider variety of foods to help attract new customers. In 1992, KFC began offering their new Rotisserie Gold chicken as an alternative to regular or extra crispy chicken. In April 1994, KFC's Rotisserie Gold won one of *Marketing News*'s 1993 Edison Best New Products Awards. Its success has been attributed to strong advertising and superior taste. Its introduction has attracted new customers to the restaurant and has helped KFC maintain its leadership of the chicken fast-food restaurant segment.

Overall, the restaurant business has been very profitable for PepsiCo. The following tables depict the profitability of the combined restaurant sales (Table 3) as well as the individual sales (Table 4) in 1992.

Snack Foods

Finally, at PepsiCo's Frito-Lay division, marketing research has produced such winners as Fritos, Lay's, Cheetos, Ruffles, Tostitos, and Rold Gold Pretzels. Frito-

TABLE 4

Individual Restaurant Sales and Profitability: 1992 (in millions of dollars)

	Pizza Hut	Taco Bell	KFC
Sales	$3,604	$2,460	$2,169
Percent change	+11%	+21%	+18%
Profits	$335	$214	$169
Percent change	+7%	+19%	+110%
System sales	$5,700	$3,300	$6,700
Percent change	+8%	+18%	+8%

Lay has been an important part of the PepsiCo mix, producing approximately 40% of its corporate earnings for 1992. For this reason, PepsiCo will continue to use marketing research techniques in its Frito-Lay division as well as in its many other divisions. This is not surprising because the magic wand of marketing research and marketing instinct has served PepsiCo well in the past and appears likely to do so in the future.

QUESTIONS

1. Discuss the role of marketing research in:
   a. Instigating the "Pepsi Challenge."
   b. Revealing a market for a diet cola made with 100% NutraSweet.
   c. Leading to the introduction of Pizza Hut's five-minute pan pizzas.

2. Discuss the role of MDS in assessing advertising effectiveness.

3. Does Pepsi's advertising appear to be effective (see Figure 1)? If so, what products or groups is it exerting the biggest effect on?

4. Based on your answer to question 3 and examination of Figure 1, do the results seem reasonable? What other factors might lend a different interpretation to the results?

5. How can MDS, factor analysis, and discriminant analysis be used to match brands with celebrities?

6. Could a regression model be constructed to predict the lunchtime sales of Pizza Hut? If so, what independent variables should be included in this model? Express this model in the form of an equation.

REFERENCES

1. Winer, R. and W. Moore. "Evaluating the Effects of Marketing-Mix Variables on Brand Positioning." *Journal of Advertising Research* (February–March 1989): 42.

TABLE 3

Combined Restaurant Sales and Profitability: 1992 (in millions of dollars)

	Domestic	International	Total
Sales	$7,115	$1,117	$8,232
Percent Change	+14%	+29%	+16%
Profits	$598	$121	$719
Percent change	+25%	+25%	+25%

2. Deveny, Kathleen. "How Country's Biggest Brands Are Faring at the Supermarket." *Wall Street Journal* (March 24, 1994): B1, B3.

3. Zinn, Laura. "Does Pepsi Have Too Many Products?" *Business Week* (February 14, 1994): 64–66.

4. "1993 Edison Best New Products Awards Winners." *Marketing News* (April 25, 1994): E7.

5. Ono, Yumiko. "Pepsi, Coke Seek Territory Held by Sports-Drink Leader Gatorade." *Wall Street Journal* (April 26, 1994): B10.

6. Janofsky, Michael. "Pepsi Tries New Diet Cola Abroad." *New York Times* (March 2, 1993): 15.

CASE 4.4

Can Gleem Shine in the Toothpaste Market?

Procter & Gamble promoted its revamped Gleem toothpaste as a tooth whitener just when the $1.5 billion dentifrice industry was deeply involved in plaque and tartar-control toothpastes. Gleem was repackaged in a metallic gold box with lettering in bright blue and orange. Gleem was promoted at the same time that Colgate-Palmolive was expected to introduce its tartar-control Colgate brand, and P & G hoped to pull the rug out from under Colgate's introduction.

P & G spent an estimated $7 million on the Gleem campaign, far less than the $50 million spent on the Crest Tartar-Control Formula campaign. The company, however, was confident that its Gleem campaign "would reaffirm Gleem's whitening superiority." This was important, because the market for Gleem toothpaste was composed of people who were concerned with the whitening properties of toothpaste. This segment of the market had the potential of including a large chunk of the U.S. population. The people in this segment of the market were interested in their appearance and in improving the color of their teeth, had middle to high income levels, and tended to be single and socially active.

Also, consumers of products that caused teeth to become stained, such as coffee and tea drinkers and heavy smokers, were interested in this particular toothpaste attribute. The ages of this market vary from 16 to 60. The market for Gleem and other whitener brands stretched across the entire country and encompassed many different people and places.

Although the potential market was large, the actual market share of whitener toothpastes was small compared with toothpastes with other attributes: 10.5% of the entire toothpaste market. Although Gleem held a respectable segment of the whitener market, its market share was low compared with brands in the fresh-breath market and the overall toothpaste market. Gleem also did poorly compared with Crest, which was Procter & Gamble's only other toothpaste. Crest, with a 32.4% share for its four varieties, led the entire market. Of the various whitener brands in the market, Gleem held 1% of the market share. Its other competitors included Lever Brothers' Close Up and Colgate's Ultra Brite, which held 5% and 2% market shares, respectively (Table 1).

In 1993, the total number of promotional toothpaste ads had increased 23%. P & G, which is still the number one toothpaste marketer, ran 59 promotions in the first half of 1993 compared with 38 for the number two, Colgate-Palmolive. Promotions in 1993 included toll-free 800 numbers that invited consumers to call for information, magazine insertions, newspaper ads, coupons, and direct mailings. Promotions specifically by P & G included eight that used coupons and ten that mentioned donations to charities. Gleem was part of one of the charity offerings. Donations were made to the Caring Program for Children when consumers purchased Gleem. P & G also offered four free weeks of *USA Today* with proofs of purchase of Gleem.

More recent data indicate that dollar sales of Procter & Gamble brand toothpaste increased 1.9% in the 52 weeks ending January 2, 1994. Procter & Gamble currently holds an estimated 34.4% of the toothpaste market (Table 2). In contrast Colgate-Palmolive's market share declined approximately 2.3% and dollar sales decreased approximately 2.9%. Procter & Gamble's increased dollar sales has been attributed to recent innovative marketing and advertising techniques.

TABLE 1

Top 10 Toothpaste Brands

Brand	Percent of Share of Market 1992	1991	Measured Advertising 1992	1991
1 Crest	32.4%	34.3%	$54.3	$44.7
2 Colgate	21.6	21.8	22.1	20.9
3 Arm & Hammer	9.4	7.8	15.9	13.7
4 Aqua-Fresh	8.5	9.5	13.7	12.9
5 Close Up	5.3	6.1	5.0	12.4
6 Sensodyne	3.6	3.4	6.5	5.1
7 Rembrandt	2.1	0.3	5.9	2.1
8 Ultra Brite	2.1	2.1	0.0	0.0
9 Aim	1.8	2.1	0.0	0.0
10 Private Label	1.6	1.4	NA	NA
All others	11.4	11.2	19.5	19.6
Total Market	$1,428.7	$1,297.8	$142.9	$131.3

Note: Total market figures and advertising expenditures are in millions of dollars.

TABLE 2

A Snapshot of Toothpaste Sales for 52 Weeks Ending January 2, 1994 (sales in millions of dollars)

	Sales	Percent Change from Year Earlier	Percent Share of Category
Procter & Gamble	$492.2	1.9	34.4
Colgate-Palmolive	330.8	–2.9	23.1
Unilever	155.8	16.1	10.9
Church & Dwight	140.7	5.9	9.8

Because the market has become so segmented, it has become essential for marketers to target a particular niche. To do this, they must know the positions their products hold in the marketplace. One way for marketers to examine their product positions in the market, relative to competing products, is via a brand positioning map generated through MDS techniques. Figure 1 by Shugan is a brand position map for five kinds of toothpaste on the dimensions of texture and taste and on anticavity abilities. Figure 2 is a perceptual map of the toothpaste brands, including Gleem, on the dimensions of fresh breath and decay prevention and whitening ability and tartar control.

These maps have proven to be useful to marketers when deciding how to position a product. Gleem may find that these kinds of MDS techniques help it in the future, especially since it recently has faced threats in its own whitening segment. Close Up has been emphasizing its enhanced whitening power and mouthwash protection as well as the cosmetic aspects of breath freshening, whiteness, and sex appeal. Given this close competition, it remains to be seen whether Gleem can outshine Close Up, Ultra Brite, and other brands in the whitening segment of the toothpaste market.

QUESTIONS

1. Describe the market research P & G could have conducted before revamping Gleem.

2. How can factor analysis be used to determine the underlying dimensions or attributes on which the consumers evaluate toothpaste brands?

3. Discuss the role of regression analysis in determining the relative importance of the variables consumers use to evaluate various toothpaste brands.

4. How would you use discriminant analysis to determine which variables distinguish between toothpaste brands that offer cavity protection and those brands that offer whitening of teeth benefit?

FIGURE 1

Toothpaste Market Map

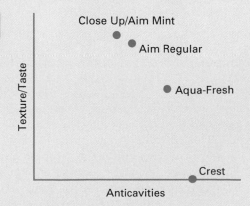

755

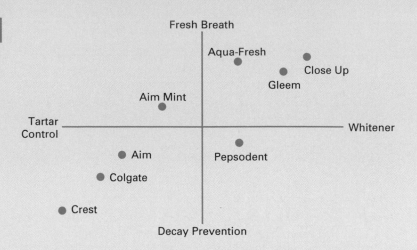

FIGURE 2

Perceptual Mapping of Toothpaste Brands

5. Discuss the role of cluster analysis in developing benefit segments for the toothpaste market.

6. How can conjoint analysis be used to determine the relative importance of the various attributes consumers use to evaluate toothpaste brands?

7. Discuss the role of MDS in determining consumers' perceptions of Gleem relative to other toothpaste brands. How could MDS be used to determine consumer preferences for Gleem relative to other toothpaste brands?

8. In Figure 1, which brand is regarded by consumers as being higher on the dimension of texture/taste? Anticavity ability? Which brand is perceived by consumers as incorporating both dimensions well?

9. According to Figure 2, which two brands are most similar? Least similar? What qualitative inferences can be drawn from Figure 2?

REFERENCES

1. Shugan, S. "Estimating Brand Positioning Maps Using Supermarket Scanning Data." *Journal of Marketing Research* (February 1987): 1–18.

2. Freeman, Laurie. "Leaders' Ad Dollars Build Dental-Care Sales." *Advertising Age* (September 29, 1993): 6.

3. Aho, Debra. "Toothpaste Promos Shoot up 68%." *Advertising Age* (August 16, 1993): 26.

4. Hwang, Suein L. "Some Colgate Brands Are Losing Market Share to Innovative Rivals." *Wall Street Journal* (April 19, 1994): B6.

CASE 4.5 Matsushita Retargets the U.S.A.

Matsushita, a large Japanese electronics producer renowned for its Panasonic, Quasar, and Technics brands, exported personal computers to the United States as a part of its overall program for the PC and PC peripherals market. This segment of the Japanese electronic giant's business was managed by the Panasonic Industrial Company's office automation group. Through 1987,

Panasonic PCs had achieved only modest success in the U.S. market, which was dominated by IBM, Apple, and Compaq. In April 1987, however, the U.S. government began charging antidumping duties on PCs made in Japan. The duties made Panasonic noncompetitive with domestic manufacturers and led to its withdrawal from the market that year.

Despite this setback, Panasonic was still a major player in PC peripherals, especially printers, displays, and floppy disk drives. Sales stagnated in 1988, however, and the company decided that it had to return to the PC market to support its position in peripherals. To circumvent the tariff on Japanese PC imports, Panasonic agreed to purchase eight models of IBM-compatible PCs from Tandy Corporation of Ft. Worth, Texas. The new Panasonic computers were ready for distribution in 1989. Matsushita continued to expand in the United States, reaching 12 manufacturing plants and six R & D facilities in 1991.

This agreement marked the first time a Japanese company purchased PCs made in the United States to sell in the U.S. market. Tandy and Panasonic had a mutually beneficial relationship in the past because Tandy's Radio Shack chain was one of Panasonic's retailers for fax machines and tape recorders, and the new agreement allowed both companies to pursue their interests in the U.S. PC market.

The agreement was a shot in the arm for Tandy as it struggled to become a major player in the U.S. PC market. Through 1987 and 1988, Tandy had taken decisive action to strengthen its weak market position. It acquired new channels of distribution distinct from its 7,000 Radio Shack outlets and their traditional retail focus. To obtain access to government contracts, it acquired a small computer manufacturer with a strong government sales history. To reach the average consumer around the country and gain market exposure, it test marketed Tandy PCs in Wal-Mart stores. Finally, to increase production of more sophisticated machines, it

agreed to supply Digital Equipment Corporation with computers to be sold under the DEC label. In 1990, Tandy released a new family-oriented PC, the 1000 RL, to reposition itself in the PC market. Finally, to gain a foothold in Europe, Tandy acquired the Victor and Micronic PC lines from Sweden's Datatronic AB.

The agreement with Matsushita followed on the heels of the DEC agreement and had the potential to place Tandy in one of the preeminent positions in the personal computer industry, according to Jack Freeman, senior analyst for the Yankee Group. Tandy's PCs had long been regarded as second rate in the world of IBM-compatible machines and had suffered from poor sales. The agreement with well-respected Matsushita would bolster Tandy's reputation throughout the industry and would allow for significant production and pricing advantages from volume purchases of Matsushita memory chips. Thus, Tandy would not only be associated with a quality product that had immense market potential, but the spin-off effects for its own brand, already one of the lowest-cost producers in the PC industry, could be significant. This would help bring a turnaround at Tandy (see Figures 1 and 2)

Following the Tandy-Panasonic agreement, the marketing department of Panasonic's office automation group designed a promotional campaign for their new PCs. Although the computers were suited to both the household and business markets, depending on the model, Panasonic wished to determine executives' willingness to buy Panasonic PCs. Management particularly wanted information in three areas: the reactions of businesses of various sizes, the impact of familiarity with Panasonic PCs

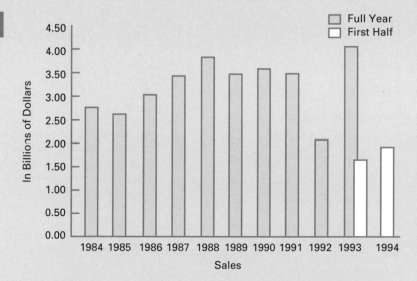

° FIGURE 1

Sales of Tandy Corporation

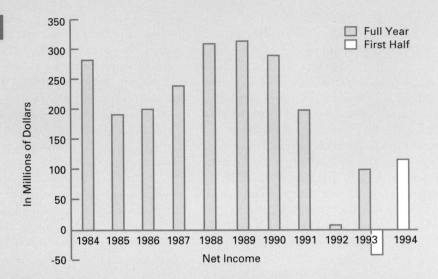

FIGURE 2

Net Income of Tandy Corporation

□ Full Year
□ First Half

In Millions of Dollars

350
300
250
200
150
100
50
0
-50

1984 1985 1986 1987 1988 1989 1990 1991 1992 1993 1994

Net Income

on willingness to buy, and how American businesses were using PCs in the workplace. This led to the related question of whether sales of peripherals to technically competent PC users could be increased.

To address these issues, 1,080 companies throughout the United States were selected from a list of subscribers to *PC Week* magazine and were sent a questionnaire designed to uncover executives' willingness to purchase a Panasonic PC, assuming that they were in the market for a PC. The companies were classified for research purposes along three variables: company size, familiarity with Panasonic PCs, and business application of PCs. Each of these variables could assume one of three values as listed below.

Variable	Value
Company size	
Small/entrepreneurial	1
Medium/private	2
Division of major corporation	3
Familiarity with Panasonic PCs	
No experience	1
Has purchased peripherals/has no knowledge	
of Panasonic PCs	2
Has purchased or is familiar with Panasonic PCs	3
Business Applications	
Word processing only	1
Word processing and data analysis	2
Word processing, data analysis, and networking	3

Forty respondents were randomly assigned to each of the 27 possible combinations of variables (40 respondents with low-low-low ratings, 40 with low-low-medium rat-

ings, etc.). The respondents' stated willingness to purchase a Panasonic PC was measured on an 11-point scale.

This design was chosen to allow for subsequent data analysis. Using SPSS, SAS, or BMDP (or a similar statistical software package), you have been assigned to write program files and analyze the data using the following procedures.

1. *Frequency distribution.* Ensure that the frequency distributions of all variables are appropriate for further analysis.

2. *Cross-tabulations.* Recode the dependent variable, willingness to buy, into three relatively equal groups corresponding (low, medium, and high). Run cross-tabulations on the dependent variable with each of the independent variables (company size, familiarity, and business application) for Panasonic PCs. Then, run cross-tabulations on the dependent variable with familiarity with Panasonic PCs controlling for business application; on company size controlling for business application; and on company size controlling for familiarity with Panasonic PCs. Interpret the results for management.

3. *Regression.* Regress the dependent variable on two dummy variables each for Company Size, Familiarity with Panasonic PCs, and business application. (Note that each independent variable has three categories and will therefore be represented by two dummy variables.) Interpret the results for management.

4. *One-way analysis of variance.* Explain the variation in the dependent variable by running three ANOVAs of the dependent variable with each of the predictor variables (company size, familiarity with Panasonic PCs, and business application).

5. *Three-way analysis of variance.* Explain the variation in the dependent variable by running a three-way ANOVA to determine interaction effects between the predictor variables.

6. *Discriminant analysis.* Group the dependent variable into three relatively equal groups based on the distribution, run discriminant analysis on the grouped data with the dummy variables created for regression, and interpret the results for management.

The data for this case are provided. In the enclosed data, the first variable represents the stated willingness to purchase a Panasonic PC. The next three variables, in the order listed in the case, represent the variables used to classify the companies. Each field occupies six columns.

The principal consultant of your firm has asked you to analyze the data using a significance level of .05 and to prepare a thorough report detailing the results of the analysis and offering recommendations for Panasonic management on their promotional program for the PCs made by Tandy. Remember that your target is U.S. business executives. Your mission, while not impossible, is a difficult one: help Panasonic retarget its market.

REFERENCES

1. "Tandy Corp., Matsushita Plan Computer Pact." *Wall Street Journal* (November 14, 1988): B4.
2. "Tandy in PC Deal with Matsushita." *The New York Times* (November 15, 1988): D5.
3. "How a Picture Tube Made in the U.S.A. Is Helping Americans Enjoy a Brighter Picture of Life." *Forbes* (January 7, 1991): S1.
4. Lappen, Alyssa A. "We're Still Here." *Forbes* (November 26, 1990): 191–95.
5. McCartney, Scott. "Tandy, After Resisting Calls for CEO's Head, Enjoys a Comeback." *Wall Street Journal* (October 18, 1994): A1, A13.

Note: This case was prepared for class discussion purposes only and does not represent the views of Matsushita, Tandy, or their affiliates. The problem scenario is hypothetical and the data provided are simulated.

CASE 4.6 Pampers Develops a Rash, A Rash of New Products

The $3.5 billion disposable diaper industry had always seemed to belong to one brand, Pampers. Procter & Gamble had dominated the market through the 1970s and into the 1980s with Pampers as its flagship offering. In the late 1970s, Luvs was added as a secondary offering to compete with Kimberly-Clark's Huggies brand. But by 1985, Huggies controlled 32.6% of the market and was a major threat to P & G's industry leadership.

To regain market dominance, P & G elected to modify both Pampers and Luvs in 1985. Accepting the widely held belief that consumers would pay more for better-quality diapers, P & G spent $500 million to update its production equipment to produce contoured diapers, a marked divergence from the rectangular diapers it had always offered. The new Pampers, named "Ultra Pampers," were introduced with great fanfare at a New York City hospital. Scientific studies on diaper rash were cited, an endorsement from a national association of pediatric nurses was announced, and simulation tests of the newly designed diapers were conducted to tout their superiority.

The only negative aspect noted about Ultra Pampers was their size; they were thinner than conventional diapers, thus leading to a perception that they were less absorbent despite their certified product qualities.

Luvs was also modified by adding premium brand attributes such as better absorbency, contoured design, and new packaging. These same modifications were highly successful in building Ultra Pampers' market share, but much of the gain was at the expense of Luvs, rather than Huggies.

As Luvs continued to flounder despite reformulation, in 1988 P & G replaced Luvs with Luvs Deluxe, a sex-specific, pastel-colored diaper offering the latest in technology and convenience. To increase absorbency, the pink diapers for girls had extra padding in the center, and the blue for boys had more padding in the front. Although these changes were heavily promoted, industry analysts were unimpressed by P & G's latest move. The general feeling was that P & G was undecided in how to best position their two brands effectively against Huggies and that

759

the introduction of Luvs Deluxe was simply a temporary measure until a new strategy could be implemented. In addition, Kimberly-Clark, continued to be aggressive in the market, introducing three significant modifications in the diaper business in 1989: the multi-ply, stay-dry transport layer; the foamed elastic waistband; and the upstanding cuffs. Sales in 1989 bore out the analysts' conclusions: Luvs Deluxe did rebound, but almost entirely at the expense of Pampers, because consumers responded favorably to the sex-specific diapers (see Table 1). But, in an industry renowned for economy of shelf space, carrying two lines forced distributors and retailers to trade off shelf space between the P & G products, rather than take it from Huggies. Clearly, P & G's two-product strategy was not succeeding against Huggies.

Huggies continued to increase the pressure against P & G in 1991, when it introduced its Huggies Baby Steps line. This line offered five diaper sizes instead of the previously offered four. In response to this, P & G quickly introduced its Pampers Phases, which had seven diaper sizes instead of the standard three. Huggies, however, was not to be outdone, and unveiled Huggies Pull-Ups, a combination between disposable diapers and underwear—in other words, disposable training pants—in late 1991. This line represented a radical new innovation in the diaper market and a very profitable one for Kimberly-Clark, because Pull-Ups sold for about twice the price of standard baby diapers and the competition, including P & G, was unable to introduce a similar product. Sales for Pull-Ups reached $500 million a year by 1992.

Midyear 1993 brought with it a deemphasis of marketing and a concentration on price. P & G began slashing prices of its premium brand Pampers to compete with the private label entries, which gained ground in the first half of the year. The fall of 1992 saw P & G introduce an everyday low-pricing strategy while eliminating consumer coupons. This move is a direct assault on private label brands that have been lower priced and quick to adopt product changes. P & G is citing a "new environment" with an emphasis on value-oriented consumers as the push behind this recent change in marketing.

In May of 1993, P & G adopted a two-tiered pricing strategy aimed at making Luvs a bargain brand, cutting 16% in the list price. The price cuts in Luvs have been supported by eliminating such extras as printed backsheets, package handles, consumer promotions, and a variety of package sizes. Pampers is still being maintained as a top-of-the-line brand and carries a higher price with only a marginal price cut of 5% in 1993. Kimberly-Clark quickly followed suit with a price cut on Huggies at the same time.

The recent price and positioning changes have been accompanied by product line introductions. Pampers introduced Pampers Ultra Dry Thins as a rebuttal to Kimberly-Clark's first entry into the thin market, Huggies UltraTrim, which went into national distribution in the late months of 1992. These thinner diapers provide better absorbency while being less bulky than other diapers. P & G is also expected to introduce a new Pampers "training pant" product to rival Kimberly-Clark's lone entry into the market segment, Huggies' Pull-Ups.

In this increasingly competitive diaper market, P & G's marketing department desired to formulate new approaches to the construction and marketing of Pampers to position them effectively against Huggies without cannibalizing Luvs. To do so, 300 mothers of infants were surveyed. Each was given a randomly selected brand of diaper (Pampers, Luvs, or Huggies) and asked to rate that diaper on nine

TABLE 1

Disposable Diaper Market Share (in percent)

	1988	1989	1990	1991	1992	1993
Pampers	29.0	24.8	24.4	27.2	29.2	28.0
Luvs	17.8	22.3	23.2	20.0	14.3	13.1
Total Procter & Gamble	46.8	47.1	47.6	47.2	43.5	41.1
Huggies (Kimberly-Clark)	30.7	30.1	30.9	36.3	37.2	38.4
Private Labels	*	*	*	12.1	14.3	15.6

Notes: *means not available.

The totals do not add to 100% because of the market shares of other brands.

attributes and to give her overall preference for the brand. These ratings were obtained on seven-point Likert scales. The study was designed so that each of the three brands appeared 100 times. The goal of the study was to learn which attributes of diapers were most important in influencing purchase preference (Y). The nine attributes used in the study were as follows:

Variable	Attribute	Marketing Options
X_1	Count per box	Desire large counts per box?
X_2	Price	Pay a premium price?
X_3	Value	Promote high value
X_4	Unisex	Unisex versus separate-sex diapers
X_5	Style	Prints/colors versus plain diapers
X_6	Absorbency	Regular versus super absorbency
X_7	Leakage	Narrow/tapered versus regular crotch
X_8	Comfort/size	Extra padding and form-fitting gathers
X_9	Taping	Resealable tape versus regular tape

Data were collected at a suburban mall using the mall-intercept technique and are enclosed. The first variable represents brand preference (Y). The next nine variables represent the ratings of the brands on the nine attributes in the order listed in the case (X_1 to X_9). Each field occupies three columns.

QUESTIONS

You must analyze the data and prepare a report for the marketing department. The one-page memo you received suggested that you use the following procedures:

1. *Frequency distribution.* Show bar graphs of all variables.
2. *Cross-tabulations.* Group brand preference as low, medium, and high under the formula low = 1 or 2, medium = 3 to 5, and high = 6 or 7. Group all independent variables as: low = 1 to 3, medium = 4, and high = 5 to 7. Run two-variable cross-tabulations of preference with each independent variable. Run the following three-variable cross-tabulations: preference with count per box, controlling for price; preference with unisex, controlling for style; and preference with comfort, controlling for taping. Interpret these results for management.
3. *Regression.* Find a regression equation for brand preference that includes all independent variables for the

model and describe how meaningful the model is. Interpret the results for management.

4. *One-way analysis of variance.* Group all independent variables into low, medium, and high groups as you did for cross-tabulations. Run a one-way analysis of variance on each independent variable with brand preference. Explain the results to management.
5. *Discriminant analysis.* Group brand preference into two relatively equal groups based on its distribution. Run discriminant analysis on the grouped data and interpret the results for management. Repeat this analysis by grouping brand preference into three relatively equal groups.
6. *Factor analysis.* Determine any underlying factors inherent in the data by running a factor analysis using principal components extraction with varimax rotation. Print all available statistics. Save the factor scores and regress these on brand preference. Interpret these results for management.
7. *Cluster analysis.* Use a nonhierarchical procedure to cluster the respondents, based on the independent variables, into two, three, four, and five clusters. Also run a hierarchical procedure to obtain five clusters using Ward's procedure and creating a dendrogram. Interpret all these results for management.

Interpret the results of the survey and make recommendations based on your findings to the marketing department. They want your opinion about which of the nine attributes mothers value most highly as well as your ideas for specific actions that can increase market share for Pampers in today's market. The marketing department is counting on your recommendations to provide them with ways to improve Pampers' image and cure the rash of new products from competitors.

REFERENCES:

1. Freeman, Laurie. "Procter & Gamble, Case Study: Pampers Disposable Diapers." *Advertising Age* (January 29, 1991): 16–17.
2. "Kimberly-Clark Bets, Wins on Innovation." *Wall Street Journal* (November 22, 1991): A5(E).
3. "For the Record: Kimberly-Clark Corp." *Advertising Age* (September 2, 1991): 41.
4. "P & G Rushes on Global Diaper Rollout." *Advertising Age* (October 14, 1991): 6.
5. "In Diapers, It's a Price Fight for P & G, K-C." *Advertising Age* (September 29, 1993): 36.

"I'd trade in my Corvette convertible in a minute to buy this car," exclaimed an excited observer at an advance showing of Chrysler Motors Corporation's design ideas for the 1990s. Since battling back from the brink of bankruptcy in the late 1970s, Chrysler had continued to run a distant third to General Motors and Ford in the U.S. automobile market, and even that position was challenged by Honda in 1990 and 1991 (see Table 1). Chrysler dramatically rebounded in the early 1980s and gained almost two percentage points over the first five years of the 1980s by adding more economical, middle-class cars to its line of luxury sedans. But increased competition from Japanese imports, poor product quality, and unimaginative design led to falling market share in the latter half of the decade.

Chrysler did, however, succeed with its minivan. Because of the triumph with the minivan, Chrysler was even more determined to succeed in the car market, so engineers and managers tried to design automobiles that would fit the stylish, high-quality image Chrysler needed. Chrysler continued to maintain its business strategy of focusing on profit instead of market share, avoiding global alliances, and thriving on a shortage of capital. In 1989, Chrysler held an advance showing of concept cars for the 1990s that included a V-10 engine for both trucks and cars. Two stylish yet pragmatic concepts were released, the Chrysler Millennium and the tiny Plymouth Speedster. Both cars featured an eye-catching design but failed to deliver performance because underneath they were based on the traditional Chrysler platform and powertrain. The reviewers, however, did take note of the rear-drive two-seat sports car, made available in 1992, which incorporated the V-10 engine. Code-named the Dodge TBD (To Be Determined) and later named the Dodge Viper, it looked like a Chevrolet Corvette, but carried a price tag of $55,000.

Even though some call the Dodge Viper the "sexiest yet silliest" car around, it appears that the introduction of the Dodge Viper was a success. Although modest, sales through November 1993 totaled 1,199. Recently, Chrysler Corporation President John Lutz stated that the company will keep Viper production lower than the number of Vipers that are demanded. Currently, annual production

runs approximately 2,000 cars per year, but this number could increase to 3,000 per year since it appears that demand for the car has increased from the time of its introduction. Chrysler also revealed that it will offer the Viper in two new colors, emerald green and yellow. Previously, the first 250 cars were red, and the rest were painted black. Improvements are also planned for the interior of the Viper. For example, Chrysler plans to add factory-installed air-conditioning systems to the Vipers. Chrysler is also considering the introduction of a coupe version of the Viper, which will feature a roof and be called the Prowler. With the success of the Dodge Viper, the LH cars, the Concorde, the Dodge Intrepid, and Eagle Vision, Chrysler has surpassed Honda and Toyota to once again become the third-ranking car company in the United States.

For continued success, the Viper must attract the yuppie crowd—highly educated, affluent baby boomers who tend to prefer imported vehicles. Because this group would be the prime target group for such a high-performance car, Chrysler needed to ensure that it could compete in a mar-

TABLE 1

U.S. Automobile Market Shares (in percent)

Year	Chrysler	Ford	General Motors	Honda	Other
1980	10.7	16.6	46.8	4.3	21.6
1981	11.6	16.2	44.5	4.3	23.4
1982	11.7	16.9	44.0	4.5	22.9
1983	12.6	17.1	44.2	4.4	21.7
1984	12.3	19.0	44.3	4.9	19.5
1985	12.5	18.8	42.5	5.0	21.2
1986	12.1	18.2	41.0	6.1	22.6
1987	10.7	20.2	36.5	7.2	25.4
1988	11.3	21.6	36.1	7.3	23.7
1989	10.4	22.2	34.9	7.8	24.7
1990	9.3	23.9	35.5	9.4	21.9
1991	8.6	23.2	35.0	9.8	23.4
1992	13.0	25.0	34.0	6.0	22.0
1993	15.0	26.0	34.0	5.0	20.0

ket traditionally dominated by Corvette, Nissan 300-ZX, and Porsche 944. Primary concerns for Chrysler were overcoming its boxcar image with this group, determining if they should appeal to patriotism or offer incentives on the Dodge Viper, and focusing on the importance of styling and prestige when promoting to this market.

To accomplish this task, 30 statements were constructed to measure attitudes toward these factors and to classify the respondents. The respondents used a nine-point Likert scale (1 = definitely disagree, 9 = definitely agree). The respondents were obtained from the mailing lists of *Car and Driver*, *Business Week*, and *Inc.* magazines and they were telephoned at their homes by an independent surveying company. The statements used in the survey of 400 respondents are listed below.

1. I am in very good physical condition.
2. When I must choose between the two, I usually dress for fashion, not comfort.
3. I have more stylish clothes than most of my friends.
4. I want to look a little different from others.
5. Life is too short not to take some gambles.
6. I am not concerned about the ozone layer.
7. I think the government is doing too much to control pollution.
8. Basically, society today is fine.
9. I don't have time to volunteer for charities.
10. Our family is not too heavily in debt today.
11. I like to pay cash for everything I buy.
12. I pretty much spend for today and let tomorrow bring what it will.
13. I use credit cards because I can pay the bill off slowly.
14. I seldom use coupons when I shop.
15. Interest rates are low enough to allow me to buy what I want.
16. I have more self-confidence than most of my friends.
17. I like to be considered a leader.
18. Others often ask me to help them out of a jam.
19. Children are the most important thing in a marriage.
20. I would rather spend a quiet evening at home than go out to a party.
21. American-made cars can't compare with foreign-made cars.
22. The government should restrict imports of products from Japan.
23. Americans should always try to buy American products.
24. I would like to take a trip around the world.
25. I wish I could leave my present life and do something entirely different.
26. I am usually among the first to try new products.
27. I like to work hard and play hard.
28. Skeptical predictions are usually wrong.
29. I can do anything I set my mind to.
30. Five years from now, my income will be a lot higher than it is now.

In addition, the criterion variable—attitude toward Dodge Viper—was measured by asking each person to respond to the statement, "I would consider buying the Dodge Viper made by Chrysler." This statement was measured on the same nine-point scale as the 30 predictor statements.

The data for the case are provided. In the enclosed data, the first variable represents attitude toward a Chrysler sportscar. The next 30 variables, in the order listed in the case, represent the ratings of the lifestyle statements. Each field occupies three columns.

QUESTIONS

The director of marketing for Chrysler is interested in knowing the psychological characteristics of the yuppies to configure the Dodge Viper program. You have been presented with the responses from the survey outlined above. Analyze the data according to the following guidelines:

1. *Frequency distribution.* Ensure that each variable is appropriate for analysis by running a frequency distribution for each variable.

2. *Regression.* Using a stepwise regression analysis, locate those variables that best explain the criterion variable. Evaluate the strength of the model and assess the impact of each variable included on the criterion variable.

3. *Factor analysis.* Determine the underlying psychological factors that characterize the respondents by means of factor analysis of all 30 independent variables. Use principal component extraction with varimax rotation for ease of interpretation. Save the factor scores and then regress them on the criterion variable, forcing all predictor variables to be included in the analysis. Evaluate the strength of this model and compare it with the initial regression. Use the factor scores to cluster the respondents into three groups. Discuss the significance of the groups based on the underlying factors. Repeat this cluster analysis for four groups.

4. *Cluster analysis.* Cluster the respondents on the original variables into three and four clusters. Which is a better model? Compare these cluster results with the cluster results on the factor scores. Which is easier to interpret? Which explains the data better?

Based on the analysis, prepare a report to management explaining the yuppie consumer and offering recommendations on the design of the Dodge Viper. Your recommendations should aid Chrysler in achieving what they seek: an image for the Viper that is attractive to the yuppie market and that helps them outperform the competition in the performance car market.

REFERENCES:

1. "Viper Vitality." *Automotive News* (February 15, 1993): 2.
2. McCormick, John. "Coupe DeViper Remains a Distinct Possibility." *Ward's Auto World* (July, 1993): 114.
3. "Two New Viper Colors." *Industrial Finishing* (July 1993): 32–34.
4. Taylor, Alex. "Will Success Spoil Chrysler?" *Fortune* (January 10, 1994): 88–92.
5. "1993 Edison Best New Products Awards Winners." *Marketing News* (April 25, 1994): E4.
6. *Automotive News* (January 10, 1994): 50.

Note: This case was prepared for class discussion purposes only and does not represent the views of Chrysler or its affiliates. The problem scenario is hypothetical and the data provided are simulated.

PART V

Communicating the Research Project

◆

Communicating the research by preparing and presenting a formal report constitutes the sixth step in a marketing research project. This part describes the importance and process of report preparation and presentation. Written with a practical orientation, it provides guidelines for writing reports and preparing tables and graphs. We also discuss oral presentation of the report and offer several useful tips.

CHAPTER TWENTY-TWO

Report Preparation and Presentation

The quality of the report and presentation are often used as major indicators of the quality of the entire marketing research project.

OBJECTIVES

After reading this chapter, the student should be able to:

1. Discuss the basic requirements of report preparation including report format, report writing, graphs, and tables.
2. Discuss the nature and scope of the oral presentation and describe the "tell 'em" and "KISS 'em" principles.
3. Describe the approach to the marketing research report from the client's perspective and the guidelines for reading the research report.
4. Explain the reason for follow-up with the client and describe the assistance that should be given to the client and the evaluation of the research project.
5. Understand the report preparation and presentation process in international marketing research.
6. Identify the ethical issues related to the interpretation and reporting of the research process and findings to the client and the use of these results by the client.
7. Explain the use of microcomputers and mainframes in report preparation and presentation.

OVERVIEW

Report preparation and presentation constitutes the sixth and final step in a marketing research project. It follows problem definition, developing an approach, research design formulation, field work, and data preparation and analysis. This chapter describes the importance of this last step as well as a process for report preparation and presentation. We provide guidelines for report preparation, including report writing and preparing tables and graphs, and we discuss oral presentation of the report. Research follow-up, including assisting the client and evaluating the research process, is described. The special considerations for report preparation and presentation in international marketing research are discussed, and relevant ethical issues are identified. We conclude by explaining the role of microcomputers and mainframes in report preparation and presentation.

We begin with some examples describing the nature and importance of report preparation and presentation.

DEPARTMENT STORE PATRONAGE PROJECT
Report Preparation and Presentation

In the department store patronage project, a formal report was prepared for the client's vice-president of marketing. The first volume, the main body of the report, had a title page; table of contents; executive summary; details of problem definition, approach, research design, methodology used to analyze the data; results; limitations of the project; and conclusions and recommendations. Volume 2 contained a title page, list of figures, and all the figures and graphs. Finally, all the statistical details, including all the tables, were given in Volume 3. The writing of the report was influenced by the style preferences of the vice-president for marketing and other key executives. Volume 1 had a nontechnical orientation and was easy to follow. In addition to the written report, an oral presentation of the entire project was made to the top management. Several of the recommendations made to management in the report were eventually implemented. ◆

EXAMPLE
Interim Report Yields Satisfaction

The marketing research firm of Elrick and Lavidge measured consumer satisfaction with a telecommunications firm's products and sales force in a phased manner in 20 markets. When the research had been conducted in four markets, an interim report about satisfaction levels and product usage in each of the four markets was prepared. This report identified factors that affected satisfaction levels and were common across markets. It was presented to the client management group, consisting of the vice-president of marketing, director of marketing, director of marketing research, and other managers. As a result of this presentation and subsequent discussions, several modifications were made in the project in the remaining 16 markets.[1] ◆

The department store example illustrates how the main body of the report follows the format of the earlier steps of the marketing research process. The Elrick and Lavidge example highlights the importance of interim reporting.

IMPORTANCE OF THE REPORT AND PRESENTATION

For the following reasons, the report and its presentation are important parts of the marketing research project:

1. They are the tangible products of the research effort. After the project is complete and management has made the decision, there is little documentary evidence of the project other than the written report. The report serves as a historical record of the project.

2. Management decisions are guided by the report and the presentation. If the first five steps in the project are carefully conducted but inadequate attention is paid to the sixth step, the value of the project to management will be greatly diminished.

3. The involvement of many marketing managers in the project is limited to the written report and the oral presentation. These managers evaluate the quality of the entire project on the quality of the report and presentation.

4. Management's decision to undertake marketing research in the future or to use the particular research supplier again will be influenced by the perceived usefulness of the report and the presentation.

THE REPORT PREPARATION AND PRESENTATION PROCESS

Figure 22.1 illustrates report preparation and presentation. The process begins by interpreting the results of data analysis in light of the marketing research problem, approach, research design, and field work. Instead of merely summarizing the statistical results, the researcher should present the findings in such a way that they can be used directly as input into decision making. Wherever appropriate, conclusions should be drawn and recommendations made. Recommendations should be actionable. Before writing the report, the researcher should discuss the major findings, conclusions, and recommendations with the key decision makers. These discussions play a major role in ensuring that the report meets the client's needs and is ultimately accepted. These discussions should confirm specific dates for the delivery of the written report and other data.

The entire marketing research project should be summarized in a single written report or in several reports addressed to different readers. Generally, an oral presentation supplements the written documents. The client should be given an opportunity to read the report. After that, the researcher should take necessary follow-up actions. The researcher should assist the client in understanding the report, implementing the findings, undertaking further research, and evaluating the research process in retrospect. The importance of the researcher being intimately involved in the report preparation and presentation process is highlighted by the following example.

FIGURE 22.1

The Report Preparation and Presentation Process

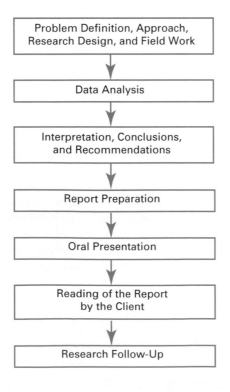

Problem Definition, Approach, Research Design, and Field Work

↓

Data Analysis

↓

Interpretation, Conclusions, and Recommendations

↓

Report Preparation

↓

Oral Presentation

↓

Reading of the Report by the Client

↓

Research Follow-Up

EXAMPLE

Focus Group Moderators' Ghostwriters Can Shortchange Clients _____

Thomas Greenbaum, president of a market research company focusing on qualitative research, notes a disturbing trend in recent years in the focus group service sector. Greenbaum of Groups Plus Inc. of Wilton, Connecticut, asserts that some moderators of focus groups misrepresent their work to clients because their reports are actually written by ghostwriters who did not participate in the focus group sessions.

According to Greenbaum, perhaps more than half of moderators use ghostwriters to develop their reports for clients; often, junior researchers learning the business or part-time employees write these reports. Greenbaum criticizes such ghostwriting because the nonverbal reactions of focus group participants, or group synergy, cannot always be accurately reported by those who merely listen to audiotapes or who view videotapes of focus group sessions. Greenbaum calls upon moderators to be forthright with clients about the authorship of focus group reports and calls upon clients to be more demanding of their contracted research teams.

"Although some people in the industry defend ghostwriting by saying they always review the reports before they are sent to the client, or perhaps even write certain key sections, this practice must be looked at carefully by clients who use focus group research," Greenbaum said. "If the clients know in advance that their reports will be written by someone else, it is clearly less of a problem, but they still do not get the best effort from their research consultants."

In addition to the likelihood of degrading a report, Greenbaum observes that the ghostwriting system delays the submission of the final report. "Moderators who write their own reports try to complete them within a week or 10 days of the last group, so the information is still fresh in their minds when they do the writing," Greenbaum said. "However, most moderators (using ghostwriters) are not able to provide clients with final reports for three to four weeks after the last group, due to the process they use with ghostwriters." [2] ◆

REPORT PREPARATION

Researchers differ in the way they prepare a research report. The personality, background, expertise, and responsibility of the researcher, along with the decision maker (DM) to whom the report is addressed, interact to give each report a unique character. Yet there are guidelines for formatting and writing reports and designing tables and graphs.[3]

Report Format

Report formats are likely to vary with the researcher or the marketing research firm conducting the project, the client for whom the project is being conducted, and the nature of the project itself. Hence, the following is intended as a guideline from which the researcher can develop a format for the research project at hand. Most research reports include the following elements:

    I. Title page
   II. Letter of transmittal
  III. Letter of authorization
  IV. Table of contents

    V. List of tables
    VI. List of graphs
    VII. List of appendices
    VIII. List of exhibits
    IX. Executive summary
        a. Major findings
        b. Conclusions
        c. Recommendations
    X. Problem definition
        a. Background to the problem
        b. Statement of the problem
    XI. Approach to the problem
    XII. Research design
        a. Type of research design
        b. Information needs
        c. Data collection from secondary sources
        d. Data collection from primary sources
        e. Scaling techniques
        f. Questionnaire development and pretesting
        g. Sampling techniques
        h. Field work
    XIII. Data analysis
        a. Methodology
        b. Plan of data analysis
    XIV. Results
    XV. Limitations and caveats
    XVI. Conclusions and recommendations
    XVII. Exhibits
        a. Questionnaires and forms
        b. Statistical output
        c. Lists

This format closely follows the earlier steps of the marketing research process. The results may be presented in several chapters of the report. For example, in a national survey, data analysis may be conducted for the overall sample and then the data for each geographic region may be analyzed separately. If so, the results may be presented in five chapters instead of one.

Title Page   The title page should include the title of the report, information (name, address and telephone) about the researcher or organization conducting the research, the name of the client for whom the report was prepared, and the date of release. The title should indicate the nature of the project, as illustrated in Research in Practice 22.1.

Letter of Transmittal   A formal report generally contains a letter of transmittal that delivers the report to the client and summarizes the researcher's overall experience with the project, without mentioning the findings. The letter should also identify the need for further action on the part of the client, such as implementation of the findings or further research that should be undertaken.

RESEARCH IN PRACTICE 22.1

Elrick and Lavidge Guidelines on The Title Page

Use client language in title; avoid "research-eze"

> "Practices Followed in Selecting Long-Distance Carriers" is better than "Long-Distance Service Study"

> "Customers' Reactions to an Expanded Financial/Insurance Relationship" is better than "Relationship Study"

Letter of Authorization   A letter of authorization is written by the client to the researcher before work on the project begins. It authorizes the researcher to proceed with the project and specifies its scope and the terms of the contract. Often, it is sufficient to refer to the letter of authorization in the letter of transmittal. It is sometimes necessary to include a copy of the letter of authorization in the report, however.

Table of Contents   The table of contents should list the topics covered and the appropriate page numbers. In most reports, only the major headings and subheadings are included. The table of contents is followed by a list of tables, list of graphs, list of appendices, and list of exhibits.

Executive Summary   The executive summary is an extremely important part of the report, because this is often the only portion of the report that executives read. The summary should concisely describe the problem, approach, and research design that was adopted. A summary section should be devoted to the major results, conclusions, and recommendations. The executive summary should be written after the rest of the report.

Problem Definition   The problem definition section of the report gives the background to the problem; highlights the discussions with the decision makers and industry experts; and discusses the secondary data analysis, the qualitative research that was conducted, and the factors that were considered. Moreover, it should contain a clear statement of the management decision problem and the marketing research problem (see Chapter 2).

Approach to the Problem   The approach to the problem section should discuss the broad approach that was adopted in addressing the problem. The process of developing an approach—including discussions with executives, examination of analogous situations, secondary data analysis, qualitative research, and pragmatic constraints—should be described (see Chapter 2). This section should also contain a description of the theoretical foundations that guided the research, any analytical models formulated, research questions, hypotheses, and the factors that influenced the research design.

Research Design   The section on research design should specify the details of how the research was conducted (see Chapters 3 through 13). This should include the nature of the research design adopted, information needed, data collection from secondary and primary sources, scaling techniques, questionnaire development and pretesting, sampling techniques, and field work. These topics should be presented in a nontechnical, easy-to-understand manner. The technical details should be included in an appendix. This section of the report should justify the specific methods selected.

Data Analysis   The section on data analysis should describe the plan of data analysis and justify the data analysis strategy and techniques used. The techniques used for analysis should be described in simple, nontechnical terms.

Results   The results section is normally the longest part of the report and may entail several chapters. Often, the results are presented not only at the aggregate level but also at the subgroup (market segment, geographical area, etc.) level. The results should be organized in a coherent and logical way. For example, in a health care marketing survey of hospitals, the results were presented in four chapters. One chapter presented the overall results, another examined the differences between geographical regions, a third presented the differences between for-profit and nonprofit hospitals, and a fourth presented the differences according to bed capacity. The presentation of the results should be geared directly to the components of the marketing research problem and the information needs that were identified. The details should be presented in tables and graphs, with the main findings discussed in the text.

Limitations and Caveats   All marketing research projects have limitations caused by time, budget, and other organizational constraints. Furthermore, the research design adopted may be limited in terms of the various types of errors (see Chapter 3), and some of these may be serious enough to warrant discussion. This section should be written with great care and a balanced perspective. On one hand, the researcher must make sure that management does not overly rely on the results or use them for unintended purposes, such as projecting them to unintended populations. On the other hand, this section should not erode their confidence in the research or unduly minimize its importance.

Conclusions and Recommendations   Presenting a mere summary of the statistical results is not enough. The researcher should interpret the results in light of the problem being addressed to arrive at major conclusions. Based on the results and conclusions, the researcher may make recommendations to the decision makers. Sometimes, marketing researchers are not asked to make recommendations because they research only one area but do not understand the bigger picture at the client firm. If recommendations are made, they should be feasible, practical, actionable, and directly usable as inputs into managerial decision making. Research in Practice 22.2 contains guidelines on conclusions and recommendations.

Report Writing

Readers   A report should be written for a specific reader or readers: the marketing managers who will use the results. The report should take into account the readers' technical sophistication and interest in the project as well as the circumstances under which they will read the report and how they will use it.[4]

Technical jargon should be avoided. As expressed by one expert, "The readers of your reports are busy people; and very few of them can balance a research report, a cup of coffee, and a dictionary at one time."[5] Instead of technical terms like maximum likelihood, heteroscedasticity, and nonparametric, use descriptive explanations. If some technical terms cannot be avoided, briefly define them in an appendix. When it comes

RESEARCH IN PRACTICE 22.2

Elrick and Lavidge Guidelines on Conclusions and Recommendations

CONCLUSIONS

- Conclusions
  - Conclusions concerning, for example:
    - customer behavior
    - customer attitudes or perceptions
    - the nature of the markets studied
  - Generally, in studies with samples designed to represent the market
  - Avoid interesting results that are not relevant to the conclusions
- May be in form of statement or paragraphs
- Use subheadings to identify conclusions covering different subjects or market segments

RECOMMENDATIONS

- Recommendations regarding actions that should be taken or considered in light of the research results:
  - Add/drop a product
  - What to say in advertising—advertising positioning
  - Market segments to select as primary targets
  - How to price product
  - Further research that should be considered
- Should be related to the stated purpose of the research
- Sometimes omitted, for example
  - Client staff members want to author the recommendations
  - Study designed merely to familiarize client with a market
- Most clients are interested in our suggestions, even though we may not be familiar with internal financial issues and other internal corporate factors

to marketing research, people would rather live with a problem they cannot solve than accept a solution they cannot understand.

Often the researcher must cater to the needs of several audiences with different levels of technical sophistication and interest in the project. Such conflicting needs may be met by including different sections in the report for different readers or separate reports entirely.

Easy to follow   The report should be easy to follow.[6] It should be structured logically and written clearly. The material, particularly the body of the report, should be structured in a logical manner so that the reader can easily see the inherent connections and linkages. Headings should be used for different topics and subheadings for subtopics.

A logical organization also leads to a coherent report. Clarity can be enhanced by using well-constructed sentences that are short and to the point. The words used should express precisely what the researcher wants to communicate. Difficult words, slang, and clichés should be avoided. An excellent check on the clarity of a report is to have two or three people who are unfamiliar with the project read it and offer critical comments. Several revisions of the report may be needed before the final document emerges.

Presentable and Professional Appearance   The looks of a report are important. The report should be professionally reproduced with quality paper, typing, and binding. The typography should be varied. Variation in type size and skillful use of white space can greatly contribute to the appearance and readability of the report.

Objective   Objectivity is a virtue that should guide report writing. Researchers can become so fascinated with their project that they overlook their scientific role. The report should accurately present the methodology, results, and conclusions of the project, without slanting the findings to conform to the expectations of management. Decision makers are unlikely to receive with enthusiasm a report that reflects unfavorably on their judgment or actions. Yet the researcher must have the courage to present and defend the results objectively. The rule is, "Tell it like it is."

Reinforce Text with Tables and Graphs   It is important to reinforce key information in the text with tables, graphs, pictures, maps, and other visual devices. Visual aids can greatly facilitate communication and add to the clarity and impact of the report. Guidelines for tabular and graphical presentation are discussed later.

Terse   A report should be terse and concise. Anything unnecessary should be omitted. If too much information is included, important points may be lost. Avoid lengthy discussions of common procedures. Yet brevity should not be achieved at the expense of completeness.

Guidelines for Tables

Statistical tables are a vital part of the report and deserve special attention. We illustrate the guidelines for tables using the data for U.S. automobile sales reported in Table 22.1. The numbers in parentheses in the following paragraphs refer to the numbered sections of the table.

Title and Number   Every table should have a number (1a) and title (1b). The title should be brief yet clearly descriptive of the information provided. Arabic numbers are used to identify tables so that they can be referenced in the text.[7]

Arrangement of Data Items   The arrangement of data items in a table should emphasize the most significant aspect of the data. Thus, when the data pertain to time, the items should be arranged by appropriate time period. When order of magnitude is most important, the data items should be arranged in that order (2a). If ease of locating items is critical, an alphabetical arrangement is most appropriate.

Basis of Measurement   The basis or unit of measurement should be clearly stated (3a).

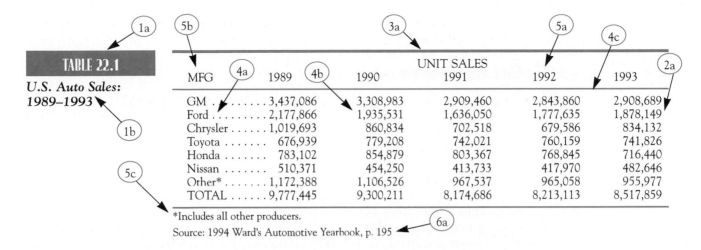

TABLE 22.1

U.S. Auto Sales: 1989–1993

| MFG | 1989 | UNIT SALES | | | |
		1990	1991	1992	1993
GM	3,437,086	3,308,983	2,909,460	2,843,860	2,908,689
Ford	2,177,866	1,935,531	1,636,050	1,777,635	1,878,149
Chrysler	1,019,693	860,834	702,518	679,586	834,132
Toyota	676,939	779,208	742,021	760,159	741,826
Honda	783,102	854,879	803,367	768,845	716,440
Nissan	510,371	454,250	413,733	417,970	482,646
Other*	1,172,388	1,106,526	967,537	965,058	955,977
TOTAL	9,777,445	9,300,211	8,174,686	8,213,113	8,517,859

*Includes all other producers.

Source: 1994 Ward's Automotive Yearbook, p. 195

Leaders, Rulings, Spaces   *Leaders*, dots or hyphens used to lead the eye horizontally, impart uniformity and improve readability (4a). Instead of ruling the table horizontally or vertically, white spaces (4b) are used to set off data items. Skipping lines after different sections of the data can also assist the eye. Horizontal rules (4c) are often used after the headings.

Explanations and Comments: Headings, Stubs, and Footnotes   Explanations and comments clarifying the table can be provided in the form of captions, stubs, and footnotes. Designations placed over the vertical columns are called headings (5a). Designations placed in the left-hand column are called stubs (5b). Information that cannot be incorporated in the table should be explained by footnotes (5c). Letters or symbols should be used for footnotes rather than numbers. The footnotes that are part of the original source should come after the main table, but before the source note.

Despite loss of sales and market share, General Motors remains the leader in automobiles with cars like Saturn. ◆ General Motors.

Sources of the Data   If the data contained in the table are secondary, the source of data should be cited (6a).

Guidelines for Graphs

As a general rule, graphic aids should be employed whenever practical. Graphical display of information can effectively complement the text and tables to enhance clarity of communication and impact.[8] As the saying goes, a picture is worth a thousand words. The guidelines for preparing graphs are similar to those for tables. Therefore, this section focuses on the different types of graphical aids.[9] We illustrate several of these using the U.S. automobile sales data from Table 22.1.

Geographic and Other Maps   Geographic and other maps, such as product positioning maps, can communicate relative location and other comparative information. Geographic maps can pertain to countries, states, counties, sales territories, and other divisions. For example, suppose that the researcher wanted to present information on the relative number of Coca-Cola Company bottlers versus the bottlers for PepsiCo and other competitors for each state in the United States. This information could be effectively communicated in a map in which each state was divided into three areas—proportionate to the number of Coca-Cola, PepsiCo, and other bottlers—with each area in a different color. Chapter 21 showed examples of product-positioning maps.

pie chart A round chart divided into sections.

Round or Pie Charts   In a **pie chart**, the area of each section, as a percentage of the total area of the circle, reflects the percentage associated with the value of a specific variable. A pie chart is not useful for displaying relationships over time or relationships among several variables. As a general guideline, a pie chart should not require more than seven sections.[10] Figure 22.2 shows a pie chart for U.S. automobile sales.

line chart A chart that connects a series of data points using continuous lines.

Line Charts   A **line chart** connects a series of data points using continuous lines. This is an attractive way of illustrating trends and changes over time. Several series can be

FIGURE 22.2

*Pie Chart of 1993
U.S. Car Sales*

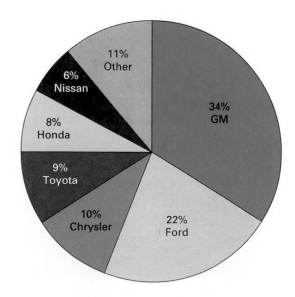

compared on the same chart, and forecasts, interpolations, and extrapolations can be shown. If several series are displayed simultaneously, each line should have a distinctive color or form (see Figure 22.3).[11]

stratum chart A set of line charts in which the data are successively aggregated over the series. Areas between the line charts display the magnitudes of the relevant variables.

A **stratum chart** is a set of line charts in which the data are successively aggregated over the series. Areas between the line charts display the magnitudes of the relevant variables (see Figure 22.4).

pictograph A graphical depiction that makes use of small pictures or symbols to display the data.

Pictographs   A **pictograph** uses small pictures or symbols to display the data. As Figure 22.5 shows, pictographs do not depict results precisely. Hence, caution should be exercised when using them.[12]

bar chart A chart that displays data in bars positioned horizontally or vertically.

Histograms and Bar Charts   A **bar chart** displays data in various bars that may be positioned horizontally or vertically. Bar charts can be used to present absolute and relative magnitudes, differences, and change. A **histogram** is a vertical bar chart in which the height of the bars represents the relative or cumulative frequency of occurrence of a specific variable (see Figure 22.6).

histogram A vertical bar chart in which the height of the bars represents the relative or cumulative frequency of occurrence.

Schematic Figures and Flowcharts   Schematic figures and flowcharts take on a number of different forms. They can be used to display the steps or components of a process, as in Figure 22.1. Another useful form of these charts is classification diagrams. Examples of classification charts for classifying secondary data were provided in Chapter 4 (Figures 4.1 to 4.4). An example of a flowchart for questionnaire design was given in Chapter 10 (Figure 10.2).[13]

ORAL PRESENTATION

The entire marketing research project should be presented to the management of the client firm. This presentation will help management understand and accept the written report. Any preliminary questions that the management may have can be addressed in the presentation. Because many executives form their first and lasting impressions about the project based on the presentation, its importance cannot be overemphasized.[14]

FIGURE 22.3

Line Chart of Total U.S. Car Sales

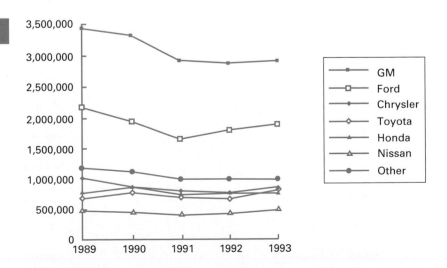

FIGURE 22.4

*Stratum Chart
of Total U.S. Car
Sales*

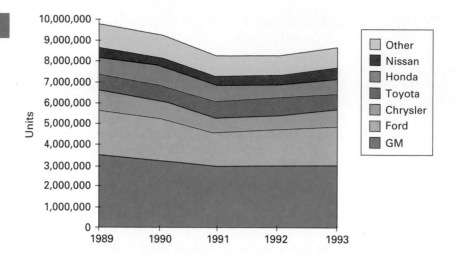

The key to an effective presentation is preparation. A written script or detailed outline should be prepared following the format of the written report. The presentation must be geared to the audience. For this purpose, the researcher should determine the backgrounds, interests, and involvement of those in the project, as well as the extent to which they are likely to be affected by it. The presentation should be rehearsed several times before it is made to the management.

Visual aids such as tables and graphs should be displayed with a variety of media. Chalkboards enable the researcher to manipulate numbers. They are particularly useful in communicating answers to technical questions. Although not as flexible, magnetic boards and felt boards allow for rapid presentation of previously prepared material. Flip charts are large pads of blank paper mounted on an easel. Visual aids are drawn on the pages in advance, and the speaker flips through the pages during the presentation. Overhead projectors can present simple charts as well as complex overlays produced by the successive additions of new images to the screen. Several computer programs are available for producing attractive overhead transparency (acetate sheet) masters. Color transparencies can also be prepared. Slides are useful for projecting photographs on the screen. Videotape

FIGURE 22.5

*Pictograph for 1993
U.S. Car Sales*

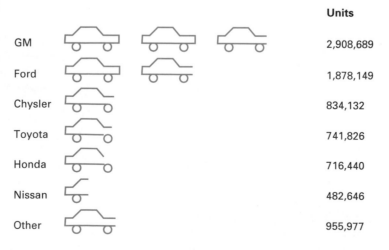

FIGURE 22.6

Histogram of 1993 U.S. Car Sales

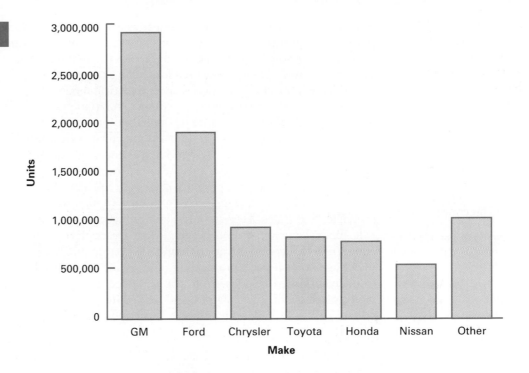

Burke gives its clients the best report graphics, bar none. ◆ Burke Marketing Research.

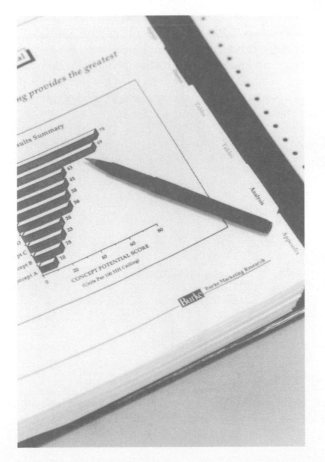

recorders (VCRs) and large-screen projectors are particularly effective in presenting focus groups and other aspects of field work that are dynamic in nature. Computer projectors attached to personal computers, which project the monitor image onto the screens, may also be employed. They can be used for making computer-controlled presentations or for presenting technical information such as analytical models.

It is important to maintain eye contact and to interact with the audience during the presentation. Sufficient opportunity should be provided for questions, both during and after the presentation.[15] The presentation should be made interesting and convincing with the use of appropriate stories, examples, experiences, and quotations. Filler words like "uh," "y'know," and "all right," should not be used. The **"tell 'em" principle** is effective for structuring a presentation. This principle states: (1) tell 'em what you're going to tell 'em, (2) tell 'em, and (3) tell 'em what you've told 'em. Another useful guideline is the **"KISS 'em" principle**, that states: Keep It Simple and Straightforward (hence the acronym KISS).

Body language should be employed. Descriptive gestures are used to clarify or enhance verbal communication. Emphatic gestures are used to emphasize what is being said. Suggestive gestures are symbols of ideas and emotions. Prompting gestures are used to elicit a desired response from the audience. The speaker should vary the volume, pitch, voice quality, articulation, and rate while speaking. The presentation should terminate with a strong closing. To stress its importance, the presentation should be sponsored by a top level manager in the client's organization, as in the following example.

tell 'em principle An effective guideline for structuring a presentation. This principle states: (1) tell 'em what you're going to tell 'em, (2) tell 'em, and (3) tell 'em what you've told 'em.

KISS 'em principle A principle of report presentation that states: Keep It Simple and Straightforward.

EXAMPLE
Taking It to the Top _____

Elrick and Lavidge conducted a research project to measure the relative effectiveness of television, print, and radio as advertising media for a client firm. In addition, the effec-

The importance of the oral presentation cannot be overemphasized since many executives form their first and lasting impressions about the project based on it. ◆ Elrick and Lavidge.

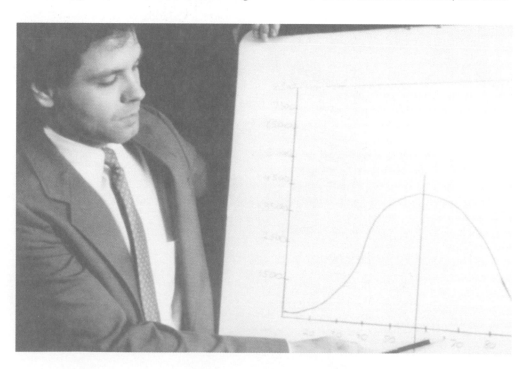

tiveness of ten TV commercials, radio commercials, and print ads was assessed. Given the nature of the project, the oral presentation of the report was particularly important in communicating the findings. In addition to an overhead projector and slide projector, a VCR (for playing TV commercials), a tape recorder (for playing radio commercials), and a story board (for showing print ads) were used. The presentation was made to the client's top corporate officers—consisting of the president, all the vice-presidents, and all the assistant vice-presidents—at one of their monthly meetings.[16] ◆

After the presentation, key executives in the client firm should be given time to read the report in detail. Some guidelines are available for report reading.

READING THE RESEARCH REPORT

Guidelines for reading the report and evaluating the marketing research project have been developed by the Advertising Research Foundation.[17]

Addresses the Problem

The problem being addressed should be clearly identified and the relevant background information should be provided. The organization sponsoring the research, as well as the one conducting the research, should be clearly identified. The report should not assume that the reader has prior knowledge of the problem situation, but should give all the relevant information. A report that does not provide such information has missed its mark, as well as its readers.

Research Design

The research design should be clearly described in nontechnical terms. If readers in the target audience of the report cannot understand the research design procedure, the fault lies with the researcher. The report should include a discussion of the information needs, data collection methods, scaling techniques, questionnaire design and pretesting, sampling techniques, and field work. Justification should be provided for the specific methods used. Reports that do not contain, or otherwise make available, methodological details should be viewed with caution.

Execution of the Research Procedures

The reader should pay special attention to the manner in which the research procedures were executed. The people working on the project should be well qualified and properly trained. Proper supervision and control procedures should be followed. This is particularly important with respect to data collection, data preparation, and statistical analysis.

Numbers and Statistics

Numbers and statistics reported in tables and graphs should be examined carefully by the reader. Inappropriate numbers and statistics can be highly misleading. Consider, for example, percentages based on small samples or means reported for ordinal data. Unfortunately, the occurrence of these types of misleading statistics in reports is not uncommon.

Interpretations and Conclusions

The findings should be reported in an objective and candid way. The interpretation of the basic results should be differentiated from the results per se. Any assumptions made in interpreting the results should be clearly identified. The limitations of the research should be discussed. Any conclusions or recommendations made without a specification of the underlying assumptions or limitations should be treated cautiously by the reader.

Generalizability

It is the responsibility of the researcher to provide evidence regarding the reliability, validity, and generalizability of the findings. The report should clearly identify the target population to which the findings apply. Factors that limit the generalizability of the findings—such as the nature and representativeness of the sample, mode and time of data collections, and various sources of error—should be clearly identified. The reader should not attempt to generalize the findings of the report without explicit consideration of these factors.

Disclosure

Finally, the reader should carefully examine whether the spirit in which the report was written indicates an honest and complete disclosure of the research procedures and results. It is particularly important that procedures—for example, those used for the treatment of missing values or for weighting—that call for subjective judgment on the part of the researcher, be made known. If any negative or unexpected findings were obtained, they should be reported. The reader should feel free to ask for any relevant information that is not contained in the report.

A careful reading of the report using these guidelines will help the client to participate in research follow-up effectively.

RESEARCH FOLLOW-UP

The researcher's task does not end with the oral presentation. Two other tasks remain. The researcher should help the client understand and implement the findings and take follow-up action. Second, while it is still fresh in the researcher's mind, the entire marketing research project should be evaluated.

Assisting the Client

After the client has read the report in detail, several questions may arise. Parts of the report, particularly those dealing with technical matters, may not be understood and the researcher should provide the help needed. Sometimes the researcher helps implement the findings. Often, the client retains the researcher to help with the selection of a new product or advertising agency, development of a pricing policy, market segmentation, or other marketing actions. An important reason for client follow-up is to discuss further research projects. For example, the researcher and management may agree to repeat the study after two years. Finally, the researcher should help the client firm make the information generated in the marketing research project a part of the firm's marketing (management) information system (MIS) or decision support system (DSS), as discussed in Chapter 1.

Evaluation of the Research Project

Although marketing research is scientific, it also involves creativity, intuition, and expertise. Hence, every marketing research project provides an opportunity for learning, and the researcher should critically evaluate the entire project to obtain new insights and knowledge. The key question to ask is, "Could this project have been conducted more effectively or efficiently?" This question, of course, raises several more specific questions. Could the problem have been defined differently so as to enhance the value of the project to the client or reduce the costs? Could a different approach have yielded better results? Was the research design that was used the best? How about the mode of data collection? Should mall-intercept interviews have been used instead of telephone interviews? Was the sampling plan employed the most appropriate? Were the sources of possible design error correctly anticipated and kept under control, at least in a qualitative sense? If not, what changes could have been made? How could the selection, training, and supervision of field workers be altered to improve data collection? Was the data analysis strategy effective in yielding information useful for decision making? Were the conclusions and recommendations appropriate and useful to the client? Was the report adequately written and presented? Was the project completed within the time and budget allocated? If not, what went wrong? The insights gained from such an evaluation will benefit the researcher and the subsequent projects conducted.

INTERNATIONAL MARKETING RESEARCH

The guidelines presented earlier in this chapter apply to international marketing research as well, although report preparation may be complicated by the need to prepare reports for management in different countries and in different languages. In such a case, the researcher should prepare different versions of the report, each geared to specific readers. The different reports should be comparable, although the formats may differ. The guidelines for oral presentation are also similar to those given earlier, with the added proviso that the presenter should be sensitive to cultural norms. For example, making jokes, which is frequently done in the United States, is not appropriate in all cultures. Most marketing decisions are made from facts and figures arising out of marketing research. But these figures have to pass the test and limits of logic, subjective experience, and gut feelings of decision makers. The subjective experience and gut feelings of managers could vary widely across countries necessitating that different recommendations be made for implementing the research findings in different countries. This is particularly important when making innovative or creative recommendations such as advertising campaigns.

EXAMPLE
Camry Chicken Fries Ford

The ad campaign designed for Toyota Camry in Australia was very different from the one in Japan. "Why did the chicken cross the road?" Toyota asks in a continuing series of TV commercials aired recently in Australia. The answer: "To sell more Toyota Camrys, of course." The spots showing an animated chicken trying to cross the road and getting its feathers blown off by a passing Camry were created by Saatchi and Saatchi Advertising. When Bob Miller, Toyota's general manager for marketing, tried to explain the ad to their counterpart in Japan, they thought he was insane. This may be so, but the commercial did unbelievably well. Even though it was an old joke, the gag helped Toyota topple Ford's dominance in Australia. As a continuing series, the next ad showed the featherless chicken sitting on a pile of eggs in the middle of the road and hatching chicks as the Camry speeds past. Although such use of humor would have been offensive to the Japanese, it solicited a favorable response from Australians.[18] ◆

ETHICS IN MARKETING RESEARCH

Many issues pertaining to research integrity arise during report preparation and presentation. A survey of 254 marketing researchers found that 33% believed that the most difficult ethical problems they face pertain to issues of research integrity. These issues included ignoring pertinent data, compromising the research design, deliberately misusing statistics, falsifying figures, altering research results, and misinterpreting the results with the objective of supporting a personal or corporate point of view, and withholding information.[19] It is important that researchers deal with these issues in a satisfactory manner and prepare a report which accurately and fully discloses the details of all the procedures and findings.

Objectivity should be maintained throughout the research process. For example, when data are analyzed and no meaningful results are found, researchers are tempted to see findings which are not supported by the analysis. One example is meaningfully interpreting a regression equation when all the independent variables turn out to be nonsignificant (Chapter 17). Ethical dilemmas can arise in these instances. The researchers are being paid for their expert interpretation of data, and can nothing meaningful be said? "[T]o arrive at some rational, logical, and convincing conclusion is so much more satisfying intellectually than to admit that the findings are inconsistent and inconclusive—no wonder we find ourselves mentally selecting and shaping what might otherwise be shapeless into a coherent, well-defined story."[20] Such temptations must be resisted to avoid unethical conduct.

Like researchers, clients also have the responsibility for full and accurate disclosure of the research findings and are obligated to employ these findings honorably. For example, the public can be negatively affected by a client who distorts the research findings to develop a more favorable television advertising campaign. Such activities are condemned by the American Marketing Association's code of ethics. "A user of research shall not knowingly disseminate conclusions from a given research project or service that are inconsistent with or not warranted by the data."[21] Ethical issues also arise when client firms, such as tobacco companies, use marketing research findings to formulate questionable marketing programs.

EXAMPLE
Tobacco Industry is "Smoking Gun"

Examination of secondary data sources uncovered the facts that tobacco smoking is responsible for 30% of all cancer deaths in the United States and is a leading cause of heart disease, along with being associated with problems such as colds, gastric ulcers, chronic bronchitis, and emphysema. Do tobacco companies share an ethical responsibility for this situation? Is it ethical for these companies to employ marketing research to create glamorous images for cigarettes that have a strong appeal to the target market? It is estimated that advertising by the tobacco industry based on systematic research has a part in creating more than 3,000 teenage smokers each day in the United States. Advertising for Camel cigarettes through the Old Joe cartoon advertisements increased Camel's share of the illegal children's cigarette market segment from .5% to 32.8%, representing sales estimates at $476 million per year. These detrimental effects are not limited to the United States. Not only is the tobacco industry enticing children to smoke, but it also targets other less informed populations such as Third World countries because this is a way for tobacco companies to replace those smokers who quit or die.[22] ◆

COMPUTER APPLICATIONS

Report preparation and presentation can benefit greatly from the use of microcomputers and mainframes. Originally, the main application of microcomputers was in word processing. With great developments in processor and software technology, however, a variety of word processors and other tools have evolved that allow for professional preparation and presentation of marketing research reports at reasonable costs.

For example, not only do word-processing software such as Microsoft Word and WordPerfect include a dictionary, thesaurus, and grammar checkers, they also have the ability to incorporate graphs, tables, and images created with other software such as spreadsheets, graphics packages, and image-processing tools. For further flexibility in text and image layout design, page layout programs such as QuarkXPress and PageMaker can be used. Page layout programs allow the user to manipulate the positioning of text boxes and are used quite frequently in designing printed advertisements. Often, word-processing and page layout programs come with templates for designing reports that only need to be modified by adding the information relevant to the current marketing report.

In addition to the word-processing packages, several software and hardware advances are available for better presentation of the report. Spreadsheet programs such as Microsoft Excel or Lotus 1-2-3 allow for the development and presentation of tables as discussed earlier in the chapter. Later versions of these spreadsheet programs have built-in statistical analysis tools for analyzing and displaying data. Furthermore, spreadsheet programs have the ability to create a majority of the graphs detailed in this chapter. All these items are easily transferred into one of the word-processing or page layout documents.

Another important addition for reports and presentations is the inclusion of graphics. These can be in the form of clip art, scanned and manipulated images, and original graphics. Several companies offer a multitude of clip art images that are available for royalty-free distribution in reports. If, however, the images that need to be included in a report are not available as clip art, images can be scanned in using a flatbed or slide scanner and an image modification package such as Adobe Photoshop or Aldus Photostyler. Not only can a picture be copied into the computer with these devices, it can be modified with the image modification software in several unique fashions for a more powerful presentation. Finally, images can be created from scratch, if necessary, using any of a number of graphics packages including CorelDraw, Canvas, Harvard Graphics, and many others.

Finally, a vast number of software programs are available for developing remarkable presentations with great ease. For example, Microsoft Powerpoint allows for the development of a slide show as a presentation. The development process is very simple, but the final product can be very intricate. Some of the tools that are available with the presentation software include a variety of transitions between slides including fade, dissolve, fly in from various directions, and many other visual effects. In addition, some presentation programs also allow for the addition of sound and video clips for a more complete representation of data. This means that news reports or audio commentaries can be easily added to a presentation. With a little more effort, presentation software such as Director or Authorware can be used to fully animate a presentation. The animation is achieved via a timeline or other programming scenario and adds another dimension to the presentation beyond that of a slide show. As with most of the word-processing software programs, graphs, tables, and text are easily imported into any of these presentation packages.

Most of these presentation programs allow for the presentation to be printed to paper or transparencies. With the decreasing costs of laptop microcomputers and projection equipment, however, it is feasible to deliver a presentation straight from the computer with color, animation, and audio for the highest impact. Also, infrared remote control technology allows for the presentation to be delivered from any position in the room.

The mainframe and microcomputer versions of the three major statistical packages have reporting procedures. In SPSS, the program REPORT can be used to present results in the desired format. TABLE(S) is particularly suited for formatting data for an on-page presentation. In SAS, procedures like PRINT, FORMS, CHARTS, PLOT, CALENDAR, and TIMEPLOT display information for reporting purposes. The PRINT paragraph in BMDP allows control of the width of the output panel format of printed data and verbosity of output. The tables and graphs produced from these packages can be directly incorporated into the report.

SUMMARY

Report preparation and presentation is the final step in the marketing research project. This process begins with interpretation of data analysis results and leads to conclusions and recommendations. Next, the formal report is written and an oral presentation made. After management has read the report, the researcher should conduct a follow-up, assisting management and undertaking a thorough evaluation of the marketing research project.

In international marketing research, report preparation may be complicated by the need to prepare reports for management in different countries and in different languages. Several ethical issues are pertinent, particularly those related to the interpretation and reporting of the research process and findings to the client and the use of these results by the client. The use of microcomputers and mainframes can greatly facilitate report preparation and presentation.[23]

ACRONYMS

The guidelines for report writing may be expressed by the acronym REPORT:

R eaders: written for specific readers
E asy to follow
P resentable and professional appearance
O bjective
R einforce text with tables and graphs
T erse: concise, yet complete

The guidelines for constructing tables may be described by the acronym TABLES:

T itle and number
A rrangement of data items
B asis of measurement
L eaders, rulings, spaces
E xplanations and comments: headings, stubs, and footnotes
S ources of data

GRAPHS can be used as an acronym for guidelines for constructing graphs:

G   eographic and other maps
R   ound or pie chart
A   ssembly or line charts
P   ictographs
H   istograms and bar charts
S   chematic figures and flow charts

The guidelines for making a presentation can be summarized by the acronym PRESENTATION:

P   reparation
R   ehearse your presentation
E   ye contact
S   tories, experiences, examples, and quotations
E   quipment: multimedia
N   o filler words
T   ell 'em principle
A   udience analysis
T   erminate with a strong closing
I   nteract with the audience
O   utline or script should be prepared
N   umber one level manager should sponsor it

The guidelines for reading and evaluating a report may be specified by the acronym READING:

R   esearch design
E   xecution of the research procedures
A   ddresses the problem
D   isclosure
I   nterpretation and conclusion
N   umbers and statistics
G   eneralizability

EXERCISES

QUESTIONS

1. Describe the process of report preparation.
2. Describe a commonly used format for writing marketing research reports.
3. Describe the following parts of a report: title page, table of contents, executive summary, problem definition, research design, data analysis, conclusions and recommendations.
4. Why is the "limitations and caveats" section included in the report?
5. Discuss the importance of objectivity in writing a marketing research report.
6. Describe the guidelines for report writing.
7. How should the data items be arranged in a table?
8. What is a pie chart? For what type of information is it suitable? For what type of information is it not suitable?
9. Describe a line chart. What kind of information is commonly displayed using such charts?
10. Describe the role of pictographs. What is the relationship between bar charts and histograms?
11. What is the purpose of an oral presentation? What guidelines should be followed in an oral presentation?

12. Describe the "tell 'em" and "KISS 'em" principles.
13. Describe the evaluation of a marketing research project in retrospect.

PROBLEMS

1. The following passage is taken from a marketing research report prepared for a group of printers and lithographers without much formal education who run a small family-owned business.

   To measure the image of the printing industry, two different scaling techniques were employed. The first was a series of semantic differential scales. The second consisted of a set of Likert scales. The use of two different techniques for measurement could be justified based on the need to assess the convergent validity of the findings. Data obtained using both these techniques were treated as interval scaled. Pearson product moment correlations were computed between the sets of ratings. The resulting correlations were high, indicating a high level of convergent validity.

   Rewrite this paragraph so that it is suitable for inclusion in the report.

2. Graphically illustrate the consumer decision-making process described in the following paragraph:

   The consumer first becomes aware of the need. Then the consumer simultaneously searches for information from several sources: retailers, advertising, word of mouth, and independent publications. After that a criterion is developed for evaluating the available brands in the marketplace. Based on this evaluation, the most preferred brand is selected.

COMPUTER EXERCISES

1. For the data given in Table 22.1, use a graphics package or a spreadsheet, such as Lotus 1-2-3 or Excel, to construct the following graphs:
   a. Pie chart
   b. Line chart
   c. Bar chart
2. Using one of the report-generation programs discussed in this chapter or a similar package, write a report explaining the data in and the charts constructed in microcomputer exercise 1.

NOTES

1. Information provided by Roger L. Bacik, senior vice-president, Elrick and Lavidge, Atlanta.
2. Thomas Greenbaum, "Using 'Ghosts' to write Reports Hurts Viability of Focus Group," *Marketing News* 27(19) (September 13, 1993): 25.
3. B. D. Sorrels, *Business Communication Fundamentals* (New York: Merrill Publishing, 1984).
4. Kenneth Roman and Joel Raphaelson, *Writing That Works* (New York: HarperCollins, 1985).
5. S. H. Britt, "The Writing of Readable Research Reports," *Journal of Marketing Research* (May 1971): 265.
6. Jock Elliott, "How Hard It Is to Write Easily," *Viewpoint: By, For, and About Ogilvy & Mather* 2 (1980): 18.
7. A. S. C. Ehrenberg, "Rudiments of Numeracy," *Journal of the Royal Statistical Society*, series A, 140 (1977): 277–97; and A. S. C. Ehrenberg, "The Problem of Numeracy," *American Statistician* 35 (May 1981): 67–71.
8. H. Takeuchi and A. H. Schmidt, "New Promise of Computer Graphics," *Harvard Business Review* (January–February 1980): 122–31.
9. William Jackson Lord, Jr., and Jessamon Dawe, *Functional Business Communication*, 3rd ed. (Englewood Cliffs, NJ: Prentice Hall, 1983).
10. Edward R. Tufte, *The Visual Display of Quantitative Information* (Cheshire, CT: Graphics Press, 1983).
11. Gene Zelazny, *Say It with Charts* (Homewood, IL: Business One Irwin, 1991).

12. Patricia Ramsey and Louis Kaufman, "Presenting Research Data: How to Make Weak Numbers Look Good," *Industrial Marketing* 67 (March 1982): 66, 68, 70, 74.

13. For an example of how graphs can enhance the presentation of research findings, see Figures 1 and 2 of Eugene W. Anderson, Claes Fornell, and Donald R. Lehmann, "Customer Ssatisfaction, Market Share, and Profitability: Findings from Sweden," *Journal of Marketing* 58 (July 1994): 53–66.

14. H. A. Murphy and H. W. Hildebrandt, *Effective Business Communications*, 5th ed. (New York: McGraw-Hill, 1988).

15. Dorothy Sarnoff, *Never be Nervous Again: Time-Tested Techniques for the Foolproof Control* (New York: Ivy Books, 1989); and Dorothy Sarnoff, *Make the Most of Your Best: A Complete Program for Presenting Yourself and Your Ideas with Confidence and Authority* (Garden City, NY: Doubleday, 1983).

16. Information provided by Roger L. Bacik, senior vice-president, Elrick and Lavidge, Atlanta.

17. Public Affairs Council, *Guidelines for the Public Use of Market and Opinion Research* (New York: Advertising Research Foundation, 1981).

18. Geoffrey Lee Martin, "Aussies Chicken Fries Ford," *Advertising Age* (January 18, 1993).

19. S. D. Hunt, L. B. Chonko, and J. B. Wilcox, "Ethical Problems of Marketing Researchers," *Journal of Marketing Research* 1 (1984): 309–24.

20. R. L. Day, "A Comment on 'Ethics in Marketing Research,'" *Journal of Marketing Research* 2 (1974): 232–33.

21. As given in Appendix 3A of Gene R. Laczniak and Patrick E. Murphy, *Ethical Marketing Decisions: The Higher Road* (Needham Heights, MA: Allyn & Bacon, 1993), pp. 76-77.

22. S. Rapp, "Cigarettes: A Question of Ethics," *Marketing* (November 5, 1992): 17.

23. The assistance of James Agarwal with the international marketing research example, the assistance of Mark Leach and Gina Miller in writing the ethics section, and the assistance of Mark Peterson in writing the computer applications section is gratefully acknowledged.

PROFESSIONAL PERSPECTIVES

Report Preparation and Presentation

FOCUSING ON THE MARKETING DECISION

It cannot be emphasized enough how important it is to keep the management decision problem and the marketing research problem in clear focus as the research report is being developed. Most practitioners of marketing research would say they agree with this statement, or would even argue that it is self-evident. However, the most common reason that research studies fail to contribute productively to a business decision is that this principle is forgotten sometime after the initial research planning meeting.

Inexperienced researchers often become engrossed in issues relating to the "science" of marketing research methodology during the research design phase and lose touch with the basic process and criteria by which the decision maker will act. That orientation then usually carries through to the report and presentation. As researchers gain more experience, they typically spend more time during the problem definition stage sitting down with decision makers and trying to understand the criteria by which they make decisions.

The report and presentation should reflect this clear focus on the management decision problem and on the variables that are relevant to it. Frequently, researchers feel compelled to discuss at length every variable that was addressed in the research, regardless of whether it contributed insight or not, simply for the sake of "completeness." In many cases, some of the issues and variables in the research design are not helpful. They should either be left out of the report and presentation or relegated to an appendix.

To maintain this kind of discipline, a simple principle should be applied to everything you put in the report

Joe Whelchel

Joe Whelchel is Senior Consultant with Weber Management Consultant, Inc. At the time of writing this article, he was an account director at Elrick and Lavidge, working with clients in the design and implementation of quantitative research projects. Prior to joining Elrick and Lavidge, Whelchel had 15 years of experience in marketing research, management science, and strategic planning in the soft drink and food service industries. For 13 years, he held positions in these three areas with the Coca-Cola Company in Atlanta. Following that, he managed a marketing research and strategic planning group with General Mills Restaurants in Orlando, Florida, for two years.

and presentation. Consider that you are making a presentation to senior management, and one of them asks you the following: "Now that you've told me that fact, how do you propose that I use it in making this decision?" If you can't answer that question, that particular fact shouldn't be included in the presentation.

USE A HIERARCHICAL APPROACH TO REPORT WRITING

It is difficult to overemphasize the importance of brevity and nontechnical language in the report, if the researcher truly wants the study to have a meaningful impact on the *real* decision makers. At the same time, however, the researcher wants to show that a complete job was done, that every angle to the issue was explored, and that proper statistical and analytical methods were used.

A report writing format that works well is one with a three part structure. The first page or two (no more) should be a concise executive summary designed for quick reading by senior management. This summary can include references to sections or page numbers in the main body of the report where more detail can be found. For example:

- The first test ad generated the highest level of recall and trial intent among the three tested (pp. 12–14 and Appendix 2).

The reader can then decide whether to obtain more information on that particular point.

The executive summary is designed for senior management. The second section, a more detailed report of findings and conclusions, is typically geared to middle managers: brand managers, advertising managers, advertising directors. This section should assume the format of a traditional report, including graphs and charts. However, this section should not include detailed, technical explanations about the analytical issues in the research. Those should be relegated to the third part, a set of appendices at the end of the report. Again, the body of the report should include cross-references to the appropriate appendix. For example, statistical design and technical analysis issues or details relating to the sample design should be covered in the appendices. There should be a management-oriented explanation of the research design and methodology in the main body of the report. Just save the technical language for the appendices.

This three-part format, together with a clear focus on the management decision problem and the marketing research problem, will help the researcher prepare a coherent and meaningful report. Such a report will lend itself to a sound presentation, which, in combination with the report, will provide the client with a solid base for making management decisions.

Preparing and Presenting the Marketing Research Report

In report writing and presentation, we take all the art and all the science of marketing research and not only attempt to interpret what they really mean but also to communicate them to others outside our field of expertise, others who may be relying on this information to make decisions involving many millions of dollars.

Chapter 22 of this text is an excellent framework within which the student or professional practitioner of marketing research can find direction and guidance for writing and organizing effective reports and presentations. Often, there are pragmatic constraints that affect the final report. Although these constraints may be pressing, it is possible to overcome them creatively and produce a report that is professional and that meets the needs of the management. These constraints include time constraints, budget limitations, decentralized decision making, management indifference, and increasing scope and complexity of research projects. These constraints are discussed first. Then, an example illustrates how these constraints can be accommodated without sacrificing the quality or usefulness of the report.

TIME CONSTRAINTS

In today's information age, we as information providers are often pressured to hurry up the results of a study and to minimize formality. The time window for decision making is becoming smaller and smaller. Management wants specific answers from the marketing research project, and it wants them quickly. The world's competitive environment very often leads management to move more quickly than any of us would like, imposing the risk of making decisions from less-than-fully analyzed and thoughtfully considered information.

BUDGET LIMITATIONS

This particular problem takes its toll in two areas. First, world competition and the recent wave of leveraged buyouts have put extreme pressure on corporations to be cost conscious and consequently to reduce the size of all corporate staff organizations, including marketing research staffs. Yet there remains as much pressure as ever to deliver actionable and timely results. Second, budgets available for marketing research projects have also come under close corporate scrutiny. Even though most firms' market information needs are growing, the researcher is being asked to do more with the same budget or even with less. To balance these pressures there is a tendency to shortcut the scope, the depth, or both, of the final report and presentation.

DECENTRALIZED DECISION MAKING

Many of our clients have undergone significant reorganizations during the past few years. The primary focus of the reorganization is to push decision making to the lowest possible line manager within an identifiable product, service, or business group. These line managers are interested primarily in the information that will answer their specific questions and help them move forward with a decision. Because they have responsibility for bottom-line profit, these line managers often do not like the formal, corporate-appearing research report, and they question whether the money spent to produce such a report is worthwhile.

MANAGEMENT INDIFFERENCE

The blood and toil put into a formal research report sometimes goes unnoticed by management. To prevent this from happening, marketing researchers must make the information they deliver to managers easy to understand and digest, using a minimum of words and a maximum of charts, diagrams, and summary tables of relevant data. The goal is to make the report stand on its own and its worth self-evident.

INCREASING SCOPE AND COMPLEXITY OF RESEARCH PROJECTS

The old adage that says, "The more I know, the more I know that I don't know" is true. In the field of marketing research, the trend is to ask all the questions and get all the answers that one can possibly squeeze into a research study. The smarter managers become, the more questions they ask. Management, in an effort to get more bang for the buck, frequently tries to load several projects on to one study of the same respondent group. This often means that the researcher is tempted to shortcut the formal reporting and presentation process.

OVERCOMING THE CONSTRAINTS: AN EXAMPLE

Although these constraints can be pressing, researchers should withstand the tendency to compromise the report preparation and presentation process. Often the researcher can creatively overcome the constraints without sacrificing the professional quality of the report and deliver the information in a form that can be used directly as input into decision making. An example from our experience is cited to illustrate this point.

Burke was asked to design and implement a customer satisfaction and problem tracking monitor for a major gasoline company. The client company operated retail service stations in 40 major markets and wanted a survey conducted among its retail service station customers in every market on a quarterly basis. To further complicate matters, the service stations themselves fell into six different ownership and service delivery configurations. Some were dealer owned, whereas others were managed by the company. Some offered gasoline only, whereas others had minimarkets or auto service bays. We had to run surveys

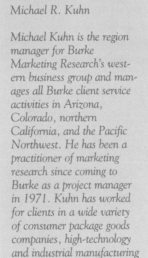

Michael R. Kuhn

Michael Kuhn is the region manager for Burke Marketing Research's western business group and manages all Burke client service activities in Arizona, Colorado, northern California, and the Pacific Northwest. He has been a practitioner of marketing research since coming to Burke as a project manager in 1971. Kuhn has worked for clients in a wide variety of consumer package goods companies, high-technology and industrial manufacturing concerns, and the travel and leisure industry. He also serves as director of Burke's customer satisfaction and external quality control programs for clients in the western United States.

in a total of 3,950 service stations in 40 markets and report to three levels of nonresearch management within two weeks of the close of each quarterly period.

We were charged with designing a reporting scheme that would satisfactorily communicate the results of the quarterly surveys. It was important to illustrate the progress made by our client's retail gasoline stations in improving customer satisfaction. These reports were to be used by three levels of management: service station owners/managers, field marketing representatives, and corporate managers in charge of the retail marketing operations. None were professional marketing researchers.

Given the constraints, it was necessary to create documents that could be understood and used by a service station manager as well as by a corporate officer. Our answer to this dilemma is shown in Figures 1 and 2 on page 793. Data were downloaded directly into a Burke-designed automated chart-making system. The figures are two examples of the charts we designed to show results from the quarterly customer surveys. A short, written introduction was also provided, explaining how to read the chart and interpret the information for decision making and program development. Corporate charts included summaries of this same information by region and for the total United States. From these charts, managers could read the following key performance information:

1. Incidence of problem occurrences this period
2. Performance trend, each problem, this period to past four periods
3. Performance relative to same period one year ago
4. Performance relative to group norms

CONCLUDING COMMENTS

Timing and cost considerations will continue to intensify, putting ever greater pressure on the marketing research professional to become more creative and efficient in delivering easy-to-understand and easy-to-digest research information. This information must be a tool that management can use with confidence to enhance the marketing and production decisions of the firm.

FIGURE 1

Problem Impact Analysis

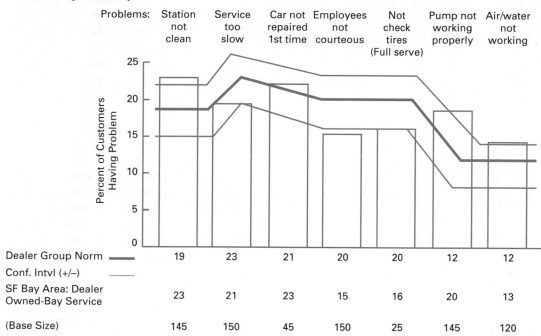

	Station not clean	Service too slow	Car not repaired 1st time	Employees not courteous	Not check tires (Full serve)	Pump not working properly	Air/water not working
Dealer Group Norm	19	23	21	20	20	12	12
Conf. Intvl (+/–)							
SF Bay Area: Dealer Owned-Bay Service	23	21	23	15	16	20	13
(Base Size)	145	150	45	150	25	145	120

FIGURE 2

Problem Trend Analysis

Market: SF/San Jose Bay Area
Store Type: Dealer-Owned Bay Service

Problem: "Station Not Clean"

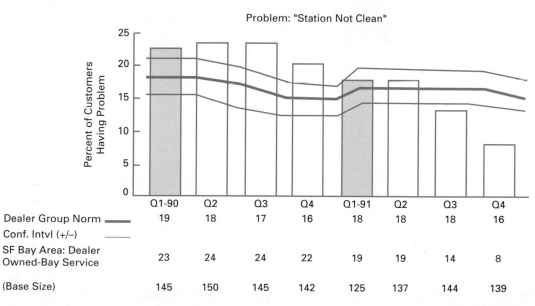

	Q1-90	Q2	Q3	Q4	Q1-91	Q2	Q3	Q4
Dealer Group Norm	19	18	17	16	18	18	18	16
Conf. Intvl (+/–)								
SF Bay Area: Dealer Owned-Bay Service	23	24	24	22	19	19	14	8
(Base Size)	145	150	145	142	125	137	144	139

Through innovative marketing, packaging, and distribution, the Coca-Cola Company has evolved from its origin in 1886 into one of the world's most prestigious international companies. In 1992 company sales of Coke totaled $2890.0 million, whereas in 1993, sales totaled approximately $2808.1 million dollars. The company sales of Minute-Maid totaled approximately $1076.1 million in 1992 and $1088.5 million in 1993, which represents a 1.1% increase over 1992 sales. The Coca-Cola trademark is probably one of the most successful in the history of marketing. The company's brands include Coca-Cola, Fanta, Sprite, Diet Sprite, Tab, caffeine-free Tab, Fresca, Mr. Pibb, Mello Yello, Diet Coke, caffeine-free Diet Coke, Cherry Coke, Diet Cherry Coke, New Coke, Minute-Maid, and Hi-C. These brands have been within reach of almost every domestic consumer, as well as the majority of international consumers. Eighty percent of Coke's earnings are derived from overseas. Coke currently operates in 160 countries.

Coca-Cola's history of finely tuned innovation, advertising, and marketing was reflected in its total control of the market in the late 1800s. In 1899, however, Pepsi was introduced. Coke's 13-year lead on Pepsi gave Coke a commanding lead in the soft drink industry. Coke soared until the late 1960s, unsurpassed by any other cola company.

By the late 1970s, however, although Coke still outsold Pepsi internationally, Coke's domestic market share was diminishing rapidly. Pepsi's growing success was largely based on its aggressive marketing tactics. Pepsi focused on the growing market of cola drinkers in the younger generation, a group that the Coca-Cola Company had often overlooked. In 1977, Pepsi introduced the "Pepsi Challenge" campaign, which challenged consumers of all ages to taste and then state whether they preferred Coke or Pepsi. This aggressive marketing tactic forced Coke to redesign its products and marketing techniques.

Companies usually conduct market research and blind taste tests and then test-market a product before launching it nationally. But these stages were not followed for Coca-Cola's new flagship, New Coke. The concept of New Coke had actually been conceived some years ago, when Coca-Cola chemists accidentally stumbled upon a syrup that tasted "smoother" than regular Coke. Over the course of two and one-half years, $4 million was spent on about 180,000 to 200,000 blind taste tests, pitting three or more new Coca-Cola recipes against old Coca-Cola, as well as archrival Pepsi-Cola. Some tests posed such questions as, "What if this were a new Coke taste?" No research, however, was done to study consumers' reactions to the replacement of regular Coke by New Coke.

Additionally, Roy Stout, then senior vice-president of marketing research at Coca-Cola USA, stated that only 30,000 to 40,000 of these blind tests actually involved the specific formula of New Coke. Further, of the four test waves conducted, only one identified the sodas being tested. The rest were devoid of any emotional brand name attachments.

In May 1985, market research at Coca-Cola showed that consumers preferred the "smoother" taste of New Coke. Hence, with all the pomp and grandeur befitting the king of colas, Coca-Cola launched its new flagship, New Coke, on the 99th birthday of the company. Chairman Roberto Goizueta introduced New Coke as "the most significant soft drink development in the company's history." He further added, "The best has been made even better." Coke pundits thought they had a winner. They were giving the consumers what they wanted, and Coke had finally met the Pepsi Challenge!

Coke management was swiftly awakened to a brutal nightmare, however. Coca-Cola headquarters in Atlanta, received a daily total of 1,500 angry calls as well as protest notes such as, "Dear Chief Dodo: What ignoramus decided to change the formula of Coke?" The most common theme of the complaints was that New Coke was dull and watery and tasted distressingly like Pepsi. The growing outbursts over a period of three months led Brian Dyson, then president of Coca-Cola USA, to believe that "people had fallen in love with the memory of Coke" and hence wanted to have as little as possible to do with New Coke. Faced with the ever-increasing cries of old Coke loyalists, top Coke executives asked themselves the following questions, "Will it go away? Is it logical? How do we address it?" Surveys showed that only 30% of consumers now preferred New Coke. Despite all the time, money, and skill that went into market research, Coke had not foreseen the emotional attachments to its 99-year-old favorite. Coca-Cola addressed the issue by bringing back regular Coke with a new name: "Coca-Cola Classic." Its market share shot up from 6% to 28.4% in 1989. The market share of New Coke dropped from 15%, at the time of its introduction, to 1.5% in 1989. Coca-Cola then considered a relaunch of New Coke under the name Coke II, with advertising that would stress that Coke II gives a "real cola taste" with the sweetness of Pepsi. This was done in the hopes that a new name and a new look would enable Coca-Cola to do what it wanted to do in 1985: directly challenge Pepsi's sweeter taste, which had haunted Coke executives for more than a decade.

All this just goes to show that market research, blind taste tests, and test marketing must be properly conducted and interpreted to be of any significance. To begin with, blind taste tests showed that 61% of consumers preferred the new taste of Coke. Unfortunately, Coke failed to probe further and see exactly what percentage of these new taste lovers were old Coke addicts and what percentage of the Coke loyalists made up the 39% who preferred the old taste. Industry pundits have expressed the belief that Coke's taste tests did not discriminate between Coke lovers and occasional sippers. In fact, Coke management totally ignored the old faithfuls. According to an insider, "Taste results were not consistent from one wave to another. The widely reported results—61% preferring 'new Coke'—versus 39% for 'old Coke'—did not hold up over all four waves in the testing."

Part of the reason Coke miscalculated was that it succumbed to the "one man, one vote" malaise. Often, 20% of buyers consume 80% of the volume in a product category. If Coke had weighted its results accordingly, the 39% who disliked the new formula would have been found to be much greater, and the new taste would have been rejected.

In addition, Coke conducted no research to determine the attitude of consumers to the replacement of old Coke. They missed the significance of the emotional attachments that people had with the product that they had grown up to believe was the "Real Thing." Management failed to anticipate how the public would react to the end of a 99-year-old symbol of American spirit. Coke's research design missed the human element—the emotional attachments and the psychological aspects of the consumer—altogether. Coke's defense was that they could not determine consumers' attitudes toward New Coke without disclosing that New Coke would replace regular Coke, a fact that it wanted to keep secret.

This has puzzled market researchers, however, because there are ways to measure quantitatively the symbolic and emotional significance of brands. Coke management was too narrow in their research, even though they poured so much money into it and interviewed many, many people. Coke could have masked the issue by developing a battery of attitude statements with which respondents could agree or disagree. Their survey could have included such statements as, "I would like to have a choice of both flavors in the supermarket," "I would be very upset if I couldn't find the Coke I'm already drinking," or "I don't care which flavor they sell." Available research techniques could have identified the emotional attachments people had to old Coke. Similarly, the negative consumer attitude should have shown up in the research. Products of every company are improved over the years to upgrade the product for consumer benefits and ward off the competition, and it is not uncommon to use research to determine the consumer attitude toward the new brand and the attachment to the old.

If Coke had employed some qualitative techniques, such as focus groups, depth interviews or psychodrama, it might have been able to avert the disaster that occurred. For example, in a psychodrama consumers are supplied with a list of soft drinks, asked to choose a beverage, and then asked to describe themselves and their behavior as that beverage. Such techniques can elicit information on why consumers prefer a particular product. For example, if visual or packaging cues elicited their conclusions, the manufacturer would not want to alter the packaging or other salient cues.

More recently, Coca-Cola USA has been introducing Coke II into major markets as a direct competitor of Pepsi. The first test market was in Spokane, Washington, and the second was Chicago. Both of these cities showed favorable results for Coke II, and because the second test market showed positive results, rollouts in the New York cities of Albany, Syracuse, Utica, and Watertown were planned. Coca-Cola has said that they will continue to support the soft drink and will continue to find new markets in which to position it against Pepsi. In mid-1992, Coke II had approximately 0.6% of the national market share. The market introductions of Coke II were supported by TV spots touting it to have "real cola taste, plus the sweetness of Pepsi."

In Coca-Cola's 1992 annual report, the company disclosed that brand Coca-Cola products such as Coke, Diet Coke, and Coke II account for approximately 73% of the Company's unit case volume of soft drinks. Of this amount, the company sold about six billion unit cases of Coca-Cola (Coke II) and Coca-Cola Classic. Approximately one and one-quarter billion unit cases of Diet

Coke were sold in 1992. The remaining 27% of unit case volume resulted from the sales of the company's allied brands, which include Sprite, Diet Sprite, TAB, Fanta, Fresca, Mr. Pibb, Hi-C, Mello Yello, Diet Mello Yello, Ramblin' root beer, and specialty overseas brands.

In 1994, Coke introduced its new $600 million marketing campaign, "Always Coca-Cola." Upon the launch, marketing chief Sergio Zyman made it clear that Coke had a lot more than just this advertisement on its mind. According to Zyman, Coke does not think that its marketing is only synonymous with its advertising. In fact, "Always Coke" will not always mean advertising. One of the world's largest advertisers is deemphasizing traditional print and television advertisements and will tend to focus on an arsenal of new marketing strategies. A new form of marketing strategy that Coke will try is interactive in-store promotions. So far, many of their bottlers have had very favorable reactions.

During 1994, Coca-Cola's first quarter earnings rose an estimated 18%. Net income was reported at $521 million, or 40¢ per share. Revenue rose 9.5% to $3.35 billion.

A quote that gets considerable lip service inside the Coca-Cola Company is that Coke is the "sublimated essence of all America stands for—a decent thing, honestly made, universally distributed, conscientiously improved with the years." Perhaps this complacency was the reason why Coke management failed to take a good, hard look at the research results for New Coke and took the naive view that Coca-Cola was simply a thirst-quenching liquid. One hopes that Coke management will avoid such mistakes in the future by pursuing more thoroughly tested avenues to ensure that they add fizz to Coke's sales rather than cause them to go flat.

QUESTIONS

1. Write a detailed report about the research conducted by the Coca-Cola Company. Follow the format suggested in the book. Your report should cover all the phases of the marketing research process. The problem definition, approach, and research design sections should be based on the perspective adopted by the Coca-Cola Company. The data analysis and interpretation sections should focus on the results of the taste tests. Your report should clearly discuss the limitations of the research conducted by the Coca-Cola Company. The conclusions and recommendations section of your report should present your personal viewpoints.

REFERENCES

1. Fahey, Alison. "Coke II Sneaks into Cola Combat Zone." *Advertising Age* (May 11, 1992): 1.
2. "Company Lines of Business." Coca-Cola Company 1992 Annual Report (1992): Financial Topics Supplement.
3. Deveny, Kathleen. "How Biggest Brands Are Faring at the Supermarket." *Wall Street Journal* (March 24, 1994): B1, B3.
4. Mallory, Maria. "At Coke, Marketing Is It." *Business Week* (February 21, 1994): 39.
5. "Coca-Cola Co.'s 1st Quarter Earnings Increased 18%; Revenues Rose 9.5%." *Wall Street Journal* (April 19, 1994): B3.

CASE 5.2

Money Can't Buy Image, but It Can Help Create It

With the large number of savings and loan failures in the late 1980s and early 1990s and the downturn of the U.S. economy in the 1990s, the entire financial industry was beginning to feel a squeeze. Reports of losses, layoffs, closings, and consolidations in the financial industry began to appear almost daily in the business press. Competition had always been strong, but now it was fierce. Like many industries, the financial industry underwent rapid deregulation. Prior to deregulation, U.S. banks were isolated from other world markets, but now these boundaries no longer existed. The series of consolidations began forcing even the largest players to focus on their customers' needs and to develop long-term markets and relationships as well as to overcome a negative image. The industry realized that by making marketing an integral part of its culture it would find a substantial competitive advantage, especially through image management.

CivicBank of Commerce, an independent bank located in the heart of the San Francisco East Bay region, offered a range of banking services and grew from an asset base of $212 million in 1988 to about $400 million in 1995. It conducted an image study in cooperation with the University of California, Berkeley, business school to collect information that could be used in its marketing and sales efforts. It was important for the bank to know not only "How are we doing?" but also "How are we doing relative to other banks?" Knowing what image a bank possessed, what image it wanted to possess, and how to go about creating that image is crucial in the bank industry, because the products that banks provide to their consumers are intangible. A bank can differentiate itself from other banks only with a unique and appealing image. At the time of the study, CivicBank was four years old and had experienced continuous growth. Its target market was owners and operators of businesses with annual sales from $500,000 to $30 million.

The image study was conducted through a survey sent to a random sample of current CivicBank clients and prospects. The origin of the survey was hidden by asking for ratings of two additional statewide banks and two independent banks along with CivicBank. CivicBank mailed 1,875 surveys and had a response rate of 219, or 11.5%. The survey revealed that the majority of the firms in the various industry sectors had annual sales between $500,000 and $25 million. They had been in business more than five years. Forty percent of the businesses were service related, 10% construction, 16% retail, 7% wholesale, 16% manufacturing, 4% transportation and communication, and 7% other.

The banking relationship section of the survey asked respondents to rank the importance of various characteristics in selecting their bank. The results revealed the following order of importance: (1) responsiveness, (2) personal attention, (3) friendliness, (4) safety of funds, (5) convenient location, and (6) capital base.

These results contradicted the belief that convenience, safety of funds, and a strong capital base were the primary determinants of customers' choice of a bank. Responsiveness and personal attention proved to be much more important to clients than capital size and location. Additionally, the survey revealed that the two statewide banks scored low in every area except for convenience. These banks had numerous locations. On the other end, independent banks ranked high in the areas of personal attention, responsiveness, and friendliness.

The survey also revealed that many businesses had been dissatisfied with their previous banking relationships and that 51% had changed banks within the last three years. Almost three-fourths of the respondents said that they intended to change banks within the next year: 37% planned on adding an additional banking relationship, 25% planned on dropping one or more of their existing banks, and 10% planned to change their entire banking relationship in the next year. Based on this information, CivicBank was able to construct an image for itself and design advertising and promotions that appealed to its customers. This just goes to show that although image cannot be bought, it can put money in the bank.

QUESTIONS

1. Write a detailed report about the research conducted by the CivicBank of Commerce. Modify the format suggested in the text as necessary. Your report should cover all phases of the marketing research process. Your conclusion section should address the issue of whether the research conducted by CivicBank was effective. Your recommendations should focus on future research that the bank might undertake.

REFERENCES

1. "How a California Bank Uses Image Research." *Bank Marketing* (March 1989): 20–22.
2. Gridley, H. M., and N. L. Brenner. "Trust Marketing: It Should Start with Consumer Research." *Bank Marketing* (April 1991): 56–57.
3. Tynan, K. B. "Staying Alive in a Hostile Environment." *Bank Marketing* (May 1991): 38–39.

PART VI

International and Ethical Dimensions

This final part focuses on the international and ethical dimensions of marketing research. Although both these topics have been discussed in a pervasive way in the previous chapters, this part presents additional details. We discuss the complex process of international marketing research. We present a conceptual framework for international marketing research and illustrate, in detail, how the environment prevailing in the countries, cultural units, or international markets being researched influences the way the marketing research process should be performed. We also emphasize the necessity for ethics in marketing research and discuss some of the leading methods that aid managers and researchers alike in ethical decision making. A framework for ethics in marketing research is proposed. The way in which ethics influences each step of the marketing research process is discussed. In keeping with the rest of the book, our orientation continues to be applied and managerial.

CHAPTER TWENTY-THREE

International Marketing Research

In international marketing research, it is critical to take into account the environment of the country or cultural unit in which the research is being conducted.

◆

OBJECTIVES

After reading this chapter, the student should be able to:

1. Develop a framework for conducting international marketing research.
2. Explain in detail the marketing, governmental, legal, economic, structural, informational and technological, and sociocultural environmental factors and how they have an impact on international marketing research.
3. Describe the use of telephone, personal, and mail survey methods in different countries.
4. Discuss how to establish the equivalence of scales and measures including construct, operational, scalar, and linguistic equivalence.
5. Describe the processes of back translation and parallel translation in translating a questionnaire into a different language.
6. Discuss the ethical considerations in international marketing research.
7. Explain the use of microcomputers and mainframes in international marketing research.

OVERVIEW

This chapter discusses the environment in which international marketing research is conducted, focusing on the marketing, government, legal, economic, structural, informational and technological, and sociocultural environment.[1] Although discussions of how the six steps of the marketing research process should be implemented in an international setting took place in earlier chapters, here we present additional details on survey methods, scaling techniques, and questionnaire translation. The relevant ethical issues in international marketing research are identified and the use of mainframes and microcomputers discussed. We begin with some examples illustrating the role of marketing research in international marketing.

EXAMPLE
Best In the West, and Around the World

Best Western, with its 3,300 independently owned and operated hotels, is the world's largest chain in terms of number of hotels. As the following chart shows, business travelers make up 36% of the market, the largest single share. Best Western has found through marketing research that business travelers often resist trying less expensive hotels and appreciate the security of a well known brand. This information has helped the chain attract business travelers.

Composition of Worldwide Hotel Market

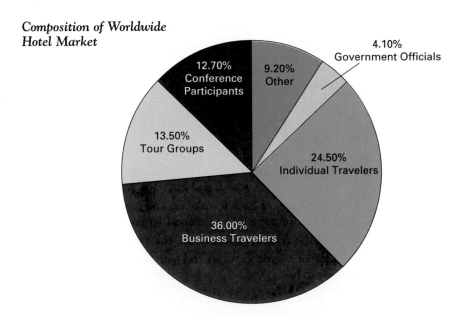

Through marketing research, Best Western has learned the sources of hotel business in different regions of the world and geared its marketing strategy accordingly (see the following table). For example, the chain emphasizes domestic business in North America, focuses on both domestic and international business in Europe, and emphasizes foreign business in the Far East, Australia, Africa, and the Middle East.[2]

Sources of Worldwide Hotel Business by Region

Source of Hotel Business	All Hotels Worldwide	Africa and the Middle East	Asia and Australia	North America	Europe
Domestic	50.7%	24.6%	35.0%	84.6%	47.3%
Foreign	49.3%	75.4%	65.0%	15.4%	52.7%
TOTAL	100.0%	100.0%	100.0%	100.0%	100.0% ◆

International marketing research has helped Best Western to become the world's largest hotel chain. ◆ Best Western International.

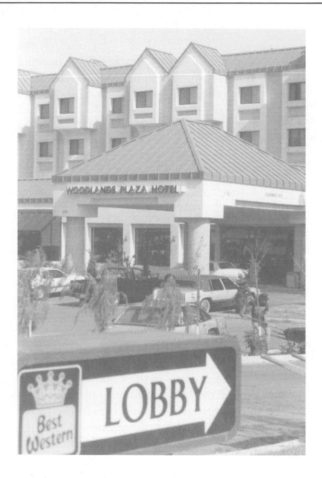

EXAMPLE
Blue Diamond Maintains Cutting Edge

One of the most successful U.S. advertising campaigns ever was, "A can a week, that's all we ask," by Blue Diamond Growers. The goal was to change U.S. consumers' perception of almonds from a special-occasion treat to an everyday snack food. The domestic goal was reached, but the campaign was not used in other countries. Rather, through extensive marketing research, Blue Diamond (BD) tailored its message to each market it selected for a campaign.

Before entering a new foreign market, BD conducts extensive secondary data analysis and even collects primary data. For example, before entering the Russian market, BD learned that the Russian government was undertaking a plan to improve its citizens' diet. BD commissioned a study of the nutritive qualities of almonds and found that almonds contain no cholesterol but provide as much protein per pound as cooked lean beef. By 1995, Russia was BD's third-largest overseas customer. In India, where almonds are thought to be brain food and an aphrodisiac, BD is considering the possibilities.[3] ◆

Both these examples point out that marketing research can contribute significantly to the formulation of successful international marketing strategies. The term *international marketing research* is used very broadly. It denotes research for true international products (international research), research carried out in a country other than the country of the research-commissioning organization (foreign research), research conducted in all or all important countries where the company is represented (multinational research), and research conducted in and across different cultures (cross-cultural research).

MARKETING RESEARCH GOES INTERNATIONAL

In the 1990s, revenue generated outside the United States has become important to the top market research firms in the United States. Several of the top 50 research firms in the United States reported revenue from work through subsidiaries, branch offices, or affiliates that are located outside the United States. This revenue amounted to approximately $1.3 billion, or 35% of the top 50 firm's total revenue (see Chapter 1).[4]

Because overseas expansion is a hot topic in the 1990s, many marketers will begin to expand into the overseas market. This expansion is primarily due to economic integration and the lowering of trade barriers. Overseas expansion will mean increased opportunities for market research companies inside and outside of the United States. When consumers outside the United States begin to spend their money, they give far greater attention to price and quality than to the country of origin. To many firms, regional markets represent the "international order of the day."[5]

As attractive as foreign markets are, companies must realize that setting up for operations in these markets does not guarantee success. Many economists warn that the economic conditions are at best sluggish. Others argue that it is unrealistic to expect aggressive consumerism in the near future even in markets with a taste for foreign concepts. The greatest problem that many firms will face in foreign markets is red tape. Many governments have implemented laws and policies that will protect their countries' businesses.

Since the demise of the Cold War, the world's economy is no longer a simple three-way battle between the United States, Japan, and Germany. Stiffer competition will force many companies inside the United States to try and gain competitive advantages outside of the United States. Three massive markets have developed since the end of the Cold War, some of which will require significant amounts of market research before entrance into that market can occur. The three markets are the Americas, Europe, and the Pacific Rim nations.

Since the passage of the North American Free Trade Agreement (NAFTA), a "veritable free market revolution" has begun to take place in Mexico. The passage of NAFTA created the world's largest market. This market is 23% larger in terms of economics than the European Union. In some Latin American countries, trade barriers are being reduced. Companies entering these changing markets will be forced to change the ways in which they do business. Quality standards will increase and prices will become more competitive due to greater selection. As product choices widen, consumer awareness and sophistication will increase. Latin Americans will become shoppers, and companies can no longer hide behind the protective barriers of their countries and will face more competition due to the greater selection in the marketplace. As a result, market researchers will be faced with two significant challenges. First, as manufacturing and markets assume a regional focus, service providers will be forced to do the same to achieve consistent results and quality. Researchers, both those internal to product operations and their outside suppliers, must follow this trend for a regional, quality approach. A top-down approach to marketing research will result, meaning that company executives will become increasingly involved in marketing research. Second, marketing researchers must remain flexible to handle local conditions.[6] Appropriate methodologies will not be the same, as indicated by Research in Practice 23.1.[7]

RESEARCH IN PRACTICE 23.1

Marketing Research Opportunities and Challenges of NAFTA

The North American Free Trade Agreement (NAFTA) presents U.S. market researchers with freer access to Mexican and Canadian markets. Yearly spending for market research services is estimated to be U.S. $55 million in Mexico and U.S. $250 million in Canada. By comparison, the top 50 U.S. market research firms tallied revenues of $2.4 billion from domestic research in 1993.

In Mexico, a subsidiary of Nielsen Marketing Research is the dominant marketing research firm, accounting for more than half of all revenues from market research. One

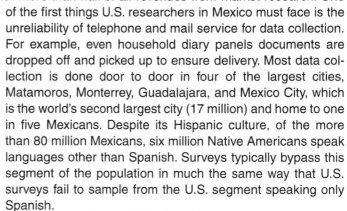

of the first things U.S. researchers in Mexico must face is the unreliability of telephone and mail service for data collection. For example, even household diary panels documents are dropped off and picked up to ensure delivery. Most data collection is done door to door in four of the largest cities, Matamoros, Monterrey, Guadalajara, and Mexico City, which is the world's second largest city (17 million) and home to one in five Mexicans. Despite its Hispanic culture, of the more than 80 million Mexicans, six million Native Americans speak languages other than Spanish. Surveys typically bypass this segment of the population in much the same way that U.S. surveys fail to sample from the U.S. segment speaking only Spanish.

Because of common language and long-standing ties between U.S. and Canadian research firms, a gauge of the Canadian research market is easier than that of Mexico. Annual revenues for Canadian research firms are about U.S. $250 million, about one-tenth the size of the U.S. market for research services (Canada's 25 million population stands in

(continued)

Personal interviews are most suited for determining shopper preferences in Mexico. ◆ Christopher Brown/Stock Boston.

the same 1:10 proportion to the U.S. population of about 250 million). As in Mexico and in the United States, Nielsen boasts the largest research operation with U.S. $44 million.

Although the Mexican research community formed a trade association in February 1993—Asociacion Mexicana de Agencias de Investigacion de Mercados y Opinion Publica (AMAI)—two trade associations have existed in Canada since 1975: the Professional Marketing Research Society (PMRS) and the Canadian Association of Marketing Research Organizations (CAMRO). PMRS regional and national conferences provide a valuable means to become familiar with Canada's research practitioners and to understand the special nuances of doing research in Canada.

With the number of U.S. products that are currently available in Europe, one can see that many manufacturers and researchers will not have to alter their marketing plans and objectives radically. The European Union is perhaps the source of the greatest economic potential in the world. The Western European market is roughly the size of the North American market, but the total size of the European market will increase due to the opening of the Eastern bloc area of Europe. Companies must remain cognizant of the significantly lower level of disposable income, however. Therefore, they must find ways in which to cope with this particular problem. A particular opportunity that should be explored is the potential for smaller and medium-sized companies to expand in the European market.

Many believe that the Pacific Rim is the fastest growing part of the world. This growth is paced by a rapid rate of investment and an abundance of trained human capital. Countries that are included here range from Australia to Indonesia to China. This region's average real economic growth is more than 5% per year and is expected to continue throughout the 1990s. China is being called the next great Mecca for marketing research because it has a consumer population of over 1.2 billion. Recently, Gallup announced the formation of Gallup China, the first foreign research firm in China. To conduct successful research, Gallup China will undoubtedly face many challenges such as rapidly increasing competition, governmental regulation, and the forming of bonds with the Chinese people. Chinese research firms have begun to form within China, and American companies have begun to form alliances with these companies so as to penetrate the Chinese market.[8] International marketing research can be very complex, however. We present a framework for understanding and dealing with the complexities involved.

A FRAMEWORK FOR INTERNATIONAL MARKETING RESEARCH

Conducting international marketing research is much more complex than domestic marketing research.[9] Although the six-step framework for domestic marketing research (Chapter 1) is applicable, the environment prevailing in the countries, cultural units, or international markets that are being researched influences the way the six steps of the marketing research process should be performed. Figure 23.1 presents a framework for conducting international marketing research.

FIGURE 23.1

**A Framework
for International
Marketing Research**

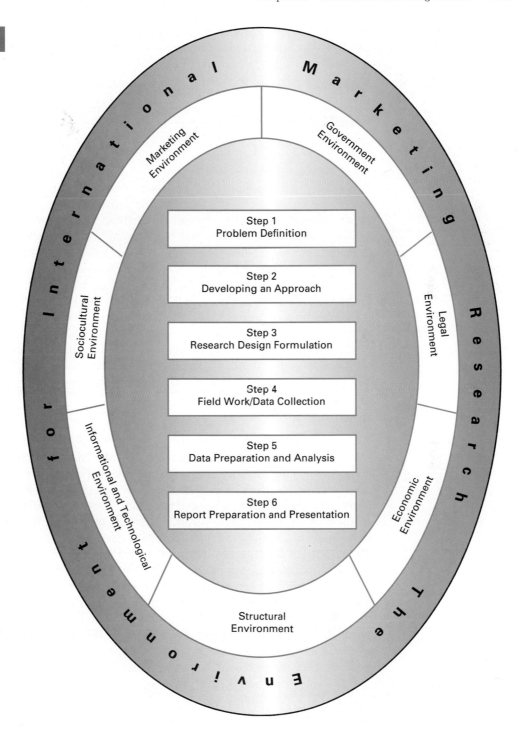

The Environment

The differences in the environments of countries, cultural units, or foreign markets should be considered when conducting international marketing research. These differences may arise in the marketing environment, government environment, legal environment, economic environment, structural environment, informational and techno-logical environment, and sociocultural environment, as shown in Figure 23.1.

Marketing Environment

The role of marketing in economic development varies in different countries. For example, developing countries are frequently oriented toward production rather than marketing. Demand typically exceeds supply, and there is little concern about customer satisfaction, especially because the level of competition is low. In assessing the market-ing environment, the researcher should consider the variety and assortment of products available, pricing policies, government control of media and the public's attitude toward advertising, the efficiency of the distribution system, the level of marketing effort undertaken, and the unsatisfied needs and behavior of consumers. For example, surveys conducted in the United States usually involve questions on the variety and selection of merchandise. These questions would be inappropriate in many countries, such as in Eastern Europe, which are characterized by shortage economies. Likewise, questions about pricing may have to incorporate bargaining as an integral part of the exchange process. Questions about promotion should be modified as well. Television advertising, an extremely important promotion vehicle in the United States, is restricted or prohibited in many countries where TV stations are owned and operated by the government. Certain themes, words, and illustrations used in the United States are taboo in some countries. The types of retailers and intermediary institutions avail-able and the services these institutions offer vary from country to country.

Government Environment

An additional relevant factor is the government environment. The type of government has a bearing on the emphasis on public policy, regulatory agencies, government incentives and penalties, and investment in government enterprises. Some governments, particularly in developing countries, do not encourage foreign competition. High tariff barriers create disincentives to the efficient use of marketing research approaches. Also, the role of gov-ernment in setting market controls, developing infrastructure, and acting as an entrepre-neur should be carefully assessed. The role of government is also crucial in many advanced countries, such as Germany and Japan, where government has traditionally worked with industry toward a common national industrial policy. At the tactical level, the government determines tax structures, tariffs, and product safety rules and regulations and often imposes special rules and regulations on foreign multinationals and their marketing prac-tices. In many countries, the government may be an important member of the distribution channel. The government purchases essential products on a large scale and then sells them to consumers, perhaps on a rationed basis. The following example shows how government may influence international marketing research.

EXAMPLE
Red Tape in Red China _____

In international marketing research, data collection and politics may go hand in hand. One Western industrial marketing researcher on a short, hurried trip through China learned this when attempting to interview officials of the Chinese automobile industry. Although they agreed to an interview, the automobile executives refused to answer any questions of substance. Instead, they continually referred the researcher to the Ministry of Foreign Affairs (MFA) as the first step in learning about the industry. After the researcher met with the MFA, the automobile executives would grant a detailed interview. When the researcher became somewhat frustrated, the Chinese auto executives gave their assurance that this process would only take a few days.[10] ◆

Legal Environment

The legal environment encompasses common law, code law, foreign law, international law, transaction law, antitrust, bribery, and taxes. From the standpoint of international marketing research, particularly salient are laws related to the elements of the marketing mix. Product laws include those dealing with product quality, packaging, warranty and after-sales service, patents, trademarks, and copyright. Laws on pricing deal with price fixing, price discrimination, variable pricing, price controls, and retail price maintenance. Distribution laws relate to exclusive territory arrangements, type of channels, and cancellation of distributor or wholesaler agreements. Likewise, laws govern the type of promotional methods that can be employed. Although all countries have laws regulating marketing activities, some countries have only a few laws that are loosely enforced and others have many complicated laws that are strictly enforced. In many countries the legal channels are clogged and the settlement of court cases is prolonged. In addition, home-country laws may also apply while conducting business or marketing research in foreign countries. For example, a U.S. citizen is subject to certain U.S. laws regardless of the country where business is being done. These laws relate to national security, antitrust, and ethical considerations.

Economic Environment

Economic environmental characteristics include economic size (gross domestic product, or GDP); level, source, and distribution of income; growth trends; and sectoral trends. A country's stage of economic development determines the size, the degree of modernization, and the standardization of its markets. Consumer, industrial, and commercial markets become more standardized and consumers' work, leisure, and lifestyles become more homogenized by economic development and advances in technology.

Structural Environment

Structural factors relate to transportation, communication, utilities, and infrastructure. For example, telephone usage in Europe is much lower than in the United States, and many households do without telephones. Mail service is inefficient in many developing countries. Personal contact with respondents is difficult because city people work during the day and rural residents are inaccessible. Block statistics and maps are not available or can be obtained only with great difficulty. Many dwelling units are unidentified.

Informational and Technological Environment

Elements of the informational and technological environment include information and communication systems, computerization, use of electronic equipment, energy, production technology, science, and invention. For example, in India, South Korea, and many Latin American countries, advances in science and technology have not had a proportionate impact on the lifestyle of the common citizens. Computers and electronic information transfer have still to make an impact at the grassroots level. Information handling and record keeping are performed in the traditional way. Again, this has an impact on the type of information that can be solicited from consumers, businesses, and other enterprises.

Differences in the marketing environment of countries should be considered when conducting international marketing research. Open-air markets like this one in Paris are quite common in France. ◆ Stuart Cohen/Comstock.

Sociocultural Environment

Sociocultural factors include values, literacy, language, religion, communication patterns, and family and social institutions. Relevant values and attitudes toward time, achievement, work, authority, wealth, scientific method, risk, innovation, change, and the Western world should be considered. The marketing research process should be modified so that it does not conflict with the cultural values. In many developing countries, 60% or more of the population is illiterate. In tradition-directed, less-developed societies, the ability of respondents to formulate opinions of their own seems to be all but absent; consequently, it is difficult to solicit information from these respondents. As a result, the sophisticated rating scales employed in the United States are not useful. Also, there may be several distinct spoken languages and dialects in a given nation or region.

A country with a homogeneous family structure is likely to be more culturally homogeneous than a country with multiple family structures. For example, Japan is culturally more homogeneous than either the United States or many African countries, which have many different kinds of family structures. The importance of designing products to be consistent with the sociocultural factors prevailing in a country is brought home by the success of BurgerLand in Saudi Arabia.

EXAMPLE
Arabian Appetites

BurgerLand has succeeded in Saudi Arabia where the major hamburger chains have failed. By combining fast-food experience with an understanding of the sociocultural environment in the Middle East, the owners of BurgerLand International hope to expand their operations throughout the Middle East. "Arabs like new things. Their life at home is often so restricted that when they have the chance to try new things, they're very much in favor of it," says a director of the company, Fuad El-Hibri. Special seating areas are provided for family groups. Arabs like children, and if the children like the restaurants, then their parents may be attracted also. Although "the Saudi culture does not permit dating, the family section is also a place where brothers might wish to take their sisters and, possibly, meet other brothers with their sisters." Arabs also do not worry about calories, so "the heavier the food, the better," remarks El-Hibri.[11] ◆

Each country's environment is unique, so international marketing research must take into consideration the environmental characteristics of the countries or foreign markets involved. Chapters 1 through 22 discussed how we can adapt the marketing research process to international situations. In the following sections, we provide additional details for implementing survey methods, scaling techniques, and questionnaire translation in international marketing research.[12]

SURVEY METHODS

The following sections discuss the major interviewing methods in light of the challenges of conducting research in foreign countries, especially Europe and developing countries.[13]

Telephone Interviewing and CATI

In the United States and Canada, the telephone has achieved almost total penetration of households. As a result, telephone interviewing is the dominant mode of questionnaire administration. The same situation exists in some of the European countries. In Sweden, the number of telephones per 1,000 inhabitants exceeds 900, and in Stockholm, the figure is even higher.[14] Along with low cost, this has led to a sharp increase in the use of telephone interviews, which now account for 46% of the interviews conducted and constitute the dominant interviewing method. In countries such as the Netherlands, the number of telephone interviews exceeds the number of personal interviews.[15] Even in these countries, the sampling of respondents for telephone interviewing may pose serious problems. (See Chapter 6 for a discussion of the issues related to the selection of probability samples in telephone interviewing.)

In many of the other European countries, telephone penetration is still not complete. Telephone penetration in Great Britain is only about 80%, and many practitioners are still skeptical of the value of telephone interviewing, especially for voting intention measurement.[16] In Finland, only 11.2 % of interviews are administered over the telephone.[17] In Portugal, telephone penetration is still low (33.6%), except in the Lisbon area (76.0%). For this reason, only 17% of interviews conducted are telephone interviews.[18]

In Hong Kong, 96% of households (other than those on outlying islands and on boats) can be contacted by telephone. With some persistence, evening telephone interviewing can successfully achieve interviews with 70 to 75% of selected respondents. Residents are uninhibited about using telephones and relaxed about telephone interviews. Yet given the culture, this is not the most important mode of data collection.[19]

In developing countries, only very few households have telephones. Telephone incidence is low in most countries in Africa. India is a predominantly rural society where the penetration of telephones is less than 1% of households.[20] In Brazil, the proportion of households with telephones is low (30% in large cities).[21] Even in countries like Saudi Arabia, where telephone ownership is extensive, telephone directories tend to be incomplete and outdated. In many developing countries, telephone interviewing may present additional problems. Daytime calls to households may be unproductive if social customs prohibit the housewife from talking with strangers. This situation can be somewhat alleviated by using female telephone interviewers, but the employment of women creates many obstacles in such countries. In many cultures, face-to-face relationships are predominant. These factors severely limit the use of telephone interviewing.

Telephone interviews are most useful with relatively upscale consumers who are accustomed to business transactions by phone or with consumers who can be reached by phone and can express themselves easily. With the decline of costs for international telephone calls, multicountry studies can be conducted from a single location.[22] This greatly reduces the time and costs associated with the organization and control of the research project in each country. Furthermore, international calls obtain a high response rate, and the results have been found to be stable (i.e., the same results are obtained from the first 100 interviews as from the next 200 or 500). It is necessary to find interviewers fluent in the relevant languages, but in most European countries this is not a problem.

Computer-assisted telephone interviewing (CATI) facilities are well developed in the United States, Canada, and some European countries, such as Germany.[23] As the use of telephone interviewing is growing, they are becoming popular in other countries.[24]

In-Home Personal Interviews

In-home interviews require a large pool of qualified interviewers. Contractual arrangements with interviewers vary considerably. For example, in France, there are three categories of interviewers: interviewers with annual guarantee for a specified duration, interviewers with annual guarantee for an unspecified duration, and freelance interviewers with no salary guarantee. Overheads can also vary. In France, the employer and the interviewer must pay large social security contributions; in Belgium, the interviewers are self-employed and pay their own social security contributions; but in the United Kingdom, although both the employer and the interviewer pay national insurance contributions, they tend to be small.[25]

Due to high cost, the use of in-home personal interviews has declined in the United States and Canada, but this is the dominant mode of collecting survey data in many parts of Europe and the developing world.[26] In-home personal interviewing is the dominant interviewing method in Switzerland.[27] In Portugal, face-to-face interviews are 77% of the total interviews conducted.[28] The majority of the surveys are done door to door, whereas some quick sociopolitical polls are carried out in the street using accidental routes. Likewise, in-home interviews are also popular in many Latin American countries.

EXAMPLE
Sweet Memories _____

In one of the research surveys conducted by Gallup Organization, the objective was to assess consumers' recall of different ads they had seen in the past month. In-home personal surveys were conducted by Gallup and its affiliates in the United States, Canada, Uruguay, Chile, Argentina, Brazil, Mexico, and Panama. In all, 7,498 people were surveyed. Unaided recall was used to get responses. Questions like, "What brands of soft drink advertisements seen in the past month first comes to mind?" were asked. Results show that Coca-Cola ads are the choice of a new generation of both North and South Americans. Coca-Cola ads were among the top six ads mentioned in seven of the eight

Western Hemisphere nations and were cited the most often in four countries. Ads of archrival PepsiCo were named among the top six in four countries, and McDonald's Corporation appeared in the top six in two countries. None of these three, however, made it to the top six in Brazil.[29] ◆

Mall-Intercept Interviews and CAPI

In North America, many marketing research organizations have permanent facilities equipped with interviewing rooms, kitchens, observation areas, and other devices in malls. Mall-intercept interviews constitute 15.2% of the interviews in Canada and 19% in the United States.[30] Although mall-intercept interviews are being conducted in some European countries, such as Sweden, they are not popular in many European or developing countries.[31] In contrast, central location and street interviews constitute the dominant method of collecting survey data in France and the Netherlands.[32]

Some interesting developments with respect to computer-assisted personal interviewing (CAPI) are taking place in Europe, however. An interviewing program for the home computer has been developed in the Netherlands and is used in panel studies and at central locations using CAPI.[33]

Mail Interviews

Because of low cost, mail interviews continue to be used in most developed countries where literacy is high and the postal system is well developed. Mail interviews constitute 6.2% of the interviews in Canada and 7% in the United States.[34] In countries where the educational level of the population is extremely high (Denmark, Finland, Iceland, Norway, Sweden, and the Netherlands), mail interviews are common.[35] In Africa, Asia, and South America, however, the use of mail surveys and mail panels is low because of illiteracy and the large proportion of population living in rural areas. In Hong Kong, mail surveys have been tried with varied success. Mail surveys are, typically, more effective in industrial international marketing research, although it is difficult to identify the appropriate respondent within each firm and to personalize the address. Nevertheless, mail surveys are used internationally, as illustrated by the following example.

EXAMPLE
World-Wide Achievers

Global Scan is a detailed survey conducted annually by Backer Spielvogel Bates to measure the attitudes and behaviors of 15,000 respondents in 14 countries. The questionnaire contains 120 attitudinal statements and is customized for each country by insertion of attitudes, lifestyles, and purchases (both product and brands).

The questionnaire is administered by mail, with local country offices responsible for distributing, meeting sampling requirements, and then transcribing the returned questionnaires to computer tape, which is shipped to the home office in New York. Global Scan averages a 50% response rate.

Based on the data, five lifestyle segments have emerged and have remained constant over time: strivers, achievers, pressureds, adapters, and traditionals. Thus, marketers have a common set of attitudes and behaviors for defining consumers all over the world. For example, the similarities between achievers in the United States, England, Australia, and Finland are greater than those between achievers and strivers in the United States.

Global Scan collects detailed brand and category information on more than 1,000 products. Marketers can then use this information to develop specific strategies.[36] ◆

Mail Panels

Mail panels are extensively used in the United Kingdom, France, Germany, and the Netherlands.[37] Mail and diary panels are also available in Finland, Sweden, Italy, Spain, and other European countries. Use of panels may increase with the advent of new technology. For example, in Germany, two agencies (A. C. Nielsen and GfK-Nurnberg) have installed fully electronic scanner test markets based on the Behavior Scan model from the United States. Nielsen will use on-the-air television; GfK will use cable.[38] Panels of this kind have not yet been developed in Hong Kong and most of the developing countries.[39]

The criteria for the selection of survey methods were discussed in Chapter 6. As discussed and illustrated in Chapter 6, an important consideration in selecting the methods of administering questionnaires is to ensure equivalence and comparability across countries. Issues of equivalence are also salient in measurement and scaling.

MEASUREMENT AND SCALING

construct equivalence A type of equivalence that deals with the question of whether the marketing constructs have the same meaning and significance in different countries.

conceptual equivalence A construct equivalence issue that deals specifically with whether the interpretation of brands, products, consumer behavior, and the marketing effort are the same in different countries.

In international marketing research, it is critical to establish the equivalence of scales and measures used to obtain data from different countries.[40] As illustrated in Figure 23.2, this requires an examination of construct equivalence, operational equivalence, scalar equivalence, and linguistic equivalence.[41]

Construct equivalence deals with the question of whether the marketing constructs (for example, opinion leadership, variety seeking, and brand loyalty) have the same meaning and significance in different countries. In many countries, the number of brands available in a given product category is limited. In some countries, the dominant brands have become generic labels symbolizing the entire product category. Consequently, a different perspective on brand loyalty may have to be adopted in these countries.

Construct equivalence is comprised of conceptual equivalence, functional equivalence, and category equivalence. **Conceptual equivalence** deals with the interpretation of brands, products, consumer behavior, and marketing effort. For example, promotional sales are an integral component of marketing effort in the United States. On the other hand, in countries with shortage economies, where the market is dominated by the sellers, consumers view sales with suspicion because they believe that the product being promoted is of poor quality. **Functional equivalence** examines whether a given concept or

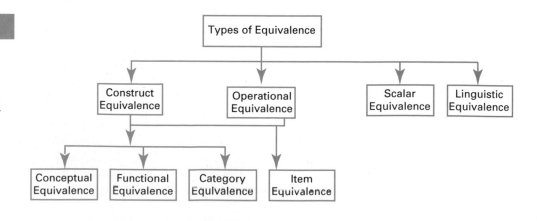

functional equivalence
A construct equivalence issue that deals specifically with whether a given concept or behavior serves the same role or function in different countries.

category equivalence A construct equivalence issue that deals specifically with whether the categories in which brands, products, and behavior are grouped is the same in different countries.

operational equivalence
A type of equivalence that measures how theoretical constructs are operationalized in different countries to measure marketing variables.

item equivalence
Proposes that the same instrument should be used in different countries.

behavior serves the same role or function in different countries. For example, in many developing countries, bicycles are predominantly a means of transportation rather than of recreation. Marketing research related to the use of bicycles in these countries must examine different motives, attitudes, behaviors, and even different competing products than such research would in the United States. **Category equivalence** refers to the category in which stimuli like products, brands, and behaviors are grouped. In the United States, the category of the principal shopper may be defined as either the male or female head of household. This category may be inappropriate in countries where routine daily shopping is done by a domestic servant. Furthermore, the category "household" itself varies across countries.

Operational equivalence concerns how theoretical constructs are operationalized to make measurements. In the United States, leisure may be operationalized as playing golf, tennis, or other sports; watching television; or basking in the sun. This operationalization may not be relevant in countries where people do not play these sports or do not have round-the-clock TV transmission. Lying in the sun is not normal behavior in countries with hot climates or where people have brown skin. **Item equivalence**, which is closely connected to operational equivalence, presupposes both construct and operational equivalence. To establish item equivalence, the construct should be measured by the same instrument in different countries.

Scalar equivalence, also called metric equivalence, is established if the other types of equivalence have been attained. This involves demonstrating that two individuals from different countries with the same value on some variable, such as brand loyalty, will score at the same level on the same test. Scalar equivalence has two aspects. The specific scale or scoring procedure used to establish the measure should be equivalent. The equivalence of response to a given measure in different countries should be considered. For example, do scores from the top box or from the top two boxes on a purchase-intent scale reflect similar likelihood of purchase in different countries? Finally, **linguistic equivalence** refers to both the spoken and the written language forms used in scales, questionnaires, and interviewing. The scales and other verbal stimuli should be translated so that they are readily understood by respondents in different countries and have equivalent meaning.[42]

QUESTIONNAIRE TRANSLATION

scalar equivalence The demonstration that two individuals from different countries with the same value on some variable will score at the same level on the same test; also called metric equivalence.

linguistic equivalence
The equivalence of both spoken and written language forms used in scales and questionnaires.

The questions may have to be translated for administration in different cultures. Direct translation, in which a bilingual translator translates the questionnaire directly from a base language to the respondent's language, is frequently used. If the translator is not fluent in both languages and is not familiar with both cultures, however, direct translation of certain words and phrases may be erroneous. Procedures like back translation and parallel translation have been suggested to avoid these errors. In **back translation**, the questionnaire is translated from the base language by a bilingual speaker whose native language is the language into which the questionnaire is being translated. This version is then retranslated back into the original language by a bilingual whose native language is the initial or base language. Translation errors can then be identified. Several repeat translations and back translations may be necessary to develop equivalent questionnaires, and this process can be cumbersome and time-consuming.[43]

An alternative procedure is **parallel translation**. A committee of translators, each of whom is fluent in at least two of the languages in which the questionnaire will be administered, discusses alternative versions of the questionnaire and makes modifications until

back translation A translation technique that translates a questionnaire from the base language by a translator whose native language is the one into which the questionnaire is being translated. This version is then retranslated back into the original language by someone whose native language is the base language. Translation errors can then be identified.

parallel translation A translation method in which a committee of translators, each of whom is fluent in at least two languages, discusses alternative versions of a questionnaire and makes modifications until consensus is reached.

consensus is reached. In countries where several languages are spoken, the questionnaire should be translated into the language of each respondent subgroup. It is important that any nonverbal stimuli (pictures and advertisements) also be translated using similar procedures. The following example underscores the importance of correct translation.

EXAMPLE

Researchers Can't Get Self-Respect in Germany

A common questionnaire used to measure consumer values is the list of values (LOV). In North America, it has revealed nine basic value segments of consumers. The most widely held values of Americans are self-respect, security, and warm relationships with others. To conduct a comparative study in Germany, the LOV had to be translated into a German version (GLOV). Through the process of translation and back translation, a suitable form was created, yet some inconsistencies remained. For example, it was very difficult to translate the English concepts of "warm relationships with others" and "self-respect" into German. As a result, the data revealed that significantly fewer Germans than Americans hold these as their most important values. The researchers concluded that the imprecise translation was more responsible for these results than actual differences in value orientations. The table shows the distribution of the top four values for each culture, with the rank in parentheses.[44]

Values	Germany		United States	
Self-respect	13%	(3)	21%	(1)
Security	24	(2)	21	(2)
Warm relationships	8	(4)	16	(3)
Sense of belonging	29	(1)	8	(7) ◆

ETHICS IN MARKETING RESEARCH

Ethical responsibilities for marketing research conducted abroad are very similar to those for research conducted domestically. For each of the six stages of the marketing research design process the same four stakeholders (client, researcher, respondent, and public) must act honorably and respect their responsibilities to one another. As Research in Practice 23.2 indicates, the ethical constraints facing marketing researchers abroad are fairly similar to those at home.[45] For all the similarities, some ethical issues become more difficult. Conducting marketing research in a foreign country can easily become a political issue. They must be careful to adopt the ethical guidelines of not only the domestic country but the host country as well.

COMPUTER APPLICATIONS

Microcomputers and mainframes can be extensively used in all phases of the international marketing research process. These uses parallel those discussed in Chapters 1 through 22 and hence will not be repeated here. Rather, software programs that can facilitate cross-cultural research will be considered. More programs such as Interviewer and PC GLOBE MAPS 'N' FACTS should become more widely available in the future to meet the challenges of international marketing research.

RESEARCH IN PRACTICE 23.2

Europeans Legislate Data Privacy

There is widespread implementation of data privacy laws in the 12 EC nations. A prototype of European nations' data privacy laws is the United Kingdom's Data Protection Act (DPA) embodying eight guidelines.

1. Personal data will be obtained and processed fairly and lawfully.
2. Personal data will be held only for specified and lawful purposes.
3. Personal data will not be used for any reason other than the specified purpose.
4. Personal data for specified purposes will not be excessive in amount.
5. Personal data will be accurate and will be kept current.
6. Personal data will not be kept longer than necessary for the specified purpose.
7. Users of personal data must provide non-delayed access to personal data (at no expense) when individuals make requests to examine their personal data over reasonable intervals. Where appropriate, data users must correct or erase erroneous data.
8. Data users must take appropriate security measures against unauthorized access, alteration, disclosure, destruction, or loss of personal data.

As can be seen, the guidelines of the British DPA are similar to those espoused by the domestic codes of ethics.

INTERVIEWER by Info Zero Un of Montreal (Québec) Canada provides bilingual interviewing capability for computer-assisted telephone interviewing (CATI). With two keystrokes, operators can switch from a questionnaire written in English to the same questionnaire written in Spanish (see Exhibits 23.1 and 23.2). This can even be done during the course of the interview in a matter of seconds. The first accompanying figure presents the English version of the telephone interviewer's screen for the question about food items consumed each day. The second accompanying figure presents the Spanish version of the same screen.

EXHIBIT 23.1

English Version

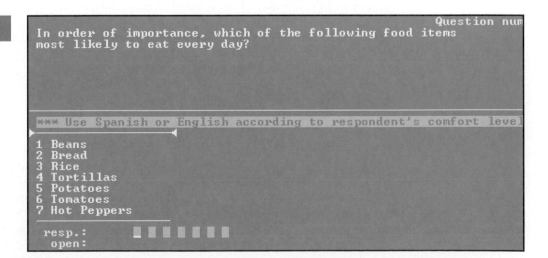

```
                                                        Question num
In order of importance, which of the following food items
most likely to eat every day?




*** Use Spanish or English according to respondent's comfort level

1 Beans
2 Bread
3 Rice
4 Tortillas
5 Potatoes
6 Tomatoes
7 Hot Peppers

resp.:   ■ ■ ■ ■ ■ ■
 open:
```

EXHIBIT 23.2

Spanish Version

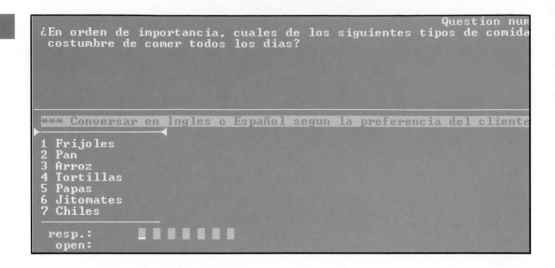

Although INTERVIEWER does not perform language translation (two separate questionnaires must be composed and loaded into the system), it does provide the power to rapidly change from one interviewing language to another. Screen prompts and menus for operators would correspond to the language of the selected questionnaire. Such help avoids the demand for repetitive and instantaneous alternating between languages for bilingual interviewers. This feature markedly reduces the mental strain for bilingual interviewers. Such interviewing features prove useful in areas with nested cultures, such as in Miami, Los Angeles, or New York. In areas of the world where market areas spread beyond political or cultural boundaries, such as in Basel, Switzerland (near the three borders of Switzerland, France, and Germany), INTERVIEWER could be used with modification. In anticipation of lower transnational telecommunication charges and political agreements permitting more open markets around the world, future plans of Info Zero Un call for switching capability between ten languages.

PC GLOBE MAPS 'N' FACTS by Bruderbund of San Francisco provides extensive information on 208 countries of the world. The program proves useful for background learning about countries or for standardizing survey elements between countries. Researchers can edit currency conversions to reflect the most current exchange rates. Users of PC GLOBE can also toggle between metric and nonmetric measures.

Importantly, this program receives frequent updates to keep pace with the dynamic geography of the post-Cold War era. Whereas PC GLOBE MAPS 'N' FACTS screens can be exported to other programs, this program does not permit the exporting of raw data to other programs. Nevertheless, PC GLOBE MAPS 'N' FACTS can provide the international marketing researcher with a rapid orientation to hundreds of locales around the world.

SUMMARY

With the globalization of markets, international marketing research is burgeoning rapidly. The environment prevailing in the international markets being researched influences all six steps of the marketing research process. Important aspects of this environment include the marketing, government, legal, economic, structural, informational and technological, and sociocultural environment.

In collecting data from different countries, it is desirable to use survey methods with equivalent levels of reliability rather than the same method. It is critical to establish the equivalence of scales and measures in terms of construct equivalence, operational equivalence, scalar equivalence, and linguistic equivalence. The questionnaire should be adapted to the specific cultural environment and should not be biased in favor of any one culture or language. Back translation and parallel translation are helpful in detecting translation errors.

The ethical concerns facing international marketing researchers are similar in many ways to the issues confronting domestic researchers. Some of the responsibilities of the researchers become more difficult in the international arena, however. Specialized software has been developed to facilitate international marketing research.[46]

ACRONYMS

In international marketing research, the components of the environment may be summarized by the acronym CULTURE:

C   ultural and social (sociocultural) environment
U   nsatisfied consumer needs: marketing environment
L   egal environment
T   echnological and information environment
U   tilities: structural environment
R   egulatory: government environment
E   conomic environment

EXERCISES

QUESTIONS

1. Describe the aspects of the environment of each country that should be taken into account in international marketing research.
2. Describe the importance of considering the marketing environment in conducting international marketing research.
3. What is meant by the structural environment? How do the variables comprising the structural environment influence international marketing research?
4. What is meant by the informational and technological environment? How do the variables comprising the informational and technological environment influence international marketing research?
5. What is meant by the sociocultural environment? How do the variables comprising the sociocultural environment influence international marketing research?
6. Describe the status of telephone interviewing and CATI in foreign countries.
7. Describe the status of in-home personal interviewing in foreign countries.
8. Describe the status of mail interviewing in foreign countries.
9. How should the equivalence of scales and measures be established when the data are to be obtained from different countries or cultural units?
10. What problems are involved in the direct translation of a questionnaire into another language? How should these problems be addressed?

PROBLEMS

1. Develop a short questionnaire to measure consumers' attitudes toward air travel. Have some foreign students do a direct translation to this questionnaire into their native language, and then do a back translation. What translation errors occurred? Correct these errors.
2. Formulate a research design for assessing consumer preferences for designer jeans in the United States, Sweden, Hong Kong, and China. Identify the sources of secondary data, decide whether any qualitative research should be carried out, recommend which survey

method to use in each country, recommend one or more scaling techniques, develop a questionnaire in English, and suggest appropriate sampling procedures for use in each country.

COMPUTER EXERCISES

1. Compile data on GDP, level of literacy, and percentage of households with telephones for 20 different countries. Using SPSS, SAS, or BMDP, run a regression analysis with GDP as the dependent variable and the other two variables as the independent variables. Interpret your results.

2. Compile data on consumption and expenditures for the following categories in 30 different countries: (1) food and beverages, (2) clothing and footwear, (3) housing and home operations, (4) household furnishings, (5) medical care and health, (6) transportation, and (7) recreation. Using SPSS, SAS, or BMDP, determine if these variables are correlated. Run a factor analysis. Interpret your results.

NOTES

1. See N. K. Malhotra, "Administration of Questionnaires for Collecting Quantitative Data in International Marketing Research," *Journal of Global Marketing* 4(2) (1991): 63–92; and N. K. Malhotra, "Designing an International Marketing Research Course: Framework and Content," *Journal of Teaching in International Business* 3 (1992): 1–27.

2. "Hotel Chains Capitalize on International Travel Market," *Hotels and Restaurants International* (June 1989): 81S–86S; and "Target Marketing Points to Worldwide Success," *Hotels and Restaurants International* (June 1989): 87S.

3. "Every Market Needs a Different Message," *IABC Communication World* (April 1990): 16–18.

4. Jack Honomichl, "Three Factors Drive Growth of Top 50 Research Firms," *Marketing News* (March 1, 1993): H2.

5. Associated Press, "Regional Markets are International Order of the Day," *Marketing News* (March 1, 1993): IR–10; and Thomas T. Semon, "Red Tape Is Chief Problem in Multinational Research," *Marketing News* (March 1, 1993): 7.

6. David C. Brezic, "Can Marketing Researchers Adapt to Free Trade in the Americas?" *Marketing News* (May 10, 1993): 8.

7. Jack Honomichl, "Research Cultures Are Different in Mexico, Canada," *Marketing News* 27(10) (May 10, 1993): 12–13.

8. Cyndee Miller, "China Emerges as Latest Battleground for Marketing Researchers," *Marketing News* (February 14, 1994): 1.

9. For a recent example of international marketing research, see Eugene H. Fram and Riad Ajami, "Globalization of Markets and Shopping Stress: Cross-Country Comparisons," *Business Horizons* 37 (January–February 1994): 17–23.

10. L. W. Foster and L. Tosi, "Business in China after Tiananmen," *Journal of Business Strategy* (May–June 1990): 22–27.

11. "Will Sheiks Take to Burgers and Fries?" *D&B Reports* (January–February 1986): 10–13.

12. See Niraj Dawar and Philip Parker, "Marketing Universals: Consumers' Use of Brand Name, Price, Physical Appearance, and Retailer Reputation as Signals of Product Quality," *Journal of Marketing* 58 (April 1994): 81–95.

13. The section on survey methods is drawn from Naresh K. Malhotra, "Administration of Questionnaires for Collecting Quantitative Data in International Marketing Research," *Journal of Global Marketing* 4(2) (1991): 63–92.

14. Jack J. Honomichl, "Survey Results Positive," *Advertising Age* 55 (November 1984): 23; D. Monk, "Marketing Research in Canada," *European Research* (November 1987): 271–74; and B. P. Kaiser, "Marketing Research in Sweden," *European Research* (February 1988): 64–70.

15. J. C. J. Oostveen, "The State of Marketing Research in Europe," *European Research* (1986): 100–35.

16. R. M. Worcester, "Political Opinion Polling in Great Britain: Past, Present and Future," *European Research* (August 1987): 143–51.

17. T. Vahvelainen, "Marketing Research in Finland," *European Research* (August 1987): 62–66.

18. L. Queiros and J. L. Santos Lima, "Marketing Research in Portugal," *European Research* (August 1988): 185–91.

19. R. W. B. Davies, C. J. W. Minter, M. Moll, and D. T. Bottomley, "Marketing Research in Hong Kong," *European Research* (May 1987): 114–20.

20. D. Sopariwala, "India: Election Polling in the World's Largest Democracy," *European Research* (August 1987): 174–77.

21. P. Pinheiro de Andrade, "Market Research in Brazil," *European Research* (August 1987): 188–97.

22. M. De Houd, "Internationalized Computerized Telephone Research: Is It Fiction?" *Marketing Research Society Newsletter* 190 (January 1982): 14–15.

23. T. Marcotty, "Mysterious Germany," *European Research* (October 1985): 148–150.

24. W. E. Saris and Marius W. de Pijper, "Computer Assisted Interviewing Using Home Computers," *European Research* (1986): 144–51.

25. J. Bigant and Y. Rickebusch, "Marketing Research in France," *European Research* (January 1985): 4–11.

26. D. Monk, "Marketing Research in Canada," *European Research* (November 1987): 271–274; and Jack J. Honomichl, "Survey Results Positive," *Advertising Age* 55 (November 1984): 23.

27. E. H. Demby, "ESOMAR Urges Changes in Reporting Demographics, Issues Worldwide Report," *Marketing News* 24(1) (January 8, 1990): 24–25.

28. L. Queiros and J. L. Santos Lima, "Marketing Research in Portugal," *European Research* (August 1988): 185–91.

29. Julie Skur Hill, "Coke Tops in Americas," *Advertising Age* (November 12, 1990).

30. Honomichl, p. 23; and D. Monk, "Marketing Research in Canada," *European Research* (November 1987): 271–74.

31. B. P. Kaiser, "Marketing Research in Sweden," *European Research* (February 1988): 64–70.

32. E. H. Demby, "ESOMAR Urges Changes in Reporting Demographics, Issues Worldwide Report," *Marketing News* 24(1) (January 8, 1990): 24–25.

33. W. E. Saris and Marius W. de Pijper, "Computer Assisted Interviewing Using Home Computers," *European Research* (1986): 144–51.

34. Jack J. Honomichl, "Survey Results Positive," *Advertising Age* 55 (November 1984): 23; and D. Monk, "Marketing Research in Canada," *European Research* (November 1987): 271–74.

35. T. Vahvelainen, "Marketing Research in the Nordic Countries," *European Research* (April 1985): 76–79; T. Vahvelainen, "Marketing Research in Finland," *European Research* (August 1987): 62–66; and E. H. Demby, "ESOMAR Urges Changes in Reporting Demographics, Issues Worldwide Report," *Marketing News* 24(1) (January 8, 1990): 24–25.

36. "We Are the World," *American Demographics* (May 1990): 42–43.

37. J. Bigant and Y. Rickebusch, "Marketing Research in France," *European Research* (January 1985): 4–11.

38. T. Marcotty, "Mysterious Germany," *European Research* (October 1985): 148–50.

39. R. W. B. Davies, C. J. W. Minter, M. Moll, and D. T. Bottomley, "Marketing Research in Hong Kong," *European Research* (May 1987): 114–20.

40. See also C. Min-Han, Byoung-Woo Lee, and Kong-Kyun Ro, "The Choice of a Survey Mode in Country Image Studies," *Journal of Business Research* 29 (February 1994): 151–62.

41. See G. Bhalla and L. Lin, "Cross-Cultural Marketing Research: A Discussion of Equivalence Issues and Measurement Strategies," *Psychology and Marketing* 4(4) (1987): 275–85. A similar discussion is also found in Susan P. Douglas and C. Samuel Craig, *International Marketing Research* (Englewood Cliffs, NJ: Prentice Hall, 1983).

42. J. Craig Andrews, Srinivas Durvasula and Richard G. Netemeyer, "Testing the Cross-National Applicability of U.S. and Russian Advertising Belief and Attitude Measures," *Journal of Advertising* 23 (March 1994): 17–26.

43. For a recent application of back translation, see Robert Wharton, Inga S. Baird, and Marjorie A. Lyles, "Conceptual Frameworks Among Chinese Managers: Joint Venture Management and Philosophy," *Journal of Global Marketing* 5 (1–2) (1991): 163–81.

44. S. C. Grunert and G. Scherhorn, "Consumer Values in West Germany: Underlying Dimensions and Cross-Cultural Comparison with North America," *Journal of Business Research* 20 (1990): 97–107.

45. Simon Chadwick, "Data Privacy Legislation All the Rage in Europe," *Marketing News* 27(17) (August 16, 1993): A7.

46. The assistance of James Agarwal with the international marketing research example, the assistance of Mark Leach and Gina Miller in writing the ethics section, and the assistance of Mark Peterson in writing the computer applications section is gratefully acknowledged.

CHAPTER TWENTY-FOUR

Ethics in Marketing Research

Ethical decision making should pervade all aspects of the marketing research process, from beginning to end.

OBJECTIVES

After reading this chapter, the student should be able to:

1. Discuss the importance of ethics in the marketing research process and explain why ethical conduct is crucial to the survival of marketing research.
2. Describe the ethical vulnerability of the various stakeholders in the marketing research process: the public, respondents, clients, and marketing researchers.
3. Describe the ethical guidelines that have been proposed in the literature.
4. Understand how ethics provide an overall framework for the marketing research process and describe the various approaches to ethical decision making.
5. Explain how ethical issues impact each step of the marketing research process.
6. Understand the ethical issues in international marketing research.
7. Explain the ethical issues related to the use of microcomputers and mainframes.

Overview

Throughout the previous chapters we have identified specific ethical issues and discussed the importance of adhering to ethical practices at each step of the marketing research process. In this capstone chapter, we begin by emphasizing the necessity for ethics in research and identifying the stakeholders in marketing research. We discuss some of the guidelines that aid managers and researchers alike in ethical decision making. A framework for ethics in marketing research is then proposed. The way in which ethics influence each step of the marketing research process is summarized. Finally, the ethical issues in international marketing research and the use of microcomputers and mainframes are examined. To give the reader some exposure to ethical dilemmas in marketing research, we provide a few introductory examples.[1]

EXAMPLE
Earthquakes Shake Marketing Ethics

Research on cognitive heuristics (mental rules of thumb) has revealed that consumers frequently use the availability heuristic. Simply put, this heuristic means that the judged probability of an event is proportional to the ease of imaging that event. Marketers of earthquake insurance have increased sales by providing consumers with vivid images of earthquakes (i.e., "fear appeals") in advertising. These images increase anxiety about the occurrence of earthquakes and thus the perception that their occurrence is more likely than it is in reality.[2] ◆

EXAMPLE
When Is a Sale Not a Sale?

Special sales are common with retailers in the United States. But when is a sale not a sale? May D & F, a division of the May Department Stores operating 12 department stores in Colorado, was forced to prove in court that its sale prices were actually sale prices. The ethical issue: If a price for an item is marked as "sale," does it have to be lower than the price of the item that is in effect most of the year?

May D & F had been accused by the Colorado attorney general's office of violating the Colorado Consumer Protection Act, specifically the section dealing with deceptive practices. Prices in the Home Store department were originally set at one price and then placed on sale. The attorney general objected because the original price was in effect for only ten days every six months while a variety of sale prices existed over the remainder of the time. Consumers responding to advertising claims of sale prices of 30% off were likely to find the price they had seen the week before. May D & F's response to the attorney general was to research what constituted a sale price in the minds of consumers. Two surveys were conducted by May D & F's marketing research supplier. The first was a random sample of 500 Denver households by telephone that attempted to assess May D & F's reputation among retailers and some specific advertising practices. In the second survey, 331 individuals were surveyed in a number of malls in Denver. A series of yes/no questions was asked to show what the term *original price* meant to them and whether respondents' perceptions of the term were influenced by the amount of merchandise actually sold at that price.

Consumers believe May D & F's sale prices to be higher than those of other area merchants. ◆ Phil Lauro/Profiles West.

The results of this research showed that consumers viewed May D & F as a store that had higher prices than competitors, good-quality products, and good service. Also, consumers believed May D & F's sale prices to be higher than those of other area merchants. Consumers went on to say that a 50% off sale at May D & F did not mean the price was lower than at other area retailers. It was also clear from the research that most Denver-area consumers feel that the most important thing to look for when trying to judge a price is to compare that price with other stores. Few felt that the store's reference or original price held great importance. Thus, May D & F advertising is not misleading for households in the Denver metropolitan area.

May D & F used the research findings to counter claims made regarding its pricing and sales policies. The public seems to understand that a sale at one store may not mean prices lower than those available at other stores. On the other hand, May D & F did advertise a "sale price" that differed little from the price of the product for most of the year (sometimes a sale price was the price in effect most of the year). Clearly, this is an accepted practice in retailing, but does that mean it is an ethical practice? It is also clear that the attorney general in this case perceived the practice to be not only unethical, but illegal.[3] ◆

These two examples help illustrate why the consideration of ethical issues is important in marketing. If research is to be done well and to provide useful information for marketing decision making, it must be conducted within guidelines of ethical behavior.

IMPORTANCE OF ETHICS IN MARKETING RESEARCH

Ethics address whether a particular action is right or wrong, good or bad. The topic of ethics is extremely pertinent for marketing and for marketing research because of the amount and variety of contact marketers have with the public. Of all the aspects of business, "marketing is closest to the public view and, consequently, is subject to consider-

ethics The process of evaluating and addressing whether a particular action is right or wrong, good or bad.

able societal analysis and scrutiny."[4] This has created a perception that, within business, marketing is the area most prone to unethical practices. It is therefore imperative that marketers, and marketing researchers in particular, adhere to ethical practices because public perceptions of the field determine how and even whether marketing research can continue. Volunteer participants are the very heart of marketing research. Consumer research would practically cease to continue without the cooperation of the public from which the respondents in marketing research are drawn.

Even though the need for ethics is clear, the subject itself is somewhat complex. Although this complexity is due to a variety of factors, five major characteristics describing ethical decisions have been identified.[5] First, most ethical decisions have extended or long-term effects. Second, ethical decisions are rarely black and white; rather, there are multiple alternatives that are acceptable to varying degrees. Third, these alternatives have both positive and negative outcomes, depending on the viewpoint of the evaluator. Fourth, what the positive or negative outcomes will be is always uncertain and not completely predictable. Finally, most ethical decisions have personal implications. This may result in many types of costs: personal, social, financial, and so forth.[6]

Identifying those affected by unethical marketing research practices, the stakeholders, enables us to be aware of some easily avoidable ethical pitfalls. The **stakeholder** concept is a method of looking at ethical relationships by identifying any group or individual who is, or can be, affected by the process under scrutiny. When that process is marketing research, there are four stakeholders: the public at large, the actual respondents used in a study, the client, and the researcher. Each of the four stakeholders is in some way vulnerable to the others. For the relationships to work ethically, each group has certain responsibilities and must be trusted to act honorably. Ethical dilemmas surrounding marketing research frequently revolve around the stakeholders' responsibilities and rights.

stakeholders Any group or individual who is, or can be, affected by the process under scrutiny. When that process is marketing research, there are four stakeholders: the public at large, the actual respondents used in a study, the client, and the researcher.

STAKEHOLDERS IN MARKETING RESEARCH

We examine each of the marketing research stakeholders in turn. To identify ethical dilemmas, attention will be focused on instances where each stakeholder is vulnerable to the others and where each can be harmed.

Public

With regard to the general public, ethical concerns revolve primarily around the methods of generating and reporting research results. The public often relies on marketing research for information on products. When this information is distorted by either the marketing researcher or the client, the public is at a disadvantage. It is the responsibility of the researcher and the client to ensure that the research findings are being disseminated accurately. In particular, care should be taken by both the market researcher and the client to avoid incomplete reporting, misleading reporting, and biased research.[7]

incomplete reporting Whenever a client firm or researcher does not reveal the research results in their entirety.

Incomplete Reporting   As the name implies, whenever a client firm or researcher does not reveal the research results in their entirety, **incomplete reporting** has occurred. This unethical act is more likely to take place when a researcher uncovers negative information that might not be favorably received by the client or the public at large.

misleading reporting
The distortion of research information. By distortion, it is meant that although the information presented to the public is correct, it leaves the public with an erroneous impression.

Misleading Reporting   **Misleading reporting**, on the other hand, involves the distortion of information. Although the information presented to the public may not be falsified, it nevertheless leaves the public with an erroneous impression. For example, suppose that a research project attempts to find out which brand of toothpaste is preferred by most dentists and arrives at the following results: 90% of dentists surveyed express no preference, 5% prefer Brand A, 3% Brand B, and 2% prefer some brand other than A or B. It is misleading if the client firm, which manufactures Brand A, claims in its advertising that more dentists prefer Brand A than any other toothpaste, not because it is necessarily untrue, but because it leaves the public with an inaccurate conclusion that most of dentists prefer Brand A, when this is clearly not the case. The overwhelming majority of the dentists do not have a preference for any brand.

biased research Research performed in a nonobjective manner that results in misleading findings.

Biased Research   **Biased research** occurs when the research process is performed improperly, resulting in incorrect findings. Errors of this nature can occur when the problem is incorrectly defined, the approach or the research design are faulty, the scales are lacking in validity, the questionnaire is poorly designed or administered, the sample is inappropriately selected, improper statistical methods are employed, or any other type of failure to execute properly the steps in the marketing research process takes place. Examples might include leading the respondents to answer in a certain way during data collection, throwing out selected respondents to produce the desired result, or using a simple average when a weighted average would have been more appropriate. When the research is biased in this manner, the ultimate loser is the public. Anyone conducting and publishing market research results should treat the public honorably. Otherwise, the public's trust of marketers will be further eroded.

Respondent

Few would argue that it is perhaps the ethical concerns of the respondents that deserve the most attention. Without their involvement there could be little research. Therefore, it is to the marketing researcher's advantage to protect the respondents from unethical research practices. The ethical issues in the researcher-respondent relationship are highlighted in Table 24.1.[8] It has been suggested that two of these deserve special attention: conducting a survey as a guise to sell products and the invasion of the privacy of the respondent.[9]

sugging The use of marketing research as a guise in the deliberate deception of respondents to sell products.

frugging The use of marketing research as a guise in the deliberate deception of respondents to improve fund-raising activities.

Conducting a Survey to Sell Products   Unfortunately, respondents have been deliberately deceived under the guise of marketing research so as to sell products. Some unethical marketers have been known to tell respondents that they were conducting a survey as a lead to a sales presentation or as an attempt to get information that could be used for sales leads or mailing lists. This practice, called **sugging** in trade language, is illegal as well as unethical. A similar practice, fund-raising under the guise of research, is called **frugging** and is also unethical. These practices violate the respondents' trust and willingness to support legitimate surveys.

Invasion of the Privacy of Respondents   The privacy of respondents is a legitimate right that must be protected. This means, among other things, that respondents who are promised anonymity or confidentiality must be provided just that. It also means that

TABLE 24.1
 	
Ethical Concerns in the Researcher-Respondent Relationship
	Deceptive Practices
	  Unrealized promise of anonymity
	  Falsified sponsor identification
	  Selling under the guise of research
	  Misrepresenting research procedures
	    Questionnaire or interview length
	    Possible follow-up contacts
	    Purpose of study
	    Uses made of results
	    Undelivered compensation (premiums, summaries or results)
	
	Invasion of Privacy
	  Observation studies without informed consent
	  Use of qualitative research techniques
	  Merging data from several sources
	  Overly personal questions and topics
	
	Lack of Concern for Subjects or Respondents
	  Contacting respondents at inconvenient times
	  Incompetent or insensitive interviewers
	  Failure to debrief after deception or disguise
	  Research producing a depression effect on respondents
	  Too frequent use of public in research
	  Nondisclosure of research procedures (length, follow-up, purpose, use)

respondents should not be contacted at times that are inconvenient, such as late at night when most might be expected to be in bed, or during mealtimes when they might be interrupted. Another concern is the prevalent practice of buying and selling mailing lists, especially those compiled through somewhat deceptive means, such as returned product warranty cards and frequent shopper programs.

EXAMPLE
Informed Consent and the Uninformed Respondents

A supermarket has instituted a frequent shoppers program where shoppers can receive discount on weekly specials by obtaining frequent shoppers cards. Each card has a UPC code that identifies the customer by name, address, and relevant demographic information provided when applying for the card. This card is scanned before grocery products when checking out every time the customer shops. Thus, the customer's identity and actual purchases are recorded. The supermarket may sell this information to syndicated services. Marketers can purchase this information from the syndicated service companies and use it to determine the purchase habits of their customers and target their marketing effect.

This example points to the principle of informed consent that states, "Researchers should try to avoid both uninformed and misinformed participation by subjects in research."[10] Shoppers in this example were participating in a scanner panel without their knowledge or consent. They were not informed that their purchases were going to be recorded and analyzed. Thus, the supermarket can be considered as invading the privacy of the consumer. ◆

Some supermarket shoppers may be participating in a scanner panel without their knowledge or consent. ◆ Richard Falco/Photo Researchers, Inc.

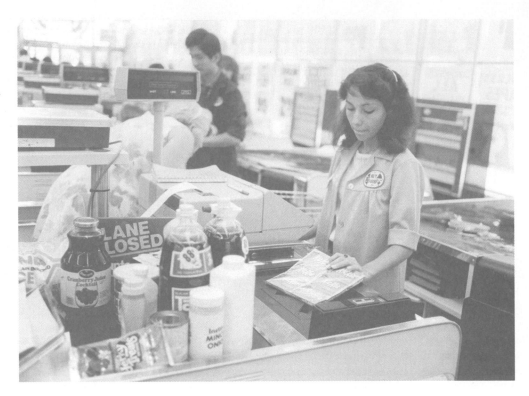

Client

Given the complexity involved, it is not surprising that the ethical issues surrounding the researcher-client relationship are somewhat numerous (see Table 24.2).[11] Areas that deserve special attention from an ethical standpoint are abuse of position arising from specialized knowledge, unnecessary research, an unqualified researcher, disclosure of identity, treating data as nonconfidential, and misleading presentation of data.[12]

Abuse of Position   Because the marketing researcher, rather than the marketing manager, possesses the research expertise, the researcher has a responsibility not to take unfair advantage of this position. In other words, the researcher should make every effort to follow correct research procedures and adopt a suitable approach and research design. In short, the researcher must conduct quality research while respecting the clients' resources of time and money.

Unnecessary Research   The researcher has the ethical duty not to perform unnecessary research. Such situations may arise when the client wishes to conduct research that would serve no useful purpose, has already been done, or does not need to be carried out to the degree specified (e.g., primary research may not be necessary as secondary data provide the required information).

Unqualified Researcher   In some instances, the researcher may not have the necessary skills or technical expertise or may not have the necessary resources to conduct the research. In these situations, the researcher should explain these limitations to the prospective client and refuse the project.

TABLE 24.2 *Ethical Concerns in the Researcher-Client Relationship*	**Abuse of Research Design, Methodology, or Results** Conducting unnecessary research Researching wrong or irrelevant problems Using unwarranted shortcuts to secure contracts or save expenses Misrepresenting limitations of research design Inappropriate analytical techniques Lack of sufficient expertise to conduct required research Overly technical language in research report Overstating validity or reliability of conclusions **Researcher Abuse of the Researcher-Client Relationship** Overbilling the project Failing to maintain client confidentiality Failing to avoid possible conflict of interest **Client Abuse of the Researcher-Client Relationship** Inappropriate use of research proposals Disclosure or use of the researcher's specialized techniques and models Cancellation of products (refusal to pay) without cause Conducting research solely to support a priori conclusions Failing to act upon dangerous or damaging findings

Disclosure of Identity   A client firm has the right to expect that its identity will be protected before, during, and after the completion of the research project. The researcher is ethically bound not to reveal the client's identity to competitors, respondents, or any other firms or individuals without the express consent of the client.

Nonconfidential Data   The client has a right to expect that any data collected or results obtained will belong to the client firm and will be held in strict confidence by the researcher. Proprietary data should not be released to the competition and should not be reused in a subsequent research project for another firm without the original firm's explicit knowledge and consent.

Misleading Presentations   The misleading presentation of research results can take many forms, such as leading the client to believe that the results are more precise than they actually are. The researcher should avoid the use of unnecessarily technical terms that only serve to confuse or convey a false sense of complexity to the client and should present numerical results only to the level of precision warranted by the study (e.g., if a numerical result is only accurate to the nearest $5, it should be reported as such and not be broken down into dollars and cents). Additionally, the researcher should not mislead the client by presenting incomplete research results or failing to provide the whole picture.

Researcher

The researcher (or the research firm) has the right to be treated ethically as well. Ethical treatment by clients involves several issues: improper solicitation of proposals, disclosure of proprietary techniques, and misrepresentation of findings.[13]

Improper Solicitation   When a research firm submits a proposal to a prospective client, it should be confident that the client is seriously considering employing it to conduct the research project. Furthermore, should the potential client decide to employ another research firm, the client will not attempt to misuse its proposal by turning it over to another firm for execution. The research proposal is the property of the research firm that developed it, unless it is paid for by the client.

proprietary techniques
Research techniques that are considered intellectual property of a research firm.

Proprietary Techniques   A researcher also has the right to expect that any of its **proprietary techniques** will not be revealed by the client to other researchers or firms. The client firm should also refrain from using such techniques for their own future use—even if the technique was used in a project previously commissioned from the researcher in question—without the express permission of the researcher who developed the technique.

Misrepresentation of Findings   The client firm should not distort the research findings to their own benefit at the expense of the researcher's reputation. Returning to the earlier example of dentists' toothpaste preference, suppose that the researcher (say Burke Marketing Research) who conducted the study made it clear to the client firm that although more of those dentists that expressed a preference preferred Brand A (5%), the majority of dentists did not express a preference (90%). It would be unethical for the client to distort this information and advertise that Burke Marketing Research found that more dentists prefer Brand A than any other brand without revealing that most dentists did not have a preference.

The researcher is also vulnerable to the unethical behaviors of the respondents. When respondents are recruited for a research project, the researcher assumes that they will provide truthful and well-thought-out responses. Respondents who fail to do so may be engaging in unethical behavior.

GUIDELINES FOR ETHICAL DECISION MAKING

Now that the stakeholders in marketing research have been identified and the more obvious ethical issues have been pointed out, we come to the more difficult task of ethical decision making. The very words *decision making* imply that a more complex process is at work, that the boundaries are not well defined, and that a clear-cut answer does not exist for every situation. So how do we approach such a monumental task?

One approach is to formulate some general guidelines for ethical behavior. To this purpose, the AMA has developed a marketing research code of ethics given in Research in Practice 24.1.[14] Other associations have developed similar codes. Research in Practice 24.2 ranks the core moral values in the various associations' codes.[15] Although this code, along with an awareness of the stakeholders in marketing research, provides a good starting point for ethical decision making, further guidelines are still needed.

A sound ethical framework, especially as it pertains to marketing research, has yet to be developed. Although various simplistic philosophies have been espoused—such as the golden rule, the utilitarian principle, Kant's categorical imperative, the professional ethic, and the TV test—they are vague and not sufficiently rigorous to provide a solid basis for ethical decision making.[16] Therefore, to aid all types of businesspersons, including marketing researchers, checklists for ethical decision making have been developed in an attempt to improve the process. One such checklist is Laczniak's and Murphy's ethical decision making checklist:[17]

1. Does action A violate the law?
2. Does action A violate any moral obligations?
3. Does action A violate any special obligations stemming from the type of marketing organization in question (for example, the special duty of pharmaceutical firms to provide safe products)?

RESEARCH IN PRACTICE 24.1

Marketing Research Code of Ethics of the AMA

The American Marketing Association, in furtherance of its central objective of the advancement of science in marketing and recognition of its obligation to the public, has established these principles of ethical practice of marketing research for the guidance of its members.

For Research Users, Practitioners and Interviewers:

1. No individual or organization will undertake any activity which is directly or indirectly represented to be marketing research, but which has as its real purpose the attempted sale of merchandise or services to some or all of the respondents interviewed in the course of the research.

2. If a respondent has been led to believe, directly or indirectly, that he is participating in a marketing research survey and that his anonymity will be protected, his name shall not be made known to anyone outside the research organization or research department, or used for other than research purposes.

For Research Practitioners:

1. There will be no intentional or deliberate misrepresentation of research methods or results. An adequate description of methods employed will be made available upon request to the sponsor of the research. Evidence that fieldwork has been completed according to specifications will, upon request, be made available to buyers of research.

2. The identity of the survey sponsor and/or the ultimate client for whom a survey is being done will be held in confidence at all times, unless this identity is to be revealed as part of the research design. Research information shall be held in confidence by the research organization or department and not used for personal gain or made available to any outside party unless the client specifically authorizes such release.

3. A research organization shall not undertake studies for competitive clients when such studies would jeopardize the confidential nature of client-agency relationships.

For Users of Marketing Research:

1. A user of research shall not knowingly disseminate conclusions from a given research project or service that are inconsistent with or not warranted by the data.

2. To the extent that a unique design involving techniques, approaches or concepts not commonly available to research practitioners is used, prospective user of research shall not solicit such a design from one practitioner and deliver it to another for execution without the approval of the design originator.

For Field Interviewers:

1. Research assignments and materials received, as well as information obtained from respondents, shall be held in confidence by the interviewer and revealed to no one except the research organization conducting the marketing study.

2. No information gained through a marketing research activity shall be used, directly or indirectly, for the personal gain or advantage of the interviewer.

3. Interviews shall be conducted in strict accordance with specifications and instructions received.

4. An interviewer shall not carry out two or more interviewing assignments simultaneously unless authorized by all contractors or employers concerned.

Members of the American Marketing Association will be expected to conduct themselves in accordance with provisions of this Code in all of their marketing research activities.

4. Is the intent of action A evil?

5. Are any major evils likely to result from or because of action A?

6. Is a satisfactory alternative B, which produces equal or more good with less evil than A, being knowingly rejected?

7. Does action A infringe upon the inalienable liberties of the consumer?

8. Does action A leave another person or group less well off? Is this person or group already relatively unprivileged?

A more straightforward list of twelve questions to help clarify ethical problems was proposed by Laura Nash:[18]

1. Have you defined the problem accurately?

2. How would you define the problem if you stood on the other side of the fence?

3. How did this situation occur in the first place?

4. To whom and to what do you give your loyalty as a person and as a member of the corporation?

5. What is your intention in making this decision?

6. How does this intention compare with the probable results?

7. Whom could your decision or action injure?

8. Can you discuss the problem with the affected parties before you make your decision?

9. Are you confident that your decision will be as valid over a long period of time as it seems now?

10. Could you disclose without qualm your decision or action to your boss, your CEO, the board of directors, your family, or society as a whole?

11. What is the symbolic potential of your action if understood? If misunderstood?

12. Under what conditions would you allow exceptions to your stand?

RESEARCH IN PRACTICE 24.2

Core Moral Values as Ranked in Research Associations' Codes

Values[a]	Advertising Research Foundation	American Marketing Association	Council of American Survey Research Organizations	Marketing Research Association	Qualitative Research Council of America
Nondeception	1	1	2	2	
Keeping promises	2		1	1	2
Serving others		2[a]	3	3[a]	1
Not harming others				3[a]	3
Justice		2[a]			
Other values	3				

[a]Values are tied in ranking.

Even more simplistic are the six questions used in ethics training programs at the Center for Business Ethics at Bentley College:[19]

1. Is it right?
2. Is it fair?
3. Who gets hurt?
4. Would you be comfortable if the details of your decision were reported on the front page of your local newspaper?
5. What would you tell your child to do?
6. How does it feel?

Marketing researchers may find the Wade system of evaluating sources of information particularly useful (see Table 24.3).[20] These checklists are by no means completely exhaustive, nor are the questions in their entirety appropriate for every situation. They do, however, provide a set of external directions to guide marketing researchers and other decision makers through ethical dilemmas.

AN ETHICAL FRAMEWORK

In an effort to move toward development of an ethical framework, we have developed an integrated model for ethical decision making in marketing research that takes into account the various ethical theories and perspectives (Figure 24.1). The integrated model also includes the various stakeholders of marketing research, that is, the client, the researcher, the respondent, and the public.

TABLE 24.3

The Wade System for Judging Sources of Information

Ethical

1. Published material and public documents such as court records.
2. Disclosures made by competitors' employees and obtained without subterfuge.
3. Market surveys and consultants' reports.
4. Financial reports and brokers' research reports.
5. Trade fairs, exhibits, and competitors' brochures.
6. Analysis of competitor's products.
7. Legitimate employment interviews with people who worked for competitor.

Arguably Unethical

8. Camouflaged questioning and "drawing out" of competitor's employees at technical meeting.
9. Direct observation under secret conditions.
10. False job interviews with a competitor's employee (i.e., without real intent to hire).
11. Hiring a professional investigator to obtain a specific piece of information.
12. Hiring an employee away from the competitor to get specific know-how.

Illegal

13. Trespassing on a competitor's property.
14. Bribing a competitor's supplier or employee.
15. "Planting" your agent on a competitor's payroll.
16. Eavesdropping on competitors (e.g., via wiretapping).
17. Theft of drawings, samples, documents, and similar property.
18. Blackmail and extortion.

Note: The numbers in the list are ranked in descending degree of ethicality or legality.

FIGURE 24.1

An Integrated Model for Ethical Decisions in Marketing Research

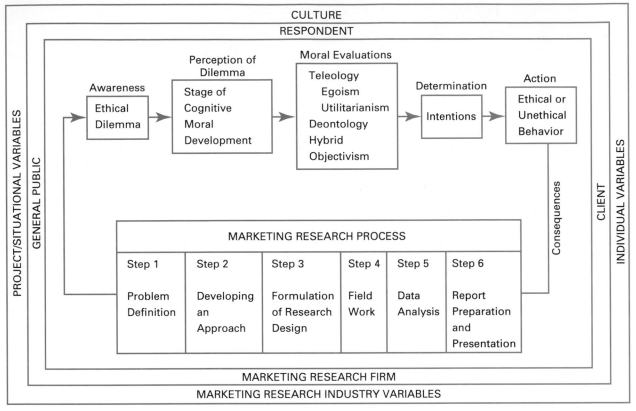

We begin with a description of the heart of the model (interior box, Figure 24.1). As in many other models, the process is activated when awareness of an ethical dilemma occurs. Then the ethical decision maker's stage of **cognitive moral development** (CMD) influences how the ethical issues will be handled. CMD theory postulates that in similar ethical dilemmas, different people make different decisions because they are in different stages of CMD.[21] One's moral development occurs through six stages, which can be simplified into three levels of two stages each. At the first level, preconventional morality, one is concerned with oneself and the external rewards or punishments that come about as a result of one's actions. The second level, conventional morality, moves beyond the individual's needs and permits one to make decisions based on society's or other significant reference group's expectations of what is right. Movement beyond individual and group expectations defines the third level, postconventional morality. Here rights that are beyond individual or group values and laws are used to make decisions.[22] Individuals advance through these stages toward a better understanding of moral obligations. Thus, people in stage six should demonstrate the ability to reason through moral dilemmas more effectively than individuals in stages one through five. How ethical situations are dealt with (individual, group, global) depends first on the level and stage of CMD that the decision maker has attained.

At this point, the decision maker identifies a set of alternative solutions to the dilemma and evaluates each one on each of five approaches: teleology (egoism and util-

cognitive moral development Moral development occurs through three levels: (1) preconventional morality—concern with oneself and the external rewards or punishments, (2) conventional morality—society's or other significant reference group's expectations of what is right, and (3) postconventional morality—rights that are beyond individual or group values. Each level consists of two stages.

itarianism) deontology (e.g., Kantian Formalism); hybrid (i.e., combination of teleological and deontological views, such as Ross's prima facie framework); and objectivism.

Teleology

teleology The degree of ethicalness depends on the outcomes or actions that result from the decisions. In other words, the end justifies the means.

The teleological perspective is also known as a consequential theory. Broadly, **teleology** states that the evaluation of the degree of ethicalness depends on the outcomes or actions that result from the decisions. The objective is to select the outcome that results in the greatest good. In other words, the end justifies the means. More specifically, the teleological perspective can be further divided into egoism and utilitarianism. The difference is that whereas the egoist viewpoint focuses on the individual, the utilitarian considers all parties involved. **Egoism** means that one takes the actions that result in the greatest good for oneself (be it short- or long-term perspective). For instance, one decides to be nice to the boss (even though the boss is not liked), not necessarily because it brings immediate "good" or happiness to one, but because in the long run it is likely to lead to a promotion that is a greater good than the more immediate good one would get from not being nice to the boss.

egoism An individualist perspective of teleology where one takes the actions that results in the greatest good for oneself (be it short- or long-term perspective).

utilitarianism A global perspective of teleology that one should take the action that results in the maximization of good for all concerned, regardless that the goodness might not be equally distributed.

Utilitarianism suggests that one should take the action (i.e., make the decision) that results in the maximization of good for all concerned, regardless that the goodness might not be equally distributed. For example, if action A results in three units of good for person 1, four units of good for person 2, and three units of good for person 3; whereas action B results in nine units of good for person 1, two units of good for person 2 and no units for person 3, action B should be taken because it results in the greatest amount of good for all parties involved.[23]

Deontology

deontology A nonconsequentialist approach to ethical evaluation focusing on the intentions behind the decision to pursue a particular alternative, rather than on the results.

Contrary to the teleological approach, **deontology** is a nonconsequentialist approach.[24] It focuses on the intention or the means behind the decision to pursue a particular alternative, rather than on the results of a decision (ends) to evaluate how an action stacks up ethically. The classical example of this school of thought is exemplified by **Kant's categorical imperative**, which states that the only ethical courses of action are those where the action taken could serve as a universal law. In other words, what makes a decision right or ethical is that the decision maker would be willing to be so treated were the positions of the parties reversed. A recent study found that managers' decisions either to discipline or to reward the behavior of salespeople are guided primarily by the inherent rightness or wrongness of the salespeople's behaviors (deontological considerations) and only secondarily by the consequences of the behaviors on the organizations (teleological factors).[25]

Kant's categorical imperative A deontological view which states that the only ethical courses of action are those where the action taken could serve as a universal law.

Hybrid

hybrid An approach that combines aspects of both teleology and deontology.

Oddly enough, although it seems that teleology and deontology are diametrically opposed, some have argued that the true decision-making behavior of people encompasses some **hybrid** of both approaches. In other words, decision makers frequently focus on both the effects of carrying out the decision (means) as well as the result of the decision (end). For example, suppose that a research firm is approached by a client who wishes to test several TV commercials to determine which one is most effective for selling a new product. Suppose, however, that this product is a new brand of cigarette that touts as its primary benefit reduced tar (giving the impression that the new brand is "healthier" to smoke), but does not mention that medical tests have suggested that the cigarette is not "healthier" because the reduced tar content causes the smoker to draw more frequently and harder on the cigarette to get the flavor of a regular cigarette, and thus all the tar of a regular cigarette. Should the research firm engage in such a project?

From the teleological perspective, it could be argued that engaging in such research would be ethical if it brings about the general good. The egoistic perspective would focus on the good for the research firm: it gains a new client. The utilitarian would consider the greatest good for all: the good resulting from the research firm gaining a new client, the client finding the most effective way to advertise, and current smokers being made aware of a new brand of cigarette they may like better. The utilitarian perspective would argue that this is a greater good than any negative effects, such as that new smokers may be cultivated and that existing smokers are encouraged to endanger their health. From a strict deontological perspective, this research is not ethical because it results in the deception of smokers and endangerment of their health, thus violating the rights of the individual through the imperative that it is wrong to endanger the health of people knowingly.

This leads to the observation that the world, and thus decisions, are not black and white and that they frequently involve trade-offs, which are accounted for in hybrid approaches such as **Ross's prima facie framework**, which notes that imperatives frequently conflict. To make decisions, one has to prioritize or determine which imperative is more crucial or important than others.

Objectivism

Objectivism holds that although ethics and completely ethical behavior are nice, for the most part they exist only in a perfect world. Ethics are determined by whatever is occurring in the real world. Thus, realizing that unethical behaviors exist, one should attempt to deal with or eliminate the unethical behaviors that do exist, rather than worry about what ought to be. One place to start is to attempt to lay down general guidelines for ethical behavior. To this purpose, the AMA and many other marketing organizations have developed marketing research codes of ethics. But even though this along with an awareness of the stakeholders in marketing research provides a good starting point for ethical decision making, further guidelines are still needed.

Next the intentions, or final decisions by the decision maker with regard to which course of action to take, is made, followed by the action or behavior itself. Consequences of the action feed into the six steps of the marketing research process. It should be recognized that ethical dilemmas may be reflected throughout all six steps of the marketing research process, just a few steps, or even one step. In other words, the number of steps affected by the decision-making process depends on the nature of the ethical dilemma itself. Regardless of how many or how few of the steps are involved, once the consequences of the actions chosen reveal their effects on the marketing research process, the behavior is evaluated and the evaluation is stored to be retrieved and fed back into future decision-making activities. Ethics and the six steps of marketing research are discussed later in the chapter.

Now that the heart of the model has been described, we can move on to the next level outward: perspective. Here the model assumes particular significance for ethical decision making in marketing research because the perspective box allows the decision process to be considered from all angles, namely the viewpoints of the four stakeholders in marketing research: the public, the respondents, the client, and the researcher. (See the earlier discussion on each of these roles.)

The final, exterior box of the model includes the consideration of variables external to the decision maker but essential in the decision-making process. These variables have an effect on the decision-making process in all the stakeholder roles in the marketing research process. Cultural variables may include the corporate culture of the

Ross's prima facie theory A hybrid view that notes that imperatives frequently conflict. To make decisions, one has to prioritize or determine which imperative is more crucial or important.

objectivism A view that instead of worrying about what ought to be, one should attempt to deal with or eliminate the unethical behaviors that do exist.

client or the national culture of a respondent. These variables affect whether ethical dilemmas are perceived at all by these role players as well as their strategies for moral evaluations. Second, and somewhat related, are individual variables, namely knowledge, values, attitudes, intentions, ego strength, field dependence, and focus of control.

Situation/project variables include resources and constraints. Things like limited time available to complete the research project or a limited budget to spend may impose certain constraints on the project, introducing ethical dilemmas into the marketing research process. Marketing research industry variables such as what types of research practices are acceptable and what technologies are available also exert a significant impact on ethical decision making in marketing research.

ETHICS AND THE MARKETING RESEARCH PROCESS

A detailed examination of ethical issues pertaining to the marketing research process was included in each of the earlier chapters. These issues are summarized in Table 24.4 and briefly discussed in the following.

Ethical issues arising in the first step, problem definition, include the misuse of research as a guise for selling and fundraising, and the personal agendas of the client (decision maker) and the researcher. For example, the client may not disclose all the pertinent information to the researcher because of personal agendas such as using the research to justify a decision already made. Likewise, if the researcher is unduly motivated by profit objectives, there may be a tendency to conduct unnecessary research or to avoid research which is not very profitable. Step two, developing an approach to the problem, includes the development of theories, models, research questions, and hypotheses. Ethical concerns at this stage include the use, in the current project, of findings and models developed for specific clients. Also, the solicitation of research proposals by the client, when the intent is not to award the research project but to gain the expertise of the researcher without pay, is fraught with ethical problems.

Research design, the third step in the marketing research process, encompasses a variety of activities from deciding on an exploratory, descriptive, or causal design to secondary data sources, qualitative techniques, measurement and scaling, questionnaire design, and sampling techniques. Many ethical dilemmas can arise including those related to the type of research design adopted and the nature of secondary data used, disguising the purpose of the research, and soliciting unfair concessions from the researcher. Several ethical issues related to the respondents are pertinent, such as maintaining anonymity, respecting privacy, observing unaware respondents, embarrassing or putting stress on respondents (Table 24.4). Other issues concern the use of reliable and valid scales, overly long questionnaires, and appropriate sampling procedures and techniques.[26] When conducting field work, the fourth step, field workers must make the respondents feel comfortable and ensure that they have a positive experience. Also, acceptable field work procedures should be followed and validation checks should be conducted to ensure the quality of the data. This information should then be made available to the client.

Data analysis is the fifth step. Ethical issues that commonly arise here include identifying and discarding unsatisfactory respondents, using statistical techniques when the underlying assumptions are violated, interpreting the results, and making conclusions and recommendations. The final step in the marketing research process is report preparation and presentation. Here, ethical decisions may have to be made about disclosing the limitations of the project to the client, avoiding misrepresentation of the findings, or inaccurate reporting.

TABLE 24.4
 	
Ethics and the Marketing Research Process
	I Problem definition
	  • Using surveys as a guise for selling or fundraising
	  • Following personal agendas of the researcher or client
	  • Conducting unnecessary research
	
	II Developing an approach
	  • Using findings and models developed for specific clients or projects for other projects
	  • Soliciting proposals to gain research expertise without pay
	
	III Research Design
	  • Formulating a research design more suited to the researcher's rather than the client's needs
	  • Using secondary data that are not applicable or have been gathered through questionable means
	  • Disguising the purpose of the research
	  • Soliciting unfair concessions from the researcher
	  • Not maintaining anonymity of respondents
	  • Disrespecting privacy of respondents
	  • Misleading respondents
	  • Disguising observation of respondents
	  • Embarrassing or putting stress on respondents
	  • Using measurement scales of questionable reliability and validity
	  • Designing overly long questionnaires, overly sensitive questions, piggybacking
	  • Using inappropriate sampling procedures and sample size
	
	IV Field Work
	  • Increasing (dis)comfort level of respondents
	  • Following (un)acceptable field work procedures
	
	V Data Preparation and Analysis
	  • Identifying and discarding unsatisfactory respondents
	  • Using statistical techniques when the underlying assumptions are violated
	  • Interpreting the results and making incorrect conclusions and recommendations
	
	VI Report Preparation and Presentation
	  • Using incomplete reporting
	  • Using biased reporting
	  • Using inaccurate reporting

INTERNATIONAL MARKETING RESEARCH

As more and more international marketing research is conducted due to the globalization of markets, new ethical issues must be addressed. Areas of concern include showing sensitivity to ethical differences among different cultures, determining whose ethical guidelines apply to what areas of marketing research, and taking into account inherent political and research integrity factors.[27]

Cultural Differences

Culture, philosophy, and morality determine what is considered as acceptable behavior and thus have an impact on ethical conduct. It has been hypothesized that the degree of individualism or collectivism of a culture can influence ethical decision making. In support of this hypothesis, it was found that business practitioners in countries high on individualism (i.e., the United States or Canada) were more likely to consider themselves as a more important stakeholder than owners or stockholders and other employees. In contrast, business practitioners in countries high in collectivism (i.e., Japan) were likely to consider the owners or stockholders and other employees as more important stakeholders than themselves.[28] Cultures can differ in other ways as well. Four major cultural dimensions have been identified and shown to influence ethical decision making: power distance, individualism, masculinity, and uncertainty avoidance.[29] Identifying how and why ethical concerns differ across cultures is important in overcoming ethical barriers to international trade, as illustrated by the following example.

EXAMPLE
Surveys Reveal Ethical Barriers to International Trade _____

Companies trying to crack international markets often find themselves in ethical dilemmas due to differences in culture. This problem can be most troublesome for smaller companies because ethical issues become another barrier these companies must overcome to be successful overseas. Many small companies simply cannot afford another barrier and, as a result, decide against expanding overseas.

A recent study in the *Journal of Small Business Management* examined the most difficult ethical questions faced by small businesses operating overseas. A two-section mail questionnaire and follow-up phone survey named bribery, government intervention, customs clearance, questionable transfer of funds, and cultural differences as the top five ethical problems. The questionnaire asked respondents to identify those aspects of international marketing that posed the most difficult marketing problems. The questionnaire format allowed the respondents to identify up to three ethical problems and rate them according to frequency and the impact on the firm. Ethical problems were seen to impact a small business' ability to compete effectively overseas negatively. Additionally, these problems may not be evident before the decision to enter the market is made, resulting in time and money losses.[30] ◆

Precedence of Ethical Guidelines

The question of whose ethical guidelines should take precedence becomes relevant when conducting research in a foreign country. Should American researchers act ethically by domestic guidelines, or by local guidelines, or by guidelines of both countries? It is difficult to come up with an emphatic answer to this rather fundamental question. This difficulty arises partly because there is no truly international research organization whose ethical guidelines are universally accepted.

A conservative stance would be to adhere to the ethical guidelines of both countries. One reason that American researchers must adhere to ethical guidelines established in the United States and those of the foreign country is that many foreign countries, particularly developing nations, often have fewer ethical guidelines. The freedom these countries offer researchers can be easily abused. Is it ethical for researchers to establish operations in lesser developed countries with fewer ethical and legal restrictions, just to conduct projects that would not be allowed in the United States? Adherence to domestic ethical guidelines can check such motives and the tendency to take advantage of the fewer ethical guidelines in some foreign countries. When the two sets of guidelines conflict, precedence should be given to the local guidelines. For example, in the United

States, children's opinions are obtained for several products that are consumed by them (e.g., cereals). In certain countries, however, interviewing children may be considered tantamount to inciting rebellion. Therefore, children should not be interviewed when conducting research in these countries. Other situations of conflicting norms are not as easily resolved, and general guidelines may not be available. If a broad set of guidelines is available, however, these should be applied to resolve the conflict. For example, the International Code of Marketing and Social Research Practice is a detailed and comprehensive code of ethical research behavior that is widely recognized in Europe.

Political and Research Integrity Concerns

The main political and research integrity concerns that pertain to international marketing research include respecting the political concerns of the host country, respecting naive foreign respondents, and full disclosure of sensitive findings. From the choice of topic to the choice of method, and dissemination of the findings and results, international research may cause political concerns in the host country. For example, the topic of birth control in Latin America is a sensitive issue with political ramifications. A researcher has a responsibility to address the political concerns of the host country and should be willing to make the necessary changes in the problem definition, approach, or the research design.

In the United States, people have participated in marketing research extensively and so are familiar with the process. In contrast, respondents in many foreign countries are naive and researchers should not take advantage of them, such as by asking questions that are overly sensitive according to local norms. Likewise, research integrity can be compromised when researchers are hesitant to disclose sensitive findings for fear that they will not be allowed back into the foreign country. As more research involves people from differing cultural backgrounds, ethical concerns and the guidelines for addressing them will evolve.

COMPUTER APPLICATIONS

The two ethical issues relevant to computer applications are researchers letting the software drive the research instead of a theoretical framework and a sound approach and researchers having the expertise to use the technology correctly. As previous chapters have demonstrated, when research is conducted, a definite approach should be followed. When data are funneled into a statistical computer program and analyzed without this theoretical backing, the findings are exploratory in nature and should not be treated as conclusive.

The second ethical question pertains to the use of statistical computer packages by researchers who do not have appropriate knowledge of, or experience with, the underlying statistical techniques. In such situations, there are too many possibilities for errors. Before using high-powered software, a researcher should be well trained and feel comfortable that no mistakes will be made. If not, these shortcomings should be admitted to the client.

SUMMARY

Ethics must become a priority of marketing research. Marketing is highly visible to the public, and it can be misperceived as highly unethical. This general poor opinion can be detrimental to marketing research, which relies on the voluntary cooperation of the public.

When examining ethical issues, it is important to consider the rights and responsibilities of four stakeholders: the public, the respondents, the client, and the marketing researcher. All these stakeholders must act in the best interest of the marketing research project. When there are conflicts between what is best for the project and what is best for the stakeholders, ethical dilemmas arise.

Common ethical issues in marketing research can be identified by examining the ways each stakeholder can suffer because of undue advantages taken by the other three. The public can suffer because of incomplete reporting, misleading reporting, and biased research. Respondents volunteer their time and opinions, which should not be abused. Specifically, surveys should not be used as a guise to sell products, and researchers should respect the privacy of respondents. Researchers also have ethical responsibilities to the clients and should not abuse their position, conduct unnecessary research, or undertake projects that they are not qualified to perform. Researchers are also obligated to maintain confidentiality, to disclose all relevant information, and to analyze and interpret data accurately. Finally, researchers deserve to be treated ethically by their clients and respondents. Clients should not solicit proposals from researchers that are not seriously being considered, should refrain from using proprietary techniques developed by the researcher without consent, and should not misrepresent the research findings to the public. Likewise, respondents should take the interviewing seriously and give honest responses.

Several codes of conduct and ethical checklists have been developed. Their limitations motivate the development of an ethical framework that describes an ethical decision as a process a stakeholder undergoes. Dilemmas are evaluated with respect to five approaches: teleology (egoism and utilitarianism), deontology, hybrid, and objectivism. Then the consequences are evaluated with reference to the six stages of the marketing research process. The six-stage marketing research process can be a useful way of exploring the ethical problems faced in marketing research.

In international marketing research, additional issues must be addressed including ethical differences among different cultures, determining whose ethical guidelines apply to what areas of marketing research, and taking into account political and research integrity concerns. Two ethical issues relevant to the use of computers are researchers letting the software, rather than a theoretical framework or approach, drive the research, and researchers lacking the knowledge and expertise to use the technology correctly.

ACRONYMS

The steps of decision making and evaluations of the ethical framework can be summarized by the acronym ETHICS.

E thical dilemma is discovered leading to awareness
T heory of cognitive moral development indicates how a decision resolving the dilemma is made
H ybrid or another one of the approaches is used to evaluate the dilemma
I ntentions or final decisions
C onsequences of ethical behavior
S takeholders: public, respondent, client, and researcher

EXERCISES

QUESTIONS

1. Discuss the importance of ethics to marketing managers and researchers.
2. What are the common characteristics describing most ethical decisions?

3. Identify the stakeholders of marketing research. How do the ethical issues in marketing research relate to the various stakeholders?

4. What responsibilities do the client and the researcher have to each other and to the marketing research project?

5. What responsibilities do the client and the respondent have to each other and to the marketing research project?

6. What responsibilities do the researcher and the respondent have to each other and to the marketing research project?

7. Describe the responsibilities of the client, researcher, or the respondent to the public?

8. How are teleology and deontology different from each other and from the hybrid approach?

9. Describe the stages of cognitive moral development and the role they play in ethical decision making?

10. What ethical issues arise in the problem definition stage of the marketing research process?

11. Discuss the ethical considerations involved in report preparation and presentation.

PROBLEMS

1. Identify a marketing research question that would require primary data gathering. Describe the ethical dilemmas you would face in gathering these data and how you would resolve them.

2. What unethical behaviors might describe a researcher who was solely trying to increase his or her billings? To answer this problem, identify at least one behavior for each of the six steps of the marketing research process.

COMPUTER EXERCISES

1. Run factor analysis for the computer exercise in Chapter 19. Eliminate at random several data values. Then run factor analysis eliminating missing values. How similar were the results to those produced with the entire data? What ethical issues does this analysis raise regarding the treatment of missing values?

NOTES

1. This chapter draws heavily from Naresh K. Malhotra and Gina Miller, "An Integrated Model for Ethical Decisions in Marketing Research," Working Paper, May 1994. Additonally, the assistance of Gina Miller and Mark Leach in writing this chapter is acknowledged.

2. A. E. Singer, S. Lysonski, M. Singer, and David Hayes, "Ethical Myopia: The Case of 'Framing' by Framing," *Journal of Business Ethics* 10 (1991): 29–36.

3. Gwendolyn K. Ortmeyer, "Ethics in Marketing, Retail Promotion Pricing: When Is A Sale Really a Sale?" *Harvard Business School Case* N9-591-111 (1991).

4. Gene R. Laczniak and Patrick E. Murphy, "Fostering Ethical Marketing Decisions," *Journal of Business Ethics* 11 (1991): 259–71.

5. L. T. Hosmer, *The Ethics of Management*, 2nd ed. (Homewood, IL: Richard D. Irwin, 1991), pp. 13–15.

6. Lynn Sharp Paine, "Managing for Organizational Integrity," *Harvard Business Review* 94 (March–April 1994): 106–17.

7. G. R. Laczniak and P. E. Murphy, *Marketing Ethics: Guidelines for Managers* (Lexington, MA: Lexington Books, 1985), p. 57.

8. Patrick E. Murphy and Gene R. Laczniak, "Traditional Ethical Issues Facing Marketing Researchers," *Marketing Research: A Magazine of Management and Applications* 4 (March 1992): 8–19. Adapted from Kenneth C. Schneider, "Ethics and Marketing Research," in James E. Nelson (ed.), *The Practice of Marketing Research* (Boston: Kent Publishing, 1982), p. 594.

9. Gene R. Laczniak and Patrick E. Murphy, *Ethical Marketing Decisions: The Higher Road* (Needham Heights, MA: Allyn and Bacon, 1993), p. 61; and N. C. Smith and J. A. Quelch, *Ethics in Marketing* (Homewood, IL: Richard D. Irwin, 1993), pp. 161–73.

10. R. Jowell, "The Codification of Statistical Ethics," *Journal of Official Statistics* 2 (1986): 3.

11. Patrick E. Murphy and Gene R. Laczniak, "Traditional Ethical Issues Facing Marketing Researchers," *Marketing Research: A Magazine of Management and Applications* 4 (March 1992): 8–19. Adapted from Kenneth C. Schneider, "Ethics and Marketing Research," in James E. Nelson (ed.), *The Practice of Marketing Research* (Boston: Kent Publishing, 1982), p. 608.

12. Gene R. Laczniak and Patrick E. Murphy, *Ethical Marketing Decisions: The Higher Road* (Needham Heights, MA: Allyn and Bacon, 1993), pp. 64–66; and N. C. Smith and J. A. Quelch, *Ethics in Marketing* (Homewood, IL: Richard D. Irwin, 1993), p. 177.

13. Gene R. Laczniak and Patrick E. Murphy, *Ethical Marketing Decisions: The Higher Road* (Needham Heights, MA: Allyn and Bacon, 1993), pp. 66–68; and N. C. Smith and J. A. Quelch, *Ethics in Marketing* (Homewood, IL: Richard D. Irwin, 1993), pp. 180–81.

14. As given in Appendix 3A of Gene R. Laczniak and Patrick E. Murphy, *Ethical Marketing Decisons: The Higher Road* (Needham Heights, MA: Allyn and Bacon, 1993), pp. 76-77.

15. Patrick E. Murphy and Gene R. Laczniak, "Emerging Ethical Issues Facing Marketing Researchers," *Marketing Research: A Magazine of Management and Applications* 4 (June 1992): 6–11; and Stephen B. Castleberry and Warren French, "The Ethical Framework of Advertising/Marketing Research Practitioners: A Moral Development Perspective," Working Paper (August 1991).

16. Gene R. Laczniak and Patrick E. Murphy, *Ethical Marketing Decisions: The Higher Road* (Needham Heights, MA: Allyn and Bacon, 1993), p. 61.

17. Adapted from N. C. Smith and J. A. Quelch, *Ethics in Marketing* (Homewood, IL: Richard D. Irwin, 1993), pp. 161–73.

18. Laura Nash, "Ethics without the Sermon," *Harvard Business Review* (November–December 1981): 88.

19. J. Bowditch and A. Buono, *A Primer on Organizational Behavior*, 2nd ed. (New York: Wiley, 1990).

20. Patrick E. Murphy and Gene R. Laczniak, "Emerging Ethical Issues Facing Marketing Researchers," *Marketing Research: A Magazine of Management and Applications* 4 (June 1992): 6–11. Adapted from Wade Worth, *Industrial Espionage and Mis-Use of Trade Secrets* (Ardmore, PA: Advance House, 1965).

21. John Fraedrich, Debbie M. Thorne, and O. C. Ferrell, "Assessing the Application of Cognitive Moral Development Theory to Business Ethics," *Journal of Business Ethics* 13 (October 1994): 829–38.

22. O. C. Ferrell and J. Fraedrich, *Business Ethics: Ethical Decision Making and Cases* (Boston: Houghton Mifflin, 1991).

23. W. H. Shaw and V. Barry, *Moral Issues in Business* (Belmont, CA: Wadsworth, 1992).

24. James E. Macdonald and Caryn L. Beck-Dudley, "Are Deontology and Teleology Mutually Exclusive?" *Journal of Business Ethics* 13 (August 1994): 615–24.

25. Shelby D. Hunt and Arturo Z. Vasquez-Parraga, "Organizational Consequences, Marketing Ethics, and Salesforce Supervision," *Journal of Marketing Research* 30 (February 1993): 78–90.

26. R. Eric Reidenbach and Donald P. Robin, "A Response to 'On Measuring Ethical Judgments,'" *Journal of Business Ethics* 14 (February 1995): 159–62.

27. Robert W. Armstrong and Jill Sweeney, "Industry Type, Culture, Mode of Entry, and Perceptions of International Marketing Ethics Problems: A Cross-Cultural Comparison," *Journal of Business Ethics* 13 (October 1994): 787–94.

28. S. J. Vitell, S. L. Nwachukwu, and J. H. Barnes, "The Effects of Culture on Ethical Decision-Making: An Application of Hofstede's Typology," *Journal of Business Ethics* 12 (1993): 753–60.

29. G. Hofstede, "The Cultural Relativity of the Quality of Life Concept," *Academy of Management Review* 3 (1984): 389–98.

30. Michael A. Mayo, "Ethical Problems Encountered by U.S. Small Businesses in International Marketing," *Journal of Small Business Management* (April 1991): 51–59.

PROFESSIONAL PERSPECTIVES

International Marketing Research: Challenge of the 1990s

Marketing research is continuously asked to describe "the consumer" of a particular product or service to help marketing managers in developing targeted communications and programs. To accomplish this goal, the six steps of marketing research must be adhered to. However, these steps must be adapted to the environment in which the research is to be conducted. Differences in the various aspects of environment (marketing, government, legal, economic, structural, information and technological, and sociocultural environments) are the primary factors that distinguish international marketing research from domestic marketing research. Therefore, these seven factors and their impact on international marketing research are the focus of this paper.

To begin our examination of the effects of these factors, consider the challenge the United States presents with its many cultures, regional biases, dialects, and slang. In spite of these differences, marketing research has succeeded in identifying commonalities that cross these cultural and regional borders. These commonalities can, in part, be attributed to the tendency of cultures to assimilate into an American mold (sociocultural environment) and to the established communication network that provides common messages nationally.

In other countries, cultures are more distinct and commonalities more subtle. For example, an examination of Malaysia's sociocultural environment reveals that its population is composed of three primary microcultures: Malays, Chinese, and Indians. There is no defined national culture, and people have little incentive to assimilate into a single culture, as they have in the United States. Inspection of the structural environment leads to the realization that there is no single popular national communications network. In spite of this, marketing

Sandra Kay Broaddus

Kay Broaddus was vice president of marketing for Turner Broadcasting Systems. Before joining Turner, Broaddus worked for the Coca-Cola Company for almost ten years in a variety of international and domestic marketing positions. Recently, Broaddus has returned to her earlier career as an international marketing consultant.

research is called on to identify the common threads shared by the total population with respect to their usage of a specific product or service. This task naturally requires consideration of not only the sociocultural and structural environments, but all seven aspects of environment. Thus, identifying consumers on a national level is difficult, but becomes even more formidable as marketing researchers are asked to expand this task (requiring researchers to take into account more variation within the seven environmental aspects) and profile the global consumer.

Because of increased complexity of the environment at a global level, many multinational corporations strive to strengthen their world position by adopting the approach, "Thing globally—act locally." In "thinking globally," management must develop a world vision, setting a global direction for the corporation and its trademarks. For those companies fortunate enough to have products with universal appeal, thinking globally naturally leads to marketing globally. Global marketing recognizes the existence of a global consumer by focusing on similarities that cross geographic and cultural borders; thus transcending environmental differences among cultures and countries. By identifying these common threads through the study of the relevant environments, marketing research provides the foundation for marketers to develop one image and one message, worldwide.

The one-image–one-message concept is illustrated in the context of the so-called global teenager. In the world marketplace, there is a global teenager who wears blue jeans, carries a backpack, probably speaks English, and drinks a Coke. Although this description is helpful to the global marketer in creating that single worldwide image and message, the local marketer must know more. Where does the teenager buy the Coke, how often, and is it consumed with or without food? The answers to these and many other questions will differ according to the seven aspects of environment.

In addition to profiling consumers, yet another dimension of marketing research arises as marketing continues to grow to global proportions. Researchers are questioning the role of geographic boundaries in marketing products because, in most of the world, the sociocultural environment variables of religion and ethnic background are primary and that of nationality secondary.

Furthermore, marketing research plays a key role in determining the most effective means to communicate the message to consumers. When rolling out a global advertising campaign based on the successful U.S. campaign "You Can't Beat The Feeling," Coca-Cola Company's research indicated the basic elements of the theme had wide universal appeal, but the message required adapting and localizing in many countries to maximize effectiveness. To fit in with the sociocultural environment in the Caribbean, Africa, and the South Pacific, the music was changed to a distinctive reggae beat. In Japan, the theme was translated to "I Feel Coke" and in Chile, to "The Feeling of Life" to reflect the influence of the relevant environment.

The above examples show the need to incorporate the seven environmental factors into international marketing research. Differences in these factors may result in differences in the formation of consumers' perceptions, attitudes, preferences, and choice behavior. Clearly, as multinational corporations move toward a more global perspective, viewing the world rather than a country as their marketplace, the challenges of international marketing research become more formidable and the results more critical.

CASE 6.1

Will KFC Fry the Competition in China?

It was an irony of great proportion. In 1985, the Chinese Ministry of Light Industry approached the international division of KFC (formerly Kentucky Fried Chicken) to see if the company would be interested in opening an outlet in the People's Republic of China. The Chinese were interested in acquiring advanced boiler technologies and fast-food processing systems to upgrade the level of Chinese food production. In return, they were offering KFC first access to the major markets of the world's most populous nation.

In 1979, with the emergence of leader Deng Xiao Ping, the business environment in China opened to foreigners. China began to pursue the policy of the four modernizations, the cornerstone of which was actively courting Western investment so as to industrialize their economy. Foreigners and foreign products were welcomed, especially if production sites were built in China. In a typical agreement, a foreign firm would enter into a joint venture with a Chinese company under the guidance of the government. After a negotiated period of time, usually 10 to 20 years, the Chinese partner would assume full control of the operations. In exchange, the foreign company was guaranteed preferential treatment for obtaining government approvals and, as always, the promise of a large market with profits for everyone.

Fast-food outlets had been considering China for several years. During the early 1980s, McDonald's, Pizza Hut, and Taco Bell had considered making the first plunge into China. Everyone felt that a tremendous market awaited the first entrant into China, as long as relations with the West remained stable, but no one had the hard data to support such a move. Government economic data, typically aggregated at the industry or provincial level, was available, but no one had prior experience in China or detailed information on which to base a decision. The government did not release data on the restaurant industry, but it was believed that people in China dined out only on special occasions or for business entertaining.

Despite this lack of information, KFC felt that it had to follow up on this opportunity. The Chinese offered ten sites, all in major metropolitan areas like Beijing (seven million people), Shanghai (12 million people) and Guangzhou (five million people). In addition, the proposed locations were exceptional. For example, in Beijing, a three-story building across the street from Tiananmen Square was offered, plus at least one other site to be determined later. From preliminary research, KFC determined that it could offer a two-piece chicken dinner with cole slaw, potatoes, and a drink for approximately U.S. $2. Yet the company lacked solid market data on the consumption habits and preferences of the Chinese. In addition, marketing research had seldom been conducted in China, so the company was not sure how the Chinese would respond to typical research techniques. KFC realized that this opportunity would be either a tremendous boom or a tremendous bust, but it did not know which.

KFC was encouraged because it had successful units in Japan for over 20 years. Therefore, KFC moved into mainland China with the opening of its outlet on Tiananmen Square in Beijing on November 12, 1987. This was the largest fast-food store in the world, and it grossed $3 million in its first year of operation. By 1990, KFC had opened four more Chinese units and had formed a joint venture to build in Shanghai.

In addition to being the first U.S. chain to break into China, KFC virtually dominated the Pacific Rim. In 1990, through joint ventures and other arrangements, KFC operated in ten of the Pacific Rim's 15 nations. The company had 70 units in Malaysia, 40 in Indonesia, 30 in South Korea, 28 in Singapore, 25 in Taiwan, 20 in the Philippines, 12 in Hong Kong, and 10 in Thailand. Japan, of course, had more than 900 units, where the average store grossed $890,000 in 1989, substantially more than the $635,000 average for U.S. units. In fact, in 1990, international sales accounted for $2.6 billion, or 45% of the company's worldwide sales. More dramatically, international operations accounted for 50% of worldwide profits.

By 1991, KFC had experienced tremendous success in the Pacific Rim, and with more than one-third (1,140 units) of its international stores located in this region, it decided to drive its expansion into this market even further. KFC Corporation recently announced plans in 1993 to expand its overseas operations in Asia by increasing the number of directly owned and franchised outlets. Currently, KFC Corporation has 1600 outlets, and it expects to increase this number to 2500 by 1999. An estimated $600 million will be allocated to finance the growth of the restaurant chain in Asia.

KFC Corporation plans to focus its expansion in China and India because many predict that China will be one of KFC's largest markets in the next ten years. In fact, the fast-food sector in China alone is growing at about 20% per year. KFC Corporation plans to spend approximately $200 million in the next four years in China. This will expand the number of KFC outlets in China from 28 to at least 200. Growth has been particularly rapid in the markets of Beijing and Shanghai. Since KFC entered Shanghai, 300 fast-food restaurants have opened, and many of these restaurants credit KFC for their success.

The KFC outlets in China are clean, cool, and brightly lit. Customers are described as aspirational with enough disposable income to spend between $2.50 and $3.50 on a fast-food meal. Many customers like the new atmosphere because most of the other restaurants that serve chicken have walls that are splattered with grease and floors that are littered with chicken bones. Competition is already becoming intense, especially with the latest entry into the Asian market by Kenny Rogers Roasters, a "pricier rotisserie restaurant." Although KFC may continue to encounter difficulties with local laws and customs, two things never change: the secret blend of 11 herbs and spices and its determination to fry the competition in whatever market it chooses to enter.

QUESTIONS

1. As a member of the KFC marketing research team, what secondary data sources would you consult to evaluate the opportunity in China?

2. Do you believe that qualitative research is needed in this case? If so, which techniques would you suggest?

3. Do you believe that quantitative research is needed in this case? If so, which techniques would you suggest? How would you go about gathering data?

4. What obstacles would need to be overcome in conducting research in China? How would you overcome these obstacles?

5. Based on the information you have, do you think that it is wise to invest in an operation in China? If you could have one more piece of information, what would it be? Why? What factors must be considered that are not important in domestic marketing?

6. What kind of research should be undertaken to assess the demand potential for fast foods in the Pacific Rim countries? How should such research be conducted?

7. Discuss the ethical aspects of undertaking research to assess the demand potential for fast foods in the Pacific Rim countries.

REFERENCES

1. Hayes, J. "Pacific Rim: Kentucky Fried Chicken Leads U.S. Operators into the Orient with More Than 1,100 Outlets from Tiananmen Square to the Philippines." *Nation's Restaurant News* (October 1, 1990): 144.

2. "Weak U.S. Results Cut KFC's 1st Q Profits." *Nation's Restaurant News* (May 27, 1991): 14.

3. Henriette, Catherine. "Dancing for Fast Food Dollars." *U.S. News and World Report*" (July 18, 1994): 46.

4. Goll, Sally D. "Pepsico's KFC Plans Expansion into Asia." *Asian Wall Street Journal Weekly* (May 30, 1994): 17.

CASE 6.2 Is Tylenol Strong Enough to Overcome Multiple Headaches?

Described as "an act of terrorism, pure and simple," the death of a young New York woman in February 1986 by a cyanide-tainted Tylenol capsule led Johnson & Johnson to remove Tylenol from the marketplace. Its 14 million capsule users were urged to switch to caplets, which were solid oval tablets with a smooth coating.

Johnson & Johnson had faced a similar product sabotage of its Tylenol capsules in 1982, when seven similar

845

deaths occurred in Chicago. At that time, the company urged consumers to trust them, and they did. The company put in three new barriers in Tylenol capsules packaging—a glued flap on the box, a plastic neck seal, and an inner foil seal over the mouth—the triple defense—to prevent any further sabotage. Tylenol capsules were then placed back on the shelves. The recalled Tylenol capsules were replaced, free of charge, with new capsules packaged in the new tamper-resistant packs. Millions of free coupons were redeemed, and three months after the poisoning, Tylenol had recaptured most of its 35% share of the $1.6 billion annual nonprescription pain-relief market.

The 1986 incident, however, proved to be a tougher problem for the company than the 1982 scare. Not only was the company asking for consumers' trust, but it was also asking them to change from capsules to caplets. Johnson & Johnson spent between $100 and $150 million on this project. It bought full-page advertisements in about 400 newspapers, offering a free exchange of caplets for capsules. It sent more than 100,000 Mailgrams to doctors, hospitals, and pharmacists promoting the caplets. A total of 2,500 salespeople, four times more than the usual salesforce, canvassed doctors and druggists and dropped off free samples of Tylenol caplets. The company even ran prime-time public service ads on TV asking people to give the caplets a try. The company strongly believed that their single most-valued asset is credibility, and they were anxious not to lose the faith that they had earned over the years. Their efforts were rewarded with renewed brand loyalty that enabled Johnson & Johnson to expand the Tylenol name to other products in the domestic market,

notably cold relief and sleeping aids. Table 1 is an excerpt from an A. C. Nielsen survey of market shares in 1993.

In 1993 and 1994, the sale of lower-cost, private brands of painkillers continued to climb steadily. The sales of the "no name" painkillers grew approximately 14.8% during the 52 weeks ending January 30, 1994. Sales totaled approximately $508 million, making them a collective number two, behind only Tylenol. Tylenol's sales grew approximately 5.4% to reach the $699.3 million level.

Tylenol's continued success has been attributed to several factors. Johnson & Johnson has been able to extend its product line into remedies for ailments that range from allergies to the sniffles of children. Johnson & Johnson has stayed with its main ingredient, acetaminophen, however, and has not tried other main ingredients like many other painkiller companies. Tylenol also has the advantage of being the number one analgesic brand, which gives it the ability and marketing power to build its product line with such tactics as the Tylenol Store. The Tylenol Store is a new in-store display that features a broad line of Tylenol products and brochures that relate to the products. Tylenol seems to realize that for lasting relief in the painkiller market it takes more than just copying the competition.

Even though Johnson & Johnson resolved its problem with cyanide-tainted capsules domestically, it had to deal with its international operations. The world market for analgesics had grown over the years (see Table 2), but Tylenol had never earned the popularity and brand recognition abroad as it had in the United States. Therefore, at the time of the cyanide scare, Johnson & Johnson felt that it would

TABLE 1

Leading Headache Remedies (sales in millions of dollars for part of 1993)

Rank 1992	Rank 1993	Brand	Partial Sales 1993	Partial Sales Percent change	Market Share 1993	Market Share 1992
1	1	Tylenol	$ 284.9	3.4	27.6	28.9
2	2	Private label	192.6	1.7	18.7	17.2
3	3	Advil	154.8	12.2	15.0	14.5
4	4	Excedrin	42.9	−2.9	4.2	4.7
5	5	Motrin IB	42.8	7.6	4.1	4.1
6	7	Tylenol PM	41.8	27.0	4.1	3.5
7	6	Bayer Genuine	5.0	−8.3	3.4	4.0
8	8	Anacin	28.7	−10.1	2.8	3.4
9	9	Nuprin	24.5	−15.2	2.2	2.4
10	11	Excedrin PM	22.9	−0.9	2.2	2.4
		Total	1,030.1	8.2	100.0	100.0

Note: Market shares do not add to 100% because of other brands not considered here.

TABLE 2

U.S. Export of Analgesics to Selected Foreign Countries (volume in thousands of dollars)

Country	1991	1990
Australia	102	27
Belgium	879	1
Brazil	1	1
Canada	4,424	2,319
China	1,515	174
France	1,784	1
Germany	1,660	124
Hong Kong	83	133
Malaysia	32	7
Netherlands	72	3
South Africa	96	13
Spain	729	230
Switzerland	1	3
Taiwan	21	5
Thailand	40	16
United Kingdom	571	42
Other countries	4,808	5,405
World	16,818	8,504

be more difficult to repair the damage overseas than at home because of the different distribution methods that were used: over-the-counter drugs and prescription drugs.

In ten countries, including Australia, Hong Kong, Brazil, and South Africa, Tylenol capsules were sold directly to the consumer. In these markets, capsules were pulled from the shelves immediately after the poisoning, and the incident affected operations in much the same way it had in the United States.

In most markets, however, Tylenol was a prescription drug. For example, in seven countries, Tylenol was sold by prescription, as in Switzerland (2% market share), or from behind the counter by pharmacists, as in Spain (2.2% market share) and France (1% market share). These countries had laws prohibiting over-the-counter sales of Tylenol. Therefore, the company had to gain the endorsement of doctors as a means of reaching the consumer. This strategy paralleled the tactics by which Tylenol became the leading pain reliever in America. In addition, in France, drug sales were reimbursable by the government provided that the producer did not advertise the brand; hence, nonadvertised brands dominated the market. Nevertheless, in an effort to distinguish themselves from the competition, approximately 30% of analgesic products, including Tylenol, were advertised. In most of these markets, capsules remained available because they were sold through pharmacists and

quality control was not questioned. In France, however, caplets had been planned for introduction in 1986, while in Australia, Tylenol was in the process of going national with capsules when the incident occurred, and had to scrap all plans of national distribution for both capsules and tablets when the poisoning occurred.

In another 12 countries, only Tylenol tablets were available. In most of these markets, Johnson & Johnson did not expect any long-lasting aftershocks from the poisoning incident but still suffered from low market share and poor brand recognition.

In 1994, Johnson & Johnson faced another situation threatening its dominance of the painkiller market. A jury awarded $8.8 million to a man who blamed Tylenol for his liver damage (see Table 3). He claimed that the damage occurred as a result of his taking Tylenol with wine at dinner for several days. This incident did not elicit from J & J the vigorous advertising and reassurance for which the company had been known in the past. In part, this may have been due to Johnson & Johnson's divided stand on the issue. On the one hand, J & J said that it would appeal the verdict, claiming that the liver damage was actually caused by a virus. On the other hand, it agreed to prepare alcohol-warning labels for all its products after a recommendation by the Food and Drug Administration advisory panel.

Johnson & Johnson stated, however, that there was no need for an advertising campaign to reassure consumers because the product was safely used by millions of people. Although several image consultants questioned the company's low-key response, industry analysts agreed that this most current incident would not affect sales. One analyst at Sanford C. Berstein said, "The whole outcome might be that 10 people will stop using Tylenol. Ten out of a billion is not a trend." Despite new competition from Procter &

TABLE 3

History of Tylenol Incidents

1960: Johnson & Johnson introduces Tylenol.

September 1982: Someone laces Extra-Strength Tylenol with cyanide; seven people die. Leads to nationwide recall.

1983: James E. Lewis convicted of demanding $1 million to stop tampering. Sentenced to ten years in jail.

February 1986: A death in Yonkers, New York linked to tainted capsules. Tylenol stops making capsules.

October 1994: Federal court awards $8.8 million to man who blames Tylenol and its lack of alcohol warnings for destroying his liver.

Gamble's Aleve grabbing market share, Johnson & Johnson was confident in its approach to the problem. It was supported in its decision by evidence that Americans have become inured to claims against corporations because of the deluge of frivolous lawsuits filed in the last few years.

Thus, Johnson & Johnson, facing increasing competition and continued growth of the world analgesic market, may have to focus its attention on the international market. Additionally, the company will have to deal with reports of negative side effects associated with acetaminophen, Tylenol's active ingredient. As a result, Johnson & Johnson may have to concentrate on alleviating the headaches confronting its Tylenol brand before it can focus its energies on international consumers' pain relief.

QUESTIONS

1. As a member of the Johnson & Johnson marketing research team, what kind of domestic market research would you conduct to determine if Tylenol capsule users would indeed switch to caplets? Justify your answer.

2. What parameters would differ if you wanted to know if consumers in Hong Kong would switch? Consumers in France?

3. What additional international research would uncover the causes of the poor performance overseas? What special precautions must you take in conducting this research?

4. Do you think that Johnson & Johnson responded in an ethical manner to the various Tylenol incidents listed in Table 3?

5. What ethical issues will be salient when researching consumer preferences for pain relievers in the U.S.? In Hong Kong? In France?

REFERENCES

1. "Tylenol 'Damage Control' Tested Overseas." *Advertising Age* (March 10, 1986): 26.

2. "Tylenol Fights Back on Aspirin Heart Claims." *Wall Street Journal* (February 21, 1989): B1.

3. Winters, Patricia. "J & J Sets Nighttime Tylenol." *Advertising Age* (February 18, 1991): 1, 46.

4. "Brand Scorecard." *Advertising Age* (August 23, 1993): 12.

5. Schiller, Zachary, and Joseph Weber. "Painkillers Are about to O. D." *Business Week* (April 11, 1994): 54–55.

6. Enrico, Dottie, and Bruce Horovitz. "Tylenol Takes Different Tack on Safety Image." *USA Today* (October 24, 1994): 3B

CASE 6.3

Kmart and its Problems in Eastern Europe

America's second largest retailer, Kmart, is encountering some new problems as it attempts to expand into the former Communist bloc of Eastern Europe. One problem that the company is repeatedly facing is the resistance of Eastern European employees to modern merchandising. For example, many employees refuse to wear the familiar red badge of Kmart that states, "I'm Here for You." The employees feel that the slogan is degrading and invites sexual harassment.

Kmart decided to expand rapidly into Eastern Europe because it felt that domestic expansion had slowed in the United States. Last year alone, Kmart purchased 13 of the best discount stores in the Czechoslovak government's Prior Chain. Unfortunately, Czechoslovakia split into the Czech Republic and Slovakia, leaving Kmart with only two stores remaining. The cost of these stores was an estimated $120 million dollars.

There was some good news for Kmart. Their largest store that is located in the Slovak capital, Bratislava, earned more than $40 million dollars in 1993. This more than topped any of the earnings reported in the United States. Although the store reported very strong earnings, it was still unprofitable due to its huge inefficiencies, high costs, and low margins. Kmart realized that they must make changes in the way Eastern European people sell products if the store were to turn a profit.

The first thing that the company must do is convince manufacturers to produce and ship products that meet the standards of the retailer rather than the standards of the manufacturer. The stores as well as the selling philosophies of the store employees need to be renovated. Kmart also hopes to extend its shopping hours.

In addition, the redesign of the stores resulted in a more open and relaxed atmosphere in which customers could touch, wander, feel and try out the merchandise. To create a higher volume of sales, more shelves were added. In the short term, this created a problem for Kmart in that there were not enough Czech goods available to fill the additional space. This ties back into the manufacturing problem. The company realized that it had to find some way to get the local manufacturers to increase the quantity, quality, and speed of production. In an attempt to do just this, Kmart collected samples from various Czech manufacturers and shipped these products to the United States for introduction into its U.S. stores. Ten of the 20 samples won consumer orders. The Czech manufacturers were pleased with the new orders, but admitted that they did not know how to react to the changes in the quantity demanded.

One of the most difficult changes that the corporation will have to make is to make a change in the relationship between the salesperson and the customer. This will mean changing the salesperson's attitudes and personal behavior. The "concept of the customer" is a difficult concept for most of the salespeople to practice. They understand the concept, but they do not always practice what they know. Kmart understands that most of their employees have lived in a socialist system now for over 40 years and have never had to function as a salesperson or a consumer.

As consumer expectations continue to rise, Kmart must continue to strive to adjust to the needs of the market. The corporation must also continue to reshape the attitudes and beliefs of its Eastern European employees and its Eastern European consumers. Perhaps most important is that the company must continue to push and assists its manufacturers in increasing and adjusting their production schedules.

QUESTIONS

1. What environmental factors need to be considered when researching consumer preferences for Kmart stores in the Czech Republic?

2. Suppose that a survey is to be conducted to determine consumer preferences for Kmart stores in the Czech Republic. Which method of survey administration would you recommend and why? How would you administer such a survey in the United States?

3. In a comparative study of consumer preferences for Kmart stores in the United States and the Czech Republic, what special considerations would be involved in designing the appropriate measures and scales?

4. Identify the salient ethical issues in researching consumer preferences for Kmart stores in the United States. Would the ethical issues be different if the research were to be carried out in the Czech Republic?

REFERENCES

1. Perlez, Jane. "In East Europe, Kmart Faces an Attitude Problem." *New York Times* (July 7, 1993): 3.

Appendix

STATISTICAL TABLES

TABLE 1 *Simple Random Numbers*

Line/Col.	(1)	(2)	(3)	(4)	(5)	(6)	(7)	(8)	(9)	(10)	(11)	(12)	(13)	(14)
1	10480	15011	01536	02011	81647	91646	69179	14194	62590	36207	20969	99570	91291	90700
2	22368	46573	25595	85393	30995	89198	27982	53402	93965	34095	52666	19174	39615	99505
3	24130	48390	22527	97265	76393	64809	15179	24830	49340	32081	30680	19655	63348	58629
4	42167	93093	06243	61680	07856	16376	39440	53537	71341	57004	00849	74917	97758	16379
5	37570	39975	81837	16656	06121	91782	60468	81305	49684	60072	14110	06927	01263	54613
6	77921	06907	11008	42751	27756	53498	18602	70659	90655	15053	21916	81825	44394	42880
7	99562	72905	56420	69994	98872	31016	71194	18738	44013	48840	63213	21069	10634	12952
8	96301	91977	05463	07972	18876	20922	94595	56869	69014	60045	18425	84903	42508	32307
9	89579	14342	63661	10281	17453	18103	57740	84378	25331	12568	58678	44947	05585	56941
10	85475	36857	53342	53988	53060	59533	38867	62300	08158	17983	16439	11458	18593	64952
11	28918	69578	88231	33276	70997	79936	56865	05859	90106	31595	01547	85590	91610	78188
12	63553	40961	48235	03427	49626	69445	18663	72695	52180	20847	12234	90511	33703	90322
13	09429	93969	52636	92737	88974	33488	36320	17617	30015	08272	84115	27156	30613	74952
14	10365	61129	87529	85689	48237	52267	67689	93394	01511	26358	85104	20285	29975	89868
15	07119	97336	71048	08178	77233	13916	47564	81056	97735	85977	29372	74461	28551	90707
16	51085	12765	51821	51259	77452	16308	60756	92144	49442	53900	70960	63990	75601	40719
17	02368	21382	52404	60268	89368	19885	55322	44819	01188	65255	64835	44919	05944	55157
18	01011	54092	33362	94904	31273	04146	18594	29852	71685	85030	51132	01915	92747	64951
19	52162	53916	46369	58586	23216	14513	83149	98736	23495	64350	94738	17752	35156	35749
20	07056	97628	33787	09998	42698	06691	76988	13602	51851	46104	88916	19509	25625	58104
21	48663	91245	85828	14346	09172	30163	90229	04734	59193	22178	30421	61666	99904	32812
22	54164	58492	22421	74103	47070	25306	76468	26384	58151	06646	21524	15227	96909	44592
23	32639	32363	05597	24200	13363	38005	94342	28728	35806	06912	17012	64161	18296	22851
24	29334	27001	87637	87308	58731	00256	45834	15398	46557	41135	10307	07684	36188	18510
25	02488	33062	28834	07351	19731	92420	60952	61280	50001	67658	32586	86679	50720	94953
26	81525	72295	04839	96423	24878	82651	66566	14778	76797	14780	13300	87074	79666	95725
27	29676	20591	68086	26432	46901	20849	89768	81536	86645	12659	92259	57102	80428	25280
28	00742	57392	39064	66432	84673	40027	32832	61362	98947	96067	64760	64584	96096	98253
29	05366	04213	25669	26422	44407	44048	37937	63904	45766	66134	75470	66520	34693	90449
30	91921	26418	64117	94305	26766	25940	39972	22209	71500	64568	91402	42416	07844	69618
31	00582	04711	87917	77341	42206	35126	74087	99547	81817	42607	43808	76655	62028	76630
32	00725	69884	62797	56170	86324	88072	76222	36086	84637	93161	76038	65855	77919	88006
33	69011	65795	95876	55293	18988	27354	26575	08625	40801	59920	29841	80150	12777	48501
34	25976	57948	29888	88604	67917	48708	18912	82271	65424	69774	33611	54262	85963	03547
35	09763	83473	73577	12908	30883	18317	28290	35797	05998	41688	34952	37888	38917	88050
36	91567	42595	27958	30134	04024	86385	29880	99730	55536	84855	29088	09250	79656	73211
37	17955	56349	90999	49127	20044	59931	06115	20542	18059	02008	73708	83517	36103	42791
38	46503	18584	18845	49618	02304	51038	20655	58727	28168	15475	56942	53389	20562	87338
39	92157	89634	94824	78171	84610	82834	09922	25417	44137	48413	25555	21246	35509	20468
40	14577	62765	35605	81263	39667	47358	56873	56307	61607	49518	89656	20103	77490	18062

(continued)

TABLE 1   (continued)

Line/Col.	(1)	(2)	(3)	(4)	(5)	(6)	(7)	(8)	(9)	(10)	(11)	(12)	(13)	(14)
41	98427	07523	33362	64270	01638	92477	66969	98420	04880	45585	46565	04102	46880	45709
42	34914	63976	88720	82765	34476	17032	87589	40836	32427	70002	70663	88863	77775	69348
43	70060	28277	39475	46473	23219	53416	94970	25832	69975	94884	19661	72828	00102	66794
44	53976	54914	06990	67245	68350	82948	11398	42878	80287	88267	47363	46634	06541	97809
45	76072	29515	40980	07391	58745	25774	22987	80059	39911	96189	41151	14222	60697	59583
46	90725	52210	83974	29992	65831	38857	50490	83765	55657	14361	31720	57375	56228	41546
47	64364	67412	33339	31926	14883	24413	59744	92351	97473	89286	35931	04110	23726	51900
48	08962	00358	31662	25388	61642	34072	81249	35648	56891	69352	48373	45578	78547	81788
49	95012	68379	93526	70765	10592	04542	76463	54328	02349	17247	28865	14777	62730	92277
50	15664	10493	20492	38301	91132	21999	59516	81652	27195	48223	46751	22923	32261	85653
51	16408	81899	04153	53381	79401	21438	83035	92350	36693	31238	59649	91754	72772	02338
52	18629	81953	05520	91962	04739	13092	97662	24822	94730	06496	35090	04822	86774	98289
53	73115	35101	47498	87637	99016	71060	88824	71013	18735	20286	23153	72924	35165	43040
54	57491	16703	23167	49323	45021	33132	12544	41035	80780	45393	44812	12515	98931	91202
55	30405	83946	23792	14422	15059	45799	22716	19792	09983	74353	68668	30429	70735	25499
56	16631	35006	85900	98275	32388	52390	16815	69293	82732	38480	73817	32523	41961	44437
57	96773	20206	42559	78985	05300	22164	24369	54224	35083	19687	11052	91491	60383	19746
58	38935	64202	14349	82674	66523	44133	00697	35552	35970	19124	63318	29686	03387	59846
59	31624	76384	17403	53363	44167	64486	64758	75366	76554	31601	12614	33072	60332	92325
60	78919	19474	23632	27889	47914	02584	37680	20801	72152	39339	34806	08930	85001	87820
61	03931	33309	57047	74211	63445	17361	62825	39908	05607	91284	68833	25570	38818	46920
62	74426	33278	43972	10119	89917	15665	52872	73823	73144	88662	88970	74492	51805	99378
63	09066	00903	20795	95452	92648	45454	69552	88815	16553	51125	79375	97596	16296	66092
64	42238	12426	87025	14267	20979	04508	64535	31355	86064	29472	47689	05974	52468	16834
65	16153	08002	26504	41744	81959	65642	74240	56302	00033	67107	77510	70625	28725	34191
66	21457	40742	29820	96783	29400	21840	15035	34537	33310	06116	95240	15957	16572	06004
67	21581	57802	02050	89728	17937	37621	47075	42080	97403	48626	68995	43805	33386	21597
68	55612	78095	83197	33732	05810	24813	86902	60397	16489	03264	88525	42786	05269	92532
69	44657	66999	99324	51281	84463	60563	79312	93454	68876	25471	93911	25650	12682	73572
70	91340	84979	46949	81973	37949	61023	43997	15263	80644	43942	89203	71795	99533	50501
71	91227	21199	31935	27022	84067	05462	35216	14486	29891	68607	41867	14951	91696	85065
72	50001	38140	66321	19924	72163	09538	12151	06878	91903	18749	34405	56087	82790	70925
73	65390	05224	72958	28609	81406	39147	25549	48542	42627	45233	57202	94617	23772	07896
74	27504	96131	83944	41575	10573	03619	64482	73923	36152	05184	94142	25299	94387	34925
75	37169	94851	39117	89632	00959	16487	65536	49071	39782	17095	02330	74301	00275	48280
76	11508	70225	51111	38351	19444	66499	71945	05422	13442	78675	84031	66938	93654	59894
77	37449	30362	06694	54690	04052	53115	62757	95348	78662	11163	81651	50245	34971	52974
78	46515	70331	85922	38329	57015	15765	97161	17869	45349	61796	66345	81073	49106	79860
79	30986	81223	42416	58353	21532	30502	32305	86482	05174	07901	54339	58861	74818	46942
80	63798	64995	46583	09785	44160	78128	83991	42865	92520	83531	80377	35909	81250	54238
81	82486	84846	99254	67632	43218	50076	21361	64816	51202	88124	41870	52689	51275	83556
82	21885	32906	92431	09060	64297	51674	64126	62570	26123	05155	59194	52799	28225	85762
83	60336	98782	07408	53458	13564	59089	26445	29789	85205	41001	12535	12133	14645	23541
84	43937	46891	24010	25560	86355	33941	25786	54990	71899	15475	95434	98227	21824	19535
85	97656	63175	89303	16275	07100	92063	21942	18611	47348	20203	18534	03862	78095	50136
86	03299	01221	05418	38982	55758	92237	26759	86367	21216	98442	08303	56613	91511	75928
87	79626	06486	03574	17668	07785	76020	79924	25651	83325	88428	85076	72811	22717	50585
88	85636	68335	47539	03129	65651	11977	02510	26113	99447	68645	34327	15152	55230	93448
89	18039	14367	61337	06177	12143	46609	32989	74014	64708	00533	35398	58408	13261	47908
90	08362	15656	60627	36478	65648	16764	53412	09013	07832	41574	17639	82163	60859	75567
91	79556	29068	04142	16268	15387	12856	66227	38358	22478	73373	88732	09443	82558	05250
92	92608	82674	27072	32534	17075	27698	98204	63863	11951	34648	88022	56148	34925	57031
93	23982	25835	40055	67006	12293	02753	14827	23235	35071	99704	37543	11601	35503	85171
94	09915	96306	05908	97901	28395	14186	00821	80703	70426	75647	76310	88717	37890	40129
95	59037	33300	26695	62247	69927	76123	50842	43834	86654	70959	79725	93872	28117	19233
96	42488	78077	69882	61657	34136	79180	97526	43092	04098	73571	80799	76536	71255	64239
97	46764	86273	63003	93017	31204	36692	40202	35275	57306	55543	53203	18098	47625	88684
98	03237	45430	55417	63282	90816	17349	88298	90183	36600	78406	06216	95787	42579	90730
99	86591	81482	52667	61582	14972	90053	89534	76036	49199	43716	97548	04379	46370	28672
100	38534	01715	94964	87288	65680	43772	39560	12918	80537	62738	19636	51132	25739	56947

TABLE 2

**Area Under
the Normal Curve**

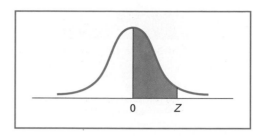

Entry represents area under the standard normal distribution from the mean to Z

Z	.00	.01	.02	.03	.04	.05	.06	.07	.08	.09
0.0	.0000	.0040	.0080	.0120	.0160	.0199	.0239	.0279	.0319	.0359
0.1	.0398	.0438	.0478	.0517	.0557	.0596	.0636	.0675	.0714	.0753
0.2	.0793	.0832	.0871	.0910	.0948	.0987	.1026	.1064	.1103	.1141
0.3	.1179	.1217	.1255	.1293	.1331	.1368	.1406	.1443	.1480	.1517
0.4	.1554	.1591	.1628	.1664	.1700	.1736	.1772	.1808	.1844	.1879
0.5	.1915	.1950	.1985	.2019	.2054	.2088	.2123	.2157	.2190	.2224
0.6	.2257	.2291	.2324	.2357	.2389	.2422	.2454	.2486	.2518	.2549
0.7	.2580	.2612	.2642	.2673	.2704	.2734	.2764	.2794	.2823	.2852
0.8	.2881	.2910	.2939	.2967	.2995	.3023	.3051	.3078	.3106	.3133
0.9	.3159	.3186	.3212	.3238	.3264	.3289	.3315	.3340	.3365	.3389
1.0	.3413	.3438	.3461	.3485	.3508	.3531	.3554	.3577	.3599	.3621
1.1	.3643	.3665	.3686	.3708	.3729	.3749	.3770	.3790	.3810	.3830
1.2	.3849	.3869	.3888	.3907	.3925	.3944	.3962	.3980	.3997	.4015
1.3	.4032	.4049	.4066	.4082	.4099	.4115	.4131	.4147	.4162	.4177
1.4	.4192	.4207	.4222	.4236	.4251	.4265	.4279	.4292	.4306	.4319
1.5	.4332	.4345	.4357	.4370	.4382	.4394	.4406	.4418	.4429	.4441
1.6	.4452	.4463	.4474	.4484	.4495	.4505	.4515	.4525	.4535	.4545
1.7	.4554	.4564	.4573	.4582	.4591	.4599	.4608	.4616	.4625	.4633
1.8	.4641	.4649	.4656	.4664	.4671	.4678	.4686	.4693	.4699	.4706
1.9	.4713	.4719	.4726	.4732	.4738	.4744	.4750	.4756	.4761	.4767
2.0	.4772	.4778	.4783	.4788	.4793	.4798	.4803	.4808	.4812	.4817
2.1	.4821	.4826	.4830	.4834	.4838	.4842	.4846	.4850	.4854	.4857
2.2	.4861	.4864	.4868	.4871	.4875	.4878	.4881	.4884	.4887	.4890
2.3	.4893	.4896	.4898	.4901	.4904	.4906	.4909	.4911	.4913	.4916
2.4	.4918	.4920	.4922	.4925	.4927	.4929	.4931	.4932	.4934	.4936
2.5	.4938	.4940	.4941	.4943	.4945	.4946	.4948	.4949	.4951	.4952
2.6	.4953	.4955	.4956	.4957	.4959	.4960	.4961	.4962	.4963	.4964
2.7	.4965	.4966	.4967	.4968	.4969	.4970	.4971	.4972	.4973	.4974
2.8	.4974	.4975	.4976	.4977	.4977	.4978	.4979	.4979	.4980	.4981
2.9	.4981	.4982	.4982	.4983	.4984	.4984	.4985	.4985	.4986	.4986
3.0	.49865	.49869	.49874	.49878	.49882	.49886	.49889	.49893	.49897	.49900
3.1	.49903	.49906	.49910	.49913	.49916	.49918	.49921	.49924	.49926	.49929
3.2	.49931	.49934	.49936	.49938	.49940	.49942	.49944	.49946	.49948	.49950
3.3	.49952	.49953	.49955	.49957	.49958	.49960	.49961	.49962	.49964	.49965
3.4	.49966	.49968	.49969	.49970	.49971	.49972	.49973	.49974	.49975	.49976
3.5	.49977	.49978	.49978	.49979	.49980	.49981	.49981	.49982	.49983	.49983
3.6	.49984	.49985	.49985	.49986	.49986	.49987	.49987	.49988	.49988	.49989
3.7	.49989	.49990	.49990	.49990	.49991	.49991	.49992	.49992	.49992	.49992
3.8	.49993	.49993	.49993	.49994	.49994	.49994	.49994	.49995	.49995	.49995
3.9	.49995	.49995	.49996	.49996	.49996	.49996	.49996	.49996	.49997	.49997

TABLE 3

Chi-Square Distribution

For a particular number of degrees of freedom,
entry represents the critical value of χ^2
corresponding to a specified upper tail area, α

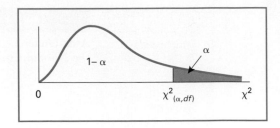

Degrees of Freedom	Upper Tail Areas (α)											
	.995	.99	.975	.95	.90	.75	.25	.10	.05	.025	.01	.005
1			0.001	0.004	0.016	0.102	1.323	2.706	3.841	5.024	6.635	7.879
2	0.010	0.020	0.051	0.103	0.211	0.575	2.773	4.605	5.991	7.378	9.210	10.597
3	0.072	0.115	0.216	0.352	0.584	1.213	4.108	6.251	7.815	9.348	11.345	12.838
4	0.207	0.297	0.484	0.711	1.064	1.923	5.385	7.779	9.488	11.143	13.277	14.860
5	0.412	0.554	0.831	1.145	1.610	2.675	6.626	9.236	11.071	12.833	15.086	16.750
6	0.676	0.872	1.237	1.635	2.204	3.455	7.841	10.645	12.592	14.449	16.812	18.548
7	0.989	1.239	1.690	2.167	2.833	4.255	9.037	12.017	14.067	16.013	18.475	20.278
8	1.344	1.646	2.180	2.733	3.490	5.071	10.219	13.362	15.507	17.535	20.090	21.955
9	1.735	2.088	2.700	3.325	4.168	5.899	11.389	14.684	16.919	19.023	21.666	23.589
10	2.156	2.558	3.247	3.940	4.865	6.737	12.549	15.987	18.307	20.483	23.209	25.188
11	2.603	3.053	3.816	4.575	5.578	7.584	13.701	17.275	19.675	21.920	24.725	26.757
12	3.074	3.571	4.404	5.226	6.304	8.438	14.845	18.549	21.026	23.337	26.217	28.299
13	3.565	4.107	5.009	5.892	7.042	9.299	15.984	19.812	22.362	24.736	27.688	29.819
14	4.075	4.660	5.629	6.571	7.790	10.165	17.117	21.064	23.685	26.119	29.141	31.319
15	4.601	5.229	6.262	7.261	8.547	11.037	18.245	22.307	24.996	27.488	30.578	32.801
16	5.142	5.812	6.908	7.962	9.312	11.912	19.369	23.542	26.296	28.845	32.000	34.267
17	5.697	6.408	7.564	8.672	10.085	12.792	20.489	24.769	27.587	30.191	33.409	35.718
18	6.265	7.015	8.231	9.390	10.865	13.675	21.605	25.989	28.869	31.526	34.805	37.156
19	6.844	7.633	8.907	10.117	11.651	14.562	22.718	27.204	30.144	32.852	36.191	38.582
20	7.434	8.260	9.591	10.851	12.443	15.452	23.828	28.412	31.410	34.170	37.566	39.997
21	8.034	8.897	10.283	11.591	13.240	16.344	24.935	29.615	32.671	35.479	38.932	41.401
22	8.643	9.542	10.982	12.338	14.042	17.240	26.039	30.813	33.924	36.781	40.289	42.796
23	9.260	10.196	11.689	13.091	14.848	18.137	27.141	32.007	35.172	38.076	41.638	44.181
24	9.886	10.856	12.401	13.848	15.659	19.037	28.241	33.196	36.415	39.364	42.980	45.559
25	10.520	11.524	13.120	14.611	16.473	19.939	29.339	34.382	37.652	40.646	44.314	46.928
26	11.160	12.198	13.844	15.379	17.292	20.843	30.435	35.563	38.885	41.923	45.642	48.290
27	11.808	12.879	14.573	16.151	18.114	21.749	31.528	36.741	40.113	43.194	46.963	49.645
28	12.461	13.565	15.308	16.928	18.939	22.657	32.620	37.916	41.337	44.461	48.278	50.993
29	13.121	14.257	16.047	17.708	19.768	23.567	33.711	39.087	42.557	45.722	49.588	52.336
30	13.787	14.954	16.791	18.493	20.599	24.478	34.800	40.256	43.773	46.979	50.892	53.672

(continued)

TABLE 3

(continued)

Degrees of Freedom	Upper Tail Areas (α)											
	.995	.99	.975	.95	.90	.75	.25	.10	.05	.025	.01	.005
31	14.458	15.655	17.539	19.281	21.434	25.390	35.887	41.422	44.985	48.232	52.191	55.003
32	15.134	16.362	18.291	20.072	22.271	26.304	36.973	42.585	46.194	49.480	53.486	56.328
33	15.815	17.074	19.047	20.867	23.110	27.219	38.058	43.745	47.400	50.725	54.776	57.648
34	16.501	17.789	19.806	21.664	23.952	28.136	39.141	44.903	48.602	51.966	56.061	58.964
35	17.192	18.509	20.569	22.465	24.797	29.054	40.223	46.059	49.802	53.203	57.342	60.275
36	17.887	19.233	21.336	23.269	25.643	29.973	41.304	47.212	50.998	54.437	58.619	61.581
37	18.586	19.960	22.106	24.075	26.492	30.893	42.383	48.363	52.192	55.668	59.892	62.883
38	19.289	20.691	22.878	24.884	27.343	31.815	43.462	49.513	53.384	56.896	61.162	64.181
39	19.996	21.426	23.654	25.695	28.196	32.737	44.539	50.660	54.572	58.120	62.428	65.476
40	20.707	22.164	24.433	26.509	29.051	33.660	45.616	51.805	55.758	59.342	63.691	66.766
41	21.421	22.906	25.215	27.326	29.907	34.585	46.692	52.949	56.942	60.561	64.950	68.053
42	22.138	23.650	25.999	28.144	30.765	35.510	47.766	54.090	58.124	61.777	66.206	69.336
43	22.859	24.398	26.785	28.965	31.625	36.436	48.840	55.230	59.304	62.990	67.459	70.616
44	23.584	25.148	27.575	29.787	32.487	37.363	49.913	56.369	60.481	64.201	68.710	71.893
45	24.311	25.901	28.366	30.612	33.350	38.291	50.985	57.505	61.656	65.410	69.957	73.166
46	25.041	26.657	29.160	31.439	34.215	39.220	52.056	58.641	62.830	66.617	71.201	74.437
47	25.775	27.416	29.956	32.268	35.081	40.149	53.127	59.774	64.001	67.821	72.443	75.704
48	26.511	28.177	30.755	33.098	35.949	41.079	54.196	60.907	65.171	69.023	73.683	76.969
49	27.249	28.941	31.555	33.930	36.818	42.010	55.265	62.038	66.339	70.222	74.919	78.231
50	27.991	29.707	32.357	34.764	37.689	42.942	56.334	63.167	67.505	71.420	76.154	79.490
51	28.735	30.475	33.162	35.600	38.560	43.874	57.401	64.295	68.669	72.616	77.386	80.747
52	29.481	31.246	33.968	36.437	39.433	44.808	58.468	65.422	69.832	73.810	78.616	82.001
53	30.230	32.018	34.776	37.276	40.308	45.741	59.534	66.548	70.993	75.002	79.843	83.253
54	30.981	32.793	35.586	38.116	41.183	46.676	60.600	67.673	72.153	76.192	81.069	84.502
55	31.735	33.570	36.398	38.958	42.060	47.610	61.665	68.796	73.311	77.380	82.292	85.749
56	32.490	34.350	37.212	39.801	42.937	48.546	62.729	69.919	74.468	78.567	83.513	86.994
57	33.248	35.131	38.027	40.646	43.816	49.482	63.793	71.040	75.624	79.752	84.733	88.236
58	34.008	35.913	38.844	41.492	44.696	50.419	64.857	72.160	76.778	80.936	85.950	89.477
59	34.770	36.698	39.662	42.339	45.577	51.356	65.919	73.279	77.931	82.117	87.166	90.715
60	35.534	37.485	40.482	43.188	46.459	52.294	66.981	74.397	79.082	83.298	88.379	91.952

For larger values of degrees of freedom (DF) the expression $z = \sqrt{2\chi^2} - \sqrt{2(DF) - 1}$ may be used and the resulting upper tail area can be obtained from the table of the standardized normal distribution

TABLE 4

t Distribution

For a particular number of degrees of freedom, entry represents the critical value of t corresponding to a specified upper tail area α

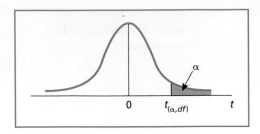

Degrees of Freedom	Upper Tail Areas					
	.25	.10	.05	.025	.01	.005
1	1.0000	3.0777	6.3138	12.7062	31.8207	63.6574
2	0.8165	1.8856	2.9200	4.3027	6.9646	9.9248
3	0.7649	1.6377	2.3534	3.1824	4.5407	5.8409
4	0.7407	1.5332	2.1318	2.7764	3.7469	4.6041
5	0.7267	1.4759	2.0150	2.5706	3.3649	4.0322
6	0.7176	1.4398	1.9432	2.4469	3.1427	3.7074
7	0.7111	1.4149	1.8946	2.3646	2.9980	3.4995
8	0.7064	1.3968	1.8595	2.3060	2.8965	3.3554
9	0.7027	1.3830	1.8331	2.2622	2.8214	3.2498
10	0.6998	1.3722	1.8125	2.2281	2.7638	3.1693
11	0.6974	1.3634	1.7959	2.2010	2.7181	3.1058
12	0.6955	1.3562	1.7823	2.1788	2.6810	3.0545
13	0.6938	1.3502	1.7709	2.1604	2.6503	3.0123
14	0.6924	1.3450	1.7613	2.1448	2.6245	2.9768
15	0.6912	1.3406	1.7531	2.1315	2.6025	2.9467
16	0.6901	1.3368	1.7459	2.1199	2.5835	2.9208
17	0.6892	1.3334	1.7396	2.1098	2.5669	2.8982
18	0.6884	1.3304	1.7341	2.1009	2.5524	2.8784
19	0.6876	1.3277	1.7291	2.0930	2.5395	2.8609
20	0.6870	1.3253	1.7247	2.0860	2.5280	2.8453
21	0.6864	1.3232	1.7207	2.0796	2.5177	2.8314
22	0.6858	1.3212	1.7171	2.0739	2.5083	2.8188
23	0.6853	1.3195	1.7139	2.0687	2.4999	2.8073
24	0.6848	1.3178	1.7109	2.0639	2.4922	2.7969
25	0.6844	1.3163	1.7081	2.0595	2.4851	2.7874
26	0.6840	1.3150	1.7056	2.0555	2.4786	2.7787
27	0.6837	1.3137	1.7033	2.0518	2.4727	2.7707
28	0.6834	1.3125	1.7011	2.0484	2.4671	2.7633
29	0.6830	1.3114	1.6991	2.0452	2.4620	2.7564
30	0.6828	1.3104	1.6973	2.0423	2.4573	2.7500
31	0.6825	1.3095	1.6955	2.0395	2.4528	2.7440
32	0.6822	1.3086	1.6939	2.0369	2.4487	2.7385
33	0.6820	1.3077	1.6924	2.0345	2.4448	2.7333
34	0.6818	1.3070	1.6909	2.0322	2.4411	2.7284
35	0.6816	1.3062	1.6896	2.0301	2.4377	2.7238
36	0.6814	1.3055	1.6883	2.0281	2.4345	2.7195
37	0.6812	1.3049	1.6871	2.0262	2.4314	2.7154

(continued)

TABLE 4

(continued)

Degrees of Freedom	Upper Tail Areas					
	.25	.10	.05	.025	.01	.005
38	0.6810	1.3042	1.6860	2.0244	2.4286	2.7116
39	0.6808	1.3036	1.6849	2.0227	2.4258	2.7079
40	0.6807	1.3031	1.6839	2.0211	2.4233	2.7045
41	0.6805	1.3025	1.6829	2.0195	2.4208	2.7012
42	0.6804	1.3020	1.6820	2.0181	2.4185	2.6981
43	0.6802	1.3016	1.6811	2.0167	2.4163	2.6951
44	0.6801	1.3011	1.6802	2.0154	2.4141	2.6923
45	0.6800	1.3006	1.6794	2.0141	2.4121	2.6896
46	0.6799	1.3002	1.6787	2.0129	2.4102	2.6870
47	0.6797	1.2998	1.6779	2.0117	2.4083	2.6846
48	0.6796	1.2994	1.6772	2.0106	2.4066	2.6822
49	0.6795	1.2991	1.6766	2.0096	2.4049	2.6800
50	0.6794	1.2987	1.6759	2.0086	2.4033	2.6778
51	0.6793	1.2984	1.6753	2.0076	2.4017	2.6757
52	0.6792	1.2980	1.6747	2.0066	2.4002	2.6737
53	0.6791	1.2977	1.6741	2.0057	2.3988	2.6718
54	0.6791	1.2974	1.6736	2.0049	2.3974	2.6700
55	0.6790	1.2971	1.6730	2.0040	2.3961	2.6682
56	0.6789	1.2969	1.6725	2.0032	2.3948	2.6665
57	0.6788	1.2966	1.6720	2.0025	2.3936	2.6649
58	0.6787	1.2963	1.6716	2.0017	2.3924	2.6633
59	0.6787	1.2961	1.6711	2.0010	2.3912	2.6618
60	0.6786	1.2958	1.6706	2.0003	2.3901	2.6603
61	0.6785	1.2956	1.6702	1.9996	2.3890	2.6589
62	0.6785	1.2954	1.6698	1.9990	2.3880	2.6575
63	0.6784	1.2951	1.6694	1.9983	2.3870	2.6561
64	0.6783	1.2949	1.6690	1.9977	2.3860	2.6549
65	0.6783	1.2947	1.6686	1.9971	2.3851	2.6536
66	0.6782	1.2945	1.6683	1.9966	2.3842	2.6524
67	0.6782	1.2943	1.6679	1.9960	2.3833	2.6512
68	0.6781	1.2941	1.6676	1.9955	2.3824	2.6501
69	0.6781	1.2939	1.6672	1.9949	2.3816	2.6490
70	0.6780	1.2938	1.6669	1.9944	2.3808	2.6479
71	0.6780	1.2936	1.6666	1.9939	2.3800	2.6469
72	0.6779	1.2934	1.6663	1.9935	2.3793	2.6459
73	0.6779	1.2933	1.6660	1.9930	2.3785	2.6449
74	0.6778	1.2931	1.6657	1.9925	2.3778	2.6439
75	0.6778	1.2929	1.6654	1.9921	2.3771	2.6430
76	0.6777	1.2928	1.6652	1.9917	2.3764	2.6421
77	0.6777	1.2926	1.6649	1.9913	2.3758	2.6412
78	0.6776	1.2925	1.6646	1.9908	2.3751	2.6403
79	0.6776	1.2924	1.6644	1.9905	2.3745	2.6395
80	0.6776	1.2922	1.6641	1.9901	2.3739	2.6387
81	0.6775	1.2921	1.6639	1.9897	2.3733	2.6379
82	0.6775	1.2920	1.6636	1.9893	2.3727	2.6371

(continued)

TABLE 4

(continued)

Degrees of Freedom	Upper Tail Areas					
	.25	.10	.05	.025	.01	.005
83	0.6775	1.2918	1.6634	1.9890	2.3721	2.6364
84	0.6774	1.2917	1.6632	1.9886	2.3716	2.6356
85	0.6774	1.2916	1.6630	1.9883	2.3710	2.6349
86	0.6774	1.2915	1.6628	1.9879	2.3705	2.6342
87	0.6773	1.2914	1.6626	1.9876	2.3700	2.6335
88	0.6773	1.2912	1.6624	1.9873	2.3695	2.6329
89	0.6773	1.2911	1.6622	1.9870	2.3690	2.6322
90	0.6772	1.2910	1.6620	1.9867	2.3685	2.6316
91	0.6772	1.2909	1.6618	1.9864	2.3680	2.6309
92	0.6772	1.2908	1.6616	1.9861	2.3676	2.6303
93	0.6771	1.2907	1.6614	1.9858	2.3671	2.6297
94	0.6771	1.2906	1.6612	1.9855	2.3667	2.6291
95	0.6771	1.2905	1.6611	1.9853	2.3662	2.6286
96	0.6771	1.2904	1.6609	1.9850	2.3658	2.6280
97	0.6770	1.2903	1.6607	1.9847	2.3654	2.6275
98	0.6770	1.2902	1.6606	1.9845	2.3650	2.6269
99	0.6770	1.2902	1.6604	1.9842	2.3646	2.6264
100	0.6770	1.2901	1.6602	1.9840	2.3642	2.6259
110	0.6767	1.2893	1.6588	1.9818	2.3607	2.6213
120	0.6765	1.2886	1.6577	1.9799	2.3578	2.6174
130	0.6764	1.2881	1.6567	1.9784	2.3554	2.6142
140	0.6762	1.2876	1.6558	1.9771	2.3533	2.6114
150	0.6761	1.2872	1.6551	1.9759	2.3515	2.6090
∞	0.6745	1.2816	1.6449	1.9600	2.3263	2.5758

TABLE 5

F Distribution

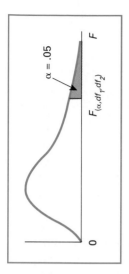

For a particular combination of numerator and denominator degrees of freedom, entry represents the critical values of F corresponding to a specified upper tail area α.

	Numerator df_1																		
Denominator df_2	1	2	3	4	5	6	7	8	9	10	12	15	20	24	30	40	60	120	∞
1	161.4	199.5	215.7	224.6	230.2	234.0	236.8	238.9	240.5	241.9	243.9	245.9	248.0	249.1	250.1	251.1	252.2	253.3	254.3
2	18.51	19.00	19.16	19.25	19.30	19.33	19.35	19.37	19.38	19.40	19.41	19.43	19.45	19.45	19.46	19.47	19.48	19.49	19.50
3	10.13	9.55	9.28	9.12	9.01	8.94	8.89	8.85	8.81	8.79	8.74	8.70	8.66	8.64	8.62	8.59	8.57	8.55	8.53
4	7.71	6.94	6.59	6.39	6.26	6.16	6.09	6.04	6.00	5.96	5.91	5.86	5.80	5.77	5.75	5.72	5.69	5.66	5.63
5	6.61	5.79	5.41	5.19	5.05	4.95	4.88	4.82	4.77	4.74	4.68	4.62	4.56	4.53	4.50	4.46	4.43	4.40	4.36
6	5.99	5.14	4.76	4.53	4.39	4.28	4.21	4.15	4.10	4.06	4.00	3.94	3.87	3.84	3.81	3.77	3.74	3.70	3.67
7	5.59	4.74	4.35	4.12	3.97	3.87	3.79	3.73	3.68	3.64	3.57	3.51	3.44	3.41	3.38	3.34	3.30	3.27	3.23
8	5.32	4.46	4.07	3.84	3.69	3.58	3.50	3.44	3.39	3.35	3.28	3.22	3.15	3.12	3.08	3.04	3.01	2.97	2.93
9	5.12	4.26	3.86	3.63	3.48	3.37	3.29	3.23	3.18	3.14	3.07	3.01	2.94	2.90	2.86	2.83	2.79	2.75	2.71
10	4.96	4.10	3.71	3.48	3.33	3.22	3.14	3.07	3.02	2.98	2.91	2.85	2.77	2.74	2.70	2.66	2.62	2.58	2.54
11	4.84	3.98	3.59	3.36	3.20	3.09	3.01	2.95	2.90	2.85	2.79	2.72	2.65	2.61	2.57	2.53	2.49	2.45	2.40
12	4.75	3.89	3.49	3.26	3.11	3.00	2.91	2.85	2.80	2.75	2.69	2.62	2.54	2.51	2.47	2.43	2.38	2.34	2.30
13	4.67	3.81	3.41	3.18	3.03	2.92	2.83	2.77	2.71	2.67	2.60	2.53	2.46	2.42	2.38	2.34	2.30	2.25	2.21
14	4.60	3.74	3.34	3.11	2.96	2.85	2.76	2.70	2.65	2.60	2.53	2.46	2.39	2.35	2.31	2.27	2.22	2.18	2.13
15	4.54	3.68	3.29	3.06	2.90	2.79	2.71	2.64	2.59	2.54	2.48	2.40	2.33	2.29	2.25	2.20	2.16	2.11	2.07
16	4.49	3.63	3.24	3.01	2.85	2.74	2.66	2.59	2.54	2.49	2.42	2.35	2.28	2.24	2.19	2.15	2.11	2.06	2.01
17	4.45	3.59	3.20	2.96	2.81	2.70	2.61	2.55	2.49	2.45	2.38	2.31	2.23	2.19	2.15	2.10	2.06	2.01	1.96
18	4.41	3.55	3.16	2.93	2.77	2.66	2.58	2.51	2.46	2.41	2.34	2.27	2.19	2.15	2.11	2.06	2.02	1.97	1.92
19	4.38	3.52	3.13	2.90	2.74	2.63	2.54	2.48	2.42	2.38	2.31	2.23	2.16	2.11	2.07	2.03	1.98	1.93	1.88
20	4.35	3.49	3.10	2.87	2.71	2.60	2.51	2.45	2.39	2.35	2.28	2.20	2.12	2.08	2.04	1.99	1.95	1.90	1.84
21	4.32	3.47	3.07	2.84	2.68	2.57	2.49	2.42	2.37	2.32	2.25	2.18	2.10	2.05	2.01	1.96	1.92	1.87	1.81
22	4.30	3.44	3.05	2.82	2.66	2.55	2.46	2.40	2.34	2.30	2.23	2.15	2.07	2.03	1.98	1.94	1.89	1.84	1.78
23	4.28	3.42	3.03	2.80	2.64	2.53	2.44	2.37	2.32	2.27	2.20	2.13	2.05	2.01	1.96	1.91	1.86	1.81	1.76
24	4.26	3.40	3.01	2.78	2.62	2.51	2.42	2.36	2.30	2.25	2.18	2.11	2.03	1.98	1.94	1.89	1.84	1.79	1.73
25	4.24	3.39	2.99	2.76	2.60	2.49	2.40	2.34	2.28	2.24	2.16	2.09	2.01	1.96	1.92	1.87	1.82	1.77	1.71
26	4.23	3.37	2.98	2.74	2.59	2.47	2.39	2.32	2.27	2.22	2.15	2.07	1.99	1.95	1.90	1.85	1.80	1.75	1.69
27	4.21	3.35	2.96	2.73	2.57	2.46	2.37	2.31	2.25	2.20	2.13	2.06	1.97	1.93	1.88	1.84	1.79	1.73	1.67
28	4.20	3.34	2.95	2.71	2.56	2.45	2.36	2.29	2.24	2.19	2.12	2.04	1.96	1.91	1.87	1.82	1.77	1.71	1.65
29	4.18	3.33	2.93	2.70	2.55	2.43	2.35	2.28	2.22	2.18	2.10	2.03	1.94	1.90	1.85	1.81	1.75	1.70	1.64
30	4.17	3.32	2.92	2.69	2.53	2.42	2.33	2.27	2.21	2.16	2.09	2.01	1.93	1.89	1.84	1.79	1.74	1.68	1.62
40	4.08	3.23	2.84	2.61	2.45	2.34	2.25	2.18	2.12	2.08	2.00	1.92	1.84	1.79	1.74	1.69	1.64	1.58	1.51
60	4.00	3.15	2.76	2.53	2.37	2.25	2.17	2.10	2.04	1.99	1.92	1.84	1.75	1.70	1.65	1.59	1.53	1.47	1.39
120	3.92	3.07	2.68	2.45	2.29	2.17	2.09	2.02	1.96	1.91	1.83	1.75	1.66	1.61	1.55	1.50	1.43	1.35	1.25
∞	3.84	3.00	2.60	2.37	2.21	2.10	2.01	1.94	1.88	1.83	1.75	1.67	1.57	1.52	1.46	1.39	1.32	1.22	1.00

(continued)

TABLE 5
(continued)

$\alpha = .025$

$F_{(\alpha, df_1, df_2)}$

	Numerator df_1																		
Denominator df_2	1	2	3	4	5	6	7	8	9	10	12	15	20	24	30	40	60	120	∞
1	647.8	799.5	864.2	899.6	921.8	937.1	948.2	956.7	963.3	968.6	976.7	984.9	993.1	997.2	1001	1006	1010	1014	1018
2	38.51	39.00	39.17	39.25	39.30	39.33	39.36	39.37	39.39	39.40	39.41	39.43	39.45	39.46	39.46	39.47	39.48	39.49	39.50
3	17.44	16.04	15.44	15.10	14.88	14.73	14.62	14.54	14.47	14.42	14.34	14.25	14.17	14.12	14.08	14.04	13.99	13.95	13.90
4	12.22	10.65	9.98	9.60	9.36	9.20	9.07	8.98	8.90	8.84	8.75	8.66	8.56	8.51	8.46	8.41	8.36	8.31	8.26
5	10.01	8.43	7.76	7.39	7.15	6.98	6.85	6.76	6.68	6.62	6.52	6.43	6.33	6.28	6.23	6.18	6.12	6.07	6.02
6	8.81	7.26	6.60	6.23	5.99	5.82	5.70	5.60	5.52	5.46	5.37	5.27	5.17	5.12	5.07	5.01	4.96	4.90	4.85
7	8.07	6.54	5.89	5.52	5.29	5.12	4.99	4.90	4.82	4.76	4.67	4.57	4.47	4.42	4.36	4.31	4.25	4.20	4.14
8	7.57	6.06	5.42	5.05	4.82	4.65	4.53	4.43	4.36	4.30	4.20	4.10	4.00	3.95	3.89	3.84	3.78	3.73	3.67
9	7.21	5.71	5.08	4.72	4.48	4.32	4.20	4.10	4.03	3.96	3.87	3.77	3.67	3.61	3.56	3.51	3.45	3.39	3.33
10	6.94	5.46	4.83	4.47	4.24	4.07	3.95	3.85	3.78	3.72	3.62	3.52	3.42	3.37	3.31	3.26	3.20	3.14	3.08
11	6.72	5.26	4.63	4.28	4.04	3.88	3.76	3.66	3.59	3.53	3.43	3.33	3.23	3.17	3.12	3.06	3.00	2.94	2.88
12	6.55	5.10	4.47	4.12	3.89	3.73	3.61	3.51	3.44	3.37	3.28	3.18	3.07	3.02	2.96	2.91	2.85	2.79	2.72
13	6.41	4.97	4.35	4.00	3.77	3.60	3.48	3.39	3.31	3.25	3.15	3.05	2.95	2.89	2.84	2.78	2.72	2.66	2.60
14	6.30	4.86	4.24	3.89	3.66	3.50	3.38	3.29	3.21	3.15	3.05	2.95	2.84	2.79	2.73	2.67	2.61	2.55	2.49
15	6.20	4.77	4.15	3.80	3.58	3.41	3.29	3.20	3.12	3.06	2.96	2.86	2.76	2.70	2.64	2.59	2.52	2.46	2.40
16	6.12	4.69	4.08	3.73	3.50	3.34	3.22	3.12	3.05	2.99	2.89	2.79	2.68	2.63	2.57	2.51	2.45	2.38	2.32
17	6.04	4.62	4.01	3.66	3.44	3.28	3.16	3.06	2.98	2.92	2.82	2.72	2.62	2.56	2.50	2.44	2.38	2.32	2.25
18	5.98	4.56	3.95	3.61	3.38	3.22	3.10	3.01	2.93	2.87	2.77	2.67	2.56	2.50	2.44	2.38	2.32	2.26	2.19
19	5.92	4.51	3.90	3.56	3.33	3.17	3.05	2.96	2.88	2.82	2.72	2.62	2.51	2.45	2.39	2.33	2.27	2.20	2.13
20	5.87	4.46	3.86	3.51	3.29	3.13	3.01	2.91	2.84	2.77	2.68	2.57	2.46	2.41	2.35	2.29	2.22	2.16	2.09
21	5.83	4.42	3.82	3.48	3.25	3.09	2.97	2.87	2.80	2.73	2.64	2.53	2.42	2.37	2.31	2.25	2.18	2.11	2.04
22	5.79	4.38	3.78	3.44	3.22	3.05	2.93	2.84	2.76	2.70	2.60	2.50	2.39	2.33	2.27	2.21	2.14	2.08	2.00
23	5.75	4.35	3.75	3.41	3.18	3.02	2.90	2.81	2.73	2.67	2.57	2.47	2.36	2.30	2.24	2.18	2.11	2.04	1.97
24	5.72	4.32	3.72	3.38	3.15	2.99	2.87	2.78	2.70	2.64	2.54	2.44	2.33	2.27	2.21	2.15	2.08	2.01	1.94
25	5.69	4.29	3.69	3.35	3.13	2.97	2.85	2.75	2.68	2.61	2.51	2.41	2.30	2.24	2.18	2.12	2.05	1.98	1.91
26	5.66	4.27	3.67	3.33	3.10	2.94	2.82	2.73	2.65	2.59	2.49	2.39	2.28	2.22	2.16	2.09	2.03	1.95	1.88
27	5.63	4.24	3.65	3.31	3.08	2.92	2.80	2.71	2.63	2.57	2.47	2.36	2.25	2.19	2.13	2.07	2.00	1.93	1.85
28	5.61	4.22	3.63	3.29	3.06	2.90	2.78	2.69	2.61	2.55	2.45	2.34	2.23	2.17	2.11	2.05	1.98	1.91	1.83
29	5.59	4.20	3.61	3.27	3.04	2.88	2.76	2.67	2.59	2.53	2.43	2.32	2.21	2.15	2.09	2.03	1.96	1.89	1.81
30	5.57	4.18	3.59	3.25	3.03	2.87	2.75	2.65	2.57	2.51	2.41	2.31	2.20	2.14	2.07	2.01	1.94	1.87	1.79
40	5.42	4.05	3.46	3.13	2.90	2.74	2.62	2.53	2.45	2.39	2.29	2.18	2.07	2.01	1.94	1.88	1.80	1.72	1.64
60	5.29	3.93	3.34	3.01	2.79	2.63	2.51	2.41	2.33	2.27	2.17	2.06	1.94	1.88	1.82	1.74	1.67	1.58	1.48
120	5.15	3.80	3.23	2.89	2.67	2.52	2.39	2.30	2.22	2.16	2.05	1.94	1.82	1.76	1.69	1.61	1.53	1.43	1.31
∞	5.02	3.69	3.12	2.79	2.57	2.41	2.29	2.19	2.11	2.05	1.94	1.83	1.71	1.64	1.57	1.48	1.39	1.27	1.00

(continued)

Table 5
(continued)

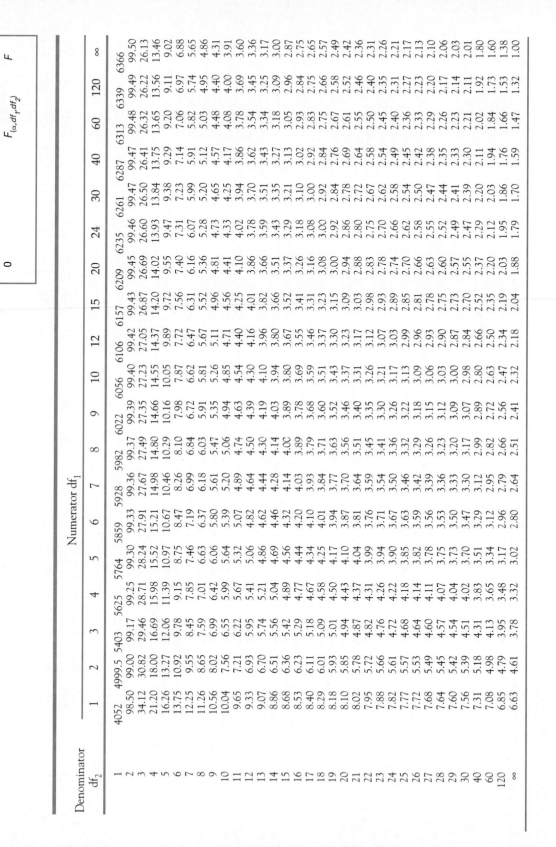

$\alpha = .01$

$F_{(\alpha, df_1, df_2)}$

Denominator	Numerator df_1																		
df_2	1	2	3	4	5	6	7	8	9	10	12	15	20	24	30	40	60	120	∞
1	4052	4999.5	5403	5625	5764	5859	5928	5982	6022	6056	6106	6157	6209	6235	6261	6287	6313	6339	6366
2	98.50	99.00	99.17	99.25	99.30	99.33	99.36	99.37	99.39	99.40	99.42	99.43	99.45	99.46	99.47	99.47	99.48	99.49	99.50
3	34.12	30.82	29.46	28.71	28.24	27.91	27.67	27.49	27.35	27.23	27.05	26.87	26.69	26.60	26.50	26.41	26.32	26.22	26.13
4	21.20	18.00	16.69	15.98	15.52	15.21	14.98	14.80	14.66	14.55	14.37	14.20	14.02	13.93	13.84	13.75	13.65	13.56	13.46
5	16.26	13.27	12.06	11.39	10.97	10.67	10.46	10.29	10.16	10.05	9.89	9.72	9.55	9.47	9.38	9.29	9.20	9.11	9.02
6	13.75	10.92	9.78	9.15	8.75	8.47	8.26	8.10	7.98	7.87	7.72	7.56	7.40	7.31	7.23	7.14	7.06	6.97	6.88
7	12.25	9.55	8.45	7.85	7.46	7.19	6.99	6.84	6.72	6.62	6.47	6.31	6.16	6.07	5.99	5.91	5.82	5.74	5.65
8	11.26	8.65	7.59	7.01	6.63	6.37	6.18	6.03	5.91	5.81	5.67	5.52	5.36	5.28	5.20	5.12	5.03	4.95	4.86
9	10.56	8.02	6.99	6.42	6.06	5.80	5.61	5.47	5.35	5.26	5.11	4.96	4.81	4.73	4.65	4.57	4.48	4.40	4.31
10	10.04	7.56	6.55	5.99	5.64	5.39	5.20	5.06	4.94	4.85	4.71	4.56	4.41	4.33	4.25	4.17	4.08	4.00	3.91
11	9.65	7.21	6.22	5.67	5.32	5.07	4.89	4.74	4.63	4.54	4.40	4.25	4.10	4.02	3.94	3.86	3.78	3.69	3.60
12	9.33	6.93	5.95	5.41	5.06	4.82	4.64	4.50	4.39	4.30	4.16	4.01	3.86	3.78	3.70	3.62	3.54	3.45	3.36
13	9.07	6.70	5.74	5.21	4.86	4.62	4.44	4.30	4.19	4.10	3.96	3.82	3.66	3.59	3.51	3.43	3.34	3.25	3.17
14	8.86	6.51	5.56	5.04	4.69	4.46	4.28	4.14	4.03	3.94	3.80	3.66	3.51	3.43	3.35	3.27	3.18	3.09	3.00
15	8.68	6.36	5.42	4.89	4.56	4.32	4.14	4.00	3.89	3.80	3.67	3.52	3.37	3.29	3.21	3.13	3.05	2.96	2.87
16	8.53	6.23	5.29	4.77	4.44	4.20	4.03	3.89	3.78	3.69	3.55	3.41	3.26	3.18	3.10	3.02	2.93	2.84	2.75
17	8.40	6.11	5.18	4.67	4.34	4.10	3.93	3.79	3.68	3.59	3.46	3.31	3.16	3.08	3.00	2.92	2.83	2.75	2.65
18	8.29	6.01	5.09	4.58	4.25	4.01	3.84	3.71	3.60	3.51	3.37	3.23	3.08	3.00	2.92	2.84	2.75	2.66	2.57
19	8.18	5.93	5.01	4.50	4.17	3.94	3.77	3.63	3.52	3.43	3.30	3.15	3.00	2.92	2.84	2.76	2.67	2.58	2.49
20	8.10	5.85	4.94	4.43	4.10	3.87	3.70	3.56	3.46	3.37	3.23	3.09	2.94	2.86	2.78	2.69	2.61	2.52	2.42
21	8.02	5.78	4.87	4.37	4.04	3.81	3.64	3.51	3.40	3.31	3.17	3.03	2.88	2.80	2.72	2.64	2.55	2.46	2.36
22	7.95	5.72	4.82	4.31	3.99	3.76	3.59	3.45	3.35	3.26	3.12	2.98	2.83	2.75	2.67	2.58	2.50	2.40	2.31
23	7.88	5.66	4.76	4.26	3.94	3.71	3.54	3.41	3.30	3.21	3.07	2.93	2.78	2.70	2.62	2.54	2.45	2.35	2.26
24	7.82	5.61	4.72	4.22	3.90	3.67	3.50	3.36	3.26	3.17	3.03	2.89	2.74	2.66	2.58	2.49	2.40	2.31	2.21
25	7.77	5.57	4.68	4.18	3.85	3.63	3.46	3.32	3.22	3.13	2.99	2.85	2.70	2.62	2.54	2.45	2.36	2.27	2.17
26	7.72	5.53	4.64	4.14	3.82	3.59	3.42	3.29	3.18	3.09	2.96	2.81	2.66	2.58	2.50	2.42	2.33	2.23	2.13
27	7.68	5.49	4.60	4.11	3.78	3.56	3.39	3.26	3.15	3.06	2.93	2.78	2.63	2.55	2.47	2.38	2.29	2.20	2.10
28	7.64	5.45	4.57	4.07	3.75	3.53	3.36	3.23	3.12	3.03	2.90	2.75	2.60	2.52	2.44	2.35	2.26	2.17	2.06
29	7.60	5.42	4.54	4.04	3.73	3.50	3.33	3.20	3.09	3.00	2.87	2.73	2.57	2.49	2.41	2.33	2.23	2.14	2.03
30	7.56	5.39	4.51	4.02	3.70	3.47	3.30	3.17	3.07	2.98	2.84	2.70	2.55	2.47	2.39	2.30	2.21	2.11	2.01
40	7.31	5.18	4.31	3.83	3.51	3.29	3.12	2.99	2.89	2.80	2.66	2.52	2.37	2.29	2.20	2.11	2.02	1.92	1.80
60	7.08	4.98	4.13	3.65	3.34	3.12	2.95	2.82	2.72	2.63	2.50	2.35	2.20	2.12	2.03	1.94	1.84	1.73	1.60
120	6.85	4.79	3.95	3.48	3.17	2.96	2.79	2.66	2.56	2.47	2.34	2.19	2.03	1.95	1.86	1.76	1.66	1.53	1.38
∞	6.63	4.61	3.78	3.32	3.02	2.80	2.64	2.51	2.41	2.32	2.18	2.04	1.88	1.79	1.70	1.59	1.47	1.32	1.00

INDEXES

Subject Index

Name Index

Company Index